P9-CRU-588

Trademark and Unfair Competition Law

Trademark and Unfair Competition Law

Cases and Materials

SIXTH EDITION

Jane C. Ginsburg
Morton L. Janklow Professor of
Literary and Artistic Property Law
Columbia Law School

Jessica Litman
John F. Nickoll Professor of Law
University of Michigan Law School

Mary Kevlin
Cowan, Liebowitz & Latman
New York, NY

Carolina Academic Press
Durham, North Carolina

eISBN 978-1-53100-115-5
Looseleaf ISBN 978-1-53100-173-5
ISBN 978-1-53100-114-8
LCCN 2016959316

Carolina Academic Press, LLC
700 Kent Street
Durham, North Carolina 27701
Telephone (919) 489-7486
Fax (919) 493-5668
www.cap-press.com

Printed in the United States of America

We dedicate the Sixth Edition to Arthur J. Greenbaum and Paul Alan Levy,
two outstanding trademark lawyers who have taught and inspired us.

Summary of Contents

Contents

Table of Cases

Preface

In the four years since we published the fifth edition of *Trademark and Unfair Competition Law,* the First Amendment has joined the Internet in shaping the law of trademarks, raising issues from registration to the scope of trademark and related rights and defenses to infringement. As trademarks (or the claims of their owners) have encroached on the subject matter of patents and copyrights, and have been brought to bear on a variety of expressive uses of marks, so have defenses to infringement expanded. The Sixth Edition gives these developments particular attention.

We have retained many of the successful features of earlier editions. The Casebook begins with a Prelude case that captures many of the issues that will recur throughout the course. We then provide introductory case law and secondary material on the concepts and policies underlying trademark law, and incorporate trademark policy concerns throughout the book. We have substantially reorganized the Dilution chapter not only to take account of recent developments, but to make it more teachable. We have continued to include in-depth coverage of important advanced topics in the second half of the Casebook. Thus, along with Domain Names, False Advertising and Remedies receive their own chapters.

We wish to express appreciation to Professors Barton Beebe, Robert Bone, Stacy Dogan, Rochelle Dreyfuss, William Landes, Mark Lemley, Jacqueline Lipton, Jeremy Sheff, Sara Stadler, Rebecca Tushnet, and Jonathan Weinberg; to Judges Alex Kozinski and Richard Posner; and to William M. Borchard, Esq., and Stephen Gaffigan, Esq., for consenting to the use of excerpts of their work. Professors Wendy Gordon, Tyler Ochoa, Jeremy Sheff and Rebecca Tushnet have called our attention to ambiguities and typographical and similar errors in the previous edition, which we hope we have rectified in the current edition. For research assistance, we are especially grateful to Jacob Grubman, Columbia Law School class of 2016. For secretarial assistance, we thank Rosa Arenas, Laura Harlow, and Colleen Regan.

September 2016

Trademark and Unfair Competition Law

Prelude

Top Tobacco, L.P v. North Atlantic Operating Company, Inc.

509 F.3d 380 (7th Cir. 2007)

Easterbrook, Chief Judge.

This case illustrates the power of pictures. One glance is enough to decide the appeal.

Top Tobacco, L.P., sells tobacco to people who want to roll cigarettes by hand or make them using a cranked machine. This is known as the roll-your-own, make-your-own or RYO/MYO business. Top Tobacco and its predecessors have been in this segment of the cigarette market for more than 100 years, and the mark TOP®, printed above a drawing of a spinning top, is well known among merchants and customers of cigarette tobacco. North Atlantic Operating Company and its predecessors also have been in the roll-your-own, make-your-own business for more than 100 years, though initially only as manufacturers of cigarette paper. Not until 1999 did North Atlantic bring its own tobacco to market. The redesigned can that it introduced in 2001 bears the phrase Fresh-Top™ Canister. Top Tobacco maintains in this suit under the Lanham Act that none of its rivals may use the word "top" as a trademark.

Trademarks are designed to inform potential buyers who makes the goods on sale. See *KP Permanent Make-Up, Inc. v. Lasting Impression I, Inc.*, 543 U.S. 111 (2004); *Dastar Corp. v. Twentieth Century Fox Film Corp.*, 539 U.S. 23 (2003). Knowledge of origin may convey information about a product's attributes and quality, and consistent attribution of origin is vital when vendors' reputations matter. Without a way to know who makes what, reputations cannot be created and evaluated, and the process of competition will be less effective. See generally William M. Landes & Richard A. Posner, *The Economic Structure of Intellectual Property Law* 166–209 (2003).

Top Tobacco insists that it has exclusive rights to the word "top" for use on tobacco in this market. But many words have multiple meanings: "Top" may mean the best, or a spinning toy, or a can's lid. Top Tobacco uses the word "top" in the second sense and may hope that consumers will hear the first as well; North Atlantic uses the word in its third sense, to refer to a pull-tab design that keeps tobacco fresh. If English used different words to encode these different meanings, there could not be a trademark problem. Because our language gives the word "top" so many different meanings, however, there is a potential for confusion. But no one who saw these cans side by side could be confused about who makes which:

The phrase "Fresh-Top Canister" on North American's can does not stand out; no consumer could miss the difference between Top Tobacco's TOP brand, with a spinning top, and North Atlantic's ZIG-ZAG® brand, with a picture of a Zouave soldier. The trade dress (including colors and typography) of each producer's can is distinctive. Here is a larger version of the ZIG-ZAG brand can.

The left panel shows the can as it was between 2001 and 2004, when Fresh-Top Canister was on the front (right under "Classic American Blend"), and the two right panels show the can as it was from 2004 through 2006, when the phrase Fresh-Top Canister was on the side. The phrase was removed in 2006 when North Atlantic replaced the aluminum pull-tab design with a plastic lid. (This change does not make the case moot, because the possibility of damages remains.)

The district court granted summary judgment for the defendants, 2007 U.S. Dist. LEXIS 2838 (N.D. Ill. Jan. 4, 2007), and the pictures show why. It is next to impossible to believe that any consumer, however careless, would confuse these products. "Next to impossible" doesn't mean "absolutely impossible"; judges are not perceptual psychologists or marketing experts and may misunderstand how trade dress affects purchasing decisions. But the pictures are all we have. Top Tobacco did not conduct a survey of consumers' reactions to the cans and did not produce an affidavit from even a single consumer or merchant demonstrating confusion.

What Top Tobacco wants us to do is to ignore the pictures and the lack of any reason to believe that anyone ever has been befuddled. Like other courts, this circuit has articulated a multi-factor approach to assessing the probability of confusion. See, e.g., *Barbecue Marx, Inc. v. 551 Ogden, Inc.*, 235 F.3d 1041 (7th Cir. 2000). These factors include whether the trademarks use the same word, whether they sound alike, and so on. Top Tobacco insists that "Fresh Top" is spelled and sounds the same as fresh "TOP", and thus it traipses through the list. It conveniently omits the fact that the phrase on the ZIG-ZAG can is "Fresh-Top Canister", with "Fresh-Top" serving as a phrasal adjective modifying the word "canister" rather than as the product's brand. But it's unnecessary to belabor the point. A list of factors designed as *proxies* for the likelihood of confusion can't supersede the statutory inquiry. If we know for sure that consumers are not confused about a product's origin, there is no need to consult even a single proxy.

Top Tobacco says that merchants may have been confused, because a few of the price lists that North Atlantic sent to its wholesalers and retailers omitted the ZIG-ZAG brand and gave prices for a "6 oz. Fresh-Top TM Can" and a ".75 oz. Pocket Pouch TM". Yet all of these lists prominently include the seller's name (North Atlantic or National Tobacco), and if any commercial buyer thought that North Atlantic was selling the TOP brand the record does not contain a shred of evidence to that effect.

Finally, only a few words are required to address Top Tobacco's claim that it has a "famous" brand that was diluted by the "Fresh-Top Canister" phrase. See 15 U.S.C. § 1125(c)(2)(A) (special protection for famous marks "widely recognized by the general public of the United States as a designator of source of the goods or services of the mark's owner"). There can be no doubt that TOP is an old and recognized brand in the loose-cigarette-tobacco market. There is also no doubt that "top" is commonly used in the tobacco business, so that the appearance of that word on a package does not affect the reputation of Top Tobacco. One brand of chewing tobacco bears a large "Top Leaf" stamp. "Top Hat" is a well-known brand of cigar tobacco. Marlboro sells cigarettes in a "Flip-Top® Box". Another brand of cigarettes is sold under the mark "Top Score". The "Tip-Top" brand of cigarette paper is available from the same sources as Top Tobacco's tobacco. When Top Tobacco obtained a federal registration for its brand of loose cigarette tobacco, it assured the Patent and Trademark Office that it was claiming only limited rights in the word "top." It could hardly be otherwise: the word "top" is too common, and too widely used to refer to the lids of packages—as well as parts of clothing ensembles, masts of ships, summits of mountains, bundles of wool used in spinning, half-innings of baseball, positions in appellate litigation (the top-side brief), and flavors of quark—to be appropriated by a single firm.

The portion of § 1125 from which we have quoted was amended in October 2006 to use "the general public" as the benchmark. This change eliminated any possibility of "niche fame," which some courts had recognized before the amendment. See *Syndicate Sales, Inc. v. Hampshire Paper Corp.*, 192 F.3d 633 (7th Cir. 1999). Top Tobacco insists that even if the amendment (and North Atlantic's new packaging) preclude equitable relief, it is still entitled to damages under the old version of § 1125. But what we have said is enough to show that the word "top" is not famously distinctive "as a designator of source" in any sensibly specified niche of tobacco products.

Affirmed.

Questions

1. What might Top have hoped to accomplish by bringing this lawsuit?

2. Should Top be able to prevent other tobacco producers from using its mark on their packaging without regard to whether consumers are confused? Why or why not?

3. How should a court evaluate whether the use of a word is likely to confuse consumers? Judge Easterbrook notes that the 7th Circuit, like other circuits, "has articulated a multi-factor approach to assessing the probability of confusion." What factors might be relevant to the assessment?

4. After alluding to the multi-factor test, Judge Easterbrook remarks that "If we know for sure that consumers are not confused about a product's origin, there is no need to consult" it. On what basis did the judges conclude that they "know for sure that customers are not confused"? Is there any evidence that Top could have introduced that would have persuaded them that they were mistaken about that?

5. Top also claimed that it was a famous brand, which entitled it to protect its trademark from dilution. Should trademark law treat famous marks differently from marks that are less well known? If so, how should a court decide whether a trademark is famous?

6. How important to the decision was the observation that the word "top" was commonly used in the tobacco business? Should trademarks consisting of common words be treated differently from trademarks that are unusual or unique?

7. As the court notes, many words have multiple meanings. Should competitors always be free to use a trademarked word so long as they use it to express a meaning that's different from the meaning invoked in the trademark? Can you think of examples?

8. In what circumstances should competitors be entitled to use a trademarked word to express the same meaning as the meaning associated with the mark? In what circumstances should they be permitted to use a trademark to refer to the product sold under the mark?

The *Top Tobacco* case addresses many of the major issues central to trademark and unfair competition law, and therefore offers a useful introduction as well as a point of reference throughout the Casebook.

Chapter 1

Concepts of Trademarks and Unfair Competition

A. Competition

Restatement of the Law (Third), Unfair Competition

(Chapter 1. The Freedom to Compete)*

§ 1. GENERAL PRINCIPLES

One who causes harm to the commercial relations of another by engaging in a business or trade is not subject to liability to the other for such harm unless:

(a) the harm results from acts or practices of the actor actionable by the other under the rules of this Restatement relating to:

(1) deceptive marketing, as specified in Chapter Two;

(2) infringement of trademarks and other indicia of identification, as specified in Chapter Three;

(3) appropriation of intangible trade values including trade secrets and the right of publicity, as specified in Chapter Four; or from other acts or practices of the actor determined to be actionable as an unfair method of competition, taking into account the nature of the conduct and its likely effect on both the person seeking relief and the public; or

(b) the acts or practices of the actor are actionable by the other under federal or state statutes, international agreements, or general principles of common law apart from those considered in this Restatement.

COMMENT:

a. The freedom to compete. The freedom to engage in business and to compete for the patronage of prospective customers is a fundamental premise of the free enterprise system. Competition in the marketing of goods and services creates incentives to offer quality products at reasonable prices and fosters the general welfare by promoting the efficient allocation of economic resources. The freedom to compete necessarily contemplates the probability of harm to the commercial relations of other participants in the market. The fundamental rule stated in the introductory clause of this Section promotes competition by insuring that neither new entrants nor existing competitors will be subject to liability for harm resulting solely from the fact of their participation in the market.

The freedom to compete implies a right to induce prospective customers to do business with the actor rather than with the actor's competitors. This Section permits a seller to seek to divert business not only from competitors generally, but also from a particular competitor. This Section is applicable to harm incurred by persons with whom the actor directly competes and to harm incurred by other persons affected by the actor's decision to enter or continue in business. Thus, the actor is not subject to liability to indirect competitors or to employees or suppliers of others who may be harmed by the actor's presence in the market. Liability is imposed under this Section, and under this Restatement generally, only in connection with harm resulting from particular methods of competition determined to be unfair.

The principle embodied in this Section is often loosely described as a "privilege" to compete. That characterization, however, is sometimes taken to imply that any intentional interference in the commercial relations of another is prima facie tortious, with the burden on the actor to establish an applicable privilege as an affirmative defense. There is as yet no consensus with respect to the allocation of the burdens of pleading and proof under the general tort of intentional interference with prospective economic relations. See Restatement, Second, Torts § 767, Comment k. However, in the case of harm resulting from competition in the marketplace, the privilege rationale appears inconsistent with the basic premise of our free enterprise system. Rather than adopting the view that such harm is prima facie tortious subject to a competitive privilege, this Restatement rejects the privilege rationale in favor of a general principle of non-liability. A person alleging injury through competition must therefore establish facts sufficient to subject the actor to liability under one or more of the rules enumerated in this Section.

International News Service v. Associated Press, 248 U.S. 215 (1918). In this landmark decision, the Supreme Court announced a "quasi-property" right in the dissemination of uncopyrightable information. At issue were news reports, published by AP on the East Coast, where they were copied by rival INS and relayed to INS's Midwest and West Coast papers, simultaneously or even ahead of their receipt by AP's local counterparts. The "quasi-" quality of the right derived from the scope of its enforceability: According to the Supreme Court majority, the right might be effective against competitors, but not against the public at large. In the course of the majority opinion, the Court invoked some agricultural metaphors that have remained firmly planted in the rhetoric of unfair competition:

> [D]efendant ... admits that it is taking material that has been acquired by complainant as the result of organization and the expenditure of labor, skill and money, and which is salable by complainant for money, and that defendant in appropriating it and selling it as its own is endeavoring to reap where it has not sown, and by disposing of it to newspapers that are competitors of complainant's members is appropriating to itself the harvest of those who have sown....
>
> ....
>
> It is said that the elements of unfair competition are lacking because there is no attempt by defendant to palm off its goods as those of the complainant, characteristic of the most familiar, if not the most typical, cases of unfair competition. [Citation.] But we cannot concede that the right to equitable relief is confined to that class of cases.

The actual holding of *INS* was narrow: it granted AP protection against its competitor during the period of initial dissemination of the information to AP's members. Nonetheless, because of the Court's willingness to find unfair competition beyond the traditional context of "passing off," as well as the opinion's fertile allusions, *INS* has come to stand for a general common law property right against "misappropriation" of commercial value. *See generally* Douglas G. Baird, *The Story of* INS v. AP*: Property, Natural Monopoly, and the Uneasy Legacy of a Concocted Controversy, in* Jane C. Ginsburg and Rochelle Cooper Dreyfuss, eds., Intellectual Property Stories 9 (2006).

Cheney Bros. v. Doris Silk Corp.

35 F.2d 279 (2d Cir. 1929)

L. Hand, Circuit Judge:

The plaintiff, a corporation, is a manufacturer of silks, which puts out each season many new patterns, designed to attract purchasers by their novelty and beauty. Most of these fail in that purpose, so that not much more than a fifth catch the public fancy. Moreover, they have only a short life, for the most part no more than a single season of eight or nine months. It is in practice impossible, and it would be very onerous if it were not, to secure design patents upon all of these; it would also be impossible to know in advance which would sell well, and patent only those. Besides, it is probable that for the most part they have no such originality as would support a design patent. Again, it is impossible to copyright them under the Copyright Act (17 USCA § 1 et seq.), or at least so the authorities of the Copyright Office hold. So it is easy for any one to copy such as prove successful, and the plaintiff, which is put to much ingenuity and expense in fabricating them, finds itself without protection of any sort for its pains.

Taking advantage of this situation, the defendant copied one of the popular designs in the season beginning in October, 1928, and undercut the plaintiff's price. This is the injury of which it complains. The defendant, though it duplicated the design in question, denies that it knew it to be the plaintiff's, and there thus arises an issue which might be an answer to the motion. However, the parties wish a decision upon the equity of the bill, and, since it is within our power to dismiss it, we shall accept its allegation, and charge the defendant with knowledge.

The plaintiff asks for protection only during the season, and needs no more, for the designs are all ephemeral. It seeks in this way to disguise the extent of the proposed innovation, and to persuade us that, if we interfere only a little, the solecism, if there be one, may be pardonable. But the reasoning which would justify any interposition at all demands that it cover the whole extent of the injury. A man whose designs come to harvest in two years, or in five, has prima facie as good right to protection as one who deals only in annuals. Nor could we consistently stop at designs; processes, machines, and secrets have an equal claim. The upshot must be that, whenever any one has contrived any of these, others may be forbidden to copy it. That is not the law. In the absence of some recognized right at common law, or under the statutes—and the plaintiff claims neither—a man's property is limited to the chattels which embody his invention. Others may imitate these at their pleasure. [Citations.]

....

Of the cases on which the plaintiff relies, the chief is *International News Service v. Associated Press*, 248 U.S. 215. Although that concerned another subject-matter—printed news dispatches—we agree that, if it meant to lay down a general doctrine, it would cover this case; at least, the language of the majority opinion goes so far. We do not believe that it did. While it is of course true that law ordinarily speaks in general terms, there are cases where the occasion is at once the justification for, and the limit of, what is decided. This appears to us such an instance; we think that no more was covered than situations substantially similar to those then at bar. The difficulties of understanding it otherwise are insuperable. We are to suppose that the court meant to create a sort of common-law patent or copyright for reasons of justice. Either would flagrantly conflict with the scheme which Congress has for more than a century devised to cover the subject-matter.

Qua patent, we should at least have to decide, as *tabula rasa*, whether the design or machine was new and required invention; further, we must ignore the Patent Office whose action has always been a condition upon the creation of this kind of property. Qua copyright, although it would be simpler to decide upon the merits, we should equally be obliged to dispense with the conditions imposed upon the creation of the right. Nor, if we went so far, should we know whether the property so recognized should be limited to the periods prescribed in the statutes, or should extend as long as the author's grievance. It appears to us incredible that the Supreme Court should have had in mind any such consequences. To exclude others from the enjoyment of a chattel is one thing; to prevent any imitation of it, to set up a monopoly in the plan of its structure, gives the author a power which the Constitution allows only Congress to create.

....

Questions

1. Does not the protection sought in *Doris Silk* match that granted in *INS* itself: exclusive reproduction rights for the very brief time of peak commercial value? Is there a principled distinction between the two? *See* Douglas G. Baird, *Common Law Intellectual Property and the Legacy of* International News Service v. Associated Press, 50 U. CHI. L. REV. 411, 419 (1983) (reporting that Judge Learned Hand "told other members of the panel in *Cheney* privately that although *INS* 'is somewhat of a stumbling block,' and although 'on principle it is hard to distinguish, and … the language applies, I cannot suppose that any principle of such far-reaching consequence was intended.'").

2. Precedent aside, did Judge Hand voice the better policy in his determination to favor the public domain of unpatented, uncopyrighted articles over plaintiff's claim to relief from parasitic competitors? Why, or why not?

3. Under the current copyright statute, 17 U.S.C. §§ 101–1205, original fabric designs are automatically protected as pictorial, graphic or sculptural works for a term that lasts until 70 years after the death of the author of the design. *See, e.g., L.A. Printex Industries v. Aeropostale, Inc.*, 676 F.3d 841 (9th Cir. 2012). Is that a superior approach to the problem? Why or why not?

Sears, Roebuck & Co. v. Stiffel Co.

376 U.S. 225 (1964)

MR. JUSTICE BLACK delivered the opinion of the Court:

The question in this case is whether a State's unfair competition law can, consistently with the federal patent laws, impose liability for or prohibit the copying of an article which is protected by neither a federal patent nor a copyright. The respondent, Stiffel Company, secured design and mechanical patents on a "pole lamp"—a vertical tube having lamp fixtures along the outside, the tube being made so that it will stand upright between the floor and ceiling of a room. Pole lamps proved a decided commercial success, and soon after Stiffel brought them on the market Sears, Roebuck & Company put on the market a substantially identical lamp, which it sold more cheaply, Sears' retail price being about the same as Stiffel's wholesale price. Stiffel then brought this action against Sears in the United States District Court for the Northern District of Illinois, claiming in its first count that by copying its design Sears had infringed Stiffel's patents and in its second count that by selling copies of Stiffel's lamp Sears had caused confusion in the trade as to the source of the lamps and had thereby engaged in unfair competition under Illinois law. There was evidence that identifying tags were not attached to the Sears lamps although labels appeared on the cartons in which they were delivered to customers, that customers had asked Stiffel whether its lamps differed from Sears', and that in two cases customers who had bought Stiffel lamps had complained to Stiffel on learning that Sears was selling substantially identical lamps at a much lower price.

The District Court, after holding the patents invalid for want of invention, went on to find as a fact that Sears' lamp was "a substantially exact copy" of Stiffel's and that the two lamps were so much alike, both in appearance and in functional details, "that confusion between them is likely, and some confusion has already occurred." On these findings the court held Sears guilty of unfair competition, enjoined Sears "from unfairly competing with [Stiffel] by selling or attempting to sell pole lamps identical to or confusingly similar to" Stiffel's lamp, and ordered an accounting to fix profits and damages resulting from Sears' "unfair competition."

The Court of Appeals affirmed, 313 F.2d 115. That court held that, to make out a case of unfair competition under Illinois law, there was no need to show that Sears had been "palming off" its lamps as Stiffel lamps; Stiffel had only to prove that there was a "likelihood of confusion as to the source of the products"—that the two articles were sufficiently identical that customers could not tell who had made a particular one. Impressed by the "remarkable sameness of appearance" of the lamps, the Court of Appeals upheld the trial court's findings of likelihood of confusion and some actual confusion, findings which the appellate court construed to mean confusion "as to the source of the lamps." The Court of Appeals thought this enough under Illinois law to sustain the trial court's holding of unfair competition, and thus held Sears liable under Illinois law for doing no more than copying and marketing an unpatented article. We granted certiorari to consider whether this use of a State's law of unfair competition is compatible with the federal patent law. 374 U.S. 826.

Before the Constitution was adopted, some States had granted patents either by special act or by general statute, but when the Constitution was adopted provision for a federal patent law was made one of the enumerated powers of Congress because, as Madison put it in The Federalist No. 43, the States "cannot separately make effectual provision" for either patents or copyrights. That constitutional provision is Art. I, § 8, cl. 8, which empowers Congress "To promote the Progress of Science and useful Arts, by securing for limited Times to Authors and Inventors the exclusive Right to their respective Writings and Discoveries." Pursuant to this constitutional authority, Congress in 1790 enacted the first federal patent and copyright law, 1 Stat. 109, and ever since that time has fixed the conditions upon which patents and copyrights shall be granted, see 17 U.S.C. §§ 1-216; 35 U.S.C. §§ 1-293. These laws, like other laws of the United States enacted pursuant to constitutional authority, are the supreme law of the land. *See Sperry v. Florida*, 373 U.S. 379 (1963). When state law touches upon the area of these federal statutes, it is "familiar doctrine" that the federal policy "may not be set at naught, or its benefits denied" by the state law. *Sola Elec. Co. v. Jefferson Elec. Co.*, 317 U.S. 173, 176 (1942). This is true, of course, even if the state law is enacted in the exercise of otherwise undoubted state power.

The grant of a patent is the grant of a statutory monopoly; indeed, the grant of patents in England was an explicit exception to the statute of James I prohibiting monopolies. Patents are not given as favors, as was the case of monopolies given by the Tudor monarchs, see *The Case of Monopolies (Darcy v. Allein)*, 11 Co. Rep. 84 b., 77 Eng. Rep. 1260 (K.B. 1602), but are meant to encourage invention by rewarding the inventor with the right, limited to a term of years fixed by the patent, to exclude others from the use of his invention. During that period of time no one may make, use, or sell the patented product without the patentee's authority. 35 U.S.C. § 271. But in rewarding useful invention, the "rights and welfare of the community must be fairly dealt with and effectually guarded." *Kendall v. Winsor*, 21 How. 322, 329 (1859). To that end the prerequisites to obtaining a patent are strictly observed, and when the patent has issued the limitations on its exercise are equally strictly enforced.... Finally, and especially relevant here, when the patent expires the monopoly created by it expires, too, and the right to make the article—including the right to make it in precisely the shape it carried when patented—passes to the public. *Kellogg Co. v. National Biscuit Co.*, 305 U.S. 111, 120–122 (1938); *Singer Mfg. Co. v. June Mfg. Co.*, 163 U.S. 169, 185 (1896).

Thus the patent system is one in which uniform federal standards are carefully used to promote invention while at the same time preserving free competition. Obviously a State could not, consistently with the Supremacy Clause of the Constitution, extend the life of a patent beyond its expiration date or give a patent on an article which lacked the level of invention required for federal patents. To do either would run counter to the policy of Congress of granting patents only to true inventions, and then only for a limited time. Just as a State cannot encroach upon the federal patent laws directly, it cannot, under some other law, such as that forbidding unfair competition, give protection of a kind that clashes with the objectives of the federal patent laws.

In the present case the "pole lamp" sold by Stiffel has been held not to be entitled to the protection of either a mechanical or a design patent. An unpatentable article, like an article on which the patent has expired, is in the public domain and may be made and sold by whoever chooses to do so. What Sears did was to copy Stiffel's design and to sell lamps almost identical to those sold by Stiffel. This it had every right to do under the federal patent laws. That Stiffel originated the pole lamp and made it popular is immaterial. "Sharing in the goodwill of an article unprotected by patent or trade-mark is the exercise of a right possessed by all—and in the free exercise of which the consuming public is deeply interested." *Kellogg Co. v. National Biscuit Co., supra*, 305 U.S. at 122. To allow a State by use of its law of unfair competition to prevent the copying of an article which represents too slight an advance to be patented would be to permit the State to block off from the public something which federal law has said belongs to the public. The result would be that while federal law grants only 14 or 17 years' protection to genuine inventions, *see* 35 U.S.C. §§ 154, 173, States could allow perpetual protection to articles too lacking in novelty to merit any patent at all under federal constitutional standards. This would be too great an encroachment on the federal patent system to be tolerated.

Sears has been held liable here for unfair competition because of a finding of likelihood of confusion based only on the fact that Sears' lamp was copied from Stiffel's unpatented lamp and that consequently the two looked exactly alike. Of course there could be "confusion" as to who had manufactured these nearly identical articles. But mere inability of the public to tell two identical articles apart is not enough to support an injunction against copying or an award of damages for copying that which the federal patent laws permit to be copied. Doubtless a State may, in appropriate circumstances, require that goods, whether patented or unpatented, be labeled or that other precautionary steps be taken to prevent customers from being misled as to the source, just as it may protect businesses in the use of their trademarks, labels, or distinctive dress in the packaging of goods so as to prevent others, by imitating such markings, from misleading purchasers as to the source of the goods. But because of the federal patent laws a State may not, when the article is unpatented and uncopyrighted, prohibit the copying of the article itself or award damages for such copying. *Cf. G. Ricordi & Co. v. Haendler*, 194 F.2d 914, 916 (2d Cir. 1952). The judgment below did both and in so doing gave Stiffel the equivalent of a patent monopoly on its unpatented lamp. That was error, and Sears is entitled to a judgment in its favor.

Reversed.

Compco Corp. v. Day-Brite Lighting, Inc., 376 U.S. 234 (1964). In this companion case to *Sears, Roebuck v. Stiffel Lamp*, plaintiff's product, also a lighting fixture, had received a design patent, which a court subsequently invalidated. In holding the state unfair competition claim preempted, the Court stated:

> Here Day-Brite's fixture has been held not to be entitled to a design or mechanical patent. Under the federal patent laws it is, therefore, in the public domain and can be copied in every detail by whoever pleases. It is true that the trial court found that the configuration of Day-Brite's fixture identified Day-Brite to the trade because the arrangement of the ribbing had, like a trademark, acquired a "secondary meaning" by which that particular design was associated with Day-Brite. But if the design is not entitled to a design patent or other federal statutory protection, then it can be copied at will.
>
> As we have said in *Sears*, while the federal patent laws prevent a State from prohibiting the copying and selling of unpatented articles, they do not stand in the way of state law, statutory or decisional, which requires those who make and sell copies to take precautions to identify their products as their own. A State of course has power to impose liability upon those who, knowing that the public is relying upon an original manufacturer's reputation for quality and integrity, deceive the public by palming off their copies as the original. That an article copied from an unpatented article could be made in some other way, that the design is "nonfunctional" and not essential to the use of either article, that the configuration of the article copied may have a "secondary meaning" which identifies the maker to the trade, or that there may be "confusion" among purchasers as to which article is which or as to who is the maker, may be relevant evidence in applying a State's law requiring such precautions as labeling; however, and regardless of the copier's motives, neither these facts nor any others can furnish a basis for imposing liability for or prohibiting the actual acts of copying and selling. [Citation.]

Question

Is the conflict articulated in *Sears* and *Compco* "constitutional" or "statutory," i.e., was state unfair competition law found to conflict with the Patent and Copyright Clause of the federal Constitution, or with the federal patent law? What is the consequence of the distinction?

Bonito Boats v. Thunder Craft Boats

489 U.S. 141 (1989)

[Plaintiff, a boat manufacturer, sought to enjoin defendant's use of a "direct molding process" to duplicate the design of plaintiff's unpatented boat hulls. Plaintiff invoked a Florida statute that made "[i]t ... unlawful for any person to use the direct molding process to duplicate for the purpose of sale any manufactured vessel hull or component part of a vessel made by another without the written permission of that other person." Fla. Stat. § 559.94(2) (1987). The statute also made it unlawful for a person to "knowingly sell a vessel duplicated in violation of subsection (2)." The Florida Supreme Court held that the statute conflicted with the federal patent law and was therefore invalid under the Supremacy Clause of the Federal Constitution. The Supreme Court affirmed.]

Justice O'Connor delivered the opinion for a unanimous Court:

[The federal patent law requires a] backdrop of free competition in the exploitation of unpatented designs and innovations. The novelty and nonobviousness requirements of patentability embody a congressional understanding, implicit in the Patent Clause itself, that free exploitation of ideas will be the rule, to which the protection of a federal patent is the exception. Moreover, the ultimate goal of the patent system is to bring new designs and technologies into the public domain through disclosure. State law protection for techniques and designs whose disclosure has already been induced by market rewards may conflict with the very purpose of the patent laws by decreasing the range of ideas available as the building blocks of further innovation. The offer of federal protection from competitive exploitation of intellectual property would be rendered meaningless in a world where substantially similar state law protections were readily available. To a limited extent the federal patent laws must determine not only what is protected but also what is free for all to use. [Citation.]

Thus, our past decisions have made clear that state regulation of intellectual property must yield to the extent that it clashes with the balance struck by Congress in our patent laws. The tension between the desire to freely exploit the full potential of our inventive resources and the need to create an incentive to deploy those resources is constant. Where it is clear how the patent laws strike that balance in a particular circumstance, that is not a judgment the states may second guess....

....

We believe that the Florida statute at issue in this case so substantially impedes the public use of the otherwise unprotected design and utilitarian ideas embodied in unpatented boat hulls as to run afoul of the teaching of our decisions in *Sears*, [*Roebuck & Co. v. Stiffel Co.*, 376 U.S. 225 (1964),] and *Compco* [*Corp. v. Day-Brite Lighting, Inc.*, 376 U.S. 234 (1964)]. It is readily apparent that the Florida statute does not operate to prohibit "unfair competition" in the usual sense that the term is understood. The law of unfair competition has its roots in the common-law tort of deceit: its general concern is with protecting *consumers* from confusion as to source. While that concern may result in the creation of "quasi-property rights" in communicative symbols, the focus is on the protection of consumers, not the protection of producers as an incentive to product innovation....

With some notable exceptions, including the interpretation of the Illinois law of unfair competition at issue in *Sears* and *Compco, see Sears, supra*, at 227–28 n.2, the common-law tort of unfair competition has been limited to protection against copying of nonfunctional aspects of consumer products which have acquired secondary meaning such that they operate as a designation of source. [Citation.] The "protection" granted a particular design under the law of unfair competition is thus limited to one context where consumer confusion is likely to result; the design "idea" itself may be freely exploited in all other contexts.

In contrast to the operation of unfair competition law, the Florida statute is aimed directly at preventing the exploitation of the design and utilitarian conceptions embodied in the product itself.... Like the patentee, the beneficiary of the Florida statute may prevent a competitor from "making" the product in what is evidently the most efficient manner available and from "selling" the product when it is produced in that fashion. [Citation.] The Florida scheme offers this protection for an unlimited number of years to all boat hulls and their component parts, without regard to their ornamental or technological merit. Protection is available for subject matter for which patent protection has been denied or has expired, as well as for designs which have been freely revealed to the consuming public by their creators....

....

The Florida statute is aimed directly at the promotion of intellectual creation by substantially restricting the public's ability to exploit ideas that the patent system mandates shall be free for all to use. Like the interpretation of Illinois unfair competition law in *Sears* and *Compco*, the Florida statute represents a break with the tradition of peaceful coexistence between state market regulation and federal patent policy. The Florida law substantially restricts the public's ability to exploit an unpatented design in general circulation, raising the specter of state-created monopolies in a host of useful shapes and processes for which patent protection has been denied or is otherwise unobtainable. It thus enters a field of regulation which the patent laws have reserved to Congress. The patent statute's careful balance between public right and private monopoly to promote certain creative activity is a "scheme of federal regulation ... so pervasive as to make reasonable the inference that Congress left no room for the States to supplement it." *Rice v. Santa Fe Elevator Corp.*, 331 U.S. 218, 230 (1947).

Congress has considered extending various forms of limited protection to industrial design either through the copyright laws or by relaxing the restrictions on the availability of design patents. *See generally* Brown, *Design Protection: An Overview*, 34 UCLA L. Rev. 1341 (1987). Congress explicitly refused to take this step in the copyright laws, *see* 17 U.S.C. § 101; H. R. Rep. No. 94-1476, p. 55 (1976), and despite sustained criticism for a number of years, it has declined to alter the patent protections presently available for industrial design. [Citations.] It is for Congress to determine if the present system of design and utility patents is ineffectual in promoting the useful arts in the context of industrial design. By offering patent-like protection for ideas deemed unprotected under the present federal scheme, the Florida statute conflicts with the "strong federal policy favoring free competition in ideas which do not merit patent protection." *Lear, Inc.* [*v. Adkins*, 395 U.S. 653 (1969)], at 656. We therefore agree with the majority of the Florida Supreme Court that the Florida statute is preempted by the Supremacy Clause, and the judgment of that court is hereby affirmed.

It is so ordered.

Questions

1. Could a federal statute validly prohibit the copying of boat hulls and other unpatented utilitarian designs? *Cf.* 17 U.S.C. §§ 1301–1322 (Protection of Original Designs). Could such a law prohibit copying of designs that had been protected by a now-expired utility patent? *See TrafFix Devices v. Marketing Displays*, 532 U.S. 23 (2001), *infra* Chapter 2[A].

2. Is it "unfair competition" to list as a work's author a person who did not in fact write the book? For example, for an unknown writer of thrillers to present her work as Stephen King's? Or to publish Stephen King's work under the unknown writer's name? Is it unfair competition for Stephen King to publish a ghost-written work under his name? Does it matter whether or not King's work is still protected by copyright? *See Dastar v. Twentieth Century Fox*, 539 U.S. 23 (2003), *infra* Chapter 7[C].

3. You are a federal judge called to decide a case presenting facts similar to those in *Cheney Bros. v. Doris Silk*. In light of *Bonito Boats*, what would you hold, and why?

National Basketball Association v. Motorola, 105 F.3d 841 (2d Cir. 1997). Plaintiff NBA attempted to prevent Motorola and Sports Team Analysis and Tracking Systems (STATS) from divulging the scores of ongoing basketball games to users of Motorola's SportsTrax paging device. Defendants did not divert broadcast or computer feeds from the NBA or its licensees; instead, STATS's own reporters watched the games on television or listened to them on the radio, and keyed the relevant information into personal computers relayed by modem to STATS's host computer, which retransmitted the information. The court held that the information at issue did not qualify as "hot news," and that any protection of the information beyond the limited "hot news" context would be preempted by the federal copyright act. The court detailed its understanding of "hot news":

> We hold that the surviving "hot-news" *INS*-like claim is limited to cases where: (i) a plaintiff generates or gathers information at a cost; (ii) the information is time-sensitive; (iii) a defendant's use of the information constitutes free-riding on the plaintiff's efforts; (iv) the defendant is in direct competition with a product or service offered by the plaintiffs; and (v) the ability of other parties to free-ride on the efforts of the plaintiff or others would so reduce the incentive to produce the product or service that its existence or quality would be substantially threatened.

The NBA met the first two elements of this five-part test, the Second Circuit held, and made a credible showing under the fourth that SportsTrax would compete with a new NBA-licensed service, "Gamestats," that in the future would offer pager access. But the NBA's failure under the third and fifth elements proved dispositive. Defendants did not free-ride, the court determined, because defendants do their own fact gathering, and "have their own network and assemble and transmit data themselves."

Questions

1. How narrow is the "hot news" *INS*-like claim that the Court of Appeals for the Second Circuit held survives federal preemption? What other fact patterns can you imagine that would fit the test articulated in *NBA v. Motorola*?

2. As readers and advertising dollars migrate to online publications, newspapers across the country are finding their previously profitable business models unsustainable and ceasing publication. Is the availability of a common law "hot news" misappropriation suit likely to help conventional news organizations stay in business?

Barclays Capital, Inc. v. Theflyonthewall.com

650 F.3d 876 (2d Cir. 2011)

[Theflyonthewall.com, Inc. ("Fly") is an Internet subscription news service that aggregates and publishes news for investors, including news, rumors, and research analysts' stock recommendations. Three financial services firms sued Fly for hot news misappropriation of facts and analyses from their research reports. The district court concluded that Fly was liable for "hot news" misappropriation under the *NBA v. Motorola* five-factor test. The court enjoined Fly from disseminating the Firms' daily recommendations until 30 minutes after the opening of the New York Stock Exchange, if the recommendation was released before the market opened, or two hours after release for recommendations issued after the market opened. Fly appealed, and the Court of Appeals for the Second Circuit reversed.]

We conclude that applying *NBA* and copyright preemption principles to the facts of this case, the Firms' claim for "hot news" misappropriation fails because it is preempted by the Copyright Act. First, the Firms' reports culminating with the Recommendations satisfy the "subject matter" requirement because they are all works "of a type covered by section[] 102," i.e., "original works of authorship fixed in a[] tangible medium of expression." 17 U.S.C. § 102.... Second, the reports together with the Recommendations fulfill the "general scope" requirement because the rights "'may be abridged by an act which, in and of itself, would infringe one of the exclusive rights' provided by federal copyright law," [citations].

Third and finally, the Firms' claim is not a so-called *INS*-type non-preempted claim because Fly is not, under *NBA*'s analysis, "free-riding." It is collecting, collating and disseminating factual information—the facts that Firms and others in the securities business have made recommendations with respect to the value of and the wisdom of purchasing or selling securities—and attributing the information to its source. The Firms are making the news; Fly, despite the Firms' understandable desire to protect their business model, is breaking it....

The use of the term "free-riding" in recent "hot news" misappropriation jurisprudence exacerbates difficulties in addressing these issues. Unfair use of another's "labor, skill, and money, and which is salable by complainant for money," *INS*, 248 U.S. at 239, sounds like the very essence of "free-riding," and, the term "free-riding" in turn seems clearly to connote acts that are quintessentially unfair.

It must be recalled, however, that the term free-riding refers explicitly to a requirement for a cause of action as described by *INS*. As explained by the *NBA* Court, "[a]n indispensable element of an *INS* 'hot news' claim is free-riding by a defendant on a plaintiff's product." *NBA*, 105 F.3d at 854.

The practice of what *NBA* referred to as "free-riding" was further described by *INS*. The *INS* Court defined the "hot news" tort in part as "taking material that has been acquired by complainant as the result of organization and the expenditure of labor, skill, and money, and which is salable by complainant for money, and ... appropriating it and selling it as [the defendant's] own...." *INS*, 248 U.S. at 239. That definition fits the facts of *INS*: The defendant was taking news gathered and in the process of dissemination by the Associated Press and selling that news as though the defendant itself had gathered it. But it does not describe the practices of Fly. The Firms here may be "acquiring material" in the course of preparing their reports, but that is not the focus of this lawsuit. In pressing a "hot news" claim against Fly, the Firms seek only to protect their Recommendations, something they create using their expertise and experience rather than acquire through efforts akin to reporting.

Moreover, Fly, having obtained news of a Recommendation, is hardly selling the Recommendation "as its own," *INS*, 248 U.S. at 239. It is selling the information with specific attribution to the issuing Firm. Indeed, for Fly to sell, for example, a Morgan Stanley Recommendation "as its own," as *INS* sold the news it cribbed from AP to INS subscribers, would be of little value to either Fly or its customers. If, for example, Morgan Stanley were to issue a Recommendation of Boeing common stock changing it from a "hold" to a "sell," it hardly seems likely that Fly would profit significantly from disseminating an item reporting that "Fly has changed its rating of Boeing from a hold to a sell." It is not the identity of Fly and its reputation as a financial analyst that carries the authority and weight sufficient to affect the market. It is Fly's accurate attribution of the Recommendation to the creator that gives this news its value.

....

We do not mean to be parsing the language of *INS* as though it were a statement of law the applicability of which determines the outcome of this appeal. As we have explained, the law that *INS* itself established was overruled many years ago. But in talking about a "'hot-news' *INS*-like claim," as we did in *NBA*, 105 F.3d at 845, or "the *INS* tort," as the district court did in this case, [citation], we are mindful that the *INS* Court's concern was tightly focused on the practices of the parties to the suit before it: news, data, and the like, gathered and disseminated by one organization as a significant part of its business, taken by another entity and published as the latter's own in competition with the former. The language chosen by the *INS* Court seems to us to make clear the substantial distance between that case and this one.

Here, like the defendants in *NBA* and unlike the defendant in *INS*, Fly "[has its] own network and assemble[s] and transmit[s] data [it]sel[f]." *NBA*, 105 F.3d at 854. In *NBA*, Motorola and STATS employees watched basketball games, compiled the statistics, scores, and other information from the games, and sold the resulting package of data to their subscribers. We could perceive no non-preempted "hot news" tort. Here, analogous to the defendant's in *NBA*, Fly's employees are engaged in the financial-industry equivalent of observing and summarizing facts about basketball games and selling those packaged facts to consumers; it is simply the content of the facts at issue that is different.

And, according to our decision in *NBA*: "An indispensable element of a [non-preempted] *INS* 'hot-news' claim is free-riding by a defendant on a plaintiff's product, enabling the defendant to produce a directly competitive product for less money because it has lower costs." *See id.* In *NBA*, we concluded that the defendant's SportsTrax service was not such a product, in part because it was "bearing [its] own costs of collecting factual information on NBA games." *Id.* In this case, as the district court found, approximately half of Fly's twenty-eight employees are involved in the collection of the Firms' Recommendations and production of the newsfeed on which summaries of the Recommendations are posted. [Citation.] Fly is reporting financial news—factual information on Firm Recommendations—through a substantial organizational effort. Therefore, Fly's service—which collects, summarizes, and disseminates the news of the Firms' Recommendations—is not the "*INS*-like" product that could support a non-preempted cause of action for misappropriation.

....

CONCLUSION

We conclude that in this case, a Firm's ability to make news—by issuing a Recommendation that is likely to affect the market price of a security—does not give rise to a right for it to control who breaks that news and how. We therefore reverse the judgment of the district court to that extent and remand with instructions to dismiss the Firms' misappropriation claim.

Raggi, J. concurring:

....

It bears noting that, like the district court, I view Fly's conduct as strong evidence of free-riding, or worse depending on how it came into possession of the Recommendations. Although Fly expends some effort to gather and aggregate the Recommendations, Fly is usurping the substantial efforts and expenses of the Firms to make a profit without expending any time or cost to conduct research of its own. I cannot celebrate such practices, which allow Fly "to reap where it has not sown." *INS*, 248 U.S. at 239. As the majority notes, however, such apparent unfairness does not control preemption analysis. Although Fly free-rides on the Firms' efforts, Fly's attribution of aggregate Recommendations demonstrates the crucial difference between the businesses: while the Firms disseminate only their own Recommendations to select clients most likely to follow the advice and place trades with the Firms, Fly aggregates and disseminates sixty-five firms' Recommendations and other financial information to anyone willing to pay for it without regard to whether clients accept or trade on particular Recommendations....

Questions

1. The majority and Judge Raggi disagree about whether Fly is free-riding, but agree that Barclay's misappropriation claim is preempted by the copyright law. What place should the defendant's free-riding have in analyzing whether a claim is preempted?

2. In The Knockoff Economy: How Imitation Sparks Innovation (2012), Professors Christopher Sprigman and Kai Raustiala present case studies of several creative fields in which copying is generally legal, yet creativity thrives. Sprigman and Raustiala examine copying in fashion, food, stand-up comedy, and football. They argue that industries can adapt to low-protection environments, and will often benefit from allowing widespread imitation. Should courts deciding unfair competition cases take these benefits into account?

B. Trademarks

Until the enactment of the Lanham Act in 1946, United States trademark law was primarily a common law creature. The common law mark was acquired by use. If you used "ACME" as a mark for cheese in Pittsburgh, you acquired common law rights in the mark ACME for cheese sold in Pittsburgh. If you expanded your sale of ACME cheese to Akron and then Cleveland, your trademark rights expanded along with your use. In the Nineteenth Century, as businesses expanded their geographic reach, they increasingly collided with other businesses that had common law rights in the same or similar trademarks. In 1870, as part of a wholesale overhaul of copyright and patent laws, Congress enacted a statute purporting to give federal trademark rights to individuals or corporations who registered their marks in the Patent Office. In 1879, the Supreme Court held that law unconstitutional.

Trade-Mark Cases

100 U.S. 82 (1879)

Mr. Justice Miller delivered the opinion of the court.

....

The entire legislation of Congress in regard to trade-marks is of very recent origin. It is first seen in sects. 77 to 84, inclusive, of the act of July 8, 1870, entitled "An Act to revise, consolidate, and amend the statutes relating to patents and copyrights." 16 Stat. 198. The part of this act relating to trade-marks is embodied in chap. 2, tit. 60, sects. 4937 to 4947, of the Revised Statutes.

It is sufficient at present to say that they provide for the registration in the Patent Office of any device in the nature of a trade-mark to which any person has by usage established an exclusive right, or which the person so registering intends to appropriate by that act to his exclusive use; and they make the wrongful use of a trade-mark, so registered, by any other person, without the owner's permission, a cause of action in a civil suit for damages. Six years later we have the act of Aug. 14, 1876 (19 Stat. 141), punishing by fine and imprisonment the fraudulent use, sale, and counterfeiting of Trademarks registered in pursuance of the statutes of the United States, on which the informations and indictments are founded in the cases before us.

The right to adopt and use a symbol or a device to distinguish the goods or property made or sold by the person whose mark it is, to the exclusion of use by all other persons, has been long recognized by the common law and the chancery courts of England and of this country, and by the statutes of some of the States. It is a property right for the violation of which damages may be recovered in an action at law, and the continued violation of it will be enjoined by a court of equity, with compensation for past infringement. This exclusive right was not created by the act of Congress, and does not now depend upon it for its enforcement. The whole system of trade-mark property and the civil remedies for its protection existed long anterior to that act, and have remained in full force since its passage.

These propositions are so well understood as to require neither the citation of authorities nor an elaborate argument to prove them.

As the property in trade-marks and the right to their exclusive use rest on the laws of the States, and, like the great body of the rights of person and of property, depend on them for security and protection, the power of Congress to legislate on the subject, to establish the conditions on which these rights shall be enjoyed and exercised, the period of their duration, and the legal remedies for their enforcement, if such power exist at all, must be found in the Constitution of the United States, which is the source of all the powers that Congress can lawfully exercise.

In the argument of these cases this seems to be conceded, and the advocates for the validity of the acts of Congress on this subject point to two clauses of the Constitution, in one or in both of which, as they assert, sufficient warrant may be found for this legislation.

The first of these is the eighth clause of sect. 8 of the first article. That section, manifestly intended to be an enumeration of the powers expressly granted to Congress, and closing with the declaration of a rule for the ascertainment of such powers as are necessary by way of implication to carry into efficient operation those expressly given, authorizes Congress, by the clause referred to, "to promote the progress of science and useful arts, by securing for limited times, to authors and inventors, the exclusive right to their respective writings and discoveries."

....

Any attempt, however, to identify the essential characteristics of a trade-mark with inventions and discoveries in the arts and sciences, or with the writings of authors, will show that the effort is surrounded with insurmountable difficulties.

The ordinary trade-mark has no necessary relation to invention or discovery. The trade-mark recognized by the common law is generally the growth of a considerable period of use, rather than a sudden invention. It is often the result of accident rather than design, and when under the act of Congress it is sought to establish it by registration, neither originality, invention, discovery, science, nor art is in any way essential to the right conferred by that act. If we should endeavor to classify it under the head of writings of authors, the objections are equally strong. In this, as in regard to inventions, originality is required. And while the word writings may be liberally construed, as it has been, to include original designs for engravings, prints, & c., it is only such as are original, and are founded in the creative powers of the mind. The writings which are to be protected are the fruits of intellectual labor, embodied in the form of books, prints, engravings and the like. The trade-mark may be, and generally is, the adoption of something already in existence as the distinctive symbol of the party using it. At common law the exclusive right to it grows out of its use, and not its mere adoption. By the act of Congress this exclusive right attaches upon registration. But in neither case does it depend upon novelty, invention, discovery, or any work of the brain. It requires no fancy or imagination, no genius, no laborious thought. It is simply founded on priority of appropriation. We look in vain in the statute for any other qualification or condition. If the symbol, however plain, simple, old, or well-known, has been first appropriated by the claimant as his distinctive trade-mark, he may by registration secure the right to its exclusive use. While such legislation may be a judicious aid to the common law on the subject of trade-marks, and may be within the competency of legislatures whose general powers embrace that class of subjects, we are unable to see any such power in the constitutional provision concerning authors and inventors, and their writings and discoveries.

The other clause of the Constitution supposed to confer the requisite authority on Congress is the third of the same section, which, read in connection with the granting clause, is as follows: "The Congress shall have power to regulate commerce with foreign nations, and among the several States, and with the Indian tribes."

The argument is that the use of a trade-mark—that which alone gives it any value—is to identify a particular class or quality of goods as the manufacture, produce, or property of the person who puts them in the general market for sale; that the sale of the article so distinguished is commerce; that the trade-mark is, therefore, a useful and valuable aid or instrument of commerce, and its regulation by virtue of the clause belongs to Congress, and that the act in question is a lawful exercise of this power.

Every species of property which is the subject of commerce, or which is used or even essential in commerce, is not brought by this clause within the control of Congress....

....

When, therefore, Congress undertakes to enact a law, which can only be valid as a regulation of commerce, it is reasonable to expect to find on the face of the law, or from its essential nature, that it is a regulation of commerce with foreign nations, or among the several States, or with the Indian tribes. If not so limited, it is in excess of the power of Congress. If its main purpose be to establish a regulation applicable to all trade, to commerce at all points, especially if it be apparent that it is designed to govern the commerce wholly between citizens of the same State, it is obviously the exercise of a power not confided to Congress.

We find no recognition of this principle in the chapter on trade-marks in the Revised Statutes.... If, for instance, the statute described persons engaged in a commerce between the different States, and related to the use of trade-marks in such commerce, it would be evident that Congress believed it was acting under the clause of the Constitution which authorizes it to regulate commerce among the States.... But no such idea is found or suggested in this statute....

It is therefore manifest that no such distinction is found in the act, but that its broad purpose was to establish a universal system of trade-mark registration, for the benefit of all who had already used a trade-mark, or who wished to adopt one in the future, without regard to the character of the trade to which it was to be applied or the residence of the owner, with the solitary exception that those who resided in foreign countries which extended no such privileges to us were excluded from them here.

....

The questions in each of these cases being an inquiry whether these statutes can be upheld in whole or in part as valid and constitutional, must be answered in the negative....

Questions

1. Does Justice Miller's analysis merely require Congress to identify the appropriate constitutional source for its authority to regulate trademarks, or does it place substantive limitations on the provisions of any trademark law Congress may enact? If it imposes substantive limitations, what are they?

2. Current views of the scope of Congress's Commerce Clause power are more expansive than the views articulated in Justice Miller's decision. If Congress sought today to reenact the trademark laws it adopted in 1870 and 1876, as described in the opinion, would the constitution as it is currently understood pose any obstacle?

After the *Trade-Mark Cases*, Congress enacted a series of trademark registration statutes based on its Commerce Clause authority. Following the First World War, the trademark bar began efforts to draft a comprehensive federal trademark statute that would pass constitutional muster. See Edward S. Rogers, *The Lanham Act and the Social Function of Trademarks*, 14 L. & Contemp. Probs. 173, 177–84 (Spring 1949). It was not until 1946 that Congress finally enacted the Lanham Trademark Protection Act, which drew many of its substantive rules from years of common law trademark decisions. Twenty-first century trademark law in the United States still bears many signs of its common law origins.

William M. Borchard, *A Trademark Is Not a Copyright or a Patent*

(2016) (excerpts)*

Although trademarks, copyrights, patents, and trade secrets all concern intangible property rights and overlap to some extent, they differ from each other significantly.... It may help to distinguish them by remembering that:

- Trademarks protect source identifications (marks of trade);
- Copyrights protect original creative expressions;
- Patents protect new and useful inventions; and
- Trade Secrets protect valuable secret information.

....

While originally part of the radiator cap, the Rolls-Royce "Flying Lady" mascot hood ornament has features suitable for simultaneous protection as a registered trademark, a copyrighted sculptural work and a patented design.

What is a Trademark?

A **trademark** is a brand name, logo or package design, or a combination of them, used by a manufacturer or merchant to identify its goods or services and distinguish them from others. Trademarks include **brand names** identifying goods (*Dole* for canned pineapple) and **trade dress** consisting of the graphics, color or shape of packaging or, after sufficient use, of goods (*Coca-Cola Bottle* for a soft drink); **service marks** identifying services (*McDonald's* for a restaurant service); **certification marks** identifying goods or services meeting specified qualifications (*Woolmark* for apparel made of 100% wool); and **collective marks** identifying goods, services or members of a collective organization (*The International Game Fish Association* for a game fishing organization). The same legal principles generally apply to all of these terms, often simply called "marks."

....

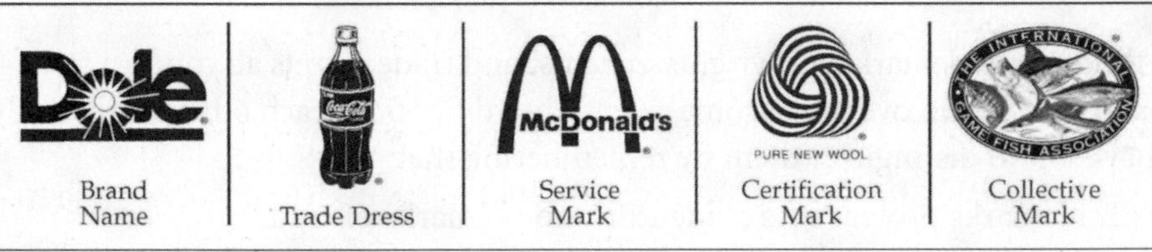

What is a Copyright?

A copyright seeks to promote literary and artistic creativity by protecting, for a limited time, what the U.S. Constitution broadly calls the "writings" of "authors." Copyrightable works include:

- literary, musical and dramatic works;
- pantomimes and choreographic works;
- pictorial, graphic and sculptural works (including the nonutilitarian design features of useful articles);
- motion pictures and other audiovisual works;
- sound recordings;
- computer programs;
- certain architectural works; and
- compilations of works and derivative works.

Copyright only protects particular expressions of ideas, not the ideas themselves. And a protectible work must be "original," i.e., not copied from another source (although two separately protectible works theoretically could be identical by coincidence). The work also must not be so elementary that it lacks sufficient creativity to be copyrightable (such as a common shape or a short phrase).

Copyright owner's rights.

The creator basically has the exclusive rights to reproduce the work, to distribute the reproductions, to display and perform the work publicly, to make derivative works, and to authorize others to do any of these things. The creator of certain works of fine art also may have rights to control their attribution or modification. The performance right in a sound recording is limited to digital transmissions, such as webcasting, with lower royalty rates for small webcasters.

....

What is a Patent?

A patent gives the patentee (patent owner) the right to exclude others from making, using, offering for sale or selling an invention within the U.S. or importing it into the U.S. It does not carry the affirmative right to make, use, sell or offer an item covered by the patent since one or more other patents may cover aspects of the same invention.

You can obtain a **utility patent** for the following statutory classes of new and useful inventions:

- processes (a chemical, mechanical or electrical procedure, such as a method for refining petroleum; or a business method of processing or displaying data or making calculations if it uses computer assisted implementation or it physically transforms an article and is not directed to a law of nature, physical phenomena or an abstract idea);
- machines (mechanisms with moving or interactive parts, such as a motor or computer system);
- articles of manufacture (man-made products, such as a hand tool); and
- compositions of matter (chemical compounds, combinations or mixtures, such as a plastic).

In addition, you can obtain a **design patent** for a new original and ornamental design for an article of manufacture, and a **plant patent** for a new variety of seed or plant or any of its parts....

Whether an invention is made by a flash of genius or painstaking research, to be patentable it also must meet all of the following hard-to-satisfy criteria:

- "novelty" in that it was neither previously known to the public, nor in public use, nor patented, nor described in a printed publication, anywhere;
- "non-obviousness" to a person having ordinary skill in the relevant art; and
- "utility" in that it has a useful purpose, actually works, and is not frivolous or immoral....

....

Summary Table

	Trademarks	Copyrights	Patents
Nature	Commercial identifications of source such as words, designs, slogans, symbols, trade dress.	Original literary and artistic expressions such as books, paintings, music, records, plays, movies, software.	New and useful inventions and configurations of useful articles.
Scope	Protects against creating a likelihood of confusion; or diluting a famous mark.	Protects against unauthorized use or copying.	Excludes others from making, using, offering for sale or selling the invention in the U.S. or by importation into the U.S.
Purpose	Protects owners and public from unfair competition.	Encourages and rewards creative expression.	Encourages and rewards innovation.
How to Obtain Rights	Use mark in commerce or apply for federal registration.	Create work and fix it in tangible form. Registration confirms rights.	Invent first and apply for federal grant. (After March 16, 2013 be first-inventor-to-file.)
Principal Advantages of Registration	Nationwide priority rights; possibly conclusive evidence of validity and ownership; U.S. Customs and Border Protection recordation; increased anti-counterfeiting remedies.	Statutory damages and attorney's fees; prima facie evidence of validity; U.S. Customs and Border Protection recordation.	Protection for non-secret inventions. May complement know-how that is a trade secret.
Basis for Registration	(1) Bona fide intention to use in commerce followed by actual use; (2) Non-U.S. owner's country of origin registration or application filed within 6 months prior to U.S. application, or extension to the U.S. of international registration, plus bona fide intention to use in commerce; or (3) Actual use in commerce.	Originality.	Novelty, non-obviousness, utility.
Notice Requirements	Optional. "TM" or "SM" if unregistered; "®" or "Reg. U.S. Pat. & Tm. Off." if registered.	Optional after March 1, 1989. © or "Copyright" with year of first publication and name of owner.	Optional. "Patent applied for" or "Pat. Pending" after application; "Patent" or "Pat." plus registration number, or website reference, after grant.
Term of Rights	As long as used; registrations must be maintained by filing use declaration before the 6th and each 10th anniversary and by renewing before each 10th anniversary (plus 6 month grace period for each filing).	Creations after January 1, 1978: author's lifetime plus 70 years, or if anonymous or work made for hire, earlier of 95 years from publication or 120 years from creation.	20 years from filing date (or sometimes 17 years from grant) for utility or plant patents, subject to periodic maintenance fees; 14 years from registration for design patents.
Infringement Prerequisites	Registration optional.	Registration required for U.S. nationals; optional for foreign nationals.	Issued patent required.
Infringement Standard	Likelihood of confusion, mistake or deception as to source or sponsorship; or dilution by blurring or tarnishment.	Unauthorized use or copying (access plus substantial similarity).	Unauthorized manufacture, use, sale, or offer for sale of devices or processes embodying the invention.
International Protection	(1) Individual countries or regions; (2) Community Trade Mark registration; or (3) Madrid Protocol centralized filing.	Usually protected without registration through international treaties.	Usually granted on a country-by-country basis with centralized filing available under the Patent Cooperation Treaty or European Patent Convention.

This summary is highly simplified and should only be used for a general comparison. •

Hanover Star Milling Co. v. Metcalf

240 U.S. 403 (1916)

[Petitioner and Respondent independently adopted the brand "Tea Rose" for flour in the 1880s. Both printed the brand name and a rose design on their flour sacks and barrels. When one of the manufacturers sold flour to a retailer in the other's geographic region, each of them filed a trademark suit seeking to enjoin the sale of the other's flour.]

Mr. Justice Pitney delivered the opinion of the Court:

....

The redress that is accorded in trademark cases is based upon the party's right to be protected in the goodwill of a trade or business. The primary and proper function of a trademark is to identify the origin or ownership of the article to which it is affixed. Where a party has been in the habit of labeling his goods with a distinctive mark, so that purchasers recognize goods thus marked as being of his production, others are debarred from applying the same mark to goods of the same description, because to do so would in effect represent their goods to be of his production and would tend to deprive him of the profit he might make through the sale of the goods which the purchaser intended to buy. Courts afford redress or relief upon the ground that a party has a valuable interest in the goodwill of his trade or business, and in the trademarks adopted to maintain and extend it. The essence of the wrong consists in the sale of the goods of one manufacturer or vendor for those of another. *Canal Co. v. Clark*, 13 Wall. 311, 322; *McLean v. Fleming*, 96 U.S. 245, 251; *Manufacturing Co. v. Trainer*, 101 U.S. 51, 53; *Menendez v. Holt*, 128 U.S. 514, 520; *Lawrence Mfg. Co. v. Tennessee Mfg. Co.*, 138 U.S. 537, 546.

This essential element is the same in trademark cases as in cases of unfair competition unaccompanied with trademark infringement. In fact, the common law of trademarks is but a part of the broader law of unfair competition. *Elgin Watch Co. v. Illinois Watch Co.*, 179 U.S. 665, 674; *G. & C. Merriam Co. v. Saalfield*, 198 Fed. Rep. 369, 372; *Cohen v. Nagle*, 190 Massachusetts, 4, 8, 15; 5 A. & E. Ann. Cas. 553, 555, 558.

Common-law trademarks, and the right to their exclusive use, are of course to be classed among property rights, *Trademark Cases*, 100 U.S. 82, 92, 93; but only in the sense that a man's right to the continued enjoyment of his trade reputation and the goodwill that flows from it, free from unwarranted interference by others, is a property right, for the protection of which a trademark is an instrumentality. As was said in the same case (p. 94), the right grows out of use, not mere adoption. In the English courts it often has been said that there is no property whatever in a trademark, as such. [Citations.] But since in the same cases the courts recognized the right of the party to the exclusive use of marks adopted to indicate goods of his manufacture, upon the ground that "[a] man is not to sell his own goods under the pretense that they are the goods of another man; he cannot be permitted to practise such a deception, nor to use the means which contribute to that end. He cannot therefore be allowed to use names, marks, letters, or other *indicia*, by which he may induce purchasers to believe, that the goods which he is selling are the manufacture of another person" [citation]; it is plain that in denying the right of property in a trademark it was intended only to deny such property right except as appurtenant to an established business or trade in connection with which the mark is used. This is evident from the expressions used in these and other English cases. Thus, in *Ainsworth v. Walmsley*,

L.R. 1 Eq. Cas. 518, 524, Vice Chancellor Sir Wm. Page Wood said: "This court has taken upon itself to protect a man in the use of a certain trademark as applied to a particular description of article. He has no property in that mark *per se*, any more than in any other fanciful denomination he may assume for his own private use, otherwise than with reference to his trade. If he does not carry on a trade in iron, but carries on a trade in linen, and stamps a lion on his linen, another person may stamp a lion on iron; but when he has appropriated a mark to a particular species of goods, and caused his goods to circulate with this mark upon them, the court has said that no one shall be at liberty to defraud that man by using that mark, and passing off goods of his manufacture as being the goods of the owner of that mark."

In short, the trademark is treated as merely a protection for the goodwill, and not the subject of property except in connection with an existing business. The same rule prevails generally in this country, and is recognized in the decisions of this court already cited. [Citations.]

Stork Restaurant, Inc. v. Sahati

166 F.2d 348 (9th Cir. 1948)

Garrecht, Circuit Judge.

The appellant seeks to enjoin the appellees from using its trade name, "The Stork Club," and its insigne, consisting of a stork standing on one leg and wearing a high hat and a monocle. The complaint likewise asked for damages in the sum of $5,000, but that prayer was waived.

The court below entered judgment denying injunctive relief. From that judgment the present appeal has been taken.

1. The Facts

....

The appellant owns and operates a cafe and night club at No. 3 East 53d Street, New York, N.Y., known as "The Stork Club," described in a newsreel as "the best and most publicized night club in the entire world." The name had been used in New York by the appellant's two predecessor corporations since 1929.

As found by the court below, the appellant has been operating that establishment since on or about August 15, 1934. The cafe supplies "expensive food, beverages, music and dancing facilities," employs approximately 240 persons, and yields an average annual gross income of more than $1,000,000.

The appellant has spent more than $700,000 during the past eleven years in advertising on a nation-wide scale. This advertising was conducted through various media, including radio, newspapers, magazines, books, motion pictures, and established mailing lists. Another form of the publicity technique used by the appellant has been "cash advertising"—gifts to customers which included automobiles, 400 radios, one of which is an exhibit in this case; thousand dollar bills, none of which are exhibits here; five hundred dollar bottles of perfume; and "thousands" of thirty-five dollar bottles of perfume. Still another form of promotion has been "house advertising"—food and liquor given away to newspaper people, to radio, stage, and screen celebrities, and to "men in prominent and public life in the industrial world."

Newspapers throughout the country publish articles and photographs relating to the Stork Club. Many of America's leading syndicate writers mention it in their columns. Articles and advertisements relating to it appear in magazines of national circulation, and books have been written about it.

The club has been mentioned in many national hook-up radio programs, such as those of Bing Crosby, Frank Sinatra, Eddie Cantor, Walter Winchell, Jack Benny, Jimmy Durante, and Fred Allen.

A motion picture entitled "The Stork Club," produced by Paramount Pictures at a cost of nearly $1,700,000 and starring Betty Hutton and Barry Fitzgerald, was given 14,457 exhibitions throughout the United States, during a run of fifty-nine weeks, at a rental of $3,018,676.26. In northern California and adjacent territory, that picture was given 532 showings, during a run of sixty weeks, at a rental of $126,588.89. And in San Francisco alone, during a ten-day run at the Fox Theater, it was viewed by 83,729 persons. According to the deposition of George A. Smith, western sales manager for Paramount, one of the reasons for popularity of the picture was that "it had a very salable title, the popularity of the Stork Club was spread all over the United States." The Stork Club was paid $27,500 for the use of its name. Pathe News and "March of Time" have shown scenes from the Stork Club.

....

[The court below found that] on or about April 6, 1945, the appellees "began the operation of, and continuously since that date have been operating and conducting a small bar, tavern and cocktail lounge at No. 200 Hyde Street, in * * * San Francisco * * * under the name of 'Stork Club' * * *." In another finding, the court indicated that a predecessor of the appellees had used the name at that location since March 1, 1943. The establishment has about ten stools at the bar, and will accommodate about fifty persons. It has about four steady employees, and serves only such food as is necessary to "conform with the law regulating the operation of bars." There are a few tables. There is no dancing, although the match pads distributed by the appellee for advertising purposes depict a dancing couple.

The appellees had a pianist "at one time," and when they "took over from the previous ownership there was a three-piece orchestra that they had on their payroll for probably two years." This orchestra continued with the appellees for about a month after the latter took over. The appellees have displayed a panel, suspended from the marquee and extending all around its three sides, with the word "Entertainment" emblazoned on each of the three sides. Napkins used in the appellee's establishment carried the picture of a stork standing on one leg and wearing a high hat, with the legend, "Stork Club * * * Finest Liquors. Expertly Blended Entertainment (sic)." Nicholas M. Sahati, one of the appellees, testified in this connection: "There might have been a few leftover napkins that the former owners had in the place when we took over, with the picture of a stork, which we used up, but never did order any napkins of that type. * * * I couldn't say exactly, maybe a few dozen. * * * There might have been a larger quantity; I have no method of knowing."

....

10. "Confusion of Source."

We reach now what is perhaps the controlling principle in the instant case—that of "confusion of source," with its corollary, "dilution of good-will." ...

In a situation where there is no direct competition between the parties, confusion of source may be defined as a misleading of the public by the imitation of "An attractive, reputable trade-mark or trade-name * * * not for the purpose of diverting trade from the person having the trade-mark or trade name to the imitator, but rather for the purpose of securing for the imitator's goods some of the good-will, advertising and sales stimulation of the trade-mark or trade name." Restatement, *id.*, at page 597.

> "One's interest in a trade-mark or trade name came to be protected, therefore, not only on competing goods, but on goods so related in the market to those on which the trade-mark or trade name is used that the good or ill repute of the one type of goods is likely to be visited upon the other. Thus one's interest in a trade-mark or trade name is protected against being subjected to the hazards of another's business." Restatement, *id.*, at pages 597–598.

The doctrine is well recognized in California. In [*Academy of Motion Picture Arts and Sciences v. Benson*, 15 Cal.2d 685, 689], the Supreme Court of the State said: "The decisions of the courts for the most part are concerned with the principle's application in respect to businesses which are directly competitive. But we perceive no distinction which, as a matter of law, should be made because of the fact that the plaintiff and the defendant are engaged in non-competing businesses..."

Again, in *Winfield v. Charles*, 77 Cal.App.2d 64, 70, the court reached the very heart of the problem when it observed: "Plaintiff has established a reputation for reliability and meritorious products. If articles which are not produced by him are attributed to him or associated with his name, the injury is obvious."

The rule has been repeatedly expounded by this and other Federal courts.

(a) "Reaping Where One Has Not Sown."

The decisions frequently refer to this sort of imitation as "reaping where one has not sown" or as "riding the coat-tails" of a senior appropriator of a trade name.

By whatever name it is called, equity frowns upon such business methods, and in proper cases will grant an injunction to the rightful user of the trade name.

....

(c) Mere Geographical Distance Does Not Obviate Danger of Confusion

The court found that, because of its business methods and its extensive publicity, the appellant's establishment, "conducted and operated under the name 'The Stork Club' and with the aforesaid insignia used in conjunction therewith, beca[me] and now is known to many persons in and about * * * San Francisco, * * * as a club in New York;" and that it "is patronized by visitors to New York * * * from * * * the metropolitan area of San Francisco * * *."

In these days of chain restaurants, one would not have to be uncommonly naive to assume that even a "humble" cafe at Turk and Hyde Streets, San Francisco, might be an unpretentious branch of a glittering New York night spot. A branch unit is usually less elaborate and impressive than the "mother house." As we shall see in a moment, however, equity will protect even the uncommonly naive against deception from unfair competition.

In any event, mere geographical distance is not of itself sufficient to preclude the possibility that a given establishment is a branch of an enterprise having its principal place of business elsewhere.

....

(d) As to False Statements Obviously False

During the oral argument, it was suggested that any one driving by an unpretentious night club displaying the sign "Stork Club" in or near San Francisco, would hardly assume that the place was in any way affiliated with the celebrated New York establishment. It may well be true that a prudent and worldly-wise passerby would not be so deceived. The law, however, protects not only the intelligent, the experienced, and the astute. It safeguards from deception also the ignorant, the inexperienced, and the gullible.

That is the teaching of the Supreme Court of the United States, and it has been followed in this and in other circuits.

....

11. Actual Loss of Trade Need Not be Shown to Warrant an Injunction.

The appellees stress the fact that the appellant has failed to show "that appellees' operation in any way has injured appellant," etc.

Neither under the California jurisprudence nor under the general law is such showing necessary. The California decisions, indeed, are overwhelmingly in accord on this point.

....

[I]n the recent case of *Winfield v. Charles, supra*, 77 Cal.App.2d at page 70, 175 P.2d at page 73, we find the following succinct statement: "It is unnecessary, in such an action, to show that any person has been confused or deceived. It is the likelihood of deception which the remedy may be invoked to prevent."

This is undoubtedly the Federal rule. In *Adolph Kastor & Bros. v. Federal Trade Commission*, 2 Cir., 138 F.2d 824, 826, the court thus summarized the doctrine: "No one need expose his reputation to the trade practices of another, even though he can show no pecuniary loss."

....

16. Conclusion

....

The appellant is not here seeking to have the appellees mulcted in damages, nor is it striving to drive them out of business. It asks merely that its adversaries be compelled to desist from an unfair trade practice that threatens to "nibble away," "whittle away," or "dilute" the value of its dearly-bought prestige.

The appellant begs that the appellees, with an "infinity" of other names to choose from, divest themselves of plumage borrowed from the Stork.

In a word, the appellant is making a plea peculiarly calculated to move the conscience of a chancellor. It prays not for a sword, but for a shield.

The judgment is reversed, and the case is remanded to the lower court, with directions to grant to the appellant an injunction as prayed for in the complaint.

Questions

1. In what sense are consumers likely to be confused about the "source" of defendant's Stork Club?

2. If a company named its diaper service "The Stork Club," would plaintiff be entitled to force it to choose a different name? If not, why not?

Robert G. Bone, *Hunting Goodwill: A History of the Concept of Goodwill in Trademark Law*

86 B.U. L. Rev. 547 (2006) [excerpt]*

....

It is customary to refer to trademark law as protecting a seller's goodwill in its mark. This familiar and well-accepted proposition has been part of the law since the latter half of the nineteenth century. There is, however, a serious problem with this proposition. Characterizing trademark law in terms of goodwill protection ultimately conflicts with the well-recognized consumer-oriented goals of trademark law. The

* Copyright 2006. Reprinted by permission. [*Footnotes omitted—Eds.*]

resulting conflict frustrates efforts to achieve doctrinal coherence, misleads judges, and pushes trademark law in troubling directions....

The core of trademark law, as it is understood today, is based on a model which I shall call the "information transmission model." This model views trademarks as devices for communicating information to the market and sees the goal of trademark law as preventing others from using similar marks to deceive or confuse consumers.

The idea of protecting goodwill fits this model rather poorly. Goodwill protection has nothing directly to do with facilitating consumer choice or safeguarding the quality of market information. It has to do instead with protecting sellers from misappropriation. Goodwill on this view denotes the special value that attaches to a mark when the seller's advertising and investments in quality generate consumer loyalty—a capacity to attract consumers over time. Trademarks are repositories or symbols of this goodwill, and trademark law prevents others from appropriating it by using a similar mark.

Put simply, the information transmission model aims to prevent misleading representations, while the misappropriation model aims to prevent unauthorized appropriations. In fact, the information transmission model has no need for the idea of goodwill at all. It is concerned solely with the quality of market information, whether or not that information has crystallized into something called goodwill.

Given this, it seems strange that judges implementing an information transmission model would even mention goodwill protection as a goal, let alone invoke misappropriation arguments to justify liability expansions. Yet that is exactly what they have done. And the result is an internally inconsistent body of law that resists efforts to achieve doctrinal coherence.

....

A. Flaws in the Moral Argument

The moral argument for misappropriation-based liability assumes that it is morally wrong to free ride on goodwill. The question is why. One might answer that free riding involves taking goodwill that belongs to the trademark owner, but that answer only invites another question: why does goodwill "belong to" the trademark owner as opposed to, say, everyone in common? One possible answer to this second question is that the trademark owner is the one who invested in creating the goodwill. This invokes the familiar Lockean labor-desert theory of natural property rights that recognizes a natural right to control the fruits of one's own labor.

However, as the legal realists recognized in the 1930s and too many judges have forgotten today, the labor-desert argument proves too much. It would condemn all competition as morally wrong because all competition involves taking customers from a competitor and thus taking value that the competitor has created through its investment in product quality and marketing. Suppose that A invents the food processor and starts selling its own brand. A's early advertising and promotion efforts build brand goodwill in A's food processor and also product goodwill in the food processor as a new kitchen device. When a second firm, B, enters the food processor market with its own brand, it necessarily benefits from the product goodwill that A has created. Yet B's free ride is encouraged and certainly not condemned as unfair.

One might try to defend the moral argument on the ground that the unfairness inheres in the defendant's motive or reason for acting. In my food processor example, B had a legitimate reason to take product goodwill; it was essential for B to compete in the food processor market. Perhaps the cases where free riding is condemned are those in which the defendant has no legitimate reason.

This argument, however, fares no better than the previous one. First, it is circular because an intent to free ride can make free riding morally wrongful only if free riding is already deemed to be morally wrong. Second, it is incorrect to suppose that defendants in trademark cases want only to profit from the plaintiff's goodwill. They also want to communicate the information that the mark conveys. As long as consumers are not confused or misled—so the information that the defendant communicates is accurate—using the plaintiff's mark saves social resources that would otherwise have to be invested in building the same meanings into a different mark. For example, a firm that uses TIFFANY as a mark for luxury cars communicates the message of luxury and high quality without spending the resources necessary to build the same message into a different mark.

Perhaps the crux of the moral problem instead lies in the fact that the defendant benefits without contributing. The focus here is not on who owns goodwill or why the defendant takes it, but instead on the asymmetry of benefit and burden. However, this variation on the argument makes no more sense than the others. Free riding is about benefiting without being burdened and free riding can be morally acceptable, as in the food processor example. Moreover, there is often benefit-burden reciprocity in trademark cases. When the defendant sells quality products and promotes those products with the same mark, it adds to the goodwill value of the mark, which confers a reciprocal benefit on the plaintiff.

B. Flaws in the Economic Argument

The economic argument for condemning goodwill appropriation is based on incentives: the assumption is that a firm will invest optimally in producing goodwill when it expects to be able to capture all the benefits. However, this argument fares no better than the moral argument in justifying a blanket prohibition on free riding.

First, an economic incentive analysis does not, in fact, support giving a firm the right to capture all the benefits of a socially desirable activity; it only supports a right to capture enough of the benefits to cover the costs of engaging in the activity. Second, it is difficult to see how the incentive argument can justify broad expansions of trademark law. For example, it seems implausible that letting Tiffany & Company capture the goodwill value of its TIFFANY mark in the automobile market will cause it to invest significantly more than it otherwise would in the jewelry market with greater benefits in terms of reduced search costs for jewelry customers.

Third, and perhaps most important, there are social costs to allowing a firm to monopolize a mark on a broad misappropriation principle. In the merchandising rights cases, for example, the trademark owner can charge a higher than competitive price with resulting deadweight loss. In other cases, trademark protection can burden First Amendment values and generate enforcement and rent-seeking costs, as well as interfere with the proper operation of the patent and copyright statutes. All of these social costs must be balanced against the social benefits.

....

In sum, my general point is quite simple: there is no economic justification for a general rule, principle, or presumption prohibiting free riding on goodwill.... [I]t is not the taking of a firm's goodwill that is problematic from an economic point of view. What is problematic is the adverse effect on the mark's capacity to communicate information to the market. One must balance this cost against the benefit of allowing the use, and the legal rights that result will necessarily be more limited than those misappropriation alone would justify.

Questions

1. Does the analysis in the *Stork Club* case derive from what Bone characterizes as an "information transmission" model or a "protection of goodwill" model?

2. If Bone is correct that a misappropriation model of trademark infringement makes neither moral nor economic sense, what accounts for its persuasiveness to courts?

Champion Spark Plug Co. v. Sanders

331 U.S. 125 (1947)

Opinion of the Court by Mr. Justice Douglas, announced by Mr. Justice Black:

Petitioner is a manufacturer of spark plugs which it sells under the trade mark "Champion." Respondents collect the used plugs, repair and recondition them, and resell them. Respondents retain the word "Champion" on the repaired or reconditioned plugs. The outside box or carton in which the plugs are packed has stamped on it the word "Champion," together with the letter and figure denoting the particular style or type. They also have printed on them "Perfect Process Spark Plugs Guaranteed Dependable" and "Perfect Process Renewed Spark Plugs." Each carton contains smaller boxes in which the plugs are individually packed. These inside boxes also carry legends indicating that the plug has been renewed. But respondent company's business name or address is not printed on the cartons. It supplies customers with petitioner's charts containing recommendations for the use of Champion plugs. On each individual plug is stamped in small letters, blue on black, the word "Renewed," which at times is almost illegible.

Petitioner brought this suit in the District Court, charging infringement of its trade mark and unfair competition. [Citation.] The District Court found that respondents had infringed the trade mark. It enjoined them from offering or selling any of petitioner's plugs which had been repaired or reconditioned unless (a) the trade mark and type and style marks were removed, (b) the plugs were repainted with a durable grey, brown, orange, or green paint, (c) the word "REPAIRED" was stamped into the plug in letters of such size and depth as to retain enough white paint to display distinctly each letter of the word, (d) the cartons in which the plugs were packed carried a legend indicating that they contained used spark plugs originally made by petitioner and repaired and made fit for use up to 10,000 miles by respondent company. The District Court denied an accounting. [Citation.]

The Circuit Court of Appeals held that respondents not only had infringed petitioner's trade mark but also were guilty of unfair competition. It likewise denied an accounting but modified the decree in the following respects: (a) it eliminated the provision requiring the trade mark and type and style marks to be removed from the repaired or reconditioned plugs; (b) it substituted for the requirement that the word "REPAIRED" be stamped into the plug, etc., a provision that the word "REPAIRED" or "USED" be stamped and baked on the plug by an electrical hot press in a contrasting color so as to be clearly and distinctly visible, the plug having been completely covered by permanent aluminum paint or other paint or lacquer; and (c) it eliminated the provision specifying the precise legend to be printed on the cartons and substituted therefor a more general one. 156 F.2d 488. The case is here on a petition for certiorari which we granted because of the apparent conflict between the decision below and *Champion Spark Plug Co. v. Reich*, 121 F.2d 769, decided by the Circuit Court of Appeals for the Eighth Circuit.

There is no challenge here to the findings as to the misleading character of the merchandising methods employed by respondents, nor to the conclusion that they have not only infringed petitioner's trade mark but have also engaged in unfair competition. The controversy here relates to the adequacy of the relief granted, particularly the refusal of the Circuit Court of Appeals to require respondents to remove the word "Champion" from the repaired or reconditioned plugs which they resell.

We put to one side the case of a manufacturer or distributor who markets new or used spark plugs of one make under the trade mark of another. *See Bourjois & Co. v. Katzel*, 260 U.S. 689. Equity then steps in to prohibit defendant's use of the mark which symbolizes plaintiff's good will and "stakes the reputation of the plaintiff upon the character of the goods." *Bourjois & Co. v. Katzel, supra*, p. 692.

We are dealing here with second-hand goods. The spark plugs, though used, are nevertheless Champion plugs and not those of another make. There is evidence to support what one would suspect, that a used spark plug which has been repaired or reconditioned does not measure up to the specifications of a new one. But the same would be true of a second-hand Ford or Chevrolet car. And we would not suppose that one could be enjoined from selling a car whose valves had been reground and whose piston rings had been replaced unless he removed the name Ford or Chevrolet. *Prestonettes, Inc. v. Coty*, 264 U.S. 359, was a case where toilet powders had as one of their ingredients a powder covered by a trade mark and where perfumes which were trade marked were rebottled and sold in smaller bottles. The Court sustained a decree denying an injunction where the prescribed labels told the truth. Mr. Justice Holmes stated, "A trade mark only gives the right to prohibit the use of it so far as to protect the owner's good will against the sale of another's product as his. When the mark is used in a way that does not deceive the public we see no such sanctity in the word as to prevent its being used to tell the truth. It is not taboo." [Citation.]

Cases may be imagined where the reconditioning or repair would be so extensive or so basic that it would be a misnomer to call the article by its original name, even though the words "used" or "repaired" were added. [Citation.] But no such practice is involved here. The repair or reconditioning of the plugs does not give them a new design. It is no more than a restoration, so far as possible, of their original condition. The type marks attached by the manufacturer are determined by the use to which the plug is to be put. But the thread size and size of the cylinder hole into which the plug is fitted are not affected by the reconditioning. The heat range also has relevance to the type marks. And there is evidence that the reconditioned plugs are inferior so far as heat range and other qualities are concerned. But inferiority is expected in most second-hand articles. Indeed, they generally cost the customer less. That is the case here. Inferiority is immaterial so long as the article is clearly and distinctly sold as repaired or reconditioned rather than as new. The result is, of course, that the second-hand dealer gets some advantage from the trade mark. But under the rule of *Prestonettes, Inc. v. Coty, supra*, that is wholly permissible so long as the manufacturer is not identified with the inferior qualities of the product resulting from wear and tear or the reconditioning by the dealer. Full disclosure gives the manufacturer all the protection to which he is entitled.

Questions

1. Which disclaimer, the District Court's or the Court of Appeals', would be more likely to forestall consumer confusion?

2. If "full disclosure gives the manufacturer all the protection to which he is entitled," should relief in all trademark infringement and unfair competition cases be limited to disclaimers and accurate labeling? If not, why not?

3. Is the court's analogy to the sale of used cars persuasive?

4. Imagine that you represent a client who wants to publish a how-to book on using Microsoft Windows 10 operating system software. She would like to call the book "*Microsoft Windows 10 and the Windows 10 mobile phone platform: An Unauthorized Guide.*" She plans to post a website to accompany the launch of the book; the site will include digital downloads of helpful add-on macros and shortcuts that she wrote herself, and that she maintains will help the novice user make the most of Windows 10 and Windows 10 mobile phones. Microsoft has an aggressive licensing program for its products, and your client neither meets Microsoft's specifications nor is willing to pay its licensing fee. What do you advise?

5. Auto Gold sells car accessories decorated with the trademarks and logos of particular brands of cars. For its Volkswagen marquee plates, it purchases VW emblems from Volkswagen, which sells them for use as replacements for Volkswagen hood ornaments. Auto Gold gold-plates the purchased emblems and mounts them on decorative marquee license plates. It packages the plates with labels that explain that

Volkswagen neither produced nor sponsored them. After *Champion Spark Plug*, has Volkswagen any basis for complaint? *See Au-Tomotive Gold v. Volkswagen of America*, 603 F.3d 1133 (9th Cir. 2010), *infra* Chapter 8[B][3].

Ralph S. Brown, Jr., *Advertising and the Public Interest: Legal Protection of Trade Symbols*

57 Yale L.J. 1165 (1948) [excerpts]*

The law of trade symbols is of modern development, largely judge-made and only partly codified. Its impetus comes from the demands of modern advertising, a black art whose practitioners are part of the larger army which employs threats, cajolery, emotions, personality, persistence and facts in what is termed aggressive selling. Much aggressive selling involves direct personal relationships; advertising depends on the remote manipulation of symbols, most importantly of symbols directed at a mass audience through mass media, or imprinted on mass-produced goods. The essence of these symbols is distilled in the devices variously called trade-marks, trade names, brand names, or trade symbols. To the courts come frequent claims for protection, made by those who say they have fashioned a valuable symbol, and that no one else should use it. Very recently, for example, the vendors of Sun-Kist oranges lost a court battle to prevent an Illinois baker from selling Sun-Kist bread. The highest court, in its most recent encounter with a like case, upheld the power of a manufacturer of rubber footwear to prevent the use of a red circle mark by a seller of rubber heels, which the plaintiff did not manufacture.

In these cases, a choice of premises and techniques is still open. One set of premises, which seems to subsume Justice Frankfurter's felicitous dictum, recognizes a primary public interest in protecting the seller who asks the court to enjoin "another [who] poaches upon the commercial magnetism of a symbol he has created." This expansive conception merits critical attention. Are all forms of poaching forbidden? Should they be, consistent with another premise? This one asserts, in the words of Judge Frank, "the basic common law policy of encouraging competition, and the fact that the protection of monopolies in names is but a secondary and limiting policy." The legal ties which bind together some apparently inconsistent decisions may be found, but not simply in an indiscriminate prohibition of poaching, nor yet in a presumption in favor of competition, no matter how compelling. Rather, courts move from these and other premises to refinements of doctrine.

It is proposed here to seek, in the milieu in which trade symbols are created and used, for data underlying both premises and dogma. This will require an independent evaluation of the institution of advertising. What do we get for the three billions of current annual outlay? Do we want it? Unfortunately, there is little consensus as to what values advertising serves. Its votaries have poured their most skillful symbols back in the soil from which they sprang. Its detractors, maddened by the success of this propaganda, would purge Radio City with fire and sword.

* *[Footnotes omitted—Eds.]*

One thing the examination will reveal is that what appear to be private disputes among hucksters almost invariably touch the public welfare. We shall therefore be concerned to ask, when courts protect trade symbols, whether their decisions further public as well as private goals.

The principal reason for advertising is an economic one—to sell goods and services. We can describe this process, and its economic effects, with relative confidence, compared to the obscurity which surrounds the psychological, cultural, or other social consequences of modern advertising. These may turn out to be more portentous than the affairs of the market-place. But the materials are uncollected or unrefined. In this survey we can only drop a handful of problems into a footnote. The reader must make his own judgments from his own observations, remembering, as we turn almost exclusively to economic discussion, that man does not live by bread alone.

Informative and Persuasive Advertising

The buying public submits to a vast outpouring of words and pictures from the advertisers, in which, mingled with exhortations to buy, is a modicum of information about the goods offered. From the point of view of the economic purist, imparting information is the only useful function of advertising. A perfect market demands a perfect enlightenment of those who buy and sell. One of the many imperfections of the real world is that, absent advertising, most buyers would have to go to a great deal of trouble to discover what is offered for sale. To the extent that the blandishments of sellers inform buyers what is to be bought, and at what price, advertising undoubtedly helps to quicken the stream of commerce.

Most advertising, however, is designed not to inform, but to persuade and influence. What is the occasion for such tremendous outlays on persuasion and influence in a well-ordered economic system? If we consider first the total stream of production and consumption, persuasive advertising seems only to consume resources that might be put to better use producing more goods and services. It does not increase total demand, it only increases wants. Effective demand arises, not from what we would like to have; but from the purchasing power of the community created by its productive power. We consume what we produce, and no more. Considering the economic welfare of the community as a whole, to use up part of the national product persuading people to buy product A rather than product B appears to be a waste of resources.

....

The Sovereign Consumer

Defenders of the institution have two additional lines of defense. The first is that persuasive advertising creates a cluster of values, no less real because they are intangible. The second, related to the first, argues that the sovereign consumer has made a free election between those values and the austerities of price competition.

These considerations bring us to the consumer as an individual. As an individual, instead of a faceless component of mass purchasing power, he is a creature of infinite diversity, with, moreover, a soul. To make a complete analysis of what he gets from advertising, the relations of material rewards and spiritual values, as affected by advertising, would have to be considered. That task we must leave to the philosophers and the psychologists. As was indicated earlier, they have not yet performed it. The only arena which is at all adequately staked out is that of the economic conflict between seller and buyer. The agreed goal is the maximum satisfaction of each consumer, as determined by his free choice in disposing of his income. In a roundabout way, problems of aggregate output and investment, already discussed, bear on the same goal. Now we have to consider how persuasive advertising adds to or subtracts from the sum of the individual's satisfied wants.

What are the intangible values? One is said to be the assurance of reliability, because the advertiser wants to build up repeat sales, and cannot afford to sell patently unsatisfactory goods. Admitting, for the sake of getting on, that unadvertised brands offer a greater opportunity for "hit-and-run" frauds, the difficulty with this contention is that the hope of continued custom is quite unrelated to the magnitude of persuasive advertising. Nothing more than information as to source is necessary for the consumer to be able to repeat a satisfactory purchase.

Other values derive from the proposition that cheapness is not enough. The buyer of an advertised good buys more than a parcel of food or fabric; he buys the pause that refreshes, the hand that has never lost its skill, the priceless ingredient that is the reputation of its maker. All these may be illusions, but they cost money to create, and if the creators can recoup their outlay, who is the poorer? Among the many illusions which advertising can fashion are those of lavishness, refinement, security, and romance. Suppose the monetary cost of compounding a perfume is trivial; of what moment is this if the ads promise, and the buyer believes, that romance, even seduction, will follow its use? The economist, whose dour lexicon defines as irrational any market behavior not dictated by a logical pecuniary calculus, may think it irrational to buy illusions; but there is a degree of that kind of irrationality even in economic man; and consuming man is full of it.

The taint of irrationality may be dispelled by asserting flatly that the utility of a good, that is, its capacity to satisfy wants, is measured exactly by what people will pay for it. If, as is undeniably the case, consumers will pay more for an advertised brand than for its unheralded duplicate, then consumers must get more satisfaction out of the advertised brand. The nature of the satisfaction is of concern only to the moralist. Though this argument can easily be pushed to absurdity—suppose it was to the interest of the advertisers to consume half the national product in persuasion?—it seems plausible if it is based on the dogma of consumer autonomy. Then anyone who questions the untrammelled use of influence by the seller and its uncoerced acceptance by the buyer is at best a Puritan, at worst a Fascist. The debate seems to end in a defense of freedom, for the advertiser as well as for the consumer.

But does the sovereign consumer have real freedom of choice? The first requisite of choice is an adequate presentation of alternatives. The classical economists who enthroned the consumer never dreamed that he would make his decisions under a bombardment of stupefying symbols. He should be informed, and willing to pay the necessary price for information. But the most charitable tabulations reveal relatively little information in advertising directed to consumers outside the classified columns and local announcements. National advertising is dominated by appeals to sex, fear, emulation, and patriotism, regardless of the relevance of those drives to the transaction at hand. The purchase of many advertised articles, then, has a raw emotional origin. Many others are compelled by the endless reiteration of the advertisers' imperative: eat lemons, drink milk, wear hats. Pseudo-information fills any gaps. It takes many forms. There is the bewildering manipulation of comparatives and superlatives: "No other soap washes cleaner"; "The world's most wanted pen." In the atomic age, precise scientific data are helpful. Bayer's Aspirin tells us that the tablet dissolves in two seconds. Whether the analgesic effect is then felt in one hour or two hours will no doubt be explained in time. Buick lists among its features such well-understood engineering terms as "Dynaflow Drive, Taper-thru Styling, Vibra-Shielded Ride, Hi-Poised Fireball Power." The reader, after ten minutes with a magazine or the radio, can select his own examples of the types of influence that are thought to move the sovereign consumer.

The foundation of free choice, to repeat, is an adequate presentation of alternatives. Admittedly, many choices, for example in politics or religion, are presented under a smoke screen of exaggeration and emotion. But there are usually at least two sides to the argument. The choice between one highly advertised dentifrice and another is, in important respects, no choice at all. It cannot register a decision to support or reject institutional arrangements which, as has been shown, contribute to monopolistic waste of resources; it cannot reflect a preference to get more or less for one's money, to take an illusion or leave it. It is only a choice between one illusion and another. That advertisers, despite their intramural rivalry, are aware that they stand on common ground, is shown by their united opposition to institutions which enlarge the consumer's alternatives. An instance is the forays and reprisals against the consumers' movement.

The forces which counter advertising propaganda may be listed as follows. First, as an individual protest, is the sentiment described as "sales resistance," a compound of realism, skepticism, and apathy. Second is organized sales resistance, the pressure for reform by the slow-moving consumers' organizations. Third, most important economically, is the still small voice of the lower price tag on an unadvertised substitute. Fourth, the nub of the present discussion, comes the shaping of legal institutions, either to curb the excesses of advertising or to foster the second and third forces just listed. It is intended to discuss in a later article the enforcement of truth in advertising, as an indication that freedom to persuade and influence has its boundaries, and the possible use of antitrust, taxation, or other devices to set new boundaries. The law also has to take a stand when the use or misuse of advertising has created measurable values for the advertiser, and "another poaches upon the commercial magnetism of the symbol." How much protection will be given the advertiser against the poacher? The answer is sought in the law of trade-marks and trade names.

Summary

Before assessing the relevance of that body of doctrine to the good and bad in advertising, it may be desirable to summarize the conclusions reached thus far.

Advertising has two main functions, to inform and to persuade. With qualifications that need not be repeated, persuasive advertising is, for the community as a whole, just a luxurious exercise in talking ourselves into spending our incomes. For the individual firm, however, it is a potent device to distinguish a product from its competitors, and to create a partial immunity from the chills and fevers of competition. The result of successful differentiation is higher prices than would otherwise prevail. The aim, not always achieved, is higher profits. Whether persuasive advertising enhances the total flow of goods by promoting cost reductions is disputable. Whether it swells the flow of investment by the lure of monopoly profits is doubtful.

For the consumer who desires to get the most for his money, persuasive advertising displays a solid front of irrelevancy. The alternatives to what the advertisers offer are not adequately presented, and the choice among advertised products is loaded with a panoply of propaganda for which the buyer pays, whether he wants it or not. However, both buyer and seller profit from informative advertising. In a complex society, it is an indispensable adjunct to a free traffic in goods and services. The task before the courts in trade symbol cases, it may therefore be asserted, should be to pick out from the tangle of claims, facts, and doctrines they are set to unravel, the threads of informative advertising, and to ignore the persuasive. The two functions are very much intertwined in trade symbols, how confusingly will appear when we try to separate them.

....

William M. Landes & Richard A. Posner, *Trademark Law: An Economic Perspective*

30 J. L. & Econ. 265 (1987) (excerpts)*

II. The Economics of Trademarks

A. Introduction

To oversimplify somewhat, a trademark is a word, symbol, or other signifier used to distinguish a good or service produced by one firm from the goods or services of other firms. Thus "Sanka" designates a decaffeinated coffee made by General Foods and "Xerox" the dry copiers made by Xerox Corporation. "Bib"—the "Michelin Man"—is the symbol of tires made by the Michelin Company. A stylized penguin is the symbol of a line of paperback books published by Penguin Books; a distinctively shaped green bottle is a trademark of the producer of Perrier bottled water; the color pink is a trademark for residential insulation manufactured by Owens-Corning.

1. Benefits of Trademarks

Suppose you like decaffeinated coffee made by General Foods. If General Foods' brand had no name, then to order it in a restaurant or grocery store you would have to ask for "the decaffeinated coffee made by General Foods." This takes longer to say, requires you to remember more, and requires the waiter or clerk to read and

* Copyright 1987 University of Chicago Press. Reprinted by permission. [*Footnotes omitted—Eds.*]

remember more than if you can just ask for "Sanka." The problem would be even more serious if General Foods made more than one brand of decaffeinated coffee, as in fact it does. The benefit of the brand name is analogous to that of designating individuals by last as well as first names, so that, instead of having to say "the Geoffrey who teaches constitutional law at the University of Chicago Law School—not the one who teaches corporations," you can say "Geoffrey Stone—not Geoffrey Miller."

To perform its economizing function a trademark or brand name (these are rough synonyms) must not be duplicated. To allow another maker of decaffeinated coffee to sell its coffee under the name "Sanka" would destroy the benefit of the name in identifying a brand of decaffeinated coffee made by General Foods (whether there might be offsetting benefits is considered later). It would be like allowing a second rancher to graze his cattle on a pasture the optimal use of which required that only one herd be allowed to graze. The failure to enforce trademarks would impose two distinct costs—one in the market for trademarked goods and the other in the distinct (and unconventional) market in language.

(a) The Market for Trademarked Goods. The benefits of trademarks in reducing consumer search costs require that the producer of a trademarked good maintain a consistent quality over time and across consumers. Hence trademark protection encourages expenditures on quality. To see this, suppose a consumer has a favorable experience with brand X and wants to buy it again. Or suppose he wants to buy brand X because it has been recommended by a reliable source or because he has had a favorable experience with brand Y, another brand produced by the same producer. Rather than investigating the attributes of all goods to determine which one is brand X or is equivalent to X, the consumer may find it less costly to search by identifying the relevant trademark and purchasing the corresponding brand. For this strategy to be efficient, however, not only must it be cheaper to search for the right trademark than for the desired attributes of the good, but also past experience must be a good predictor of the likely outcome of current consumption choices—that is, the brand must exhibit consistent quality. In short, a trademark conveys information that allows the consumer to say to himself, "I need not investigate the attributes of the brand I am about to purchase because the trademark is a shorthand way of telling me that the attributes are the same as that of the brand I enjoyed earlier."

Less obviously, a firm's incentive to invest resources in developing and maintaining (as through advertising) a strong mark depends on its ability to maintain consistent product quality. In other words, trademarks have a self-enforcing feature. They are valuable because they denote consistent quality, and a firm has an incentive to develop a trademark only if it is able to maintain consistent quality. To see this, consider what happens when a brand's quality is inconsistent. Because consumers will learn that the trademark does not enable them to relate their past to future consumption experiences, the branded product will be like a good without a trademark. The trademark will not lower search costs, so consumers will be unwilling to pay more for the branded than for the unbranded good. As a result, the firm will not earn a sufficient return on its trademark promotional expenditures to justify making them. A similar argument shows that a firm with a valuable trademark would be reluctant to lower the quality of its brand because it would suffer a capital loss on its investment in the trademark.

It should be apparent that the benefits of trademarks in lowering consumer search costs presuppose legal protection of trademarks. The value of a trademark is the saving in search costs made possible by the information or reputation that the trademark conveys or embodies about the brand (or the firm that produces the brand). Creating such a reputation requires expenditures on product quality, service, advertising, and so on. Once the reputation is created, the firm will obtain greater profits because repeat purchases and word-of-mouth references will generate higher sales and because consumers will be willing to pay higher prices for lower search costs and greater assurance of consistent quality. However, the cost of duplicating someone else's trademark is small—the cost of duplicating a label, design, or package where the required inputs are widely available. The incentive to incur this cost (in the absence of legal regulation) will be greater the stronger the trademark. The free-riding competitor will, at little cost, capture some of the profits associated with a strong trademark because some consumers will assume (at least in the short run) that the free rider's and the original trademark holder's brands are identical. If the law does not prevent it, free riding will eventually destroy the information capital embodied in a trademark, and the prospect of free riding may therefore eliminate the incentive to develop a valuable trademark in the first place.

....

2. The Costs of Legally Enforceable Trademarks

These costs are modest, at least in the simple case of the "fanciful" mark, such as "Exxon" and "Kodak," which has no information content except to denote a specific producer or brand. Since the mark "goes with" the brand (in a sense explained later), the transfer of the mark is automatically effected by a transfer of the rights to make the branded product, as by a sale, or licensing, of production rights or assets. Rent seeking to stake out a trademark is not much of a problem either. Prior to establishing a trademark, the distinctive yet pronounceable combinations of letters to form words that will serve as a suitable trademark are as a practical matter infinite, implying a high degree of substitutability and hence a slight value in exchange. Finally, the costs of enforcement, though not trivial (especially where there is a danger of a brand name's becoming a generic name), are modest and (again putting aside the generic problem) do not include the cost in inefficient resource allocation from driving a wedge between price and marginal cost. A proper trademark is not a public good; it has social value only when used to designate a single brand.

We may seem to be ignoring the possibility that, by fostering product differentiation, trademarks may create deadweight costs, whether of monopoly or (excessive) competition. We have assumed that a trademark induces its owner to invest in maintaining uniform product quality, but another interpretation is that it induces the owner to spend money on creating, through advertising and promotion, a spurious image of high quality that enables monopoly rents to be obtained by deflecting consumers from lower-price substitutes of equal or even higher quality. In the case of products that are produced according to an identical formula, such as aspirin or household liquid bleach, the ability of name-brand goods (Bayer aspirin, Clorox bleach) to command higher prices than generic (nonbranded) goods has seemed to some economists and more lawyers an example of the power of brand advertising to bamboozle the public and thereby promote monopoly; and brand advertising presupposes trademarks—they are what enable a producer readily to identify his brand to the consumer. Besides the possibility of creating monopoly rents, trademarks may transform rents into costs, as one firm's expenditure on promoting its mark cancels out that of another firm. Although no monopoly profits are created, consumers may pay higher prices, and resources may be wasted in a sterile competition.

The short answer to these arguments is that they have gained no foothold at all in trademark law, as distinct from antitrust law. The implicit economic model of trademarks that is used in that law is our model, in which trademarks lower search costs and foster quality control rather than create social waste and consumer deception. A longer answer, which we shall merely sketch, is that the hostile view of brand advertising has been largely and we think correctly rejected by economists. The fact that two goods have the same chemical formula does not make them of equal quality to even the most coolly rational consumer. That consumer will be interested not in the formula but in the manufactured product and may therefore be willing to pay a premium for greater assurance that the good will actually be manufactured to the specifications of the formula. Trademarks enable the consumer to economize on a real cost because he spends less time searching to get the quality he wants. If this analysis is correct, the rejection by trademark law of a monopoly theory of trademarks is actually a mark in favor of the economic rationality of that law.

Jeremy N. Sheff, *Biasing Brands*

32 Cardozo L. Rev. 1245 (2011) [excerpts]*

In June of 2006, Miralus Healthcare launched a multi-million dollar television advertising campaign. The company's ten-second advertisement, which ran repeatedly in syndicated programming, late-night television, and basic cable, featured video of a young woman rubbing Miralus's product—a glue-stick-like applicator—against her forehead, while a female narrator urgently read the following script in voiceover:

> HeadOn: Apply directly to the forehead. HeadOn: Apply directly to the forehead. HeadOn: Apply directly to the forehead. HeadOn is available without a prescription at retailers nationwide.

Obviously, this advertisement did not provide any information to viewers as to the precise purpose or function of the HeadOn product. Nor was that its intent. Miralus's marketing department had conducted focus group testing of various advertisements and learned that maximizing repetition led to the greatest consumer recall

* Copyright 2011. Reprinted by permission. [*Footnotes omitted—Eds.*]

of the ad, and as Dan Charron, Miralus's Vice President of Sales and Marketing explained: "It's all about recall. It's all about recall."

This deliberately uninformative marketing strategy was likely rendered even more attractive by the questionable properties of the HeadOn product itself. Miralus intended to sell HeadOn as a topical headache remedy, but the product contained only trace amounts of its claimed effective ingredients, none of which had been found in any published study to alleviate headaches. As a result, in March of 2006, the National Advertising Division of the Council of Better Business Bureaus cautioned Miralus against claiming that HeadOn provided headache relief, under threat of referral to the Food and Drug Administration. Miralus's repetitive but uninformative ad campaign followed soon thereafter.

The HeadOn ad was quickly derided in the national press as "mind-numbing," "bizarre," and "the most annoying commercial on television," but Miralus's Charron was unapologetic: "We're just trying to build a brand by getting people to remember it." And people did remember: While the ad spawned a host of parodies on late-night comedy shows and the Internet, it also generated a huge boost in Miralus's revenues. Sales of HeadOn grew by 234% from 2005 to 2006, and their torrid growth pace continued at least through the first six months of 2007; meanwhile, spinoff products generated millions of dollars in additional revenue for the company. Medical experts argued consistently and repeatedly on the broadcast networks and in major daily newspapers that any perceived headache relief delivered by HeadOn was due to the placebo effect, but millions of tubes of the product were nevertheless purchased by consumers at prices between five and eight dollars per unit.

The HeadOn example, in which a branded product objectively does not perform its intended function, is marketed to the public by simply repeating the brand name without disclosing the function of the underlying product, and yet generates millions of dollars in revenues for its manufacturer, represents more than the latest confirmation of a phrase attributed to P.T. Barnum. It also has serious implications for the legal regulation of consumer markets—and particularly for the theoretical underpinnings of our system of trademark law. The project of this Article is to analyze the features of consumer psychology and behavior that make episodes like the HeadOn phenomenon possible, and to discuss resulting challenges posed to conventional trademark law theory.

....

For decades, trademark law theory has been dominated by the economic analysis of the Chicago School.... The economic justification for trademark protection, as described in the models of Chicago School commentators, is twofold. First, giving individual producers an exclusive right to access the consumer goodwill that attaches to a particular word or symbol is said to provide those producers with an incentive to produce products of a high and consistent quality....

Second—and more importantly for present purposes—it is argued that trademark protection lowers consumer search costs, thereby facilitating welfare-increasing transactions. Most products will have some features or qualities that will be relevant to the consumer's decision whether or not to purchase, but that cannot be measured without either engaging in costly information gathering or, if this is not possible, consuming the product. Because the seller who manufactured the product typically has more information about such unobservable product qualities than potential buyers have, it will be more efficient for sellers to provide that information to buyers than for buyers to attempt to seek out the information themselves—if buyers were even capable of obtaining the information. Trademarks allow a convenient and efficient means of executing this information transfer, allowing producers to quickly and inexpensively convey a wealth of information about the unobservable qualities of their products to consumers in order to inform their decision whether or not to purchase. Because sellers can convey this information through a trademark at a lower cost than the cost to consumers of acquiring such information for themselves, trademarks are said to lower consumer search costs—a type of transactions cost—thereby facilitating welfare-increasing voluntary transactions and increasing aggregate social welfare.

The proposition that the function of trademarks is to inform consumers is at the heart of the dominant theoretical model of trademark law. In this view, the consumer's mind runs a kind of matching algorithm, testing the consumer's own preferences against all sources of information—whether derived from the consumer's own search or from the informational content of a trademark—about the available purchase options, in order to determine which purchase option is most likely to satisfy his preferences. And on its face, this second justification for trademark protection is attractive. Producers will obviously have better information about the qualities of their products and services than prospective purchasers. Consumers will obviously rely on information about those qualities in deciding whether to make a purchase, and in deciding which product or service to select from a range of options. As modern consumers, we can all think of numerous examples of trademarks that bring to our minds particular information about the attributes of the associated product that would be relevant to our decision to make a purchase. Such information would be difficult or impossible to obtain without consuming the product: the taste of a soft drink, the reliability of a car, or the safety and efficacy of a drug. In short, the search-costs rationale has great intuitive appeal.

... Despite its intuitive appeal, this model does not describe actual consumer decision-making very well. It is unlikely that any modern consumer can, on reflection, honestly characterize their myriad and varied purchasing decisions as a series of calculations to determine likelihood of preference-satisfaction based on a synthesis of product information conveyed by a trademark with product information obtained independently. Many, if not most, consumer transactions—from purchasing a pack of gum at a drugstore checkout, to ordering a beer at a bar, to pre-ordering the latest tech gadget online—are considerably less systematic and analytical than the search-costs model can account for. Two questions therefore arise: First, is a more descriptively accurate model of consumer decision-making available; and second, does that model, if it exists, provide the same normative support for the current system of legal protection for trademarks?

With respect to the first question, there is an entire field of academic and professional study devoted to analyzing, predicting, and influencing the consumer decision-making process: marketing. The marketing literature has developed tools for analyzing consumer decision-making, and particularly for analyzing the effect of trademarks (and of the related construct, brands) on that decision-making. In particular, marketing researchers have directed considerable attention to the question of what makes consumers willing to pay more for a branded product than for an equivalent unbranded product—the question of "brand equity." Academic development of the concept of brand equity has given rise to a model of consumer decision-making that shares some overlap with the search-costs model, but also contradicts it in important ways.

... Trademarks have multiple effects on consumers, each of which has different normative implications. First, and consistent with the search-costs model, trademarks inform consumers: They provide consumers with objective information about the products and services to which they are affixed. Second, trademarks persuade consumers: Marketing efforts can generate or change consumer preferences to align with whatever qualities—including subjective qualities—are perceived to be offered by a marked product. The persuasive function of trademarks and advertising has long been a subject of intense debate in the economic and legal academic literatures.

[T]his Article will focus on a third, under-appreciated effect of trademarks: their ability to bias consumers. By "bias," I mean that trademarks, supported by marketing activities (a combination this Article will refer to as a "brand"), can give rise to consumer beliefs about objective product qualities that are objectively mistaken, and yet resistant to correction by exposure of the consumer to objective evidence. I refer to this phenomenon as "brand bias," and I situate it as an example of the type of boundedly rational decision-making behavior that undergirds the behavioralist critique of neoclassical law and economics models (such as the search-costs model).

The behavioralist critique does not so much invalidate traditional economic models of behavior (such as the search-costs model) as it requires their qualification. Specifically, it raises the possibility that strategic actors can compromise the efficiencies of a system (such as the trademark system) by manipulating the divergence between rational and boundedly rational behavior. As the Miralus example above illustrates, ... marketing techniques can be and are in fact deployed strategically by brand owners to manipulate brand bias in welfare-reducing ways. Moreover, this strategic behavior is enabled by the very trademark protection that the search-costs model purports to justify in the name of efficiency.

For this reason, trademark law may, in some circumstances, demand support from complementary legal regimes—consumer protection regimes—in order to minimize the ability of strategic actors (like Miralus in the example above) to compromise the efficiencies of the trademark system. Whether such legal intervention is desirable depends on a comparison of the costs of strategic manipulation of brand bias with the costs of the intervention in question....

Questions

1. Have Landes and Posner adequately responded to the policy questions raised by Brown and Sheff? How would you respond?

2. Economist Jonathan Aldred suggests that the argument that trademarks actually reduce consumer search costs is circular:

> What precisely is guaranteed to the consumer by a guarantee of origin? There is no guarantee regarding the product's function or fitness for purpose, nor that it has been made in a particular way or at a particular location.... To a cynical economist, it seems that the only thing *guaranteed* to the consumer is that the trade mark owner will take a share of the profits on the sale of the product.

While Landes and Posner suggest that a trademark will give the owner of the mark an incentive to maintain a reputation for high quality products, Aldred responds that a mark owner has an interest in building its reputation but also has an interest in reducing its costs.

> Often the best way of achieving this combination is through sophisticated marketing, rather than making high quality products. Consumers come to *believe* the trade mark signals high quality, and may continue to do so even after purchase if the quality defects are hidden or debatable. As the central device in a marketing strategy, the trade-marked sign may be used by firms to mislead consumers rather than convey useful information, reputation arguments notwithstanding.

Aldred goes on to argue that Landes and Posner are too ready to accept that if consumers are willing to pay higher prices for products with well-known trademarks, that fact, without more, demonstrates that the trademarked products are better than their lower priced competitors. *See* Jonathan Aldred, *The Economic Rationale of Trademarks: An Economist's Critique, in* LIONEL BENTLY, JENNIFER DAVIS AND JANE C. GINSBURG, EDS., TRADE MARKS AND BRANDS: AN INTERDISCIPLINARY CRITIQUE (Cambridge U. Press 2008). Do Landes and Posner have a persuasive response?

Jessica Litman, *Breakfast with Batman: The Public Interest in the Advertising Age*

108 YALE L.J. 1717 (1999) (excerpts)*

The expansion of the law of trade symbol protection has tracked two distinct but related trends. First has been an evolution in widely held views of the public interest. Ralph Brown argued in *Advertising and the Public Interest* that just because people

* Copyright 1999. Reprinted with permission. [*Footnotes omitted — Eds.*]

paid more for products did not mean there had been any actual increase in productivity and welfare—rather, we had let ourselves be talked into paying more money for the same stuff. That, he insisted, was obviously in the interest of the producers whose advertising had persuaded the public to pay a higher price, but was wasteful for the public at large. Today, that once self-evident point is controversial. Productivity seems to be measured less by what people make than by what people are inclined to buy. What consumers are willing to pay has become synonymous with value. Commodification is the preeminent engine of progress. Transforming ephemeral figments into saleable property is a patriotic act, and the fact, without more, that an offer to sell something will find customers is reason enough to sanction its appropriation from the commons. There has been inexorable pressure to recognize as an axiom the principle that if something appears to have substantial value to someone, the law must and should protect it as property. Recent years have seen an explosion of cases in which courts have relied on trademark-like rubrics to uphold claims to exclusive rights in names, faces, voices, gestures, phrases, artistic style, marketing concepts, locations, and references.

Second, the descriptive proposition that trade symbols have no intrinsic value has come to seem demonstrably inaccurate. The use of trademarks on promotional products has evolved from an advertising device for the underlying product line to an independent justification for bringing a so-called underlying product to market. Elvis Presley's estate has earned more annually in license fees than it did in the late singer's most profitable year. Warner Brothers has brought out a seemingly endless series of lackluster Batman sequels. Critics disliked the sequels, and their box office performances were mediocre, but the sales of Batman toys have more than made up for it. It is hard to maintain a straight face when asserting that the "Batman" mark has value only as an indicator that Batman-branded products are licensed by Warner Brothers. The worth of such valuable trade symbols lies less in their designation of product source than in their power to imbue a product line with desirable atmospherics.

Indeed, in the new orthodoxy, marketing *is* value. American industry seems to proceed on the assumption that we can make the consumer richer simply by revising a product's packaging, without having to make any changes in the product itself.

Consider the effort and expense that goes into distinguishing a Ford Taurus from a Mercury Sable and persuading customers to buy one rather than the other, when, after all, they're essentially the same car. Buying a truck? Agonize over whether you'd rather drive a Mazda B-Series (*Get in. Be moved.*), "the official truck of the AMA Motorcross Nationals," or haul your friends to the river, kayaks in tow, in a Ford Ranger (*Built Tough. Built To Last.*). The only major difference between them is the marketing. Auto companies can pitch their vehicles to specialized, niche markets without needing to redesign anything but the ad campaigns for their cars.

But why not? If the illusion of a vehicle custom-built for a particular sort of buyer is worth a couple of thousand dollars to a couple of million consumers, the customers will be happier, the auto companies will be wealthier, and the American economy will keep chugging along, picking up speed without burning additional coal. Anecdotal evidence suggests that many consumers don't feel duped, or, in any event, don't mind being duped. It isn't as if anyone has tried to conceal that the Sable and the Taurus are twins, that Advil and Motrin and generic ibuprofen are the exact same stuff, or that the reason that Tylenol and not some other brand of acetaminophen is "the pain reliever hospitals use most" is that McNeil sets the hospital price of Tylenol low enough to enable it to make that claim. At some level, most consumers know that; most of them have nonetheless settled on their own favorite advertised brands.

Moreover, there is something more going on than producers and consumers agreeing with each other to pretend that the atmospherics of product advertising are somehow reflected in the advertised products. Ask a child, and he'll persuade you that the difference between a box of Kellogg's Corn Flakes with a picture of Batman on it and some other box without one is real. There is nothing imaginary about it. It has nothing to do with the way the cereal tastes. What kids want isn't a nutritious part of a complete breakfast; they want Batman to have breakfast with them. One box supplies that; the other doesn't.

An important premise underlying Ralph Brown's analysis was that trade symbols themselves had no legitimate intrinsic value except insofar as they symbolized information about the products they accompanied. As a normative proposition, that would strike many consumers today as questionable; as a descriptive one, it is demonstrably untrue. Consumers have come to attach enormous value to trade symbols, and it is no longer uncommon to see the symbols valued far in excess of the worth of the underlying products they identify. In a very real sense, trade symbols are themselves often products: Toys are designed, perfumes are compounded, and breakfast cereals are devised for no better reason than to serve as a vehicle for the trade symbol du jour. If we have come to value the atmospherics embodied in advertising, shouldn't our law be reformed to protect them from unauthorized imitation?

At first glance, the syllogism seems to pack powerful intuitive appeal. Ralph Brown's argument relied on the axiom that what he called the persuasive function of trade symbols was of no value to the public at large; indeed, from the viewpoint of the public interest, the persuasive value of advertising was at best irrelevant and at worst pernicious. Affording it strong legal protection, therefore, seemed perverse. Whether or not that axiom described the U.S. economy in 1948, it seems naive in 1999. In today's world, the public has invested considerable spending dollars and a significant chunk of intangible goodwill in the atmospherics purveyed by advertisers. If society now values the persuasive function of trade symbols more than it used to, then perhaps it ought to protect that persuasive function more powerfully than it used to.

To say that many consumers seem to attach real value to atmospherics, however, doesn't itself demonstrate that those atmospherics should be afforded legal protection. Many things have value. As Ralph Brown reminded us often, the essence of any intellectual property regime is to divide the valuable stuff subject to private appropriation from the valuable stuff that, precisely because of its importance, is reserved for public use. In the law of trade symbols, for instance, it has long been the rule that functional product features may not be protected, because they have too much value, not too little. Value, without more, does not tell us whether a particular item for which protection is sought belongs in the proprietary pile or the public one.

To agree to treat a class of stuff as intellectual property, we normally require a showing that, if protection is not extended, bad things will happen that will outweigh the resulting good things. But it would be difficult to argue that the persuasive values embodied in trade symbols are likely to suffer from underprotection. Indeed, the Mattels, Disneys, and Warner Brothers of the world seem to protect their atmospherics just fine without legal assistance. Not only can their target audiences tell the difference between, say, a Barbie doll and some other thirteen-inch fashion doll, but, regardless of features, they seem well-trained in the art of insisting on the Mattel product. Nor is the phenomenon limited to the junior set. The popularity of Ralph Lauren's Polo brand shirts or Gucci handbags is an obvious example.

To the extent that consumers want to purchase the higher-priced spread, they ought to be able to be sure that they are paying the higher price for the genuine branded article. If the concept of branding is itself legitimate, then we want to ensure consumers' protection against confusion or deception. Conventional trademark law does that. But, to stick with Lauren's Polo for a minute, what about consumers who want to pick up a polo shirt with some design on the chest at a good price? What if, instead, they want to buy this month's issue of *Polo* magazine (which follows the sport, not the fashion)? It seems obvious why Lauren might want to hinder the first and collect a license fee from the second, so it would hardly be perplexing if his company threatened to sue. There seems, nonetheless, to be no good reason why we should help him.

If competition is still the American way of doing business, then before we give out exclusive control of some coin of competition, we need, or should need, a justification. Protecting consumers from deception is the justification most familiar to trademark law, but it does not support assigning broad rights to prevent competitive or diluting use when no confusion seems likely. Supplying incentives to invest in the item that's getting the protection is another classic justification for intellectual property, and it is equally unavailing here. An argument that we would have an undersupply of good commercials if advertisers were not given plenary control over the elements in their ads cannot be made with a straight face. Finally, there is the perennially popular justification of desert. Producers have invested in their trade symbols, the argument goes; they have earned them, so they're entitled to them.

But so have we. The argument that trade symbols acquire intrinsic value—apart from their usefulness in designating the source—derives from consumers' investing those symbols with value for which they are willing to pay real money. We may want our children to breakfast with Batman. It may well increase the total utils in our society if every time a guy drinks a Budweiser or smokes a Camel, he believes he's a stud. We may all be better off if, each time a woman colors her hair with a L'Oreal product, she murmurs to herself "*and I'm worth it.*" If that's so, however, Warner Brothers, Anheuser-Busch, R.J. Reynolds, and L'Oreal can hardly take all the credit. They built up all that mystique with their customers' money and active collaboration.

If the customers want to move on, to get in bed with other products that have similar atmospherics, why shouldn't they? It's not very sporting to try to lock up the atmospherics.

To the extent, moreover, that the impulse to protect something beyond any prevention of consumer confusion derives from the perception that this thing has value, that it is something people want to buy, then giving its purveyor intellectual property protection is the wrong response. If the thing itself is valuable, if it is in some sense itself a product, then we want other purveyors to compete in offering it to consumers in their own forms and on their own terms. Competition is, after all, the premise of the system. Without competition, none of the rest of the rules make any practical sense.

Questions

1. On balance, do you see either benefit or harm from encouraging the public to perceive equivalent products as materially different from each other?

2. Articulate the justifications for protecting trademarks and other trade symbols from non-confusing use by others. Should it make a difference whether the use is commercial or non-commercial?

3. If kids want to eat breakfast with Batman, should any cereal manufacturer be entitled to put pictures of Batman on its cereal boxes without Time Warner's permission?

Chapter 2

What Is a Trademark?

A. Subject Matter of Trademark Protection

Restatement of the Law (Third), Unfair Competition*

§ 9. DEFINITIONS OF TRADEMARK AND SERVICE MARK

A trademark is a word, name, symbol, device, or other designation, or a combination of such designations, that is distinctive of a person's goods or services and that is used in a manner that identifies those goods or services and distinguishes them from the goods or services of others. A service mark is a trademark that is used in connection with services.

COMMENT:

....

b. Historical origins of trademarks. The use of identifying marks on goods dates to antiquity. The original purpose of such marks was to indicate ownership. With the development of commercial trade the marks came to serve a different function—identification of the source of goods offered for sale in the marketplace.

The use of trademarks was well-known in Roman times, although it was apparently left to the defrauded purchaser to bring an action against a trademark infringer. The guild system of medieval England produced the first widespread use of trademarks. Distinctive production marks were required on goods manufactured by the local guilds. The purpose of such compulsory marking was primarily regulatory since the marks fixed responsibility for defective merchandise and facilitated enforcement of the territorial monopolies enjoyed by the guilds. The geographic expansion of markets and the development of more complex distribution systems eventually resulted in a new function for production marks. The marks served to identify the source of the goods to prospective purchasers who could then make their selections based upon the reputation, not merely of the immediate vendor, but also of the manufacturer. Manufacturers began to adopt marks expressly for the purpose of identifying their goods to prospective customers. The medieval production mark thus evolved into the modern trademark used by manufacturers, distributors, and other sellers to identify their goods and services in the marketplace.

....

f. "Trademark"; "Trade name"; "Service mark". The term "trademark" as originally employed at common law described only inherently-distinctive designations such as fanciful or arbitrary marks. The term "trade name" was used to denote other designations such as descriptive terms or personal names that through use had come to identify the goods of a particular seller. During the first half of the 20th century the substantive rules governing the protection of "trademarks" and "trade names" became essentially identical, and the significance of the distinction diminished. Passage of the Lanham Act in 1946 hastened the abandonment of the former terminology. The statutory definition of "trademark" subsumes all designations that are distinctive of the user's goods....

The Lanham Act and the Model State Trademark Bill limit the term "trademark" to marks used to identify the source of goods. A mark used to identify the source of services is denominated a "service mark." The substantive rules applicable to both types of marks are fundamentally identical, however, and the term "trademark" is generally understood to include marks used in the marketing of either goods or services. The definitions in this Section adopt this convenient usage. The term "service mark" as defined here thus denotes a specific type of trademark.

g. Subject matter. The subject matter of trademark law was initially limited to fanciful or arbitrary words and symbols. This limitation excluded not only descriptive words and symbols, but also other devices that could identify the source of goods, such as the physical appearance of the goods or the appearance of labels, wrappers, containers, or advertising materials that accompany the goods in the marketplace. When such features in fact served to distinguish the goods of a particular producer, they were protected, together with descriptive marks, in an action for unfair competition. As the distinctions between the actions for trademark infringement and unfair competition diminished, the law of trademarks eventually subsumed descriptive designations that had acquired significance as indications of source. Although the protection of product and packaging designs that are indicative of source remains subject to special limitations not applicable to other marks, they too have now been subsumed under the law of trademarks....

The definition of "trademark" adopted in this Section does not incorporate any technical limitations on the nature of the subject matter that may qualify for protection. Words remain the most common type of trademark, such as the word FORD used in connection with the sale of automobiles or KODAK used in connection with cameras. Numbers, letters, and slogans are also eligible for protection as trademarks, as are pictures, symbols, characters, sounds, graphic designs, product and packaging features, and other matter capable of identifying and distinguishing the goods or services of the user....

Kellogg Co. v. National Biscuit Co.

305 U.S. 111 (1938)

Mr. Justice Brandeis delivered the opinion of the Court:

This suit was brought in the federal court for Delaware by National Biscuit Company against Kellogg Company to enjoin alleged unfair competition by the manufacture and sale of the breakfast food commonly known as shredded wheat. The competition was alleged to be unfair mainly because Kellogg Company uses, like the plaintiff, the name shredded wheat and, like the plaintiff, produces its biscuit in pillow-shaped form.

Shredded wheat is a product composed of whole wheat which has been boiled, partially dried, then drawn or pressed out into thin shreds and baked. The shredded wheat biscuit generally known is pillow-shaped in form. It was introduced in 1893 by Henry D. Perky, of Colorado; and he was connected until his death in 1908 with companies formed to make and market the article. Commercial success was not attained until the Natural Food Company built, in 1901, a large factory at Niagara Falls, New York. In 1908, its corporate name was changed to "The Shredded Wheat Company;" and in 1930 its business and goodwill were acquired by National Biscuit Company.

Kellogg Company has been in the business of manufacturing breakfast food cereals since its organization in 1905. For a period commencing in 1912 and ending in 1919 it made a product whose form was somewhat like the product in question, but whose manufacture was different, the wheat being reduced to a dough before being pressed into shreds. For a short period in 1922 it manufactured the article in question. In 1927, it resumed manufacturing the product.... On June 11, 1932, the present suit was brought. Much evidence was introduced; but the determinative facts are relatively few; and as to most of these there is no conflict.

In 1935, the District Court dismissed the bill. It found that the name "Shredded Wheat" is a term describing alike the product of the plaintiff and of the defendant; and that no passing off or deception had been shown. It held that upon the expiration of the Perky patent No. 548,086 issued October 15, 1895, the name of the patented article passed into the public domain. In 1936, the Circuit Court of Appeals affirmed that decree. Upon rehearing, it vacated, in 1937, its own decree and reversed that of the District Court, with direction "to enter a decree enjoining the defendant from the use of the name 'Shredded Wheat' as its trade-name and from advertising or offering for sale its product in the form and shape of plaintiff's biscuit in violation of its trade-mark; and with further directions to order an accounting for damages and profits."...

....

The plaintiff concedes that it does not possess the exclusive right to make shredded wheat. But it claims the exclusive right to the trade name "Shredded Wheat" and the exclusive right to make shredded wheat biscuits pillow-shaped. It charges that the defendant, by using the name and shape, and otherwise, is passing off, or enabling others to pass off, Kellogg goods for those of the plaintiff. Kellogg Company denies that the plaintiff is entitled to the exclusive use of the name or of the pillow-shape; denies any passing off; asserts that it has used every reasonable effort to distinguish its product from that of the plaintiff; and contends that in honestly competing for a part of the market for shredded wheat it is exercising the common right freely to manufacture and sell an article of commerce unprotected by patent.

First. The plaintiff has no exclusive right to the use of the term "Shredded Wheat" as a trade name. For that is the generic term of the article, which describes it with a fair degree of accuracy; and is the term by which the biscuit in pillow-shaped form is generally known by the public. Since the term is generic, the original maker of the product acquired no exclusive right to use it. As Kellogg Company had the right to make the article, it had, also, the right to use the term by which the public knows it. [Citations.] Ever since 1894 the article has been known to the public as shredded wheat....

Moreover, the name "Shredded Wheat," as well as the product, the process and the machinery employed in making it, has been dedicated to the public. The basic patent for the product and for the process of making it, and many other patents for special machinery to be used in making the article, issued to Perky. In those patents the term "shredded" is repeatedly used as descriptive of the product. The basic patent expired October 15, 1912; the others soon after. Since during the life of the patents "Shredded Wheat" was the general designation of the patented product, there passed to the public upon the expiration of the patent, not only the right to make the article as it was made during the patent period, but also the right to apply thereto the name by which it had become known. As was said in *Singer Mfg. Co. v. June Mfg. Co.*, 163 U.S. 169, 185:

> "It equally follows from the cessation of the monopoly and the falling of the patented device into the domain of things public, that along with the public ownership of the device there must also necessarily pass to the public the

generic designation of the thing which has arisen during the monopoly.... To say otherwise would be to hold that, although the public had acquired the device covered by the patent, yet the owner of the patent or the manufacturer of the patented thing had retained the designated name which was essentially necessary to vest the public with the full enjoyment of that which had become theirs by the disappearance of the monopoly."

It is contended that the plaintiff has the exclusive right to the name "Shredded Wheat," because those words acquired the "secondary meaning" of shredded wheat made at Niagara Falls by the plaintiff's predecessor. There is no basis here for applying the doctrine of secondary meaning. The evidence shows only that due to the long period in which the plaintiff or its predecessor was the only manufacturer of the product, many people have come to associate the product, and as a consequence the name by which the product is generally known, with the plaintiff's factory at Niagara Falls. But to establish a trade name in the term "shredded wheat" the plaintiff must show more than a subordinate meaning which applies to it. It must show that the primary significance of the term in the minds of the consuming public is not the product but the producer. This it has not done. The showing which it has made does not entitle it to the exclusive use of the term shredded wheat but merely entitles it to require that the defendant use reasonable care to inform the public of the source of its product.

The plaintiff seems to contend that even if Kellogg Company acquired upon the expiration of the patents the right to use the name shredded wheat, the right was lost by delay. The argument is that Kellogg Company, although the largest producer of breakfast cereals in the country, did not seriously attempt to make shredded wheat, or to challenge plaintiff's right to that name until 1927, and that meanwhile plaintiff's predecessor had expended more than $17,000,000 in making the name a household word and identifying the product with its manufacture. Those facts are without legal significance. Kellogg Company's right was not one dependent upon diligent exercise. Like every other member of the public, it was, and remained, free to make shredded wheat when it chose to do so; and to call the product by its generic name. The only obligation resting upon Kellogg Company was to identify its own product lest it be mistaken for that of the plaintiff.

Second. The plaintiff has not the exclusive right to sell shredded wheat in the form of a pillow-shaped biscuit—the form in which the article became known to the public. That is the form in which shredded wheat was made under the basic patent. The patented machines used were designed to produce only the pillow-shaped biscuits. And a design patent was taken out to cover the pillow-shaped form. Hence, upon expiration of the patents the form, as well as the name, was dedicated to the public. As was said in *Singer Mfg. Co. v. June Mfg. Co., supra*, p. 185:

"It is self evident that on the expiration of a patent the monopoly granted by it ceases to exist, and the right to make the thing formerly covered by the patent becomes public property. It is upon this condition that the patent is granted. It follows, as a matter of course, that on the termination of the patent there passes to the public the right to make the machine in the form in which it was constructed during the patent. We may, therefore, dismiss without further comment the complaint, as to the form in which the defendant made his machines."

Where an article may be manufactured by all, a particular manufacturer can no more assert exclusive rights in a form in which the public has become accustomed to see the article and which, in the minds of the public, is primarily associated with the article rather than a particular producer, than it can in the case of a name with similar connections in the public mind. Kellogg Company was free to use the pillow-shaped form, subject only to the obligation to identify its product lest it be mistaken for that of the plaintiff.

Third. The question remains whether Kellogg Company in exercising its right to use the name "Shredded Wheat" and the pillow-shaped biscuit, is doing so fairly. Fairness requires that it be done in a manner which reasonably distinguishes its product from that of plaintiff.

Each company sells its biscuits only in cartons. The standard Kellogg carton contains fifteen biscuits; the plaintiff's twelve. The Kellogg cartons are distinctive. They do not resemble those used by the plaintiff either in size, form, or color. And the difference in the labels is striking. The Kellogg cartons bear in bold script the names "Kellogg's Whole Wheat Biscuit" or "Kellogg's Shredded Whole Wheat Biscuit" so sized and spaced as to strike the eye as being a Kellogg product. It is true that on some of its cartons it had a picture of two shredded wheat biscuits in a bowl of milk which was quite similar to one of the plaintiff's registered trademarks. But the name Kellogg was so prominent on all of the defendant's cartons as to minimize the possibility of confusion.

Some hotels, restaurants, and lunchrooms serve biscuits not in cartons and guests so served may conceivably suppose that a Kellogg biscuit served is one of the plaintiff's make. But no person familiar with plaintiff's product would be misled. The Kellogg biscuit is about two-thirds the size of plaintiff's; and differs from it in appearance. Moreover, the field in which deception could be practiced is negligibly small. Only 2? per cent of the Kellogg biscuits are sold to hotels, restaurants and lunchrooms. Of those so sold 98 per cent are sold in individual cartons containing two biscuits. These cartons are distinctive and bear prominently the Kellogg name. To put upon the individual biscuit some mark which would identify it as the Kellogg product is not commercially possible. Relatively few biscuits will be removed from the individual cartons before they reach the consumer. The obligation resting upon Kellogg Company is not to insure that every purchaser will know it to be the maker but to use every reasonable means to prevent confusion.

It is urged that all possibility of deception or confusion would be removed if Kellogg Company should refrain from using the name "Shredded Wheat" and adopt some form other than the pillow-shape. But the name and form are integral parts of the goodwill of the article. To share fully in the goodwill, it must use the name and the pillow-shape. And in the goodwill Kellogg Company is as free to share as the plaintiff. *Compare William R. Warner & Co. v. Eli Lilly & Co.*, 265 U.S. 526, 528, 530. Moreover, the pillow-shape must be used for another reason. The evidence is persuasive that this form is functional—that the cost of the biscuit would be increased and its high quality lessened if some other form were substituted for the pillow-shape.

Kellogg Company is undoubtedly sharing in the goodwill of the article known as "Shredded Wheat"; and thus is sharing in a market which was created by the skill and judgment of plaintiff's predecessor and has been widely extended by vast expenditures in advertising persistently made. But that is not unfair. Sharing in the goodwill of an article unprotected by patent or trade-mark is the exercise of a right possessed by all—and in the free exercise of which the consuming public is deeply interested. There is no evidence of passing off or deception on the part of the Kellogg Company; and it has taken every reasonable precaution to prevent confusion or the practice of deception in the sale of its product.

....

Questions

1. The "Shredded Wheat" decision concerned the trademark protection available to the design of a product, and to its name, following expiration of patents covering the product and the processes and special machinery needed to manufacture it. Is the Court holding that once such a patent expires, neither the product's shape nor its name can *ever* be the subject of a trademark? If not, under what circumstances is the assertion of trademark rights permissible?

2. Is trademark protection available for a word that accurately describes an article? For one that partially describes an article?

3. Is trademark protection available for a design for which a patent still subsists? For an unpatented design?

4. Justice Brandeis acknowledges that by adopting its predecessor's name and design, the second-comer

> is undoubtedly sharing in the goodwill of the article known as "Shredded Wheat"; and thus is sharing in a market which was created by the skill and judgment of plaintiff's predecessor and has been widely extended by vast expenditures in advertising persistently made. But that is not unfair. Sharing in the goodwill of an article unprotected by patent or trademark is the exercise of a right possessed by all—and in the free exercise of which the consuming public is deeply interested.

In other words, one may share in the goodwill of the product, but not in that of the producer. What is the difference between these two kinds of "sharing"? How would you demonstrate the difference?

5. For a full exploration of the history and implications of the "Shredded Wheat" decision, see Graeme Dinwoodie, *The Story of* Kellogg v. National Biscuit*: Breakfast with Brandeis, in* JANE C. GINSBURG & ROCHELLE COOPER DREYFUSS, EDS., INTELLECTUAL PROPERTY STORIES 222 (2005).

1. Word Marks

Coca-Cola Co. v. Koke Co. of America

254 U.S. 143 (1920)

MR. JUSTICE HOLMES delivered the opinion of the Court:

This is a bill in equity brought by the Coca-Cola Company to prevent the infringement of its trade-mark Coca-Cola and unfair competition with it in its business of making and selling the beverage for which the trade-mark is used. The District Court gave the plaintiff a decree. 235 Fed. Rep. 408. This was reversed by the Circuit Court of Appeals. *Koke Co. v. Coca-Cola Co.*, 255 Fed. Rep. 894. Subsequently a writ of certiorari was granted by this Court.

It appears that after the plaintiff's predecessors in title had used the mark for some years it was registered under the Act of Congress of March 3, 1881, c. 138, 21 Stat. 502, and again under the Act of February 20, 1905, c. 592, 33 Stat. 724. Both the Courts below agree that subject to the one question to be considered the plaintiff has a right to equitable relief. Whatever may have been its original weakness, the mark for years has acquired a secondary significance and has indicated the plaintiff's product alone. It is found that defendant's mixture is made and sold in imitation of the plaintiff's and that the word "Koke" was chosen for the purpose of reaping the benefit of the advertising done by the plaintiff and of selling the imitation as and for the plaintiff's goods. The only obstacle found by the Circuit Court of Appeals in the way of continuing the injunction granted below was its opinion that the trade-mark in itself and the advertisements accompanying it made such fraudulent representations to the public that the plaintiff had lost its claim to any help from the Court. That is the question upon which the writ of certiorari was granted and the main one that we shall discuss.

Of course a man is not to be protected in the use of a device the very purpose and effect of which is to swindle the public. But the defects of a plaintiff do not offer a very broad ground for allowing another to swindle him. The defense relied on here should be scrutinized with a critical eye. The main point is this: Before 1900 the beginning of the good will was more or less helped by the presence of cocaine, a drug that, like alcohol or caffeine or opium, may be described as a deadly poison or as a valuable item of the pharmacopoeia according to the rhetorical purposes in view. The amount seems to have been very small, but it may have been enough to begin a bad habit and after the Food and Drug Act of June 30, 1906, c. 3915, 34 Stat. 768, if not earlier, long before this suit was brought, it was eliminated from the plaintiff's compound. Coca leaves still are used, to be sure, but after they have been subjected to a drastic process that removes from them every characteristic substance except a little tannin and still less chlorophyll. The cola nut, at best, on its side furnishes but a small portion of the caffeine, which now is the only element that has appreciable effect. That comes mainly from other sources. It is argued that the continued use of the name imports a representation that has ceased to be true … and that thus the very thing sought to be protected is used as a fraud.

The argument does not satisfy us. We are dealing here with a popular drink not with a medicine, and although what has been said might suggest that its attraction lay in producing the expectation of a toxic effect the facts point to a different conclusion. Since 1900 the sales have increased at a very great rate corresponding to a like increase in advertising. The name now characterizes a beverage to be had at almost any soda fountain. It means a single thing coming from a single source, and well known to the community. It hardly would be too much to say that the drink characterizes the name as much as the name the drink. In other words "Coca-Cola" probably means to most persons the plaintiff's familiar product to be had everywhere rather than a compound of particular substances.… [I]t has acquired a secondary meaning in which perhaps the product is more emphasized than the producer but to which the producer is entitled. The coca leaves and whatever of cola nut is employed may be used to justify the continuance of the name or they may affect the flavor as the plaintiff contends, but before this suit was brought the plaintiff had advertised to the public that it must not expect and would not find cocaine, and had eliminated everything tending to suggest cocaine effects except the name and the picture of the leaves and nuts, which probably conveyed little or nothing to most who saw it. It appears to us that it would be going too far to deny the plaintiff relief against a palpable fraud because possibly here and there an ignorant person might call for the drink with the hope for incipient cocaine intoxication. The plaintiff's position must be judged by the facts as they were when the suit was begun, not by the facts of a different condition and an earlier time.

…

Question

Should the law protect trademarks that describe products deceptively? Why or why not?

a. Slogans

It is no longer disputed that slogans can function as trademarks. In 1955, the Commissioner of Patents held the slogan MOVING AIR IS OUR BUSINESS registrable on the Principal Register. In 1990, Jimmy Johns registered the slogan FREE SMELLS for restaurant services. In 1995, Nike registered the slogan, JUST DO IT for sportswear. More recently, Coca Cola registered the slogan OPEN HAPPINESS for soft drinks, General Motors registered FIND NEW ROADS for automobiles, Whole Foods Markets registered the slogan AMERICA'S HEALTHIEST GROCERY STORE for retail grocery store services, the Smucker Company registered CHOOSY MOMS CHOOSE JIF for peanut butter, and Proctor & Gamble registered the slogan ENJOY THE GO for toilet paper.

What if the slogan is straightforwardly descriptive? Like other descriptive terms, a descriptive slogan can acquire secondary meaning through extensive, continuous and substantially exclusive use. One such slogan was at issue in *Roux Labs. v. Clairol, Inc.*, 427 F.2d 823 (C.C.P.A. 1970), where the court dismissed an opposition to registration on the Principal Register of the slogan "HAIR COLOR SO NATURAL ONLY HER HAIR DRESSER KNOWS FOR SURE" for "hair tinting, dyeing and coloring preparation." In rejecting opposer's mere descriptiveness challenge, the court emphasized the pervasiveness of applicant's advertising and sales: from 1956–66, applicant sold over 50 million dollars worth of the product, and expended 22 million dollars in advertising containing the disputed slogan. In *In re Boston Beer*, 198 F.3d 1370 (Fed. Cir. 1999), however, the Court of Appeals for the Federal Circuit upheld the Board's refusal to register THE BEST BEER IN AMERICA despite evidence of 85 million dollars of sales and 10 million dollars of advertising. The court observed: "The record shows that 'The Best Beer in America' is a common phrase used descriptively by others before and concurrently with Boston Beer's use, and is nothing more than a claim of superiority." 198 F.3d at 1374. More recently, the Trademark Trial and Appeal Board upheld the trademark examiner's refusal to register the slogan ONCE A MARINE, ALWAYS A MARINE for clothing on the ground that the slogan did not function as a trademark. *In re Eagle Crest, Inc.*, 96 U.S.P.Q.2d (BNA) 1227 (T.T.A.B. 2010):

> There is no dispute that the phrase ONCE A MARINE, ALWAYS A MARINE is an old and familiar Marine expression, and as such it is the type of expression that should remain free for all to use. In fact, the evidence shows that the slogan is commonly used in an informational and ornamental manner on t-shirts and various other retail items produced and/or sold by others.... The function of a trademark is to identify a single commercial source. Because consumers would be accustomed to seeing this phrase displayed on clothing items from many different sources, they could not view the slogan as a trademark indicating source of the clothing only in applicant. It is clear

that clothing imprinted with this slogan will be purchased by consumers for the message it conveys. Applicant is not entitled to appropriate the slogan to itself and thereby attempt to prevent competitors from using it to promote the sale of their own clothing.

b. Personal Names

Peaceable Planet, Inc. v. Ty, Inc.

362 F.3d 986 (7th Cir. 2004)

POSNER, J.

....

... Like the defendant, the much larger and better known Ty Inc...., Peaceable Planet makes plush toys in the shape of animals, filled with bean-like materials to give the toys a soft and floppy feel. Ty's plush toys are, of course, the famous "Beanie Babies."

In the spring of 1999, Peaceable Planet began selling a camel that it named "Niles." The name was chosen to evoke Egypt, which is largely desert except for the ribbon of land bracketing the Nile. The camel is a desert animal, and photos juxtaposing a camel with an Egyptian pyramid are common. The price tag fastened to Niles's ear contains information both about camels and about Egypt, and the Egyptian flag is stamped on the animal.

A small company, Peaceable Planet sold only a few thousand of its camels in 1999. In March of the following year, Ty began selling a camel also named "Niles." It sold a huge number of its "Niles" camels—almost two million in one year—precipitating this suit. The district court ruled that "Niles," being a personal name, is a descriptive mark that the law does not protect unless and until it has acquired secondary meaning, that is, until there is proof that consumers associate the name with the plaintiff's brand. Peaceable Planet did not prove that consumers associate the name "Niles" with its camel.

....

The reluctance to allow personal names to be used as trademarks reflects valid concerns... One of the concerns is a reluctance to forbid a person to use his own name in his own business. [Citations.] Supposing a man named Brooks opened a clothing store under his name, should this prevent a second Brooks from opening a clothing store under his own (identical) name even though consumers did not yet associate the name with the first Brooks's store? It should not. [Citations.]

Another and closely related concern behind the personal-name rule is that some names are so common—such as "Smith," "Jones," "Schwartz," "Wood," and "Jackson"—that consumers will not assume that two products having the same name therefore have the same source, and so they will not be confused by their bearing the same name. [Citations.] If there are two bars in a city that are named "Steve's," people will not infer that they are owned by the same Steve.

The third concern, which is again related but brings us closest to the rule regarding descriptive marks, is that preventing a person from using his name to denote his business may deprive consumers of useful information. Maybe "Steve" is a well-known neighborhood figure. If he can't call his bar "Steve's" because there is an existing bar of that name, he is prevented from communicating useful information to the consuming public. [Citations.]

....

The personal-name "rule," it is worth noting, is a common law rather than statutory doctrine. All that the Lanham Act says about personal names is that a mark that is "primarily merely a surname" is not registrable in the absence of secondary meaning. 15 U.S.C. §§ 1052(e)(4), (f). There is no reference to first names. The reason for the surname provision is illustrated by the Brooks example. The extension of the rule to first names is a judicial innovation and so needn't be pressed further than its rationale, as might have to be done if the rule were codified in inflexible statutory language. Notice too the limitation implicit in the statutory term "primarily."

In thinking about the applicability of the rationale of the personal-name rule to the present case, we should notice first of all that camels, whether real or toy, do not go into business. Peaceable Planet's appropriation of the name "Niles" for its camel is not preventing some hapless camel in the Sahara Desert who happens to be named "Niles" from going into the water-carrier business under its own name. The second thing to notice is that "Niles" is not a very common name; in fact it is downright rare. And the third thing to notice is that if it were a common name, still there would be no danger that precluding our hypothetical Saharan water carrier from using its birth name "Niles" would deprive that camel's customers of valuable information. In short, the rationale of the personal-name rule is wholly inapplicable to this case.

What is more, if one wants to tie the rule in some fashion to the principle that descriptive marks are not protectable without proof of second meaning, then one must note that "Niles," at least when affixed to a toy camel, is a suggestive mark, like "Microsoft" or "*Business Week*," or—coming closer to this case—like "Eeyore" used as the name of a donkey, or the proper names in *Circuit City Stores, Inc. v. CarMax, Inc., supra*, 165 F.3d [1047 (6th Cir. 1999)] at 1054, rather than being a descriptive mark. Suggestive marks are protected by trademark law without proof of secondary meaning. [Citations.] Secondary meaning is not required because there are plenty of alternatives to any given suggestive mark. There are many more ways of suggesting than of describing. Suggestive names for camels include "Lawrence [of Arabia]" (one of Ty's other Beanie Babies *is* a camel named "Lawrence"); "Desert Taxi," "Sopwith" (the Sopwith Camel was Snoopy's World War I fighter plane), "Camelia," "Traveling Oasis," "Kamelsutra," "Cameleon," and "Humpy-Dumpy."

If "Niles" cannot be a protected trademark, it must be because to give it legal protection would run afoul of one of the purposes of the common law rule that we have identified rather than because it is a descriptive term, which it is not. But we have seen that it does not run afoul of any of those purposes. "Niles" is not the name of the defendant—it's not as if Peaceable Planet had named its camel "Ty Inc." or "H. Ty Warner." It also is not a common name, like "Smith" or "Jackson." And making

Ty use a different name for its camel would not deprive the consumer of valuable information about Ty or its camel.

. . . .

Questions

1. How should the law balance an individual's interest in using her personal name as the name of her business with the public's interest in protection from confusing and deceptive marks?

2. Orville Clarence Redenbacher grew up in Indiana and founded a tremendously successful popcorn brand, which he sold under his name. Redenbacher died in 1995; his popcorn company (now owned by ConAgra) lives on. If someone else with the Redenbacher surname now wants to start a snack food business under his own name, does ConAgra have a legitimate basis for complaint? *Cf. Taylor Wine Co. v. Bully Hill Vineyards*, 569 F.2d 731 (2d Cir. 1977) (affirming injunction prohibiting the grandson of Walter Taylor from using his name as a trademark for wine).

2. Symbols

Mishawaka Rubber & Woolen Manufacturing Co. v. S.S. Kresge Co.

316 U.S. 203 (1942)

Mr. Justice Frankfurter delivered the opinion of the Court.

The petitioner, which manufactures and sells shoes and rubber heels, employs a trade-mark, registered under the Trade-Mark Act of 1905, 33 Stat. 724, 15 U.S.C. § 81 *et seq.*, consisting of a red circular plug embedded in the center of a heel. The heels were not sold separately, but were attached to shoes made by the petitioner. It has spent considerable sums of money in seeking to gain the favor of the consuming public by promoting the mark as assurance of a desirable product. The respondent sold heels not made by the petitioner but bearing a mark described by the District Court as "a circular plug of red or reddish color so closely resembling that of the plaintiff [petitioner] that it is difficult to distinguish the products sold by the defendant from the plaintiff's products." The heels sold by the respondent were inferior in quality to those made by the petitioner, and "this tended to destroy the good will created by the plaintiff in the manufacture of its superior product." Although there was no evidence that particular purchasers were actually deceived into believing that the heels sold by the respondent were manufactured by the petitioner, the District Court found that there was a "reasonable likelihood" that some purchases might have been induced by the purchaser's belief that he was obtaining the petitioner's product. "The ordinary purchaser, having become familiar with the plaintiff's trade-mark, would naturally be led to believe that the heels marketed by the defendant were the product of the plaintiff company." Concluding that the petitioner's mark had thus been infringed, the court enjoined future infringement and also ordered that the respondent account to the petitioner for profits made from sales "to purchasers who were induced to buy because they believed the heels to be those of plaintiff and which sales plaintiff would otherwise have made."

....

The protection of trade-marks is the law's recognition of the psychological function of symbols. If it is true that we live by symbols, it is no less true that we purchase goods by them. A trade-mark is a merchandising short-cut which induces a purchaser to select what he wants, or what he has been led to believe he wants. The owner of a mark exploits this human propensity by making every effort to impregnate the atmosphere of the market with the drawing power of a congenial symbol. Whatever the means employed, the aim is the same—to convey through the mark, in the minds of potential customers, the desirability of the commodity upon which it appears. Once this is attained, the trade-mark owner has something of value. If another poaches upon the commercial magnetism of the symbol he has created, the owner can obtain legal redress. And in this case we are called upon to ascertain the extent of the redress afforded for infringement of a mark registered under the Trade-Mark Act of 1905.

....

If it can be shown that the infringement had no relation to profits made by the defendant, that some purchasers bought goods bearing the infringing mark because of the defendant's recommendation or his reputation or for any reason other than a response to the diffused appeal of the plaintiff's symbol, the burden of showing this is upon the poacher. The plaintiff of course is not entitled to profits demonstrably not attributable to the unlawful use of his mark. [Citations.] The burden is the infringer's to prove that his infringement had no cash value in sales made by him. If he does not do so, the profits made on sales of goods bearing the infringing mark properly belong to the owner of the mark. [Citation.] There may well be a windfall to the trade-mark owner where it is impossible to isolate the profits which are attributable to the use of the infringing mark. But to hold otherwise would give the windfall to the wrongdoer. In the absence of his proving the contrary, it promotes honesty and comports with experience to assume that the wrongdoer who makes profits from the sales of goods bearing a mark belonging to another was enabled to do so because he was drawing upon the good will generated by that mark. And one who makes profits derived from the unlawful appropriation of a mark belonging to another cannot relieve himself of his obligation to restore the profits to their rightful owner merely by showing that the latter did not choose to use the mark in the particular manner employed by the wrongdoer.

....

Questions

1. What has the "psychological function of symbols" to do with consumer protection? Is poaching upon the commercial magnetism of a symbol the same thing as confusing consumers about the source or origin of a product?

2. Justice Frankfurter speaks of the power of trademarks as embodying the "drawing power of a congenial symbol." To what degree should the law take into account the fact that some symbols may be intrinsically more congenial than others?

3. Trade Dress

Qualitex Co. v. Jacobson Products Co., Inc.

514 U.S. 159 (1995)

JUSTICE BREYER delivered the opinion of the Court:

The question in this case is whether the Trademark Act of 1946 (Lanham Act), 15 U.S.C. §§ 1051–1127 (1988 ed. and Supp. V), permits the registration of a trademark that consists, purely and simply, of a color. We conclude that, sometimes, a color will meet ordinary legal trademark requirements. And, when it does so, no special legal rule prevents color alone from serving as a trademark.

I

The case before us grows out of petitioner Qualitex Company's use (since the 1950's) of a special shade of green-gold color on the pads that it makes and sells to dry cleaning firms for use on dry cleaning presses. In 1989, respondent Jacobson Products (a Qualitex rival) began to sell its own press pads to dry cleaning firms; and it colored those pads a similar green-gold. In 1991, Qualitex registered the special green-gold color on press pads with the Patent and Trademark Office as a trademark. Registration No. 1,633,711 (Feb. 5, 1991). Qualitex subsequently added a trademark infringement count, 15 U.S.C. § 1114(1), to an unfair competition claim, § 1125(a), in a lawsuit it had already filed challenging Jacobson's use of the green-gold color.

Qualitex won the lawsuit in the District Court. 21 U.S.P.Q.2d (BNA) 1457 (C.D. Cal.1991). But, the Court of Appeals for the Ninth Circuit set aside the judgment in Qualitex's favor on the trademark infringement claim because, in that Circuit's view, the Lanham Act does not permit Qualitex, or anyone else, to register "color alone" as a trademark. 13 F.3d 1297, 1300, 1302 (1994).

The Courts of Appeals have differed as to whether or not the law recognizes the use of color alone as a trademark. Compare *NutraSweet Co. v. Stadt Corp.*, 917 F.2d 1024, 1028 (C.A.7 1990) (absolute prohibition against protection of color alone), with *In re Owens-Corning Fiberglas Corp.*, 774 F.2d 1116, 1128 (C.A. Fed. 1985) (allowing registration of color pink for fiberglass insulation), and *Master Distributors, Inc. v. Pako Corp.*, 986 F.2d 219, 224 (C.A.8 1993) (declining to establish *per se* prohibition against protecting color alone as a trademark). Therefore, this Court granted certiorari. 512 U.S. 1287 (1994). We now hold that there is no rule absolutely barring the use of color alone, and we reverse the judgment of the Ninth Circuit.

II

The Lanham Act gives a seller or producer the exclusive right to "register" a trademark, 15 U.S.C. § 1052 (1988 ed. and Supp. V), and to prevent his or her competitors from using that trademark, § 1114(1). Both the language of the Act and the basic underlying principles of trademark law would seem to include color within the universe of things that can qualify as a trademark. The language of the Lanham Act describes that universe in the broadest of terms. It says that trademarks "include[e] any word, name, symbol, or device, or any combination thereof." § 1127. Since human beings might use as a "symbol" or "device" almost anything at all that is capable of carrying meaning, this language, read literally, is not restrictive....

A color is also capable of satisfying the more important part of the statutory definition of a trademark, which requires that a person "us[e]" or "inten[d] to use" the mark

> "to identify and distinguish his or her goods, including a unique product, from those manufactured or sold by others and to indicate the source of the goods, even if that source is unknown." 15 U.S.C. § 1127.

True, a product's color is unlike "fanciful," "arbitrary," or "suggestive" words or designs, which almost *automatically* tell a customer that they refer to a brand. *Abercrombie & Fitch Co. v. Hunting World, Inc.*, 537 F.2d 4, 9–10 (C.A.2 1976) (Friendly, J.); see *Two Pesos, Inc. v. Taco Cabana, Inc.*, 505 U.S. 763, 768 (1992). The imaginary word "Suntost," or the words "Suntost Marmalade," on a jar of orange jam immediately would signal a brand or a product "source"; the jam's orange color does not do so. But, over time, customers may come to treat a particular color on a product or its packaging (say, a color that in context seems unusual, such as pink on a firm's insulating material or red on the head of a large industrial bolt) as signifying a brand. And, if so, that color would have come to identify and distinguish the goods—*i.e.*, "to indicate" their "source"—much in the way that descriptive words on a product (say, "Trim" on nail clippers or "Car-Freshner" on deodorizer) can come to indicate a product's origin. See, *e.g.*, *J. Wiss & Sons Co. v. W.E. Bassett Co.*, 462 F.2d 567, 569 (1972); *Car-Freshner Corp. v. Turtle Wax, Inc.*, 268 F. Supp. 162, 164 (S.D.N.Y. 1967). In this circumstance, trademark law says that the word (*e.g.*, "Trim"), although not inherently distinctive, has developed "secondary meaning." See *Inwood Laboratories, Inc. v. Ives Laboratories, Inc.*, 456 U.S. 844, 851, n. 11 (1982) ("[S]econdary meaning" is acquired when "in the minds of the public, the primary significance of a product feature ... is to identify the source of the product rather than the product itself"). Again, one might ask, if trademark law permits a descriptive word with secondary meaning to act as a mark, why would it not permit a color, under similar circumstances, to do the same?

We cannot find in the basic objectives of trademark law any obvious theoretical objection to the use of color alone as a trademark, where that color has attained "secondary meaning" and therefore identifies and distinguishes a particular brand (and thus indicates its "source"). In principle, trademark law, by preventing others from copying a source-identifying mark, "reduce[s] the customer's costs of shopping and making purchasing decisions," 1 J. McCarthy, McCarthy on Trademarks and Unfair Competition § 2.01[2], p. 2–3 (3d ed. 1994) (hereinafter McCarthy), for it quickly and easily assures a potential customer that *this* item—the item with this mark—is made by the same producer as other similarly marked items that he or she liked (or disliked) in the past. At the same time, the law helps assure a producer that it (and not an imitating competitor) will reap the financial, reputation-related rewards associated with a desirable product. The law thereby "encourage[s] the production of quality products," *ibid.*, and simultaneously discourages those who hope to sell inferior products by capitalizing on a consumer's inability quickly to evaluate the quality of an item offered for sale. [Citations.] It is the source—distinguishing ability of a mark—not its ontological status as color, shape, fragrance, word, or sign—that permits it to serve these basic purposes. See Landes & Posner, *Trademark Law: An Economic Perspective*, 30 J. Law & Econ. 265, 290 (1987). And, for that reason, it is difficult to find, in basic trademark objectives, a reason to disqualify absolutely the use of a color as a mark.

Neither can we find a principled objection to the use of color as a mark in the important "functionality" doctrine of trademark law. The functionality doctrine prevents trademark law, which seeks to promote competition by protecting a firm's reputation, from instead inhibiting legitimate competition by allowing a producer to control a useful product feature. It is the province of patent law, not trademark law, to encourage invention by granting inventors a monopoly over new product designs or functions for a limited time, 35 U.S.C. §§ 154, 173, after which competitors are free to use the innovation. If a product's functional features could be used as trademarks, however, a monopoly over such features could be obtained without regard to whether they qualify as patents and could be extended forever (because trademarks may be renewed in perpetuity). See *Kellogg Co. v. National Biscuit Co.*, 305 U.S. 111, 119–120 (1938) (Brandeis, J.); *Inwood Laboratories, Inc., supra*, at 863 (White, J., concurring in result) ("A functional characteristic is 'an important ingredient in the commercial success of the product,' and, after expiration of a patent, it is no more the property of the originator than the product itself") (citation omitted). Functionality doctrine therefore would require, to take an imaginary example, that even if customers have come to identify the special illumination-enhancing shape of a new patented light bulb with a particular manufacturer, the manufacturer may not use that shape as a trademark, for doing so, after the patent had expired, would impede competition—not by protecting the reputation of the original bulb maker, but by frustrating competitors' legitimate efforts to produce an equivalent illumination-enhancing bulb. See, *e.g.*, *Kellogg Co., supra*, at 119–120 (trademark law cannot be used to extend monopoly over "pillow" shape of shredded wheat biscuit after the patent for that shape had expired). This Court consequently has explained that, "[i]n general terms, a product feature is functional," and cannot serve as a trademark, "if it is essential to the use or purpose of the article or if it affects the cost or quality of the article," that is, if exclusive use of the feature would put competitors at a significant non-reputation-related disadvantage.

Inwood Laboratories, Inc., 456 U.S. at 850, n. 10. Although sometimes color plays an important role (unrelated to source identification) in making a product more desirable, sometimes it does not. And, this latter fact—the fact that sometimes color is not essential to a product's use or purpose and does not affect cost or quality—indicates that the doctrine of "functionality" does not create an absolute bar to the use of color alone as a mark. See *Owens-Corning*, 774 F.2d at 1123 (pink color of insulation in wall "performs no nontrademark function").

It would seem, then, that color alone, at least sometimes, can meet the basic legal requirements for use as a trademark. It can act as a symbol that distinguishes a firm's goods and identifies their source, without serving any other significant function. [Citations.] Indeed, the District Court, in this case, entered findings (accepted by the Ninth Circuit) that show Qualitex's green-gold press pad color has met these requirements. The green-gold color acts as a symbol. Having developed secondary meaning (for customers identified the green-gold color as Qualitex's), it identifies the press pads' source. And, the green-gold color serves no other function. (Although it is important to use *some* color on press pads to avoid noticeable stains, the court found "no competitive need in the press pad industry for the green-gold color, since other colors are equally usable." 21 U.S.P.Q.2d (BNA) at 1460.) Accordingly, unless there is some special reason that convincingly militates against the use of color alone as a trademark, trademark law would protect Qualitex's use of the green-gold color on its press pads.

III

Respondent Jacobson Products says that there are four special reasons why the law should forbid the use of color alone as a trademark. We shall explain, in turn, why we, ultimately, find them unpersuasive.

First, Jacobson says that, if the law permits the use of color as a trademark, it will produce uncertainty and unresolvable court disputes about what shades of a color a competitor may lawfully use. Because lighting (morning sun, twilight mist) will affect perceptions of protected color, competitors and courts will suffer from "shade confusion" as they try to decide whether use of a similar color on a similar product does, or does not, confuse customers and thereby infringe a trademark. Jacobson adds that the "shade confusion" problem is "more difficult" and "far different from" the "determination of the similarity of words or symbols."

We do not believe, however, that color, in this respect, is special. Courts traditionally decide quite difficult questions about whether two words or phrases or symbols are sufficiently similar, in context, to confuse buyers. They have had to compare, for example, such words as "Bonamine" and "Dramamine" (motion-sickness remedies); "Huggies" and "Dougies" (diapers); "Cheracol" and "Syrocol" (cough syrup); "Cyclone" and "Tornado" (wire fences); and "Mattres" and "1-800-Mattres" (mattress franchisor telephone numbers). See, *e.g., G.D. Searle & Co. v. Chas. Pfizer & Co.*, 265 F.2d 385, 389 (C.A.7 1959); *Kimberly-Clark Corp. v. H. Douglas Enterprises, Ltd.*, 774 F.2d 1144, 1146–1147 (C.A. Fed.1985); *Upjohn Co. v. Schwartz*, 246 F.2d 254, 262 (C.A.2 1957); *Hancock v. American Steel & Wire Co. of N.J.*, 203 F.2d 737, 740–741 (1953); *Dial-A-*

Mattress Franchise Corp. v. Page, 880 F.2d 675, 678 (C.A.2 1989). Legal standards exist to guide courts in making such comparisons. See, *e.g.*, 2 McCarthy § 15.08; 1 McCarthy §§ 11.24–11.25 ("[S]trong" marks, with greater secondary meaning, receive broader protection than "weak" marks). We do not see why courts could not apply those standards to a color, replicating, if necessary, lighting conditions under which a colored product is normally sold. See Ebert, *Trademark Protection in Color: Do It By the Numbers!*, 84 T.M. Rep. 379, 405 (1994). Indeed, courts already have done so in cases where a trademark consists of a color plus a design, *i.e.*, a colored symbol such as a gold stripe (around a sewer pipe), a yellow strand of wire rope, or a "brilliant yellow" band (on ampules). See, *e.g.*, *Youngstown Sheet & Tube Co. v. Tallman Conduit Co.*, 149 U.S.P.Q. (BNA) 656, 657 (TTAB 1966); *Amsted Industries, Inc. v. West Coast Wire Rope & Rigging Inc.*, 2 U.S.P.Q.2d (BNA) 1755, 1760 (TTAB 1987); *In re Hodes-Lange Corp.*, 167 U.S.P.Q. (BNA) 255, 256 (TTAB 1970).

Second, Jacobson argues, as have others, that colors are in limited supply. See, *e.g.*, *NutraSweet Co.*, 917 F.2d at 1028; *Campbell Soup Co. v. Armour & Co.*, 175 F.2d 795, 798 (C.A.3 1949). Jacobson claims that, if one of many competitors can appropriate a particular color for use as a trademark, and each competitor then tries to do the same, the supply of colors will soon be depleted. Put in its strongest form, this argument would concede that "[h]undreds of color pigments are manufactured and thousands of colors can be obtained by mixing." L. Cheskin, Colors: What They Can Do For You 47 (1947). But, it would add that, in the context of a particular product, only some colors are usable. By the time one discards colors that, say, for reasons of customer appeal, are not usable, and adds the shades that competitors cannot use lest they risk infringing a similar, registered shade, then one is left with only a handful of possible colors. And, under these circumstances, to permit one, or a few, producers to use colors as trademarks will "deplete" the supply of usable colors to the point where a competitor's inability to find a suitable color will put that competitor at a significant disadvantage.

This argument is unpersuasive, however, largely because it relies on an occasional problem to justify a blanket prohibition. When a color serves as a mark, normally alternative colors will likely be available for similar use by others. See, *e.g.*, *Owens-Corning*, 774 F.2d at 1121 (pink insulation). Moreover, if that is not so—if a "color depletion" or "color scarcity" problem does arise—the trademark doctrine of "functionality" normally would seem available to prevent the anticompetitive consequences that Jacobson's argument posits, thereby minimizing that argument's practical force.

The functionality doctrine, as we have said, forbids the use of a product's feature as a trademark where doing so will put a competitor at a significant disadvantage because the feature is "essential to the use or purpose of the article" or "affects [its] cost or quality." *Inwood Laboratories, Inc.*, 456 U.S. at 850, n. 10. The functionality doctrine thus protects competitors against a disadvantage (unrelated to recognition or reputation) that trademark protection might otherwise impose, namely, their inability reasonably to replicate important non-reputation-related product features. For example, this Court has written that competitors might be free to copy the color of a medical pill where that color serves to identify the kind of medication (*e.g.*, a type of blood medicine) in addition to its source. See *id.*, at 853, 858, n. 20 ("[S]ome patients commingle medications in a container and rely on color to differentiate one from another"); see also J. Ginsburg, D. Goldberg, & A. Greenbaum, Trademark and Unfair Competition Law 194–195 (1991) (noting that drug color cases "have more to do with public health policy" regarding generic drug substitution "than with trademark law"). And, the federal courts have demonstrated that they can apply this doctrine in a careful and reasoned manner, with sensitivity to the effect on competition. Although we need not comment on the merits of specific cases, we note that lower courts have permitted competitors to copy the green color of farm machinery (because customers wanted their farm equipment to match) and have barred the use of black as a trademark on outboard boat motors (because black has the special functional attributes of decreasing the apparent size of the motor and ensuring compatibility with many different boat colors). See *Deere & Co. v. Farmhand, Inc.*, 560 F. Supp. 85, 98 (S.D. Iowa 1982), aff'd, 721 F.2d 253 (C.A.8 1983); *Brunswick Corp. v. British Seagull Ltd.*, 35 F.3d 1527, 1532 (C.A. Fed.1994), cert. pending, No. 94-1075; see also *Nor-Am Chemical v. O.M. Scott & Sons Co.*, 4 U.S.P.Q.2d (BNA) 1316, 1320 (E.D. Pa. 1987) (blue color of fertilizer held functional because it indicated the presence of nitrogen). The Restatement (Third) of Unfair Competition adds that, if a design's "aesthetic value" lies in its ability to "confe[r] a significant benefit that cannot practically be duplicated by the use of alternative designs," then the design is "functional." Restatement (Third) of Unfair Competition § 17, Comment *c*, pp. 175–176 (1995). The "ultimate test of aesthetic functionality," it explains, "is whether the recognition of trademark rights would significantly hinder competition." *Id.*, at 176.

The upshot is that, where a color serves a significant nontrademark function—whether to distinguish a heart pill from a digestive medicine or to satisfy the "noble instinct for giving the right touch of beauty to common and necessary things," G. Chesterton, Simplicity and Tolstoy 61 (1912)—courts will examine whether its use as a mark would permit one competitor (or a group) to interfere with legitimate (nontrademark-related) competition through actual or potential exclusive use of an important product ingredient. That examination should not discourage firms from creating esthetically pleasing mark designs, for it is open to their competitors to do the same. See, *e.g.*, *W.T. Rogers Co. v. Keene*, 778 F.2d 334, 343 (C.A.7 1985) (Posner, J.). But, ordinarily, it should prevent the anticompetitive consequences of Jacobson's hypothetical "color depletion" argument, when, and if, the circumstances of a particular case threaten "color depletion."

Third, Jacobson points to many older cases—including Supreme Court cases—in support of its position. In 1878, this Court described the common-law definition of trademark rather broadly to "consist of a name, symbol, figure, letter, form, or device, if adopted and used by a manufacturer or merchant in order to designate the goods he manufactures or sells to distinguish the same from those manufactured or sold by another." *McLean v. Fleming*, 96 U.S. 245, 254. Yet, in interpreting the Trademark Acts of 1881 and 1905, 21 Stat. 502, 33 Stat. 724, which retained that common-law definition, the Court questioned "[w]hether mere color can constitute a valid trade-mark," *A. Leschen & Sons Rope Co. v. Broderick & Bascom Rope Co.*, 201 U.S. 166, 171 (1906), and suggested that the "product including the coloring matter is free to all who make it." *Coca-Cola Co. v. Koke Co. of America*, 254 U.S. 143, 147 (1920). Even though these statements amounted to dicta, lower courts interpreted them as forbidding protection for color alone. See, *e.g.*, *Campbell Soup Co.*, 175 F.2d at 798, and n. 9; *Life Savers Corp. v. Curtiss Candy Co.*, 182 F.2d 4, 9 (C.A.7 1950) (quoting *Campbell Soup*, *supra*, at 798).

These Supreme Court cases, however, interpreted trademark law as it existed before 1946, when Congress enacted the Lanham Act. The Lanham Act significantly changed and liberalized the common law to "dispense with mere technical prohibitions," S. Rep. No. 1333, 79th Cong., 2d Sess., 3 (1946), most notably, by permitting trademark registration of descriptive words (say, "U-Build-It" model airplanes) where they had acquired "secondary meaning." See *Abercrombie & Fitch Co.*, 537 F.2d at 9 (Friendly, J.). The Lanham Act extended protection to descriptive marks by making clear that (with certain explicit exceptions not relevant here),

> "nothing ... shall prevent the registration of a mark used by the applicant which has become distinctive of the applicant's goods in commerce." 15 U.S.C. § 1052(f) (1988 ed., Supp. V).

This language permits an ordinary word, normally used for a nontrademark purpose (*e.g.*, description), to act as a trademark where it has gained "secondary meaning." Its logic would appear to apply to color as well. Indeed, in 1985, the Federal Circuit considered the significance of the Lanham Act's changes as they related to color and held that trademark protection for color was consistent with the

> "jurisprudence under the Lanham Act developed in accordance with the statutory principle that if a mark is capable of being or becoming distinctive of [the] applicant's goods in commerce, then it is capable of serving as a trademark." *Owens-Corning*, 774 F.2d at 1120.

In 1988 Congress amended the Lanham Act, revising portions of the definitional language, but left unchanged the language here relevant. § 134, 102 Stat. 3946, 15 U.S.C. § 1127....

This history undercuts the authority of the precedent on which Jacobson relies. Much of the pre-1985 case law rested on statements in Supreme Court opinions that interpreted pre-Lanham Act trademark law and were not directly related to the holdings in those cases. Moreover, we believe the Federal Circuit was right in 1985 when it found that the 1946 Lanham Act embodied crucial legal changes that liberalized the law to permit the use of color alone as a trademark (under appropriate circumstances). At a minimum, the Lanham Act's changes left the courts free to reevaluate the pre-existing legal precedent which had absolutely forbidden the use of color alone as a trademark. Finally, when Congress re-enacted the terms "word, name, symbol, or device" in 1988, it did so against a legal background in which those terms had come to include color, and its statutory revision embraced that understanding.

Fourth, Jacobson argues that there is no need to permit color alone to function as a trademark because a firm already may use color as part of a trademark, say, as a colored circle or colored letter or colored word, and may rely upon "trade dress" protection, under § 43(a) of the Lanham Act, if a competitor copies its color and thereby causes consumer confusion regarding the overall appearance of the competing products or their packaging, see 15 U.S.C. § 1125(a) (1988 ed., Supp. V). The first part of this argument begs the question. One can understand why a firm might find it difficult to place a usable symbol or word on a product (say, a large industrial bolt that customers normally see from a distance); and, in such instances, a firm might want to use color, pure and simple, instead of color as part of a design. Neither is the second portion of the argument convincing. Trademark law helps the holder of a mark in many ways that "trade dress" protection does not. See 15 U.S.C. § 1124 (ability to prevent importation of confusingly similar goods); § 1072 (constructive notice of ownership); § 1065 (incontestable status); § 1057(b) (prima facie evidence of validity and ownership). Thus, one can easily find reasons why the law might provide trademark protection in addition to trade dress protection.

IV

Having determined that a color may sometimes meet the basic legal requirements for use as a trademark and that respondent Jacobson's arguments do not justify a special legal rule preventing color alone from serving as a trademark (and, in light of the District Court's here undisputed findings that Qualitex's use of the green-gold color on its press pads meets the basic trademark requirements), we conclude that the Ninth Circuit erred in barring Qualitex's use of color as a trademark. For these reasons, the judgment of the Ninth Circuit is

REVERSED.

Questions

1. Color can be a highly distinctive feature of a product or its packaging. Hawaiian Punch® fruit juice drink, Pepto Bismol® medicine, and Windex® glass cleaner are examples of products with distinctive coloration; Philadelphia® Cream Cheese and Coca Cola® are examples of products with widely recognized package colors. Color may also, however, function as an efficient symbol for conveying important information about the product. Sprite® soda is only one example of a citrus-flavored soft drink that has long been sold in a green can; over-the-counter drugs promoted as especially effective for night-time use, like Vick's NyQuil® and Tylenol® PM, are sold in boxes adorned with soothing blue tones. The Court in *Qualitex* determined that "color may sometimes meet the basic legal requirements for use as a trademark...." How would you articulate the test to determine whether a particular use of color in fact meets those legal requirements?

2. In Justice Breyer's view, can color alone ever qualify as a trademark without first acquiring secondary meaning?

3. Christian Louboutin has sold high heeled pumps with a contrasting high-gloss red lacquer sole since 1992, and claims a trademark on red lacquer soles on footwear. Yves St. Laurent has recently introduced a line of monochrome high heels in bright shades of purple, green, yellow, and red. The YSL red shoe is red all over, including its sole. Louboutin insists that the red monochrome shoe infringes his trademark; Yves St. Laurent contends that the trademark is invalid. How should the court rule? *See Louboutin v. Yves St. Laurent Am. Holding*, 709 F.3d 140 (2d Cir. 2012), *infra* Chapter 8[A].

Traffix Devices, Inc. v. Marketing Displays, Inc.

532 U.S. 23 (2001)

Justice Kennedy delivered the opinion of the Court.

Temporary road signs with warnings like "Road Work Ahead" or "Left Shoulder Closed" must withstand strong gusts of wind. An inventor named Robert Sarkisian obtained two utility patents for a mechanism built upon two springs (the dual-spring design) to keep these and other outdoor signs upright despite adverse wind conditions. The holder of the now-expired Sarkisian patents, respondent Marketing Displays, Inc. (MDI), established a successful business in the manufacture and sale of sign stands incorporating the patented feature. MDI's stands for road signs were recognizable to buyers and users (it says) because the dual-spring design was visible near the base of the sign.

This litigation followed after the patents expired and a competitor, TrafFix Devices, Inc., sold sign stands with a visible spring mechanism that looked like MDI's. MDI and TrafFix products looked alike because they were. When TrafFix started in business, it sent an MDI product abroad to have it reverse engineered, that is to say copied....

MDI brought suit under the Trademark Act of 1964 (Lanham Act), 60 Stat. 427, as amended, 15 U.S.C. 1051 *et seq.*, against TrafFix for trademark infringement (based on the similar names), trade dress infringement (based on the copied dual-spring design) and unfair competition....

I

We are concerned with the trade dress question. The District Court ruled against MDI on its trade dress claim. 971 F. Supp. 262 (E.D. Mich. 1997). After determining that the one element of MDI's trade dress at issue was the dual-spring design, *id.* at 265, it held that "no reasonable trier of fact could determine that MDI has established secondary meaning" in its alleged trade dress, *id.* at 269. In other words, consumers did not associate the look of the dual-spring design with MDI. As a second, independent reason to grant summary judgment in favor of TrafFix, the District Court determined the dual-spring design was functional. On this rationale secondary meaning is irrelevant because there can be no trade dress protection in any event....

The Court of Appeals for the Sixth Circuit reversed the trade dress ruling. 200 F.3d 929 (1999). The Court of Appeals held the District Court had erred in ruling

MDI failed to show a genuine issue of material fact regarding whether it had secondary meaning in its alleged trade dress, *id.* at 938, and had erred further in determining that MDI could not prevail in any event because the alleged trade dress was in fact a functional product configuration, *id.* at 940.... In its criticism of the District Court's ruling on the trade dress question, the Court of Appeals took note of a split among Courts of Appeals in various other Circuits on the issue whether the existence of an expired utility patent forecloses the possibility of the patentee's claiming trade dress protection in the product's design. [Citations]. To resolve the conflict, we granted certiorari.

II

It is well established that trade dress can be protected under federal law. The design or packaging of a product may acquire a distinctiveness which serves to identify the product with its manufacturer or source; and a design or package which acquires this secondary meaning, assuming other requisites are met, is a trade dress which may not be used in a manner likely to cause confusion as to the origin, sponsorship, or approval of the goods. In these respects protection for trade dress exists to promote competition.... Congress confirmed this statutory protection for trade dress by amending the Lanham Act to recognize the concept. Title 15 U.S.C. § 1125(a)(3) (1994 ed., Supp. V) provides: "In a civil action for trade dress infringement under this chapter for trade dress not registered on the principal register, the person who asserts trade dress protection has the burden of proving that the matter sought to be protected is not functional." This burden of proof gives force to the well-established rule that trade dress protection may not be claimed for product features that are functional. *Qualitex*, 514 U.S. at 164–165; *Two Pesos, Inc. v. Taco Cabana, Inc.*, 505 U.S. 763, 775 (1992). And in [*Wal-Mart Stores, Inc. v. Samara Brothers, Inc.*, 529 U.S. 205 (2000)], *supra*, we were careful to caution against misuse or over-extension of trade dress. We noted that "product design almost invariably serves purposes other than source identification." 529 U.S. at 213.

Trade dress protection must subsist with the recognition that in many instances there is no prohibition against copying goods and products. In general, unless an intellectual property right such as a patent or copyright protects an item, it will be subject to copying. As the Court has explained, copying is not always discouraged or disfavored by the laws which preserve our competitive economy. *Bonito Boats, Inc. v. Thunder Craft Boats, Inc.*, 489 U.S. 141, 160 (1989). Allowing competitors to copy will have salutary effects in many instances. "Reverse engineering of chemical and mechanical articles in the public domain often leads to significant advances in technology." *Ibid.*

The principal question in this case is the effect of an expired patent on a claim of trade dress infringement. A prior patent, we conclude, has vital significance in resolving the trade dress claim. A utility patent is strong evidence that the features therein claimed are functional. If trade dress protection is sought for those features the strong evidence of functionality based on the previous patent adds great weight to the statutory presumption that features are deemed functional until proved otherwise by the party seeking trade dress protection. Where the expired patent claimed the features in question, one who seeks to establish trade dress protection must carry the heavy burden of showing that the feature is not functional, for instance by showing that it is merely an ornamental, incidental, or arbitrary aspect of the device.

In the case before us, the central advance claimed in the expired utility patents (the Sarkisian patents) is the dual-spring design; and the dual-spring design is the essential feature of the trade dress MDI now seeks to establish and to protect. The rule we have explained bars the trade dress claim, for MDI did not, and cannot, carry the burden of overcoming the strong evidentiary inference of functionality based on the disclosure of the dual-spring design in the claims of the expired patents.

....

The rationale for the rule that the disclosure of a feature in the claims of a utility patent constitutes strong evidence of functionality is well illustrated in this case. The dual-spring design serves the important purpose of keeping the sign upright even in heavy wind conditions; and, as confirmed by the statements in the expired patents, it does so in a unique and useful manner. As the specification of one of the patents recites, prior art "devices, in practice, will topple under the force of a strong wind." U.S. Patent No. 3,662,482, col. 1. The dual-spring design allows sign stands to resist toppling in strong winds. Using a dual-spring design rather than a single spring achieves important operational advantages. For example, the specifications of the patents note that the "use of a pair of springs ... as opposed to the use of a single spring to support the frame structure prevents canting or twisting of the sign around a vertical axis," and that, if not prevented, twisting "may cause damage to the spring structure and may result in tipping of the device." U.S. Patent No. 3,646,696, col. 3. In the course of patent prosecution, it was said that "[t]he use of a pair of spring connections as opposed to a single spring connection ... forms an important part of this combination" because it "forc[es] the sign frame to tip along the longitudinal axis of the elongated ground-engaging members." The dual-spring design affects the cost of the device as well; it was acknowledged that the device "could use three springs but this would unnecessarily increase the cost of the device." These statements made in the patent applications and in the course of procuring the patents demonstrate the functionality of the design. MDI does not assert that any of these representations are mistaken or inaccurate, and this is further strong evidence of the functionality of the dual-spring design.

III

In finding for MDI on the trade dress issue the Court of Appeals gave insufficient recognition to the importance of the expired utility patents, and their evidentiary significance, in establishing the functionality of the device. The error likely was caused by its misinterpretation of trade dress principles in other respects. As we have noted, even if there has been no previous utility patent the party asserting trade dress has the burden to establish the nonfunctionality of alleged trade dress features. MDI could not meet this burden. Discussing trademarks, we have said "'[i]n general terms, a product feature is functional,' and cannot serve as a trademark, 'if it is essential to the use or purpose of the article or if it affects the cost or quality of the article.'" *Qualitex*, 514 U.S. at 165 (quoting *Inwood Laboratories, Inc. v. Ives Laboratories, Inc.*,

456 U.S. 844, 850, n. 10 (1982)). Expanding upon the meaning of this phrase, we have observed that a functional feature is one the "exclusive use of [which] would put competitors at a significant non-reputation-related disadvantage." 514 U.S. at 165. The Court of Appeals in the instant case seemed to interpret this language to mean that a necessary test for functionality is "whether the particular product configuration is a competitive necessity." 200 F.3d at 940. [Citation.] This was incorrect as a comprehensive definition. As explained in *Qualitex, supra*, and *Inwood, supra*, a feature is also functional when it is essential to the use or purpose of the device or when it affects the cost or quality of the device. The *Qualitex* decision did not purport to displace this traditional rule. Instead, it quoted the rule as *Inwood* had set it forth. It is proper to inquire into a "significant non-reputation-related disadvantage" in cases of esthetic functionality, the question involved in *Qualitex*. Where the design is functional under the *Inwood* formulation there is no need to proceed further to consider if there is a competitive necessity for the feature. In *Qualitex*, by contrast, esthetic functionality was the central question, there having been no indication that the green-gold color of the laundry press pad had any bearing on the use or purpose of the product or its cost or quality.

....

There is no need, furthermore, to engage, as did the Court of Appeals, in speculation about other design possibilities, such as using three or four springs which might serve the same purpose. 200 F.3d at 940. Here, the functionality of the spring design means that competitors need not explore whether other spring juxtapositions might be used. The dual-spring design is not an arbitrary flourish in the configuration of MDI's product; it is the reason the device works. Other designs need not be attempted.

Because the dual-spring design is functional, it is unnecessary for competitors to explore designs to hide the springs, say by using a box or framework to cover them, as suggested by the Court of Appeals. *Ibid.* The dual-spring design assures the user the device will work. If buyers are assured the product serves its purpose by seeing the operative mechanism that in itself serves an important market need. It would be at cross-purposes to those objectives, and something of a paradox, were we to require the manufacturer to conceal the very item the user seeks.

....

... The judgment of the Court of Appeals is reversed, and the case is remanded for further proceedings consistent with this opinion.

It is so ordered.

Questions

1. Why does the Court decline to hold that a utility patent is conclusive evidence that the product feature covered by the patent is functional? Can you think of an example of a patented product feature that should be entitled to trademark protection?

2. In his discussion of the *Qualitex* case, Justice Kennedy suggests that a product feature might sometimes be aesthetically functional. If plaintiff claims a feature that affects neither the cost nor quality of its product as protectable trade dress, can defendant argue that the attractiveness of plaintiff's design is itself a product feature, and that prohibiting defendant from copying it would impose a significant non-reputation-related disadvantage on plaintiff's competitors? In particular, can ornamental product features be protected as trade dress? *See infra* Chapter 8[A].

3. Lepton markets the dietary supplement AllDaySlim through a website at www.alldayslim.com. The website features a blue and orange color scheme; a background image of a cloudy blue sky; before and after photos; charts graphically comparing customers' appearance, appetite, and energy before and after taking the supplement; a trial offer; and language guaranteeing customers' satisfaction. Lepton's competitor markets a competing supplement, SlimBlastFast, through its website, which Lepton claims copies all of these elements and therefore infringes Lepton's protected trade dress. Which of the elements of Lepton's website should be protected as trade dress? *See Lepton Labs LLC v. Walker*, 55 F. Supp. 3d 1230 (C.D. Cal. 2014).

4. Other Identifying Indicia

If the protection of visual marks is well established, what about marks that appeal to the other senses? Can a musical chime serve as a trademark? What about a scent? A flavor? A touch? As Justice Breyer observed in *Qualitex*, the statutory definition of trademarks is not limited to words, logos or pictures, but extends to "any word, name, symbol, or device" used to indicate the source of goods. So long as a symbol or device in fact functions as a trademark in the marketplace, in the sense that it distinguishes a product from products of other producers and is perceived by consumers as an indicator of product source, is there any reason why it should not be protected as a trademark under the Lanham Act? The preamble of Section 2 of the Lanham provides that:

> No trademark by which the goods of the applicant may be distinguished from the goods of others shall be refused registration on the principal register *on account of its nature* ... (emphasis added).

Courts and the PTO interpret this flexible definition of a trademark as allowing protection of non-graphic marks that have come to identify and distinguish the source of a service or a product. *See generally* Jane C. Ginsburg, *"See Me, Feel Me, Touch Me, Hea[r] Me," I am a Trademark—A U.S. Perspective, in* TRADE MARKS AND BRANDS: AN INTERDISCIPLINARY CRITIQUE 92 (Lionel Bently, Jennifer Davis & Jane C. Ginsburg, eds., Cambridge University Press 2008). For example, businesses have registered distinctive sounds as trademarks. Pillsbury succeeded in registering its DoughBoy character's high-pitched giggle as a trademark for baked goods. Intel registered a sequence of five audio tones (D♭, D♭, G♭, D♭, A♭) as a trademark for computer hardware. The American Family Life Assurance Company has registered the sound of a duck quacking the word "AFLAC."

The registrability of an arbitrary, nonfunctional scent was addressed in *In re Clarke*, 17 U.S.P.Q.2d 1238 (T.T.A.B. 1990). The Trademark Examining Attorney refused to register a mark for "sewing thread and embroidery yarn" that comprised "a high impact, fresh floral fragrance reminiscent of Plumeria blossoms." The examining attorney claimed that the "fragrance mark is analogous to other forms of product ornamentation in that it is not the type of matter which consumers would tend to perceive as an indication of origin." Analogies were made to other products that contain scents, such as cosmetics and cleaning products, where there is no showing that consumers regard the scent as an indication of source as opposed to a mere "pleasant feature of the goods." The Trademark Trial and Appeal Board held that the scented fragrance did function as a trademark for thread and embroidery yarn and found that:

> It is clear from the record that applicant is the only person who has marketed yarns and threads with a fragrance. That is to say, fragrance is not an inherent attribute or natural characteristic of applicant's goods but is rather a feature supplied by applicant. Moreover, applicant has emphasized this characteristic of her goods in advertising, promoting the scented feature of her goods. Applicant has demonstrated that customers, dealers and distributors of her scented yarns and threads have come to recognize applicant as the source of these goods.

The T.T.A.B. limited this holding to exclude "scents or fragrances of products which are noted for those features, such as perfumes, colognes or scented household products." *Compare In re Star Pharmaceuticals, Inc.*, 225 U.S.P.Q. 209 (T.T.A.B. 1985) (where applicant failed to demonstrate that the colors sought to be registered had been promoted as a source indicator).

Marks directed to the sense of taste have fared less well. *See, e.g., Perk Scientific, Inc. v. Ever Scientific, Inc.*, 77 U.S.P.Q.2d 1412 (E.D. Pa. 2005) (lack of carbonation and flavor selection held functional for glucose tolerant beverage products); *In re N.V. Organon*, 79 U.S.P.Q.2d 1639 (T.T.A.B. 2006) (orange flavor for antidepressants in quick-dissolving tablets and pills held functional for masking the unpleasant tastes of certain medicines). In *Organon*, the Board also held that consumers would not perceive the flavor as an indicator of source rather than a feature of the product. The Board expressed considerable doubt that flavor would ever be capable of serving as a trademark:

> [W]e are not blind to the practical considerations involved in the registration of flavor marks. Flavor perception is very subjective; what applicant considers to be a unique and distinctive orange flavor may be considered by patients as simply an orange flavor. Moreover, the Office's examination of flavor marks, not to mention litigation at the Board, would be very problematic.
>
> Further, it is not clear how taste would as a practical matter function as a trademark. A consumer generally has no access to the product's flavor prior to purchase. A trademark is defined as a word, name, symbol, or device that is used by a person "to identify and distinguish his or her goods, including a unique product, from those manufactured or sold by others and to indicate the source of the goods." Section 45 of the Trademark Act, 15 U.S.C. § 1127. Unlike color, sound and smell, there generally is no way for consumers routinely

> to distinguish products by sampling them before they decide which one to purchase. Generally, it would not be expected that prescribed antidepressants would be tasted prior to purchase so that a consumer, in conjunction with a physician, could distinguish one antidepressant from another on the basis of taste. Thus, the consumer, in making a purchasing decision involving either a prescribed medication or an over-the-counter medication, is unable to distinguish one pharmaceutical from another based on flavor. Consequently, it is difficult to fathom exactly how a flavor could function as a source indicator in the classic sense, unlike the situation with other nontraditional trademarks such as color, sound and smell, to which consumers may be exposed prior to purchase.

In *In re Pohl-Boskamp GmbH & Co. KG*, 106 U.S.P.Q.2d 1042 (T.T.A.B. 2013), the Trademark Trial and Appeal Board rejected the scent and flavor of peppermint as trademarks for medication. "Most substances that are introduced into the mouth will create sensations of flavor and scent. Consumers are not predisposed to equate either flavor or scent with the source of the product ingested," the Board ruled. "Rather, they are predisposed to view such features as mere attributes of the product itself." In *New York Pizzeria v. Syal*, 56 F. Supp. 3d 875 (S.D. Tex. 2014), plaintiff claimed that its "specially sourced branded ingredients and innovative preparation and preservation techniques" gave its pizza a distinctive flavor, which should be protected as its trademark. Plaintiff argued that defendant had used those ingredients and processes to produce a pizza with an infringingly similar flavor. The court declined to recognize the flavor of plaintiff's pizza as a trademark, concluding that "The flavor of food undoubtedly affects its quality, and is therefore a functional element of the product."

By contrast, the Trademark Office has registered a "sensory, touch mark," consisting of a "velvet textured covering on the surface of a bottle of wine." *See* Registration Number 3155702 (October 17, 2006).

Note: Service Marks

As the Restatement sections excerpted at the beginning of this chapter explain, service marks are trademarks used to distinguish the source of services rather than goods. STORK CLUB was a service mark for restaurant services rather than a trademark for food or liquor; AT&T's slogan, MOBILIZING YOUR WORLD, is a service mark for telecommunications services rather than a trademark for hardware. The Federal Circuit has broadly defined a "service" as "the performance of labor for the benefit of another." *In re Advertising & Marketing Development Inc.*, 821 F.2d 614, 619 (Fed. Cir. 1987). Services performed only for the benefit of the owner of the mark, such as advertising the owner's own goods, are not considered a service. *See, e.g., In re Dr. Pepper Co.*, 836 F.2d 508 (Fed. Cir. 1987).

Note: Trademark Actions before the Trademark Tribunals and before the Federal Judicial Courts

The Trademark Trial and Appeal Board (T.T.A.B. or "Board") is a specialized body within the Patent and Trademark Office, an administrative agency. Claims arising out of trademark registration proceedings must first be brought before the T.T.A.B. If a Trademark Examiner has refused to register a mark, the applicant may appeal the refusal to the Board. 15 U.S.C. § 1070 (Lanham Act § 20). If this tribunal sustains the examiner's decision, the applicant may further appeal to the United States Court of Appeals for the Federal Circuit (Fed. Cir.) or may have the Board's decision reviewed by a federal district court. 15 U.S.C. § 1071(a), (b) (Lanham Act § 21(a), (b)). Before creation of the Federal Circuit in 1982, a substantially equivalent appellate tribunal was known as the Court of Customs and Patent Appeals (C.C.P.A.).

If the Examiner accepts the mark, it is published in the "Official Gazette" of the Patent and Trademark Office, a publication that the P.T.O. posts on its website every week. At this point, owners of trademarks who believe the mark proposed for registration is likely to be confused with their marks may initiate opposition proceedings before the T.T.A.B. 15 U.S.C. § 1067 (Lanham Act § 17). The Board's decision may be appealed either to the Federal Circuit, or to any United States District Court that has jurisdiction over the parties. In addition, petitions to cancel a trademark registration, for example on the ground that the mark has become generic (*see* Chapter 5[A]) or been abandoned (*see* Chapter 5[B]), are brought to the T.T.A.B., whose decision may be appealed either to the Federal Circuit or to the appropriate U.S. District Court.

Trademark infringement actions may be initiated before federal district courts, if a federally registered mark is at issue or if the claim alleges a violation of Section 43 of the Lanham Act, a broad liability provision covering, inter alia, unregistered marks. In addition, federal courts hear state law based trademark and unfair competition claims, either as claims joined to the federal trademark claim, *see* 28 U.S.C. § 1338(b), or, in the absence of a federal claim, pursuant to their diversity jurisdiction, if the amount in controversy exceeds $75,000, *see* 28 U.S.C. § 1332. Federal courts do not have exclusive jurisdiction over federal trademark infringement claims, unlike patent and copyright claims. *See* 28 U.S.C. § 1338(a). State courts therefore may also hear federal trademark infringement claims, as well as state law based trademark and unfair competition claims.

Because the Federal Circuit has exclusive jurisdiction over all appeals from patent tribunals and all appeals of patent infringement decisions emanating from United States District Courts of general jurisdiction, it will also adjudicate a trademark appeal from a federal district court of general jurisdiction when the trademark claim was joined with a patent claim. However, when the Federal Circuit hears a trademark appeal from a federal district court, the Federal Circuit does not rule on the basis of its own trademarks precedents, but applies the trademark law as developed in the circuit including the district court. *See, e.g., Cicena Ltd. v. Columbia Telecommunications Group*, 900 F.2d 1546 (Fed. Cir. 1990).

B. Distinctiveness

1. Arbitrary, Fanciful, Suggestive and Descriptive Terms

Abercrombie & Fitch Co. v. Hunting World, Inc.

537 F.2d 4 (2d Cir. 1976)

FRIENDLY, CIRCUIT JUDGE.

[Abercrombie & Fitch claimed trademark rights in SAFARI for a variety of clothing items and accessories. The trial court found the term failed to distinguish Abercrombie's goods from other retailers' similar apparel. The Second Circuit upheld the lower court with respect to certain items, notably hats, but reversed as to others, for example, shoes and boots.]

It will be useful at the outset to restate some basic principles of trademark law, which, although they should be familiar, tend to become lost in a welter of adjectives.

The cases, and in some instances the Lanham Act, identify four different categories of terms with respect to trademark protection. Arrayed in an ascending order which roughly reflects their eligibility to trademark status and the degree of protection accorded, these classes are (1) generic, (2) descriptive, (3) suggestive, and (4) arbitrary or fanciful. The lines of demarcation, however, are not always bright. Moreover, the difficulties are compounded because a term that is in one category for a particular product may be in quite a different one for another,[6] because a term may shift from one category to another in light of differences in usage through time,[7] because a term may have one meaning to one group of users and a different one to others,[8] and because the same term may be put to different uses with respect to a single product. In various ways, all of these complications are involved in the instant case.

A generic term is one that refers, or has come to be understood as referring, to the genus of which the particular product is a species. At common law neither those terms which were generic nor those which were merely descriptive could become valid trademarks, *see Delaware & Hudson Canal Co. v. Clark*, 80 U.S. (13 Wall.) 311, 323 (1872) ("Nor can a generic name, or a name merely descriptive of an article or its qualities, ingredients, or characteristics, be employed as a trademark and the exclusive use of it be entitled to legal protection"). The same was true under the Trademark Act of 1905, *Standard Paint Co. v. Trinidad Asphalt Mfg. Co.*, 220 U.S. 446 (1911), except for marks which had been the subject of exclusive use for ten years prior to its enactment, 33 Stat. 726. While, as we shall see, [citation] the Lanham Act makes an important exception with respect to those merely descriptive terms which have acquired secondary meaning, *see* § 2(f), 15 U.S.C. § 1052(f), it offers no

---

6. To take a familiar example, "Ivory" would be generic when used to describe a product made from the tusks of elephants but arbitrary as applied to soap.

7. *See, e.g., Haughton Elevator Co. v. Seeberger*, 85 U.S.P.Q. 80 (1950), in which the coined word "Escalator," originally fanciful, or at the very least suggestive, was held to have become generic.

8. *See, e.g., Bayer Co. v. United Drug Co.*, 272 F. 505 (S.D.N.Y. 1921).

such exception for generic marks. The Act provides for the cancellation of a registered mark if at any time it "becomes the common descriptive name of an article or substance," § 14(c).* This means that even proof of secondary meaning, by virtue of which some "merely descriptive" marks may be registered, cannot transform a generic term into a subject for trademark. As explained in *J. Kohnstam, Ltd. v. Louis Marx and Company*, 280 F.2d 437, 440 (C.C.P.A. 1960), no matter how much money and effort the user of a generic term has poured into promoting the sale of its merchandise and what success it has achieved in securing public identification, it cannot deprive competing manufacturers of the product of the right to call an article by its name. [Citations.] ... The pervasiveness of the principle is illustrated by a series of well-known cases holding that when a suggestive or fanciful term has become generic as a result of a manufacturer's own advertising efforts, trademark protection will be denied save for those markets where the term still has not become generic and a secondary meaning has been shown to continue. *Bayer Co. v. United Drug Co.*, 272 F. 505 (S.D.N.Y. 1921) (L. Hand, D.J.); *DuPont Cellophane Co. v. Waxed Products Co.*, 85 F.2d 75 (2 Cir.) (A.N. Hand, C.J.), *cert. denied*, 299 U.S. 601 (1936); *King-Seeley Thermos Co. v. Aladdin Industries, Inc.*, 321 F.2d 577 (2 Cir.1963). A term may thus be generic in one market and descriptive or suggestive or fanciful in another.

The term which is descriptive but not generic stands on a better basis. Although § 2(e) of the Lanham Act, 15 U.S.C. § 1052, forbids the registration of a mark which, when applied to the goods of the applicant, is "merely descriptive," § 2(f) removes a considerable part of the sting by providing that "except as expressly excluded in paragraphs (a)–(d) of this section, nothing in this chapter shall prevent the registration of a mark used by the applicant which has become distinctive of the applicant's goods in commerce"** and that the Commissioner may accept, as prima facie evidence that the mark has become distinctive, proof of substantially exclusive and continuous use of the mark applied to the applicant's goods for five years preceding the application. As indicated in the cases cited in the discussion of the unregistrability of generic terms, "common descriptive name," as used in §§ 14(c) and 15(4), refers to generic terms applied to products and not to terms that are "merely descriptive." In the former case any claim to an exclusive right must be denied since this in effect would confer a monopoly not only of the mark but of the product by rendering a competitor unable effectively to name what it was endeavoring to sell. In the latter case the law strikes the balance, with respect to registration, between the hardships to a competitor in hampering the use of an appropriate word and those to the owner who, having invested money and energy to endow a word with the good will adhering to his enterprise, would be deprived of the fruits of his efforts.

* [*Editors' Note*: After the 1988 amendments to the Lanham Act, § 14(3) provides for cancellation "at anytime if the registered mark becomes the generic name for the goods or services...."]

** [*Editors' Note*: Section 2(f) of the current statute provides: "Except as expressly excluded in subsections (a), (b), (c), (d), (e)(3), and (e)(5) of this section, nothing in this chapter shall prevent the registration of a mark used by the applicant which has become distinctive of the applicant's goods in commerce...."]

The category of "suggestive" marks was spawned by the felt need to accord protection to marks that were neither exactly descriptive on the one hand nor truly fanciful on the other—a need that was particularly acute because of the bar in the Trademark Act of 1905, 33 Stat. 724, 726, (with an exceedingly limited exception noted above) on the registration of merely descriptive marks regardless of proof of secondary meaning. *See Orange Crush Co. v. California Crushed Fruit Co.*, 297 F. 892 (D.C. Cir. 1924). Having created the category the courts have had great difficulty in defining it.

....

If a term is suggestive, it is entitled to registration without proof of secondary meaning....

It need hardly be added that fanciful or arbitrary terms[12] enjoy all the rights accorded to suggestive terms as marks—without the need of debating whether the term is "merely descriptive" and with ease of establishing infringement.

....

In the Matter of the Application of Quik-Print Copy Shops, Inc., 616 F.2d 523 (C.C.P.A. 1980). The Court of Customs and Patent Appeals affirmed the T.T.A.B.'s refusal to register the mark QUIK PRINT for printing and duplication services, on the ground that the mark was merely descriptive under section 2(e)(1):

> A mark is merely descriptive if it immediately conveys to one seeing or hearing it knowledge of the ingredients, qualities, or characteristics of the goods or services with which it is used; whereas, a mark is suggestive if imagination, thought, or perception is required to reach a conclusion on the nature of the goods or services. *In re Abcor Development Corp.*, 588 F.2d 811, 813–14 (CCPA 1978). Registration will be denied if a mark is merely descriptive of any of the goods or services for which registration is sought. *In re American Society of Clinical Pathologists*, 442 F.2d 1404 (1971). Therefore, the dispositive question is whether the mark QUIK-PRINT is merely descriptive of any of appellant's services.
>
> Appellant argues that although the words "quick" and "print" used individually are well-known, mundane words useful to the trade, the term QUIK-PRINT is a fanciful and distinctive term not ordinarily usable in the trade to describe any quality, characteristic, or ingredient of the service; that, at most, the mark suggests to the consumer, after perception and analysis, that appellant can perform printing services within a short period of time; and that the board's use of perception, logical analysis, and mental gymnastics

12. As terms of art, the distinctions between suggestive terms and fanciful or arbitrary terms may seem needlessly artificial. Of course, a common word may be used in a fanciful sense; indeed one might say that only a common word can be so used, since a coined word cannot first be put to a bizarre use. Nevertheless, the term "fanciful," as a classifying concept, is usually applied to words invented solely for their use as trademarks. When the same legal consequences attach to a common word, i.e., when it is applied in an unfamiliar way, the use is called "arbitrary."

to prove that QUIK-PRINT is merely descriptive actually demonstrates that the mark is suggestive.

We do not agree. One of the services provided by appellant is printing. Clearly the term "QUIK" describes one of the qualities or characteristics of this service, namely: the speed with which it is done. Such speed is emphasized in appellant's advertising brochure, which offers a "SAME-DAY SERVICE." Because this quality or characteristic of appellant's service comes immediately to mind, we are satisfied that the mark QUIK-PRINT is merely descriptive. The board, contrary to appellant's argument, did not make use of perception, logical analysis, and mental gymnastics to prove that QUIK-PRINT is merely descriptive. Rather, it set forth a reasonable explanation in support of its finding that QUIK-PRINT would immediately convey knowledge of the essential character of appellant's service.

The decision of the board is *affirmed.*

Zobmondo Entertainment, LLC. v. Falls Media, LLC

602 F.3d 1108 (9th Cir. 2010)

Gould, Circuit Judge:

Appellants Falls Media, LLC, Justin Heimberg, and David Gomberg (collectively "Falls Media") appeal the district court's summary judgment for Appellee Zobmondo Entertainment, LLC ("Zobmondo") rejecting Falls Media's action for trademark infringement, unfair competition, and related claims arising from Zobmondo's use of Falls Media's federally registered trademark, "WOULD YOU RATHER ...?". The district court held that "WOULD YOU RATHER ...?" is not entitled to federal trademark protection because the mark is "merely descriptive" and lacks secondary meaning, and the district court ordered the mark cancelled from the federal trademark registry. We have jurisdiction under 28 U.S.C. § 1291. We conclude that there is a genuine issue of material fact whether "WOULD YOU RATHER ...?" is merely descriptive. Hence we reverse the summary judgment and remand for further proceedings consistent with this opinion.

I

This appeal involves a persistent dispute between two competitors, Falls Media and Zobmondo, over the right to sell products using the "WOULD YOU RATHER ...?" mark. Both competitors use similar marks to identify board games and books that incorporate questions posing humorous, bizarre, or undesirable choices.[2] As of 2008, both competitors had established successful businesses earning millions of dollars in revenues from sales of "WOULD YOU RATHER ...?" products.

... Falls Media published its first book using the mark, *Would You Rather ...? Over 200 Absolutely Absurd Dilemmas to Ponder*, in October of 1997. It published a sequel

2. For example, a sample question posed by Falls Media asks, "Would you rather be able to expedite the arrival of an elevator by pressing the button multiple times or have the ability to sound incredibly natural and sincere on answering machines?"

to the book, *Would You Rather 2, Electric Boogaloo*, in 1999. These books were carried by retailers including Borders, Barnes & Noble, and Urban Outfitters. To promote the books, Falls Media also established a website, www.wouldyourather.com, which as of 2008 was receiving about 30,000 unique visitors per month. Although the books were not the subject of a paid advertising campaign at the time of their publication, they received unpaid print, radio, and television publicity, including mention in magazines such as *Rolling Stone* and comment on television shows such as *Oprah* and *The Tonight Show with Jay Leno*. Heimberg and Gomberg also made personal appearances to promote their books. As of 2002—when Zobmondo began using "WOULD YOU RATHER ...?" as a mark on its board games—Falls Media had sold about 91,000 total copies of its two "WOULD YOU RATHER ...?" books.

....

[When Falls Media introduced a "Would You Rather?" board game, Zobmondo filed a trademark suit. Falls Media responded by filing a trademark infringement suit against Zobmondo. The two cases were consolidated, and the parties filed cross-motions for summary judgment. The district court granted Zobmondo summary judgment on Falls Media's trademark infringement claims, on the ground that the mark, "WOULD YOU RATHER ...?" was merely descriptive and lacked secondary meaning.]

Falls Media timely appealed. On appeal, Falls Media contends that it raised genuine issues of material fact regarding whether "WOULD YOU RATHER ...?" is a valid, protectable mark.

....

III

Falls Media first contends that the district court erred by concluding that there was no genuine issue of material fact whether "WOULD YOU RATHER ...?" is suggestive, concluding instead that the mark is merely descriptive. A suggestive mark is one for which "a consumer must use imagination or any type of multistage reasoning to understand the mark's significance ... the mark does not *describe* the product's features, but *suggests* them." *Kendall-Jackson Winery, Ltd. v. E. & J. Gallo Winery*, 150 F.3d 1042, 1047 n.8 (9th Cir. 1998). By contrast, a merely descriptive mark "describes the qualities or characteristics of a good or service." *Park 'n Fly, Inc. v. Dollar Park & Fly, Inc.*, 469 U.S. 189, 194 (1985)....

....

We have generally applied one or two "tests" to differentiate between suggestive and merely descriptive marks. Because the district court found the application of these tests, the imagination test and the competitors' needs test, important to its summary judgment inquiry, we examine each in turn. We stress that these tests are only "criteria offer[ing] guidance," *Self-Realization Fellowship Church v. Ananda Church of Self-Realization*, 59 F.3d 902, 911 (9th Cir. 1995), and that the burden to show that there is no genuine issue of material fact is on the moving party, Zobmondo, while the non-moving party, Falls Media, gets the benefit of reasonable inferences.

The first, and clearly the most-used, test is known as the "imagination" test, and asks whether "imagination or a mental leap is required in order to reach a conclusion as to the nature of the product being referenced." *Rudolph Int'l, Inc. v. Realys, Inc.*, 482 F.3d 1195, 1198 (9th Cir. 2007) (quotation marks omitted). For example, the mark "ENTREPRENEUR" as applied to a magazine was descriptive, not suggestive, because "an entirely unimaginative, literal-minded person would understand the significance of the reference." *Entrepreneur Media* [*v. Smith*], 279 F.3d [1135 (9th Cir. 2002)] at 1142. On the other hand, "ROACH MOTEL" was held suggestive because "an ordinary consumer having read or heard on television the words 'roach motel' would remember the conception ... a fanciful abode for roaches in an establishment normally frequented by human [travelers]." *Am. Home Prods. Corp. v. Johnson Chem. Co.*, 589 F.2d 103, 107 (2d Cir. 1978). We have said that the imagination test is our "primary criterion" for evaluating distinctiveness. *Self-Realization*, 59 F.3d at 911.

The district court determined that the imagination test indicated that "WOULD YOU RATHER ...?" is merely descriptive as a matter of law because it requires "no imaginative or interpretive leap to understand that this phrase is the main aspect of the game to which it is affixed." Falls Media argues that the district court erred because multistage reasoning is needed to link the mark to the "essential nature of these products ... that the choices are ridiculous, bizarre, or themed and that they are limited to a two-option format."

We reject Falls Media's argument in part. The imagination test does not ask what information about the product *could* be derived from a mark, but rather whether "a mental leap is *required*" to understand the mark's relationship to the product. *Rudolph Int'l*, 482 F.3d at 1198 (quotation omitted and emphasis added). Our prior precedent makes it clear that merely descriptive marks need not describe the "essential nature" of a product; it is enough that the mark describe some aspect of the product. *See, e.g.*, [*Bada Co. v. Montgomery Ward & Co.*], 426 F.2d [8 (9th Cir. 1970)] at 11 (holding the mark "Micro-Precision" merely descriptive when applied to wheel balancers and weights).

But we conclude that the district court erred in concluding that the imagination test indicates that "WOULD YOU RATHER ...?" is merely descriptive as a matter of law. We cannot look the entire mark up in a dictionary; there is no literal meaning of the "WOULD YOU RATHER ...?" phrase, given that the words precede an ellipse; one may infer that there is a question, but only imagination can tell us that the question will serve up a bizarre or humorous choice. [Citations.] On the one hand, consumers who already understand the phrase "WOULD YOU RATHER ...?" to refer specifically to a game of questions involving bizarre or humorous choices might not consider the mark very suggestive as the name of a board game, but to consumers who do not share such an understanding, "WOULD YOU RATHER ...?" is simply the first three words of an open-ended question. For those consumers, the mark "WOULD YOU RATHER ...?" may not "describe" anything, except that a question is asked, and may indeed require imagination and multistage reasoning to understand the mark's relationship to the game to which it is affixed. *See Rudolph Int'l*, 482 F.3d at 1198; *Self-Realization*, 59 F.3d at 911 (observing that the mark "recovery" in the self-help context is descriptive, but the same mark is suggestive when used as the name of a business teaching counselors to teach self-help because "[the] extra step constitutes the difference between descriptiveness and suggestiveness"). Given the record before us, which lacks comprehensive consumer surveys, we cannot say with confidence precisely what consumers will understand the phrase "WOULD YOU RATHER ...?" to mean, nor are we confident that our own understanding of the phrase is an adequate substitute.[9] ... When we give all reasonable inferences to Falls Media, and credit its evidence as true, we conclude that the imagination test is inconclusive by itself to determine if the challenged mark is descriptive or suggestive of a board game.

The second test, known as the "competitors' needs" test, "focuses on the extent to which a mark is actually needed by competitors to identify their goods or services." *Rodeo Collection, Ltd. v. W. Seventh*, 812 F.2d 1215, 1218 (9th Cir. 1987). If competitors have a great need to use a mark, the mark is probably descriptive; on the other hand, if "the suggestion made by the mark is so remote and subtle that it is really not likely to be needed by competitive sellers to describe their goods or services[,] this tends to indicate that the mark is merely suggestive." *Id.* (internal punctuation omitted). The competitors' needs test is related to the imagination test, "because the more imagination that is required to associate a mark with a product or service, the less likely the words used will be needed by competitors to describe their products or services." *Id.* (internal punctuation omitted).

The district court concluded that the competitors' needs test was "difficult to apply in this case" and declined to consider it because these tests "are merely factors to consider" and other tests favored Zobmondo. Falls Media argues that this was error, and in this case we agree. Drawing all inferences in favor of Falls Media, the competitors' needs test strongly favored Falls Media's argument that "WOULD YOU RATHER ...?" is suggestive. Falls Media proffered significant evidence suggesting that its competitors do not need to use "WOULD YOU RATHER ...?" to fairly describe their products. Perhaps most important is the experience of Zobmondo itself. Zobmondo identified 135 possible alternative names for its game during development. Also, Zobmondo marketed and sold its game and a related book for a period of time without using the phrase "WOULD YOU RATHER ...?" (instead using the name "The Outrageous Game of Bizarre Choices"), and another board game company used the name "Would You Prefer?" during the same time period. These titles are not linguistically inferior

9. The underlying issue is the standard of meaning "prevalent among prospective purchasers of the article." *Bada*, 426 F.2d at 11. On that basis, some terms may not be susceptible to abstract "imagination test" analysis at summary judgment, and instead the application of the imagination test will be informed by expert testimony offered at trial suggesting how consumers will view this phrase on a board game.

to "WOULD YOU RATHER . . . ?". *Cf. Entrepreneur Media*, 279 F.3d at 1143 (observing that others need the term "entrepreneur" because "[w]e are not aware of, nor has EMI suggested, any synonym for the word"). In the face of this evidence, credited as true on summary judgment, it's difficult to say that Zobmondo necessarily needs to use "WOULD YOU RATHER . . . ?" for its version of the board game of bizarre or humorous choices.

Zobmondo argues that "WOULD YOU RATHER . . . ?" is needed to fairly describe its products because the meaning of the phrase "WOULD YOU RATHER . . . ?" is entrenched in the minds of consumers in a way that renders other possible marks inherently inferior. This argument, however, depends on a disputed issue of fact regarding the meaning of the phrase to consumers, an issue that we have already suggested cannot adequately be decided at summary judgment on the basis of abstract theorizing alone. Giving all reasonable inferences from the evidence in favor of Falls Media, competitors do not need to use "WOULD YOU RATHER . . . ?" to describe their products. They can say "Would you prefer" or "Would you most like" or use some other verbal formula to convey a choice of alternatives.

. . . .

. . . [G]iving all reasonable inferences to Falls Media, we conclude that there is a genuine issue of material fact whether "WOULD YOU RATHER . . . ?" is suggestive or merely descriptive as a mark for a board game. The issue of descriptiveness or suggestiveness in this case cannot correctly be resolved by summary judgment, and we remand for trial.

. . . .

Question

Which of the two tests described by the court is a better measure of whether a mark is descriptive or suggestive?

In re Vertex Group, LLC, 89 U.S.P.Q.2d (BNA) 1694 (T.T.A.B. 2009). Applicant sought to register the sound of a personal security alarm for children. The Board upheld the refusal to register on the ground that, while sounds could serve as trademarks, the alarm sound at issue failed to function as a trademark.

> Would the sound sought to be registered be perceived as a source indicator or merely as a sound emitted by the personal alarm to call public attention to the conduct prompting the alarm? Applicant argues that the sound would be perceived as an indication of the source of its product.
>
> . . . .
>
> . . . [A]larms . . . are somewhat ubiquitous. Applicant has shown this by placing in the record evidence of numerous other producers of personal alarms, all of which are described as loud, and most of which, according to applicant, "utilize differing frequencies and differing arrangements of frequencies," just as applicant's alarm does. Sound pulses are not at all an

> uncommon way for a phone to ring, an alarm clock to sound, an appliance timer to go off, a smoke alarm to signal the possibility of fire, or for any number of other products to provide an audible signal designed to attract attention. As *General Electric* [*Broadcasting Co., Inc.*, 199 U.S.P.Q. 560, 563 (T.T.A.B. 1978),] instructs, "a distinction must be made between unique, different, or distinctive sounds and those that resemble or imitate 'commonplace' sounds or those to which listeners have been exposed under different circumstances." 199 USPQ at 563. Clearly, alarm sounds consisting of a series of sound pulses, including those at frequency or decibel levels approximating those employed by applicant's alarms, are commonplace and the types of sounds to which prospective consumers of applicant's products would have been exposed in various circumstances. To state the obvious, every audible alarm emits some sort of sound, many similar to that of applicant's product; and we do not find that consumers are predisposed to equate such sounds with the sources of the products that emit them.

Questions

1. The *Abercrombie* decision supplies an often quoted enumeration and description of the four categories of terms in trademark law. Are you satisfied with the court's elaboration? What does the court mean when it denominates a generic term as "referring to the genus of which the particular product is a species"? How do you know whether you are confronting a "genus" or a "species"? Does trademark law include a Linnean classification of goods and services?

2. Which of the following terms are suggestive? Which are merely descriptive? Which are generic?

a. BIG STAR for internet retailer of movie products. *See BigStar Entertainment, Inc. v. Next Big Star, Inc.*, 105 F. Supp. 2d 185 (S.D.N.Y. 2000) (*suggestive*).

b. PET PALS for pet safety program. *See P.A.W. Safety Charities v. Petco Animal Supplies, Inc.*, 2000 U.S. Dist. LEXIS 3110 (N.D. Tex. Mar. 15, 2000) (*descriptive*).

c. WWW.FIRSTJEWELRY.COM for internet jewelry store. *See First Jewellery, Inc. v. Internet Shopping Network*, 53 U.S.P.Q.2d 1838 (S.D.N.Y. 2000) (*suggestive*).

d. CHANGING FOR THE BETTER EVERY DAY for retail store slogan. *See K's Merchandise Mart v. Kmart Corporation*, 81 F. Supp. 2d 923 (C.D. Ill. 2000) (*descriptive*).

e. BETTER-N-BUTTER for oil-based butter substitute. *See Blendco v. Conagra*, 132 Fed. Appx. 520 (5th Cir. 2005) (*suggestive*).

f. BATTERY TENDER for battery recharger. *See Deltona Transformer Corp. v. Wal-Mart Stores, Inc.*, 115 F. Supp. 2d 1361 (M.D. Fla. 2000) (*descriptive*).

g. TUMBLEBUS for a "mobile gym on wheels" (school buses retrofitted with gymnastics equipment). *See Tumblebus v. Cranmer*, 399 F.3d 754 (6th Cir. 2005) (*suggestive*).

h. LAWOFFICES for a database of attorneys. *See DeGidio v. West Group Corp.*, 355 F.3d 506 (6th Cir. 2004) (*descriptive*).

i. FARMACY for retail store selling organics and herbs. *See In re Tea & Sympathy*, 88 U.S.P.Q.2d (BNA) 1062 (T.T.A.B. 2008) (*suggestive*).

j. TEXAS TOAST for oversize croutons. *See T. Marzetti Co. v. Roskam Baking Co.*, 680 F.3d 629 (6th Cir. 2012) (*generic*).

k. LABRADOR for search engine services. *See Labrador Software, Inc. v. Lycos, Inc.*, 32 F. Supp. 2d 31 (D. Mass. 1999) (*descriptive*).

l. SWAP for interchangeable watchbands and faces. *See Swatch AG v. Beehive Wholesale, LLC*, 739 F.3d 150 (4th Cir. 2014) (*suggestive*).

m. NOPALEA for nutritional supplements containing nopal cactus juice. *See In re Trivita, Inc.*, 783 F.3d 872 (Fed. Cir. 2015) (*descriptive*).

n. SECRETS OF THE MILLIONAIRE MIND for self-improvement books and tapes. *See Learning Annex Holdings, LLC v. True Power International, Ltd.*, 2009 TTAB LEXIS 112 (TTAB 2009) (suggestive).

Rock and Roll Hall of Fame and Museum v. Gentile, 134 F.3d 749 (6th Cir. 1998). Cleveland's Rock and Roll Hall of Fame Foundation hired world-famous architect I.M. Pei to design a building to house its Museum. The resulting building is a striking combination of steel and glass. The Museum sells posters, tee shirts, and postcards featuring different photographs of its building, and had filed an application with the Patent and Trademark Office to register the shape of its building as a service mark.

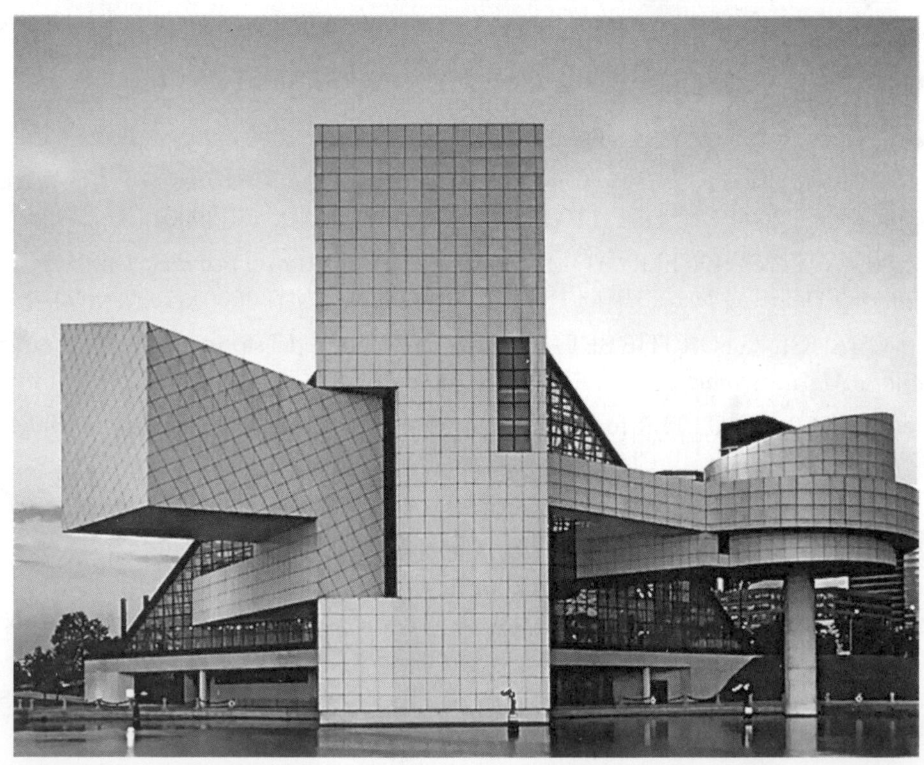

Charles Gentile is a professional photographer who sells photographs and posters commercially. In 1996, he began to sell a poster showing a photograph of the Rock and Roll Hall of Fame and Museum building at sunset. The Museum sued him for trademark infringement. The trial court concluded that the Museum building was a fanciful mark and entered a preliminary injunction enjoining further sales of the poster and ordering Gentile to deliver all copies of the poster to the Museum's lawyers for destruction. The Court of Appeals for the Sixth Circuit reversed:

> [A]lthough no one could doubt that the Museum's building design is fanciful, it is less clear that a picture or a drawing of the Museum is fanciful in a trademark sense.... Although the plaintiffs "invented" the Museum, the Museum's existence as a landmark in downtown Cleveland undermines its "fancifulness" *as a trademark.* A picture or a drawing of the Museum is not fanciful in the same way that a word like Exxon is when it is coined as a service mark. Such a word is distinctive as a mark because it readily appears to a consumer to have no other purpose. In contrast, a picture of the Museum on a product might be more readily perceived as ornamentation than as an identifier of source.
>
> We recognize, of course, that a designation may serve both ornamental and source-identifying purposes, *see, e.g., WSM, Inc. v. Tennessee Sales Co.*, 709 F.2d 1084, 1087 (6th Cir. 1983), and this brings us to our principal difficulty with the Museum's argument and the district court's judgment. As we described *supra*, although the Museum has used drawings or pictures of its building design on various goods, it has not done so with any consistency.... Several items marketed by the Museum display only the rear of the Museum's building, which looks dramatically different from the front. Drawings of the front of the Museum on the two T-shirts in the record are similar, but they are quite different from the photograph featured in the Museum's poster. And, although the photograph from the poster is also used on a postcard, another postcard displays various close-up photographs of the Museum which, individually and perhaps even collectively, are not even immediately recognizable as photographs of the Museum.
>
> ...
>
> In reviewing the Museum's disparate uses of several different perspectives of its building design, we cannot conclude that they create a consistent and distinct commercial impression as an indicator of a single source of origin or sponsorship....
>
> In the end, then, we believe that the district court abused its discretion by treating the "Museum's building design" as a single entity, and by concomitantly failing to consider whether and to what extent the Museum's use of its building design served the source-identifying function that is the essence of a trademark. As we have noted, we find no support for the factual finding that the public recognizes the Museum's building design, in any form, let alone in all forms,

as a trademark. In light of the Museum's irregular use of its building design, then, we believe that it is quite unlikely, on the record before us, that the Museum will prevail on its claims that Gentile's photograph of the Museum is an infringing trademark use of the Museum's building design.

Wal-Mart Stores, Inc. v. Samara Brothers, Inc.

529 U.S. 205 (2000)

JUSTICE SCALIA delivered the opinion of the Court.

In this case, we decide under what circumstances a product's design is distinctive, and therefore protectible, in an action for infringement of unregistered trade dress under § 43(a) of the Trademark Act of 1946 (Lanham Act), 60 Stat. 441, as amended, 15 U.S.C. § 1125(a).

I

Respondent Samara Brothers, Inc., designs and manufactures children's clothing. Its primary product is a line of spring/summer one-piece seersucker outfits decorated with appliques of hearts, flowers, fruits, and the like. A number of chain stores, including JCPenney, sell this line of clothing under contract with Samara.

Petitioner Wal-Mart Stores, Inc., is one of the Nation's best known retailers, selling among other things children's clothing. In 1995, Wal-Mart contracted with one of its suppliers, Judy-Philippine, Inc., to manufacture a line of children's outfits for sale in the 1996 spring/summer season. Wal-Mart sent Judy-Philippine photographs of a number of garments from Samara's line, on which Judy-Philippine's garments were to be based; Judy-Philippine duly copied, with only minor modifications, 16 of Samara's garments, many of which contained copyrighted elements. In 1996, Wal-Mart briskly sold the so-called knockoffs, generating more than $1.15 million in gross profits.

In June 1996, a buyer for JCPenney called a representative at Samara to complain that she had seen Samara garments on sale at Wal-Mart for a lower price than JCPenney was allowed to charge under its contract with Samara. The Samara representative told the buyer that Samara did not supply its clothing to Wal-Mart. Their suspicions aroused, however, Samara officials launched an investigation, which disclosed that Wal-Mart and several other major retailers — Kmart, Caldor, Hills, and Goody's — were selling the knockoffs of Samara's outfits produced by Judy-Philippine.

After sending cease-and-desist letters, Samara brought this action in the United States District Court for the Southern District of New York against Wal-Mart, Judy-Philippine, Kmart, Caldor, Hills, and Goody's for copyright infringement under federal law, consumer fraud and unfair competition under New York law, and — most relevant for our purposes — infringement of unregistered trade dress under § 43(a) of the Lanham Act, 15 U.S.C. § 1125(a). All of the defendants except Wal-Mart settled before trial.

After a weeklong trial, the jury found in favor of Samara on all of its claims. Wal-Mart then renewed a motion for judgment as a matter of law, claiming, *inter alia*, that there was insufficient evidence to support a conclusion that Samara's clothing designs could be legally protected as distinctive trade dress for purposes of § 43(a).

The District Court denied the motion, 969 F. Supp. 895 (S.D.N.Y. 1997), and awarded Samara damages, interest, costs, and fees totaling almost $1.6 million, together with injunctive relief. The Second Circuit affirmed the denial of the motion for judgment as a matter of law, 165 F.3d 120 (1998), and we granted certiorari, 528 U.S. 808 (1999).

II

The Lanham Act provides for the registration of trademarks, which it defines in § 45 to include "any word, name, symbol, or device, or any combination thereof [used or intended to be used] to identify and distinguish [a producer's] goods ... from those manufactured or sold by others and to indicate the source of the goods...." 15 U.S.C. § 1127. Registration of a mark under § 2 of the Act, 15 U.S.C. § 1052, enables the owner to sue an infringer under § 32, 15 U.S.C. § 1114; it also entitles the owner to a presumption that its mark is valid, see § 7(b), 15 U.S.C. § 1057(b), and ordinarily renders the registered mark incontestable after five years of continuous use, see § 15, 15 U.S.C. § 1065. In addition to protecting registered marks, the Lanham Act, in § 43(a), gives a producer a cause of action for the use by any person of "any word, term, name, symbol, or device, or any combination thereof ... which ... is likely to cause confusion ... as to the origin, sponsorship, or approval of his or her goods...." 15 U.S.C. § 1125(a). It is the latter provision that is at issue in this case.

The breadth of the definition of marks registrable under § 2, and of the confusion-producing elements recited as actionable by § 43(a), has been held to embrace not just word marks, such as "Nike," and symbol marks, such as Nike's "swoosh" symbol, but also "trade dress"—a category that originally included only the packaging, or "dressing," of a product, but in recent years has been expanded by many Courts of Appeals to encompass the design of a product. See, *e.g.*, *Ashley Furniture Industries, Inc. v. Sangiacomo N.A., Ltd.*, 187 F.3d 363 (C.A.4 1999) (bedroom furniture); *Knitwaves, Inc. v. Lollytogs, Ltd.*, 71 F.3d 996 (C.A.2 1995) (sweaters); *Stuart Hall Co., Inc. v. Ampad Corp.*, 51 F.3d 780 (C.A.8 1995) (notebooks). These courts have assumed, often without discussion, that trade dress constitutes a "symbol" or "device" for purposes of the relevant sections, and we conclude likewise. "Since human beings might use as a 'symbol' or 'device' almost anything at all that is capable of carrying meaning, this language, read literally, is not restrictive." *Qualitex Co. v. Jacobson Products Co.*, 514 U.S. 159, 162 (1995). This reading of § 2 and § 43(a) is buttressed by a recently added subsection of § 43(a), § 43(a)(3), which refers specifically to "civil action[s] for trade dress infringement under this chapter for trade dress not registered on the principal register." 15 U.S.C. § 1125(a)(3) (Oct. 1999 Supp.).

The text of § 43(a) provides little guidance as to the circumstances under which unregistered trade dress may be protected. It does require that a producer show that the allegedly infringing feature is not "functional," see § 43(a)(3), and is likely to cause confusion with the product for which protection is sought, see § 43(a)(1)(A), 15 U.S.C. § 1125(a)(1)(A). Nothing in § 43(a) explicitly requires a producer to show that its trade dress is distinctive, but courts have universally imposed that requirement, since without distinctiveness the trade dress would not "cause confusion as to the origin, sponsorship, or approval of [the] goods," as the section requires. Distinctiveness is, moreover, an explicit prerequisite for registration of trade dress under § 2, and "the general principles qualifying a mark for registration under § 2 of the Lanham Act are for the most part applicable in determining whether an unregistered mark is entitled to protection under § 43(a)." *Two Pesos, Inc. v. Taco Cabana, Inc.*, 505 U.S. 763, 768 (1992) (citations omitted).

In evaluating the distinctiveness of a mark under § 2 (and therefore, by analogy, under § 43(a)), courts have held that a mark can be distinctive in one of two ways. First, a mark is inherently distinctive if "[its] intrinsic nature serves to identify a particular source." *Ibid.* In the context of word marks, courts have applied the now-classic test originally formulated by Judge Friendly, in which word marks that are "arbitrary" ("Camel" cigarettes), "fanciful" ("Kodak" film), or "suggestive" ("Tide" laundry detergent) are held to be inherently distinctive. See *Abercrombie & Fitch Co. v. Hunting World, Inc.*, 537 F.2d 4, 10–11 (C.A.2 1976). Second, a mark has acquired distinctiveness, even if it is not inherently distinctive, if it has developed secondary meaning, which occurs when, "in the minds of the public, the primary significance of a [mark] is to identify the source of the product rather than the product itself." *Inwood Laboratories, Inc. v. Ives Laboratories, Inc.*, 456 U.S. 844, 851, n. 11 (1982).*

The judicial differentiation between marks that are inherently distinctive and those that have developed secondary meaning has solid foundation in the statute itself. Section 2 requires that registration be granted to any trademark "by which the goods of the applicant may be distinguished from the goods of others"—subject to various limited exceptions. 15 U.S.C. § 1052. It also provides, again with limited exceptions, that "nothing in this chapter shall prevent the registration of a mark used by the applicant which has become distinctive of the applicant's goods in commerce"—that is, which is not inherently distinctive but has become so only through secondary meaning. § 2(f), 15 U.S.C. § 1052(f). Nothing in § 2, however, demands the conclusion that *every* category of mark necessarily includes some marks "by which the goods of the applicant may be distinguished from the goods of others" *without* secondary meaning—that in every category some marks are inherently distinctive.

Indeed, with respect to at least one category of mark—colors—we have held that no mark can ever be inherently distinctive. See *Qualitex*, 514 U.S. at 162–163. In *Qualitex*, petitioner manufactured and sold green-gold dry-cleaning press pads. After respondent began selling pads of a similar color, petitioner brought suit under § 43(a), then added a claim under § 32 after obtaining registration for the color of its pads. We held that a color could be protected as a trademark, but only upon a showing of secondary meaning. Reasoning by analogy to the *Abercrombie & Fitch* test developed

* The phrase "secondary meaning" originally arose in the context of word marks, where it served to distinguish the source-identifying meaning from the ordinary, or "primary," meaning of the word. "Secondary meaning" has since come to refer to the acquired, source-identifying meaning of a nonword mark as well. It is often a misnomer in that context, since nonword marks ordinarily have no "primary" meaning. Clarity might well be served by using the term "acquired meaning" in both the word-mark and the nonword-mark contexts—but in this opinion we follow what has become the conventional terminology.

for word marks, we noted that a product's color is unlike a "fanciful," "arbitrary," or "suggestive" mark, since it does not "almost *automatically* tell a customer that [it] refers to a brand," *ibid.*, and does not "immediately ... signal a brand or a product 'source,'" 514 U.S. at 163. However, we noted that, "over time, customers may come to treat a particular color on a product or its packaging ... as signifying a brand." 514 U.S. at 162–163. Because a color, like a "descriptive" word mark, could eventually "come to indicate a product's origin," we concluded that it could be protected *upon a showing of secondary meaning. Ibid.*

It seems to us that design, like color, is not inherently distinctive. The attribution of inherent distinctiveness to certain categories of word marks and product packaging derives from the fact that the very purpose of attaching a particular word to a product, or encasing it in a distinctive packaging, is most often to identify the source of the product. Although the words and packaging can serve subsidiary functions—a suggestive word mark (such as "Tide" for laundry detergent), for instance, may invoke positive connotations in the consumer's mind, and a garish form of packaging (such as Tide's squat, brightly decorated plastic bottles for its liquid laundry detergent) may attract an otherwise indifferent consumer's attention on a crowded store shelf—their predominant function remains source identification. Consumers are therefore predisposed to regard those symbols as indication of the producer, which is why such symbols "almost *automatically* tell a customer that [it] refer[s] to a brand," 514 U.S. at 162–163, and "immediately ... signal a brand or a product 'source,'" 514 U.S. at 163. And where it is not reasonable to assume consumer predisposition to take an affixed word or packaging as indication of source—where, for example, the affixed word is descriptive of the product ("Tasty" bread) or of a geographic origin ("Georgia" peaches)—inherent distinctiveness will not be found. That is why the statute generally excludes, from those word marks that can be registered as inherently distinctive, words that are "merely descriptive" of the goods, § 2(e)(1), 15 U.S.C. § 1052(e)(1), or "primarily geographically descriptive of them," see § 2(e)(2), 15 U.S.C. § 1052(e)(2). In the case of product design, as in the case of color, we think consumer predisposition to equate the feature with the source does not exist. Consumers are aware of the reality that, almost invariably, even the most unusual of product designs—such as a cocktail shaker shaped like a penguin—is intended not to identify the source, but to render the product itself more useful or more appealing.

The fact that product design almost invariably serves purposes other than source identification not only renders inherent distinctiveness problematic; it also renders application of an inherent-distinctiveness principle more harmful to other consumer interests. Consumers should not be deprived of the benefits of competition with regard to the utilitarian and esthetic purposes that product design ordinarily serves by a rule of law that facilitates plausible threats of suit against new entrants based upon alleged inherent distinctiveness. How easy it is to mount a plausible suit depends, of course, upon the clarity of the test for inherent distinctiveness, and where product design is concerned we have little confidence that a reasonably clear test can be devised. Respondent and the United States as *amicus curiae* urge us to adopt for product design relevant portions of the test formulated by the Court of Customs and Patent Appeals for product packaging in *Seabrook Foods, Inc. v. Bar-Well Foods, Ltd.*, 568 F.2d 1342 (1977). That opinion, in determining the inherent distinctiveness of a product's packaging, considered, among other things, "whether it was a 'common' basic shape or design, whether it was unique or unusual in a particular field, [and] whether it was a mere refinement of a commonly-adopted and well-known form of ornamentation for a particular class of goods viewed by the public as a dress or ornamentation for the goods." *Id.* at 1344 (footnotes omitted). Such a test would rarely provide the basis for summary disposition of an anticompetitive strike suit. Indeed, at oral argument, counsel for the United States quite understandably would not give a definitive answer as to whether the test was met in this very case, saying only that "this is a very difficult case for that purpose."

It is true, of course, that the person seeking to exclude new entrants would have to establish the nonfunctionality of the design feature, see § 43(a)(3), 15 U.S.C. § 1125(a)(3) (Oct. 1999 Supp.)—a showing that may involve consideration of its esthetic appeal, see *Qualitex*, 514 U.S. at 170. Competition is deterred, however, not merely by successful suit but by the plausible threat of successful suit, and given the unlikelihood of inherently source-identifying design, the game of allowing suit based upon alleged inherent distinctiveness seems to us not worth the candle. That is especially so since the producer can ordinarily obtain protection for a design that *is* inherently source identifying (if any such exists), but that does not yet have secondary meaning, by securing a design patent or a copyright for the design—as, indeed, respondent did for certain elements of the designs in this case. The availability of these other protections greatly reduces any harm to the producer that might ensue from our conclusion that a product design cannot be protected under § 43(a) without a showing of secondary meaning.

. . . .

Question

How should courts distinguish between product packaging and product design? In *In re Slokevage,* 441 F.3d 957 (Fed. Cir. 2006), the manufacturer of Flash Dare brand sportswear sought to register a mark consisting of the phrase "Flash Dare" flanked by two peek-a-boo holes in the rear hip area of the garment. The applicant argued that the mark was packaging; the court concluded that it was product design:

> Slokevage urges that her trade dress is not product design because it does not alter the entire product but is more akin to a label being placed on a garment. We do not agree. The holes and flaps portion are part of the design of the clothing—the cut-out area is not merely a design placed on top of a garment, but is a design incorporated into the garment itself. Moreover, while Slokevage urges that product design trade dress must implicate the entire product, we do not find support for that proposition. Just as the product design in *Wal-Mart* consisted of certain design features featured on clothing, Slokevage's trade dress similarly consists of design features, holes and flaps, featured in clothing, revealing the similarity between the two types of design.

In addition, the reasoning behind the Supreme Court's determination that product design cannot be inherently distinctive is also instructive to our case. The Court reasoned that, unlike a trademark whose "predominant function" remains source identification, product design often serves other functions, such as rendering the "product itself more useful or more appealing." *Wal-Mart*, 529 U.S. at 212, 213. The design at issue here can serve such utilitarian and aesthetic functions. For example, consumers may purchase Slokevage's clothing for the utilitarian purpose of wearing a garment or because they find the appearance of the garment particularly desirable. Consistent with the Supreme Court's analysis in *Wal-Mart*, in such cases when the purchase implicates a utilitarian or aesthetic purpose, rather than a source-identifying function, it is appropriate to require proof of acquired distinctiveness.

Finally, the Court in *Wal-Mart* provided guidance on how to address trade dress cases that may be difficult to classify: "To the extent that there are close cases, we believe that courts should err on the side of caution and classify ambiguous trade dress as product design, thereby requiring secondary meaning." 529 U.S. at 215. Even if this were a close case, therefore, we must follow that precedent and classify the trade dress as product design. We thus agree with the Board that Slokevage's trade dress is product design and therefore that she must prove acquired distinctiveness in order for her trade dress mark to be registered.

2. Secondary Meaning

American Waltham Watch Co. v. United States Watch Co.

173 Mass. 85 (Mass. 1899)

Holmes, J:

This is a bill brought to enjoin the defendant from advertising its watches as the "Waltham Watch" or "Waltham Watches," and from marking its watches in such a way that the word "Waltham" is conspicuous. The plaintiff was the first manufacturer of watches in Waltham, and had acquired a great reputation before the defendant began to do business. It was found at the hearing that the word "Waltham," which originally was used by the plaintiff in a merely geographical sense, now, by long use in connection with the plaintiff's watches, has come to have a secondary meaning as a designation of the watches which the public has become accustomed to associate with the name. This is recognized by the defendant so far that it agrees that the preliminary injunction, granted in 1890, against using the combined words "Waltham Watch" or "Waltham Watches" in advertising its watches, shall stand and shall be embodied in the final decree.

The question raised at the hearing, and now before us, is whether the defendant shall be enjoined further against using the words "Waltham," or "Waltham, Mass.," upon plates of its watches without some accompanying statement which shall distinguish clearly its watches from those made by the plaintiff. The judge who heard the case found that it is of considerable commercial importance to indicate where the defendant's business of manufacturing is carried on, as it is the custom of watch manufacturers so to mark their watches, but nevertheless found that such an injunction ought to issue. He also found that the use of the word "Waltham," in its geographical sense, upon the dial, is not important, and should be enjoined.

The defendant's position is that, whatever its intent and whatever the effect in diverting a part of the plaintiff's business, it has a right to put its name and address upon its watches; that to require it to add words which will distinguish its watches from the plaintiff's in the mind of the general public is to require it to discredit them in advance; and that, if the plaintiff, by its method of advertisement, has associated the fame of its merits with the city where it makes its wares instead of with its own name, that is the plaintiff's folly, and cannot give it a monopoly of a geographical name, or entitle it to increase the defendant's burden in advertising the place of its works.

In cases of this sort, as in so many others, what ultimately is to be worked out is a point or line between conflicting claims, each of which has meritorious grounds and would be extended further were it not for the other. [Citation.] It is desirable that the plaintiff should not lose custom by reason of the public mistaking another manufacturer for it. It is desirable that the defendant should be free to manufacture watches at Waltham, and to tell the world that it does so. The two desiderata cannot both be had to their full extent, and we have to fix the boundaries as best we can. On the one hand, the defendant must be allowed to accomplish its desideratum in some way, whatever the loss to the plaintiff. On the other, we think the cases show that the defendant fairly may be required to avoid deceiving the public to the plaintiff's harm, so far as is practicable in a commercial sense. It is true that a man cannot appropriate a geographical name, but neither can he a color, or any part of the English language, or even a proper name to the exclusion of others whose names are like his. Yet a color in connection with a sufficiently complex combination of other things may be recognized as saying so circumstantially that the defendant's goods are the plaintiff's as to pass the injunction line. [Citation.] So, although the plaintiff has no copyright on the dictionary or any part of it, he can exclude a defendant from a part of the free field of the English language, even from the mere use of generic words, unqualified and unexplained, when they would mislead the plaintiff's customers to another shop. So the name of a person may become so associated with his goods that one of the same name coming into the business later will not be allowed to use even his own name without distinguishing his wares. [Citations.] And so, we doubt not, may a geographical name acquire a similar association with a similar effect. [Citation.]

Whatever might have been the doubts some years ago, we think that now it is pretty well settled that the plaintiff, merely on the strength of having been first in the field, may put later comers to the trouble of taking such reasonable precautions as are commercially practicable to prevent their lawful names and advertisements from deceitfully diverting the plaintiff's custom.

We cannot go behind the finding that such a deceitful diversion is the effect and intended effect of the marks in question. We cannot go behind the finding that it is practicable to distinguish the defendant's watches from those of the plaintiff, and that it ought to be done. The elements of the precise issue before us are the importance of indicating the place of manufacture and the discrediting effect of distinguishing words on the one side, and the importance of preventing the inferences which the public will draw from the defendant's plates as they now are, on the other. It is not possible to weigh them against each other by abstractions or general propositions. The question is specific and concrete. The judge who heard the evidence has answered it, and we cannot say that he was wrong.

Restatement of the Law (Third), Unfair Competition*

§ 13. DISTINCTIVENESS; SECONDARY MEANING

A word, name, symbol, device, or other designation, or a combination of such designations, is "distinctive" under the rules stated in §§ 9–12 if:

(a) the designation is "inherently distinctive," in that, because of the nature of the designation and the context in which it is used, prospective purchasers are likely to perceive it as a designation that, in the case of a trademark, identifies goods or services produced or sponsored by a particular person, whether known or anonymous, or in the case of a trade name, identifies the business or other enterprise of a particular person, whether known or anonymous, or in the case of a collective mark, identifies members of the collective group or goods or services produced or sponsored by members, or in the case of a certification mark, identifies the certified goods or services; or

(b) the designation, although not "inherently distinctive," has become distinctive, in that, as a result of its use, prospective purchasers have come to perceive it as a designation that identifies goods, services, businesses, or members in the manner described in Subsection (a). Such acquired distinctiveness is commonly referred to as "secondary meaning."

COMMENT:

e. Secondary meaning. A designation that is not inherently distinctive, such as a word that describes the nature of the product on which it appears, nevertheless may become, as a result of its use by a specific person, uniquely associated with that person's goods, services, or business. Such acquired distinctiveness is called "secondary meaning." Secondary meaning does not connote a subordinate or rare meaning. It refers instead to a subsequent significance added to the original meaning of the term. Secondary meaning exists only if a significant number of prospective purchasers understand the term, when used in connection with a particular kind of good, service, or business, not merely in its lexicographic sense, but also as an indication of

---

association with a particular, even if anonymous, entity. The concept of secondary meaning is also applicable to designations such as graphic designs, symbols, packaging features, and product designs. In these contexts secondary meaning denotes that the feature, although not inherently distinctive, has come through use to be uniquely associated with a particular source. A designation that has acquired secondary meaning thus distinguishes the goods, services, or business of one person from those of others.

When a designation has become distinctive through the acquisition of secondary meaning, it is protected under the same principles applicable to inherently distinctive designations. Protection extends, however, only to the secondary meaning that has attached to the designation. The trademark owner acquires no exclusive right to the use of the term in its original, lexicographic sense.

Board of Supervisors for Louisiana State University Agricultural and Mechanical College v. Smack Apparel Co.

550 F.3d 465 (5th Cir. 2008)

Reavley, Circuit Judge:

These consolidated appeals concern a trademark dispute between four universities and an apparel company and its principal. The Universities alleged in the district court that the defendants violated the Lanham Act and infringed their trademarks by selling t-shirts with the schools' color schemes and other identifying indicia referencing the games of the schools' football teams. The district court granted summary judgment to the Universities for trademark infringement and conducted a jury trial as to damages, with the jury returning a verdict favoring the plaintiffs. The defendants appeal the summary judgment order, and the Universities appeal the district court's denial of their post-verdict motion for attorneys' fees. We conclude that the colors, content, and context of the offending t-shirts are likely to cause confusion as to their source, sponsorship, or affiliation, and we AFFIRM.

I. Background

The plaintiffs are Louisiana State University (LSU), the University of Oklahoma (OU), Ohio State University (OSU), the University of Southern California (USC), and Collegiate Licensing Company (CLC), which is the official licensing agent for the schools. The defendants are Smack Apparel Company and its principal, Wayne Curtiss (collectively Smack).

Each university has adopted a particular two-color scheme as its school colors (purple and gold for LSU, crimson and creme for OU, scarlet and gray for OSU, and cardinal and gold for USC). The Universities have used their respective color combinations for over one hundred years, and the color schemes are immediately recognizable to those who are familiar with the Universities. The schools use these color schemes in many areas associated with university life, including on campus signs and buildings, on printed brochures, journals, and magazines, and on materials sent to potential donors. The Universities also use the color schemes extensively in connection with their athletic programs, particularly on team uniforms, resulting in wide-spread recognition of the colors among college sports fans. Each university operates a successful collegiate football program, and the respective football teams have appeared on numerous occasions in nationally televised football games that have been viewed by millions of people.

The schools also grant licenses for retail sales of products, including t-shirts, that bear the university colors and trademarks. In recent years, the total annual sales volume of products bearing the school colors along with other identifying marks has exceeded $93 million for all the Universities combined. The Universities hold registered trademarks in their respective names and commonly used initials. They do not, however, possess registered trademarks in their color schemes.

Smack Apparel Company is located in Tampa, Florida. Since 1998 Smack has manufactured t-shirts targeted toward fans of college sports teams, and it uses school colors and printed messages associated with the Universities on its shirts. Smack sells some of the shirts over the Internet, but most are sold wholesale to retailers and t-shirt vendors. The shirts frequently appear alongside those that have been officially licensed by the Universities. The instant case involves six of Smack's t-shirt designs that concern the appearance of the OU and LSU football teams in the 2004 Sugar Bowl in New Orleans, Louisiana, and the number of national championships previously won by OSU and USC....

The Universities sued Smack, alleging that the above six shirt designs infringed their trademark rights....

....

II. Discussion

....

A. Protectible trademark and secondary meaning

....

The protectibility of unregistered marks is governed generally by the same principles that qualify a mark for registration under the Lanham Act. *Two Pesos, Inc. v. Taco Cabana, Inc.* The key is whether the mark is "capable of distinguishing the applicant's goods from those of others." Marks are generally classified as (1) generic, (2) descriptive, (3) suggestive, (4) arbitrary, or (5) fanciful. The parties here do not articulate a classification for the marks at issue, but the briefs show that they, and indeed the district court, have treated the marks as descriptive. This type of mark is not inherently distinctive because it does not inherently identify a particular source of the product; instead, it requires secondary meaning to be protected under the Lanham Act.

The parties correctly agree that a color scheme can be protected as a trademark when it has acquired secondary meaning and is non-functional. *Qualitex Co. v. Jacobson Prods. Co.* Although the parties discuss color at length in their briefs, the Universities do not claim that every instance in which their team colors appear violates their respective trademarks. Instead, the claimed trademark is in the colors on merchandise that combines other identifying indicia referring to the Universities. It is appropriate therefore to consider not only the color but also the entire context in which the color and other indicia are presented on the t-shirts at issue here.

... [T]he first step here is to ask whether the Universities' claimed marks have acquired secondary meaning.

Secondary meaning "occurs when, 'in the minds of the public, the primary significance of a [mark] is to identify the source of the product rather than the product itself.'" *Wal-Mart Stores, Inc. v. Samara Bros., Inc.* The inquiry is one of the public's mental association between the mark and the alleged mark holder. *Sno-Wizard Mfg., Inc. v. Eisemann Prods. Co.*[26] A mark has acquired secondary meaning when it "has come through use to be uniquely associated with a specific source." *Pebble Beach Co. v. Tour 18 I Ltd.*[27] We have applied a multi-factor test for determining secondary meaning. The factors include: "(1) length and manner of use of the mark or trade dress, (2) volume of sales, (3) amount and manner of advertising, (4) nature of use of the mark or trade dress in newspapers and magazines, (5) consumer-survey evidence, (6) direct consumer testimony, and (7) the defendant's intent in copying the trade dress."[28] These factors in combination may show that consumers consider a mark to be an indicator of source even if each factor alone would not prove secondary meaning.

There is no dispute in this case that for a significant period of time the Universities have been using their color schemes along with other indicia to identify and distinguish themselves from others. Smack admits in its brief that the Universities' colors are well known among fans "as a shorthand nonverbal visual means of identifying the universities." But according to Smack, the longstanding use of the school colors to adorn licensed products is not the same as public recognition that the school colors identify the Universities as a unique source of goods. We think, however, that the factors for determining secondary meaning and an examination of the context in which the school colors are used and presented in this case support the conclusion that the secondary meaning of the marks is inescapable.

The record shows that the Universities have been using their color combinations since the late 1800s.[30] The color schemes appear on all manner of materials, including brochures, media guides, and alumni materials associated with the Universities. Significantly, each university features the color schemes on merchandise, especially apparel connected with school sports teams, and such prominent display supports a finding of secondary meaning. The record also shows that sales of licensed products

---

26. 791 F.2d 423, 427 (5th Cir. 1986) ("[T]he prime element of secondary meaning is 'a mental association in buyers' minds between the alleged mark and a single source of the product.'" (citation omitted)).

27. 155 F.3d 526, 536 (5th Cir. 1998) (internal quotation marks omitted), abrogation on other grounds recognized by Eppendorf-Netheler-Hinz GMBH v. Ritter GMBH, 289 F.3d 351, 356 (5th Cir. 2002).

28. *Pebble Beach*, 155 F.3d at 541.

30. OSU adopted its school colors in 1878, while LSU has been using its colors since 1893, and OU and USC since 1895.

combining the color schemes with other references to the Universities annually exceed the tens of millions of dollars. As for advertising, the district court held that the Universities "advertise items with their school colors in almost every conceivable manner...." It is not clear from the summary judgment evidence where and how the Universities advertise their merchandise, but they certainly do use their color schemes and indicia in numerous promotional materials aimed at students, faculty, alumni, and the public in general, which strengthens the conclusion that the color schemes and indicia viewed in context of wearing apparel also serves as an indicator of the Universities as the source or sponsor of the apparel. Furthermore, the district court correctly observed that the school color schemes have been referenced multiple times in newspapers and magazines and that the schools also frequently refer to themselves using the colors. The district court did not specifically refer to any consumer-survey evidence or direct consumer testimony, but it noted that Smack admitted it had incorporated the Universities' color schemes into its shirts to refer to the Universities and call them to the mind of the consumer. Thus, Smack itself believed that the Universities' color schemes had secondary meaning that could influence consumers, which further supports the conclusion that there is secondary meaning here. Given the longstanding use of the color scheme marks and their prominent display on merchandise, in addition to the well-known nature of the colors as shorthand for the schools themselves and Smack's intentional use of the colors and other references, there is no genuine issue of fact that when viewed in the context of t-shirts or other apparel, the marks at issue here have acquired the secondary meaning of identifying the Universities in the minds of consumers as the source or sponsor of the products rather than identifying the products themselves.

....

Smack argues that because photographs of businesses near the campuses of the Universities show use of school colors by those businesses, consumers in college towns merely associate school colors with "support of the home team." Smack cites no authority or supporting evidence for its contention, however. Moreover, the fact that other businesses in college towns may use the same colors as a local university does not create an issue of fact as to the secondary meaning of the colors used in merchandise that the Universities indisputably produce, especially given Smack's admission of intentional use of the colors to influence consumers.

Smack also argues that because the Universities grant licenses to many licensees, a consumer may not identify a university as the *single* source of the product. The fact that the Universities may grant licenses to many licensees to sell authorized products does not negate the fact that the schools are still the sources of the marks. We conclude that the record establishes secondary meaning in the marks here.

....

Questions

1. The court lists seven factors that it considers in deciding whether the owner of the mark has established secondary meaning. Which of those factors strike you as

the most probative of trademark distinctiveness? Which ones seemed most persuasive to the court in this case?

2. When you buy a garment showing a university's school colors, do you believe that the school has licensed the use of its colors on the garment? Do you care? If offered the choice of a licensed tee shirt bearing your school's colors and an unlicensed shirt at a lower price, which one would you buy?

3. Is the showing required for secondary meaning different when the mark is a trade dress mark rather than a word mark? Should it be different? Why or why not?

4. Beginning in 1998, the Blue Springs Water Company marketed bottled water under the name "Naturally Zero Canadian Natural Spring Water" in Illinois, Wisconsin, and Indiana. When the Coca Cola Company adopted COKE ZERO and SPRITE ZERO as marks for its zero-calorie sodas in 2004, Blue Springs filed suit for trademark infringement. Blue Springs concedes that its mark was initially merely descriptive. It insists, however, that the fact that it used the mark on bottled water for more than five years demonstrates that the mark acquired secondary meaning; that showing is buttressed by evidence that Coca Cola was aware of and intentionally copied the "Zero" mark. Coca Cola argues that Blue Springs' tiny market share and negligible advertising expenditures were insufficient to establish secondary meaning. How should the court rule? *See Baig v. Coca Cola*, 607 Fed. Appx. 557 (7th Cir. 2015).

Adidas Am., Inc. v. Skechers USA, Inc. 149 F. Supp. 3d 1222 (D. Or. 2016). Adidas sued Skechers, claiming that three different Skechers shoes infringed Adidas' trademarks and trade dress. The court found that "Adidas is likely to succeed in establishing its right to enforce the marks and trade dress asserted here, including the unregistered Stan Smith trade dress" (shown below):

i) Whether adidas Holds Valid and Enforceable Marks

....

The key question is whether adidas's unregistered Stan Smith trade dress is valid and enforceable under the Lanham Act. An unregistered mark or trade dress, while not entitled to a presumption of validity, may still be protectable if its holder can demonstrate it is both 1) distinctive, and 2) non-functional. [Citations.]

(1) Whether the Stan Smith Trade Dress is Distinctive

....

A mark is distinctive if it is either 1) inherently distinctive, or 2) has acquired distinctiveness through secondary meaning. [*Walmart v. Samara Brothers*, 529 U.S. at] 210–11. "[A] a mark is inherently distinctive if its intrinsic nature serves to identify a particular source," such as "Camel" cigarettes, "Kodak" film, or "Tide" laundry detergent. *Id.* at 210 (internal quotation omitted). A mark acquires secondary meaning when "in the minds of the public, the primary significance of a mark is to identify the source of the product rather than the product itself." *Id.* at 211 (quotation and alteration omitted)....

Whether a particular trade dress has acquired secondary meaning is a question of fact. [Citation.] That inquiry is guided by a number of factors, including (1) whether actual purchasers associate the dress with the source, which can be shown through customer surveys; (2) the degree and manner of advertising of the trade dress; (3) the length and manner of use of the dress; (4) whether the party seeking protection has used the trade dress exclusively; (5) sales success of the trade dress; and (6) attempts by others to imitate. [Citations.]

Adidas is likely to succeed in showing that the Stan Smith has acquired distinctiveness through secondary meaning. Since the early 1970s, Adidas has used the Stan Smith mark exclusively and has expended significant capital and human resources promoting the shoe and its appearance. Adidas executive Mr. Beaty testified about Adidas's extensive marketing and promotion of the Stan Smith; in the past two years, Adidas spent over $1 million in online and traditional advertising for the shoe. Adidas engages in extensive social media and other online campaigns to drive consumer engagement around the Stan Smith. Adidas also reaps significant but difficult-to-quantify value from placing the Stan Smith with celebrities, musicians, athletes, and other "influencers" to drive consumer hype....

Mr. Beaty testified that Adidas has sold 40 million pairs of Stan Smiths worldwide, totaling tens of millions in sales. In 2014 and 2015 alone, Adidas sold nearly 430,000 pairs of Stan Smiths, with a wholesale value of almost $20 million. These significant sales and advertising expenditures are evidence of the Stan Smith's secondary meaning. [Citations.]

Adidas submitted numerous earned media articles and other clips from a range of sources as evidence of the iconic nature of the Stan Smith. One article announces the Stan Smith as 2014's "Shoe of the Year." Another explains "Why the Adidas Stan Smith is the Most Important Sneaker of All-Time." Yet another spotted celebrities like David Beckham, Kendall Jenner, and Gwen Stefani sporting the Stan Smith as their sneaker of choice in the summer of 2015. The Stan Smith popped up as number four on a list of the "50 Greatest Tennis Sneakers of All Time," as one of the most Influential Sneaker Sponsorships in Sports History, and as number one on a list of the "10 Greatest Ever Trainers".... The Stan Smith even got a shout out from hip-hop mogul Jay-Z on his album *The Blueprint*: "Lampin' in the Hamptons, the weekends man; the Stan Smith Adidas and the Campus." These articles and pop culture references lend further support to the conclusion that the Stan Smith has acquired distinctiveness through secondary meaning. [Citations.]

Notably, Skechers own conduct suggests the Stan Smith has acquired distinctiveness through secondary meaning. The Skechers website was programmed in such a way that users who searched for "adidas stan smith" were directed to the page featuring the Skechers Onix shoe. The only reason "adidas stan smith" is a useful search term is that consumers associate the term with a distinctive and recognizable shoe made by Adidas. [Citation.]

Finally, the Ninth Circuit has noted that "[p]roof of exact copying, without any opposing proof, can be sufficient to establish secondary meaning [since] there is no logical reason for the precise copying save an attempt to realize upon a secondary meaning that is in existence." [Citation.] Although Skechers points out minor differences between its Onix shoe and the Stan Smith—that the Onix has five, not three, rows of perforations which extend in a different direction, and that its colored heel patch is a slightly darker shade of green—the unmistakable overall impression is two nearly identical shoes. The reasonable inference to draw is that Skechers copied the overall look of the Adidas shoe to realize upon the Stan Smith's secondary meaning. [Citation.]

....

Chrysler Group LLC v. Moda Group LLC

796 F. Supp. 2d 866 (E.D. Mich. 2011)

Tarnow, J.

I. INTRODUCTION

....

Plaintiff seeks a preliminary injunction to enjoin Defendants Moda Group, LLC dba Pure Detroit, Kevin Borsay, and Shawn Santo (collectively, "Pure Detroit") from using the phrase "IMPORTED FROM DETROIT" ("IFD") during the pendency of this lawsuit. The Court, for the following reasons, denies the motion for preliminary injunction.

II. BACKGROUND

....

The Parties

Plaintiff primarily manufactures automobiles, but also sells products online. Its principal place of business is in Auburn Hills, MI. Chrysler's automobiles are produced, manufactured, and assembled outside of Detroit. Its assembly plants are located in Sterling Heights, Michigan; Windsor, Ontario; and Brampton, Ontario.

Defendant, Pure Detroit, is a family owned business that specializes in selling products that promote and/or are made in Detroit. All of Pure Detroit's stores are located in landmark Detroit buildings: the Fisher Building, the Guardian Building, and the Renaissance Center. Pure Detroit sells its products on the internet also. Pure Detroit contends that its whole purpose is "amping up" local culture. Pure Detroit is involved in numerous residential, neighborhood, and urban development projects in Detroit.

The Products

In an effort to increase its sales and compete with foreign car companies, Plaintiff hired an outside marketing agency to develop a "repositioning campaign." Plaintiff has spent more than fifty million dollars on its campaign. Plaintiff introduced its campaign during the Superbowl with a two minute *Born of Fire* commercial. *Born of Fire* (Chrysler commercial broadcast on FOX Feb. 6, 2011).

....

The only Chrysler product featured in the commercial is the Chrysler 200 model. There are no products with the IFD phrase on them in the commercial. At the end of the commercial, the screen fades to black, and the words "IMPORTED FROM DETROIT" appear on the screen for seven seconds. The Chrysler name and wing badge appear after the words fade.

After the commercial aired, Chrysler's website hits went from fewer than 500 hits per second to 13,244 hits per second. Chrysler began selling t-shirts with the IFD phrase through its website. After the commercial, Defendants began making shirts featuring the IFD phrase. Defendants' shirts do not have the Chrysler logo or the Chrysler name on the shirt. Pure Detroit's shirts have its own signature stamp of the Spirit of Detroit on the back. One of the Defendants' ads for the shirts said:

> Imported From Detroit—Women's—Black: A tagline that is making headlines across America! Get your very own Imported From Detroit T-Shirt today. Grey Letters on a Ladies Black Tee. A Pure Detroit Exclusive!

Plaintiff contacted Defendants shortly after finding out about the IFD shirts. Plaintiff requested that Pure Detroit cease and desist using the IFD phrase. Defendants refused and continue to sell shirts. Defendants also began selling tote bags and other variations of the t-shirt.

....

IV. DISCUSSION

....

2. IFD as a Protectable Trademark

....

a. Whether Plaintiff Has a Protectable Trademark

Plaintiff has not shown that it has a protectable trademark. Plaintiff has not shown that the IFD phrase is inherently distinctive. Nor has it shown that it has acquired distinctiveness through a second meaning.

"Inherently Distinctive" or Geographically Descriptive

Only trademarks that are "distinctive" as a matter of law are protectable. *Leelanau Wine Cellars, Ltd. v. Black and Red, Inc.*, 502 F.3d 504, 512 (6th Cir. 2007). Descriptive terms that are not inherently distinctive may only be protected if they are proven to have acquired a secondary meaning. *DeGidio v. W. Grp. Corp.*, 355 F.3d 506, 510 (6th Cir. 2004).

The line between a "descriptive" mark and a "suggestive" mark is thinly drawn. *Tumblebus* [*v. Cranmer*, 399 F.3d 754 (6th Cir. 2005)] at 763. In determining whether a mark is suggestive, the court should consider "the degree of inferential reasoning necessary for a consumer to discern" the goods provided in connection with the mark. *Tumblebus*, 399 F.3d at 763. Inferential reasoning is required if seeing the mark in isolation would not necessarily identify the goods offered. *See id.*

"The Lanham Act does not protect primarily geographically descriptive marks." *Burke-Parsons-Bowlby Corp. v. Appalachian Log Homes, Inc.*, 871 F.2d 590, 594 (6th Cir. 1989). "Where it is determined that a mark as perceived by potential purchasers describes the geographical origin of the goods the mark is primarily geographically descriptive." *Id.* at 595; *Leelanau*, 502 F.3d at 513 ("A geographically descriptive term or phrase is one that designates a geographical location and would tend to be regarded by buyers as descriptive of the geographic location of origin of the goods or services.").

Plaintiff contends that the IFD phrase is inherently distinctive. Plaintiff argues that it is impossible for an American to "import" a vehicle from "Detroit." Plaintiff argues that the IFD phrase is a "clever commentary underlying the play on words," requiring a "mental leap" to identify the underlying goods. The Court disagrees.

The IFD phrase is not inherently distinctive; it is geographically descriptive. There is no mental leap required to understand the phrase, as Plaintiff suggests. The phrase describes that the product is "imported from Detroit," simply describing the geographical origin of the goods as the city of Detroit. *Burke-Parsons-Bowlby Corp.*, 871 F.2d at 594 ("Where it is determined that the mark as perceived by potential purchasers describes the geographic origin of the goods the mark is primarily geographically descriptive.") (internal citation omitted); *see also Ligotti v. Garofalo*, 562 F. Supp. 2d 204, 215 (D. N.H. 2008) (finding the phrase ["THE GUY FROM BOSTON"] is not protectable because it simply describes a regular guy from Boston with no inference required at all).

Plaintiff's own testimony was that the IFD phrase is used to influence Americans to buy cars from the Motor City—Detroit—instead of foreign imports. IFD serves exactly that purpose. It lets buyers know that its cars are from the Motor City. There is no mental leap or inference required.

....

Therefore, the Court finds that it is unlikely that Plaintiff will show that the IFD phrase is inherently distinctive. It is likely geographically descriptive and not protectable.

Distinctiveness Acquired by Secondary Meaning

Plaintiff argues, in the alternative, that the IFD phrase has acquired distinctiveness through secondary meaning at this early stage of the litigation. The Court disagrees.

....

To determine secondary meaning, the court looks at seven factors: 1) direct consumer testimony; 2) consumer surveys; 3) exclusivity, length, and manner of use; 4) amount and manner of advertising; 5) amount of sales and number of customers; 6) established place in the market; and 7) proof of intentional copying. [*Leelanau*, 502 F.3d at 504]. No single factor is determinative and not all factors must be proven. *Midwest Guaranty Bank* [*v. Guar. Bank*], 270 F. Supp. 2d [900 (E.D. Mich. 2003)] at 911–12. "The duration of use of the mark can establish secondary meaning where the duration is more than a relatively short period." *Burke-Parsons*, 871 F.2d at 596.

The first two factors will not be considered; Plaintiff has not presented consumer testimony or consumer surveys. As to the third factor—exclusivity, length, and manner of use—Plaintiff mentions that "only a short time has passed since Chrysler unveiled the [IFD phrase]...." This statement by Plaintiff does not support its position, as more than a short period of time is required to establish secondary meaning. *See Burke-Parsons*, 871 F.2d at 596. This factor weighs against the finding of the acquisition of a secondary meaning.

Plaintiff argues that the amount and manner of advertising is proof of acquisition of secondary meaning. Plaintiff argues that the commercial and campaign ensured that the IFD phrase was well-known instantaneously with over 94 million viewers seeing the commercial. Plaintiff spent over fifty million dollars on the repositioning campaign.

While expense is an indication of an attempt to establish a secondary meaning, it is not proof alone that a secondary meaning exists. *Citizens Banking Corp. v. Citizens Fin. Grp., Inc.*, No. 07-11514, 2008 U.S. Dist. LEXIS 36800, at *4 (E.D. Mich. May 6, 2008) (internal citations omitted), *aff'd*, 320 Fed. App'x 341 (6th Cir. 2009). Therefore, Plaintiff's millions of dollars spent are surely an indication that it wanted to establish secondary meaning. It is not conclusive. As Defendants argue, Plaintiff's commercial was only one of many car commercials during the Superbowl. The advertising expenditures are required to survive in the market and are not conclusive proof of secondary meaning. *See* 2008 U.S. Dist. LEXIS 36800 at *4. Nevertheless, this factor likely weighs in Plaintiff's favor.

As to the amount of sales and number of customers, Plaintiff argues that as a result of the popularity of the *Born of Fire* commercial, it sold out of more than 1,750 t-shirts bearing the phrase in a few hours. Since then Plaintiff has sold more than 5,800 items with the IFD phrase. This factor weighs in Plaintiff's favor.

As to the sixth factor, Plaintiff fails to show that the IFD phrase was established in the marketplace prior to Defendants' use of the phrase. "Secondary meaning must be established prior to [another's] use...." *Burke-Parsons*, 871 F.2d at 596 (citing *Saratoga Vichy Spring Co. v. Lehman*, 625 F.2d 1037, 1043 (2d Cir. 1980)).

Defendants began making t-shirts the day after the commercial aired and prior to Plaintiff making shirts. Plaintiff would essentially have to show that IFD acquired secondary meaning overnight. Plaintiff points to the high traffic on its website, articles, and online references that spiked in the few weeks after the commercial aired to show that secondary meaning was acquired. As a matter of law, secondary meaning cannot be established instantaneously, as Plaintiff suggests. *See Burke-Parsons*, 871 F.2d at 596.

Finally, Plaintiff argues that Defendants intentionally copied the phrase from the Superbowl Commercial. "Intentional copying may be used to show secondary meaning..., but it is only one of many considerations in that test and does not alone establish secondary meaning." *Gen. Motors Corp.* [*v. Lanard Toys, Inc.*], 468 F.3d [405 (6th Cir. 2006)] at 419. While Defendants knew of the Chrysler commercial before making the shirts, "mere knowledge of the competitor's mark is insufficient as a matter of law to prove intentional copying." *DeGidio*, 355 F.3d at 514. "Intentional copying is not actionable under the Lanham Act absent evidence that the copying was done with the intent to derive a benefit from the reputation of another." *DeGidio*, 355 F.3d at 514.

Pure Detroit argues that it never intended or attempted to derive a benefit from Chrysler's reputation. Pure Detroit contends that it used the IFD phrase to promote a social movement—pride in Detroit—which is the purpose of its entire company. Here, the Court finds Defendants' testimony to be credible. However, as Plaintiff points out, Defendants specifically stated in their t-shirt advertisements that the t-shirt contained "A tagline that is making headlines across America!," allegedly referencing Plaintiff's commercial. The Court finds that as to this factor, it is a close call. The factor slightly weighs on Plaintiff's side.

Considering the seven factors, Plaintiff has not shown the acquisition of a secondary meaning. Plaintiff has shown that three out of the seven factors weigh on its side. As to two of those factors—1) amount and manner of advertising and 2) proof of intentional copying—Defendants have presented meritorious responses. Plaintiff has not met its "substantial burden" in establishing the secondary meaning of the IFD phrase. *See Burke-Parsons*, 871 F.2d at 596. Therefore, Plaintiff has not shown that there is a strong likelihood of success on the merits.

....

Questions

1. The courts in *Board of Supervisors v. Smack Apparel*, *Adidas v. Skechers*, and *Chrysler v. Moda* all use multi-factor tests to determine whether a mark has acquired secondary meaning. The factors overlap considerably, but are not identical. Is there a meaningful difference among the three tests? Which of the facts strike you as most nearly probative of secondary meaning?

2. If, as Chrysler argues, the exceptional buzz surrounding the commercial caused the phrase to acquire secondary meaning within hours or days, how could Chrysler have shown that?

3. During the 1980s, a handful of district courts protected newly adopted unregistered trademarks and service marks against deliberate imitation under a theory called "secondary meaning in the making." *See, e.g., Jolly Good Industries, Inc. v. Elegra, Inc.*, 690 F. Supp. 227, 230–31 (S.D.N.Y. 1988); *Metro Kane Imports, Ltd. v. Federated Dept. Stores, Inc.*, 625 F. Supp. 313, 316 (S.D.N.Y. 1985), *aff'd*, 800 F.2d 1128 (2d Cir. 1986). The theory was rejected by Courts of Appeals, on the ground that it made no sense to protect marks that lacked inherent distinctiveness before they gained acquired distinctiveness. *See Laureyssens v. Idea Group, Inc.*, 964 F.2d 131 (2d Cir. 1992); *Lang v. Retirement Living Pub. Co.*, 949 F.2d 57 (2d Cir. 1991); *Cicena, Ltd. v. Columbia Telecommunications Group*, 900 F.2d 1546 (Fed. Cir. 1990); *Black & Decker Mfg. v. Ever-Ready Appliance Mfg. Co.*, 684 F.2d 546, 550 (8th Cir. 1982). Would such a theory have made sense in *Chrysler v. Moda*?

4. For the past thirty years, Louisiana Fish Fry Products has been using the following mark, and the slogan "Louisiana Fish Fry Products Bring the Taste of Louisiana Home," for its marinades, sauces and sauce mixes:

When the company sought to register the mark, the Trademark Examiner refused registration unless the application disclaimed any exclusive rights in the phrase "Fish Fry Products," because the phrase was either generic or highly descriptive, and the applicant had failed to show distinctiveness. Is the phrase "fish fry products" generic or descriptive? If "Fish Fry Products" is descriptive, what evidence would the company need to show to demonstrate secondary meaning? *See In re Louisiana Fish Fry Products, Ltd.* 797 F.3d 1332 (Fed Cir. 2015).

C. Collective and Certification Marks and Other Group Designations

The marks we have looked at so far designate a single source for a product. Collective marks, certification marks, and geographic indications indicate instead that the product bearing the mark belongs to a group of products that share particular characteristics. Collective marks communicate that a product comes from a member of the collective entity that owns the mark. Certification marks communicate that a product has been evaluated and found to meet the standards established by the entity that owns the mark. Geographic indications communicate that a product originated in a defined geographic territory.

---

15 U.S.C. § 1054 [Lanham Act § 4]

Subject to the provisions relating to the registration of trademarks, so far as they are applicable, collective and certification marks, including indications of regional origin, shall be registrable under this chapter, in the same manner and with the same effect as are trademarks, by persons, and nations, States, municipalities, and the like, exercising legitimate control over the use of the marks sought to be registered, even though not possessing an industrial or commercial establishment, and when registered they shall be entitled to the protection provided in this chapter in the case of trademarks, except in the case of certification marks when used so as to represent falsely that the owner or a user thereof makes or sells the goods or performs the services on or in connection with which such mark is used. Applications and procedure under this section shall conform as nearly as practicable to those prescribed for the registration of trademarks.

---

15 U.S.C. § 1127 [Lanham Act § 45]

Collective Mark

The term "collective mark" means a trademark or service mark—

(1) used by the members of a cooperative, an association, or other collective group or organization, or

(2) which such cooperative, association, or other collective group or organization has a bona fide intention to use in commerce and files an application to register on the principal register established by this Act, and includes marks indicating membership in a union, an association, or other organization.

Certification Mark

The term "certification mark" means any word, name, symbol, or device, or any combination thereof—

(1) used by a person other than its owner, or

(2) which its owner has a bona fide intention to permit a person other than the owner to use in commerce and files an application to register on the principal register established by this chapter,

to certify regional or other origin, material, mode of manufacture, quality, accuracy, or other characteristics of such person's goods or services or that the work or labor on the goods or services was performed by members of a union or other organization.

---

15 U.S.C. § 1064 [Lanham Act § 14]

[Provides for cancellation of certification mark:]

(5) At any time in the case of a certification mark on the ground that the registrant (A) does not control, or is not able legitimately to exercise control over, the use of such mark, or (B) engages in the production or marketing of any goods or services to which the certification mark is applied, or (C) permits the use of the certification mark for purposes other than to certify, or (D) discriminately refuses to certify or to continue to certify the goods or services of any person who maintains the standards or conditions which such mark certifies[.]

... Nothing in paragraph (5) shall be deemed to prohibit the registrant from using the certification mark in advertising or promoting recognition of its certification program or of the goods or services meeting the certification standards of the registrant....

1. Collective and Certification Marks

There are two different types of collective marks: collective trademarks and service marks, and collective membership marks. Collective service marks are used by members of an organization to identify and distinguish their services. For example, REALTOR is the collective service mark of a trade association of real estate agents named the National Association of Realtors. (In both *Zimmerman v. National Association of Realt*ors, 70 U.S.P.Q.2d 1425 (T.T.A.B. 2004), and *Freeman v. National Association of Realtors*, 64 U.S.P.Q.2d 1700 (T.T.A.B. 2002), the Board rejected petitions to cancel the REALTOR collective mark on the asserted ground that it had become a generic term for real estate agent.) Collective membership marks, by contrast, are designations used by individual members to indicate that they are members of a group. Collective membership marks may be owned by collective organizations that never use the symbols of their organizations in connection with the commercialization of goods or services, such as fraternal benefit societies.

A certification mark, unlike a trademark or service mark, does not indicate the producer of the goods or services. Indeed, the owner of a certification mark is prohibited from using it as a mark to identify the source of its own goods or services. Rather, a certification mark functions as a symbol of guarantee or certification that the goods or services bearing the mark meet certain criteria or conditions or that products meet certain standards. The UL of Underwriter's Laboratory is a certification mark that indicates compliance with safety standards. The Union of Orthodox Jewish Congregations of America's kosher certification mark, Ⓤ, indicates that the food inside the package has been certified as kosher. The federal Environmental Protection Agency's Energy Star logo certifies that products bearing the mark are more energy efficient than most items sold in the same category. Designations of regional origin, such as ROQUEFORT for cheese produced in Roquefort, France, from blue-mold sheep's milk, can be certification marks; as may designations that certify that labor on goods was performed by members of a union or organization, such as the UNITE

HERE! label. Because a certification mark certifies the quality or regional origin of goods, its owner must control the mark's use in order to ensure that the goods in connection with which the mark appears in fact conform to the characteristics that the mark is supposed to certify.

Further, the owner of a certification mark may not arbitrarily choose whom it will permit to use the mark, unlike the trademark or service mark owner who can choose its licensees. Indeed, the certification mark is subject to cancellation if the certifying organization excludes a potential user who meets the certifier's criteria. The Lanham Act's "certification mark cancellation provisions illustrate the legislative intent to protect a further public interest in free and open competition among producers and distributors of the certified product. By requiring certification mark holders to license all individuals who meet the certification criteria, the Lanham Act ensures that the market will include as many participants as can produce conforming goods. By preventing mark holders from becoming market participants, it removes incentives for mark holders to engage in anti-competitive conduct. The Lanham Act's cancellation provisions thus appear designed to promote free competition in the market for certified products." *Idaho Potato Comm'n v. G & T Terminal Packaging, Inc.*, 425 F.3d 708 (9th Cir. 2005) (citation omitted) (internal quotation marks omitted).

Like trademarks and service marks, collective and certification marks are protectable whether or not they are registered. Section 45 of the Lanham Act defines the term "mark" as "any trademark, service mark, collective mark, or certification mark entitled to registration under this Act *whether registered or not*" (emphasis added). Common law certification marks have been recognized by the Trademark Trial and Appeal Board, *see, e.g. Institut National Des Appellations d'Origine v. Brown-Forman Corp.*, 47 U.S.P.Q.2d 1875 (T.T.A.B. 1998) (finding that COGNAC is a common law certification mark indicating brandy produced in the Cognac region of France and declining to dismiss opposition filed by French government agency charged with protecting national indications of origin, against registration of CANADIAN MIST AND COGNAC), and by the courts, *see, e.g., Florida v. Real Juices, Inc.*, 330 F. Supp. 428 (M.D. Fla. 1971) (use by defendant of plaintiff's unregistered SUNSHINE TREE certification mark for citrus fruits a violation of Section 43(a) of Lanham Act).

Regional certification marks are sometimes challenged as being generic terms rather than as certifying the regional origin of goods. For example, ROQUEFORT for cheese and COGNAC for brandy have survived generic challenges. *See Community of Roquefort v. Faehndrich*, 303 F.2d 494 (2d Cir. 1962); *Institut National Des Appellations d'Origine v. Brown-Forman Corp.*, 47 U.S.P.Q.2d 1875 (T.T.A.B. 1998). Other terms such as "Swiss cheese" have been considered generic terms in the U.S. In the COGNAC case, the Board described the difference between a valid regional certification mark and a generic term as follows:

> In determining whether a designation, the use of which in fact is controlled by the certifier and is limited to products meeting the standards of regional

> origin established by the certifier, is a protectible regional certification mark, as opposed to an unprotectible generic name for the product, the issue is not whether the public is expressly aware of the certification function of the mark or the certification process underlying use of the mark, but rather is whether the public understands that goods bearing the mark come only from the region named in the mark. If use of the designation in fact is controlled by the certifier and limited to products meeting the certifier's standards of regional origin, and if purchasers understand the designation to refer only to products which are produced in the particular region, and not to products produced elsewhere, then the designation functions as a regional certification mark. Neither the statute nor the case law requires that purchasers also be expressly aware of the term's certification function, *per se.* [Citations.]
>
> In short, a regional certification mark will not be deemed to have become a generic term as applied to particular goods unless it appears that it has lost its significance as an indication of regional origin for those goods, e.g., by virtue of its having been used on goods which originate somewhere other than the place named in the mark.

Institut National Des Appellations d'Origine, 47 U.S.P.Q.2d at 1885 (citations omitted).

Questions

1. Section 4 of the Lanham Act extends the general provisions relating to trademarks to collective and certification marks "so far as the[se provisions] are applicable." Which provisions would not be applicable, and why?

2. Section 14(5) of the Lanham Act makes discriminatory refusal to certify the "goods or services of any person who maintains the standards or conditions which such mark certifies" a ground for cancellation of the registration of a certification mark. There is no equivalent provision for cancellation of a collective mark. Should there be?

2. Geographic Indications

The 1994 World Trade Organization Agreement on Trade Related Aspects of Intellectual Property (TRIPs), which the United States ratified in 1994 obliges Member States to protect "geographical indications." Article 22(1) defines these as:

> indications which identify a good as originating in the territory of a Member, or a region or locality in that territory, where a given quality, reputation, or other characteristic of the good is essentially attributable to its geographical origin.

Thus, not only must the goods originate in a particular place, but the goods would be (or would be perceived to be) qualitatively different if they came from some other place. For example, "Cuba" plays such a role in relation to tobacco, but not with respect to other goods grown or produced there, such as corn.

Article 22(2) obliges member states to prevent

> the use of any means in the designation or presentation of a good that indicates or suggests that the good in question originates in a geographical area other than the true place of origin in a manner which misleads the public as to the geographical origin of the good

As a result, not all use of a geographic term violates international norms. In particular, if to the national public, the term is generic—for example, Swiss cheese—its use cannot mislead as to the goods' geographical origin. Even terms, such as Feta, which some countries recognize as geographic indications (in this case, the EU) may not enjoy that status in others. TRIPs does not generally oblige one member State to adopt another's geographic indications.

Member States may implement TRIPs norms in a variety of ways, including application, and where necessary adaptation, of extant domestic trademark laws. Excerpts from the TRIPs Agreement appear in Appendix E of this Casebook.

Chapter 3

Use and Ownership

A. Trademark Use

Thoroughbred Legends, LLC v. Walt Disney Co.

2008 U.S. Dist. LEXIS 19960 (N.D. Ga. Feb. 12, 2008)

MARTIN, J.

This trademark case is before the court on the Motion for Summary Judgment ... filed by Defendants The Walt Disney Company ("Disney"), American Broadcasting Companies, Inc. ("ABC"), and ESPN Productions, Inc. ("ESPN") (collectively, "Defendants")....

....

This case involves the story of the famous filly racehorse Ruffian. Plaintiff Jacinto Vasquez ("Mr. Vasquez") is a retired professional jockey who rode Ruffian in nine of her eleven career races, including her final race. Plaintiff Frank Whiteley, Jr. ("Mr. Whiteley") was Ruffian's trainer. Ruffian won her first ten races by significant margins, breaking records previously held by colts. Recognizing her achievements, the New York Racing Association offered a large sum of money for Ruffian to race one-on-one against the 1975 Kentucky Derby winner, a colt named Foolish Pleasure, in a nationally televised match on July 6, 1975 at Belmont Park. A quarter of a mile into the race, Ruffian broke her right foreleg. She underwent surgery to correct the injury. Ruffian awoke from the procedure earlier than anticipated and upon regaining consciousness, thrashed around, further damaging her injured leg. After consultation with trainers and veterinarians, Ruffian's owners ultimately decided to euthanize her.

In 2004, Defendants ESPN and ABC (both owned by Defendant Disney) decided to make a movie about Ruffian. Defendants hired Orly Adelson Productions ("OAP") to produce the film. Defendants asked Mr. Whiteley and Mr. Vasquez to participate in the project. They each declined around May 12, 2004, and advised OAP or ESPN that they would not permit the use of their names or likenesses in the film.

On May 10, 2004, Plaintiff Thoroughbred Legends, LLC ("Legends"), a Georgia limited liability corporation, applied to the United States Patent and Trademark Office ("PTO") to register "RUFFIAN" as a service mark. The application, submitted May 10, 2004, was for a mark in "[e]ntertainment services, namely, production of theatrical plays, motion picture films, television shows, and documentaries." On October 31,

2006, Legends' owner Peter Blum ("Mr. Blum") offered to license the "RUFFIAN" mark to ESPN, an invitation that ESPN declined.

Defendants proceeded to make a film entitled "Ruffian," about Ruffian. When Legends heard of the production, it notified Defendants by letter that any use of the "RUFFIAN" mark in the film would violate Legends' rights. ESPN's counsel responded that Legends' claims were without merit and that it intended to proceed with production of the film. On June 9, 2007, the film aired on ABC and is currently available for purchase in DVD format.

....

In Counts One through Three of the Second Amended Complaint, Plaintiffs assert that the film "Ruffian" infringes their trademark "RUFFIAN." They point out that the mark and movie's title are identical, which they contend will confuse viewers as to the movie's source. Plaintiffs also argue that the film deceives viewers into thinking Mr. Whiteley and Mr. Vasquez participated in it or sponsored it....

....

III. Analysis

A. Trademark Infringement Claims

To survive summary judgment on a claim of trademark infringement, a plaintiff must present evidence that (i) the plaintiff has a valid trademark, and (ii) the defendant adopted a similar mark such that consumers would be likely to confuse the two. *Leigh* [*v. Warner Bros*, 212 F.3d 1210 (11th Cir. 2000)] at 1216; *see Welding Servs.* [*v. Forman*, 509 F.3d 1351 (11th Cir. 2007)] at 1356. Plaintiffs have neither pointed to evidence showing a genuine issue of material fact as to whether Defendants infringed on rights validly claimed in the mark "RUFFIAN," nor established that they are entitled to discovery on that matter. Therefore, the court grants summary judgment in favor of Defendants on Counts I–III of the Second Amended Complaint as to the claims of trademark infringement, and denies the Rule 56(f) Motion as to those claims.

1. Plaintiffs have not shown that "RUFFIAN" is entitled to protection

a. Plaintiffs have shown no trademark use of "RUFFIAN"

A plaintiff in a trademark infringement lawsuit must not only show that it used its mark in commerce, but also that it used the mark as a *trademark*, whether the mark is registered or not. *Rock & Roll Hall of Fame & Museum, Inc. v. Gentile Prods.*, 134 F.3d 749, 753 (6th Cir. 1998) ("[I]n order to be protected as a valid trademark, a designation must create a separate and distinct commercial impression, which ... performs the trademark function of identifying the source of the merchandise to the customers.") (citation and internal quotations omitted); *Aini v. Sun Taiyang Co., Ltd.*, 964 F. Supp. 762, 773 (S.D.N.Y. 1997) ("One ... may not 'own' a trademark unless one uses the mark as a designation of origin on or in connection with goods or services made or furnished by or under one's control."); 1 MCCARTHY ON TRADEMARKS AND UNFAIR COMPETITION § 3:3 (4th ed. 2007) ("[T]o create trademark ... rights, a designation must be proven to perform the job of identification:

to identify one source and distinguish it from other sources. If it does not do this, then it is not protectable as a trademark, service mark, trade dress or any similar exclusive right."); *see Leigh*, 212 F.3d at 1217–18 (photographer had no trademark when he used photograph as example of art and not as a mark to identify his photographic services). A trademark's primary function is to signify origin to potential customers and competitors. *Leigh*, 212 F.3d at 1216–17 ("Trademarks ... answer the question 'Who made it?' rather than 'What is it?'"). A valid service mark must be used to identify or distinguish the services being offered. *Lone Star Steakhouse & Saloon, Inc. v. Longhorn Steaks, Inc.*, 106 F.3d 355, 361 (11th Cir. 2007) (upholding the district court's decision that a sign displayed on the interior wall of the plaintiff's restaurant was not a valid service mark as a matter of law, citing 15 U.S.C. § 1127).

Plaintiffs fail to show trademark use of "RUFFIAN." Plaintiffs desired to make a movie about Ruffian, and took steps toward that goal by attempting to license what they called a service mark, among other things. But Plaintiffs fail to show that the alleged "RUFFIAN" mark was in fact ever *used to signify origin to customers and competitors*. *See Leigh*, 212 F.3d at 1216–17. As Plaintiffs note, the requirement of use does not necessarily require Plaintiffs to show any sales. *See Planetary Motion, Inc. v. Techsplosion, Inc.*, 261 F.3d 1188, 1194, 1195–96 (11th Cir. 2001). However, none of the "uses" Plaintiffs list qualify as a bona fide use in commerce to signify the source of a product or service.

In Mr. Blum's affidavit, he states that he took many actions in furtherance of the goal of producing a film about Ruffian. In addition to attempting to license "RUFFIAN" to ESPN, he held discussions with various television networks, television producers, and other individuals. He states that these conversations were aimed toward the goal of creating a movie about Ruffian "to be produced and marketed under the RUFFIAN mark." He directed a well-known horse racing broadcaster to film interviews of Mr. Whiteley, Mr. Vasquez, and Ruffian's assistant trainer, Mike Bell. He obtained commitments from most relevant individuals involved in Ruffian's racing career. He gathered information from a large number of sources. He acquired historic memorabilia like the saddle Ruffian wore during her final match. Generally speaking, these actions fall in one of two categories: engaging parties to participate in the production of a Ruffian film, or soliciting parties interested in making a Ruffian film to purchase the stories of Mr. Vasquez and Mr. Whiteley.

In taking these actions, Legends did not use the "RUFFIAN" mark to identify the source of any service, but merely described it and claimed rights to the mark. For example, Mr. Blum's October 31, 2006 e-mail attempting to license "RUFFIAN" to ESPN claims ownership of "RUFFIAN." The message, which appears to be from Mr. Blum's personal e-mail address and displays no logo or corporate header, states: "I own Thoroughbred Legends, LLC, an entity that has obtained the trademarks for a number of famous thoroughbred racehorses—among them Ruffian, Alydar, Man O'War, Citation, and Whirlaway." The word "Ruffian" is not distinguishable or set apart in any way from the rest of the message. Put simply, one cannot acquire rights in a trademark by asserting he owns it. *See Sengoku Works Ltd. v. RMC Int'l, Ltd.*, 96

F.3d 1217, 1219 (9th Cir. 1996) ("To acquire ownership of a trademark it is not enough to have invented the mark first or even to have registered it first; the party claiming ownership must have been the first to actually use the mark in the sale of goods or services."); *AB Electrolux v. Bermil Indus. Corp.*, 481 F. Supp. 2d 325, 330 (S.D.N.Y. 2007) ("In determining ownership of a trademark ... creation or invention of the mark is irrelevant. The critical question is which party first used the mark in the sale of goods or services."). Therefore, the attempts to license and similar actions Mr. Blum took in order to produce a film about Ruffian cannot save Plaintiffs' infringement claims.

Mr. Blum also states that "Legends has tried to further its RUFFIAN project by generating and distributing advertising materials through Paradies Shops." He attaches those materials, including a letter dated August 22, 2007 from an executive assistant at The Paradies Shops to an attorney named Michael Hobbs. The letter encloses a copy of a license agreement between Legends and The Paradies Shops, in which Legends grants The Paradies Shops a license to use several alleged marks in the names of famous racehorses, including "RUFFIAN." The license agreement permitted The Paradies Shops to use those marks "for clothing and printed matter and paper goods for marketing, distribution and sale in [The Paradies Shops]." Without more, this does not create a genuine issue of material fact as to whether Plaintiffs used "RUFFIAN" as a trademark. Though one may acquire protection in a service mark through its use by licensees, *see Turner v. HMH Publ'g Co.*, 380 F.2d 224, 229 (5th Cir. 1967), the proffered documents do not show that The Paradies Shops ever used the mark. Indeed, the version of the license agreement provided to the court has not been executed by Legends. Additionally, the use specified in the agreement pertained to clothing, printed matter, and paper goods, with no discernible connection to film production.

Mr. Blum also discusses a charity he founded called the Ruffian Foundation, but fails to allege commercial trademark use of "RUFFIAN" in connection with that organization. Furthermore, the Ruffian Foundation's mission is not to produce movies or television shows but "to further equine medical research, and the preservation of thoroughbred racing history." As such, plaintiffs have failed to establish that any materials related to the Ruffian Foundation amount to trademark use of the film-production-related mark Plaintiffs claim to own.

....

In conclusion, Plaintiffs have not shown a genuine issue of material fact as to whether they have acquired rights in the trademark "RUFFIAN." ... The court dismisses Plaintiffs' trademark infringement claims because Plaintiffs have not shown valid trademark rights.

....

Questions

1. As noted in the opinion, plaintiffs included Ruffian's trainer and jockey. Her owners, Stuart and Barbara Janney, do not appear to have been involved in either the movie or the plaintiffs' efforts to license Ruffian's name. Would plaintiffs have had a stronger case if they had sought the Janneys' participation? Why or why not?

2. Why does the law require that a mark actually be used to signify the origin of goods or services to customers or competitors before it can be a valid trademark or service mark?

American Express Co. v. Goetz, 515 F.3d 156 (2d Cir. 2008). Goetz, a consultant for an advertising agency, devised a slogan, "MY LIFE, MY CARD," which it proposed to several credit card companies, including American Express. Amex did not reply to Goetz' solicitation. Several months later, however, after working with a different advertising agency, Amex began to air advertisements incorporating the "MY LIFE, MY CARD" slogan. In response to Goetz' demand that Amex cease and desist its ad campaign, Amex sought a declaration that Goetz had no trademark rights in the slogan because he had not used the slogan as a trademark. The Second Circuit agreed:

> Under the Lanham Act, 15 U.S.C. §§ 1051 *et seq.*, a trademark or service mark is any combination of words, names, symbols or devices that are used to identify and distinguish goods or services and to indicate their source. [Citation.] While copyright law protects the content of a creative work itself, [citation] it is trademark law that protects those symbols, elements or devices which identify the work in the marketplace and prevent confusion as to its source. [Citations.] For example, the title of a song might identify that song in the marketplace, but the musical composition itself would not perform that function; thus, while the title may be protectable by trademark, the composition would not be. [Citation.] Further, a mark that does not perform the role of identifying a source is not a trademark.
>
> Notably, the same mark that performs this source-identifying role in one set of hands may constitute the creative work itself in another. Such distinction often is appropriate when an advertising agency licenses a slogan to a client for the client's use in marketing a product. In this scenario, the slogan is part of the advertising agency's creative work, but it may become a source identifier when used by the client. [Citation.]
>
> The Patent and Trademark Office's Trademark Trial and Appeal Board has long recognized, in such situations, that the slogans cannot be registered as marks by the advertising agency, even if they would be subject to registration by the end users of the marks....
>
> In the present case, construing all the facts in Goetz's favor, the only reasonable conclusion that can be drawn is that My Life, My Card was a component of Goetz's business proposal to the credit card companies rather than a mark designating the origin of any goods or services he offered to them.
>
> According to Goetz, he believed that the phrase My Life, My Card would "perfectly embody what card consumers sought." Yet, for the obvious reason that Goetz did not sell credit cards, he never displayed the slogan to card

consumers. Instead, he offered the slogan as a complement to the card personalization concept and software he proposed to sell and, in this respect, his claim is no better than that of an advertising agency that offers its clients a marketing concept to enhance their sales.

Our review of Goetz's letters and proposals to card companies reinforces that conclusion. Every use of the tagline My Life, My Card is immediately followed by the name of a credit card company which might choose to deliver personalized cards with such a slogan. My Life, My Card never appears as a standalone logo and the phrase is never followed by a reference to Goetz himself or his company. It is thus clear that Goetz did not intend the phrase My Life, My Card to ensure MasterCard, American Express or Citigroup would associate the card personalization concept with him, but instead to interest these companies in a slogan that would identify personalized cards with whichever company elected to make this product available to its customers.

....

In sum, Goetz employed the slogan My Life, My Card to generate interest among potential licensee credit card companies and not to differentiate or identify the origin of his goods or services. In such circumstances, the slogan served as "a mere advertisement for itself as a hypothetical commodity." [Citation.] Consequently, Goetz's trademark claim was properly dismissed.

....

Question

Does trademark law provide a basis for advertising agencies to assert ownership or control over clever marketing ideas they devise for potential clients? If not, why not?

B. Ownership

Crystal Entertainment & Filmworks, Inc. v. Jurado

643 F.3d 1313 (11th Cir. 2011)

Pryor, Circuit Judge:

This appeal is from a judgment against an entertainment company that sued the current members of "Exposé," an American girl dance band, about the trademark name of the band. Crystal Entertainment & Filmworks, Inc., is the purported assignee of the trademark rights of Pantera Group Enterprises and Pantera Productions, Inc., which created the original Exposé band in 1984. The current members of Exposé, Jeanette Jurado, Ann Curless, and Gioia Bruno, replaced the original members of the band in 1986, and the current members, along with Kelly Moneymaker, have produced several albums and intermittently performed as Exposé since then. In 2006, in a written agreement with Crystal, the current members obtained a license to use the Exposé mark when the band resumed performing. Before the agreement expired, the members of the band ceased paying licensing fees to Crystal and informed Crystal that they planned to seek federal registration of the Exposé mark through their own company, Walking Distance Entertainment, LLC. Crystal filed a complaint for breach of contract and violations of federal and state statutes and sought damages and injunctive relief. The district court conducted a bench trial and determined that Jurado, Curless, Bruno, and Walking Distance were the common-law owners of the Exposé mark. Because the record supports the findings by the district court, we affirm.

I. BACKGROUND

Crystal Entertainment & Filmworks, Inc., and Crystal Entertainment & Filmworks II, Inc., are music and film entertainment businesses based in Miami, Florida. Ismael Garcia and Joe Maenza … incorporated Crystal I in 1994 to manage performers and artists, and they incorporated Crystal II in 2003 to manage income from record companies.…

Garcia has also served as an officer of two other companies, Pantera Group Enterprises and Pantera Productions, Inc., and Crystal asserts that these companies were its predecessors-in-interest.… Garcia and Francisco Diaz were the only shareholders of Pantera.…

In 1984, Pantera formed the American girl dance band "Exposé." Garcia, Diaz, and Roy Lott from Arista Records created the name. Garcia testified that, as an officer of Pantera, he had "financed the production, the equipment, the offices, everything, the whole show." Pantera hired Lewis Martineé to write and to produce the songs and lyrics for Exposé, and Martineé received royalties for his efforts.

Exposé originally consisted of three female singers who released a recording of a song entitled "Point of No Return" that was played on radio stations and in dance clubs in Miami, New York, and Los Angeles. Exposé also made several live performances, and at least one member of the band purportedly collected royalties, but the likenesses of the members of the band did not appear on any Exposé albums or commercially available recordings. Garcia testified that the original members of Exposé did not enjoy commercial success: "They started with us when ["Point of No Return"] was not popular, so most of the shows that they did were for free. They did a lot of freebies. It didn't make much money."

In 1986, Jeanette Jurado, Ann Curless (now Ann Curless Weiss), and Gioia Bruno replaced the original members of Exposé and released with Arista Records a debut album entitled *Exposure* that reached "triple platinum status," which means that the band sold at least three million copies of the album. The album cover featured photographs of Jurado, Curless, and Bruno. Jurado, Curless, and Bruno did not compose songs or write lyrics for the band, but Bruno testified that they "became the name and the face and the voices of Exposé." Garcia conceded that the new members of the band have been the "face of Exposé since 1986." Garcia also testified that the new members "were critical to the look of the image that we wanted, the concept that we wanted to go out with on the road."

....

Jurado, Curless, and Bruno continued to experience success as the band Exposé. In 1989, Exposé released a second album entitled *What You Don't Know* that "went gold," which means that the band sold at least 500,000 copies of the album. The album cover featured Jurado, Curless, and Bruno. In 1992, Kelly Moneymaker temporarily replaced Bruno, and Exposé released a third album entitled *Exposé* with Moneymaker as a member of the group. This album depicted Jurado, Curless, and Moneymaker as the members of the band. The members of Exposé disbanded in 1995, but sales of their music continued; from 1995 until 2005, Arista Records released five compilation albums of pre-recorded music by Exposé.

Crystal contends that, when it was incorporated, ... Pantera assigned its purported rights to the Exposé mark to Crystal.... Based on this purported assignment, Crystal ... claims ownership of the Exposé mark....

....

In August 2003, Jurado and Curless executed a trademark and licensing agreement with Crystal I because they wanted to resume performing as Exposé. In the 2003 Agreement, the two singers acknowledged that Crystal I owned the Exposé mark exclusively and controlled its use. The two singers cancelled a tour of performances after one show because Curless had become pregnant.

Jurado, Curless, and Bruno executed a second trademark and licensing agreement with Crystal I in 2006 in anticipation of another tour. In the 2006 Agreement, the three singers acknowledged that Crystal I owned and controlled the Exposé mark. The 2006 Agreement gave Jurado, Curless, and Bruno the discretion to decide when Moneymaker would serve as a replacement. Jurado, Curless, and Bruno selected Paradise Artists, Inc., as their booking agent to schedule their tour dates, and Crystal approved this selection. Without the consent of Crystal, Jurado, Curless, and Bruno advertised the tour on the Internet at two web addresses: "exposeonline.net" and "myspace.com/exposeonline."

In 2007, the relationship between the band members and Crystal reached a "Point of No Return." *See* Exposé, *Point of No Return, on* Exposure (Arista Records 1987). Jurado, Curless, and Bruno tired of paying licensing fees to Crystal because Crystal had not promoted or scheduled any performances of Exposé under the 2006 Agreement. Bruno and Jurado testified that they, along with Curless, had directed and controlled everything since the band began performing again in 2006 with no assistance from Crystal. On August 10, 2007 ... Jurado, Curless, and Bruno ceased paying Crystal licensing fees under the 2006 Agreement, which expired on December 31, 2007, and instead deposited them with an escrow agent. They continued to perform on tour as Exposé during 2007, 2008, and 2009.

Crystal filed a complaint against the members of the band. Crystal sought a preliminary and permanent injunction, damages, and ... the licensing fees that Jurado's counsel had placed in escrow....

....

After a three-day bench trial, the district court made several findings of fact in favor of Jurado, Curless, and Bruno: all of the Exposé albums contained photographs of Jurado, Curless, and Bruno as the band Exposé, except for the album where Moneymaker temporarily replaced Bruno; Jurado, Curless, and Bruno created the goodwill associated with the Exposé mark; like the band members in *Bell v. Streetwise Records, Ltd.*, 640 F. Supp. 575 (D. Mass. 1986), Jurado, Curless, and Bruno "are the product that is denoted by the mark Exposé"; a member of the public who purchased a ticket to an Exposé concert would expect to see Jurado, Curless, and Bruno; and Moneymaker's involvement was at the discretion of Jurado, Curless, and Bruno. The district court also made several findings of fact against Crystal: Crystal failed to prove that it had selected Moneymaker, that it had exercised control over Jurado, Curless, and Bruno, or that it had taken an active role in scheduling their performances; ... Garcia conceded that he had been unable to put a different group together to perform as Exposé since 1986; and Garcia's testimony contained inconsistencies that rendered him less credible than the other witnesses.

The district court found that Crystal had failed to prove that it owned the Exposé mark or that the use of the mark by Jurado, Curless, Bruno, and Walking Distance was likely to cause consumer confusion. The district court ruled that Jurado, Curless, and Bruno were the "common law owners of the mark" because they had used the mark publicly since 1986. The district court reasoned that "the public's interest [was] best served by exclusively awarding [rights to the mark] to [Jurado, Curless, Bruno, and Walking Distance]," and "[t]o do otherwise would leave the name available to anyone who wanted to perform under the name Exposé, and cause unnecessary consumer confusion." The district court granted judgment in favor of Jurado, Curless, Bruno, and Walking Distance and against Crystal on its claims under the Lanham Act....

....

III. DISCUSSION

....

A. *The District Court Did Not Err When It Determined That Jurado, Curless, and Bruno Were the Common-Law Owners of the Exposé Mark.*

....

1. The Record Supports the Finding That Crystal Has No Enforceable Rights in the Exposé Mark.

The parties recognize the bedrock principle of trademark law that a mark can identify and distinguish only a single commercial source, see 2 J. McCarthy, Trademarks and Unfair Competition § 16:40, p. 16-77 (4th ed. 2011), and the opposing parties request this Court to "Let Me Be the One" who obtains rights to the Exposé mark, *see* Exposé, *Let Me Be the One, on* Exposure (Arista Records 1987). Crystal argues that it is the rightful owner because Pantera first appropriated the mark in 1984, but the record supports the finding to the contrary by the district court.

....

As the Federal Circuit has explained, trademark law permits a corporate entity to own the right to the name of a musical group, and the public need not associate the mark with the name of the corporate entity:

> [The corporate entity] submitted a license evidencing its right to control the quality of the sound recordings [of the band]. Since [the corporate entity] controls the quality of the goods, it is the source of the goods. Any trademark for the sound recordings can therefore only indicate source in [the corporate entity] since no other entity is the source. The source of the goods does not depend on the public's perception; the public need not know [the] role [of the corporate entity].

In re Polar Music Int'l AB, 714 F.2d 1567, 1571 (Fed. Cir. 1983) (footnote omitted). We consider whether Crystal (or, more precisely, its predecessor Pantera) satisfied the requirement of "'use in a way sufficiently public to identify or distinguish the marked goods in an appropriate segment of the public mind,'" [citation] ever mindful that the public need not have known the role of the corporate entity, *Polar Music*, 714 F.2d at 1571.

The district court determined that Crystal failed to prove that it had enforceable rights in the Exposé mark, and that finding is not clearly erroneous. Crystal failed to present evidence sufficient to establish that Pantera appropriated the Exposé mark "'in a way sufficiently public to identify or distinguish the marked goods in an appropriate segment of the public mind'" before Jurado, Curless, and Bruno joined the band....

Because Crystal failed to prove that it first appropriated the Exposé mark, the district court was required to determine the owner of the mark "where prior ownership by one of several claimants cannot be established." *Bell*, 640 F. Supp. at 580. The *Bell* court aptly described this controversy as a "case of joint endeavors." *Id.* We have yet to address a trademark dispute of this type, but other courts have consistently resolved such disputes by awarding trademark rights to the claimant who controls the nature and quality of the services performed under the mark. *See Robi v. Reed*, 173 F.3d 736, 740 (9th Cir. 1999); *Polar Music*, 714 F.2d at 1571; *Ligotti v. Garofalo*, 562 F. Supp. 2d 204, 227 (D.N.H. 2008); *Bell*, 640 F. Supp. at 580; *Rick v. Buchansky*, 609 F. Supp. 1522, 1537–38 (S.D.N.Y. 1985).

The *Bell* court applied a two-step approach in this circumstance: "[T]o determine ownership in a case of this kind, a court must first identify that quality or characteristic for which the group is known by the public. It then may proceed to the second step of the ownership inquiry, namely, who controls that quality or characteristic." *Bell*, 640 F. Supp. at 581 (footnotes omitted). *See also Ligotti*, 562 F. Supp. 2d at 217–27; 2 McCarthy, *supra*, § 16:45, pp. 16-85 to -86 ("Whether the service mark or name [of a performing group] identifies and distinguishes that particular performer combination or just style and quality [is] an issue of fact.... The issue to be resolved is whether the mark signifies personalities, or style and quality regardless of personalities."). In *Bell*, the members of the band "New Edition" and the companies that had produced, recorded, and marketed their first album disputed the rights to the name of the band. The *Bell* court ruled that the band members owned the mark because they had first appropriated it, and alternatively they owned the mark under the "joint endeavors" test. 640 F. Supp. at 580–82. The court explained that "the quality which the mark New Edition identified was first and foremost the [band members] with their distinctive personalities and style as performers." *Id.* at 582.

The district court reasonably applied the "joint endeavors" test to determine that Jurado, Curless, and Bruno owned the Exposé mark at common law. The district court found that Crystal failed to prove that it had selected Moneymaker, had exercised control over Jurado, Curless, and Bruno, or had "taken any active role in scheduling any of the group's performances"; Garcia had conceded that he had been unable to put a different group together to perform as Exposé since 1986; the involvement of Crystal with Exposé was limited to collecting royalties from the sale of records; and the private agreements upon which Crystal relied disclosed nothing to the public to change this perception. The district court also found that Exposé had been consistently portrayed to the public as Jurado, Curless, and Bruno since 1986; they were the product denoted by the Exposé mark; they owned the goodwill associated with the mark; and a member of the public who purchased a ticket to an Exposé concert would clearly expect to see Jurado, Curless, and Bruno perform. The record supports these findings that Jurado, Curless, and Bruno controlled the qualities and characteristics that the public associates with the Exposé mark.

....

IV. CONCLUSION

We AFFIRM the judgment in favor of Jurado, Weiss, Bruno, and Walking Distance.

Commodores Entertainment Corporation v. McClary, 648 Fed. Appx. 771 (11th Cir. 2016). In the 1970s, Lionel Ritchie, Thomas McClary, and four other musicians formed the funk/soul band, The Commodores. In the early 1980s, both Richie and McClary left the band to pursue other opportunities. Other musicians replaced them, and the band continued to perform and record. The Commodores Entertainment Corporation [CEC] registered the THE COMMODORES mark as both a service mark for entertainment services and a trademark for recorded music in 2001. In 2014, McClary began to perform with a band he called "The Commodores featuring Thomas McClary," playing music that included old Commodores hits. CEC filed suit against McClary; McClary then filed a petition in the USPTO to cancel CEC's registration of the COMMODORES marks. The district court granted CEC's motion for a preliminary injunction, finding that the members of the group who continued to perform as The Commodores owned the common law mark, because the musicians who stayed with the group continued to control the nature and quality of the mark, and that McClary's continued use of the mark was likely to cause confusion. McClary appealed. The Court of Appeals for the 11th Circuit affirmed:

> [W]e find no error in the district court's finding that the members who remained with the group and controlled the quality and reputation of the

> marks had the common law rights to the marks, not Appellants. *See Crystal [Entertainment v. Jurado]*, 643 F.3d at 1320 (holding that a company that originally formed a band did not own rights to the band's mark because, *inter alia*, the company failed to exercise control over the band); *see also Robi v. Reed*, 173 F.3d 736, 740 (9th Cir. 1999) (noting that an original founding member of the group who "remained and performed with it from its inception" retained the right to use the mark to the exclusion of a band member who left).

Lunatrex, LLC v. Cafasso, 674 F. Supp. 2d 1060 (S.D. Ind. 2009). The parties in this case were members of the "LunaTrex" team competing in the Google Lunar X Prize competition, which offers a prize of as much as $20 million for a private effort to land a robot on the surface of the moon. The LunaTrex team members had a falling out. In this lawsuit, each side claimed exclusive rights to the LUNATREX service mark, and sought a preliminary injunction under federal trademark law to block the other side from using the LUNATREX mark. Plaintiff Pete Bitar supplied all of the initial funding for the effort, and directed the money-raising aspects of the project. Defendant Mary Cafasso was the technical team leader, and oversaw research and development of the lunar rocket and robot. With the help of a marketing firm hired by Bitar, the team agreed on the LUNATREX mark and associated logo.

> ... Bitar then quickly arranged to have that logo used on the X Prize website for the competition, on the LunaTrex team's own website, and on business cards and other promotional items (including 1000 small rubber "squeeze balls" to relieve stress, painted and shaped like the moon, with the LunaTrex logo printed on it). Team members, including Cafasso, distributed their LunaTrex business cards (and the squeeze balls) widely among space and aerospace businesses in the United States and Europe. The name and logo were used in numerous contacts with the news media to publicize the team's efforts....
>
> ....
>
> The X Prize Foundation expected the competing teams to post at least weekly updates on a blog feature of the foundation's website. In February 2008, Bitar began posting blog entries for the LunaTrex team on the foundation website, and he posted similar materials on the team's own website. Cafasso also had codes that allowed her to post on the blog, but she rarely did so.

The group's initial work was well received: In 2008, the Lunar X Prize website sponsored a "poll" in which visitors were invited to vote for their favorite team from among the 12 registered teams. The poll attracted several hundred votes. LunaTrex came in first with 65 percent of the votes cast. In 2009, Bitar presented the group's plans to the Stihl Corporation, and received informal assurances of a $1 million sponsorship. Cafasso and Bitar could not agree on strategic and financial decisions, and came into increasing conflict. Eventually, the dispute became public. The Stihl Corporation declined to pursue sponsorship of LunaTrex until the conflict was resolved. The X Prize Foundation sent a letter to both Bitar and Cafasso saying that the dispute between them put the foundation in "an untenable position" and that the LunaTrex team was suspended effective immediately.

Plaintiffs have shown that the LunaTrex team was using the mark in commerce at least as early as February 2008, when the team used the mark to designate its entry in the Google Lunar X Prize competition. That use was sufficiently prominent to seize the attention of the small relevant market of participants in the competition and those following it. The use was sufficient to alert interested persons that the mark had a definite referent, the LunaTrex team. After the publicity concerning the new team in February 2008, the team expanded its use of the mark to publicity in advertising brochures, the squeeze balls, in many conferences and symposiums all over the United States and in Europe, and in efforts to seek sponsors to support the team's entry. Different team members used the mark in different ways and at different times and places, but all of them used the mark to refer to the same thing: the LunaTrex team and its entry in the Lunar X Prize competition. The use was genuine and continuous; there is no indication here that the LunaTrex team was merely seeking to reserve the mark for some future use.

....

The evidence before the court indicates that the LunaTrex team amounted to a joint venture or de facto partnership with at least four partners: Air Buoyant, LLC, MC Squared, Inc., Orbit Frontiers, LLC, and High Altitude Research Corporation. Those four companies are associated with Bitar, Cafasso, Gangestad, and Allison, respectively, and those four people were the leadership team of the LunaTrex team. Each team member contributed substantially to the team's efforts and reputation. Because there is no contractual agreement governing the membership and legal control of the team's assets, the name or trademark is best treated as the asset of a de facto partnership.

The plaintiffs, however, contend that they alone own the mark. They rely on the roles that Bitar and Air Buoyant played in developing and then exploiting the mark: Bitar paid the out-of-pocket expenses incurred in developing and exploiting the mark. He used the mark in his efforts to publicize the team and to seek sponsors. Bitar was also identified as the team leader and spokesman in the team's Google Lunar X Prize registration package and on the X Prize website.

Without diminishing at all Bitar's significant contributions to the team, including bearing most of the out-of-pocket expenses, the problem with the plaintiffs' theory is that the entire team contributed to the creation of the mark's value and protected status. Awarding control of the mark to the plaintiffs alone would ignore the contributions that the rest of the team made to the value of the LunaTrex name. Perhaps most important, awarding sole ownership to the plaintiffs would require the court to conclude that Bitar and Air Buoyant had made such visible and disproportionately valuable contributions to the team's efforts that the relevant public associates the LunaTrex name with Bitar and Air Buoyant to a much greater degree than with any other team members. The evidence here simply will not support such a conclusion.

Bitar played a key leadership role for the team, but he is not the only person to have done so. Bitar paid for most of the advertising or promotional activities. He was identified as team leader, but the promotional materials appear to have focused on the team as a whole. They certainly did not suggest that Bitar was the technical leader or otherwise had an exceptionally prominent role in the team. He was not personally responsible for inventing the mark or affixing it to any promotional materials; those were team efforts in the January 2008 meeting and later meetings. None of the team members put their own names on the team or its promotional materials. No one team member appears to have had principal responsibility for maintaining the quality and uniformity of the team efforts, and Cafasso was the technical team leader. There is no evidence that the relevant public believes that any one team member in particular stood behind the LunaTrex team and the quality of its effort.

Bitar seems to argue that the fact that he laid out the cash gives him the strongest claim to the LunaTrex mark. His payment of those expenses is surely an important factor, but it is not the only factor. Cash is not the only way to contribute to the team effort. Cafasso devoted a great deal of time and talent to the effort, as did other team members. Gangestad estimated that he had spent roughly 1000 hours on LunaTrex business. Cafasso estimated that she had spent roughly 2500 hours on LunaTrex business. There is no evidence here that team members thought that Bitar was entitled to special prominence and individual rights to the trademark.

On this record, therefore, it appears that the LunaTrex trademark belongs to all members of the team. None of the four members of the leadership team—Bitar's Air Buoyant, Cafasso's MC Squared, Gangestad's Orbit Frontiers, or Allison's High Altitude Research Corporation—is entitled to use the mark to the exclusion of any of the others.

....

The original LunaTrex team is no longer operating as a de facto partnership, and it seems to have broken up permanently. Typically, when a partnership breaks up, the assets are distributed among the partners. A trademark, however, is not divisible. If it were shared among the different splintered partners, the resulting confusion would destroy the value that each partner worked so hard to create. Organizers of the Google Lunar X Prize are well aware of this risk and seem committed to preventing this confusion: they say they will disqualify the entire team if this dispute is not resolved, and they will not allow two "LunaTrex" teams to compete. Both plaintiffs and defendants have shown that they have an ownership interest in the mark and a right to veto unauthorized uses of the mark. Neither side has shown that it is likely to succeed in showing that the other side is not equally entitled to use the mark. To prevent confusion to the public, the best solution under the law is to prevent all parties from using the mark without the consent of all other parties who are entitled to share control of its use. In other words, the court will take the unusual step of granting each side's motion for preliminary injunction to prevent the other from using the LunaTrex trademark without the moving side's consent.[8]

....

Questions

1. In 1953, musicians Alex Hodge, Cornell Gunter, David Lynch, Joe Jefferson, Gaynel Hodge and Herb Reed formed the vocal group, "The Platters," and signed a recording contract with Federal Records. Later that year, Tony Williams replaced Gunter. In 1954, Zola Taylor joined the group and Paul Robi replaced Hodge. In 1955, the Platters switched labels from Federal to Mercury Records. In 1960, Sonny Turner replaced Williams. In 1964, Barbara Randolph replaced Taylor. Paul Robi left in 1965. Herb Reed left the group in 1969. Turner left in 1970, and Monroe Powell joined The Platters and continued to sing with the group for more than 20 years. After leaving The Platters, Reed, Robi, Taylor, Turner, and Powell each toured with a vocal group under the name "The Platters," and were in and out of state and federal courts contesting each other's right to use the name. Robi died of cancer in 1989 and left his interest in The Platters to his widow Martha. Reed died in 2012, after assigning his rights to a corporation. Who owns the service mark? *See Robi v. Reed*, 173 F.3d 736 (9th Cir.1999). For other cases disputing ownership of the PLATTERS service mark, see *Herb Reed Enterprises, LLC v. Florida Entertainment Management,* 736 F.3d 1239 (9th Cir. 2013), *infra* Chapter 12[A]; *Herb Reed Enterprises LLC v. Florida Entertainment Management, Inc.*, 2014 US Dist LEXIS 45564 (D. Nev. 2014); *Herb Reed Enterprises, LLC v. The World Famous Platters Road Shows I LLC,* 2014 U.S. Dist LEXIS 22046 (M.D. Fla 2014); *Herb Reed Enterprises, Inc. v. Monroe Powells Platters, LLC,* 842 F. Supp. 2d 1282 (D. Nev. 2012).

2. In 1995, Walter Mercado-Salinas, a popular psychic, agreed with Bart Enterprises to provide psychic services in return for a monthly salary and Bart's efforts to promote the services. As part of that agreement, Mercado-Salinas assigned the right to use the service mark WALTER MERCADO to Bart. Ten years later, Mercado-Salinas ceased to provide the contractual services and Bart ceased to pay the contractual salary. Both parties claim to own the WALTER MERCADO mark: Bart insists the assignment was valid and transferred any of Mercado-Salinas's rights; Mercado-Salinas argues that the public understands the mark WALTER MERCADO to refer to services performed by him. How should the court rule? *See Mercado-Salinas v. Bart Enterprises,* 671 F.3d 12 (1st Cir 2011).

---

8. Nothing in this decision would necessarily prevent the parties from resolving the dispute by agreement, so long as they can avoid confusion for the relevant public as to the origin of an ongoing LunaTrex effort.

C. "Use In Commerce"

15 U.S.C. § 1127 [Lanham Act § 45]

In the construction of this Act, unless the contrary is plainly apparent from the context—

....

Commerce. The word "commerce" means all commerce which may lawfully be regulated by Congress.

....

Trademark. The term "trademark" includes any word, name, symbol, or device, or any combination thereof—

(1) used by a person, or

(2) which a person has a bona fide intention to use in commerce and applies to register on the principal register established by this chapter,

to identify and distinguish his or her goods, including a unique product, from those manufactured or sold by others and to indicate the source of the goods, even if that source is unknown.

....

Use in Commerce. The term "use in commerce" means the bona fide use of a mark in the ordinary course of trade, and not made merely to reserve a right in a mark. For purposes of this chapter, a mark shall be deemed to be in use in commerce—

(1) on goods when—

(A) it is placed in any manner on the goods or their containers or the displays associated therewith or on the tags or labels affixed thereto, or if the nature of the goods makes such placement impracticable, then on documents associated with the goods or their sale, and

(B) the goods are sold or transported in commerce, and

(2) on services when it is used or displayed in the sale or advertising of services and the services are rendered in commerce, or the services are rendered in more than one State or in the United States and a foreign country and the person rendering the services is engaged in commerce in connection with the services.

Note: Token Use

In amending the Lanham Act's definition of "use in commerce" in 1989 to specify that the use be made "in the ordinary course of trade, and not made merely to reserve a right in a mark," Congress sought to end the prior practice of "token use" through which a trademark claimant would make essentially fictitious use of the selected marks in order to create a record sufficient to support an assertion to the Patent and Trademark Office that the mark had been used in interstate commerce and therefore was eligible for registration. For example, in *Procter & Gamble v. Johnson & Johnson*, 485 F. Supp. 1185 (S.D.N.Y. 1979), *aff'd*, 636 F.2d 1203 (2d Cir. 1980), Procter & Gamble had devised a "minor brands" program to attempt to maintain registrations of hundreds of trademarks for goods that P & G was not in fact selling. Under the program, P & G would affix a label bearing the trademark to other, similar, goods in its product lines (or even to a rival company's goods of the type for which the trademark would be claimed), and then ship them for sale out of state; no advertising accompanied these sales, the sales were not accounted together with P & G's non-minor brands, and P & G's sales personnel were generally unaware of the minor brands. The program enabled P & G to have registered trademarks at the ready when it developed a new product; in fact, however, P & G rarely chose from the minor brands when a new product in fact emerged. The maintenance of hundreds of minor brands registrations had the incidental, if not intended, effect of warning competitors away from adopting those marks for their relevant goods. As a result, notwithstanding the widespread practice of "token use," the Second Circuit affirmed Judge Leval's district court opinion holding that P & G's Minor Brands program failed to establish any trademark rights in the selected brands.

Recognizing that product development may be long and costly, and that waiting till the goods were ready to market brought the risk that in the interim a third party might in good faith adopt the same or similar trademark for the same or similar goods or services, the 1989 amendments sought to achieve one of the objectives of "token use" by allowing claimants to apply for registration before making actual use of the marks. We will explore the resulting "intent to use" system in Chapter 4. At the same time, by requiring "bona fide use of a mark in the ordinary course of trade," the 1989 amendments aimed to end the anticompetitive abuses engendered by "token use."

Couture v. Playdom, 778 F.3d 1379 (Fed. Cir. 2015). In 2009, David Couture registered the PLAYDOM mark as a service mark for entertainment services. As proof of use in commerce, Couture submitted a screen capture of a website at playdominc.com that included a "website under construction" notice, and also said, "Welcome to PlaydomInc.com. We are proud to offer writing and production services for motion picture film, television, and new media. Please feel free to contact us if you are interested: playdominc@gmail.com." Although Couture offered to provide entertainment services before applying to register the mark, he didn't actually render the services until 2010. In the meantime, a different service had adopted the PLAYDOM mark for entertainment services. That company petitioned to cancel Couture's registration, arguing that because he had offered but not yet rendered services under the PLAYDOM mark, he had failed to use the service mark in commerce at the time of his registration application. The Court of Appeals for the Federal Circuit agreed:

> We have not previously had occasion to directly address whether the offering of a service, without the actual provision of a service, is sufficient to constitute use in commerce under Lanham Act § 45, 15 U.S.C. § 1127.... On its face, the statute is clear that a mark for services is used in commerce only

when *both* [1] "it is used or displayed in the sale or advertising of services and [2] the services are rendered...." 15 U.S.C. § 1127 (emphasis added). This statutory language reflects the nature of trademark rights:

> There is no such thing as property in a trademark except as a right appurtenant to an established business or trade in connection with which the mark is employed.... [T]he right to a particular mark grows out of its use, not its mere adoption....

United Drug Co. v. Theodore Rectanus Co., 248 U.S. 90, 97 (1918).

Other circuits have interpreted Lanham Act § 45 as requiring actual provision of services.... The Board in this case and the leading treatise on trademarks also agree that rendering services requires actual provision of services. *See* McCarthy on Trademarks and Unfair Competition § 19:103 (4th ed. Supp. 2013) ("To qualify for registration, the Lanham Act requires that the mark be both used in the sale or advertising of services *and* that the services themselves have been rendered in interstate or foreign commerce." (emphasis in original)).

Here, there is no evidence in the record showing that appellant rendered services to any customer before 2010, and the cancellation of appellant's registration was appropriate.

In re Dell Inc., 71 U.S.P.Q.2d (BNA) 1725 (T.T.A.B. 2004). The Dell Computer Corporation sought to register QUIETCASE as a trademark for computer workstation hardware. To show use in commerce, Dell submitted a printout of a page taken from its website showing an image of its Precision Workstation 530, with bullet points describing the computer. One of the bullet points said: "QuietCase™ acoustic environment, provides easy access to system interior and supports tool-less upgrades and maintenance of key internal components." The trademark examiner refused registration on the ground that Dell had failed to show actual trademark use. The Trademark Trial and Appeal Board reversed:

> Section 45 of the Trademark Act states, in part, that:
>
> For purposes of this Act, a mark shall be deemed to be in use in commerce—
>
> (1) on goods when—
>
> (A) it is placed in any manner on the goods or their containers or the displays associated therewith or on the tags or labels affixed thereto, or if the nature of the goods makes such placement impracticable, then on documents associated with the goods or their sale....
>
> ....
>
> With respect to the question of whether a website page can constitute a display associated with the goods, it is true, as the Examining Attorney points out, that traditionally "displays associated with the goods" have been banners, shelf-talkers and other point-of-sale material. However, in *Lands' End* [*Inc. v. Manbeck*, 797 F. Supp. 511 (E.D. Va. 1992)], the Court held that a catalog

could also be a display associated with the goods. *Lands' End* was attempting to register KETCH as a trademark for purses, and

> submitted a page of its catalogue showing the picture of a purse, a verbal description, and the term "KETCH" as they allege constitutes trademark usage. The alleged trademark "KETCH" appears prominently in large bold lettering on the display of purses in the Lands' End specimen in a manner which closely associates the term with the purses.

[Citation.]

As the Court reiterated in that decision, citing *In re Shipley Co.*, 230 U.S.P.Q. at 694 (T.T.A.B. 1986), "A point of sale location provides a customer with the opportunity to look to the displayed mark as a means of identifying and distinguishing the source of goods." [Citation.] In *Shipley*, the Board found that a specimen showing the mark at a trade show booth was an acceptable "display associated with the goods" because the trade show booth was a sales counter for the applicant's products, even though the chemicals being sold were not physically present at the booth. The Court found this situation analogous to the catalog involved in *Lands' End*; the customer could associate this display of the mark with the goods in deciding whether to buy the product. Using the catalog, a customer could associate the product with the trademark in the display, and make a decision to purchase by filling out the sales form and sending it in or by calling in a purchase by phone.

Following the reasoning of the *Lands' End* decision, we hold that a website page which displays a product, and provides a means of ordering the product, can constitute a "display associated with the goods," as long as the mark appears on the webpage in a manner in which the mark is associated with the goods. It is a well-recognized fact of current commercial life that many goods and services are offered for sale on-line, and that on-line sales make up a significant portion of trade....

In today's commercial environment, we must recognize that the banners, shelf-talkers and other point of purchase displays that are associated with brick and mortar stores are not feasible for the on-line shopping setting. Web pages which display goods and their trademarks and provide for the on-line ordering of such goods are, in fact, electronic displays which are associated with the goods. Such uses are not merely advertising, because in addition to showing the goods and the features of the goods, they provide a link for ordering the goods. In effect, the website is an electronic retail store, and the webpage is a shelf-talker or banner which encourages the consumer to buy the product. A consumer using the link on the webpage to purchase the goods is the equivalent of a consumer seeing a shelf-talker and taking the item to the cashier in a brick and mortar store to purchase it.

The Examining Attorney has asserted that a single webpage does not fit within the *Lands' End* determination of a display associated with the goods because it is not an actual catalog nor is it an electronic catalog. However, the point made in *Lands' End* was not that, to be a display associated with the goods, the specimen had to be a catalog (whether actual or electronic). The single webpage submitted in the present case is used as a vehicle for ordering the product shown on the webpage....

The single webpage is, thus, a point of sale display, a display by which the actual sale is made.

....

In the context of the specimen webpage, we find that QUIETCASE is sufficiently prominent that consumers will recognize it as a trademark for the computer hardware shown on the webpage....

....

Questions

1. Why does the statutory definition of "use in commerce" require that the trademark be attached to goods or associated displays or documents of sale? Why doesn't the definition impose a similar requirement for service mark use in commerce?

2. The TTAB opinion stresses the importance of displaying the trademark on the same part of a website that allows customers to purchase the goods. Recall your last few online shopping experiences. Does the Board's analysis accord with your perceptions as a customer of what words and symbols were trademarks and what were informational advertising? What factors influenced your impressions?

3. Why does the Lanham Act require that goods actually be sold or transported in commerce and that services actually be rendered in commerce?

4. The Lanham Act defines "use in commerce" on services to require that the mark be "used or displayed in the sale or advertising of services" and the services be "rendered in commerce, or the services are rendered in more than one State or in the United States and a foreign country and the person rendering the services is engaged in commerce in connection with the services." If a person in central Nebraska owned and operated a single grocery store named "Nebraska Bill's" that sold food exclusively to local residents, would his activities constitute "use in commerce" under the Lanham Act? What more do you need to know to address this question?

Larry Harmon Pictures Corp. v. Williams Restaurant Corp., 929 F.2d 662 (Fed. Cir. 1991). Plaintiff, a corporation owned by Larry Harmon, a.k.a. Bozo the Clown, opposed registration of the mark "BOZO'S" for restaurant services. Applicant owned a single restaurant in Mason, Tennessee. Harmon asserted, inter alia, that registration should be denied because operation of a single restaurant did not constitute "use in commerce" within the meaning of the Lanham Act. The Court affirmed the Board's dismissal of the opposition.

... Williams has operated BOZO'S pit barbecue restaurant in Mason, Tennessee, since 1932. Mason is about a 50 or 60 minute drive from Memphis, Tennessee, which is a large city and a major commercial center for the Mid-South region. The Memphis metropolitan statistical area comprises not only a portion of Tennessee, but also portions of Mississippi and Arkansas. As conceded by Harmon before the board, BOZO'S "restaurant is obviously popular with Memphis residents.... It is close enough (50–60 minutes) to make a pleasant outing from the city. Articles ... from Memphis newspapers and magazines also refer to the restaurant's popularity with Memphis residents." In addition, BOZO'S restaurant has been at least mentioned in publications originating in New York, New York; Washington, D.C.; Dallas, Texas; Gila Bend, Arizona; and Palm Beach, Florida. Further, according to the board's opinion, "[t]here is no dispute that BOZO'S restaurant services are rendered to interstate travelers" and Harmon "acknowledges that applicant's restaurant ... serves some interstate travelers."

....

The only issue in this appeal is whether the board correctly concluded that the "use in commerce" requirement set forth in Section 3 of the Lanham Act is satisfied by the service in a single-location restaurant of interstate customers. Harmon argues that the use in commerce requirement of Section 3 cannot be satisfied by a single-location restaurant, such as BOZO'S, that serves only a minimal number of interstate travelers. In support of its argument, Harmon relies on *In re Bookbinder's Restaurant, Inc.*, 240 F.2d 365 (1957), in which a single-location restaurant in Philadelphia was not permitted to register its service mark. Harmon further contends that if the *Bookbinder's* rule—which it interprets to be that single-location restaurants, not located on an interstate highway, cannot be considered as rendering services in commerce—seems too restrictive, this court should adopt the test that a single-location restaurant is not entitled to register its service mark unless (1) it is located on an interstate highway, (2) at least 50% of its meals are served to interstate travelers, or (3) it regularly advertises in out-of-state media. We decline to circumscribe the statute in the manner suggested.

....

Harmon's position is based primarily on *In re Bookbinder's*, but in that case the court's decision reflects clearly the failure to prove any use in commerce. The court observed that "[t]he record indicates that appellant operates a single restaurant in Philadelphia, Pennsylvania, and the services relied on are rendered in that city," and that "[t]here are no affidavits or testimony of record and the application states merely that the mark is used 'for restaurant, catering and banquet services.'" The court also discounted as not probative the "unverified statement [by the applicant's attorney] that the services were offered to customers and prospective customers in states adjoining Pennsylvania." 240 F.2d at 368.

In *In re Gastown, Inc.*, 326 F.2d 780 (C.C.P.A. 1964), decided seven years after *Bookbinder's*, the CCPA again discussed the "use in commerce" requirement set forth in Section 3 of the Lanham Act. In *Gastown*, the appellant operated a chain of automobile and truck service stations, some of which were located on federal highways. Although the services rendered by the appellant were confined to the State of Ohio, some of appellant's customers had their legal situs in other states, were engaged in interstate commerce when served by appellant in Ohio, and were extended credit and billed in their respective domiciliary states. The court held that those circumstances established that the services had a direct effect on interstate commerce and were sufficient to show that applicant's mark was used in commerce within the meaning of Sections 3 and 45 of the Lanham Act.

....

While the facts supporting Williams' contention that its service mark is used in commerce are not as extensive, or as persuasive, as those in *Gastown*, we are convinced they are sufficient to satisfy the statutory requirement for registration. In *Gastown*, the court approved the Fifth Circuit's observation that in enacting the Lanham Act "[i]t would seem that ... Congress intended to regulate interstate and foreign commerce to the full extent of its constitutional powers." *Gastown*, 326 F.2d at 784 (quoting the Fifth Circuit's decision in *Bulova Watch v. Steele*, 194 F.2d 567, 571 (5th Cir.), *aff'd*, 344 U.S. 280 (1952)).

....

The record here established that the BOZO'S mark has been used in connection with services rendered to customers traveling across state boundaries. It is not required that such services be rendered in more than one state to satisfy the use in commerce requirement. [Citations.] Harmon does not dispute that there has been some use in commerce of Williams' mark. It contends only that the volume of such activity was less than Williams' affidavit would indicate. Harmon, however, has produced no evidence to counter the proof of interstate activity by Williams....

We therefore reject Harmon's argument that a certain increased threshold level of interstate activity is required before registration of the mark used by a single-location restaurant may be granted. The Lanham Act by its terms extends to all commerce which Congress may regulate. This court does not have the power to narrow or restrict the unambiguous language of the statute. Accordingly, we affirm the decision of the board.

Questions

1. Does the *Larry Harmon Pictures* decision afford sufficient guidance in determining whether the "use is in commerce" for Lanham Act purposes? If the goods are sold or the services are rendered in anything plausibly affecting interstate commerce, and the

user wants to register the mark, is there a good policy reason *not* to register the mark? Once federally registered, the mark's existence is easily ascertained. Registration thus diminishes the likelihood of a national second-comer's unpleasant surprise at finding a local user of the same mark; registration affords notice to all potential adopters of the mark. Federal registration also confers nation-wide rights against subsequent adopters and users; would these be inappropriate if the registrant is truly local?

2. Pure Detroit, Inc. (the defendant in *Chrysler Group v. Moda Group*, 796 F. Supp. 2d 866 (E.D. Mich. 2011), *supra* Chapter 2[B]) operates three stores selling Detroit-themed merchandise designed and manufactured in Detroit. All three stores are located in landmark buildings in downtown Detroit. Visitors to one of the Pure Detroit stores may buy works by local artists, hub cap clocks, locally-made Pewabic tiles, Red Pelican mustard, tote bags made from automotive seat belt webbing, historic photographs, books, gift baskets, and hats, jewelry, posters, and tee shirts that celebrate the city. The company sponsors cultural events in the city, and invests in urban development projects within Detroit city limits. Has the company used the PURE DETROIT mark in commerce?

3. In January, a new company is formed to manufacture sports gear and apparel and to sell and distribute it online. The company, formed under the name Sports Galore, immediately registers a domain name for its Internet site under the name Sports-Galore.com. By February, Sports Galore has manufactured an initial line of t-shirts, bearing a plain-type Sports Galore label. Before bringing the inventory online, the company holds a contest to promote its launch by inviting website visitors to design a new logo for the company. The logo will emblazon the website and future clothing labels. In March, a winner is selected and promotional efforts are undertaken with the company name, web address, and logo to advertise the impending launch. The marketing encourages website visitors to register for prizes and gift certificates. In April, the website officially opens and makes its first sale. When did Sports Galore establish use in commerce for its name? For its logo?

Note: Foreign Commerce

The Lanham Act, § 45, defines "commerce" as "all commerce which may lawfully be regulated by Congress." What does this suggest about trademark uses occurring outside the U.S.? Congress's power extends to commerce between the United States and a foreign country, *see* U.S. Const. art. I, § 8, cl. 3, but the Trademark Manual of Examining Procedures (8th edition) § 901.03 cautions: "Unless the 'foreign commerce' involves the United States, Congress does not have the power to regulate it. Use of a mark in a foreign country does not give rise to rights in the United States if the goods or services are not sold or rendered in the United States."

Grupo Gigante SA de CV v. Dallo & Co., Inc., 391 F.3d 1088 (9th Cir. 2004). Plaintiff Grupo Gigante opened its first GIGANTE market in Mexico in 1962, and expanded to a large and well-known chain of nearly 100 grocery stores, all of them in Mexico. It operated two GIGANTE stores in Tijuana, just south of the US-Mexican border in San Diego. In the 1990s, defendant Dallo opened two stores in San Diego named "Gigante Market." Meanwhile, Grupo Gigante pursued plans to expand into the United States. It discovered Dallo's stores, and sought without success to persuade him to cease using the GIGANTE mark. In 1999, it opened three GIGANTE stores in Los Angeles. Litigation ensued. The district court held that the fame of the GIGANTE mark in Mexico entitled it to assert trademark rights in California. Dallo appealed:

> A fundamental principle of trademark law is first in time equals first in right. But things get more complicated when to time we add considerations of place, as when one user is first in time in one place while another is first in time in a different place. The complexity swells when the two places are two different countries, as in the case at bar.
>
> Under the principle of first in time equals first in right, priority ordinarily comes with earlier *use* of a mark in commerce. It is "not enough to have invented the mark first or even to have registered it first." If the first-in-time principle were all that mattered, this case would end there. It is undisputed that Grupo Gigante used the mark in commerce for decades before the Dallos did. But the facts of this case implicate another well-established principle of trademark law, the "territoriality principle." The territoriality principle, as stated in a treatise, says that "[p]riority of trademark rights in the United States depends solely upon priority of use in the United States, not on priority of use anywhere in the world."[9] Earlier use in another country usually just does not count. Although we have not had occasion to address this principle, it has been described by our sister circuits as "basic to trademark law," in large part because "trademark rights exist in each country solely according to that country's statutory scheme." While Grupo Gigante used the mark for decades before the Dallos used it, Grupo Gigante's use was in Mexico, not in the United States. Within the San Diego area, on the northern side of the border, the Dallos were the first users of the "Gigante" mark. Thus, according to the territoriality principle, the Dallos' rights to use the mark would trump Grupo Gigante's.

The court recognized an exception to the territoriality principle for famous foreign marks:

> ... While the territoriality principle is a long-standing and important doctrine within trademark law, it cannot be absolute. An absolute territoriality rule without a famous-mark exception would promote consumer confusion and fraud. Commerce crosses borders. In this nation of immigrants, so do people. Trademark is, at its core, about protecting against consumer confusion and "palming off." There can be no justification for using trademark law to fool immigrants into thinking that they are buying from the store they liked back home.

9. J. Thomas McCarthy, *McCarthy on Trademarks and Unfair Competition*, § 2 9:2, at 29-6 (4th ed. 2002) (internal footnote omitted).

To qualify for the exception, the court held, the foreign mark owner must persuade the court "that a *substantial* percentage of consumers in the relevant American market is familiar with the foreign mark." The Ninth Circuit continued:

> ... The relevant American market is the geographic area where the defendant uses the alleged infringing mark. In making this determination, the court should consider such factors as the intentional copying of the mark by the defendant, and whether customers of the American firm are likely to think they are patronizing the same firm that uses the mark in another country. While these factors are not necessarily determinative, they are particularly relevant because they bear heavily on the risks of consumer confusion and fraud, which are the reasons for having a famous-mark exception.

ITC Ltd. v. Punchgini

518 F.3d 159 (2d Cir. 2008)

Raggi, Circuit Judge:

[Plaintiff ITC Limited operated a famous high-end Indian restaurant in a New Delhi hotel under the mark BUKHARA, and operated or licensed other Bukhara restaurants in hotels in Singapore, Kathmandu, and Ajman. When defendants, some of whom had worked at the Delhi Bukhara restaurant, decided to open an Indian restaurant in Manhattan, they adopted the name "Bukhara Grill," and used logos, décor, staff uniforms and other trade dress that were markedly similar to plaintiff's. ITC sued for trademark infringement and unfair competition. The district court granted summary judgment to defendants, holding that even if U.S. law recognized a famous mark exception to the territoriality principle, ITC had failed to prove sufficient fame to trigger the exception. On appeal, the Court of Appeals for the Second Circuit concluded that Congress had not incorporated a famous foreign marks exception into the Lanham Act, and that the policy arguments favoring such an exception did not justify its judicial recognition. The court however, suggested that state law might recognize such an exception, and certified to the New York Court of Appeals the questions whether New York Law permitted the owner of a famous foreign mark to recover in a state law action for unfair competition, and, if so, how famous the foreign mark must be to support such a claim. *ITC Ltd. v. Punchgini, Inc.*, 482 F.3d 135 (2d Cir. 2007). Upon receipt of the New York Court of Appeals' response, the Second Circuit affirmed the grant of summary judgment to defendants:]

I. The New York Court of Appeals' Answers to the Certified Questions

To explain our decision, we first summarize the Court of Appeals' answers to our certified questions. The Court of Appeals responded to our first question in the affirmative, see *ITC Ltd. v. Punchgini*, 9 N.Y.3d 467, but, in doing so, specifically stated that it did not recognize the famous marks doctrine as an independent theory of liability under state law. Rather, the court explained that its affirmative response was intended only to reaffirm established state law prohibiting unfair competition, specifically, the principle that "when a business, through renown in New York, possesses goodwill constituting property or commercial advantage in this state, that goodwill is protected from misappropriation under New York unfair competition law. This is so whether the business is domestic or foreign." 9 N.Y.3d at 479.

In response to our second question, the Court of Appeals wrote as follows:

> Protection from misappropriation of a famous foreign mark presupposes the existence of actual goodwill in New York. If a foreign plaintiff has no goodwill in this state to appropriate, there can be no viable claim for unfair competition under a theory of misappropriation. At the very least, a plaintiff's mark, when used in New York, must call to mind its goodwill.... Thus, at a minimum, consumers of the good or service provided under a certain mark by a defendant in New York must primarily associate the mark with the foreign plaintiff.

9 N.Y.3d at 479 (citations omitted). Although the court cautioned that the relevant inquiry would necessarily vary with the facts of each case, it identified the following factors as potentially relevant: (1) evidence that "the defendant intentionally associated goods with those of the foreign plaintiff in the minds of the public, such as public statements or advertising stating or implying a connection with the foreign plaintiff"; (2) "direct evidence, such as consumer surveys, indicating that consumers of defendant's goods or services believe them to be associated with the plaintiff"; and (3) "evidence of actual overlap between customers of the New York defendant and the foreign plaintiff." 9 N.Y.3d at 479–80.

The Court of Appeals concluded its response to our certified inquiry by observing that,

> to prevail against defendants on an unfair competition theory, under New York law, ITC would have to show first, as an independent prerequisite, that defendants appropriated (i.e., deliberately copied), ITC's Bukhara mark or dress for their New York restaurants. If they make that showing, [ITC] would then have to establish that the relevant consumer market for New York's Bukhara restaurant primarily associates the Bukhara mark or dress with those Bukhara restaurants owned and operated by ITC.

9 N.Y.3d at 480. In short, to pursue an unfair competition claim, ITC must adduce proof of both deliberate copying and "secondary meaning." [Citation.]

II. ITC's Failure to Raise a Genuine Issue of Material Fact as to Secondary Meaning

Reviewing the challenged summary judgment award on ITC's state law claim of unfair competition in light of this response, we easily conclude, as the district court did [citation], that ITC adduced sufficient evidence of deliberate copying to satisfy that element of this claim. Thus, we focus in this opinion on the sufficiency of defendants' showing of secondary meaning.

The district court concluded that ITC "failed even to establish a triable issue as to the existence of 'secondary meaning' in the New York market in which defendants operate." [Citation.] In challenging this conclusion, ITC has abandoned its original appellate argument that no proof of secondary meaning is required when a New York unfair competition claim is based on intentional copying. Recognizing that the New York Court of Appeals' opinion ruled otherwise, ITC now contends that the district court erred in concluding that it could not establish secondary meaning....

....

... ITC's proffered evidence of goodwill derived entirely from foreign media reports and sources and was unaccompanied by any evidence that would permit an inference that such reports or sources reach the relevant consumer market in New York. [Citation.] ITC proffered no evidence that it had "directly targeted advertising of its Indian or other foreign 'Bukhara' restaurants to the United States." [Citation.] It made no attempt to prove its goodwill in the relevant market through consumer study evidence linking the Bukhara mark to itself, and it presented no research reports demonstrating strong brand name recognition for the Bukhara mark anywhere in the United States. [Citation.] Moreover, the record is devoid of any evidence of actual overlap between customers of defendants' restaurant and ITC's Bukhara, aside from ITC's own inadmissible speculation. Absent admissible evidence, however, a reasonable factfinder could not conclude that potential customers of defendants' restaurant would primarily associate the Bukhara mark with ITC, particularly in light of evidence that numerous Indian restaurants in Massachusetts, Washington, Virginia, and around the world have used the name "Bukhara," all without any affiliation or association with ITC.

ITC's belated efforts to identify admissible evidence of secondary meaning are unavailing. First, ITC points to record evidence that a significant number of defendants' customers are Indian or "well-traveled [people who] know what authentic Indian food tastes like." Even if these facts support a reasonable inference that this consumer market is "more knowledgeable about India than the general New York population," ITC provides no evidence—apart from its own conjecture—to support the conclusion that, as a consequence, these persons "primarily associate" the name "Bukhara" with ITC. Conjecture, of course, is insufficient to withstand summary judgment. [Citation.] Second, ITC argues that the district court failed to consider evidence of "public statements or advertising stating or implying a connection with the foreign plaintiff." We are not persuaded. The district court plainly considered this evidence and concluded that it supported ITC's claim of intentional copying. Moreover, the district court recognized that "there may be some circumstances in which intentional copying is sufficient to show 'secondary meaning.'" *ITC Ltd. v. Punchgini, Inc.*, 373 F. Supp. 2d at 291. But it cogently explained why this was not such a case: "it would be tautological to conclude that copying alone demonstrates 'secondary meaning' sufficient to permit an unfair competition claim as to a foreign mark here, where that copying is only prohibited by the 'well known' or 'famous' mark exception if the mark has 'secondary meaning.'" *Id.* We adopt this reasoning as consistent with the New York Court of Appeals' conclusion that more than copying is necessary for a famous foreign mark holder to pursue a state law claim for unfair competition. That foreign holder must further offer evidence that the defendant's potential customers "primarily associate" the mark with the foreign holder. *ITC Ltd. v. Punchgini*, 9 N.Y. 3d at 479. ITC cannot satisfy this burden simply by pointing to evidence of obvious similarities between defendants' Bukhara Grill and ITC's own Bukhara restaurant, because such evidence is no proof that defendants' potential customers were even aware of the existence of ITC's Bukhara.

. . . .

Questions

1. If ITC had a website, accessible in the U.S., that allowed U.S. residents to book tables at the Bukhara restaurants in Delhi, Singapore, Kathmandu, and Ajman, would this be a "use in commerce"?

2. If a foreign mark must have generated goodwill in New York, what is the relevant segment of the New York public? Suppose plaintiff's establishment is a famous sushi restaurant in Tokyo, which is not known to most New Yorkers. The Tokyo restaurant is, however, certainly known to Japanese business people who visit or temporarily reside in New York City, and to New Yorkers who frequently travel to Tokyo. Plaintiff has no restaurant in New York City. Defendant decides to open a New York sushi restaurant with the same name as the famous Tokyo restaurant. Does plaintiff have a claim under New York law on the ground that the local establishment is targeting customers who are familiar with the Tokyo original? Does it matter if the New York restaurant's clientele includes not only Japanese business people, but New Yorkers who are unaware of the Tokyo restaurant?

3. Under the NY Court of Appeals' and Second Circuit's approach, is there any basis on which to hold liable a merchant who identifies a trademark and/or trade dress well-known in its country of origin, but not in the U.S., and then assiduously copies the mark and/or trade dress in purveying identical goods or rendering identical services? *See Person's Co., Ltd. v. Christman*, 900 F.2d 1565 (Fed. Cir. 1990), *infra* Chapter 4[C]. On the shortcomings of territorially-based theories of protection in a world of cross-border consumer mobility, advertising and Internet promotion and sales, see Graeme Austin, *The Story of* Steele v Bulova*: Trademarks on the Line, in* Jane C. Ginsburg & Rochelle Cooper Dreyfuss, Intellectual Property Stories 395 (2006).

4. As commercial activity becomes increasingly global, does it make sense for courts to continue to apply a territorial model of trademark rights? *See* Graeme W. Austin, "The Consumer in Cross-Border Passing Off Cases" (2016) 47(2) Victoria University of Wellington Law Review Special Issue: Papers from the 2016 New Zealand Private Law Roundtable pp 191–208.

5. Article 6*bis* of the Paris Convention for the Protection of Industrial Property (*see infra* Chapter 4[A][1]; excerpts from the Convention appear in Appendix D) requires member States, to "prohibit the use[] of a trademark which constitutes a reproduction, an imitation, or a translation, liable to create confusion, of a mark considered by the competent authority of the country of ... use to be well known in that country as being already the mark of a person entitled to the benefits of this Convention and used for identical or similar goods." Article 16.2 of the 1994 World Trade Organization Agreement on Trade Related Aspects of Intellectual Property (TRIPs), which extends Paris Conv. art. 6*bis* to services, further specifies, "In determining whether a trademark is well-known, Members shall take account of the knowledge of the trademark in the relevant sector of the public, including knowledge in the Member concerned which has been obtained as a result of promotion of the trademark." Is the Second Circuit's decision (which cites neither international agreement) consistent with these standards?

Paleteria La Michoacana v. Productos Lacteos Tocumbo, 69 F. Supp. 3d 175 (D.D.C. 2014), *reconsideration denied*, 79 F. Supp. 3d 60 (D.D.C. 2015), *subsequent opinion at* 2016 U.S. Dist. LEXIS 69621 (D.D.C. 2016). Two companies sought to use similar marks for Mexican-style ice cream treats. One of the companies, Prolacto, claimed to have used its mark in Mexico since the 1940s, and had licensed some United States sales under the mark beginning in 1999. The other company, Paleteria La Michoacana [PLM], had sold ice cream products within the United States under its mark since 1991. Prolacto claimed that the famous mark doctrine recognized in *Grupo Gigante v. Dallo* entitled it to prevail over PLM. The District Court disagreed:

> It is axiomatic that under United States trademark law, a party establishes valid ownership of a mark by being the first to use that mark in commerce. [Citations.] It also is a basic tenet of American trademark law that foreign use of a mark creates no cognizable right to use that mark within the United States. [Citations]. This is known as the "territoriality principle," through which "trademark rights exist in each country solely according to that country's statutory scheme." *Person's Co., Ltd. v. Christman*, 900 F.2d 1565, 1568–69 (Fed. Cir. 1990); *see also Aktieselskabet AF 21. Nov. 2001 v. Fame Jeans, Inc.*, 511 F. Supp. 2d 1, 12 n.5 (D.D.C. 2007). As such, the "'[p]riority of trademark rights in the United States depends solely upon priority of use in the United States, not on priority of use anywhere in the world.'" *See Grupo Gigante SA De CV v. Dallo & Co., Inc.*, 391 F.3d 1088, 1093 (9th Cir. 2004) (quoting 3 McCarthy on Trademarks § 29:2 (4th ed.) (internal footnote omitted)).
>
> There is, however, a narrow yet divisive disturbance to the force of the territoriality principle. This is the so-called "famous mark" or "well-known mark" doctrine, under which a mark may be deemed so well-known in a particular American market—despite no actual commercial use in the market—that the territoriality principle is disregarded and priority is established through reputation rather than actual use in the United States. *See id.* at 1094. The gist of the famous mark doctrine is that "even those who use marks in other countries can sometimes—when their marks are famous enough—gain exclusive rights to the marks in this country." *Id.* at 1095.

But to date, this exception has been adopted only within one federal circuit following a decision by the U.S. Court of Appeals for the Ninth Circuit. The Ninth Circuit panel justified embracing the doctrine in *Grupo Gigante* largely on policy grounds: "An absolute territoriality rule without a famous-mark exception would promote consumer confusion and fraud. Commerce crosses borders. In this nation of immigrants, so do people. Trademark is, at its core, about protecting against consumer confusion and 'palming off.'" *Grupo Gigante*, 391 F.3d at 1094. Before and since *Grupo Gigante*, however, no other federal circuit court has adopted such a doctrine, though the exception has been recognized in the past by the T.T.A.B.

The U.S. Court of Appeals for the Second Circuit, on the other hand, has explicitly rejected the doctrine. *See generally ITC Ltd. v. Punchgini, Inc.*, 482 F.3d 135 (2d Cir. 2007).... In *ITC v. Punchgini*, the Second Circuit concluded that the Lanham Act lacked an express recognition of the famous mark doctrine as embodied in the Paris Convention and the Agreement on Trade-Related Aspects of Intellectual Property Rights. Because the operative American trademark statute did not recognize the rule in so many words, the court concluded that it was not part of federal law. In reaching this conclusion, the court rejected an argument that the famous mark rule is implicit in the structure of the Lanham Act, as advocated by Professor McCarthy. Finally, although the court acknowledged the strong policy rationales for incorporating the doctrine into federal law, it concluded that those arguments must be directed to Congress, not the courts.

Though there are robust arguments on both sides regarding the famous mark doctrine—including legitimate concerns over the need to protect famous international marks as commerce becomes increasingly globalized and interconnected—the Court need not decide whether to recognize the rule at this time because PROLACTO does not come close to establishing the necessary fame of its marks within the United States for the doctrine to apply. Without doubt, absent the famous mark doctrine, foreign trademark owners are at risk of having their marks adopted in the United States by a seller who wants American consumers to believe they are buying the products of a well-known foreign company. But there must be a limit to the reach of such a doctrine, as not every foreign mark is famous enough within the United States to warrant legal protection.

PROLACTO spends significant portions of its already-extensive summary judgment briefing and statement of facts discussing the company's long history in Mexico and how PLM allegedly knew of this history when it adopted the relevant marks. But such facts are, of course, irrelevant even under the famous mark doctrine: although the rule alters the historical requirement that only use within the United States establishes priority, it still demands that a mark achieve some level of awareness within this country. Thus, even assuming this Court was to recognize the doctrine, prior use and fame within

> a foreign country are immaterial under the famous mark doctrine except insofar as that familiarity actually permeates into the United States at such a critical level that it qualifies for legal protection.
>
> ....
>
> Returning to the evidence in the present case, ... PROLACTO appears to seek nationwide priority of its marks through the famous mark doctrine. But PROLACTO fails to provide evidence demonstrating sufficient familiarity with the marks in any relevant United States market, let alone across the entire country.

Paleteria La Michoacana v. Productos Lacteos Tocumbo, 69 F. Supp. 3d at 201–04.

At the ensuing bench trial, Prolacto offered a fall-back argument: It claimed that PLM could not itself have acquired rights in the contested trademarks, because it adopted and used them knowing that they had been used for similar products in Mexico. It argued that PLM's use of the marks was therefore a bad faith attempt to capitalize on Prolacto's goodwill among customers familiar with its Mexican products. The court found that PLM was the senior U.S. user of the mark. Although PLM had been aware of the use of similar marks in Mexico, and had chosen its marks because of their use in Mexico, the court concluded that PLM had nonetheless adopted the marks in good faith because it believed that the marks were used by multiple Mexican ice cream treat producers, and did not designate any single source. *See Paleteria La Michoacana v. Productos Lacteos Tocumbo*, 2016 U.S. Dist. LEXIS 69621 (D.D.C. 2016).

Questions

1. Should it matter whether PLM believed that the marks denoted a single product source in Mexico when the company adopted them in the United States? Why or why not?

2. Bayer has marketed FLANAX brand analgesic in Mexico since the 1970s, but does not sell any FLANAX brand product in the United States. Belmora introduced a line of analgesic products in the United States under the FLANAX brandname in 2002. Belmora's packaging of its FLANAX products greatly resembles the trade dress of Bayer's Mexican FLANAX. Bayer argues that Belmora's use of the FLANAX mark and similar trade dress deceives the public by implying that its product is the same as Bayer's. Belmora argues that since Bayer has never marketed FLANAX analgesic in the United States, it owns no cognizable trademark interest in the word or associated packaging. How should the court rule? *See Belmora LLC v. Bayer Consumer Care AG*, 819 F.3d 697 (4th Cir. 2016), *infra* Chapter 7[A][3].

D. Analogous Use

Many producers of goods and services begin to advertise their products long before they are available for purchase. Every summer, television networks run commercials promoting their new fall shows. Microsoft and Apple promote new versions of their operating systems software months before that software is released. Automobile manufacturers run teaser ads to spur interest in upcoming car models. New shopping centers, sports venues, and amusement parks announce themselves to the public while they are still under construction. Since the goods and services are not yet on sale (and may not yet exist) even an extensive advertising campaign won't meet the statutory definition of use-in-commerce. What happens when the public comes to associate a mark with a particular source before the product is available? The courts and the PTO have developed the concept of "analogous use" to help address that problem.

Aktieselskabet AF 21. November 2001 v. Fame Jeans, Inc.

525 F.3d 8 (D.C. Cir. 2008)

Brown, Circuit Judge.

For some reason, a pair of jeans labeled Jack & Jones will sell for the equivalent of $96. Clearly there is magic in the name, and Fame Jeans tried to capture that magic by registering Jack & Jones as a trademark in the United States. Aktieselskabet (Bestseller), which generated the magic by selling Jack & Jones jeans elsewhere in the world, opposed Fame's trademark application....

Bestseller, a Danish corporation, has been selling Jack & Jones jeans since 1990. By 2005, its business with the brand had expanded to include jeans, T-shirts and jackets, distributed in Europe, the Middle East, South America, and Asia. In the European Union alone, Bestseller sold nineteen million articles of branded clothing in 2005. It has registered Jack & Jones and related marks in forty-six countries, and it owns twenty-one domain names incorporating variations of the name.

In 2003, Bestseller decided to expand into North America; its competitor Fame Jeans appears, so far, to have stalled that expansion into the United States by assiduous effort at the U.S Patent and Trademark Office (PTO). Bestseller planned to begin operations in Canada, from which it would develop the brand into the United States. Accordingly, it applied to register the Jack & Jones mark in Canada in August 2004 and in the United States on December 6, 2004. Unfortunately for Bestseller, Fame had already applied to register Jack & Jones in the United States on January 9, 2004. As of their respective filing dates, neither party had tested the susceptibility of American consumers to the allure of Jack & Jones by actually trying to sell any jeans under the brand. Fame, therefore, filed its application under Lanham Act § 1(b), 15 U.S.C. § 1051(b), avowing its intent to use the trademark in commerce. Bestseller, on its part, filed under Lanham Act § 44(e), 15 U.S.C. § 1126(e), swearing it intended to use the mark and citing its 1990 Danish registrations.

Nine days after filing its U.S. application to register Jack & Jones, Bestseller filed an opposition to Fame's application to register the mark, alleging that Fame's registration was likely to cause confusion with Bestseller's Jack & Jones mark and interfere with Bestseller's application to register the mark. On January 30, 2006, the TTAB granted summary judgment on Bestseller's opposition. First, the TTAB pointed out

Bestseller had admitted it never used the mark in commerce in the United States, and it explained foreign use alone gave Bestseller no right of priority here. Second, the TTAB held Bestseller's December 6, 2004, application junior to Fame's January 9, 2004, application.

Bestseller sought district court review of the TTAB decision, under Lanham Act § 21(b), 15 U.S.C. § 1071(b).... The district court dismissed all the claims....

....

B

Since Fame Jeans filed its application on January 9, 2004, Bestseller must establish use, either actual or constructive, before that date.... Bestseller has adequately alleged actual use. Although the complaint does not set forth trademark use to earn Bestseller rights in the Jack & Jones mark, an opposer who has made enough "analogous" use can still defeat a registration. *See Malcolm Nicol & Co. v. Witco Corp.*, 881 F.2d 1063, 1065 (Fed. Cir. 1989) (quoting 3 McCarthy, *supra*, § 20:4 (1984)).

First, Bestseller fails to allege actual use in the most straightforward way, by showing its own protectible right to the Jack & Jones trademark in the United States. At common law, "prior ownership of a mark is only established as of the first actual use of a mark in a genuine commercial transaction." *Allard Enters., Inc. v. Adv. Programming Res., Inc.*, 146 F.3d 350, 358 (6th Cir. 1998). The 1988 amendments to the Lanham Act codified a standard of "use in commerce," necessary for a valid trademark registration, which means "the bona fide use of a mark in the ordinary course of trade," including, for a trademark, attaching the trademark to goods. 15 U.S.C. § 1127. In any case, "sporadic or minimal" sales are not sufficient. *Allard Enters.*, 146 F.3d at 359; *see also Zazu Designs v. L'Oreal, S.A.*, 979 F.2d 499, 503 (7th Cir. 1992) ("A few bottles sold over the counter ... and a few more mailed to friends" are not sufficient use.). While a single sale may indicate the first use of a mark, it must be the beginning of "continuous commercial utilization." *Allard*, 146 F.3d at 358. Obviously, as § 1052(d) requires, such use must also be "in the United States." *See Person's Co. v. Christman*, 900 F.2d 1565, 1568–69 (Fed. Cir. 1990) (T-shirt sales in Japan are not "use in United States commerce").

However, Bestseller need not "meet the technical statutory requirements to register ... [a mark] to have a basis for objection to another's registration." *Nat'l Cable Television Ass'n v. Am. Cinema Editors, Inc.*, 937 F.2d 1572, 1578 (Fed. Cir. 1991). Section 2(d) requires only "use[] in the United States," and adoption of the mark by use analogous to strict trademark use will therefore suffice. *T.A.B. Sys., Inc. v. PacTel Teletrac*, 77 F.3d 1372, 1375 (Fed. Cir. 1996). An opposer may rely on myriad forms of activity besides sales themselves, including, among others, regular business contacts, after-sales services, advertising of various forms, and marketing. *First Niagara Ins. Brokers, Inc. v. First Niagara Fin. Group*, 476 F.3d 867, 868–69 (Fed. Cir. 2007); *Johnny Blastoff, Inc. v. L.A. Rams Football Co.*, 188 F.3d 427, 434 (7th Cir. 1999); *Malcolm Nicol*, 881 F.2d at 1064. Even marketing of a trademarked product before the product is ready for sale has the potential to defeat a rival's registration. *See Old Swiss House*,

Inc. v. Anheuser-Busch, Inc., 569 F.2d 1130, 1133 (C.C.P.A. 1978). Still, desultory marketing such as sending out occasional press releases is not enough. *Id.* Analogous use must be "of such a nature and extent as to create public identification of the target term with the opposer's product." *T.A.B. Sys.*, 77 F.3d at 1375.

Bestseller's allegations fall short of showing a sale, whether in the United States or to an American abroad, as the beginning of a continuous commercial exploitation of the Jack & Jones mark in the United States; but they do give fair notice of a claim to analogous use. While Bestseller clearly sells millions of dollars worth of Jack & Jones branded clothing elsewhere in the world, it fails to allege any sales in the United States or to Americans. The closest Bestseller comes is saying this clothing "has been available to U.S. consumers through Bestseller's foreign customers and stores as well as through re-sales on eBay.com." This allegation does not imply any American sales at all, much less continuous commercial sales.

By contrast, Bestseller actually does say it conducted "research and marketing for use of the mark within the United States." The complaint does not say this marketing was sufficiently extensive to create an awareness of the Jack & Jones brand among American consumers, but it is reasonable to infer such an awareness from Bestseller's other allegations. Presumably, Bestseller will need to produce more substantial evidence if Fame contests this conclusion.... Simply put, the allegation of marketing in the United States, together with the inference of public association, is enough to give Fame fair notice of what it must contest. No more is required of a complaint.

....

Questions

1. How persuasive is the claim of analogous use? If Fame Jeans was trying to usurp the fame of the Jack & Jones brand, but the foreign trademark owner had not yet sold jeans under the mark in the United States, what other recourse would Bestseller have?

2. Recall *Grupo Gigante v. Dallo, supra.* Could the Ninth Circuit have found that Grupo Gigante had made analogous use of the GIGANTE mark in the U.S.? Would such a finding have aided Grupo Gigante's claim against Dallo?

E. Priority

Blue Bell, Inc. v. Farah Manufacturing Co.

508 F.2d 1260 (5th Cir. 1975)

Gewin, Circuit Judge:

In the spring and summer of 1973 two prominent manufacturers of men's clothing created identical trademarks for goods substantially identical in appearance. Though the record offers no indication of bad faith in the design and adoption of the labels, both Farah Manufacturing Company (Farah) and Blue Bell, Inc. (Blue Bell) devised the mark "Time Out" for new lines of men's slacks and shirts. Both parties market their goods on a national scale, so they agree that joint utilization of the same trademark would confuse the buying public. Thus, the only question presented for our review is which party established prior use of the mark in trade. A response to that seemingly innocuous inquiry, however, requires us to define the chameleonic term "use" as it has developed in trademark law.[1]

After a full development of the facts in the district court both parties moved for summary judgment. The motion of Farah was granted and that of Blue Bell denied. It is not claimed that summary judgment procedure was inappropriate; the controversy presented relates to the application of the proper legal principles to undisputed facts. A permanent injunction was granted in favor of Farah but no damages were awarded, and Blue Bell was allowed to fill all orders for garments bearing the Time Out label received by it as of the close of business on December 5, 1973. For the reasons hereinafter stated we affirm.

Farah conceived of the Time Out mark on May 16, after screening several possible titles for its new stretch menswear. Two days later the firm adopted an hourglass logo and authorized an extensive advertising campaign bearing the new insignia. Farah presented its fall line of clothing, including Time Out slacks, to sales personnel on June 5. In the meantime, patent counsel had given clearance for use of the mark after scrutiny of current federal registrations then on file. One of Farah's top executives demonstrated samples of the Time Out garments to large customers in Washington, D.C. and New York, though labels were not attached to the slacks at that time. Tags containing the new design were completed June 27. With favorable evaluations of marketing potential from all sides, Farah sent one pair of slacks bearing the Time Out mark to each of its twelve regional sales managers on July 3. Sales personnel paid for the pants, and the garments became their property in case of loss.

Following the July 3 shipment, regional managers showed the goods to customers the following week. Farah received several orders and production began. Further shipments of sample garments were mailed to the rest of the sales force on July 11 and 14. Merchandising efforts were fully operative by the end of the month. The first shipments to customers, however, occurred in September.

Blue Bell, on the other hand, was concerned with creating an entire new division of men's clothing, as an avenue to reaching the "upstairs" market.... On June 18 Blue Bell management arrived at the name Time Out to identify both its new division and its new line of men's sportswear. Like Farah, it received clearance for use of the mark from counsel. Like Farah, it inaugurated an advertising campaign. Unlike Farah, however, Blue Bell did not ship a dozen marked articles of the new line to its sales personnel. Instead, Blue Bell authorized the manufacture of several hundred labels

1. *Compare* Western Stove Co. v. George D. Roper Corp., 82 F. Supp. 206 (S.D. Cal. 1949) (first commercial sale controls, despite opposing party's prior conception and advertisement of the mark) *with* Charles Pfizer & Co. v. R.J. Moran Co., 125 U.S.P.Q. 201 (1960) (prior commercial sale is not determinative; drug manufacturer who first conceived of the mark and appended it to drugs for experimental purposes has rights superior to drug producer who initially placed goods on the market).

bearing the words Time Out and its logo shaped like a referee's hands forming a T. When the labels were completed on June 29, the head of the embryonic division ... instructed shipping personnel to affix the new Time Out labels to slacks that already bore the "Mr. Hicks" trademark. The new tags, of varying sizes and colors, were randomly attached to the left hip pocket button of slacks and the left hip pocket of jeans. Thus, although no change occurred in the design or manufacture of the pants, on July 5 several hundred pair left [the division] with two tags.

Blue Bell made intermittent shipments of the doubly-labeled slacks thereafter, though the out-of-state customers who received the goods had ordered clothing of the Mr. Hicks variety. Production of the new Time Out merchandise began in the latter part of August, and Blue Bell held a sales meeting to present its fall designs from September 4–6. Sales personnel solicited numerous orders, though shipments of the garments were not scheduled until October.

By the end of October Farah had received orders for 204,403 items of Time Out sportswear, representing a retail sales value of over $2,750,000. Blue Bell had received orders for 154,200 garments valued at over $900,000. Both parties had commenced extensive advertising campaigns for their respective Time Out sportswear.

Soon after discovering the similarity of their marks, Blue Bell sued Farah for common law trademark infringement and unfair competition, seeking to enjoin use of the Time Out trademark on men's clothing. Farah counter-claimed for similar injunctive relief. The district court found that Farah's July 3 shipment and sale constituted a valid use in trade, while Blue Bell's July 5 shipment was a mere "token" use insufficient at law to create trademark rights.[3] While we affirm the result reached

---

3. Specifically, the district court made the following factual determinations:

c. On July 3, 1973, Defendant, Farah Manufacturing Company, Inc., made interstate shipment of men's slacks bearing "TIME OUT" labels, and the shipment on such date was a good faith step in a continuous and uninterrupted program of marketing of "TIME OUT" slacks. The shipment of July 3, 1973, was to Farah's regional sales managers also employed by Farah Sales Corporation, a wholly owned subsidiary of Farah Manufacturing Company, Inc. The garments shipped were sold to and paid for by the regional sales managers. The shipment was made to enable sales personnel to exhibit the labeled garments to customers to solicit orders. The garments shipped were exhibited to customers and orders were solicited and obtained therefor. As a result of such shipment and marketing program, orders for Farah's TIME OUT slacks were received in substantial volume such that prior to submission hereof, Farah had received orders from retail stores for some 204,403 units of TIME OUT garments, representing retail sales value of some $2,751,935.00.

d. The Plaintiff, Blue Bell, Inc., sought to establish a new TIME OUT division within the company and to this end incorporated a new corporation under the name TIME OUT, INC. At the time of Plaintiff's claimed first use of the trademark on July 5, 1973, the new corporation had not been formed and there was no established business in the new division nor did Plaintiff have any established line of garments known or identified as TIME OUT garments. In an effort to reserve the trademark "TIME OUT" for a contemplated new line of garments and/or for a contemplated new division within the company, Plaintiff randomly tagged and shipped with a supplemental "TIME OUT" label, garments manufactured by its HICKS-PONDER division, which garments had been ordered, shipped and sold bearing the "MR. HICKS" trademark.

by the trial court as to Farah's priority of use, the legal grounds upon which we base our decision are somewhat different from those undergirding the district court's judgment.

Federal jurisdiction is predicated upon diversity of citizenship, since neither party has registered the mark pursuant to the Lanham Act. Given the operative facts surrounding manufacture and shipment from El Paso, the parties agree the Texas law of trademarks controls. In 1967 the state legislature enacted a Trademark Statute. Section 16.02 of the Act explains that a mark is "used" when it is affixed to the goods and "the goods are sold, displayed for sale, or otherwise publicly distributed." Thus the question whether Blue Bell or Farah established priority of trademark use depends upon interpretation of the cited provision. Unfortunately, there are no Texas cases construing § 16.02. This court must therefore determine what principles the highest state court would utilize in deciding such a question. In view of the statute's stated purpose to preserve common law rights, we conclude the Texas Supreme Court would apply the statutory provision in light of general principles of trademark law.

A trademark is a symbol (word, name, device or combination thereof) adopted and used by a merchant to identify his goods and distinguish them from articles produced by others. [Citations.] Ownership of a mark requires a combination of both appropriation and use in trade, *United Drug Co. v. Theodore Rectanus Co.*, 248 U.S. 90 (1918). Thus, neither conception of the mark [citations], nor advertising alone establishes trademark rights at common law. [Citations.] Rather, ownership of a trademark accrues when goods bearing the mark are placed on the market. [Citation.]

The exclusive right to a trademark belongs to one who first uses it in connection with specified goods. *McClean v. Fleming*, 96 U.S. 245 (1877); 3 R. CALLMAN, UNFAIR COMPETITION, TRADEMARKS AND MONOPOLIES § 76.2(c) (3d ed. 1969). Such use need not have gained wide public recognition [citation], and even a single use in trade may sustain trademark rights if followed by continuous commercial utilization. [Citation.]

The initial question presented for review is whether Farah's sale and shipment of slacks to twelve regional managers constitutes a valid first use of the Time Out mark.

The trial court reached the following conclusions of law:

4. Defendant Farah's shipment of TIME OUT labeled garments in interstate commerce on July 3, 1973, was a good faith step in a continuous and uninterrupted program of placing labeled goods on the market and soliciting orders therefor, and constituted a valid first use of the trademark. Such actions on the part of the Defendant Farah constituted use of the mark within the meaning of Art. 16.02, Business and Commerce Code of the State of Texas, in that TIME OUT labels were placed on tags or labels affixed to the goods and the goods were sold, displayed for sale, and otherwise publicly distributed in the state. Such use preceded any use of the trademark by Plaintiff Blue Bell.

5. Plaintiff Blue Bell's shipment of "MR. HICKS" garments carrying a supplemental "TIME OUT" label on July 5, 1973, was an attempt to reserve the trademark for a line of garments or line of business not yet established or existing. Such shipment was a token use insufficient in law to give Plaintiff prior rights to the trademark. Moreover, Plaintiff's claimed first use on such date came after Defendant's first use of the trademark.

Blue Bell claims the July 3 sale was merely an internal transaction insufficiently public to secure trademark ownership. After consideration of pertinent authorities, we agree.

Secret, undisclosed internal shipments are generally inadequate to support the denomination "use." Trademark claims based upon shipments from a producer's plant to its sales office, and vice versa, have often been disallowed. [Citations.] Though none of the cited cases dealt with sales to intra-corporate personnel, we perceive that fact to be a distinction without a difference. The sales were not made to customers, but served as an accounting device to charge the salesmen with their cost in case of loss. The fact that some sales managers actively solicited accounts bolsters the good faith of Farah's intended use, but does not meet our essential objection: that the "sales" were not made to the public.

The primary, perhaps singular purpose of a trademark is to provide a means for the consumer to separate or distinguish one manufacturer's goods from those of another. Personnel within a corporation can identify an item by style number or other unique code. A trademark aids the public in selecting particular goods. As stated by the First Circuit:

> But to hold that a sale or sales are the *sine qua non* of a use sufficient to amount to an appropriation would be to read an unwarranted limitation into the statute, for so construed registration would have to be denied to any manufacturer who adopted a mark to distinguish or identify his product, and perhaps applied it thereon for years, if he should in practice lease his goods rather than sell them, as many manufacturers of machinery do. It seems to us that although evidence of sales is highly persuasive, the question of use adequate to establish appropriation remains one to be decided on the facts of each case, and that evidence showing, first, adoption, and, second, *use in a way sufficiently public to identify or distinguish the marked goods in an appropriate segment of the public mind as those of the adopter of the mark*, is competent to establish ownership....

New England Duplicating Co. v. Mendes, 190 F.2d 415, 418 (1st Cir. 1951) (emphasis added). Similarly, the Trademark Trial and Appeal Board has reasoned:

> To acquire trademark rights there has to be an "open" use, that is to say, a use has to be made to the relevant class of purchasers or prospective purchasers since a trademark is intended to identify goods and distinguish those goods from those manufactured or sold by others. There was no such "open" use, rather the use can be said to be an "internal" use, which cannot give rise to trademark rights.

Sterling Drug, Inc. v. Knoll A.G. Chemische Fabriken, [159 U.S.P.Q. 628 (T.T.A.B. 1988)] at 631.

Farah nonetheless contends that a recent decision of the Board so undermines all prior cases relating to internal use that they should be ignored. In *Standard Pressed Steel Co. v. Midwest Chrome Process Co.*, 183 U.S.P.Q. 758 (T.T.A.B. 1974), the agency held that internal shipment of marked goods from a producer's manufacturing plant to its sales office constitutes a valid "use in commerce" for registration purposes.

An axiom of trademark law has been that the right to register a mark is conditioned upon its actual use in trade. [Citations.] Theoretically, then, common law use in trade should precede the use in commerce upon which Lanham Act registration is predicated. Arguably, since only a trademark owner can apply for registration, any activity adequate to create registrable rights must perforce also create trademark rights. A close examination of the Board's decision, however, dispels so mechanical a view. The tribunal took meticulous care to point out that its conclusion related solely to registration use rather than ownership use.

> It has been recognized and especially so in the last few years that, in view of the expenditures involved in introducing a new product on the market generally and the attendant risk involved therein prior to the screening process involved in resorting to the federal registration system and in the absence of an "intent to use" statute, a token sale or a single shipment in commerce *may be sufficient to support an application to register a trademark* in the Patent Office notwithstanding that the evidence may not show what disposition was made of the product so shipped. That is, the fact that a sale or a shipment of goods bearing a trademark was *designed primarily to lay a foundation for the filing of an application for registration* does not, per se, invalidate any such application or subsequent registration issued thereon.
>
> ....
>
> Inasmuch as it is our belief that a most liberal policy should be followed in a situation of this kind [*in which dispute as to priority of use and ownership of a mark is not involved*], applicant's initial shipment of fasteners, although an intra-company transaction in that it was to a company sales representative, was a bona fide shipment....

Standard Pressed Steel Co. v. Midwest Chrome Process Co., supra at 764–65 (emphasis added).

Priority of use and ownership of the Time Out mark are the only issues before this court. The language fashioned by the Board clearly indicates a desire to leave the common law of trademark ownership intact. The decision may demonstrate a reversal of the presumption that ownership rights precede registration rights, but it does not affect our analysis of common law use in trade. Farah had undertaken substantial preliminary steps toward marketing the Time Out garments, but it did not establish ownership of the mark by means of the July 3 shipment to its sales managers. The gist of trademark rights is actual use in trade. *Modular Cinemas of America, Inc. v. Mini Cinemas Corp.*, 348 F. Supp. 578 (S.D.N.Y. 1972). Though technically a "sale", the July 3 shipment was not "publicly distributed" within the purview of the Texas statute.

Blue Bell's July 5 shipment similarly failed to satisfy the prerequisites of a bona fide use in trade. Elementary tenets of trademark law require that labels or designs be affixed to the merchandise actually intended to bear the mark in commercial transactions. *Persha v. Armour & Co.*, 239 F.2d 628 (5th Cir. 1957). Furthermore, courts have recognized that the usefulness of a mark derives not only from its capacity to identify a certain manufacturer, but also from its ability to differentiate between different classes of goods produced by a single manufacturer. *Western Stove Co. v. George D. Roper Corp.*, 82 F. Supp. 206 (S.D. Cal. 1949). Here customers had ordered slacks of the Mr. Hicks species, and Mr. Hicks was the fanciful mark distinguishing these slacks from all others. Blue Bell intended to use the Time Out mark on an entirely new line of men's sportswear, unique in style and cut, though none of the garments had yet been produced.

While goods may be identified by more than one trademark, the use of each mark must be bona fide. [Citation.] Mere adoption of a mark without bona fide use, in an attempt to reserve it for the future, will not create trademark rights. [Citations.] In the instant case Blue Bell's attachment of a secondary label to an older line of goods manifests a bad faith attempt to reserve a mark. We cannot countenance such activities as a valid use in trade. Blue Bell therefore did not acquire trademark rights by virtue of its July 5 shipment.

We thus hold that neither Farah's July 3 shipment nor Blue Bell's July 5 shipment sufficed to create rights in the Time Out mark. Based on a desire to secure ownership of the mark and superiority over a competitor, both claims of alleged use were chronologically premature. Essentially, they took a time out to litigate their differences too early in the game. The question thus becomes whether we should continue to stop the clock for a remand or make a final call from the appellate bench. While a remand to the district court for further factual development would not be improper in these circumstances, we believe the interests of judicial economy and the parties' desire to terminate the litigation demand that we decide, if possible, which manufacturer first used the mark in trade.

Careful examination of the record discloses that Farah shipped its first order of Time Out clothing to customers in September of 1973. Blue Bell, approximately one month behind its competitor at other relevant stages of development, did not mail its Time Out garments until at least October. Though sales to customers are not the *sine qua non* of trademark use, *see New England Duplicating Co. v. Mendes, supra*, they are determinative in the instant case. These sales constituted the first point at which the public had a chance to associate Time Out with a particular line of sportswear. Therefore, Farah established priority of trademark use; it is entitled to a decree permanently enjoining Blue Bell from utilization of the Time Out trademark on men's garments.

The judgment of the trial court is *affirmed.*

Hana Financial v. Hana Bank, 135 S. Ct. 907 (2015). Two financial services companies used the HANA service mark. Hana Bank began using the HANA mark in Korea in 1991. In 1994, it began offering services to Korea expatriates in the United States under the mark HANA OVERSEAS KOREAN CLUB. In 2000, Hana Bank changed the name of that service to HANA WORLD CENTER. In 2006, it opened a bank in the United States under the name HANA BANK. Hana Financial first rendered services in commerce under the HANA FINANCIAL mark in 1995, and registered the service mark in 1996. In 1997, it sued Hana Bank for trademark infringement. Hana Bank argued that it should be able to rely on its prior uses of marks incorporating HANA to establish priority over Hana Financial. The district court instructed the jury that:

> A party may claim priority in a mark based on the first use date of a similar but technically distinct mark where the previously used mark is the legal equivalent of the mark in question.

The jury returned a verdict in favor of Hana Bank, and Hana Financial appealed, arguing that the question of tacking should be determined as a matter of law by a judge rather than by a jury. The Court of Appeals for the 9th Circuit upheld the jury verdict, and Hana Financial petitioned the Supreme Court for certiorari. A unanimous Supreme Court affirmed:

> Rights in a trademark are determined by the date of the mark's first use in commerce. The party who first uses a mark in commerce is said to have priority over other users. Recognizing that trademark users ought to be permitted to make certain modifications to their marks over time without losing priority, lower courts have provided that, in limited circumstances, a party may clothe a new mark with the priority position of an older mark. This doctrine is called "tacking," and lower courts have found tacking to be available when the original and revised marks are "legal equivalents" in that they create the same, continuing commercial impression. The question presented here is whether a judge or a jury should determine whether tacking is available in a given case. Because the tacking inquiry operates from the perspective of an ordinary purchaser or consumer, we hold that a jury should make this determination....

Questions

1. Your client, Ruprecht Murky, a media mogul, planned to launch a new periodical, *New Greed.* In January 2015, Murky, Inc. announced the impending publication to potential advertisers and sought their purchase of advertising space in the new venture. In February 2015, Murky, Inc. sent mailings to subscribers of its other periodicals, describing the kind of magazine *New Greed* would be, and offering special charter subscription rates. In March 2015, Murky, Inc. published a prototype issue of *New Greed* as a special center insert in one of Murky's nationally distributed magazines, *New Wealth.* The inaugural full issue of *New Greed* hit the newsstands in April 2015.

At the same time Murky, Inc. began elaborating its plans, Market Magazines (a smaller publisher) also determined to release a new publication, coincidentally called *New Greed.* Although Market Magazines was initially unaware of Murky's intended publication, Market learned of it by February. Market accordingly rushed its own production schedule. Later in February, it placed an advertisement in the national financial newspaper, the *Easy Street Journal*, announcing Market's forthcoming *New Greed.* In March, it sent to newsstands a hastily put-together photocopied issue of *New Greed*, and released conventional four-color professionally printed issues beginning in May 2015.

Who owns the *New Greed* trademark? (Assume no one has filed for federal registration.) Would it make a difference if the periodical Market Magazines released in March were a fully professionally produced issue? *See, e.g., The New West Corp. v. NYM Company of California, Inc.*, 595 F.2d 1194 (9th Cir. 1979); *Marvel Comics Ltd. v. Defiant*, 837 F. Supp. 546 (S.D.N.Y. 1993).

2. In October 2008, Polyplus began field-testing a system for tracking fleet vehicles over cellular telephone networks, and recovering lost or stolen vehicles. In June 2009, Polyplus adopted the name CELLTRAK. In July 2009, Polyplus began a comprehensive public relations campaign to market its new service, including distributing press releases and giving interviews to print and electronic media. It also made presentations to prospective customers. In April 2010, Polyplus began making its service available on a commercial basis. Polyplus's first customer signed on in April 2010, although it did not begin paying for the service until December. From mid-2010 onward, Polyplus developed customers among various vehicle fleet operating enterprises and had agreements with at least twenty-four of them.

Meanwhile, in mid-2009, Adam Allan came up with the idea for a lost and found service using attachable tags with unique serial numbers. Finders of lost tagged items could report their discovery by calling a toll-free number, and his company would send a text message to the owner of the tag. In June 2009, Allan coined the name "CEL-TRAC" for the service.

In late summer 2009, Allan obtained a toll free number under the name "Cel-Trac Lost and Found Hotline." He also printed up postcards advertising his service, and drew up a business plan. In October 2009, an unrelated company, Locksmith Ledger, included Allan's postcard in its own bulk mailing to 35,000 locksmiths. This post card announced the Cel-Trac World Wide Toll Free Lost and Found Hotline, and Cel-Trac "never-lost" tags. Allan received 128 responses from the mailing, but made no sales as a result.

In February 2010, Allan sold a Cel-Trac tag to a long time friend. Allan produced a one page typewritten registration form he prepared for the tag, number 11229, dated February 23, 2010. Allan could not state, however, how much the friend paid for the tag, how he paid for the tag, nor is there any record reflecting payment.

In January 2011, Allan saw advertisements for Polyplus's Celltrak service. He conducted a trademark search and discovered no pending application on file with the United States Patent and Trademark Office (PTO). He filed a service mark application for "Cel-Trac Lost and Found" and a trademark application for "Cel-Trac" claiming first use of the marks in October 2009, the time of the postcard mailer.

Polyplus has challenged the registration applications filed by Allan. Who first used the mark, as of when? Has either party established use analogous to trademark use sufficient to claim priority? *See Chance v. Pac-Tel Teletrac Inc.*, 242 F.3d 1151 (9th Cir. 2001).

3. The U.S. National Park Service operates Yosemite National Park. From 1993 to 2016, private company DNC provided hotel, restaurant, retail shop and other concession services at the park under a contract with the National Park Service. DNC operated a number of tourist sites at Yosemite, including a hotel and downhill ski resort at Yosemite's Badger Pass and rustic cabins at the park's Curry Village. Before DNC took over, concession services had been provided by the Curry Company. After being awarded the contract, DNC purchased the Curry Company in 1993 in order to acquire possession of the buildings and other property that Curry had built over many years of providing concession services at Yosemite. In 2003, without informing the park Service, DNC registered YOSEMITE NATIONAL PARK, BADGER PASS, and CURRY VILLAGE as service marks for hotel, golf, and restaurant services and trademarks for pens, stickers, coffee mugs and apparel, claiming that the Curry Company had established ownership of the marks by using them in commerce for many years. The concession contract with DNC expired in February of 2016, and the Park Service awarded the concessions to a different company. DNC insists that the new company must either purchase its valuable trademarks and service marks, or call the concession services and souvenirs sold at the park by different names. What legal advice would you give to the Park Service? *See DNC Parks & Resorts at Yosemite, Inc. v. United States*, No. 15-cv-1034 (Ct. Claims, filed Sept. 17, 2015). *Cf. City of New York v. Tavern on the Green*, 427 B.R. 233 (S.D.N.Y. 2010).

F. Concurrent Use

United Drug Co. v. Theodore Rectanus Co.

248 U.S. 90 (1918)

Mr. Justice Pitney delivered the opinion of the Court:

This was a suit in equity brought September 24, 1912, in the United States District Court for the Western District of Kentucky, by the present petitioner, a Massachusetts corporation, against the respondent, a Kentucky corporation, together with certain individual citizens of the latter State, to restrain infringement of trade-mark and unfair competition.

....

The essential facts are as follows: About the year 1877 Ellen M. Regis, a resident of Haverhill, Massachusetts, began to compound and distribute in a small way a preparation for medicinal use in cases of dyspepsia and some other ailments, to which she applied as a distinguishing name the word "Rex"—derived from her surname. The word was put upon the boxes and packages in which the medicine was placed upon the market, after the usual manner of a trade-mark. At first alone, and afterwards in partnership with her son under the firm name of "E.M. Regis & Company," she continued the business on a modest scale; in 1898 she recorded the word "Rex" as a trademark under the laws of Massachusetts (Acts 1895, p.519, ch. 462 § 1); in 1900 the firm procured its registration in the United States Patent Office under the Act of March 3, 1881, c. 138, 21 Stat. 502; in 1904 the Supreme Court of Massachusetts sustained their trade-mark right under the state law as against a concern that was selling medicinal preparations of the present petitioner under the designation of

"Rexall remedies" (*Regis v. Jaynes*, 185 Massachusetts, 458); afterwards the firm established priority in the mark as against petitioner in a contested proceeding in the Patent Office; and subsequently, in the year 1911, petitioner purchased the business with the trade-mark right, and has carried it on in connection with its other business, which consists in the manufacture of medicinal preparations, and their distribution and sale through retail drug stores, known as "Rexall stores," situate in the different States of the Union, four of them being in Louisville, Kentucky.

Meanwhile, about the year 1883, Theodore Rectanus, a druggist in Louisville, familiarly known as "Rex," employed this word as a trade-mark for a medicinal preparation known as a "blood purifier." He continued this use to a considerable extent in Louisville and vicinity, spending money in advertising and building up a trade, so that—except for whatever effect might flow from Mrs. Regis' prior adoption of the word in Massachusetts, of which he was entirely ignorant—he was entitled to use the word as his trade-mark. In the year 1906 he sold his business, including the right to the use of the word, to respondent; and the use of the mark by him and afterwards by respondent was continuous from about the year 1883 until the filing of the bill in the year 1912.

Petitioner's first use of the word "Rex" in connection with the sale of drugs in Louisville or vicinity was in April, 1912, when two shipments of "Rex Dyspepsia Tablets," aggregating 150 boxes and valued at $22.50, were sent to one of the "Rexall" stores in that city. Shortly after this the remedy was mentioned by name in local newspaper advertisements published by those stores. In the previous September, petitioner shipped a trifling amount—five boxes—to a drug store in Franklin, Kentucky, approximately 120 miles distant from Louisville. There is nothing to show that before this any customer in or near Kentucky had heard of the Regis remedy, with or without the description "Rex," or that this word ever possessed any meaning to the purchasing public in that State except as pointing to Rectanus and the Rectanus Company and their "blood purifier." That it did and does convey the latter meaning in Louisville and vicinity is proved without dispute. Months before petitioner's first shipment of its remedy to Kentucky, petitioner was distinctly notified (in June, 1911,) by one of its Louisville distributors that respondent was using the word "Rex" to designate its medicinal preparations, and that such use had been commenced by Mr. Rectanus as much as 16 or 17 years before that time.

There was nothing to sustain the allegation of unfair competition, aside from the question of trade-mark infringement. As to this, both courts found, in substance, that the use of the same mark upon different but somewhat related preparations was carried on by the parties and their respective predecessors contemporaneously, but in widely separated localities, during the period in question—between 25 and 30 years—in perfect good faith, neither side having any knowledge or notice of what was being done by the other. The District Court held that because the adoption of the mark by Mrs. Regis antedated its adoption by Rectanus, petitioner's right to the exclusive use of the word in connection with medicinal preparations intended for dyspepsia and kindred diseases of the stomach and digestive organs must be sustained, but without accounting for profits or assessment of damages for unfair trade. [Citations.] The Circuit Court of Appeals held that in view of the fact that Rectanus had used the mark for a long period of years in entire ignorance of Mrs. Regis' remedy or of her trade-mark, had expended money in making his mark well known, and had established a considerable though local business under it in Louisville and vicinity, while on the other hand during the same long period Mrs. Regis had done nothing, either by sales agencies or by advertising, to make her medicine or its mark known outside of the New England States, saving sporadic sales in territory adjacent to those States, and had made no effort whatever to extend the trade to Kentucky, she and her successors were bound to know that, misled by their silence and inaction, others might act, as Rectanus and his successors did act, upon the assumption that the field was open, and therefore were estopped to ask for an injunction against the continued use of the mark in Louisville and vicinity by the Rectanus Company.

The entire argument for the petitioner is summed up in the contention that whenever the first user of a trade-mark has been reasonably diligent in extending the territory of his trade, and as a result of such extension has in good faith come into competition with a later user of the same mark who in equal good faith has extended his trade locally before invasion of his field by the first user, so that finally it comes to pass that the rival traders are offering competitive merchandise in a common market under the same trade-mark, the later user should be enjoined at the suit of the prior adopter, even though the latter be the last to enter the competitive field and the former have already established a trade there. Its application to the case is based upon the hypothesis that the record shows that Mrs. Regis and her firm, during the entire period of limited and local trade in her medicine under the Rex mark, were making efforts to extend their trade so far as they were able to do with the means at their disposal. There is little in the record to support this hypothesis; but, waiving this, we will pass upon the principal contention.

The asserted doctrine is based upon the fundamental error of supposing that a trade-mark right is a right in gross or at large, like a statutory copyright or a patent for an invention, to either of which, in truth, it has little or no analogy. [Citations.] There is no such thing as property in a trade-mark except as a right appurtenant to an established business or trade in connection with which the mark is employed. The law of trade-marks is but a part of the broader law of unfair competition; the right to a particular mark grows out of its use, not its mere adoption; its function is simply to designate the goods as the product of a particular trader and to protect his good will against the sale of another's product as his; and it is not the subject of property except in connection with an existing business. *Hanover Milling Co. v. Metcalf*, 240 U.S. 403, 412–414.

The owner of a trade-mark may not, like the proprietor of a patented invention, make a negative and merely prohibitive use of it as a monopoly. [Citations.]

In truth, a trade-mark confers no monopoly whatever in a proper sense, but is merely a convenient means for facilitating the protection of one's goodwill in trade by placing a distinguishing mark or symbol—a commercial signature—upon the merchandise or the package in which it is sold.

It results that the adoption of a trade-mark does not, at least in the absence of some valid legislation enacted for the purpose, project the right of protection in advance of the extension of the trade, or operate as a claim of territorial rights over areas into which it thereafter may be deemed desirable to extend the trade. And the expression, sometimes met with, that a trade-mark right is not limited in its enjoyment by territorial bounds, is true only in the sense that wherever the trade goes, attended by the use of the mark, the right of the trader to be protected against the sale by others of their wares in the place of his wares will be sustained.

Property in trade-marks and the right to their exclusive use rest upon the laws of the several States, and depend upon them for security and protection; the power of Congress to legislate on the subject being only such as arises from the authority to regulate commerce with foreign nations and among the several States and with the Indian tribes. *Trade-Mark Cases*, 100 U.S. 82, 93.

Conceding everything that is claimed in behalf of the petitioner, the entire business conducted by Mrs. Regis and her firm prior to April, 1911, when petitioner acquired it, was confined to the New England States with inconsiderable sales in New York, New Jersey, Canada, and Nova Scotia. There was nothing in all of this to give her any rights in Kentucky, where the principles of the common law obtain. [Citations.] We are referred to no decision by the courts of that State, and have found none, that lays down any peculiar doctrine upon the subject of trade-mark law. There is some meager legislation, but none that affects this case....

It is not contended, nor is there ground for the contention, that registration of the Regis trade-mark under either the Massachusetts statute or the act of Congress, or both, had the effect of enlarging the rights of Mrs. Regis or of petitioner beyond what they would be under common-law principles. Manifestly, the Massachusetts statute (Acts 1895, p. 519, c. 462) could have no extraterritorial effect. And the Act of Congress of March 3, 1881, c. 138, 21 Stat. 502, applied only to commerce with foreign nations or the Indian tribes, with either of which this case has nothing to do. [Citation.] Nor is there any provision making registration equivalent to notice of rights claimed thereunder. The Act of February 20, 1905, c. 592, 33 Stat. 724, which took the place of the 1881 Act, while extending protection to trade-marks used in interstate commerce, does not enlarge the effect of previous registrations....

Undoubtedly, the general rule is that, as between conflicting claimants to the right to use the same mark, priority of appropriation determines the question. [Citations.] But the reason is that purchasers have come to understand the mark as indicating the origin of the wares, so that its use by a second producer amounts to an attempt to sell his goods as those of his competitor. The reason for the rule does not extend to a case where the same trade-mark happens to be employed simultaneously by two manufacturers in different markets separate and remote from each other, so that the mark means one thing in one market, an entirely different thing in another. It would be a perversion of the rule of priority to give it such an application in our broadly extended country that an innocent party who had in good faith employed a trade-mark in one State, and by the use of it had built up a trade there, being the first appropriator in that jurisdiction, might afterwards be prevented from using it, with consequent injury to his trade and good-will, at the instance of one who theretofore had employed the same mark but only in other and remote jurisdictions, upon the ground that its first employment happened to antedate that of the first-mentioned trader.

In several cases federal courts have held that a prior use of a trade-mark in a foreign country did not entitle its owner to claim exclusive trade-mark rights in the United States as against one who in good faith had adopted a like trade-mark here prior to the entry of the foreigner into this market. [Citations.]

The same point was involved in *Hanover Milling Co. v. Metcalf*, 240 U.S. 403, 415, where we said: "In the ordinary case of parties competing under the same mark in the same market, it is correct to say that prior appropriation settles the question. But where two parties independently are employing the same mark upon goods of the same class, but in separate markets wholly remote the one from the other, the question of prior appropriation is legally insignificant, unless at least it appears that the second adopter has selected the mark with some design inimical to the interests of the first user, such as to take the benefit of the reputation of his goods, to forestall the extension of his trade, or the like."

In this case, as already remarked, there is no suggestion of a sinister purpose on the part of Rectanus or the Rectanus Company; hence the passage quoted correctly defines the status of the parties prior to the time when they came into competition in the Kentucky market. And it results, as a necessary inference from what we have said, that petitioner, being the newcomer in that market, must enter it subject to whatever rights had previously been acquired there in good faith by the Rectanus Company and its predecessor. To hold otherwise—to require Rectanus to retire from the field upon the entry of Mrs. Regis' successor—would be to establish the right of the latter as a right in gross, and to extend it to territory wholly remote from the furthest reach of the trade to which it was annexed, with the effect not merely of depriving Rectanus of the benefit of the good-will resulting from his long-continued use of the mark in Louisville and vicinity, and his substantial expenditures in building up his trade, but of enabling petitioner to reap substantial benefit from the publicity that Rectanus has thus given to the mark in that locality, and of confusing if not misleading the public as to the origin of goods thereafter sold in Louisville under the Rex mark, for, in that market, until petitioner entered it, "Rex" meant the Rectanus product, not that of Regis.

....

Here the essential facts are so closely parallel to those that furnished the basis of decision in the *Allen & Wheeler Case*, reported *sub nom. Hanover Milling Co. v. Metcalf*, 240 U.S. 403, 419–420, as to render further discussion unnecessary. Mrs. Regis and her firm, having during a long period of years confined their use of the "Rex" mark to a limited territory wholly remote from that in controversy, must be held to have taken the risk that some innocent party might in the meantime hit upon the same mark, apply it to goods of similar character, and expend money and effort in building up a trade under it; and since it appears that Rectanus in good faith, and without notice of any prior use by others, selected and used the "Rex" mark, and by the expenditure of money and effort succeeded in building up a local but valuable trade under it in Louisville and vicinity before petitioner entered that field, so that "Rex" had come to be recognized there as the "trade signature" of Rectanus and of respondent as his successor, petitioner is estopped to set up their continued use of the mark in that territory as an infringement of the Regis trade-mark. Whatever confusion may have arisen from conflicting use of the mark is attributable to petitioner's entry into the field with notice of the situation; and petitioner cannot complain of this....

Decree *affirmed.*

Questions

1. The *Rectanus* opinion concerns concurrent terrestrial use. What, if any, difference would it make if the senior user of the mark offered its goods via a website accessible throughout the U.S., and the junior user purveyed its goods from bricks-and-mortar stores located in a small number of states? What if the junior user also had a website? *See also* Chapter 4[B], *infra.*

2. Are there circumstances in which a junior user of a mark in a given territory should get priority over a senior user? As we will see in Chapter 4, the first user's priority of rights yields to prior applicants for registration in two circumstances. First, an application filed under the § 1(b) intent-to-use procedure will trump a first user if the application's filing date predates the senior user's actual use. Second, an application to register a foreign mark based on an application filed in a foreign Paris convention member country of origin up to six months before the U.S. filing will be given priority over a trademark first used in the U.S. before the U.S. filing, but after the date of the original foreign filing.

Thrifty Rent-a-Car System v. Thrift Cars, Inc.

831 F.2d 1177 (1st Cir. 1987)

Davis, Circuit Judge:

In this trademark infringement suit brought by Thrifty Rent-a-Car System, Inc. (Thrifty), that firm and defendant Thrift Cars, Inc. (Thrift Cars) both appeal the decision of the district court for the District of Massachusetts (Young, J.), 639 F. Supp. 750. After a bench trial, the court enjoined Thrift Cars from conducting a car or truck rental or leasing business outside of Taunton, Massachusetts under the "Thrift Cars" name, and limited Thrift Cars' advertising to those media it had used prior to July 26, 1964, the date that Thrifty obtained federal registration of its own mark. Concomitantly, the court prohibited Thrifty from operating any of its business establishments in East Taunton, Massachusetts or from advertising in any media principally intended to target the East Taunton community. We affirm.

I. *Background*

A. *Thrifty Rent-a-Car System, Inc.*

Thrifty Rent-a-Car System traces its beginnings to March 3, 1958 when L.C. Crow, an individual, began renting cars in Tulsa, Oklahoma, under the trade name "Thrifty." In 1962, Stemmons, Inc., an Oklahoma corporation, purchased Crow's business and expanded the business to Houston, Texas, renting automobiles to customers under the "Thrifty" trade name. Stemmons subsequently changed its name to The Thrifty Rent-a-Car System, Inc. and expanded the business to Wichita, Kansas, Dallas, Texas and St. Louis, Missouri. On July 30, 1962 Thrifty Rent-a-Car made an application to the United States Patent Office to register the service mark "Thrifty Rent-a-Car System" and was granted that mark in July 1964. Thrifty expanded the business through both franchises and directly-owned rental agencies. In December 1967, a Thrifty Rent-a-Car outlet opened in Massachusetts. By the time of trial, Thrifty had become the fifth largest car rental agency worldwide, and operated car rental outlets in 23 locations in Massachusetts.

B. *Thrift Cars, Inc.*

Thrift Cars' rental business began in October 1962 and was incorporated in Massachusetts as Thrift Cars, Inc. Thrift Cars' owner and proprietor, Peter A. Conlon, at first began a modest car-rental service out of his home in East Taunton, Massachusetts. The East Taunton business was largely limited to what the car-rental industry considers a "tertiary market," that is, the market that serves individuals needing replacement cars to bridge the short term car rental and the longer term automobile lease. Thrift Cars provided customized service, arranging delivery of the rental car to the customer as well as pick-up at the termination of the rental period. In the years immediately following 1962, Thrift Cars delivered automobiles to Boston's Logan Airport and to various cities on Cape Cod and to Nantucket. Prior to Thrifty's federal registration in July 1964, Thrift Cars advertised in the Taunton area yellow pages telephone directory, in *The Taunton Daily Gazette, The Cape Cod Times* (a newspaper of general circulation servicing Cape Cod, Martha's Vineyard, and Nantucket) and in *The Anchor* (the newspaper of the Roman Catholic Diocese of Fall River). In 1963 Thrift Cars also advertised in The *Inquirer and Mirror*, a Nantucket newspaper. In 1970, some six years after Thrifty had obtained federal registration of its mark, Thrift Cars received a license to operate a car rental facility at the Nantucket airport, and Conlon, Thrift Cars' Chief Executive Officer, moved the major portion of the business to Nantucket.

The Nantucket facility, unlike the operation at East Taunton, was operated largely as a traditional car rental service, servicing the resort market. Customers came directly to the airport to arrange for rental and pick-up of the automobile. Thrift Cars' post-1970 Nantucket operation thus came into a direct clash with Thrifty, which was also operating a car rental facility directed to the resort market in the Cape Cod area.

C. *Litigation below.*

Thrifty brought this action against Thrift Cars in federal district court, alleging trademark infringement and false designation of title under the Lanham Act. 15 U.S.C. § 1125(a) and §§ 1051–1127. The parties stipulated that the Thrift and Thrifty names are confusingly similar—as, of course, they are. The trial court found that Thrift Cars' business activities as of the critical date of July 26, 1964 (the date of Thrifty's registration) did not extend to areas beyond East Taunton, Massachusetts. The district court then enjoined Thrift Cars from using "Thrift" in conducting a car rental business outside of Taunton. The court also enjoined Thrift Cars from advertising in media directed outside of East Taunton, except in publications in which Thrift Cars had advertised prior to July 26, 1964.

Conversely, the court enjoined Thrifty from operating any business establishment in East Taunton and prohibited it from advertising in any media principally intended to target the East Taunton area.

Both parties appealed. Thrift Cars claims that the court erred by limiting its car rental activities under the "Thrift" name to Taunton, urging that this court expand its permissible business activities to southeastern Massachusetts, including Nantucket. Thrifty's cross-appeal argues that the district court erred in allowing Thrift Cars to conduct business in any locality under the Thrift Cars name because the business had not been continuous until trial, as required under the Lanham Act. In the alternative, Thrifty urges that the scope of Thrift Cars' business activities should be limited to East Taunton, not Taunton, because the record indicates that Thrift Cars' business had been limited to East Taunton, not to Taunton, prior to Thrifty's 1964 federal registration. Thrifty also says that the district court allowed Thrift Cars too broad an advertising base since it permitted Thrift Cars to advertise in publications directed outside of East Taunton.

II. *Discussion*

....

Section 15 of the Lanham Act, 15 U.S.C. § 1065, provides that a party like Thrifty, which has successfully registered and continued using a federal service mark, has an incontestable right to use the mark throughout the United States in connection with the goods or services with which it has been used. *See Giant Food, Inc. v. Nation's Foodservice, Inc.*, 710 F.2d 1565, 1568 (Fed. Cir. 1983). Lanham Act registration also puts all would-be users of the mark (or a confusingly similar mark) on constructive notice of the mark. 15 U.S.C. § 1072.

A. "*Limited area exception.*"

However, Lanham Act § 33(b), 15 U.S.C. § 1115(b)(5), declares a "limited area" exception to that general premise of incontestability, an exception which the district court concluded was applicable in this case. The essence of the exception embodied in § 1115(b)(5) is based on common law trademark protection for remote users established by the Supreme Court in *Hanover Star Milling Co. v. Metcalf*, 240 U.S. 403 (1916), and *United Drug Co. v. Theodore Rectanus Co.*, 248 U.S. 90 (1918). Subsection

(5) confers upon a junior user, such as Thrift Cars, the right to continued use of an otherwise infringing mark in a remote geographical area if that use was established prior to the other party's federal registration.* The junior user is permitted to maintain a proprietary interest in the mark even though it has no general federal protection through registration. To be able to invoke the § 1115(b)(5) exception, however, the junior user must have used the mark continuously in that location and initially in good faith without notice of an infringing mark. [Citation.]

To sustain its "limited area" defense of 15 U.S.C. § 1115(b)(5), Thrift Cars was required to demonstrate (1) that it adopted its mark before Thrifty's 1964 registration under the Lanham Act, and without knowledge of Thrifty's prior use; (2) the extent of the trade area in which Thrift Cars used the mark prior to Thrifty's registration; and (3) that Thrift Cars has continuously used the mark in the pre-registration trade area. [Citation.] There is no issue that Thrift Cars had adopted its mark in good faith and without notice prior to Thrifty's registration. Rather, the questions are whether Thrift Cars had established a market presence in any locality, the extent of that market presence, and whether that market presence had been continuous within the meaning of § 1115(b)(5). The district court found that Thrift Cars' use of the service mark had been continuous in East Taunton within the meaning of § 1115(b)(5), but also found that it had not established a sufficient market presence outside of East Taunton (*i.e.*, in Nantucket or other areas of southeastern Massachusetts) to establish there a continuous market presence sufficient to confer on Thrift Cars trademark protection under the statute.

As the district court held, the scope of protection afforded by § 1115(b)(5) is limited. A pre-existing good faith user's rights are frozen to the geographical location where the user has established a market penetration as of the date of registration. Such users are unable thereafter to acquire additional protection superior to that obtained by the federal registrant. [Citations.] The district court therefore held that Thrift Cars' expansion into new market areas after the 1964 date of Thrifty's federal registration is not protected under § 1115(b)(5).

....

B. *Thrift Cars did not demonstrate a continuous presence outside of East Taunton within the meaning of § 1115(b)(5)*

The district court found that Thrift Cars had not established a continuous presence in any area outside of East Taunton—prior to July 1964—adequate to satisfy the requirements of § 1115(b)(5). That finding was necessarily based on the hard facts and the inferences drawn from the trial evidence. The limited advertising Thrift Cars had done was not deemed sufficient to establish a presence outside East Taunton; nor were Thrift Cars' sporadic rentals in Nantucket and elsewhere in southeastern Massachusetts enough to sustain Thrift Cars' claim that it had already expanded out of

* [*Editors' Note:* Under section 7(c) of the current statute, the nationwide priority date for a registered mark is the date on which the application to register the mark is filed. See 17 U.S.C. § 1057(c); *infra* Chapter 4[A].]

East Taunton prior to Thrifty's federal registration. [Citations.] These findings are not clearly erroneous and we do not overturn the district court's findings on this matter.

We also note that the fact that Thrift Cars had desired to expand into the Nantucket market prior to July 1964 by unsuccessfully applying for a license to operate at the airport is not sufficient to meet the requirements of § 1115(b)(5). A mere desire, without more, will not confer upon Thrift Cars the ability to exclude Thrifty from Nantucket. [Citation.] The policy behind the Lanham Act is very strong and the party challenging the federal registrant has the burden of showing a continued and actual market presence in order to qualify for the "limited area" exception under the statute. The trial court permissibly found that Thrift Cars did not meet its burden in this respect.

C. *Thrift Cars' activities in East Taunton fall into the "limited area" defense of § 1115(b)(5).*

The more difficult question is whether Thrift Cars has established and maintained a continuous market presence in East Taunton so as to sustain an injunction against Thrifty in that region. Under § 1115(b)(5), the junior user must show that it has made continuous use of the mark prior to the issuance of the senior user's registration and must further prove continued use up until trial. [Citations.] Otherwise, the defense "dries up" and the junior user cannot assert rights in the limited trade area. [Citations.]

Here, the district court properly found that Thrift Cars established a significant enough market share in East Taunton prior to Thrifty's 1964 federal registration to constitute continuous use there at least until May 1970, when Conlon opened business operations in Nantucket. The pivotal issue is, however, whether Thrift Cars continued enough of a market presence in East Taunton after May 1970 (to the time of trial) to qualify for the § 1115(b)(5) defense. The district court made no specific findings on this precise matter (though its opinion reveals an implicit affirmative finding), and we think it is a close call whether Thrift Cars conducted a significant amount of business in East Taunton up until trial. Nevertheless, we believe that on this record Thrift Cars should be entitled to continue doing business in East Taunton and Thrifty should be enjoined from establishing a franchise there. First, the record shows that Thrift Cars continually advertised in media directed specifically to the East Taunton area such as the Taunton area telephone yellow pages, even after opening the Nantucket facility. The record also reveals that Thrift Cars made a showing of general reputation in the East Taunton area throughout the period involved by maintaining an East Taunton address and an East Taunton telephone number. We cannot say that the district court's inherent finding of continuous use should be upset.

....

E. *The district court did not abuse its discretion by allowing Thrift Cars to advertise in those publications it had used prior to Thrifty's registration.*

The district court allowed Thrift Cars to continue advertising in those media it had used prior to the critical date of July 26, 1964. Thrifty now urges that the court allowed Thrift Cars too broad an advertising distribution base, because it extended outside East Taunton to Cape Cod and Nantucket. Thrifty says that by permitting both parties to advertise in the major resort area publications, the court abused its discretion because substantial consumer confusion is likely to result.

We reject Thrifty's arguments and agree with the district court that to contract Thrift Cars' advertising base would be a punitive move. The district court did not allow Thrift Cars to advertise in any publications that it had not used prior to Thrifty's registration. On the contrary, the court simply authorized Thrift Cars to use only the same newspapers it had used prior to that critical date. While we recognize that some consumer confusion may result because there will be some overlap in advertising, the Lanham Act does not require the complete elimination of all confusion. [Citation.] We think, moreover, that the confusion spawned as a result of Thrift Cars' advertising will be minimal and should not significantly interfere with Thrifty's proprietary rights in its mark. [Citation.] Each party shall bear its own costs.

Affirmed.

Dudley v. HealthSource Chiropractic Inc., 883 F. Supp. 2d 377 (W.D.N.Y. 2012). Plaintiff Dudley established his practice as a chiropractor in Rochester, New York, in 2003, doing business as HEALTHSOURCE CHIROPRACTIC. Dudley registered the domain name healthsourcechiropractic.com and created a web site to promote his practice. He advertised locally and regionally in the *Yellow Pages*, magazines, newspapers, restaurants, and on local radio. At trial, Dudley claimed that his practice extended to the five-county area surrounding Rochester. Defendant HealthSource is an Ohio corporation that franchises 325 chiropractic offices nationwide under the HEALTHSOURCE CHIROPRACTIC mark; its first franchise opened in 2006. In April 2007, defendant Stephen Divito opened a HEALTHSOURCE CHIROPRACTIC office in Rochester as HealthSource's franchisee. When Dudley complained, defendants agreed to use the mark "HealthQuest Chiropractic" for the Rochester franchise to avoid confusion. Dudley sued, arguing that he was the senior user of HEALTHSOURCE CHIROPRACTIC both in the five county area and on the Internet. On cross motions for summary judgment, the court concluded that Dudley was the senior user of mark in Rochester, but that there were disputed issues of material fact as to the geographic extent of his trademark rights. The court then turned to Dudley's claim to be the senior user of the service mark on the Internet:

> By claiming exclusivity to the HealthSource Chiropractic mark on the internet, the Plaintiff assumes that the internet is a territory in which he can establish exclusive rights. The internet is not, however, a geographic territory to be subdivided; instead, it is a global communication medium that is accessible from anywhere on the planet. The internet has become vital for local, regional, national, and international communication. It is used for selling, advertising, and marketing products and services as well as communicating with clients and customers. An internet presence has become crucial for businesses of all sizes, whether they operate locally or nationally.

The rights of concurrent users would be substantially harmed if one user were able to monopolize the internet to the exclusion of other lawful users of the same mark. If, as the Plaintiff suggests, a senior common law user could claim exclusive use on the internet, then it would undermine the benefits and security provided by federal registration. A federal registrant could never be certain that its rights extended to the internet and that a senior user would not come forward claiming priority and exclusivity to the internet. Similarly, allowing a federal registrant exclusive use of the mark on the internet would undermine the territorial rights of a senior user. Unlike national advertising which would often be cost-prohibitive for a local or regional user, the internet is an almost-necessary tool for a user to develop its business and remain competitive within its exclusive territory. Restricting internet use to the federal registrant would therefore equally undermine the territorial rights of a senior common law user. Consequently, this Court concludes that neither party can claim exclusive rights to the internet. [Citation.]

....

In this case, the Defendants have taken reasonable measures to ensure that they are not using the HealthSource Chiropractic mark on the internet to intrude into the Plaintiff's territory. The Defendants have removed Dr. Divito's practice completely from HealthSource Inc.'s web site. Dr. Divito maintains his own web site, rochesterspinalcare.com, for his Rochester practice and only uses the HealthQuest mark on his web site. The Plaintiff has presented no evidence that indicates the Defendants have used the HealthSource mark on the internet to specifically target the Rochester market.

....

A trademark owner cannot reasonably expect to have exclusive use of a term on the internet. Defendants presented evidence that as of 2008 there were 754 registered domain names with that included the term "healthsource." Users of a mark must develop ways to distinguish themselves on the internet beyond resorting to the trademark laws. *See Lockheed Martin Corp. v. Network Solutions, Inc.*, 985 F. Supp. 949, 968 (C.D. Cal. 1997) aff'd, 194 F.3d 980 (9th Cir. 1999) (stating that the solution to difficulties faced by trademark owners on the internet is innovation). Accordingly, because he cannot establish exclusive rights on the internet, the Plaintiff's claim for trademark infringement under 15 U.S.C. § 1125(a) with respect to the Defendants' use of the HealthSource Chiropractic mark on the internet is dismissed.

....

Question

Can you imagine circumstances in which a trademark owner could reasonably claim exclusive trademark rights in connection with use on the Internet? If not, why not? Does use of the Internet to advertise a product expand the scope of the geographic territory in connection with which one can be deemed to be using the mark? How would one ascertain the extent of the expansion?

Dawn Donut Co. v. Hart's Food Stores, Inc., 267 F.2d 358 (2d Cir. 1959). Dawn Donut had continuously used the trademark "Dawn" on bags of doughnut mix, which it sold and shipped to bakers in various states from its Michigan warehouse. Plaintiff also furnished advertising and packaging material bearing the trademark "Dawn" and permitted these bakers to sell goods made from the mixes to the consuming public under that trademark. The licensing of plaintiff's mark in connection with retail sales of doughnuts in New York had been confined to areas not less than 60 miles from defendant's trading area of Rochester, NY. While sales of Dawn Donut mix had been made to bakers in defendant's trading area, these bakers had not employed plaintiff's mark in connection with retail sales.

Defendant, Hart Food Stores, owned and operated a retail grocery chain in New York. The defendant's bakery distributed doughnuts with the imprint "Dawn" through these stores within the 45 mile radius of Rochester, NY. Defendant adopted the mark "Dawn" because of a slogan "Baked at midnight, delivered at Dawn." Defendant's adoption was subsequent to plaintiff's registration but without actual knowledge of plaintiff's use.

Plaintiff's marks were registered federally in 1927, and their registration was renewed in 1947. Therefore, by virtue of the Lanham Act, 15 U.S.C. § 1072, the defendant had constructive notice of plaintiff's marks as of July 5, 1947, the effective date of the Act.

The Second Circuit nonetheless affirmed the district court's dismissal of plaintiff's complaint.

> As long as plaintiff and defendant confine their use of the mark "Dawn" in connection with the retail sale of baked goods to their present separate trading areas it is clear that no public confusion is likely.
>
> . . . .
>
> The decisive question then is whether plaintiff's use of the mark "Dawn" at the retail level is likely to be confined to its current area of use or whether in the normal course of its business, it is likely to expand the retail use of the mark into defendant's trading area. If such expansion were probable, then the concurrent use of the marks would give rise to the conclusion that there was a likelihood of confusion.
>
> . . . .
>
> Accordingly, because plaintiff and defendant use the mark in connection with retail sales in distinct and separate markets and because there is no present prospect that plaintiff will expand its use of the mark at the retail level into defendant's trading area, we conclude that there is no likelihood of public confusion arising from the concurrent use of the marks and therefore

the issuance of an injunction is not warranted.... However, because of the effect we have attributed to the constructive notice provision of the Lanham Act, the plaintiff may later, upon a proper showing of an intent to use the mark at the retail level in defendant's market area, be entitled to enjoin defendant's use of the mark.

....

Guthrie Healthcare Sys. v. ContextMedia, Inc., 826 F.3d 27 (2d Cir. 2016). The Court of Appeals for the Second Circuit distinguished *Dawn Donut* in a case involving two healthcare businesses, which had adopted very similar logos. Plaintiff Guthrie HealthCare Systems operated more than 30 medical facilities in Pennsylvania and New York, and recruited its doctors, nurses, and students nationwide. Defendant ContextMedia delivered health-related video content to doctors' officers in all 50 states. In 2001, Guthrie adopted a logo featuring a stylized human figure superimposed on a three-color shield. In 2008, ContextMedia began using a very similar logo. The district court found that there was a likelihood of confusion between the marks within Guthrie's service area, but no likelihood of confusion outside of New York and Pennsylvania. The court therefore enjoined ContextMedia from using the logo in plaintiff's service area, but refused to enjoin its use of the logo outside of that area. Guthrie appealed and the Second Circuit reversed:

It is correct that a senior user must prove a probability of confusion in order to win an injunction. But it does not follow that the injunction may extend only into areas for which the senior user has shown probability of confusion. It is not as if the senior user must prove a new claim of infringement for each geographic area in which it seeks injunctive relief. Once the senior user has proven entitlement to an injunction, the scope of the injunction should be governed by a variety of equitable factors—the principal concern ordinarily being providing the injured senior user with reasonable protection from the junior user's infringement. Of course, if the junior user demonstrates that in a particular geographic area there is no likelihood of confusion, ordinarily no useful purpose would be served by extending the injunction into that area, potentially inflicting great harm on the junior user without meaningful justification. *See Dawn Donut Co. v. Hart's Food Stores, Inc.*, 267 F.2d 358, 364–65 (2d Cir. 1959) (upholding the district court's finding that, "in view of the plaintiff's inactivity for about thirty years in exploiting its trademarks in defendant's trading area at the retail level ... there was no reasonable expectation that plaintiff would extend its retail operations into defendant's trading area").

....

Defendant's reliance on *Dawn Donut* is misplaced for several reasons. In that case, the absence of likelihood of confusion was *proven by the defendant* by showing that in 30 years of operation the plaintiff had never sought to use its mark in the defendant's area. The court noted that there was "ample evidence" supporting the absence of likelihood of confusion. *Dawn Donut Co.*, 267 F.2d at 365. Furthermore, the court ruled that, if the plaintiff later made a showing of intent to use the mark in the defendant's market area, then the plaintiff "may later ... be entitled to enjoin defendant's use of the mark." *Id.* Finally, *Dawn Donut*, did not present the problem, like this case, of a plaintiff who has shown entitlement to an injunction in one geographic area and seeks to have the injunction extend beyond as well. It therefore has no pertinence to the question at issue here.*

Questions

1. How would the court have ruled in *United Drug* had § 33(b) of the Lanham Act [15 U.S.C. § 1115(b)] been in effect at the time of the Court's decision?

2. Was the court in *Dawn Donut* correct in concluding that there will be no confusion of the mark "Dawn" in the Rochester area? Had there been a likelihood of confusion in the *Dawn Donut* case, would the court have enjoined the defendant from using the mark? Does § 33(b)(5) of the Lanham Act help the defendant here?

3. Is *Dawn Donut* distinguishable from *Stork Club, supra*, Chapter 1? Suppose a Michigan resident drives through Western New York State? Is that traveler's potential confusion less cognizable than the New Yorker's who visits San Francisco?

4. Pegasus Pizza has a federally registered trademark for its retail pizza chain stores. It franchises hundreds of pizzerias in the southwest United States, and the company maintains a website on which it advertises its company. The website contains information on its pizzas, special Internet deals, and a store locator pointing website visitors to the pizzeria nearest them. Aside from the website, the company engages in no national advertising.

Pizza di Pegasus is an Italian restaurant that serves pizza and pasta. Its sole location is in Ithaca, New York. It advertises exclusively within its local college community through fliers and ads in newspapers.

Pegasus Pizza plans to expand its operations in the southeast United States, but it has no current plans to open pizzerias in New York.

Does the analysis in *Dawn Donut* protect the junior user Pizza di Pegasus under these facts? Would the result be different if Pegasus Pizza also sold frozen pizzas available in its pizzerias throughout the United States over its website?

5. Was the court in *Thrifty Rent-a-Car* correct in allowing the defendant to continue to advertise in the same media in which it had advertised prior to the plaintiff's federal registration? Does § 33(b)(5) of the Lanham Act dictate this result? Is this ruling consistent with *Dawn Donut*? With *Guthrie Healthcare*?

---

* *Editors' Note: See also Guthrie Healthcare Sys. v. ContextMedia, Inc, infra*, Chapter 12[A][1] for more on the proper scope of the injunction.

Chapter 4

Registration of Trademarks

A. The Bases And Process

1. Bases of Registration

There are five bases of registration in the U.S., i.e., use in commerce (under section 1(a) of the Lanham Act), a bona fide intent to use the mark in commerce (under section 1(b) of the Lanham Act), ownership of a qualified foreign registration (under section 44(e) of the Lanham Act), ownership of a qualified foreign application (under section 44(d) of the Lanham Act) or ownership of an International Registration that has been extended to the U.S. (under section 66 of the Lanham Act). Domestic applicants generally can apply either based on having made use of the mark in commerce in connection with the goods/services prior to filing or based on a bona fide intent to use the mark in commerce for such goods/services. In addition to these two bases, foreign applicants generally can also apply under section 44(d) or (e) of the Lanham Act or can extend an International Registration to the U.S. under the Madrid Protocol. Each of these bases is discussed below.

Use-Based Applications

Section 1(a) of the Lanham Act, 15 U.S.C. § 1051(a), provides for filing applications for marks that have been used in commerce as follows:

15 U.S.C. § 1051(a) [Lanham Act § 1(a)]

(1) The owner of a trademark used in commerce may request registration of its trademark on the principal register hereby established by paying the prescribed fee and filing in the Patent and Trademark Office an application and a verified statement, in such form as may be prescribed by the Director, and such number of specimens or facsimiles of the mark as used as may be required by the Director.

(2) The application shall include specification of the applicant's domicile and citizenship, the date of the applicant's first use of the mark, the date of the applicant's first use of the mark in commerce, the goods in connection with which the mark is used, and a drawing of the mark.

(3) The statement shall be verified by the applicant and specify that—

(A) the person making the verification believes that he or she, or the juristic person in whose behalf he or she makes the verification, to be the owner of the mark sought to be registered;

(B) to the best of the verifier's knowledge and belief, the facts recited in the application are accurate;

(C) the mark is in use in commerce; and

(D) to the best of the verifier's knowledge and belief, no other person has the right to use such mark in commerce either in the identical form thereof or in such near resemblance thereto as to be likely, when used on or in connection with the goods of such other person, to cause confusion, or to cause mistake, or to deceive....

A use-based application must allege use in commerce, must set forth the first use dates anywhere and the first use date of the mark in commerce for each class of goods or services, and must attach specimens showing use of the mark in commerce in connection with each class of goods or services. For what constitutes use in commerce, see the discussion in Chapter 3[C], *supra.* The Trademark Office interprets "use in commerce" to mean "lawful use in commerce" and thus will refuse registration to a mark when it would be illegal under federal law to sell or distribute products or services that fall within the applied-for goods or services. *See In re Morgan Brown*, 119 U.S.P.Q.2d 1350 (T.T.A.B. 2016) (HERBAL ACCESS refused registration for retail services featuring herbs where specimen of use showed one product sold was marijuana, an illegal product under federal law; fact that state law permitted sale did not change analysis).

Intent to Use

15 U.S.C. § 1051(b) [Lanham Act § 1(b)]

(b) Application for bona fide intention to use trademark

(1) A person who has a bona fide intention, under circumstances showing the good faith of such person, to use a trademark in commerce may request registration of its trademark on the principal register hereby established by paying the prescribed fee and filing in the Patent and Trademark Office an application and a verified statement, in such form as may be prescribed by the Director.

(2) The application shall include specification of the applicant's domicile and citizenship, the goods in connection with which the applicant has a bona fide intention to use the mark, and a drawing of the mark.

(3) The statement shall be verified by the applicant and specify—

(A) that the person making the verification believes that he or she, or the juristic person in whose behalf he or she makes the verification, to be entitled to use the mark in commerce;

(B) the applicant's bona fide intention to use the mark in commerce;

...

(D) that, to the best of the verifier's knowledge and belief, no other person has the right to use the mark in commerce either in the identical form thereof or in such near resemblance thereto as to be likely, when used on or in connection with the goods of such person, to cause confusion, or cause mistake, or to deceive....

M.Z. Berger & Co., Inc. v. Swatch AG

787 F.3d 1368 (Fed. Cir. 2015)

CHEN, CIRCUIT JUDGE.

M.Z. Berger & Co., Inc. (Berger) appeals from the ... decision to sustain an opposition on grounds that Berger, at the time of its application for the mark "iWatch," lacked a bona fide intent to use the mark in commerce under Section 1(b)(1) of the Lanham Act, 15 U.S.C. § 1051(b)(1). The Board concluded that Berger merely intended to reserve a right in the mark and thus lacked the requisite intent. Because substantial evidence supports the Board's determination, we affirm.

I. BACKGROUND

Berger is a business that manufactures, imports, and sells watches, clocks, and personal care products. On July 5, 2007, it filed an intent-to-use application at the Patent and Trademark Office (PTO), ... to register the mark "iWatch" for over thirty different goods, each of which belongs to one of three general categories: watches, clocks, and goods related to watches and/or clocks (e.g., clock dials, watch bands, and watch straps).

....

... With respect to Berger's intent to use the iWatch mark on two of the categories, clocks and goods related to watches/clocks, the Board considered the testimony of Berger's owner and CEO, Bernard Mermelstein. Mr. Mermelstein not only created the iWatch mark and instructed that the trademark application be filed, but he was Berger's sole witness designated under Federal Rule of Civil Procedure 30(b)(6). The Board thus treated Mr. Mermelstein's testimony as representing the views of the company at the time the application was filed.

... Mr. Mermelstein testified ... :

Q. Are there other products other than watches that you anticipate for use with the iWatch mark?

A. No.

Mr. Mermelstein further testified:

Q. At the time you filed the application you didn't expect the iWatch mark to be used for clocks and personal care products?

A. No. Correct.

Berger's paralegal who filed the application, Monica Titera, testified that Mr. Mermelstein instructed her to register the mark only for watches and clocks. When asked why the other related goods were identified in the application, Ms. Titera claimed that the list was "standard" and used to "leave all doors open." Based on Mr. Mermelstein's and Ms. Titera's testimonies, the Board concluded that Berger lacked a genuine intent to use the mark on clocks and related goods.

... [T]he Board also concluded that Berger lacked a genuine plan to commercialize the iWatch mark on [watches]. The Board ... found that such [documentary] evidence did not demonstrate intent because the documents related solely to prosecution of the trademark application. As for the testimonial evidence presented by Berger, the Board found that Berger's employees failed to tell a consistent story about the company's intent at the time the application was filed. The Board lastly considered the company's long history in the watch business, but found that Berger's inaction with respect to a potential iWatch product diminished the value of such evidence.

....

II. Discussion

....

B

The Trademark Law Revision Act of 1988 (TLRA) contemplated the very scenario presented by this case. The TLRA changed the Lanham Act by permitting applicants to begin the registration process before actual use of the mark in commerce at the time of filing, so long as the applicant had a "*bona fide intention* ... to use [the] mark in commerce" at a later date. 15 U.S.C. § 1051(b)(1) (emphasis added).

The prior version of the Lanham Act required that a trademark applicant already be using the mark in commerce at the time of the application's filing to qualify for trademark registration. [Citation.] This requirement, however, led to the practice of some applicants engineering a "token use," which refers to the most minimal use of a trademark, designed purely to secure rights in that mark before an applicant is truly prepared to commercialize a good or service in connection with a given mark. In the legislative record of the TLRA, Congress noted that token use was problematic for a number of reasons, including that such uses were not uniformly available across industries. S. Rep. No. 100-515 ("Senate Report"), at 6 (1988), *reprinted in* 1988 U.S.C.C.A.N. 5577, 5582. For example, token use for large or expensive products, such as airplanes, or for service industries was "virtually impossible." *Id.* Another problem was that the rules allowed registration based on minimal use, which led to an undesirable surplus of registered but virtually unused marks. *Id.* On the other hand, Congress also recognized that the use requirement placed "significant legal risks on the introduction of new products and services" and disadvantaged certain industries and smaller companies in the marketplace. *Id.* at 5. An applicant already using a mark in commerce risks, for example, potential infringement of a competitor's pre-existing mark prior to being able to begin the process of securing its own rights.

... To address the problem of "token use," the TLRA heightened the burden for use applications by requiring that an applicant's use be "*bona fide use* of [the] mark in the ordinary course of trade." [Citation.] Concurrently, the TLRA lowered the bar to starting registration by allowing applicants to proceed on the basis that they have a "bona fide intention to use the mark in commerce" at a later date. 15 U.S.C. § 1051(b)(1); *see* H.R. REP. No. 100-1028 ("House Report"), at 8–9 (1988) ("By permitting applicants to seek protection of their marks through an 'intent to use' system, there should be no need for 'token use' of a mark simply to provide a basis for an application. The use of the term 'bona fide' is meant to eliminate such 'token use' and to require, based on an objective view of the circumstances, a good faith intention to eventually use the mark in a real and legitimate commercial sense."); [citation].

....

C

... Because a bona fide intent to use the mark in commerce is a statutory requirement of a valid intent-to-use trademark application under Section 1(b), the lack of such intent is a basis on which an opposer may challenge an applicant's mark. We note that the one other circuit court to address this issue has likewise so held. *Aktieselskabet AF 21. Nov. 2001 v. Fame Jeans Inc.*, 525 F.3d 8, 21, 381 U.S. App. D.C. 76 (D.C. Cir. 2008).

D

....

There is no statutory definition of the term "bona fide," but the language is clear on its face that an applicant's intent must be "under circumstances showing the good faith of such person." *Id.* Th[is] reference ... strongly suggests that the applicant's intent must be demonstrable and more than a mere subjective belief. Both the PTO and the leading treatise on trademark law have arrived at this same understanding. *See Lane*, 33 U.S.P.Q.2d at 1355; 3 *McCarthy on Trademarks* § 19.14, at 19.48 ("Congress did not intend the issue to be resolved simply by an officer of the applicant later testifying, 'Yes, indeed, at the time we filed that application, I did truly intend to use the mark at some time in the future.'").

This interpretation is confirmed by the legislative history, where Congress made clear that whether an applicant's intent is "bona fide" should be assessed on an objective basis:

> ... In connection with this bill, *"bona fide" should be read to mean a fair, objective determination of the applicant's intent* based on all the circumstances.

Senate Report at 24 (emphasis added); *see also id.* at 23 ("Bona fide intent is measured by objective factors."); House Report at 8–9 ("The use of the term 'bona fide' is meant to ... require, based on an objective view of the circumstances, a good faith intention to eventually use the mark in a real and legitimate commercial sense."). In addition, an applicant's intent must reflect an intention to use the mark consistent with the Lanham Act's definition of "use in commerce":

> [T]he bona fide use of a mark in the ordinary course of trade, and not made merely to reserve a right in a mark.

15 U.S.C. § 1127; *see also* Senate Report at 24–25 (quoting the definition). The applicant's intention to use the mark in commerce must have been "firm." Senate Report at 24.

Neither the statute nor the legislative history indicates the specific quantum or type of objective evidence required to meet the bar. Indeed, Congress expressly rejected inclusion of a statutory definition for "bona fide" in order to preserve "the flexibility which is vital to the proper operation of the trademark registration system." *Id.*

Accordingly, we hold that whether an applicant had a "bona fide intent" to use the mark in commerce at the time of the application requires objective evidence of intent. 15 U.S.C. § 1051(b)(1). Although the evidentiary bar is not high, the circumstances must indicate that the applicant's intent to use the mark was firm and not merely intent to reserve a right in the mark. *See id.* § 1127; *see also* Senate Report at 24–25. The Board may make such determinations on a case-by-case basis considering the totality of the circumstances.

III. M.Z. Berger's Appeal

A

... Berger's arguments hinge on its belief that the Board should have found the intent requirement satisfied because Berger offered *some* objective evidence in support of its position. Viewed in isolation, the evidence Berger prefers to focus on could perhaps lead a reasonable fact-finder to conclude there was bona fide intent. As discussed above, however, all circumstances regarding an applicant's bona fide intent must be considered, including those facts that would tend to disprove that Berger had the requisite intent. 15 U.S.C. § 1051(b)(1); [citation].

Here ... we find that substantial evidence supports the Board's conclusion ... [W]e agree ... that the documentary evidence offered by Berger appears to relate only to the prosecution of the trademark application. *See Opinion* at 1474–75 (citing *Research In Motion Ltd. v. NBOR Corp.*, 92 U.S.P.Q.2d (BNA) 1926, 1931 (T.T.A.B. 2009) ("If the filing and prosecution of a trademark application constituted a bona fide intent to use a mark, then in effect, lack of a bona fide intent to use would never be a ground for opposition or cancellation, since an *inter partes* proceeding can only be brought if the defendant has filed an application.")). The paralegal who performed the trademark search testified that such searches are routinely conducted before Berger files a trademark so that Berger does not waste time filing an application on an unavailable mark. It is undisputed that the internal email relaying the substance of a discussion with the trademark examining attorney also relates to the application. The other internal emails, which forwarded the images of two watches and a clock bearing the mark, were undisputedly submitted to the PTO in response to the trademark examining attorney's request for documents showing how the mark would be used.

Faced with conflicting statements from Berger witnesses about whether the images were created for prosecution or for business reasons evidencing intent, the Board exercised its discretion in crediting the testimony of Mr. Mermelstein, Berger's Rule 30(b)(6) witness, over that of other Berger employees. (relying on Mr. Mermelstein's admissions that the images were created for the trademark application).... [T]he Board reasonably determined that such images were likely created with an intention to advance the prosecution of the trademark application rather than an intention to move forward on an actual product in commerce.... Mr. Mermelstein admitted that there was no intent to use the iWatch mark for clocks, and Ms. Titera conceded that the other accessories and related goods were only designated to leave Berger's options open.

With respect to watches, the Board considered conflicting testimony about Berger's alleged meeting with a buyer, as well as whether the watch would be technological in nature. The Board was within its discretion to disagree with Berger's bottom-line position that it possessed a bona fide intent, given the inability of the Berger witnesses to pull together a consistent story on a number of issues, e.g., would the watch be technological, did actual physical samples exist, were potential customers ever consulted. Critically, Mr. Mermelstein all but conceded that Berger had not yet made a firm decision to use the mark in commerce at the time of its application. ("[I]f [Berger] decided to do a—either a technology watch or information watch or something that would have that type of characteristics that [iWatch] would be a good mark for it."). *See, e.g., Research in Motion*, 92 U.S.P.Q.2d at 1931 (applicant's stated belief that the mark would be "a good mark for future use" does not establish a bona fide intent to use).

We also find unavailing Berger's contention that the Board ignored Berger's history in the watch industry. The Board did consider Berger's past but noted that even though the iWatch mark was allegedly to be used with a "smart" watch, Berger had never made such a watch and took no steps following the application to develop such a watch. We find no error with the Board's determination that there was no nexus between Berger's general capacity to produce watches and the capacity required to produce a "smart" watch.

....

The bar for showing a bona fide intent is not high. But in our view, considering the inconsistent testimony offered by Berger employees and the general lack of documentary support, substantial evidence supports the Board's conclusion that Berger's intent at the time of the application was merely to reserve a right in the mark, and not a bona fide intent to use the mark in commerce.

B

... Berger contends the Board erred by applying a more stringent threshold for bona fide intent than required by statute or by the PTO's regulations and procedures.

We disagree. Nowhere did the Board state that the applicable standard requires an applicant to have actually promoted, developed, and marketed the mark at the time of the application.... To the contrary, the Board's opinion reflects that it reached its conclusions by considering all the relevant facts and circumstances, including those that indicated Berger lacked intent. This is indeed the proper inquiry under the Lanham Act. 15 U.S.C. § 1051(b)(1) (intent to use must be "under circumstances showing the good faith of such person").

....

We find that the Board did not err in its application of the standard for bona fide intent. As discussed *supra*, whether an applicant has a bona fide intent to use a mark in commerce is an objective inquiry based on the totality of the circumstances. The Board conducted such an inquiry.

....

AFFIRMED

After an ITU application is approved by the Trademark Office and either no oppositions are filed or, if filed, are overcome, a Notice of Allowance issues. In order to obtain a registration, an ITU applicant must use the mark in commerce for the covered goods/services. After a Notice of Allowance issues, the applicant has 6 months to file a Statement of Use for the goods or services for which the mark is being used in which it states the first use dates in commerce and anywhere and provides specimens of use for each class of goods or services. If it cannot do so, the ITU applicant can apply for six-month extensions of time up to a total of 5 times, for a possible maximum of 3 years from the date of the Notice of Allowance. If a Statement of Use is not filed within the allowable time, the application will be deemed abandoned.

Question

An intent-to-use application may not be assigned "except to the successor to the business of the applicant, or portion thereof, to which the mark pertains." 15 U.S.C. § 1060. If an ITU application is assigned (together with other trademarks and applications) as collateral to a loan, does the assignment invalidate the ITU application? *See Clorox Co. v. Chemical Bank*, 40 U.S.P.Q.2d 1098 (T.T.A.B. 1996). What if a subsidiary company assigns an ITU application to its parent company without assigning any part of the business? Should the fact that the parent in some sense owns the business of the subsidiary make a difference as to whether the assignment is valid? *See Central Garden & Pet Co. v. Doskocil Mfg. Co.*, 108 U.S.P.Q.2d 1134 (T.T.A.B. 2013) (Board held assignment invalid).

Note: U.S. Registration Under Section 44

The United States is a member of the Paris Convention for the Protection of Industrial Property. *See* Appendix D, *infra*. This is the leading multilateral treaty covering patents and trademarks. First promulgated in 1883 and originally ratified by eleven nations in 1884, it numbers over 170 members, including all the industrialized nations. The current text of the Convention is that of the 1967 Stockholm revision, and has been incorporated into the 1994 Agreement on Trade Related aspects of Intellectual Property (TRIPs). *See* art. 1.3. The Paris Convention rests primarily upon the principle of national treatment. This is a nondiscrimination principle: member nations must treat the nationals or domiciliaries of other members as they would their own citizens (*see* art. 2). The Paris Convention does not automatically protect the trademark in all Paris Union countries once it is protected in one country. Rather, in most cases, protection depends upon securing a trademark registration in each of the other member countries. The national treatment principle operates primarily to oblige member countries to grant trademark owners from other member countries equal access to local trademark registration procedures. *See, e.g., In re Rath*, 402 F.3d 1207 (Fed. Cir. 2005) (Paris Convention is not self-executing in the U.S.; accordingly, applications for RATH and DR. RATH based on German registrations under section 44(e) are subject to scrutiny under Lanham Act's statutory bars to registration).

An applicant from a Paris Convention or WTO country may register a trademark in the United States in various ways. First, under the principle of national treatment, any foreign applicant who can allege use or a bona fide intent to use in commerce can file an application on the same basis as a U.S. applicant under section 1(a) [use] or section 1(b) [intent to use] of the Lanham Act.

In addition, applicants can obtain a registration in the United States on the basis of a prior registration in the applicant's country of origin. The country of origin is either the country in which the applicant "has a bona fide and effective industrial or commercial establishment,"* or, in the absence of a business establishment, the country of which the applicant is a domiciliary or a national. Lanham Act § 44(c), 15 U.S.C. § 1126(c). Neither contractual relations with an independent company nor shipment of product to a third-party distributor located in a country qualify that country as a location for an "effective industrial or commercial establishment." *See Kallamni v. Khan*, 101 U.S.P.Q.2d 1864 (T.T.A.B. 2012) (Pakistani national could not rely on business of independent contractor or third-party distributor located in the European Union; Community Trademark was thus not adequate basis for registration under section 44(e)). A mark duly registered in the country of origin may be registered on the Principal Register if eligible, otherwise, on the Supplemental Register, both of which are discussed, *infra*, this Chapter. As of the 1988 Lanham Act Amendments, the application must state the applicant's bona fide intention to use the mark in commerce, but actual use is not required prior to registration. Together with the application, the 44(e) applicant must submit a true copy of the registration in the country of origin. Lanham Act § 44(e), 15 U.S.C. § 1126(e).

* Typically, applicants under section 44 are not U.S. nationals; however, if a U.S. company has an effective industrial or commercial establishment outside the U.S. and otherwise satisfies the requirements of section 44, it may also apply under this basis.

Moreover, an applicant may apply to register the mark in the United States based on an application to register the mark in the country of origin under section 44(d). The U.S. application must be filed within six months of the date on which the application was first filed abroad. Such an application must comply in other ways with the requirements of the Lanham Act, including a statement that the applicant has a bona fide intention to use the mark in commerce. The U.S. application will receive the same force and effect as if it had been filed in the U.S. on the date on which it was first filed abroad, which can be up to 6 months prior to the U.S. filing. *See* Lanham Act § 44(d), 15 U.S.C. § 1126(d). However, the registration in the U.S. will not issue on this basis until the foreign registration has issued and a true copy has been sent to the USPTO.

Once obtained, the U.S. registration based on section 44 will be independent of the registration in the country of origin. The Lanham Act will govern the duration, validity, and transfer of rights under the U.S. registration. Lanham Act § 44(f), 15 U.S.C. § 1126(f). As a result, while applicants may obtain a U.S. registration without prior use in U.S. commerce, the applicant must commence use in the United States within three years of issuance of the registration, or the statutory presumption of abandonment (discussed in Chapter 5[B], *infra*) may be triggered.

Question

A Cuban company sells its COHIBA cigars all over the world but cannot sell them in the U.S. due to the Cuban Assets Control Regulations, which remain in effect despite the move toward normalization of relations between the U.S. and Cuba. Should it be able to register its COHIBA mark in the U.S. under section 44(e) based on its Cuban registration? Would it have the requisite bona fide intent to use the mark in commerce? *See generally Empresa Cubana del Tobaco v. General Cigar Co.*, 753 F.3d 1270 (Fed. Cir. 2014) (court noted propriety of section 44(e) application but did not address bona fide intent question).

Note: Madrid Protocol Extensions to the U.S.

The Madrid Protocol is an international trademark filing treaty among over 85 countries.* The treaty allows non-U.S. applicants from member countries to extend their international registrations to the United States and allows domestic mark owners to obtain international registrations extending to member countries based upon the owner's U.S. applications or registrations. The international registration system is administered by the World Intellectual Property Organization ("WIPO") located in Geneva. The mark owner can select the member countries to which the international registration will extend, and those countries then have the ability to accept or refuse the extension. The international registration offers several benefits, such as the ability

* *Editors' Note*: The text of the Madrid Protocol can be found at http://www.wipo.int/madrid/en/legal_texts/.

to renew registrations and to record assignments in one place for a single registration that covers many countries.

A holder of a non-U.S. mark can extend the international registration ("IR") it obtains from WIPO to the United States based on the international registration holder's "basic application" or "basic registration" in a Protocol country (other than the U.S.) in which it is a national, is domiciled or has a real and effective industrial or commercial establishment. The extension of the registration to the United States is submitted to the USPTO by WIPO and must be accompanied by a verified declaration that the international registration holder has a bona fide intent to use the mark in commerce. The date of the international registration (if the request for extension is filed in the international application) or the date the request for extension is recorded by WIPO (if the request is made after the international registration issued) is analogous to constructive first use date under section 7(c) of the Lanham Act (discussed in Section [B] of this Chapter, *infra*). The USPTO examines the application as it normally does, and if it is approved, the application is published for opposition. In the event that no oppositions are filed or, if filed, are overcome, the USPTO will issue a certificate of extension of protection that will have the same effect as a registration on the Principal Register. If the application is either not approved by the USPTO or if an opposition is filed, the USPTO will issue a notice of refusal within 18 months from the date on which WIPO transmits the request for extension to the USPTO, stating the grounds. In addition, the USPTO will issue a notice of the possibility of refusal within 18 months if an opposition is possible, for example if a request for an extension of time to oppose is filed.

A unique feature of an international registration under the Protocol is the possibility of central attack. If the basic application or registration upon which the IR is based is restricted, abandoned or cancelled with respect to some or all of the covered goods or services within 5 years (or more than 5 years if the change resulted from an action within the 5 years), then all the extensions of the IR to various countries, including to the United States, will be similarly restricted, abandoned or cancelled. For example, if a French application is the basis for the IR and is successfully opposed in France, then the IR and all extensions of the IR to other countries will be cancelled. If an IR is cancelled in whole or in part, the IR holder has the option to transform its extension to the U.S. into a U.S. application under section 70(c) by filing, within 3 months of the cancellation of the IR, an application in the U.S. for the same mark and goods or services covered by the cancelled registration. This application can be made pursuant either to section 1 or section 44 of the Lanham Act and will be accorded the same filing date as that of the IR or recordal of the extension.

Once an extension of protection has issued, the IR holder is not required to renew the IR at the USPTO since renewal of the IR takes place centrally through WIPO. However, the IR holder is nevertheless required to submit to the USPTO declarations of use (or of excusable nonuse) under section 71 of the Lanham Act within 5 to 6 years after the certificate of extension to the U.S. has been issued and within a year prior to the 10th year and successive 10 year periods thereafter with a grace period of 6 months for each such deadline.

Question

Applicants that file based on a foreign application or registration under section 44 or that extend an international registration to the U.S. under section 66 are also required to declare a bona fide intention to use the mark in commerce for the covered goods or services. Should evidence about activities outside the U.S. be considered in determining such applicants' bona fide intent to use in mark in U.S. commerce? *See Honda Motor Co. v. Winkelmann*, 90 U.S.P.Q.2d 1660 (T.T.A.B. 2009).

2. The Process

William M. Borchard, *How to Get and Keep a Trademark*

Trademarks and the Arts (2d Ed. 2000) (Excerpt)*

A. How to Clear a Proposed Mark

The best way to learn whether a conflicting mark is being used is to order a search report through one of the independent searching companies.** The search report will purport to disclose all federal trademark registrations currently in effect, or which have been cancelled or have expired, for identical or similar marks applied to identical or closely related goods. It also will list state trademark registrations of interest, pertinent references in various relevant trade directories and on-line databases, and similar business names found in telephone directories or trade lists.

....

B. How to Establish Rights in a Mark

Once you have cleared the trademark for adoption, the next step is either to start using the mark in the ordinary course of trade on or in connection with the goods or services or to file an intent-to-use application for federal registration (which will not be issued until the mark has been put into bona fide use). To use the trademark, it could be applied to labels or affixed to the goods or to containers for the goods. In the alternative, it could be applied directly to the goods themselves, or it could be shown on point-of-sale displays associated with the goods. Use of a trademark solely in invoices, bills of lading, packing slips [except in rare situations due to the

---

** *Editors' Note:* Searching prospective marks prior to adoption is important for a number of reasons. Conducting a search can save the time and expense in investing in a mark that is unavailable. Moreover, defendants in infringement litigations can rely on a counsel's opinion based on a search in establishing their good faith in adopting a mark, one factor that can be considered in determining likelihood of confusion. *See, e.g., Lang v. Retirement Living Publishing Co., Inc.*, 949 F.2d 576 (2d Cir. 1991). Moreover, some courts have found a failure to search to be a factor in determining whether a party acted in bad faith, which in turn can lead to an award of profits, enhanced damages and/or attorney's fees. *See, e.g., Int'l Star Class Yacht Racing Assn v. Tommy Hilfiger, U.S.A., Inc.*, 80 F.3d 749 (2d Cir. 1996) (failure of defendant to conduct full search of mark after recommendation by attorney a factor in assessing bad faith). Parties or their counsel can conduct preliminary searches on the Trademark Office's TESS database, proprietary databases and search engines such as Google. If a proposed mark is not knocked out, a full availability search can be ordered from a searching company.

impracticality of placing the mark on goods, packaging or point-of-sale displays due to the nature of the goods] or advertisements for the goods would not meet the technical requirements for obtaining trademark ownership rights.

The types of use for securing rights in a service mark are slightly different from those described above. The service mark may be used in advertisements, brochures, letterheads, signs or any other item used in either advertising or rendering the service.

In addition, the service must actually be rendered in federal commerce to be federally registrable. Generally, this means that the service must be rendered in more than one state. But if the service is in a location where its patrons are traveling from state to state such as on an interstate highway [or travel to the location of the service from another state in response to advertising], the use in commerce requirement will be satisfied....

C. How to Obtain a Federal Registration of a Mark*

1. *Preparing the Application*

Once you have used the mark in commerce as described above, or once you have a bona fide intention to use the mark in commerce,[8] you can file an application to register it in the United States Patent and Trademark Office (hereinafter "PTO")....

The *minimum requirements* to receive a filing date for the application are as follows:

(a) *Applicant's Name*....

(b) *A Name and Address for Correspondence*....

(c) *Drawing.* Clear drawing of the mark suitable for printing on the certificate of registration must be part of the application or must accompany it. If the mark is not used in a stylized form of display, it may be registered in block-letter form and the drawing may be typed. However, if the mark has a particular style of lettering or incorporates a design, a pen and ink drawing may have to be prepared by a draftsman.

A sound mark—such as a musical signature—must be presented in an appropriate written description. A three-dimensional mark—such as a sculpture outside of a restaurant—must be presented in a line-drawing, not a photograph....

(d) *Identification of Goods or Services.* Identify in fairly specific ordinary terms the goods or services for which the mark has been or will be used, for example, t-shirts; prerecorded musical CD's and tapes; prerecorded

---

* *Editors' Note:* This discussion does not apply to requests for extensions of an International Registration to the United States under the Madrid Protocol, which have different procedures and requirements. See Note Madrid Protocol Extensions to the U.S., *supra*, this Chapter.

8. This intention must be more than a "wish list." It must be somewhat concrete, although it can be subject to one or more contingencies, and it is helpful if there is written evidence of this intent. *Commodore Electronics Ltd. v. Cbm KK*, 26 U.S.P.Q.2d 1503, 1507 (T.T.A.B.1993) (lack of documentary evidence is sufficient to prove that the applicant lacks a bona fide intention to use the mark in commerce).

video cassettes featuring motion pictures; entertainment services rendered by a vocal and instrumental group; motion picture distributorship services; restaurant services, etc. (At some point, you also must specify the official class in which the goods or services fall. The PTO follows the International Classification System which has 34 classes of trademarks and 11 classes of service marks.... A single application can cover the same mark in more than one class.)

(e) *Filing Fee.* The fee [is] $600 per class if the application is filed on paper. [I]f the application is filed electronically, there is a reduced fee of [from $225 to $400] per class [depending on] if the goods/services description complies with the Trademark Office's Acceptable Identification of Goods and Services and if the application meets certain other conditions.

Other requirements that can be satisfied later, are as follows:

(f) *Dates of Use.* If the application is based on use of the mark, state the date the mark was first used anywhere, even in intrastate commerce, for each PTO class being covered. In addition, state the date the mark was first used in federal commerce in each PTO class. These two dates may or may not be the same.

If the application is based on intent-to-use, the use information will be included when the amendment or statement of use is filed during the prosecution of the application.

If the application is based on a Paris Convention country of origin application (filed during the previous 6 months) or a country of origin registration, no use information will be required. A true copy of the country of origin registration (with English translation) eventually will be needed, however.

(g) *Specimens of Use.* When the dates of use are required and are submitted, you also must submit one specimen showing the mark as actually used in each PTO class being covered....

(h) *Color Features of the Mark.* If the mark always appears in a particular color which is to be regarded as a feature of the mark, explain where the colors appear and the nature of the colors.

(i) *Declaration.* The application at some point must be dated and signed immediately below a specified statement to the effect that the statements made in the application are true under penalties of perjury....

....

3. Examination by the PTO

... [T]he application is examined by a Trademark Attorney on the PTO's staff who reviews the application for form, completeness and registrability.

A mark may be considered unregistrable if it consists of or comprises: (1) immoral, deceptive or scandalous matter; or matter which may disparage or falsely suggest a connection with persons, living or dead, institutions, beliefs, or national symbols, or bring them into contempt or disrepute; (2) a name, portrait, or signature identifying a particular living individual except by his written consent; or (3) a mark which so resembles a mark registered in the PTO or a mark previously used in the United States by another and not abandoned, as to be likely to cause confusion when applied to your goods or services.

If the mark is merely descriptive of the goods or services, such as the term "Non-Stop Music" for "radio broadcasting services," it is not registrable on the Principal Register without proof that it has had sufficient use and advertising to have become recognized as designating a source in addition to its descriptive connotation. This is sometimes known as acquiring a "secondary meaning." The same is true if the mark is deceptively misdescriptive, such as the term "The Jones Sisters" for a musical group having members with no family relationship; or geographically descriptive, such as the term "New York's Own" for handicrafts that come from New York State; or a surname such as "Smith's" for a dance company.[21]

....

Often, the application encounters ... objections which can be dealt with through correspondence [or a telephone conversation with the Trademark Attorney]. The PTO issues an Office Action. The Office Action is dated and the applicant has six months from that date within which to respond....

A technical objection might be, for example, to identify the goods or services more precisely; to change the class; to add a disclaimer of a descriptive term incorporated in the mark; to prove that the mark has become distinctive through use, if that is appropriate; or to provide additional literature which will help the examination of the application. If the mark is refused registration because of a previously registered mark, an extended argument often is made, usually citing similar previously decided cases involving analogous facts or legal points.

4. Publication for Opposition

If the application is approved, it is then published in a weekly publication entitled the "Official Gazette of the U.S. Patent and Trademark Office." Publication ... means that it has satisfied all of the requirements of the PTO's Trademark Attorney. However, it also enables anyone who believes he or she will be damaged by application of the mark to oppose its registration.

An opposition, or request for extension of time to oppose, must be filed within thirty days from the date of publication. If an opposition is filed, a proceeding will be conducted before the Trademark Trial and Appeal Board of the PTO. The proceeding

21. [Lanham Act] §§ 2(e) and (f). Without proof of "secondary meaning," such a mark still can be registered on the Supplemental Register if it is in lawful use in commerce. *Id.* § 23. A Supplemental Register registration provides no substantive rights, but it ensures that the mark will appear on search reports, prevents anyone else from getting a Principal Register registration of the same mark for the same goods or services, and carries with it the right to use the same statutory notice of registration as applies to a Principal Register registration. A deceptive or geographically deceptively misdescriptive mark, such as "Viennese" for an orchestra from New Jersey, cannot be registered.

comes close to being a full trial with pre-trial discovery, testimony of witnesses, documentary evidence, legal briefs and possibly oral argument, and legal fees that can run very high.

If no opposition is filed and if the application is an intent-to-use application (that was not previously amended to a use application), the PTO will issue a Notice of Allowance. The applicant has six months in which to file a Statement of Use (with dates of first use and three specimens of use) accompanied by a filing fee of $100 per class [if filed electronically]. The deadline for filing the Statement of Use can be extended for six month intervals for up to 36 months after the Notice of Allowance was issued provided there is a reason for each extension after the first, there still is a bona fide intention to use the mark, and each [electronic] extension request is accompanied by a filing fee of [$125] per class covered....

The application will mature to registration and a certificate will be issued within approximately three months from the date of publication (if no opposition is filed) or from acceptance of the Statement of Use. The entire registration process can take as long as one to two years from the date of filing, and substantially longer if there is an opposition proceeding or there are extensions for filing the Statement of Use.

D. How to Obtain State Registrations of a Mark

It sometimes is desirable to file an application with the Department of State in each state in which the mark has been used because it takes so long to obtain a federal registration, or because the mark may not have been used on goods or services in federally regulated commerce.

State registrations are not given much weight in infringement actions because the applications are not examined for prior conflicts. But you generally can obtain a state registration in a matter of weeks and it will turn up on search reports so that subsequent users of the same or a similar mark will be alerted to the mark's existence. Moreover, a state registration constitutes evidence of a claim to exclusive trademark rights within all or at least part of the state, although that evidence is subject to rebuttal.

....

The Trademark Manual of Examining Procedure [TMEP] is a Patent and Trademark Office publication designed to give trademark examining attorneys and applicants guidance on the trademark examining process and relevant statutes, regulations and case law. The PTO has in recent years revised the TMEP frequently. It posts the current edition of the Manual online at its website. *See* Trademark Manual of Examining Procedure (April 2016), at https://tmep.uspto.gov/RDMS/TMEP/current.

Note: Advantages of Trademark Registration on the Principal Register

1. *Nationwide protection from the date of the application.* Once a mark is federally registered, the registrant's trademark rights relate back to the date of the trademark application, and give the registrant nationwide priority against a party adopting the

same or similar mark after the filing date of the registrant's application. If a mark is left unregistered, common law protection may be limited to those areas in which the mark had actually been in use or become known. If a registrant does not apply for registration immediately upon use in commerce (or does not file an intent-to-use application), and another user innocently adopts a similar mark following the registrant's use, but prior to registrant's application, the registrant's entitlement to use the mark in the entire United States may be limited by the area of use in which the other user in good faith exploited the mark prior to the registrant's application.

2. *Incontestability.* If the registered mark is used continuously for five years, it may become incontestable. This means that the statute limits the defenses alleged infringers may assert to certain specified defenses in the statute. The other defenses are no longer available. *See* Chapter 8[A], *infra.*

3. *Warning to others.* The registered mark will easily be found in trademark searches. Therefore, third parties should not blunder into adopting a similar mark for similar goods or services. Such blunders can result in expensive litigation if the second-comer refuses to relinquish its use of the mark. Moreover, if the mark is registered, its constructive date of first use will be the date the application for registration was filed. Because priority of use can be important in determining the rights of conflicting claimants to a mark, the registrant's constructive use date can make the difference in a priority conflict. This is particularly true for registrations made on the basis of intent to use applications. Moreover, the Patent and Trademark Office will protect a registered mark by refusing to register any other mark that the Trademark Examiner considers likely to cause consumer confusion.

4. *Barring imports.* Goods produced abroad bearing infringing marks may be blocked at Customs, provided that the registrant is a U.S. citizen, and is not related in certain ways to the producer of the imported goods.

5. *Protection against counterfeiting.* Enhanced remedies are available against counterfeiters of trademarks registered on the Principal Register. *See* Chapter 12[C], *infra.*

6. *Evidentiary advantages.* A registered mark is prima facie valid and enjoys other evidentiary presumptions, such as relieving the registrant of the burden of proof on nonfunctionality. *See International Watchman, Inc. v. NATO Strap Co.*, 62 F. Supp. 3d 674 (N.D. Ohio 2014) (denied defendant's summary judgment motion on the ground that plaintiff's NATO mark for watches was not generic; court relied on presumption of validity of plaintiff's registrations and insufficient rebuttal evidence proffered by defendant).

7. *Use of the R symbol, or of the phrases "Registered in U.S. Patent Office" or "U.S. Pat. Off." to denote federal registration.* This notice informs the public that proprietary rights are recognized in the mark. The notice can be of importance with respect to marks which some might consider descriptive, generic, or merely ornamental.

8. *Confirms ownership and validity.* Trademarks can be important factors in the sale of a product line or of a company itself. Trademark registration greatly simplifies auditing and clearing title.

9. *Basis of Foreign Filings.* A U.S. application or registration can form the basis of an International Registration. *See* Note on Madrid Protocol, *supra* this section. Additionally, a U.S. application can be used as a basis for Paris Convention filing priority in Paris Convention countries.

10. *Preemption of State Regulation.* 15 U.S.C. § 1121(b) [Lanham Act § 39(b)]:

> No state or other jurisdiction of the United States or any political subdivision or any agency thereof may require alteration of a registered mark, or require that additional trademarks, service marks, trade names, or corporate names that may be associated with or incorporated into the registered mark be displayed in the mark in a manner differing from the display of such additional trademarks, service marks, trade names or corporate names contemplated by the registered mark as exhibited in the certificate of registration issued by the United States Patent and Trademark Office.

This rarely-invoked provision preserves the integrity of federal trademarks from state law interference. In effect, the Lanham Act preempts state truth-in-labeling laws, when these would compel the registrant to change the trademark's presentation. The provision has been applied against state labeling measures that would have required alteration of trademarks, *see, e.g. Beatrice Foods Co. v. State of Wisconsin*, 223 U.S.P.Q. 75 (W.D. Wis. 1983) (challenge by producer of BUTTERMATCH margarine against state dairy protection regulation that barred use of word "butter" in label of product not containing butter).

State and local zoning laws have presented a source of § 39(b) challenges to state regulation. A locality's "aesthetic zoning" regulations may, for example, require all merchants to display their store logos in a uniform style and color scheme. If the merchant is a franchisee, and the aesthetic ordinance commands changes to the appearance of the source-identifying symbols (think of pink arches for a McDonalds outlet in a shopping center regulated under the ordinance) does the ordinance violate § 39(b)? A divided Ninth Circuit addressed this issue in *Blockbuster Videos, Inc. v. City of Tempe*, 141 F.3d 1295 (9th Cir. 1998), and held that Tempe's local zoning ordinances, which required Video Updates to use a different color scheme on an exterior sign in a Tempe shopping mall from its federally registered mark, violated § 1121(b). The dissenting opinion interpreted § 1121(b) more narrowly as prohibiting across-the-board restrictions on displays of registered marks, rather than restriction only of exterior signage in a particular location to conform to aesthetic zoning regulations. *See also Lisa's Party City, Inc. v. Town of Henrietta*, 185 F.3d 12 (2d Cir. 1999) (Second Circuit adopted interpretation in the *Blockbuster Videos* dissent and held a local ordinance that required coordinated exterior signage did not require "alteration" of a registered trademark in violation of section 39(b)).

Note: The Supplemental Register

In addition to the Principal Register, Section 23 of the Lanham Act, 15 U.S.C. § 1091, directs the Director to maintain a Supplemental Register. Marks "not registrable on the Principal Register" may be registered on the Supplemental Register if they are "capable of distinguishing the applicant's goods or services." So long as the mark is "capable" of distinctiveness, it need not in fact distinguish applicant's goods or services from those of others. Thus, terms that are descriptive or geographic, or are surnames, may find a home on the Supplemental Register.

Section 27 of the Lanham Act, 15 U.S.C. § 1095, provides: "Registration of a mark on the supplemental register shall not constitute an admission that the mark has not acquired distinctiveness." Nonetheless, does the amendment permit the argument that a supplemental registration constitutes an admission that the mark is not *inherently* distinctive? *See, e.g., Perma Ceram Enterprises, Inc. v. Preco Industries Ltd.*, 23 U.S.P.Q.2d 1134, 1137 n.11 (T.T.A.B. 1992); *In re Rosemount Inc.*, 86 U.S.P.Q.2d 1436 (T.T.A.B. 2008).

Under Section 23, a domestic applicant's mark is now eligible for supplemental registration upon lawful use in commerce. May an application based on intent-to-use be filed on the Supplemental Register? The intent-to-use regime applies only to the Principal Register. However, an intent-to-use application can be amended to the Supplemental Register upon the filing of an amendment to the application alleging use. Trademark Rule 2.75(b), 37 C.F.R. § 2.75(b). In addition, applications based on a foreign registration in the country of origin need not allege use in order to be eligible for supplemental registration. Section 44 of the Lanham Act, 15 U.S.C. § 1126, permits registration by foreign applicants upon a claim of bona fide intention to use the mark. Section 26 of the Lanham Act, 15 U.S.C. § 1094, explicitly provides that registrations on the Supplemental Register do not receive the same powerful statutory advantages as registrations on the Principal Register do, such as constituting prima facie evidence of validity of the mark, providing constructive notice and nationwide priority or providing a basis to stop infringing goods via Customs. Why then would applicants wish to register on the Supplemental Register? One reason is that the registration appears on search reports and may accordingly deter others from choosing a confusingly similar mark. Additionally, the PTO may cite a prior registration on the Supplemental Register against a mark considered confusingly similar. Finally, the registrant is permitted to use the registration notice and to sue in federal court.

Note: The Notice of Registration

Although use of a notice of registration is permissive, important benefits attach to use of a notice "by displaying with the mark the words 'Registered in U.S. Patent and Trademark Office' or 'Reg. U.S. Pat. & Tm. Off.' or the letter R enclosed within a circle, thus ®" 15 U.S.C. § 1111. Failure to use such notice results in a bar to an award of profits or damages in an infringement suit involving a registered trademark absent a finding that a defendant had actual notice of the registration. *Id.*

The language "displaying with the mark" was interpreted in *Kransco Mfg. Inc. v. Hayes Specialties Corp.*, 33 U.S.P.Q.2d 1999 (E.D. Mich. 1994), *aff'd in relevant part and vacated in part*, 77 F.3d 503 (Fed. Cir. 1996), which involved a registered trademark in the sinuous seam of a two-panel footbag. The ® notice followed the registered word mark HACKY SACK, which was also near the sinuous seam. The back side of the packaging stated: "HACKY SACK is a brand name and registered trademark of [plaintiff]."

Judge Churchill in *Kransco* noted:

> In the opinion of the Court, the plaintiff's footbag and package does a poor job of communicating to anyone that the encircled "R" refers to the sinuous seam as well as to the name "HACKY SACK," particularly in light of the statement on the package.
>
> The defendant, however, has provided the Court with no authority whatsoever for its position that a statutory notice should be used in connection with each of several federally registered marks on one product. The defendant cannot claim estoppel based upon the limited words on the back of the package because its managing officers deny knowledge of the existence of the plaintiff's product and package.
>
> As a matter of law, the encircled "R" on the plaintiff's footbag is displayed "with the mark" within the meaning of 15 U.S.C. § 1111 and the plaintiff would be entitled to recover profits even without proof that the defendant had actual notice of the registration.

Note: Maintenance and Renewal of Registration: Sections 8 and 9 of the Lanham Act

Section 8 of the Lanham Act, 15 U.S.C. § 1058, requires a registrant to file an affidavit that the mark is in use for at least some of the goods or services covered in the registration between the fifth and sixth year after the registration date (or within a six-month grace period thereafter for an additional fee). Goods or services not included in the use affidavit will be deleted from the registration. Absent any filing, the registration will be automatically cancelled by the PTO. The kind of "use" necessary is actual use in commerce, not mere token use designed nominally to preserve the mark. "Special circumstances" may excuse non-use of a mark where the registrant did not intend to abandon the mark. Examples of the "special circumstances" excusing non-use include governmental regulation or prohibition, and illness, fire or other catastrophe. *See* TMEP § 1604.11.

Section 9 of the Lanham Act, 15 U.S.C. § 1059, provides that "each registration may be renewed for periods of ten years from the end of the expiring period upon payment of the prescribed fee and the filing of a verified application therefor." The registrant is now also required to file an affidavit under Section 8 in each 10th year (or within a 6 month grace period) that the mark is still in use in commerce for at least some of the goods or services covered in the registration, and attach a specimen or facsimile showing current use of the mark every ten years after a registration issues. Any goods or services not included in the use affidavit will be deleted from the registration. Failure to file the renewal and use affidavit will result in the registration's being automatically cancelled by the PTO.

The chart on the following page summarizes the process of registration and maintenance for the five bases of trademark applications.

	1(a) Use	1(b) ITU	44(e) Foreign Registration	44(d) Foreign Application	66 Protocol Extension
Application	application includes 1st use dates & specimens	application states bona fide ITU mark in commerce	application states bona fide ITU & includes a copy of foreign registration	application states bona fide ITU & includes copy of foreign application	WIPO sends request for extension of Int'l. Reg.[1] to U.S. which states bona fide ITU
Examination	Office Action or approved for Publication	Office Action or approved for Publication	Office Action or approved for Publication	Office Action or approved for Publication then suspended pending foreign reg.	Office Action or approved for Publ.—18 mos. deadline to notify WIPO of refusal
Publication	Official Gazette	Official Gazette	Official Gazette	Official Gazette	Official Gazette
Opposition	either opposed successfully or reg. issues	either opposed successfully or Notice of Allowance issues	either opposed successfully or reg. issues	either opposed successfully or reg. issues if foreign reg. issues and is filed	either opposed successfully or Certificate of Extension of Protection issues[2]
Post Publication		S/U & specimens w/in 3 yrs. after N/A[3]—then Office Action or reg. issues			
Post Registration	§ 8 Use Aff. 5–6 yrs. after reg. (or w/in 6 mos. grace period)	§ 8 Use Aff. 5–6 yrs. after reg. (or w/in 6 mos. grace period)	§ 8 Use Aff. 5–6 yrs. after reg. (or w/in 6 mos. grace period)	§ 8 Use Aff. 5–6 yrs. after reg. (or w/in 6 mos. grace period)	§ 71 Use Aff. 5–6 yrs. after Cert. of Ext. of Protection (or 6 mos. grace period)
Renewal	§ 8 Use Aff. & renewal 9–10 yrs. after reg. (or 6 mos. grace period) & then every 10 yrs.	§ 8 Use Aff. & renewal 9–10 yrs. after reg. (or 6 mos. grace period) & then every 10 yrs.	§ 8 Use Aff. & renewal 9–10 yrs. after reg. (or 6 mos. grace period) & then every 10 yrs.	§ 8 Use Aff. & renewal 9–10 yrs. after reg. (or 6 mos. grace period) & then every 10 yrs.	§ 71 Use Aff. 9–10 yrs. after Cert. of Ext. (or 6 mos. grace period) & then every 10 yrs.[4]

1. If the underlying Basic Registration or Application in the home country on which the International Registration is based is cancelled in whole or in part within 5 years, the extension to the U.S. is similarly void or cancelled, but within 3 months, the applicant has the right of transformation under § 70(c) to file an application under § 1 or § 44 with the same priority filing date.

2. Extensions to oppose and oppositions against the Madrid extensions must be filed electronically—no amendments to grounds in oppositions are allowed.

3. An Applicant can seek extensions of time to file a Statement of Use in 6 month intervals after the Notice of Allowance. After the first extension, good cause must be stated in addition to a bona fide intent to use the mark.

4. The International Registration must be renewed through WIPO every 10 years. The section 71 use affidavit requirements are additional to maintain the U.S. extension and date from the Certificate of Extension of Protection rather than from the International Registration date.

B. Priority of ITUs and Applications Claiming Paris Convention Priority

Note: Constructive Use as of Filing Date

Every application, regardless of the basis, receives a constructive first use date as of the date of filing (or as of the date of filing of the underlying foreign application under the Paris Convention). Granting constructive first use to such applications where there has been no use in U.S. commerce can be important in establishing priority.

Section 7(c) of the Lanham Act provides:

Contingent on the registration of a mark on the principal register provided by this chapter, the filing of the application to register such mark shall constitute constructive use of the mark, conferring a right of priority, nationwide in effect, on or in connection with the goods or services specified in the registration against any other person except for a person whose mark has not been abandoned and who, prior to such filing—

(1) has used the mark;

(2) has filed an application to register the mark which is pending or has resulted in registration of the mark; or

(3) has filed a foreign application to register the mark on the basis of which he or she has acquired a right to priority, and timely files an application under section 1126(d) of this title to register the mark which is pending or has resulted in registration of the mark.

Larami Corp. v. Talk To Me Programs, Inc.

36 U.S.P.Q.2d 1840 (T.T.A.B. 1995)

By The Board:

[Talk To Me Programs, Inc. ("TTMP") filed an ITU application on July 31, 1990 to register the mark THE TOTALLY RAD SOAKER for toy water guns. Larami Corp. opposed, alleging that it had used the mark SUPER SOAKER for toy water guns. TTMP filed a civil action against Larami, claiming infringement because Larami's first use was after TTMP's constructive first use date based on its ITU filing date. Meanwhile, the Board suspended the opposition pending the civil action. The District Court granted Larami's summary judgment motion and dismissed TTMP's infringement claims. The District Court reasoned that since TTMP did not yet have a registration, it could not rely on its constructive first use date of its ITU application to support an infringement claim. Further, it could not establish prior common law rights in the mark. The District Court also concluded that TOTALLY RAD SOAKER was merely descriptive and had not acquired the requisite secondary meaning to be protectable. On appeal, the Second Circuit affirmed. The opposition proceeding then resumed. Larami moved for summary judgment claiming TOTALLY RAD SOAKER was merely descriptive as found by the court. Although the Board agreed that collateral estoppel applied to the issue of descriptiveness, it disagreed that it applied to the issue of secondary meaning.]

... [E]ven if its mark is merely descriptive, applicant contends that in seeking registration of its mark, rather than in asserting infringement of the same, applicant should not be required to show secondary meaning prior to use by opposer. Applicant argues that in this proceeding applicant is entitled to the benefit of the constructive use provisions of Section 7(c) and to rely upon this date to demonstrate priority of use. As a result, applicant argues, it need only show the acquisition of secondary meaning as of the present date. Thus applicant urges that opposer has failed to meet its burden of showing that no genuine issues of material fact remain or that opposer is entitled to summary judgment.

....

The interrelated issues of priority and distinctiveness (secondary meaning), ... are not so readily resolved. The Court found that TTMP could not establish priority because (1) it could not base its claim of priority on the filing date of its application for registration and (2) under Second Circuit law, a plaintiff charging infringement of a descriptive mark must establish that the mark had acquired secondary meaning prior to the first use by the alleged infringer, an impossible burden for TTMP, whose first actual use of the mark in commerce, other than a token use, was later than Larami's first use. These findings by the Court concerning priority, for purposes of the infringement action, are not binding for purposes of this opposition proceeding.

First of all, the Board and the Court treat differently the constructive use provisions of Section 7(c). In *Zirco Corp. v. American Telephone and Telegraph Co.*, 21 USPQ2d 1542 (TTAB 1991), the Board described the operation of the constructive use provision of Section 7(c) (added to the Lanham Act by the Trademark Law Revision Act of 1988) in inter partes proceedings before the Board. Relying upon the legislative history and commentaries thereon, as well as its own reading of Section 7(c) in conjunction with concurrent amendments to other portions of the Lanham Act implementing this provision, the Board held that the right of an intent-to-use applicant to rely upon its constructive use date in Board proceedings comes into existence with the filing of its intent-to-use application, and that the intent-to-use applicant can rely upon this date in an opposition for purposes of establishing priority (albeit entry of final judgment in favor of the intent-to-use applicant must be deferred until the mark is registered), if that applicant cannot prevail without establishing constructive use pursuant to Section 7(c). Thus, an intent-to-use applicant was held to be entitled, under this provision, to rely upon the filing date of its application in an opposition filed by a party alleging common law rights based on use prior to any actual use which might be asserted by the applicant [but after the filing date]. The Board pointed out that if the constructive use provision only came into play after the issuance of a registration, an intent-to-use applicant would never be able to defend its application in an opposition based on likelihood of confusion, brought by a third party asserting common law rights. Such was not, in the Board's view, the intent behind the adoption of the constructive use provision, since the legislative history clearly indicated the goal of fostering the filing of intent-to-use applications and giving an applicant under Section 1(b) superior rights over a subsequent user of a similar mark, provided the applicant's mark was ultimately used and registered. To require registration of an applicant's mark prior to realization of its rights under Section 7(c) would defeat the purpose of filing applications based on intent-to-use.

The District Court concluded that a different interpretation should be accorded to Section 7(c), when relied upon by an intent-to-use applicant bringing an infringement suit against a competitor. Under these circumstances the Court determined that the priority rights conferred by Section 7(c) were contingent upon registration of the mark and thus not available to TTMP, whose intent-to-use application remained pending. The Court explicitly pointed out that the Board's interpretation was rendered in the course of an opposition proceeding in which the party relying upon the contingency portion of Section 7(c), the common law user, was attempting to defeat registration of the mark filed by the intent-to-use applicant, whereas, in the action before it, the common law user was attempting to defend itself in an infringement suit brought by the intent-to-use applicant, prior to the registration of its mark.

We find no difficulty in reconciling these two interpretations of Section 7(c), depending upon the circumstances under which the provision has been invoked. In a proceeding before the Board, whose jurisdiction is limited solely to the registration of a party's mark, it would defeat the purpose of filing an intent-to-use application if an applicant were not able to rely upon its constructive use date in defending its right to registration, as pointed out in the *Zirco* decision. On the other hand, in a civil action involving a party's right to use a mark, such as TTMP's infringement action, it would not be equitable for an intent-to-use applicant to be entitled to rely upon a constructive use date prior to registration of its mark, and thus potentially prior to any use whatsoever, to defeat the common law rights of a first actual user of its mark.[7] Accordingly, in this proceeding before the Board, applicant is entitled

7. ... In the commentary provided for the final version of the amended Lanham Act by the U.S. Trademark Association, it was pointed out that although Sections 18, 21 and 24 were amended to defer entry of final judgment in intent-to-use cases originating before the Board, a similar provision was not included in Section 34, which is directed to injunctive relief in actions brought under Section 43(a). The reason given for this omission was the concern of the House Judiciary Committee that, if such a provision were included, the courts would be hearing cases not ripe for decision and applicants who have not perfected their rights would be filing suit. [Citation.] It is clear therefrom that Congress intended Section 7(c) to operate differently in the district courts than it does in proceedings before the Board.

Finally, we want to emphasize that, although in *Zirco* (as in the case now before us) it was the applicant for registration—that is, the party in the position of defendant—who sought to rely on the constructive use provisions of Section 7(c) to defeat the opposer's priority claim, a party in the position of opposer may, likewise, rely on the constructive use provisions of Section 7(c) to establish its priority for purposes of Section 2(d). An opposer may rely on Section 7(c) to establish priority if it owns a registration for the mark it is asserting under Section 2(d) or if it has filed an application for registration of that mark. We might put the matter more simply by saying that in proceedings before the Board the constructive use provisions of Section 7(c) may be used both defensively and offensively. (Of course, as we have noted, Section 7(c) provides that any judgment entered in favor of a party relying on constructive use—whether that party is in the position of plaintiff or defendant in a Board proceeding—is contingent upon the ultimate issuance of a registration to that party.)

to rely upon its constructive use date, namely, its filing date of July 31, 1990, and to assert priority of use based thereupon.

....

Moreover, in this opposition proceeding, if applicant establishes that its mark has acquired distinctiveness, it may, for purposes of establishing its priority, rely upon the filing date of its application.[9] Congress made Section 7(c) applicable to all applications for registration on the Principal Register. That statutory section does not bestow the benefits of constructive use on only those marks that are inherently distinctive and those marks that, though not inherently distinctive, had become distinctive as of the filing date of the application for registration. Nor are we willing to find such a limitation implicit in Section 7(c). Indeed, Section 2(f), in setting out the showing that the Commissioner may take as a prima facie case of distinctiveness, provides that

> [t]he Commissioner may accept as prima facie evidence that the mark has become distinctive, as used on or in connection with the applicant's goods in commerce, proof of substantially exclusive and continuous use therefor as a mark by the applicant in commerce *for the five years before the date on which the claim of distinctiveness is made.* (emphasis added)

Thus, a mark may be registered—and receive the benefits of constructive use under Section 7(c)—even if the claim of acquired distinctiveness was made after the filing date of the application and even if the use on which the claim of distinctiveness was predicated was made mostly after the filing date of the application.

Accordingly, opposer has failed to establish that no genuine issues of material fact remain with respect to the distinctiveness of applicant's mark. Applicant is entitled to an opportunity to plead and to prove, if it so desires, that its mark, though initially merely descriptive, has acquired secondary meaning. Moreover, applicant is correct in its arguments that, in demonstrating its right to registration, it is not restricted to any limitations on the time period in which it must show the acquisition of secondary meaning, but instead is entitled to prove the same as of the present date. Although applicant has not pleaded the acquisition of secondary meaning as an affirmative defense in its answer to the amended notice, the Board will allow applicant time to amend its pleadings to include allegations of this nature.

In summary, opposer's motion for summary judgment is granted as to the issue of descriptiveness, retrial being precluded on the basis of issue preclusion. Opposer's motion is denied as to the issue of secondary meaning, with applicant being allowed

9. The Board has held that, where neither party's mark in an opposition proceeding is inherently distinctive, priority lies with the party whose mark is the first to become distinctive through use in commerce. *Perma Ceram Enterprises Inc. v. Preco Industries Ltd.*, 23 USPQ2d 1134 (TTAB 1992). In *Perma Ceram*, the applicant had used its mark long prior to the filing date of its application for registration and claimed distinctiveness from a date long prior to the filing date of that application. Therefore, it was not relying on its constructive use date to establish priority. For that reason, we do not believe our decision in *Perma Ceram* is at odds with our present holding.

until twenty days from the date hereof to amend its answer to the amended notice to assert as an affirmative defense the acquired distinctiveness of its mark.

....

Questions

1. Is the justification of the different approaches by the Board and the courts to offensive use of an ITU application as set forth in *Larami Corp. v. Talk To Me Programs, Inc.* persuasive? Should an ITU applicant be able to obtain a contingent judgment in an infringement action based on its unperfected priority? *See Fila Sport S.p.A. v. Deadora America Inc.*, 21 U.S.P.Q.2d 1063 (N.D. Ill. 1991) (motion to dismiss infringement and unfair competition claims granted where, although ITU applicant's constructive first use date preceded defendant's use of a similar mark, it neither had a registration nor use in the U.S.); *cf. Warner Vision Ent. Inc. v. Empire Carolina, Inc.*, 101 F.3d 259 (2d Cir. 1996) (user of mark subsequent to constructive first use date of ITU applicant could not enjoin use by ITU applicant as such an injunction would prevent the ITU applicant from perfecting its superior priority in contradiction to the purpose of the ITU provisions). Is there anything an ITU applicant, such as in *Fila*, can do short of suing a user of an infringing mark prior to perfecting its registration?

2. Eventually, Talk to Me abandoned its application and Laramie registered the mark, which it had been using for long enough by then to have accumulated secondary meaning. Until Talk to Me decided not to use the mark, Laramie was using its mark at its peril. The majority of ITU applications don't mature to actual use and registration. What advice would you give to a client who discovers that another business has filed an ITU for a mark she has adopted, but that the other business hasn't yet made actual use?

Problems

1. Early Bird Corp. filed an intent-to-use application for EARLY BIRD Brand shampoo in January 2010. Early Bird had been testing the product and expected to release it within the next year. In May of 2011, the Patent and Trademark Office sent Early Bird a notice of allowance. Sparrow Corp. began using the mark EARLY BIRD for shampoo on June 1, 2011. On October 15, 2011, Early Bird Corp. began selling large quantities of EARLY BIRD shampoo in interstate commerce and filed a statement of actual use with the PTO. What are the respective rights of Early Bird and Sparrow?

2. Same as above, except that Early Bird Corp., did not begin selling large quantities of EARLY BIRD shampoo in interstate commerce until January 2016. Beginning in April of 2014, however, having filed for all available extensions, Early Bird Corp. test markets the shampoo in interstate commerce.

3. Same as #2, except that, instead of test marketing, Early Bird shipped two cases of a different brand shampoo, overlaid with EARLY BIRD labels, in interstate commerce.

4. Ginger Spirits, Inc. filed an intent-to-use application on June 28, 1993 for the mark SOUTH BEACH BEER for "alcoholic beverages, namely beer." Ginger Spirits alleges that it first used the mark in commerce on October 4, 1994. The registration was issued on March 7, 1995.

Frank Salacuse filed an intent-to-use application on March 22, 1993 for the mark SOUTH BEACH for "brewed drinks, namely, beer and ale." Between March and August of 1993, Salacuse filed a total of 8 intent-to-use applications for the mark SOUTH BEACH. These applications were for products including wine and wine drinks; frozen drinks; pencil cases and other desk accessories; luggage; lingerie; furniture; motor vehicles; plastic sports bottles, portable insulated coolers, and insulated lunch boxes; school notebooks, calendars, diaries, and address books. Salacuse has also filed intent-to-use applications for SOBE and SO-BE-IT!, which are variations of SOUTH BEACH. With respect to these expanded applications, Salacuse did not have any documents bearing upon or supporting his intention to use the SOUTH BEACH mark in commerce.

In 1997, Salacuse filed a petition to cancel respondent's registration, alleging priority of use and likelihood of confusion under Trademark Act Section 2(d).

What affirmative defenses can Ginger Spirits assert? Does it matter that at the time he filed suit, Salacuse had not used the mark in commerce? Do the other seven intent-to-use applications have any bearing on this case? What effect does his lack of documentary evidence have on his claim of bona fide intent? *See Salacuse v. Ginger Spirits*, 44 U.S.P.Q.2d 1415 (T.T.A.B. 1997); *Commodore Electronics Ltd. v. CBM Kabushiki Kaisha*, 26 U.S.P.Q.2d 1503 (T.T.A.B. 1993); *Dunn Computer Corp. v. Loudcloud, Inc.*, 133 F. Supp. 2d 823 (E.D. Va. 2001) (350 ITU applications of words incorporating the term "cloud"); *Boston Red Sox Baseball Club LP v. Sherman*, 88 U.S.P.Q.2d 1581 (T.T.A.B. 2008).

5. WebStream Inc. operates websites offering website design services under the domain names web-stream.com and web-stream.net. The domain names were registered on July 14, 2008; the websites were up and running by July 24, 2008. On August 3, 2008, SongNetwork filed an ITU application for WEB STREAM for streaming music services, and began use in September 2008. WebStream's websites and domain name registration had not appeared on the trademark search report commissioned by SongNetwork, but SongNetwork learned of WebStream's sites shortly after filing its ITU applications. SongNetwork requested that WebStream include on its websites a disclaimer of affiliation with SongNetwork, but WebStream refused, and, after converting the Webstream.com site to offer music streaming services, ultimately initiated a trademark infringement action against SongNetwork. WebStream's websites have generated no income, and received no visitors when they first went up. WebStream has been unable to attract traffic to the websites through well-placed links on the major search engines because SongNetwork had already obtained those placements for its websites. Who has prior use of the WebStream mark? *See Burns v. RealNetworks*, 359 F. Supp. 2d 1187 (W.D. Okla. 2004).

Compagnie Gervais Danone v. Precision Formulations, LLC

89 U.S.P.Q.2d 1251 (T.T.A.B. 2009)

BY THE BOARD:

Precision seeks to register the mark FRUITOLOGY for various cosmetic products in International Class 3, various nutritional goods and medicated skin creams in International Class 5, and various beverage goods in International Class 32.

Danone has moved for summary judgment ... on its claim of priority and likelihood of confusion regarding Precision's nutritional goods of International Class 5 and the goods of International Class 32. Danone has not opposed Precision's application to register the mark in International Class 3.

....

There are no questions as to standing or similarity of the marks and goods in these cases, as the parties' submissions show they have filed trademark applications for nearly identical marks, for overlapping or legally identical goods, and each party has claimed there is a likelihood of confusion. Moreover, in its answer to the notice of opposition Precision admitted that the parties' marks are "identical in sight, sound, connotation and commercial impression" and that "there is direct overlap between some" of the parties' goods. The parties have therefore effectively conceded that confusion is likely between the opposed goods in each opposed class. The sole issue that remains is one of priority.

....

We begin by looking at Precision's priority date. A party that has filed an intent-to-use application may rely on the filing date of its application to establish priority. *See Larami Corp. v. Talk To Me Programs Inc.*, 36 USPQ2d 1840, 1845 n.7 (TTAB 1995) (constructive use provisions may be used both defensively and offensively to establish priority); *see also, Zirco Corp. v. American Telephone & Telegraph Co.*, 21 USPQ2d 1542, 1544 (TTAB 1991) (right to rely on constructive use date comes into existence with filing of intent-to-use application). Precision may, therefore, claim priority back to the February 21, 2007 date on which it filed the intent-to-use application. Precision has not relied on any earlier date for priority purposes.

We next consider Danone's priority date. We note that Danone filed its application on May 22, 2007 pursuant to Section 66, 15 U.S.C. § 1141f, of the Trademark Act.[3] Section 66(b), 15 U.S.C. § 1141f(b), provides that a Section 66(a) application:

> ... shall constitute constructive use of the mark, conferring the same rights as those specified in section 7(c), as of the earliest of the following:
>
> (1) The international registration date, if the request for extension of protection was filed in the international application.

---

3. The filing date of Danone's § 66(a) application is the international registration date of May 22, 2007. *See* TMEP § 1940.01(b).

(2) The date of recordal of the request for extension of protection, if the request for extension of protection was made after the international registration date.

(3) The date of priority claimed pursuant to section 67.

Section 67 of the Trademark Act, 15 U.S.C. § 1141g, states that an applicant is entitled to claim a date of priority when it holds an international registration, makes a request for extension of protection (application) to the U.S., includes a claim of priority based on a right of priority under Article 4 of the Paris Convention for the Protection of Industrial Property, and the date of the international registration is within six months of the filing date of the application underlying the international registration. Danone's International Registration No. 0930814 issued May 22, 2007. The International Registration is based on an underlying French application (No. 06 3 467 672) filed December 6, 2006, which issued on May 11, 2007, as French Registration No. 06 3 467 672. Danone claimed priority based on the December 6, 2006 filing date of the French application. Thus, pursuant to Sections 66(b) and 67, Danone is entitled to a priority date of December 6, 2006. *See General Motors Corp. v. Aristide & Co., Antiquaire de Marques*, 87 USPQ2d 1179, 1181 (TTAB 2008).

Because Danone's application has an effective filing date of December 6, 2006, and that date is earlier than Precision's filing date of February 21, 2007, Danone may rely on its effective filing date to establish priority. Thus, we find that there are no genuine issues of material fact as to the issue of priority.

Accordingly, Danone's motion for summary judgment is granted, contingent upon application Serial No. 79041120 maturing into a registration.[4] If application Serial No. 79041120 matures into a registration, the Board will enter judgment against Precision, sustain the opposition, and refuse registration to Precision for International Classes 5 and 32.

Question

If Precision rather than Danone had priority and received a contingent judgment, Danone could potentially be forced to wait up to 3 years if Precision submitted all available extensions of time to file a statement of use. After that time, it might nevertheless allow the application to go abandoned. Would it be fair to make Danone wait so long before it knew whether it could register its mark? A study of the outcome of applications filed from 1981 through 2007 showed that the overall grant rate for use-based applications was 75% as compared with 37% of intent to use applications from 1989 through 2007. B. Beebe, *Is the Trademark Office a Rubber Stamp?*, 48

4. Section 66(b), 15 U.S.C. § 1141f(b), confers the same rights as those specified in Section 7(c) of the Trademark Act, 15 U.S.C. § 1057(c). Section 7(c) provides that filing an application for registration on the Principal Register establishes constructive use and nationwide priority, contingent upon issuance of a registration. Thus, we do not enter judgment at this time, but rather grant Danone's summary judgment motion contingent on the issuance of a registration in application Serial No. 79041120.

HOUSTON L. REV. 751 (2011). Given the much lower success rate for ITU applications, is it fair to make others desirous of adopting a similar mark wait potentially more than 3 years to see if such rights will be perfected?* What would be the alternative(s)?

Problems

Consider the following problems: who has priority and why?

1. On January 10, 2016, Koala Corp., an Australian company, filed an application in Australia for OUTDOORS for beer. On January 15, 2016, Armadillo Corp, a U.S. company, filed an intent-to-use application in the U.S. Patent and Trademark Office for OUTDOORS for beer. On March 1, 2016, Armadillo began to promote the impending arrival on the U.S. market of its OUTDOORS beer. On April 15, 2016, Koala began selling OUTDOORS beer in the U.S. On May 1, 2016, Armadillo began selling its OUTDOORS beer, and filed its Statement of Use in the PTO. On May 10, 2016, Koala filed a trademark application in the PTO citing its January 10 Australian filing. If Armadillo opposes issuance of Koala's registration:

a. Armadillo will prevail because it filed first in the U.S.

b. Armadillo will prevail because it has prior analogous use in the U.S.

c. Koala will prevail because it used first in the U.S.

d. Koala will prevail because it filed first.

2. Same facts as #1 above, except that Armadillo began promoting the arrival of its OUTDOORS beer on January 1, 2016.

a. Armadillo will prevail because it filed first in the U.S.

b. Armadillo will prevail because it has prior analogous use in the U.S.

c. Koala will prevail because it used first in the U.S.

d. Koala will prevail because it filed first.

3. Same facts as #1 above, except that Armadillo first sold its OUTDOORS beer on April 1, 2016.

a. Armadillo will prevail because it filed first in the U.S.

b. Armadillo will prevail because it has prior analogous use in the U.S.

c. Armadillo will prevail because it used first in the U.S.

d. Koala will prevail because it filed first.

4. Same facts as #1 above, except that Koala does not file in the PTO until July 15, 2016.

a. Armadillo will prevail because it filed first in the U.S.

b. Armadillo will prevail because it has prior analogous use in the U.S.

---

* *Editors' Note:* In fact, Danone's registration issued without proving use as it was based on a Madrid extension. The registration was cancelled in 2015 for failure to file the required declaration of use.

c. Koala will prevail because it used first in the U.S.

d. Koala will prevail because it filed first.

5. Same facts as #4 above, except that Koala began selling its OUTDOORS beer in the U.S. on January 1, 2016.

a. Armadillo will prevail because it filed first in the U.S.

b. Armadillo will prevail because it has prior analogous use in the U.S.

c. Koala will prevail because it used first in the U.S.

d. Koala will prevail because it filed first.

C. Bars to Registration

1. Section 2(a) of the Lanham Act: Immoral, Scandalous, Disparaging or Deceptive Matter and False Suggestion of a Connection

Section 2(a) of the Lanham Act prohibits registration of a mark that

> (a) consists of or comprises immoral, deceptive, or scandalous matter, or matter which may disparage or falsely suggest a connection with persons, living or dead, institutions, beliefs, or national symbols, or bring them into contempt, or disrepute....

Proof of distinctiveness cannot avail an applicant who is refused registration under Section 2(a); the bar is absolute. The four distinctive prongs of Section 2(a)—immoral or scandalous, disparaging, deceptive and false suggestion of a connection—are discussed below.

a. Immoral, Scandalous or Disparaging Marks

In Re Fox

702 F.3d 633 (Fed. Cir. 2012)

DYK, CIRCUIT JUDGE:

Marsha Fox appeals from a decision of the Trademark Trial and Appeal Board ("Board") affirming the refusal of the examiner to register her mark. The Board concluded that the mark was unregistrable under 15 U.S.C. § 1052(a). We affirm, holding that a mark that creates a double entendre falls within the proscription of § 1052(a) where, as here, one of its meanings is clearly vulgar.

BACKGROUND

I

Section 2 of the Lanham Act, as amended, provides that "[n]o trademark by which the goods of the applicant may be distinguished from the goods of others shall be refused registration on the principal register on account of its nature unless it[] (a) [c]onsists of or comprises immoral, deceptive, or scandalous matter." 15 U.S.C. § 1052.

... This court and its predecessor have long assumed that the prohibition "is not an attempt to legislate morality, but, rather, a judgment by the Congress that [scandalous] marks not occupy the time, services, and use of funds of the federal government." *In re Mavety Media Grp. Ltd.*, 33 F.3d 1367, 1374 (Fed. Cir. 1994) (quotation marks omitted). Because a refusal to register a mark has no bearing on the applicant's ability to use the mark, we have held that § 1052(a) does not implicate the First Amendment rights of trademark applicants. *See id.*

... [W]hat constitutes "immoral ... or scandalous matter" has evolved over time. *See id.* at 1372. The formal legal framework, however, has remained consistent: in order to refuse a mark, "the [Patent and Trademark Office (PTO)] must demonstrate that the mark is 'shocking to the sense of truth, decency, or propriety; disgraceful; offensive; disreputable; ... giving offense to the conscience or moral feelings; ... [or] calling out [for] condemnation.'" *Id.* at 1371 (second and third alterations in original) (quoting *In re Riverbank Canning Co.*, 95 F.2d 327, 328, 25 C.C.P.A. 1028, 1938 Dec. Comm'r Pat. 442 (CCPA 1938)).... [T]he PTO may prove scandalousness by establishing that a mark is "vulgar." *In re Boulevard Entm't, Inc.*, 334 F.3d 1336, 1340 (Fed. Cir. 2003). This demonstration must be made "in the context of contemporary attitudes," "in the context of the marketplace as applied to only the goods described in [the] application," and "from the standpoint of not necessarily a majority, but a substantial composite of the general public." *Mavety*, 33 F.3d at 1371 (quotation marks omitted).

Where the meaning of a mark is ambiguous, mere dictionary evidence of a possible vulgar meaning may be insufficient to establish the vulgarity of the mark. *See id.* at 1373–74. But where it is clear from dictionary evidence "that the mark[] as used by [the applicant] in connection with the [products] described in [the] application" invokes a vulgar meaning to a substantial composite of the general public, the mark is unregistrable. *See Boulevard*, 334 F.3d at 1341.

II

The mark at issue here has two parts: a literal element, consisting of the words COCK SUCKER, and a design element, consisting of a drawing of a crowing rooster. Since 1979, Fox has used this mark to sell rooster-shaped chocolate lollipops, which she "displays ... in retail outlets in small replicas of egg farm collecting baskets to emphasize the country farmyard motif." The consumers targeted by Fox's business are, primarily, fans of the University of South Carolina and Jacksonville State University, both of which employ gamecocks as their athletic mascots.

In September 2001, Fox applied to register her mark for use in connection with "[c]hocolate suckers molded in the shape of a rooster." ... In December 2001, the PTO examiner determined that the mark "consists of or comprises immoral or scandalous matter," and is therefore unregistrable under § 1052(a). Specifically, the examiner found that a dictionary defined "cocksucker" as "someone who performs an act of fellatio."

In June 2002, Fox filed a response, noting that that "Webster's Dictionary defines ... a cock as a rooster, and ... a sucker as a lollipop," and asserting that these non-vulgar definitions, which match both the product design and the design element of the mark, are "more relevant" than the vulgar definition....

In July 2008, ... the PTO issued a final refusal. The examiner conceded that Fox had presented "evidence potentially supporting an equally relevant non-scandalous meaning," but concluded that "due to the strong meaning of 'cock-sucker' in society in general," a "substantial composite of the general public will ... assign the scandalous meaning to the wording/mark."

Fox filed a motion for reconsideration, in which she clarified that "the intended term to be trademarked was COCK SUCKER [(with a space)], not COCKSUCKER," and included a revised image of her mark in which the two words were clearly separated. Fox protested that by "driv[ing the words] together," the examiner had "stripp[ed] the mark of any possibility of double entendre from which the relevant humor of the mark is derived," and also reiterated that the rooster design was intended to "guid[e] the potential purchaser to the less risqué of the two definitions."

In August 2009, the examiner responded, noting that "COCK is defined ... as '*penis*,' and SUCKER as, '*one that sucks*,'" and that both words are considered vulgar "as used in context." Conceding that this vulgar meaning is not the primary meaning of "cock," the examiner asserted that "taking COCK in context with SUCKER, the primary meaning of this wording as a whole is 'one who sucks a penis,'" and that "the strong and commonly known meaning of COCKSUCKER in the general public" ensures that the two component words, when used together, will "un-equivocal[ly]" assume their vulgar meanings....

....

Fox appealed to the Board, which affirmed the examiner's refusal.... The Board concluded that "[t]he word portion of applicant's mark..., when used in connection with applicant's products, creates a double entendre[, where] one meaning is one who performs fellatio[] and the other meaning is a rooster lollipop." The Board noted that "[t]he term 'Cocksucker' is uniformly identified as a vulgar term in dictionaries," and "g[a]ve very little weight to [Fox's] argument [that] COCK SUCKER has a different meaning than COCKSUCKER." The Board concluded that "the evidence supports the fact that the term COCK SUCKER is vulgar and, therefore, is precluded from registration under [§ 1052(a)]."

Fox timely appealed....

Discussion

....

I

Fox first argues that the Board lacked substantial evidence to support its finding that her mark has a vulgar meaning. Properly interpreted, Fox argues, the literal element of her mark means *only* "rooster lollipop."

This argument is without merit. As an initial matter, Fox concedes that "cocksucker" is a vulgar term in its common usage, and the dictionary evidence is devoid of an alternate, non-vulgar definition for that word. Fox urges, however, that "[i]n the present case, the space between the words makes all the difference." However, Fox concedes that a mark's "sound" is central to its "commercial impression" for purposes of § 1052. Fox, moreover, has admitted that her mark at least in part has a vulgar meaning. She acknowledged that "the ... humor of the mark is derived" from "[the] possibility of [a] double entendre," consisting of a vulgar and a non-vulgar meaning. At oral argument, she conceded that her mark, if used to sell sweaters, would be unregistrable as vulgar. We think that the Board did not err in concluding that the distinction between COCKSUCKER and COCK SUCKER is a distinction without a difference. So too the association of COCK SUCKER with a poultry-themed product does not diminish the vulgar meaning—it merely establishes an additional, non-vulgar meaning and a double entendre. This is not a case in which the vulgar meaning of the mark's literal element is so obscure or so faintly evoked that a context that amplifies the non-vulgar meaning will efface the vulgar meaning altogether. Rather, the mark is precisely what Fox intended it to be: a double entendre, meaning both "rooster lollipop" and "one who performs fellatio."

II

....

[T]here is no requirement in the statute that a mark's vulgar meaning must be the only relevant meaning—or even the most relevant meaning. Rather, as long as a "substantial composite of the general public" perceives the mark, in context, to have a vulgar meaning, the mark as a whole "consists of *or comprises* ... scandalous matter." *See* 15 U.S.C. § 1052(a) (emphasis added); *Boulevard*, 334 F.3d at 1340. The word "comprises," at the time of the statute's enactment in 1905, meant "includes." *See Webster's Academic Dictionary* 121 (Springfield, Mass., G. & C. Merriam Co. 1895). Congress thus chose to extend the prohibition not only to marks that "[c]onsist[]

of … scandalous matter," but also to marks that *include* scandalous matter. Fox concedes that the mark's effect as a humorous double entendre requires the consumer to "understand[ ]" the risqué as well as the banal meaning of the mark. We therefore see no reason why the PTO is required to prove anything more than the existence of a vulgar meaning to a substantial composite of the general public in order to justify its refusal.

Nor do we agree with Fox that the precedent excludes double entendres from the statutory bar. Fox attempts to derive this rule from two of our cases: *Mavety*, 33 F.3d 1367, [citation].

In *Mavety*, the court considered the mark BLACK TAIL as applied to "an adult entertainment magazine featuring photographs of both naked and scantily-clad African-American women." *Mavety*, 33 F.3d at 1368–69. The Board affirmed the examiner's refusal to register the mark, citing a vulgar dictionary definition of "tail" as "a female sexual partner." *Id.* at 1369–70. The applicant appealed, citing the ambiguity created by the presence of two alternative, non-vulgar meanings: "a woman's rear end," and "a type of evening coat … worn by men at formal occasions." *Id.* The court reversed, holding that "[i]n view of the existence of … an alternate, non-vulgar definition" (a woman's rear end), the Board erred by refusing registration based solely on the existence of a vulgar dictionary definition, without identifying any "[extrinsic] evidence as to which of these definitions the substantial composite would choose." *Id.* at 1373–74. Nowhere in its opinion did the court describe the constellation of meanings at issue as a "double entendre"; to the contrary, it described the different meanings as "alternate[s]." *Id. Mavety* is thus a case about ambiguous marks, and does not control a case, such as this one, in which the conceded effect of the mark is to invoke a "double meaning." [Citation.]

….

We recognize that there are "whimsical" and humorous aspects to Fox's mark. But the fact that something is funny does not mean that it cannot be "scandalous." Indeed, the Supreme Court in *Pacifica*, in determining that the use of the word "cocksucker" is generally patently "indecent" under 18 U.S.C. § 1464, made a point of noting that "[t]he transcript of [humorist George Carlin's] recording … indicates frequent laughter from the audience." *FCC v. Pacifica Found.*, 438 U.S. 726, 729 (1978).

Nothing in this decision precludes Fox from continuing to sell her merchandise under the mark at issue, or from seeking trademark protection for some other, otherwise registrable element of her product's design, dress, or labeling. If Fox is correct that the mark at issue "bring[s] [nothing] more than perhaps a smile to the face of the prospective purchaser," then the market will no doubt reward her ingenuity. But this does not make her mark registrable.

….

Conclusion

We find that substantial evidence supports the Board's determination that Fox's mark, taken as a whole and in context, has a vulgar meaning that will be perceived by a substantial composite of the general public. The Board did not err in concluding that this finding is sufficient to establish that the mark "[c]onsists or comprises ... scandalous matter" within the meaning of 15 U.S.C. § 1052(a), and is not registrable.

AFFIRMED

Questions

1. In concluding that COCK SUCKER would be perceived as vulgar by a substantial portion of the public, is it adequate to rely exclusively on dictionary definitions? Should the type of evidence required be different for a Trademark Examiner than for an opposer?

2. Did the court in *In re Fox* consider applicant's target group of fans of two universities' teams in determining the vulgarity of the COCK SUCKER design mark for lollipops? Should it? In stating that "We recognize that there are 'whimsical' and humorous aspects to Fox's mark. But the fact that something is funny does not mean that it cannot be 'scandalous,'" did the Federal Circuit fail to consider whether, for the likely purchasers of the goods, the humor would outweigh the mark's vulgarity?

3. The meaning of a mark to a substantial composite of the public must be evaluated in the context of the goods. In *In re Fox*, the goods were lollipops in the shape of a rooster, and Fox's mark included a depiction of a rooster crowing. Given these goods and the design component of Fox's mark, did the Federal Circuit correctly conclude that the vulgar meaning should preclude registration?

4. The Federal Circuit in *Fox* noted that its decision did not stop Fox from using her mark, just from registering it. Recall the advantages of registration discussed *supra* this Chapter. Does the decision adequately justify depriving applicant of these advantages?

In *Harjo v. Pro-Football, Inc.*, 30 U.S.P.Q.2d 1828 (T.T.A.B. 1994), the Board found that the football team's REDSKINS marks should be cancelled as the term is disparaging to a substantial composite of Native Americans and was so at the time the registrations issued, the oldest of which dates back to 1967. A long saga ensued, starting with Pro-Football's appeal to the D.C. district court. Ultimately, the D.C. Circuit found that the cancellation action was barred by laches. *See Pro Football v.* Harjo, 565 F.3d 880 (D.C. Cir. 2009), *infra* Chapter 8[A][2][d]. Undeterred, another group of Native Americans (who were younger than the Harjo Native American petitioners and thus who reached their majority later for laches purposes) filed another petition to cancel the REDSKINS registrations. The Board once again found that the term is disparaging and rejected the laches defense and found that the registrations should be cancelled. *Blackhorse v. Pro-Football, Inc.*, 111 U.S.P.Q.2d (T.T.A.B. 2014). Pro-Football appealed the case to the Eastern District of Virginia and challenged the constitutionality of section 2(a) as violative of the First Amendment, due process and the Takings Clause, and as void for vagueness. The district court rejected these claims and a laches claim as a matter of law and addressed the merits of disparagement in the following case.

Blackhorse v. Pro-Football, Inc.

112 F. Supp. 3d 439 (E.D. Va. 2015)

Lee, United States District Judge.

....

The TTAB has established a two-part test to determine whether a mark contains matter that "may disparage." The parties agree that the test in this case is as follows:

1. What is the meaning of the matter in question, as it appears in the marks and as those marks are used in connection with the goods and services identified in the registrations?

2. Is the meaning of the marks one that may disparage Native Americans?

[Citations.] Here, the registration dates are 1967, 1974, 1978, and 1990.

When answering the second question, ... courts should look to the views of Native Americans, not those of the general public. Moreover, Blackhorse Defendants are only required to show that the marks "may disparage" a "substantial composite" of Native Americans. A substantial composite is not necessarily a majority. [Citations.]

....

1. The Meaning of the Matter in Question is a Reference to Native Americans

The Court finds that the meaning of the matter in question in all six Redskins Marks—the term "redskins" and derivatives thereof—is a reference to Native Americans. PFI admits that "redskins" refers to Native Americans. The team has consistently associated itself with Native American imagery. First, two of the Redskins Marks contain an image of a man in profile that alludes to Native Americans, including one that also has a spear that alludes to Native Americans. Second, the team's helmets contain an image of a Native American in profile. Third, the team's marching band wore Native American headdresses as part of their uniforms from at least 1967–1990. Fourth, ... the cheerleaders, the "Redskinettes," also dressed in Native American garb and wore black braided-hair wigs. Lastly, Washington Redskins' press guides displayed Native American imagery.

....

... The Court ... finds that because PFI has made continuous efforts to associate its football team with Native Americans during the relevant time period, the meaning of the matter in question is a reference to Native Americans.

2. The Redskins Marks "May Disparage" a Substantial Composite of Native Americans During the Relevant Time Period

The Court finds that the meaning of the marks is one that "may disparage" a substantial composite of Native Americans in the context of the "Washington Redskins" football team. The relevant period for the disparagement inquiry is the time at which the marks were registered. Here, the Court focuses on the period between 1967 and 1990.... [T]hree categories of evidence are weighed to determine whether a term may "disparage": (1) dictionary definitions and accompanying editorial designations;

(2) scholarly, literary, and media references; and (3) statements of individuals or group leaders of the referenced group regarding the term. [Citations.]

....

a. Dictionary Evidence

First, the record evidence contains dictionary definitions and accompanying designations of "redskins" that weigh in favor of finding that the Redskins Marks consisted of matter that "may disparage" a substantial composite of Native Americans when each of the six marks was registered. Dictionary evidence is commonly considered when deciding if a term is one that "may disparage." [Citations.]

The record contains several dictionaries defining "redskins" as a term referring to North American Indians and characterizing "redskins" as offensive or contemptuous ...

....

b. Scholarly, Literary, and Media References

....

Here, ... the Court finds that the scholarly, literary, and media references evidence weighs in favor of finding that the Redskins Marks ... "may disparage" a substantial composite of Native Americans between 1967 and 1990. For example, as early as 1911, sources such as Encyclopedia Britannica contemplated the poor standing of the term "redskins." The Court finds that Encyclopedia Britannica is a well-respected source....

Prior to the first mark's registration in 1967, there were two renowned journals and an Encyclopedia Britannica reference that illustrate the term's disfavor among Native Americans. Taken altogether, the Court finds that these three pieces of evidence establish that in 1967, ... evidence existed that showed that the Redskins Marks consisted of matter that "may disparage" a substantial composite of Native Americans during the relevant time period.

c. Statements of Individuals or Group Leaders

Third, the record evidence contains statements of Native American individuals or leaders of Native American groups that weigh in favor of finding that the Redskins Marks consisted of matter that "may disparage" a substantial composite of Native Americans during the relevant time period....

....

Additional evidence that the marks consisted of matter that "may disparage" is found in NCAI Resolution.... NCAI bills itself as "the oldest and largest intertribal organization nationwide representative of, and advocate for national, regional, and local tribal concerns." The [1993] resolution provided, in pertinent part, that, "[T]he term REDSKINS is not and has never been one of respect, but instead has always been and continues to be a pejorative, derogatory, denigrating, offensive, scandalous, contemptuous, disreputable, disparaging and racist designation for Native American[s]." The Court finds that this resolution is probative of NCAI's constituent members' collective opinion of the term "redskin" and PFI's marks for many years, including when the last REDSKINS mark was registered. [Citation.]

PFI objects to this evidence ... because the resolution was passed outside of the relevant time period. However, ... this is just like any other testimony from individuals that was taken after the fact: witnesses testify about what they perceived in the past. PFI may challenge the weight this evidence is afforded but the words of the resolution are indisputable: this national organization of Native Americans declared that the term "REDSKINS" has always been derogatory, offensive, and disparaging.... [T]he Court ... finds the resolution is probative ...

....

Here, the Court finds that the record contains evidence ... demonstrating that between 1967 and 1990, the Redskins Marks consisted of matter that "may disparage" a substantial composite of Native Americans. The dictionary evidence included multiple definitions describing the term "redskin" in a negative light, including one from 1898—almost seventy years prior to the registration of the first Redskins Mark—characterizing "redskin" as "often contemptuous." The record evidence also includes references in renowned scholarly journals and books showing that "redskin" was offensive prior to 1967. Encyclopedia Britannica described its poor repute in 1911. The record evidence also shows that in 1972 NCAI a National Native American organization ... sent its president to accompany leaders of other Native American organizations at a meeting with the president of PFI to demand that the team's name be changed. NCAI also passed a resolution which provided that it has found the term and team name "Redskins" to be derogatory, offensive, and disparaging.

... [T]he case law is clear: when all three categories contain evidence that a mark consists of matter that "may disparage" a substantial composite of the referenced group, the TTAB and the Federal Circuit have denied or cancelled the mark's registration.

This remains true even when there is also dictionary evidence that does not characterize the term as offensive, literary references using the term in a non-disparaging fashion, and statements from members of the referenced group demonstrating that they do not think the mark consists of matter that "may disparage." That is because Section 2(a) does not require a finding that every member of the referenced group thinks that the matter "may disparage." Nor does it mandate a showing that a majority of the referenced group considers the mark one that consists of matter that "may disparage." Instead, Section 2(a) allows for the denial or cancellation of a registration of any mark that consists of or comprises matter that "may disparage" a substantial composite of the referenced group.

The Court finds that Blackhorse Defendants have shown by a preponderance of the evidence that there is no genuine issue of material fact as to the "may disparage" claim: the record evidence shows that the term "redskin," in the context of Native Americans and during the relevant time period, was offensive and one that "may disparage" a substantial composite of Native Americans, "no matter what the goods or services with which the mark is used." [Citation.] "Redskin" certainly retains this meaning when used in connection with PFI's football team; a team that has always associated itself with Native American imagery, with nothing being more emblematic of this association than the use of a Native American profile on the helmets of each member of the football team.

Accordingly, the Court finds that the Redskins Marks consisted of matter that "may disparage" a substantial composite of Native Americans during the relevant time period, 1967–1990, and must be cancelled. Also, consistent with the parties' concession that Section 2(a)'s "may disparage" and "contempt or disrepute" provisions use the same legal analysis, the Court further finds that the Redskins Marks consisted of matter that bring Native Americans into "contempt or disrepute." Thus, Blackhorse Defendants are entitled to summary judgment....

....

Questions

1. The measure of scandalous and immoral marks is the perception of a substantial composite of the general public; whereas, marks disparaging to a particular group are viewed through the lens of a substantial composite of that group. What if the disparaged group consists of a religion with 1,000 adherents, will the negative perceptions of 400 of them be sufficient to block a registration?

2. Where there is conflicting evidence as to the perception of the term HEEB as disparaging or not among different groups within the Jewish community, what should be the measure of a substantial composite of the referenced group? Should it matter that the applicant is targeting its goods/services to the group that does not regard the term as offensive or disparaging? *See In re Heeb Media*, 89 U.S.P.Q.2d 1071 (T.T.A.B. 2008).

3. *Blackhorse* involves registrations that date back to the 1960s. The Board and district court analyzed the meaning of the REDSKINS marks as of the time the owner registered them. Does this make sense if the meaning changes over time?

4. Pro-Football has appealed the *Blackhorse* decision to the Fourth Circuit and has renewed its claims of the unconstitutionality of the disparagement prong of Section 2(a). How should the Fourth Circuit rule? Consider how the Federal Circuit dealt with a similar challenge in the *In re Tam* decision below.

5. When disparagement is directed to an individual or an institution rather than a group such as Native Americans, the Board applies a different standard, *i.e.*, that the communication reasonably would be understood as referring to the individual or institution and that the communication "would be considered offensive or objectionable by a reasonable person or ordinary sensibilities." *Boston Red Sox Baseball Club LP v. Sherman*, 88 U.S.P.Q.2d 1581 (T.T.A.B. 2008). In that case, Applicant mixed the letters in opposer's Red Sox mark for its well-known baseball team and also mimicked the stylization of that mark as follows:

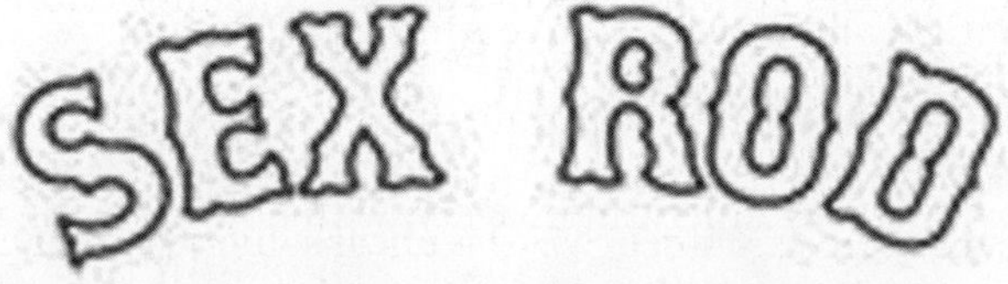

The Red Sox stylization appears as follows:

Applying the standard articulated above, how should the Board rule?

6. In *Shammas v. Focarino*, 990 F. Supp. 2d 587 (E.D. Va. 2014), *aff'd*, 784 F.3d 219 (4th Cir. 2015), the applicant sought review of an *ex parte* refusal to register his mark by a district court, which held that section 21(b)(3) of the Lanham Act provides that all expenses of such an *ex parte* appeal to a court, including attorney's fees, must be paid by the applicant whether or not the applicant is successful in the appeal. The statute does not apply to appeals to the Federal Circuit of *ex parte* refusals. What, if any, is the rationale for awarding expenses to the party who prevails in an appeal to the Federal Circuit, but not to a successful applicant who chooses to bring a new action before a district court?

In re Tam

808 F.3d 1321 (Fed. Cir. 2016) (En Banc), *cert. granted*, *Lee v. Tam*, 195 L. Ed.2d 202 (U.S. 2016).

MOORE, CIRCUIT JUDGE.

Section 2(a) of the Lanham Act bars the Patent and Trademark Office ("PTO") from registering scandalous, immoral, or disparaging marks. 15 U.S.C. § 1052(a). The government enacted this law and defends it today—because it disapproves of the messages conveyed by disparaging marks. It is a bedrock principle underlying the First Amendment that the government may not penalize private speech merely because it disapproves of the message it conveys. That principle governs even when the government's message-discriminatory penalty is less than a prohibition.

... Mr. Simon Shiao Tam named his band THE SLANTS to make a statement about racial and cultural issues in this country. With his band name, Mr. Tam conveys more about our society than many volumes of undisputedly protected speech. Another rejected mark, STOP THE ISLAMISATION OF AMERICA, proclaims that Islamisation is undesirable and should be stopped. Many of the marks rejected as disparaging convey hurtful speech that harms members of oft-stigmatized communities. But the First Amendment protects even hurtful speech.

The government cannot refuse to register disparaging marks because it disapproves of the expressive messages conveyed by the marks. It cannot refuse to register marks because it concludes that such marks will be disparaging to others. The government regulation at issue amounts to viewpoint discrimination, and under the strict scrutiny review appropriate for government regulation of message or viewpoint, we conclude that the disparagement proscription of § 2(a) is unconstitutional. Because the government has offered no legitimate interests justifying § 2(a), we conclude that it would also be unconstitutional under the intermediate scrutiny traditionally applied to regulation of the commercial aspects of speech. We therefore vacate the Trademark Trial and Appeal Board's ("Board") holding that Mr. Tam's mark is unregistrable, and remand this case to the Board for further proceedings.

Background

I. The Lanham Act

....

Under the Lanham Act, the PTO must register source-identifying trademarks unless the mark falls into one of several categories of marks precluded from registration. [Citation.] Many of these categories bar the registration of deceptive or misleading speech, because such speech actually undermines the interests served by trademark protection and, thus, the Lanham Act's purposes in providing for registration. For example, a mark may not be registered if it resembles a registered mark such that its use is likely to "cause confusion, or to cause mistake, or to deceive," § 2(d), or if it is "deceptively misdescriptive," § 2(e). These restrictions on registration of deceptive speech do not run afoul of the First Amendment. [Citations.]

Section 2(a), however, is a hodgepodge of restrictions. Among them is the bar on registration of a mark that "[c]onsists of or comprises immoral, deceptive, or scandalous matter; or matter which may disparage or falsely suggest a connection with persons, living or dead, institutions, beliefs, or national symbols, or bring them into contempt or disrepute." Section 2(a) contains proscriptions against deceptive speech, for example, the prohibition on deceptive matter or the prohibition on falsely suggesting a connection with a person or institution. But other restrictions in § 2(a) differ in that they are based on the expressive nature of the content, such as the ban on marks that may disparage persons or are scandalous or immoral. These latter restrictions cannot be justified on the basis that they further the Lanham Act's purpose in preventing consumers from being deceived. These exclusions ... deny the protections of registration for reasons quite separate from any ability of the mark to serve the consumer and investment interests underlying trademark protection. In fact, § 2(a)'s exclusions can undermine those interests because they can even be employed in cancellation proceedings challenging a mark many years after its issuance and after the markholder has invested millions of dollars protecting its brand identity and consumers have come to rely on the mark as a brand identifier.

This case involves the disparagement provision of § 2(a).[1] ... Only in the last several decades has the disparagement provision become a more frequent ground of rejection or cancellation of trademarks. Marks that the PTO has found to be

---

1. We limit our holding in this case to the constitutionality of the § 2(a) disparagement provision. Recognizing, however, that other portions of § 2 may likewise constitute government regulation of expression based on message, such as the exclusions of immoral or scandalous marks, we leave to future panels the consideration of the § 2 provisions other than the disparagement provision at issue here. To be clear, we overrule *In re McGinley*, 660 F.2d 481 (C.C.P.A. 1981), and other precedent

disparaging include: REDSKINS, *Pro-Football, Inc. v. Blackhorse,* No. 1-14-CV-01043-GBL, 112 F. Supp. 3d 439, 2015 U.S. Dist. LEXIS 90091, 2015 WL 4096277 Va. (July 8, 2015) (2014 PTO cancellation determination currently on appeal in Fourth Circuit); STOP THE ISLAMISATION OF AMERICA, *In re Geller,* 751 F.3d 1355 (Fed. Cir. 2014); THE CHRISTIAN PROSTITUTE (2013); AMISHHOMO (2013); MORMON WHISKEY (2012); KHORAN for wine, *In re Lebanese Arak Corp.,* 94 U.S.P.Q.2d 1215 (T.T.A.B. Mar. 4, 2010); ... HEEB, *In re Heeb Media, LLC,* 89 U.S.P.Q.2d 1071 (T.T.A.B. Nov. 26, 2008); SEX ROD, *Boston Red Sox Baseball Club L.P. v. Sherman,* 88 U.S.P.Q.2d 1581 (T.T.A.B. Sept. 9, 2008) (sustaining an opposition on multiple grounds, including disparagement); MARRIAGE IS FOR FAGS (2008); DEMOCRATS SHOULDN'T BREED (2007); REPUBLICANS SHOULDN'T BREED (2007); 2 DYKE MINIMUM (2007); WET BAC/WET B.A.C. (2007); URBAN INJUN (2007); SQUAW VALLEY, *In re Squaw Valley Dev. Co.,* 80 U.S.P.Q.2d 1264 (T.T.A.B. June 2, 2006); DON'T BE A WET BACK (2006); FAG-DOG (2003); N.I.G.G.A. NATURALLY INTELLIGENT GOD GIFTED AFRICANS (1996); a mark depicting a defecating dog, *Greyhound Corp. v. Both Worlds, Inc.,* 6 U.S.P.Q.2d 1635 (T.T.A.B. Mar. 30, 1988) (found to disparage Greyhound's trademarked running dog logo); an image consisting of the national symbol of the Soviet Union with an "X" over it, *In re Anti-Communist World Freedom Cong., Inc.,* 161 U.S.P.Q. 304 (T.T.A.B. Feb. 24, 1969); DOUGH-BOY for "a prophylactic preparation for the prevention of venereal diseases," *Doughboy Indus., Inc. v. Reese Chem. Co.,* 88 U.S.P.Q. 227 (T.T.A.B. Jan. 25, 1951).

... If the examiner "make[s] a prima facie showing that a substantial composite, although not necessarily a majority, of the referenced group would find the proposed mark, as used on or in connection with the relevant goods or services, to be disparaging in the context of contemporary attitudes," the burden shifts to the applicant for rebuttal. If the applicant fails to rebut the prima facie case of disparagement, the examiner refuses to register the mark.... A single examiner ... can reject a mark as disparaging by determining that it would be disparaging to a substantial composite of the referenced group.

II. Facts of This Case

Mr. Tam is the "front man" for the Asian-American dance-rock band The Slants. Mr. Tam named his band The Slants to "reclaim" and "take ownership" of Asian stereotypes. The band draws inspiration for its lyrics from childhood slurs and mocking nursery rhymes, and its albums include "The Yellow Album" and "Slanted Eyes, Slanted Hearts." The band "feel[s] strongly that Asians should be proud of their cultural heri[ta]ge, and not be offended by stereotypical descriptions." With their lyrics, performances, and band name, Mr. Tam and his band weigh in on cultural and political discussions about race and society that are within the heartland of speech protected by the First Amendment.

---

insofar as they could be argued to prevent a future panel from considering the constitutionality of other portions of § 2 in light of the present decision.

....

The Board affirmed the examiner's refusal to register the mark [and] wrote that "it is abundantly clear from the record not only that THE SLANTS ... would have the 'likely meaning' of people of Asian descent but also that such meaning has been so perceived and has prompted significant responses by prospective attendees or hosts of the band's performances." *In re Tam,* No. 85472044, 2013 TTAB LEXIS 485, 2013 WL 5498164, at *5 (T.T.A.B. Sept. 26, 2013) ("*Board Opinion*").... [T]he Board pointed to dictionary definitions, the band's website, which displayed the mark next to "a depiction of an Asian woman, utilizing rising sun imagery and using a stylized dragon image," and a statement by Mr. Tam that he selected the mark in order to "own" the stereotype it represents. The Board also found that the mark is disparaging to a substantial component of people of Asian descent because "[t]he dictionary definitions, reference works and all other evidence unanimously categorize the word 'slant,' when meaning a person of Asian descent, as disparaging," and because there was record evidence of individuals and groups in the Asian community objecting to Mr. Tam's use of the word. The Board therefore disqualified the mark for registration under § 2(a).

[The initial Federal Circuit panel affirmed in a 2–1 decision and rejected Tam's First Amendment arguments based on prior Federal Circuit precedent in *In re McGinley,* 660 F.2d 481 (C.C.P.A. 1981). The Federal Circuit granted rehearing *en banc*, concluding that the disparagement prong is unconstitutional.]

....

Discussion

I. Section 2(a)'s Denial of Important Legal Rights to Private Speech Based on Disapproval of the Message Conveyed Is Subject to, and Cannot Survive, Strict Scrutiny

Strict scrutiny is used to review any governmental regulation that burdens private speech based on disapproval of the message conveyed. Section 2(a), which denies important legal rights to private speech on that basis, is such a regulation.... [I]t cannot survive strict scrutiny.

A. The Disparagement Provision, Which Discriminates Based on Disapproval of the Message, Is Not Content or Viewpoint Neutral

"Content-based regulations are presumptively invalid." *R.A.V. v. City of St. Paul,* 505 U.S. 377, 382, 112 S. Ct. 2538, 120 L. Ed. 2d 305 (1992); [citation]. "Content-based laws—those that target speech based on its communicative content—are presumptively unconstitutional and may be justified only if the government proves that they are narrowly tailored to serve compelling state interests." [Citations.]

Viewpoint-based regulations, targeting the substance of the viewpoint expressed, are even more suspect. They are recognized as a particularly "egregious form of content discrimination." ... "The First Amendment requires heightened scrutiny whenever the government creates 'a regulation of speech because of disagreement with the message it conveys.'" *Sorrell,* 131 S. Ct. at 2664 (quoting *Ward v. Rock Against Racism,* 491 U.S. 781, 791, 109 S. Ct. 2746, 105 L. Ed. 2d 661 (1989)). This is true whether the regulation bans or merely burdens speech....

... Section 2(a) prevents the registration of disparaging marks ... And the test for disparagement—whether a substantial composite of the referenced group would find the mark disparaging—makes clear that it is the nature of the message conveyed by the speech which is being regulated. If the mark is found disparaging by the referenced group, it is denied registration....

And § 2(a) ... also discriminates on the basis of message conveyed, ... it targets "viewpoints [in] the marketplace," *Simon & Schuster*, 502 U.S. at 116. It does so as a matter of avowed and undeniable purpose, and it does so on its face.

....

... The PTO rejects marks under § 2(a) when it finds the marks refer to a group in a negative way, but it permits the registration of marks that refer to a group in a positive, non-disparaging manner.... Yet the government registers marks that refer to particular ethnic groups or religions in positive or neutral ways—for example, NAACP, THINK ISLAM, NEW MUSLIM COOL, MORMON SAVINGS, JEWISHSTAR, and PROUD 2 B CATHOLIC.

The government argues ... that under § 2(a), two marks with diametrically opposed viewpoints will both be refused, so long as those marks use the same disparaging term. It points to Mr. Tam—who does not seek to express an anti-Asian viewpoint—as proof....

... The government[] ... is incorrect. The PTO looks at what message the referenced group takes from the applicant's mark in the context of the applicant's use, and it denies registration only if the message received is a negative one. Thus, an applicant can register a mark if he shows it is perceived by the referenced group in a positive way, even if the mark contains language that would be offensive in another context. For example, the PTO registered the mark DYKES ON BIKES ... after the applicant showed the term was often enough used with pride among the relevant population. In *Squaw Valley*, the Board allowed the registration of the mark SQUAW VALLEY in connection with one of the applied-for classes of goods (namely, skiing-related products), but not in connection with a different class of goods. 80 U.S.P.Q.2d at *22.... It is thus the viewpoint of the message conveyed which causes the government to burden the speech....

... STOP THE ISLAMISATION OF AMERICA and THINK ISLAM express two different viewpoints. Under § 2(a), one of these viewpoints garners the benefits of registration, and one does not. The government enacted § 2(a), and defends it today, because it is hostile to the messages conveyed by the refused marks. Section 2(a) is a viewpoint-discriminatory regulation of speech, created and applied in order to stifle the use of certain disfavored messages. Strict scrutiny therefore governs its First Amendment assessment—and no argument has been made that the measure survives such scrutiny.

....

II. Section 2(a) Is Not Saved From Strict Scrutiny Because It Bans No Speech or By Government-Speech or Government-Subsidy Doctrines

... [T]he government argues ... § 2(a) ... prohibits no speech, but leaves Mr. Tam free to name his band as he wishes and use this name in commerce.... [T]he government suggests that trademark registration is government speech, and thus the government can grant and reject trademark registrations without implicating the First Amendment ... and the government argues that § 2(a) merely withholds a government subsidy for Mr. Tam's speech and is valid as a permissible definition of a government subsidy program. We reject each of the government's arguments.

A. Strict Scrutiny Applies to § 2(a), Which Significantly Chills Private Speech on Discriminatory Grounds, Though It Does Not Ban Speech

The government argues that § 2(a) does not implicate the First Amendment because it does not prohibit any speech.... But the First Amendment's standards, including those broadly invalidating message discrimination, are not limited to such prohibitions. [Citation.]

....

[W]hile it is true that a trademark owner may use its mark in commerce even without federal registration, it has been widely recognized that federal trademark registration bestows *truly* significant and financially valuable benefits upon markholders. *B&B Hardware*, 135 S. Ct. at 1300; *Park 'n Fly, Inc. v. Dollar Park & Fly, Inc.*, 469 U.S. 189, 199–200, 105 S. Ct. 658, 83 L. Ed. 2d 582 (1985) (valuable new rights were created by the Lanham Act); [citations].

Denial of these benefits creates a serious disincentive to adopt a mark which the government may deem offensive or disparaging. [Citations.]

For those reasons, the § 2(a) bar on registration creates a strong disincentive to choose a "disparaging" mark. And that disincentive is not cabined to a clearly understandable range of expressions. The statute extends the uncertainty to marks that "may disparage." 15 U.S.C. § 1052(a). The uncertainty as to what *might be deemed* disparaging is not only evident on its face, given the subjective-reaction element and shifting usages in different parts of society. It is confirmed by the record of PTO grants and denials over the years, from which the public would have a hard time drawing much reliable guidance.

....

B. Trademark Registration Is Not Government Speech

....

[T]he government appears to argue that trademark registration and the accoutrements of registration ... amount to government speech. This argument is meritless. Trademark registration is a regulatory activity.... [M]anifestations of government registration do not convert the underlying speech to government speech. And if they do, then copyright registration would likewise amount to government speech....

In *Walker v. Texas Division, Sons of Confederate Veterans, Inc.*, the Supreme Court detailed the indicia of government speech. 135 S. Ct. 2239, 192 L. Ed. 2d 274 (2015). The Court concluded that specialty license plates were government speech, even though a state law allowed individuals, organizations, and nonprofit groups to request certain designs. The Court ... stressed that "[t]he State places the name 'TEXAS' in large letters at the top of every plate," that "the State requires Texas vehicle owners to display license plates, and every Texas license plate is issued by the State," that "Texas also owns the designs on its license plates," and that "Texas dictates the manner in which drivers may dispose of unused plates." *Id.* As a consequence, the Court reasoned, "Texas license plate designs 'are often closely identified in the public mind with the State.'" *Id.* (quoting *Summum*, 555 U.S. at 472 (alteration omitted)). Amidst all of its other aspects of control, moreover, "Texas maintains direct control over the messages conveyed on its specialty plates." *Id.* at 2249. "Indeed, a person who displays a message on a Texas license plate likely intends to convey to the public that the State has endorsed that message." *Id.*

... When the government registers a trademark, the only message it conveys is that a mark is registered. The vast array of private trademarks are not created by the government, owned or monopolized by the government, sized and formatted by the government, immediately understood as performing any government function (like unique, visible vehicle identification), aligned with the government, or (putting aside any specific government-secured trademarks) used as a platform for government speech. There is simply no meaningful basis for finding that consumers associate registered private trademarks with the government.

....

In short, the act of registration, which includes the right (but not the obligation) to put an ® symbol on one's goods, receiving a registration certificate, and being listed in a government database, simply cannot amount to government speech. The PTO's processing of trademark registrations no more transforms private speech into government speech than when the government issues permits for street parades, copyright registration certificates, or, for that matter, grants medical, hunting, fishing, or drivers licenses, or records property titles, birth certificates, or articles of incorporation. To conclude otherwise would transform every act of government registration into one of government speech and thus allow rampant viewpoint discrimination. When the government registers a trademark, it regulates private speech. It does not speak for itself.

C. Section 2(a) Is Not a Government Subsidy Exempt from Strict Scrutiny

We reject the government's argument that § 2(a)'s message-based discrimination is merely the government's shaping of a subsidy program.... The Supreme Court has repeatedly invalidated denials of "benefits" based on message-based disapproval of private speech that is not part of a government-speech program. In such circumstances, denial of an otherwise-available benefit is unconstitutional at least where, as here, it has a significant chilling effect on private speech. [Citations.]

....

III. Section 2(a) Is Unconstitutional Even Under the *Central Hudson* Test for Commercial Speech

....

Even if we were to treat § 2(a) as a regulation of commercial speech, it would fail to survive. In *Central Hudson*, the Supreme Court laid out the intermediate-scrutiny framework for determining the constitutionality of restrictions on commercial speech. 447 U.S. at 566. First, commercial speech "must concern lawful activity and not be misleading." *Id.* If this is the case, we ask whether "the asserted governmental interest is substantial," *id.*, and whether the regulation "directly and materially advanc[es]" the government's asserted interest and is narrowly tailored to achieve that objective. *Lorillard Tobacco Co. v. Reilly,* 533 U.S. 525, 555–56, 121 S. Ct. 2404, 150 L. Ed. 2d 532 (2001). "Under a commercial speech inquiry, it is the State's burden to justify its content-based law as consistent with the *First Amendment.*" *Sorrell,* 131 S. Ct. at 2667.

First, we ask whether the regulated activity is lawful and not misleading. *Cent. Hudson,* 447 U.S. at 563–64. Unlike many other provisions of § 2, the disparagement provision does not address misleading, deceptive, or unlawful marks. There is nothing illegal or misleading about a disparaging trademark like Mr. Tam's mark.

Next, ... a substantial government interest must justify the regulation. *Id.* at 566. But ... [t]he entire interest of the government in § 2(a) depends on disapproval of the message. That is an insufficient interest to pass the test of intermediate scrutiny, as the Supreme Court made clear in *Sorrell.* 131 S. Ct. at 2668 (law must not "seek to suppress a disfavored message"); [citations].

The government ... argues ... that the United States is "entitled to dissociate itself from speech it finds odious." ... [T]hat disapproval is not a legitimate government interest where, as here, ... there is no plausible basis for treating the speech as government speech or as reasonably attributed to the government by the public.

The government also argues that it has a legitimate interest in "declining to expend its resources to facilitate the use of racial slurs as source identifiers in interstate commerce." The government's interest in directing its resources does not warrant regulation of these marks.... [T]rademark registration is user-funded, not taxpayer-funded. The government expends few resources registering these marks. Its costs are the same costs that would be incidental to any governmental registration: articles of incorporation, copyrights, patents, property deeds, etc....

....

We conclude that the government has not presented us with a substantial government interest justifying the § 2(a) bar on disparaging marks. All of the government's proffered interests boil down to permitting the government to burden speech it finds offensive. This is not a legitimate interest. With no substantial government interests, the disparagement provision of § 2(a) cannot satisfy the *Central Hudson* test. We hold the disparagement provision of § 2(a) unconstitutional under the First Amendment.

....

Questions

1. The Supreme Court granted certiorari from the Federal Circuit's *In re Tam* decision. The Fourth Circuit has suspended its consideration of the *Blackhorse v. Pro-Football, Inc.* appeal pending the Supreme Court's decision, which may or may not alter the landscape of disparagement under Section 2(a). Professor Rebecca Tushnet has contended that section 2(a) is generally constitutional as set forth below:

> I conclude that § 2(a) is generally constitutional as a government determination about what speech it is willing to approve, if not endorse. If the Supreme Court disagrees, it will face a difficult job distinguishing other aspects of trademark law. And these difficulties signal a greater problem: the Court has lost touch with the reasons that some content-based distinctions might deserve special scrutiny. Often, perfectly sensible and by no means censorious regulations that depend on identifying the semantic content of speech would fall afoul of a real application of heightened scrutiny, to no good end.

Rebecca Tushnet, *The First Amendment Walks into a Bar: Trademark Regulation and Free Speech*, 92 Notre Dame L. Rev. ___ (forthcoming 2016). Which way do you think the Supreme Court should rule?

2. Although the *In re Tam* decision limits its holding to the unconstitutionality of the disparagement prong of section 2(a), the language nevertheless appears to suggest that the "scandalous and immoral" prong also impermissibly targets expressive content without a justification of preventing deceptive or misleading material. The Federal Circuit currently has an appeal before it from the Board's decision that FUCT, Serial No. 85/310,960, is scandalous and immoral. *In re Brunetti*, 2014 TTAB LEXIS 328 (T.T.A.B. 2014). Is there any basis to argue a difference in the First Amendment analysis that the Federal Circuit should apply? What if the matter rises to the level of obscenity? Would the provision be facially invalid in that case?

3. The majority decision differentiates the validity of the provisions barring registration of deceptive or misleading marks from disparaging, scandalous and/or immoral marks. Is this persuasive? Would, for example, the bars against geographically misdescriptive marks or against marks that incorporate the name of dead presidents if their spouse is still alive survive strict scrutiny analysis?

b. Deceptive Terms

Bayer Aktiengesellschaft v. Stamatios Mouratidis

2010 TTAB LEXIS 218 (T.T.A.B. May 21, 2010)

Bergsman, Administrative Trademark Judge:

Bayer Aktiengesellschaft ("opposer") filed an opposition to the application of Stamatios Mouratidis ("applicant") to register the mark ORGANIC ASPIRIN on the Principal Register, in standard character form, for "dietary supplements for human consumption," in International Class 5. As grounds for opposition, opposer asserted that the mark ORGANIC ASPIRIN as applied to dietary supplements is deceptive under Section 2(a) of the Trademark Act of 1946, 15 U.S.C. § 1052(a), and is deceptively misdescriptive under Section 2(e)(1) of the Trademark Act, 15 U.S.C. § 1052(e)(1). In its answer, applicant admitted that its dietary supplements do not contain acetylsalicylic acid but otherwise denied the salient allegations in the opposition.

....

Elements for Proving a Mark is Deceptive and Deceptively Misdescriptive

... The Court of Appeals for the Federal Circuit has articulated the following test for whether a mark consists of or comprises deceptive matter:

1. Is the term misdescriptive of the character, quality, function, composition or use of the goods?

2. If so, are prospective purchasers likely to believe that the description actually describes the goods?

3. If so, is the misdescription likely to affect a significant portion of the relevant consumers' decision to purchase?

In re Budge Mfg. Co. Inc., 857 F.2d 773, 8 USPQ2d 1259, 1260 (Fed. Cir. 1988).

If the first two questions are answered affirmatively, the mark is deceptively misdescriptive of the goods under Section 2(e)(1) of the Trademark Act. *In re Quady Winery Inc.*, 221 USPQ 1213, 1214 (TTAB 1984). The third question, whether the misdescription is likely to affect the decision to purchase, distinguishes marks that are deceptive from marks that are merely deceptively misdescriptive. *Id; see also In re Shniberg*, 79 USPQ2d 1309, 1311 (TTAB 2006) ("If the misdescription is more than simply a relevant factor that may be considered in purchasing decisions but *is* a material factor, the mark would also be deceptive") (emphasis in the original).

A. Whether the mark ORGANIC ASPIRIN is misdescriptive of the character, quality, function, composition or use of dietary supplements?

Aspirin is "[a] white, crystalline compound ... derived from salicylic acid and commonly used in tablet form to relieve pain and reduce fever and inflammation. It is also used as an antiplatelet agent. Also called *acetylsalicylic acid.*" (Emphasis in the original). In its brief, applicant concedes that "aspirin is a generic term for the chemical acetylsalicylic acid."

"Organic" has the following relevant definitions:

1. Of, relating to, or derived from living organisms: *organic matter.*

....

3b. Raised or conducted without the use of drugs, hormomes, or synthetic chemicals: *organic chicken; organic cattle farming.*

In his brief, applicant succinctly defines the word "organic" as "produced without synthetic chemicals."

... [F]or a term to misdescribe goods, the term must be merely descriptive of a significant aspect of the goods which the goods could plausibly possess but in fact do not. *In re Phillips-Van Heusen Corp.*, 63 USPQ2d 1047, 1051 (TTAB 2002). We find that it is plausible that dietary supplements could contain aspirin for its cardiovascular and other health benefits.... Applicant's dietary supplements do not contain acetylsalicylic acid otherwise known as aspirin. Thus, the term "Aspirin" is misdescriptive of applicant's goods. *See In re ALP of South Beach Inc.*, 79 USPQ2d 1009, 1010 (TTAB 2006) (CAFETERIA used in connection with restaurant services that explicitly excludes cafeterias is misdescriptive); *In re Shapely, Inc.*, 231 USPQ 72, 73 (TTAB 1986) ("There is no question that the presence of the noun 'silk' as a prefix renders the mark SILKEASE misdescriptive of appellant's blouses and dresses which contain no silk fibers").

B. Whether prospective purchasers are likely to believe ORGANIC ASPIRIN describes applicant's goods?

Reasonably prudent consumers are likely to believe that applicant's ORGANIC ASPIRIN dietary supplements contain aspirin derived without synthetic chemicals. In fact, excerpts from applicant's website, shown below, liken its product to aspirin, thus, leading consumers to mistakenly believe that applicant's dietary supplements include a naturally occurring aspirin (emphasis added).

> Studies have shown that aspirin (acetylsalicylic acid) consumption benefits the heart. *Salicylates like aspirin have been used in various forms since antiquity.* Actually, *the first salicylates consumed were all botanical.* The use of naturally occurring salicylates from plant extracts prompted the chemical synthesis of aspirin. Today, all aspirin is synthesized industrially from phenol (a byproduct or coal of benzene).
>
> ....
>
> *Organic Aspirin capsules provide you with salicylates for your heart's protection.... Organic Aspirin products contain exclusively naturally occurring phytochemicals and salicylates which later convert into salicylic acid* in our bodies and allow for gentler digestion than harsher synthetic medications while at the same time providing a wider range of benefits.

....

Finally, applicant advertises that its ORGANIC ASPIRIN is similar to a botanical predecessor of aspirin.

> Organic Aspirin capsules contain salicin from both forerunners of aspirin and should not be used by those who are allergic to aspirin, have a gastrointestinal disorder, tinnitus, are pregnant, and/or breast-feeding.
>
> ....
>
> Organic Aspirin capsules contain naturally occurring salicin, calcium and phytochemicals, including heparin-like compounds and tannins.

Applicant argues ... that ORGANIC ASPIRIN is not misdescriptive and not deceptively misdescriptive because the combination of the words "Organic" and "Aspirin" is incongruous, thus, creating an inherently distinctive mark. This argument is based on the facts that there is no such thing as organically grown aspirin, that the term ORGANIC ASPIRIN is not synonymous with aspirin, and that ORGANIC ASPIRIN has no meaning.

However, we find that the term ORGANIC ASPIRIN conveys the literal commercial impression that applicant's products are, or contain, a natural aspirin product. The text of applicant's websites and advertising noted above reinforces this commercial impression by contrasting applicant's products with synthetic aspirin. As we noted above, applicant's advertising leads consumers to believe that there are two types of aspirin: organic and synthetic.

Furthermore, we do not agree with applicant's argument that the incongruous combination of the words "Organic" and "Aspirin" to form ORGANIC ASPIRIN "reliably dissuades consumers from believing the goods are made of aspirin, since such a belief is not plausible." Applicant's conclusion is based on the premise that consumers know that there is no such thing as organic aspirin. Presumably, dietary supplements are available to all consumers some of whom may not know that there is no such thing as organic aspirin. Moreover, because applicant is advertising that its dietary supplements are naturally occurring phytochemicals and salicylates which form salicylic acid and that they contain salicin from botanical forerunners of aspirin, applicant is leading consumers to mistakenly believe that its product is, or contains, aspirin derived from natural products.

Applicant contends that ORGANIC ASPIRIN is similar to the facts in *In re Robert Simmons, Inc.*, 192 USPQ 331 (TTAB 1976) where that applicant sought to register the mark WHITE SABLE for artist's paint brushes. According to applicant, "[t]he terms 'WHITE' and 'SABLE' are similarly at odds with each other, and the term 'WHITE SABLE' is not deceptive on artist's paint brushes, in view of the fact that [the] characteristic color of sable fur is black and the brush is made of synthetic brush filament." However, in *Simmons*, the Board found that the word "sable" when used in connection with artist's paint brushes does not "mean literally a brush whose bristles are made from the hair or fur of a sable animal." 192 USPQ at 333. Thus, the term "White Sable" would not deceive consumers because they do not believe that brushes would be made from sable fur. In other words, the Board found that by merely contemplating the goods involved [paint brushes], consumers reasonably would be able to draw a correct conclusion about the nature of the goods. [Citation.] In this case, however, we find that when consumers consider applicant's goods [dietary supplements], they will believe that applicant's products contain aspirin and, thus, the term ORGANIC ASPIRIN mistakenly leads consumers to believe that applicant's dietary supplements contain aspirin derived without the use of synthetic chemicals.

C. Whether the use of term ORGANIC ASPIRIN is likely to affect the purchasing decision?

We find that the use of the term "aspirin" in applicant's mark ORGANIC ASPIRIN is likely to affect the purchasing decision because consumers will purchase applicant's dietary supplements in the mistaken belief that the products contain aspirin and, thus, provide the health benefits of aspirin. The heart-health and cancer preventing benefits of aspirin have been reported in the *Kansas City Star, Obesity, Fitness & Wellness Week*, and *USA Today.* Also, the U.S. Food and Drug Administration notes that aspirin may be recommended for treating heart attack, stroke, certain other cardiovascular conditions, rheumatologic diseases, and for pain relief. Applicant advertises its ORGANIC ASPIRIN as providing anti-inflammatory and cardiovascular benefits without the gastrointestinal problems that aspirin can cause. Accordingly, the use of the term ORGANIC ASPIRIN to identify applicant's dietary supplements is likely to affect the purchasing decision of consumers who want the benefits of aspirin from a natural source, as opposed to synthetic chemicals, without the problems that traditional aspirin may cause.

In view of the foregoing we find that applicant's mark ORGANIC ASPIRIN for dietary supplements for human consumption is both deceptively misdescriptive under Section 2(e)(1) and deceptive under Section 2(a).

Question

Was it appropriate for the Board to rely on Applicant's promotional material in determining whether purchasers were likely to believe that Organic Aspirin described Applicant's product?

Note: The Difference between Deceptive Terms and "Deceptively Misdescriptive" Terms

Section 2(a) of the Lanham Act bars registration of any mark which "comprises ... deceptive ... matter...." This is an absolute bar and cannot be rescued under section 2(f) of the Lanham Act by showing that a mark "has become distinctive" through a showing of secondary meaning. Marks which are considered "merely deceptively misdescriptive" of the goods or services of an applicant are also barred from registration under section 2(e)(1) of the Lanham Act. Such marks are registrable, however, if secondary meaning under section 2(f) can be demonstrated. The distinction between deceptive marks and merely deceptively misdescriptive marks thus can be significant.

If the answers to the first two questions in the *In re Budge* test are affirmative (that is that the mark is misdescriptive of the goods/services and prospective purchases are likely to believe the misdescription), but the answer to the third question is negative (that the misdescription is not material to the purchasing decision), then the mark is deceptively misdescriptive. *See, e.g., In re Woodward & Lothrop Inc.*, 4 U.S.P.Q.2d 1412 (T.T.A.B. 1987). If only the first question is answered in the affirmative, then the mark may be arbitrary or suggestive since belief in the misdescription is key to a finding of deceptiveness.

Questions

Which of the following marks are deceptive? Which are deceptively misdescriptive? Arbitrary? Suggestive? Why?

1. ORGANIK for garments made of untreated, 100% natural cotton from plants that were not necessarily grown without chemicals or pesticides. *See In re Organik Technologies*, 41 U.S.P.Q.2d 1690 (T.T.A.B. 1997).

2. BLANC DE CHINE for "porcelain, namely lamp bases, pots and figurines." Blanc de Chine is a term used to identify a valuable type of porcelain, made between

the 15th and 19th centuries, in China. Antique Blanc de Chine figurines sell for over $10,000, although dishes may sell for $100 to $200. Applicant's porcelain goods contain no Blanc de Chine; its small bowls will be priced at $125, and a footed bowl will sell for $245. The Examining Attorney has rejected the mark as deceptive. Applicant contends that consumers cannot be deceived, either because they have never heard of Blanc de Chine, or because those who are familiar with the term know that it cannot apply to applicant's goods. How should the Board rule? *See In re Volk Art*, 1998 TTAB LEXIS 140 (T.T.A.B. July 8, 1998).

3. TITANIUM for recreational vehicles. *See Glendale Int'l Corp. v. U.S.P.T.O.*, 374 F. Supp. 2d 479 (E.D. Va. 2005).

4. THCTea for tea-based beverages that do not contain THC (*i.e.*, marijuana). *See In re Hinton*, 116 U.S.P.Q.2d 1051 (T.T.A.B. 2015).

c. False Suggestion of a Connection

Hornby v. TJX Companies, Inc.

87 U.S.P.Q.2d 1411 (T.T.A.B. 2008)

SEEHERMAN, ADMINISTRATIVE TRADEMARK JUDGE:

Lesley Hornby a/k/a Lesley Lawson a/k/a Twiggy, an individual (hereafter "petitioner") has petitioned to cancel a registration owned by TJX Companies, Inc. (hereafter "respondent") for the mark TWIGGY for "clothing, namely, children's pants, tops, slacks, skirts, vests, sweaters, shirts and blouses." The grounds asserted in the petition to cancel ... are likelihood of confusion (one element of which, of course, is priority of use), false suggestion of a connection, fraud, and dilution.

....

[The Board found against petitioner on the grounds of fraud, likelihood of confusion and likelihood of dilution and found against respondent as to its laches defense].

False Suggestion of a Connection

The final ground which we must decide is whether respondent's use of the mark TWIGGY for children's clothing may falsely suggest a connection with petitioner. The Federal Circuit explained in *University of Notre Dame du Lac v. J.C. Gourmet Food Imports Co., Inc.*, 703 F.2d 1372, 217 USPQ 505, 508 (Fed. Cir. 1983), that the purpose of the false suggestion of a connection language of Section 2(a) was to protect "the name of an individual or institution which was not a 'technical' trademark or 'trade name' upon which an objection could be made under Section 2(d)," and that this statutory section embraces the concepts of the right of privacy and the related right of publicity. *See In re White*, 80 USPQ2d 1654 (TTAB 2006). The Federal Circuit further stated that to succeed on such a ground the plaintiff must demonstrate that the name or equivalent thereof claimed to be appropriated by another must be unmistakably associated with a particular personality or "persona" and must point uniquely to the plaintiff. The Board, in *Buffett v. Chi-Chi's, Inc.*, 226 USPQ 428 (TTAB 1985), in accordance with the principles set forth in *Notre Dame*, required that a plaintiff asserting a claim of a false suggestion of a connection demonstrate 1) that the defendant's mark is the same or a close approximation of plaintiff's previously used name or identity; 2) that the mark would be recognized as such; 3) that the plaintiff is not connected with the activities performed by the defendant under the mark; and 4) that the plaintiff's name or identity is of sufficient fame or reputation that when the defendant's mark is used on its goods or services, a connection with the plaintiff would be presumed.... However, in some of the decisions involving the false suggestion of a connection ground, the language of the second factor has been modified somewhat, to state "that the marks would be recognized as [the same as, or a close approximation of, the name or identity previously used by the other person], in that they point uniquely and unmistakably to that person." *See L. & J.G. Stickley Inc. v. Cosser*, [81 U.S.P.Q.2d 1956,] at 1972; *In re White*, [80 U.S.P.Q.2d 1654]; *In re Urbano*, 51 USPQ2d 1776 (TTAB 1999); *In re Wielinski*, 49 USPQ2d 1754 (TTAB 1998). This modified language recognizes the requirement set forth by the Federal Circuit that the name claimed to be appropriated by the defendant must point uniquely to the plaintiff.

There is no real dispute in this case as to factors one and three. The evidence clearly shows that petitioner is known, both personally and professionally, as "Twiggy," and that respondent's mark TWIGGY is identical to petitioner's name. It is also clear that she is not connected with respondent, and did not give respondent permission to use her name as a trademark for its goods.

With respect to the fourth factor, respondent asserts that its mark TWIGGY would not be recognized as petitioner's name because petitioner's name or identity is not of sufficient fame or reputation that consumers seeing it on children's clothing would presume a connection with petitioner. Petitioner, obviously, takes the opposite position.

... [T]he fame or reputation of petitioner must be determined as of the time respondent's registration for TWIGGY issued. Thus, although petitioner may have been a major celebrity in the late 1960s, the burden on petitioner is to show that she had sufficient fame and/or reputation as of July 4, 2000.

There is no question that petitioner was a huge sensation in the late 1960s, a model who was also a celebrity. Certainly if her fame and reputation were considered during the period of 1967–1970, that fame would easily satisfy the prong of the *Buffett* test.... What we must consider, then, is whether since that time she has retained a sufficient degree of fame or reputation that, as of July 4, 2000, a connection with her would still be presumed by consumers seeing the mark TWIGGY on children's clothing. We find that she has.

Petitioner is not simply a model who made a name for herself more than 30 years ago and then disappeared from public view. On the contrary, through the years she has continued to play a public role.... [D]uring the 1970s she starred in a U.S. film called "The Boyfriend," for which she won two Golden Globe awards, and appeared on various television shows that were broadcast nationally in the United States, including "The Sonny and Cher Show" and the "Mike Douglas Show," on which she was a co-host for a week. In the 1980s she starred in a major Broadway hit and

Tony-award winning show for 18 months, and was herself nominated for a Tony award. She performed on one of the Academy Award telecasts, and was also a presenter. She also made many appearances on nationally seen television interview shows, including "Johnny Carson" and "Merv Griffin." She starred in movies opposite such "name" actors as Robin Williams and Shirley Maclaine. In the 1990s she had a presence on U.S. television, starring for one year (1991) in a U.S. television series, and in a TV movie in 1996. She also performed in theatrical productions in the United States, starring in a 1997 summer theater production that was reviewed in "The New York Times" (a newspaper with national circulation), and starring for five months in 1999 in an off-Broadway production that was positively reviewed.

She did interviews through the years, for example, when she had a show coming out, and she also did a publicity tour of U.S. cities to publicize her film "Madame Sousatzka." In connection with the sitcom "Princesses," she had interviews in "People," "Vogue" and "US" magazine.

These various entertainment activities, and the promotional efforts surrounding them, have successfully kept her name before the U.S. public, and have built on the extraordinary initial reputation and celebrity that was created in the period from 1967–1970. We do not say that her post-1970 activities would, on their own, be sufficient to demonstrate the requisite recognition, but they are sufficient when taken together with the phenomenal amount of publicity and recognition she received in that initial period. As further evidence of her reputation and recognition in 2000, the year that respondent's registration issued, we take judicial notice that the fourth edition of The American Heritage Dictionary of the English Language, published in 2000, listed "Twiggy" as an entry, as follows:

> Originally Lesley Hornby. British model who epitomized the ultrathin look popular from 1966 to 1976.

In addition, we think it is significant that in 1999 the Franklin Mint asked petitioner to license her name and likeness for a collectible doll. The other dolls in this collection were Jackie Kennedy, Princess Diana, Marilyn Monroe and Elvis Presley. Although the doll did not go on the market until after respondent's mark was registered, the fact that the Franklin Mint asked petitioner to be part of its doll collection, and the stature of the other dolls in the collection, indicates that her fame was considerable and still ongoing during 1999, the year prior to the issuance of respondent's registration, and that consumers would, at that time, recognize her name. The subsequent sale of a million TWIGGY dolls confirms this. Although the sales of the dolls occurred shortly after the issuance of respondent's registration, they are still indicative of her reputation in 2000.

In sum, we find that petitioner and her name, Twiggy, had sufficient fame and reputation in 1999 and 2000, both prior to and at the time respondent's mark was registered, that purchasers of children's clothing would, upon seeing the mark TWIGGY on such goods, presume an association with her....

Respondent has argued that purchasers of children's clothing would not be aware of petitioner's activities in 1967–1970, when she was a phenomenon. Essentially respondent is asserting that people who knew of petitioner in that time period are now too old to buy children's clothing, and that there is no evidence that "a new generation of adult consumers" would be aware of the 1960s model Twiggy. We accept that purchasers who were too young to have been exposed to the "Twiggy phenomenon," or were born after 1970, would not necessarily be aware of petitioner or her name through her various entertainment activities subsequent to 1970.... However, girls who were 8–17 years old in 1970 would have been aware of petitioner at that time, and, at least at the younger age range, would have been the purchasers of the board game Twiggy the Queen of Models, the dress-up paper dolls and the other licensed products. These same girls would have been 38–47 years old in 2000, and are likely to have had children at that time who would wear "children's clothing," since such clothing can be worn by 12–13 year olds. In other words, these women could have given birth when they were in the age range of 25 to 34 and, therefore, have been purchasers of children's clothing in 2000. And not to belabor the point, but it is not unusual for women to continue to have children when in their late 30s or early 40s, and therefore even women who were in their late teens or early 20s in 1967–1970 could have been consumers of respondent's goods in 2000. Further, even if their own children were too old in 2000 to wear children's clothing, the people who knew of petitioner in 1967–1970 are still potential purchasers of children's clothing, for their friends' children or even for their own grandchildren. Moreover, while we have addressed our comments to women as the purchasers of children's clothing, we must also recognize that fathers may purchase clothing for their children, and they do not have the biological issues that women do. Because of petitioner's great celebrity during 1967–1970, men as well as women, and boys as well as girls, would have been very aware of her, and may, in 2000, have been purchasing clothing for their children.

Accordingly, petitioner has satisfied the fourth factor set forth in *Buffett*, that petitioner's name is of sufficient fame or reputation that when the respondent's mark is used on children's clothing, a connection with petitioner would be presumed.

Finally, we consider the second factor, whether respondent's mark would be recognized as pointing uniquely and unmistakably to the petitioner. As we have discussed at length, "Twiggy" had been the personal and professional name of petitioner for more than 30 years at the time respondent's registration issued, and her name was of sufficient fame or reputation that consumers would make a connection between children's clothing sold under the mark TWIGGY and petitioner. The evidence supporting our finding that her name has fame and/or reputation also demonstrates that the name "Twiggy" is unmistakably associated with petitioner. Further, on this record, we find that TWIGGY points uniquely to petitioner. Respondent has pointed out that "twiggy" has a dictionary meaning and, although it has not submitted a copy of it, we take judicial notice that "twiggy" means "1. Resembling a twig or twigs, as in slenderness or fragility. 2. Abounding in twigs: *a twiggy branch.*" Respondent has also submitted three third-party registrations, two for the mark TWIGGY for bicycles and for entertainment services presenting a live squirrel water skiing behind a boat, and one for the mark TWIGGY STARDOM for entertainment services consisting of live musical performances and a web site featuring musical performances, etc.

The requirement that a respondent's mark point "uniquely" to petitioner does not mean that TWIGGY must be a unique term. Rather, in the context of the respondent's goods, we must determine whether consumers would view the mark as pointing only to petitioner, or whether they would perceive it to have a different meaning. Thus, if the respondent's goods were a plant food or a plant, the mark TWIGGY used on them could very well be understood as having the dictionary meaning quoted above. However, there is nothing in the record from which we can conclude that TWIGGY for children's clothing would have such a meaning.... In fact, the obvious connection between models and clothing is further support for our conclusion that respondent's mark for children's clothing points uniquely to petitioner.[19]

....

... [T]he three registrations submitted by respondent are not for goods or services even remotely related to clothing, so they are of no value in showing that TWIGGY for children's clothing would have a meaning that does not point to petitioner. In short, the three third-party registrations have no probative value in showing that the name "Twiggy" does not point uniquely to petitioner.

After considering all of the evidence of record in connection with the Section 2(a) false suggestion of a connection factors, we find that respondent's mark TWIGGY for children's clothing may falsely suggest a connection with petitioner.

Questions

1. Can the persona of an institution be embodied in a design for purposes of establishing a false suggestion of a connection under section 2(a)? Consider a business that sells tags to trace goods and that provides lost property tracking and return services and applies to register a design that consists of a hand inserting a key into a blue mailbox as shown below:

19. In saying this, we want to be clear that it is not necessary, in order to succeed on a Section 2(a) false suggestion of a connection ground, that the plaintiff show that consumers would believe

Should the U.S. Postal Service be able to claim that its blue collection boxes in the shape shown below are a part of its identity or persona?

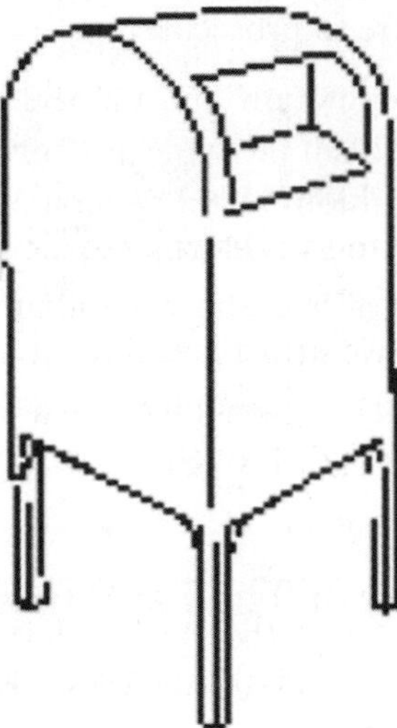

Is the above design synonymous with USPS's identity under the first factor articulated in *Hornby*? See *U.S. Postal Service v. Lost Key Rewards, Inc*, 102 U.S.P.Q.2d 1595 (T.T.A.B. 2010).

2. In *Hornby*, the Board differentiates a false suggestion of a connection claim under section 2(a) and a likelihood of confusion claim under section 2(d). If relevant purchasers falsely believe there may be a connection, would they also not be likely to be confused as to the sponsorship of such goods/services? Is the real difference in the claims found in the Board's statement that false suggestion of a connection also protects a name or institution that is not a "technical" trademark or trade name? Should false suggestion of a connection apply where a person does not use the name at issue but others refer to her that way? Kate Middleton's title is Duchess of Cambridge. Should PRINCESS KATE be refused registration for cosmetics, apparel and other goods as falsely suggesting a connection with her if that is not her title? *See In re Nieves & Nieves*, 113 U.S.P.Q.2d 1629 (T.T.A.B. 2015). Should MARATHON MONDAY be found to suggest a false suggestion of a connection with the organizers of the BOSTON MARATHON if the latter term is found to be an identity of the organizer? *See Boston Athletic Assn. v. Velocity, LLC*, 117 U.S.P.Q.2d 1492 (T.T.A.B. 2015).

3. The false suggestion of a connection prong of section 2(a) applies *inter alia* to "persons, living or dead." How long after a person dies should this provision be

---

the defendant's goods emanate from the plaintiff. That is a requirement for a Section 2(d) likelihood of confusion claim, but not a Section 2(a) claim. We point to petitioner's fame as a model not to show that consumers would expect her to be associated with the sale of clothing, but because consumers are likely to associate clothing and models, and therefore to view the mark TWIGGY as pointing to petitioner.

applicable? Does it matter if the deceased person has no heirs or estate managing rights to the name? *See In re MC MC S.r.l.*, Application No. 79022561 for MARIA CALLAS (T.T.A.B. Sept. 26, 2008) and *Strathopoulos v. MC MC S.r.l.*, Opp. No. 91187914 (dismissed for failure to prosecute).

4. What level of "fame or reputation" must a person or institution possess to establish a false suggestion claim? Is it the same level of fame required for a federal dilution claim, i.e., a wide recognition "by the general consuming public of the United States"? *See Association pour la Defense de Marc Chagall v. Bondarchuk*, 82 U.S.P.Q.2d 1838 (T.T.A.B. 2007) (applying a lesser standard of fame than the dilution standard). Does MARC CHAGALL for vodka suggest a false association with the post-impressionist, Russian artist Marc Chagall, who died in 1985, where the mark owner has no connection with the artist or his heirs?

2. Sections 2(b) and 2(c) of The Lanham Act

15 U.S.C. § 1052(b) and (c) [Lanham Act § 2(b) and (c)]

No trademark by which the goods of the applicant may be distinguished from the goods of others shall be refused registration on the principal register on account of its nature unless it—

. . . .

(b) Consists of or comprises the flag or coat of arms or other insignia of the United States, or of any State or municipality, or of any foreign nation, or any simulation thereof.

(c) Consists of or comprises a name, portrait, or signature identifying a particular living individual except by his written consent, or the name, signature, or portrait of a deceased President of the United States during the life of his widow, if any, except by the written consent of the widow.

Note: Refusals under 2(b)

Refusals to register a mark because the mark "consists of or comprises the flag or coat of arms, or other insignia of the United States, of any state or municipality, or of any foreign nation, or any simulation thereof" constitute an absolute bar. Moreover, unlike refusals based on Section 2(a), there is no requirement to show any additional element, such as disparagement or false association. TMEP § 1204. It is also not necessary that the mark consist exclusively of a governmental flag, coat of arms or other insignia if the mark includes such an element. *Id.* Do you believe that the following mark for condoms should be refused under Section 2(b)?

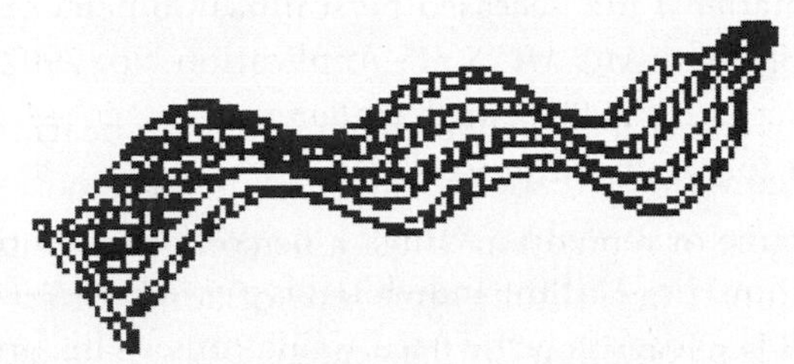

Is the design element a "simulation" of the American flag under Section 2(b)? Is the mark immoral or scandalous under Section 2(a)? *See In re Old Glory Condom Corp.*, 26 U.S.P.Q.2d 1216 (T.T.A.B. 1993). A perusal of registered marks shows many with a flag design, suggesting that "simulation" has been interpreted to require fairly exact copying. *See Re/Ma LLC v. M.L. Jones & Assocs.*, 114 U.S.P.Q.2d 1139 (E.D.N.C. 2014) (registration for flag design that copied Netherlands flag with 3 rectangles of red-over-white-over blue was ordered cancelled). Section 2(b) prohibits registration of insignia of the U.S., any state or municipality or foreign nation. What if the governmental body itself applies to register its own insignia? Does it matter whether the registration is for the governmental services provided by that entity?

In re City of Houston; In re the Government of the District of Columbia, 731 F.3d 1326 (Fed. Cir. 2013). In upholding the TTAB's refusal to register official insignia under section 2(b) both by the city of Houston for tourism, business administration and public utility services and by the District of Columbia for promotional items such as shirts and cups, the Federal Circuit relied on the unambiguous language of section 2(b) that prohibits registration of such insignia without any exceptions. In response to the argument that this interpretation prevented a municipality from protecting the public from deception, the court noted:

> ... Houston has other means to prevent "pirates and cheats" from using its city seal to deceive the public. Presumably the city of Houston could pass an ordinance prohibiting such activity. Other legal protections under the Lanham Act may exist as well. *See* 15 U.S.C. § 1125. But if Houston feels that the legal protections available to it under the Lanham Act are insufficient, and Houston desires a rewriting of § 2(b) to permit it to register its city seal, Houston must take the matter up with Congress; this court is not the proper forum for rewriting of Congressional acts.

Should Congress clarify the language of 2(b) to except governmental entities?

In re Richard M. Hoefflin, 97 U.S.P.Q.2d 1174 (T.T.A.B. 2010). In affirming the Examiner's refusal to register *inter alia* OBAMA BAHAMA PAJAMAS and OBAMA PAJAMA for pajamas under Section 2(c) of the Lanham Act because the application did not include the consent of President Obama, the Board rejected the Applicant's argument that the marks did not specifically refer to Barack Hussein Obama as follows:

> In determining whether a particular living person bearing the "name" would be associated with the mark as being used on the goods, we must consider (1) if the person is so well known that the public would reasonably assume the connection, or (2) if the individual is publicly connected with the business in which the mark is being used. [Citations.] This provision is intended to protect the intellectual property right of privacy and publicity that a living person has in his/her identity. [Citations.]
>
> In support of her position, the Trademark Examining Attorney cites to a "Morning Edition" story on January 12, 2009 (after the election of President Obama and days before his inauguration as the 44th President of the United States—and just weeks after the date on which these applications were filed) from National Public Radio (NPR) reporter Steve Inskeep. The news report highlighted many examples of "Obamification" which the nation had experienced over the preceding year. Inskeep and members of the American Dialect Society whom he interviewed defined "Obamifications" as "words manufactured from Barack Obama's name." According to those interviewed, some of these words originated with supporters and others with detractors. Many were used in a political sense only, while others tried to capitalize on the surging demand for Obama merchandise.
>
> Perhaps it is not surprising that an early online favorite was the rhyming "Obama pajama." ...
>
> ... [A]pplicant takes a number of different tacks in an attempt to overcome the Section 2(c) bar. One of applicant's arguments is that ... "Obama," as used in his marks, do[es] not represent any particular individual, and certainly not "the United States President Barack Hussein Obama II." Of course, the fact that applicant filed these ... particular applications together just weeks before President Obama's historical swearing-in would seem to belie this representation. In any case, given that registration is being sought during the presidency of Mr. Obama, and that the record shows the "obamafication" discussed above, we have no doubt but that purchasers would recognize that OBAMA BAHAMA PAJAMAS [and] OBAMA PAJAMA ... are referring to the Forty-Fourth President of the United States. To the extent that applicant is suggesting that Section 2(c) prohibits only registration of the entire names of individuals, we disagree. Rather, this statutory sub-section operates to bar the registration of marks containing not only full names, but also surnames, shortened names, nicknames, etc., so long as the name in question does, in fact, "identify" a particular living individual. *In re Sauer*, 27 USPQ2d at 1074.
>
> Applicant also takes the position that the record does not support the conclusion that President Obama is in any way connected with pajamas....

> Without this showing, applicant argues, there is no bar under Section 2(c) of the Act. However, we agree with the Trademark Examining Attorney that in making our § 2(c) determination as to these ... claimed marks, we find that President Barack Obama, *because* he is the President of the United States, is so well known and famous that members of the purchasing public will associate the individual name "Obama" as used in applicant's marks with the President and will reasonably assume that President Obama is being identified. *Martin v. Carter Hawley Hale Stores, Inc.*, 206 USPQ at 933 [No evidence to indicate that "Neil Martin" enjoys a reputation of such fame as to be recognizable by the public at large, or that he has been publicly connected with the clothing field]; and *Ross v. Analytical Technology Inc.*, 51 USPQ2d 1269 (TTAB 1999) [record fails to show that Dr. James W. Ross, Jr. is so well-known that the mark ROSS would lead to an assumption that the mark referred to him, and that he is associated with the electrodes on which the mark ROSS is being used]. While lesser-known figures (like Mr. Martin or Dr. Ross) may have to show that the consuming public connects them with the manufacturing or marketing of shirts or electrodes, for example, well-known individuals such as celebrities and world-famous political figures are entitled to the protection of Section 2(c) without having to evidence a connection with the involved goods or services. *See In re Masucci*, 179 USPQ 829 (TTAB 1973) [In spite of any common law rights applicant may have, EISENHOWER for greeting cards was refused on the ground that it consisted of the name of the late President Eisenhower during the life of his widow, and application for registration was filed without her consent]; and *In re Steak and Ale Restaurants of America, Inc.*, 185 USPQ 447 (TTAB 1975) [PRINCE CHARLES for meat was refused on the ground it identified a particular living individual whose consent was not of record].

Questions

1. May a third party register MARILYN MONROE for hosiery, or JAMES DEAN for motorcycle jackets under Section 2(c)? Would Section 2(a) of the Lanham Act bar registration?

2. Could an applicant register BILL CLINTON for neckties? RONALD REAGAN?

3. Section 2(d) of the Lanham Act: Likely Confusion

Section 2(d) of the Lanham Act provides, in relevant part, that a mark shall be refused registration if it

> (d) consists of or comprises a mark which so resembles a mark registered in the Patent and Trademark Office, or a mark or trade name previously used in the United States by another and not abandoned, as to be likely, when used on or in connection with the goods of the applicant, to cause confusion, or to cause mistake, or to deceive....

Stone Lion Capital Partners, L.P. v. Lion Capital LP

746 F.3d 1317 (Fed. Cir. 2014)

Wallach, Circuit Judge.

Stone Lion Capital Partners, L.P. ("Stone Lion") appeals from the Trademark Trial and Appeal Board's ("Board") decision refusing registration of the mark "STONE LION CAPITAL" due to a likelihood of confusion with opposer Lion Capital LLP's ("Lion") registered marks, "LION CAPITAL" and "LION." Because the Board's decision is supported by substantial evidence and in accordance with the law, this court affirms.

Background

I. The Parties

Both Stone Lion and Lion are investment management companies. Appellant Stone Lion ... manages a hedge fund that focuses on credit opportunities. Appellee Lion is a private equity firm ... that invests primarily in companies that sell consumer products.

Lion has two registered marks ... "LION CAPITAL" and "LION." ... The services ... include "financial and investment planning and research," "investment management services," and "capital investment consultation" for "LION"; and "equity capital investment" and "venture capital services" for "LION CAPITAL." There is no dispute that Lion has priority over Stone Lion with respect to these marks.

II. Proceedings Before the Board

On August 20, 2008, Stone Lion filed an intent-to-use application to register the mark "STONE LION CAPITAL" ... in connection with "financial services, namely investment advisory services, management of investment funds, and fund investment services." [Citation]. Lion opposed the registration under section 2(d) of the Lanham Act, 15 U.S.C. § 1052(d) (2006), alleging Stone Lion's proposed mark would be likely to cause confusion with Lion's registered marks when used for Stone Lion's recited financial services.

The Board conducted the likelihood of confusion inquiry pursuant to the thirteen factors set forth in *In re E.I. du Pont de Nemours & Co.*, 476 F.2d 1357, 1361 (C.C.P.A. 1973):

(1) The similarity or dissimilarity of the marks in their entireties as to appearance, sound, connotation and commercial impression.

(2) The similarity or dissimilarity and nature of the goods or services as described in an application or registration or in connection with which a prior mark is in use.

(3) The similarity or dissimilarity of established, likely-to-continue trade channels.

(4) The conditions under which and buyers to whom sales are made, i.e. "impulse" vs. careful, sophisticated purchasing.

(5) The fame of the prior mark (sales, advertising, length of use).

(6) The number and nature of similar marks in use on similar goods.

(7) The nature and extent of any actual confusion.

(8) The length of time during and conditions under which there has been concurrent use without evidence of actual confusion.

(9) The variety of goods on which a mark is or is not used (house mark, "family" mark, product mark).

(10) The market interface between applicant and the owner of a prior mark....

(11) The extent to which applicant has a right to exclude others from use of its mark on its goods.

(12) The extent of potential confusion, i.e., whether *de minimis* or substantial.

(13) Any other established fact probative of the effect of use.

Id. The parties presented evidence regarding factors one through six. The Board found that factors one through four weighed in favor of finding a likelihood of confusion, and that the remaining factors were neutral....

Upon weighing all of the pertinent *DuPont* factors, the Board found Lion met its burden to establish a likelihood of confusion by a preponderance of the evidence, and refused Stone Lion's application.

Stone Lion filed this timely appeal....

Discussion

Section 2(d) of the Lanham Act provides that a trademark may be refused registration if it so resembles a prior used or registered mark "as to be likely, when used on or in connection with the goods of the applicant, to cause confusion, or to cause mistake, or to deceive." 15 U.S.C. § 1052(d). Likelihood of confusion is a question of law with underlying factual findings made pursuant to the *DuPont* factors. *M2 Software, Inc. v. M2 Commc'ns, Inc.*, 450 F.3d 1378, 1381 (Fed. Cir. 2006). This court reviews the Board's factual findings on each *DuPont* factor for substantial evidence, *In re Pacer Tech.*, 338 F.3d 1348, 1349 (Fed. Cir. 2003), and its legal conclusion of likelihood of confusion de novo, *On-Line Careline, Inc. v. Am. Online, Inc.*, 229 F.3d 1080, 1084 (Fed. Cir. 2000)....

On appeal, Stone Lion challenges the Board's findings with respect to *DuPont* factors one, three, and four. It contends the Board: (1) "conducted an erroneous comparison of the marks," pursuant to factor one, (2) "erred in analyzing the purchasers and trade channels" in factor three, and (3) "committed legal error in dismissing purchaser sophistication and conditions of sale" in factor four. Each argument is considered in turn.

I. The Board Properly Compared the Marks Pursuant to the First *DuPont* Factor

The similarity of the marks is determined by focusing on "'the marks in their entireties as to appearance, sound, connotation, and commercial impression.'" *Palm*

Bay Imps. Inc. v. Veuve Clicquot Ponsardin Maison Fondee En 1772, 396 F.3d 1369 1371 (Fed. Cir. 2005) (quoting *DuPont*, 476 F.2d at 1361). With respect to the Board's reasoning that Stone Lion's mark "incorporates the entirety of [Lion's] marks," Stone Lion contends "the Board's analysis rests on the faulty assumption that incorporating an opposer's mark necessarily results in a likelihood of confusion," which, it says, "is not the law."[2] Stone Lion further criticizes the Board's finding that the noun "LION" was "the dominant part of both parties' marks." "'[L]ikelihood of confusion cannot be predicated on dissection of ... only part of a mark,'" and Stone Lion argues "the Board's analysis undertook the very dissection of the mark that this Court forbids." According to Stone Lion, the Board improperly "fail[ed] to assess the commercial impression made by STONE LION CAPITAL as a whole." *Id.* at 33.

These arguments misconstrue the Board's analysis. The Board properly considered whether the marks were "similar in sight, sound, meaning, and overall commercial impression." Although it reasoned that "LION" was "dominant" in both parties' marks, "there is nothing improper in stating that ... more or less weight has been given to a particular feature of a mark, provided the ultimate conclusion rests on consideration of the marks in their entireties." *In re Nat'l Data Corp.*, 753 F.2d at 1059. Nor did the Board err by according little weight to the adjective "STONE," on the ground that it did not "distinguish the marks in the context of the parties' services." 3 J. Thomas McCarthy, *McCarthy on Trademarks and Unfair Competition* § 23:50 (4th ed.) ("[A]ddition of a suggestive or descriptive element is generally not sufficient to avoid confusion."); *see also In re Rexel Inc.*, 223 U.S.P.Q. 830 (T.T.A.B. 1984) (finding likelihood of confusion between GOLIATH for pencils and LITTLE GOLIATH for a stapler). The Board properly rested its "ultimate conclusion" of similarity "on consideration of the marks in their entireties." *See In re Nat'l Data Corp.*, 753 F.2d at 1059.

Stone Lion also ... contends that "STONE LION" "is the most communicative and evocative aspect of the mark," and "contains an initial sibilant sound not found in either of Lion Capital's marks." Its "meaning [is] also quite different," according to Stone Lion, and connotes "patience, courage, fortitude and strength" as opposed to "just LION, which communicates no such lithic significance." *Id.* The record adequately supports the Board's contrary conclusions, however, and the Board did not err in finding that "STONE LION CAPITAL" is "similar in sight, sound, meaning, and overall commercial impression" to "LION CAPITAL" and "LION."

Finally, Stone Lion argues the Board gave inadequate weight to Lion's statements during prosecution of its "LION CAPITAL" registration distinguishing the third-party mark "ROARING LION." A party's prior arguments may be considered as "illuminative of shade and tone in the total picture," but do not alter the Board's obligation to reach its own conclusion on the record. *Interstate Brands Corp. v. Celestial*

2. Stone Lion argues the Board's "incorporation" analysis is improper for the additional reason that it gave "CAPITAL" meaningful weight, even though both parties "disclaimed the exclusive right to the term." The Board recognized the parties' disclaimer, however, and accordingly attached less significance to that term.

Seasonings, Inc., 576 F.2d 926, 929 (C.C.P.A. 1978). The Board's findings under the first *DuPont* factor are affirmed.[3]

II. The Board Properly Compared the Relevant Trade Channels Pursuant to the Third *DuPont* Factor

... The Board found the application and the registrations contained "no limitations" on the channels of trade and classes of purchasers and therefore "presume[d] that the parties' services travel through all usual channels of trade and are offered to all normal potential purchasers." The parties' recited services were in part legally identical, so the Board concluded the "channels of trade and classes of purchasers are the same." Because the application and registrations shared the same channels of trade and classes of purchasers, the Board determined the third *DuPont* factor weighed in favor of finding a likelihood of confusion.

On appeal, Stone Lion contends the Board "fail[ed] to examine the record to determine *which types of persons* within these organizations the parties normally dealt with." It contends the Board's findings on the third *DuPont* factor are unsupported by substantial evidence because there was no overlap between the parties' actual investors.

It was proper, however, for the Board to focus on the application and registrations rather than on real-world conditions, because "the question of registrability of an applicant's mark must be decided on the basis of the identification of goods set forth in the application." *Octocom Sys., Inc. v. Houston Comp. Servs. Inc.*, 918 F.2d 937, 942 (Fed. Cir. 1990). This is so "regardless of what the record may reveal as to the particular nature of an applicant's goods, the particular channels of trade or the class of purchasers to which sales of the goods are directed." *Id.* Even assuming there is no overlap between Stone Lion's and Lion's current customers, the Board correctly declined to look beyond the application and registered marks at issue. An application with "no restriction on trade channels" cannot be "narrowed by testimony that the applicant's use is, in fact, restricted to a particular class of purchasers." *Id.* at 943. The Board thus properly found Stone Lion's application and Lion's registrations covered the same potential purchasers and channels of trade.

III. The Board Properly Considered the Sophistication of Potential Customers Under the Fourth *DuPont* Factor

The fourth *DuPont* factor considers "[t]he conditions under which and buyers to whom sales are made, i.e. 'impulse' vs. careful, sophisticated purchasing." *DuPont*, 476 F.2d at 1361. Although recognizing that Stone Lion and Lion in fact require large

3. ... According to Stone Lion, "having concluded that the Lion Capital marks are not strong or well-known in the financial services field, the Board overlooked that the level of renown of an opposer's mark is supposed to play a 'dominant role in the process of balancing the *DuPont* factors.'" The Board never found that Lion's marks were weak. It found that in spite of news about Lion's investments featured in, e.g., The Wall Street Journal and The New York Times, the marks were not "well-known." Stone Lion does not challenge these fact-findings on appeal, and the Board did not err in declining to give this neutral factor determinative weight in its likelihood of confusion analysis.

minimum investments and target sophisticated investors, the Board focused on the sophistication of all *potential* customers of "the parties' services as they are recited in the application and registrations, respectively." Stone Lion's application includes all "investment advisory services," and Lion's registrations include "capital investment consultation." Such services, the Board found, "are not restricted to high-dollar investments or sophisticated consumers," but rather "could be offered to, and consumed by, anyone with money to invest, including ordinary consumers seeking investment services."

Stone Lion ... nevertheless argues the Board erred in considering the sophistication of potential customers. Both parties agree their current investors are sophisticated. In light of the services currently offered by Stone Lion and Lion, securities regulations require substantive, preexisting relationships with potential investors before they may invest. Stone Lion contends the Board failed to give proper weight to this clientele sophistication.[4]

Stone Lion effectively asks this court to disregard the broad scope of services recited in its application, and to instead rely on the parties' current investment practices. This would be improper because the services recited in the application determine the scope of the post-grant benefit of registration. "[R]egistration provides the registrant with prima facie evidence of ... the registrant's 'exclusive right' to use the mark on or in connection with *the goods and services specified in the certificate of registration.*" *U.S. Search LLC v. U.S. Search.com Inc.*, 300 F.3d 517, 524 (4th Cir. 2002) (emphasis added); *see also* 15 U.S.C. § 1115(a) (the registration is prima facie evidence of the registrant's exclusive right to use the mark "in connection with the goods or services specified in the registration"). Other benefits of registration are likewise commensurate with the scope of the services recited in the application, not with the applicant's then-existing services. *See, e.g.*, 15 U.S.C. § 1072 (federal registrants enjoy nationwide constructive notice of their ownership of the registered mark); *id.* § 1117 (allowing recovery of defendant's profits, plaintiff's damages, and the costs of the action for violation of a registered mark). It would make little sense for the Board to consider only the parties' current activities when the intent-to-use application, not current use, determines the scope of this post-grant benefit. Parties that choose to recite services in their trademark application that exceed their actual services will be held to the broader scope of the application. *See Octocom Sys.*, 918 F.2d at 943 (stating that a broad application "is not narrowed by testimony that the applicant's use is, in fact, restricted").

At oral argument, Stone Lion contended that ... limiting the investor sophistication analysis to the four corners of the application is contrary to *DuPont*, where our predecessor court considered "all of the evidence" on sophistication, not only the services

4. ... Stone Lion maintains there is no likelihood of confusion at the point of sale, because any potential confusion would be resolved during the lengthy qualification process for qualified investors....

There is no need to address these contentions.... As discussed below, the Board properly held the recited services may be offered to ordinary consumers and Stone Lion does not contest that such consumers may be confused at the point of sale. This finding is sufficient to affirm the Board's conclusion that the fourth *DuPont* factor favored opposer Lion.

recited in the application. In *DuPont*, the Board found likelihood of confusion between DuPont's applied-for mark, RALLY, for "combination polishing, glazing and cleaning agent for use on automobiles," and the ... "registered mark RALLY for an all-purpose detergent." *DuPont,* 476 F.2d at 1359. While DuPont's appeal was pending before the Board, DuPont had purchased Horizon's mark in the context of automobile products and the parties entered into an agreement allowing DuPont to use the mark in the "automotive aftermarket" and "incidentally usable" products, and limiting Horizon to the "commercial building or household market." *Id.*

Our predecessor court reversed the Board's refusal of DuPont's application, holding that substantial weight should be given to the parties' "detailed agreement[]." *Id.* at 1362. Although such reasoning reaches beyond the application, it does so only to the extent that the parties legally bound themselves to using the mark in their respective product category. *See id.* at 1363 (explaining that if either party strays beyond their product category set forth in the agreement, they would be subject to a breach of contract action). Such a binding agreement limits the benefits of registration. For instance, the agreement's provision limiting each party to different product categories would rebut the evidentiary value of a registered mark provided in 15 U.S.C. § 1115(a) ... The *DuPont* court contrasted such a binding agreement to "a naked 'consent,'" which it found would merit little weight because "the consenter may continue or expand his use." *Id.* at 1362.

Stone Lion has not provided a naked consent, much less contractually restricted itself to its current high-minimum-investment services.... Granting Stone Lion's application would entitle it to the full scope of services recited therein, and Stone Lion cannot now distance itself from such breadth when faced with an opposition.

Accordingly, the Board properly considered *all* potential investors for the recited services, including ordinary consumers seeking to invest in services with no minimum investment requirement. Although the services recited in the application also encompass sophisticated investors, Board precedent requires the decision to be based "on the least sophisticated potential purchasers." [Citations.] Substantial evidence supports the Board's finding that such ordinary consumers "will exercise care when making financial decisions," but "are not immune from source confusion where similar marks are used in connection with related services." The Board's conclusion that the fourth *DuPont* factor weighs in opposer Lion's favor is consistent with Stone Lion's application, Lion's registrations, and with applicable law.

Conclusion

The Board properly determined that the first four *DuPont* factors weighed in favor of finding a likelihood of confusion and that the remaining factors were neutral. The refusal of Stone Lion's application for trademark registration is therefore affirmed.

AFFIRMED

Coach Services, Inc. v. Triumph Learning LLC, 668 F.3d 1356 (Fed. Cir. 2012). The Federal Circuit affirmed a finding of no likelihood of confusion between Coach's

COACH marks for handbags, luggage and accessories and Applicant's COACH mark and design mark for software, tapes and printed materials aimed at students and teachers preparing for standardized tests. In applying the *DuPont* factor analysis, the court rejected the argument that the fame of Opposer's mark was sufficient to outweigh the differences in the marks' commercial impressions and in the parties' goods. With respect to the strength of Opposer's COACH mark, the court noted:

> The fame of the registered mark plays a "dominant" role in the *DuPont* analysis, as famous marks "enjoy a wide latitude of legal protection." *Recot, Inc. v. M.C. Becton,* 214 F.3d 1322, 1327 (Fed. Cir. 2000); [citation]. A famous mark is one that has "extensive public recognition and renown." *Bose Corp. v. QSC Audio Prods. Inc.,* 293 F.3d 1367, 1371 (Fed. Cir. 2002); [citation].
>
> Fame for purposes of likelihood of confusion is a matter of degree that "varies along a spectrum from very strong to very weak." [Citation.] Relevant factors include sales, advertising, length of use of the mark, market share, brand awareness, licensing activities, and variety of goods bearing the mark. [Citations.]
>
> It is well-established that fame is insufficient, standing alone, to establish likelihood of confusion. *Univ. of Notre Dame Du Lac v. J.C. Gourmet Food Imports Co.,* Inc., 703 F.2d 1372, 1374 (Fed. Cir. 1983) ("Likely ... to cause confusion means more than the likelihood that the public will recall a famous mark on seeing the same mark used by another.") (internal quotations omitted). Although fame cannot overwhelm the other *DuPont* factors, we are mindful that it "deserves its full measure of weight in assessing likelihood of confusion." *Recot,* 214 F.3d at 1328 (noting that "fame alone cannot overwhelm the other *DuPont* factors as a matter of law").
>
> To show the strength and fame of its mark, CSI introduced the following evidence before the Board:
>
> - CSI began using the COACH mark at least as early as December 28, 1961.
> - There are approximately 400 COACH retail stores throughout all 50 states.
> - CSI's COACH products are sold by approximately 1,000 third-party retailers throughout the US.
> - In 2008, CSI's annual sales were roughly $3.5 billion.
> - In 2008, CSI spent "about $30–60 million a year" on advertising.
> - CSI has advertised in magazines such as Elle, Vogue, Vanity Fair, and The New Yorker.
> - CSI has advertised in newspapers in major metropolitan areas.
> - CSI's COACH products have received unsolicited publicity from newspapers and magazines discussing fashion trends.
> - CSI has been the subject of articles that refer to the renown of its products.

- CSI's internal brand awareness study, which issued in March 2008, showed a high level of awareness of the COACH brand for women between the ages of 13–24.
- CSI's COACH products are the subject of counterfeiting.

Based on this evidence, the Board found that CSI's COACH mark is famous for purposes of likelihood of confusion. Substantial evidence supports this finding....

On the similarity of marks factor, although the court found that the parties' marks were identical as to sight and sound, it emphasized the differences in meaning and commercial impression as follows:

> As noted, Triumph's applications seek to register COACH in standard character form, COACH in a stylized font, and COACH with a mascot and the tagline "America's Best for Student Success." It is undisputed that the word marks for both parties are identical in sound and appearance: they both use the word "Coach." This fact is significant to the similarity inquiry. We, nevertheless, agree with the Board that, despite their undisputed similarity, the marks have different meanings and create distinct commercial impressions. This is particularly true given that the word "coach" is a common English word that has many different definitions in different contexts.
>
> Specifically, we find that substantial evidence supports the Board's determination that Triumph's COACH mark, when applied to educational materials, brings to mind someone who instructs students, while CSI's COACH mark, when used in connection with luxury leather goods, including handbags, suitcases, and other travel items, brings to mind traveling by carriage. We agree with the Board that these distinct commercial impressions outweigh the similarities in sound and appearance, particularly since, as discussed below, the parties' goods are unrelated. [Citation.] Accordingly, this factor favors Triumph.

With respect to the other *DuPont* factors considered by the Board and the overall balance, the court also agreed with the Board:

> 3. Similarity of the Goods
>
> ... [T]he Board found, and we agree, that the parties' goods are unrelated ...
>
> 4. Channels of Trade and Classes of Customers
>
> ... [T]he Board did not err in concluding that the goods are not related and the channels of trade are distinct. Although there could be some overlap in the classes of purchasers for the parties' products, we agree it is unlikely that, in the circumstances in which the products are sold, customers would associate CSI's COACH brand products with educational materials used to prepare students for standardized tests. And, there is nothing in the record to suggest that a purchaser of test preparation materials who also purchases a luxury handbag would consider the goods to emanate from the same source.

> [Citation.] Accordingly, substantial evidence supports the Board's decision that this factor favors Triumph.
>
> ....
>
> ... On the record before us, and after weighing the relevant *DuPont* factors de novo, we agree with the Board that customer confusion is not likely between the parties' respective COACH marks. Although CSI's COACH mark is famous for likelihood of confusion purposes, the unrelated nature of the parties' goods and their different channels of trade weigh heavily against CSI. Absent overlap as to either factor, it is difficult to establish likelihood of confusion. Because the *DuPont* factors favoring Triumph outweigh the factors favoring CSI, the Board was correct in finding no likelihood of confusion.

The court went on to affirm the Board's finding of no likely dilution, but vacated and remanded on the question of whether Applicant's mark was merely descriptive without secondary meaning.

Questions

1. As to similarity of marks, the court found this factor weighed in favor of the plaintiff asserting the similarity of the LION versus STONE LION marks, but against the plaintiff asserting the COACH versus COACH marks. Is this divergence justified?

2. The court in *Coach Services* found that plaintiff's COACH mark is famous for the purpose of its likelihood of confusion analysis. Should the test of fame be the same as the test of fame for dilution under section 43(c)(1)? *See Palm Bay Imports, Inc. v. Veuve Clicquot Ponsardin Maison Fondee en 1722*, 396 F.3d 1369 (Fed. Cir. 2005) ("While dilution fame is an either/or proposition—fame either does or does not exist—likelihood of confusion fame 'varies along a spectrum from very strong to very weak'").

3. What effect does third-party use of a term have on the evaluation of fame? For example, where the term MOTOWN had originated as a mark for musical sound recordings, should the fact that people subsequently referred to the city of Detroit, where the mark owner is located, as "Motown" diminish the strength of the MOTOWN mark? *See UMG Recordings Inv. v. Mattel Inc.*, 100 U.S.P.Q.2d 1868 (T.T.A.B. 2011).

4. How should the Board rule in an appeal of an Examiner's finding of likelihood of confusion between JAWS and JAWS DEVOUR YOUR HUNGER for "streaming of audiovisual material via an Internet channel providing programming related to cooking," based on the registered mark JAWS for "video recordings in all formats all featuring motion pictures" and on the fame of the JAWS movie? Recall the statement in *Stone Lion* that the marks are compared for the goods and services identified in the application or registration and not "real world conditions." *See In re Mr. Recipe*, 118 U.S.P.Q.2d 1084 (T.T.A.B. 2016).

Note: Differences in Likely Confusion Analysis for Registration and for Infringement Purposes

Because a registration covers a mark in the formats and for the goods or services applied for, while an infringement determination focuses on how parties are actually using their marks in the marketplace for particular goods/services and in specific trade channels, the analysis for the purposes of determining likelihood of confusion differs. Both analyses assess the likelihood of confusion by applying multi-factor tests, such as the *DuPont* factors used by Examiners and the Board. See *Stone Lion Capital Partners L.P. v. Lion Capital, L.P., supra*, this Chapter for a listing of the *DuPont* factors. Although many of the factors applied by the courts, *see* Chapter 6[B], *infra*, are similar to those in registrability decisions, the method of analysis for some of them differs depending on whether the question is registration or infringement. For example, in the *Stone Lion Capital* case above, the focus in the similarity of the goods and the channel of trade factors was on how the goods were described in the pertinent application and registrations and the channels of trade in which such goods would normally travel. If there is no limitation in the application or registration, Examining Attorneys and the Board will consider the channels of trade in which such goods or services could be expected to move because an unrestricted registration could theoretically cover such channels. Courts determining infringement, by contrast, look at the actual goods/services on which the parties use their respective marks and at the actual channels of trade employed. Analysis of the similarity of the marks factor also can differ. Although both the Trademark Office and the courts look to similarities in sight, sound and meaning of marks, where an application or registration covers a mark in standard character form without any stylization or design features, the Examining Attorneys and Board will look at a variety of formats in which a mark might appear. *See, e.g., In re Viterra*, 671 F.3d 1358 (Fed. Cir. 2012) (standard character XCEED confusingly similar to XSEED and Design for agricultural seeds). XSEED and design was displayed as:

The court reasoned that the standard character XCEED mark could be considered in a variety of stylizations and displays in which it may appear. Courts in determining infringement, by contrast, assess how the parties' marks actually appear in the marketplace because they are trying to determine whether there is a likelihood of confusion in fact, not in just in theory. The Supreme Court considered the differences in registration decisions by the Board and infringement decisions by the court in the following case.

B&B Hardware, Inc. v. Hargis Industries, Inc.

135 S. Ct. 1293, 191 L. Ed.2d 222 (2015)

Justice Alito delivered the opinion of the Court:

Sometimes two different tribunals are asked to decide the same issue. When that happens, the decision of the first tribunal usually must be followed by the second, at least if the issue is really the same. Allowing the same issue to be decided more than once wastes litigants' resources and adjudicators' time, and it encourages parties who lose before one tribunal to shop around for another. The doctrine of collateral estoppel or issue preclusion is designed to prevent this from occurring.

This case concerns the application of issue preclusion in the context of trademark law. Petitioner, B&B Hardware, Inc. (B&B), and respondent Hargis Industries, Inc. (Hargis), both use similar trademarks; B&B owns SEALTIGHT while Hargis owns SEALTITE. Under the Lanham Act, ... an applicant can seek to register a trademark through an administrative process within the United States Patent and Trademark Office (PTO). But if another party believes that the PTO should not register a mark because it is too similar to its own, that party can oppose registration before the Trademark Trial and Appeal Board (TTAB). Here, Hargis tried to register the mark SEALTITE, but B&B opposed SEALTITE's registration. After a lengthy proceeding, the TTAB agreed with B&B that SEALTITE should not be registered.

In addition to permitting a party to object to the registration of a mark, the Lanham Act allows a mark owner to sue for trademark infringement. Both a registration proceeding and a suit for trademark infringement, moreover, can occur at the same time. In this case, while the TTAB was deciding whether SEALTITE should be registered, B&B and Hargis were also litigating the SEALTIGHT versus SEALTITE dispute in federal court. In both registration proceedings and infringement litigation, the tribunal asks whether a likelihood of confusion exists between the mark sought to be protected (here, SEALTIGHT) and the other mark (SEALTITE).

The question before this Court is whether the District Court in this case should have applied issue preclusion to the TTAB's decision that SEALTITE is confusingly similar to SEALTIGHT. Here, the Eighth Circuit rejected issue preclusion ... We disagree [and] hold that a court should give preclusive effect to TTAB decisions if the ordinary elements of issue preclusion are met. We therefore reverse the judgment of the Eighth Circuit and remand for further proceedings....

....

To obtain the benefits of registration, a mark owner files an application with the PTO....

If a trademark examiner believes that registration is warranted, the mark is published in the Official Gazette of the PTO. § 1062. At that point, "[a]ny person who believes that he would be damaged by the registration" may "file an opposition." § 1063(a). Opposition proceedings occur before the TTAB (or panels thereof). § 1067(a). The TTAB consists of administrative trademark judges and high-ranking

PTO officials, including the Director of the PTO and the Commissioner of Trademarks. § 1067(b).

Opposition proceedings before the TTAB are in many ways "similar to a civil action in a federal district court." [Citation.] These proceedings, ... are largely governed by the Federal Rules of Civil Procedure and Evidence. [Citation.] The TTAB also allows discovery and depositions. [Citation.] The party opposing registration bears the burden of proof, ... and if that burden cannot be met, the opposed mark must be registered, [citation].

The primary way in which TTAB proceedings differ from ordinary civil litigation is that ... there is no live testimony. Even so, the TTAB allows parties to submit transcribed testimony, taken under oath and subject to cross-examination, and to request oral argument. [Citation].

When a party opposes registration because it believes the mark proposed to be registered is too similar to its own, the TTAB evaluates likelihood of confusion by applying some or all of the 13 factors set out in *In re E.I. DuPont de Nemours & Co.*, 476 F.2d 1357 (CCPA 1973). After the TTAB decides whether to register the mark, a party can seek review in the U.S. Court of Appeals for the Federal Circuit, or it can file a new action in district court. *See* 15 U.S.C. § 1071. In district court, the parties can conduct additional discovery and the judge resolves registration *de novo*. [Citations.]

The Lanham Act, of course, also creates a federal cause of action for trademark infringement. The owner of a mark, whether registered or not, can bring suit in federal court if another is using a mark that too closely resembles the plaintiff's. The court must decide whether the defendant's use of a mark in commerce "is likely to cause confusion, or to cause mistake, or to deceive" with regards to the plaintiff's mark. *See* 15 U.S.C. § 1114(1)(a) (registered marks); § 1125(a)(1)(A) (unregistered marks). In infringement litigation, the district court considers the full range of a mark's usages, not just those in the application.

B

Petitioner B&B and respondent Hargis both manufacture metal fasteners. B&B manufactures fasteners for the aerospace industry, while Hargis manufactures fasteners for use in the construction trade. Although there are obvious differences between space shuttles and A-frame buildings, both aerospace and construction engineers prefer fasteners that seal things tightly ...

....

For purposes here, we pick up the story in 2002, when the PTO published SEALTITE in the Official Gazette. This prompted opposition proceedings before the TTAB, complete with discovery, including depositions....

Invoking a number of the *DuPont* factors, the TTAB sided with B&B. The Board considered, for instance, whether SEALTIGHT is famous (it's not, said the Board), how the two products are used (differently), how much the marks resemble each other (very much), and whether customers are actually confused (perhaps sometimes). Concluding that "the most critical factors in [its] likelihood of confusion analysis are the similarities of the marks and the similarity of the goods," the TTAB determined that SEALTITE—when "used in connection with 'self-piercing and self-drilling metal screws for use in the manufacture of metal and post-frame buildings'"—could not be registered because it "so resembles" SEALTIGHT when "used in connection with fasteners that provide leakproof protection from liquids and gases, fasteners that have a captive o-ring, and 'threaded or unthreaded metal fasteners and other related hardware ... for use in the aerospace industry' as to be likely to cause confusion." Despite a right to do so, Hargis did not seek judicial review in either the Federal Circuit or District Court.

All the while, B&B had sued Hargis for infringement. Before the District Court ruled on likelihood of confusion, however, the TTAB announced its decision. After a series of proceedings not relevant here, B&B argued to the District Court that Hargis could not contest likelihood of confusion because of the preclusive effect of the TTAB decision. The District Court disagreed, reasoning that the TTAB is not an Article III court. The jury returned a verdict for Hargis, finding no likelihood of confusion.

B&B appealed to the Eighth Circuit. Though accepting for the sake of argument that agency decisions can ground issue preclusion, the panel majority affirmed for three reasons: first, because the TTAB uses different factors than the Eighth Circuit to evaluate likelihood of confusion; second, because the TTAB placed too much emphasis on the appearance and sound of the two marks; and third, because Hargis bore the burden of persuasion before the TTAB, while B&B bore it before the District Court. 716 F. 3d 1020 (2013). Judge Colloton dissented, concluding that issue preclusion should apply. After calling for the views of the Solicitor General, we granted certiorari. 573 U.S. ___, 134 S. Ct. 2899, 189 L. Ed. 2d 854 (2014).

....

IV

[W]e turn to whether there is a categorical reason why registration decisions can never meet the ordinary elements of issue preclusion ... Although many registrations will not satisfy those ordinary elements, that does not mean that none will. We agree with Professor McCarthy that issue preclusion applies where "the issues in the two cases are indeed identical and the other rules of collateral estoppel are carefully observed." 6 McCarthy § 32:99, at 32–244; see also 3 *Gilson* § 11.08[4][i][iii][B], p. 11-319 ("Ultimately, Board decisions on likelihood of confusion ... should be given preclusive effect on a case-by-case basis").

A

The Eighth Circuit's primary objection to issue preclusion was that the TTAB considers different factors than it does. Whereas the TTAB employs some or all of the *DuPont* factors to assess likelihood of confusion, the Eighth Circuit looks to similar, but not identical, factors identified in *SquirtCo v. Seven-Up Co.,* 628 F. 2d 1086, 1091 (CA8 1980). The court's instinct was sound: "[I]ssues are not identical if the second action involves application of a different legal standard, even though the factual setting of both suits may be the same." 18 C. Wright, A. Miller, & E. Cooper, Federal Practice & Procedure §4417, p. 449 (2d ed. 2002) (hereinafter Wright & Miller). Here, however, the same likelihood-of-confusion standard applies to both registration and infringement.

To begin with, it does not matter that registration and infringement are governed by different statutory provisions. Often a single standard is placed in different statutes; that does not foreclose issue preclusion. [Citation.] Neither does it matter that the TTAB and the Eighth Circuit use different factors to assess likelihood of confusion. For one thing, the factors are not fundamentally different.... More important, if federal law provides a single standard, parties cannot escape preclusion simply by litigating anew in tribunals that apply that one standard differently. A contrary rule would encourage the very evils that issue preclusion helps to prevent.

The real question, therefore, is whether likelihood of confusion for purposes of registration is the same standard as likelihood of confusion for purposes of infringement. We conclude it is, for at least three reasons. First, the operative language is essentially the same; the fact that the registration provision separates "likely" from "to cause confusion, or to cause mistake, or to deceive" does not change that reality.[3] [Citation.] Second, the likelihood-of-confusion language that Congress used in these Lanham Act provisions has been central to trademark registration since at least 1881.... And third, district courts can cancel registrations during infringement litigation, just as they can adjudicate infringement in suits seeking judicial review of registration decisions. [Citation]. There is no reason to think that the same district judge in the same case should apply two separate standards of likelihood of confusion.

Hargis responds that the text is not actually the same because the registration provision asks whether the marks "resemble" each other, 15 U.S.C. §1052(d), while the infringement provision is directed towards the "use in commerce" of the marks, §1114(1) ... There is some force to this argument. It is true that "a party opposing an application to register a mark before the Board often relies only on its federal registration, not on any common-law rights in usages not encompassed by its registration," and "the Board typically analyzes the marks, goods, and channels of trade only as set forth in the application and in the opposer's registration, regardless of whether the actual usage of the marks by either party differs." Brief for United States as *Amicus Curiae* 23; see also *id.*, at 5 (explaining that "the Board typically reviews only the

---

3. Compare 15 U.S.C. §1114(1) ("Any person who shall ... use in commerce any ... mark in connection with the sale, offering for sale, distribution, or advertising of any goods or services on or in connection with which such use is *likely to cause confusion, or to cause mistake, or to deceive* ... shall be liable in a civil action by the registrant for the remedies hereinafter provided" (emphasis added)) with §1052(d) ("No trademark ... shall be refused registration ... unless it ... [c]onsists of or comprises a mark which so resembles a mark registered in the Patent and Trademark Office ... as to be *likely*, when used on or in connection with the goods of the applicant, *to cause confusion, or to cause mistake, or to deceive* ..." (emphasis added)).

usages encompassed by the registration") (citing 3 *Gilson* § 9.03[2][a][ii]); 3 McCarthy § 20:15, at 20–45 (explaining that for registration "it is the mark as shown in the application and as used on the goods described in the application which must be considered, not the mark as actually used"). This means that unlike in infringement litigation, "[t]he Board's determination that a likelihood of confusion does or does not exist will not resolve the confusion issue with respect to non-disclosed usages." Brief for United States as *Amicus Curiae* 23.

Hargis' argument ... mistakes a reason not to apply issue preclusion in some or even many cases as a reason never to apply issue preclusion. Just because the TTAB does not always consider the *same usages* as a district court does, it does not follow that the Board applies a *different standard* to the usages it does consider. If a mark owner uses its mark in ways that are materially the same as the usages included in its registration application, then the TTAB is deciding the same likelihood-of-confusion issue as a district court in infringement litigation. By contrast, if a mark owner uses its mark in ways that are materially unlike the usages in its application, then the TTAB is not deciding the same issue. Thus, if the TTAB does not consider the marketplace usage of the parties' marks, the TTAB's decision should "have no later preclusive effect in a suit where actual usage in the marketplace is the paramount issue." 6 McCarthy § 32:101, at 32–246.

....

A fortiori, if the TTAB considers a different mark altogether, issue preclusion would not apply. Needless to say, moreover, if the TTAB has not decided the same issue as that before the district court, there is no reason why any deference would be warranted.

For a similar reason, the Eighth Circuit erred in holding that issue preclusion could not apply here because the TTAB relied too heavily on "appearance and sound." Undoubtedly there are cases in which the TTAB places more weight on certain factors than it should. When that happens, an aggrieved party should seek judicial review. The fact that the TTAB may have erred, however, does not prevent preclusion. As Judge Colloton observed in dissent, "'issue preclusion prevent[s] relitigation of wrong decisions just as much as right ones.'" 716 F.3d, at 1029 (quoting *Clark v. Clark*, 984 F.2d 272, 273 (CA8 1993)); see also *Restatement (Second) of Judgments* § 28, Comment j, at 284 (explaining that "refusal to give the first judgment preclusive effect should not ... be based simply on a conclusion that [it] was patently erroneous").

B

Hargis also argues that ... the TTAB uses procedures that differ from those used by district courts. Granted, "[r]edetermination of issues is warranted if there is reason to doubt the quality, extensiveness, or fairness of procedures followed in prior litigation." *Montana*, 440 U.S., at 164, n. 11, 99 S. Ct. 970, 59 L. Ed. 2d 210; *see also Parklane Hosiery*, 439 U.S., at 331, and n. 15, 99 S. Ct. 645, 58 L. Ed. 2d 552 (similar). But again, this only suggests that sometimes issue preclusion might be inappropriate, not that it always is.

No one disputes that the TTAB and district courts use different procedures. Most notably, district courts feature live witnesses. Procedural differences, by themselves, however, do not defeat issue preclusion … Rather than focusing on whether procedural differences exist—they often will—the correct inquiry is whether the procedures used in the first proceeding were fundamentally poor, cursory, or unfair. *See Montana*, 440 U.S., at 164, n. 11, 99 S. Ct. 970, 59 L. Ed. 2d 210.

Here, there is no categorical "reason to doubt the quality, extensiveness, or fairness," *ibid.*, of the agency's procedures. In large part they are exactly the same as in federal court. *See* 37 CFR §§2.116(a), 2.122(a). For instance, although "[t]he scope of discovery in Board proceedings.… is generally narrower than in court proceedings"—reflecting the fact that there are often fewer usages at issue—the TTAB has adopted almost the whole of Federal Rule of Civil Procedure 26. [Citation.] It is conceivable, of course, that the TTAB's procedures may prove ill-suited for a particular issue in a particular case, *e.g.*, a party may have tried to introduce material evidence but was prevented by the TTAB from doing so, or the TTAB's bar on live testimony may materially prejudice a party's ability to present its case. The ordinary law of issue preclusion, however, already accounts for those "rare" cases where a "compelling showing of unfairness" can be made. *Restatement (Second) of Judgments* §28, Comments g and j, at 283–284.

….

C

Hargis also contends that the stakes for registration are so much lower than for infringement that issue preclusion should never apply to TTAB decisions. Issue preclusion may be inapt if "the amount in controversy in the first action [was] so small in relation to the amount in controversy in the second that preclusion would be plainly unfair." *Restatement (Second) of Judgments* §28, Comment j, at 283–284. After all, "[f]ew … litigants would spend $50,000 to defend a $5,000 claim." Wright & Miller §4423, at 612. Hargis is wrong, however, that this exception to issue preclusion applies to every registration. To the contrary: When registration is opposed, there is good reason to think that both sides will take the matter seriously.

The benefits of registration are substantial. Registration is "prima facie evidence of the validity of the registered mark," 15 U.S.C. §1057(b), and is a precondition for a mark to become "incontestable," §1065. Incontestability is a powerful protection. *See, e.g., Park 'n Fly, Inc. v. Dollar Park & Fly, Inc.*, 469 U.S. 189, 194, 105 S. Ct. 658, 83 L. Ed. 2d 582 (1985) (holding that an incontestable mark cannot be challenged as merely descriptive); (citation).

The importance of registration is undoubtedly why Congress provided for *de novo* review of TTAB decisions in district court. It is incredible to think that a district court's adjudication of particular usages would not have preclusive effect in another district court. Why would unchallenged TTAB decisions be different? Congress' creation of this elaborate registration scheme, with so many important rights attached and backed up by plenary review, confirms that registration decisions can be weighty enough to ground issue preclusion.

V

For these reasons, the Eighth Circuit erred in this case. On remand, the court should apply the following rule: So long as the other ordinary elements of issue preclusion are met, when the usages adjudicated by the TTAB are materially the same as those before the district court, issue preclusion should apply.

The judgment of the United States Court of Appeals for the Eighth Circuit is reversed, and the case is remanded for further proceedings consistent with this opinion.

It is so ordered.

JUSTICE GINSBURG, concurring.

The Court rightly recognizes that "for a great many registration decisions issue preclusion obviously will not apply." That is so because contested registrations are often decided upon "a comparison of the marks in the abstract and apart from their marketplace usage." 6 J. McCarthy, Trademarks and Unfair Competition § 32:101, p. 32-247 (4th ed. 2014). When the registration proceeding is of that character, "there will be no [preclusion] of the likel[ihood] of confusion issue ... in a later infringement suit." *Ibid.* On that understanding, I join the Court's opinion.

Questions

1. B&B registered SEALTIGHT for metal fasteners and hardware for use in the aerospace industry; while Hargis sought to register SEALTITE for metal screws for use in the manufacture of metal and post-frame buildings. Does the fact that the parties' respective registration and application reflected the actual uses of their products suggest that the Board's analysis of likely confusion would mirror that of the court's? How should the case be decided on remand? *See B & B Hardware, Inc. v. Hargis Indus.*, 800 F.3d 427 (8th Cir. 2015).

2. In assessing the similarity of marks, the Board compares the similarity of their sight, sound and meaning. Where the sight and sound of two marks are different, but the meaning of the challenged mark is the foreign language equivalent of the other, how heavily should this similarity of meaning weigh? *See, e.g., In re La Peregrina Ltd.*, 86 U.S.P.Q.2d 1645 (T.T.A.B. 2008) (LA PEREGRINA for jewelry found confusingly similar to PILGRIM for jewelry where la peregrina means "the pilgrim" in Spanish); *In re American Safety Razor Co.*, 2 U.S.P.Q.2d 1459 (T.T.A.B. 1987) (BUENOS DIAS for soap confusingly similar to GOOD MORNING for shaving cream); *In re Aquamar, Inc.*, 115 U.S.P.Q.2d 1122 (T.T.A.B. 2015) (MARAZUL for fish and seafood products confusingly similar to BLUE SEA for fish and frozen fish where MAR AZUL means "blue sea" in Spanish).

3. Is it legitimate to compare different portions of a mark to two separate marks of another if those marks are often used on the same product and in its advertising? *See Schering-Plough Healthcare Products, Inc. v. Huang*, 84 U.S.P.Q.2D (BNA) 1323 (T.T.A.B. 2007) (DR. AIR for shoe insoles as compared with DR. SCHOLL'S and AIR PILLO for the same products).

To establish a 2(d) claim, a threshold issue is that another has prior rights in a mark before a determination of likelihood of confusion is made. Recall the principle of territoriality articulated by the Second Circuit in *ITC Ltd. v. Punchgini*, 518 F.3d 159 (2d Cir. 2008), and the priority of a good faith remote junior user articulated in *United Drug Co. v. Theodore Rectanus Co.*, 248 U.S. 90 (1918), *supra* Chapter 3[F]. Consider the following two cases in light of these principles in the context of establishing a 2(d) claim for registration purposes where one of the users is a non-U.S. entity.

In **Person's Co. v. Christman**, 900 F.2d 1565 (Fed. Cir. 1990), Christman, a U.S. national, traveled to Japan where he observed use of the PERSON'S mark and logo by Person's Co., a Japanese company. On return to the U.S., Christman consulted an attorney who cleared the PERSON'S mark for use in the U.S. Christman commenced use of the mark and copied some of the clothing designs and logo of the Japanese company. He filed a trademark application, at which time he was unaware that the Japanese company intended to introduce its line in the U.S., which in fact the Japanese company started to do before Christman's registration issued. The Japanese company argued that it was the senior user and that Christman had adopted the mark in bad faith. In rejecting this argument, the Federal Circuit stated:

> In the present case, appellant Person's Co. relies on its use of the mark in Japan in an attempt to support its claim for priority in the United States. Such foreign use has no effect on U.S. commerce and cannot form the basis for a holding that appellant has priority here. The concept of territoriality is basic to trademark law; trademark rights exist in each country solely according to that country's statutory scheme. Christman was the first to use the mark in United States commerce and the first to obtain a federal registration thereon. Appellant has no basis upon which to claim priority and is the junior user under these facts.
>
> ....
>
> ... Person's Co. argues that a "remote junior user" of a mark obtains no right superior to the "senior user" if the "junior user" has adopted the mark with knowledge of the "senior user's" prior use.
>
> ... In the case at bar, appellant Person's Co., while first to adopt the mark, was not the first user in the United States. Christman is the senior user, and we are aware of no case where a senior user has been charged with bad faith. The concept of bad faith adoption applies to remote junior users seeking concurrent use registrations; in such cases, the likelihood of customer confusion in the remote area may be presumed from proof of the junior user's knowledge. In the present case, when Christman initiated use of the mark, Person's Co. had not yet entered U.S. commerce. The Person's Co. had no goodwill in the United States and the "PERSON'S" mark had no reputation here. Appellant's argument ignores the territorial nature of trademark rights.
>
> Appellant next asserts that Christman's knowledge of its prior use of the mark in Japan should preclude his acquisition of superior trademark rights

in the United States. The Board found that, at the time of registration, Christman was not aware of appellant's intention to enter the U.S. clothing and accessories market in the future. Christman obtained a trademark search on the "PERSON'S" mark and an opinion of competent counsel that the mark was "available" in the United States. Since Appellant had taken no steps to secure registration of the mark in the United States, Christman was aware of no basis for Person's Co. to assert superior rights to use and registration here. Appellant would have us infer bad faith adoption because of Christman's awareness of its use of the mark in Japan, but an inference of bad faith requires something more than mere knowledge of prior use of a similar mark in a foreign country.

First Niagara Ins. v. First Niagara Financial, 476 F.3d 867 (Fed. Cir. 2007). First Niagara Insurance, a Canadian corporation whose use of the mark in Canada dated to 1984, invoked § 2(d) to oppose a US company's ITU registration of First Niagara for financial services, including insurance brokerage. The Board dismissed the opposition on the ground that Opposer did not use its marks "in a type of commerce regulable by Congress." The Federal Circuit reversed.

FN-Canada operates entirely out of Niagara Falls and Niagara-on-the-Lake, in Ontario, Canada, and has no physical presence (e.g., offices, employees, assets, etc.) in the United States. Moreover, FN-Canada is not licensed to act as an insurance broker in any country other than Canada. Nevertheless, FN-Canada's business does have connections to the United States. For example, FN-Canada sells insurance policies issued by United States-based underwriting companies. FN-Canada also sells, through insurance brokers in this country, policies to United States citizens having Canadian property. In other words, if an American owns property in Canada and needs insurance for that property, a domestic broker will contact FN-Canada, who will then provide an appropriate policy issued by one of FN-Canada's underwriters. The domestic broker and FN-Canada share the commission generated by the transaction.... FN-Canada does not own any registered United States marks; however, in its advertising (including advertising that "spills over" into the United States) and correspondence (including correspondence to customers and other business contacts in the United States) FN-Canada regularly uses several unregistered marks: "First Niagara," "First Niagara Insurance Brokers." ...

In the proceedings below, the Board based its analysis on the assumption that an "opposer's claim of prior use can succeed only if it has proved use of its marks in connection with services rendered in commerce lawfully regulated by Congress, as required under Section 45 of the Trademark Act, 15 U.S.C. § 1127." Such an assumption was unwarranted, however, in light of the plain language of the statute, which merely requires the prior mark to have been "used in the United States by another." 15 U.S.C. § 1052(d).... Indeed, as the Board observed in a footnote in its opinion, "[a]n opposer claiming priority under Section 2(d) may rely on use that is strictly intrastate and not regulable by Congress." That privilege attaches to all opposers, regardless of whether they are foreign or domestic. Thus, a foreign opposer can present its opposition on the merits by showing only use of its mark in the United States....

Under the correct test, it is clear that the Board erred in dismissing FN-Canada's oppositions. The record unquestionably reveals more than ample use of FN-Canada's marks in the United States to satisfy the use requirements of Section 2(d). Therefore, we are compelled to reverse the decision below. [The court declined to determine whether FN-Canada's US use was also "use in commerce."]

Questions

1. Is *Person's* still good law after *First Niagara*? If the PERSONS mark were known to U.S. tourists and Persons had first sold to buyers in Japan for resale in the U.S. before Christman had sold goods in the U.S. under the PERSONS mark, would the Japanese company have been entitled to register PERSONS in the U.S.? Would it have been able to oppose Christman's US registration of the same mark for the same goods?

2. Do you agree with the *Person's* court's distinction between knowingly adopting a mark already in use in a limited geographic area within the U.S. (bad faith), and knowingly adopting a mark already in use outside the U.S. (good faith)? Is such a distinction good policy? For a general examination of the concept of trademark territoriality that underlies the distinction, *see, e.g.*, Graeme B. Dinwoodie, *Trademarks and Territoriality: Detaching Trademark Law from the Nation-State*, 41 Hous. L. Rev. 885 (2004).

Sections 13 and 14 of the Lanham Act, 15 U.S.C. §§ 1063 and 1064, were amended in 1999 to permit oppositions and cancellations to be brought on the ground of dilution as set forth in Section 43(c), 15 U.S.C. § 1125(c). Dilution is not a bar to registration under section 2, and an Examiner cannot rely on dilution as a ground to refuse registration. Interested third parties, however, can institute an opposition or cancellation action on this basis. Examine the language in Section 13, 15 U.S.C. §§ 1063, which states that "any person who believes that he would be damaged by the registration of a mark..., including as a result of dilution under Section 43(c)" may file an opposition. Could an opposition rely upon dilution under state law as a ground to oppose an application? *See Enterprise Rent-A-Car Co. v. Advantage Rent-A-Car, Inc.*, 330 F.3d 1333 (Fed. Cir. 2003) (state dilution not a ground for opposition). See Chapter 9, *infra*, for a discussion of dilution cases.

4. Section 2(e)(2) and (3) of the Lanham Act: Geographic Terms

Section 2(e) of the Lanham Act offers a variety of grounds for refusal to register. We have already encountered refusals on the basis that the mark is "merely descriptive," *see In re Quik-Print Copy Shops, Inc.*, 616 F.2d 523 (C.C.P.A. 1980), Chapter 2[B], *supra*, and that it is "deceptively misdescriptive," *see* this Chapter, *supra.* Section 2(e) also bars from registration a mark which, *inter alia*

(e) consists of a mark which ...

(2) when used on or in connection with the goods of the applicant is primarily geographically descriptive of them, except as indications of regional origin may be registrable under section 1054 of this title,

(3) when used on or in connection with the goods of the applicant is primarily geographically deceptively misdescriptive of them....

Note that section 2(e)(2) refusals may be overcome by a showing pursuant to section 2(f) that the mark as used "has become distinctive of the applicant's goods in commerce." However, since the 1993 amendments to the Lanham Act, a showing of distinctiveness will no longer overcome a rejection on the ground that the mark is "primarily geographically deceptively misdescriptive" under section 2(e)(3):

(f) Except as expressly excluded in paragraphs (a), (b), (c), (d), (e)(3) and (e)(5) of this section, nothing in this chapter shall prevent the registration of a mark used by the applicant which has become distinctive of the applicant's goods in commerce. The Director may accept as prima facie evidence that the mark has become distinctive, as used on or in connection with the applicant's goods in commerce, proof of substantially exclusive and continuous use thereof as a mark by the applicant in commerce for the five years before the date on which the claim of distinctiveness is made. Nothing in this section shall prevent the registration of a mark which, when used on or in connection with the goods of the applicant, is primarily geographically deceptively misdescriptive of them, and which became distinctive of the applicant's goods in commerce before [December 8, 1993]....

In re The Newbridge Cutlery Co.

776 F.3d 854 (Fed. Cir. 2015)

LINN, CIRCUIT JUDGE.

The Newbridge Cutlery Company (the "applicant") appeals from the decision of the Trademark Trial and Appeal Board (the "Board") affirming the Trademark Examiner's refusal to register applicant's NEWBRIDGE HOME mark as being primarily geographically descriptive. [Citation.] Because substantial evidence fails to support the Examiner's refusal, we reverse and remand.

BACKGROUND

Applicant is an Irish company headquartered in Newbridge, Ireland, that designs, manufactures and sells housewares, kitchen ware and silverware in the United States and elsewhere around the world under the mark NEWBRIDGE HOME. Applicant designs its products in Newbridge, Ireland, and manufactures some, but not all, of its products there....

....

... [W]hile the genesis of the refusal to register geographical names was to prevent a first registrant from preempting all other merchants from identifying the source of their goods, the focus of the 1946 Lanham Act moved to a more nuanced restriction that considered the primary significance of the mark when applied to the goods.

....

This court's predecessor provided considerable guidance in interpreting the statutory language relating to primarily geographical marks in *Nantucket*, a pre-NAFTA case dealing with primarily geographically deceptively misdescriptive marks. *See* 677 F.2d 95. The PTO rejected the mark NANTUCKET for shirts because it considered the mark primarily geographically deceptively misdescriptive, as the "term NANTUCKET has a readily recognizable geographic meaning, and no alternative non-geographic significance." *Id.* at 97; [citation]. The Court of Customs and Patent Appeals reversed, concluding that there was no showing of an association in the public's mind between the place, i.e., Nantucket, and the marked goods, i.e., the shirts. *See id.* at 101. The court explained:

> "The wording of [§ 1052(e)] makes it plain that not all terms which are geographically suggestive are unregistrable. Indeed, the statutory language declares nonregistrable only those words which are 'primarily geographically descriptive.' The word 'primarily' should not be overlooked, for it is not the intent of the federal statute to refuse registration of a mark where the geographic meaning is minor, obscure, remote, or unconnected with the goods. Thus, if there be no connection of the geographical meaning of the mark with the goods in the public mind, that is, if the mark is arbitrary when applied to the goods, registration should not be refused under § 2(e)(2)."

Id. at 99; [citation].

... The rationale for allowing registration of marks that relevant consumers do not view as primarily geographic is that the consumer would consider such marks "arbitrary." [Citations.] That the phrase "when applied to the goods of the applicant" was replaced, in 1988, with the phrase "when used on or in connection with," did not change the law. *Nantucket*'s interpretation of § 1052(e) is bolstered by the legislative history, which indicates that this section was introduced to eliminate rejections of geographical trademarks made without reference to their connotations to consumers in association with the goods or services for which the marks are used.

... As the statute uses the phrase "primarily geographically" in both the descriptive and deceptively misdescriptive subsections, this court's decisions relating to one subsection inform the meaning of the other and make clear that to refuse registration under either subsection the Trademark Examiner must show that: (1) "the mark sought to be registered is the name of a place known generally to the public," *Vittel*, 824 F.2d at 959, and (2) "the public would make a goods/place association, i.e., believe that the goods for which the mark is sought to be registered originate in that place." *Id. Accord In re Miracle Tuesday, LLC*, 695 F.3d 1339, 1343 (Fed. Cir. 2012) (describing analogous factors for primarily geographically deceptively misdescriptive marks) (citing *Cal. Innovations*, 329 F.3d at 1341).

To refuse registration of a mark as being primarily geographically descriptive, the PTO must also show that (3) "the source of the goods is the geographic region named in the mark." *Bernier*, 894 F.2d at 391. [Citation]. In applying prongs (1) and (2) of this test, our precedent establishes that the relevant public is the purchasing public in the United States of these types of goods. As we made clear in *Vittel*, "we are not concerned with the public in other countries." [Citation.]

Regarding the first prong of the test, that the population of the location is sizable and/or that members of the consuming public have ties to the location (to use the example in *Loew's*: that Durango, Mexico, would be recognized by "the Mexican population of this country") is evidence that a location is generally known. *See Loew's*, 769 F.2d at 766, 768. By contrast, that the geographic meaning of a location is "minor, obscure [or] remote" indicates that the location is not generally known....

In establishing the goods/place association required by the second prong of the test, we have explained that the PTO only needs to show "a *reasonable predicate* for its conclusion that the public would be *likely* to make the particular goods/place association on which it relies." *Miracle Tuesday*, 695 F.3d at 1344. [Citation.] It need not show an "actual" association in consumers' minds. [Citation.] A goods/place association can be shown even where the location is not " 'well known' " or " 'noted' " for the relevant goods. *Cal. Innovations*, 329 F.3d at 1338 (quoting *Loew's*, 769 F.2d at 767). If the Trademark Examiner establishes such a *prima facie* case, an applicant may rebut this showing with evidence "that the public would not actually believe the goods derive from the geographic location identified by the mark." *In re Save Venice New York, Inc.*, 259 F.3d 1346, 1354 (Fed. Cir. 2001).

The PTO has long held that where: (1) a location is generally known; (2) the term's geographic significance is its primary significance; and (3) the goods do, in fact, originate from the named location, a goods/place association can be presumed. [Citations.] This presumption may well be proper, but, as this case can be decided on other grounds, we do not address its propriety and leave it for another day.

III. The Examiner's Refusal

The Examiner found that the primary significance of the word "Newbridge" is a "generally known geographic place," i.e., Newbridge, Ireland, and that the goods originated there. The Examiner then applied the TMEP's presumption that a goods/place association existed. The word "home," according to the Examiner, was "generic or highly descriptive" and, therefore, did not affect the geographic significance of the term. Accordingly, the Examiner rejected the mark under § 1052(e)(2).

....

The conclusion that Newbridge, Ireland, a town of less than twenty thousand people, is a place known generally to the relevant American public is not supported by substantial evidence. That Newbridge is the second largest town in County Kildare and the seventeenth largest in the Republic of Ireland reveals nothing about what the relevant American purchaser might perceive the word "Newbridge" to mean and is too insignificant to show that Newbridge is a place known generally to the American purchasing public. Similarly, while the Board relied on the *Columbia Gazetteer of the World* listing, what is missing is any evidence to show the extent to which the relevant American consumer would be familiar with the locations listed in this gazetteer.

Likewise, the fact that Newbridge, Ireland, is mentioned on some internet websites does not show that it is a generally known location. The internet (and websites such as Wikipedia) contains enormous amounts of information: some of it is generally known, and some of it is not. [Citation.] There is simply no evidence that the relevant American consumer would have any meaningful knowledge of all of the locations mentioned in the websites cited by the PTO.

Further, it is simply untenable that any information available on the internet should be considered known to the relevant public. The fact that potential purchasers have enormous amounts of information instantly available through the internet does not evidence the extent to which consumers of certain goods or services in the United States might use this information to discern the primary significance of any particular term....

To be clear, we do not foreclose the PTO from using gazetteer entries or internet websites to identify whether a location is generally known. [Citation.] For example, we have credited gazetteer entries as part of the evidence used to establish that Durango, Mexico, was generally known. [Citation.] But the gazetteer showing was just one piece of evidence that together with other evidence was sufficient to establish a *prima facie* case that Durango is known generally to the relevant public. Gazetteer entries and internet websites are valuable for the information they provide. But the mere entry in a gazetteer or the fact that a location is described on the internet does not necessarily evidence that a place is known generally to the relevant public. *See Vittel*, 824 F.2d at 959 ("In dealing with all of these questions of the public's response to word symbols, we are dealing with the supposed reactions of a segment of the American public, in this case the mill-run of cosmetics purchasers, not with the unusually well-travelled, the aficionados of European watering places, or with computer operators checking out the meaning of strange words on NEXIS.").

... That Newbridge, Ireland, is not generally known is supported by the fact that certain maps and atlases do not include it. That "Newbridge" has other meanings, both geographical and non-geographical, also makes it less likely that Newbridge, Ireland, is generally known as the name of a place....

In sum, the facts here are similar to those of the Board's decision in *Bavaria*, ... which held that Jever, West Germany, a town of 10,342, was not generally known, despite being mentioned in a geographical index ... *Bavaria*, 222 U.S.P.Q. 926. Here, as in *Bavaria*, the evidence as a whole suggests that Newbridge, Ireland, is not generally known. Thus, to the relevant public the mark NEWBRIDGE is not *primarily* geographically descriptive of the goods, which is what matters. [Citation.] Prong one of the test for primarily geographically descriptive marks is therefore not met. Accordingly, we need not and do not separately consider whether a goods/place association exists.

Conclusion

For the foregoing reasons, we reverse the Board's refusal to register applicant's mark under § 1052(e)(2) and remand for further proceedings consistent with this opinion.

Question

The *Newbridge* decision notes that the Board routinely presumes a goods/place association if the goods come from the named place and the primary significance of the named place is a generally known geographic term. The decision, however, takes no position on the propriety of such a presumption. What do you think?

In re Miracle Tuesday, LLC

695 F.3d 1339 (Fed. Cir. 2012)

O'Malley, Circuit Judge:

Miracle Tuesday LLC ("Miracle Tuesday") appeals from a decision of the Trademark Trial and Appeal Board ("the Board") which affirmed the … refusal to register the mark JPK PARIS 75 and design on grounds that it is primarily geographically deceptively misdescriptive under Section 2(e)(3) of the Lanham Act, 15 U.S.C. § 1052(e)(3). [Citation.] Because we find that the Board's refusal to register the mark was based on substantial evidence, we affirm.

Background

… Miracle Tuesday filed … to register the mark JPK PARIS 75 and design, shown below, in connection with sunglasses, wallets, handbags and purses, travel bags, suitcases, belts, and shoes:

The letters "JPK" are the initials of Jean-Pierre Klifa, who is the manager of Miracle Tuesday and designer of the goods at issue.

….

… [T]he Board rejected Miracle Tuesday's argument that the monogram "JPK" is the dominant portion of the mark.…

Discussion

Under Section 2(e)(3) of the Lanham Act, a mark may not be registered on the principal register if the mark, "when used on or in connection with the goods of the applicant is primarily geographically deceptively misdescriptive of them." 15 U.S.C. § 1052(e)(3). A mark is primarily geographically deceptively misdescriptive, and thus barred from registration, if: (1) "the primary significance of the mark is a generally known geographic location"; (2) "the consuming public is likely to believe the place identified by the mark indicates the origin of the goods bearing the mark, when in fact the goods do not come from that place"; and (3) "the misrepresentation was a material factor in the consumer's decision" to purchase the goods. *In re Cal. Innovations, Inc.*, 329 F.3d 1334, 1341 (Fed. Cir. 2003).

....

On appeal, Miracle Tuesday does not challenge the Board's finding that the primary significance of the mark is Paris; it focuses its arguments on the second and third elements of the Board's Section 2(e)(3) refusal. Specifically, Miracle Tuesday argues that the Board erred when it: (1) found that the goods identified do not originate in Paris even though the designer of the goods has significant ties to Paris; (2) applied the wrong standard in concluding that the use of the word Paris in the mark is deceptive; and (3) failed to consider certain material evidence in reaching its decision. For the reasons explained below, each of these arguments lacks merit.

A. Association & Origin

... [W]e turn directly to the second element which asks "whether the public would reasonably identify or associate the goods sold under the mark with the geographic location contained in the mark." [*In re*] *Save Venice N.Y.*, 259 F.3d [1346] at 1353–54 [(Fed. Cir. 2003)]. This element involves two questions: (1) whether there is an association between the goods and the place identified ("a goods/place association"); and (2) whether the applicant's goods in fact come from that place. *See Cal. Innovations*, 329 F.3d at 1341 (the PTO must ask whether "the consuming public is likely to believe the place identified by the mark indicates the origin of the goods bearing the mark, when in fact the goods do not come from that place").

... [T]he examiner has the initial burden of submitting evidence to establish a goods/place association and the burden then shifts to the applicant to rebut this showing with evidence "that the public would not actually believe the goods derive from the geographic location identified by the mark." *Save Venice N.Y.*, 259 F.3d at 1354.... [T]he PTO is not required to establish an "*actual* goods/place association." [*In re*] *Pacer Tech.*, 338 F.3d [1348 (Fed. Cir. 2003),] at 1351 (emphasis added). Instead, the PTO need only "establish 'a *reasonable predicate* for its conclusion that the public would be *likely* to make the particular goods/place association on which it relies.'" *Id.* (emphasis in original) (quoting *In re Loew's Theatres, Inc.*, 769 F.2d 764, 768 (Fed. Cir. 1985)).

Where ... a case involves goods rather than services, we have held that "the goods-place association often requires little more than a showing that the consumer identifies the place as a known source of the product." *In re Les Halles de Paris J.V.*, 334 F.3d 1371, 1374 (Fed. Cir. 2003). [Citations.] Therefore, to establish a goods/place association, "the case law permits an inference that the consumer associates the product with the geographic location in the mark because that place is known for producing the product." *Id.* [Citation.]

It is undisputed that Paris is famous for fashion and fashion accessories, including the types of goods identified in the application. Because relevant purchasers are likely to think of Paris as a known source for fashion accessories, we agree with the Board that there is sufficient evidence of a goods/place association between Paris and the goods listed.

The second inquiry under this element asks whether the goods will in fact originate from the named place. It is undisputed that goods may be deemed to originate in a geographic location if they are manufactured there. Origin can be predicated on factors other than manufacture, however, where the circumstances justify such a connection. [Citation.] Indeed, at oral argument, the PTO conceded that, in appropriate circumstances, "the place of design can be enough." Similarly, if the goods contain a main component or ingredient from the place identified in the mark, that connection can be sufficient to find that the goods originate from that place. *See Corporacion Habanos*, 88 U.S.P.Q.2d [1785,] at 1791 [(TTAB 2008)] ("[A] product might be found to originate from a place where the main component or ingredient was made in that place." (citation omitted)); *see also Loew's Theatres*, 769 F.2d [764 (Fed. Cir. 1985),] at 768 (evidence that tobacco is "one in a short list of principal crops" in Durango, Mexico was sufficient to show that the public would likely believe that chewing tobacco under the mark DURANGO originated there). And, a product might be found to originate from a place where the applicant has its headquarters or research and development facilities, even when the manufacturing facilities are elsewhere. *See In re Nantucket Allserve, Inc.*, 28 U.S.P.Q.2d 1144, 1145–46 (TTAB 1993) (identifying Nantucket as the principal origin of applicant's products, even though the goods were manufactured elsewhere, because the company had its headquarters and research and development center on Nantucket).

Here, the Board found that Miracle Tuesday is located in Miami, its designer is not located in Paris, and the goods at issue are designed and produced somewhere other than Paris. The Board rejected Miracle Tuesday's argument that the fact that Mr. Klifa lived and worked in Paris for twenty-two years is sufficient to justify the conclusion that the products originated in Paris. The Board concluded that, "[a]lthough Mr. Klifa may still consider himself to be Parisian, the goods that applicant seeks to register are not because there is no current connection between the goods and Paris." [Citation.]

On appeal, Miracle Tuesday argues ... that its designer — Mr. Klifa — has a significant connection with Paris and that customers are more interested in the designer's origin than the origin of the goods themselves. In support of this position, Miracle Tuesday references red carpet events where interviewers ask celebrities "who are you wearing?" rather than "where was it made?"

Regardless of whether today's consumers consider and care about the origin of the designer of the goods they purchase, the relevant inquiry under the statute is whether there is a connection between the *goods* and Paris—not between the designer and Paris. *See* 15 U.S.C. § 1052(e)(3) (a mark is not registrable if, "when used on or in connection with the *goods* of the applicant is primarily geographically deceptively misdescriptive of them") (emphasis added). Accordingly, the fact that Mr. Klifa lived in Paris over twenty-five years ago is insufficient to establish that the goods to now be marketed under the proposed mark originate there. On this record, there is no evidence that Mr. Klifa's activities while he lived in Paris had anything to do with designing handbags or the other goods identified in the application. Nor is there any evidence that Mr. Klifa exhibited any of the types of goods at issue at the Parisian trade shows he attended. Given the statutory focus on the geographic origin of the goods, Miracle Tuesday's attempts to shift the inquiry to the historical origin of the designer must fail.

Although there is support for the proposition that goods need not be manufactured in the named place to originate there—and we do not endorse application of a contrary rule here—it is clear that there must be some other direct connection between the goods and the place identified in the mark (*e.g.*, the place identified is where the goods are designed or distributed, where the applicant is headquartered or has its research and development facility, or where a main component of the good originates). Here, Miracle Tuesday concedes that the goods identified in the application do not originate in Paris.... The record further reveals that the goods identified are designed in Miami, and there is no evidence that a main component of the goods, or even any component of the goods, comes from Paris. Simply put, there is no evidence of a current connection between the goods and Paris.

Given that Paris is a world-renowned fashion center and is well-known as a place where fashion goods and accessories are designed, manufactured, and sold, we agree with the Board that "the relevant public would likely believe that [Miracle Tuesday's] products offered under the mark JPK PARIS 75 and design come from Paris (*i.e.*, that a goods/place association exists) when in fact the goods will not come from that place." And, because there is no evidence showing a direct connection between Miracle Tuesday's goods and Paris, the Board properly found that there is insufficient evidence that the goods originate in Paris.

B. Materiality

The third and final element of a Section 2(e)(3) refusal focuses on materiality and asks "whether a substantial portion of the relevant consumers is likely to be deceived" by the mark's misrepresentation of a goods/place association. *In re Spirits Int'l, N.V.*, 563 F.3d 1347, 1353 (Fed. Cir. 2009). In *Spirits International*, we held that, "to establish a prima facie case of materiality there must be some indication that a substantial portion of the relevant consumers would be materially influenced in the decision to purchase the product or service by the geographic meaning of the mark." *Id.* at 1357. We have also held that "the PTO may raise an inference in favor of materiality with evidence that the place is famous as a source of the goods at issue." *Les Halles de Paris*, 334 F.3d at 1374.[5]

Applying these standards, the Board stated that:

> Because we have determined that the primary significance of Paris to the relevant public is the geographic place, and in view of the renown and reputation of fashion designs originating in Paris, we may infer that at least a substantial portion of consumers who encounter applicant's mark featuring the word "Paris" on applicant's products are likely to be deceived into believing that those products come from or were designed in Paris.

Board Decision, 2011 TTAB LEXIS 32, at *9. Accordingly, the Board found that the materiality factor was satisfied.

On appeal, Miracle Tuesday argues that the Board ... was required to find that the use of the word Paris "does in fact deceive the public." According to Miracle Tuesday, because there is a substantial connection between Mr. Klifa and Paris, the reference to Paris in the mark is a true statement that is not deceptive. Miracle Tuesday's arguments are without merit.

First, Miracle Tuesday points to our decision in *Les Halles de Paris* as evidence that the PTO "must show some heightened standard to show a false association between the services and the relevant geographic location." Miracle Tuesday's argument is fundamentally flawed, however, given that this case involves a mark to identify goods whereas *Les Halles de Paris* involved an application to register a mark for restaurant services. Indeed, in *Les Halles de Paris*, we specifically recognized that: (1) "the standard under section 2(e)(3) is more difficult to satisfy for service marks than for marks on goods"; and (2) "geographic marks in connection with services are less likely to mislead the public than geographic marks on goods." *Les Halles de Paris*, 334 F.3d at 1374.[6] Given these differences, we drew a distinction between the evidence necessary to give rise to an inference of materiality for goods and that necessary to give rise to that same inference for services. Although for *goods*, evidence that a place is famous as a source of those goods is sufficient to raise an inference of materiality, when dealing with *service* marks, we held that there must be a heightened association between the services and geographic location. *See id.* at 1374–75 ("In other words, an inference of materiality arises in the event of a very strong services-place association. Without a particularly strong services-place association, an inference would not arise, leaving the PTO to seek direct evidence of materiality."). Because this case involves

5. Although *Les Halles de Paris* was decided before this court clarified the materiality standard in *Spirits International*, nothing in *Spirits International* suggests that there must be actual evidence of deception rather than an inference of materiality drawn from the evidence.

6. In *Les Halles de Paris*, we explained that a "customer typically receives services, particularly in the restaurant business, at the location of the business." 334 F.3d at 1373. "Having chosen to come to that place for the services, the customer is well aware of the geographic location of the service. This choice necessarily implies that the customer is less likely to associate the services with the geographic location invoked by the mark rather than the geographic location of the service, such as a restaurant." *Id.*

goods—rather than services—Miracle Tuesday's reliance on the portion of *Les Halles de Paris* creating a heightened standard for service marks is misplaced.

As the Board correctly noted, the fact that Paris is famous for fashion and design gives rise to an inference that a substantial portion of relevant customers would be deceived into thinking the goods identified came from Paris. Miracle Tuesday points to no evidence that would rebut this inference. Instead, as noted above, Miracle Tuesday maintains that customers care more about the origin of the designer than the origin of the goods and seems to argue that, where the mark involves a fashion designer, it should be treated as a service mark, with an attendant heightened level of materiality required. *See* Appellant's Br. 16 ("The relationship of the designer to Paris [is] not so far from a service performed by the designer, much as a restaurant service where a heightened materiality test is required."). Miracle Tuesday cites no authority for this proposition and ignores the fact that its application for registration is directed to goods, not services. Because our analysis must focus on the information provided in the application, Mr. Klifa's early years in Paris are effectively irrelevant, and certainly insufficient to overcome a proper inference of materiality.

....

Questions

1. The applicant in *Miracle Tuesday* did not press its argument on appeal that the dominant element of its marks was the JPK portion and thus the primary significance was not geographic. Do you agree that this was a losing argument? The Federal Circuit in *In re California Innovations, Inc.*, 329 F.3d 1334 (Fed. Cir. 2003), noted the following in evaluating the first prong of the test for the mark CALIFORNIA INNOVATIONS and Design:

> Under the first prong of the test—whether the mark's primary significance is a generally known geographic location—a composite mark ... must be evaluated as a whole.... It is not erroneous, however, for the examiner to consider the significance of each element within the composite mark in the course of evaluating the mark as a whole.

2. Do you agree that the historical association of the designer with Paris in *Miracle Tuesday* was irrelevant to evaluating whether consumers would be deceived as to the origin of the goods? What if the designer resided in Paris but the goods were manufactured in Asia, would the result have been different? Should it have been? Suppose the designer was both more famous than JPK and was closely associated with Paris. If that designer subsequently moved to New York City, but kept the Paris workshop, would a mark containing the term "Paris" be misdescriptive? What if the workshop were no longer in Paris?

3. The Federal Circuit drew a distinction between service marks and trademarks. Is this justified? For example, the mark at issue in *Les Halles de Paris* was LE MARAIS for restaurant services. The New York City restaurant served French kosher cuisine. Le Marais is a predominantly Jewish neighborhood in Paris. Would patrons of the

New York City restaurant mistakenly believe the New York City restaurant was part of a chain originating in Paris? Would this belief be material to their decision to dine there?

4. Fage Yogurt secured an interim injunction in the UK against Danone, prohibiting Danone's use of the phrase GREEK YOGURT on DANIO high-protein, low-fat yogurt packaging. Fage argues that yogurt made outside of Greece should not be able to use this term; whereas, Danone claims that the term refers to a manufacturing process. How would this situation be analyzed in the U.S. under section 2(e)(3)?

In *Miracle Tuesday*, the Federal Circuit stated that the third prong of materiality can be inferred when the place named is famous for the particular goods. Yet previously, in **In re Spirits International, N.V.**, 563 F.3d 1347 (Fed. Cir. 2009), the Federal Circuit vacated a refusal to register MOSKOVSKAYA for vodka neither manufactured or produced in Moscow nor with another connection with Moscow even though Moscow is well known for vodka. The Federal Circuit remanded to apply the correct standard of materiality in determining that the mark was geographically deceptively misdescriptive and stated:

> *California Innovations* did not address the question of whether the materiality test of subsection (e)(3) embodies a requirement that a significant portion of the relevant consumers be deceived. We hold that subsection (e)(3) does incorporate such a requirement, and that the appropriate inquiry for materiality purposes is whether a substantial portion of the relevant consumers is likely to be deceived, not whether any absolute number or particular segment of the relevant consumers (such as foreign language speakers) is likely to be deceived.
>
> ....
>
> Under the circumstances it is clear that section (e)(3) ... requires that a significant portion of the relevant consuming public be deceived. That population is often the entire U.S. population interested in purchasing the product or service. We note that, in some cases, the use of a non-English language mark can be evidence that the product in question is targeted at the community of those who understand that language. In such cases, the relevant consuming public will be composed of those who are members of that targeted community, and, as a result, people who speak the non-English language could comprise a substantial portion of the relevant consumers. [Citation.] There is no such contention here.
>
> ... The problem with the Board's decision is that it ... rejected a requirement of proportionality, and discussed instead the fact that Russian is a "common, modern language[] of the world [that] will be spoken or understood by an appreciable number of U.S. consumers for the product or service at issue," such number being in this case 706,000 people, according to the 2000 Census. *Id.* The Board, however, failed to consider whether Russian

speakers were a "substantial portion of the intended audience." Because the Board applied an incorrect test, a remand is required.

We express no opinion on the ultimate question of whether a substantial portion of the intended audience would be materially deceived. We note that only 0.25% of the U.S. population speaks Russian. If only one quarter of one percent of the relevant consumers was deceived, this would not be, by any measure, a substantial portion. However, it may be that Russian speakers are a greater percentage of the vodka-consuming public; that some number of non-Russian speakers would understand the mark to suggest that the vodka came from Moscow; and that these groups would together be a substantial portion of the intended audience.

Questions

1. What evidence can an Examiner rely on to show the proportion of the relevant purchasing group for a particular product? How would the Examiner show that vodka purchasers in the U.S. are aware of Russia's connections to vodka or that even non-Russian speakers would understand Moskovskaya to mean somewhere in Russia? *Cf. Corporacion Habanos, S.A. v. Guantamera Cigars Co.*, 102 U.S.P.Q.2d 1085 (T.T.A.B. 2012) (record included census data about number of Spanish speakers, federal studies of Spanish study in schools and applicant's ads and website in Spanish; GUANTANAMERA held primarily geographically deceptive misdescriptive for cigars not from Cuba).

2. Should the mark LA GIANNA HAVANA be considered geographically deceptively misdescriptive for cigars not from Cuba where the only possible connection with Cuba is that the cigars may have been grown from seeds descended from Cuban seeds more than 45 years earlier? *See Corporacion Habanos, S.A. v. Garofalo*, Opp. No. 91186535 (Jan. 2, 2009 T.T.A.B.).

Note: The Cuban Embargo and Havana Club Rum

A long-running dispute between two claimants for the HAVANA CLUB mark in the United States for rum has taken another twist, perhaps due to the thawing of Cuban-U.S. relations. The Arechabala family manufactured rum in Cuba and sold HAVANA CLUB rum in the U.S. starting in the 1930s. In exile after seizure of the Cuban business during the Cuban Revolution, the family nevertheless owned a U.S. registration, but the registration lapsed in 1973. Cubaexport, owned by the Cuban government, applied for and received a U.S. registration for the same mark in 1976, which it renewed in 1996. Bacardi bought the rum business from the Arechebalas in 1994 and applied to register the mark, which application is still pending. Most recently, in 2011, the Court of Appeals for the District of Columbia ruled in Bacardi's favor and upheld the prior denial to Cubaexport of an exception to the Cuban Assets Control Regulations of 1998 and thus its ability to further renew the registration. *Empresa Cuban Exportadora de Alimentos y Productos Varios, dba Cubaexport v. Dept. of the Treasury*, 638 F.3d 794 (D.C. Cir. 2011). The Supreme Court denied certiorari.

Cubaexport then re-sought an exception, which this time was granted. It then petitioned to renew the registration as of 2006 based on excusable nonuse due to the embargo. The USPTO granted the petition and the renewal. The grace period for this renewal will run out on July 27, 2016. To be continued.

Note: Special Protection for Wines and Spirits

The TRIPS Agreement obliges Member States to accord additional protection to geographical indications for wines and spirits. While the general provision on geographic indications, art. 22(2), *see* Appendix E, *infra,* addresses uses that mislead the public as to geographical origin, art. 23(1) condemns a much broader scope of use of the designation, but only with respect to wines and spirits:

> Each member shall provide the legal means for interested parties to prevent use of a geographical indication identifying wines for wines not originating in the place indicated by the geographical indication in question or identifying spirits for spirits not originating in the place indicated by the geographical indication in question, even where the true origin of the goods is indicated or the geographical indication is used in translation or accompanied by expressions such as "kind," "type," "tyle," "imitation," or the like.

The United States has implemented art. 23(1) through the following amendment to Lanham Act § 2(a):

> [A trademark shall be denied registration if it consists of] a geographical indication which, when used on or in connection with wines or spirits, identifies a place other than the origin of the goods and is first used on or in connection with wines or spirits by the applicant on or after [1996].

Questions

1. Does § 2(a) fully satisfy the United States' international obligations under TRIPs?

2. May any of the following be registered? May any of the following be used? The mark for which registration is sought is set out in quotation marks. The goods are marketed using the entire phrase.

a. "Fabulous Fizz New York State Champagne." First use: 1990.

b. "Fabulous Fizz New York State Champagne." First use: 2010.

c. "Fabulous Fizz" New York State Champagne. First use: 2010.

d. "Fabulous Fizz Champagne Method" New York State Sparkling Wine. First use: 2010.

Note: "Geographically Suggestive" Marks

Some place names convey general qualities in whose aura a trademark proprietor might wish her goods or services to bask. For example, "Paris" evokes high fashion and style, "California" evokes a laid back life style, "Park Avenue" evokes wealth and luxury, "Wall Street" evokes wealth and power, "Dodge City" evokes the Wild West.

"Hollywood" evokes the razzle dazzle of the entertainment industry. These kinds of marks might be dubbed "geographically suggestive," because they do not describe the place of the goods' origin, but they do (or are intended to) conjure up a variety of desirable associations with the place whose name the goods or services bear. Were you a Trademark Examiner, how would you rule on the following marks (assume in all cases that the goods are not in fact produced at the named locations):

A. "California Innovations" for thermal insulated bags. *Cf. In re California Innovations*, 329 F.3d 1334 (Fed. Cir. 2003);

B. "Paris" for disposable diapers;

C. "Park Avenue" for cigarettes, *cf. Philip Morris Inc. v. Reemtsma Cigarettenfabriken Gmbh*, 14 U.S.P.Q.2d 1487 (T.T.A.B. 1990);

D. "Wall Street" for desk organizers;

E. "Dodge City" for chewing tobacco, *cf. In re Loew's Theatres, Inc.*, 769 F.2d 764 (Fed. Cir. 1985);

F. "Dodge City" for leather goods;

G. "Swiss Army" for multiple-implement pocket knives, *cf. Forschner Group v. Arrow Trading*, 30 F.3d 348 (2d Cir. 1994);

H. "Hollywood Fries" for fast food restaurants, *cf. In re International Taste Inc.*, 53 U.S.P.Q.2d 1604 (T.T.A.B. 2000);

I. "Vegas" for playing cards, *cf. United States Playing Card Co. v. Harbro*, 81 U.S.P.Q.2d 1537 (T.T.A.B. 2006).

Some courts have addressed the commercial advantage a trademark claimant may reap by linking itself to the desirable qualities associated with particular locales, even where there is no precise "goods-place association." In *Haagen-Dazs, Inc. v. Frusen Gladje*, 493 F. Supp. 73 (S.D.N.Y. 1980), the court rejected a trademark infringement claim brought by the originator of an ersatz-Scandinavian ice cream brand against a competitor who also adopted a name with "Scandinavian flair." The court declined to protect "plaintiff's unique Scandinavian marketing theme." By contrast, in another frozen confection controversy, despite the strong attraction of the suggestive power of ALASKA for ice cream, the court held that geographic designation susceptible to private appropriation. *See Alaska Incorporated v. Alaska Ice Cream Co.*, 34 U.S.P.Q.2d 1145 (E.D. Pa. 1995).

5. Section 2(e)(4) of the Lanham Act: Surnames and Other Issues

15 U.S.C. § 1502 [Lanham Act § 2(e)(4)]

No trademark by which the goods of the applicant may be distinguished from the goods of others shall be refused registration on the principal register on account of its nature unless it—

1. Consists of a mark which … (4) is primarily merely a surname.

Trademark Manual of Examining Procedure
§ 1211 Refusal on Basis of Surname

... The Trademark Act, in § 2(e)(4), reflects the common law that exclusive rights in a surname per se cannot be established without evidence of long and exclusive use which changes its significance to the public from that of a surname of an individual to that of a mark for particular goods or services. The common law also recognizes that surnames are shared by more than one individual, each of whom may have an interest in using his surname in business and, by the requirement for evidence of distinctiveness, in effect, delays appropriation of exclusive rights in the name. *In re Etablissements Darty et Fils*, 759 F.2d 15, 16 (Fed. Cir. 1985).

The question of whether a mark is primarily merely a surname depends on the mark's primary significance to the purchasing public. *See, e.g., Ex Parte Rivera Watch Corp.*, 106 U.S.P.Q. 145, 149 (Comm'r Pats. 1955). Each case must be decided on its own facts, based upon the evidence in the record.

In re Quadrillion Publishing Ltd.

2000 TTAB LEXIS 562 (Aug. 9, 2000)

Bucher, Administrative Trademark Judge:

An intent-to-use application has been filed by Quadrillion Publishing Limited to register the mark "BRAMLEY" for a wide variety of books, magazines and stationery items in International Class 16.

The Trademark Examining Attorney has refused registration under Section 2(e)(4) of the Trademark Act, 15 U.S.C. § 1052(e)(4), on the ground that applicant's mark is primarily merely a surname

We *affirm* the refusal to register.

In support of her surname refusal, the Trademark Examining Attorney has made of record the results of her search of a database containing eighty million names, finding 433 "BRAMLEY" surname listings from PHONEDISC POWERFINDER USA ONE 1997 (3rd ed.), as well as an excerpt from *Webster's Unabridged Third New International Dictionary*, 1986, showing that there is no listing of the term "Bramley" in that dictionary.

Applicant argues that the Trademark Examining Attorney has failed to establish a prima facie surname case. Applicant challenges the Trademark Examining Attorney's PHONEDISC evidence on the ground that the quantum of evidence submitted by the Examining Attorney is indeterminate of the primary significance of the term to purchasers. Applicant asserts that "Bramley" is also the name of a small village in England. In support of its position, applicant has submitted a map showing the village of Bramley in the county of Surrey, as well as a picture post card seeming to represent images of several buildings in the village of Bramley. Finally, applicant has also provided a copy of the *Oxford English Dictionary* where the term "Bramley" is defined as "a large green variety of cooking apple."

The test for determining whether a mark is primarily merely a surname is the primary significance of the mark to the purchasing public. [Citations.] The initial burden is on the Trademark Examining Attorney to establish a prima facie case that a mark is primarily merely a surname. See *In re Etablissements Darty et Fils*, 759 F.2d 15, 16, 225 U.S.P.Q. 652, 653 (Fed. Cir. 1985). After the Trademark Examining Attorney establishes a *prima facie* case, the burden shifts to the applicant to rebut this finding.

The Board, in the past, has considered several different factors in making a surname determination under Section 2(e)(4): (i) the degree of surname rareness; (ii) whether anyone connected with applicant has the surname; (iii) whether the term has any recognized meaning other than that of a surname; and (iv) the structure and pronunciation or "look and sound" of the surname. *In re Benthin Management GmbH*, 37 U.S.P.Q.2d 1332 (T.T.A.B. 1995).

There is no doubt that the Trademark Examining Attorney has met her initial burden of establishing that "BRAMLEY" would be perceived by consumers as primarily merely a surname. In particular, the Trademark Examining Attorney has presented over four hundred "BRAMLEY" surname references from the PHONEDISC database, along with proof that the word "Bramley" does not appear in an unabridged, English-language dictionary. The Court of Appeals for the Federal Circuit has held that this type of evidence is sufficient to establish a *prima facie* surname case. [Citations.]

The Trademark Examining Attorney's PHONEDISC evidence is collected from telephone directories and address books across the country. There is no magic number of directory listings required to establish a prima facie surname case. *In re Cazes*, 21 U.S.P.Q.2d 1796, 1797 (T.T.A.B. 1991); *In re Industrie Pirelli Societa per Azioni*, 9 U.S.P.Q.2d 1564, 1566 (T.T.A.B. 1988), *aff'd unpublished decision*, No. 89-1231 (Fed. Cir. 1989). It is reasonable to conclude from these submissions that "BRAMLEY," while obviously not as common as some other surnames, has had measurable public exposure.[2] Even if "BRAMLEY" is an uncommon surname, it is by no means a decidedly rare surname.[3] From more than four hundred "BRAMLEY" surname references in the PHONEDISC database, we conclude that "BRAMLEY" is a surname even if there are relatively few people in the United States having this name.

---

2. To the extent applicant contends that BRAMLEY is an uncommon surname, we would point out that even uncommon surnames may not be registrable on the Principal Register. *See Industrie Pirelli*, 9 U.S.P.Q.2d at 1566.

3. This evidence is far more significant than the number of listings presented in other cases where the surname has been categorized as "rare." *See e.g. Kahan & Weisz*, 508 F.2d at 832, 184 U.S.P.Q. at 422 (six DUCHAMP surname telephone directory listings); *In re Sava Research Corp.*, 32 U.S.P.Q. 2d 1380 (T.T.A.B. 1994) (one hundred SAVA surname telephone directory listings); *Benthin Management*, 37 U.S.P.Q.2d at 1333 (one hundred BENTHIN surname telephone directory listings); *In re Garan, Inc.*, 3 U.S.P.Q.2d 1537 (T.T.A.B. 1987) (six GARAN telephone directory listings and one NEXIS listing). This is one of four factors. Hence, the quantum of PHONEDISC evidence which may be persuasive for finding surname significance in one case may be insufficient in another because of differences in the surnames themselves and/or consideration of the other relevant surname factors. *Darty, supra.*

Applicant dismisses the hundreds of listings from the PHONEDISC database as representing "1/10,000 of 1%," or an "imperceptible sliver of the American population." However, we find this "percentage-of-the-entire population" argument to be a hollow reed. The rich diversity of surnames in this country is amply reflected in the PHONEDISC computer database evidence. If one were to take a statistical measurement of this database for common names like "Smith" or "Jones," each would constitute a relatively small fraction of the total database content.

As to the second *Benthin* factor, we recognize that no one connected to applicant's organization has been shown to have the "Bramley" surname. If a Bramley were associated in some way with applicant, it could well indicate the public's recognition of the term as a surname. However, logic tells us that the converse is not necessarily true, i.e., the mere fact that this query comes up negative herein cannot compel the conclusion that consumers will perceive the term as a non-surname.

In weighing the third *Benthin* factor, we have considered applicant's contention that "Bramley" has recognized meanings other than that of a surname. However, both the *Benthin* decision and our primary reviewing court clearly require that the other meanings be "recognized" by a significant number of people. We do not believe that a significant number of people would recognize the other meanings proffered in this case because they are remote or obscure. Thus, they do not rebut the Examining Attorney's prima facie surname case. The mere fact that the word "Bramley" has two obscure or remote meanings is insufficient to show that it will not be perceived as "primarily merely a surname." Even applicant concedes that "Bramley" is " ... the name of a very small village outside Guildford, Surrey in England, which consists of a few houses, a post office and a general store." *See Harris-Intertype*, 518 F.2d at 631 n.4, 186 U.S.P.Q. at 239 n.4 (Harris, Missouri, population 174, and Harris, Minnesota, population 559 held obscure). Applicant certainly has not demonstrated that consumers in the United States would recognize that "Bramley" is the name of a tiny, rural village in England.[4]

Similarly, as to its other alleged non-surname meaning (i.e., a variety of apple), we note that according to applicant's own dictionary entry, the designation "Bramley's seedlings" comes from "M. Bramley, English butcher in whose garden it [the apple variety] may have first grown." Moreover, an entry from the *Oxford English Dictionary* combined with the absence of entries in several unabridged English language dictionaries commonly used in the United States suggests to us that this alleged non-surname significance is remote in the United Kingdom, that this alternate meaning is directly derived from an English surname, and that this particular non-surname meaning is nonexistent in the United States.

---

4. Surnames are routinely used as key parts of the names of streets, neighborhoods, towns, mountains and so forth, indicating the surnames of the people for whom they are named. Given that it is a common practice to name places after individuals, it would be surprising if the village of "Bramley" in Surrey could not also trace the historical origins of the village name to the surname of an English family that once lived there.

Finally, as to the fourth *Benthin* factor, contrary to applicant's contention, it is the view of the Board that "BRAMLEY" has the structure and pronunciation of a surname, not of an arbitrary designation. In fact, judging this matter simply by its look and feel, "BRAMLEY" seems to fit the archetype of British surnames having an "-ley" suffix, such as Bailey, Bradley, Buckley, Brantley or Barkley, and differs only in a single vowel from American surnames, Bromley, Brumley and Brimley.

Decision: The refusal to register the mark "BRAMLEY" under Section 2(e)(4) is affirmed.

In re Joint-Stock Company "Baik," 84 U.S.P.Q.2d 1921 (T.T.A.B. 2007). In a decision holding that BAIK, a relatively rare surname, is not primarily merely a surname, Judge Seeherman's concurring opinion discusses how the "look and feel" of a surname factor should be interpreted in assessing whether a mark is primarily merely a surname:

> ... if a term does not have the "look and feel" of a surname, it should not be refused registration even if there is evidence to show that it is, in fact, a surname.
>
> However, I do not think that, in the converse situation, registration should be refused simply because the mark at issue is similar in sound or appearance to other surnames. The purpose behind prohibiting the registration of marks that are primarily merely surnames is not to protect the public from exposure to surnames, as though there were something offensive in viewing a surname. Rather, the purpose behind Section 2(e)(4) is to keep surnames available for people who wish to use their own surnames in their businesses, in the same manner that merely descriptive terms are prohibited from registration because competitors should be able to use a descriptive term to describe their own goods or services.
>
> Because the purpose of Section 2(e)(4) is not to protect the public from being exposed to surname marks, the fact that the public may view a mark as a surname because it has the "look and feel" of a surname should not be the basis for refusing registration of rare surnames. If a surname is extremely rare, it is also extremely unlikely that someone other than the applicant will want to use the surname for the same or related goods or services as that of the applicant. Therefore, if the Office is not able to muster sufficient evidence to show that the mark is the surname of a reasonable number of people, and must instead resort to finding other surnames which rhyme with the mark or differ from the mark by one or two letters, I believe that it is not proper to refuse registration. Interpreting the "look and feel" factor to refuse registration of marks simply because they are similar to recognized surnames does not serve the intention of the statute.

Do you agree with Judge Seeherman's analysis? Why or why not?

Questions

1. Recall the discussion of personal names in *Peaceable Planet v. Ty, Inc.*, 362 F.3d 986 (7th Cir. 2004), *supra*, Chapter 2[A], in which the court noted that courts frequently require a showing of secondary meaning to protect personal names. Does Section 2(e)(4) bar registration of, for example, STEVE'S for ice cream shops without a showing of secondary meaning? Is STEVE primarily merely a surname? Is there a greater interest in using a surname than a first name in business?

2. Fiore, which has over 5,000 telephone listings as a surname, means "flower" in Italian. Should Isabella Fiore be able to register FIORE for bags, luggage and other goods or should the application be refused as being primarily merely a surname? *See In re Isabella Fiore, LLC*, 75 U.S.P.Q.2d 1564 (T.T.A.B. 2005).

3. Should BIRD for binoculars be barred as primarily a surname? How about WASHINGTON?

Note: Numerals, Letters and Initials

Various products may carry model, grade or style designations that are helpful in identifying the goods to their producers and sellers, as well as to consumers. For example, most household appliances will carry a model number in addition to the brand name. As a general rule, "A word, phrase, symbol, numeral or letter that merely differentiates between various grades, styles, colors or types of products, and does not designate their source, is not a protectable trademark.... Grade designations are analogous to descriptive terms, in that they serve the primary without secondary meaning function of describing or supplying information about the product to the consumer." A. Lalonde et al., Gilson on Trademarks, sec. 2.03[4][a] (2011).

A grade or style designation may nevertheless warrant protection as a trademark if, in addition to specifying the quality, style, or type of product, it also, and "primarily," designates the source of the goods. This is a fact question requiring analysis of the manner of use, the intent of the user, and the meaning understood by the consumer. *See, e.g., Ex Parte International Nickel Co., Inc.*, 115 U.S.P.Q. 365 (Com. Pat. 1957) (registration allowed for "135" because it "identifies and distinguishes applicant's welding electrodes for welding particular alloys"); *Ex Parte Esterbrook Pen Co.*, 109 U.S.P.Q. 368 (Com. Pat. 1956) (registration denied "2668" for penpoints for failure to demonstrate recognition "either in the trade or by consumers as a pen point made only by applicant"). Well-known model or style designations that consumers are likely to recognize as source designations include "747" for airplanes, and "501" for a model of LEVI'S jeans.

Combinations of letters or initials may also function as trademarks. *See, e.g., ECI Division of E-Systems, Inc. v. Environmental Communications Inc.*, 207 U.S.P.Q. 443 (T.T.A.B.1980) ("In fact, the marketing area is replete with well-known trademarks consisting of letters and, in particular, acronyms or nicknames derived from initial letters of the words forming their corporate names, such a 'GM,' 'GE,' 'RCA,' and 'NBC,' to name a few of which judicial notice may be taken.").

6. Section 2(e)(5) of the Lanham Act: Functionality

15 U.S.C. § 1052(e)(5) [Lanham Act § 2(e)(5)]

No trademark by which the goods of the applicant may be distinguished from the goods of others shall be refused registration on the principal register on account of its nature unless it....

(e) consists of a mark which ...

(5) comprises any matter that, as a whole, is functional.

Congress added Section 2(e)(5), 15 U.S.C. § 1052(e)(5), to the Lanham Act, barring the registration of functional features, in 1998. The amendment codified the long-standing practice of the PTO and the courts of holding functional features ineligible for trademark protection even if such features developed secondary meaning.

In re Becton, Dickinson and Co.

675 F.3d 1368 (Fed. Cir. 2012)

Clevenger, Circuit Judge (for the majority):

Gibson Becton, Dickinson and Company ("BD") appeals from the final decision of the Trademark Trial and Appeal Board ("Board") affirming the examining attorney's refusal to register BD's design of a closure cap for blood collection tubes as a trademark on the ground that the design is functional.... [W]e affirm the Board's conclusion that the mark as a whole is functional.

I

BD applied to register with the United States Patent and Trademark Office ("PTO") the following mark on the Principal Register for "closures for medical collection tubes":

... The required description of the mark, as amended, reads as follows:

> The mark consists of the configuration of a closure cap that has [1] an overall streamlined exterior wherein the top of the cap is slimmer than at the bottom and the cap features [2] vertically elongated ribs set out in combination sets of numerous slim ribs bordered by fatter ribs around most of the cap circumference, where [3] a smooth area separates sets of ribs. [4] The slim ribs taper at their top to form triangular shapes which intersect and blend together at a point where [5] a smooth surface area rings the top of the cap above the ribs, thus [6] extending the cap's vertical profile. At the bottom, [7] a flanged lip rings the cap and protrudes from the sides in two circumferential segments with the bottom-most segment having [8] a slightly curved contour. The matter in dotted lines is not claimed as a feature of the mark, but shows the tube on which the closure is positioned.

The numbers in brackets ... were used by BD in conjunction with the following illustration to illustrate key features of the mark:

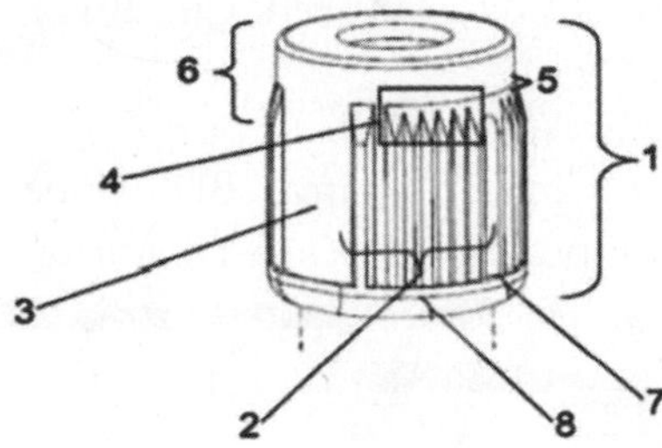

....

The Board considered the four factors from *In re Morton-Norwich Prods., Inc.*, 671 F.2d 1332 (CCPA 1982), in finding that the cap design, considered in its entirety, is functional. The Board found that the first factor—the existence of a utility patent (e.g., the '446 patent) disclosing the utilitarian advantages of the design sought to be registered—weighed in favor of finding the cap design functional. The Board found that the '446 patent explained the utilitarian advantages of at least two prominent features of the cap design, namely, the circular opening and the ribs.

The second factor—advertising by the applicant that touts the utilitarian advantages of the design—also weighed in favor of a functionality finding. The Board agreed with the examining attorney that several parts of BD's advertising "extol the utilitarian advantages of several design features of the proposed mark," including (1) the ridges on the side of the cap that allow for a more secure grip, (2) the flanged lip at the bottom that inhibits the handler's ability to roll their thumb to pop off the cap, thereby reducing the risk of splattering, and (3) the hooded feature of the cap whereby the bottom of the cap extends over the top of the tube and thus prevents the user's gloves from getting pinched between the stopper and tube when closing the tube.

Next, the Board considered the third factor, assessing whether the cap design results from a comparatively simple or inexpensive method of manufacture. With little argument or evidence on this factor, the Board found that it did not favor a finding of functionality. *Id.* Finally, the Board considered the fourth factor, regarding the availability of alternative designs, and found that "the record does not establish that there are alternative designs for collection tube closure caps." The Board considered BD's evidence: website printouts featuring three third-party collection tube products. The Board found one product did not perform the same function as BD's goods and therefore was not relevant. Regarding the two remaining third-party products, the Board found them difficult to characterize as alternative designs because they shared the same utilitarian features as BD's cap design, including ribs on the side to allow for a better grip and an opening on the top, rather than discernible contrasting features.

Thus, the Board concluded that "the closure cap configuration mark, considered in its entirety, is functional." ...

BD posits legal error by the Board in its determination that certain features of the mark, which are admittedly nonfunctional, will not serve to remove the mark as a whole from the realm of functionality. BD asserts that the elongated shape of the closure cap, the spacing of the ribs and their particular shapes, as well as the design relationship of those features to the whole of the closure cap are the design embraced by the mark. BD does not contest that the ribs themselves are functional, as is the opening in the top of the closure cap. These prominent and important functional features, which are common to the closure caps made by BD's competitors, led the Board to conclude that admitted non-functional features could not save the mark from being deemed overall functional. BD contends that the Board committed reversible error by discounting the significance of the non-functional elements.

....

A

... Whenever a proposed mark includes both functional and non-functional features, as in this case, the critical question is the degree of utility present in the overall design of the mark. This court recognized as much in *Morton-Norwich*, 671 F.2d at 1338, where ... this court reiterated the importance of the "degree of utility" proposition, and explained how the distinction between de facto and de jure functionality gives shape to a court's inquiry into a mark's "degree of utility."

De facto functionality simply means that a design has a function, like the closure cap in this case. Such functionality is irrelevant to the question of whether a mark as a whole is functional so as to be ineligible for trademark protection. De jure functionality "means that the product is in its particular shape because it works better in this shape." *Id.* Further, ... *Textron* instructs that where a mark is composed of functional and non-functional features, whether "an overall design is functional should be based on the superiority of the design as a whole, rather than on whether each design feature is 'useful' or 'serves a utilitarian purpose.'" *Textron v. ITC*, 753 F.2d [1019] at 1026 [(Fed. Cir. 1985)]. *Textron* cited as an example the Coca-Cola® bottle, noting that the bottle's significant overall non-functional shape would not lose trademark protection simply because "the shape of an insignificant element of the design," such as the lip of the bottle, is arguably functional." *Id.* at 1027. Likewise, a mark possessed of significant functional features should not qualify for trademark protection where insignificant elements of the design are non-functional.

The foregoing authority makes clear that the Board committed no legal error by weighing the functional and non-functional features of BD's mark against each other. As the court explained in *Morton-Norwich*, "we must strike a balance between the 'right to copy' and the right to protect one's method of trade identification." 671 F.2d at 1340. To decide as a matter of fact "whether the 'consuming public' has an interest in making use of [one's design], superior to [one's] interest in being [its] sole vendor," we are guided by the *Morton-Norwich* factors. *Id.*

B

....

.... As to the first *Morton-Norwich* factor, the Board did not err in finding that this factor weighs in favor of finding functionality. In *TrafFix Devices, Inc. v. Marketing Displays, Inc.*, 532 U.S. 23, 31 (2001), the Supreme Court stated that "the disclosure of a feature in the claims of a utility patent constitutes strong evidence of functionality." As discussed by the Board, claim 4 of the '446 patent shows the utilitarian nature of at least two prominent features of BD's mark: (1) the two concentric circles at the top of the closure cap, which allow a needle to be inserted, and (2) the ribs, which serve as a gripping surface.

... The Board correctly read the '446 patent to indicate that at least two of the important elements of the proposed mark were functional.

....

As to the second *Morton-Norwich* factor, ... BD's advertising touts the utilitarian advantages of the prominent features of the mark, such as the top's circular opening (which maximizes the possible useful area of the opening), the side's ribs, and the bottom's flanged lip. The advertisements emphasize that the "ridges on the outer surface permit for a more secure grip," and praise the "enhanced handling features" that are "inherent in the design." The advertisements explain that the top's "plastic shield" is an "important design innovation that keeps the blood safely contained within the closure" and "encourages safer opening—discourages use of the thumb roll technique, which can result in spattering of the specimen," and that the "hooded feature of closure reduces the possibility of catching glove between stopper and tube on reclosing." ... BD argues that the designs shown in the advertisements are not exactly the same as the proposed mark's design.... While the spire-like tops of the ribs may not be shown in the advertisements, the arrangement of the ribs along the side of the top and the shape of the opening are sufficiently like the features of the claimed mark to show an identity of functionality between the articles shown in the advertising and the proposed mark's prominent features.... BD would characterize the advertisements as "look for" advertising—the kind that pulls out of an overall article a few features to catch the viewer's attention.... This argument fails.... [T]he enlarged photographs of parts of the device actually highlight the functional aspects of the mark.

As to the third factor, if functionality is found based on other considerations, there is "no need to consider the availability of alternative designs, because the feature cannot be given trade dress protection merely because there are alternative designs available." *Valu Eng'g* [*v. Rexnord Corp.*], 278 F.3d [1268] at 1276 [(Fed. Cir. 2002)]. Thus, since the patent and advertising evidence established functionality, the Board did not need to analyze whether alternative designs exist. Nonetheless, the Board ... found that one of the proposed designs was irrelevant and the other two could not be characterized as alternative designs because they shared the same utilitarian features of BD's design....

Finally, as to the fourth factor, there was little record evidence before the Board to establish whether the cap design results from a comparatively simple or inexpensive method of manufacture. The sole evidence in the record on this factor consists of the declarations of ... two BD witnesses, who both averred that the design features did not lower the cost of manufacture. Given this scarce evidence, the Board did not err in refusing to weigh this factor in its analysis.

... The record in this case shows that BD's competitors in the closure cap industry also feature ribs for sure gripping and similar functional openings on their products. The Board thus concluded that the record failed to establish that there are meaningful alternative designs for collection tube closure caps. Substantial evidence supports this conclusion, which underscores the competitive need to copy the functional features of BD's proposed mark.

Because the Board committed no legal error in its assessment of the functionality of BD's proposed mark, and because substantial evidence supports the Board's findings of fact under the *Morton-Norwich* factors, we affirm the final decision of the Board.

LINN, CIRCUIT JUDGE, dissenting:

....

... It is undisputed that certain individual features of BD's closure cap design are functional, but the evidence falls short in supporting a conclusion that the mark, as a whole and as shown in the drawing, is in essence utilitarian, and thus de jure functional.... [D]e jure functionality is directed to the appearance of the design (not the thing itself) and is concerned with whether the design is "made in the form it must be made if it is to accomplish its purpose"; in other words, whether the appearance is dictated by function. *Morton-Norwich*, 671 F.2d at 1338–39; [citation].

I agree with the majority that the degree of design utility must be considered in determining de jure functionality. I part company with the majority, however, when it approves the Board's "weigh[ing] the elements of a mark against one another to develop an understanding of whether the mark as a whole is essentially functional and thus non-registrable." The presence of functional features may be relevant, but not in the sense of comparing dissociated functional features against non-functional features. The proper inquiry is to examine the degree to which the mark as a whole is dictated by utilitarian concerns (functional or economic superiority) or is arbitrary ("without complete deference to utility"). *See Morton-Norwich*, 671 F.2d at 1338–39, 1342–43.

Weighing individual elements of a mark against each other is analytically contrary to the consideration of the mark as a whole. As this court has previously held, "[s]imply dissecting appellant's alleged trademark into its design features and attributing to each a proven or commonly known utility is not, without more, conclusive that the design, considered as a whole, is de jure functional and not registrable." *In re Teledyne Indus., Inc.*, 696 F.2d 968, 971 (Fed. Cir. 1982).

This court's decision in *Morton-Norwich* is instructive. *Morton-Norwich* sought to register the following design:

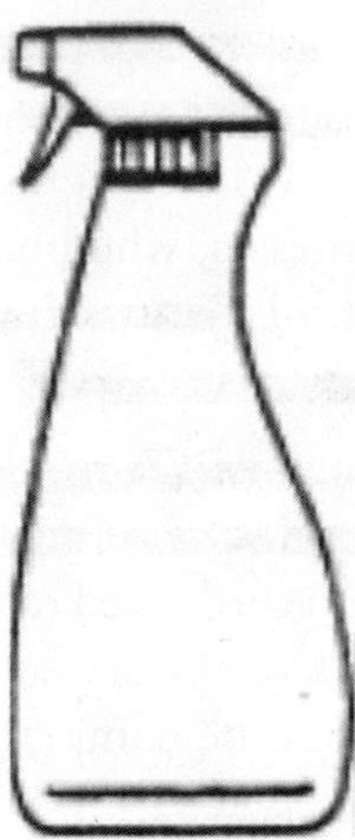

671 F.2d at 1334. The attorney rejected the mark on the basis that the design "is no more than a nondistinctive purely functional container for the goods plus a purely functional spray trigger controlled closure ... essentially utilitarian and non-arbitrary." *Id.* at 1335. The Board similarly concluded that the mark "is dictated primarily by functional (utilitarian) considerations, and is therefore unregistrable." *Id.* (original emphasis omitted).

Our predecessor court reversed, finding that the applicant sought to register "no single design feature or component but the overall composite design comprising both bottle and spray top." *Id.* at 1342. Thus, the degree of design utility was analyzed for the whole mark, not the dissociated functional elements. Although the bottle and spray top each served a function, there was a complete absence of evidence to show that the shape of the bottle and spray top were required to look as they did to serve those functions. *Id.* Indeed, the evidence before the Board established that the bottle and spray top could take a number of diverse forms, equally as suitable from a functional standpoint. *Id.* The court concluded that there would be no injury to competition if Morton-Norwich were entitled to protection of this particular design; competitors could obtain the functions of the container without copying the trade dress. *Id.* at 1342–43. In sum, the evidence failed to prove that the overall design was "the best or one of a few superior designs available." *Id.* at 1341.

As in *Morton-Norwich*, there is no evidence that the overall design of the BD closure cap is required to look the way it does or that the design is "the best or one of a few superior designs available." *Id.* at 1341–42. The Board and the majority place principal focus on the function served by certain features of the mark, including, *inter alia*, the top's opening (to allow for the insertion of a needle), the ribs on the side of the cap (to allow for increased grip), and the bottom's flanged lip (to allow for a safer opening). These considerations relate to the de facto functionality of individual product features and not the de jure functionality of the overall design—whether the design as a whole must look this way to serve some identified function. In focusing on the functional attributes of individual components, the Board and the majority overlook the arbitrary nature of BD's overall design.

....

Because the Board committed legal error in failing to analyze the functionality of BD's mark as a whole and lacked substantial evidence for its findings, I would reverse the Board's decision on functionality. On the functionality determination, I therefore respectfully dissent.

Question

The overall configuration of the spray bottle at issue in the *Morton-Norwich* case is depicted in the dissent. The CCPA in that case found that, although the overall configuration accommodated de facto purposes, such as holding liquid, having a neck to grip and possessing a housing for the spray mechanism (the pump mechanism inside of which was covered by a utility patent), the record did not show that the particular shape of these features was dictated by functional considerations, especially in light of possible alternative designs. Both the majority and the dissenting opinion in *In re Becton Dickinson* purport to follow *Morton-Norwich.* With which opinion do you agree?

In re Vertex Group LLC

89 U.S.P.Q.2d 1694 (T.T.A.B. 2009)

ROGERS, ADMINISTRATIVE TRADEMARK JUDGE:

Applicant Vertex Group LLC seeks to register as a trademark on the Principal Register a sound described as follows:

> ... a descending frequency sound pulse (from 2.3kHz to approximately 1.5kHz) that follows an exponential, RC charging curve, wherein said descending frequency sound pulse occurs four to five times per second, and that over a one second period of time, there is alternating sound pulses and silence with each occurring approximately 50% of the time during a one second period of time.[2]

Registration of the sound is sought for goods identified as a "Personal security alarm in the nature of a child's bracelet to deter and prevent child abductions," in

2. A recording of the sound can be heard by accessing an audio file through the USPTO website, at the following address: http://www.uspto.gov/go/kids/soundex/78940163_0001.mp3.

Class 9 (application Serial No. 76601697; the "child's bracelet application") and as "Personal security alarms," in Class 9 (application Serial No. 78940163; the "personal alarms application")....

....

Functionality

The Trademark Act provides that a proposed mark may be refused registration if it "comprises any matter that, as a whole, is functional." Section 2(e)(5), 15 U.S.C. § 1052(e)(5). The Supreme Court has stated "'[i]n general terms, a product feature is functional,' and cannot serve as a trademark, 'if it is essential to the use or purpose of the article or if it affects the cost or quality of the article,' that is, if exclusive use of the feature would put competitors at a significant non-reputation-related disadvantage." *Qualitex v. Jacobson*, 34 USPQ2d at 116–364, quoting *Inwood Laboratories, Inc. v. Ives Laboratories, Inc.*, 456 U.S. 844, 214 USPQ 1, 4 n.10 (1982). *See also, TrafFix Devices Inc. v. Marketing Displays Inc.*, 532 U.S. 23, 58 USPQ2d 1001, 1006 (2001). We note that this standard contemplates at least two possible bases upon which a finding of functionality may be made. First, if the product feature is essential to the use or purpose of the article it may be found functional. *See TrafFix Devices*, 58 U.S.P.Q.2d at 1006 ("Where the design is functional under the *Inwood* formulation there is no need to proceed further to consider if there is a competitive necessity for the feature."). Second, if the product feature affects the cost or quality of the article, so that exclusive right to use it would put a competitor at a disadvantage, this, too, may support a conclusion that the product feature is functional.

The Federal Circuit, our primary reviewing court, looks at [the] four [*Morton-Norwich*] factors, originally set out by a predecessor court, when it considers the issue of functionality, and the factors are particularly helpful for analyzing functionality under the second approach.... *In re Morton-Norwich Products, Inc.*, 671 F.2d 1332, 213 USPQ 9, 15–16 (CCPA 1982). [Citation.]

In the cases at hand, we conclude that the sound proposed for registration is functional and not entitled to registration under either view of functionality. Quite simply, the use of an audible alarm is essential to the use or purpose of applicant's products. It is clear, for example, that applicant touts the loud volume of the sound emitted by its alarm watch (and emphasizes the loudness much more than the flashing LEDs). Similarly, the evidence regarding competitive personal security devices that applicant put into the record also shows the predominant use of loud sound as an alarm. In addition, the sound involves alternating sound pulses and silence, which the ... evidence shows is a more effective way to use sound as an alarm than is a steady sound.

Applicant has argued that it is not seeking to register a sound of any particular loudness. Equally significant, however, is that the description of the sound is not limited to a particular volume. Thus, we must consider it to encompass all reasonable degrees of loudness for an alarm sound. *Cf. Phillips Petroleum Co. v. C.J. Webb, Inc.*, 442 F.2d 1376, 58 C.C.P.A. 1255, 170 USPQ 35, 36 (CCPA 1971) ("Webb's application is not limited to the mark depicted in any special form. In trying to visualize what other forms the mark might appear in, we are aided by the specimens submitted with Webb's application."). Moreover, it is clear from the record that applicant's alarm emits a loud sound and that the loudness of the sound is an essential feature of the product. For example, the specimen of use shows that applicant's sound is typically used in a loud manner. In addition, applicant has admitted "[t]he volume of the alarm is critical." See September 14, 2005 response to office action, child's bracelet application. Indeed, a soft alarm sound would not draw much attention.

In short, the ability of applicant's products to emit a loud, pulsing sound is essential to their use or purpose. For that reason alone, the functionality refusal must be affirmed in regard to each application. However, we shall also consider the question whether the proposed mark is functional under the *Morton-Norwich* analysis.

The first *Morton-Norwich* factor focuses on whether a utility patent exists disclosing the advantages of the proposed mark. Applicant argues that it has a utility patent application for its product, not for its sound. This argument, however, is undercut by the application's focus on a digital wristwatch with a "loud alarm" as an exemplary embodiment for the product, and the application's description of an alarm of 80–125 decibels. The application does not note the degree of brightness for lights that could potentially be utilized in a visual alarm, or the types of odors that could be used for an olfactory alarm; but it does specify a decibel range for the audible alarm that would be characterized as loud. Moreover, even if applicant is correct in its argument that the existence of its patent application for its product is not relevant to a *Morton-Norwich* analysis regarding the registrability of its sound, the absence of a patent for the sound would only mean this factor would be neutral in the analysis of functionality. *See TrafFix Devices*, 58 USPQ2d at 1006, and *In re N.V. Organon*, 79 USPQ2d at 1646.

The second *Morton-Norwich* factor focuses on whether advertising materials tout utilitarian advantages. Applicant's advertising clearly extols the loudness of the alarm sound, much more than the engineering of the product that produces the sound. Applicant has admitted as much. See January 22, 2008 response, child's bracelet application ("the advertising touts the degree of *loudness*") (emphasis in original). The advertising material does not tout the particular frequencies of the sound pulses or the pattern of the pulses, but applicant has admitted "[t]he volume of the alarm is critical." See September 14, 2005 response to office action, child's bracelet application. Thus, applicant's advertising touts a critical feature of its sound, as emitted by the identified goods. This factor favors a finding of functionality.

The third *Morton-Norwich* factor focuses on whether competitors would have functionally equivalent sounds available to them if applicant were accorded the exclusive rights attendant to registration. Of course, as already noted, when a proposed mark has been found functional on other grounds, it is not necessary for the record to also show use of applicant's particular sound would be a competitive necessity. *See Valu Engineering*, 61 USPQ2d at 1427. Nonetheless, it is clear from the record that alarm sounds work best when they alternate pulses of sound and silence, when the sound pulses fall within a particular range of frequencies, and when the sound is loud. Applicant argues that there are thousands of specific frequencies within the range that is most suitable for use in alarms. That range may be taken as between 1000 and 3000 Hz, based on the information of record. Thus, under applicant's analysis the thousands of frequencies within this range can be combined into countless variations and therefore applicant's particular combination of frequencies need not be employed by other makers of personal alarms. What applicant's argument fails to appreciate, however, is that the description of its mark only specifies that its sound pulses will be between 1500 Hz and 2300 Hz. Based on this description, applicant would be free to combine sound pulses for any of the frequencies within this range, a large swath of the optimal range of 1000 Hz to 3000 Hz. While there may indeed be countless combinations of frequencies available for personal alarms utilizing the frequencies within the optimal range, registration of applicant's sound as described would deprive competitors of many of those options. It matters not that applicant's actual sound may currently use only a handful of particular frequencies, for it would be free to change the combinations at any time and still have its sound fall within the ambit of the description. This factor favors a finding of functionality.

The final *Morton-Norwich* factor considers whether the sound yields applicant a comparatively simple or cheap method of manufacturing personal alarms. Applicant has explained, and the record shows, that the sound of its product has no bearing on the cost or ease of manufacture of its alarms. This factor is neutral.

Weighing all the *Morton-Norwich* factors in the balance, we conclude that the mark applicant has described in its application and proposes to register is functional and unregistrable. The functionality refusal is affirmed in each application, based on both the *Inwood* formulation of the sound being essential to the use or purpose of applicant's goods and under the *Morton-Norwich* analysis.

Question

Would the applicant have fared any better under the Board's functionality analysis if it had specified the volume and pulsing more narrowly? Under the *Inwood* test? Under the *Morton-Norwich* factors?

Chapter 5

Loss of Trademark Rights

A. Genericism

1. Development of the Standard

Recall the "Shredded Wheat" case, *Kellogg Co. v. National Biscuit Co.*, 305 U.S. 111 (1938), *supra*, Chapter 2[A]. The court held Nabisco had no trademark rights in "Shredded Wheat," because that was "the term by which the biscuit in pillow shaped form is generally known by the public. As Kellogg Company had the right to make the article, it had, also, the right to use the term by which the public knows it." If the name claimed as the brand is (or becomes) the "generic" name of the goods or services, principles of competition require that the name remain (or become) free for all purveyors to use. The cases that follow address both terms that initially served as trademarks but came to lose their source-denoting significance, and terms that aptly described the goods from the start, and may (or should) never have been trademarks.

Bayer Co. v. United Drug Co.

272 F. 505 (S.D.N.Y. 1921)

Learned Hand, J:

[Plaintiff Bayer Co. was the holder of a recently-expired patent for acetylsalicylic acid, a pharmaceutical product that Bayer marketed under the name "Aspirin."

Defendant, a competitor, was not only selling acetylsalicylic acid, but was doing so under the Aspirin designation. In response to Bayer's common-law trademark infringement suit, defendant asserted, *inter alia*, that Aspirin had become a commonly recognized name for the drug, and that once the patent expired, any person could not only manufacture and sell the drug, but could call it the name by which the public had come to know the goods.]

....

The single question, as I view it, ... is merely one of fact: What do the buyers understand by the word for whose use the parties are contending? If they understand by it only the kind of goods sold, I take it, it makes no difference whatever what efforts the plaintiff has made to get them to understand more. He has failed, and he cannot say that, when the defendant uses the word, he is taking away customers who wanted to deal with him, however closely disguised he may be allowed to keep his identity. So here the question is whether the buyers merely understood that the word "Aspirin" meant this kind of drug, or whether it meant that and more than that; i.e., that it came from the same single, though, if one please anonymous, source from which they had got it before. Prima facie I should say, since the word is coined and means nothing by itself, that the defendant must show that it means only the kind of drug to which it applies. The fact that it was patented until 1917 is indeed a material circumstance, but it is not necessarily controlling.

....

In the case at bar the evidence shows that there is a class of buyers to whom the word "Aspirin" has always signified the plaintiff, more specifically indeed than was necessary for its protection. I refer to manufacturing chemists, to physicians, and probably to retail druggists. From 1899 it flooded the mails with assertions that "Aspirin" meant its own manufacture. This was done in pamphlets, advertisements in trade papers, on the packages and cartons, and by the gratuitous distribution of samples. True, after 1904 it abandoned the phrase "acetyl salicylic acid" for "monoaceticacidester of salicylicacid," but even that extraordinary collocation of letters was intelligible to these classes of buyers who, except possibly the more ignorant of the retail druggists, were measurably versed in the general jargon of pharmaceutical chemistry. Moreover, the drug continued to be generally known by the more tolerable phrase "acetyl salicylic acid," which also adequately described its chemical organization. As to these buyers the plaintiff has therefore, I think, made out a case at least to compel the addition of some distinguishing suffix, even though its monopoly had been more perfect than in fact it was.

The crux of this controversy, however, lies not in the use of the word to these buyers, but to the general consuming public, composed of all sorts of buyers from those somewhat acquainted with pharmaceutical terms to those who knew nothing of them. The only reasonable inference from the evidence is that these did not understand by the word anything more than a kind of drug to which for one reason or another they had become habituated. It is quite clear that while the drug was sold as powder this must have been so. It was dispensed substantially altogether on prescription during this period, and, although physicians appear to have used the terms, "Aspirin" or "acetyl salicylic acid" indifferently, it cannot be that such patients as read their prescriptions attributed to "Aspirin" any other meaning than as an ingredient in a general compound, to which faith and science might impart therapeutic virtue. Nor is there any evidence that such as may have seen both terms identified them as the same drug. I cannot speculate as to how many in fact did so. No packages could possibly have reached the consumer, nor was any advertising addressed to them; their only acquaintance with the word was as the name for a drug in whose curative properties they had got confidence.

In 1904, however, they began to get acquainted with it in a different way, for then all the larger manufacturing chemists began to make tablets, and the trade grew to extraordinary proportions. The consumer, as both sides agree, had long before the autumn of 1915 very largely abandoned consultation with physicians and assumed the right to drug himself as his own prudence and moderation might prescribe. In all cases—omitting for the moment the infringing product—the drug was sold in bottles labeled "Aspirin" with some indication of the name of the tablet maker, but none of the plaintiff. It is probable that by far the greater part of the tablets sold were in dozens or less, and that the bottles so labeled did not generally reach the hands of the consumer, but, even so, a not inconsiderable number of bottles of 100 were sold, and as to the rest they were sold only under the name "Aspirin." The consumer did not know and could not possibly know the manufacturer of the drug which he got, or whether one or more chemists made it in the United States. He never heard the name "acetyl salicylic acid" as applied to it, and without some education could not possibly have kept it in his mind, if he had. So far as any means of information at all were open to him, they indicated that it was made by most large chemists indiscriminately.

This being the situation up to the autumn of 1915, the defendant seems to me to have effectually rebutted any presumption which the coined word might carry....

After the autumn of 1915 the plaintiff totally changed its methods, and thereafter no tablets reached the consumer without its own name. But it is significant that even then it used the word "Aspirin" as though it was a general term, although it is true that there was ample notice upon the bottles and boxes that "Aspirin" meant its manufacture. The most striking part of the label read, "Bayer—Tablets of Aspirin." While this did not show any abandonment of the name, which there has never been, it did show how the plaintiff itself recognized the meaning which the word had acquired, because the phrase most properly means that these tablets were Bayer's make of the drug known as "Aspirin." It presupposes that the persons reached were using the word to denote a kind of product. Were it not so, why the addition of "Bayer," and especially why the significant word "of"?

Disregarding this, however, it was too late in the autumn of 1915 to reclaim the word which had already passed into the public domain. If the consuming public had once learned to know "Aspirin" as the accepted name for the drug, perhaps it is true that an extended course of education might have added to it some proprietary meaning, but it would be very difficult to prove that it had been done in 17 months, and in any case the plaintiff does not try to prove it. The issue in this aspect, indeed, becomes whether during that period the word had obtained a secondary meaning, and I do not understand that any such thing is claimed. If it is, I own I cannot find any basis for it in the record. Probably what really happened was that the plaintiff awoke to the fact that on the expiration of the patent its trade-mark would be questioned, and strove to do what it could to relieve it of any doubts. Yet, had it not been indifferent to the results of selling to the consumer, it could have protected itself just as well as the time when consumers began to buy directly as in 1915. Nothing would have been easier than to insist that the tablet makers should market the drug in small tin boxes bearing the plaintiff's name, or to take over the sale just as it did later. Instead of this, they allowed the manufacturing chemists to build up this part of the demand without regard to the trade-mark. Having made that bed, they must be content to lie in it. Hence it appears to me that nothing happening between October, 1915, and March, 1917, will serve to turn the word into a trade-mark.

....

The case, therefore, presents a situation in which, ignoring sporadic exceptions, the trade is divided into two classes, separated by vital differences. One, the manufacturing chemists, retail druggists, and physicians, has been educated to understand that "Aspirin" means the plaintiff's manufacture, and has recourse to another and an intelligible name for it, actually in use among them. The other, the consumers, the plaintiff has, consciously I must assume, allowed to acquaint themselves with the drug only by the name "Aspirin," and has not succeeded in advising that the word means the plaintiff at all. If the defendant is allowed to continue the use of the word of the first class, certainly without any condition, there is a chance that it may get customers away from the plaintiff by deception. On the other hand, if the plaintiff is allowed a monopoly of the word as against consumers, it will deprive the defendant, and the trade in general, of the right effectually to dispose of the drug by the only description which will be understood. It appears to me that the relief granted cannot in justice to either party disregard this division; each party has won, and each has lost.

....

[The court granted injunctive relief against selling the product under the designation "Aspirin" to physicians, manufacturing chemists and retail druggists, but permitted use of "Aspirin" for bottles intended for direct sale to consumers.]

Questions

1. A factor that may have influenced the court in the Aspirin case was the trademark proprietor's merely denominative use of the terms. Plaintiff's failure to use the terms in trademark fashion, or adequately to police others' use of the terms, resulted in the term's loss of trademark significance. Is there anything Bayer could have done to prevent this result? A similar fate met the term "cellophane." *See DuPont Cellophane Co. v. Waxed Products Co.*, 85 F.2d 75 (2d Cir. 1936).

2. We have encountered the curtailment of trademark rights in a "limited geographic area" in Lanham Act section 33(b)(5), entitling good faith junior users to continue to operate where they were doing business prior to the effective date of the federal trademark owner's registration. *See Thrifty Rent-a-Car System v. Thrift Cars, Inc.*, 831 F.2d 1177 (1st Cir. 1987), *supra*, Chapter 3[F]. Does the concept of "limited geographic area" apply to other bases on which a trademark owner might lose rights in a mark (whether or not registered)? For example, if studies show that a majority of consumers in the states of Alabama, Mississippi, and Georgia use the word "Coke" to describe all carbonated soft drinks, should a court rule that the mark "Coke" is generic within that limited geographic area? (On the studies, see, e.g., http://www.popvssoda.com/statistics/ALL.html). *Cf. Primary Children's Med. Ctr. Foundation v. Scentsy, Inc.*, 104 U.S.P.Q.2d 1124 (D. Utah 2012) (FESTIVAL OF TREES not generic as a matter of law for fundraising devices benefitting children's medical center despite showing that terms are common in some parts of the country where there were genuine issues as to whether terms functioned as a mark in Utah).

Note: Protecting Trademarks against Genericism

As *Bayer* and other cases show, a trademark holder may lose trademark rights if the term ceases to indicate the source of the goods or services, and instead becomes synonymous with the goods or services. Companies employ various strategies to maintain trademark awareness, including placing advertisements directed toward the relevant public, and stressing the trademark significance of the term. Consider the examples on the following pages. Do you think they are an effective means of maintaining brand awareness?

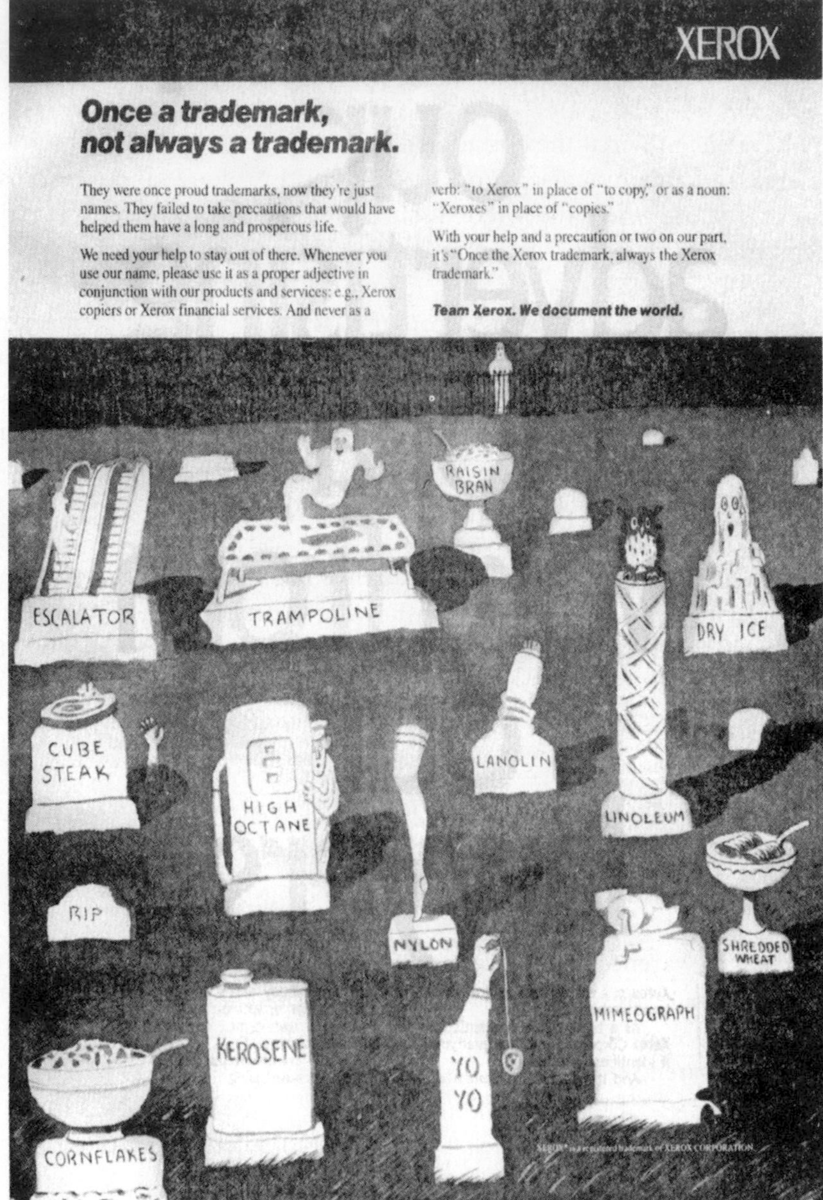

Keeping company personnel and other business people attuned to proper trademark use is as important as maintaining public awareness, and can require its own education measures. For example, those with permission to use the GOOGLE mark are provided with the following usage rules:

Permissions – Google Page 1 of 1

Google

Permissions

Rules for proper usage

When you use any of our Brand Features, you must always follow the Rules for Proper Usage included in these Guidelines. In addition, Google may provide you with written requirements as to the size, typeface, colors, and other graphic characteristics of the Google Brand Features. If we provide these requirements to you at the time of our approval, you must implement them before using our Brand Features. If we provide these requirements to you after we initially gave our permission, you must implement them within a commercially reasonable timeframe.

Things you must do when given permission to use a Google trademark:

- If you are using a Google trademark, distinguish the trademark from the surrounding text in some way. Capitalize the first letter, capitalize or italicize the entire mark, place the mark in quotes, use a different type style or font for the mark than for the generic name.
- If you do not capitalize the entire mark, always spell and capitalize the trademark exactly as they are shown in the Google Trademarks and Suggested Accepted Generic Terms below.
- Use the trademark only as an adjective, never as a noun or verb, and never in the plural or possessive form.
- Use a generic term following the trademark, for example: GOOGLE search engine, Google search, GOOGLE web search.
- Use only Google-approved artwork when using Google's logos.
- If you are using a Google logo on a web page, there must exist a minimum spacing of 25 pixels between each side of the logo and other graphic or textual elements on your web page.

http://www.google.com/permissions/trademark/rules.html 11/20/2012

In *Kleenex is a Registered Trademark (And Other Desperate Appeals)*, THE ATLANTIC (Sept. 25, 2014), Megan Garber reproduced several advertisements seeking to forestall generic uses of marks:

THE WORD FRIGIDAIRE ALWAYS ENDS WITH A CAPITAL "R."

The capital "R" has a circle around it, too. Because Frigidaire® is more than an ordinary word, it's our registered trademark.

To many, it means the finest quality refrigerator available. It's a name that's so popular some people call every refrigerator a Frigidaire®. Unfortunately, that's wrong.

Only Frigidaire® refrigerators have the quality, engineering and heritage to bear the name.

So if a refrigerator really is a Frigidaire®, say so.

If it's not, use the other word that ends with an "R." Refrigerator.

We would appreciate it.

Frigidaire®
HERE TODAY. HERE TOMORROW.

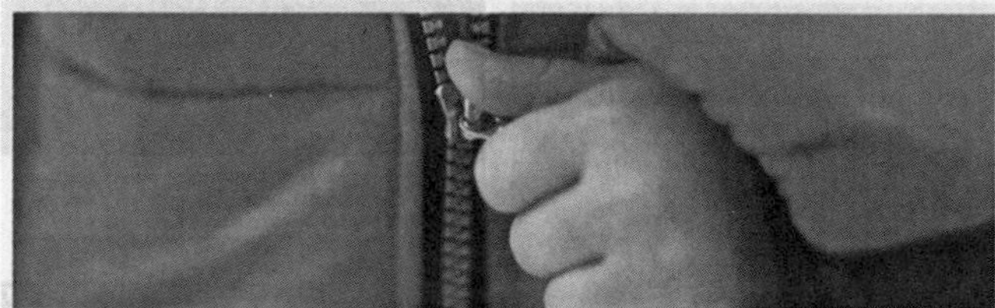

If a trademark is misused it could come undone.

If you didn't know zipper was a trademark, don't worry, it's not. But it used to be. It was lost because people misused the name. And the same could happen to ours, Xerox. Please help us ensure it doesn't. Use Xerox only as an adjective to identify our products and services, such as Xerox copiers, not a verb, "to Xerox," or a noun, "Xeroxes." Something to keep in mind that will help us keep it together.

xerox.com

Ready For Real Business xerox

BOTOX® isn't a nickname. It isn't generic for botulinum toxin, and it isn't a verb.

BOTOX® Purified Neurotoxin Complex is a drug that has made significant differences in many patients' lives.

And, BOTOX® is a registered trademark of Allergan, Inc.

So when you write about BOTOX® therapy, don't make the mistake of forgetting the proper way to use the BOTOX® trademark: as an adjective, and as a brand name.

Purified Neurotoxin Complex

ALLERGAN

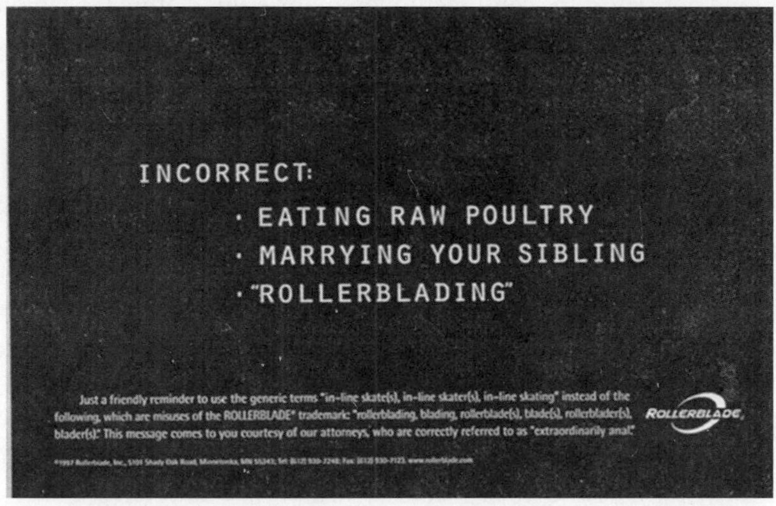

In *How to Use a Trademark Properly*, from Trademark Problems and How to Avoid Them (rev. ed. 1981), Sidney Diamond offered useful tips to prevent a trademark from degenerating into a generic term. He stressed that the product's generic name should accompany the trademark. A trademark is an adjective; it should never be used as a noun or as a verb. Thus, proper promotion of a GREMLIN brand washing machine would proclaim that "clothes come cleaner with a GREMLIN washing machine," rather than "clothes come cleaner with a Gremlin." Similarly, the trademark owner should not exhort the consumer to "gremlinize" his clothing. Diamond counseled: "A simple test to apply to advertising copy is this: Would a complete thought be expressed if the trademark were omitted from the sentence?" Do the advertising materials you have just perused meet this test?

Elliot v. Google, Inc., 45 F. Supp. 3d 1156 (D. Ariz. 2014). Google's guidelines caution not to use "Google" as a verb. Sidney Diamond gives the same advice to brand owners. The question as to whether widespread use of a mark as a verb renders it generic arose with respect to the GOOGLE mark in this case. Plaintiffs had acquired over 700 domain names that coupled "google" with another brand, person or place, e.g. googledisney.com, googlebarackobama.com and googlemexicocity.com. Google brought a UDRP proceeding in which the arbitrator ordered transfer of the domain names to Google. *See generally* Chapter 11, *infra*. The plaintiffs instituted the court action seeking a declaration that GOOGLE is generic and cancellation of two GOOGLE registrations. Google counterclaimed for trademark dilution and cybersquatting as well as state claims. Plaintiffs moved for summary judgment to cancel the registrations as generic.

The plaintiffs' primary argument centered on widespread usage of "Google" as a verb. The district court forcefully rejected this argument and noted that there are two kinds of uses of a mark as a verb.

> Verb use of a trademark is not fundamentally incapable of identifying a producer or denoting source. A mark can be used as a verb in a discriminate sense so as to refer to an activity with a particular product or service, e.g., "I will PHOTOSHOP the image" could mean the act of manipulating an image by using the trademarked Photoshop graphics editing software developed and sold by Adobe Systems. This discriminate mark-as-verb usage clearly performs the statutory source-denoting function of a trademark.
>
> However, a mark can also be used as a verb in an indiscriminate sense so as to refer to a category of activity in general, e.g., "I will PHOTOSHOP the image" could be understood to mean image manipulation by using graphics editing software other than Adobe Photoshop. This use commandeers PHOTOSHOP to refer to something besides Adobe's trademarked product. Such indiscriminate mark-as-verb usage does not perform the statutory trademark function; instead, it functions as a synecdoche describing both a particular species of activity (e.g. using Adobe's PHOTOSHOP brand software) and the genus of services to which the species belongs (e.g. using image manipulation software in general).

The district court rejected that prevalence of even the second type of usage necessarily renders a mark generic, because the proper test is the primary significance of the term to the public.

> It cannot be understated that a mark is not rendered generic merely because the mark serves a synecdochian "dual function" of identifying a particular species of service while at the same time indicating the genus of services

> to which the species belongs. S. Rep. No. 98-627,4 at 5 (1984), *reprinted in* 1984 U.S.C.C.A.N. 5718, 5722 (explaining "dual function" use "is not conclusive of whether the mark is generic"); *accord* 15 U.S.C. § 1064(3) ("A registered mark shall not be deemed to be the generic name of goods or services solely because such mark is also used as a name of or to identify a unique product or service."). Nor is a mark "generic merely because it has *some significance* to the public as an indication of the nature or class of an article.... In order to become generic the *principal significance* of the word must be its indication of the nature or class of an article, rather than an indication of its origin." *Feathercombs, Inc. v. Solo Prods. Corp.*, 306 F.2d 251, 256 (2d Cir. 1962) (emphasis added). Moreover, "casual, non-purchasing uses of [marks] are not evidence of generic usage" because primary significance is determined by "'the use and understanding of the [mark] in the context of purchasing decisions.'" 2 J. Thomas McCarthy, McCarthy on Trademarks and Unfair Competition § 12:8 (4th ed. 2014) (*quoting* Restatement (Third) of Unfair Competition § 15 cmt. c (1995)).

After considering the evidence of record, which contained expert and survey evidence offered by the parties, including a Teflon study proffered by Google that showed over 90% of the respondents identified GOOGLE as a brand name, the district court granted judgment for Google as a matter of law on the genericism issue, stating:

> ... Plaintiffs cannot supplant the primary-significance test with a frequency-of-verb-use test to cancel the GOOGLE mark, which they admit refers to "one of the largest, most recognized, and widely used internet search services in the world."

2. Implementing the Standard: Survey Evidence

King-Seeley Thermos Co. v. Aladdin Industries, Inc., 321 F.2d 577 (2d Cir. 1963). King-Seeley owned eight trademark registrations for "Thermos." Aladdin Industries tried to sell its own vacuum-insulated containers as "thermos bottles," a term that it regarded as generic. King-Seeley sought to enjoin Aladdin Industries from using the term, and defendant countered seeking to cancel the registration of the word "thermos" for having become "a generic descriptive word in the English language ... as a synonym for 'vacuum insulated' container."

According to the District Court, King-Seeley's promotional campaign directed at the public for the "Thermos bottle" had the effect of making "thermos" a generic term descriptive of the product rather than its origin. For example, a catalogue used "Thermos" as a noun with phrases like: "Thermos is sold and recommended by every good store everywhere." Subsequent efforts by King-Seeley to police its trademark succeeded within the trade but failed to change public perception. The District Court, 207 F. Supp. 9, n.8 (S.D.N.Y. 1962), relied in part on defendant's survey that included the following questions:

> Are you familiar with the type of container that is used to keep liquids, like soup, coffee, tea and lemonade, hot or cold for a period of time?
>
> ....
>
> If you were going to buy one of these containers tomorrow—that is, the type that keeps food and beverages hot or cold—what type of store would you select to make your purchase?
>
> What would you ask for—that is, what would you tell the clerk you wanted?
>
> Can you think of any other words that you would use to ask for a container that keeps liquids hot or cold?
>
> If you were going to describe one of these containers to a friend of yours—what words would come to your mind first to describe a container that keeps liquids hot or cold?
>
> ....
>
> Do you know the names of any manufacturers who make these containers that keep liquids hot or cold?
>
> Can you name any trade-marks or brand names that are used on these containers?

The District Court summarized the survey results as follows:

> The results of the survey were that about 75% of adults in the United States who were familiar with containers that keep the contents hot or cold, call such a container a "thermos"; about 12% of the adult American public know that "thermos" has a trade-mark significance, and about 11% use the term "vacuum bottle." This is generally corroborative of the court's conclusions drawn from the other evidence, except that such other evidence indicated that a somewhat larger minority than 12% was aware of the trade-mark meaning of "thermos"; and a somewhat larger minority than 11% used the descriptive term "vacuum" bottle or other container.

However, as there was an appreciable, though minority, segment of consumers who recognized plaintiff's trademarks, the District Court imposed certain restrictions on use of the word "thermos" by defendant, which were upheld by the 2d Circuit as follows:

> Since in this case, the primary significance to the public of the word "thermos" is its indication of the nature and class of an article rather than as an indication of its source, whatever duality of meaning the word still holds for a minority of the public is of little consequence except as a consideration in the framing of a decree. Since the great majority of those members of the public who use the word "thermos" are not aware of any trademark significance, there is not enough dual use to support King-Seeley's claims to monopoly of the word as a trademark.
>
> No doubt, the Aspirin and Cellophane doctrine can be a harsh one for it places a penalty on the manufacturer who has made skillful use of advertising

and has popularized his product. However, King-Seeley has enjoyed a commercial monopoly of the word "thermos" for over fifty years. During that period, despite its efforts to protect the trademark, the public has virtually expropriated it as its own. The word having become part of the public domain, it would be unfair to unduly restrict the right of a competitor of King-Seeley to use the word.

The court below, mindful of the fact that some members of the public and a substantial portion of the trade still recognize and use the word "thermos" as a trademark, framed an eminently fair decree designed to afford King-Seeley as much future protection as was possible. The decree provides that defendant must invariably precede the use of the word "thermos" by the possessive of the name "Aladdin"; that the defendant must confine its use of "thermos" to the lower-case "t"; and that it may never use the words "original" or "genuine" in describing its product. *See Bayer Co. v. United Drug Co.*, 272 F. 505 (S.D.N.Y. 1921); *DuPont Cellophane Co. v. Waxed Products Co.*, 85 F.2d 75 (2d Cir. 1936). In addition, plaintiff is entitled to retain the exclusive right to all of its present forms of the trademark "Thermos" without change. These conditions provide a sound and proper balancing of the competitive disadvantage to defendants arising out of plaintiff's exclusive use of the word "thermos" and the risk that those who recognize "Thermos" as a trademark will be deceived.

Questions

1. The "thermos" survey requested respondents to supply a name for a container that keeps liquids hot or cold. Do you see any problems with this survey? Recall Judge Hand's statement: "If they understand by it only the kind of goods sold ... [plaintiff's effort] makes no difference to get them to understand more." Judge Hand suggests that terms can function both as marks, an indication of source, and as identifying a type of product. Does the survey question: "What would you ask for—that is what would you tell the clerk you wanted?" adequately account for the dual-functioning nature of marks? Does it distinguish the primary significance of the term?

2. In "thermos," although (according to the survey) 75% of the public perceived no trademark significance in the term, 25% did view the term as a trademark. Did the court's relief adequately balance the interests of protecting against confusion of the minority of the public that recognized "thermos" as a mark with the competitor's need to use the designation as a generic term?

E.I. Dupont de Nemours & Co. v. Yoshida International, Inc.

393 F. Supp. 502 (E.D.N.Y. 1975)

NEAHER, J.:

[DuPont, trademark proprietors of the TEFLON mark for non-stick cookware coating, brought a trademark infringement action against YKK, the manufacturers of the EFLON easy-glide zipper. Among other defenses, YKK asserted that TEFLON was a generic term. Both parties introduced surveys purporting to show that the public did or did not perceive TEFLON to be the common noun for non-stick cookware coatings.]

YKK's principal proof of generic usage by the public comes from a second survey introduced into evidence. That survey, actually two nationwide studies ... is entitled "Awareness and Name Identification of Non-Stick Coating Concept."

The first study ("Survey I") was conducted among adult women, 90.6% of whom expressed awareness of "kitchen pots and pans that have their inside surfaces coated by chemical substances to keep grease or food from sticking to them." Of the aware[51] respondents, 86.1% apparently mentioned only "TEFLON" or "TEFLON II" as their sole answer when asked, "What is the name ... or names of these pots and pans ...?" Further, 71.7% of the aware women gave only "TEFLON" or "TEFLON II" as the name they would use to describe the pots and pans to a store clerk or friend. The figure was 79.3%, counting those who gave responses in addition to TEFLON or TEFLON II. Only 7.3% of the aware women identified DuPont as the manufacturer of the pots and pans.

The second study ("Survey II") was conducted among adult women, 89.4% of whom expressed some sort of awareness of "substances that manufacturers sometimes apply to the surfaces of certain products in order to prevent things from sticking to them." Of the aware respondents, 81.4% apparently mentioned only "TEFLON" or "TEFLON II" as their sole answer when asked, "What name or names are these substances called ...?" Further, 60% of the aware women gave only "TEFLON" or "TEFLON II" as the name they would use to describe the pots and pans to a store clerk or friend. The figure was 70% counting those who gave other responses in addition to TEFLON or TEFLON II. Only 9.1% of the aware women identified DuPont as the manufacturer of the substances. Understandably enough, no one in either survey apparently ever mentioned polytetrafluoroethylene.

In response to these two surveys, DuPont introduced a second Burke survey, conducted telephonically.... It also contained two separate studies. In the first of these ("Survey A"), respondents of either sex who represented over the telephone to be over 18 years of age were told: "Protective coatings are sometimes applied by manufacturers to the inside of household utensils in order to prevent food and grease from sticking." They were then asked, "Do you know a brand name or trademark for one of these coatings?" Pursuing affirmative answers only, respondents were then asked, "What is that brand name or trademark?"

The results of the survey were that of the 60% of the respondents who reached the latter question, 80% of them—or 48% of the entire sample—answered "TEFLON." All respondents were then asked, "Can you think of any other words or terms to describe these coatings?" Among the TEFLON respondents to the prior

51. "Aware" respondents were only those who indicated an awareness of the subject matter of the survey by responding in some affirmative fashion to an initial question, "Have you ever heard about these kitchen pots and pans....?"

question, 32% were able to supply an additional term, the most frequently expressed of which was "Non-Stick." Sixty-eight percent knew no other words.

The second study ("Survey B") was conducted among adults in a similar fashion. By using the example of "Chevrolet—automobile" the interviewer first explained the difference between a brand name and a common name, and then asked whether each of eight names, including TEFLON, was a brand name or a common name. The results, as shown in more detail in the margin,[54] were that 68% of the respondents identified TEFLON as a brand name and 31% as a common name.

... YKK contends that DuPont's Survey A confirms its own findings, because 68% of those who identified "TEFLON" as a brand name or trademark had no other word or term to describe the coatings. Accordingly, say defendants, this 68% regards "TEFLON" as the descriptive name of the non-stick substances, a figure that compares closely with their own. In response, DuPont argues that YKK's own studies are invalid because the way Survey I and Survey II questions were worded, it was not possible to determine "what percentage of the women who gave a TEFLON response did so in the belief or on the assumption that they were being asked for a brand name." ...

On a review of the exhibits, and especially the cross-examination of the author of YKK's surveys, ... the court is satisfied that those surveys are ambiguous on the question of whether the responses truly reflect generic use of the TEFLON mark to the extent indicated.[56]

The fact is that the surveys do not really focus on the issue of the absence of *trademark* significance in public use of the word TEFLON. This is made clear by DuPont's own Survey A, which asked essentially the same question as did Survey II—name for non-stick coatings—but used the expression "brand name or trademark" rather than "name or names." It seems clear from the results that in all three surveys (I, II and A), respondents were, by the design of the questions, more often than not focusing on supplying the inquirer a "name," without regard to whether the principal significance

---

54.

NAME	BRAND	COMMON	DON'T KNOW
	%	%	%
STP	90	5	5
THERMOS	51	46	3
MARGARINE	9	91	1
TEFLON	68	31	2
JELLO	75	25	1
REFRIGERATOR	6	94	—
ASPIRIN	13	86	—
COKE	76	24	—

Pl. Exh. 61, Table 2.

56. This is not wholly to reject defendants' contention that the surveys reveal some evidence and examples of generic use of TEFLON by the public. DuPont admits that they do. But as the discussion makes clear, "some evidence" of generic usage is not sufficient. Moreover, references, for example, to "Teflon pots and pans" are at best only ambiguous illustration of generic use and hardly furnish the convincing proof required to overcome trademark or brand name usage for a non-stick coated pot or pan.

of the name supplied was "its indication of the nature or class of an article, rather than an indication of its origin." *King-Seeley Thermos Co., supra*, 321 F.2d at 580.

The only survey which really gets down to this critical element of the case is Survey B. It stands unrebutted as evidence that, to the extent it accurately reflects public opinion, a substantial majority of the public continues to believe that TEFLON is a brand name. YKK criticizes the survey not for being unrepresentative, but for its failure to be tied to a particular product, and argues it is thus no evidence that TEFLON has trademark significance. That contention is without merit. In fact, the responses of the survey reveal that the public is quite good at sorting out brand names from common names, and, for TEFLON, answers the critical question left unanswered by the ambiguities inherent in Surveys I, II and A—that of the *principal significance* of the TEFLON mark to the public.[57] Not only have defendants failed to show that TEFLON's principal significance is as a common noun, plaintiff has succeeded in showing it to be a "brand name"—an indicator, in the words of DuPont's questionnaire, of a product "made by one company."

....

The foregoing makes clear that, on the facts of this case, YKK was required to make a rather clear and convincing showing that the principal significance of the word TEFLON to the public is as a term for non-stick coatings and finishes rather than its trademark significance. But no matter how defendants' burden is described, it simply has not been met on this record and the defense must fail.

....

Princeton Vanguard, LLC v. Frito-Lay North America, Inc., 786 F.3d 960 (Fed. Cir. 2015). The Federal Circuit vacated the Board's decision in **Frito-Lay North America, Inc. v. Princeton Vanguard, LLC**, 109 U.S.P.Q.2d 1949 (T.T.A.B. 2014), and remanded for further proceedings. The Board held PRETZEL CRISPS is generic for "pretzel crackers." Both parties had submitted dueling Teflon studies with opposite results. Plaintiff's survey asked 250 respondents who were purchasers of salty snacks at supermarkets/grocery stores within 6 months or likely such purchasers in the next 6 months the following questions:

> Participants who said they understood the difference between a category name and brand name were then read a list of names individually for food and some unrelated products and asked whether they thought each name was a category name, a brand name, "don't know", or "not sure." The list, with results, follows:

---

57. Also, ... the court finds no significance in the evidence in Surveys I and II of the large proportion of the public unaware of the identify of DuPont as the manufacturer of TEFLON. As has been noted, such evidence has no bearing on the likelihood of confusion issue. It would be pertinent on the genericization issue only if the mark itself were an important component of the name of the manufacturing company, e.g., Coca-Cola Bottling Co. But where, as here, the mark is entirely distinct from the identity of the manufacturer, such evidence is of no value.

Results By Name:

Name	Brand	Category	Don't Know/ Not Sure
RITZ BITZ	82%	12%	7%
LUCKY CHARMS	87%	10%	3%
I-POD	61%	28%	11%
AMERICAN AIRLINES	89%	9%	2%
TRISCUIT	80%	13%	7%
PRETZEL CRISPS	41%	41%	18%
GINGER ALE	25%	72%	3%
AUTOMOBILE	9%	91%	1%
POTATO CHIPS	8%	90%	2%
NEWSPAPER	5%	93%	2%
POPCORN	6%	93%	1%

The Board credited defendant's expert's critique of this survey. It also reported the results of defendant's survey but took no position with respect to its validity:

> Initially 500 adults were screened, but only 222 were found eligible after meeting the screening criteria in a "double-blind" survey, conducted by phone. As a screening gateway, in the *Teflon* format, respondents were given an explanation of the difference between brand and common names, and then asked both whether BAKED TOSTITOS is a brand or common name, and whether TORTILLA CHIPS is a brand or common name. Only those who answered both correctly proceeded with the survey. Those respondents then were questioned about a number of "brand" or "common" names with the option of "don't know."
>
> … [T]he results were as follows:

Name	Brand	Common	Don't Know/ Haven't Heard
SUN CHIPS	96%	3%	<1%
CHEESE NIPS	85%	13%	2%
PRETZEL CRISPS	55%	36%	9%
FLAVOR TWISTS	48%	34%	18%
GOURMET POPCORN	25%	72%	3%
ONION RINGS	8%	91%	1%
MACADAMIA NUT	7%	92%	<1%

The Federal Circuit reversed and remanded, criticizing the Board's treatment of the survey evidence:

> ... We ... have recognized that "consumer surveys may be a preferred method of proving genericness." *BellSouth Corp. v. DataNational Corp.*, 60 F.3d 1565, 1570 (Fed. Cir. 1995).
>
> ....
>
> ... [T]he Board ... can[not] disregard the results of survey evidence without explanation....
>
> ... [T]he Board expressly agreed with [the] criticisms of [plaintiff's] survey." ... In particular, the Board concluded that the two "don't know" and "not sure" answers "potentially were confusing to survey participants, and may have le[d] those who understood the survey question to elect to indicate they did not." As to [defendant's] survey, which found that 55% of respondents thought that PRETZEL CRISPS was a brand name.... The Board did not agree with [plaintiff's] critique ... [n]or ... call into question [defendant's expert's] conclusion that "the primary significance of the name 'PRETZEL CRISPS' to past and prospective purchasers of salty snacks is as a brand name." Nevertheless, in finding the mark generic, the Board indicated that it considered the evidence of record "including the surveys (which in any event arrive at different conclusions)," but gave controlling weight to dictionary definitions, evidence of use by the public, and evidence of use by Princeton Vanguard. The Board seems to have treated the surveys as though they cancelled each other out, but failed to offer any explanation for doing so. The Board thus overlooked or disregarded a genericness survey as to which it apparently found no flaw. On remand, the Board will have the opportunity to make the relevant factual findings based on all of the evidence of record, and must give appropriate consideration to the proffered survey evidence.

Tiffany and Co. v. Costco Wholesale Corp., 127 F. Supp. 3d 241 (S.D.N.Y. 2015). Tiffany sued Costco for its use of Tiffany on display case signage for the sale of rings, such as, "605880—Platinum Tiffany .70 VS2, 1 Round Diamond Ring." Costco counterclaimed that Tiffany was generic for a particular type of ring setting. The court dismissed the counterclaim as a matter of law and credited plaintiff's Teflon-type survey:

> Dr. Jacoby administered the survey to ... 464 men and women ages 21 and older who said that they would consider purchasing certain types of jewelry over the course of two years.... The population was ... split into groups ... some respondents were shown the word Tiffany in isolation, others were shown point of sale signage like that used by Costco....
>
> ... [I]n isolation, approximately 9 out of 10 of likely consumers considered it to be a brand identifier.... [I]n the context of point of sale signage..., nearly 4 out of 10 consumers ... believed it was being used as a brand name, and another 3 out of 10 ... thought it was both brand name and descriptive word.... Dr. Jacoby ... conclu[ded] that "regardless of whether used in isolation

> or shown the way it appeared on the tags affixed to diamond engagement rings sold by Costco, the term Tiffany is understood and used by the relevant consuming public not as a descriptive or generic term, but as a brand or source identifier." ...

The district court rejected Costco's contention that Tiffany has two independent meanings, as a brand name and as a descriptor of a type of ring setting, depending on the context:

> ... Dr. Nunberg notes that the foundational question of Jacoby's study "presupposes that Tiffany must be either a trademark for jewelry or a generic term for a ring setting, and cannot be both—that is, we could not be dealing with two homonymous words, one a brand name and the other an independent adjective applying to certain jewelry settings that has no logical or historical relation to the brand.... Professor Nunberg also offers his own genericism report, which consists of a lexicographical study of the word Tiffany. After studying an array of dictionary treatments, specialized jewelry guides, advertisements drawn from newspapers and ads produced by Tiffany, Nunberg concludes that "[a]ll available evidence overwhelmingly indicates that Tiffany is and for more than 100 years has been a generic name for a type or style of jewelry setting in which a single gemstone is held by several prongs ... the style name Tiffany and the trademark Tiffany are and for more than 100 years have been two different words having two very different meanings."
>
> ....
>
> ... Costco has proffered no affirmative evidence that raises a material issue of fact with respect to the issue of whether the primary significance of the Tiffany mark to the relevant public is as a generic descriptor or a brand identifier. The question of "primary significance" is the key to a determination of genericism, [citation] and none of the evidence that Costco has proffered on this point contravenes the results of Dr. Jacoby's study. The Court therefore holds that Costco has not raised a genuine issue of material fact with respect to its genericism counterclaim, and finds that Tiffany is entitled to summary judgment dismissing it.

Questions

1. Do you agree with the *Teflon* court that DuPont's second survey was superior to the Thermos-type study in measuring the primary significance of a term to consumers?

2. Given the Federal Circuit's statement that "consumer surveys may be a preferred method of proving genericness," is the Board free to decide either way on remand of the PRETZEL CRISPS case? Did the court in *Tiffany* properly dismiss Costco's counterclaim of genericness as a matter of law based on the survey evidence despite the lexicographic evidence to the contrary?

For further debate over survey evidence of genericism, *see, e.g.*, Itamar Simonson, *An Empirical Investigation of the Meaning and Measure of "Genericness,"* 84 TMR 199 (1994); Folsom & Teply, *Surveying "Genericness" in Trademark Litigation*, 78 TRADEMARK REP. 1 (1988); Swann & Palladino, *Surveying "Genericness": A Critique of Folsom and Teply*, 78 TRADEMARK REP. 179 (1988); Folsom & Teply, *A Reply to Swann and Palladino's Critique of Folsom and Teply's Model Survey*, 78 TRADEMARK REP. 197 (1988); Greenbaum, Ginsburg & Weinberg, *A Proposal for Evaluating Genericism after "Anti-Monopoly,"* 73 TRADEMARK REP. 101 (1983).

Note: Legislative "Clarification" of Standards to Assess Genericism

In *Anti-Monopoly, Inc. v. General Mills Fun Group*, 684 F.2d 1316 (9th Cir. 1982), the creator of the "Anti-Monopoly" board game brought an antitrust declaratory judgment claim against the producers of the "Monopoly" real estate trading game. In adjudicating the trademark infringement counterclaim, the Ninth Circuit reviewed several surveys, ultimately crediting a "motivation survey" that inquired into whether consumers purchased "Monopoly" because they liked Parker Brothers' products, or because they were "interested in playing 'Monopoly,' [they] don't much care who makes it." This ruling provoked a great outcry for disregarding the "single, if anonymous, source" rule, and for failing to recognize that trademarks serve a "dual purpose" of identifying both the producer of the goods, and the goods themselves. This is particularly true for "unique" goods, where the mark inevitably conveys product information as well as source information. That does not necessarily mean, however, that consumers do not perceive the trademark as a brand name. (Indeed, brand advertising endeavors to convince consumers that the trademark stands for goods whose qualities consumers should believe are unique.)

Congress responded with the "Trademark Clarification Act of 1984." This legislation supplemented section 14 of the Lanham Act's provision on cancellation of trademark registrations of marks that had become the "common descriptive name" of the goods or services, with the following specifications (in italics):

> *A registered mark shall not be deemed to be the common descriptive name of goods or services solely because such mark is also used as a name of or to identify a unique product or service. The primary significance of the registered mark to the relevant public rather than purchaser motivation shall be the test for determining whether the registered mark has become the common descriptive name of goods or services in connection with which it has been used.*

The legislation also modified the section 45 definitions of "trademark," "service mark" and "abandoned" as indicated in italics:

> The term "trademark" includes any word, name, symbol, or device or any combination thereof adopted and used by a manufacturer or merchant to identify and distinguish his goods, *including a unique product* from those manufactured or sold by others and to indicate the source of the goods, *even if that source is unknown.*

The term "service mark" means a mark used in the sale or advertising of services to identify and distinguish the services of one person, *including a unique service*, from the services of others and to indicate the source of the services, *even if that source is unknown*....

....

A mark shall be deemed to be "abandoned"—

....

(b) When any course of conduct of the registrant, including acts of omission as well as commission, causes the mark to lose its significance as an indication of origin. *Purchaser motivation shall not be a test for determining abandonment under this subparagraph.*

3. Genericism and Confusion

Note: "De Facto Secondary Meaning"

A trademark designates source. When the consuming public comes to recognize the term as identifying goods or services coming from a single, if anonymous, source, the term has acquired "secondary meaning," and is entitled to trademark status. Sometimes, however, as the "Shredded Wheat" decision exemplifies, the public may identify a term with a single source of origin, but the term is nonetheless not accorded trademark status. This phenomenon is, perhaps unhelpfully, known as "de facto secondary meaning."

There are two types of de facto secondary meaning. The first type arises in those situations in which the public does not recognize the term at issue as a brand name, but nonetheless may know that there is a single source for the goods. This occurs when the producer is the single source of the goods because it enjoys a patent monopoly, or because others are otherwise unable or unwilling to compete, and the producer has not been using the term applied to the goods in a proper trademark fashion. The other type of de facto secondary meaning occurs in those instances, such as the LITE beer case, *Miller Brewing Co. v. G. Heileman Brewing Co.*, 561 F.2d 75 (7th Cir. 1977), where a producer selects as a trademark a term that is deemed already to have been the commonly recognized, i.e., generic, name of the goods, but through substantial advertising, proper trademark use, and market dominance, succeeds in establishing public trademark recognition for this otherwise common name. In this case, there is real secondary meaning, because the public has come to understand the term as the producer's brand name. Nonetheless, the judicial result is the same—no trademark protection. *Anheuser-Busch v. Labatt*, 89 F.3d 1339 (8th Cir. 1996), *cert. denied*, 519 U.S. 1109 (1997), affords a more recent, but still beer-related example of selection of a mark deemed generic *ab initio*, in that case, "ice" beer.

Courts have held that a generic term cannot be converted into a trademark by means of de facto secondary meaning. The rationale for the statement is plain: if the term initially was, or has become, the common name of the goods, persons endeavoring to compete once the patent has expired—or once the market allows for competition—must be able to call the goods by their commonly recognized names. To permit a producer the exclusive use of a term that either was initially generic, or that has become generic, but that enjoys either type of de facto secondary meaning, would in effect afford that producer an improper monopoly in the goods. Thus, at bottom, the de facto secondary meaning doctrine reflects the legal conclusion that even if the public is aware that there has been only one source for the goods whose term is at issue, or even if the public further perceives the term as a brand name, that term must be held free for competitive use if it is in fact the commonly recognized name of the goods.

For examples of judicial treatment of trademark claims in terms perhaps born generic, but arguably associated with a single producer, consider the following decisions.

America Online, Inc. v. AT&T Corp.

243 F.3d 812 (4th Cir. 2001)

Niemeyer, Circuit Judge:

America Online, Inc. ("AOL") commenced this action against AT&T Corporation ("AT&T") for AT&T's alleged infringements of three trademarks that AOL claims in connection with its Internet services—"Buddy List," "You Have Mail," and "IM." The district court entered summary judgment in favor of AT&T with respect to each mark, concluding that, as a matter of law, the alleged marks are generic and cannot be enforced as the exclusive property of AOL. For the reasons that follow, we conclude that the question whether "Buddy List" is a valid mark raises disputed issues of material fact and therefore cannot be resolved on summary judgment. With respect to the two other claimed marks, we affirm for the reasons given herein.

I.

....

In connection with its chat service, AOL uses "Buddy List" and "IM" to describe features of the service. The "Buddy List" enables the subscriber to create a list of identified screen names employed by other users with whom the subscriber wishes to communicate and displays which of those pre-selected users is currently using the AOL service. If a "Buddy" is identified by the "Buddy List" as online, the subscriber may then click a button labeled "IM," which are the initials of "instant messaging," and initiate a real-time chat session with the subscriber so identified on the "Buddy List." AOL has used "Buddy List" and "IM" since at least 1997. It has promoted these terms extensively, and it asserts now that it has a proprietary interest in them. In addition, with respect to "Buddy List," AOL obtained a certificate of registration on June 23, 1998, from the Patent and Trademark Office, indicating that the mark has been registered on the Principal Register and that AOL has used the mark as a service mark since August 31, 1995.

Also, in connection with its e-mail service, AOL advises its subscribers that they have received e-mail by displaying the words "You Have Mail," by playing a recording that announces, "You've got mail," and by depicting an icon of a traditional mailbox with the red flag raised. AOL contends that it has used these marks to describe its e-mail service since 1992, that it has promoted them extensively, and that it now has a proprietary interest in them.

AT&T, a competing Internet service provider, uses marks or phrases similar to those claimed by AOL in connection with its service to subscribers. It uses the terms "Buddy List," "You have Mail!," and "I M Here."

In December 1998, AOL commenced this action, seeking preliminary and permanent injunctive relief against AT&T to prohibit it from using marks similar to those asserted by AOL. [In response] AT&T ... filed a counterclaim seeking a declaratory judgment that AOL's marks are not valid trademarks and requesting an order directing the Patent and Trademark Office to cancel the registration for "Buddy List."

The district court denied preliminary injunctive relief and, following discovery, granted AT&T summary judgment.... The district court rested its decision on evidence in the record obtained from third-party sources, including Internet dictionaries, published users' guides to both the Internet and to AOL services, use of the alleged marks by competitors, and use by AOL of the alleged marks in a manner suggesting their generic character. Although AOL proffered survey evidence in support of its contention that the marks "You Have Mail" and "Buddy List" were protected trademarks, the court considered the survey evidence irrelevant because it had concluded that the marks were generic and that words used generically cannot become trademarks by association....

II. "Buddy List"

AOL's principal argument for the validity of "Buddy List" as a "suggestive" mark rests on ... having obtained a certificate of registration from the Patent and Trademark Office ("PTO"). It argues that the district court erred in failing to give deference to the expert decision of the PTO to register the mark without requiring evidence of secondary meaning.

... When the Commissioner of Patents and Trademarks ... lists a mark on the Principal Register, he issues a certificate of registration which provides the registrant with prima facie evidence of (1) the validity of the mark and its registration; (2) the registrant's ownership; and (3) the registrant's "exclusive right" to use the mark on or in connection with the goods and services specified in the certificate of registration. *See* 15 U.S.C. § 1057(b).... With a certificate of registration, therefore, the registrant obtains prima facie evidence that its mark is not generic in the eyes of the relevant public, *see* 15 U.S.C. § 1064(3), and that its mark is not "merely" descriptive, but at a minimum is descriptive and has obtained secondary meaning, *see* 15 U.S.C. § 1052(e)....

....

... Of particular importance to the [District] Court was the fact that "virtually every third party which has used the phrase, including so many of AOL's competitors, use it as a generic phrase." AT&T ... maintains that the benefit accorded by AOL's registration of "Buddy List" was not "sufficient in light of the overwhelming evidence presented by AT&T. AT&T's 'compelling' and 'overwhelming' evidence of genericism amply supports the district court's ruling that no reasonable jury could find 'buddy list' anything other than generic." ...

Although we have observed that a district court should not freely substitute its opinion for that of the PTO, this observation was not made because the PTO was entitled to deference, but rather because its decision to register a mark, without requiring evidence of secondary meaning, was "powerful evidence that the registered mark is suggestive and not merely descriptive," *id.* (emphasis added); *see also Petro Stopping Ctrs. L.P. v. James River Petroleum Inc.*, 130 F.3d 88, 93 (4th Cir. 1997) (holding that the PTO's determination is "only prima facie evidence that the mark is suggestive," and, for that reason, "may be rebutted").

Accordingly, we conclude that in deciding whether "Buddy List" was generic, the district court ... was required to receive the certification of registration for "Buddy List" into evidence and treat that certificate as prima facie evidence of the validity of the mark—and, in this case, as prima facie evidence that it was suggestive. [The court held that the validity of "Buddy List" could not be determined on summary judgment.] ...

III. "You Have Mail"

....

AOL has not registered "You Have Mail" with the PTO, and therefore it must carry the burden of establishing the validity and its ownership of the mark as part of its larger burden in a trademark infringement action. That burden is to prove that it has a valid, protectable trademark and that the defendant is infringing its mark by creating confusion, or a likelihood thereof, by causing mistake, or by deceiving as to the attributes of its mark. *See* 15 U.S.C. §§1114, 1125. We agree with the district court that AOL did not meet this burden.

First, the record establishes, without contradiction, that "You Have Mail" has been used to inform computer users since the 1970s, a decade before AOL came into existence, that they have electronic mail in their electronic "mailboxes." ... In the context of computer-based electronic communications across networked computers, the phrase "You Have Mail" has been used for the common, ordinary purpose of informing users of the arrival of electronic mail in their electronic mailboxes. In addition, books describing how a computer user is informed that he has e-mail on [the] UNIX [operating system] similarly reveal the functional nature of the phrase. For example, the following explanations for the presence of mail are described with "You Have Mail." ...

—"Accessing your mail: Immediately upon logging in, should you have mail, you will see a message indicating: You Have Mail." Peter M. Birns et al., UNIX for People 242 (1985).

—"When you login your system, you are told whether you have electronic mail waiting for you. If there is mail waiting, you'll see a line like the following: You Have Mail." Kevin Reichard, *UNIX: The Basics* 160 (2d ed. 1998).

Furthermore, other companies that provide e-mail services have used "You Have Mail," or derivations thereof, to notify their subscribers of the arrival of e-mail messages. Prodigy Communications has used the spoken phrase, "You Have New Mail," since 1993 in connection with its online service. Netcom, an Internet service provider, uses "You Have Mail" to inform users that they have e-mail. [Qualcomm, Banyan's "Beyond Mail Program," Care-Mail (a web-based e-mail provider), and "Internet Relay Chat" (a software program) all use "You Have New Mail" to notify users when they have e-mail.]

It is significant in the context of this usage that AOL has never registered "You Have Mail," nor has it attempted to enforce it as a mark prior to this action.

Second, in addition to the long and uninterrupted use by others of "You Have Mail," AOL's own use of "You Have Mail" has been inconsistent with its claim that the phrase is a trademark. Rather than describing a service that AOL offers—and indicating that it is describing such a service—AOL simply uses "You Have Mail" when the subscriber in fact has mail in the electronic mailbox. Once the user opens the new message, the phrase "You Have Mail" disappears from the user's screen. Moreover, if the subscriber does not have mail when he logs on, the screen does not display "You Have Mail." AOL's use of the phrase, conditioned on whether mail is present, does not describe AOL's e-mail service, but rather simply informs subscribers, employing common words to express their commonly used meaning, of the ordinary fact that they have new electronic mail in their mailboxes.

This functional manner in which AOL uses "You Have Mail" is consistent with a public perception of the phrase as describing whether or not mail is in an electronic mailbox, rather than as describing a service associated with AOL. For example, *America Online for Dummies*™ states, "You have two ways to see your new mail. One is pretty obvious.... The obvious one is the big picture button of a hand holding up some letters, emblazoned with a subtle notation You Have Mail. (I have seen obvious before and it looked a lot like this.)" John Kaufeld, *America Online for Dummies*™ 99 (1995)....

Indeed, AOL itself has made no claim that "You Have Mail" has been used to indicate anything but the information that the subscriber has mail. Even in its complaint, it asserts little more, alleging that it has used "You Have Mail ... in connection with its automatic e-mail notification services for AOL Service members." The scope of this asserted use—to give notice of mail to subscribers—is no broader than the words' common meaning.

We agree with the district court that when words are used in a context that suggests only their common meaning, they are generic and may not be appropriated as exclusive property. But a debate over whether a word or phrase is being used in a context that communicates merely its common meaning can quickly become as metaphysical as the study of language itself....

The task of distinguishing words or phrases functioning as trademarks from words or phrases in the "linguistic commons" begins with the development of an understanding of the common meaning of words and their common usage and then proceeds to a determination of whether the would-be trademark falls within this heartland of meaning and usage. The farther a would-be mark falls from the heartland of common meaning and usage, the more "distinctive" the would-be mark can become. At one level, this determination of word meaning and usage can be a question of law, but at another, it becomes a factual question as to what the relevant public perceives. The dichotomy between the legal question and the factual question is similar to that which exists in construing contracts—when meaning and usage are unambiguous, the court construes the contract, but when they are ambiguous, the factual question must be resolved by the factfinder....

In the case before us, the record context of "You Have Mail" permits us to conclude as a matter of law that AOL's usage of the would be mark falls within the heartland of common meaning and usage and therefore that AOL may not exclude others from using the same words in connection with their e-mail service. This is indicated by two significant facts that remain undisputed. First, AOL uses "You Have Mail" functionally—consistently with that phrase's common meaning—to tell its subscribers they have mail. Second, others in the relevant industry have used and continue to use "you have mail," or a similar phrase, to announce the presence of an e-mail message in an electronic mailbox.... We therefore agree with the district court that AOL may not enforce "You Have Mail" as a trademark in connection with its e-mail notification service.

AOL argues that its survey evidence indicates an association in the public's eye between "You Have Mail" and AOL and that this association is sufficient to permit a reasonable factfinder to conclude that "You Have Mail" is a trademark descriptive of its e-mail service that has acquired secondary meaning. AOL contends, therefore, that only a jury can decide whether "You Have Mail" is a trademark. Its evidence for secondary meaning consisted of a random survey of 507 Internet users whose households were "very likely paying to be receiving an Internet access service or an online service during the three months following the survey." The 507 respondents were divided into four groups: Group A, 250 respondents; Group B, 85; Group C, 86; and, Group D, 86. The respondents in Group A were first asked whether they had heard or seen the expression "You Have Mail." Those who answered affirmatively were then asked whether they associated that expression with one specific Internet or online service provider, or more than one provider. Those who associated the expression with one specific provider were then asked to identify the particular provider with whom they associated the phrase. Respondents in Groups B, C, and D were asked similar questions about different phrases. Instead of being queried for their reaction to "You Have Mail," respondents in Group B were asked about "New Mail Has Arrived"; respondents in Group C were asked about "Mail Is Here"; and, respondents in Group D were asked about "Mail Call." The results obtained from the answers given by the respondents in Groups B, C, and D were termed the "Control Condition," which, according to the design of the survey, was to provide "an important baseline against which to judge the strength of people's associations with the expression 'You Have Mail.'"

Out of the group that heard "You Have Mail," 41% of the respondents associated the phrase with a single Internet or online service provider, and 37% of the respondents associated the phrase with AOL. In Groups B, C, and D, only 9% of the respondents were able to associate the phrase they heard with a single Internet or online service provider, and only 5% were able to name a specific Internet or online service provider with which to associate the phrase they heard....

At this summary-judgment stage of the proceedings, we must accept AOL's assertion that a portion of the public associates "You Have Mail" with AOL, the most widespread user of the phrase. But this fact does not reveal that the primary significance of the term "You Have Mail" to announce the arrival of new e-mail is not the functional, heartland usage of the phrase.... AOL's evidence of association may establish what is called "de facto secondary meaning," but such secondary meaning does not entitle AOL to exclude others from a functional use of the words. Stated otherwise, the repeated use of ordinary words functioning within the heartland of their ordinary meaning, and not distinctively, cannot give AOL a proprietary right over those words, even if an association develops between the words and AOL....

We therefore conclude that "You Have Mail" has been and continues to be used by AOL and by others to alert online subscribers that there is electronic e-mail in their electronic mailboxes, and no more. This functional use of words within the heartland of their ordinary meaning cannot give rise to a trademark for the e-mail service when it is no more than the announcement of the arrival of a message. Because AOL has failed to establish its exclusive right to "You Have Mail," we affirm the district court's conclusion that AOL may not exclude others from use of those words in connection with its e-mail service.

IV. "IM"

... The district court ... concluded that "IM" is "an initialism" for "instant message," and that, despite their management's admonitions against using "IM" as a noun or a verb, AOL employees used "IM" as a noun or a verb in lieu of "instant message," such as in "They had an IM pending" or "Stop IM'ing me." The court also pointed to books, dictionaries, and glossaries defining "instant message" with the "IM" designation such as: "instant message, IM for short," or "instant message (IM)." It noted that Yahoo!, in promoting its pager service, claimed that it was providing "IMs." Based on these and similar facts, as well as the fact that AOL does not claim any proprietary interest in the phrase "instant messaging," the district court held that "IM stands for 'instant message' (as AOL admits), and because the primary significance of 'instant message' is to stand for an 'instant message,' the term ... is generic."

AOL bases its claim to "IM" on its assertions that "IM" has frequently been associated by the media with AOL and that no other online or Internet service provider calls its real-time communications feature "IM." It argues that because it was one of the first companies to provide "IM," a jury could conclude that "IM" denotes the source, not the feature. But AOL has offered no evidence to support that contention. It can only contend in a conclusory manner that "IM" is a trademark rather than simply the product at issue. Accordingly, while we do not determine that "IM" is generic, we nevertheless agree with the district court's decision, based on this record, to deny AOL enforcement of "IM" as its trademark.

V.

In sum, we conclude that the validity of "Buddy List" cannot be resolved on summary judgment in view of genuine issues of material fact. Accordingly, we vacate the district court's order finding "Buddy List" generic, as well as its order directing cancellation of the certificate of registration for that mark, and remand for further proceedings. With respect to the district court's rulings denying enforcement of "You Have Mail" and "IM" as the trademarks of AOL, we affirm.

AFFIRMED IN PART, VACATED IN PART, AND REMANDED.

[Judge Luttig dissented in part on the ground that whether or not the phrase "YOU HAVE MAIL" was generic, AOL has in fact been using the phrase "YOU'VE GOT MAIL." This phrase, Judge Luttig urged, was "sufficiently different from the phrase 'YOU HAVE MAIL' in both its grammatical dysfunctionality and likely secondary meaning, and possibly its genericness as well, as to render a decision on its protection a separate matter altogether from a decision as to protection for the feature that includes the phrase 'YOU HAVE MAIL.'"]

Facebook, Inc. v. Teachbook.com, 819 F. Supp. 2d 764 (N.D. Ill. 2011). Teachbook.com is a social networking site aimed at teachers. Facebook, Inc. alleged trademark infringement, and Teachbook defended on the ground that the marks were dissimilar apart from the suffix "-book," and the suffix was a generic term. The court disagreed:

> First of all, we are not convinced that disaggregating the FACEBOOK mark and focusing on the suffix -BOOK is appropriate in this case. The Seventh Circuit has indicated that it is sometimes appropriate to vary the weight accorded to the different components of a mark when one component may be more salient than another or when one component is generic or descriptive. [Citation.] But nothing in our reading of the relevant case law suggests that this splicing is mandatory, especially in light of the highly fact specific contexts in which trademark infringement claims arise. Here, Facebook contends that it is not asserting blanket trademark rights in the suffix -BOOK but is instead relying on the composite FACEBOOK. We accept this contention as true for the time being. Indeed, upon initial reading, nothing about the two component parts of the FACEBOOK mark makes one more salient than the other. Rather, it is the aggregate effect of the conjoined parts that gives the mark its distinctiveness. And given the ubiquity Facebook claims its mark has achieved, one could reasonably infer that the choice of the TEACHBOOK mark—which, like the FACEBOOK mark, is a curt, two-syllable conjunction of otherwise unremarkable words—to offer a similar service in the same medium was no accident. Thus, we agree with Facebook that Teachbook's attempt to make Facebook's trademark infringement claim

exclusively about the suffix -BOOK is an inaccurate characterization of the complaint.

In any event, even if we were to focus exclusively on the suffix -BOOK in Facebook's and Teachbook's marks, Facebook has still made sufficient allegations to preclude a finding of genericness at this point.... Facebook is using the suffix -BOOK to offer social networking services via the internet. Even in this age of "e-books," social networking services do not fall within the category of what one would traditionally call "books." Thus, accepting the complaint as true, Facebook is not using the suffix -BOOK to designate the product itself and the usage is not generic.[2]

Questions

1. Was the phrase "you have mail" held generic because it fulfilled the function of notifying subscribers that they had mail? Because AOL had used it generically? Because others had? Can a coined word or phrase be born generic?

2. On remand, were you representing AT&T, how would you rebut the presumption that "Buddy List" is a valid trademark? If you were representing AOL, what would you show in support of the presumption?

3. The *Facebook* court deferred determination of whether "-book" was or had become generic for social networking services. To advance that defense, what would Teachbook.com need to show?

Harley Davidson v. Grottanelli

164 F.3d 806 (2d Cir. 1999)

Newman, Circuit Judge:

[Harley Davidson, the well-known producer of motorcycles, brought a trademark infringement action against a garage and motorcycle repair business under the name the "Hog Farm." Harley-Davidson claimed that HOG was a common law trademark for their motorcycles. The court determined that the term Hog was generic for large motorcycles.]

1. The Word "Hog" Applied to Motorcycles

Public use of the word "hog". In the late 1960s and early 1970s, the word "hog" was used by motorcycle enthusiasts to refer to motorcycles generally and to large motorcycles in particular. The word was used that way in the press at least as early as

2. In its motion to stay discovery during the pendency of this motion to dismiss, Teachbook indicates that it intends to argue that the suffix -BOOK is generic "for directory and networking services." But this argument requires proof and goes beyond the appropriate grounds for a motion to dismiss. Facebook also points to allegations in the complaint that, thanks to its efforts, the suffix -BOOK in the internet-based social networking context is distinctive. Thus, whether the suffix -BOOK is generic for online "directory and networking services" can not be definitively resolved at this stage.

1965, and frequently thereafter, prior to the 1980s when Harley first attempted to make trademark use of the term. Several dictionaries include a definition of "hog" as a motorcycle, especially a large one. The October 1975 issue of Street Chopper contained an article entitled "Honda Hog,"[4] indicating that the word "hog" was generic as to motorcycles and needed a tradename adjective....

Harley-Davidson's use of the word "hog". In 1981, Harley-Davidson's new owners recognized that the term "hog" had financial value and began using the term in connection with its merchandise, accessories, advertising, and promotions. In 1983, it formed the Harley Owners' Group, pointedly using the acronym "H.O.G." In 1987, it registered the acronym in conjunction with various logos. It subsequently registered the mark "HOG" for motorcycles. That registration lists Harley-Davidson's first use as occurring in 1990.

Grottanelli's use of the word "hog". Grottanelli opened a motorcycle repair shop under the name "The Hog Farm" in 1969. Since that time his shop has been located at various sites in western New York. At some point after 1981, Grottanelli also began using the word "hog" in connection with events and merchandise. He has sponsored an event alternatively known as "Hog Holidays" and "Hog Farm Holidays," and sold products such as "Hog Wash" engine degreaser and a "Hog Trivia" board game.

....

Discussion

I. Use of the Word "Hog"

... Harley-Davidson acknowledged at oral argument that its state law claim fails if "hog" is generic as applied to large motorcycles. No manufacturer can take out of the language a word, even a slang term, that has generic meaning as to a category of products and appropriate it for its own trademark use....

Though the Magistrate Judge made no ultimate finding as to whether "hog" was generic as applied to large motorcycles prior to Harley-Davidson's trademark use of the word, his subsidiary findings point irresistibly toward that conclusion. He found that there was "substantial evidence which would indicate that in those years the term referred to motorcycles (or motorcyclists) generally." He cited the various press and dictionary usages of the word that we have set forth above. Though not conclusive, dictionary definitions of a word to denote a category of products are significant evidence of genericness because they usually reflect the public's perception of a word's meaning and its contemporary usage. In this case, one dictionary cites a generic use of "hog" to mean a large motorcycle as early as 1967, long before Harley's first trademark use of the word, and the recent dictionary editions continuing to define the word to mean a large motorcycle indicate that the word has not lost its generic meaning. We have observed that newspaper and magazine use of a word in a generic sense is "a strong indication of the general public's perception" that the word is generic. In

4. *See The Oxford Dictionary of Modern Slang* (1992) ("hog, noun U.S. A large, often old, car or motorcycle. 1967–.").

this case, media use of "hog" to mean a large motorcycle began as early as 1935 and continued thereafter.

. . . .

Harley-Davidson suggests, . . . that it is entitled to trademark use of "HOG" as applied to motorcycles because a substantial segment of the relevant consumers began to use the term specifically to refer to Harley-Davidson motorcycles before the company made trademark use of the term. Some decisions have invoked this principle to accord a company priority as to its subsequent trademark use of a term. *See National Cable Television Ass'n, Inc. v. American Cinema Editors, Inc.*, 937 F.2d 1572 (Fed. Cir. 1991) (mark "ACE"); *Volkswagenwerk AG v. Hoffman*, 489 F.Supp. 678 (D.S.C.1980) (mark "BUG"). Whether or not we would agree with these decisions, they present a significantly different situation. Neither "ACE" nor "BUG" was a generic term in the language as applied, respectively, to a category of film editors or a category of automobiles prior to the public's use of the terms to refer to the American Cinema Editors and Volkswagen cars. By contrast, "hog" was a generic term in the language as applied to large motorcycles before the public (or at least some segments of it) began using the word to refer to Harley-Davidson motorcycles. The public has no more right than a manufacturer to withdraw from the language a generic term, already applicable to the relevant category of products, and accord it trademark significance, at least as long as the term retains some generic meaning.

For all of these reasons, Harley-Davidson may not prohibit Grottanelli from using "hog" to identify his motorcycle products and services. Like any other manufacturer with a product identified by a word that is generic, Harley-Davidson will have to rely on all or a portion of its tradename (or other protectable marks) to identify its brand of motorcycles, e.g., "Harley Hogs."

H-D Michigan v. Top Quality Serv., 496 F.3d 755 (7th Cir. 2007). Harley-Davidson motorcycle owners Dean and Debbie Anderson formed Top Quality Services, and organized a cruise for fellow Harley owners, which they advertised as HOGS ON THE HIGH SEAS.

> [The advertisement] said, "1st Annual Harley Owners' Cruise Rally" in large print immediately above a circular logo that contained the words "HOGS ON THE HIGH SEAS" and a cartoon pig riding a large motorcycle on an ocean wave. Top Quality's website said, "Bring your Harley friends, HOG group members, riding buddies, there won't be a stranger on the ship." Top Quality advised potential vendors that the trip was an "all Harley Owners Cruise Ship Rally." Ninety-seven percent of the passengers on the first cruise owned Harley motorcycles.

When the Andersons sought to register HOGS ON THE HIGH SEAS, Harley-Davidson both filed an opposition proceeding and a trademark infringement action. The District Court ruled for the Andersons, holding the issue of the protectability of HOG precluded by the judgment in *Grottanelli*. The Seventh Circuit reversed.

... In this case, the parties only dispute whether the issue litigated in *Grottanelli* is the same as the one here. Harley contends that the issues are different because in *Grottanelli*, the Second Circuit evaluated whether the word "hog" was generic as applied to large motorcycles, whereas in this case, the issue is whether "hog" was generic as applied to a motorcyclist club. Top Quality contends that *Grottanelli* held that "hog" is generic as applied to all motorcycle products and services, thus precluding Harley's infringement claim....

The first sentence in *Grottanelli* strongly suggests that the issue in that case was different than the one here. The court said, "This appeal primarily involves trademark issues as to whether the mark 'HOG' *as applied to large motorcycles* is generic...." *Id.* at 808 (emphasis added). The court then summarized its holding by stating, "[W]e conclude that the word 'hog' had become generic *as applied to large motorcycles* before Harley-Davidson began to make trademark use of 'HOG.'" *Id.* (emphasis added). A few paragraphs later, the court discussed the history of "The Word 'Hog' Applied to Motorcycles" and, in the remainder of the opinion, referred to the generic nature of the word "hog" "as applied to motorcycles" or "as applied to large motorcycles" at least ten different times. The court never stated that "hog" was generic as applied to a motorcyclist club or to motorcycle products or services.

The Second Circuit also noted that Harley conceded that its claim failed if the word "hog" was generic as applied to large motorcycles, further suggesting that the court had no occasion to decide the issue in this case. *Id.* at 810. Finally, the parties' Second Circuit briefs did not discuss whether "hog" was generic as applied to a motorcyclist club, focusing instead on whether "hog" means large motorcycle. [Citation.]

Grottanelli did mention that the "HOG" trademark was used to refer to Harley's motorcyclist club, but the court did not state, or even suggest, that Harley's use of the word "hog" was generic as applied to the Harley Owners Group. In short, the *Grottanelli* opinion and the parties' briefs convince us that the Second Circuit did not resolve the issue here: whether "hog" is a generic word for a motorcyclist club. Accordingly, Harley is not collaterally estopped from bringing the claims in this case.

Top Quality argues that *Grottanelli* must have held that "hog" was generic for all motorcycle products and services because it allowed Grottanelli to continue using the word "hog" when promoting his "Hog Holiday" motorcycle rally, "Hog Wash" engine degreaser, and "Hog Trivia" board game. Top Quality seems to suggest that by allowing Grottanelli's continued use of his trade names, the Second Circuit found that both Harley's and Grottanelli's use of the word "hog" was generic. However, that is simply not the case. The Second Circuit had no occasion to decide whether Grottanelli's use of the word "hog" was generic, because it already had held that Harley's mark as applied to large motorcycles was not protectable, and Harley conceded that this doomed its claim. A plaintiff's generic use of a word has no bearing on whether the defendant's use of the word is also generic.

B. Protectability

Having resolved that collateral estoppel does not preclude Harley's suit, we must address the merits. From our previous discussion, it should be evident that Harley's use of the word "hog" is not generic as applied to its motorcyclist club. As noted above, a generic term is commonly used as a name for the seller's goods, while a descriptive term names a characteristic of a particular product or service. [Citations.] The word "hog" is not commonly used as a name for a motorcyclist club. It is a name for a motorcycle. As such, Harley's use of the word "hog" to refer to the Harley Owners Group is not generic; rather, it is descriptive because it describes the club's members: people who enjoy motorcycles. [Citation.]

Top Quality argues that it uses the word "hogs" generically, and thus cannot be infringing on Harley's mark. However, this argument lacks merit as well. Though a consumer might conclude that Top Quality's trade name means "Motorcycles on the High Seas," that is not what Top Quality is selling. Top Quality's service does not invite motorcycles to travel on the ocean; it invites motorcyclists to travel on the ocean. As a result, its mark is not generic. [Citations.]

Questions

1. How persuasive is the court's distinction between HOG as a generic term for a large motorcycle, and HOG as a descriptive term when used to mean owners of large motorcycles (or of Harley-Davidson motorcycles)? Would Bayer have a claim against the (fictitious) Association of Aspirin Advocates, an organization that urges ingestion of acetylsalicylic acid to diminish the risk of blood clots?

2. Is genericism a question of law or of fact? The prominence of survey evidence in cases of "genericide" (a once-distinctive mark's loss of trademark significance) suggests that courts see the issue of a mark's "primary significance" to require factual inquiry. Is genericism also a question of fact when the trademark claimant has adopted a term allegedly "born generic"? *See Autodesk, Inc. v. Dassault Systemes*, 685 F. Supp. 2d 1001 (N.D. Cal. 2009) (deeming both initial and acquired genericism to be questions for the jury).

In what circumstances is it appropriate to hold the acronym for a generic phrase to be generic? Must the court find that the phrase itself is used generically, or is it enough that the initials stand for a generic phrase? In *Blinded Veterans Association v. Blinded American Veterans Foundation*, 872 F.2d 1035 (D.C. Cir. 1989), the court determined that the term "Blinded Veterans" was generic for "formerly sighted former servicemen." The court then stated: "We need not deal separately with the question whether the initials 'BVA' are generic; if the full name is generic, an abbreviation is treated similarly." How, if at all, does the approach applied in *AOL* differ? Consider the following:

Welding Services Inc. v. Forman, 509 F.3d 1351 (11th Cir. 2007). Having held the plaintiff's claimed mark "Welding Services, Inc." to be generic for welding services, the court next considered whether a different analysis should apply to a claimed mark consisting of the initials of the company name, WSI:

> Although we conclude that the words "welding services" are not protectable, this does not decide the precise question before us because Welding Services, Inc. does not seek protection for the words themselves, but for the abbreviation "WSI" and the stylized logo using that abbreviation. The protectability of the initials and of the stylized logo present different issues, so we will consider them in turn.
>
> Abbreviations of generic words may become protectable if the party claiming protection for such an abbreviation shows that the abbreviation has a meaning distinct from the underlying words in the mind of the public. *G. Heileman Brewing Co. v. Anheuser-Busch, Inc.*, 873 F.2d 985, 993–94 (7th Cir. 1989) ("heavy burden" on trademark claimant seeking to show an independent meaning for initials of descriptive words apart from the fact that they are abbreviations for the descriptive words); 2 McCarthy, *supra*, § 12:37 (distinguishing between abbreviations "which still convey[] to the buyer the original generic connotation of the abbreviated name" and those which are "not recognizable as the original generic term"). *But cf. Anheuser-Busch, Inc. v. Stroh Brewery Co.*, 750 F.2d 631, 635–36 (8th Cir. 1984) (abbreviation of generic words protectable if "some operation of the imagination is required to connect the initials with the product"); *Modern Optics, Inc. v. Univis Lens Co.*, 234 F.2d 504, 506, 43 C.C.P.A. 970, 1956 Dec. Comm'r Pat. 350 (C.C.P.A. 1956) ("[I]nitials cannot be considered descriptive unless they have become so generally understood as representing descriptive words as to be accepted as substantially synonymous therewith.").
>
> Welding Services introduced the affidavit of its marketing director, Michael Welch, stating that the company had used the abbreviation since 1990 and the stylized logo for nine years before Welding Technologies began using its marks. Welch said Welding Services had spent $5 million advertising its marks over the course of fourteen years (from 1990 to 2004) and had generated more than $1 billion in revenues. Welch said that the WSI marks are recognized as a "highly significant indicator of WSI's welding services." On the basis of this evidence, the district court declined to hold that Welding Services' marks were not protectable.
>
> But Welch's affidavit does not address the question of whether the company's investment in advertising its marks served to give the abbreviation "WSI" a meaning distinct from the words "Welding Services Inc." While investment in advertising is relevant to the question of secondary meaning

generally, *Investacorp, Inc. v. Arabian Inv. Banking Corp.*, 931 F.2d 1519, 1525 (11th Cir. 1991), the question of whether the abbreviation has a discrete meaning in the minds of the public from the generic words for which it stands requires a different kind of evidence. The only evidence in the record relevant to this question shows Welding Services has not created a separate meaning for the abbreviation. Crucially, exhibit B to Welding Services' statement of material facts shows the logo with the initials on advertising material displayed immediately next to the words "Welding Services Inc." Thus, Welding Services' own motion papers indicate that the abbreviation is used in association with the generic words, rather than being used in a way that would give rise to a meaning distinct from those words. Accordingly, we hold that Welding Services had not shown "WSI" to be protectable.

Should it make a difference if the term is generic in a foreign language? In *Otokoyama Co. v. Wine of Japan Import*, 175 F.3d 266 (2d Cir. 1999), the court reversed the district court's refusal to consider evidence of the generic meaning of "Otokoyama" in Japanese because:

> If Otokoyama in Japanese signifies a type of sake, and one United States merchant were given the exclusive right to use that word to designate its brand of sake, competing merchants would be prevented from calling their product by the word which designates that product in Japanese. Any Japanese-speaking customers and others who are familiar with the Japanese terminology would be misled to believe that there is only one brand of otokoyama available in the United States.
>
> The meaning of otokoyama in Japanese, and particularly whether it designates sake, or a type or category of sake, was therefore highly relevant to whether plaintiff may assert the exclusive right to use that word as a mark applied to sake. Defendant should have been allowed to introduce evidence of otokoyama's meaning and usage in Japan to support its claim that the mark is generic and therefore ineligible for protection as a trademark.

See also Orto Conserviera Sameranese di Giacchetti Marino & C. v. Bioconserve S.R.L., 49 U.S.P.Q.2d 2013 (S.D.N.Y. 1999) (court rejected plaintiff's assertion of trademark rights in "Bella di Cerignola," a type of olive known in Italy, but not then widely known in the U.S.); *Enrique Bernat F., S.A. v. Guadalajara, Inc.*, 210 F.3d 439 (5th Cir. 2000) (CHUPA is Spanish word for lollipops and thus is generic in plaintiff's CHUPA CHUPS mark for ice cream flavored lollipops); *Vista India v. Raaga, LLC*, 501 F. Supp. 2d 605 (D.N.J. 2007) (preliminary injunction against RAAGA for website providing downloads and streaming of Indian music denied where RAAGA in plaintiff's RAAGA ENTERTAINMENT SUPERSTORES mark for Indian and South Asian music stores is generic Indian word for Indian music).

Recapturing Generic Terms?

Whether the term was "born generic" or became generic through misuse or other loss of public recognition of the term as a trademark, can it ever regain, or if initially generic, acquire, source identification? Consider the following:

Miller's Ale House v. Boynton Carolina Ale House, 702 F.3d 1312 (11th Cir. 2012). Plaintiff Miller's asserted trademark rights in "ale house." In an earlier litigation against a different competitor, Miller's claim failed when the court held the term to be generic for a drinking establishment. In its suit against Boynton Carolina, Miller's argued that in the intervening ten years, the term had ceased to be generic, thanks to Miller's expanded operations throughout Florida. The district court acknowledged the possibility that a generic term could be recaptured as a mark, but ruled that the prior decision precluded relitigation of the issue of genericism because the evidence of genericism had not sufficiently changed in the interval. The Eleventh Circuit affirmed.

> Under the Lanham Act, "the primary significance of the registered mark to the relevant public ... shall be the test for determining whether the registered mark has [lost trademark protection by] becom[ing] the generic name of goods or services on or in connection with which it has been used." 15 U.S.C. § 1064(3). There is no clear standard for the inverse situation, when a previously generic term may gain trademark protection. In only two cases, *Singer Mfg. Co. v. Briley*, 207 F.2d 519 (5th Cir. 1953), and *Goodyear Tire & Rubber Co. v. H. Rosenthal Co.*, 246 F. Supp. 724 (D. Minn. 1965), have courts held that a term previously found to be generic had been "reclaimed from the public domain by a change in public usage," 2 J. Thomas McCarthy, McCarthy on Trademarks & Unfair Competition § 12:30 (4th ed. 2012). Both cases involved personal names that were introduced originally as a mark and later fell into generic usage only to be ultimately reclaimed by the original coiner. *Id.* Some courts have gone so far as to suggest that even where evidence of changed consumer perception exists, it is irrelevant in determining whether a once-generic term has acquired distinctiveness. See *Welding Services [v. Forman*, 509 F.3d 1351, 1356 (11th Cir. 2007),] at 1358 ("[E]ven if the name becomes in some degree associated with the source, a generic mark cannot achieve true secondary meaning."); *Boston Duck Tours, LP v. Super Duck Tours, LLC*, 531 F.3d 1, 21 (1st Cir. 2008) (trademark law does not protect a producer who "has acquired a 'de facto secondary meaning' through its exclusive use of a generic term that causes customers to associate the term with that specific source"). Were changed perception sufficient to warrant the elevation of a non-coined, generic term to trademark status, such change would have to be radical. See 2 McCarthy, *supra*, § 12:30.
>
> Miller's evidence is wholly inadequate to indicate that, after the Fourth Circuit's decision, such a drastic change occurred in the public's perception of the term "ale house." Miller's offered declarations by two of its customers from Boca Raton, a community located south of Boynton Beach. Unlike a

random consumer survey, these statements fail to offer evidence of general public perception. See 2 McCarthy, *supra*, § 12:14 ("Consumer surveys have become almost de rigueur in litigation over genericness."). These two customers stated that they refer to the Miller's locations where they have eaten as "Ale Houses" and to their local location as "the Ale House" and that they only use the term for Miller's restaurants. Neither, though, stated that he had ever even visited Miller's Ale House or Carolina Ale House in Boynton Beach. In fact, these customers appear to reside in an area in which Miller's is the only user of the term "ale house," which renders their statements not inconsistent with generic use of the term "ale house."

Miller's also presented employee statements that customers routinely confuse the two restaurants. Such evidence is irrelevant to our inquiry. The prominent use of a generic term by two competitors may understandably confuse consumers; however, this does not make the term any less generic. See *Gift of Learning Found., Inc. v. TGC, Inc.*, 329 F.3d 792, 801 (11th Cir. 2003) ("[C]onfusion ... is irrelevant unless the mark is protectible in the first instance."); *Boston Duck Tours*, 531 F.3d at 21 ("[T]rademark law ... is not intended to prevent confusion between two similar, generic marks.").

Finally, the fact that Miller's expanded its locations and spent more advertising provides little to no indication of public perception, because it has no bearing on how that expansion and advertising was received. See *Abercrombie* [*& Fitch Co. v. Hunting World, Inc.*, 537 F.2d 4 (2d Cir. 1976),] at 9 (stating that advertising may not remove a generic term from the public domain).

Miller's evidence fails to indicate any change at all in the public perception of the term "ale house," and the uncontested fact that restaurants and bars unaffiliated with either party use the term "ale house" points in the opposite direction. *See Boston Duck Tours*, 531 F.3d at 19 (stating that generic use by third parties is evidence that the term is generic).

Question

What type of evidence would satisfy the high evidentiary burden to reclaim a mark from being generic? A survey?

B. Abandonment

15 U.S.C. § 1127 [Lanham Act § 45]

....

Abandonment. A mark shall be deemed to be "abandoned" when either of the following occurs:

(1) When its use has been discontinued with intent not to resume such use. Intent not to resume may be inferred from circumstances. Nonuse for three consecutive

years shall be prima facie evidence of abandonment. "Use" of a mark means the bona fide use of that mark made in the ordinary course of trade, and not made merely to reserve a right in a mark.

(2) When any course of conduct of the owner, including acts of omission as well as commission, causes the mark to become the generic name for the goods or services on or in connection with which it is used or otherwise to lose its significance as a mark. Purchaser motivation shall not be a test for determining abandonment under this paragraph.

1. Non Use

Silverman v. CBS, Inc.

870 F.2d 40 (2d Cir. 1989)

Newman, Circuit Judge:

This appeal presents somewhat novel issues of both copyright and trademark law arising from the efforts of appellant Stephen M. Silverman to develop a musical based on the "Amos 'n' Andy" characters....

Facts

The "Amos 'n' Andy" characters were created in 1928 by Freeman F. Gosden and Charles J. Correll, who wrote and produced for radio broadcasting "The Amos 'n' Andy Show." The show became one of the country's most popular radio programs. The characters in the Amos 'n' Andy programs were Black. Gosden and Correll, who were White, portrayed Amos and Andy on radio. The authors appeared in blackface in publicity photos. Black actors played the parts in the subsequent television programs.

Gosden and Correll assigned all of their rights in the "Amos 'n' Andy Show" scripts and radio programs to CBS Inc. in 1948. Gosden and Correll continued to create new "Amos 'n' Andy" scripts, which formed the basis for CBS radio programs. The radio programs continued until 1955. Beginning in 1951 CBS also broadcast an "Amos 'n' Andy" television series. The television series was aired on CBS affiliate stations until 1953 and continued in reruns and non-network syndication until 1966. CBS has not aired or licensed for airing any of the radio or television programs since 1966.

In 1981, Silverman began writing a script for a Broadway musical based on the "Amos 'n' Andy" characters.... Silverman sought a license to use the "Amos 'n' Andy" characters, but CBS refused.

Silverman filed this lawsuit seeking a declaration that the "Amos 'n' Andy" radio programs broadcast from March 1928 through March 1948 (the "pre-1948 radio programs") are in the public domain and that he is therefore free to make use of the content of the programs, including the characters, character names, and plots. He also sought a declaration that CBS has no rights in these programs under any body of law, including statutory and common law copyright law and trademark law. CBS asserted five counterclaims: (1) that Silverman's scripts infringed CBS's copyrights in the scripts for three post-1948 radio programs; (2) that the Silverman scripts violated section 43(a) of the Lanham Act, 15 U.S.C. § 1125(a) (1982), by infringing various CBS trademarks, including "AMOS 'N' ANDY," the names of various characters such as "George ('Kingfish') Stevens," "Madame Queen," and "Lightnin'," and various phrases such as "Scuse me for protruding," "splain dat," and "Holy mackral" (perhaps Amos's best-known contribution to the language)....

On the trademark side of the case, Judge Goettel ruled that the name "Amos 'n' Andy," as well as the names and appearances of "Amos 'n' Andy" characters and "other distinctive features of the ... radio and television shows" are protectable marks. *Id.* at 1356. He then set down for trial the issue of whether CBS's non-use of the marks constituted abandonment. Finally, he ruled that the issue of trademark infringement, as well as the related issues of unfair competition and dilution, were premature in the absence of a staging of Silverman's musical. *Id.* at 1357–58.

After a bench trial on the issue of abandonment, Judge Goettel concluded that CBS had not abandoned its trademarks. *Silverman v. CBS*, 666 F. Supp. 575 (S.D.N.Y.1987) (*Silverman II*)....

....

Discussion

1. Trademark Issues

... We find it unnecessary to decide which features of the programs might give rise to protectable marks because we agree with Silverman that CBS has abandoned the marks.

... There are ... two elements for abandonment: (1) non-use and (2) intent not to resume use. *See Saratoga Vichy Spring Co. v. Lehman*, 625 F.2d 1037, 1043 (2d Cir. 1980). Two years of non-use* creates a rebuttable presumption of abandonment. *Id.* at 1044.

On the undisputed facts of this case, CBS made a considered decision to take the "Amos 'n' Andy" television programs off the air ... in response to complaints by civil rights organizations, including the NAACP, that the programs were demeaning to Blacks. By the time the abandonment issue came before the District Court, non-use of the AMOS 'N' ANDY marks had continued for 21 years. Although CBS has no current plans to use the marks within the foreseeable future, CBS asserts that it has always intended to resume using them at some point in the future, should the social climate become more hospitable.

Ordinarily, 21 years of non-use would easily surpass the non-use requirement for finding abandonment. *See, e.g., I.H.T. Corp. v. Saffir Publishing Corp.*, 444 F. Supp. 185 (S.D.N.Y. 1978) (denying preliminary injunction to protect trademark after 12 years of non-use). The District Court concluded, however, that CBS had successfully rebutted the presumption of abandonment arising from its prolonged non-use by offering a reasonable explanation for its decision to keep the programs off the air and

* [*Editors' Note:* Section 45 of the Lanham Act was later amended to state "Nonuse for *three* consecutive years shall be prima facie evidence of abandonment" (emphasis added).]

by asserting its intention to resume use at some indefinite point in the future. This conclusion raises a question as to the proper interpretation of the statutory phrase "intent not to resume": Does the phrase mean intent never to resume use or does it merely mean intent not to resume use within the reasonably foreseeable future?

We conclude that the latter must be the case. The statute provides that intent not to resume may be inferred from circumstances, and two consecutive years of non-use is prima facie abandonment. Time is thereby made relevant. Indeed, if the relevant intent were intent never to resume use, it would be virtually impossible to establish such intent circumstantially. Even after prolonged non-use, and without any concrete plans to resume use, a company could almost always assert truthfully that at some point, should conditions change, it would resume use of its mark.

We do not think Congress contemplated such an unworkable standard. More likely, Congress wanted a mark to be deemed abandoned once use has been discontinued with an intent not to resume within the reasonably foreseeable future. This standard is sufficient to protect against the forfeiture of marks by proprietors who are temporarily unable to continue using them, while it also prevents warehousing of marks, which impedes commerce and competition.

We are buttressed in this conclusion by the fact that the statute requires proof of "intent not to resume," rather than "intent to abandon." The statute thus creates no state of mind element concerning the ultimate issue of abandonment. On the contrary, it avoids a subjective inquiry on this ultimate question by setting forth the circumstances under which a mark shall be "deemed" to be abandoned. Of course, one of those circumstances is intent not to resume use, which is a matter of subjective inquiry. But we think the provision, by introducing the two concepts of "deemed" abandonment and intent not to resume use, contemplates a distinction, and it is a distinction that turns at least in part on duration of the contemplated non-use.

Congress's choice of wording appears to have been deliberate. One early version of what became section 45 of the Lanham Act had provided that "[i]ntent to *abandon* may be inferred from the circumstances." H.R. Rep. 4744, 76th Cong., 1st Sess. (1939) (emphasis added). However, shortly thereafter a new bill modified this phrase by substituting "[i]ntent not to resume" for "[i]ntent to abandon." H.R. Rep. 6618, 76th Cong., 1st Sess. (1939). We think that Congress, by speaking of "intent not to resume" rather than "intent to abandon" in this section of the Act meant to avoid the implication that intent never to resume use must be shown.[4]

This approach is consistent with our recent decisions concerning trademark abandonment. [I]n *Defiance Button Machine Co. v. C & C Metal Products Corp.*, 759 F.2d

4. An early Supreme Court case involving abandonment under pre-Lanham Act, common law trademark said that proof of abandonment must include proof of an "intent to abandon." *Saxlehner v. Eisner & Mendelson Co.*, 179 U.S. 19, 31 (1900). In cases applying the Act, we have also on occasion used the phrase "intent to abandon," *see Saratoga Vichy Spring Co. v. Lehman, supra*, 625 F.2d at 1044, but decisions using the phrase have not faced the issue whether the requisite intent is never to resume use or not to resume in the reasonably foreseeable future. Where that choice matters, as in this case, the statutory phrase "intent not to resume" better describes the requisite mental element.

1053 (2d Cir.), *cert. denied*, 474 U.S. 844 (1985), we rejected an abandonment claim where, during a brief period of non-use, the proprietor tried to sell the mark, its associated goodwill, and some other assets and, upon failing to find a buyer, became a subsidiary of a company in its original line of trade and prepared to resume its business. In [that] case[], the proprietor of the mark had an intention to exploit the mark in the reasonably foreseeable future by resuming its use or permitting its use by others.

The undisputed facts of the pending case are entirely different. Unlike the proprietor[] in ... *Defiance Button*, CBS has not been endeavoring to exploit the value of its marks, failing to do so only because of lack of business opportunities. Instead, it has decided, albeit for socially commendable motives, to forgo whatever business opportunities may currently exist in the hope that greater opportunities, unaccompanied by adverse public reaction, will exist at some undefined time in the future.

... [A] proprietor may not protect a mark if he discontinues using it for more than 20 years and has no plans to use or permit its use in the reasonably foreseeable future. A bare assertion of possible future use is not enough.

We recognize the point, forcefully made by Judge Goettel, when he wrote:

> It would be offensive to basic precepts of fairness and justice to penalize CBS, by stripping it of its trademark rights, merely because it succumbed to societal pressures and pursued a course of conduct that it reasonably believes to be in the best interests of the community.

Silverman II, 666 F. Supp. at 581. Nonetheless, we believe that however laudable one might think CBS's motives to be, such motives cannot overcome the undisputed facts that CBS has not used its marks for more than 20 years and that, even now, it has no plans to resume their use in the reasonably foreseeable future. Though we agree with Judge Goettel that CBS should not be penalized for its worthy motive, we cannot adjust the statutory test of abandonment to reward CBS for such motive by according it protection where its own voluntary actions demonstrate that statutory protection has ceased. Moreover, we see nothing in the statute that makes the consequence of an intent not to resume use turn on the worthiness of the motive for holding such intent.

We are also mindful of the facts, relied on by the District Court, that show some minor activities by CBS regarding its properties, allegedly sufficient to rebut abandonment of the marks. These are CBS's actions in licensing the programs for limited use in connection with documentary and educational programs, challenging infringing uses brought to its attention, renewing its copyrights, and periodically reconsidering whether to resume use of the programs. But challenging infringing uses is not use, and sporadic licensing for essentially non-commercial uses of a mark is not sufficient use to forestall abandonment. *Cf. Exxon Corp. v. Humble Exploration Co., supra*, 695 F.2d at 102 (use must be "commercial use" to avoid abandonment). Such uses do not sufficiently rekindle the public's identification of the mark with the proprietor, which is the essential condition for trademark protection, nor do they establish an intent to resume commercial use....

An adjudication of trademark rights often involves a balancing of competing interests. *See La Société Anonyme des Parfums Le Galion v. Jean Patou, Inc.*, 495 F.2d 1265, 1274 n. 11 (2d Cir. 1974). In weighing the competing interests and reaching our conclusion concerning abandonment, we are influenced in part by the context in which this dispute arises—one in which the allegedly infringing use is in connection with a work of artistic expression. Just as First Amendment values inform application of the idea/expression dichotomy in copyright law, *see Harper & Row, Publishers, Inc. v. Nation Enterprises*, 471 U.S. 539, 556 (1985), in similar fashion such values have some bearing upon the extent of protection accorded a trademark proprietor against use of the mark in works of artistic expression.

Ordinarily, the use of a trademark to identify a commodity or a business "is a form of commercial speech and nothing more." *Friedman v. Rogers*, 440 U.S. 1, 11 (1979). Requiring a commercial speaker to choose words and labels that do not confuse or deceive protects the public and does not impair expression. [Citations.]

In the area of artistic speech, however, enforcement of trademark rights carries a risk of inhibiting free expression, *cf. L.L. Bean, Inc. v. Drake Publishers, Inc.*, 811 F.2d 26, 28–29 (1st Cir.), *cert. denied*, 107 S. Ct. 3254 (1987), not only in the case at hand but in other situations where authors might contemplate use of trademarks in connection with works of artistic expression. These risks add some weight to Silverman's claims.

From the standpoint of the proprietor of a mark in a work of artistic expression, there is also an interest in expression, along with the traditional trademark interest in avoiding public confusion as to source. Trademark law can contribute to a favorable climate for expression by complementing the economic incentive that copyright law provides to create and disseminate artistic works, *see Harper & Row Publishers, Inc. v. Nation Publishers, supra*, 471 U.S. at 558. In this case, however, the expression interest on CBS's side is markedly diminished by its decision to withhold dissemination of the works with which its marks are associated.

The interest of CBS, and the public, in avoiding public confusion, an interest obviously entitled to weight in every trademark case, is also somewhat diminished in the context of this case. This interest is not as weighty as in a case involving a non-artistic product whose trademark is associated with high quality or other consumer benefits. Though Silverman undoubtedly hopes that some of his audience will be drawn from those who favorably recall the "Amos 'n' Andy" programs, we doubt if many who attend Broadway musicals are motivated to purchase tickets because of a belief that the musical is produced by the same entity responsible for the movie, book, or radio or television series on which it is based. That is not to say that the musical is in a sufficiently distinct line of commerce to preclude all protection; the holder of a mark associated with a television series would normally be entitled to "bridge the gap" and secure some protection against an infringing use of the mark in connection with a Broadway musical. It is to say, however, that most theater-goers have sufficient awareness that the quality of a musical depends so heavily on a combination of circumstances, including script, score, lyrics, cast, and direction, that they are not likely to be significantly influenced in their ticket-purchasing decision by an erroneous belief that the musical emanated from the same production source as the underlying work.

The point must not be overstated. Trademark protection is not lost simply because the allegedly infringing use is in connection with a work of artistic expression. But in determining the outer limits of trademark protection—here, concerning the concept of abandonment—the balance of risks just noted is relevant and in some cases may tip the scales against trademark protection. These considerations are especially pertinent in the pending case where some aspects of the material claimed to be protected by trademark are in the public domain as far as copyright law is concerned.

For all of these reasons, we conclude that the undisputed facts establish abandonment of the AMOS 'N' ANDY marks.

....

ITC Limited v. Punchgini, 482 F.3d 135 (2d Cir. 2007). The plaintiff ITC Hotels and Restaurants owns a chain of world-renowned Indian restaurants under the name Bukhara. (See *supra*, Chapter 3[C]) "The restaurant's look is pure Flintstones: walls of boulders, solid-wood tables and menus printed on laminated sections of tree." ITC licensed the Bukhara trademark, for which it had obtained a U.S. registration, and trade dress to several franchisees, including one in New York City. The New York branch opened in 1986 and closed in 1991. In 1999, the defendants, former employees of the New York restaurant, opened a Bukhara Grill in New York. In addition to the name, defendants also allegedly emulated aspects of the prior restaurant's trade dress, including the rustic decor, heavy wooden menus, use of checkered bibs in lieu of napkins, and logo font. In 2000, ITC sent a cease and desist letter; the New York restaurant replied that the mark had been abandoned, and thus was legitimately taken up by the New York entrepreneurs. ITC ultimately sued in 2003. In response to defendants' motion for summary judgment, ITC conceded that it had not used the mark in the United States for over three years before defendants' appropriation, but it claimed a genuine issue of material fact as to its intent to resume use, sufficient to rebut the statutory presumption at trial and precluding summary judgment.

The Second Circuit affirmed the district court's findings that ITC had not rebutted the presumption of abandonment that arises from three years of nonuse. The court found that neither ITC's internal memoranda, nor its dealings with potential business partners, nor its plans to market packaged foods under the "Bukhara" brand evidenced a concrete intent to resume use of the mark in the U.S. It also found that while ITC had pursued franchise agreements around the world, none of the potential franchisees were located in the U.S.

> (4) Bukhara Restaurants Outside the United States
>
> Finally, ITC cites *La Société Anonyme des Parfums le Galion v. Jean Patou, Inc.* to support its argument that the continued operation of its Bukhara restaurants outside the United States demonstrates "an ongoing program to exploit the mark commercially," giving rise to an inference of an intent to resume

the mark's use in this country, 495 F.2d 1265, 1272 (2d Cir. 1974). In fact, ITC's reliance on *Societe Anonyme* is misplaced. In that case, this court ruled that a "meager trickle" of perfume sales within the United States—89 bottles sold over a period of 20 years—was insufficient to establish trade-mark rights in the United States. *Id.* Nothing in that case suggests that ongoing foreign use of a mark, by itself, supports an inference that the owner intends to re-employ a presumptively abandoned mark in the United States. *Cf. id.* at 1271 n.4 (noting "well-settled" view "that foreign use is ineffectual to create trademark rights in the United States"). Indeed, we identify no authority supporting that conclusion.

Specht v. Google, Inc.

747 F.3d 929 (7th Cir. 2014)

Rovner, Circuit Judge

....

Background

Inspired by the recent success of a number of technology start-ups, Erich Specht decided in 1998 to enter the business world himself. He designed a suite of e-commerce software and formed Android Data Corporation (ADC), through which he intended to license the software to clients. ADC also performed a number of other web-based services to clients, including website hosting and design, and computer consulting services. Two years later, Specht applied to register the trademark "Android Data" with the United States Patent and Trademark Office. The application was approved in 2002.

Despite the trademark's approval, by the end of 2002 ADC stopped major operations. That year, the company lost five clients, prompting Specht to lay off his only employee, cancel ADC's internet service contract, and move the business into his home. Signifying the end of ADC's life, he transferred all of ADC's assets, including its software and the registered "Android Data" mark, to another of his wholly-owned companies, The Android's Dungeon, Incorporated (ADI). Specht spent all of the next year unsuccessfully seeking a buyer for ADC's assets. As ADC was idle, he also shut off its phone line that year.

After 2002, Specht's business activities were limited. He continued to host ADC's website a while longer and conducted some hosting services for others. But he let the registration for the company's URL (androiddata.com) lapse in 2005, at which time he could no longer be reached at his associated email address. Specht passed out business cards in 2005 bearing the Android Data mark, but the record does not disclose how many, to whom, or why.

In 2007, about five years after he first began to wind down ADC's operations, Specht attempted to revive the use of the Android Data mark. First, to promote his software suite to catalog companies, Specht sent out a mass mailing in December 2007 with the Android Data mark. These mailings garnered no sales. Second, two months later, Specht attempted to license his software to a healthcare consulting firm, also to no avail. He made no other use of "Android Data" in 2007 or the next year. In April 2009, he used the mark once again when he resurrected his website, albeit with a slightly different URL (android-data.com) because his previous URL had by then been registered by a third party. He also assigned the Android Data mark to ADI, retroactive to the December 2002 asset transfer.

Meanwhile, during the years that Specht struggled with his shrinking business, another technology start-up calling itself "Android, Incorporated" began developing what would become known as the Android operating system for smart phones. Google purchased Android, Inc., in 2005. Two years after the purchase, Google released to the public a beta version of its Android software. This release, in November 2007, occurred about a month before Specht had attempted to revive his use of the Android Data mark in his mail mailing that December.

....

Specht, ADC, and ADI sued Google, the founders of Android, Inc., and the Open Handset Alliance ... over the use of the Android mark. The plaintiffs (whom we will, except where necessary, refer to simply as "Specht") raise two claims under the Lanham Act: one for trademark infringement, *see* 15 U.S.C. § 1114(1), and one for unfair competition, *see id.* § 1125(a)....

....

... Google ... sought a declaration that Specht had abandoned the mark, depriving him and his companies of any rights to it ... [and] asked the district court to cancel the plaintiff's mark.

... Google moved for summary judgment, ... [T]he district court ruled that all of Specht's claims failed as a matter of law. The district court also issued Google's requested declaration, and canceled Specht's registration.

....

... A trademark is abandoned if its "use in commerce" has been discontinued with no intent to resume use. 15 U.S.C. § 1127; [citation]. Under the Lanham Act, "[n]onuse for 3 consecutive years shall be prima facie evidence of abandonment," 15 U.S.C. § 1127. A prima facie showing of abandonment may be rebutted with evidence excusing the nonuse or demonstrating an intent to resume use. [Citation.] But the intent to resume use in commerce must be formulated within the three years of nonuse. *ITC Ltd. v. Punchgini, Inc.*, 482 F.3d 135, 149 n.9 (2d Cir. 2007); *Imperial Tobacco Ltd., Assignee of Imperial Group PLC v. Philip Morris, Inc.*, 899 F.2d 1575, 1581 (Fed. Cir. 1990). Furthermore, the use must pertain to the sale of goods or provision of services. *See* 15 U.S.C. § 1127; *United Drug Co. v. Theodore Rectanus Co.*, 248 U.S. 90, 97, 39 S. Ct. 48, 63 L. Ed. 141, 1918 Dec. Comm'r Pat. 369 (1918); *Rearden LLC v. Rearden Commerce, Inc.*, 683 F.3d 1190, 1204 (9th Cir. 2012); *Int'l Bancorp, LLC v. Societe des Bains de Mer et du Cercle des Estrangers a Monaco*, 329 F.3d 359, 364 (4th Cir. 2003).

Under these principles, this appeal turns on three dates: the date (if any) that Specht discontinued using the Android Data mark, the date Google began using the

Android mark in commerce and acquired rights to it, and the date (if any) that Specht intended to resume use of the mark....

With respect to Specht's discontinued use of the mark, the evidence is conclusive that Specht ceased using the Android Data mark at the end of 2002. That is the year that ADC essentially shut down after losing five clients, laying off its one employee, and transferring its assets to ADI. Specht cites to four activities that he believes show his continued use of the Android Data mark after 2002, but they are insufficient.

First Specht notes that he attempted to sell his business's assets in 2003 and 2004. But an effort to sell the assets of a business is different from trading on the goodwill of a trademark to sell a business's goods or services and therefore does not constitute a use of the mark in commerce. *See Electro Source, LLC v. Brandess-Kalt-Aetna Grp., Inc.*, 458 F.3d 931, 938 n.5 (9th Cir. 2006). Second, Specht observes that ADC's phone service was not canceled until 2003. But Specht included any phone expenses from 2003 on ADC's 2002 balance sheet precisely because, in his view, ADC did not operate in 2003.

The remaining two activities are also insufficient to show a resumption of use. Specht points out that ADC's website was operating until 2005, and a website that bears a trademark may constitute a bona fide use in commerce. [Citation.] But Specht did not identify any goods or services ADC could have provided through or in connection with the website after 2002. [Citations]. As such, the website was not a use in commerce. Specht's reply that the site averaged 2,925 monthly visitors (actually the record shows only 808 monthly visits), goes nowhere because he furnished no evidence of any commercial interest associated with the visits. Finally, Specht maintains that his two sales efforts in 2007 (the mass mailing and his failed bid to license software to a healthcare firm) are evidence of commercial use of the mark. But these two efforts were isolated and not sustained; sporadic attempts to solicit business are not a "use in commerce" meriting the protection of the Lanham Act. *See Zazu Designs v. L'Oreal, S.A.*, 979 F.2d 499, 503 (7th Cir. 1992); *Aktieselskabet AF 21. November 2001 v. Fame Jeans Inc.*, 525 F.3d 8, 20, 381 U.S. App. D.C. 76 (D.C. Cir. 2008). The district court, therefore, correctly determined that Specht had abandoned the mark at the end of 2002.

....

... Google became the senior user of the Android mark when it used the mark in commerce in November 2007. By then, the Android mark lay abandoned. Once a mark is abandoned, it returns to the public domain, and may be appropriated anew. *See Indianapolis Colts, Inc. v. Metro. Baltimore Football Club Ltd. P'Ship*, 34 F.3d 410, 412 (7th Cir. 1994); *ITC Ltd.*, 482 F.3d at 147. By adopting the abandoned mark first, Google became the senior user, entitled to assert rights to the Android mark against the world. Its use since November 2007 has been uninterrupted and continuous. That is enough to warrant trademark protection. *See Zazu Designs*, 979 F.2d at 503; *Blue Bell, Inc. v. Farah Mfg. Co., Inc.*, 508 F.2d 1260, 1265 (5th Cir. 1975) ("even a single use in trade may sustain trademark rights if followed by continuous commercial utilization"); *see also Planetary Motion, Inc. v. Techsplosion, Inc.*, 261 F.3d 1188, 1194–95

(11th Cir. 2001) (release of software to end users is use in commerce even though no sale was made).

Specht replies that, even if he had abandoned the mark after 2002, he either resumed using or developed an intent to resume using the Android Data mark by December 2007, again citing his mass mailing. But by then it was too late. Specht had abandoned the mark by the end of 2002, and more than three years had passed before Google publicized its release of the Android operating system in November 2007. With the mark permanently abandoned by November 2007, Specht could not reclaim it the following month. The district court therefore correctly granted summary judgment on all of Specht's claims. *See TMT N. Amer. v. Magic Touch GmbH*, 124 F.3d 876, 885 (7th Cir. 1997) … ("abandonment … result[s] in the loss of trademark rights against the world").

Questions

1. Non-use for three years creates a rebuttable presumption of abandonment. Is the *Specht* court correct in finding that intent to resume use must be evidenced in the same three-year period?

2. Were ITC's US contacts less extensive than those deemed to constitute "use in commerce" in *First Niagara Ins. v. First Niagara Financial, supra*, Chapter 4[C]? Is there a reason to require a stronger showing of use in order to avoid abandonment of U.S. trademark rights than to establish U.S. trademark rights, or to have standing to oppose another's U.S. trademark registration?

3. Nicole Bédé authors a successful French comic book series, *Les triplés*. In 1998, Nicole obtained a U.S. trademark registration on the basis of her French registration and her declaration of an intent to use the triplés mark in the U.S. (regarding U.S. registrations based on foreign registrations, *see supra*, Chapter 4[A]) Although Nicole has sought and continues to seek U.S. licensees for an English-language version of her comic books, or for other merchandizing properties, she has so far been unsuccessful. Color Comics seeks to register the mark Triplets for a series of its own. Denied registration on the ground that Color's mark is likely to cause confusion with Nicole's, Color brings a cancellation action alleging abandonment. How should the Board rule? *See Cromosoma S.A. v. Nicole Lambert*, 2005 TTAB LEXIS 101 (T.T.A.B. Feb. 23, 2005).

4. Vincent George sold his eponymous family widget manufacturing business to Barton Robert, and returned home to Albania, his health shattered by long years of work. Fully recovered, George later returned to the U.S. and resumed manufacturing widgets under the same name. George's Widgets, Inc. brings a trademark infringement action, and George defends on the ground that he cannot "abandon" his own name. How should the court rule? *See Vais Arms, Inc. v. Vais*, 383 F.3d 287 (5th Cir. 2004).

5. An applicant's failure to submit a statement of use in connection with an intent-to-use application for trademark registration results in "abandonment" of the application. Does it also show abandonment of any rights in the mark? *See Who Dat Yat Chat v. Who Dat*, 2012 U.S. Dist. LEXIS 46733 (E.D. La. Apr. 3, 2012) (holding abandonment of application may be evidence of, but does not itself suffice to show, abandonment of mark).

6. What type of use can be considered to show that an abandonment has not occurred? Should a member of a former band that ceased recording many years earlier be able to rely on receipt of royalties for sales of the older recordings in order to prove use? *See Herb Reed Enterprises, LLC v. Florida Entertainment Management, Inc.*, 736 F.3d 1239 (9th Cir. 2013), *infra*, Chapter 12.A.

*Note: "The Song Is Ended (but the Melody Lingers On)"**

Even long after a producer has ceased exploiting a mark, the term may continue to carry considerable residual goodwill. Most often, the mark's goodwill continues to redound to the benefit of the producer; even though the mark is no longer being used, the public continues to associate it with its former user. A new entrant's adoption of the mark for the same or related goods may thus prompt suspicion that it is seeking to reap the benefits of the goodwill remaining in the mark. In such a situation, a court may strain to avoid finding that an abandonment has occurred. For example, in *Exxon Corp. v. Humble Exploration Co.*, 695 F.2d 96 (5th Cir. 1983), discussed in *Silverman*, the Fifth Circuit, having rejected an intent-not-to-abandon standard, remanded to the district court to determine if Exxon had an intent to resume use of the HUMBLE mark. The district court, 592 F. Supp. 1226 (N.D. Tex. 1984), after surveying several abandonment decisions and observing that "each case is founded on its own facts," found certain special considerations underlying Exxon's three-year non-use of the HUMBLE mark. In particular, the court cited Exxon's efforts to replace its three regional marks, HUMBLE, ESSO, and ENCO, in the public mind with a single national mark, EXXON. Establishing the national brand required non-use of the regional brands, because "the very strength of the HUMBLE mark made it difficult to find a use for HUMBLE which would not contaminate the EXXON mark." Nonetheless, the court found that Exxon had an "intent to make more than token use of HUMBLE," principally through its inclusion of the HUMBLE mark, along with the EXXON mark, on drums of petroleum products. The court held that "during the period of non-use, Exxon did not have an intent not to resume use of the HUMBLE mark and, further, that Exxon intended to resume commercial use of HUMBLE."

Even when the mark has been abandoned, courts may require the new adopter to take reasonable precautions to prevent confusion during the period of "residual significance" during which the "mark that has been abandoned ... is still associated by the public with its former holder." *Cumulus Media, Inc. v. Clear Channel*, 304 F.3d 1167 (11th Cir. 2002) (upholding a preliminary injunction against a radio station which had adopted the name abandoned by a rival station thirteen months earlier). *Cf.* "Genericism and Confusion," *supra*, this Chapter, Subsection A[3].

Not all lingering goodwill evokes the reputation of the prior trademark owner. Sometimes the goodwill takes on a life of its own, no longer signaling the producer.

* *Editors' Note:* Irving Berlin wrote his famous song, "The Song Is Ended ..." in the late 1920s.

This situation has arisen in the context of sports teams that relocate to a different city. *Indianapolis Colts Inc. v. Metropolitan Baltimore Football Club Limited Partnership*, 34 F.3d 410 (7th Cir. 1994), and *Major League Baseball Props. v. Sed Non Olet Denarius*, 817 F. Supp. 1103 (S.D.N.Y. 1993), *vacated pursuant to settlement*, 859 F. Supp. 80 (S.D.N.Y. 1994), represent different approaches to this problem. The latter case involved the unauthorized adoption of the term "Brooklyn Dodger" by a restaurant located in Brooklyn, New York. Decorated with Brooklyn Dodgers memorabilia, the restaurant sought to evoke the happy days of the baseball team's residence in the borough of Brooklyn—before the team's still-resented 1958 departure for Los Angeles. In response to the Los Angeles Dodgers' and Major League Baseball's suit for an injunction, the restaurant claimed that the "Brooklyn Dodgers" mark had been abandoned. The restaurant also disparaged any suggestion that it was seeking to capitalize on the Los Angeles' organization's goodwill: as the court described the testimony of one witness, "a life-long Brooklyn resident," "given the acrimonious abandonment of Brooklyn by Los Angeles, the idea of trading on Los Angeles' 'goodwill' in Brooklyn is almost 'laughable.'"

Although plaintiffs had not used the mark "Brooklyn Dodgers" between 1958 and 1981 (when plaintiffs began a limited licensing program for the mark), plaintiffs contended that the protected mark was simply "Dodgers," and that this mark had been in continuous use. The court rejected plaintiff's characterization of the mark:

> [I]n this context, "Brooklyn" is more than a geographic designation or appendage to the word "Dodgers." The "*Brooklyn* Dodgers" was a non-transportable cultural institution separate from the "Los Angeles Dodgers" or the "Dodgers" who play in Los Angeles. It is not simply the "Dodgers" (and certainly not the "Los Angeles Dodgers") that defendants seek to invoke in their restaurant; rather, defendants specifically seek to recall the nostalgia of the cultural institution that was the "Brooklyn Dodgers." It was the "*Brooklyn* Dodgers" name that had acquired secondary meaning in New York in the early part of the century, prior to 1958. It was that cultural institution that Los Angeles abandoned.

The court held that plaintiffs' non-use of "*Brooklyn* Dodgers" for thirty-two years constituted an abandonment. Moreover, plaintiffs' partial resumption of use through the sporadic granting of licenses beginning in 1981 created only common-law rights in the term. Thus, plaintiffs could claim rights only in those locations and in those kinds of uses for which it had granted licenses. Because plaintiffs had not previously granted a license for restaurant use in Brooklyn (and because the court had already found that defendants' use was not likely to be confused with plaintiffs'), defendants were entitled to continue using the "Brooklyn Dodger" mark. By contrast, in *Indianapolis Colts*, Judge Posner viewed the mark as "COLTS," independently of urban affiliation. Hence, the equally resented abandonment of Baltimore in 1984 by its former football team did not entitle the Canadian Football League (CFL) to adopt the name "Colts" in connection with its new team in Baltimore. Judge Posner declined to pair the goodwill of the team with its former home town:

> [Defendants] make a tremendous to-do over the fact that the district judge found that the Indianapolis Colts abandoned the trademark "Baltimore Colts" when they moved to Indianapolis. Well, of course; they were no longer playing football under the name "Baltimore Colts," so could not have used the name as the team's trademark.... The Colts' abandonment of a mark confusingly similar to their new mark neither broke the continuity of the team in its different locations—it was the same team, merely having a different home base and therefore a different geographical component in its name—nor entitled a third party to pick it up and use it to confuse [consumers]... with regard to the identity, sponsorship, or league affiliation of the third party, that is, the new Baltimore team.
>
> A professional sports team is like Heraclitus's river: always changing, yet always the same.... [A]s far as the record discloses there is as much institutional continuity between the Baltimore Colts of 1984 and the Indianapolis Colts of 1994 as there was between the Baltimore Colts of 1974 and the Baltimore Colts of 1984.... There is, in contrast, no continuity, no links contractual or otherwise, nothing but a geographical site in common, between the Baltimore Colts and the Canadian Football League team that would like to use its name. Any suggestion that there is such continuity is false and potentially misleading.

The following decision is a more recent example of the problem of residual goodwill:

Wells Fargo & Co. v. ABD Insurance & Financial Services, Inc. 758 F.3d 1069 (9th Cir. 2014). Wells Fargo moved for a preliminary injunction against the defendant for use of the mark ABD. Wells Fargo had previously acquired the original ABD Insurance company and changed the name to Wells Fargo, but continued to use the ABD mark in various ways. Former ABD employees started a new company and changed its name to ABD when Wells Fargo did not renew the registration for the mark. The Ninth Circuit reversed the district court's denial of a preliminary injunction and remanded for a reconsideration under the correct abandonment analysis.

> The district court also abused its discretion by misapplying the law in its abandonment analysis when it considered evidence of prospective intent to abandon the mark to determine whether Wells Fargo's uses were bona fide and in the ordinary course of business. To prove abandonment of a mark as a defense to a claim of trademark infringement, a defendant must show that there was: "(1) discontinuance of trademark use *and* (2) intent not to resume such use." *Electro Source, LLC v. Brandess-Kalt-Aetna Grp., Inc.*, 458 F.3d 931, 935 (9th Cir. 2006). The phrase "trademark use" means "the bona fide use of a mark in the ordinary course of trade, and not merely to reserve a right in a mark." *Id.* at 936 (quoting 15 U.S.C. § 1127). Even a "single instance of use is sufficient against a claim of abandonment of a mark if such use is made in good faith." *Carter-Wallace, Inc. v. Procter & Gamble Co.*, 434 F.2d 794, 804 (9th Cir. 1970). All bona fide uses in the ordinary course of business must cease before a mark is deemed abandoned.

We have said that "unless the trademark use is actually terminated the intent not to resume use prong of abandonment does not come into play." *Electro Source,* 458 F.3d at 937–38. "[A] prospective intent to abandon says nothing about whether use of the mark has been discontinued." *Id.* at 937.

The district court held that Wells Fargo abandoned the ABD mark, reasoning that Wells Fargo's continued uses of the ABD mark were not bona fide and in the ordinary course of trade because such uses were "residual ... or in the context of a historical background" given Wells Fargo's rebranding efforts. The district court's abandonment findings were flawed for two significant reasons. First, prospective intent to abandon is not properly considered when examining whether bona fide uses of the mark in the ordinary course of business have ceased, and the district court erred when it considered Wells Fargo's intent to rebrand ABD in that context. Second, the district court misconstrued the breadth of uses included within the scope of a "bona fide use in the ordinary course of trade." Courts must consider the totality of the circumstances surrounding the use, and "even a declining business retains, may benefit from, or may continue to build its goodwill until it shuts its doors or ceases use of its marks." *Id.* at 938. In this case, Wells Fargo continued to use the mark in several ways, most notably in customer presentations and solicitations. Such uses demonstrate Wells Fargo's business calculation that it could continue to benefit from the goodwill and mark recognition associated with ABD, and we conclude that Wells Fargo continued its bona fide use of the mark in the ordinary course of business through these uses. Thus, the district court erred by concluding that Wells Fargo abandoned the ABD mark, contrary to the principles of *Electro Source.*

Jack Wolfskin Ausrustung Fur Draussen GmbH v. New Millenium Sports, S.L.U., 797 F.3d 1363 (Fed. Cir. 2015). Mark owners sometimes modify or modernize their marks over time. Such changes can lead to challenges that the original mark has been abandoned, which can have an impact on priority. The court articulated when an abandonment occurs so that a mark owner cannot tack back to the priority of the original mark. New Millenium's original mark was

Since 2004, it has used a modified mark shown here:

The Federal Circuit found that the standard for tacking is the same whether the question is abandonment or priority.

> In both contexts—priority and abandonment—the fundamental inquiry is the same: has the original mark been so substantially altered such that third parties would not expect that presently used mark to be used under and protected by the registration. Our case law recognizes that it would be wrong to allow a trademark owner to claim priority to a mark that creates a different commercial impression from the mark currently in use. This same inequity exists when a trademark owner seeks to avoid abandonment of the originally registered mark even though the current mark is a materially different version. We hold that the same legal standard applies in both contexts. Accordingly, when a trademark owner uses a modified version of its registered trademark, it may avoid abandonment of the original mark only if the modified version "create[s] the same, continuous commercial impression."

In applying this standard to the KELME and Design mark, the Federal Circuit noted:

> Despite the stylistic modifications, the mark that New Millennium currently uses still consists of the literal KELME element and the paw print design element. The KELME portion still appears in all capital, block style lettering. The minor adjustment to the font is not sufficient to warrant a finding that consumers would view these as different marks. Likewise, Jack Wolfskin presents no persuasive reason why the alterations to the design element change the commercial impression that the mark creates. As the Board stated, "[i]t appeared to be a paw before, and now it still appears to be a paw." *Id.* For these reasons, we conclude that the Board's finding that New Millennium did not abandon its registered mark by migrating to a modernized version of its mark is supported by substantial evidence. A reasonable fact-finder could conclude that the new version creates the same continuing commercial impression as the registered mark. We therefore affirm the Board's dismissal of Jack Wolfskin's cancellation counterclaim.

Questions

1. Abandonment casts a mark into the public domain. It becomes free for another's adoption. However, if a mark held to have been abandoned nonetheless in fact continues to symbolize the producer's goodwill, how would you protect the interests of the public, and of the producer, in avoiding confusion?

2. Examine the current Lanham Act definition of "abandonment." The statute now provides that a mark shall be deemed abandoned "[w]hen its use has been discontinued with intent not to resume *such use.*" How does the addition of the italicized words affect analysis of abandonment claims? For example, how would you decide the *Humble* case given the current definition? Does this definition preclude protection on the basis of residual goodwill?

3. Recall the Second Circuit's *Silverman* statement: "Though Silverman undoubtedly hopes that some of his audience will be drawn from those who favorably recall the

'Amos 'n Andy' programs, we doubt if many who attend Broadway musicals are motivated to purchase tickets because of a belief that the musical is produced by the same entity responsible for the movie, book, or radio or television series on which it is based." What is the relevance of the "motivation" test to abandonment? To infringement?

4. Ferrari, the automobile manufacturer, ceased producing its well-known DAYTONA SPYDER model sports car in 1974. At that time and thereafter, Ferrari has had no plans to resume producing the sports car. However, Ferrari has continued to manufacture mechanical and body parts for the repair and servicing of existing DAYTONA SPYDER automobiles. Ferrari sells these parts through exclusive licensees who continue to service the DAYTONA cars. Moreover, these cars are still widely driven.

McBurnie specializes in manufacturing car assembly kits and completed cars, including a model it calls the "California Daytona Spyder." If Ferrari brings a trade dress infringement claim against McBurnie, how should the court rule on the issue of abandonment? How much weight would you place on the continuing service activities? How much on the strong residual goodwill in the DAYTONA SPYDER? *See Ferrari S.p.A. Esercizio Fabbriche Automobili e Corse v. McBurnie*, 11 U.S.P.Q.2d 1843 (S.D. Cal. 1989).

5. The uses by Wells Fargo that the court considered bona fide uses in commerce were presumably transitional. If Wells Fargo ceases such uses, would the defendant then be free to adopt the ABD mark again? If Wells Fargo believed it was making bona fide use of the ABD mark, why did it not renew its registration?

6. In 2008, Lehman Brothers, a financial investment powerhouse for over a century, filed for bankruptcy and sold its investment business to Barclay's. Lehman Brothers was granted a perpetual license by Barclays to use the mark in connection with certain businesses, including liquidating the highly valuable assets of Lehman Brothers, such as commercial real estate. Lehman Brothers emerged from bankruptcy and uses the Lehman Brothers name on business cards, stationery and signage at its offices at a prestigious Times Square building. Although Barclay's did not maintain the numerous LEHMAN BROTHERS registrations that it acquired in 2008, Barclays filed an ITU application to register the mark LEHMAN BROTHERS for various Class 36 financial services on October 2, 2013. Meanwhile, Tiger Lily, a UK company, filed an ITU application for LEHMAN BROTHERS on March 6, 2013 for beer and spirits and on June 2, 2014 for bar and restaurant services. Tiger Lily's intended SNAPFIRE, ASHES OF DISASTER and EVERGREEN (with nose: "wicked suggestion of burning banknotes") products are shown below:

Tiger Lily's website shows the products against photos of New York City buildings, including one with money floating in the air. Both entities have opposed the other's application(s). What arguments would you make for each to prevail?

7. Recall that applicants for marks based on foreign registrations or on extensions of International Registrations do not have to make use before registration. If no use is made in U.S. commerce thereafter, at what point would their registration become vulnerable to a non-use claim? *See Dragon Bleu (SARL) v. VENM, LLC*, 112 U.S.P.Q.2d 1925 (T.T.A.B. 2014).

2. Assignment in Gross

Clark & Freeman Corp. v. Heartland Co. Ltd.

811 F. Supp. 137 (S.D.N.Y. 1993)

Martin, J:

This case involves the competing claims of two companies to the exclusive right to use the name "Heartland" in connection with their business operations. Defendants have been using the name since July of 1985 in connection with their sales of shirts, sweaters, trousers and jackets. Plaintiffs first commenced using the name "Heartland" on April 26, 1986 in connection with the sale of men's shoes and boots.

Had each of the parties continued with their original operations, plaintiffs selling men's shoes and boots and defendants selling shirts, trousers and jackets, there would have been little need for either to seek the intervention of the Court. While some evidence of confusion was introduced at trial, such confusion was limited and not sufficient to justify interfering with the parties' continued operating in their separate lines of merchandise. Recently, however, plaintiffs have decided that they wish to launch a clothing line under the "Heartland" name and, thus, this lawsuit.

Although plaintiffs began using the name "Heartland" after defendants, plaintiffs claim priority because in 1987 they obtained an assignment of the "Heartland" name from Sears, Roebuck & Co. which had used the name since 1983 in connection with the sale of women's boots. Plaintiffs filed an application to register the "Heartland" mark with the U.S. Patent and Trademark Office on July 3, 1986. On November 25, 1986, the application was allowed and published in the Official Gazette. Nine days later on December 4, 1986, Sears notified plaintiffs of their prior use of the "Heartland" name and threatened to bring opposition proceedings. Ultimately, Sears agreed to settle the matter by assigning the "Heartland" name to plaintiffs in exchange for $15,000. The settlement was effected on April 6, 1987, and, on July 28, 1987, plaintiffs' mark was registered by the U.S. Patent and Trademark Office.

Since plaintiffs' own use of the name "Heartland" did not commence until after defendants' use of that trademark, plaintiffs can prevail in this action only if they have succeeded to the priority rights in the trademark "Heartland" which were enjoyed by Sears. Defendants contend, however, that the assignment of the trademark from Sears to plaintiffs was an assignment in gross and, therefore, plaintiffs may not tack on the period of Sears' prior use to defeat defendants' claim of priority.

Generally, an assignment of a trademark and its accompanying goodwill will entitle the assignee to "step into the shoes" of the assignor, gaining whatever priority the assignor might have had in the mark [citations omitted]; *accord* 15 U.S.C. § 1060.[2] However, where a trademark has been assigned "in gross," i.e. without the accompanying goodwill, then the assignment is invalid, and the "assignee" must instead rely upon his or her own use to establish priority.

Marshak v. Green, 746 F.2d 927 (2d Cir. 1984), discusses the rationale behind the assignment in gross rule: "Use of the mark by the assignee in connection with a different goodwill and different product would result in a fraud on the purchasing public who reasonably assume that the mark signifies the same thing, whether used by one person or another." *Id.* at 929.

Plaintiffs claim that the assignment is valid for two reasons: (1) Because Sears immediately ceased manufacture and marketing of its "Heartland" boots, there was an ipso facto transfer of goodwill to plaintiffs; (2) Because plaintiffs were applying the trademark to "substantially similar" goods, they had acquired the goodwill as well as the mark.

Plaintiffs' first argument can be easily dismissed. Plaintiffs cite no case establishing the proposition that forbearance by the assignor operates to transfer goodwill ipso facto. *Hy-Cross Hatchery, Inc. v. Osborne*, 303 F.2d 947, 950 (C.C.P.A. 1962) (using

---

2. Although § 1060 applies only to registered trademarks, it parallels the common law rules of trademark assignment. [Citations.] Thus, no distinction is made herein between cases discussing assignability of registered trademarks and those involving unregistered trademarks.

forbearance only as one element in transfer of goodwill determination). Indeed, if forbearance alone were sufficient, then discussion of "consumer deception" would be irrelevant, since an assignee could use the mark for any product desired as long as the assignor halted operations. Goodwill is not such a mechanistic concept.

Plaintiffs' second contention presents a closer question. It is well established that "courts have upheld such assignments if they find that the assignee is producing a product or performing a service substantially similar to that of the assignor and that the customers would not be deceived or harmed." *Marshak*, 746 F.2d at 930.[3] This is the case even if no physical or tangible assets have been transferred. The key question is whether plaintiffs produced a product "substantially similar" to that of Sears such that "the customers would not be deceived or harmed."

For these purposes, it is not dispositive that plaintiffs' footwear is of high quality. It is not merely the quality of the product, but its similarity to that produced by the assignor that determines whether goodwill has been transferred. "[A] trademark may be validly transferred without the simultaneous transfer of any tangible assets, as long as the recipient continues to produce goods of the same quality *and nature* previously associated with the mark." *Defiance Button*, 759 F.2d at 1059 (emphasis added). Plaintiffs' argument that customers cannot be harmed or deceived either because their shoes are of such high quality or because they are available for inspection prior to purchase misses the mark; by that rationale, plaintiffs could have produced the finest quality jet engines under the mark "Heartland" and claimed to have acquired Sears' goodwill in ladies' boots. Substantial similarity demands more than quality.

Case law on "substantial similarity" is only moderately instructive, since the facts of each case are distinct and dispositive. Some courts have found "substantial similarity" even though the products differed in some respects. In *Main Street Outfitters v. Federated Dep't Stores*, 730 F. Supp. 289 (D. Minn. 1989), "substantial similarity" was found to establish a goodwill transfer where the assignor had sold "all-weather coats and women's coats" and the assignee was using the mark on "various items of clothing including jackets, rain wear and various items of apparel." *Id.* at 290. The court found dispositive that "[assignee] conducted a business of selling apparel, especially women's apparel, as had its assignor. The goods sold by [assignee] had substantially the same characteristics, that is: apparel, as those of the assignor." *Id.* at 292.

In *Mulhens & Kropff v. Ferd Muelhens, Inc.*, 38 F.2d 287, 293 ([S.]D.N.Y. 1929), the district court found assignor's and assignee's colognes to be "substantially similar" even though the assignor retained the secret formula to its cologne. But the court of appeals reversed, stating that "a majority of the court believe that assignment of the recipe is essential to give the assignee the exclusive right to a mark which denotes a

3. Goodwill may also be transferred if "the purchaser is able to 'go on in real continuity with the past,'" *Bambu Sales, Inc. v. Sultana Crackers, Inc.*, 683 F. Supp. 899 (E.D.N.Y. 1988), or if "there is a continuity of management," *Marshak*, 746 F.2d at 930. Neither of these occurrences has been alleged by plaintiffs.

product manufactured thereunder." 43 F.2d 937, 939 (2d Cir.), *cert. denied*, 282 U.S. 881, 51 S. Ct. 84 (1930).

In *Warner-Lambert Pharm. Co. v. General Foods Corp.*, 164 U.S.P.Q. 532 (T.T.A.B. 1970), the court found that assignor's mineral-vitamin pharmaceutical was not similar enough to assignee's anti-caries (tooth decay preventative) preparation in chewable tablet and capsule form to establish a transfer of goodwill.

Even minor differences can be enough to threaten customer deception. In the oft-cited *Pepsico, Inc. v. Grapette Co.*, 416 F.2d 285 (8th Cir. 1969), the court found that assignor's cola-flavored syrup and assignee's pepper-flavored syrup were sufficiently different to prevent a transfer of goodwill, and thus invalidate the assignment: "[The assignee]'s intended use of the mark is one simply to describe its new pepper beverage. The evidence is clear that [the assignee] did not intend to adopt or exploit any 'goodwill' from the [trademark] and [the assignor]'s long association and use of it with a cola syrup." *Id.* at 289–90.

The facts of record in this case support a finding of assignment in gross here. Sears sold only women's pixie boots under the mark "Heartland," while plaintiffs immediately applied it only to men's shoes, then later to men's hiking boots. The markets for the two goods are substantially distinct; it is unlikely that men buying plaintiffs' "Heartland" shoes would be considering a reputation for footwear generally that Sears built by selling women's boots. That plaintiffs [were] using the "Heartland" mark before the assignment is also relevant, in that it tends to show that plaintiffs sought only to gain the ability to use the name "Heartland" rather than the goodwill associated with it. *Cf. Pepsico.* This is further supported by the fact that plaintiffs did not attempt to obtain the assignment from Sears until after Sears threatened to bring opposition proceedings to prevent plaintiffs from registering the "Heartland" trademark.

Since the assignment from Sears was an assignment in gross, defendants have shown priority in the use of the name "Heartland" and, therefore, plaintiffs may not enjoin defendants from using the "Heartland" name for the sale of its current line of products....

Questions

1. Sugarbusters, Inc., was an Indiana corporation operating a retail store named "Sugarbusters" in Indianapolis that provided products and information for diabetics. The corporation obtained a federal service mark registration for "retail store services featuring products and supplies for diabetic people; namely, medical supplies, medical equipment, food products, informational literature and wearing apparel featuring a message regarding diabetes." Sugarbusters, Inc. later sold "any and all rights to the mark" to the publisher of a best-selling book titled "SUGAR BUSTERS! Cut Sugar to Trim Fat." Under the terms of the sale, the plaintiff publisher purchased "all the interests" in the mark and "the goodwill of all business connected with the use of and symbolized by" the mark. The store also agreed that it would "cease all use of the mark, name and trademark interests within one hundred eighty (180) days." Defendant, a former consultant to plaintiff, published a cookbook titled "SUGAR BUST

For Life!" and resisted the ensuing trademark infringement suit on the ground that the trademark had been abandoned because plaintiff's acquisition was a transfer in gross. Plaintiff contends that it nonetheless enjoys common law protection for the book title, and that defendant's book title is likely to confuse consumers. How should the court rule? *See Sugar Busters LLC v. Brennan*, 177 F.3d 258 (5th Cir. 1999).

2. What is the rationale behind prohibiting trademarks from being assigned in gross? As you study the next cases, consider whether the reason for such a prohibition is the same as or different from the rationale for holding that naked licensing can work a trademark abandonment.

3. Is transfer of a domain name, without the business formerly conducted under the domain name, an assignment in gross? *See InterState Net Bank v. NetB@nk*, 348 F. Supp. 2d 340 (D.N.J. 2004) (despite increase in value of domain names, they may not constitute a "tangible asset" necessary to accompany the transfer of a trademark; in any event, the acquirer of the domain name did not offer a service "substantially similar" to the services offered by the previous domain name holder).

4. Boathouse Group Inc. and TigerLogic Corp. both claim rights in the mark POSTPOST for services in connection with social networking. Boathouse began using the mark in August 2010, TigerLogic since December 2010. Boathouse's service allows a user to conduct keyword searches of historical content of the user's social circle stored on social network sites (albeit, at the time of the litigation, not Facebook) and then to create a subset of those results to post to the user's profile page for display. TigerLogic describes its service as a "real-time personal social newspaper" which compiles links, pictures and videos posted on Facebook and presents them to users in newspaper format. Boathouse asserts that the services are essentially the same, and that it is the senior user. After Boathouse filed its suit, TigerLogic obtained a trademark assignment from (and granted a license back to) a company which since February, 2007 used POSTPOST in connection with a "plugin" on a blog platform that enables a blogger to append a preface or footnote to a blog entry so the text appears in a certain location on the computer screen. Boathouse claims that the assignor's product does not search for content and "ha[s] nothing to do with" social networking sites. Does the assignment validly convey prior rights to TigerLogic?

3. Naked Licensing

Eva's Bridal Ltd. v. Halanick Enterprises, Inc.

639 F.3d 788 (7th Cir. 2011)

Easterbrook, Chief Judge:

In 1966 Eva Sweis established in Chicago a shop that she called "Eva's Bridal." It sold dresses for brides and bridal parties. The venture was a success; Sweis allowed her children to open their own shops under the same name. The business passed to Said and Nancy Ghusein (née Sweis), who operate an "Eva's Bridal" shop in Oak Lawn, one of Chicago's suburbs. They have continued the pattern of licensing the name to relatives. Three years after opening a shop in Orland Park, another of Chicago's suburbs, Said and Nancy Ghusein sold that operation to Nayef Ghusein for $10. The agreement required Nayef to pay $75,000 a year for the right to use the "Eva's Bridal" name and marks.

The license agreement expired in 2002. Nayef and his corporation Halanick Enterprises have continued to operate the store under the Eva's Bridal name (see http://www.evasbridalsoforlandpark.com/) but no longer remit a royalty. In 2007 Said and his firm Eva's Bridal Ltd. filed this suit under the Lanham Act, contending that Nayef and Halanick have violated the Act by using the "Eva's Bridal" mark without payment (or, for that matter, a current license agreement).

The district judge did not decide whether plaintiffs waited too long before suing. Instead the court dismissed the suit, on the ground that plaintiffs abandoned the "Eva's Bridal" mark by engaging in naked licensing—that is, by allowing others to use the mark without exercising "reasonable control over the nature and quality of the goods, services, or business on which the [mark] is used by the licensee". Restatement (Third) of Unfair Competition § 33 (1995); *see also id.* § 30 (discussing abandonment); [citation]. The written agreement did not require Nayef and Halanick to operate the Orland Park store in any particular way and did not give the licensor any power of supervision over how the business was conducted. Nancy conceded during her deposition that she and her husband Said never tried to control any aspect of how defendants' shop operated or how the mark was used. The district judge concluded that the mark has been abandoned and that defendants therefore may use it without payment. Plaintiffs do not dispute the proposition that a naked license abandons a mark. Instead they observe that many decisions say that a licensor must supervise to ensure quality control, and they insist that they have never doubted the high standards of Nayef and his firm, so they had no reason to superintend any aspects of defendants' business. Plaintiffs maintain that Nayef and Halanick sell dresses from the same designers that the shop carried when it opened in 1988 and when ownership changed in 1991. Because consumers care about who designs and makes the clothing, which determines how the dresses look when worn, plaintiffs maintain that there was no need for any form of regulation. Doubtless consumers also care about the quality of service, whether the dressing rooms are clean and the staff helpful, whether alterations are performed accurately and on time, and so forth—matters about which plaintiffs left defendants to their own devices—but it is not necessary to decide which aspects of a retail bridal business contribute most to customers' satisfaction.

This argument that licensors may relinquish all control of licensees that operate "high quality" businesses misunderstands what judicial decisions and the Restatement mean when they speak about "quality." There is no rule that trademark proprietors must ensure "high quality" goods or that "high quality" permits unsupervised licensing. "Kentucky Fried Chicken" is a valid mark, *see Kentucky Fried Chicken Corp. v. Diversified Packaging Corp.*, 549 F.2d 368 (5th Cir. 1977), though neither that chain nor any other fast-food franchise receives a star (or even a mention) in the Guide Michelin. The sort of supervision required for a trademark license is the sort that produces consistent quality. "Trademarks [are] indications of consistent and predictable quality assured through the trademark owner's control over the use of the designation". Restatement § 33 comment b. [Citation.]

A person who visits one Kentucky Fried Chicken outlet finds that it has much the same ambiance and menu as any other. A visitor to any Burger King likewise enjoys a comforting familiarity and knows that the place will not be remotely like a Kentucky Fried Chicken outlet (and is sure to differ from Hardee's, Wendy's, and Applebee's too). The trademark's function is to tell shoppers what to expect—and whom to blame if a given outlet falls short. The licensor's reputation is at stake in every outlet, so it invests to the extent required to keep the consumer satisfied by ensuring a repeatable experience. [Citation.]

How much control is enough? The licensor's self-interest largely determines the answer. Courts are apt to ask whether "the control retained by the licensor [is] sufficient under the circumstances to insure that the licensee's goods or services would meet the expectations created by the presence of the trademark." Restatement § 33 comment a (summarizing doctrine); *see also id.* at Reporter's Note comment c (collecting authority, which we need not set out). It isn't necessary to be more specific here, because plaintiffs did not retain any control—not via the license agreement, not via course of performance. A person who visited Eva's Bridal of Oak Lawn and then Eva's Bridal of Orland Park might not have found a common ambiance or means of doing business. And though the shops may have had many designers in common, this would not distinguish an "Eva's Bridal" shop from any other bridal shop; the trademark would not be doing any work if identical dresses could be purchased at Macy's or Nordstrom, and the "Eva's Bridal" shops were dissimilar except for some products that many retailers carried. Safeway could not license its marks to a corner grocery store, while retaining no control over inventory, appearance, or business methods, just because every grocery store is sure to have Coca-Cola and Wheaties on the shelf.

Trademark law requires that "decision making authority over quality remains with the owner of the mark." Restatement § 33 comment c. How much authority is enough can't be answered generally; the nature of the business, and customers' expectations, both matter. Ours is the extreme case: plaintiffs had, and exercised, no authority over the appearance and operations of defendants' business, or even over what inventory to carry or avoid. That is the paradigm of a naked license.

Questions

1. The court in *Eva's Bridal* intimated that the amount of quality control that is sufficient varies with the circumstances and consumer expectations. Would use of a mark on collateral merchandise, such as a mug bearing NEW YORK YANKEES logos, require less quality control than licensing MCDONALD'S for fast food services? *See* J. Thomas McCarthy 3 *McCarthy on Trademarks and Unfair Competition* § 18:55 (2016).

2. Barcamerica licensed its LEONARDO DA VINCI mark for wine to a vineyard. The agreement had no quality control provisions although Barcamerica's principal testified he occasionally informally tasted the wine and relied on the reputation of the vineyard's well-known winemaker (who subsequently died). Does this arrangement constitute naked licensing before the winemaker died? After he died? *See Barcamerica Int'l USA Trust v. Tyfield Importers, Inc.*, 289 F.3d 589 (9th Cir. 2002).

Freecycle Sunnyvale v. Freecycle Network, 626 F.3d 509 (9th Cir. 2010). The Freecycle Network ("TFN") is an organization devoted to facilitating the recycling of goods. The term "freecycling" combines the words "free" and "recycling" and refers to the practice of giving an unwanted item to a stranger so that it can continue to be used for its intended purpose, rather than be discarded. Freecycling is primarily a local activity conducted by means of internet groups, which are created by volunteers; most TFN member groups use Yahoo! Groups as a forum for members to coordinate their freecycling activities. TFN also maintains its own website, www.freecycle.org, which provides a directory of member groups as well as resources for volunteers to create new groups. The website also includes a section devoted to etiquette guidelines. Following a trademark licensing dispute, local member Freecycle Sunnyvale (FS) moved for summary judgment to declare that TFN had failed to control the quality of its members' use, and therefore no longer had enforceable rights in the mark.

> When deciding summary judgment on claims of naked licensing, we first determine whether the license contained an express contractual right to inspect and supervise the licensee's operations. *See Barcamerica* [*Int'l USA Trust v. Tyfield Importers, Inc.*, 289 F.3d 589] at 596 [(9th Cir. 2002)]. The absence of an agreement with provisions restricting or monitoring the quality of goods or services produced under a trademark supports a finding of naked licensing. [Citations.]
>
> TFN concedes that it did not have an express license agreement with FS regarding FS's use of the trademarks. Without an express license agreement, TFN necessarily lacks express contractual rights to inspect and supervise FS. However, TFN argues that the October 9, 2003 email, in which [TFN] advised [FS] that: "You can get the neutral logo from www.freecycle.org, just don't use it for commercial purposes...," reflects an implied license.
>
> Even assuming that [TFN]'s emailed admonition ... not to use the trademarks for commercial purposes constitutes an implied licensing agreement, it contained no express contractual right to inspect or supervise FS's services and no ability to terminate FS's license if FS used the trademarks for commercial purposes. *See Barcamerica*, 289 F.3d at 597 (determining that a license agreement lacking similar controls was insufficient). We therefore hold that, by TFN's own admission, there is no disputed issue of material fact as to whether TFN maintained an express contractual right to control quality.

The court next held that TFN had failed to maintain actual control over its members' activities.

> ... [W]e conclude that TFN's non-commercial requirement says nothing about the quality of the services provided by member groups and therefore

does not establish a control requiring member groups to maintain consistent quality. Thus, it is not an actual control in the trademark context. Third, because member groups may freely adopt and adapt TFN's listed rules of etiquette and because of the voluntary and amorphous nature of these rules, they cannot be considered an actual control. For example, FS modified the etiquette that was listed on TFN's website and TFN never required FS to conform to TFN's rules of etiquette. Fourth, TFN admits that a central premise of its "Freecycle Ethos" is local enforcement with local variation. By definition, this standard does not maintain consistency across member groups, so it is not an actual control.

Even assuming that TFN's asserted quality control standards actually relate to the quality of its member groups' services, they were not adequate quality controls because they were not enforced and were not effective in maintaining the consistency of the trademarks. Indeed, TFN's alleged quality controls fall short of the supervision and control deemed inadequate in other cases in which summary judgment on naked licensing has been granted to the licensee. [Citations.]

....

TFN contends that even if it did not exercise actual control, it justifiably relied on its member groups' quality control measures. Although "courts have upheld licensing agreements where the licensor is familiar with and relies upon the licensee's own efforts to control quality," *Barcamerica*, 289 F.3d at 596 (internal quotation marks and brackets omitted), we, like the other circuits that have considered this issue, have required that the licensor and licensee be involved in a "close working relationship" to establish adequate quality control in the absence of a formal agreement, [citations]. In *Barcamerica*, we cited four examples of "close working relationships" that would allow the licensor to rely on the licensee's own quality control: (1) a close working relationship for eight years; (2) a licensor who manufactured ninety percent of the components sold by a licensee and with whom it had a ten year association and knew of the licensee's expertise; (3) siblings who were former business partners and enjoyed a seventeen-year business relationship; and (4) a licensor with a close working relationship with the licensee's employees, and the pertinent agreement provided that the license would terminate if certain employees ceased to be affiliated with the licensee. 289 F.3d at 597.

Here, TFN and FS did not enjoy the type of close working relationship that would permit TFN to rely on FS's quality control measures.... Furthermore, we have held that, while reliance on a licensee's own quality control efforts is a relevant factor, such reliance is not alone sufficient to show that a naked license has not been granted. [Citations.] Because sole reliance on a licensee's own control quality efforts is not enough to overcome a finding of naked licensing without other indicia of control, and because TFN lacked a close working relationship with FS and failed to show any other indicia of actual control, we conclude that TFN could not rely solely on FS's own quality control efforts.

Questions

1. The Ninth Circuit in *Freecycle* noted that there was no formal license with Freecycle Sunnydale. If there had been a license with formal quality control but TFN exercised no actual control, would the result have been different? Should it?

2. Patsy's Italian Restaurant on W. 56th in Manhattan coexisted with Patsy's Pizzeria in E. Harlem for many decades until the late 1990s, when the Pizzeria licensed locations in Staten Island and in Syosset, Long Island. The ensuing litigation resulted in a jury finding of abandonment of the Pizzeria's mark through naked licensing of the two new locations. Should that finding result in a total abandonment of the Pizzeria's mark or only in the two new locations? *See Patsy's Italian Restaurant v. Banas*, 658 F.3d 254 (2d Cir. 2011).

3. Licensor offers Internet services. A two-page trademark licensing agreement specifies the following:

> Licensee shall employ reasonable commercial efforts to maintain the positive business value of the mark; it will limit mark use to that substantially as shown in the pending applications and with services substantially as recited; and, it shall cooperate with licensor to mitigate the confusion or likelihood of confusion between the parties' respective marks.

Does this language establish quality control sufficient to ward off charges of "naked licensing"? The license does not include a right to inspect or supervise the services rendered under the mark. *See Halo Mgmt. v. Interland*, 76 U.S.P.Q.2d 1199 (N.D. Cal. 2004).

Exxon Corp. has vigorously policed its "interlocking xx" mark against third party usage, including with respect to remote goods. As part of the settlement agreements it enters into with unauthorized users, Exxon permits the users to phase out their use of the mark by selling off their stock of goods bearing the "interlocking xx" mark. Exxon does not exercise quality control over the goods thus sold off. Oxxford Clothes, Inc. employs an interlocking xx design similar to Exxon's. When pursued by Exxon for dilution, Oxxford interposed the affirmative defense that the absence of quality control in Exxon's prior settlement agreements entails naked licensing by Exxon, and that Exxon has therefore forfeited its rights in the "interlocking xx" mark. After observing that it knew of no case arising under the Texas dilution statute at issue in which the defense of naked licensing had been discussed, the Fifth Circuit held that even if the settlement agreements constituted "licenses," Exxon's actions did not lead to an abandonment of its mark. The court declined to presume that licensing without quality control leads to a loss of trademark significance. Moreover, the court stressed, "We would find it wholly anomalous to presume a loss of trademark significance merely because Exxon, in the course of diligently protecting its mark, entered into agreements designed to preserve the distinctiveness and strength of that mark." *See Exxon v. Oxxford*, 109 F.3d 1070 (5th Cir.), *cert. denied*, 522 U.S. 915 (1997). *See also Fuel Clothing Co., Inc. v. Nike, Inc.*, 7 F. Supp. 3d 594 (D.S.C. 2014) (defendant's motion for summary judgment based on naked licensing defense denied as to three settlement-type agreements entered into by Fuel Clothing since "a reasonable jury could interpret the agreement to restrict [the other party's] use of the 'fuel' mark and thus prevent an infringing use"; such agreements would not be categorized as licenses even if they contain a phase-out period for certain uses).

Question

In *Dawn Donut Co. v. Hart's Food Stores, Inc.*, 267 F.2d 358 (2d Cir. 1959), *supra*, Chapter 3[F], in addition to addressing priority of trademark use, the court considered whether the registrant and senior user had properly policed its licensees. The court observed:

> Without the requirement of control, the right of a trademark owner to license his mark separately from the business in connection with which it has been used would create the danger that products bearing the same trademark might be of diverse qualities. If the licensor is not compelled to take some reasonable steps to prevent misuses of his trademark in the hands of others the public will be deprived of its most effective protection against misleading uses of a trademark. The public is hardly in a position to uncover deceptive uses of a trademark before they occur and will be at best slow to detect them after they happen. Thus, unless the licensor exercises supervision and control over the operations of its licensees the risk that the public will be unwittingly deceived will be increased and this is precisely what the Act is in part designed to prevent. Clearly, the only effective way to protect the public where a trademark is used by licensees is to place on the licensor the affirmative duty of policing in a reasonable manner the activities of his licensees.

Given the wide variety of products for which trademarks today are licensed, does this rationale still make sense?

Dzhunaydov v. Emerson Electric Co., 2016 U.S. Dist. LEXIS 34747 (E.D.N.Y Mar. 17, 2016). In order to be valid, a trademark license must include quality control. However, if a licensor is responsible for quality of a product, that fact can make it a target in a product liability suit. The plaintiff Dzhunaydov sued for injury to his hand caused by a table saw and included Emerson, the licensor of the trademark for the saw, as a defendant. The district court granted summary judgment to Emerson based on its limited role in quality control of the product.

> Under New York law, "[a] trademark licensor cannot be held liable for injuries caused by a defective product bearing its label where the licensor did not design, manufacture, sell, distribute or market the allegedly defective item." *D'Onofrio v. Boehlert,* 221 A.D.2d 929, 635 N.Y.S.2d 384, 385 (4th

Dep't 1995); *see also Bova v. Caterpillar, Inc.*, 305 A.D.2d 624, 761 N.Y.S.2d 85, 87 (2d Dep't 2003) ("Liability cannot be imposed on a party that was outside the chain of manufacturing, selling, or distributing a product."); *Auto. Ins. Co. of Hartford Connecticut v. Murray, Inc.*, 571 F. Supp. 2d 408, 422–23 (W.D.N.Y. 2008) ("Although the actual exercise of control is not required by [case law], the requisite 'capacity' of exercising control must exceed the mere existence of a licensing arrangement....")

....

Under the licensing agreement, Emerson retained limited authority over the Ridgid mark, akin to a right to approve for quality control. See Defs.' Mot. Sum. J. ("Home Depot ... agrees that [Emerson] reserves all rights of approval, such approvals not to be unreasonably withheld, which are necessary" to "protect and enhance the reputation and integrity" of the mark). There is no evidence, however, that Emerson exercised control over the design of the saw. In fact, the evidence is to the contrary.

....

... [A] Home Depot representative attested to Emerson's limited role as a trademark licensor. "[W]ith respect to the subject [table saw], Emerson was merely the licensor[] of the 'Ridgid' trademark to Home Depot.... Emerson did not design, manufacture, assemble, test and/or certify the subject table saw, nor did Emerson exercise any significant role in the table saw's final quality or the warnings that accompanied it."

Nonetheless, Dzuhnaydov argues that the licensing agreement demonstrates sufficient control by Emerson to warrant liability under *Automobile Insurance Company of Hartford v. Murray, Inc.*, 571 F. Supp. 2d 408 (W.D.N.Y. 2008). However, in *Murray*, unlike here, the trademark licensor exercised its authority to control and inspect the products bearing its mark, performed quality control visits, and approved the specifications for the product at issue. Even if the present licensing agreement authorized Emerson to exercise such authority, there is no evidence that Emerson actually exercised such authority. *See id.* ("[T]he requisite 'capacity' of exercising control must exceed the mere existence of a licensing agreement.").

Accordingly, the defendants' motion for summary judgment is granted as to all claims against Emerson.

Question

Does a trademark licensor face a potential dilemma over exercising too much or too little quality control?

Trademark Licensing Provisions

Reproduced below are one complete trademark licensing agreement and quality-control clauses from another license agreement. Study these contracts, and think about the kinds of situations in which a licensor would wish to exercise the most stringent quality control, and those in which a more summary agreement may suffice. Are any of these agreements or provisions too summary?

Sample Trademark Licensing Agreement*

TRADEMARK LICENSE

This will confirm our understanding as follows:

1. We hereby grant to you upon the terms and conditions of this agreement a non-exclusive license to use the trade name "________________" (hereinafter referred to as the "Licensed Name") as part of the trade and corporate name "________________" and a non-exclusive license to use the trademark "________________" (hereinafter referred to as the "Licensed Mark").

2. The Licensed Name and the Licensed Mark shall be used by you only on and in connection with such business operations and goods as shall be approved by us.

3. You agree to maintain such quality standards as shall be prescribed by us in the conduct of the business operations with which the Licensed Name is used and for the goods on which the Licensed Mark is used.

4. You agree that you will display the Licensed Name and the Licensed Mark only in such form or manner as shall be specifically approved by us. You also shall cause to appear on all materials on or in connection with which the Licensed Name or Licensed Mark is used, such legends, markings and notices as we may request in order to give appropriate notice of any trademark, trade name or other rights therein or pertaining thereto.

5. We shall have the right to inspect your business operations conducted under the Licensed Name and the goods on which the Licensed Mark is used in order to assure ourselves that the provisions of this agreement are being observed.

6. You confirm our ownership of the Licensed Name and the Licensed Mark, and you agree that all use by you of the Licensed Name and the Licensed Mark shall inure to our benefit.

7. This agreement supersedes all prior agreements between us relating to the subject-matter hereof and shall remain in effect until terminated as provided herein. If you shall violate or fail to perform any of your obligations hereunder, we shall have the right to give written notice of such default to you, and this license shall terminate thirty (30) days after such notice unless you shall have completely remedied the default within the thirty-day period. In addition, if we should at any time cease to own, directly or indirectly, at least fifty percent (50%) of your outstanding capital stock this agreement shall terminate automatically, and promptly upon written notice from us, you shall change your corporate name so as to eliminate the Licensed Name therefrom, and shall cease all use of the Licensed Name and Licensed Mark.

* The financial provisions and terms have been removed from the sample agreement.

8. All rights in the Licensed Name and the Licensed Mark other than those specifically granted herein are reserved by us for our own use and benefit. Upon the termination of this agreement for any reason whatsoever, all rights in the Licensed Name and the Licensed Mark shall automatically revert to us. You shall at any time execute any documents reasonably required by us to confirm our ownership of all such rights.

Please signify your assent by signing at the indicated place below.

Very truly yours,

By ____________________

Accepted and Agreed to:

By ____________________

Sample Quality Control Clauses

3. *Quality Control*

3.1 The Licensed Products and all tags, labels, cartons, containers, wrappings and other materials in which or with which Licensed Products are packaged (collectively, "Packaging Materials") shall be of high standards and of such style, appearance, distinctiveness and quality as to protect and enhance the prestige of Licensor and of the Trademark and the goodwill pertaining thereto. The Licensed Products will be manufactured, packaged, sold, advertised and distributed in accordance with all applicable national and local laws and regulations. The policy of sale, marketing and distribution by Licensee shall be of high standards so that the same shall in no manner reflect adversely upon the good name of Licensor or the Trademark. Licensee acknowledges that the control by Licensor over the nature and quality of all Licensed Products and all Packaging Materials are essential elements of the license herein granted. Accordingly, all aspects of the use of the Trademark and the manufacture, sale, marketing and distribution of Licensed Products and Packaging Materials shall be subject to the prior written approval of Licensor, it being specifically understood and agreed that Licensor's approval may be based solely on Licensor's subjective standards.

3.2 In furtherance of the purpose and intent expressed in Paragraph 3.1, prior to the production of any Licensed Product or Packaging Materials, Licensee shall submit to Licensor, during regular business hours, all preliminary and final designs, specifications, fabrics and color details relating thereto and, in the case of each finished Licensed Product or Packaging Material, a sample, for approval with such completed forms as Licensor may from time to time require. In order to avoid piecemeal submittals and provide Licensor, among other things, with the opportunity to review sample submittals in the context of an entire line, Licensee agrees that initial sample submittals shall consist of not less than ninety (90%) percent of the Licensed Products representing each particular line. Licensee shall submit to Licensor, for its approval, samples of Licensed Products representing each particular line. Licensee shall submit to Licensor, for its approval, samples of Licensed Products from all production runs from every production source prior to the first production run. Thereafter upon request made by Licensor, Licensee shall furnish Licensor with current production samples of the Licensed Products conforming to the samples approved by Licensor. Licensee shall conduct its normal tests and verification procedures on samples of each Licensed Product prior to the sale thereof to assure that the quality thereof is at least equal to the quality required hereunder.

3.3 Promptly following inspection by Licensor of submittals made by Licensee pursuant to Paragraph 3.2, Licensor shall advise Licensee of its approval, or shall advise Licensee of its reasons for denial of approval; provided, however, that if Licensor fails to disapprove of any item submitted to it within two (2) weeks after the receipt thereof (provided that with respect to the submission of samples of finished Licensed Products, Licensor is in receipt of not less than ninety (90%) percent of a particular line), Licensor shall be deemed to have approved such item. Any disapproved sample shall not be manufactured by or for Licensee. Each Licensed Product must be approved for each season, regardless of whether it was approved for a prior season. For purposes of this provision, a season shall be deemed to be no more than one six-month shipping period.

3.4 Licensee shall provide Licensor with the addresses of all facilities, including third-party manufacturers, at which the Licensed Products and Packaging Materials are manufactured and/or distributed by or for Licensee. Licensor shall have the right, during regular business hours, upon reasonable notice, to inspect all such facilities controlled by Licensee and Licensee shall use its best efforts to obtain permission for Licensor to inspect all third-party facilities. Inspections may include any reasonable actions necessary to assure Licensor that the Licensed Products and Packaging Materials are being manufactured consistent with approved standards.

3.5 Licensee warrants that the Licensed Products and Packaging Materials manufactured and sold shall be substantially similar to the samples submitted to and approved by Licensor. If at any time Licensor is of the opinion that Licensee is not properly using the Trademark on Licensed Products or Packaging Materials, or that the standard of quality of any Licensed Product or Packaging Material does not conform to the standards approved by Licensor, Licensor may give Licensee notice to this effect, identifying in such notice the situation to which it objects. Upon receipt of such notice, Licensee shall immediately and forthwith cease its sale and distribution of such items and request and direct its customers to cease the sale and distribution of such items. Licensor and Licensee shall then make a good faith effort to promptly resolve the objections made by Licensor. Notice by Licensor to Licensee of its objection to or disapproval of Licensed Products or Packaging Materials shall not relieve Licensee from its obligation to pay royalties on such Licensed Products for sales made by Licensee to the date of disapproval or thereafter.

4. *Use of Trademark*

4.1 Licensee shall not use the Trademark, in any manner whatsoever (including, without limitation, for advertising, promotional and publicity proposes, but excluding normal business correspondence), without obtaining the prior approval of Licensor. Such approval will be deemed given if such use is in strict conformity with the trademark specifications referred to in Paragraph 4.2 below: provided, however, that such approval shall apply only to the manner in which the Trademark is used and shall not be construed as approval of any Licensed Product, Packaging Material, advertisement, promotion or publicity campaign, or that the approved material complies with any applicable laws.

4.2 Licensor shall furnish or cause to be furnished to Licensee from time to time, trademark specifications containing samples of its approved standard formats and modes of use of the Trademark then in force, including, without limitation, styles, scripts, colors and size specifications (the "TM Specifications"). Licensor may, in its sole discretion, revise the TM Specifications from time to time during the term of this Agreement and shall furnish Licensee with a copy of any such revision. Licensee shall comply with all such revisions. Licensor's failure to furnish Licensee the TM Specifications shall not excuse Licensee from obtaining Licensor's prior approval of use of the Trademark.

4.3 Licensee shall affix or apply to all Licensed Products, tags or labels bearing or using the Trademark and agrees that such use of the Trademark shall be strictly in conformity with the TM Specifications or as otherwise set forth in any approval of Licensor then in effect. No Licensed Products shall be sold or otherwise distributed under any trademark other than the Trademark, unless otherwise permitted herein. All Licensed Products shall contain Licensee's identifying mark so that the origin of the Licensed Products can be determined.

4.4 Licensee shall cause to appear on or within each Licensed Product, and in all Packaging Materials and advertising using the Trademark, all appropriate or necessary trademark legends, markings and notices as may be required by law or regulation in the Territory, and all in the name of Licensor as set forth in any notice received from Licensor.

4.5 Licensee shall not use any name or names other than the Trademark in any labeling, packaging or advertising utilized by Licensee in connection with Licensed Products, without Licensor's prior approval, except that Licensee shall be permitted to use its name on labels and hang tags used on the Licensed Products in a non-prominent manner which has been approved in advance by Licensor.

4.6 Licensee shall use its best efforts to supervise the use of the Trademark by Licensee's customers to ensure that its customers advertise, display, and promote the Licensed Products in a manner consistent with the terms and conditions of this Agreement.

5. *Advertising and Promotion*

5.1 With the view towards protecting the prestige of the Trademark and Licensor, all advertising materials to be used by Licensee in connection with the Licensed Products, including Licensee's trade releases announcing the introduction of Licensed Products bearing the Trademark and any other trade release concerning the Licensed Products, must be provided, at Licensee's cost and expense, by The Ad Group, Inc. (an affiliate of Licensor) or such other advertising agency as Licensor may designate from time to time, provided, however, that the rates charged by said agency are competitive. Consistent with the intent of the immediately preceding provision, Licensee shall not retain any public relations firm in connection with the Licensed Products, without Licensor's prior approval, which approval shall not be unreasonably withheld. The intended use by Licensee of any advertising, promotional or publicity materials or campaigns (including, without limitation, placement and scheduling thereof) must be approved in advance by Licensor.

Chapter 6

Infringement

15 U.S.C. § 1114 [Lanham Act § 32(1)]

Any person who shall, without the consent of the registrant—

(a) use in commerce any reproduction, counterfeit, copy, or colorable imitation of a registered mark in connection with the sale, offering for sale, distribution, or advertising of any goods or services on or in connection with which such use is likely to cause confusion, or to cause mistake, or to deceive ... shall be liable in a civil action by the registrant for the remedies hereinafter provided....

In Chapter 6, we look at infringement of registered trademarks under section 32 of the Lanham Act. In earlier chapters, we have focused on what trademarks receive legal protection. Here, we examine the scope of that protection, and what uses of a registered mark or a designation similar to a registered mark count as trademark infringement. (We postpone until Chapter 7 consideration of infringement of unregistered trademarks, which is actionable under section 43(a).)

A. Defendant's Use in Commerce

"... use in commerce any reproduction, counterfeit, copy, or colorable imitation of a registered mark in connection with the sale, offering for sale, distribution, or advertising of any goods or services...."

Naked Cowboy v. CBS

844 F. Supp. 2d 510 (S.D.N.Y. 2010)

[New York's "Naked Cowboy" sued CBS over an episode of *The Bold and the Beautiful* that featured a character dressed in briefs, a cowboy hat and cowboy boots, singing and playing a guitar for several seconds. CBS also posted a clip of the scene on YouTube, and purchased the adwords "naked cowboy" from YouTube in connection with the posting of the clip. Plaintiff claimed that the broadcast, YouTube posting, and adword purchase violated his registered NAKED COWBOY service mark. The court granted CBS's motion to dismiss the complaint.]

Plaintiff is an "enormously successful and popular" street performer who "dresses as a cowboy—only a virtually Naked one." When performing, he wears only briefs, cowboy boots, a cowboy hat, and a guitar. The words "Naked Cowboy" are displayed across the back of his briefs, on his hat, and on his guitar. The word "Tips" or the symbol "$" is painted on his boots. Wearing this costume, Plaintiff "meet[s] and greet[s] the public in New York City's Times Square," and has been doing so since 1997. Plaintiff "can be seen on any given day in Times Square." Plaintiff has also appeared throughout the country and in movies, radio, magazines, and newspapers. Plaintiff has already made roughly fifteen television appearances as himself. According to the New York State tourism department, Plaintiff is "more recognizable than The Statue of Liberty."

Plaintiff registered the word mark "Naked Cowboy" on April 9, 2002, and reregistered the same mark on May 25, 2010. Plaintiff has obtained "numerous corporate sponsorships" and sells licensed merchandise, "includ[ing] T-Shirts, Postcards, Keychains, Shot Glasses, Music CDs, Pencils, Photos and more" throughout New York City. Plaintiff also has distribution and endorsement agreements with New York Popular & Robin Ruth and with Blue Island Shellfish Farms.

CBS is the network that broadcasts "The Bold and the Beautiful," a thirty-minute daytime television series. Bell-Phillip is the producer of the television program. Bell-Phillip's well-known "B&B" logo is displayed during the opening credits of the show, and "Bell-Phillip Television Productions, Inc." appears in large bold letters at the end of each episode. "CBS Television City" and the famous CBS "Eye" logo are also displayed during the closing credits.

The Complaint arises from the November 1, 2010, episode of "The Bold and the Beautiful" (the "Episode"). The Episode featured a character named Oliver who, for several seconds, appeared only in his briefs, cowboy boots, and a cowboy hat, while singing and playing the guitar. The words "Naked Cowboy" did not appear anywhere during the Episode nor were they spoken by any of the characters. "Naked Cowboy" was not written on Oliver's underwear, his hat or his guitar, and his boots did not display the words "Tips" or "$".

....

An audience of roughly 3,049,000 people viewed the original airing of the Episode. During both the original airing of the Episode, and the November 5 recap episode, Defendants profited from paid commercial advertisements.

CBS posted a clip of the Episode on CBS's YouTube channel.... CBS titled its YouTube clip "The Bold and the Beautiful—Naked Cowboy," and "began selling advertising with that video immediately." The CBS and CBS "Eye" logos were displayed prominently on CBS's YouTube page. The caption "Oliver has a surprise for Amber" appeared beneath the clip. "CBS.com" and CBS's "Eye" logo appear at the end of the clip.

YouTube pages often include "tags" which are words that describe a particular video and help viewers find the content for which they are searching. Roughly 30 tags were listed beneath the clip on the Clarence B&B Update page, including the words "naked" and "cowboy." "Defendants also purchased adword advertising from youtube for the specific search term 'naked cowboy,' which gave [the clips] top page visibility as a 'Featured Video' on youtube." If a user typed the search term "naked cowboy" into the YouTube search engine, "the page would repeatedly refresh with the Defendants' videos" among the top search results.

The Complaint asserts nine causes of action arising from Defendants' alleged use of the Naked Cowboy costume, as well as the use of the words "naked," "cowboy," and "Naked Cowboy" in connection with the YouTube clips of the Episode and the Clarence B&B Update. Defendants have moved to dismiss the Complaint under Federal Rule 12(b)(6) for failure to state a claim on which relief may be granted.

....

A. Trademark Infringement Claim

The Lanham Act prohibits the "use in commerce [of] any reproduction, counterfeit, copy, or colorable imitation of a registered mark in connection with the sale, offering for sale, distribution, or advertising of any goods or services on or in connection with which such use is likely to cause confusion, or to cause mistake, or to deceive." 15 U.S.C. § 1114(1)(a). To prevail on a trademark infringement claim, Plaintiff must establish that: (1) it has a valid registered mark; and that (2) Defendants used the mark, (3) in commerce, (4) in connection with the sale or advertising of goods or services, and (5) without Plaintiff's consent. *1-800 Contacts, Inc. v. WhenU.com, Inc.*, 414 F.3d 400, 406–07 (2d Cir. 2005). In addition, Plaintiff must allege facts sufficient to establish that Defendants' use of the registered mark "is likely to cause confusion ... as to the affiliation, connection, or association of [Defendants] with [Plaintiff], or as to the origin, sponsorship, or approval of [Defendants'] goods, services, or commercial activities by [Plaintiff]." *Id.* at 407.

"Naked cowboy" is a registered mark and Plaintiff is thus afforded trademark rights in the phrase. However, there could have been no infringement of those rights if Defendants did not make use of the word mark in commerce. A mark is used in commerce for trademark infringement purposes when (1) "it is placed in any manner on the goods ... or the displays associated therewith or on the tags or labels affixed thereto, or if the nature of the goods makes such placement impracticable, then on documents associated with the goods or their sale," and (2) "the goods are sold or transported in commerce[.]" 15 U.S.C. § 1127. None of the contents of the Episode could have violated Plaintiff s trademark rights because the word mark "Naked Cowboy" does not appear anywhere in it. Similarly, inclusion of "naked" and "cowboy" as separate tags associated with the YouTube video clips is not "use" of Plaintiff's word mark "Naked Cowboy."

The purchase from YouTube of adword advertising for the term "naked cowboy" likewise does not constitute "use in commerce" because Defendants did not "place [the 'naked cowboy' term] on any goods or containers or displays or associated documents, nor do they use them in any way to indicate source or sponsorship." *Merck & Co., Inc. v. Mediplan Health Consulting, Inc.*, 425 F. Supp. 2d 402, 415 (S.D.N.Y. 2006). The only use of Plaintiff's registered word mark in commerce—and therefore the only potential source of trademark infringement—is CBS's use of the term "Naked Cowboy" in the title of its YouTube video clip.

[The court concluded that the use of the Naked Cowboy term in the YouTube clip, while a use in commerce, was not actionable because it came within an exception in section 33(b)(4) of the statute permitting "use, otherwise than as a mark, ... which is descriptive of and used fairly and in good faith only to describe" the user's product. We will explore section 33(b)(4) *infra* in Chapter 8[A][2][b].]

Born to Rock Design, Inc. v. CafePress.com, Inc., 104 U.S.P.Q.2d 1538 (S.D.N.Y. 2012). Born to Rock Design, Inc., owns two trademark registrations for the phrase BORN TO ROCK. It uses the mark in connection with the sale of electric guitars, guitar picks, and T-shirts. Born to Rock sued CafePress for infringing its registered marks by selling user-designed T-shirts and other merchandise bearing the phrase "Born to Rock." Following discovery, CafePress moved for summary judgment, arguing that BTR had failed to show that CafePress used BTR's mark in commerce. The court denied the motion:

> Defendant Cafepress Inc.... ("CafePress") operates a virtual online marketplace that allows its users to set up virtual "shops." CafePress users upload graphic designs to the CafePress.com website; by doing so, the users grant CafePress a license to "design, produce, market and sell" products bearing the users' designs.
>
> Once the design is uploaded, the website causes it to appear on images of merchandise, such as (otherwise blank) T-shirts, coffee mugs, or key chains. Visitors to the CafePress.com website can browse designs, and if they find a design they like, they can select the kind of merchandise they would like printed with the design. Once a visitor places an order, CafePress prints the design on the selected merchandise and ships it to the customer. CafePress collects the payment, a portion of which is remitted to the CafePress.com user who created and uploaded the design.... The parties sometimes refer to CafePress' business as a "print-on-demand service."
>
> Plaintiff Born to Rock Design Incorporated ("BTR") owns trademarks that it says CafePress infringes through its print-on-demand service. In particular, BTR obtained a trademark for the words BORN TO ROCK, Reg. No. 1,846,642 in Class 15 for electric guitars, in 1994....
>
> ....
>
> BTR alleges that CafePress infringes its trademarks by selling merchandise bearing designs uploaded to the CafePress.com website that incorporate BTR's marks.
>
> Since at least 2003, CafePress.com users have uploaded designs to the website that use the phrase "Born to Rock," either alone or in conjunction with other words or images....
>
> ....
>
> B. Trademark infringement

....

1. *BTR's prima facie case*

CafePress first argues that it is entitled to summary judgment because BTR has failed to make out its *prima facie* case for trademark infringement. CafePress is incorrect.

To prevail on a trademark infringement claim, BTR must establish the following: (1) that it has a valid mark that is entitled to protection under the Lanham Act; and that (2) CafePress used the mark, (3) in commerce, (4) in connection with the sale or advertising of goods or services, (5) without BTR's consent. *1-800 Contacts. Inc. v. WhenU.Com, Inc.*, 414 F.3d 400, 406–407 (2d Cir. 2005) (citing 15 U.S.C. § 1114(1)(a)) (other citations omitted).

In addition to these elements, BTR must show that CafePress' use of the mark "is likely to cause confusion ... as to the affiliation, connection, or association of [CafePress] with [BTR], or as to the origin, sponsorship, or approval of [CafePress'] goods, services, or commercial activities by [BTR]." [Citations.]

CafePress concedes for the purpose of its motion that a reasonable jury could find in BTR's favor on every element of its *prima facie* case, except one. Of particular importance, CafePress assumes that a jury could find that BTR has valid trademarks that are entitled to protection; and CafePress declines to argue that BTR cannot show a likelihood of confusion.

CafePress argues that, nevertheless, it is entitled to summary judgment because BTR has not presented evidence from which a jury could conclude that CafePress "used" BTR's mark "in commerce." CafePress argues that it does not use the words "Born to Rock" in commerce when it displays the words on its website, for instance in connection with its search function. When a visitor to the website types "Born to Rock" into CafePress' search function, a page will appear, displaying the phrase in connection with identifying designs and merchandise. The page may show pictures of designs that incorporate "Born to Rock," and links that read "Born to Rock gifts" or "Born to Rock T-shirts." CafePress argues that under recent caselaw addressing the issue of "use in commerce," CafePress' presentation of the words "Born to Rock" in these circumstances does not meet the threshold use in commerce requirement. *See 1-800 Contacts*, 414 F.3d at 407; *Rescuecom Corp. v. Google Inc.*, 562 F.3d 123 (2d Cir. 2009).

CafePress is being facetious: it is undisputed that it imprints the designs on merchandise and ships that merchandise to customers. That activity constitutes "use in commerce."

The Lanham Act defines "use in commerce," in relevant part, as follows:

> For purposes of this Chapter, a mark shall be deemed to be in use in commerce (1) on goods when—

(A) it is placed in any manner on the goods or their containers or the displays associated therewith or on the tags or labels affixed thereto, or if the nature of the goods makes such placement impracticable, then on documents associated with the goods or their sale, and

(B) the goods are sold or transported in commerce, and

(2) on services when it is used or displayed in the sale or advertising of services and the services are rendered in commerce ...

Under the foregoing definition, "use in commerce ... on goods" is readily apparent in CafePress' print-on-demand business. CafePress "uses" the words "Born to Rock" "in commerce" when it "place[s]" the words "on the goods," such as T-shirts, that CafePress imprints with its users' designs. "The goods are sold and transported in commerce" whenever the imprinted merchandise is sold and shipped to CafePress' online customers. As noted, it is undisputed on this motion that CafePress sells merchandise bearing the phrase "Born to Rock."

Thus, a jury could find this element of BTR's *prima facie* case satisfied regardless of whether CafePress also "used" the BORN TO ROCK mark when it displayed that phrase elsewhere on its website (or in its source code, or in its "URL" or "metatags") in response to search results within its website. The sort of "use" discussed in the search provider context is simply irrelevant in cases, like this one, where the alleged infringer physically places the mark on goods that it sells to its customers.

This evidence of "use in commerce," in combination with the concessions identified above, makes out BTR's *prima facie* case of trademark infringement. Thus, CafePress' motion for summary judgment on the infringement claims must be denied....

1-800 Contacts, Inc. v. Lens.com, Inc., 755 F. Supp. 2d 1151 (D. Utah 2010). This controversy arose out of Google's "AdWords" program. Google sells terms, both generic words and trademarks, as "key words" to trigger the appearance of "sponsored links" to an advertiser's website. Under the AdWords program, a seller of contact lenses might purchase the opportunity to have their links to their websites appear when searchers entered generic words such as "contact lenses" into search engines. Google also sold the opportunity to generate links to the advertiser's website when a consumer entered the advertiser's own, or a competitor's, trademark as the search term. 1-800 Contacts filed suit against its competitor, Lens.com, alleging that its Lens.com's purchase of "1800Contacts" as an ad-generating keyword infringed 1-800's trademark; Lens.com argued that purchasing an ad word was not an actionable use in commerce. The court disagreed:

B. Use in Commerce

1. Use of the Mark as a Keyword

The "use" element of trademark infringement requires proof that Defendant used Plaintiff's service mark or a confusingly similar mark in commerce.

Under the Lanham Act, a service mark is "deemed to be [a] use in commerce ... when it is used or displayed in the sale or advertising of services and the services are rendered in commerce." This case is unusual because it presents two different types of uses: one that is invisible to consumers and another that is visible. The purchase and use of keywords is invisible to consumers. Of the courts that have addressed the issue, a split exists "on the issue of whether the purchase ... of keywords that trigger advertising constitutes the type of 'use' contemplated by the Lanham Act." Because a keyword is "invisible to potential consumers," and merely operates as a "pure machine-linking function," some courts have concluded that it is not a use in commerce. In contrast, other courts have concluded that use of another's mark "to trigger internet advertisements for itself," is a use in commerce. The statutory language supports this latter conclusion.

The Lanham Act does not require use *and* display of another's mark for it to constitute "use in commerce." Rather, "use in commerce" occurs when a mark is "used *or* displayed in the sale or advertising of services and the services are rendered in commerce." Here, Plaintiff's service mark was used to trigger a sponsored link for purposes of advertising and selling the services of Defendant. In other words, Plaintiff's mark was used to promote Defendant's services and to provide a consumer with a link to a website where it could make a purchase from Defendant. The court concludes such actions constitute a "use in commerce" under the Lanham Act.

Clear evidence has been presented that certain Lens.com affiliates purchased Plaintiff's service mark as a keyword. Thus, the "use" requirement has been satisfied with respect to the identified Lens.com affiliates. Plaintiff has not presented evidence, however, that Defendant itself purchased Plaintiff's service mark as a keyword. Rather, Defendant purchased similar variations or misspellings of the mark, such as "1 800 contact lenses" and "800comtacts.com." Because infringement can occur if the mark one uses is confusingly similar to another's protected mark, if Plaintiff establishes that Defendant's use of these variations and misspellings likely would result in consumer confusion, Defendant itself may be liable under the Lanham Act for using these variations. The court therefore addresses this issue below.

2. Use of the Mark in Advertisements

The second use at issue is the use of Plaintiff's mark, or a similar variation, by a Lens.com affiliate in Internet advertisements. Approximately 65,000 impressions were generated that used Plaintiff's mark or a similar variation of it in the advertisement. Neither party disputes that such "use" falls under the Lanham Act.

On appeal, the Court of Appeals for the 10th Circuit affirmed in part and reversed in part on other grounds, assuming without deciding that the purchase of a keyword could satisfy the use in commerce requirement. *1-800 Contacts, Inc. v. Lens.com, Inc.*, 722 F.3d 1229, 1242 (10th Cir. 2013).

Questions

1. If the Naked Cowboy had registered his costume as a trade dress service mark for entertainment services, would CBS's display of the clip on YouTube have been a "use in commerce"?

2. Can the *Naked Cowboy* court's conclusion that CBS's purchase of AdWord advertising for the phrase "naked cowboy" was not a use in commerce be reconciled with the *1-800 Contacts* court's holding that Lens.com's purchase of 1-800CONTACTS to trigger advertising was a use in commerce?

3. KST manufactures rigid endoscopes, which it sells under the KARL STORZ trademark. The KARL STORZ mark is etched on each endoscope on the housing between the eyepiece and the shaft. Endoscopes cost thousands of dollars, so when they break, doctors and hospitals prefer to repair them rather than replace them. Surgi-Tech repairs and refurbishes medical equipment, including KSI endoscopes. KSI sues Surgi-Tech for trademark infringement, arguing that when Surgi-Tech purports to repair or refurbish a Karl Storz endoscope, it replaces all of the functional parts, retaining only the housing that bears KSI's trademark. KSI argues that replacing all of the essential parts but retaining the KSI housing and trademarks infringes its marks under section 32. Surgi-tech argues that repairing a broken product is not a "use in commerce" within the meaning of the Lanham Act. How should the court rule? *See Karl Storz Endoscopy-America Inc. v. Surgical Technologies, Inc.*, 285 F.3d 848 (9th Cir. 2002).

Rescuecom Corp. v. Google, Inc., 562 F.3d 123 (2d Cir. 2009). If the customers of a keyword-based advertising service use third party trademarks in commerce when they purchase those marks as triggers for advertisements to sell their products, is the keyword-based advertising service itself using the mark in commerce? What if the search engine has a tool to assist advertisers in selecting keywords, and recommends the purchase of trademarks? Google introduced a keyword tool to help its advertisers select keywords. Advertisers type words or phrases into a dialog box, and the tool returns a list of possible keywords, along with information about how many searches are performed using those words and how competitive the bidding is to purchase those words as ad triggers. The district court dismissed Rescuecom's complaint, holding that Google's sales of third party trademarks to trigger the purchaser's advertisements was not a use of those marks in commerce. The Second Circuit reversed:

> Many of Rescuecom's competitors advertise on the Internet. Through its Keyword Suggestion Tool, Google has recommended the Rescuecom trademark to Rescuecom's competitors as a search term to be purchased. Rescuecom's competitors, some responding to Google's recommendation, have purchased Rescuecom's trademark as a keyword in Google's AdWords program, so that whenever a user launches a search for the term "Rescuecom,"

seeking to be connected to Rescuecom's website, the competitors' advertisement and link will appear on the searcher's screen. This practice allegedly allows Rescuecom's competitors to deceive and divert users searching for Rescuecom's website. According to Rescuecom's allegations, when a Google user launches a search for the term "Rescuecom" because the searcher wishes to purchase Rescuecom's services, links to websites of its competitors will appear on the searcher's screen in a manner likely to cause the searcher to believe mistakenly that a competitor's advertisement (and website link) is sponsored by, endorsed by, approved by, or affiliated with Rescuecom.

....

... The allegations of Rescuecom's complaint adequately plead a use in commerce.

....

[W]hat Google is recommending and selling to its advertisers is Rescuecom's trademark.... Google displays, offers, and sells Rescuecom's mark to Google's advertising customers when selling its advertising services. In addition, Google encourages the purchase of Rescuecom's mark through its Keyword Suggestion Tool. Google's utilization of Rescuecom's mark fits literally within the terms specified by 15 U.S.C. § 1127. According to the Complaint, Google uses and sells Rescuecom's mark "in the sale ... of [Google's advertising] services ... rendered in commerce." § 1127.

....

Google, supported by amici, argues that ... the inclusion of a trademark in an internal computer directory cannot constitute trademark use.... Google's recommendation and sale of Rescuecom's mark to its advertising customers are not internal uses.... [A]n alleged infringer's use of a trademark in an internal software program [cannot] insulate[] the alleged infringer from a charge of infringement, no matter how likely the use is to cause confusion in the marketplace. If we were to adopt Google and its amici's argument, the operators of search engines would be free to use trademarks in ways designed to deceive and cause consumer confusion. This is surely neither within the intention nor the letter of the Lanham Act.

Google and its amici contend further that its use of the Rescuecom trademark is no different from that of a retail vendor who uses "product placement" to allow one vender to benefit from a competitors' name recognition. An example of product placement occurs when a store-brand generic product is placed next to a trademarked product to induce a customer who specifically sought out the trademarked product to consider the typically less expensive, generic brand as an alternative. [Citation.] Google's argument misses the point. From the fact that proper, non-deceptive product placement does not result in liability under the Lanham Act, it does not follow that the label "product placement" is a magic shield against liability, so that even a deceptive plan of product placement designed to confuse consumers would similarly escape liability. It is not by reason of absence of a use of a mark in commerce that benign product placement escapes liability; it escapes liability because it is a benign practice which does not cause a likelihood of consumer confusion. In contrast, if a retail seller were to be paid by an off-brand purveyor to arrange product display and delivery in such a way that customers seeking to purchase a famous brand would receive the off-brand, believing they had gotten the brand they were seeking, we see no reason to believe the practice would escape liability merely because it could claim the mantle of "product placement." The practices attributed to Google by the Complaint, which at this stage we must accept as true, are significantly different from benign product placement that does not violate the Act.

Questions

1. How much was the court influenced by the allegation that Google's keyword tool suggested purchase of Rescuecom's mark as an advertising trigger to Rescuecom's competitors? If Google were to eliminate its keyword suggestion tool, would the court's analysis deem the sale and display of marks to trigger advertising a use in commerce?

2. Is "product placement," such as a competitor's buying shelf space next to a specific brand of product (for example, shelving Pepsi Cola, or house brand cola, next to Coca Cola), a "use in commerce"? Is it a "use in commerce" for a sales representative to tell a consumer that its detergent is very similar to Tide, but cheaper? Is it "use in commerce" for Burger King to place an advertisement on a billboard abutting a McDonald's? If not, why not? Would your answers be different if the activities involving the trademarks occurred via the Internet? Why or why not?

3. Is it "use in commerce" for a character in a movie to wear (without the trademark owner's authorization) a sweatshirt sporting a brand name or logo?

4. Recall *Blue Bell v. Farah*, 508 F.2d 1260 (5th Cir. 1975), *supra* Chapter 3[D]. If Blue Bell had purchased "Time Out" as a keyword in a search engine ad for its own line of slacks, would that have sufficed to establish its ownership of the mark even if it had not yet produced or shipped the clothing bearing the mark? Would it make any difference if the search engine selling the keywords sold exclusive trigger rights, so that no other advertiser could acquire "Time Out" as a keyword?

5. Jordan Kahn formed a successful party band that performed under the name "Downtown Fever." Emerald City, a Texas band management business, recruited Kahn to move to Texas, join its company, and oversee its party bands. At Emerald City, Kahn formed a new "Downtown Fever" band, and managed it and the company's other bands. As part of those efforts, Kahn acted as the administrator of Facebook pages and social media accounts for "Downtown Fever" and the other bands. Five years after joining the company, Kahn resigned. After leaving the company, Kahn deactivated the "Downtown Fever" Facebook page and social media accounts, and changed the passwords so that Emerald City would be unable to access them. Emerald City claims to be the owner of the DOWNTOWN FEVER service mark. It demanded

that Kahn surrender the Facebook and social media accounts. Kahn refused. Emerald City has sued Kahn for infringement of the DOWNTOWN FEVER mark. Kahn argues that neither deactivating a Facebook account nor blocking Emerald City's access to it should be deemed a "use in commerce" within the meaning of the Lanham Act. How should the court rule? *See Emerald City Management LLC v. Kahn*, 641 Fed. Appx. 410 (5th Cir. 2016).

Note: Use in Commerce and the Debate over "Trademark Use"

As the search engine advertising cases worked their way through the courts, trademark scholars disagreed about whether the purchase or sale of trademarks as advertising triggers should count as "use in commerce ... in connection with the sale, offering for sale, distribution, or advertising of any goods or services." Professors Stacey Dogan, Mark Lemley, Margreth Barrett, and Mark McKenna, among others, argued that Section 32 required that defendants have made "trademark use" of a mark—or used the mark to identify the source of defendants' goods or services. *See, e.g.*, Margreth Barrett, *Finding Trademark Use: The Historical Foundation for Limiting Liability to Uses "in the Manner of a Mark,"* 43 Wake Forest L. Rev. (2008); Stacey L. Dogan, *Beyond Trademark Use*, 8 J. Telecomm. & High Tech. L. (2010); Stacey L. Dogan & Mark A. Lemley, *Trademarks And Consumer Search Costs on the Internet*, 41 Houston L. Rev. 777 (2004); Mark A. Lemley & Stacey L. Dogan, *Grounding Trademark Law Through Trademark Use*, 92 Iowa L. Rev. 1669 (2007); Mark P. McKenna, *Trademark Use and the Problem of Source*, 2009 Ill. L. Rev. 773 (2009). The purchase and sale of trademarks as keywords, according to these scholars, should not without more be actionable, since neither selling keywords nor buying keywords amounted to trademark use. Professors Graeme Dinwoodie, Mark Janis, and Greg Lastowka, among others, contended that the "use in commerce" language required only that defendant's activities affect commerce within Congress's authority to regulate. If buying or selling keywords engendered a likelihood of confusion, they should, in these authors' views, be deemed infringing. *See, e.g.*, Graeme B. Dinwoodie & Mark D. Janis, *Lessons from the Trademark Use Debate*, 92 Iowa L. Rev. 1703 (2007); Graeme B. Dinwoodie & Mark D. Janis, *Confusion Over Use: Contextualism in Trademark Law*, 92 Iowa L. Rev. 1597 (2007); Greg Lastowka, *Google's Law*, 73 Brooklyn L. Rev. 1327 (2008). Which view do you find more persuasive? Which view best corresponds to the courts' analyses in the cases you've read so far?

Questions

1. Why did Congress limit liability for trademark infringement to uses of a mark or a colorable imitation of the mark in commerce?

2. What is the strongest argument you can make that Congress intended the definition of "use in commerce" in section 45 to limit the scope of potential defendants' liability? What is the strongest argument you can make that Congress did not intend the definition of "use in commerce" to apply to section 32? Which argument strikes you as more sound?

Steele v. Bulova Watch Co.

344 U.S. 280 (1952)

MR. JUSTICE CLARK delivered the opinion of the Court:

The issue is whether a United States District Court has jurisdiction to award relief to an American corporation against acts of trademark infringement and unfair competition consummated in a foreign country by a citizen and resident of the United States. Bulova Watch Company, Inc., a New York corporation, sued Steele, petitioner here, in the United States District Court for the Western District of Texas. The gist of its complaint charged that "Bulova," a trade-mark properly registered under the laws of the United States, had long designated the watches produced and nationally advertised and sold by the Bulova Watch Company; and that petitioner, a United States citizen residing in San Antonio, Texas, conducted a watch business in Mexico City where, without Bulova's authorization and with the purpose of deceiving the buying public, he stamped the name "Bulova" on watches there assembled and sold. Basing its prayer on these asserted violations of the trademark laws of the United States, Bulova requested injunctive and monetary relief. Personally served with process in San Antonio, petitioner answered by challenging the court's jurisdiction over the subject matter of the suit.... The trial judge ... dismissed the complaint "with prejudice," on the ground that the court lacked jurisdiction over the cause. This decision rested on the court's findings that petitioner had committed no illegal acts within the United States. With one judge dissenting, the Court of Appeals reversed; it held that the pleadings and evidence disclosed a cause of action within the reach of the Lanham Trademark Act of 1946, 15 U.S.C. § 1051 *et seq*.... We granted certiorari, 343 U.S. 962.

Petitioner concedes, as he must, that Congress in prescribing standards of conduct for American citizens may project the impact of its laws beyond the territorial boundaries of the United States. [Citations.] Resolution of the jurisdictional issue in this case therefore depends on construction of exercised congressional power, not the limitations upon that power itself. And since we do not pass on the merits of Bulova's claim, we need not now explore every facet of this complex and controversial Act.

The Lanham Act, on which Bulova posited its claims to relief, confers broad jurisdictional powers upon the courts of the United States....

The record reveals the following significant facts which for purposes of a dismissal must be taken as true: Bulova Watch Company, one of the largest watch manufacturers in the world, advertised and distributed "Bulova" watches in the United States and foreign countries. Since 1929, its aural and visual advertising, in Spanish and English, has penetrated Mexico. Petitioner, long a resident of San Antonio, first entered the watch business there in 1922, and in 1926 learned of the trademark "Bulova." He subsequently transferred his business to Mexico City and, discovering that "Bulova" had not been registered in Mexico, in 1933 procured the Mexican registration of that mark. Assembling Swiss watch movements and dials and cases imported from that country and the United States, petitioner in Mexico City stamped his watches with "Bulova" and sold them as such. As a result of the distribution of spurious "Bulovas,"

Bulova Watch Company's Texas sales representative received numerous complaints from retail jewelers in the Mexican border area whose customers brought in for repair defective "Bulovas" which upon inspection often turned out not to be products of that company.... On October 6, 1952, the Supreme Court of Mexico rendered a judgment upholding an administrative ruling which had nullified petitioner's Mexican registration of "Bulova."

On the facts in the record we agree with the Court of Appeals that petitioner's activities, when viewed as a whole, fall within the jurisdictional scope of the Lanham Act. This Court has often stated that the legislation of Congress will not extend beyond the boundaries of the United States unless a contrary legislative intent appears. [Citations.] The question thus is "whether Congress intended to make the law applicable" to the facts of this case. [Citation.] For "the United States is not debarred by any rule of international law from governing the conduct of its own citizens upon the high seas or even in foreign countries when the rights of other nations or their nationals are not infringed. With respect to such an exercise of authority there is no question of international law, but solely of the purport of the municipal law which establishes the duty of the citizen in relation to his own government." [Citation.] As Mr. Justice Minton, then sitting on the Court of Appeals, applied the principle in a case involving unfair methods of competition: "Congress has the power to prevent unfair trade practices in foreign commerce by citizens of the United States, although some of the acts are done outside the territorial limits of the United States." ... In the light of the broad jurisdictional grant in the Lanham Act, we deem its scope to encompass petitioner's activities here. His operations and their effects were not confined within the territorial limits of a foreign nation. He bought component parts of his wares in the United States, and spurious "Bulovas" filtered through the Mexican border into this country; his competing goods could well reflect adversely on Bulova Watch Company's trade reputation in markets cultivated by advertising here as well as abroad. Under similar factual circumstances, courts of the United States have awarded relief to registered trademark owners, even prior to the advent of the broadened commerce provisions of the Lanham Act. [Citations.] Even when most jealously read, that Act's sweeping reach into "all commerce which may lawfully be regulated by Congress" does not constrict prior law or deprive courts of jurisdiction previously exercised. We do not deem material that petitioner affixed the mark "Bulova" in Mexico City rather than here, or that his purchases in the United States when viewed in isolation do not violate any of our laws. They were essential steps in the course of business consummated abroad; acts in themselves legal lose that character when they become part of an unlawful scheme. [Citations.] "[In] such a case it is not material that the source of the forbidden effects upon ... commerce arises in one phase or another of that program." [Citations.] In sum, we do not think that petitioner by so simple a device can evade the thrust of the laws of the United States in a privileged sanctuary beyond our borders.

....

AFFIRMED.

McBee v. Delica

417 F.3d 107 (1st Cir. 2005)

[Cecil McBee, a well-known American jazz musician, discovered that a Japanese clothing manufacturer had adopted the brand CECIL MCBEE for its teen clothing line. Since McBee did not own a trademark registration for his name, he filed suit under section 43(a) of the Lanham Act, which permits suits over infringement of unregistered trademarks and other false designations of origin and false representations.* Section 43(a), like section 32, requires that defendant use a false designation or representation in commerce in connection with goods or services.]

Lynch, Circuit Judge.

It has long been settled that the Lanham Act can, in appropriate cases, be applied extraterritorially. *See Steele v. Bulova Watch Co.*, 344 U.S. 280 (1952). This case, dismissed for lack of subject matter jurisdiction, requires us, as a matter of first impression for this circuit, to lay out a framework for determining when such extraterritorial use of the Lanham Act is proper.

....

* [*Editors' Note*: We will cover section 43(a) in detail in Chapter 7.]

Our framework asks first whether the defendant is an American citizen; that inquiry is different because a separate constitutional basis for jurisdiction exists for control of activities, even foreign activities, of an American citizen. Further, when the Lanham Act plaintiff seeks to enjoin sales in the United States, there is no question of extraterritorial application; the court has subject matter jurisdiction.

In order for a plaintiff to reach foreign activities of foreign defendants in American courts, however, we adopt a separate test. We hold that subject matter jurisdiction under the Lanham Act is proper only if the complained-of activities have a substantial effect on United States commerce, viewed in light of the purposes of the Lanham Act. If this "substantial effects" question is answered in the negative, then the court lacks jurisdiction over the defendant's extraterritorial acts; if it is answered in the affirmative, then the court possesses subject matter jurisdiction.

...

... We conclude that the [district] court lacked jurisdiction over McBee's claims seeking (1) an injunction in the United States barring access to Delica's Internet website, which is written in Japanese, and (2) damages for harm to McBee due to Delica's sales in Japan. McBee has made no showing that Delica's activities had a substantial effect on United States commerce....

I.

The relevant facts are basically undisputed. McBee, who lives in both Maine and New York, is a jazz bassist with a distinguished career spanning over forty-five years. He has performed in the United States and worldwide, has performed on over 200 albums, and has released six albums under his own name (including in Japan). He won a Grammy Award in 1989, was inducted into the Oklahoma Jazz Hall of Fame in 1991, and teaches at the New England Conservatory of Music in Boston. McBee has toured Japan several times, beginning in the early 1980s, and has performed in many major Japanese cities, including Tokyo. He continues to tour in Japan. McBee has never licensed or authorized the use of his name to anyone, except of course in direct connection with his musical performances, as for example on an album. In his own words, he has sought to "have [his] name associated only with musical excellence."

Delica is a Japanese clothing retailer. In 1984, Delica adopted the trade name "Cecil McBee" for a line of clothing and accessories primarily marketed to teen-aged girls. Delica holds a Japanese trademark for "Cecil McBee," in both Japanese and Roman or English characters, for a variety of product types. Delica owns and operates retail shops throughout Japan under the brand name "Cecil McBee"; these are the only stores where "Cecil McBee" products are sold. There are no "Cecil McBee" retail shops outside of Japan. Delica sold approximately $23 million worth of "Cecil McBee" goods in 1996 and experienced steady growth in sales in subsequent years; in 2002, Delica sold $112 million worth of "Cecil McBee" goods.

... It is undisputed that [Delica] has never shipped any "Cecil McBee" goods outside of Japan. As described later, Delica's policy generally is to decline orders from the United States.

Delica operates a website, http://www.cecilmcbee.net, which contains pictures and descriptions of "Cecil McBee" products, as well as locations and telephone numbers of retail stores selling those products. The website is created and hosted in Japan, and is written almost entirely in Japanese, using Japanese characters (although, like the style book, it contains some English words). The website contains news about the "Cecil McBee" line, including promotions. Customers can log onto the site to access their balance of bonus "points" earned for making past "Cecil McBee" purchases, as well as information about how to redeem those points for additional merchandise. However, the site does not allow purchases of "Cecil McBee" products to be made online. The website can be viewed from anywhere in the Internet-accessible world.

McBee produced evidence that, when searches on Internet search engines (such as Google) are performed for the phrase "Cecil McBee," Delica's website (www.cecilmcbee.net) generally comes up as one of the first few results, and occasionally comes up first, ahead of any of the various websites that describe the musical accomplishments of the plaintiff. Certain other websites associated with Delica's "Cecil McBee" product line also come up when such searches are performed; like www.cecilmcbee.net, it is evident from the search results page that these websites are written primarily in Japanese characters.

. . . .

[T]here is virtually no evidence of "Cecil McBee" brand goods entering the United States after being sold by Delica in Japan. McBee stated in affidavit that "[f]riends, fellow musicians, fans, students, and others … have reported seeing [his] name on clothing, shopping bags [and] merchandise (whether worn or carried by a young girl walking on the street in Boston or New York or elsewhere)…." But no further evidence or detail of these sightings in the United States was provided. McBee also provided evidence that Cecil McBee goods have occasionally been sold on eBay, an auction website that allows bids to be placed and items sold anywhere in the world. Most of the sellers were not located in the United States, and there is no evidence that any of the items were purchased by American buyers.

. . . .

III.

A. Framework for Assessing Extraterritorial Use of the Lanham Act

. . . .

2. Claim for Injunction Barring Access to Internet Website

McBee next argues that his claim for an injunction against Delica's posting of its Internet website in a way that is visible to United States consumers also does not call for an extraterritorial application of the Lanham Act. Here McBee is incorrect: granting this relief would constitute an extraterritorial application of the Act, and thus subject matter jurisdiction would only be appropriate if McBee could show a substantial effect on United States commerce. McBee has not shown such a substantial effect from Delica's website.

....

Delica's website, although hosted from Japan and written in Japanese, happens to be reachable from the United States just as it is reachable from other countries. That is the nature of the Internet. The website is hosted and managed overseas; its visibility within the United States is more in the nature of an effect, which occurs only when someone in the United States decides to visit the website. To hold that any website in a foreign language, wherever hosted, is automatically reachable under the Lanham Act so long as it is visible in the United States would be senseless. The United States often will have no real interest in hearing trademark lawsuits about websites that are written in a foreign language and hosted in other countries.

Our conclusion does not make it impossible for McBee to use the Lanham Act to attack a Japan-based website; it merely requires that McBee first establish that the website has a substantial effect on commerce in the United States before there is subject matter jurisdiction under the Lanham Act. We can imagine many situations in which the presence of a website would ensure (or, at least, help to ensure) that the United States has a sufficient interest. The substantial effects test, however, is not met here.

Delica's website is written almost entirely in Japanese characters; this makes it very unlikely that any real confusion of American consumers, or diminishing of McBee's reputation, would result from the website's existence. In fact, most American consumers are unlikely to be able to understand Delica's website at all. Further, McBee's claim that Americans looking for information about him will be unable to find it is unpersuasive: the Internet searches reproduced in the record all turned up both sites about McBee and sites about Delica's clothing line on their first page of results. The two sets of results are easily distinguishable to any consumer, given that the Delica sites are clearly shown, by the search engines, as being written in Japanese characters. Finally, we stress that McBee has produced no evidence of any American consumers going to the website and then becoming confused about whether McBee had a relationship with Delica.

....

Questions

1. In *Steele v. Bulova*, the defendant had targeted U.S. purchasers when it sold the spurious watches from a tourist town right across the Mexican border. *American Rice v. Arkansas Rice Growers Co-op. Ass'n*, 701 F.2d 408 (5th Cir. 1983), presented a more attenuated case for assertion of Lanham Act jurisdiction, for the purchasers resided and the packaging was created beyond U.S. borders. All parties, however, were U.S. entities. The court of appeals for the 5th Circuit concluded that the trial court had properly exercised jurisdiction over the case under the standard articulated in *Steele v. Bulova*. Is that all that is required to permit an assertion of Lanham Act jurisdiction with extraterritorial effect? The Fifth Circuit has adhered to its approach: in a more recent case involving the same plaintiff, *American Rice, Inc. v. Producers Rice Mill, Inc.*, 518 F.3d 321 (5th Cir. 2008), the court again held that the Lanham Act would apply to American Rice's claim that its American rival in Saudi Arabia had adopted a confusingly similar mark.

2. Suppose the Mexican Court had upheld the validity of the *Steele v. Bulova* defendant's Mexican registration of BULOVA. How should a U.S. court have analyzed the challenge to exercise of jurisdiction under the Lanham Act?

3. Plaintiff operates a consumer lending business in the United States under the registered service mark THE CASH STORE. Defendant operates an unrelated consumer lending business in Canada under the mark THE CASH STORE. Defendant has no U.S. customers, and does not advertise in U.S. markets, but has some American stock holders and has been listed on the New York Stock Exchange since June 2010. In addition, it has given presentations to gatherings of potential investors in the United States. Defendant argues that none of its activities constitute actionable "use in commerce." How should the court rule? *See Cottonwood Fin. Ltd. v. Cash Store Fin. Servs.*, 778 F. Supp. 2d 726 (N.D. Tex. 2011).

4. Recall the decisions addressing whether a foreign mark's "use" or "use in [U.S.] commerce" suffices to vest the foreign entrepreneur with trademark rights in the U.S., or to confer standing to oppose a U.S. registration, *supra*, Chapters 3[D], 3[E], and 4[C][3]. Are those decisions consistent with *Steele v. Bulova*? With *McBee v. Delica*?

5. Frida Kahlo was a Mexican painter whose works attracted widespread acclaim after her death in 1954. In 2005, Kahlo's family sold all of Kahlo's copyrights and trademarks to a Panamanian corporation, which does business as the Frida Kahlo Corporation. The corporation enters into licensing agreements with companies wishing to use the Frida Kahlo mark or images related to Kahlo's art. The corporation has registered FRIDA KAHLO on the principal register in the United States for a variety of consumer products (*e.g.*, women's clothing; kitchenware; beer). Upon hearing reports of an Argentine company that marketed household products bearing images from Kahlo's paintings and marked with her initials to customers in Argentina, Mexico, Costa Rica, and Guatemala, the Frida Kahlo Corporation asked a sales consultant in Mexico to purchase some of the items and mail them to the corporation's Miami offices. The Corporation then filed a trademark infringement suit against the Argentine company and its U.S. corporate parent in the Southern District of Florida. The defendants move to dismiss the complaint, arguing that they have not used any Frida Kahlo mark in commerce within the meaning of section 32 of the Lanham Act. Plaintiff argues that infringing products are displayed on defendants' Argentine and Mexican websites, which are accessible from the United States, and that purchasers of defendants' Frida Kahlo products have marketed them in the United States on eBay, YouTube, and Facebook. How should the court rule? *See Frida Kahlo Corp. v. Tupperware Corp.*, No. 13-21039 (S.D. Fla. March 31, 2014).

6. Trader Joe's is a well-known, national grocery store chain with a South Seas motif that claims to sell hard-to-find, great-tasting food at inexpensive prices. The store has registered TRADER JOE'S on the principal register as a service mark for its store and a trademark for its private brand products. Trader Joe's has no stores outside of the United States. Michael Hallatt operates a grocery store in Vancouver, B.C.,

Canada named "PIRATE JOE'S." He stocks his store, in part, with products that he buys at full price from Trader Joe's stores across the border in Washington State and then imports into Canada, paying customs duties as appropriate. Trader Joe's claims that Hallatt's store violates the Lanham Act; Hallatt insists he has not used Trader Joe's marks in commerce. How should the court rule? *See Trader Joe's Company v. Hallatt*, 835 F.3d 960 (9th Cir. Aug. 26, 2016).

B. Likelihood of Confusion

"*... is likely to cause confusion, or to cause mistake, or to deceive....*"

Restatement of the Law (Third), Unfair Competition*

§ 20 STANDARD OF INFRINGEMENT

(1) One is subject to liability for infringement of another's trademark, trade name, collective mark, or certification mark if the other's use has priority under the rules stated in § 19 and in identifying the actor's business or in marketing the actor's goods or services the actor uses a designation that causes a likelihood of confusion:

(a) that the actor's business is the business of the other or is associated or otherwise connected with the other; or

(b) that the goods or services marketed by the actor are produced, sponsored, certified, or approved by the other; or

(c) that the goods or services marketed by the other are produced, sponsored, certified, or approved by the actor....

1. Factors for Assessing Likelihood of Confusion

Polaroid Corp. v. Polarad Elects. Corp., 287 F.2d 492 (2d Cir. 1961). Polaroid, the owner of federal registrations for the POLAROID mark for optical lenses and cameras sued the Polarad Electronics Corporation over its use of the mark POLARAD for television equipment and microwave devices. The district court found no likelihood of confusion because the products did not compete with one another, and also found Polaroid's claim barred by laches. Polaroid appealed. The Second Circuit enunciated eight factors for evaluating likelihood of confusion between non-competing goods or services:

> Where the products are different, the prior owner's chance of success is a function of many variables: the strength of his mark, the degree of similarity between the two marks, the proximity of the products, the likelihood that the prior owner will bridge the gap, actual confusion, and the reciprocal of defendant's good faith in adopting its own mark, the quality of defendant's product, and the sophistication of the buyers. Even this extensive catalogue

does not exhaust the possibilities—the court may have to take still other variables into account.

Examining the factors, the court noted that Polaroid's mark was strong, and the two marks very similar, but that evidence of actual confusion was weak. The court concluded that the fact that television equipment and cameras were related products would have entitled Polaroid to injunctive relief but for the finding of laches, which the Court of Appeals affirmed.

The factors set forth above have come to be known in the Second Circuit as "the *Polaroid* factors." The *Polaroid* factors at first evolved as a measure of confusion between non-competing goods. Gradually, however, the court came to rely on the multifactor test as an all-purpose template for evaluating likelihood of confusion under the Lanham Act. The test is reminiscent of the *DuPont* factors test for confusing similarity between marks seeking registration, which we looked at *supra* chapter 4, but focuses on potential confusion caused by marks as they actually appear in the marketplace rather than potential confusion between marks in the abstract.

Other circuits have elaborated similar criteria. In the Seventh Circuit, for example, the court looks at seven factors:

1. the similarity between the marks in appearance and suggestion;
2. the similarity of the products;
3. the area and manner of concurrent use;
4. the degree of care likely to be exercised by consumers;
5. the strength of the plaintiff's mark;
6. any actual confusion; and
7. the intent of the defendant to "palm off" his product as that of another.

Autozone, Inc. v. Strick, 543 F.3d 923 (7th Cir. 2008). The Ninth Circuit's eight factor test is similar:

1. strength of the mark;
2. proximity of the goods;
3. similarity of the marks;
4. evidence of actual confusion;
5. marketing channels used;
6. type of goods and the degree of care likely to be exercised by the purchaser;
7. defendant's intent in selecting the mark; and
8. likelihood of expansion of the product lines

AMF v. Sleekcraft Boats, 599 F.2d 341, 348–49 (9th Cir. 1979). Although the factors weighed in making a determination of the likelihood of confusion vary to some degree from circuit to circuit, certain considerations seem to appear uniformly: the degree of similarity between the marks, the proximity of the products, the defendant's intent in selecting the allegedly infringing mark, evidence of actual confusion, and the strength of plaintiff's mark. The names the various circuits give their multifactor tests figure below:

First Circuit: "*Pignons*" Factors (from *Pignons S.A. de Mecanique de Precision v. Polaroid Corp.*, 657 F.2d 482 (1st Cir. 1981)), *see Peoples Fed. Sav. Bank v. People's United Bank*, 672 F.3d 1, 7 (1st Cir. 2012)

Third Circuit: "*Lapp*" Factors (from *Interpace v. Lapp*, 721 F.2d 460 (3d Cir. 1983)), *see Sabinsa Corp. v. Creative Compounds, LLC*, 609 F.3d 175, 180 (3d Cir. 2010);

Fourth Circuit: "*Pizzeria Uno*" factors (from *Pizzeria Uno Corp. v. Temple*, 747 F.2d 1522 (4th Cir. 1984)), *see George & Co. LLC v. Imagination Entertainment Ltd.*, 575 F.3d 383 (4th Cir. 2009);

Fifth Circuit: "digits of confusion," *see Xtreme Lashes v. Extended Beauty*, 576 F.3d 221 (5th Cir. 2009);

Sixth Circuit: "*Frisch's*" factors (from *Frisch's Restaurants v. Elby's Big Boy, Inc.*, 670 F.2d 642 (6th Cir. 1982)), *see Makers Mark Distillery, Inc. v. Diageo, N.A.*, 679 F.3d 410 (6th Cir. 2012);

Seventh Circuit: "*AutoZone*" factors (from *Autozone, Inc. v. Strick*, 543 F.3d 923 (7th Cir. 2008)), *see Board of Regents v. Phoenix International Software*, 653 F.3d 448 (7th Cir. 2011);

Eighth Circuit: "*SquirtCo*" factors (from *SquirtCo. v. Seven-Up Co.*, 628 F.2d 1086, 1091 (8th Cir. 1980)), *see Davis v. Walt Disney Co.*, 430 F.3d 910 (8th Cir. 2005);

Ninth Circuit: "*Sleekcraft*" factors (from *AMF v. Sleekcraft Boats*), *see Network Automation v. Advanced System Concepts*, 638 F.3d 1137 (9th Cir. 2011);

Tenth Circuit: "*Sally Beauty Co.*" factors (from *Sally Beauty Co., Inc. v. Beautyco, Inc.*, 304 F.3d 964 (10th Cir. 2002)), *see Utah Lighthouse Ministry v. Foundation for Apologetic Information and Research*, 527 F.3d 1045 (10th Cir. 2008);

Eleventh Circuit: "likelihood of confusion factors," *see Tana v. Dantanna's*, 611 F.3d 767 (11th Cir. 2012).

The appellate jurisdiction of the **Court of Appeals for the Federal Circuit** encompasses cases involving a patent question from any district court in the country. 28 U.S.C. § 1295. Because trademark claims are sometimes combined with patent claims, the Federal Circuit sometimes deals with the issue of likelihood of confusion on appeal from district courts in various circuits. In such cases, the CAFC applies the law of the regional circuit. *E.g., KeyStone Retaining Wall Systems, Inc. v. Westrock, Inc.*, 997 F.2d 1444, 1447 (Fed. Cir. 1993).

The Restatement (3d) of Unfair Competition describes the multifactor test for likelihood of confusion this way:

Restatement of the Law (Third), Unfair Competition*

§ 21 PROOF OF LIKELIHOOD OF CONFUSION: MARKET FACTORS

Whether an actor's use of a designation causes a likelihood of confusion with the use of a trademark, trade name, collective mark, or certification mark by another under the rule stated in § 20 is determined by a consideration of all the circumstances involved in the marketing of the respective goods or services or in the operation of the respective businesses. In making that determination the following market factors, among others, may be important:

(a) the degree of similarity between the respective designations, including a comparison of

(i) the overall impression created by the designations as they are used in marketing the respective goods or services or in identifying the respective businesses;

(ii) the pronunciation of the designations;

(iii) the translation of any foreign words contained in the designations;

(iv) the verbal translation of any pictures, illustrations, or designs contained in the designations;

(v) the suggestions, connotations, or meanings of the designations;

(b) the degree of similarity in the marketing methods and channels of distribution used for the respective goods or services;

(c) the characteristics of the prospective purchasers of the goods or services and the degree of care they are likely to exercise in making purchasing decisions;

(d) the degree of distinctiveness of the other's designation;

(e) when the goods, services, or business of the actor differ in kind from those of the other, the likelihood that the actor's prospective purchasers would expect a person in the position of the other to expand its marketing or sponsorship into the product, service, or business market of the actor;

(f) when the actor and the other sell their goods or services or carry on their businesses in different geographic markets, the extent to which the other's designation is identified with the other in the geographic market of the actor.

COMMENTS & ILLUSTRATIONS:

a. General. The test for infringement is whether the actor's use of a designation as a trademark, trade name, collective mark, or certification mark creates a likelihood of confusion as described in § 20. The likelihood of confusion standard applies in infringement actions at common law as well as in actions arising under the Lanham Act and under state trademark registration and unfair competition statutes. Whether the use of a particular designation causes a likelihood of confusion must be evaluated in light of the overall market context in which the designation is used. This Section addresses several market factors that are important in many cases. The factors listed in this Section are not exhaustive of the relevant circumstances, however, and any factor that is likely to influence the impression conveyed to prospective purchasers by the actor's use of the designation is relevant is assessing the likelihood of confusion. No mechanistic formula or list can set forth in advance the variety of factors that may contribute to the particular marketing context of an actor's use. Not all the factors listed here will be applicable in every case, nor can the factors be applied independently. The likelihood of confusion depends on the interplay of all the factors that constitute the marketing environment in which the designation is used.... The relative importance of any factor, including intent or actual confusion, depends on the facts of the particular case.

....

Question

How does the Restatement formulation of the multi-factor test differ from the Second Circuit's *Polaroid* factors and the Seventh Circuit's *AutoZone* factors? Is the choice of factors to examine likely to change the result of the analysis of likelihood of confusion?

2. Likelihood of Confusion in the Courts

E. & J. Gallo Winery v. Consorzio del Gallo Nero

782 F. Supp. 457 (N.D. Cal. 1991)

JENSEN, J.:

Background

This is an action for trademark infringement and dilution brought by plaintiff E. & J. Gallo Winery ("Gallo") against defendant Consorzio del Gallo Nero ("Gallo Nero"). Gallo, the largest winery in the United States, produces and sells a variety of wines featuring the "Gallo" trademark and is the owner of several federal registrations of the "Gallo" mark. Since 1933, Gallo has consistently used the "Gallo" name in relation to its wines and has sold some 2 billion bottles of wine bearing the "Gallo" mark to consumers through retail establishments of all types, including restaurants, grocery stores, wine shops, and liquor stores. Finally, over the past 50 years, Gallo has spent some $500 million in promoting the "Gallo" brand of wines, and Gallo's advertising is presently calculated to reach every consumer in the United States approximately 50–70 times a year.

Defendant Gallo Nero is an Italian trade association based in Florence, Italy, that promotes Chianti Classico wine produced by its individual members in the Chianti region of Italy. Prior to the formation of Gallo Nero in 1987, Chianti Classico producers were represented by the Consorzio Vino Chianti Classico ("CVCC"), which was formed in 1924. CVCC had consistently utilized the symbol of a black rooster, or "gallo nero," to represent its wines, a symbol with history of strong association with the Chianti region of Italy. In particular, the symbol appeared on the neck seal of its bottles, surrounded by the designation "Consorzio Vino Chianti Classico." The name of the successor organization, Consorzio del Gallo Nero, was selected on the basis of this association between the symbol and the wines of the Chianti region, and defendant has continued the tradition of using the black rooster symbol on its neck seals, substituting the designation "Consorzio del Gallo Nero" for the previous one. However, although Gallo Nero has produced such neck seals, they have not yet been used on any Gallo Nero wine distributed in the United States.

....

Discussion

....

1. *Strength of plaintiff's mark*

A registered mark is "presumed to be distinctive and should be afforded the utmost protection." [Citation.].... Therefore, in light of Gallo's current federal registration of several versions of the "Gallo" mark, plaintiff has established as an initial matter the validity and distinctiveness of the mark and Gallo's exclusive right to use the mark in promoting and selling its wines in the United States.

In addition to these statutory presumptions, the Gallo mark itself has been held by a sister court of this Circuit to have achieved "virtually universal recognition as a trademark for wine," and that it is "universally known both nationally and in California, and has become an extraordinarily strong and distinctive mark." *E. & J. Gallo Winery Cattle Co.*, 12 U.S.P.Q.2d 1657, 1661, 1667 (E.D. Cal. 1989). This conclusion is further supported by Gallo's undisputed showing that it has used the Gallo mark in relation to its wines for over 50 years; it has spent some $500 million in advertising its wines distributed under the mark; and it has sold to consumers some 2 billion bottles of wine bearing the Gallo mark. [Citation.]

Gallo Nero contests the strength of the Gallo mark by noting that there are numerous third-party uses of the "Gallo" name, and that "Gallo" itself is merely a common surname and basic element of Italian vocabulary. However, "evidence of other unrelated potential infringers is irrelevant to claims of trademark infringement," [citation] and Gallo Nero has not shown that these third-party uses are in any way connected to the production, promotion, and sale of wine, much less that any of these uses has achieved significant consumer recognition. Therefore Gallo Nero's evidence of third-party uses is neither persuasive nor relevant to the issue of the strength of the "Gallo" mark.

Secondly, a family name is entitled to protection as a mark so long as it has acquired a recognized "secondary meaning" through use, advertising, and public recognition.... "Gallo" has clearly become associated with wine in the United States such that its evolution to "secondary meaning" status may not be seriously questioned.

In conclusion, the Court finds that Gallo has established both its exclusive right to use the "Gallo" trademark under federal law and that the trademark itself is exceptionally strong when used in relation to the promotion and sale of wine in the United States. While the strength of plaintiff's mark is but one of several issues to be considered in determining whether there is likelihood of confusion between the parties' products, [citation] the Court notes that "a strong mark is 'afforded the widest ambit of protection from infringing uses.'" [Citation.]

2. *Similarity of marks used*

Similarity of marks is judged by their sound, appearance, and meaning. Gallo contends that the two marks share the total identity of the substantive term "Gallo" and are therefore substantially similar for purposes of trademark infringement.

Gallo Nero in opposition argues that its use of surrounding terms, *i.e.*, Consorzio del Gallo Nero, sufficiently distinguishes the latter from the "Gallo" mark to render the two uses dissimilar. However, it is undisputed that Gallo has valid, current federal registrations of the "Gallo" mark used in conjunction with other words, *e.g.*, "Ernest & Julio Gallo," and that Gallo has consistently combined the word "Gallo" with other descriptive terms, *e.g.*, "Gallo Premium Blush" and "Gallo Classic Burgundy." Therefore, as Gallo argues, there is a logical conclusion that consumers are accustomed to seeing the "Gallo" mark used in conjunction with other terms or surrounded by other words. The distinctive term in each instance is "Gallo," which, as discussed above, has clearly obtained a unique status when coupled with wine. Finally, this characteristic would seem to be particularly maintained with regard to non-Italian-speaking consumers when the "Gallo" mark is surrounded by the foreign terms "Consorzio" and "Nero." Again, for English speakers, the "stand out" or significant term in the phrase "Consorzio del Gallo Nero" is the word "Gallo" when the phrase is encountered on or in connection with a bottle of wine.

Gallo Nero also argues that the presentation of the terms on the bottle sufficiently distinguish the two uses such that defendant's use is dissimilar to plaintiff's. Thus, even if the subject marks are identical, "their similarity must be considered in light of the way the marks are encountered in the marketplace and the circumstances surrounding their purchase." [Citations.] Gallo Nero notes that the use of the term "Gallo" is always in conjunction with the term "Nero," and its proposed limitation to small script on the neck seal strengthens the immediate dissimilarity arising from the otherwise clearly different labels attached to the parties' bottles of wine.

Gallo does not respond to this particular argument, but the Court finds that Gallo Nero's argument, while having some merit, is neither dispositive nor persuasive on the issue of similarity between marks. As an initial matter, Gallo Nero is arguably well aware of the similarity of the "Gallo Nero" name to that of "Gallo" in light of defendant's interactions with foreign trademark offices. Specifically, in August 1984, defendant's predecessor, CVCC, sought to register the words "Gallo Nero" as a trademark in Canada. The application, however, was rejected because the Canadian trademark office concluded that "Gallo Nero" was likely to be confused with Gallo's registered marks. Moreover, just prior to commencing its U.S. marketing campaign, Gallo Nero opposed plaintiff's application to register "Ernest and Julio Gallo" in the United Kingdom on the ground that this mark would be "deceptive or confusing" with "Gallo Nero."

In conclusion, the Court finds that the continued use of the term "Gallo" as a manifestation of a federally registered mark or in conjunction with other terms establishes not only that the mark itself is strong, but that the consuming public will find the single term "Gallo" to be wholly and uniquely distinctive whenever it is used in conjunction with the promotion or sale of wine in the United States. Therefore, because "Gallo" is the single "dominant" or "substantive" term used by plaintiff on all its products—including the 2 billion bottles of wine already sold—defendant's use of the term "Gallo" even on a facially distinctive label or in conjunction with other terms does not divert this Court from its conclusion that, as a matter of law, the two terms are significantly similar for purposes of a finding of a likelihood of confusion between the two uses.

3. *Similarity of goods sold*

"When the goods produced by the alleged infringer compete for sales with those of the trademark owner, infringement usually will be found if the marks are sufficiently similar that confusion can be expected." [Citations.] Both parties are involved in the sale of wine, although of arguably different varieties. Gallo notes, however, that the Patent and Trademark Office has repeatedly found that wines of all types constitute a single class of goods. [Citations.] In fact, if Gallo Nero sought to register its name as a trademark, it would fall into the same class of goods as Gallo's trademarks. *See* 37 C.F.R. §§6.1, 6.2 (1990).

Gallo Nero in opposition contends that the wines themselves are distinct, one produced in Italy while the other in the United States. Moreover, Gallo Nero's members produce only chianti wines, whereas Gallo effectively produces everything but Italian chianti. However, Gallo Nero cites no authority for finding a distinction between the wines produced by the parties, and representatives of Gallo Nero have themselves stated that Gallo Nero wines distributed in the United States are "in competition with every red wine that is being produced."

Therefore, the Court finds that the goods produced by Gallo and Gallo Nero are substantially similar for purposes of establishing a likelihood of confusion.

4. *Similarity of marketing channels used*

Both parties market their products through retail establishments like wine shops and liquor stores, and utilize magazines for advertizing purposes. Gallo Nero effectively does not dispute Gallo's showing on this issue; indeed, Gallo Nero notes use of the same retail establishment in Washington, D.C., the Mayflower Wine & Spirits Shop, by both parties in selling their respective wines. Moreover, the above deposition testimony that Gallo Nero wines are in direct competition with those of other producers also supports a finding that the wines are marketed by similar means. Therefore the Court finds as a matter of law that both parties use similar marketing channels to distribute their wines.

5. *Degree of care exercised by purchasers*

Confusion between marks is generally more likely where the goods at issue involve relatively inexpensive, "impulse" products to which the average, "unsophisticated" consumer does not devote a great deal of care and consideration in purchasing. [Citations.] Wine has been deemed an "impulse" product, and certainly so with respect to the average consumer, effectively compelling the consumer's reliance "on faith in the maker." *Taylor Wine Co. v. Bully Hill Vineyards, Inc.*, 569 F.2d 731, 733–34 (2d Cir. 1978); *see also id.* ("The average American who drinks wine on occasion can hardly pass for a connoisseur of wines"). Indeed, Gallo Nero employees themselves have testified that the average American consumer is unlearned in the selection of wine.

The only opposition Gallo Nero offers to Gallo's characterization of the wine-buying public is a single 1959 case from the Middle District of Alabama, stating that "the wine-buying public—insofar as their selection and purchase of wine is concerned—is a highly discriminating group." *E. & J. Gallo Winery v. Ben R. Goltsman & Co.*, 172 F. Supp. 826, 830 (M.D. Ala. 1959). That case, however, involved plaintiff's "THUNDERBIRD" fortified wine—with the "Gallo" name above—versus the defendant's "THUNDERBOLT"—with the words "Private Stock" immediately below—both products arguably failing any classification as "fine wines." Moreover, with all due respect to Alabama, it would seem common knowledge that wine was not a widely appreciated beverage in the South in 1959.

On balance then, the Court finds that Gallo Nero has failed to contest either through evidence or legal support the characterization of the wine-buying public as generally unsophisticated "impulse" buyers who are an "easy mark for a [trademark] infringer." [Citation.] Therefore the Court finds that the lack of consumer sophistication significantly enhances the likelihood of confusion between the two products.

6. *Evidence of actual confusion*

While evidence of actual consumer confusion provides strong support for a finding of a likelihood of confusion, "the failure to prove instances of actual confusion is not dispositive" of an infringement claim. [Citation.] Thus evidence of actual confusion "is merely one factor to be considered ... and it is not determinative" if it is not shown. [Citation.] Therefore, at a minimum, the absence of actual confusion will not defeat an otherwise successful claim of infringement by Gallo as this Court must find only a *likelihood* of confusion.

Gallo Nero relies in significant part on the survey conducted by Dr. Jacob Jacoby, Merchants Council Professor of Consumer Behavior and Retail Management at the Stern School of Business, New York University, entitled "Consumer Perceptions of Wine Bottles Bearing the Consorzio del Gallo Nero Neck Seal" (the "Jacoby Survey"), to show that there is no likelihood of confusion between the parties' respective uses of the "Gallo" name. In the survey, individual participants were shown an array of eight bottles of red wine, including two bottles of Gallo wines and two bottles of Gallo Nero wines. Participants were then asked a series of questions designed to assess the likelihood of "point-of-sale" confusion as to the source of the respective wines. Dr. Jacoby found "only a trivial level of likely confusion as to source among these consumers," as "only three of the 216 respondents (1.4%) identified one or more E & J Gallo bottles and one or more Consorzio del Gallo Nero bottles as coming from the same source." Jacoby Survey at 3.

Gallo in response contends that the survey itself is irrelevant, and that even if it were, only 10 of the 216 respondents even referred to the neck seal. Thus Gallo argues that it is unclear whether each of the respondents even saw the critical mark being tested. Moreover, Gallo emphasizes that failure to show "actual" confusion under survey conditions is not dispositive of an infringement claim. Indeed, Gallo notes that it would be impossible at this stage to show actual confusion other than in the artificial setting of a survey as Gallo Nero has not sold a single bottle of wine in the U.S. bearing the words "Gallo Nero." Finally, Gallo proffers its own survey evidence conducted by Robert Lavidge of Elrick & Lavidge, a custom marketing research firm (the "Lavidge Survey"). In that survey, 512 respondents were shown the neck seal with the "Consorzio del Gallo Nero" designation, and another 512 were shown the advertisement which appeared in the *Wine Spectator* in 1986. Gallo reports that 43% of the respondents unequivocally associated the neck seal with the Ernest & Julio Gallo Winery, and 38% did so with regard to the advertisement. Lavidge Survey at 9–10.

Numerous courts hold a side-by-side comparison like the one conducted by Dr. Jacoby to be legally irrelevant in determining whether defendant's use of a similar mark leads to a finding of a likelihood of confusion. "The proper test for likelihood of confusion is not whether consumers would be confused in a side-by-side comparison of the products, but whether confusion is likely when a consumer, familiar with the one party's mark, is presented with the other party's goods alone." [Citations.] Based on the foregoing, it would seem that Gallo Nero's survey evidence is irrelevant to the issue of infringement and that Gallo's own evidence is both relevant and dispositive.

On the other hand, other authorities maintain that the proper survey evidence is that which attempts to most closely replicate the marketplace setting in which consumers will typically encounter the competing marks. [Citations.] Under such a view, then clearly the Gallo Nero survey has relevance in gauging a likelihood of consumer confusion when confronted with bottles of wine sporting the "Consorzio del Gallo Nero" name.

On summary judgment, drawing all inferences in the non-movant's favor, the Court finds nonetheless that there is *some* evidence of a likelihood of confusion under both surveys, even if the Jacoby Survey results in only a "trivial" showing. Moreover, even accepting that Gallo has overstated the results of its own survey, the "adjusted" statistics nonetheless establish that, again, there is *some* evidence of a likelihood of confusion as to source when a consumer is presented with allegedly infringing "Gallo Nero" name. While such showings are not overwhelming, given that no bottle of defendant's wine bearing the "Gallo Nero" name has ever been sold in the United States, and that failure to show actual confusion is not a prerequisite to finding a likelihood of confusion, the Court finds that Gallo Nero has sustained its burden on summary judgment with respect to this factor as well.

7. *Defendant's intent in adopting the "Gallo Nero" name*

Just as with actual confusion, a showing of intent is not necessary to support a finding of a likelihood of confusion. [Citation.] However, where an infringer adopts a particular name with knowledge of plaintiff's mark, courts presume that there was an intent to copy the mark. [Citations.]

The record here establishes that Gallo Nero was aware of the "Gallo" mark prior to beginning its U.S. marketing campaign in 1989, as demonstrated both by its predecessor's direct knowledge of the potentially infringing use of "Gallo" in its advertisements of "Gallo Nero" as well as the communications with the trademark offices of Canada and the United Kingdom.

Gallo Nero in opposition contends that there was no intent to infringe Gallo's marks because the adoption of the "Gallo Nero" name was made in good faith and for sound business reasons. The Court readily acknowledges the extensive and colorful tradition surrounding the relation between the "gallo nero" symbol and the Chianti region of Italy. Moreover, neither the Court nor Gallo has any qualms with Gallo Nero's continued use of the black rooster symbol to identify and distinguish its products in the U.S. marketplace. However, the present issue is not whether Gallo Nero had admirable motivations when it initially adopted its name in 1987, but whether Gallo Nero had knowledge of the potentially infringing effect its use of the "Gallo Nero" and "Consorzio del Gallo Nero" marks would have when it entered the U.S. wine market. The record establishes that Gallo Nero was so aware, and while there may be a question whether such knowledge rises to the level of willful infringement or bad faith, [citations] it shows nonetheless that Gallo Nero was at least cognizant of the potentially infringing nature of its use of the "Gallo" name.

8. *Conclusion*

Balancing the foregoing factors, the Court concludes that Gallo has established as a matter of law that it is entitled to summary judgment on its trademark infringement claim. Clearly the "Gallo" mark is a mighty fortress in the U.S. wine market, and use of that name on a bottle of competing wine marketed through similar channels leads to an initial finding of infringement. Compounded with defendant's knowledge that its use of the term "Gallo" in any combination would be deemed an infringement by Gallo—if not, in fact, by a federal district court—and some evidence showing a likelihood of confusion, the foregoing is sufficient to find that defendant's use of the term "Gallo" in conjunction with the promotion and sale of its wines in the United States would lead to a likelihood of consumer confusion with Gallo's products. Therefore Gallo is entitled to summary judgment on its infringement claim.

Banfi Products Corp. v. Kendall-Jackson Winery Ltd.

74 F. Supp. 2d 188 (E.D.N.Y. 1999)

Platt, J:

Plaintiff Banfi Products Corporation commenced this action against defendant Kendall-Jackson Winery, Ltd. on March 14, 1996, seeking a declaratory judgment of non-infringement. In the alternative, plaintiff has asserted claims for: (1) trademark infringement in violation of the Lanham Act Section 32(1), 15 U.S.C. Section 1114; (2) unfair competition/false designation of origin and false advertising, in violation of section 43(a) of the Lanham Act, 15 U.S.C. Section 1125(a); and (3) common law trademark infringement.

In response, defendant Kendall-Jackson Winery, Ltd. has asserted counterclaims for: (1) false designation of origin in violation of section 43(a) of the Lanham Act, 15 U.S.C. Section 1125(a); (2) unfair competition in violation of N.Y. Gen. Bus. Law Section 368-e; and (3) unfair business practices in violation of N.Y. Gen. Bus. Law Section 349. Additionally, Kendall-Jackson Winery, Ltd. seeks an order canceling Banfi's federal trademark registration No. 1,743,450 for COL-DI-SASSO.

... For the following reasons, this Court finds that there is no likelihood of confusion....

Findings of Fact

A. Parties

Plaintiff Banfi Products Corporation ("Banfi") is a New York corporation whose principal place of business is in the Village of Old Brookville, Nassau County, New York. At present, Banfi is the largest importer of Italian wines in the United States, importing as much as sixty to seventy percent of all Italian wines coming into this country. Banfi also imports wines produced by its affiliated companies in Montalcino and Strevi, Italy. Domestically, Banfi produces a chardonnay wine in Old Brookville, New York, distributed primarily on Long Island and in Manhattan.

Defendant Kendall-Jackson Winery, Ltd. ("Kendall-Jackson") is a California corporation with its principal place of business in Santa Rosa, California. In 1994, Kendall-Jackson purchased the Robert Pepi Winery, located in Napa Valley, California.

B. COL-DI-SASSO

Banfi imports and sells COL-DI-SASSO, which is produced by an affiliate of Banfi in the Tuscan region of Italy. Dr. Ezio Rivella, Banfi's general manager of Italian operations, conceived of the name COL-DI-SASSO in Montalcino, Italy in 1989 or 1990. COL-DI-SASSO is an Italian term meaning "hill of stone." It was named for a particular rock known as "sasso," prevalent in the region of Tuscany.

Originally, COL-DI-SASSO was introduced as a Cabernet Sauvignon wine. Soon thereafter, however, Banfi changed COL-DI-SASSO to a 50-50 blend of Sangiovese and Cabernet. Banfi began selling this new blend in early 1993.

COL-DI-SASSO's trade dress is very distinctive. Its front label includes an orange-yellow depiction of a landscape, surrounded by a green-black marbleized background. The name COL-DI-SASSO is featured prominently on the front label, as are the words "Sangiovese" and "Cabernet." The back label includes the following legends: (1) "Red Table Wine of Tuscany;" (2) "Banfi S.R.L.;" (3) "50% Sangiovese-50% Cabernet Sauvignon;" (4) "Banfi Vinters;" and (5) "Produce of Italy." Additionally, the word "Banfi" appears in black script on the cork used in bottles of COL-DI-SASSO.

In 1991, Banfi introduced COL-DI-SASSO to the Italian market, and sold substantial quantities from that point forward throughout Europe. Banfi sent its first shipment of COL-DI-SASSO, consisting of two bottles, to the United States in late 1991. Yet commercial distribution and sales of COL-DI-SASSO in the U.S. did not commence until the Spring of 1992. On or about December 29, 1992, the United States Patent and Trademark Office ("PTO") issued Banfi federal trademark registration No. 1,743,450 for COL-DI-SASSO.

By late 1993, Banfi began to experience a sharp increase in U.S. sales of COL-DI-SASSO. To date, over 27,000 cases of COL-DI-SASSO have been sold in the United States. In 1998, Banfi's total U.S. sales in dollars of COL-DI-SASSO exceeded $1.3 million.

....

Banfi sells COL-DI-SASSO to wine and spirit distributors throughout the United States, who in turn distribute the wine to restaurants and retail establishments. Banfi markets COL-DI-SASSO as an affordable, everyday Italian red wine. Accordingly, Banfi encourages its distributors to place the wine in discount liquor stores, supermarkets, and mid-range Italian restaurants such as the Olive Garden and Macaroni Grill. COL-DI-SASSO sells for between $8 and $10 per bottle in stores, and for anywhere from $16 to $23 per bottle in restaurants. Restaurants also feature COL-DI-SASSO by the glass as a promotional tool.

Since its introduction, COL-DI-SASSO has received generally favorable reviews from the media[, including the Houston Chronicle, the Providence Journal-Bulletin, the Washington Post, and the Port St. Lucie News.] ...

C. ROBERT PEPI COLLINE DI SASSI

The other wine at issue in this case is ROBERT PEPI COLLINE DI SASSI, produced by the Robert Pepi Winery in Napa Valley, California. In July 1994, defendant Kendall-Jackson Winery ("Kendall-Jackson") purchased the Pepi winery and has continued to produce COLLINE DI SASSI ever since. In late 1989 or early 1990, Robert A. Pepi and his son Robert L. Pepi, founders of the Pepi winery, arrived at the name ROBERT PEPI COLLINE DI SASSI while eating dinner together.

Directly translated, ROBERT PEPI COLLINE DI SASSI means "Robert Pepi little hills of stone." The "Colline" element of ROBERT PEPI COLLINE DI SASSI is a three-syllable word pronounced "Col-ee-ne." Although ROBERT PEPI COLLINE DI SASSI is labeled solely as a Sangiovese varietal, it contains a small amount (typically 15%) of cabernet.

....

The current trade dress of ROBERT PEPI COLLINE DI SASSI consists of a rectangular wrap-around front label. The label is orange and cream, bearing the legend "Robert Pepi" in black script in the top left corner. The words "Colline Di Sassi" and "Napa Valley Sangiovese" are centered on the front label in black print. The back label reiterates that the wine is produced and bottled in Napa Valley California.

In September 1990, ROBERT PEPI COLLINE DI SASSI labels were approved by the Bureau of Alcohol, Tobacco and Firearms ("BATF"). Of considerable significance, the label approval application listed "ROBERT PEPI" as the "brand name" and "COLLINI (sic) DI SASSI" as the so-called "fanciful name." Thereafter, in October

1990, Pepi began to distribute the 1988 vintage of ROBERT PEPI COLLINE DI SASSI throughout the United States.

Since then, distribution of ROBERT PEPI COLLINE DI SASSI has been relatively limited. Annual case sales of defendant's wine have ranged from 133 cases in 1990, to 462 in 1991, 689 in 1992, 301 in 1993, 170 in 1994, 996 in 1995, 903 in 1996, 37 in 1997, and 1345 in 1998. Pepi did not produce a 1994 vintage of ROBERT PEPI COLLINE DI SASSI due to concerns over quality. Moreover, from 1990 through 1998, advertising expenditures for ROBERT PEPI COLLINE DI SASSI, both by Pepi and Kendall-Jackson, have been minimal.

Kendall-Jackson distributes ROBERT PEPI COLLINE DI SASSI to independent distributors, who in turn sell the wine to restaurants and retail stores. ROBERT PEPI COLLINE DI SASSI has been marketed as an high-end, limited production wine. In fact, after its purchase of the Pepi winery in 1994, Kendall-Jackson included ROBERT PEPI COLLINE DI SASSI as part of its "Artisans & Estates" stable of high-end, specialty wines. Accordingly, both Pepi and Kendall-Jackson have tried to place ROBERT PEPI COLLINE DI SASSI in better or high-priced restaurants and wine shops, as opposed to chain restaurants and discount stores. ROBERT PEPI COLLINE DI SASSI sells for $20 to $25 per bottle in stores, and from $35 to $45 or more in restaurants. Due to its high cost, ROBERT PEPI COLLINE DI SASSI generally is not sold by the glass in restaurants....

D. Nature of Dispute

This dispute arose in 1994 when John Mariani, Banfi's Chairman Emeritus, saw a reference to the Pepi wine in an article published in USA Today. The article, entitled "California vineyards take on an Italian accent," listed "ROBERT PEPI COLLINO (sic) DI SASSI" as one of several California wines using such Italian grape varietals as Sangiovese. It should be noted that up until the date of the USA Today article, John Mariani had never heard of the mark ROBERT PEPI COLLINE DI SASSI....

[Banfi wrote to Pepi, claiming that the two names were confusingly similar, and requesting Pepi to rename its wine. Pepi replied that Pepi was the senior user, the names certainly were confusingly similar, and Banfi should therefore choose a different name for its wine.]

After conducting an investigation during which it reviewed sales figures, bills of lading, and trade articles relating to the two wines, Banfi concluded that there was no likelihood of confusion between COL-DI-SASSO and ROBERT PEPI COLLINE-DI-SASSI, and accordingly declined to cease using the COL-DI-SASSO mark. To further ensure that there would be no confusion, however, Banfi added the word "Banfi" in gold script along the side of COL-DI-SASSO's front label. In July 1994, defendant Kendall-Jackson purchased Pepi and continued to demand that Banfi cease using the COL-DI-SASSO mark.

In order to resolve this dispute once and for all, Banfi commenced the instant action pursuant to the Lanham Act, 15 U.S.C. Section 1051, et seq., seeking a judgment declaring that its use of the COL-DI-SASSO mark does not infringe Kendall-Jackson's use of ROBERT PEPI COLLINE DI SASSI, i.e., that there is no likelihood of confusion. In response, Kendall-Jackson asserted several counterclaims, arguing that it has priority, the marks are confusing, and therefore Banfi should be enjoined from using the COL-DI-SASSO mark.

E. Facts Relevant to Polaroid Analysis to Determine Likelihood of Confusion

Before this dispute developed, COL-DI-SASSO and ROBERT PEPI COLLINE DI SASSI co-existed for approximately four years without any evidence of actual confusion. No one associated with Banfi had ever heard of ROBERT PEPI COLLINE DI SASSI, nor had Pepi or Kendall-Jackson heard of COL-DI-SASSO. Similarly, there is no evidence that any consumer, distributor, retailer, or critic confused the two wines at issue in this case, as neither Banfi nor Kendall-Jackson ever received misdirected mail or telephone calls. Furthermore, to date, neither party has conducted a market study to determine whether there is, in fact, a likelihood of confusion. Accordingly, during oral argument on Banfi's Motion for Partial Summary Judgment on September 4, 1998, parties stipulated that there is no actual confusion between the two wines.

Moreover, it should be noted that there is widespread third-party use of names similar to COL-DI-SASSO and ROBERT PEPI COLLINE DI SASSI in the wine industry, including, inter alia, CA'DEL SOLO, COLLI SENESI, COL D'ORCIA, COLLE MANORA, COLLE SOLATO, COLLI FIORENTINI, COLLINA RIONDA DI SERRALUNGA, COLLINE DI AMA, and COLLINE NOVARESI BIANCO.

In terms of the wine industry as a whole, it is well settled that retail wine stores typically segregate wine according to geographic origin, i.e., California, Italy, and Chile. Similarly, restaurant wine lists either separate wines from different countries, or at a minimum include some indication of each wine's geographic origin, along with the vinter's name and the year and price of the wine. In addition, while serving bottles of wine, waiters almost uniformly present the bottle so that the customer can examine the label and smell the cork, which, in the case of COL-DI-SASSO is imprinted with the word "Banfi."

Lastly, with respect to the sophistication of wine consumers, studies, like the one published by The U.S. Wine Market Impact Databank Review and Forecast, have indicated that wine drinkers tend to be older, wealthier, and better educated than the average population. Specifically, wine consumers "60 and over account for some 28% of all wine volume, while those between 50 and 59 consume another 22 percent." In addition, "[t]he wine consumer is generally an affluent one—more than forty-one percent have incomes of at least $60,000." Finally, survey results indicate that "[a]t least half of the drinkers for all of the wine types (with the exception of Sangria) have some college education...."

Conclusions of Law

....

1. Strength of Kendall-Jackson's Mark

....

In the instant case, as Kendall-Jackson argues and Banfi more or less concedes, ROBERT PEPI COLLINE DI SASSI is an arbitrary mark because it has no meaning to the average consumer, nor does it suggest the qualities and features of the wine. [Citation.] However, a finding that a particular mark is arbitrary does not guarantee a determination that the mark is strong. [Citation.] Instead, this Court still must evaluate the mark's distinctiveness in the marketplace.

Courts may consider several factors in determining a particular mark's distinctiveness in the marketplace. For example, the "strength of a mark is [] often ascertained by looking at the extent of advertising invested in it, and by the volume of sales of the product." [Citation.] In addition, "extensive third-party use can dilute the strength of a mark." [Citation.]

Here, ROBERT PEPI COLLINE DI SASSI is not particularly distinctive in the marketplace. In the first instance, Kendall-Jackson's advertising expenditures for ROBERT PEPI COLLINE DI SASSI over the last several years have been minimal. Kendall-Jackson's distribution of its wine also has been limited in scale. Furthermore, numerous vinters [sic] have used variations of the words "Colline" and "Sassi" in their respective marks. Accordingly, this first *Polaroid* factor weighs in favor of Banfi.

2. The Degree of Similarity Between the Two Marks

In determining whether the two marks are similar, and therefore likely to cause consumer confusion, courts should evaluate "'the overall impression created by the logos and the context in which they are found and consider the totality of factors that could cause confusion among prospective purchasers.'" [Citation.] In doing so, courts may consider "the products' sizes, logos, typefaces and package designs, among other factors." [Citation.]

In the case at bar, the two marks are quite dissimilar. Banfi's mark, COL-DI-SASSO, is composed of three words, separated by hyphens, whereas Kendall-Jackson's ROBERT PEPI COLLINE DI SASSI is composed of five words with no hyphens. There are also phonetic differences between the two marks, to wit, the "Col" element of Banfi's COL-DI-SASSO has one syllable, while the "Colline" element of Kendall-Jackson's mark has three syllables and is pronounced "Col-ee-ne."[2] *See Buitoni Foods Corp. v. Gio. Buton*, 680 F.2d 290, 292 (2d Cir. 1982) (noting that differences in the pronunciation between the marks at issue rendered the degree of similarity insubstantial). In addition, the English translations of the two marks differ in that COL-DI-SASSO means "hill of stone," and ROBERT PEPI COLLINE DI SASSI translates into "Robert Pepi little hills of stone."

There are also several key distinctions between the products themselves and the overall impression created by the marks that would prevent consumer confusion. For instance, Banfi's front label includes an orange-yellow depiction of a landscape with a black marbleized background. The Banfi wine's front label features the COL-DI-SASSO name, along with the words "Sangiovese" and "Cabernet." Additionally, the

2. Even if a prospective purchaser were to mispronounce "Colline" as a two-syllable word, its pronunciation still would differ from that of plaintiff's COL-DI-SASSO mark.

word "Banfi" appears on the side of the front label in gold script and on the cork in black script. Banfi's back label features the legends "Produce of Italy," "Red Table Wine of Italy" and "Banfi Vinters."

By contrast, the front label of ROBERT PEPI COLLINE DI SASSI contains neither a depiction nor a marbleized background. Rather, the cream and orange label features the words "Robert Pepi" in the top left corner, with "Colline Di Sassi" and "Napa Valley Sangiovese" in the center. The back label plainly states that the wine is both produced and bottled in Napa Valley, California. Based on the foregoing, this factor also weighs in Banfi's favor.

3. The Proximity of the Products

Under this *Polaroid* factor, courts must assess whether the two products at issue compete with each other in the same market. [Citation.] In doing so, courts should evaluate "the nature of the products themselves, as well as the structure of the relevant market." [Citation.] Differences in price between the two products also should be considered in measuring product proximity. [Citations.]

Taking these criteria in turn, this Court concludes that the products in this case differ in ways that may be deemed material to consumers. First, Banfi's COL-DI-SASSO is a 50-50 blend of Sangiovese and Cabernet. On the other hand, ROBERT PEPI COLLINE DI SASSI is both labeled and marketed solely as a Sangiovese, even though it contains a small percentage of Cabernet. Additionally, COL-DI-SASSO is marketed as an affordable, everyday red wine, and as such is sold to distributors, who in turn market the wine to discount drug stores, supermarkets, and mid-range Italian restaurant chains. ROBERT PEPI COLLINE DI SASSI, marketed as a high-end, special occasion wine, is sold exclusively in fine restaurants and retail wine stores. In fact, Kendall-Jackson submitted no evidence to suggest that the two wines at issue were ever sold in the same location, be it restaurant or retail store.

Additionally, Banfi's COL-DI-SASSO is sold for $8 to $10 per bottle in stores, and $16 to $23 per bottle in restaurants. Conversely, ROBERT PEPI COLLINE DI SASSI is sold for double this price, i.e., $20 to $25 in stores, and $35 to $45 in restaurants. Banfi's wine is often sold by the glass in restaurants as a promotional tool, whereas Kendall-Jackson's is rarely, if ever, sold by the glass. Accordingly, this factor is of little help to Kendall-Jackson's claim that there is a likelihood of confusion.

4. The Likelihood That the Party Alleging Infringement Will "Bridge the Gap"

This factor considers whether Kendall-Jackson will enter Banfi's market. [Citation.] Here, Kendall-Jackson has presented no evidence to suggest that it intends to produce a 50-50 blend of Sangiovese and Cabernet, produce and bottle a wine in Italy, or reduce the price of ROBERT PEPI COLLINE DI SASSI to match that of Banfi's COL-DI-SASSO. This factor, then, favors Banfi.

5. Actual Confusion

In the instant matter, Kendall-Jackson stipulated to the absence of actual confusion between the two products. Of equal significance, however, is the fact that Kendall-Jackson was ignorant of Banfi's use of the COL-DI-SASSO mark until 1994 when this dispute arose. This co-existence further buttresses this Court's finding that not only is there no actual confusion, but no likelihood of confusion as well. [Citation.]

6. The Alleged Infringer's Good Faith in Adopting the Mark

This factor considers "whether the [alleged infringer] adopted its mark with the intention of capitalizing on [the opposing party's] reputation and goodwill and any confusion between his and the senior user's product." [Citation.] One indication of a party's good faith is "the selection of a mark that reflects the product's characteristics." [Citation.]

Here, Banfi demonstrated that it conceived its mark at approximately the same time that Kendall-Jackson adopted its own mark, albeit in Italy as opposed to Napa Valley, California. Moreover, Banfi selected the COL-DI-SASSO name because the wine was produced in Tuscany, a region in which sasso rock is prevalent. Conversely, Pepi adopted its ROBERT PEPI COLLINE DI SASSI mark at a family meal, without any relation to "little hills of stone." Banfi also adopted the COL-DI-SASSO mark without ever having heard of ROBERT PEPI COLLINE DI SASSI. Furthermore, Banfi showed its continuing good faith by initiating this instant action, seeking resolution of both party's rights to the marks at issue. Accordingly, this factor weighs against a finding of likelihood of confusion.

7. The Quality of the Alleged Infringer's Mark

Courts consistently have concluded that this factor primarily is concerned with "whether the senior user's reputation could be jeopardized by virtue of the fact that the junior user's product is of inferior quality." [Citation.] In the case at bar, the evidence establishes that Banfi's COL-DI-SASSO is not of lesser quality than ROBERT PEPI COLLINE DI SASSI. On the contrary, since it was first introduced in the United States, COL-DI-SASSO has received favorable reviews from many critics. Thus, this factor favors Banfi.

8. The Sophistication of the Buyers

This final *Polaroid* factor considers "the general impression of the ordinary consumer, buying under normal market conditions and giving the attention such purchasers usually give in purchasing the product at issue." [Citation.] In this case, the only evidence relevant to this factor suggests that wine purchasers are likely to be older, wealthier, and better educated than the general population. Because Kendall-Jackson submitted no evidence to contradict these findings, this factor weighs in Banfi's favor.

9. Balancing the Polaroid *Factors*

In sum, all eight *Polaroid* factors favor Banfi, albeit in varying degrees. Consequently, there is no likelihood that consumers will confuse Banfi's COL-DI-SASSO, with Kendall-Jackson's ROBERT PEPI COLLINE DI SASSI.

....

Conclusion

This Court has examined Kendall-Jackson's remaining claims and finds that they are without merit. Accordingly, for the reasons stated herein, this Court concludes that there is no likelihood of confusion between the two marks at issue, and directs the Clerk of the Court to enter judgment of non-infringement. In view of this conclusion, this Court dismisses as meritless both parties' remaining claims.

So ordered.

Questions

1. What are the salient differences that explain the different outcomes in the *E. & J. Gallo* and *Banfi* cases?

2. Banfi first distributed Col-Di-Sasso in the United States in 1991; Robert Pepi began to sell Colline Di Sassi in October 1990. Should Banfi's general counsel have mailed a cease-and-desist letter to Kendall-Jackson without first researching whether Banfi was the senior user?

3. In evaluating the similarity of the marks, the *E. & J. Gallo Winery* court notes that "gallo" is a common Italian word, and that, in context, plaintiff's and defendant's marks were very different in appearance, but concludes defendant's use is confusingly similar because "for English speakers, the 'stand out' or significant term in the phrase 'Consorzio del Gallo Nero' is the word 'Gallo' when the phrase is encountered on or in connection with a bottle of wine." What is the basis for the court's conclusion? Can you think of any use of the word "gallo" in connection with wine or wine-related products that would be sufficiently dissimilar to make confusion unlikely?

4. The court compares the two marks in the *Banfi* case and finds them "quite dissimilar." In addition to dissimilarities in the trade dress of the labels, the court notes that Banfi's mark is three syllables separated by hyphen while Kendall-Jackson's is five syllables; "Col" is pronounced differently from "Colline," and "the English translations of the two marks differ in that COL-DI-SASSO means 'hill of stone,' and ROBERT PEPI COLLINE DI SASSI translates into 'Robert Pepi little hills of stone.'" Is the *Banfi* court using the same standard as the *E.&J. Gallo* court for assessing the similarity of the marks? How would you articulate the difference?

5. Gallo Nero presented a survey in which subjects were shown an array of eight bottles of wine, including two bottles of Gallo and two of Gallo Nero. Gallo argued that the survey proved nothing because it was unclear that the subjects even saw defendant's mark. Why is that not probative of the absence of likely confusion?

6. Review the court's treatment of the *E. & J. Gallo Winery* defendant's intent. Does the court conclude that Gallo Nero's initial adoption of its mark was made in good faith, but that its later decision to use that mark on wine exported to the U.S. was not? Does that make any sense?

Leelanau Wine Cellars, Ltd v. Black & Red, Inc., 502 F.3d 504 (6th Cir. 2007). "In 1981, Michigan's Leelanau Peninsula was designated an Approved American Viticultural Area (AVA). 27 C.F.R. § 9.40. Federal regulation defines a 'viticultural area' as a 'delimited grape-growing region distinguishable by geographical features, the boundaries of which have been delineated....' 27 C.F.R. § 9.11. An area's designation as an AVA permits the name of the area to be used as an 'appellation of origin' on wine labels and in advertising." Both plaintiff Leelanau Wine Cellars (LWC) and defendant Black & Red (B&R) own and operate wineries located in the Leelanau Peninsula. LWC has been making wine since 1977 and, in 1997, obtained a federal trademark registration for LEELANAU CELLARS. B&R began making wine in 1999 and, in 2000, adopted the name "Chateau de Leelanau Vineyard and Winery." In 2001, LWC filed an action under federal and state trademark law seeking to enjoin B&R from using the term "Leelanau" in connection with the sale of wine. The district court found confusion unlikely; the Sixth Circuit affirmed. The court was particularly critical of plaintiff's survey:

On the issue of actual confusion, LWC, on remand from this court, produced a consumer survey conducted by Dr. Parikh at four malls throughout Michigan: two in Detroit, one in Grand Rapids, and one in Traverse City. In the study, interviewees were taken into a room and shown an advertisement for Leelanau Cellars wine. Interviewees were then asked to put the advertisement away and look at five bottles of Chardonnay, all of which originated in Michigan. The study included a "test cell" and a "control cell." The test and control cells both contained Turner Road, St. Julian, Wilhurst, and Zafarana wines. In the test cell, the fifth wine was Chateau de Leelanau. In the control cell, the fifth wine was Bel Lago. Participants in the study were, after viewing the advertisement and the wines, asked, "Do you believe there is *OR* is not a bottle of wine in this display that is the same as, or comes from the same source, that is, the same winery that puts out the wine in the advertisement that you just looked at?" Of those subjected to the test cell, 64 percent responded in the affirmative to the proposed question, and 54 percent identified Chateau de Leelanau as the wine they believed matched the ad. Of those who selected Chateau de Leelanau, 38 percent justified their belief on the basis of the use of the name "Leelanau" in both the Leelanau Cellars ad and on the Chateau de Leelanau bottle. Among the individuals who did not identify a match between the wine in the ad and a wine in the display, 10 percent nevertheless believed that there was a "relationship, sponsorship, or association" between the winery in the ad and the winery producing one of the bottles in the display. Eight percent of those individuals identified Chateau de Leelanau only as the associated wine. By contrast, only 31 percent of those individuals exposed to the control cell identified Bel Lago as coming from the same or a related source as Leelanau Cellars and reached that conclusion based on similarities in the labels. After adjusting her results for survey noise or guessing, Dr. Parikh concluded that, the "net confusion level" ranged between 27 percent and 31 percent.

The district court permitted the admission of the Parikh study, but refused to give Parikh's survey significant weight, citing three reasons: (1) the universe of respondents was overbroad and failed to include individuals who were potential purchasers of B & R's wines; (2) the survey did not replicate conditions

> that consumers would encounter in the marketplace; and (3) the survey questions were suggestive and misleading. These were legitimate bases for declining to rely heavily on the findings of the Parikh study. The district court correctly recognized that the study failed to limit the respondent population to those persons likely to purchase defendant's products. [Citation.] Although the study included adults who had or were likely to purchase a bottle of wine in the $5 to $14 price range, there was no attempt to survey only those people who would purchase moderately priced wines produced in the state of Michigan, undoubtedly a distinct group. Nor was the survey limited to wine purchasers who acquire wine through wine tasting rooms, the primary distribution source of B & R. The district court was also correct in concluding that the study failed to replicate actual market conditions. B & R sells its wines almost exclusively through its tasting rooms. Thus, it is unlikely that a purchaser of Chateau de Leelanau would find herself faced with the need to distinguish among various wines or, having walked into a B & R tasting room, erroneously believe that she was in fact at Leelanau Cellars.
>
> These deficiencies undermine the persuasiveness of the Parikh survey. Where a survey presented on the issue of actual confusion reflects methodological errors, a court may choose to limit the importance it accords the study in its likelihood of confusion analysis. [Citations.]

The court also observed that consumers were unlikely to encounter the respective wines in the same commercial setting:

> Courts consider the respective marketing channels of the parties to a trademark infringement action.... There is less likelihood of confusion where the goods are sold through different avenues. [Citation.]
>
> There is very limited overlap between the distribution channels B & R and LWC utilize. B & R sells approximately 85 percent of its wine through its tasting rooms. Indeed, Kurtz testified that B & R wine almost "never leaves our tasting room." B & R does not sell to major retail operations. LWC, by contrast, sells 25 to 30 percent of its wines through its tasting rooms and the remaining 70 to 75 percent through retail stores like Sam's Club or Meijer's. Thus, despite their operation within a common geographical area, Chateau de Leelanau and LWC are sold, for the most part, in entirely distinct environments. This factor suggests a lesser likelihood of purchaser confusion.

Kraft Foods Group Brands LLC v. Cracker Barrel Old Country Store, Inc., 735 F.3d 735 (7th Cir 2013). Kraft has sold supermarket cheddar cheese under the CRACKER BARREL mark since 1954; it registered the mark in 1957. Cracker Barrel Old Country Store (CBOCS) has operated a chain of restaurants since the 1970s. In 2013, CBOCS announced that it was introducing a line of grocery store deli meats to be sold in supermarkets under the CRACKER BARREL OLD COUNTRY STORE mark. Kraft filed a trademark infringement suit. The trial court found a likelihood of confusion and issued a preliminary injunction. The Court of Appeals for the 7th Circuit affirmed.

Judge Posner wrote that "[t]he likelihood of confusion seems substantial and the risk to Kraft of the loss of valuable goodwill and control therefore palpable." He had critical words, however, for the survey Kraft relied on to demonstrate likelihood of confusion:

> So the grant of the preliminary injunction must be affirmed. But mainly for future reference we want to say something about the consumer survey that Kraft presented in support of its claim of confusion. Consumer surveys conducted by party-hired expert witnesses are prone to bias. There is such a wide choice of survey designs, none fool-proof, involving such issues as sample selection and size, presentation of the allegedly confusing products to the consumers involved in the survey, and phrasing of questions in a way that is intended to elicit the surveyor's desired response—confusion or lack thereof—from the survey respondents. [Citations.] Among the problems identified by the academic literature are the following: when a consumer is a survey respondent, this changes the normal environment in which he or she encounters, compares, and reacts to trademarks; a survey that produces results contrary to the interest of the party that sponsored the survey may be suppressed and thus never become a part of the trial record; and the expert witnesses who conduct surveys in aid of litigation are likely to be biased in favor of the party that hired and is paying them, usually generously....
>
> Of course, judges and jurors have their own biases and blind spots.
>
> ....
>
> Nevertheless it's clear that caution is required in the screening of proposed experts on consumer surveys. Kraft's expert in this case was Hal Poret, an experienced survey researcher, and we won't hold it against him that he appears to be basically a professional expert witness.... Poret was able to obtain a random or at least representative sample of 300 American consumers of whole-ham products, email them photographs of the CBOCS sliced spiral ham, and ask them in the email whether the company that makes the ham also makes other products—and if so what products. About a quarter of the respondents said cheese. It's difficult to know what to make of this. The respondents may have assumed that a company with a logo that does not specify a particular food product doesn't make *just* sliced spiral ham. So now they have to guess what else such a company would make. Well, maybe cheese.
>
> Poret showed a control group of 100 respondents essentially the same ham, but made by Smithfield—and none of these respondents said that Smithfield also makes cheese. Poret inferred from this that the name "Cracker Barrel" on the ham shown the 300 respondents had triggered their recollection of Cracker Barrel cheese, rather than the word "ham" being the trigger. That is plausible, but its relevance is obscure. Kraft's concern is not that people will think that Cracker Barrel cheeses are made by CBOCS but that they will think that CBOCS ham is made by Kraft, in which event if they have a bad experience with the ham they'll blame Kraft.

Also it's very difficult to compare people's reactions to photographs shown to them online by a survey company to their reactions to products they are looking at in a grocery store and trying to decide whether to buy. The contexts are radically different, and the stakes much higher when actual shopping decisions have to be made (because that means parting with money), which may influence responses.

....

We can imagine other types of expert testimony that might be illuminating in a case such as this—testimony by experts on retail food products about the buying habits and psychology of consumers of inexpensive food products....

We have doubts about the probative significance of the Poret survey. But the similarity of logos and of products, and of the channels of distribution (and the advertising overlap) if CBOCS is allowed to sell its products through grocery stores under its Cracker Barrel logo, and the availability to the company of alternatives to grocery stores for reaching a large consumer public under the logo, provide adequate support for the issuance of the preliminary injunction.

Questions

1. Does "size matter"? Where defendant is a small producer, and particularly if its goods are high quality or addressed to an elite audience, is a court less likely to find confusion? *See Starbucks Corp. v. Wolfe's Borough Coffee, Inc.*, 588 F.3d 97 (2d Cir. 2009) (affirming finding, after trial, of no likelihood of confusion between STARBUCKS and BLACK BEAR MR. CHARBUCKS for coffee). For the Second Circuit's decision in the same case concerning Starbucks' dilution claim, see *infra* Chapter 9.

2. How helpful are surveys in assessing the likelihood of confusion? Compare the *Gallo* and *Leelanau* courts' analyses of the surveys. How would you redesign the Parikh survey in *Leeanau* to replicate actual marketplace conditions? *See, e.g., THOIP v. Walt Disney Company*, 788 F. Supp. 2d 168 (S.D.N.Y. 2011) (finding that both parties' surveys failed to replicate actual marketplace conditions and were therefore "largely irrelevant"). How would you redesign the CRACKER BARREL survey to provide evidence that is more probative of whether confusion is likely?

3. Who is the relevant public for the purpose of assessing whether confusion is likely? *Arrowpoint Capital Corp. v. Arrowpoint Asset Management, LLC*, 793 F.3d 313 (3d Cir. 2015), involved a dispute between two financial services companies, both of which did business using the ARROWPOINT mark. The senior user and owner of multiple registrations for the mark sought a preliminary injunction. To show actual confusion, plaintiff sought to introduce evidence that brokers and dealers had mixed up the two companies or expressed the view that they were affiliated with each other. The district court applied the Third Circuit's multifactor test, found confusion unlikely, and denied the injunction. The judge discounted the proffered evidence of actual confusion among brokers or dealers, reasoning that it did not show any basis for inferring *customer* confusion. The Court of Appeals for the Third Circuit reversed:

> In the present case, the District Court cited the correct standard when it stated that "the [Lanham] Act covers 'the use of trademarks which are likely to cause confusion, mistake, or deception *of any kind*, not merely of purchasers nor simply as to source of origin.'" [Citation.] But the Court did not then appear to apply that standard; instead it repeatedly discussed the lack of *customer* confusion. It said, for example, that "the plaintiff produced no evidence of actual customer confusion.... [I]t argues that 'broker dealers'... all have been misled." Similarly, it concluded that, as a matter of law, there was no general likelihood of confusion, "especially since the record is devoid of any inference of *customer* confusion." (emphasis added). And, rather than recognizing the special importance of identity and reputation in the financial industry, it discounted such concerns, saying that similar marks can coexist because "consumers take greater care than many others," and "'prospective purchasers are unlikely to perceive the marks before becoming familiar with the parties' businesses.'" That overly narrow interpretation of what constitutes confusion under the Lanham Act is contrary to our deeply rooted precedent.... We thus take this opportunity to reiterate that the Lanham Act protects against "the use of trademarks which are likely to cause confusion, mistake, or deception *of any kind*, not merely of purchasers nor simply as to source of origin." [Citation.] It certainly covers confusion created "'in the minds of persons in a position to influence [a] purchasing decision or persons whose confusion presents a significant risk to the sales, goodwill, *or* reputation of the trademark owner.'" [Citation.]

Note: Is Likelihood of Confusion a Question of Fact or a Question Of Law?

Judicial attempts to characterize likelihood of confusion as an issue of fact, law, or both have produced a three-way split among the federal circuits. The fact-law determination bears significantly on many aspects of a trademark case, including appeals, preliminary injunctions, and motions for summary judgment.

Perhaps most importantly, whether likelihood of confusion is an issue of fact or law affects the standard of review applied by appellate courts. If the issue is one of fact, an appellate court must adopt the conclusion of the trial court unless it determines the underlying facts to be "clearly erroneous." The "clearly erroneous" standard, set forth in Federal Rule of Civil Procedure 52(a), means that "unless an appellate court is left with [a] 'definite and firm conviction that a mistake [was] committed,' it must accept the trial court's findings." *Inwood Labs., Inc. v. Ives Labs., Inc.*, 456 U.S. 844, 855 (1982) (quoting *United States v. U.S. Gypsum Co.*, 333 U.S. 364, 395 (1948)).

The rationale for restricting appellate courts' discretion is that the trier of fact is considered best situated to evaluate the evidence before it. By contrast, appellate courts review issues of law *de novo*. Thus, if an appellate court deems likelihood of confusion a question of law, it may independently review the facts and will not be bound by the lower court's conclusions.

The Restatement (Third) of Unfair Competition (1995), in a comment to § 21 "Proof of Likelihood of Confusion: Market Factors," suggests that the better approach is to treat likelihood of confusion as a question of fact:

> *m. Question of law or fact.* Although the cases are not unanimous, whether the defendant's use of a trademark creates a likelihood of confusion is properly regarded as a question of fact. In jury trials the issue is submitted to the jury with appropriate instructions and the jury's determination is entitled to the usual deference accorded jury verdicts. In non-jury cases the findings of the trial judge concerning the likelihood of confusion should be subject to reversal only if clearly erroneous.

Indeed, the majority of circuits—the First, Third, Fourth, Fifth, Seventh, Eighth, Ninth, Tenth, and Eleventh—holds that likelihood of confusion is a question of fact subject to the "clearly erroneous" standard of review. Only one circuit, the Court of Appeals for the Federal Circuit, holds that the question is one of law.

A third approach, adopted by the Second and Sixth Circuits, treats the issue as a mixed question of fact and law. Under this two-step hybrid approach, an appellate court separates the determination as to whether each likelihood of confusion factor favors the plaintiff or defendant from the ultimate conclusion about whether the balance of all the factors together indicates a likelihood of consumer confusion. First, the appellate court reviews the lower court's conclusion about each likelihood of confusion factor, reversing the determination only if "clearly erroneous." Second, the appellate court balances the factors *de novo* to determine whether likelihood of confusion exists.

Maker's Mark Distillery, Inc. v. Diageo North America, Inc.

679 F.3d 410 (6th Cir. 2012)

Boyce F. Martin, Jr., Circuit Judge.

....

I.

All bourbon is whiskey, but not all whiskey is bourbon. Whiskey, like other distilled spirits, begins as a fermentable mash, composed of water and grains or other fermentable ingredients. The mash is heated and then cooled, yeast is introduced to ferment the sugars in the mash, and the yeast turns the sugars into alcohol and carbon dioxide. This now-alcoholic liquid is then distilled to concentrate the alcohol. Gary Regan & Mardee Haidin Regan, The Bourbon Companion 32–33 (1998). The composition of the mash, and the aging, treating, and flavoring of the distilled alcohol, determine the flavor, color, and character of the distilled spirit. In the case of bourbon, the corn-based mash and aging in charred new oak barrels impart a distinct mellow flavor and caramel color. Distillers compete intensely on flavor, but also through branding and marketing; the history of bourbon, in particular, illustrates why strong branding and differentiation is important in the distilled spirits market.

....

In recognition of bourbon's unique place in American culture and commerce, ... Congress in 1964 designated bourbon as a "distinctive product[] of the United States," 27 C.F.R. § 5.22(l)(1), and prescribed restrictions on which distilled spirits may bear the label "bourbon." Federal regulations require that bourbon whiskey to, among other things, be aged in charred new oak barrels, contain certain proportions of mash ingredients, and be barreled and bottled at certain proofs. § 5.22(b). Importantly, whiskey made for consumption within the United States cannot be called bourbon unless it is made in the United States. § 5.22(l)(1). While bourbon is strongly associated with Kentucky, and while "[ninety-five] percent of the world's supply of bourbon comes from Kentucky," Jessie Halladay, *Kentucky's Libation Vacations*, COURIER-J., Feb. 26, 2012, at D1, some notable bourbons are made in other states.

Maker's Mark occupies a central place in the modern story of bourbon. The Samuels family, founder of the Maker's Mark distillery in Loretto, Kentucky, has produced whiskey in Kentucky nearly continuously from the eighteenth century through today. REGAN & REGAN, *supra*, at 161–62. Indeed, Robert Samuels (along with Jacob Beam, Basil Hayden, and Daniel Weller, all of whose surnames are familiar to bourbon connoisseurs) was one of Kentucky's early settlers. [CHARLES K. COWDERY, BOURBON, STRAIGHT: THE UNCUT AND UNFILTERED STORY OF AMERICAN WHISKEY (2004)] at 4. Bill Samuels, Sr. formulated the recipe for Maker's Mark bourbon in 1953. His wife, Margie, conceived of the red dripping wax seal and used the family deep fryer to perfect the process of applying it. The company has bottled bourbon for commercial sale under the Maker's Mark name, and has used a red dripping wax seal on its Maker's Mark bourbon bottles, since 1958. Maker's Mark, and craft bourbon generally, garnered national attention when the *Wall Street Journal* published a front-page article about the bourbon, the red dripping wax seal, and the family behind it. David P. Garino, *Maker's Mark Goes Against the Grain to Make its Mark*, WALL ST. J., Aug. 1, 1980, at 1. In 1985, Maker's Mark registered a trademark for the dripping-wax-seal element of its trade dress, which it described as a "wax-like coating covering the cap of the bottle and trickling down the neck of the bottle in a freeform irregular pattern." The trademark is silent as to color, but Maker's Mark conceded in submissions before the district court that it sought only to enforce it as applied to the red dripping wax seal.

Jose Cuervo produced a premium tequila, "Reserva de la Familia," beginning in 1995. The tequila bottle had a wax seal that was straight-edged and did not initially feature drips. By 2001, Cuervo had begun selling this tequila in the United States in bottles with a red dripping wax seal reminiscent of the Maker's Mark red dripping wax seal. In 2003, Maker's Mark instituted this suit against Casa Cuervo S.A. de C.V., Jose Cuervo International, Inc., Tequila Cuervo La Rojeòa S.A. de C.V., and Diageo North America, Inc. claiming state and federal trademark infringement and federal trademark dilution; sometime thereafter, Cuervo discontinued use of the red dripping wax seal and reverted to a red straight-edged wax seal. In its suit, Maker's Mark sought damages, injunctions against dilution and infringement, and costs. Cuervo counterclaimed for cancellation of the Maker's Mark trademark.

After a six-day bench trial, the district court found that Maker's Mark's red dripping wax seal is a valid trademark and that Cuervo had infringed that trademark. Based on those findings, the district court enjoined Cuervo permanently "from using red dripping wax on the cap of a bottle in the sale, offering for sale, distribution or advertising of Cuervo tequila products at any locality within the United States." The district court found that Cuervo had not diluted the mark and denied Maker's Mark's claim for damages; the district court also denied Cuervo's counterclaim for cancellation of the mark. In a separate opinion, the district court awarded Maker's Mark some of its costs.

Cuervo appeals the district court's determination that the red dripping wax seal is not aesthetically functional, some of the district court's factual findings, its balancing of those findings in determining Cuervo had infringed, and its award of some of Maker's Mark's costs. Cuervo does not appeal the scope of the injunction.

II.

....

B. Factual Findings under Frisch

....

[A] court considering a claim for trademark infringement must determine the likelihood of consumer confusion. The factors the court should consider are: "1. strength of the plaintiff's mark; 2. relatedness of the goods; 3. similarity of the marks; 4. evidence of actual confusion; 5. marketing channels used; 6. likely degree of purchaser care; 7. defendant's intent in selecting the mark; [and] 8. likelihood of expansion of the product lines." *Frisch's Rests., Inc. v. Elby's Big Boy, Inc.*, 670 F.2d 642, 648 (6th Cir. 1982) (quoting *Toho Co., Ltd. v. Sears, Roebuck & Co.*, 645 F.2d 788, 790 (9th Cir. 1981)).

We review the district court's factual findings under *Frisch* for clear error. *Tumblebus Inc. v. Cranmer*, 399 F.3d 754, 764 (6th Cir. 2005). We assess each factor with respect to the relevant consumer market; potential buyers of the "junior" product (here, Cuervo's Reserva de la Familia) are the relevant consumers. *Leelanau Wine Cellars, Ltd. v. Black & Red, Inc.*, 502 F.3d 504, 518 (6th Cir. 2007). Cuervo appeals the district court's findings on only three of the eight *Frisch* factors: strength, similarity, and actual confusion.

1. Strength

To evaluate the strength factor under the *Frisch* analysis, this Court "focuses on the distinctiveness of a mark and its recognition among the public." *Therma-Scan, Inc. v. Thermoscan, Inc.*, 295 F.3d 623, 631 (6th Cir. 2002). One leading commentator usefully characterizes this evaluation as encompassing two separate components: (1) "conceptual strength," or "placement of the mark on the spectrum of marks," which encapsulates the question of inherent distinctiveness; and (2) "commercial strength" or "the marketplace recognition value of the mark." 2 J. Thomas McCarthy, McCarthy on Trademarks and Unfair Competition § 11.83 (4th ed.). In other words, "[a] mark is strong if it is highly distinctive, i.e., if the public readily accepts it as the hallmark of a particular source; it can become so because it is unique, because it has been the subject of wide and intensive advertisement, or because of a combination of both." *Homeowners Grp. v. Home Mktg. Specialists, Inc.*, 931 F.2d 1100, 1107 (6th Cir. 1991) (internal quotation marks omitted).

Because the strength of a trademark for purposes of the likelihood-of-confusion analysis depends on the interplay between conceptual and commercial strength, the existence of inherent distinctiveness is not the end of the inquiry. *See Therma-Scan, Inc.*, 295 F.3d at 631–32 (noting that a mark can be inherently distinctive but not especially strong if it fails to attain broad public recognition); *Homeowners Grp., Inc.*, 931 F.2d at 1107 ("The District Court's finding that HMS was an arbitrary and inherently distinctive mark is only a first step in determining the strength of a mark in the marketplace."); *see also* McCarthy, *supra* § 11:83 ("[T]he true relative strength of a mark can only fully be determined by weighing [both] aspects of strength."). Thus, although inherent distinctiveness may provide powerful support for the strength of a mark, the full extent of that support nonetheless depends on the scope of commercial recognition.

Here, the district court appropriately evaluated both components of the strength factor. From the physical characteristics of the mark, the district court specifically found the red dripping wax seal to be inherently distinctive based on its uniqueness and its potential to "draw in the customer" in an unusual manner.... As to commercial recognition, the district court found the seal "acquired secondary meaning through fifty years of use, extensive advertising and consumer recognition."[3] The district court also found that Maker's Mark's advertising was intensive, citing the extent of its advertising budget that "focuses almost entirely on branding the red dripping wax," as well as the significant public attention that the wax seal has received through the media. In further support of these findings, the district court also cited studies showing significant amounts of consumer dialogue about the brand, as well as a high level of recognition among both whiskey drinkers and distilled-spirits drinkers more generally.

Cuervo argues that the district court erred in its evaluation of the strength of the mark by (1) disregarding third-party use of red dripping wax seals; (2) failing to give proper weight to the lack of a survey regarding recognition of the red dripping wax seal; (3) relying in its analysis on Maker's Mark's advertisements without apparent evidence of their dates or circulation; and (4) relying on evidence of the strength of the mark in the overbroad group of distilled spirits drinkers instead of prospective Reserva purchasers.

We recognize that "extensive third-party uses of a trademark [may] substantially weaken the strength of a mark." *Homeowners Grp.*, 931 F.2d at 1108; *Herman Miller, Inc. v. Palazzetti Imps. & Exps., Inc.*, 270 F.3d 298, 317 (6th Cir. 2001) (noting the possibility that the strength of a plaintiff's mark may be " 'weakened' by widespread use in the market," causing the mark to "lose its significance as an indication of source." (quoting McCarthy, *supra* § 17:17)). Contrary to Cuervo's argument, the district

---

3. In light of the district court's finding that the mark is inherently distinctive, it did not need to consider secondary meaning. *See Two Pesos, Inc. v. Taco Cabana, Inc.*, 505 U.S. 763, 769 (1992) ("The general rule regarding distinctiveness is clear: An identifying mark is distinctive and capable of being protected if it *either* (1) is inherently distinctive *or* (2) has acquired distinctiveness through secondary meaning."). The district court's findings on secondary meaning, however, are nonetheless relevant to the broader questions of commercial recognition and overall strength. *See* McCarthy, *supra* § 11:83 (distinguishing between the analyses used to determine secondary meaning and strength).

court *did* consider evidence of third-party use of similar seals on distilled spirits, but rejected that evidence as limited and unconvincing because it concerned seals used on all distilled spirits; the court found that the relevant use of the seals is limited to the "relevant market," and not among all distilled spirits. We agree with the district court's finding and reasoning.

Next, while "survey evidence is the most direct and persuasive evidence" of whether a mark has acquired secondary meaning, "consumer surveys ... are not a prerequisite to establishing secondary meaning." *Herman Miller, Inc.*, 270 F.3d at 312, 315 (citations and internal quotation marks omitted). Nor is such evidence indispensable to the broader question of commercial recognition. In light of the abundance of other evidence demonstrating market recognition, such as Maker's Mark's extensive marketing efforts focusing on the red dripping wax seal and its widespread publicity, it was not clear error for the district court to overlook the lack of survey evidence because that evidence was not determinative of the strength of the mark.

As to the district court's consideration of advertising evidence, the district court discussed the nature of the advertising and found that advertising efforts by Maker's Mark usually focus directly on the red dripping wax seal. As the record and the district court's opinion show, the district court had before it, and considered, an abundance of Maker's Mark advertisements that specifically feature the red dripping wax seal. Moreover, these advertisements were recent, relevant, and strong enough to convince *Business Week*, in 2002, to declare the dripping wax seal "one of the most recognizable branding symbols in the world," and CBS Sunday Morning, in 2008, to refer to the process by which the seal is applied as the "famous dip in red sealing wax." These findings support the district court's ultimate conclusion regarding the breadth of market recognition of Maker's Mark's trademarked red dripping wax seal.

Finally, as to the district court's discussion of evidence of the mark's strength within the broader group of distilled spirits drinkers, the district court considered, but did not rest its holding on, this evidence. Instead, the district court based its holding primarily on the seal's "unique design and [Maker's Mark's] singular marketing efforts." We therefore find no error here.

In sum, none of Cuervo's arguments undermines the district court's finding "that the Maker's Mark red dripping wax seal is an extremely strong mark due to its unique design and the company's singular marketing efforts." We therefore conclude that the district court did not clearly err in its evaluation of the strength of the red dripping wax seal.

2. Similarity

In assessing similarity, "courts must determine whether a given mark would confuse the public when viewed alone, in order to account for the possibility that sufficiently similar marks may confuse consumers who do not have both marks before them but who may have a general, vague, or even hazy, impression or recollection of the other party's mark." *Daddy's Junky Music Stores, Inc. v. Big Daddy's Family Music Cntr.*, 109 F.3d 275, 283 (6th Cir. 1997) (internal quotation marks omitted). The district court found this factor "narrowly favor[s] Maker's Mark," and found that, though "[v]ery few consumers ... would buy one product believing it was the other," the seals were facially similar. The district court examined the two seals and found that "nothing on the products *other than* the red dripping wax ... would suggest an association between the two."

Cuervo focuses its argument on the relevance of the house marks—product labels identifying the name of the manufacturer—on the bottles. We have held that the presence of a house mark can decrease the likelihood of confusion. *Therma-Scan, Inc.*, 295 F.3d at 634 ("[T]he presence of [a house mark on a product] does not eliminate the similarity between the trademarks. Instead, this labeling diminishes the likelihood of confusion created by the comparable marks and reduces the importance of this factor."); *AutoZone, Inc. v. Tandy Corp.*, 373 F.3d 786, 797 (6th Cir. 2004) ("The co-appearance of a junior mark and a house mark is not dispositive of dissimilarity, but it is persuasive."). The district court concluded that this consideration is not "as important in an association case, when the two products are related enough that one might associate with or sponsor the other and still use their own house mark."

In *AutoZone*, we found that the proximity of the Radio Shack house mark to the "POWERZONE" mark would alleviate any confusion between POWERZONE and AUTOZONE marks. *AutoZone* does not, however, stand for the proposition that the presence of a house mark always has significant weight in the similarity analysis; it merely states that presence of a house mark is a factor to be considered in the evaluation of similarity and, depending on the facts of the case, may be significant to the overall likelihood of confusion. *AutoZone, Inc.*, 373 F.3d at 796–97. Furthermore, the district court's analysis in this case highlights two factors that diminish the significance of the house marks in the present context. First, testimony in the record indicates that many consumers are unaware of the affiliations between brands of distilled spirits, and that some companies produce multiple types of distilled spirits, which supports the district court's assessment here. Second, the presence of a house mark, as the district court correctly noted, is more significant in a palming off case than in an association case—as the district court reasoned, in an association case "when the two products are related enough ... one might associate with or sponsor the other and still use their own house mark." Accordingly, the district court did not clearly err in its factual findings under this factor, and we adopt its findings.

3. Actual Confusion

The district court stated that "neither party produced meaningful evidence related to actual confusion" and concluded that the lack of evidence was "neutral." The district court reasoned that, though evidence of actual confusion might have been obtainable if it existed, Cuervo sold Reserva for a limited time and in limited quantities, and so the district court did not place weight on the fact that Maker's Mark did not furnish "meaningful" evidence of actual confusion. Despite Cuervo's arguments to the contrary, this finding falls squarely within this Circuit's case law. Though "[e]vidence of actual confusion is undoubtedly the best evidence of likelihood of confusion ... a lack of such evidence is rarely significant." *Daddy's*, 109 F.3d at 284 (citation and internal quotation marks omitted). Here, the Reserva product was sold for a short time and in limited quantities; under these circumstances, it is reasonable that no meaningful evidence of actual confusion was available. The district court did not clearly err in finding the lack of actual confusion evidence non-determinative, and we adopt its findings.

C. Balancing the Frisch *Factors*

We "review *de novo* the legal question of whether [the district court's *Frisch* factual findings] constitute a likelihood of confusion." *Tumblebus Inc.*, 399 F.3d at 764 (quoting *Champions Golf Club, Inc. v. The Champions Golf Club, Inc.*, 78 F.3d 1111, 1116 (6th Cir. 1996)) (internal quotation marks omitted). Because we find above that the district court did not reversibly err in its factual findings on the three disputed factors—strength, similarity, and actual confusion—and because the parties do not dispute the district court's factual findings under the remaining five factors, we adopt all of the district court's factual findings and balance them de novo.

1. Strength. The district court found the evidence of the strength of the mark heavily favored Maker's Mark. We have held that the strength of the mark supplies the weight it should be accorded in balancing. In general, "[t]he stronger the mark, all else equal, the greater the likelihood of confusion." *AutoZone*, 373 F.3d at 794 (alteration in original) (quoting *Homeowners Grp., Inc.*, 931 F.2d at 1107). Because the district court found the mark at issue here to be "extremely strong," the strength factor is weighed very heavily.

2. Relatedness of the goods. The district court found the goods were somewhat related because they were part of the same broad category of high-end distilled spirits, but not fully related because the Cuervo product was priced at $100 per bottle, while Maker's Mark sold for $24 per bottle. Where the goods are "somewhat related but not competitive, the likelihood of confusion will turn on other factors." *Daddy's*, 109 F.3d at 282. Here, the district court found that the products are somewhat related. We accord this factor little weight because the products are competitive only within a very broad category and are only somewhat related; it is thus more appropriate to concentrate the weight of our balancing analysis on other factors.

3. Similarity. The district court found the similarity factor "narrowly favors Maker's [Mark]." "The similarity of the senior and junior marks is 'a factor of considerable weight.'" *AutoZone*, 373 F.3d at 795 (quoting *Daddy's*, 109 F.3d at 283).

4. Actual confusion. As discussed above, "a lack of such evidence is rarely significant, and the factor of actual confusion is weighted heavily only where there is evidence of past confusion, or perhaps, when the particular circumstances indicate such evidence should have been available." *Daddy's*, 109 F.3d at 284 (internal quotation marks omitted). The district court found that this factor was neutral. As we noted, the Reserva product was sold for a short time and in limited quantities; under these circumstances, we give the lack of evidence of actual confusion little weight.

5. *Marketing channels used by the parties.* The court found the channels "similar in some ways and dissimilar in others. Perhaps this factor marginally favors Maker's Mark." The weight of this factor will not add much to a finding of infringement because of the equivocal nature of the district court's factual findings. We accord this factor very little weight.

6. *Likely degree of purchaser care.* The district court found this factor "clearly favors" Cuervo because of the degree of care potential tequila customers would exercise in purchasing a $100 bottle of Reserva; knowledgeable bourbon customers would also exercise similar care and, further, know that Maker's Mark sells only one kind of liquor. This factor, though strongly in favor of Cuervo, is not dispositive. "[C]onfusingly similar marks may lead a purchaser who is extremely careful and knowledgeable ... to assume nonetheless that the seller is affiliated with or identical to the other party." *Id.* at 286. For these reasons, we give this factor substantial weight.

7. *Intent.* The district court found Cuervo did not intend to infringe, but we give no weight to this finding because "[i]ntent is an issue whose resolution may benefit only the cause of the senior user, not of an alleged infringer." *Leelanau*, 502 F.3d at 520 (internal quotation marks omitted).

8. *Likelihood of expansion of product lines.* The district court found this factor was neutral where neither party put forth evidence of significant expansion plans. Because a "strong possibility that either party will expand his business to compete with the other ... will weigh in favor of finding that the present use is infringing," *Daddy's*, 109 F.3d at 287 (internal quotation marks omitted), a finding of little evidence of expansion plans is accorded little to no weight, but does not weigh against Maker's Mark, who, by this test, would benefit by any significant evidentiary showing under this factor, no matter which of the parties intended to expand. For these reasons, we give this factor no weight.

The balance of the factors compels a finding of infringement. Excluding the neutral factors, the majority of the factors—strength, relatedness of the goods, similarity, and marketing channels—favor Maker's Mark. The district court found that Maker's Mark's trademark is "extremely strong," and we have adopted that finding. Further, we have said that the "most important *Frisch* factors" are similarity and strength of the mark, *Gray v. Meijer, Inc.*, 295 F.3d 641, 646 (6th Cir. 2002); both of these factors favor Maker's Mark. The "likely degree of purchaser care" factor "clearly" favors Cuervo. Though this factor is given substantial weight, this factor alone cannot override the "extreme" strength of the mark that, when coupled with similarity (which itself is given "considerable weight"), and combined with the two other factors weighing in favor of Maker's Mark, together favor a finding of infringement. Buttressing this determination is that, in its briefing, Cuervo complains of errors in the district court's factual determinations, but does not argue that, even given the factual findings made by the district court, a de novo balancing under *Frisch* should come out in Cuervo's favor. While Cuervo disputes the factual findings themselves and the related *outcome* of the balancing, it does not argue that the weight given the factors should have been different.

We conclude that there is a likelihood of confusion between the products and that Cuervo has infringed.

....

IV.

... We conclude that the *Frisch* factors weigh in Maker's Mark's favor.... The judgments of the district court are AFFIRMED.

Questions

1. In discussing Cuervo's intent, the court remarks that the trial court "found Cuervo did not intend to infringe...." The court gave "no weight to this finding because '[i]ntent is an issue whose resolution may benefit only the cause of the senior user, not of an alleged infringer.'" What might be the rationale for such a rule?

2. How effective are the likelihood of confusion factors at guiding judicial discretion? Does the multi-factor test supply meaningful boundaries, or is it a thinly disguised invitation to courts to do whatever they please? Are individual factors more probative of likelihood of confusion than others? Do some factors seem more easily manipulated than others? How much does the commercial context in which the consumer encounters the contending marks matter to the weighing of the factors? Recall the *Leelanau* court's emphasis on the different channels of distribution of the parties' wines. Does the offering of goods or services over the Internet influence the weight to be given the confusion factors? See *Network Automation Inc. v. Advanced Systems Concepts Inc.*, 638 F.3d 1137 (9th Cir. 2011), *infra* Chapter 6[B][3][a].

3. Professor Barton Beebe, in a study of multifactor likelihood of confusion tests, finds an imbalance in the significance accorded each factor and a willingness by courts to "stampede" the less-significant factors. "Judges employ fast and frugal heuristics to short-circuit the multifactor test ... [and] rely upon a few factors or combinations of factors to make their decisions. The rest of the factors are at best redundant and at worst irrelevant." *An Empirical Study of the Multifactor Tests for Trademark Infringement*, 94 Cal. L. Rev. 1581, 1586 (2006).

Professors Beebe's study highlights an underlying judicial tension with regard to the multi-factor tests. Compare the remarks of Judge Cardamone, and Judge Sprizzo's response, in *Centaur Communications, Ltd. v. A/S/M Communications, Inc.*, 830 F.2d 1217 (2d Cir. 1987). In a suit by Marketing Week against AD WEEK's Marketing Week, Judge Cardamone, writing for the majority observed:

> This appeal, from a finding of trademark infringement, necessarily implicates the legal concepts of secondary meaning and likelihood of confusion, for which our precedents establish a long list of factors that must be considered before a determination may be reached. Unfortunately, there is no shortcut. To reach a principled conclusion in a trademark case, it is just as essential to recite the right formulas as it was for Ali Baba to say "Open Sesame" in order to open the door to the treasure cave of the Forty Thieves.

830 F.2d at 1219.

Judge Sprizzo (of the Southern District of New York, sitting by designation) complained in a concurring opinion:

> I do not share the view that a proper analysis of th[e] factors can or should be properly characterized as a recital of "the right formulas" akin to Ali Baba's magical incantation "Open Sesame," nor do I believe that a proper resolution of future cases raising these issues will be aided or enhanced by encouraging district court judges to perceive their function in the mechanistic fashion which that language suggests.

Id. at 1230.

Can you design a better test? What would it look like? How would it be applied?

4. In the same study, Professor Beebe suggests that bad intent weighs powerfully in courts' assessments:

> The data ... suggest that a finding of bad faith intent creates, if not in doctrine, then at least in practice, a nearly un-rebuttable presumption of a likelihood of confusion. All but one of the fifty preliminary injunction opinions in which the court found bad faith intent resulted in a finding of a likelihood of confusion, and all but one of the seventeen bench trials in which the court found bad faith intent produced the same result....
>
> ....
>
> It is black-letter doctrine across the circuits ... that bad faith intent may be inferred solely from the fact that the parties' marks are similar and the fact that the defendant had knowledge of the plaintiff's mark when it adopted its own, similar mark. The data suggest that this circumstantial inference is the leading basis for a finding of bad faith intent. District courts found bad faith in 102 of the 331 opinions sampled. In fifty-eight of these 102 opinions, the court based its finding of bad faith at least in part on the combination of similarity and defendant's knowledge. In thirty of these fifty-eight opinions, the court also based its finding on direct evidence of bad faith, such as documents produced by the defendant or actions of the defendant after receiving a cease and desist demand from the plaintiff....
>
> Finally, what light do the data shed on the conflict among the courts concerning the proper role of intent in the multifactor analysis? ... [T]he intent factor data suggest that a finding of bad faith intent exerts excessive influence on the outcome of the multifactor test. The facile assumption, evidently quite pervasive among the courts, that if the defendant intended to confuse, then it succeeded in doing so does not do justice to the great diversity of trademark infringement fact patterns before the courts. Further, it loosens the focus of the multifactor analysis on what should be the overriding empirical question of whether consumers are likely to be confused. To be sure, in light of the defendant's bad faith, courts employ the multifactor test to

> reach what they deem to be the right result. But if trademark law seeks to prevent commercial immorality, then it should do so explicitly. An injunction should issue and damages be granted on that basis alone, and not on the basis of possibly distorted findings of fact as to the likelihood of consumer confusion.

Barton Beebe, *An Empirical Study of the Multifactor Tests for Trademark Infringement*, 94 CAL. L. REV. 1581, 1628–31 (2006).

Recall the courts' treatment of defendants' intent in the cases you have read so far. Do you agree that the courts' inferences of bad faith intent have tended to distort the determination of the likelihood of confusion? If so, is there a modification of the multifactor test that would avoid the problem?

5. Don Henley is a singer-songwriter who first became famous in the early 1970s as the drummer and lead vocalist for the Eagles, a rock and roll band. One of the Eagles' early hits was a song titled, "Take It Easy." In addition to performing and recording with the Eagles, Henley has had a successful solo career. In 2000, Henley registered DON HENLEY as a service mark for entertainment services and a trademark for music sound recordings. Duluth Trading, a Wisconsin clothing retailer, has recently marketed a cotton Henley-style (button placket) shirt with the slogan, "DON A HENLEY and Take it easy." Henley has filed suit for infringement of his registered marks. Do you see a likelihood of confusion? *See Henley v. Duluth Holdings, Inc.*, No. CV 14-7827 (C.D. Cal. filed Oct. 8, 2014).

Robert G. Bone, *Taking the Confusion Out of Likelihood of Confusion: Towards a More Sensible Approach to Trademark Infringement*

106 NW. U. L. REV. 1307 (2012) (excerpt)*

The liability standards for trademark infringement are a mess. For most trademark suits, liability turns on the likelihood that an ordinary consumer will be confused. The likelihood of consumer confusion, in turn, depends on a multifactor test, the application of which varies from circuit to circuit.[1] These multifactor tests are deeply flawed. They support an open-ended and relatively subjective approach that generates serious litigation uncertainty, chills beneficial uses of marks, and supports socially problematic expansions of trademark law. It is time to take a closer look at the likelihood of confusion test with an eye to replacing it with a more sensible approach to trademark infringement.

In recent years, trademark scholars have identified a number of problems with the likelihood of confusion test. In 2006, Professor Barton Beebe described it as "in a severe state of disrepair" and complained in particular about its inconsistent formulation

---

* Copyright 2012. Reprinted by permission. [*Some footnotes omitted—Eds.*]

1. See Barton Beebe, *An Empirical Study of the Multifactor Tests for Trademark Infringement*, 94 CALIF. L. REV. 1581, 1591 (2006) (summarizing, in chart form, the factors each circuit considers).

and application across circuits.[2] More recently, Professor William McGeveran criticized the test's uncertainty and the high litigation costs it generates.[3] He argued that trademark owners exploit this uncertainty and high cost to chill legitimate uses of marks. Professor Michael Grynberg points to problematic expansions in the types of actionable confusion—from source to sponsorship and from point-of-purchase to initial interest and post-sale—that create product monopolies, impair First Amendment interests, and interfere with creative consumer search techniques on the Internet.[5] Professors Mark Lemley and Mark McKenna argue that these problematic expansions are linked to the multifactor test's uncritical focus on likely confusion itself without regard to the materiality of the confusion to consumer choice.[6] Professor Rebecca Tushnet agrees. She draws on a comparison between trademark law and false advertising to argue for the addition of a materiality requirement to trademark infringement.[7]

These are important criticisms. At a deep level, the likelihood of confusion test rests on an inadequately justified and normatively incomplete premise. That premise assumes that the ultimate goal of trademark law is to prevent consumer confusion. But this makes no sense. People are often confused in their ordinary lives and the law does not intervene to help. Before a likelihood of confusion can trigger trademark liability, there must be a good reason why the law should prevent confusion when it involves consumers responding to marks. In short, the likelihood of confusion test suffers from a normative gap. It focuses exclusively on the probability of confusion, when it should also consider confusion-related harm and the reasons for redressing that harm.

Most of the critics who recognize the gap fill it with an economic analysis that gives short shrift to moral justifications. Moreover, they assume that the goal of trademark law is the same as the goal of false advertising: to prevent false statements of fact about product quality material to consumer choice. However, trademark law has a broader function: to protect marks as information transmission devices. This distinction is important because ... the information transmission function can be impaired in ways that have nothing to do with materiality.

The judicial response is also inadequate. Those courts that recognize problems with the likelihood of confusion test tinker with the factors without questioning the test's exclusive focus on likely confusion and its neglect of confusion-related harm. Even when courts consider the harm from confusion, they do so superficially within

2. *Id.* at 1582–84.

3. William McGeveran, *Rethinking Trademark Fair Use*, 94 Iowa L. Rev. 49 (2008).

5. Michael Grynberg, *Trademark Litigation as Consumer Conflict*, 83 N.Y.U. L. Rev. 60 (2008); *see also* Mark A. Lemley & Mark McKenna, *Irrelevant Confusion*, 62 Stan. L. Rev. 413, 414 (2010) (arguing that trademark law should be refocused away from "sponsorship and affiliation confusion ... that do[es] not affect consumers' decisionmaking process" and back to "confusion that is actually relevant to purchasing decisions").

6. *See* Lemley & McKenna, *supra* note 5, at 414, 427.

7. Rebecca Tushnet, *Running the Gamut from A to B: Federal Trademark and False Advertising Law*, 159 U. Pa. L. Rev. 1305, 1365 (2011).

the framework of a confusion-focused analysis that fails to appreciate the central importance of harm to the infringement analysis.

All these criticisms reduce to one fundamental point: There is no good reason to prevent consumer confusion when it causes very little harm and involves no morally blameworthy conduct.

....

Questions

1. The multi-factor test for likelihood of confusion has attracted criticism from all quarters. Critics complain that the test is manipulable, unpredictable, and measures the wrong things. What, then, accounts for its appeal to courts? Recall that the *Polaroid* factors arose as a test to measure the likelihood of confusion when similar marks appeared on non-competing products, and that courts eventually came to rely on it as an all-purpose test for likelihood of confusion. Why have courts come to rely on it?

2. Recall the Restatement (3d)'s articulation of the multifactor test, *supra* in [B][1]. Which of the factors common to the different Circuits' versions of the test does it omit? Based on the cases you have read so far, can you come up with a hypothesis as to why the authors of the Restatement chose to exclude them?

3. According to Prof. Bone, courts should not seek to prevent consumer confusion when it causes little harm, "and involves no morally blameworthy conduct." Why should moral blameworthiness matter? Is moral blameworthiness relevant to "information transmission"?

3. Different Varieties of Confusion

a. Initial Interest Confusion

Mobil Oil Corp. v. Pegasus Petroleum Corp.

818 F.2d 254 (2d Cir. 1987)

LUMBARD, CIRCUIT JUDGE:

Mobil Oil Corporation brought this action in the Southern District charging Pegasus Petroleum Corporation with trademark infringement and unfair competition, 15 U.S.C. § 1114(1); false designation of origin, 15 U.S.C. § 1125(a); and trademark dilution, N.Y. Gen. Bus. Law § 368-d. On July 8, 1986, after a three-day bench trial, Judge MacMahon entered judgment for Mobil on each of its claims, dismissed Pegasus Petroleum's counterclaims seeking to cancel Mobil's trademark registration, and enjoined Pegasus Petroleum from using the mark "Pegasus" in connection with the petroleum industry or related businesses. We affirm.

Mobil, one of the world's largest corporations, manufactures and sells a vast array of petroleum products to industrial consumers and to the general public. Since 1931, Mobil has made extensive use of its well-known "flying horse" symbol—representing Pegasus, the winged horse of Greek mythology—in connection with its petroleum business. Mobil displays this registered trademark, usually in red, but occasionally in blue, black, white, or outline form, at virtually all its gasoline service stations (usually on an illuminated disk four feet in diameter); in connection with all petroleum products sold at its service stations; in connection with the sale of a variety of its other petroleum products; on its oil tankers, barges, and other vehicles; and on its letterhead. As the district court explained, it is "undisputed that Mobil's extensive use of the flying horse symbol for such a long period of time in connection with all of Mobil's commercial activity has rendered it a very strong mark. Indeed, counsel for [Pegasus Petroleum] could think of few trademarks, if any, that were stronger trademarks in American commerce today."

As part of its petroleum business, Mobil buys and sells crude and refined petroleum products in bulk, an activity known as oil trading, to insure a continuous flow of oil to its refineries, and ultimately to its customers. The oil trading market is tight-knit and sophisticated: It encompasses a select group of professional buyers and brokers, representing approximately 200 oil companies, wholesalers, and oil traders; deals are in the hundreds of thousands, or millions of dollars, and in tens of tons; and, oil traders do not consummate deals with strangers except after a thorough credit check. Mobil does not use its flying horse symbol in connection with its oil trading business.

Pegasus Petroleum, incorporated in 1981, confines its activities to oil trading, and does not sell directly to the general public. Its founder, Gregory Callimanopulos, testified that he selected the name "Pegasus Petroleum" because he wanted a name with both mythical connotations and alliterative qualities. Callimanopulos admitted that he knew of Mobil's flying horse symbol when he picked the name, but claimed that he did not know that the symbol represented Pegasus or that Mobil used the word "Pegasus" in connection with its petroleum business. Shortly after the genesis of Pegasus Petroleum, Ben Pollner, then president of the company, sent a letter to 400–500 people in the oil trading business informing them about Pegasus Petroleum's formation. The letter stated that Pegasus Petroleum was part of the "Callimanopulos group of companies," and used an interlocking double P as a letterhead. Pegasus Petroleum has never used a flying horse symbol and sells no products with the name "Pegasus" on them.

In 1982, Mobil approached Pegasus Petroleum after learning of its use of the mark "Pegasus." When attempts to reach an agreement failed, Mobil filed the instant suit. The case proceeded to trial before Judge MacMahon, without a jury. After examining the criteria set forth in *Polaroid Corp. v. Polarad Electronics Corp.*, 287 F.2d 492, 495 (2d Cir.), *cert. denied*, 368 U.S. 820 (1961), Judge MacMahon concluded that "there is a sufficient likelihood of confusion between [Mobil's flying horse symbol] and [Pegasus Petroleum's use of the 'Pegasus' mark] to grant [Mobil] relief under the Lanham Act." Judge MacMahon also held for Mobil on its unfair competition, false designation, and antidilution claims; and enjoined Pegasus Petroleum's further use of the mark "Pegasus" in connection with the oil industry. With Mobil's consent, the injunction has been stayed, pending resolution of this appeal.

The Lanham Act prohibits the use of "any reproduction, counterfeit, copy, or colorable imitation of a registered mark" where "such use is likely to cause confusion, or to cause mistake, or to deceive." 15 U.S.C. § 1114(1)(a). To state a claim under this section, a plaintiff must show a "likelihood that an appreciable number of ordinarily prudent purchasers are likely to be misled, or indeed simply confused, as to the source of the goods in question." ... We agree with both the district court's determination of each of the *Polaroid* factors and its balancing of those factors to arrive at its conclusion that Pegasus Petroleum infringed upon Mobil's senior mark—the flying horse.

Pegasus Petroleum does not dispute the district court's conclusion that the strength of Mobil's flying horse mark is "without question, and perhaps without equal." As an arbitrary mark—there is nothing suggestive of the petroleum business in the flying horse symbol—Mobil's symbol deserves "the most protection the Lanham Act can provide." *Lois Sportswear, U.S.A., Inc. v. Levi Strauss & Co.*, 799 F.2d 867, 871 (2d Cir. 1986). On the other hand, Pegasus Petroleum vigorously attacks the district court's finding of similarity between the two marks. Pegasus Petroleum argues that the district court erred by blindly equating the word "Pegasus" with its pictorial representation—Mobil's flying horse. While we agree that words and their pictorial representations should not be equated as a matter of law, a district court may make such a determination as a factual matter. [Citations.] Judge MacMahon made such a determination here:

> We find that the similarity of the mark exists in the strong probability that prospective purchasers of defendant's product will equate or translate Mobil's symbol for "Pegasus" and vice versa.
>
> We find that the word "Pegasus" evokes the symbol of the flying red horse and that the flying horse is associated in the mind with Mobil. In other words, the symbol of the flying horse and its name "Pegasus" are synonymous.

That conclusion finds support in common sense as well as the record.

The third *Polaroid* factor addresses the competitive proximity between the two marks. Pegasus Petroleum points out that while Judge MacMahon correctly found that Mobil and Pegasus Petroleum both compete in the oil trading business, Mobil does not use its flying horse trademark in that field. However, "direct competition between the products is not a prerequisite to relief.... Confusion, or the likelihood of confusion, not competition, is the real test of trademark infringement." [Citation.] Both Mobil and Pegasus Petroleum use their marks in the petroleum industry. [Citations.]

Moreover, competitive proximity must be measured with reference to the first two *Polaroid* factors: The unparalleled strength of Mobil's mark demands that it be given broad protection against infringers. [Citations.] Mobil's ubiquitous presence throughout the petroleum industry further increases the likelihood that a consumer will confuse Pegasus Petroleum with Mobil. [Citation.] Finally, the great similarity between the two marks—the district court concluded that they were "synonymous"—entitles Mobil's mark to protection over a broader range of related products. [Citation.] We agree with the district court's finding of competitive proximity.

Our evaluation of the first three *Polaroid* factors, perhaps the most significant in determining the likelihood of confusion, [citation], strongly supports the district court's conclusion that such a likelihood exists. The district court's finding under the fourth *Polaroid* factor that Pegasus Petroleum did not innocently select its potentially confusing mark reinforces this conclusion: Intentional copying gives rise to a presumption of a likelihood of confusion. [Citation.] The district court discredited Gregory Callimanopulos's testimony that "he did not intentionally choose the tradename 'Pegasus' with either the symbol of Mobil's flying horse or Mobil's wordmark in mind." The court explained:

> Mr. Callimanopulos is obviously an educated, sophisticated man who, from his prior shipping business, was familiar with the flying horse and from his own background and education and awareness of Greek mythology could not have escaped the conclusion that the use of the word "Pegasus" would infringe the tradename and symbol of the plaintiff.

In response, Pegasus Petroleum first contends that this finding is clearly erroneous given the objective evidence before the court, specifically pointing to its letter to the trade of June, 1982, which stated that it was a member of the Callimanopulos group of companies. While this correspondence was one piece of evidence for the district court to consider, it falls far short of establishing, by itself, Pegasus Petroleum's good faith.... We believe the record clearly substantiates Judge MacMahon's inference of bad faith.

The existence of some evidence of actual confusion, the fifth *Polaroid* factor, further buttresses the finding of a likelihood of confusion. [Citation.] Both Mobil and Pegasus Petroleum offered surveys of consumers and of members of the oil trading industry as evidence relating to the existence of actual confusion between the two marks. The district court properly admitted these surveys into evidence, despite claims of statistical imperfections by both sides, as those criticisms affected the weight accorded to the evidence rather than its admissibility. [Citation.] After reviewing these surveys, Judge MacMahon concluded that there was "evidence of actual confusion." His decision was not clearly erroneous....

Pegasus Petroleum argues that the absence of misdirected mail and telephone calls between the parties, and the fact that Pegasus Petroleum must post a letter of credit as security during its oil trading deals while Mobil need not, prove that no actual confusion between the two firms existed. This argument misunderstands the district court's opinion. Judge MacMahon found a likelihood of confusion not in the fact that a third party would do business with Pegasus Petroleum believing it related to Mobil, but rather in the likelihood that Pegasus Petroleum would gain crucial credibility during the initial phases of a deal. For example, an oil trader might listen to a cold phone call from Pegasus Petroleum—an admittedly oft-used procedure in the oil trading business—when otherwise he might not, because of the possibility that Pegasus Petroleum is related to Mobil. The absence of misdirected phone calls and the difference in the letter of credit requirements are other matters.

Pegasus Petroleum never rebutted the inference of a likelihood of confusion. The district court did not examine the sixth *Polaroid* factor—whether Mobil would "bridge the gap" by expanding its use of the flying horse symbol into the oil trading market (Mobil presently competes, but does not use its flying horse trademark, in the oil trading field). Nevertheless, "sufficient likelihood of confusion may be established although likelihood of bridging the gap is not demonstrated." [Citation.] The absence of an intent to bridge the gap does not negate a finding of a likelihood of confusion in the market as presently constituted. [Citation.] The Lanham Act extends trademark protection to related goods in order to guard against numerous evils in addition to restraints on the possible expansion of the senior user's market, including consumer confusion, tarnishment of the senior user's reputation, and unjust enrichment of the infringer. [Citation.]

The seventh *Polaroid* factor suggests that the court examine the quality of Pegasus Petroleum's product. The district court made no findings on this issue. Pegasus Petroleum argues that its product — oil — does not differ from that sold by Mobil. However, a senior user may sue to protect his reputation even where the infringer's goods are of top quality. [Citations.]

We finally turn to the eighth *Polaroid* factor, the sophistication of purchasers. The district court concluded that, "even though defendant's business is transacted in large quantities only with sophisticated oil traders, there is still and nevertheless a likelihood of confusion." We agree. As explained above, the district court's concerns focused upon the probability that potential purchasers would be misled into an initial interest in Pegasus Petroleum. Such initial confusion works a sufficient trademark injury. [Citation.] The district court's concerns had a sufficient basis in fact despite the sophistication of the oil trading market: Pegasus Petroleum admits that it solicits business through telephone calls to potential customers. Pegasus Petroleum also acknowledges that "[t]rust, in the oil industry, is of paramount importance." Finally, Mobil's Oil Trading Department executive, Thomas Cory, testified that he did not undertake an investigation of a new company before initially dealing with it. Such an investigation was undertaken only prior to the culmination of a deal.

For the foregoing reasons, we agree with the district court's finding that Pegasus Petroleum infringed on Mobil's registered flying horse trademark and therefore affirm its judgment....

Affirmed.

Blockbuster Entertainment Group v. Laylco, Inc., 869 F. Supp. 505 (E.D. Mich. 1994). Blockbuster challenged defendant's use of the name Video Busters. Video Busters argued that its use of a name confusingly similar to "Blockbuster Video" was not actionable under the Lanham Act if customers were not likely to be confused at the time they actually rented video tapes in Video Busters' stores. Video Busters contended that while consumers might be confused initially by the similarity of the two stores' names, they were not likely to be confused once they entered Video Busters' stores to rent video cassettes because of the different appearance and layout of Video Busters and Blockbuster Video's stores.

The court held that the Lanham Act's protection was not limited to confusion at the "point of sale," *i.e.*, the moment of actual purchase or rental:

> Rather, the Act protects against confusion among potential customers and protects the reputation among the general public of trade mark holders. [Citation.] [T]he issue in a trade mark action is not limited to whether a purchaser would buy an allegedly infringing product thinking it was actually a product of or had some connection to the owner of the original mark. Instead, ... the issue is the degree of likelihood that the allegedly infringing name would attract potential customers based on the reputation earned by the owner of the original mark.
>
> Therefore, the issue in this case is the degree of likelihood that the name "Video Busters" would attract potential customers based on the reputation built by Blockbuster. That a customer would recognize that Video Busters is not connected to Blockbuster after entry into a Video Busters store and viewing the Video Busters membership application, brochure, video cassette jacket, and store layout is unimportant. The critical issue is the degree to which Video Busters might attract potential customers based on the similarity to the Blockbuster name. The court finds that Video Busters might attract some potential customers based on the similarity to the Blockbuster name. Because the names are so similar and the products sold are identical, some unwitting customers might enter a Video Busters store thinking it is somehow connected to Blockbuster. Those customers probably will realize shortly that Video Busters is not related to Blockbuster, but under *Esercizio* [*Ferrari S.P.A. v. Roberts*, 944 F.2d 1235 (6th Cir. 1991)] and *Grotrian* [*Helfferich, Schulz, Th. Steinweg Nachf. v. Steinway & Sons*, 523 F.2d 1331 (2d Cir. 1975)] that is irrelevant.

Questions

1. Note the Second Circuit's discussion of the "actual confusion" and "sophistication of purchasers" factors in *Pegasus.* The court upheld the finding of likely confusion by highly sophisticated oil traders because defendant's use of the Pegasus name might evoke Mobil Oil and thereby secure defendant initial access to purchasers. Should this kind of "confusion" be cognizable, if the initial misimpression is dispelled by the time a purchase decision is made? Why or why not? *See also Elvis Presley Enterprises, Inc. v. Capece*, 141 F.3d 188 (5th Cir. 1998) (considering the relevance of initial interest in defendant's VELVET ELVIS nightclub as a result of impressions that club might be associated with Presley or Presley merchandise).

2. Is the rationale for "initial interest confusion" stronger when plaintiff and defendant sell the same products or services? Is it stronger when the products are essentially fungible? How do the cost and availability of the products affect the analysis?

Initial Interest Confusion and Internet Advertising

In the 1990s, the initial interest confusion theory became popular in trademark infringement suits over the appearance of competitors' trademarks in Internet addresses, metatags, and keyword advertising. (We explore the distinct issues raised by trademarks in Internet domain names in Chapter 11, *infra.*) Trademark owners argued that the presence of a trademark anywhere on a competitor's website or as a keyword ad trigger might cause a consumer to click on a link and land on a page other than the page she was seeking. Early cases found initial interest confusion likely. In *Brookfield Communications, Inc. v. West Coast Entertainment Corp.*, 174 F.3d 1036 (9th Cir. 1999), for example, the Court of Appeals for the Ninth Circuit addressed the potential for confusion when someone other than the registrant for the trademark, MOVIEBUFF, used the mark in a website metatag:

> In the Internet context, in particular, entering a web site takes little effort—usually one click from a linked site or a search engine's list; thus, Web surfers are more likely to be confused as to the ownership of a web site than traditional patrons of a brick-and-mortar store would be of a store's ownership....
>
> ....
>
> Although entering "MovieBuff" into a search engine is likely to bring up a list including "westcoastvideo.com" if West Coast has included that term in its metatags, the resulting confusion is not as great as where West Coast uses the "moviebuff.com" domain name. First, when the user inputs "MovieBuff" into an Internet search engine, the list produced by the search engine is likely to include both West Coast's and Brookfield's web sites. Thus, in scanning such list, the Web user will often be able to find the particular web site he is seeking. Moreover, even if the Web user chooses the web site belonging to West Coast, he will see that the domain name of the web site he selected is "westcoastvideo.com." Since there is no confusion resulting from the domain address, and since West Coast's initial web page prominently displays its own name, it is difficult to say that a consumer is likely to be confused about whose site he has reached or to think that Brookfield somehow sponsors West Coast's web site.
>
> Nevertheless, West Coast's use of "moviebuff.com" in metatags will still result in what is known as initial interest confusion. Web surfers looking for Brookfield's "MovieBuff" products who are taken by a search engine to "westcoastvideo.com" will find a database similar enough to "MovieBuff" such that a sizeable number of consumers who were originally looking for Brookfield's product will simply decide to utilize West Coast's offerings instead. Although there is no source confusion in the sense that consumers know they are patronizing West Coast rather than Brookfield, there is nevertheless initial interest confusion in the sense that, by using "moviebuff.com" or "MovieBuff" to divert people looking for "MovieBuff" to its web site, West Coast improperly benefits from the goodwill that Brookfield developed in its mark.

As consumers, and judges, became more familiar with the Internet, though, courts began to take a more nuanced approach.

Network Automation, Inc. v. Advanced Systems Concepts, Inc., 638 F.3d 1137 (9th Cir. 2011).

> Network Automation ("Network") and Advanced Systems Concepts ("Systems") are both in the business of selling job scheduling and management software, and both advertise on the Internet. Network sells its software under

the mark Auto-Mate, while Systems' product is sold under the registered trademark ActiveBatch. Network decided to advertise its product by purchasing certain keywords, such as "ActiveBatch," which when keyed into various search engines, most prominently Google and Microsoft Bing, produce a results page showing "www.NetworkAutomation.com" as a sponsored link. Systems' objection to Network's use of its trademark to interest viewers in Network's website gave rise to this trademark infringement action.

....

The district court granted [preliminary] injunctive relief on April 30, 2010. Noting that the parties did not dispute the validity or ownership of the ActiveBatch mark, the district court ruled that Systems was likely to succeed in satisfying the Lanham Act's "use in commerce" requirement by showing that Network "used" the mark when it purchased advertisements from search engines triggered by the term "ActiveBatch." Applying the eight-factor *Sleekcraft* test for source confusion, the district court emphasized three factors it viewed as significant for "cases involving the Internet": the similarity of the marks, relatedness of the goods or services, and simultaneous use of the Web as a marketing channel. The district court concluded that all three factors favored Systems: Network used the identical mark to sell a directly competing product, and both advertised on the Internet.

....

The district court also analyzed whether Network infringed Systems' mark by creating initial interest confusion—as opposed to source confusion—which "occurs when the defendant uses the plaintiff's trademark in a manner calculated to capture initial consumer attention, even though no actual sale is finally completed as a result of the confusion." ... Because the district court found that Network's advertisements did not clearly divulge their source, it concluded that consumers might be confused into unwittingly visiting Network's website, allowing the company to "impermissibly capitalize[] on [Systems'] goodwill."

Based on its analysis of the *Sleekcraft* factors and its finding of likely initial interest confusion, the district court concluded that Systems had a strong likelihood of success on the merits of its trademark infringement claim....

....

III. Discussion

....

... Network argues that its use of Systems' mark is legitimate "comparative, contextual advertising" which presents sophisticated consumers with clear choices. Systems characterizes Network's behavior differently, accusing it of misleading consumers by hijacking their attention with intentionally unclear advertisements. To resolve this dispute we must apply the *Sleekcraft* test in a flexible manner, keeping in mind that the eight factors it recited are not exhaustive, and that only some of them are relevant to determining whether confusion is likely in the case at hand.

....

B.

Here we consider whether the use of another's trademark as a search engine keyword to trigger one's own product advertisement violates the Lanham Act. We begin by examining the *Sleekcraft* factors that are most relevant to the determination whether the use is likely to cause initial interest confusion. While the district court analyzed each of the *Sleekcraft* factors, it identified the three most important factors as (1) the similarity of the marks, (2) the relatedness of the goods or services, and (3) the simultaneous use of the Web as a marketing channel, for any case addressing trademark infringement on the Internet....

....

Given the multifaceted nature of the Internet and the ever-expanding ways in which we all use the technology, however, it makes no sense to prioritize the same three factors for every type of potential online commercial activity.... The potential infringement in this context arises from the risk that while using Systems' mark to search for information about its product, a consumer might be confused by a results page that shows a competitor's advertisement on the same screen, when that advertisement does not clearly identify the source or its product.

In determining the proper inquiry for this particular trademark infringement claim, we adhere to two long stated principles: the *Sleekcraft* factors (1) are non-exhaustive, and (2) should be applied flexibly, particularly in the context of Internet commerce. Finally, because the *sine qua non* of trademark infringement is consumer confusion, when we examine initial interest confusion, the owner of the mark must demonstrate likely confusion, not mere diversion.

....

The nature of the goods and the type of consumer is highly relevant to determining the likelihood of confusion in the keyword advertising context. A sophisticated consumer of business software exercising a high degree of care is more likely to understand the mechanics of Internet search engines and the nature of sponsored links, whereas an un-savvy consumer exercising less care is more likely to be confused. The district court determined that this factor weighed in Systems' favor because "there is generally a low degree of care exercised by Internet consumers." However, the degree of care analysis cannot begin and end at the marketing channel. We still must consider the nature and cost of the goods, and whether "the products being sold are marketed primarily to expert buyers." *Brookfield [Commc'ns, Inc. v. West Coast Entm't Corp.*, 174 F.3d 1036 (9th Cir. 1999)] at 1060.

....

We have recently acknowledged that the default degree of consumer care is becoming more heightened as the novelty of the Internet evaporates and online commerce becomes commonplace....

....

Therefore the district court improperly concluded that this factor weighed in Systems' favor based on a conclusion reached by our court more than a decade ago in *Brookfield* ... that Internet users on the whole exercise a low degree of care. While the statement may have been accurate then, we suspect that there are many contexts in which it no longer holds true.

....

The appearance of the advertisements and their surrounding context on the user's screen are similarly important here. The district court correctly examined the text of Network's sponsored links, concluding that the advertisements did not clearly identify their source. However, the district court did not consider the surrounding context.... Here, even if Network has not clearly identified itself in the text of its ads, Google and Bing have partitioned their search results pages so that the advertisements appear in separately labeled sections for "sponsored" links. The labeling and appearance of the advertisements as they appear on the results page includes more than the text of the advertisement, and must be considered as a whole.

C.

Given the nature of the alleged infringement here, the most relevant factors to the analysis of the likelihood of confusion are: (1) the strength of the mark; (2) the evidence of actual confusion; (3) the type of goods and degree of care likely to be exercised by the purchaser; and (4) the labeling and appearance of the advertisements and the surrounding context on the screen displaying the results page.

The district court did not weigh the *Sleekcraft* factors flexibly to match the specific facts of this case. It relied on the Internet "troika," which is highly illuminating in the context of domain names, but which fails to discern whether there is a likelihood of confusion in a keywords case. Because the linchpin of trademark infringement is consumer confusion, the district court abused its discretion in issuing the injunction....

Multi Time Machine, Inc. v. Amazon.com

804 F.3d 930 (9th Cir. 2015)

SILVERMAN, CIRCUIT JUDGE:

In the present appeal, we must decide whether the following scenario constitutes trademark infringement: A customer goes online to Amazon.com looking for a certain military-style wristwatch—specifically the "MTM Special Ops"—marketed and manufactured by Plaintiff Multi Time Machine, Inc. The customer types "mtm special ops" in the search box and presses "enter." Because Amazon does not sell the MTM Special Ops watch, what the search produces is a list, with photographs, of several other brands of military style watches that Amazon *does* carry, specifically identified by their brand names—Luminox, Chase-Durer, TAWATEC, and Modus.

MTM brought suit alleging that Amazon's response to a search for the MTM Special Ops watch on its website is trademark infringement in violation of the Lanham Act. MTM contends that Amazon's search results page creates a likelihood of confusion, even though there is no evidence of any actual confusion and even though the other brands are clearly identified by name. The district court granted summary judgment in favor of Amazon, and MTM now appeals.

We affirm. "The core element of trademark infringement" is whether the defendant's conduct "is likely to confuse customers about the source of the products." [Citation.] Because Amazon's search results page clearly labels the name and manufacturer of each product offered for sale and even includes photographs of the items, no reasonably prudent consumer accustomed to shopping online would likely be confused as to the source of the products. Thus, summary judgment of MTM's trademark claims was proper.

I. Factual and Procedural Background

MTM manufactures and markets watches under various brand names including MTM, MTM Special Ops, and MTM Military Ops. MTM holds the federally registered trademark "MTM Special Ops" for timepieces. MTM sells its watches directly to its customers and through various retailers. To cultivate and maintain an image as a high-end, exclusive brand, MTM does not sell its watches through Amazon.com. Further, MTM does not authorize its distributors, whose agreements require them to seek MTM's permission to sell MTM's products anywhere but their own retail sites, to sell MTM watches on Amazon.com. Therefore, MTM watches have never been available for sale on Amazon.com.

Amazon is an online retailer that purports to offer "Earth's Biggest Selection of products." Amazon has designed its website to enable millions of unique products to be sold by both Amazon and third party sellers across dozens of product categories.

Consumers who wish to shop for products on Amazon's website can utilize Amazon's search function. The search function enables consumers to navigate Amazon.com's large marketplace by providing consumers with relevant results in response to the consumer's query. In order to provide search results in which the consumer is most likely to be interested, Amazon's search function does not simply match the words in the user's query to words in a document, such as a product description in Amazon.com's catalog. Rather, Amazon's search function—like general purpose web search engines such as Google or Bing—employs a variety of techniques, including some that rely on user behavior, to produce relevant results. By going beyond exactly matching a user's query to text describing a product, Amazon's search function can provide consumers with relevant results that would otherwise be overlooked.

Consumers who go onto Amazon.com and search for the term "mtm special ops" are directed to a search results page. On the search results page, the search query used—here, "mtm special ops"—is displayed twice: in the search query box and directly below the search query box in what is termed a "breadcrumb." The breadcrumb displays the original query, "mtm special ops," in quotation marks to provide a trail for the consumer to follow back to the original search. Directly below the breadcrumb, is a "Related Searches" field, which provides the consumer with alternative search queries in case the consumer is dissatisfied with the results of the original search. Here, the Related Search that is suggested to the consumer is: "mtm special ops watch." Directly below the "Related Searches" field is a gray bar containing the text "Showing 10 Results." Then, directly below the gray bar is Amazon's product listings. The gray bar separates the product listings from the breadcrumb and the "Related Searches" field. The particular search results page at issue is displayed below:

MTM watches are not listed on the page for the simple reason that neither Amazon nor MTM sells MTM watches on Amazon.

MTM filed a complaint against Amazon, alleging that Amazon's search results page infringes MTM's trademarks in violation of the Lanham Act. Amazon filed a motion for summary judgment, arguing that (1) it is not using MTM's mark in commerce and (2) there is no likelihood of consumer confusion. In ruling on Amazon's motion for summary judgment, the district court declined to resolve the issue of whether Amazon is using MTM's mark in commerce, and, instead, addressed the issue of likelihood of confusion. In evaluating likelihood of confusion, the district court utilized the eight-factor test set forth in *AMF Inc. v. Sleekcraft Boats*, 599 F.2d 341 (9th Cir. 1979). Relying on our recent decision in *Network Automation, Inc. v. Advanced Systems Concepts*, 638 F.3d 1137 (9th Cir. 2011), the district court focused in particular on the following factors: (1) the strength of MTM's mark; (2) the evidence of actual confusion and the evidence of no confusion; (3) the type of goods and degree of care likely to be exercised by the purchaser; and (4) the appearance of the product listings and the surrounding context on the screen displaying the results page. Upon reviewing the factors, the district court concluded that the relevant *Sleekcraft* factors established "that there is no likelihood of confusion in Amazon's use of MTM's trademarks in its search engine or display of search results." Therefore, the district court granted Amazon's motion for summary judgment.

....

III. Discussion

....

Here, the district court was correct in ruling that there is no likelihood of confusion. Amazon is responding to a customer's inquiry about a brand it does not carry by doing no more than stating clearly (and showing pictures of) what brands it does carry. To whatever extent the *Sleekcraft* factors apply in a case such as this—a merchant responding to a request for a particular brand it does not sell by offering other brands clearly identified as such—the undisputed evidence shows that confusion on the part of the inquiring buyer is not at all likely. Not only are the other brands clearly labeled and accompanied by photographs, there is no evidence of actual confusion by anyone.

To analyze likelihood of confusion, we utilize the eight factor test set forth in *Sleekcraft*. However, "[w]e have long cautioned that applying the *Sleekcraft* test is not like counting beans." [Citations.] "Some factors are much more important than others, and the relative importance of each individual factor will be case-specific" [Citation.] Moreover, the *Sleekcraft* factors are not exhaustive and other variables may come into play depending on the particular facts presented. *Network Automation*, 638 F.3d at 1145–46. This is particularly true in the Internet context. [Citation]. Indeed, in evaluating claims of trademark infringement in cases involving Internet search engines, we have found particularly important an additional factor that is outside of the eight-factor *Sleekcraft* test: "the labeling and appearance of the advertisements and the surrounding context on the screen displaying the results page." *Network Automation*, 638 F.3d at 1154.

In the present case, the eight-factor *Sleekcraft* test is not particularly apt. This is not surprising as the *Sleekcraft* test was developed for a different problem—i.e., for analyzing whether two competing brands' *marks* are sufficiently similar to cause consumer confusion. [Citation.] Although the present case involves *brands* that compete with MTM, such as Luminox, Chase-Durer, TAWATEC, and Modus, MTM does not contend that the *marks* for these competing brands are similar to its trademarks. Rather, MTM argues that the design of Amazon's search results page creates a likelihood of initial interest confusion because when a customer searches for MTM Special Ops watches on Amazon.com, the search results page displays the search term used—here, "mtm special ops"—followed by a display of numerous watches manufactured by MTM's competitors and offered for sale by Amazon, without explicitly informing the customer that Amazon does not carry MTM watches.

Thus, the present case focuses on a different type of confusion than was at issue in *Sleekcraft*. Here, the confusion is not caused by the design of the competitor's mark, but by the design of the web page that is displaying the competing mark and offering the competing products for sale. *Sleekcraft* aside, the ultimate test for determining likelihood of confusion is whether a "reasonably prudent consumer" in the marketplace is likely to be confused as to the origin of the goods. [Citation.] Our case can be resolved simply by an evaluation of the web page at issue and the relevant consumer. [Citation.].... In other words, the case will turn on the answers to the following two questions: (1) Who is the relevant reasonable consumer?; and (2) What would he reasonably believe based on what he saw on the screen?

Turning to the first question, we have explained that "[t]he nature of the goods and the type of consumer is highly relevant to determining the likelihood of confusion in the keyword advertising context." *Network Automation*, 638 F.3d at 1152. "In evaluating this factor, we consider 'the typical buyer exercising ordinary caution.'" [Citation.] "Confusion is less likely where buyers exercise care and precision in their purchases, such as for expensive or sophisticated items." [Citation.] Moreover, "the default degree of consumer care is becoming more heightened as the novelty of the Internet evaporates and online commerce becomes commonplace." *Network Automation*, 638 F.3d at 1152.

The goods in the present case are expensive. It is undisputed that the watches at issue sell for several hundred dollars. Therefore, the relevant consumer in the present case "is a reasonably prudent consumer accustomed to shopping online." [Citation.]

Turning to the second question, as MTM itself asserts, the labeling and appearance of the products for sale on Amazon's web page is the most important factor in this case. This is because we have previously noted that clear labeling can eliminate the likelihood of initial interest confusion in cases involving Internet search terms....

Here, the products at issue are clearly labeled by Amazon to avoid any likelihood of initial interest confusion by a reasonably prudent consumer accustomed to online shopping. When a shopper goes to Amazon's website and searches for a product using MTM's trademark "mtm special ops," the resulting page displays several products, all of which are clearly labeled with the product's name and manufacturer in large, bright, bold letters and includes a photograph of the item. In fact, the manufacturer's name is listed twice. For example, the first result is "*Luminox Men's 8401 Black Ops Watch* by Luminox." The second result is "*Chase-Durer Men's 246.4BB7-XL-BR Special Forces 1000XL Black Ionic-Plated Underwater Demolition Team Watch* by Chase-Durer." Because Amazon clearly labels each of the products for sale by brand name and model number accompanied by a photograph of the item, it is unreasonable to suppose that the reasonably prudent consumer accustomed to shopping online would be confused about the source of the goods.

MTM argues that initial interest confusion might occur because Amazon lists the search term used—here the trademarked phrase "mtm special ops"—three times at the top of the search page. MTM argues that because Amazon lists the search term "mtm special ops" at the top of the page, a consumer might conclude that the products displayed are types of MTM watches. But, merely looking at Amazon's search results page shows that such consumer confusion is highly unlikely. None of these watches is labeled with the word "MTM" or the phrase "Special Ops," let alone the specific phrase "MTM Special Ops." Further, some of the products listed are not even watches. The sixth result is a book entitled "*Survive!: The Disaster, Crisis and Emergency Handbook* by Jerry Ahem." The tenth result is a book entitled "*The Moses Expedition: A Novel* by Juan Gómez-Jurado." No reasonably prudent consumer, accustomed to shopping online or not, would assume that a book entitled "The Moses Expedition" is a type of MTM watch or is in any way affiliated with MTM watches. Likewise, no reasonably prudent consumer accustomed to shopping online would view Amazon's search results page and conclude that the products offered are MTM watches....

MTM argues that in order to eliminate the likelihood of confusion, Amazon must change its search results page so that it explains to customers that it does not offer MTM watches for sale before suggesting alternative watches to the customer. We disagree. The search results page makes clear to anyone who can read English that Amazon carries only the brands that are clearly and explicitly listed on the web page. The search results page is unambiguous....

In light of the clear labeling Amazon uses on its search results page, no reasonable trier of fact could conclude that Amazon's search results page would likely confuse a reasonably prudent consumer accustomed to shopping online as to the source of the goods being offered....

....

The likelihood of confusion is often a question of fact, but not always. In a case such as this, where a court can conclude that the consumer confusion alleged by the trademark holder is highly unlikely by simply reviewing the product listing/advertisement at issue, summary judgment is appropriate. [Citation.] Indeed, in the similar context of evaluating claims of consumer deception when dealing with false advertising claims, we have at least twice concluded—after a review of the label or advertisement at issue—that there was no likelihood of consumer deception as a matter of law because no reasonable consumer could have been deceived by the label/advertisement at issue in the manner alleged by the plaintiff. [Citation.]

....

IV. Conclusion

In light of Amazon's clear labeling of the products it carries, by brand name and model, accompanied by a photograph of the item, no rational trier of fact could find that a reasonably prudent consumer accustomed to shopping online would likely be confused by the Amazon search results. Accordingly, we affirm the district court's grant of summary judgment in favor of Amazon.

BEA, CIRCUIT JUDGE, dissenting:

Today the panel holds that when it comes to internet commerce, judges, not jurors, decide what labeling may confuse shoppers. In so doing, the court departs from our own trademark precedent and from our summary judgment jurisprudence. Because I believe that an Amazon shopper seeking an MTM watch might well initially think that the watches Amazon offers for sale when he searches "MTM Special Ops" are affiliated with MTM, I must dissent.

If her brother mentioned MTM Special Ops watches, a frequent internet shopper might try to purchase one for him through her usual internet retail sites, perhaps Overstock.com, Buy.com, and Amazon.com. At Overstock's site, if she typed "MTM special ops," the site would respond "Sorry, your search: 'mtm special ops' returned no results." Similarly, at Buy.com, she would be informed "0 results found. Sorry. Your search for *mtm special ops* did not return an exact match. Please try your search again."

Things are a little different over at "Earth's most customer-centric company," as Amazon styles itself. There, if she were to enter "MTM Special Ops" as her search request on the Amazon website, Amazon would respond with its page showing (1) MTM Special Ops in the search field (2) "MTM Specials Ops" again—in quotation marks—immediately below the search field and (3) yet again in the phrase "Related Searches: *MTM special ops watch,*" (emphasis in original) all before stating "Showing 10 Results." What the website's response will not state is the truth recognized by its competitors: that Amazon does not carry MTM products any more than do Overstock.com or Buy.com. Rather, below the search field, and below the second and third mentions of "MTM Special Ops" noted above, the site will display aesthetically similar, multi-function watches manufactured by MTM's competitors. The shopper will see that Luminox and Chase-Durer watches are offered for sale, in response to her MTM query.

MTM asserts the shopper might be confused into thinking a relationship exists between Luminox and MTM; she may think that MTM was acquired by Luminox, or that MTM manufactures component parts of Luminox watches, for instance. As a result of this initial confusion, MTM asserts, she might look into buying a Luminox watch, rather than junk the quest altogether and seek to buy an MTM watch elsewhere. MTM asserts that Amazon's use of MTM's trademarked name is likely to confuse buyers, who may ultimately buy a competitor's goods.

MTM may be mistaken. But whether MTM is mistaken is a question that requires a factual determination, one this court does not have authority to make.

By usurping the jury function, the majority today makes new trademark law. When we allow a jury to determine whether there is a likelihood of confusion, as I would, we do not *make* trademark law, because we announce no new principle by which to adjudicate trademark disputes. Today's brief majority opinion accomplishes a great deal: the majority announces a new rule of law, resolves whether "clear labeling" favors Amazon using its own judgment, and, sub silentio, overrules this court's "initial interest confusion" doctrine.

Capturing initial consumer attention has been recognized by our court to be a grounds for finding of infringement of the Lanham Act since 1997. *Dr. Seuss Enterprises, L.P. v. Penguin Books USA, Inc.*, 109 F.3d 1394, 1405 (9th Cir. 1997) (identifying "initial consumer attention" as a basis for infringement). In 1999, citing *Dr. Seuss*, we expressly adopted the initial interest confusion doctrine in the internet context, and never repudiated it. *Brookfield Communications, Inc. v. West Coast Entertainment Corp.*, 174 F.3d 1036, 1062 (9th Cir. 1999). It may not apply where the competing goods or services are "clearly labeled" such that they cause only mere diversion, but whether such goods or services are clearly labeled so as to prevent a prudent internet shopper's initial confusion depends on the overall function and presentation of the web page. The issue is whether a prudent internet shopper who made the search request and saw the Amazon result—top to bottom—would more likely than not be affected by that "initial interest confusion." That is, an impression—when first shown the results of the requested MTM Special Ops search—that Amazon carries watches that have some connection to MTM, and that those watches are sold under the name Luminox or Chase-Durer. Whether there is likelihood of such initial interest confusion, I submit, is a jury question. Intimations in our case law that initial interest confusion is bad doctrine notwithstanding, it is the law of our circuit, and, I submit, the most fair reading of the Lanham Act.

....

On this record, a jury could infer that users who are confused by the search results are confused as to why MTM products are not listed. There is a question of fact whether users who are confused by the search result will wonder whether a competitor has acquired MTM or is otherwise affiliated with or approved by MTM. *See Brookfield Communications*, 174 F.3d at 1057. This is especially true as to a brand like MTM, as many luxury brands with distinct marks are produced by manufacturers of lower-priced, better known brands—just as Honda manufactures Acura automobiles but sells Acura automobiles under a distinct mark that is marketed to wealthier purchasers, and Timex manufactures watches for luxury fashion houses Versace and Salvatore Ferragamo. Like MTM, Luminox manufactures luxury watches, and a customer might think that MTM and Luminox are manufactured by the same parent company. The possibility of initial interest confusion here is likely much higher than if, for instance, a customer using an online grocery website typed "Coke" and only

Pepsi products were returned as results. No shopper would think that Pepsi was simply a higher end version of Coke, or that Pepsi had acquired Coke's secret recipe and started selling it under the Pepsi mark.

In any event, even as to expensive goods—for instance, pianos sold under a mark very similar to the famous Steinway and Sons brand's mark—the issue is not that a buyer might buy a piano manufactured by someone other than Steinway thinking that it was a Steinway. The issue is that the defendant's use of the mark would cause initial interest confusion by attracting potential customers' attention to buy the infringing goods because of the trademark holder's hardwon reputation. [Citation.]

A jury could infer that the labeling of the search results, and Amazon's failure to notify customers that it does not have results that match MTM's mark, give rise to initial interest confusion. If so, a jury could find that Amazon customers searching for MTM products are subject to more than mere diversion, since MTM is not required to show that customers are likely to be confused at the point of sale. *Playboy Enterprises, Inc. v. Netscape Communications Corp.*, 354 F.3d 1020, 1025 (9th Cir. 2004).

. . . .

Through its cursory review of the *Sleekcraft* factors and conclusory statements about clear labeling, the majority purports to apply this circuit's trademark law, and ignores the doctrine of initial interest confusion. In so doing, the majority today writes new trademark law and blurs the line between innovation and infringement.

More troubling, the majority ignores the role of the jury. Summary judgment law is an aid to judicial economy, but it can be so only to the extent that it comports with the Seventh Amendment. Were we to reverse and remand, MTM might well lose. The likelihood of that outcome is irrelevant to the question whether there is a genuine issue of fact. I respectfully dissent.

Questions

1. The majority concludes that Amazon's search results are unambiguous "to anyone who can read English." The dissent argues that the potential for initial interest confusion is one that requires a jury to assess. What are the advantages and disadvantages of having a jury make this determination?

2. Bricks and mortar marketplaces are rife with examples of packaging and advertising that may cause fleeting initial interest confusion. CVS and Walgreens, for example, sell house brand cosmetics and medicines packaged to resemble nationally advertised products. Typically, the house brand products appear on the shelves next to the name brand products that they imitate. *See Conopco, Inc. v. May Department Stores*, *infra* Chapter 7[A][1]. When should a trademark owner be able to recover because initial interest confusion enables the seller of competing products to capture the attention of a potential customer, and when should it be sufficient for a defendant to show that any confusion is likely to be dispelled before the customer purchases the product? Can you articulate a principle that would aid courts and juries in determining whether and when initial interest confusion is significant enough and persists long enough to be actionable?

3. If initial interest confusion is sometimes actionable in connection with bricks-and-mortar marketing, should courts treat allegations of initial interest confusion arising from online marketing by the same or different rules? *Network Automation* involved the purchase of a competitor's mark as an advertising keyword. *MTM* involved the display of third-party product listings in response to a customer's input of a trademark as a search term. Do you see any difference between the two uses that might be relevant to the likelihood of confusion?

4. In *Trademarks as Keywords: Much Ado About Something?*, 26 Harv. J. L. & Tech 481 (2013), Professors David Franklyn and David Hyman presented the results of their two-part empirical study assessing whether consumers are confused by the use of trademarks as keyword for search engine ads: "We find little evidence of consumer confusion regarding the source of goods, but only a small minority of consumers correctly and consistently distinguished paid ads from unpaid search results. We also find that the aggregate risk of consumer confusion is low, because most of the ads triggered by the use of trademarks as keywords are for authorized sellers or the trademark owners themselves. However, a sizeable percentage of survey respondents thought it was unfair and inappropriate for one company to purchase another company's trademark as a keyword, independent of confusion as to source." Should Frankyn's and Hyman's findings affect the result in initial interest confusion litigation?

5. CollegeSource and AcademyOne both provide online information sources for college students seeking to transfer to other colleges and educational institutions interested in evaluating the educational accomplishments of prospective transfer students. CollegeSource owns a service mark registration in COLLEGESOURCE and common law service mark rights in CAREER GUIDANCE FOUNDATION; it markets its services through print materials and attendance at trade shows and conferences. AcademyOne markets its services through the Internet. In particular, AcademyOne buys online banner ads from search engines using the words or phrases "college," "college source," "career guidance," and "career guidance foundation" as ad triggers. The ads themselves contain neither CollegeSource's marks nor AcademyOne's. They are headed "College Transfer Help" and contain a link to AcademyOne's website at www.collegetransfer.net. Do you see a likelihood of confusion? What more would you need to know? *See CollegeSource, Inc. v. AcademyOne, Inc.*, 2012 US Dist. LEXIS 153197 (E.D. Pa. 2012), *aff'd.*, 597 Fed. Appx. 116 (3d Cir. 2015).

b. Post-Sale Confusion

Mastercrafters Clock & Radio Co. v. Vacheron & Constantin-Le Coultre Watches, Inc.

221 F.2d 464 (2d Cir. 1955)

Frank, Circuit Judge:

Mastercrafters Clock & Radio Co., the plaintiff below, is an American manufacturer of electric clocks. Vacheron & Constantin-Le Coultre Watches, Inc. (hereinafter referred to as "Vacheron"), defendant-counterclaimant, is an American importer and distributor of Swiss watches....

In 1952, when Mastercrafters launched the production and distribution of its Model 308 clock, Vacheron wired Mastercrafters and many of its customers-distributors that Model 308 was a counterfeit of the distinctive appearance and configuration of the Atmos clock, distributed by Vacheron, and that Vacheron would commence legal action if necessary. Following these telegrams, Vacheron started state-court suits against several of Mastercrafters' distributors for damages and an injunction. Mastercrafters, faced with a cancellation of orders for its Model 308 from distributors being sued in the state courts, countered by bringing the present action seeking a declaratory judgment that its Model 308 does not unfairly compete with Vacheron, and asking damages allegedly resulting from Vacheron's suits against Mastercrafters' distributors and an injunction to restrain further prosecution of those suits. Vacheron counterclaimed for damages from alleged unfair competition and for an injunction restraining the manufacture and distribution of Model 308....

The [trial] judge found that, before plaintiff began production of its Model 308, the Atmos clock "was readily distinguishable from all other clocks then on the market by virtue of its appearance"; that plaintiff's Model 308 copied that appearance; that plaintiff "undoubtedly intended to, and did, avail itself of an eye-catching design and hoped to cater to the price-conscious purchaser who desires to own a copy of a luxury design clock regardless of mechanism or source"; that the Atmos clock sold for not less than $175 while plaintiff's sold for $30 or $40; that on "two or three occasions Model 308 has been described as 'a copy of Atmos,'" once by a representative of plaintiff at an exhibit in Chicago, on the other occasions by distributors of plaintiff's clock; that "since the introduction of the Model 308, Vacheron's salesmen have encountered considerable sales resistance" and its sales have "fallen off"; and that these facts undoubtedly prove "the uniqueness and even the aesthetic qualities of" the Atmos clock. He further found that three customers inquired as to "the lower priced Atmos" and that others "said they knew where they 'could get a clock for $30 or $40 just like the Atmos.'" But he held there was no unfair competition by plaintiff because (a) more than one person lawfully distributed the Atmos clock and therefore there was no single source, (b) there was no evidence to show that the public cared what was the ultimate source, and (c) plaintiff's clock was plainly marked and advertised as plaintiff's.

Absent a design patent or a secondary meaning, of course there would be no actionable harm by plaintiff. But the existence of a secondary meaning, attaching to the unique appearance of the Atmos clock, is not precluded by the mere fact that more than one person distributed that clock in the same area. The actionable harm, in a secondary-meaning case, may result either from the likelihood (a) of loss of customers or (b) of loss of reputation, or (c) of both. Such loss can result from the customer's belief that the competing article derives from the same source as that of the party complaining; and it matters not whether the customers know just who is the source. The ultimate source here was the Swiss manufacturer, while the intermediate sources, in this country, were the defendant and Cartier. All three had actionable claims against plaintiff, if its conduct did or was likely to injure the reputation of the ultimate source of the Atmos clock, for all three legitimately enjoyed the benefits of that reputation.

True, a customer examining plaintiff's clock would see from the electric cord, that it was not an "atmospheric" clock. But, as the judge found, plaintiff copied the design of the Atmos clock because plaintiff intended to, and did, attract purchasers who wanted a "luxury design" clock. This goes to show at least that some customers would buy plaintiff's cheaper clock for the purpose of acquiring the prestige gained by displaying what many visitors at the customers' homes would regard as a prestigious article. Plaintiff's wrong thus consisted of the fact that such a visitor would be likely to assume that the clock was an Atmos clock. Neither the electric cord attached to, nor the plaintiff's name on, its clock would be likely to come to the attention of such a visitor; the likelihood of such confusion suffices to render plaintiff's conduct actionable.

Plaintiff's intention thus to reap financial benefits from poaching on the reputation of the Atmos clock is of major importance. Of course, where there is no likelihood of confusion—as, *e.g.*, where the alleged infringing article is not in a sufficiently adjacent field—then an alleged infringer's intent becomes irrelevant, since an intent to do a wrong cannot transmute a lawful into an unlawful act. But where the copying is unlawful, if only there is a likelihood of confusion, then the intent of the copier becomes decidedly relevant: It gives rise to a powerful inference that confusion is likely, and puts on the alleged infringer the burden of going forward with proof that it is not. Here the plaintiff's intent is unmistakable; accordingly, plaintiff had the burden of going forward with proof showing an absence of such likelihood; and that burden plaintiff did not discharge. Consequently, we do not accept the judge's findings as to the absence of unfair competition by plaintiff.

....

Since plaintiff was guilty of unfair competition, the judgment against defendant must be reversed. We remand with directions to dismiss plaintiff's complaint and, on the counterclaim, to grant an injunction against plaintiff, and to ascertain the damages to defendant....

The trial judge should determine whether defendant should also be awarded a sum equal to plaintiff's profits from sales of the infringing clock. We do not now decide that such an amount should be awarded but leave that matter to be decided, in the first instance at any rate, by the trial judge. *Reversed and remanded.*

Questions

1. So long as the actual purchaser is not confused regarding the source of the goods, why should it matter under trademark and unfair competition law that the purchaser's friends may be misled (or even that the purchaser sought to mislead his friends)? How, if at all, would the trademark owner be harmed?

2. Is "copying for the purpose of acquiring prestige" trademark infringement?

3. Do you understand why "associating" goods or services with a trademark owner is "confusing"? Do you agree?

Jeremy N. Sheff, *Veblen Brands*

96 MINN. L. REV. 769 (2012) (excerpt)*

Post-sale confusion is an invention of the lower federal courts. The Supreme Court has never endorsed the theory, nor even discussed it. But for over half a century it has been the key weapon in the arsenal of luxury brand owners. Given this history, post-sale confusion as a doctrine unto itself has received surprisingly little critical attention. What literature does exist either characterizes post-sale confusion as merely one example of broader trends in intellectual property, or else discusses the economic or philosophical implications of luxury consumption without critically examining the underlying legal doctrine that facilitates that consumption. This Article makes a new contribution, first by critiquing the actual doctrine of post-sale confusion, and second by examining the relationship between that doctrine and what I claim is its unique (and heretofore overlooked) purpose: the regulation of socially expressive consumption.

The first step in this project is to try to provide a coherent doctrinal account of the post-sale confusion cases. As it turns out, this is an impossible task. There is no single coherent theory of injury in post-sale confusion cases; rather, there are three....

The first theory, which I label "bystander confusion," refers to the following factual scenario: a defendant sells its product to a non-confused purchaser; observers who see the non-confused purchaser using the defendant's product mistake it for the plaintiff's product; and those observers draw conclusions from their observations that influence their future purchasing decisions. This theory shares similarities with more conventional theories of trademark infringement, with the distinction that, in practice, it improperly reduces the burden on plaintiffs from proving a "likelihood of confusion" to proving a mere possibility of confusion.

The next theory of injury—which I label "downstream confusion"—is implicated where there is a risk that a non-confused purchaser of a knockoff or altered trademarked good might give or resell the good to a confused recipient. This variety of post-sale confusion flies in the face of long-standing Supreme Court precedent regarding contributory infringement and trademark law's first-sale doctrine. That inconsistency, in turn, allows a trademark infringement plaintiff to turn a losing case into a winning case merely by changing the name of his claim.

The problems inherent in bystander and downstream confusion can be remedied by minor doctrinal refinements, although those refinements might well result in discarding the theories as such. The more difficult issue is that both these theories are often invoked in tandem with (and potentially as a distraction from) the third theory of injury, which I label "status confusion." Status confusion is the legal theory that most often serves to justify liability against the manufacturers of knockoff luxury branded goods, even though the purchasers of those goods know full well what they are buying.

 [*Footnotes omitted—Eds.*]

Status-confusion cases often invoke an argument owing its origins to economist and social critic Thorstein Veblen: that individuals conspicuously consume some expensive products (a Fendi handbag, say) to stake a claim to social status. As the courts in these cases implicitly recognize, if the symbols used to stake such claims are freely available to anyone, a classic problem of information economics arises: the claim loses its credibility—indeed its very meaning—due to indiscriminate use. In the United States, trademark law has solved this problem by propertizing the symbols that express the claim, driving them into a market system. By incentivizing private parties to ration access to such symbols, status-confusion doctrine creates the scarcity that is required for the symbols to have social meaning.

This is an odd role for trademark law to play. Putting to one side relatively novel and unsettled doctrines like dilution, the conventional theoretical account of trademarks is that they facilitate the transfer of information between buyers and sellers regarding the source or quality of goods in the marketplace. In the status-confusion cases, however, information about the goods themselves is essentially irrelevant to all parties concerned. Rather, the courts in those cases view the trademarks at issue as a means of transferring information about people: buyers consume luxury goods in view of a social audience for the purpose of making a statement about what kind of people they are (or aspire to be). For reasons that will become clear, I refer to the luxury trademarks that serve this socially expressive function (by virtue of the artificial scarcity that trademark law permits their owners to maintain) as "Veblen brands."

This Article ultimately asks whether the trademark system has any legitimate interest in creating, maintaining, and regulating the market for Veblen brands, and if so, whether the First Amendment permits the law of trademarks to be used in that way. Status-confusion doctrine has the direct effect of "restricting the speech of some elements of our society in order to enhance the relative voice of others," an exercise of government power which the Supreme Court has stated in other contexts "is wholly foreign to the First Amendment." By establishing a system of licenses for social expression and enforcing those licenses with both monetary and injunctive remedies, the State is entering into an expressive alliance with one (powerful) segment of society, in opposition to the expressive interests of a different (weak) segment of society. Even if this alliance of interests did not offend the First Amendment (and I argue it does), it ought to offend our democratic sensibilities. I claim that whatever government interest is at stake in the status confusion cases is insufficient to justify their coercive and selective restriction of social expression. Therefore, I propose that status-confusion doctrine—and post-sale confusion doctrine as a whole—be discarded.

Munsingwear, Inc. v. Jockey International

31 U.S.P.Q.2d 1146 (D. Minn.), *aff'd*, 39 F.3d 1184 (8th Cir. 1994)

Doty, J.:

This matter is before the court on plaintiff Munsingwear's motion for a preliminary injunction and defendant Jockey's motion for summary judgment. Based on a review of the file, record, and proceedings herein, the court grants Jockey's motion and denies Munsingwear's motion.

BACKGROUND

This matter involves the marketing of a horizontal-fly version of mens' [sic] underwear by Jockey. Jockey first introduced its horizontal-fly[1] briefs under the "Jockey Pouch" ("Pouch") name in June 1992. The Pouch line consisted of briefs with the horizontal-fly and the "JOCKEY" trademark woven into the waistband. They were sold through Jockey's standard lines of commerce. The packaging consisted of standard cellophane wrapped around the brief with the "JOCKEY" trademark and Jockey Design trademark on both the front and back of the packaging.

Munsingwear instituted this action against Jockey claiming trademark infringement under § 43(a) of the Lanham Act, common law trademark infringement, and deceptive trade practices. Munsingwear based these claims on its alleged preexisting trademark rights in the horizontal-fly (or H-FLY) mark. While not having actual federal registration of the H-FLY, Munsingwear claims it is entitled to protection based upon its continuous use of the design since 1946, reinforced by millions of dollars of advertising.

Munsingwear now moves for a preliminary injunction to prevent Jockey from manufacturing, distributing and selling Pouch underwear. Jockey moves for summary judgment claiming that there is no likelihood of confusion between the two manufacturers' underwear as a matter of law.

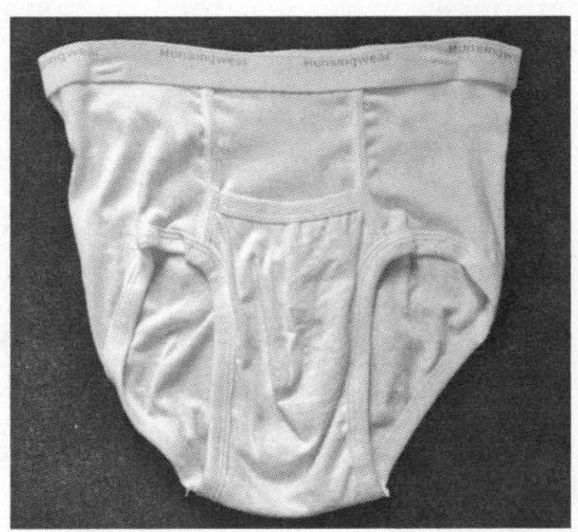

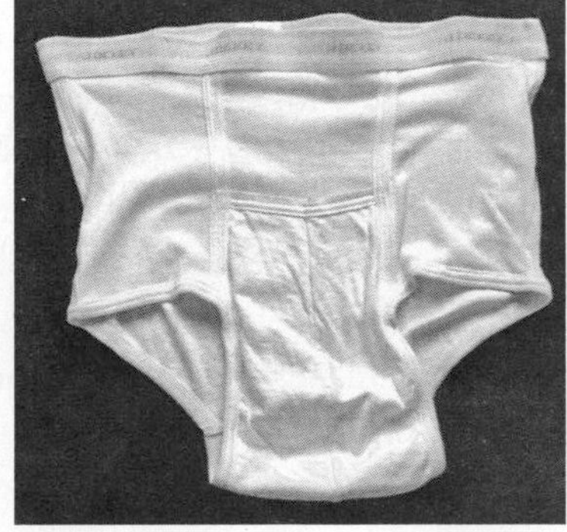

DISCUSSION

. . . .

Before undertaking the six factor *SquirtCo* analysis, the court must initially determine which products are to be compared. In this action two alternatives exist, either the pre-sale or post-sale product. The pre-sale product consists of the underwear as packaged and sold to the consuming public, seen in Figures 1 and 2 of Jockey's motion

1. A horizontal-fly is exactly as it is described. Rather than running vertical, or parallel with the leg, the horizontal-fly is perpendicular to the leg and looks generally like a pocket.

for summary judgment. The post-sale product consists of the actual individual briefs themselves.... Determination of which products are to be compared is made by referring to how consumers will encounter the two products. *Lindy Pen Co., Inc. v. Bic Pen Corp.*, 725 F.2d 1240 (9th Cir. 1984) (Similarity of marks considered in light of the way they are encountered in the marketplace and the circumstances surrounding their purchase.)

Jockey contends that the overall combination and arrangement of the package design elements, the pre-sale product, should serve as the basis of analysis. Evidence submitted in support of that contention shows that underwear is purchased in single or multi-unit cellophane wrapped packages that indicate source and style information.

Munsingwear claims that, while the products are purchased as packaged, consumers base their buying decision on other factors. Among those cited are the consumer's desire for certain styles and purchase place exposure to the product while it is on mannequins. Munsingwear contends that the combination of the two factors often leads to the subsequent purchasing decision and thus likelihood of customer confusion. Munsingwear equates this display technique to post-sale exposure which serves as the basis for its argument that consumers will be confused.

The courts that have decided the question have split as to whether pre-sale products or post-sale products provide the proper basis for analysis. The Eighth Circuit has not yet ruled on this issue. On the facts of this case, the argument for pre-sale exposure is stronger because any relevant consumer confusion will likely occur prior to sale, if at all. As customarily worn, underwear is concealed by other articles of clothing. The general public does not ordinarily see underwear in the same manner and to the extent that it views outerwear. Thus, the potential for customer confusion is not as great as it could be for other articles of clothing. *Lois Sportswear, U.S.A., Inc. v. Levi Strauss & Co.*, 631 F. Supp. 735 (S.D.N.Y. 1985), *aff'd*, 799 F.2d 867, 872–73 (2d Cir. 1986). In *Levi* the Second Circuit held that potential confusion may exist in consumers seeing appellant's jeans worn outside the retail store absent any identifying labels that may be attached at the time of purchase. *Id.* The inherently concealed nature of worn underwear diminishes the concern for post-sale confusion noted by the *Levi* court. Thus Munsingwear's reliance on *Levi* is misplaced. The lack of post-sale exposure of the product to the general public reduces the risk that any customers will be confused as to source.

....

a. Similarity

The first step in the *SquirtCo* analysis is to compare the two products as they are encountered by the consuming public. Examination of the two product packages reveals that they are not similar. The Jockey package consists of a cardboard insert that has a picture of a man wearing the style of underwear the package contains. The "JOCKEY POUCH" label is written across the top with the "JOCKEY" and Jockey logo trademarks. Finally, the material makeup of the underwear is also listed as well as the size and manufacturer's barcodes. The Munsingwear package does not have a cardboard insert but rather consists of a "band and medallion" through the middle of the package. The medallion has the kangaroo design with "MUNSINGWEAR KANGAROO BRIEF" encircling the drawing. Under the band is the Munsingwear trade mark. The Munsingwear package also lists sizes. When viewed side by side, it is obvious which package is produced by which manufacturer. Thus, the court finds that there is no substantial similarity between the two products.

b. Proximity

While competitive proximity is not controlled by the two manufactures, both products are sold in the men's department of stores. Munsingwear cites an individual instance where the two products were sold side-by-side; Jockey contends that this is not the usual course of business and is unusual. However, whether Munsingwear and Jockey are sold side-by-side becomes irrelevant when the market is viewed. In a market controlled by only a few producers it is inevitable that one brand will be located near another. Efficiency and customer assistance dictate that many stores will display and sell all similar products in relatively close proximity. Thus, the court finds that due to the nature of the product, it is highly likely that the two products will be sold in relatively close proximity, but that this is a function of market decisions made by individual stores rather than by the litigants.

c. Intent to Pass-Off

Munsingwear next argues that Jockey formed a specific intent to pass-off its "Pouch" underwear as Munsingwear's "H-Fly" underwear. Jockey contends that the existing strength of its trademark and the amount spent in advertising indicate that this is not the case. Jockey claims that its marketing of Pouch underwear is a form of competition for market share rather than an attempt to pass-off its underwear as that of Munsingwear.

Viewing the two packages together, the court finds that it is evident that there is no intent to pass off. First, the two packages prominently indicate who the manufacturer is. Second, the individual pieces of underwear have the manufacturer's name permanently stitched into the waistband. Based upon these factors, the court finds that Jockey has no intent to pass off its underwear as that of Munsingwear.

d. Actual Confusion

[The court found no evidence probative of actual confusion.]

e. Survey Evidence

[No surveys were submitted.]

f. Costs and Conditions of Purchase

Finally, the court must consider the costs and conditions surrounding the purchase of the two products. Generally, the more sophisticated the average consumer of a product is, the less likely it is that similarities in trade dress and trademarks will result in confusion concerning the source or sponsorship of the product. *Bristol-Myers Squibb Co. v. McNeil-P.P.C., Inc.*, 973 F.2d 1033 (2d Cir. 1992). In this action, both parties suggest that its products are purchased in a retail setting and that the costs are similar and relatively inexpensive. The purchasers of relatively inexpensive goods are held to a lesser standard of purchasing care and do not give much thought to the purchase of such inexpensive goods. *Specialty Brands, Inc. v. Coffee Bean Distributors, Inc.*, 748 F.2d 669 (Fed. Cir. 1984); *c.f.*, *Beer Nuts, Inc. v. Clover Club Foods, Co.*, 805 F.2d 920 (10th Cir. 1986); *Sun-Fun Products, Inc. v. Suntan Research & Development, Inc.*, 656 F.2d 186 (5th Cir. 1981). Therefore, due to the inexpensive nature of the products, the court finds that the relevant consumer is not generally sophisticated and gives little thought to the purchasing decision.

Upon review of the facts in this case, and applying the *SquirtCo* analysis, the court finds that the dissimilarity between the two products in their pre-sale condition, the lack of an intent to pass off by Jockey and the lack of actual customer confusion all weigh heavily in Jockey's favor. The relatively close proximity of the two products during retail sale, the unsophisticated decision making process of the average consumer and the lack of a survey to establish or disprove actual confusion weigh in favor of neither party. Therefore, the court finds that Jockey has established that no likelihood of confusion exists between the two products.

Questions

1. Why did Munsingwear bring this suit? Was it worried that prospective buyers of its H-Fly underwear would purchase Jockey's Pouch briefs by mistake? Was it trying to monopolize a product feature that it believed some customers preferred? Was it concerned that customers might believe it had merged with Jockey or sold its H-Fly line to another company? Which, if any, of these concerns should trademark law respond to?

2. Do you agree with Professor Sheff that post-sale confusion doctrine as applied to knock-off luxury goods is an illegitimate expansion of trademark liability? Imagine that you represent the producer of a luxury product. What argument might you make to respond to Sheff's critique?

3. Adidas makes athletic footwear, apparel, and sporting equipment. The company uses many variations of a well-known three-stripe design as trademarks on its shoes and other merchandise. It enforces those marks aggressively. Recently, it filed suit against Skechers, claiming that Skechers sneakers infringed Adidas' three-stripe mark.

adidas Ultra Boost

Skechers Relaxed Fit Cross Court TR

adidas Stan Smith

Skechers Onix

Skechers argues that all of its sneakers are prominently marked with the Skechers logo and bear tags with the Skechers brand. Adidas acknowledges that Skechers' logos, tags, and marking may diminish point-of-sale confusion, but claims that they won't prevent post-sale confusion. How should the court rule? *See Adidas America, Inc. v. Skechers U.S.A., Inc.*, 149 F. Supp. 3d 1222 (D. Ore. 2016).

c. Reverse Confusion

Dreamwerks Production, Inc. v. SKG Studio

142 F.3d 1127 (9th Cir. 1998)

Kozinski, Circuit Judge

Dreamwerks, a company hardly anyone has heard of, sues entertainment colossus DreamWorks SKG, claiming trademark infringement. This is the reverse of the normal trademark infringement case, where the well-known mark goes after a look-alike, sound-alike, feel-alike unknown which is trying to cash in on the famous mark's goodwill. The twist here is that Dreamwerks, the unknown, was doing business under that name long before DreamWorks was a twinkle in Hollywood's eye. Dreamwerks is therefore the senior mark, and it argues that its customers will mistakenly think they are dealing with DreamWorks, the junior mark.

Facts

Everyone — or most everyone — has heard of DreamWorks SKG, established in 1994 by what many consider the three hottest names in Hollywood: Steven Spielberg, Jeffrey Katzenberg and David Geffen (each of whom graciously contributed an initial to form the SKG part of the trademark). DreamWorks is a film studio, having produced such well-advertised movies as *The Peacemaker, Amistad* and *Mouse Hunt.* Like other movie studios, DreamWorks participates more generally in the entertainment business, having created DreamWorks Interactive (a joint venture with software giant Microsoft); GameWorks (described in the press as a micropub and virtual reality video arcade for the 90s); and DreamWorks Toys (a joint venture with toy maker Hasbro).

Less well known is Dreamwerks Production Group, Inc., a small Florida company that since 1984 has been in the business of organizing conventions in the Northeast and Midwest, mostly with a Star Trek theme. At a typical Star Trek convention, Dreamwerks draws customers with a star like DeForest Kelley (Bones), Leonard Nimoy (Spock) or Michael Dorn (Worf from *The Next Generation*). For an admission fee of $25 or so, customers get autographs, meet fellow trekkies, compete in costume contests, listen to pitches for upcoming movies and browse the products of vendors who have rented space at the convention. Dreamwerks sometimes presents previews of science fiction and adventure/fantasy movies produced by the major studios, such as *Batman Returns, Dracula, Aladdin* and *Jurassic Park*. Dreamwerks clearly caters to the pocket-protector niche, and its convention business has never really taken off. But the longevity of the enterprise illustrates its remarkable resilience, not unlike the starship itself.

Because Dreamwerks registered its mark with the United States Patent and Trademark Office in 1992, it holds the senior mark and is the plaintiff here. It claims that DreamWorks SKG is causing confusion in the marketplace by using a mark too similar to its own and is doing so with respect to goods and services that are too similar to those it (Dreamwerks) is offering.

Pshaw, one might say. What could be better for Dreamwerks than to have people confuse it with a mega movie studio? Many an infringer has tried to manufacture precisely such confusion and thereby siphon off the goodwill of a popular mark. *See, e.g., E. & J. Gallo Winery* v. *Gallo Cattle Co.*, 967 F.2d 1280, 1293 (9th Cir. 1992) ("Gallo" wine and "Joseph Gallo" cheese). Not so, answers Dreamwerks, apparently in earnest. It is not interested in fooling consumers, and it claims to suffer ill will when people buy tickets under the misimpression that they are dealing with DreamWorks rather than Dreamwerks. Dreamwerks also frets that its own goodwill will be washed away by the rising tide of publicity associated with the junior mark. Dreamwerks points out (somewhat wistfully) that it hopes to expand its business into related fields, and that these avenues will be foreclosed if DreamWorks gets there first. Finally, Dreamwerks notes that whatever goodwill it has built now rests in the hands of DreamWorks; if the latter should take a major misstep and tarnish its reputation with the public, Dreamwerks too would be pulled down.

These are not fanciful or unreasonable concerns, though they may be somewhat exaggerated by the hope of winning an award or settlement against an apparently very solvent DreamWorks. We are not, however, in a position to judge the extent to which these harms are likely, nor whether they are somehow offset by any extra goodwill plaintiff may inadvertently reap as a result of the confusion between its mark and that of the defendant. These are matters for the trier of fact. The narrow question presented here is whether Dreamwerks has stated a claim for trademark infringement sufficient to survive summary judgment. The district court held that Dreamwerks had not because the core functions of the two businesses are so distinct that there is no likelihood of confusion as a matter of law. Dreamwerks appeals, and it is that ruling we review de novo. [Citation.]

Discussion

The test for likelihood of confusion is whether a "reasonably prudent consumer" in the marketplace is likely to be confused as to the origin of the good or service bearing one of the marks. In *AMF Inc.* v. *Sleekcraft Boats*, 599 F.2d 341, 348–49 (9th Cir. 1979), we listed eight factors to facilitate the inquiry....

In the usual infringement case, these factors are applied to determine whether the junior user is palming off its products as those of the senior user. Would a consumer who finds a running shoe marked Mike be bamboozled into thinking that it was manufactured by Nike? In a reverse infringement case, like ours, there is no question of palming off, since neither junior nor senior user wishes to siphon off the other's goodwill. The question in such cases is whether consumers doing business with the senior user might mistakenly believe that they are dealing with the junior user. More specifically, the question here is whether a reasonable consumer attending a Dreamwerks-sponsored convention might do so believing that it is a convention sponsored by DreamWorks.[3]

Before performing a Vulcan mind meld on the "reasonably prudent consumer," we note that if this were an ordinary trademark case rather than a reverse infringement case—in other words if DreamWorks had been there first and Dreamwerks later opened up a business running entertainment-related conventions—there would be little doubt that DreamWorks would have stated a case for infringement sufficient to survive summary judgment.[4] The reason for this, of course, is that a famous mark like DreamWorks SKG casts a long shadow. Does the result change in a reverse infringement case because the long shadow is cast by the junior mark? We think not.[5]

Three of the *Sleekcraft* factors are pivotal here: (1) arbitrariness of the mark; (2) similarity of sight, sound and meaning; and (3) relatedness of the goods. "Dreamwerks" is an arbitrary and fictitious mark deserving of strong protection. Had Dreamwerks chosen a descriptive mark like Sci-Fi Conventions Inc., or a suggestive mark like Sci-Fi World, some confusion with the marks of legitimate competitors might be expected. DreamWorks argues that the word "Dream" makes the Dreamwerks mark suggestive of a company which brings sci-fi dreams to life. But "Dream" is used in too many different ways to suggest any particular meaning to the reasonable consumer. At best, "Dreamwerks" conjures images related to fantasy, hope or reverie. It's too

3. Or more precisely for our purposes, the question is whether the district court erred in holding that Dreamwerks had failed to establish a triable issue of fact with respect to this. The distinction is important because it requires us to draw reasonable inferences—about the workings of the entertainment industry, the mind set of trekkies attending conventions and so on—in favor of Dreamwerks.

4. The unusual posture of the case has caused DreamWorks SKG, the holder of the famous mark, to make an argument that is quite uncharacteristic for someone in its position. Namely, it argues that the plaintiff's mark (and therefore its own) deserves relatively narrow protection. DreamWorks may someday find itself in a case where its position is reversed, and discover that the arguments it made in our case come back to haunt it. *See, e.g., Russell v. Rolfs*, 893 F.2d 1033, 1037 (9th Cir. 1990) (applying judicial estoppel).

5. In an infringement case involving "forward" confusion, a more well-known senior mark suggests greater likelihood of confusion because a junior user's mark is more likely to be associated with a famous mark. In a reverse confusion case, however, we must focus on the strength of the junior user's mark. *See Sands, Taylor & Wood Co. v. Quaker Oats Co.*, 978 F.2d 947, 959 (7th Cir. 1992). The concern here is that convention-goers will think DreamWorks SKG is sponsoring the Star Trek conventions. So the greater the power of DreamWorks' mark in the marketplace, the more likely it is to capture the minds of Dreamwerks customers.

great a mental leap from hopes to Star Trek conventions for us to treat the mark as suggestive. The Dreamwerks mark deserves broad protection.

Sight, sound and meaning is easy. There is perfect similarity of sound, since "Dreamwerks" and "DreamWorks" are pronounced the same way. There is also similarity of meaning: Neither literally means anything, and to the extent the words suggest a fantasy world, they do so equally.[9] Similarity of sight presents a slightly closer question. The man-in-the-moon DreamWorks logo, when presented in the full regalia of a movie trailer, is quite distinctive. But "DreamWorks" often appears in the general press and in Industry magazines without the logo, leaving only the slight difference in spelling. Spelling is a lost art; many moviegoers might think that Mirimax and Colombia Pictures are movie studios. Moreover, a perceptive consumer who does notice the "e" and lower-case "w" in Dreamwerks might shrug off the difference as an intentional modification identifying an ancillary division of the same company. While we recognize that spelling matters, we're not sure substituting one vowel for another and capitalizing a middle consonant dispels the similarity between the marks.

The clincher is the relatedness of the goods. Twenty years ago DreamWorks may have had an argument that making movies and promoting sci-fi merchandise are different businesses promoting different products. But movies and sci-fi merchandise are now as complementary as baseball and hot dogs. The main products sold at Dreamwerks conventions are movie and TV collectibles and memorabilia; the lectures, previews and appearances by actors which attract customers to Dreamwerks conventions are all dependent, in one way or another, on the output of entertainment giants like DreamWorks.

The district court emphasized that Dreamwerks has carved out a narrow niche in the entertainment marketplace, while DreamWorks controls a much broader segment. Dreamwerks targets trekkies; DreamWorks targets everyone. But the relatedness of each company's prime directive isn't relevant. Rather, we must focus on Dreamwerks' customers and ask whether they are likely to associate the conventions with DreamWorks the studio. Entertainment studios control all sorts of related industries: publishing, clothing, amusement parks, computer games and an endless list of toys and kids' products. In this environment it's easy for customers to suspect DreamWorks of sponsoring conventions at which movie merchandise is sold.[10] Other studios are

---

9. "Dreamwork" seems to have two more specific but lesser-known meanings. In psychiatry, "dream-work" is a term coined by Sigmund Freud to refer to the work a dream does by bringing out one's fears, anxieties and hopes, thereby helping balance one's personality. *See* Sigmund Freud, *The Interpretation of Dreams* 174–75 (A.A. Brill trans., Random House 1950). The term "dreamwork" has even spilled over into academic film analysis, where the viewing of a film (sitting in the dark, passive) is often analogized to a dream. *See, e.g.*, Paul Coates, *The Sense of an Ending: Reflections on Kieslowski's Trilogy*, Film Quarterly, Dec. 1, 1996 (discussing dreamwork in Blue). Since we can hardly expect the reasonable consumer to discover this film-specific meaning, we think it is appropriate to also treat the DreamWorks mark as simply calling to mind vague notions of fantasy, hope or reverie.

10. According to Jeffrey Katzenberg's deposition testimony, DreamWorks has no current plans to sponsor conventions. But DreamWorks does not dispute that it plans to hawk mass quantities of commercial goods in addition to the movies themselves. People attending Dreamwerks conventions

rapidly expanding their merchandising outlets: Universal Studios has theme parks in California, Florida and Japan with dozens of stores selling movie-related products, and Disney is helping transform New York's Times Square into a G-rated shopping center. Dreamwerks convention-goers might well assume that DreamWorks decided to ride the coattails of Spielberg's unparalleled reputation for sci-fi/adventure films (Jaws, E.T., Close Encounters, Raiders, Jurassic Park) into the sci-fi merchandising business.[11]

Conclusion

We do not decide the ultimate question presented in this case, whether DreamWorks SKG infringes the trademark held by Dreamwerks Production Group, Inc. We only remand for trial. While it is somewhat unusual for a famous mark to defend its very existence against a much lesser known mark, DreamWorks is in no different a position than any other new company which must ensure that its proposed mark will not infringe on the rights of existing trademark holders.

. . . .

Fortres Grand Corp. v. Warner Brothers Entertainment, 763 F.3d 696 (7th Cir. 2014). Warner Brothers' 2012 Batman film, *The Dark Knight Rises*, included a handful of references to a fictional software program named "Clean Slate," reputed to be capable of erasing a criminal's history from every software database in the world. Either Warner Brothers or Batman fans also created two websites that purported to be the sites of the fictional software company that marketed the fictional "Clean Slate" software, complete with a fictitious patent for the fictitious program. Fortres Grand, which has marketed a software program named CLEAN SLATE since 2001 and has registered the mark on the principal register, sued Warner Brothers for trademark infringement, alleging reverse confusion. The district court dismissed the case. The Court of Appeals for the 7th Circuit affirmed:

> . . . Fortres Grand's claims depend on plausibly alleging that Warner Bros.' use of the words "clean slate" is "likely to cause confusion." . . . But general confusion "in the air" is not actionable. Rather, only confusion about "origin, sponsorship, or approval of . . . goods" supports a trademark claim. [Citations.]
>
> . . . .

---

may not know about Katzenberg's plans and could easily assume that DreamWorks has spun off a Star Trek marketing division.

11. Promoting sci-fi merchandise may or may not amount to the same thing as sponsoring conventions. But how would a Dreamwerks customer know the difference? If an entertainment studio can own the movie, the theatres which show the movie, the newspapers which list the movie, the television networks which advertise the movie, the magazines which review the movie, the stores which sell the toys, clothing and posters associated with the movie, the amusement parks with rides based on the movie and the rights to the movie-related merchandise itself, then why wouldn't a studio also sponsor a convention which celebrates movies and sells movie-related products?

> ... Fortres Grand argues that it has stated a claim via "reverse confusion" ... In reverse confusion, the *senior user's* products are mistaken as originating from (or being affiliated with or sponsored by) the *junior user*. This situation often occurs when the junior user is a well-known brand which can quickly swamp the marketplace and overwhelm a small senior user. [Citations.] The harm from this kind of confusion is that "the senior user loses the value of the trademark—its product identity, corporate identity, control over its goodwill and reputation, and ability to move into new markets." [Citation.] To state a claim for infringement based on reverse confusion, Fortres Grand must plausibly allege that Warner Bros.' use of the words "clean slate" in its movie to describe an elusive hacking program that can eliminate information from any and every database on earth has caused a likelihood that consumers will be confused into thinking that Fortres Grand's Clean Slate software "emanates from, is connected to, or is sponsored by [Warner Bros.]." [Citations.]
>
> In considering the plausibility of such an allegation of confusion we look to the applicable test for likelihood of confusion. In this circuit, we employ a seven-factor test ...

The Court first discussed the similarity of the products:

> The problem here is that Fortres Grand wants to allege confusion regarding the source of a utilitarian desktop management software based solely on the use of a mark in a movie and two advertising websites. Warner Bros ... does not sell any movie merchandise similar to Fortres Grand's software which also bears the allegedly infringing mark. Fortres Grand mentions that Warner Bros. sells video games. Desktop management software and video game software may be similar enough to make confusion plausible, but Fortres Grand does not allege that the *video games* bear the "clean slate" mark. Nor does Fortres Grand allege that desktop management software is a commonly merchandised movie tie-in (as a video game might be). Accordingly, the only products available to compare—Fortres Grand's software and Warner Bros.' movie—are quite dissimilar, even considering common merchandising practice. Fortres Grand has alleged no facts that would make it plausible that a super-hero movie and desktop management software are "goods related in the minds of consumers in the sense that a single producer is likely to put out both goods."
>
> Fortres Grand emphasizes that we have clearly stated that courts should not rely on the weakness of a single factor to dispose of a trademark infringement claim. [Citation.] But its allegation of reverse confusion is just as implausible in light of the other factors. Both the movie and Fortres Grand's software are available on the internet, but the movie was shown first and primarily in theaters and Fortres Grand's software is only available at its website, not at other places on the internet. And anyone who arrives at Fortres Grand's website is very unlikely to imagine it is sponsored by

Warner Bros. (assuming, safely, that Fortres Grand is not using Catwoman as a spokesperson for its program's efficacy). *See* FortresGrand.com, *Clean Slate 7*, http://www.fortresgrand.com/products/cls/cls.htm. And the movie websites, while on the internet, sell no products and are clearly tied to the fictional universe of Batman. Further, Warner Bros.' use of the mark is not a traditional use in the marketplace, but in the dialogue of its movie and in extensions of its fictional universe, so the "the area and manner of concurrent use" also makes confusion unlikely. Fortres Grand also asserts that consumers of "security software," similar to what it sells, are discerning and "skeptical," which is indicative of a "degree of care likely to be exercised by consumers" making confusion unlikely. Additionally, the mark "clean slate" is just one variation of a phrase that traces its origins at least as far back as Aristotle and is often used to describe fresh starts or beginnings. While the use of the term may be suggestive for security software, its use descriptively (and suggestively) is quite broad, including in reference to giving convicted criminals fresh starts, to redesigning the internet, or, indeed, to a movie about an investigator with amnesia. Accordingly, Warner Bros.' descriptive use of the words "clean slate" in the movie's dialogue to describe a program that cleans a criminal's slate is unlikely to cause confusion. [Citation.]

Finally, Fortres Grand speculates that there must have been actual confusion because of "internet chatter" and "web pages, tweets, and blog posts in which potential consumers question whether the CLEAN SLATE program, as it exists in *The Dark Knight Rises*, is real and could potentially work." But this is not an allegation of actual confusion. This is an assertion that consumers are speculating that there really could be a hacking tool that allows a user to erase information about herself from every database on earth. *Id.* At best Fortres Grand's argument is that consumers are mistakenly thinking that its software may be such a hacking tool (or an attempt at such a hacking tool), and not buying it. But this is not reverse confusion about origin. Whoever these unusually gullible hypothetical consumers are, Fortres Grand has not and could not plausibly allege that consumers are confused into thinking Fortres Grand is selling such a diabolical hacking tool *licensed by Warner Bros.* Fortres Grand's real complaint is that Warner Bros.' use of the words "clean slate" has tarnished Fortres Grand's "clean slate" mark by associating it with illicit software. But this type of harm may only be remedied with a dilution claim. *See* 15 U.S.C. § 1125(c). And it would not be appropriate to use a contorted and broadened combination of the "reverse confusion" and "related products" doctrines to extend dilution protection to non-famous marks which are explicitly excluded from such protection by statute. *Id.* ("the owner of a *famous* mark ... shall be entitled to an injunction against another person who ... commences use of a mark ... that is likely to cause ... dilution by tarnishment of the *famous* mark" (emphasis added)).

In fact, the only factor to which Fortres Grand's allegations lend any strength is the similarity of the marks—both marks are merely "clean slate" or "the clean slate." But juxtaposed against the weakness of all the other factors, this similarity is not enough. Trademark law protects the source-denoting function of words used in conjunction with goods and services in the marketplace, not the words themselves. [Citation.] Assuming all Fortres Grand's other allegations are true, its reverse confusion allegation—that consumers may mistakenly think Warner Bros. is the source of Fortres Grand's software—is still "too implausible to support costly litigation." [Citation.] Accordingly, we need not—and do not—reach Warner Bros.' argument that its descriptive use of the words "clean slate" in the dialogue of its movie is shielded by the First Amendment.

Questions

1. The Harlem Wizards is a "show" basketball team. Founded in 1962, the team plays exhibition games in which competitive basketball play is interspersed with comedic antics and tricks. The Wizards do not, typically, sell tickets to their "games"; rather, they market themselves to third party organizations, which hire them to appear at fairs, festivals and charity programs. The Harlem Wizards have performed throughout the United States and internationally. The team sells souvenir t-shirts, sweatshirts, caps, basketballs and posters bearing the Wizards logo at its games and appearances, but does not market them to retail stores. Until 1997, the NBA basketball team that made its home in Washington DC was named the Washington Bullets. Concerned that the Bullets name had violent connotations, the team changed its name to the Washington Wizards. The Harlem Wizards filed a lawsuit alleging a likelihood of reverse confusion. How should the court rule? *See Harlem Wizards Entertainment Basketball, Inc. v. NBA Properties, Inc.*, 952 F. Supp. 1084 (D.N.J. 1997).

2. Surfvivor is a coined word, and a trademark registered for Hawaiian beach-themed products, and has been in use in Hawaii for some years before the inauguration of the reality-television show, *Survivor.* The show's producers have licensed "Survivor" for a variety of consumer merchandise, including beachwear. The producers were aware of the Surfvivor mark when they adopted Survivor for the television show. There has been no evidence of actual confusion of the marks. How should the court rule on Surfvivor's reverse confusion claim? *See Surfvivor Media v. Survivor Productions*, 406 F.3d 625 (9th Cir. 2005).

3. In 1999, Byron Preiss founded a new book imprint, which he named ibooks. Preiss announced that ibooks would publish backlist novels simultaneously in paper and digital editions. Simon and Schuster agreed to distribute the print versions to bookstores, and ibooks made the digital versions available for paid download at its website, www.ibooksinc.com. ibooks released its first books in 2000. Its catalogue included classic science fiction by Isaac Asimov, Alfred Bester and Arthur C. Clarke.

All books included the ibooks logo, which featured a lightbulb containing a lowercase "i" and the word "ibooks":

Between 2000 and 2005, ibooks published science fiction, mystery, history and science books. In 2005, Preiss was killed in a traffic accident. After Preiss's death, the company foundered, and it filed for bankruptcy in 2006. Independent publisher J Boylston & Company purchased the assets of ibooks, Inc., and continued to publish books under the ibooks imprint. Sales have been modest; in some years the imprint lost money. In 2010, Apple Computer Company adopted the mark iBooks for its ereader software and its ebookstore. J Boylston & Company filed suit against Apple, claiming reverse confusion. How should the court rule? *See J Colby & Co. v. Apple, Inc.*, 586 Fed. Appx. 8 (2d Cir. 2014).

4. Uber Promotions is a marketing and event-planning agency in Gainesville, Florida, which has been operating since 2006. Its services include party planning, party transportation rental, printing and photography services and private venue rental. Uber Technologies is a transportation network company that allows customers to summon private drivers using a smartphone app. Uber Technologies launched its service and adopted the UBER service mark in 2010. Uber Technologies has expanded rapidly, offering services in many cities across the world, including Gainesville. It has recently branched out to offer delivery services, luxury car transportation, and carpool coordination. It has also introduced targeted promotions keyed to holidays, special events, and partnerships with other businesses. Uber Promotions has filed suit against Uber Technologies, alleging a likelihood of reverse confusion. Which of the factors in the multi-factor likelihood of confusion test seem most important to resolving the case? How should the court rule? *See Uber Promotions, Inc. v. Uber Technologies, Inc.*, 152 F. Supp. 3d 1253 (N.D. Fla. 2016).

5. Since 1997, Hugunin has manufactured and sold LAND O' LAKES brand fishing tackle to retail stores. In 2000, he registered LAND O' LAKES as a trademark for fishing tackle. The Land O' Lakes agricultural cooperative sells dairy products under the LAND O' LAKES trademark, which it adopted in the 1920s and registered in 1930. Recently, the dairy cooperative became the official sponsor of a sportfishing tournament and began advertising its dairy products in fishing magazines. Hugunin sued the dairy cooperative for trademark infringement, arguing that his business is the senior user in the fishing industry, and that the dairy cooperative's advertisements and event sponsorship creates a likelihood of reverse confusion. How should the court rule? *See Hugunin v. Land 'O Lakes, Inc.*, 815 F.3d 1064 (7th Cir. 2016).

d. Approval Confusion

Medic Alert Foundation v. Corel Corp., 43 F. Supp. 2d 933 (N.D. Ill. 1999). Medic Alert Foundation makes jewelry and wallet cards designed to alert emergency medical services of non-apparent medical conditions. The Foundation marks these bracelets, pendants, and cards with its logo, which consists of the words MEDIC and ALERT running from top to bottom on either side of a caduceus. It has registered the logo as a trademark and service mark. Medic Alert sued Corel for including clipart files in its mass-market software that reproduced an image of a bracelet bearing the Medic Alert logo. The Foundation argued that consumers would believe that it had authorized Corel to distribute the clip art images.

The court granted summary judgment to Corel:

> Before turning to the evidence, I want to clarify the sort of confusion the law is concerned about. In short, consumer confusion as to what? Corel argues that the proper question is whether consumers looking to buy Corel products would be confused either as to their proper source (source confusion) or as to an affiliation between the parties' respective services and products that actually aided in selling Corel's products (approval confusion). Medic Alert concedes that there is no evidence of source confusion, but argues that Corel's definition of approval confusion is overly narrow. It asserts that consumers need only think that Medic Alert authorized Corel to use its trademarked symbol in creating the medalert.eps or otherwise approved of its use, regardless of whether they see that use as an endorsement of Corel's products or whether Corel sales benefitted as a result.
>
> The answer lies somewhere in between.... Here, the relevant confusion is whether the customer would believe that Medic Alert sponsored, endorsed or was otherwise affiliated with Corel's software. *See Nike, Inc., v. "Just Did It" Enter.*, 6 F.3d 1225, 1228–29 (7th Cir. 1993). The approval at issue, therefore, is not whether Medic Alert approved of the use (or alleged use) of its trademarked image, but rather, whether Medic Alert approved of Corel's software. While perceived permission to use a trademarked image *can* amount to perceived product approval, *see Pebble Beach Co. v. Tour 18 I Ltd.*, 155 F.3d 526, 544 (5th Cir. 1998), it does not constitute *per se* evidence of such, and a finding that consumers are likely to be confused about the former would not end the ultimate factual inquiry as Medic Alert suggests. In *Pebble Beach*, the defendant golf course operator used trademarked logos of famous golf courses in promotional materials for its own less-famous course, thereby suggesting that the famous courses had permitted use of their marks in this manner and thus had endorsed defendant's course. *See id.* at 535. Here, where the use of the alleged infringing mark is not part of promotional materials, but rather hidden inside a software program, any confusion as to perceived permission does not constitute necessarily confusion as to perceived endorsement.
>
> ....

> The relevant inquiry therefore is whether consumers in the market for computer software are likely to think, upon seeing one or the other medalert.eps image in the clipart file, that Medic Alert has somehow endorsed Corel software or is otherwise affiliated with its production or offering....
>
> ....
>
> Taking all of this evidence together, there simply is no genuine issue of material fact as to whether consumers in the market for computer software would somehow be more or less inclined to purchase Corel software because it believes that Medic Alert has given its seal of approval to the product. Medic Alert essentially concedes this point: it admits that there are no facts to suggest that when a software consumer purchases a Corel software product, the consumer believes that Medic Alert endorses Corel or the Corel software product. Likewise, it is unlikely that a person seeking a provider of emergency health care information would be less likely to turn to Medic Alert because it thinks that it has endorsed computer software. I find that as a matter of law, the evidence simply does not support a finding of a likelihood of consumer confusion in this case.

Anheuser-Busch, Inc. v. Balducci Publications

28 F.3d 769 (8th Cir. 1994)

John R. Gibson, Senior Circuit Judge.

Anheuser-Busch, Inc., appeals from the judgment of the district court dismissing its federal and state trademark infringement, trademark dilution, and unfair competition claims against Balducci Publications and its publishers, Richard and Kathleen Balducci, for the use of registered Anheuser-Busch trademarks in a fictitious advertisement for "Michelob Oily." *See* 15 U.S.C. §§ 1114(1), 1125(a) (1988); Mo. Rev. Stat. §§ 417.056, 417.061 (1986). We have carefully reviewed the record before us, and we reverse.

Anheuser-Busch operates a brewery in St. Louis. Its products include the Michelob family of beers: Michelob, Michelob Dry, Michelob Light and Michelob Classic Dark. For use in its marketing of these products, Anheuser-Busch owns several federally-registered trademarks: (1) Michelob; (2) Michelob Dry; (3) A & Eagle Design; (4) Bottle and Label Configuration; (5) Bottle Configuration; (6) Vertical Stripe Design; (7) the phrase "ONE TASTE AND YOU'LL DRINK IT DRY;" and (8) Vertical Stripe and A & Eagle Design. Of these, (1) and (3) are also registered Missouri trademarks.

Balducci Publications is a publishing business owned by Richard and Kathleen Balducci, also defendants in this case. Balducci Publications has published *Snicker*, a humor magazine, since April 1987. The back cover of issue 5-1/2, published in April 1989, contains a mock advertisement for the fictitious product "Michelob Oily." A reduced copy of the advertisement is attached as Appendix A. The advertisement states in bold type, "ONE TASTE AND YOU'LL DRINK IT OILY" immediately above

"MICHELOB OILY®." The accompanying graphics include a partially-obscured can of Michelob Dry pouring oil onto a fish, an oil-soaked rendition of the A & Eagle design (with the eagle exclaiming "Yuck!") below a Shell Oil symbol, and various "Michelob Oily" products bearing a striking resemblance to appellants' Michelob family. This resemblance was quite intentional, as evidenced by the admitted use of actual Anheuser-Busch "clip-art" in replicating several of the protected trademarks. In smaller text the ad opines, "At the rate it's being dumped into our oceans, lakes and rivers, you'll drink it oily sooner or later, anyway." Finally, the following disclaimer is found in extremely small text running vertically along the right side of the page: "Snicker Magazine Editorial by Rich Balducci. Art by Eugene Ruble. Thank goodness someone still cares about quality (of life)." ...

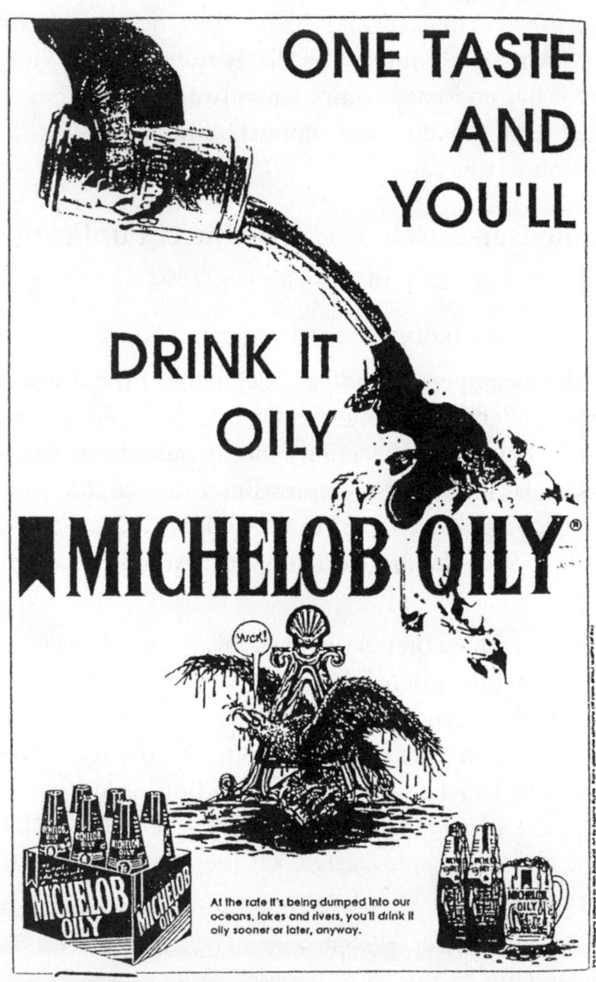

Balducci continues to sell back issues of *Snicker*—including Issue 5-1/2. Advertising for back issues of the magazine has included the words "Michelob Oily" and a blue ribbon design associated with Anheuser-Busch.

Mr. Balducci stated at trial that he used the parody to comment on: (1) the effects of environmental pollution, including a specific reference to the then-recent Shell oil spill in the Gasconade River—a source of Anheuser-Busch's water supply; (2) Anheuser-Busch's subsequent decision to temporarily close its St. Louis brewery; and (3) the proliferation of Anheuser-Busch beer brands and advertisements. The defendants concede they possessed no knowledge that any Anheuser-Busch product actually contained oil.

Anheuser-Busch, displeased with Balducci's extensive use of its trademarks and the possible implication that its products were tainted with oil, brought this suit in May 1989. It asserted five causes of action: (1) infringement of federally-registered trademarks, 15 U.S.C. § 1114(1); (2) federal unfair competition, 15 U.S.C. § 1125(a); (3) state trademark infringement, Mo. Rev. Stat. § 417.056; (4) common law unfair competition; and (5) state law trademark dilution, Mo. Rev. Stat. § 417.061. It sought one dollar in nominal damages and injunctive relief.

Other than the Balducci ad itself, the primary evidence offered by Anheuser-Busch was a study designed by Jacob Jacoby, Ph.D., and conducted under the supervision of Leon B. Kaplan, Ph.D. This survey, conducted in St. Louis shopping malls, involved 301 beer drinkers or purchasers who claimed to periodically review magazines or newspapers. The surveyors showed the Balducci ad to 200 participants and a Michelob Dry ad to the remaining 101. Of those viewing the Balducci ad, many expressed an impression of Anheuser-Busch's role in its creation. For example, fifty-eight percent felt the creators "did have to get permission to use the Michelob name." Fifty-six percent believed permission would be required for the various symbols and logos. Six percent of the classified[2] responses construed the Balducci ad to be an actual Anheuser-Busch advertisement. Almost half (45%) found nothing about the parody which suggested it was an editorial, and seventy-five percent did not perceive it as satirical. Virtually none (3.5%) noticed the tiny disclaimer on the side of the ad. Fifty-five percent construed the parody as suggesting that Michelob beer is or was in some way contaminated with oil. As a result, twenty-two percent stated they were less likely to buy Michelob beer in the future.

2

After a bench trial, the district court ruled in favor of Balducci on each of the five theories. Although the court found that "Defendants clearly used Plaintiff's marks in their ad parody, they used some of those marks without alteration, and they did so without Plaintiff's permission," it dismissed the trademark claims because "Defendants' use of [the] marks did not create a likelihood of confusion in the marketplace." *Balducci*, 814 F. Supp. 791 at 793. In reaching this decision, the court expressed the need to give "special sensitivity" to the First Amendment aspects of the case. *Id.* at 796. Accordingly, the court concluded that although "Plaintiff's statistical evidence [might] well be persuasive in the context of a classic trademark infringement case, ...

2. The staff at Princeton Research & Data Consulting Center, Inc. classified the answers to open-ended questions. Balducci objects to this classification process generally, but offers no persuasive evidence that any significant number of responses have been erroneously classified.

where the allegedly infringing use occurs in an editorial context," more persuasive evidence of confusion is required. *Id.* at 797. . . .

On appeal, Anheuser-Busch contends the district court gave inordinate weight to Balducci's First Amendment claims and erred in finding no likelihood of confusion. Balducci contends the court correctly found no likelihood of confusion and, furthermore, argues the ad parody is absolutely protected by the First Amendment.

I.

This case involves the tension between the protection afforded by the Lanham Act to trademark owners and the competing First Amendment rights of the parodist. Our analysis of the district court's decision encompasses two related, but distinct steps. We begin by considering whether the district court erred in finding no likelihood of confusion. Since a trademark infringement action requires a likelihood of confusion, this finding, if upheld, decides this case. If we conclude the court erred in finding no likelihood of confusion, we must consider Balducci's additional argument that the First Amendment protects it from liability.

Section 32(1) of the Lanham Act protects owners of registered trademarks from uses "likely to cause confusion, or to cause mistake, or to deceive." 15 U.S.C. § 1114(1). The determination of whether "likelihood of confusion" exists is a factual determination which we review under the clearly erroneous standard. *Mutual of Omaha Ins. Co. v. Novak*, 836 F.2d 397, 398 (8th Cir. 1987); *SquirtCo v. Seven-Up Co.*, 628 F.2d 1086, 1091 (8th Cir. 1980). However, our review is not so limited when, as here, the district court's "conclusions are inextricably bound up in its view of the law." *Calvin Klein Cosmetics Corp. v. Lenox Labs.*, 815 F.2d 500, 504 (8th Cir. 1987). Rather than first considering whether Balducci's ad parody was likely to confuse the public and then considering the scope of First Amendment protection, the district court conflated the two. The court essentially skewed its likelihood of confusion analysis in an attempt to give "special sensitivity" to the First Amendment, holding Anheuser Busch to a higher standard than required in a "classic trademark infringement case." *Balducci*, 814 F. Supp. at 796–97. Since we cannot separate the court's factual finding of confusion from its legal conclusions, we conduct a de novo review of the well-developed record before us. *Calvin Klein*, 815 F.2d at 504.

Many courts have applied, we believe correctly, an expansive interpretation of likelihood of confusion, extending "protection against use of [plaintiff's] mark on any product or service which would reasonably be thought by the buying public to come from the same source, or thought to be affiliated with, connected with, or sponsored by, the trademark owner." McCarthy, *Trademarks and Unfair Competition* § 24.03, at 24-13 (3d ed. 1992); *Novak*, 836 F.2d at 398; *Nike, Inc. v. "Just Did It" Enters.*, 6 F.3d 1225, 1228 (7th Cir. 1993); *Dallas Cowboys Cheerleaders, Inc. v. Pussycat Cinema, Ltd.*, 604 F.2d 200, 204–05 (2d Cir. 1979); *Jordache Enters., Inc. v. Levi Strauss*, 841 F. Supp. 506 (S.D.N.Y. 1994). This approach seems consistent with congressional intent, as evidenced by the express inclusion during the 1989 revision of the Lanham Act of protection against confusion as to "origin, sponsorship, or approval." 15 U.S.C. § 1125(a).

This court enumerated several factors pertinent to the finding of likelihood of confusion in *SquirtCo*, 628 F.2d at 1091: (1) the strength of the trademark; (2) the similarity between the plaintiff's and defendant's marks; (3) the competitive proximity of the parties' products; (4) the alleged infringer's intent to confuse the public; (5) evidence of any actual confusion; and (6) the degree of care reasonably expected of the plaintiff's potential customers. These factors are not a distinct test, but represent the sort of considerations which a court should consider in determining whether likelihood of confusion exists. We briefly consider the application of these factors to this case.

Anheuser-Busch possessed several very strong trademarks that Balducci displayed virtually unaltered in the ad parody. Thus, the first two *SquirtCo* factors weigh heavily in favor of Anheuser-Busch. The third factor, competitive proximity, is less one-sided. Balducci does not directly compete with Anheuser-Busch. Confusion, however, may exist in the absence of direct competition. *SquirtCo*, 628 F.2d at 1091. Moreover, Balducci published the parody on the back cover of a magazine—a location frequently devoted to real ads, even in *Snicker.* This location threatens to confuse consumers accustomed to seeing advertisements on the back cover of magazines.

Our analysis of Balducci's intent relies, of necessity, on circumstantial evidence. According to Richard Balducci, he sought to comment on certain social conditions through parody. "An intent to parody is not an intent to confuse." *Jordache Enters., Inc. v. Hogg Wyld, Ltd.*, 828 F.2d 1482, 1486 (10th Cir. 1987). Other factors, however, suggest Balducci had, if not an intent to confuse, at least an indifference to the possibility that some consumers might be misled by the parody. For example, no significant steps were taken to remind readers that they were viewing a parody and not an advertisement sponsored or approved by Anheuser-Busch. Balducci carefully designed the fictitious ad to appear as authentic as possible. Several of Anheuser-Busch's marks were used with little or no alteration. The disclaimer is virtually undetectable. Balducci even included a ® symbol after the words Michelob Oily. These facts suggest that Balducci sought to do far more than just "conjure up" an image of Anheuser-Busch in the minds of its readers. *Cf. Walt Disney Productions v. Air Pirates*, 581 F.2d 751, 758 (9th Cir. 1978), *cert. denied*, 439 U.S. 1132 (1979) (in copyright context, "fair use" doctrine does not entitle parodist to copy everything needed to create the "best parody;" rather, the parodist may copy only that portion of the protected work necessary to "conjure up the original"). These factors limit the degree to which Balducci's intent to parody weighs in favor of a finding of no likelihood of confusion.

Balducci's desired message, or humor, presumably hinged on consumers' ultimate realization that although this "advertisement" was based on the painstaking duplication of Anheuser-Busch's marks, it was in fact a parody or editorial parody. We have significant doubt as to whether many consumers would develop this understanding of Balducci's true purpose. There is a distinct possibility, accepted by the district court, "that a superficial observer might believe that the ad parody was approved by Anheuser-Busch." *Balducci*, 814 F. Supp. at 797. The back cover of magazines is frequently used for advertisements and cannot be expected to command the thoughtful deliberation of all or even most of the viewing public. The district court downplayed this fact, observing that "once again ... the First Amendment concerns at issue in this litigation require a closer examination of Plaintiff's claims." *Id.* When objectively viewed, the fourth and sixth *SquirtCo* factors (i.e., intent and degree of care) may not fully support Anheuser-Busch, but they are consistent with a finding that the parody presented a significant likelihood of confusing consumers.

The survey evidence, whether considered as direct or indirect evidence of actual confusion, tilts the analysis in favor of Anheuser-Busch. Over half of those surveyed thought Balducci needed Anheuser-Busch's approval to publish the ad. Many of these presumably felt that such approval had in fact been obtained. Six percent thought that the parody was an actual Anheuser-Busch advertisement. Other courts have accepted similar survey findings. *See Novak*, 836 F.2d at 400; *Nat'l Football League Props., Inc. v. New Jersey Giants, Inc.*, 637 F. Supp. 507, 517 (D.N.J. 1986) (citing decisions relying on surveys showing 8.5% to 15% confusion); *Schieffelin & Co. v. Jack Company of Boca*, 850 F. Supp. 232 (S.D.N.Y. 1994). In *Novak*, for example, "approximately ten percent of all the persons surveyed thought that Mutual 'goes along' with Novak's product." 836 F.2d at 400. The court found this persuasive despite the existence of "some ambiguity" in the survey question. *Id.* Thus, we are left with evidence, obtained by means of a valid consumer survey, that strongly indicates actual consumer confusion.

Our review of the record before the district court, including the Balducci ad and the survey evidence, convinces us that the court erred in finding no likelihood of confusion. The court reached its finding only after it mistakenly weighted its analysis in favor of Balducci in an effort to satisfy the limits set by the First Amendment. We believe the better course would have been to analyze the likelihood of confusion first and then proceed to an analysis of the First Amendment issues.

Having determined that a likelihood of confusion exists, we must next consider Balducci's argument that the First Amendment protects it from liability for its ad parody....

....

There is no simple, mechanical rule by which courts can determine when a potentially confusing parody falls within the First Amendment's protective reach....

... [W]e must weigh the public interest in protecting Balducci's expression against the public interest in avoiding consumer confusion.

Applying this standard, we are convinced that the First Amendment places no bar to the application of the Lanham Act in this case. As we have discussed, Balducci's ad parody was likely to confuse consumers as to its origin, sponsorship or approval. This confusion might have to be tolerated if even plausibly necessary to achieve the desired commentary—a question we need not decide. In this case, the confusion is wholly unnecessary to Balducci's stated purpose. By using an obvious disclaimer, positioning the parody in a less-confusing location, altering the protected marks in a meaningful way, or doing some collection of the above, Balducci could have conveyed its message with substantially less risk of consumer confusion....

....

Questions

1. About what were consumers likely to be confused?

2. The court interprets the survey evidence to show that more than half of the consumers surveyed believed that Balducci's ad was either developed or authorized by Anheuser-Busch. Look again at the ad. If consumers indeed believed that Anheuser-Busch approved of the ad, how plausible is that belief? Should plausibility affect the analysis? Should it affect the court's assessment of the reliability of the survey?

3. Should trademark law require parodists to seek their subjects' permission before creating parodies? If not, has the court created a *de facto* permission requirement by reifying consumers' misunderstandings of the law?

4. The court explains that First Amendment analysis should be separate from the analysis of likelihood of confusion. Do you agree? What are the advantages and disadvantages of considering likelihood of confusion with some attention to First Amendment considerations? For more on how courts approach this question, see *infra* Chapter 8[C].

C. Secondary Liability for Trademark Infringement

Under what circumstances may a person other than the direct infringer be held liable for the direct infinger's trademark infringing acts? In *AT&T v. Winback*, 42 F.3d 1421, 1433–34 (3d Cir. 1994), the Third Circuit recognized that indirect liability could arise under the Lanham Act:

> There is a good reason for this: the Lanham Act is derived generally and purposefully from the common law tort of unfair competition, and its language parallels the protections afforded by state common law and statutory torts.... The Act federalizes a common law tort. In construing the Act, then, court's routinely have recognized the propriety of examining basic tort liability concepts to determine the scope of liability.... Applying the analysis to the facts of this case, it is clear that liability based on agency principles is often appropriate.

Courts generally recognize two different bases of derivative liability: (1) Contributory infringement, for inducing infringement or knowingly supplying the means to infringe; and (2) vicarious liability imposed under the principles of agency law.

The Restatement (Third) of Unfair Competition would impose liability for contributory infringement when " ... (a) the actor intentionally induces the third person to engage in the infringing conduct; or (b) the actor fails to take reasonable precautions against the occurrence of the third person's infringing conduct in circumstances in which the infringing conduct can be reasonably anticipated." Restatement (Third) of Unfair Competition § 27.

Vicarious liability turns on the defendant's deriving a financial benefit from the infringement, and especially on its ability to control the conduct of the direct infringer. *See, e.g., Procter & Gamble Co. v. Haugen*, 317 F.3d 1121 (10th Cir. 2003) (declining to hold defendant corporation vicariously liable for acts of independent distributors outside corporation's control who disparaged P&G products and insinuated that P&G was in league with Satan). As you review the following materials, consider the extent to which the two bases are in fact distinct.

Inwood Labs., Inc. v. Ives Labs., Inc.

456 U.S. 844 (1982)

JUSTICE O'CONNOR delivered the opinion of the Court:

This action requires us to consider the circumstances under which a manufacturer of a generic drug, designed to duplicate the appearance of a similar drug marketed by a competitor under a registered trademark, can be held vicariously liable for infringement of that trademark by pharmacists who dispense the generic drug.

I

In 1955, respondent Ives Laboratories, Inc. (Ives), received a patent on the drug cyclandelate, a vasodilator used in long-term therapy for peripheral and cerebral vascular diseases. Until its patent expired in 1972, Ives retained the exclusive right to make and sell the drug, which it did under the registered trademark CYCLOSPASMOL. Ives marketed the drug, a white powder, to wholesalers, retail pharmacists, and hospitals in colored gelatin capsules. Ives arbitrarily selected a blue capsule, imprinted with "Ives 4124," for its 200 mg dosage and a combination blue-red capsule, imprinted with "Ives 4148," for its 400 mg dosage.

After Ives' patent expired, several generic drug manufacturers, including petitioners Premo Pharmaceutical Laboratories, Inc., Inwood Laboratories, Inc., and MD Pharmaceutical Co., Inc. (collectively the generic manufacturers), began marketing cyclandelate.[2] They intentionally copied the appearance of the CYCLOSPASMOL capsules, selling cyclandelate in 200 mg and 400 mg capsules in colors identical to those selected by Ives.

The marketing methods used by Ives reflect normal industry practice. Because cyclandelate can be obtained only by prescription, Ives does not direct its advertising to the ultimate consumer. Instead, Ives' representatives pay personal visits to physicians, to whom they distribute product literature and "starter samples." Ives initially directed these efforts toward convincing physicians that CYCLOSPASMOL is superior to other vasodilators. Now that its patent has expired and generic manufacturers have entered the market, Ives concentrates on convincing physicians to indicate on prescriptions that a generic drug cannot be substituted for CYCLOSPASMOL.

The generic manufacturers also follow a normal industry practice by promoting their products primarily by distribution of catalogs to wholesalers, hospitals, and

2. The generic manufacturers purchase cyclandelate and empty capsules and assemble the product for sale to wholesalers and hospitals. The petitioner wholesalers, Darby Drug Co., Inc., Rugby Laboratories, Inc., and Sherry Pharmaceutical Co., Inc., in turn, sell to other wholesalers, physicians, and pharmacies.

retail pharmacies, rather than by contacting physicians directly. The catalogs truthfully describe generic cyclandelate as "equivalent" or "comparable" to CYCLOSPASMOL. In addition, some of the catalogs include price comparisons of the generic drug and CYCLOSPASMOL and some refer to the color of the generic capsules. The generic products reach wholesalers, hospitals, and pharmacists in bulk containers which correctly indicate the manufacturer of the product contained therein.

A pharmacist, regardless of whether he is dispensing CYCLOSPASMOL or a generic drug, removes the capsules from the container in which he receives them and dispenses them to the consumer in the pharmacist's own bottle with his own label attached. Hence, the final consumer sees no identifying marks other than those on the capsules themselves.

II

A

Ives instituted this action in the United States District Court for the Eastern District of New York under §§ 32 and 43(a) of the Trademark Act of 1946 (Lanham Act), 60 Stat. 427, as amended, 15 U.S.C. § 1051 et seq., and under New York's unfair competition law, N.Y. Gen. Bus. Law § 368-d (McKinney 1968).

Ives' claim under § 32, 60 Stat. 437, as amended, 15 U.S.C. § 1114, derived from its allegation that some pharmacists had dispensed generic drugs mislabeled as CYCLOSPASMOL.[8] Ives contended that the generic manufacturers' use of lookalike capsules and of catalog entries comparing prices and revealing the colors of the generic capsules induced pharmacists illegally to substitute a generic drug for CYCLOSPASMOL and to mislabel the substitute drug CYCLOSPASMOL. Although Ives did not allege that the petitioners themselves applied the Ives trademark to the drug products they produced and distributed, it did allege that the petitioners contributed to the infringing activities of pharmacists who mislabeled generic cyclandelate.

Ives' claim under § 43(a), 60 Stat. 441, 15 U.S.C. § 1125(a), alleged that the petitioners falsely designated the origin of their products by copying the capsule colors used by Ives and by promoting the generic products as equivalent to CYCLOSPASMOL. In support of its claim, Ives argued that the colors of its capsules were not functional[10] and that they had developed a secondary meaning for the consumers.[11]

8. The claim involved two types of infringements. The first was "direct" infringement, in which druggists allegedly filled CYCLOSPASMOL prescriptions marked "dispense as written" with a generic drug and mislabeled the product as CYCLOSPASMOL. The second, "intermediate" infringement, occurred when pharmacists, although authorized by the prescriptions to substitute, allegedly mislabeled a generic drug as CYCLOSPASMOL. The one retail pharmacy originally named as a defendant consented to entry of a decree enjoining it from repeating such actions. 455 F.Supp., at 942.

10. In general terms, a product feature is functional if it is essential to the use or purpose of the article or if it affects the cost or quality of the article. *See Sears, Roebuck & Co. v. Stiffel Co.*, 376 U.S. 225, 232 (1964); *Kellogg Co. v. National Biscuit Co.*, 305 U.S. 111, 122 (1938).

11. To establish secondary meaning, a manufacturer must show that, in the minds of the public, the primary significance of a product feature or term is to identify the source of the product rather than the product itself. *See Kellogg Co. v. National Biscuit Co.*, *supra*, at 118.

Contending that pharmacists would continue to mislabel generic drugs as CYCLOSPASMOL so long as imitative products were available, Ives asked that the court enjoin the petitioners from marketing cyclandelate capsules in the same colors and form as Ives uses for CYCLOSPASMOL. In addition, Ives sought damages pursuant to § 35 of the Lanham Act, 60 Stat. 439, as amended, 15 U.S.C. § 1117.

B

The District Court denied Ives' request for an order preliminarily enjoining the petitioners from selling generic drugs identical in appearance to those produced by Ives. 455 F. Supp. 939 (1978). Referring to the claim based upon § 32, the District Court stated that, while the "knowing and deliberate instigation" by the petitioners of mislabeling by pharmacists would justify holding the petitioners as well as the pharmacists liable for trademark infringement, Ives had made no showing sufficient to justify preliminary relief. *Id.*, at 945. Ives had not established that the petitioners conspired with the pharmacists or suggested that they disregard physicians' prescriptions.

The Court of Appeals for the Second Circuit affirmed. 601 F.2d 631 (1979). To assist the District Court in the upcoming trial on the merits, the appellate court defined the elements of a claim based upon § 32 in some detail. Relying primarily upon *Coca-Cola Co. v. Snow Crest Beverages, Inc.*, 64 F.Supp. 980 (Mass. 1946), *aff'd*, 162 F.2d 280 (CA1), *cert. denied*, 332 U.S. 809 (1947), the court stated that the petitioners would be liable under § 32 either if they suggested, even by implication, that retailers fill bottles with generic cyclandelate and label the bottle with Ives' trademark or if the petitioners continued to sell cyclandelate to retailers whom they knew or had reason to know were engaging in infringing practices. 601 F.2d, at 636.

C

After a bench trial on remand, the District Court entered judgment for the petitioners. 488 F.Supp. 394 (1980). Applying the test approved by the Court of Appeals to the claim based upon § 32, the District Court found that the petitioners had not suggested, even by implication, that pharmacists should dispense generic drugs incorrectly identified as CYCLOSPASMOL.

In reaching that conclusion, the court first looked for direct evidence that the petitioners intentionally induced trademark infringement. Since the petitioners' representatives do not make personal visits to physicians and pharmacists, the petitioners were not in a position directly to suggest improper drug substitutions. *Cf. William R. Warner & Co. v. Eli Lilly & Co.*, 265 U.S. 526, 530–531 (1924); *Smith, Kline & French Laboratories v. Clark & Clark*, 157 F.2d 725, 731 (CA3), *cert. denied*, 329 U.S. 796 (1946). Therefore, the court concluded, improper suggestions, if any, must have come from catalogs and promotional materials. The court determined, however, that those materials could not "fairly be read" to suggest trademark infringement. 488 F.Supp. at 397.

The trial court next considered evidence of actual instances of mislabeling by pharmacists, since frequent improper substitutions of a generic drug for CYCLOSPASMOL could provide circumstantial evidence that the petitioners, merely by making available imitative drugs in conjunction with comparative price advertising, implicitly had suggested that pharmacists substitute improperly. After reviewing the evidence of incidents of mislabeling, the District Court concluded that such incidents occurred too infrequently to justify the inference that the petitioners' catalogs and use of imitative colors had "impliedly invited" druggists to mislabel. *Ibid.* Moreover, to the extent mislabeling had occurred, the court found it resulted from pharmacists' misunderstanding of the requirements of the New York Drug Substitution Law, rather than from deliberate attempts to pass off generic cyclandelate as CYCLOSPASMOL. *Ibid.*

The District Court also found that Ives failed to establish its claim based upon § 43(a). In reaching its conclusion, the court found that the blue and blue-red colors were functional to patients as well as to doctors and hospitals: many elderly patients associate color with therapeutic effect; some patients commingle medications in a container and rely on color to differentiate one from another; colors are of some, if limited, help in identifying drugs in emergency situations; and use of the same color for brand name drugs and their generic equivalents helps avoid confusion on the part of those responsible for dispensing drugs. *Id.*, at 398–399. In addition, because Ives had failed to show that the colors indicated the drug's origin, the court found that the colors had not acquired a secondary meaning. *Id.*, at 399.

Without expressly stating that the District Court's findings were clearly erroneous, and for reasons which we discuss below, the Court of Appeals concluded that the petitioners violated § 32. 638 F.2d 538 (1981). The Court of Appeals did not reach Ives' other claims. We granted certiorari, 454 U.S. 891 (1981), and now reverse the judgment of the Court of Appeals.

III

A

As the lower courts correctly discerned, liability for trademark infringement can extend beyond those who actually mislabel goods with the mark of another. Even if a manufacturer does not directly control others in the chain of distribution, it can be held responsible for their infringing activities under certain circumstances. Thus, if a manufacturer or distributor intentionally induces another to infringe a trademark, or if it continues to supply its product to one whom it knows or has reason to know is engaging in trademark infringement, the manufacturer or distributor is contributorially responsible for any harm done as a result of the deceit. *See William R. Warner & Co. v. Eli Lilly & Co., supra; Coca-Cola Co. v. Snow Crest Beverages, Inc., supra.*

It is undisputed that those pharmacists who mislabeled generic drugs with Ives' registered trademark violated § 32. However, whether these petitioners were liable for the pharmacists' infringing acts depended upon whether, in fact, the petitioners intentionally induced the pharmacists to mislabel generic drugs or, in fact, continued to supply cyclandelate to pharmacists whom the petitioners knew were mislabeling generic drugs. The District Court concluded that Ives made neither of those factual showings.

B

In reviewing the factual findings of the District Court, the Court of Appeals was bound by the "clearly erroneous" standard of Rule 52(a), Federal Rules of Civil

Procedure. *Pullman-Standard v. Swint, ante*, 456 U.S. 273. That Rule recognizes and rests upon the unique opportunity afforded the trial court judge to evaluate the credibility of witnesses and to weigh the evidence. *Zenith Radio Corp. v. Hazeltine Research, Inc.*, 395 U.S. 100, 123 (1969). Because of the deference due the trial judge, unless an appellate court is left with the "definite and firm conviction that a mistake has been committed," *United States v. United States Gypsum Co.*, 333 U.S. 364, 395 (1948), it must accept the trial court's findings.

IV

In reversing the District Court's judgment, the Court of Appeals initially held that the trial court failed to give sufficient weight to the evidence Ives offered to show a "pattern of illegal substitution and mislabeling in New York...." 638 F.2d, at 543. By rejecting the District Court's findings simply because it would have given more weight to evidence of mislabeling than did the trial court, the Court of Appeals clearly erred. Determining the weight and credibility of the evidence is the special province of the trier of fact. Because the trial court's findings concerning the significance of the instances of mislabeling were not clearly erroneous, they should not have been disturbed.

Next, after completing its own review of the evidence, the Court of Appeals concluded that the evidence was "clearly sufficient to establish a § 32 violation." *Ibid.* In reaching its conclusion, the Court of Appeals was influenced by several factors. First, it thought the petitioners reasonably could have anticipated misconduct by a substantial number of the pharmacists who were provided imitative, lower priced products which, if substituted for the higher priced brand name without passing on savings to consumers, could provide an economic advantage to the pharmacists. *Ibid.* Second, it disagreed with the trial court's finding that the mislabeling which did occur reflected confusion about state law requirements. *Id.* at 544. Third, it concluded that illegal substitution and mislabeling in New York are neither *de minimis* nor inadvertent. *Ibid.* Finally, the Court of Appeals indicated it was further influenced by the fact that the petitioners did not offer "any persuasive evidence of a legitimate reason unrelated to CYCLOSPASMOL" for producing an imitative product. *Ibid.*

Each of those conclusions is contrary to the findings of the District Court. An appellate court cannot substitute its interpretation of the evidence for that of the trial court simply because the reviewing court "might give the facts another construction, resolve the ambiguities differently, and find a more sinister cast to actions which the District Court apparently deemed innocent." *United States v. Real Estate Boards*, 339 U.S. 485, 495 (1950).

V

The Court of Appeals erred in setting aside findings of fact that were not clearly erroneous. Accordingly, the judgment of the Court of Appeals that the petitioners violated § 32 of the Lanham Act is reversed.

Although the District Court also dismissed Ives' claims alleging that the petitioners violated § 43(a) of the Lanham Act and the state unfair competition law, the Court of Appeals did not address those claims. Because § 43(a) prohibits a broader range of practices than does § 32, as may the state unfair competition law, the District Court's decision dismissing Ives' claims based upon those statutes must be independently reviewed. Therefore, we remand to the Court of Appeals for further proceedings consistent with this opinion.

Reversed and remanded.

Questions

1. Under what circumstances is it appropriate to impose liability on a business that is not itself infringing any trademark rights, but that is facilitating or profiting from trademark infringement by others? Should the landlord of a store that deals in infringing merchandise be held liable as a contributory infringer? The ad agency that prepares ads for infringing products? The celebrity who endorses infringing goods?

2. Should it make a difference whether Inwood's generic cyclandelate differs in any material way from Ives' cyclospasmol? May Inwood use blue and red capsules for generic cyclandelate in higher or lower doses than the 400 mg. capsule? If not, why not?

Life Alert Emergency Response, Inc. v. LifeWatch, Inc., 601 Fed Appx. 469 (9th Cir. 2015). Life Alert markets medical alert devices and monitoring services for the elderly. In 1989, Life Alert began running memorable television commercials and magazine ads for its service featuring an older woman on the floor saying, "I've fallen and I can't get up." In 2007, Life Alert registered I'VE FALLEN AND I CAN'T GET UP! as a service mark for emergency medical response services. In 2014, it registered HELP, I'VE FALLEN AND I CAN'T GET UP! as a trademark for security and electronic monitoring systems.

LifeWatch markets competing devices and monitoring services, using telemarketers to offer its products directly to potential customers over the telephone. In 2008, Life Alert discovered that some telemarketers for LifeWatch had used Life Alert's registered slogans in marketing LifeWatch's service. It sued LifeWatch for direct, contributory and vicarious trademark infringement. The district court entered a preliminary injunction enjoining LifeWatch from using Life Alert's trademarks and from doing business with any sales agent whom LifeWatch knows or should know was using those marks to sell LifeWatch's services. LifeWatch appealed, arguing that it lacked the ability to monitor and control the telemarketers who solicited customers for its products, and should not be held responsible for their infringing actions. The Court of Appeals for the 9th Circuit disagreed:

> The district court also correctly concluded that Life Alert is likely to succeed on the merits of its claim for trademark infringement under the theory of contributory infringement. A plaintiff can establish contributory infringement in one of two ways. *See Inwood Labs., Inc. v. Ives Labs., Inc.*, 456 U.S. 844, 853–54 (1982). Life Alert can do both.

The first way is to show that the defendant "'intentionally induced' the primary infringer to infringe." *Perfect 10, Inc. v. Visa Int'l Serv., Ass'n*, 494 F.3d 788, 807 (9th Cir. 2007) (quoting *Inwood*, 456 U.S. at 855). A reasonable inference supports the conclusion that LifeWatch intentionally induced infringement by approving scripts for its telemarketers (the primary infringers) that contained Life Alert's trademarked slogans. First, directly under the telemarketing services agreements and, at the very least, indirectly under the purchase agreements, LifeWatch engaged telemarketers to solicit customers on its behalf. Second, formally under the telemarketing services agreements and perhaps functionally under the purchase agreements, telemarketers are authorized to read only scripts approved by LifeWatch. Third, at least one telemarketer, Worldwide Info Services, used the "I've Fallen" trademark, and contacted customers who then received LifeWatch goods.

The evidence also shows that LifeWatch "continued to supply an infringing product to an infringer with knowledge that the infringer is mislabeling the particular product supplied." *Perfect 10, Inc., 494 F.3d at 807.* This is the second way to establish contributory infringement. Life Alert is likely to succeed under either the product or service version of this test.

On the product version, LifeWatch has continued to engage telemarketers and sellers to cultivate customers for its products even though it knows, or at least has reason to know, that they are using Life Alert's trademarks. *See Inwood, 456 U.S. at 853–55.* Worldwide used an infringing script during the era in which it could read only scripts approved by LifeWatch. And LifeWatch listens to the sales calls its telemarketers are required to retain and make available for LifeWatch's review.

On the service version, Life Alert can show that LifeWatch controlled and monitored the instrument (the telemarketing calls) the telemarketers and sellers used to infringe Life Alert's trademark. *See Lockheed Martin Corp. v. Network Solutions, Inc.*, 194 F.3d 980, 984 (9th Cir. 1999). For instance, there is evidence that LifeWatch had the power and practice of approving scripts when it engaged telemarketers pursuant to the old telemarketing services agreements. Pursuant to its new purchase agreements, LifeWatch continues to provide sellers "guidelines" about its products. LifeWatch also reviews sales calls, and advises sales agents to change their message when it hears something it does not like. Finally, LifeWatch could stop the infringement if it wanted to do so. *See Perfect 10*, 494 F.3d at 807. LifeWatch could exercise its right under the telemarketing services and purchase agreements to terminate its relationship with telemarketers and sellers that fail to comply with trademark law. Without these contracts, telemarketers and sellers would have no reason to make infringing calls.

The district court also correctly found that Life Alert is likely to succeed on the merits of its trademark infringement claim under the theory of vicarious liability. The same evidence of LifeWatch's control over telemarketers that supports the district court's finding on contributory infringement supports the court's finding on vicarious liability. *See id.* ("Vicarious liability for trademark infringement requires 'a finding that the defendant and the infringer have an apparent or actual partnership, have authority to bind one another in transactions with third parties or exercise joint ownership or control over the infringing product.'")....

Tiffany and Company v. eBay, Inc.

600 F.3d 93 (2d Cir. 2010)

Sack, Circuit Judge:

[Tiffany, Inc. claimed that sellers using eBay's online auction sites were offering counterfeit Tiffany silver jewelry. Although eBay responded to Tiffany by closing access to offending sites, Tiffany contended that principles of secondary liability imposed on eBay an obligation "preemptively [to] refus[e] to post any listing offering five or more Tiffany items." The Second Circuit affirmed the district court's rejection of Tiffany's claim.]

We have apparently addressed contributory trademark infringement in only two related decisions, *see Polymer Tech. Corp. v. Mimran*, 975 F.2d 58, 64 (2d Cir. 1992) ("*Polymer I*"); *Polymer Tech. Corp. v. Mimran*, 37 F.3d 74, 81 (2d Cir. 1994) ("*Polymer II*"), and even then in little detail. Citing *Inwood*, we said that "[a] distributor who intentionally induces another to infringe a trademark, or continues to supply its product to one whom it knows or has reason to know is engaging in trademark infringement, is contributorially liable for any injury." *Polymer I*, 975 F.2d at 64.

The limited case law leaves the law of contributory trademark infringement ill-defined. Although we are not the first court to consider the application of *Inwood* to the Internet, *see, e.g., Lockheed* [*Martin Corp. v. Network Solutions, Inc.*], 194 F.3d 980 [(9th Cir. 1999)] (Internet domain name registrar), we are apparently the first to consider its application to an online marketplace.

B. Discussion

....

2. Is eBay Liable Under *Inwood*?

The question ... is whether eBay is liable under the *Inwood* test on the basis of the services it provided to those who used its website to sell counterfeit Tiffany products. As noted, when applying *Inwood* to service providers, there are two ways in which a defendant may become contributorially liable for the infringing conduct of another: first, if the service provider "intentionally induces another to infringe a trademark," and second, if the service provider "continues to supply its [service] to one whom it knows or has reason to know is engaging in trademark infringement." *Inwood*, 456 U.S. at 854. Tiffany does not argue that eBay induced the sale of counterfeit Tiffany goods on its website—the circumstances addressed by the first part of the *Inwood* test. It argues instead, under the second part of the *Inwood* test, that eBay continued to supply its services to the sellers of counterfeit Tiffany goods while knowing or having reason to know that such sellers were infringing Tiffany's mark.

The district court rejected this argument. First, it concluded that to the extent the NOCIs [Notice of Claimed Infringement forms] that Tiffany submitted gave eBay reason to know that particular listings were for counterfeit goods, eBay did not continue to carry those listings once it learned that they were specious. The court found that eBay's practice was promptly to remove the challenged listing from its website, warn sellers and buyers, cancel fees it earned from that listing, and direct buyers not to consummate the sale of the disputed item. The court therefore declined to hold eBay contributorially liable for the infringing conduct of those sellers. On appeal, Tiffany does not appear to challenge this conclusion. In any event, we agree with the district court that no liability arises with respect to those terminated listings.

Tiffany disagrees vigorously, however, with the district court's further determination that eBay lacked sufficient knowledge of trademark infringement by sellers behind other, non-terminated listings to provide a basis for *Inwood* liability. Tiffany argued in the district court that eBay knew, or at least had reason to know, that counterfeit Tiffany goods were being sold ubiquitously on its website. As evidence, it pointed to, inter alia, the demand letters it sent to eBay in 2003 and 2004, the results of its Buying Programs that it shared with eBay, the thousands of NOCIs it filed with eBay alleging its good faith belief that certain listings were counterfeit, and the various complaints eBay received from buyers claiming that they had purchased one or more counterfeit Tiffany items through eBay's website. Tiffany argued that taken together, this evidence established eBay's knowledge of the widespread sale of counterfeit Tiffany products on its website. Tiffany urged that eBay be held contributorially liable on the basis that despite that knowledge, it continued to make its services available to infringing sellers.

....

The district court concluded that "while eBay clearly possessed general knowledge as to counterfeiting on its website, such generalized knowledge is insufficient under the *Inwood* test to impose upon eBay an affirmative duty to remedy the problem." The district court found the cases Tiffany relied on for the proposition that general knowledge of counterfeiting suffices to trigger liability to be inapposite. The court reasoned that *Inwood*'s language explicitly imposes contributory liability on a defendant who "continues to supply its product[—in eBay's case, its service—]to *one* whom it knows or has reason to know is engaging in trademark infringement." (emphasis in original). The court also noted that plaintiffs "bear a high burden in establishing 'knowledge' of contributory infringement," and that courts have

> been reluctant to extend contributory trademark liability to defendants where there is some uncertainty as to the extent or the nature of the infringement. In *Inwood*, Justice White emphasized in his concurring opinion that a defendant is not "require[d] ... to refuse to sell to dealers who merely *might* pass off its goods."

(quoting *Inwood*, 456 U.S. at 861 (White, J., concurring)) (emphasis and alteration in original).

Accordingly, the district court concluded that for Tiffany to establish eBay's contributory liability, Tiffany would have to show that eBay "knew or had reason to know of specific instances of actual infringement" beyond those that it addressed upon learning of them. Tiffany failed to make such a showing.

On appeal, Tiffany argues that the distinction drawn by the district court between eBay's general knowledge of the sale of counterfeit Tiffany goods through its website, and its specific knowledge as to which particular sellers were making such sales, is a "false" one not required by the law. Tiffany posits that the only relevant question is "whether all of the knowledge, when taken together, puts [eBay] on notice that there is a substantial problem of trademark infringement. If so and if it fails to act, [eBay] is liable for contributory trademark infringement."

We agree with the district court. For contributory trademark infringement liability to lie, a service provider must have more than a general knowledge or reason to know that its service is being used to sell counterfeit goods. Some contemporary knowledge of which particular listings are infringing or will infringe in the future is necessary.

We are not persuaded by Tiffany's proposed interpretation of *Inwood.* Tiffany understands the "lesson of *Inwood*" to be that an action for contributory trademark infringement lies where "the evidence [of infringing activity]—direct or circumstantial, taken as a whole— ... provide[s] a basis for finding that the defendant knew or should have known that its product or service was being used to further illegal counterfeiting activity." We think that Tiffany reads *Inwood* too broadly. Although the *Inwood* Court articulated a "knows or has reason to know" prong in setting out its contributory liability test, the Court explicitly declined to apply that prong to the facts then before it.... The Court applied only the inducement prong of the test.

We therefore do not think that *Inwood* establishes the contours of the "knows or has reason to know" prong. Insofar as it speaks to the issue, though, the particular phrasing that the Court used—that a defendant will be liable if it "continues to supply its product to one whom it knows or has reason to know is engaging in trademark infringement"—supports the district court's interpretation of *Inwood*, not Tiffany's.

We find helpful the Supreme Court's discussion of *Inwood* in a subsequent copyright case, *Sony Corp. of America v. Universal City Studios, Inc.*, 464 U.S. 417 (1984). There, defendant Sony manufactured and sold home video tape recorders. Plaintiffs Universal Studios and Walt Disney Productions held copyrights on various television programs that individual television-viewers had taped using the defendant's recorders. The plaintiffs contended that this use of the recorders constituted copyright infringement for which the defendants should be held contributorily liable. In ruling for the defendants, the Court discussed *Inwood* and the differences between contributory liability in trademark versus copyright law.

> If *Inwood's narrow standard* for contributory trademark infringement governed here, [the plaintiffs'] claim of contributory infringement would merit little discussion. Sony certainly does not "intentionally induce[ ]" its customers

> to make infringing uses of [the plaintiffs'] copyrights, nor does it supply its products to *identified individuals known by it* to be engaging in continuing infringement of [the plaintiffs'] copyrights.

(quoting *Inwood*, 456 U.S. at 855; emphases added).

Thus, the Court suggested, had the *Inwood* standard applied in *Sony*, the fact that Sony might have known that some portion of the purchasers of its product used it to violate the copyrights of others would not have provided a sufficient basis for contributory liability. *Inwood's* "narrow standard" would have required knowledge by Sony of "identified individuals" engaging in infringing conduct. Tiffany's reading of *Inwood* is therefore contrary to the interpretation of that case set forth in *Sony*.

Although the Supreme Court's observations in *Sony*, a copyright case, about the "knows or has reason to know" prong of the contributory trademark infringement test set forth in *Inwood* were dicta, they constitute the only discussion of that prong by the Supreme Court of which we are aware. We think them to be persuasive authority here.

Applying *Sony*'s interpretation of *Inwood*, we agree with the district court that "Tiffany's general allegations of counterfeiting failed to provide eBay with the knowledge required under *Inwood*." Tiffany's demand letters and Buying Programs did not identify particular sellers who Tiffany thought were then offering or would offer counterfeit goods. And although the NOCIs and buyer complaints gave eBay reason to know that certain sellers had been selling counterfeits, those sellers' listings were removed and repeat offenders were suspended from the eBay site. Thus Tiffany failed to demonstrate that eBay was supplying its service to individuals who it knew or had reason to know were selling counterfeit Tiffany goods.

Accordingly, we affirm the judgment of the district court insofar as it holds that eBay is not contributorially liable for trademark infringement.

3. Willful Blindness.

Tiffany and its amici express their concern that if eBay is not held liable except when specific counterfeit listings are brought to its attention, eBay will have no incentive to root out such listings from its website. They argue that this will effectively require Tiffany and similarly situated retailers to police eBay's website—and many others like it—"24 hours a day, and 365 days a year." Council of Fashion Designers of America, Inc. Amicus Br. 5. They urge that this is a burden that most mark holders cannot afford to bear.

First, and most obviously, we are interpreting the law and applying it to the facts of this case. We could not, even if we thought it wise, revise the existing law in order to better serve one party's interests at the expense of the other's.

But we are also disposed to think, and the record suggests, that private market forces give eBay and those operating similar businesses a strong incentive to minimize the counterfeit goods sold on their websites. eBay received many complaints from users claiming to have been duped into buying counterfeit Tiffany products sold on eBay. The risk of alienating these users gives eBay a reason to identify and remove counterfeit listings.[13] Indeed, it has spent millions of dollars in that effort.

Moreover, we agree with the district court that if eBay had reason to suspect that counterfeit Tiffany goods were being sold through its website, and intentionally shielded itself from discovering the offending listings or the identity of the sellers behind them, eBay might very well have been charged with knowledge of those sales sufficient to satisfy *Inwood*'s "knows or has reason to know" prong. A service provider is not, we think, permitted willful blindness. When it has reason to suspect that users of its service are infringing a protected mark, it may not shield itself from learning of the particular infringing transactions by looking the other way. [Citations.][14]

eBay appears to concede that it knew as a general matter that counterfeit Tiffany products were listed and sold through its website. Without more, however, this knowledge is insufficient to trigger liability under *Inwood.* The district court found, after careful consideration, that eBay was not willfully blind to the counterfeit sales. That finding is not clearly erroneous. eBay did not ignore the information it was given about counterfeit sales on its website.

Question

Would it make a difference to the analysis of contributory infringement under the *Inwood* standard if eBay had failed to respond to notices that it was hosting sites offering counterfeit merchandise? *Cf. Louis Vuitton Malletier, S.A. v. Akanoc Solutions, Inc.*, 658 F.3d 936 (9th Cir. 2011).

---

13. At the same time, we appreciate the argument that insofar as eBay receives revenue from undetected counterfeit listings and sales through the fees it charges, it has an incentive to permit such listings and sales to continue.

14. To be clear, a service provider is not contributorially liable under Inwood merely for failing to anticipate that others would use its service to infringe a protected mark. [Citation.] But contributory liability may arise where a defendant is (as was eBay here) made aware that there was infringement on its site but (unlike eBay here) ignored that fact.

Chapter 7

Section 43(a)(1)(A) of the Lanham Act

15 U.S.C. § 1125(a)(1)(A) [Lanham Act § 43(a)(1)(A)]

(1) Any person who, on or in connection with any goods or services, or any container for goods, uses in commerce any word, term, name, symbol, or device, or any combination thereof, or any false designation of origin, false or misleading description of fact, or false or misleading representation of fact, which—

(A) is likely to cause confusion, or to cause mistake, or to deceive as to the affiliation, connection, or association of such person with another person, or as to the origin, sponsorship, or approval of his or her goods, services, or commercial activities by another person,

...

shall be liable in a civil action by any person who believes that he or she is or is likely to be damaged by such act.

....

(3) In a civil action for trade dress infringement ... for trade dress not registered on the principal register, the person who asserts trade dress protection has the burden of proving that the matter sought to be protected is not functional.

A. Unregistered Marks

Note: The Expanding Scope of Section 43(a)

The language of section 43(a) as originally enacted in the 1946 Lanham Act provided:

> Any person who shall affix, apply, or annex, or use in connection with any goods or services, or any container or containers for goods, a false designation of origin, or any false description or representation, including words or other symbols tending falsely to describe or represent the same, and shall cause such goods or services to enter into commerce ... shall be liable to a civil action *by any person doing business in the locality falsely indicated as that of origin or the region in which said locality is situated*, or by any person who believes that he is or is likely to be damaged by the use of any such false description or representation.

Act of July 5, 1946, ch. 540, 60 Stat. 441 (emphasis added).

The history of section 43(a) of the Lanham Act has been one of expansion. *See, e.g.*, David Klein, *The Ever-Expanding Section 43(a): Will The Bubble Burst?*, 2 U. Balt. Intell. Prop. L.J. 65 (1993). Initially both the "false designation of origin" and the "false description or representation" provisions were intended to apply to geographic origin, for example, enabling a perfumery to recover if its competitor labeled a bottle of Canadian perfume "Parfum de France." *See* Trademarks: Hearings on H.R. 13486 Before the House Committee on Patents, 69th Cong. 87 (1927). Courts, however, broadly construed "false designation of origin" to encompass the source or sponsor of a product. *See, e.g.*, Joel W. Rees, *Defining The Elements of Trade Dress Infringement Under Section 43(a)*, 2 Tex. Intell. Prop. LJ 103 (Winter 1994). Since infringing an unregistered, common-law trademark is likely to confuse purchasers about the source (or origin) of the marked product, most courts entertained actions for infringement of unregistered marks as suits for false designation of origin of the marked products. Thus, section 43(a) quickly grew in importance as a basis for a broader federal law of unfair competition. Congress amended the language of section 43(a)(1)(A) in 1988, *supra*, that codified this interpretation. Additionally, the courts interpreted section 43(a) to cover rights that were not technically trademarks, such as titles of artistic works, elements of a celebrity's identity and authorship credit.

Some of the cases in earlier chapters, such as *McBee v. Delica*, 417 F.3d 107 (1st Cir. 2005), *supra* Chapter 6[A], *Munsingwear v. Jockey*, 31 U.S.P.Q.2d 1146 (D. Minn.), *aff'd*, 39 F.3d 1184 (8th Cir. 1994), *supra* Chapter 6[B], involved unregistered trademarks and were brought under section 43(a). Other cases, such as *Maker's Mark Distillery, Inc. v. Diageo North America, Inc.*, 679 F.3d 410 (6th Cir. 2012), and *Banfi v. Kendall-Jackson*, 74 F. Supp. 2d 188 (E.D.N.Y. 1999), *supra* Chapter 6[B][2] asserted both sections 32 and 43(a) claims. Can you think of a reason why an owner of a registered mark would also sue under section 43(a)?

The false or misleading description or representation of fact prong of section 43(a) is addressed in Chapter 10, *infra.*

1. Application to Traditional Trademark and Trade Dress Cases

DC Comics v. Powers

465 F. Supp. 843 (S.D.N.Y. 1978)

Duffy, J.:

This is a trademark action involving use of the name Daily Planet both as the title of a news publication and in connection with a myriad of consumer products. Plaintiff, DC Comics, Inc., charges that the continued use of the name Daily Planet by defendants, the Daily Planet, Inc. and its President, Jerry Powers, is violative of § 43(a) of the Lanham Act, 15 U.S.C. § 1125(a), (hereinafter "the Act") and constitutes unfair competition resulting in dilution of plaintiff's common law trademark under the law of New York....

In June of 1938, plaintiff's predecessors created the fictional character called Superman the "man of steel who, with powers and abilities beyond those of mortal men, fights a never ending battle for truth, justice and the American way." The Daily Planet serves a dual function in relation to the Superman character. Primarily, it is the name of the fictitious Metropolis newspaper which employs Superman's alter ego, together with the other central characters in the Superman story. The Daily Planet is also the title of a promotional news column appearing from time-to-time within Superman comic books.

Defendants are the moving forces behind an underground news publication called the Daily Planet. The Daily Planet appeared between the years 1969 through 1973. Since its demise in 1973, the Daily Planet lay dormant until recently when defendants demonstrated a great interest in its resuscitation.

Upon commencement of the instant action, defendants moved for a preliminary injunction to preclude plaintiff from any use of the name Daily Planet including the advertisement, promotion, distribution or sale of any products in connection with the multi-million dollar cinema production of "Superman," scheduled to be released in just a few weeks by plaintiff's parent, Warner Communications. Plaintiff has cross moved for injunctive relief seeking to preclude defendants from any use of the Daily Planet.

....

Both plaintiff and defendants claim that as a result of a prior appropriation and use of the name Daily Planet, they each possess exclusive rights to its use. What is really at issue, however, is whether either party to this action is entitled to exclusive exploitation of the name Daily Planet based on the expected wave of public interest in the Superman character calculated to result from the release of the Superman movie.

....

Merits of the Case

It is undisputed that neither plaintiff nor defendants presently hold a registered trademark in the Daily Planet and, therefore, any rights to the exclusive use thereof are to be determined solely under the common law of trademarks. [Citation.]

The Superman character has, since its creation in 1938, been featured in comic books, comic strips and on radio and television. The Daily Planet first appeared in the Superman story in 1940. Since then, the Daily Planet has played a key role, not only in the Superman story, but also in the development of the Superman character. In addition, plaintiff has gone to great effort and expense throughout the long history of Superman to utilize the Superman character in connection with a myriad of products born of the Superman story. Indeed, to this end plaintiff employed the Licensing Corporation of America to act as its agent in the licensing of the Superman character to persons wishing to use it in connection with a given product. These products have included school supplies, toys, costumes, games and clothes.

At the hearing before me, Joseph Grant, the President of the Licensing Corporation of America, explained the licensing procedures for the DC Comics, Inc. and in particular the Superman characters. He testified that his corporation ... licenses the Superman story as a package. Thus, the typical licensing agreement would permit use not only of Superman, but of all the Superman characters. Mr. Grant concluded that while the Daily Planet was never singled out in any licensing agreement, he believed it to be part and parcel of the typical licensing agreement. Indeed, it was clearly established that the Daily Planet has been prominently featured on many products emanating from these licensing agreements.

In contrast, defendants' relationship with the term Daily Planet has been both brief and, at best, sporadic. Defendants' first published their newspaper in 1969 in Miami, Florida and called it "The Miami Free Press." Thereafter, the name went through a series of changes from "The Miami Free Press and The Daily Planet", to "The Daily Planet and The Miami Free Press" and finally to "The Daily Planet." In 1970, Powers registered the name Daily Planet as the trademark for the paper. It was also during this period that Powers caused the incorporation of the Daily Planet, Inc.

There was testimony from the defendant Powers that the Daily Planet was distributed at the Woodstock Music Festival in Woodstock, New York and at the Atlanta Pop Festival in Georgia. I am willing to believe that to be true. Much of Power's other testimony, however, strains credibility.

Despite defendants' dream of creating a paper with national appeal, the Daily Planet remained throughout its brief history essentially a local affair and, as such, was published between 1969 through 1973 on an irregular basis. Powers also testified that from its inception, the Daily Planet was plagued with financial problems. Finally, in 1973, its financial woes became overwhelming and the paper folded.

Thereafter, Powers left Florida and began work on a new underground publication called "Superstar." At least two issues of "Superstar" were published at this time. It appears that the majority of defendants' time and efforts were devoted to the promotion of this new publication. Consequently, defendants permitted their trademark registration of Daily Planet to lapse and it was subsequently cancelled by the Office of Patent and Trademark Registration in 1976.

In light of the foregoing, it is apparent that only plaintiff has demonstrated an association of such duration and consistency with the Daily Planet sufficient to establish a common law trademark therein. The totality of evidence demonstrates that the Daily Planet has over the years become inextricably woven into the fabric of the Superman story.

Defendants, on the other hand, have offered very little to evidence either a substantial or genuine interest in the Daily Planet. More importantly, however, upon the demise of the Daily Planet in 1973, I find that defendants engaged in a course of conduct evidencing an intent to abandon any interests they may have acquired therein. The fact that defendants permitted their registration of the Daily Planet to lapse and thereafter began to publish another paper of the same nature as the Daily Planet under the name "Superstar" is dispositive of this intent and supports a finding of abandonment.

Turning in particular to plaintiff's claim under section 43(a) of the Lanham Act, 15 U.S.C. § 1125(a), it is not a prerequisite for remedial action thereunder that the mark in issue be registered. [Citations.] Consequently, under this section, a common law trademark is entitled to the same protection as its statutory counterpart. A plaintiff, therefore, is entitled to remedial action under this section if the defendant has affixed plaintiff's mark to his goods in such a fashion as to misrepresent to the public the source of the goods.

Although it is imperative in the instant action for plaintiff to demonstrate that defendants' use of the Daily Planet is likely to either confuse or deceive purchasers as to the source of items bearing the mark, [citation], liability will attach even though plaintiff is not in direct competition with the defendants.[5]

....

Applying these principles to the case at bar, it is evident that plaintiff has demonstrated a probability of success on the merits sufficient to warrant the equitable relief requested.

....

... I find substantial evidence indicating that the adoption by defendants of the name Daily Planet in 1969 was merely an attempt to cash in on the Superman story and its notoriety. Powers admitted that he was aware of the relationship between the Daily Planet and the Superman story when he first decided to use the name. It was also established that there were, throughout the brief history of Powers' Daily Planet, numerous references in the paper not only to the Superman character, but also to the Superman story, for example:

(i) A lead article entitled "Superman smokes super dope";

(ii) A promotional campaign to encourage new subscriptions employing the phrase "Join the Planet Army in Metropolis";[7]

(iii) Use of the phrase "Watchdog of Metropolis" as its slogan;

(iv) Numerous drawings of the Superman character;

(v) Use of a masthead which was an exact replica of the Daily Planet insignia appearing in numerous Superman comic books.

Thus, it is quite apparent that defendants, both in adopting the Daily Planet as the title of their newspaper and in its publication, intended to at least confuse, if not to deceive the public as to the origin of the publication.

---

5. Accordingly, the fact that plaintiff never published an actual paper entitled the Daily Planet is neither a barrier to the instant suit nor to preliminary equitable relief.

7. Metropolis is "the resident city of Superman and the scene of the vast majority of his adventures." *See* The Great Superman Book, The Complete Encyclopedia of the Folk Hero of America, at 223 (Plaintiff's Exhibit 14 herein).

. . . .

Moreover, while plaintiff may have been somewhat less than diligent in policing its mark, in light of the local appeal and limited distribution (geographic and numeric) of defendants' publication, I am not convinced that their lack of diligence was so great as to warrant loss of their trademark.

In light of the foregoing, the defendants' continued use of the Daily Planet is likely to cause irreparable injury to plaintiff's business reputation, good will and to its common law trademark.

Accordingly, defendants' motion for preliminary relief is denied and plaintiff's motion for a preliminary injunction is granted.

So ordered.

Questions

1. A Napa Valley wine branded with the mark CLARK KENT, Superman's alter ego, also bears indicia associated with the Superman character on its label, including a telephone booth where Superman traditionally dons his costume; eyeglasses, which Clark Kent removes when he becomes Superman; and a mock newspaper headline for *The Daily Grape* as shown below. As counsel for D.C. Comics, would you advise your client to assert a section 43(a) claim?

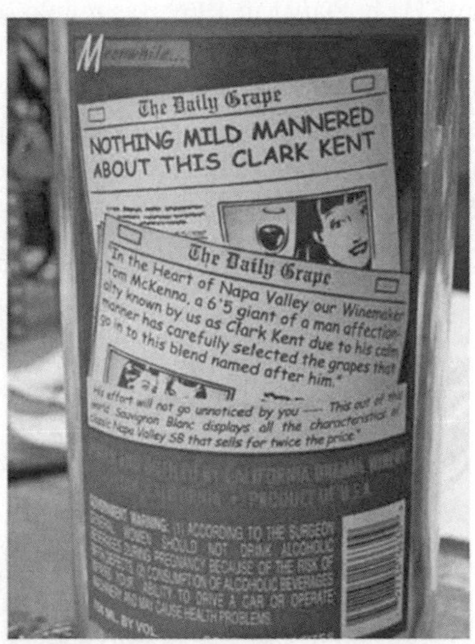

2. In the *DC Comics* case, the court found plaintiff had developed common law rights in *The Daily Planet* through its general licensing of the Superman fictional characters (although the term was not specifically mentioned in any license) and then found a likelihood of confusion with defendant's underground publication. In the Batman movie *The Dark Knight Rises*, the character of Catwoman used a program called "the Clean Slate" to hack into computers to erase criminal history material.

Fortres sells a CLEAN SLATE desktop management program and alleged that sales fell after the movie's release. It asserted a claim of reverse confusion, which was rejected by the court. Would the result have been different if Batman's licensed products, such as video games, used "the Clean Slate" term? *See Fortres Grand Corp. v. Warner Bros. Entertainment, Inc.*, 763 F.3d 696 (7th Cir. 2014), *supra* Chapter 6[B][3][c].

3. In 1999, the musical group Red Hot Chili Peppers released a song titled "Californication" on an album of the same name. The album sold 24 million copies, and both song and album were nominated for Grammy awards. The song has remained popular; the album is still available. In 2007, Showtime introduced a new original television series, which it titled "Californication," featuring the sexual adventures of a novelist portrayed by David Duchovny. The series was a success, and Showtime renewed it for the 2008–09 television season, and released the first season's episodes on DVD. Showtime also released a television soundtrack album under the title "Temptation: Music from the Showtime Series Californication." The Red Hot Chili Peppers filed suit against Showtime, claiming that Showtime's use of "Californication" as a title for its series, and the use of the word "Californication" in the title of the DVD and soundtrack CD, amount to false designations of origin under § 43(a). How should the court rule? *See Kiedis v. Showtime Networks*, 2008 U.S. Dist. LEXIS 124334 (C.D. Cal. 2008).

4. *In the Night Kitchen* is the title of an illustrated book by Maurice Sendak, which was first published by Harper Collins in 1970. The book tells the story of a young boy who wakes up in the middle of the night and falls out of his pajamas and into a bowl of batter in the night kitchen. The book has been continuously in print since it first appeared.

Your clients have opened a catering business under the name "Night Kitchen Catering." They have printed up business cards:

Your clients have also posted a website at www.inthenightkitchen.com, which describes their business and features sample menus. Do you see a likelihood of confusion?

Two Pesos, Inc. v. Taco Cabana, Inc.

505 U.S. 763 (1992)

Justice White delivered the opinion of the Court:

The issue in this case is whether the trade dress[1] of a restaurant may be protected under § 43(a) of the Trademark Act of 1946 (Lanham Act), 60 Stat. 441, 15 U.S.C. § 1125(a) (1982 ed.), based on a finding of inherent distinctiveness, without proof that the trade dress has secondary meaning.

I

Respondent Taco Cabana, Inc., operates a chain of fast-food restaurants in Texas. The restaurants serve Mexican food. The first Taco Cabana restaurant was opened

1. The District Court instructed the jury: "'Trade dress' is the total image of the business. Taco Cabana's trade dress may include the shape and general appearance of the exterior of the restaurant, the identifying sign, the interior kitchen floor plan, the decor, the menu, the equipment used to serve food, the servers' uniforms and other features reflecting on the total image of the restaurant." The Court of Appeals accepted this definition and quoted from *Blue Bell Bio-Medical v. Cin-Bad, Inc.*, 864 F.2d 1253, 1256 (C.A.5 1989): "The 'trade dress' of a product is essentially its total image and overall appearance." *See* 932 F.2d 1113, 1118 (C.A.5 1991). It "involves the total image of a product and may include features such as size, shape, color or color combinations, texture, graphics, or even particular sales techniques." *John H. Harland Co. v. Clarke Checks, Inc.*, 711 F.2d 966, 980 (C.A.11 1983).

in San Antonio in September 1978, and five more restaurants had been opened in San Antonio by 1985. Taco Cabana describes its Mexican trade dress as

> "a festive eating atmosphere having interior dining and patio areas decorated with artifacts, bright colors, paintings and murals. The patio includes interior and exterior areas with the interior patio capable of being sealed off from the outside patio by overhead garage doors. The stepped exterior of the building is a festive and vivid color scheme using top border paint and neon stripes. Bright awnings and umbrellas continue the theme." 932 F.2d 1113, 1117 (C.A.5 1991).

In December 1985, a Two Pesos, Inc., restaurant was opened in Houston. Two Pesos adopted a motif very similar to the foregoing description of Taco Cabana's trade dress. Two Pesos restaurants expanded rapidly in Houston and other markets, but did not enter San Antonio. In 1986, Taco Cabana entered the Houston and Austin markets and expanded into other Texas cities, including Dallas and El Paso where Two Pesos was also doing business.

In 1987, Taco Cabana sued Two Pesos in the United States District Court for the Southern District of Texas for trade dress infringement under § 43(a) of the Lanham Act, 15 U.S.C. § 1125(a) (1982 ed.),[2] ... The case was tried to a jury, which was instructed

2. Section 43(a) provides: "Any person who shall affix, apply, or annex, or use in connection with any goods or services, or any container or containers for goods, a false designation of origin, or any false description or representation, including words or other symbols tending falsely to describe or represent the same, and shall cause such goods or services to enter into commerce, and any person who shall with knowledge of the falsity of such designation of origin or description or representation cause or procure the same to be transported or used in commerce or deliver the same to any carrier

to return its verdict in the form of answers to five questions propounded by the trial judge. The jury's answers were: Taco Cabana has a trade dress; taken as a whole, the trade dress is nonfunctional; the trade dress is inherently distinctive;[3] the trade dress has not acquired a secondary meaning in the Texas market; and the alleged infringement creates a likelihood of confusion on the part of ordinary customers as to the source or association of the restaurant's goods or services. Because, as the jury was told, Taco Cabana's trade dress was protected if it either was inherently distinctive or had acquired a secondary meaning, judgment was entered awarding damages to Taco Cabana. In the course of calculating damages, the trial court held that Two Pesos had intentionally and deliberately infringed Taco Cabana's trade dress.[5]

The Court of Appeals ruled that the instructions adequately stated the applicable law and that the evidence supported the jury's findings. In particular, the Court of Appeals rejected petitioner's argument that a finding of no secondary meaning contradicted a finding of inherent distinctiveness.

In so holding, the court below followed precedent in the Fifth Circuit. In *Chevron Chemical Co. v. Voluntary Purchasing Groups, Inc.*, 659 F.2d 695, 702 (C.A.5 1981), the court noted that trademark law requires a demonstration of secondary meaning only when the claimed trademark is not sufficiently distinctive of itself to identify the producer; the court held that the same principles should apply to protection of trade dresses. The Court of Appeals noted that this approach conflicts with decisions of other courts, particularly the holding of the Court of Appeals for the Second Circuit in *Vibrant Sales, Inc. v. New Body Boutique, Inc.*, 652 F.2d 299 (1981), *cert. denied*, 455 U.S. 909 (1982), that § 43(a) protects unregistered trademarks or designs only where secondary meaning is shown. *Chevron, supra*, at 702. We granted certiorari to resolve the conflict among the Courts of Appeals on the question whether trade dress which is inherently distinctive is protectable under § 43(a) without a showing that it has acquired secondary meaning.[6] 112 S. Ct. 964 (1992). We find that it is, and we therefore affirm.

---

to be transported or used, shall be liable to a civil action by any person doing business in the locality falsely indicated as that of origin or in the region in which said locality is situated, or by any person who believes that he is or is likely to be damaged by the use of any such false description or representation." 60 Stat. 441.

This provision has been superseded by § 132 of the Trademark Law Revision Act of 1988, 102 Stat. 3946, 15 U.S.C. § 1121.

3. The instructions were that to be found inherently distinctive, the trade dress must not be descriptive.

5. The Court of Appeals agreed: "The weight of the evidence persuades us, as it did Judge Singleton, that Two Pesos brazenly copied Taco Cabana's successful trade dress, and proceeded to expand in a manner that foreclosed several important markets within Taco Cabana's natural zone of expansion." 932 F.2d, at 1127, n.20.

6. We limited our grant of certiorari to the above question on which there is a conflict. We did not grant certiorari on the second question presented by the petition, which challenged the Court of Appeals' acceptance of the jury's finding that Taco Cabana's trade dress was not functional.

II

The Lanham Act was intended to make "actionable the deceptive and misleading use of marks" and "to protect persons engaged in ... commerce against unfair competition." § 45, 15 U.S.C. § 1127. Section 43(a) "prohibits a broader range of practices than does § 32," which applies to registered marks, *Inwood Laboratories, Inc. v. Ives Laboratories, Inc.*, 456 U.S. 844, 858 (1982), but it is common ground that § 43(a) protects qualifying unregistered trademarks and that the general principles qualifying a mark for registration under § 2 of the Lanham Act are for the most part applicable in determining whether an unregistered mark is entitled to protection under § 43(a).

A trademark is defined in 15 U.S.C. § 1127 as including "any word, name, symbol, or device or any combination thereof" used by any person "to identify and distinguish his or her goods, including a unique product, from those manufactured or sold by others and to indicate the source of the goods, even if that source is unknown." In order to be registered, a mark must be capable of distinguishing the applicant's goods from those of others. § 1052. Marks are often classified in categories of generally increasing distinctiveness; following the classic formulation set out by Judge Friendly, they may be (1) generic; (2) descriptive; (3) suggestive; (4) arbitrary; or (5) fanciful. *See Abercrombie & Fitch Co. v. Hunting World, Inc.*, 537 F.2d 4, 9 (C.A.2 1976). The Court of Appeals followed this classification and petitioner accepts it. The latter three categories of marks, because their intrinsic nature serves to identify a particular source of a product, are deemed inherently distinctive and are entitled to protection. In contrast, generic marks—those that "refer to the genus of which the particular product is a species," *Park 'n Fly, Inc. v. Dollar Park and Fly, Inc.*, 469 U.S. 189, 194 (1985), *citing Abercrombie & Fitch, supra*, at 9—are not registrable as trademarks. *Park 'n Fly, supra*, at 194.

Marks which are merely descriptive of a product are not inherently distinctive. When used to describe a product, they do not inherently identify a particular source, and hence cannot be protected. However, descriptive marks may acquire the distinctiveness which will allow them to be protected under the Act. Section 2 of the Lanham Act provides that a descriptive mark that otherwise could not be registered under the Act may be registered if it "has become distinctive of the applicant's goods in commerce." §§ 2(e), (f), 15 U.S.C. §§ 1052(e), (f). *See Park 'n Fly, supra*, at 194, 196. This acquired distinctiveness is generally called "secondary meaning." *See ibid.; Inwood Laboratories, supra*, at 851, n. 11; *Kellogg Co. v. National Biscuit Co.*, 305 U.S. 111, 118 (1938). The concept of secondary meaning has been applied to actions under § 43(a).

The general rule regarding distinctiveness is clear: an identifying mark is distinctive and capable of being protected if it either (1) is inherently distinctive or (2) has acquired distinctiveness through secondary meaning. RESTATEMENT (THIRD) OF UNFAIR COMPETITION, § 13, pp. 37–38, and Comment a (Tent. Draft No. 2, Mar. 23, 1990). *Cf. Park 'n Fly, supra*, at 194. It is also clear that eligibility for protection under § 43(a) depends on nonfunctionality. *See, e.g., Inwood Laboratories, supra*, at 863 (White, J., concurring in result). It is, of course, also undisputed that liability under § 43(a) requires proof of the likelihood of confusion.

The Court of Appeals and ... the District Court ... ruled that Taco Cabana's trade dress was not descriptive but rather inherently distinctive, and that it was not functional. None of these rulings is before us in this case, and for present purposes we assume, without deciding, that each of them is correct.... [T]he Court of Appeals, following its prior decision in *Chevron*, held that Taco Cabana's inherently distinctive trade dress was entitled to protection despite the lack of proof of secondary meaning. It is this issue that is before us for decision, and we agree with its resolution by the Court of Appeals. There is no persuasive reason to apply to trade dress a general requirement of secondary meaning which is at odds with the principles generally applicable to infringement suits under § 43(a)....

....

The Fifth Circuit was quite right in *Chevron*, and in this case, to follow the *Abercrombie* classifications consistently and to inquire whether trade dress for which protection is claimed under § 43(a) is inherently distinctive. If it is, it is capable of identifying products or services as coming from a specific source and secondary meaning is not required. This is the rule generally applicable to trademark, and the protection of trademarks and trade dress under § 43(a) serves the same statutory purpose of preventing deception and unfair competition. There is no persuasive reason to apply different analysis to the two. The "proposition that secondary meaning must be shown even if the trade dress is a distinctive, identifying mark, [is] wrong, for the reasons explained by Judge Rubin for the Fifth Circuit in *Chevron*." *Blau Plumbing, Inc. v. S.O.S. Fix-it, Inc.*, 781 F.2d 604, 608 (C.A.7 1986). The Court of Appeals for the Eleventh Circuit also follows *Chevron, Ambrit, Inc. v. Kraft, Inc.*, 805 F.2d 974, 979 (1986), and the Court of Appeals for the Ninth Circuit appears to think that proof of secondary meaning is superfluous if a trade dress is inherently distinctive. *Fuddruckers, Inc. v. Doc's B.R. Others, Inc.*, 826 F.2d 837, 843 (1987).

It would be a different matter if there were textual basis in § 43(a) for treating inherently distinctive verbal or symbolic trademarks differently from inherently distinctive trade dress. But there is none. The section does not mention trademarks or trade dress, whether they be called generic, descriptive, suggestive, arbitrary, fanciful, or functional. Nor does the concept of secondary meaning appear in the text of § 43(a). Where secondary meaning does appear in the statute, 15 U.S.C. § 1052 (1982 ed.), it is a requirement that applies only to merely descriptive marks and not to inherently distinctive ones. We see no basis for requiring secondary meaning for inherently distinctive trade dress protection under § 43(a) but not for other distinctive words, symbols, or devices capable of identifying a producer's product.

Engrafting onto § 43(a) a requirement of secondary meaning for inherently distinctive trade dress also would undermine the purposes of the Lanham Act. Protection of trade dress, no less than of trademarks, serves the Act's purpose to "secure to the owner of the mark the goodwill of his business and to protect the ability of consumers to distinguish among competing producers. National protection of trademarks is desirable, Congress concluded, because trademarks foster competition and the maintenance of quality by securing to the producer the benefits of good reputation." *Park 'n Fly*, 469 U.S., at 198, *citing* S. Rep. No. 1333, 79th Cong., 2d Sess., 3–5 (1946) (citations omitted). By making more difficult the identification of a producer with its product, a secondary meaning requirement for a nondescriptive trade dress would hinder improving or maintaining the producer's competitive position.

Suggestions that under the Fifth Circuit's law, the initial user of any shape or design would cut off competition from products of like design and shape are not persuasive. Only nonfunctional, distinctive trade dress is protected under § 43(a). The Fifth Circuit holds that a design is legally functional, and thus unprotectable, if it is one of a limited number of equally efficient options available to competitors and free competition would be unduly hindered by according the design trademark protection. This serves to assure that competition will not be stifled by the exhaustion of a limited number of trade dresses.

On the other hand, adding a secondary meaning requirement could have anti-competitive effects, creating particular burdens on the start-up of small companies. It would present special difficulties for a business, such as respondent, that seeks to start a new product in a limited area and then expand into new markets. Denying protection for inherently distinctive nonfunctional trade dress until after secondary meaning has been established would allow a competitor, which has not adopted a distinctive trade dress of its own, to appropriate the originator's dress in other markets and to deter the originator from expanding into and competing in these areas.

. . . .

III

We agree with the Court of Appeals that proof of secondary meaning is not required to prevail on a claim under § 43(a) of the Lanham Act where the trade dress at issue is inherently distinctive, and accordingly the judgment of that court is affirmed.

It is so ordered.

Justice Stevens, concurring in the judgment:

As the Court notes in its opinion, the text of § 43(a) of the Lanham Act, 15 U.S.C. § 1125(a), "does not mention trademarks or trade dress." Nevertheless, the Court interprets this section as having created a federal cause of action for infringement of an unregistered trademark or trade dress and concludes that such a mark or dress should receive essentially the same protection as those that are registered. Although I agree with the Court's conclusion, I think it is important to recognize that the meaning of the text has been transformed by the federal courts over the past few decades. I agree with this transformation, even though it marks a departure from the original text, because it is consistent with the purposes of the statute and has recently been endorsed by Congress.

. . .

In light of the general consensus among the Courts of Appeals that have actually addressed the question, and the steps on the part of Congress to codify that consensus, stare decisis concerns persuade me to join the Court's conclusion that secondary meaning is not required to establish a trade dress violation under §43(a) once inherent distinctiveness has been established. Accordingly, I concur in the judgment, but not in the opinion of the Court.

Questions

1. In *Dirk Laureyssens v. Idea Group, Inc.*, 964 F.2d 131 (2d Cir. 1992), the Court of Appeals for the Second Circuit concluded that protecting trade dress that had not acquired secondary meaning would be inconsistent with the language and purpose of trademark law because:

> Where there is no actual secondary meaning in a trade dress, the purchasing public simply does not associate the trade dress with a particular producer. Therefore, a subsequent producer who adopts an imitating trade dress will not cause confusion, mistake, or deception as to the "origin, sponsorship, or approval" of the goods. Second, a junior producer's use of imitating trade dress bears no "false designation of origin" because, in the absence of secondary meaning in the senior producer's trade dress, the imitating trade dress suggests no particular origin to the consuming public.

What is Justice White's response to this objection?

2. Common law ownership of trademarks extended only to the geographic area of actual use. One of the advantages of registration on the principal register is that it permits the registrant to claim nationwide priority in the mark except as against actual senior users in the geographic areas of their actual use before registration. In *Two Pesos*, Justice White found "no persuasive reason" to analyze the infringement of unregistered marks under section 43(a) differently from the analysis applied to registered marks. One result of this analysis is that it permits Taco Cabana to claim priority over the actual senior user in the city of Houston, without having registered its trade dress. How might that affect the incentives Congress has put in place to encourage registration?

3. The Subway sandwich store at 2601 Highway Number 1 recently went out of business, and the landlord of the building leased the premises to Vinnie's Smokehouse. Vinnie's moved into the new building, but failed to change the interior décor. The inside of the smokehouse, therefore, sports brick-design wallpaper, a mural of vegetables, and clocks with logos that Subway identifies as Subway-themed. Subway claims that all of these features are its distinctive trade dress and sues Vinnie's Smokehouse for trade dress infringement, seeking an injunction requiring Vinnie's to redecorate. How should the court rule? *See Doctors Associates, Inc. v. Vinnie's Smokehouse*, 2011 U.S. Dist. LEXIS 75375 (E.D. La. July 13, 2011).

4. Plaintiff seeks to register a design as a trademark, but the PTO rejects the application for lack of distinctiveness. What, if any, relevance should the PTO's action have on plaintiff's section 43(a) suit to protect the design from trade dress infringement? Recall the Supreme Court's decision in *B&B Hardware, supra* Chapter 4[C], that Board decisions on likely confusion can have a preclusive effect in subsequent infringement actions. Should the Board's finding of lack of distinctiveness be preclusive? *See Dunn v. Gull*, 990 F.2d 348 (7th Cir. 1993).

5. Consider the following bottle and cap designs for SCOPE OUTLAST mouthwash.

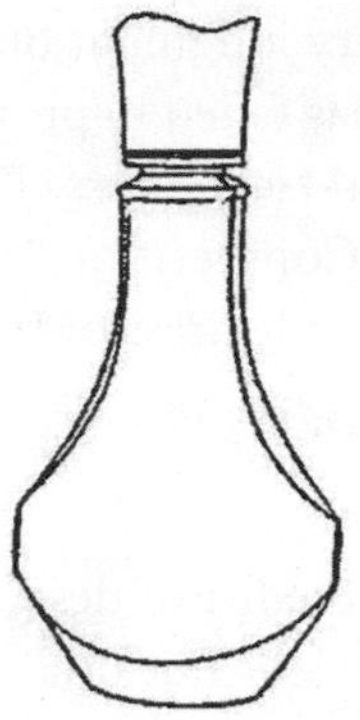

Both designs have won design awards and are subject of design patents. The Supreme Court in *Wal-Mart Stores, Inc. v. Samara Brothers, Inc.*, 529 U.S. 205 (2000), *supra*, Chapter 2[B], held that product packaging can be inherently distinctive. Do the bottle and cap images above constitute product packaging? If so, should they be considered inherently distinctive? What additional information would you want to know? *See In re Proctor & Gamble Co.*, 105 U.S.P.Q.2d 1119 (T.T.A.B. 2012).

6. In *Wal-Mart v. Samara*, *supra* Chapter 2[B][1], Justice Scalia wrote: "Respondent contends that our decision in *Two Pesos* forecloses a conclusion that product-design trade dress can never be inherently distinctive.... *Two Pesos* unquestionably establishes the legal principle that trade dress can be inherently distinctive, [citation], but it does not establish that product-design trade dress can be. *Two Pesos* is inapposite to our holding here because the trade dress at issue, the décor of a restaurant, seems to us not to constitute product design. It was either product packaging—which, as we have discussed, normally is taken by the consumer to indicate origin—or else some *tertium quid* that is akin to product packaging and has no bearing on the present case." "*Tertium quid*" is a Latin phrase that means "third thing." How can you tell whether the claimed trade dress at issue is product design, product packaging, or some third thing?

Hammerton, Inc. v. Heisterman, 2008 U.S. Dist. LEXIS 38036 (D. Utah May 8, 2008). Hammerton sued its former employee, Heisterman, alleging that defendant was "knocking off" the designs of plaintiff's expensive, handmade lighting fixtures. Heisterman had worked in plaintiff's product development department for two years before he resigned and founded a competing business. Plaintiff claimed that defendant copied the designs of its fixtures from plaintiff's catalog, infringing its trade dress in 50 different fixtures from five different lines. The court granted defendant's motion for summary judgment on the trade dress claim:

[A] plaintiff asserting trade dress rights in a product design "must articulate the design elements that compose the trade dress." The "focus on the overall look of a product [or products] does not permit a plaintiff to dispense with an articulation of the specific elements which comprise its distinct dress."

In this case, Defendants are entitled to summary judgment on Plaintiff's trade dress infringement claim because Plaintiff has failed to properly articulate the design elements that comprise its alleged trade dress. Despite two rounds of briefing and a hearing on the Unfair Competition Motion, the Court still does not know what Plaintiff's alleged trade dress or trade dresses look like.

....

Notably, even if Plaintiff had opted to rely on the list of design elements set forth in its [Interrogatory response], that list does not describe a trade dress entitled to protection under § 43(a) of the Lanham Act. Plaintiff's response reads as follows:

> ... The non-functional ornamental designs and shapes of Hammerton's said lighting fixtures. In addition, other design elements which distinguish Hammerton's products are the combination of 1) the fact that they are individually sculpted from metal, rather than being cast in a mold and mass produced, like Hammerton's other competitors; 2) how the Hammerton metals are distressed; 3) the way that Hammerton creates its unique bark texture[;] and 4) the Hammerton hand-modeled finish.

The first three of the four elements in this combination appear to claim the processes by which Plaintiff produces its light fixtures. However, § 43(a) of the Lanham Act does not offer protection for manufacturing processes, which are the exclusive province of patent law. Moreover, to the extent these elements might refer to the appearance created by Plaintiff's manufacturing processes, Plaintiff has not specified what that appearance is. Plaintiff has submitted its catalogs, which contain pictures of the products on its list of infringed products. However, these pictures show a number of distressed metals and finishes that are very different in appearance. Additionally, the majority of the allegedly infringed products do not contain both a distressed metal element and a bark texturing element and, thus, do not embody the same "overall look" (i.e., the claimed trade dress). Simply stated, even looking at pictures of the allegedly infringed products, the Court cannot discern what the trade dress vaguely described in Plaintiff's response to Interrogatory No. 2 looks like. And, remarkably, Plaintiff has made no attempt to point it out. Without knowledge of what Plaintiff's alleged trade dress looks like, the Court cannot even begin to determine whether it might be entitled to protection under the Lanham Act.

... [I]t appears to the Court that much of the confusion surrounding Plaintiff's trade dress claims stems from a fundamental misunderstanding of the protection afforded under § 43(a) of the Lanham Act. Section 43(a) does not protect manufacturers from having their products copied by competitors. "The Lanham Act does not exist to reward manufacturers for their innovation in creating a particular device; that is the purpose of the patent law and its period of exclusivity." Rather, "the underlying purpose of the Lanham Act … is protecting consumers and manufacturers from deceptive representations of affiliation and origin." Accordingly, trade dress protection is directly tied to the combination of specific features (i.e., the trade dress) embedded in a product that identifies the source of the product to the consuming public. Without a careful identification of the combination of design features that comprise the trade dress, and a showing that the trade dress has obtained secondary meaning and is nonfunctional, trade dress law could easily be used to achieve patent-like protection for products without regard to the requirements and limitations of patent law. This potential for misuse of trade dress law is of particular concern in product design cases, as "product design almost invariably serves purposes other than source identification." Thus, "courts have exercised particular 'caution' when extending protection to product designs."

In bringing its trade dress infringement claim, Plaintiff seeks to prevent Defendants from "knocking off" its products—relief that is simply not afforded under the Lanham Act.

The court in the case below considered whether Dooney & Bourke's It Bag infringed Vuitton's popular Multicolore bag, examples of which are depicted below.

Louis Vuitton Malletier v. Dooney & Bourke, Inc.

454 F.3d 108 (2d Cir. 2006)

CARDAMONE, CIRCUIT JUDGE:

. . . .

In 1896 [Vuitton] created the Toile Monogram, featuring entwined LV initials with three motifs: a curved diamond with a four-point star inset, its negative, and a circle with a four-leafed flower inset. Vuitton registered trademarks in this design pattern as well as the individual unique shapes with the United States Patent and Trademark Office. …

In October 2002 plaintiff launched a series of handbags featuring "new signature designs". … The new bags … incorporated an update on the fashion house's famous Toile marks. The fresh design—coined the Louis Vuitton Monogram Multicolore pattern …—was a modified version of the Toile marks, printed in 33 bright colors … on a white or black background.

Plaintiff states that it spent over $4 million in 2003–2004 advertising and promoting the Multicolore mark and associated handbags. In addition, the new design garnered significant media attention. CBS's *The Early Show* and publications ranging from *USA Today* and *The New York Times* to *People, Women's Wear Daily, Marie Claire,* and *Vogue* all featured the Murakami handbags. Celebrities including Jennifer Lopez, Reese Witherspoon, and Madonna were photographed with the bags in tow.

At the time plaintiff filed its complaint, it had sold nearly 70,000 handbags and accessories with the Multicolore mark design in the United States for between $360 and $3,950 each, amounting to over $40 million. Of that sum, $25 million was attributable to the white background design and $16 million to the black background design.

... Since 2001 as part of the Dooney & Bourke's "Signature" and "Mini Signature" lines, [Dooney & Bourke] has sold bags featuring the DB monogram of interlocking initials, a registered trademark, in a repeated pattern. The handbags sell for between $125 and $400.

In the fall of 2002 Peter Dooney, president and chief designer of Dooney & Bourke, began collaborating with *Teen Vogue* magazine on a joint promotional project as the magazine was being launched. The magazine selected a group of teenaged girls to travel with Dooney to Italy in March 2003 to help develop Dooney & Bourke handbags appealing to teenagers. The group, dubbed the "It Team," was photographed looking into Vuitton's store window display featuring handbags with the Multicolore marks on a white background. Another photograph taken during the trip showed the group in a factory viewing a swatch of fabric with the Multicolore mark on a black background.

... [I]n late July 2003 Dooney & Bourke introduced its "It-Bag" collection, which featured the DB monogram in an array of bright colors set against a white background. The intertwined initials, with the "D" and the "B" displayed in contrasting colors, were printed forward and backward in repeating diagonal rows. The handbags also sported a multicolor zipper, with fabric similar to that used by Vuitton, and a small pink enamel heart bearing the legend "Dooney & Bourke" on a tag hanging from the handle. In October 2003 Dooney & Bourke began selling the handbags with a black background. The It-Bag collection now includes a variety of colored backgrounds (periwinkle, bubble gum, grape) in addition to black and white.

....

II Trademark Infringement

Vuitton claims trademark infringement under both § 32 of the Trademark Act of 1946 (Lanham Act), 15 U.S.C. § 1114, and § 43(a) of that Act, 15 U.S.C. § 1125(a). Because the trademark at the core of this case—the Multicolore mark—is unregistered, we focus our discussion on the § 43(a) claim. Yet, we note that the same analysis applies to claims of trademark infringement under § 32. *See Virgin Enters. Ltd. v. Nawab*, 335 F.3d 141, 146 (2d Cir. 2003).

Section 43(a) of the Lanham Act prohibits a person from using "any word, term, name, symbol, or device, or any combination thereof ... which ... is likely to cause confusion ... as to the origin, sponsorship, or approval of his or her goods...." 15 U.S.C. § 1125(a). This section protects from infringement unregistered trademarks, *EMI Catalogue P'ship v. Hill, Holliday, Connors, Cosmopulos Inc.*, 228 F.3d 56, 61 (2d Cir. 2000), as well as trade dress and product design, *see Wal-Mart Stores, Inc. v. Samara Bros., Inc.*, 529 U.S. 205, 209 (2000).

We analyze trademark infringement claims under the familiar two-prong test described in *Gruner + Jahr USA Publ'g v. Meredith Corp.*, 991 F.2d 1072 (2d Cir. 1993). First, we look to see whether plaintiff's mark merits protection, and second, whether defendant's use of a similar mark is likely to cause consumer confusion. *Id.* at 1075. The central consideration in assessing a mark's protectability, namely its degree of distinctiveness, is also a factor in determining likelihood of confusion. [Citation.] On appeal, Vuitton contends the district court blurred Vuitton's distinctive trademark by reducing it to an undefined and unprotectable "look," and also focused improperly on a side-by-side comparison to assess likelihood of confusion. We discuss each contention in turn.

A. *Recognizing and Defining Vuitton's Trademark*

... Vuitton claims a new trademark, currently unregistered, consisting of a design plus color, that is, the traditional Vuitton Toile pattern design—entwined LV initials with the three already described motifs—displayed in the 33 Murakami colors and printed on a white or black background....

....

In "determining whether an unregistered mark is entitled to protection under § 43(a)," *Two Pesos, Inc. v. Taco Cabana, Inc.*, 505 U.S. 763, 768 (1992), "the general principles qualifying a mark for registration under § 2 of the Lanham Act are for the most part applicable," *id.*...

....

Basic geometric shapes, basic letters, and single colors are not protectable as inherently distinctive. [*Star Indus. v. Bacardi & Co.*, 412 F.3d 373,] at 381 [(2d Cir.

2005)]; *see Qualitex*, 514 U.S. at 162–63. These symbols may be protected only upon a showing of secondary meaning. *See Qualitex*, 514 U.S. at 162–63. However, "stylized letters or shapes are not 'basic,' and are protectable when original within the relevant market." *Star Indus.*, 412 F.3d at 383 (holding stylized "O" on vodka bottle protectable as inherently distinctive, but weak, mark).

Vuitton's Multicolore mark, consisting of styled shapes and letters—the traditional Toile mark combined with the 33 Murakami colors—is original in the handbag market and inherently distinctive. The Toile pattern, on which it is based, has been a famous indicator of Louis Vuitton for over a century. The new Multicolore mark was created as a source-identifier for Vuitton in the new millennium. It is a strong mark. The mark earned praise and became famous almost instantly. We agree with the district court that the Multicolore mark is protectable both because it is inherently distinctive and because it has acquired secondary meaning.

B. *Assessing the Likelihood of Confusion*

... In analyzing this second prong of the test for trademark infringement, courts apply the non-exclusive multi-factor test developed by Judge Friendly in *Polaroid Corp. v. Polarad Electronics Corp.*, 287 F.2d 492, 495 (2d Cir. 1961)....

The similarity of the marks is a key factor in determining likelihood of confusion. [Citation.] "To apply this factor, courts must analyze the mark's overall impression on a consumer, considering the context in which the marks are displayed and the 'totality of factors that could cause confusion among prospective purchasers.'" *Id.* (*quoting Gruner + Jahr USA*, 991 F.2d at 1078).

The district court ... determined that despite the similarities, the two marks were not confusingly similar. *See Dooney & Bourke*, 340 F. Supp. 2d at 440.

It appears the trial court made the ... mistake [of] inappropriately focusing on the similarity of the marks in a side-by-side comparison instead of when viewed sequentially in the context of the marketplace. The district court reasoned:

> [I]t could not be more obvious that Louis Vuitton uses the initials "LV," while Dooney & Bourke uses its trademarked "DB" logo. Thus, *a consumer seeing these trademarks printed on these bags, either up close or at a distance, is not likely to be confused....* [T]he Dooney & Bourke bags only use their "DB" initials; there are no geometric shapes interspersed with the monogram.... [T]he colors used on the Dooney & Bourke bag are noticeably toned down, and consequently fail to evoke the characteristic "friction" sparked by Murakami's bright, clashing colors, the Louis Vuitton marks create a very different overall impression (i.e., large interspersed shapes and initials in crisp, bold colors) than the Dooney & Bourke bags (i.e., tightly interlocked initials in dulled colors).

Dooney & Bourke, 340 F. Supp. 2d at 440 (emphasis added)....

Utilizing a side-by-side comparison can be a useful "heuristic means of investigating similarities and differences in ... respective designs," so long as a court maintains a "focus on the ultimate issue of the likelihood of consumer confusion." [*Louis Vuitton Malletier v. Burlington Coat Factory Warehouse Corp.*, 426 F.3d 532] at 538 [(2d Cir. 2005)]. Courts should keep in mind that in this context the law requires only confusing similarity, not identity. [Citation.] Further, where, as here, the plaintiff claims initial-interest and post-sale confusion, market conditions must be examined closely to see whether the differences between the marks are "likely to be memorable enough to dispel confusion on serial viewing." *Burlington Coat Factory*, 426 F.3d at 538.

The district court erred because it based its determination that confusion between the Vuitton and Dooney & Bourke marks was unlikely at least in part on an overemphasized side-by-side comparison. This is suggested by the district court's comment that "no amount of expert opinion, legal analysis, or demonstrative evidence can overcome the clarity that comes from direct observation." *Dooney & Bourke*, 340 F. Supp. 2d at 421.

We do not believe the district court clearly erred with respect to the other *Polaroid* factors. Nonetheless, because no single factor is dispositive, we must remand for the district court to revisit the entire analysis, under the new standard described here and in *Burlington Coat Factory*. Upon remand, the district court should keep in mind that "[n]o single factor is dispositive, nor is a court limited to consideration of only these factors." *Brennan's* [*Inc. v. Brennan's Rest.*], 360 F.3d [125] at 130 [(2d Cir. 2004)]. Accordingly, we must vacate its order insofar as it declined to issue a preliminary injunction and remand the case to allow the district court to reassess Vuitton's claim of a design plus color trademark under the Lanham Act.

....

Questions

1. How do you think the district court should rule on likelihood of confusion on remand? *See Louis Vuitton Malletier v. Dooney & Burke, Inc.*, 525 F. Supp. 2d 558 (S.D.N.Y. 2007).

2. Did the court treat Vuitton's mark as product configuration under *Wal-Mart*? Should it have done so since the pattern covered the entire surface of Vuitton's handbags?

Conopco, Inc. v. May Dept. Stores Co.

46 F.3d 1556 (Fed. Cir. 1994)

Plager, Circuit Judge:

Defendants May Department Stores Co. (May), Venture Stores, Inc. (Venture), The Benjamin Ansehl Co. (Ansehl), and Kessler Containers Ltd. (Kessler) appeal the judgment of the District Court for the Eastern District of Missouri.... *Conopco, Inc. v. May Dep't Stores Co.*, 784 F. Supp. 648, 24 U.S.P.Q.2d 1721 (E.D. Mo. 1992). The District Court ruled that defendants willfully infringed a package of proprietary rights owned by plaintiff Conopco, Inc. d/b/a Chesebrough-Pond's U.S.A. Co. (Conopco) relating to a relaunch of Conopco's Vaseline Intensive Care Lotion (VICL) product....

BACKGROUND

In 1986, Conopco decided to "relaunch" VICL, a product it had been marketing for over 20 years. Conopco wanted to enhance that product's therapeutic image and to further distance it from private label brands, which had been eroding its sales. Accordingly, it set about developing a new bottle shape and label for the product. It also set about developing a new formula for the lotion. Conopco's objective was to reduce the lotion's greasiness while maintaining its thickness and smooth skin feel.

....

... By the fall of 1989, the product was on the shelves of virtually every major retailer and drug store in the United States. Between the fall of 1989 and March of 1990, Conopco spent over $37 million to advertise and promote the product.

Ansehl is a manufacturer of private label hand lotions, which it distributes through retailers such as Venture, who also handle national brands such as the revised VICL product. Kessler is a manufacturer of containers, and May is Venture's corporate parent.

In January 1989, Ansehl became aware of Conopco's plans to relaunch VICL. Accordingly, it developed a private label product to compete with the revised VICL product. Together with Kessler, it developed a container for the product. In conjunction with Venture, it developed the labeling that would be affixed to the container. Soon after Conopco initiated the VICL relaunch, Ansehl began marketing its product through several retailers, including Venture.

... In August 1990, Conopco filed suit against the defendants in the District Court for the Eastern District of Missouri ...

....

On January 2, 1992, the court ... entered [judgment] after a bench trial in favor of plaintiff. [Citation.] The court found that ... all defendants had willfully infringed plaintiff's trademark and trade dress rights. The court found the case to be exceptional, and that enhanced damages were warranted. The court awarded ... trebled damages of $281,622 for the trademark and trade dress infringement. The court also awarded costs, attorney fees, prejudgment interest, a recall order, and an injunction. It also imposed joint and several liability on the defendants. These appeals followed.

....

DISCUSSION

B. Trade Dress and Trademark Infringement Issues

The trade dress and trademark infringement issues raise substantive legal issues over which this court does not have exclusive subject matter jurisdiction. Accordingly, it is our practice to defer to the law of the regional circuit in which the district court sits, in this case the Eighth Circuit, to resolve them. [Citation.]

1. Trade Dress

Conopco's trade dress infringement claim was brought pursuant to section 43(a) of the Lanham Act (codified as amended at 15 U.S.C. § 1125(a) (1988)). Conopco seeks injunctive and monetary relief. In the Eighth Circuit, the elements to be proved in a claim for trade dress infringement differ depending on whether injunctive or monetary relief is being sought. [Citations.] To establish entitlement to monetary relief, a plaintiff must show actual confusion, while to establish entitlement to injunctive relief, it is sufficient if the plaintiff establishes likelihood of confusion. [Citation.] The difficulty of proving actual confusion understandably is greater than that of proving likelihood of confusion. [Citations.] We consider first Conopco's claim for monetary relief, then its claim for injunctive relief.

a. Monetary Relief—Actual Confusion

In the Eighth Circuit, the question of actual confusion vel non is one of fact subject to the clearly erroneous standard of review. *Prufrock Ltd., Inc. v. Lasater*, 781 F.2d 129, 132–33, 228 U.S.P.Q. 435, 437 (8th Cir. 1986) (discussing standard of review for trade dress infringement claim). The trial court based its finding of actual confusion on two factors. The first is the testimony of a consumer, Mrs. Sickles. The second is a presumption of actual confusion arising from the "overwhelming evidence that defendants intended to deceive and confuse the public in connection with the Venture skin care lotion product."

In her testimony, Mrs. Sickles stated that she purchased a private label brand of VICL—the Target brand—thinking it to have originated from Conopco. The problem with the testimony is that Mrs. Sickles's confusion arose at least in part from her assumption, erroneous as applied to this case, that national brand manufacturers secretly market private label brands. First, there is no evidence that this assumption is widely held by the relevant consumers, the vantage point from which the confusion issue must ultimately be addressed. Second, under the circumstances of this case, in which the national brand is being sold side-by-side with the private label brand, the assumption is at best counter-intuitive—it assumes that a national brand manufacturer would embark on a scheme to deliberately erode its sales of the national brand.[8]

Thus, Mrs. Sickles's experience appears to have been atypical.... Isolated instances of actual confusion do not justify an award of monetary relief when there is a reasonable explanation in the record which serves to discount their importance. [Citations.] Accordingly, that testimony is legally insufficient to sustain the court's award of monetary relief.

Actual confusion is normally proven "through the use of direct evidence, i.e., testimony from members of the buying public, as well as through circumstantial evidence, e.g., consumer surveys or consumer reaction tests." *PPX Enters. v. Audio Fidelity*

8. The circumstance in which the private label brand is being sold through different commercial channels than the national brand might present a different case.

Enterprises, 818 F.2d 266, 271, 2 U.S.P.Q.2d 1672, 1675 (2d Cir. 1987). A presumption of actual confusion arising from an intent to deceive is neither. Thus, the question is whether such a judicially-created presumption constitutes a sufficient basis to sustain the trial court's award of monetary relief.

....

This is a case in which a retailer markets a national brand product and at the same time markets its own private label product in direct competition. The retailer packages its product in a manner to make it clear to the consumer that the product is similar to the national brand, and is intended for the same purposes. At the same time, the retailer clearly marks its product with its private logo, and expressly invites the consumer to compare its product with that of the national brand, by name.

With the rise of regional and national discount retailers with established names and logos, retailers who market both national brands and their own private label brands in direct competition, this form of competition has become commonplace and well-known in the marketplace. When such packaging is clearly labeled and differentiated—as was the case here— ... we are unwilling to attribute to the Eighth Circuit, absent clear precedent so requiring, a rule that would make such competition presumptively unlawful.

The District Court erred in concluding that under Eighth Circuit law actual confusion could be presumed from defendants' intent to copy the overall package design. Consequently, there is a complete absence of proof of actual confusion, the required element in plaintiff's claim for monetary relief. The court's award of monetary relief is thus not sustainable, and is reversed.

b. Injunctive Relief—Likelihood of Confusion

....

The trial court concluded that likelihood of confusion had been established on the basis of the following findings: that plaintiff's marks are strong, the trade dress of the two products is "extremely similar," the two products are "directly competitive," the defendants "acted with deliberate intent to imitate and infringe the revised VICL trade dress," a presumption of likelihood of confusion arising from defendants' intent to deceive and copy, and the presence of actual confusion. As noted, *supra*, the court's finding of actual confusion was erroneous because of a complete failure of proof. Thus, our task is to determine whether the other findings are sufficient to support the court's finding of likelihood of confusion.

We conclude that they are not. Even accepting these other findings as true, they are at best merely inferentially or presumptively relevant to the likelihood of confusion issue. A factor more probative of that issue, which the court in its opinion failed to address, is the significance of the black and white diagonally-striped Venture logo prominently situated on the front of the original and relaunched Venture products. Photographs comparing the original and relaunched Conopco products with the corresponding Venture products, reproduced below, show the prominent placement of that logo on the front of the Venture products:

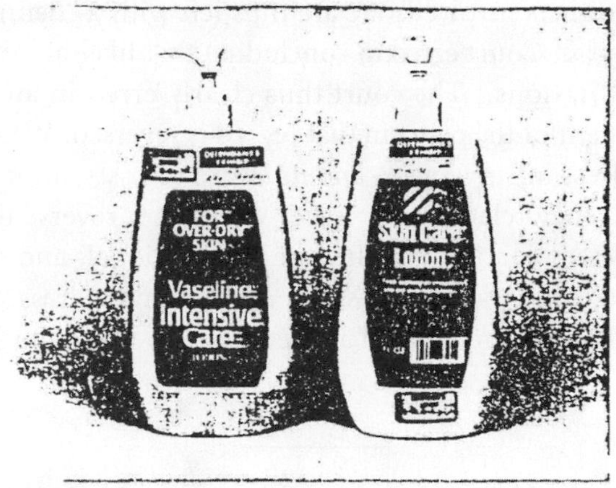

COMPARISON OF ORIGINAL VICL AND VENTURE BOTTLES

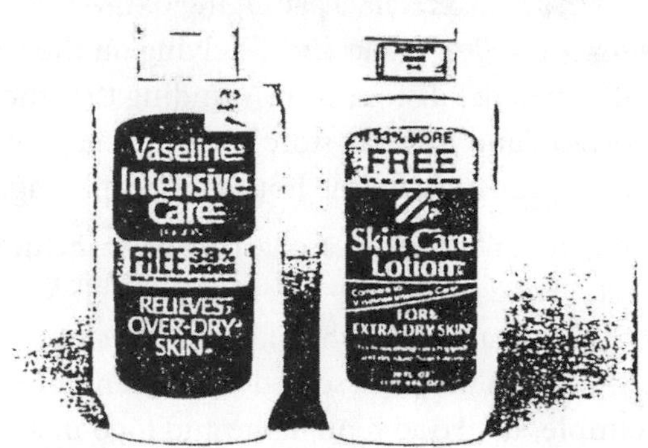

COMPARISON OF REVISED VICL AND VENTURE BOTTLES

The unique and extensive appearance of that logo in the store parking lot, on store signs, on employees' badges, in Venture's frequent and periodic print and television advertisements, and on other private label items sold by Venture, the large volume of Venture's annual sales ($1.3 billion in 1990), and the dearth of evidence that consumers ever purchased the Venture brand thinking it to have originated from Conopco despite the extended (over 10 year) period over which the original and relaunched products were sold alongside the Venture brand, give rise to the expectation that consumers identify the logo with Venture, rather than Conopco, and use that logo to successfully distinguish between the two brands.

The fact that Venture (and other retailers) compete in the manner described, which is all that the evidence establishes, is simply insufficient to amount to proof that there is in the minds of consumers a likelihood of confusion about whose product is whose....

[T]he marketing device employed by defendants in this case is neither new nor subtle. The cases have approved the general practice in a variety of settings, at least to the extent of not finding a violation of the Lanham Act absent a showing by the plaintiff that real consumers have real confusion or likelihood of it with regard to the origin of the products involved. We are thus left with a "definite and firm conviction" that the District Court erred in concluding that likelihood of confusion had been established. [Citations.] The court thus clearly erred in awarding injunctive relief, and the judgment of the court in that regard is reversed. We reverse the court's judgment of trade dress infringement, and its award of costs, attorney fees, and prejudgment interest as they relate to this issue. We further reverse the court's finding of willfulness, the determination that the case is exceptional, and the determination that enhanced damages are warranted as they relate to trade dress infringement. The injunction and recall order are vacated as they relate to this issue.

....

McNeil Nutritionals, LLC v. Heartland Sweeteners, LLC, 511 F.3d 350 (3d Cir. 2007). The producer of Splenda artificial sweetener sued the producer of multiple store brands of artificial sweetener made from sucralose, the principal ingredient in Splenda. Plaintiff argued that defendant's packaging of its store brand sweeteners infringed Splenda's distinctive yellow trade dress. Relying on the reasoning in *Conopco*, the court of appeals affirmed the district court's finding that there was no likelihood of confusion for Food Lion and Safeway store brand packaging, in which the name of the stores appeared prominently on the house brand packages:

> Applying these principles to the case at bar, we conclude that there was no clear error. First, "Food Lion" and "Safeway" are well-known because they are well-known to the consumers who shop in the stores with those same names. Second, the stores are represented prominently on their respective packages. For example, the Food Lion name and logo in black (a color with virtually no presence on the front of Splenda packages) are displayed in the top-left corner. As importantly, a vertical design element runs through the front of the package, visually dividing it between a dark yellow bar and a light yellow canvas, in a way found on other Food Lion store-brand products. The yellow color aside, these features are far more similar to other Food Lion store-brand packaging features and therefore distinguish themselves from any feature present on the Splenda packages. These distinguishing elements are also found on the Food Lion bag of granular sucralose.

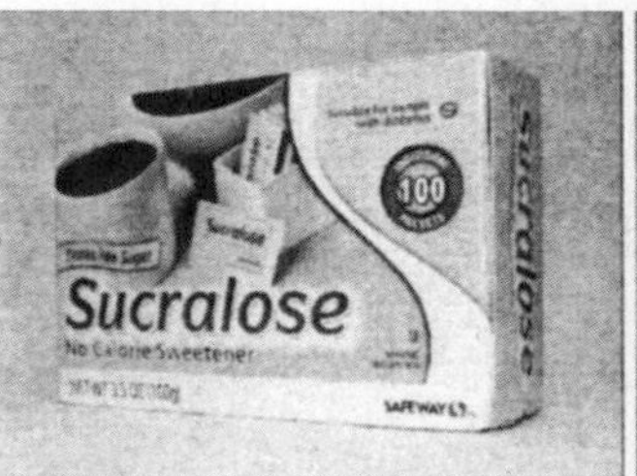

> The District Court found additional differences between the Food Lion trade dress and Splenda trade dress. First, the Food Lion product name

"Sweet Choice" is shown rather than "Splenda." Second, "Sweet Choice" is positioned at the bottom of the box, rather than at the top. Third, whereas "Sweet Choice" is not surrounded by a white cloud, "Splenda" is. Fourth, missing from the Food Lion packages is the circular element with the slogan "Made From Sugar, Tastes Like Sugar." When combined with the distinguishing use of the Food Lion name and logo, these differences are not minute ones found only upon examination with a microscope....

McNeil argues that the history of color coding in the sweetener industry increases the likelihood of consumer confusion among sucralose-based products. A restaurant consumer, for example, encounters a range of sweeteners organized by packet color: white (and possibly brown) for sugar, pink for saccharin, blue for aspartame, and yellow for Splenda. According to McNeil, these colors have become a "shorthand" by which consumers identify their sweetener of choice. Moreover, there is apparently a history of the manufacturers of Equal and Sweet 'N Low waiting too long to challenge imitators of their respective colors, whereas McNeil has been challenging its imitators since Splenda's inception. Therefore, McNeil argues that yellow does not signify sucralose; it signifies Splenda.

There are several problems with this argument.... [J]ust because a consumer sees yellow packaging in the sugar aisle does not mean that she believes McNeil or Splenda to be the source, especially because consumers are generally aware of the use of pink and blue by manufacturers other than those of Sweet 'N Low and Equal, respectively. The sugar aisle in a representative grocery store also contains yellow packages of products other than sucralose, including sugar itself. In this factual context, we cannot conclude that whenever any other sucralose producer uses yellow packaging, consumers are likely to associate that product with Splenda.

The court reached the opposite conclusion with respect to the packaging for Giant and Stop & Shop store brands of sucralose sweetener:

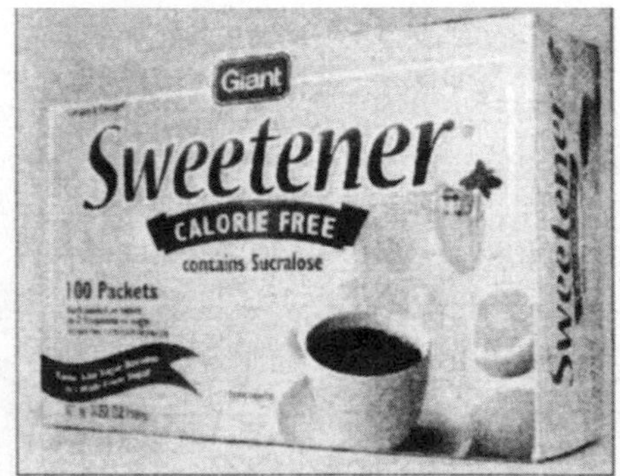

In contrast to the products in *Conopco*, the store name and logo are not prominently displayed on the [Giant and Stop & Shop] packaging. Indeed,

> as already explained, the Food Lion and Safeway packages are in this sense much closer to the *Conopco* packages because a store-specific signature is prominently displayed on them, thereby substantially reducing the degree of similarity and hence the likelihood of confusion. The same simply cannot be said for the [Giant] packages, and the District Court itself so found. To repeat, the District Court may take *Conopco* into account when analyzing the [*Polaroid*] factors, in particular the first ... factor because ..., the more a store's name and/or logo are present around that store's shoppers, the more likely those shoppers will know well that name and/or logo, which in turn may serve to differentiate materially a store-brand packaging that displays them prominently. The District Court may not, however, consider the *Conopco* reasoning as an independent defense that altogether overrides the ... factors.
>
> The nuanced distinction we make also brings the trade dress infringement issue back to its proper focus: just how similar the trade dresses are.

On remand, McNeil renewed its motion for a preliminary injunction prohibiting the distribution of sucralose in the Giant and Stop & Shop trade dress. Defendant represented to the court that it had redesigned the packaging of Giant and Stop & Shop sweeteners. It wanted, however, to use up the inventory it had already manufactured. Judge John R. Padova concluded that McNeil was likely to show that its trade dress was non-functional and had acquired secondary meaning. The court entered an injunction prohibiting use of the original Giant and Stop & Shop trade dress pending trial. *See McNeil Nutritionals v. Heartland Sweeteners LLC*, 566 F. Supp. 2d 378 (E.D. Pa. 2008).

Questions

1. Was May using the copied elements of the Vaseline Intensive Care trade dress as a trademark for its private label lotion?

2. In any large supermarket or pharmacy chain, you can find national brand products on shelves beside private brand equivalents. Some of the private brand imitations are identical in formulation to their national brand models; others are more distantly related. Some of the private brand packages merely note their comparability to a national brand product, while others have packages designed to duplicate characteristic features of the national brand trade dress. Are there policy reasons that support permitting this degree of imitation?

3. Judge Cardamone in *Dooney & Burke* disagreed with the district court's side-by-side analysis. Is such analysis more appropriate in the *Conopco* situation? Do you agree that the Venture striped logo is sufficient to avoid likely confusion even though lotion is a low-cost item that purchasers may not exercise great care in selecting? What if the product were a pharmaceutical product? *See McNeil-PPC, Inc. v. Guardian Drug Co.*, 984 F. Supp. 1066 (E.D. Mich. 1997) (court enjoined look-alike private label trade dress for lactose intolerance remedy even though product bore the ARBOR house mark; court distinguished *Conopco* on the basis that the parties' previous products in that case had co-existed for many years with similar trade dresses).

4. Footnote 8 of the *Conopco* opinion notes that "[t]he circumstance in which the private label brand is sold through different commercial channels than the national brand might present a different case." How should such a case be resolved? For many decades, Pepperidge Farm has sold MILANO oval-shaped sandwich cookies with chocolate in the middle, packaged in a gable-top bag inside of which cookies are placed in folded paper containers. Trader Joe's grocery store chain, which primarily sells its own brand of goods and does not sell MILANO cookies, introduced a sandwich cookie with chocolate in the middle in a similar package type. Though Trader Joe's cookies are placed in a plastic tray inside the package, the outside package displays the cookies in a "fluted paper tray."

Pepperidge Farm sues. As neither party wants to spend the time and money for a trial, what sort of settlement might protect both parties' interests?

2. Marketing Concepts and Techniques

Original Appalachian Artworks, Inc v. The Toy Loft, Inc., 684 F.2d 821 (11th Cir. 1982). Plaintiff sold Cabbage Patch Kids brand soft-sculpture dolls with a "birth certificate" and "adoption papers" for the purchaser. Plaintiff also sent the buyer a birthday card for the doll a year after the sale. Defendant also sold soft-sculpture dolls and utilized a similar marketing technique. Plaintiff sued for copyright infringement and for trade dress infringement. The district court ruled for the plaintiff on both counts. The Eleventh Circuit affirmed and treated the adoption and birth certificate papers accompanying plaintiff's dolls as trade dress.

> The former Fifth Circuit has held ... that § 43(a) provides a federal cause of action for trade dress infringement. [Citations.] The essential element of an action under § 43(a) is proof by the plaintiff that the alleged infringement by the defendant creates a likelihood of confusion on the part of consumers as to the source of the goods. [Citations.]

Lawson ... asserts that the adoption procedures and birth certificate marketing techniques are not protectible trade dress. Lawson cites no legal authority for this assertion and fails to explain the reasoning behind it. Nevertheless, we derive from a close reading of appellant's brief and oral argument that the essence of Lawson's position is that "trade dress" refers to the packaging or display of a product rather than a sales technique.

We recognize that the majority of trade dress claims involve a manufacturer's container or packaging for a product. *E.g., Chevron Chemical* [*Co. v. Voluntary Purchasing Groups, Inc.*, 659 F.2d 695 (5th Cir. 1981)], (packaging and containers for lawn care products); *Sun-Fun* [*Products, Inc. v. Suntan Research & Develop. Inc.*, 565 F.2d 186 (5th Cir. 1981)], (container for sun tan lotion). To the extent packaging is not utilitarian, however, it represents a sales technique designed to make the product readily identifiable to consumers and unique in the marketplace. The same is true of OAA's adoption technique. The adoption procedure truly is part of the "packaging" of OAA's product both in the sense that dolls are never sold without the adoption papers and birth certificate and because the adoption procedure is designed to make OAA's dolls distinctive in the marketplace. The courts, moreover, have recognized that an unfair competition claim can extend to marketing techniques. *E.g., Artus Corp. v. Nordic Co.*, 512 F. Supp. 1184, 1191 (W.D. Pa. 1981) ("likelihood of confusion" test extends to labelling and marketing techniques); *Menley & James Laboratories, Ltd. v. Approved Pharmaceutical Corp.*, 438 F. Supp. 1061, 1066 (N.D.N.Y. 1977) ("Unfair competition ... relates to the product as a whole, as it is marketed, and the public's general impression of it."). Consequently, we conclude that the adoption procedures used by OAA in the sale of its dolls qualify as protectible trade dress.

Lawson's second argument is that OAA failed to show a likelihood of confusion because it did not prove that Lawson intentionally intended to "palm-off" his dolls as OAA products and because the record shows that he took steps to differentiate the dolls, including directing the employees to distinguish the Lawson dolls from OAA's "if confusion occurred." This argument is not persuasive. As we noted above, the touchstone test for a violation of §43(a) is the "likelihood of confusion" resulting from the defendant's adoption of a trade dress similar to the plaintiff's. The defendant's intent to tread on the goodwill of the plaintiff, while certainly a relevant factor in establishing a likelihood of confusion, *Chevron Chemical, supra*, 659 F.2d at 703–04, is not the only factor. Instead, our precedents have held that the likelihood of consumer confusion rests on an evaluation of a variety of factors including the defendant's intent, the similarity of design, the similarity of product, the similarity of retail outlets and purchasers, the similarity of advertising media, and actual confusion. *Chevron Chemical, supra*, 659 F.2d at 703. *See Sun-Fun, supra*, 656 F.2d at 189, 192 (factors relevant to unfair competition claim are essentially the same as those for trademark infringement); [citations].

Here the trial court found that Lawson's trade dress created a likelihood of confusion.... The finding is not clearly erroneous. Both Lawson's and OAA's products are the same, soft-sculpture baby dolls, and are sold in similar retail establishments to a practically identical clientele. OAA, moreover, presented evidence of actual confusion by a potential customer, and this evidence is "patently the best evidence of likelihood of confusion." *Chevron Chemical, supra*, 659 F.2d at 704; [citations]. Finally, as to Lawson's intent, we note:

> It is so easy for a business man who wishes to sell his goods upon their merits to select marks and packaging that cannot possibly be confused with his competitor's that "courts look with suspicion upon one who, in dressing his goods for the market, approaches so near to his successful rival that the public may fail to distinguish between them."

Chevron Chemical, supra, 659 F.2d at 704 (quoting *Florence Mfg. Co. v. J.C. Dowd & Co.*, 178 F. 73, 75 (2d Cir. 1910)). We hold, therefore, that the trial court's finding that Lawson had infringed OAA's trade dress and thus had committed unfair competition was not erroneous.

Jeffrey Milstein, Inc. v. Greger, Lawlor, Roth, Inc.

58 F.3d 27 (2d Cir. 1995)

NEWMAN, CHIEF JUDGE:

This appeal, arising in the context of greeting card designs, poses issues concerning the limits of trade dress protection under section 43(a) of the Lanham Act, 15 U.S.C. § 1125(a) (1988).

Plaintiff-appellant Jeffrey Milstein, Inc., d/b/a Paper House Productions ("Paper House"), appeals from the order of the District Court ... denying Paper House's motion for a preliminary injunction enjoining defendant-appellee Greger, Lawlor, Roth, Inc., d/b/a/ Triangle Enterprises ("Triangle"), from copying the unregistered trade dress of Paper House's greeting cards. That dress in essence comprises photographs die cut to the shapes of the objects depicted on the cards. According trade dress protection to this format would effectively grant Paper House a monopoly in the idea of using die-cut photographs on greeting cards. For reasons set forth below, we affirm.

Background

Appellant['s] ... greeting cards are typically a sheet of paper, folded vertically, that has been cut to the outline of an animal, person, or object depicted in a color photograph on the front panel of the card. With this die-cutting technique, the photograph completely fills the front panel. The inside panels and the back panel of the card are usually blank. The cards are packaged in clear cellophane bags.

Appellee Triangle['s] ... products include die-cut gift bags, die-cut stand ups, and die-cut note pads. Some time between May and August 1994, Triangle began to produce and sell "tri-cut" photographic greeting cards. Unlike Paper House's greeting cards, ... Triangle's cards depict the die-cut image on the front of all three panels of each card. Like Paper House's cards, Triangle's cards have blank interiors and are packaged in clear cellophane wrapping.

Paper House instituted this action, alleging that Triangle had copied its greeting card format, in violation of section 43(a) of the Lanham Act and New York's common law of unfair competition. Of Triangle's complete line of tri-cut greeting cards, Paper House selected six that allegedly copied Paper House's trade dress, though, as the District Court noted in its opinion, Paper House is not seeking protection with respect to only the handful of cards depicting photographic images similar to those used by Triangle; rather, Paper House is alleging infringement of the general format of its entire line of die-cut greeting cards.

At the hearing on Paper House's motion for a preliminary injunction, Paper House's president, Jeffrey Milstein, acknowledged that other greeting card companies have either marketed die-cut cards or used photographic images, but he asserted that his company was the first to produce a line of greeting cards that applied the die-cutting process to photographs.

Relying on the two-part test of trade dress infringement applied in *Two Pesos, Inc. v. Taco Cabana, Inc.*, 112 S. Ct. 2753, 2758, 120 L. Ed. 2d 615 (1992), and *Paddington Corp. v. Attiki Importers & Distributors, Inc.*, 996 F.2d 577, 582 (2d Cir. 1993), the District Court concluded that Paper House had shown neither distinctiveness of its trade dress nor likelihood of consumer confusion.

... Paper House described its trade dress as "straight-on color photographs of animals, plants, people or objects, die-cut to the shape of the image of the photograph, with the inside of the card being a blank white color." *Jeffrey Milstein, Inc. v. Gregor, Lawlor, Roth, Inc.*, No. 94 Civ. 8003 (KTD), mem. dec. at 4 (S.D.N.Y. Dec. 12, 1994) *("Dist. Ct. Op.")*. Evaluating these characteristics for distinctiveness, the District Court determined that Paper House's trade dress was "generic," *id.* at 5, consisting solely of common and functional elements such as die-cutting, photographs, and blank white interiors. The District Court also found that Paper House had not demonstrated that its dress had acquired a secondary meaning.

With respect to the likelihood of confusion, the District Court applied the eight-factor test set forth in *Polaroid Corp. v. Polarad Electronics Corp.*, 287 F.2d 492, 495 (2d Cir.), *cert. denied*, 368 U.S. 820 (1961), and concluded that the only factors favoring Paper House were "proximity/bridging the gap" and the relative lack of sophistication among consumers of greeting cards. *Dist. Ct. Op.* at 7.

As to the other factors, the District Court found that Paper House's trade dress was weak at best, and any similarity between the two brands of greeting cards could be explained by "the fact that Plaintiff's and Defendant's products depict similar natural objects, die-cut to form." *Id.* at 7–8. The District Court found no support for Paper House's allegations of deliberate copying,[1] and it found no evidence of

1. Though Paper House argued that Triangle was aware of Paper House's line of cards, Triangle denied copying and provided evidence indicating that at least some of the images used on its cards

actual confusion. In addition, the District Court noted that a visual inspection of Paper House's and Triangle's greeting cards failed to disclose an appreciable disparity in quality. Because Paper House had not satisfied the standard for trade dress infringement, the District Court found, Paper House could not show a likelihood of success on the merits of its Lanham Act claim.... Accordingly, the District Court denied Paper House's motion.

B. *Lanham Act Claim*

Section 43(a) of the Lanham Act, "though enacted as part of the Trademark Act, ... functions as a federal law of unfair competition for unregistered goods ... [and] extends protection to a product's 'trade dress.'" *Coach Leatherware Co., v. AnnTaylor Inc.*, 933 F.2d 162, 168 (2d Cir. 1991)....

At one time, "trade dress" referred only to the manner in which a product was "dressed up" to go to market with a label, package, display card, and similar packaging elements. However, "trade dress" has taken on a more expansive meaning and includes the design and appearance of the product as well as that of the container and all elements making up the total visual image by which the product is presented to customers. [Citation.] Thus, trade dress is "essentially [a product's] total image and overall appearance," *Two Pesos*, 112 S. Ct. at 2755 n.1, "as defined by its overall composition and design, including size, shape, color, texture, and graphics." *AnnTaylor*, 933 F.2d at 168. To prevail in an action for trade dress infringement under section 43(a) of the Lanham Act, a plaintiff must prove (1) that its dress is distinctive and (2) that a likelihood of confusion exists between its product and the defendant's product. *See Two Pesos*, 112 S. Ct. 2753, 2758, 120 L. Ed. 2d 615; [citation]....

(1) *Distinctiveness.* We evaluate the distinctiveness of trade dresses according to the test set forth by Judge Friendly in *Abercrombie & Fitch Co. v. Hunting World, Inc.*, 537 F.2d 4, 9 (2d Cir. 1976). [Citation.] ...

Although each element of a trade dress individually might not be inherently distinctive, it is the combination of elements that should be the focus of the distinctiveness inquiry. Thus, if the overall dress is arbitrary, fanciful, or suggestive, it is distinctive despite its incorporation of generic elements. *Cf. LeSportsac*, [*Inc. v. K Mart Corp.*], 754 F.2d [71] at 76 [(2d Cir. 1985)] (despite functionality of individual elements, bag was nonfunctional "when viewed in its entirety"). Nonetheless, the fact that a trade dress is composed exclusively of commonly used or functional elements might suggest that that dress should be regarded as unprotectable or "generic," to avoid tying up a product or marketing idea. *Cf. Stormy Clime* [*v. ProGroup, Inc.*], 809 F.2d [971] at 978 [(2d Cir. 1987)] (referring to risk of monopolization of market where trade dress consists of "arrangement of predominantly functional features").[3]

---

were previously reproduced on other Triangle merchandise.

3. Paper House asserts that the District Court improperly evaluated the individual features of Paper House's trade dress in isolation rather than in combination. However, in determining that Paper House's dress was not distinctive, the District Court stated that it was "examining each card in

In evaluating claims to distinctive trade dresses, two additional considerations should be borne in mind. First, although trade dress law may supplement copyright and patent law by protecting unpatentable product configurations and novel marketing techniques, *see, e.g., LeSportsac*, 754 F.2d at 76–77, 79 (luggage design), overextension of trade dress protection can undermine restrictions in copyright and patent law that are designed to avoid monopolization of products and ideas. Consequently, courts should proceed with caution in assessing claims to unregistered trade dress protection so as not to undermine the objectives of these other laws. *See Stormy Clime*, 809 F.2d at 977–78 (noting that although patent laws "bestow[] limited periods of protection" to designs, "trademark protection extends for an unlimited period").

Second, just as copyright law does not protect ideas but only their concrete expression, neither does trade dress law protect an idea, a concept, or a generalized type of appearance. *See, e.g., Hartford House Ltd. v. Hallmark Cards Inc.*, 846 F.2d 1268, 1274 (10th Cir.) ("Blue Mountain has not been granted exclusive rights in an artistic style or in some concept, idea, or theme of expression. Rather, it is Blue Mountain's specific artistic expression, in combination with other features to produce an overall Blue Mountain look, that is being protected."), *cert. denied*, 488 U.S. 908 (1988); [citation]. Examples of ideas or concepts too general to warrant protection are the "theme" of skeletons engaging in sexual activities, which plaintiff used in its t-shirt design, *see Fashion Victim*, [*Ltd. v. Sunrise Turquoise, Inc.*], 785 F. Supp. [1302] at 1308 [(N.D. Ill. 1992)], and the "generalized concept" of grotesque figures in toys, *see Those Characters From Cleveland, Inc. v. J.J. Gams, Inc.*, No. 86 Civ. 3180, 1992 U.S. Dist. LEXIS 8424, *13 (S.D.N.Y. Apr. 12, 1992). By contrast, the concrete expression of an idea in a trade dress has received protection. *See Hartford House*, 846 F.2d at 1269, 1274 ("specific artistic expression" consisting of "non-occasion emotional messages concerning love, personal relationships, and other similar subjects, superimposed on watercolor or airbrush artwork that generally had a landscape motif or nature theme"); *Roulo v. Berrie*, 886 F.2d 931, 935 (7th Cir. 1989) (dress consisted of "beige, single-face (no fold) cards containing sentimental verses and frequently using ellipses written in Roulo's handwriting with brown ink"; "flanking the messages on the left and right borders [were] a series of four stripes, two silver foil stripes, enveloping one brown and one colored stripe in the middle"), *cert. denied*, 493 U.S. 1075 (1990).

Drawing the line between "ideas" or "concepts" on the one hand and "concrete expressions" on the other may sometimes present close questions. Often a helpful consideration will be the purpose of trade dress law: to protect an owner of a dress in informing the public of the source of its products, without permitting the owner to exclude competition from functionally similar products. The line-drawing task is analytically no different than applying Learned Hand's "abstractions" test in the copyright field, *see Nichols v. Universal Pictures Corp.*, 45 F.2d 119, 121 (2d Cir. 1930),

---

its entirety" and "taking these individual generic components as a whole." *Dist. Ct. Op.* at 5. Therefore, Paper House's objection is without merit.

cert. denied, 282 U.S. 902 (1931), to distinguish an unprotectable idea from a protectable expression of the idea. The level of generality at which a trade dress is described, as well as the fact that a similar trade dress is already being used by manufacturers of other kinds of products, may indicate that that dress is no more than a concept or idea to be applied to particular products.

In this case, Paper House alleges that its trade dress comprises "straight-on, strong photographic, glossy images of animals, persons or objects on die cut cards that are cut without bleed of any kind." Paper House also appears to include in its dress the blank interior of the cards, as well as the cellophane wrapping in which they are packaged. Paper House asserts that its card design is unique because the other die-cut cards have an "antique" look, are not glossy, are not completely die-cut, or are made from drawings rather than from photographs.

Despite its initial novelty within the greeting card industry, however, Paper House's trade dress cannot qualify for trade dress protection because Paper House is effectively seeking protection for an idea or concept—die-cut photographic greeting cards. It is clear that the first manufacturer to create a die-cut photographic product could not have claimed trade dress protection for all die-cut photographic designs, since a trade dress described as consisting solely of die-cut photographs would simply "'refer to the genus of which the particular product is a species.'" *Two Pesos*, 112 S. Ct. at 2757 (quoting *Park 'n Fly*, 469 U.S. at 194).

That Paper House seeks trade dress protection only in the greeting card industry, and not with respect to all die-cut photographic products, does not alter our conclusion. Just as the first company to depict a heart and an arrow on Valentine's cards or to produce cards depicting tabby cats could not seek protection for those designs because they are concepts, defined abstractly, so Paper House cannot obtain protection for its general idea of creating cards out of die-cut photographs.[4]

....

In sum, we agree with the District Court that Paper House is seeking trade dress protection for a generalized idea—one that has been applied, and has many applications, to products outside the greeting card context, including, for example, Triangle's die-cut photographic bags.

Since the features of Paper House's trade dress for which it seeks protection can be considered "generic," even a showing of secondary meaning could not make that dress "distinctive." *See Two Pesos*, 112 S. Ct. at 2757. In any event, Judge Duffy's determination of the secondary meaning issue was proper.... Based on [the] limited evidence, the District Court's finding as to lack of secondary meaning was not clearly erroneous.

---

4. As the District Court below correctly perceived, since the photographs Paper House uses vary from card to card, only the use of die cutting and the depiction of photographs remain constant. In addition, Paper House also consistently uses blank white interiors as well as cellophane wrapping, but, as the District Court suggested, such "functional" elements do not increase the distinctiveness of the trade dress, even considered as a whole.

....

Conclusion

The District Court did not exceed its discretion in denying the motion for preliminary relief. Accordingly, the order is affirmed.

Questions

1. The *Milstein* decision finds that plaintiff's die-cut photograph greeting card concept is too abstract to qualify for trade dress protection. Is this result consistent with that in *Original Appalachian Artworks* that found sales of dolls with birth certificates and adoption papers constituted protectable trade dress?

2. *Milstein* found Paper House's artistic style to be too abstract to constitute protectable trade dress. The well-known artist Britto filed a complaint alleging, *inter alia*, trade dress infringement against two graphic artists and Apple, Inc., which used an image created by the artists in its "Start Something New" campaign. *Britto Central, Inc. v. Redman*, 1:15 CV 21320 (S.D. Fl. April 6, 2015). The complaint describes the combination of elements making up the Britto trade dress as:

> vibrant color combinations, often dominated by bright yellow; compositions constructed by the juxtaposition of randomly shaped swaths of recurring distinctive patterns (including polka dots and stripes) to form the subject matter of the image, with each compositional element all outlined in bold black strokes; and uplifting, bright and happy visual themes.

The complaint alleges that Britto has licensed his trade dress to numerous companies and provides examples of Britto's works that embody the claimed features, including:

The graphic created by defendants for Apple is displayed below:

Has Britto alleged a protectable trade dress? If so, does the Apple graphic infringe?

3. *Milstein* requires trade dress to be a non-functional source identifier rather than consisting of generalized concepts and ideas. Fair Wind Sailing school sued a rival school started by former employees and alleged defendants copied Fair Wind's trade dress, which it described as including the following elements: only using 45-foot catamarans, following particular itineraries in teaching and using a unique teaching curriculum and procedures for student feedback. No details of the curriculum or feedback mechanism were alleged. Do such allegations satisfy Fair Wind's obligation to articulate a protectable trade dress rather than generalized or unprotectable concepts? *See Fair Wind Sailing, Inc. v. Dempster*, 764 F.3d 303 (3d Cir. 2014).

4. Philip Morris, makers of Marlboro cigarettes, sued Cowboy Cigarettes for trade dress infringement. Cowboy markets its Cowboy Cigarettes in a red package showing the silhouette of a cowboy on a horse. The Cowboy package design does not resemble the design of the Marlboro package, but Philip Morris argues that its long use of cowboy imagery to promote Marlboro is itself trade dress, and Cowboy's use of cowboy imagery and the Cowboy name constitutes trade dress infringement. How should the court rule? *See Philip Morris USA v. Cowboy Cigarette*, 70 U.S.P.Q.2d 1092 (S.D.N.Y. 2003).

3. Use in Commerce

Belmora LLC v. Bayer Consumer Care AG

819 F.3d 697 (4th Cir. 2016)

Agee, Circuit Judge.

In this unfair competition case, we consider whether the Lanham Act permits the owner of a foreign trademark ... to pursue false association, false advertising, and trademark cancellation claims against the owner of the same mark in the United States. Bayer Consumer Care AG ("BCC") owns the trademark "FLANAX" in Mexico and has sold naproxen sodium pain relievers under that mark in Mexico (and other parts of Latin America) since the 1970s. Belmora LLC owns the FLANAX trademark in the United States and has used it here since 2004 in the sale of its naproxen sodium pain relievers. BCC and its U.S. sister company Bayer HealthCare LLC ("BHC," and collectively with BCC, "Bayer") contend that Belmora used the FLANAX mark to deliberately deceive Mexican-American consumers into thinking they were purchasing BCC's product.

BCC successfully petitioned the U.S. Trademark Trial and Appeal Board ("TTAB") to cancel Belmora's registration for the FLANAX mark based on deceptive use. Belmora appealed ... to the district court. In the meantime, BCC filed a separate complaint for false association against Belmora under § 43 of the Lanham Act, 15 U.S.C. § 1125, and in conjunction with BHC, a claim for false advertising. After the two cases were consolidated, the district court reversed the TTAB's cancellation order and dismissed the false association and false advertising claims.

Bayer appeals those decisions. For the reasons outlined below, we vacate the judgment of the district court and remand this case for further proceedings consistent with this opinion.

....

... FLANAX sales by BCC [in Mexico] have totaled hundreds of millions of dollars, with a portion of the sales occurring in Mexican cities near the United States border. BCC's FLANAX brand is well-known in Mexico and other Latin American countries, as well as to Mexican-Americans and other Hispanics in the United States.... BCC's sister company, BHC, sells naproxen sodium pain relievers under the brand ALEVE in the United States market.

Belmora LLC began selling naproxen sodium tablets in the United States as FLANAX in 2004. The following year, Belmora registered the FLANAX mark in the United States. Belmora's early FLANAX packaging ... closely mimicked BCC's Mexican FLANAX packaging..., displaying a similar color scheme, font size, and typeface.

Belmora later modified its packaging..., but the color scheme, font size, and typeface remain similar to that of BCC's FLANAX packaging.

In addition..., Belmora made statements implying that its FLANAX brand was the same FLANAX product sold by BCC in Mexico. For example, Belmora circulated a brochure to prospective distributors that stated,

> For generations, Flanax has been a brand that Latinos have turned to for various common ailments. Now you too can profit from this highly recognized topselling brand among Latinos. Flanax is now made in the U.S. and continues to show record sales growth everywhere it is sold. Flanax acts as a powerful attraction for Latinos by providing them with products they know, trust and prefer.

Belmora also employed telemarketers and provided them with a script [that] stated that Belmora was "the direct producer[] of FLANAX in the US" and that "FLANAX is a very well known medical product in the Latino American market, for FLANAX is sold successfully in Mexico." Belmora's "sell sheet," used to solicit orders from retailers, likewise claimed that "Flanax products have been used [for] many, many years in Mexico" and are "now being produced in the United States by Belmora LLC."

Bayer points to evidence that these and similar materials resulted in Belmora's distributors, vendors, and marketers believing that its FLANAX was the same as or affiliated with BCC's FLANAX. For instance, Belmora received questions regarding whether it was legal for FLANAX to have been imported from Mexico. And an investigation of stores selling Belmora's FLANAX "identified at least 30 [purchasers] who believed that the Flanax products ... were the same as, or affiliated with, the Flanax products they knew from Mexico."

....

... In 2007, BCC ... sought cancellation of Belmora's registration under § 14(3) of the Lanham Act because Belmora had used the FLANAX mark "to misrepresent the source of the goods ... [on] which the mark is used." ... [The] TTAB ordered cancellation..., concluding that Belmora had misrepresented the source of the FLANAX goods ...

Shortly after the TTAB's ruling, Bayer filed suit in the Southern District of California, alleging that 1) BCC was injured by Belmora's false association with its FLANAX product in violation of Lanham Act § 43(a)(1)(A), and 2) BCC and BHC were both injured by Belmora's false advertising of FLANAX under § 43(a)(1)(B)....

Belmora meanwhile appealed the TTAB's cancellation order ... as a civil action in the Eastern District of Virginia....

The California case was transferred to the Eastern District of Virginia and consolidated with Belmora's pending action. Belmora then moved the district court to dismiss Bayer's § 43(a) claims under Rule 12(b)(6) and for judgment on the pleadings under Rule 12(c) on the § 14(3) claim.... [T]he district court issued a memorandum opinion and order ruling in favor of Belmora across the board.

... [The district court] ... "distilled" the case "into one single question":

> Does the Lanham Act allow the owner of a foreign mark that is not registered in the United States and further has never used the mark in United States commerce to assert priority rights over a mark that is registered in the United States by another party and used in United States commerce?

The district court concluded that "[t]he answer is no" based on its reading of the Supreme Court's decision in *Lexmark International, Inc. v. Static Control Components, Inc.*, 134 S. Ct. 1377, 188 L. Ed. 2d 392 (2014).* Accordingly, the district court dismissed Bayer's false association and false advertising claims for lack of standing [and] ... reversed the TTAB's § 14(3) cancellation order.

....

A. False Association and False Advertising Under Section 43(a)

....

... [T]he plain language of § 43(a) does not require that a plaintiff possess or have used a trademark in U.S. commerce as an element of the cause of action. Section 43(a) stands in sharp contrast to Lanham Act § 32, which is titled as and expressly addresses "infringement." 15 U.S.C. § 1114 (requiring for liability the "use in commerce" of "any reproduction, counterfeit, copy, or colorable imitation of a *registered* mark" (emphasis added)). Under § 43(a), it is the defendant's use in commerce—whether of an offending "word, term, name, symbol, or device" or of a "false or misleading description [or representation] of fact"—that creates the injury under the terms of the statute. And here the alleged offending "word ..." is Belmora's FLANAX mark.

---

* *Editors Note:* The Supreme Court's opinion in *Lexmark v. Static Control Components* appears *infra* Chapter 10[D].

What § 43(a) does require is that Bayer was "likely to be damaged" by Belmora's "use[] in commerce" of its FLANAX mark and related advertisements. [I]n *Lexmark*, a false advertising case ... the Supreme Court, ... observed that the real question ... was "whether Static Control has a cause of action under the statute." *Id.* at 1387....

The Court concluded that § 43(a)'s broad authorization—permitting suit by "any person who believes that he or she is or is likely to be damaged"—should not be taken "literally" to reach the limits of Article III standing, but is framed by two "background principles," which may overlap. *Id.*

First, a plaintiff's claim must fall within the "zone of interests" protected by the statute. *Id.*... Because the Lanham Act contains an "unusual, and extraordinarily helpful" purpose statement in § 45, identifying the statute's zone of interests "requires no guesswork." *Id.* Section 45 provides:

> The intent ... is to regulate commerce within the control of Congress by making actionable the deceptive and misleading use of marks in such commerce; to protect registered marks used in such commerce from interference by State, or territorial legislation; to protect persons engaged in such commerce against unfair competition; to prevent fraud and deception in such commerce by the use of reproductions, copies, counterfeits, or colorable imitations of registered marks; and to provide rights and remedies stipulated by treaties and conventions respecting trademarks, trade names, and unfair competition entered into between the United States and foreign nations.

....

The second *Lexmark* background principle is that "a statutory cause of action is limited to plaintiffs whose injuries are proximately caused by violations of the statute." *Id.* The injury must have a "sufficiently close connection to the conduct the statute prohibits." *Id.* In the § 43(a) context, this means "show[ing] economic or reputational injury flowing directly from the deception wrought by the defendant's advertising; and that that occurs when deception of consumers causes them to withhold trade from the plaintiff." *Id.* at 1391.

....

... [T]his is an unfair competition case, not a trademark infringement case. Belmora and the district court conflated the Lanham Act's infringement provision in § 32 (which authorizes suit only "by the registrant," and thereby requires the plaintiff to have used its own mark in commerce) with unfair competition claims pled in this case under § 43(a). Section 32 makes clear that Congress knew how to write a precondition of trademark possession and use into a Lanham Act cause of action when it chose to do so. It has not done so in § 43(a). [Citation.]

... [W]e lack authority to introduce a requirement into § 43(a) that Congress plainly omitted. Nothing in *Lexmark* can be read to suggest that § 43(a) claims have an unstated requirement that the plaintiff have first used its own mark ... in U.S. commerce before a cause of action will lie against a defendant who is breaching the statute.

....

... As the Supreme Court has pointed out, § 43(a) "goes beyond trademark protection." *Dastar Corp.*, 539 U.S. [23] at 29 [(2003)]. For example, a plaintiff whose mark has become generic—and therefore not protectable—may plead an unfair competition claim against a competitor that uses that generic name and "fail[s] adequately to identify itself as distinct from the first organization" such that the name causes "confusion or a likelihood of confusion." *Blinded Veterans Ass'n v. Blinded Am. Veterans Found.*, 872 F.2d 1035, 1043, 277 U.S. App. D.C. 65 (D.C. Cir. 1989); *see also Kellogg Co. v. Nat'l Biscuit Co.*, 305 U.S. 111, 118–19, 59 S. Ct. 109, 83 L. Ed. 73, 1939 Dec. Comm'r Pat. 850 (1938) (requiring the defendant to "use reasonable care to inform the public of the source of its product" even though the plaintiff's "shredded wheat" mark was generic and therefore unprotectable); [citation].

....

[T]he proper *Lexmark* inquiry is twofold. Did the alleged acts of unfair competition fall within the Lanham Act's protected zone of interests? And if so, did Bayer plead proximate causation of a cognizable injury? We examine the false association and false advertising claims in turn.

As to the zone of interests, *Lexmark* advises that "[m]ost of the [Lanham Act's] enumerated purposes are relevant to false-association cases." 134 S. Ct. at 1389. One such enumerated purpose is "making actionable the deceptive and misleading use of marks" in "commerce within the control of Congress." Lanham Act; [citation]. As pled, BCC's false association claim advances that purpose.

The complaint alleges Belmora's misleading association with BCC's FLANAX has caused BCC customers to buy the Belmora FLANAX in the United States instead of purchasing BCC's FLANAX in Mexico. For example, the complaint alleges that BCC invested heavily in promoting its FLANAX to Mexican citizens or Mexican-Americans in border areas. Those consumers cross into the United States and may purchase Belmora FLANAX here before returning to Mexico. And Mexican-Americans may forego purchasing the FLANAX they know when they cross the border to visit Mexico because Belmora's alleged deception led them to purchase the Belmora product in the United States.

In either circumstance, BCC loses sales revenue because Belmora's deceptive and misleading use of FLANAX conveys to consumers a false association with BCC's product. Further, by also deceiving distributors and vendors, Belmora makes its FLANAX more available to consumers, which would exacerbate BCC's losses.

We thus conclude that BCC has adequately pled a § 43(a) false association claim for purposes of the zone of interests prong. Its allegations reflect the claim furthers the § 45 purpose of preventing "the deceptive and misleading use of marks" in "commerce within the control of Congress."

Turning to *Lexmark's* second prong, proximate cause, BCC has also alleged injuries that "are proximately caused by [Belmora's] violations of the [false association] statute." 134 S. Ct. at 1390. The complaint can fairly be read to allege "economic or reputational injury flowing directly from the deception wrought by the defendant's" conduct. *Id.* at 1391.... BCC alleges "substantial sales in major cities near the U.S.-Mexico border" and "millions of dollars promoting and advertising" its FLANAX brand in that region. Thus, BCC may plausibly have been damaged by Belmora's alleged deceptive use of the FLANAX mark in at least two ways.... FLANAX customers in Mexico near the border may be deceived into foregoing a FLANAX purchase in Mexico as they cross the border to shop and buy the Belmora product in the United States. Second, Belmora is alleged to have targeted Mexican-Americans in the United States who were already familiar with the FLANAX mark from their purchases from BCC in Mexico. We can reasonably infer that some subset of those customers would buy BCC's FLANAX upon their return travels to Mexico if not for the alleged deception by Belmora. Consequently, BCC meets the Lexmark pleading requirement as to proximate cause.

BCC may ultimately be unable to prove that Belmora's deception "cause[d] [these consumers] to withhold trade from [BCC]" in either circumstance, *Lexmark,* 134 S. Ct. at 1391, but at the initial pleading stage we must draw all reasonable factual inferences in BCC's favor. [Citation.] Having done so, we hold BCC has sufficiently pled a § 43(a) false association claim to survive Belmora's Rule 12(b)(6) motion. The district court erred in holding otherwise.

[The court then used similar reasoning to reverse both the district court's dismissal of the claims for false advertising under § 43(a) and its overturning the cancellation under § 14(3).]

Question

Would the result in *ITC Ltd v. Punchgini, supra* Chapter 3[C], involving use of the BUKHARA service mark outside the U.S., be any different under the reasoning of *Belmora v. Bayer*?

B. False Endorsement

Note: Rights of Publicity and Section 43(a)

Recognition of a person's right of publicity (sometimes framed as a privacy right) is exclusively a matter of state law, either through state statute(s) and/or under the common law. The right of publicity is the right to control the commercialization of aspects of a person's identity. Over 30 states have recognized such a right, J. Thomas McCarthy, 5 McCarthy on Trademarks § 28.11 (2016 ed.), although there is no uniformity in the aspects of identity protected, e.g. name, signature, likeness, voice, etc., or in the duration of such rights, ranging from a person's lifetime to a specified number of years after a person's death. *See generally* J. Thomas McCarthy, The Rights of Publicity and Privacy (2016 ed.). Likelihood of confusion is not necessary to finding a violation of a right to publicity. A person needs to show use of a protected aspect of his or her identity in connection with commercial advertising without the person's consent.

Although there is no federal right of publicity, many courts have recognized a claim of false endorsement under section 43(a) of the Lanham Act, involving use in commercial advertising of aspects of a celebrity's identity, such as name, likeness or voice, that is likely to cause deception or confusion as to the celebrity's endorsement or approval of the advertised goods or services. The 1988 amendments to section 43(a), added the language "is likely to cause confusion, or to cause mistake or to deceive ... as to the ... sponsorship, or *approval* of his or her goods, services, or commercial activities by another person" (emphasis added). This language explicitly covers confusion or deception as to approval or endorsement and appears to codify prior judicial interpretations of section 43(a).

Allen v. National Video, Inc.

610 F. Supp. 612 (S.D.N.Y. 1985)

MOTLEY, CHIEF DISTRICT JUDGE:

This case arises because plaintiff, to paraphrase Groucho Marx, wouldn't belong to any video club that would have him as a member. More precisely, plaintiff sues over an advertisement for defendant National Video (National) in which defendant Boroff, allegedly masquerading as plaintiff, portrays a satisfied holder of National's movie rental V.I.P. Card. Plaintiff asserts that the advertisement appropriates his face and implies his endorsement, and that it therefore violates his statutory right to privacy, his right to publicity, and the federal Lanham Act's prohibition of misleading advertising....

....

Facts

... Plaintiff Woody Allen is a film director, writer, actor, and comedian. Among the films plaintiff has directed are "Annie Hall," which won several Academy Awards, "Manhattan," "Bananas," "Sleeper," "Broadway Danny Rose," and, most recently, "The Purple Rose of Cairo." ... Although he has not often lent his name to commercial endeavors other than his own projects, plaintiff's many years in show business have made his name and his face familiar to millions of people. This familiarity, and plaintiff's reputation for artistic integrity, have significant, exploitable, commercial value.

The present action arises from an advertisement, placed by National to promote its nationally franchised video rental chain, containing a photograph of defendant Boroff.... The photograph portrays a customer in a National Video store, an individual in his forties, with a high forehead, tousled hair, and heavy black glasses.... It is not disputed that, in general, the physical features and pose are characteristic of plaintiff.

... Sitting on the counter are videotape cassettes of "Annie Hall" and "Bananas," two of plaintiff's best known films, as well as "Casablanca" and "The Maltese Falcon." The latter two are Humphrey Bogart films of the 1940's associated with plaintiff primarily because of his play and film "Play It Again, Sam," in which the spirit of Bogart appears to the character played by Allen and offers him romantic advice. In addition, the title "Play It Again, Sam" is a famous, although inaccurate, quotation from "Casablanca."

The individual in the advertisement is holding up a National Video V.I.P. Card, which apparently entitles the bearer to favorable terms on movie rentals. The woman behind the counter is smiling at the customer and appears to be gasping in exaggerated excitement at the presence of a celebrity.

The photograph was used in an advertisement which appeared in the March 1984 issue of "Video Review," a magazine published in New York and ... in the April 1984 issue of "Take One," an in-house publication which National distributes to its franchisees across the country. The headline on the advertisement reads "Become a V.I.P. at National Video. We'll Make You Feel Like a Star." The copy goes on to explain that holders of the V.I.P. card receive "hassle-free movie renting" and "special savings" and concludes that "you don't need a famous face to be treated to some pretty famous service."

The same photograph and headline were also used on countercards distributed to National's franchisees. Although the advertisement that ran in "Video Review" contained a disclaimer in small print reading "Celebrity double provided by Ron Smith's Celebrity Look-Alike's, Los Angeles, Calif.," no such disclaimer appeared in the other versions of the advertisement.

....

... Although defendants concede that they sought to evoke by reference plaintiff's general persona, they strenuously deny that they intended to imply that the person in the photograph was actually plaintiff or that plaintiff endorsed National....

According to defendants, the idea of the advertisement is that even people who are not stars are treated like stars at National Video. They insist that the advertisement depicts a "Woody Allen fan," so dedicated that he has adopted his idol's appearance and mannerisms, who is able to live out his fantasy by receiving star treatment at National Video. The knowing viewer is supposed to be amused that the counter person actually believes that the customer is Woody Allen.

Defendants urge ... that if defendant Boroff merely appeared as someone who looks like Woody Allen, but not as Woody Allen himself, then plaintiff's rights were not violated. Defendants further seek summary judgment against plaintiff on the basis that plaintiff has offered no actual evidence that anyone was actually deceived into thinking that the photograph was of him....

....

[The court declined to award Allen summary judgment on his New York privacy claim, on the ground that the N.Y. Civil Rights statute protects rights in the plaintiff's "portrait or picture" and that when a look-alike portrays a celebrity, a reasonable jury could find that the advertisement did not display Allen's likeness, but that of the look-alike.]

Lanham Act Claim

Plaintiff seeks summary judgment on his claim under section 43(a) of the federal Lanham Act, 15 U.S.C. section 1125(a) (West 1982) ("the Act"), which prohibits false descriptions of products or their origins....

The Act has ... been held to apply to situations that would not qualify formally as trademark infringement, but that involve unfair competitive practices resulting in actual or potential deception. To make out a cause of action under the Act, plaintiff must establish three elements: 1) involvement of goods or services, 2) effect on interstate commerce, and 3) a false designation of origin or false description of the goods or services.

Application of the act is limited, however, to potential deception which threatens economic interests analogous to those protected by trademark law. One such interest is that of the public to be free from harmful deception. Another interest, which provides plaintiff here with standing, is that of the "trademark" holder in the value of his distinctive mark....

A celebrity has a ... commercial investment in the "drawing power" of his or her name and face in endorsing products and in marketing a career. The celebrity's investment depends upon the good will of the public, and infringement of the celebrity's rights also implicates the public's interest in being free from deception when it relies on a public figure's endorsement in an advertisement. The underlying purposes of the Lanham Act therefore appear to be implicated in cases of misrepresentations regarding the endorsement of goods and services.

The Act's prohibitions, in fact, have been held to apply to misleading statements that a product or service has been endorsed by a public figure. In *Geisel v. Poynter*

Products, Inc., 283 F. Supp. 261 (S.D.N.Y. 1968), plaintiff, the well-known children's book author and artist known as "Dr. Seuss," sought to enjoin the use of his distinctive pseudonym in connection with dolls based on his characters. The court held that "a 'false representation,' whether express or implied, that a product was authorized or approved by a particular person is actionable under [the Act]." The court further held that liability attached not just for descriptions that are literally false, but for those that create a "false impression." *Geisel*, 283 F. Supp. at 267. "The plaintiff is not required to prove actual palming off. A showing of the likelihood of consumer confusion as to the source of the goods is sufficient." *Id.* (citation omitted)....

In *Cher v. Forum International, Ltd.*, 213 U.S.P.Q. 96 (C.D. Cal. 1982), plaintiff, a popular singer and actress ... sued when an interview she had granted to "US" magazine was sold to "Forum" magazine, a publication of Penthouse International. "Forum" published the interview and advertised it widely, falsely implying that plaintiff read and endorsed "Forum" and had granted the magazine an exclusive interview. *Id.* at 99–100. The court held that the Act "extends to misrepresentations in advertising as well as labeling of products and services in commerce," *id.* at 102, and noted that no finding of an actual trademark is required under the Act. *Id.* "The Lanham Act proscribes any false designation or representation in connection with any goods or services in interstate commerce," a standard which plaintiff Cher had met. *Id.*

Geisel and *Cher* suggest that the unauthorized use of a person's name or photograph in a manner that creates the false impression that the party has endorsed a product or service in interstate commerce violates the Lanham Act. Application of this standard to the case at bar, however, is complicated by defendants' use of a look-alike for plaintiff, rather than plaintiff's actual photograph, as in *Cher*, or pseudonym, as in *Geisel.* Unlike the state law privacy claim..., the plaintiff's Lanham Act theory does not require the court to find that defendant Boroff's photograph is, as a matter of law, plaintiff's "portrait or picture." The court must nevertheless decide whether defendant's advertisement creates the likelihood of consumer confusion over whether plaintiff endorsed or was otherwise involved with National Video's goods and services. *See Geisel*, 283 F. Supp. at 267.[8]

This inquiry requires the court to consider whether the look-alike employed is sufficiently similar to plaintiff to create such a likelihood—an inquiry much like that made in cases involving similar, but not identical, trademarks. The court therefore

8. The court rejects defendants' argument that the perception that plaintiff appeared in National's advertisement does not give rise to an inference that he endorses their product. It is disingenuous to suggest that consumers would assume no more than that plaintiff had been hired as an actor. When a public figure of Woody Allen's stature appears in an advertisement, his mere presence is inescapably to be interpreted as an endorsement. [Citations.] Moreover, defendant's pose in National's advertisement—smiling at the camera while holding up the V.I.P. card—is the classic stance of the product spokesperson.

finds it helpful, in applying the likelihood of confusion standard to the facts of this case, to refer to traditional trademark analysis....

The first factor..., the strength of plaintiff's mark, concerns the extent to which plaintiff has developed a favorable association for his mark in the public's mind. There is no dispute that plaintiff's name and likeness are well-known to the public, and that he has built up a considerable investment in his unique, positive public image. Plaintiff's "mark," to analogize from trademark law, is a strong one.

The similarity of the "marks"—i.e., the similarity of plaintiff to defendant Boroff... has already been addressed above. While the court was unable to hold that defendant Boroff's photograph was as a matter of law plaintiff's portrait or picture, the resemblance between the two is strong and not disputed.

Under the third factor, proximity of the products, the court notes that while plaintiff does not own a video rental chain, he is involved in producing and distributing his own motion pictures, and he is strongly identified with movies in the public mind. The audience at which National Video's advertisement was aimed—movie watchers—is therefore the same audience to which plaintiff's own commercial efforts are directed. There is no requirement under the Act that plaintiff and defendant actually be in competition.

The court has declined to rely on plaintiff's proffered consumer survey, and plaintiff has submitted no other evidence of actual confusion.... [S]uch evidence, although highly probative of likelihood of confusion, is not required.

The sophistication of the relevant consuming public is measured under the fifth factor. The average reader of "Video Review" or customer of National Video is likely to be comparatively sophisticated about movies, such that a good number of them arguably would realize that plaintiff did not actually appear in the photograph. This is relevant to the question of whether the advertisement contained plaintiff's "portrait or picture." However, given the close resemblance between defendant Boroff's photograph and plaintiff, there is no reason to believe that the audience's relative sophistication eliminates all likelihood of confusion; at a cursory glance, many consumers, even sophisticated ones, are likely to be confused.

The final factor is the good or bad faith of defendants. While plaintiff has not established that defendants acted intentionally to fool people into thinking that plaintiff actually appeared in the advertisement, defendants admit that they designed the advertisement intentionally to evoke an association with plaintiff. They must therefore at least have been aware of the risk of consumer confusion, which militates against a finding that their motives were completely innocent. The failure of defendant National to include any disclaimer on all but one of the uses of the photograph also supports a finding of, at best, dubious motives.

A review of all these factors leads the court to the inescapable conclusion that defendants' use of Boroff's photograph in their advertisement creates a likelihood of consumer confusion over plaintiff's endorsement or involvement. In reaching this conclusion, the court notes several distinctions between plaintiff's Lanham Act and privacy claims which make this case more appropriate for resolution under the Lanham Act.

... [T]he likelihood of confusion standard applied herein is broader than the strict "portrait or picture" standard under the Civil Rights Law. Evocation of plaintiff's general persona is not enough to make out a violation of section 51, but it may create a likelihood of confusion under the Lanham Act. As the Second Circuit held in the trademark context, "In order to be confused, a consumer need not believe that the owner of the mark actually produced the item and placed it on the market. The public's belief that the mark's owner sponsored or otherwise approved the use satisfies the confusion requirement." *Dallas Cowboys Cheerleaders, Inc. v. Pussycat Cinema, Ltd.*, 604 F.2d 200, 204–05 (2d Cir. 1979) [citations]. *See also Estate of Elvis Presley v. Russen*, 513 F. Supp. 1339, 1371 (D.N.J. 1981). Similarly, even if the public does not believe that plaintiff actually appeared in the photograph, it may be led to believe by the intentional reference to plaintiff that he is somehow involved in or approves of their product. This broader standard is justified since the Lanham Act seeks to protect not just plaintiff's property interest in his face, but the public's interest in avoiding deception.

Second, the likelihood of confusion standard is easier to satisfy on the facts of this case. Enough people may realize that the figure in the photograph is defendant Boroff to negate the conclusion that it amounts to a "portrait or picture" of plaintiff as a matter of law. All that is necessary to recover under the Act, however, is that a likelihood of confusion exists. While defendants, as noted above, have urged an interpretation of the advertisement which might defeat a finding of "portrait or picture," the court finds that no such explanation can remove the likelihood of confusion on the part of "any appreciable number of ordinarily prudent" consumers.

....

In seeking to forestall summary judgment, defendants Smith and Boroff maintain that the disclaimer which they insisted be included in the advertisement would have avoided consumer confusion. The court disagrees. Even with regard to the one version of the advertisement in which the requisite disclaimer was included, there exists a likelihood of consumer confusion. The disclaimer, in tiny print at the bottom of the page, is unlikely to be noticed by most readers as they are leafing through the magazine. Moreover, the disclaimer says only that a celebrity double is being used, which does not in and of itself necessarily dispel the impression that plaintiff is somehow involved with National's products or services. To be effective, a disclaimer would have to be bolder and make clear that plaintiff in no way endorses National, its products, or its services. Having gone to great lengths to evoke plaintiff's image, defendants must do more than pay lip service to avoiding confusion....

....

Defendants have argued that any injunction against them must be limited in geographical scope to New York State. While such a limitation might be required for an injunction under the New York Civil Rights Law, given the differences in privacy law among different jurisdictions, an injunction under the Lanham Act need not be so limited. Plaintiff enjoys a nationwide reputation, and defendants advertised a nationally franchised business through a national magazine. The harm sought to be prevented is clearly not limited to the New York area, and the injunction must therefore be national in scope.

Plaintiff seeks an injunction preventing defendants from presenting defendant Boroff as plaintiff in advertising. Defendant Boroff argues that any such injunction would interfere impermissibly with his ability to earn a living and his First Amendment rights....

What plaintiff legitimately seeks to prevent is not simply defendant Boroff dressing up as plaintiff, but defendant passing himself off as plaintiff or an authorized surrogate. Therefore, defendant must be enjoined from appearing in advertising that creates the likelihood that a reasonable person might believe that he was really plaintiff or that plaintiff had approved of his appearance. Defendant may satisfy the injunction by ceasing his work as a Woody Allen look-alike, but he may also satisfy it by simply refusing to collaborate with those advertisers, such as National Video in this case, who recklessly skirt the edges of misrepresentation. Defendant may sell his services as a look-alike in any setting where the overall context makes it completely clear that he is a look-alike and that plaintiff has nothing to do with the project—whether that is accomplished through a bold and unequivocal disclaimer, the staging of the photograph, or the accompanying advertising copy....

Editors' Note: Woody Allen's lawsuits against look-alike Boroff and Ron Smith Celebrity Look-Alike agency did not end with this case. In *Allen v. Men's World*, 679 F. Supp. 360 (S.D.N.Y. 1988), Allen prevailed against an advertising agency and its client regarding an advertisement for Men's World depicting an Allenesque Boroff, this time with a clarinet, an instrument that Allen is known to play in public. The court rejected defendants' contention that res judicata should bar the claim; an earlier contempt action against Smith and Boroff for the Men's World advertisement alleging violation of the National Video having failed on what the court deemed "technical" grounds. *Allen v. National Video, Inc.*, No. 84 Civ. 2764 (CBM) (S.D.N.Y. June 25, 1986).

Questions

1. Judge Motley found that Woody Allen was not entitled to summary judgment on his privacy claim because a reasonable jury could find that others would interpret the advertisement as portraying a Woody Allen lookalike rather than Woody Allen himself. She also found that Woody Allen was entitled to summary judgment on his Lanham Act claim because no reasonable jury could find that the ads do not falsely represent that Allen endorsed National Video. Are those two findings consistent?

2. *Allen v. National Video* illustrates successful invocation of the Lanham Act to control rights in likeness, where New York Civil Rights Law failed to secure relief. The court applied the *Polaroid* factors to assess confusion as to personal endorsements by analogy to a trademark infringement case. How apt is this analysis?

Tom Waits v. Frito-Lay, Inc.

978 F.2d 1093 (9th Cir. 1992)

Boochever, Circuit Judge:

....

Tom Waits is a professional singer, songwriter, and actor of some renown. Waits has a raspy, gravelly singing voice, described by one fan as "like how you'd sound if you drank a quart of bourbon, smoked a pack of cigarettes and swallowed a pack of razor blades.... Late at night. After not sleeping for three days." Since the early 1970s, ... Waits has recorded more than 17 albums and has toured extensively, playing to sold-out audiences throughout the United States, Canada, Europe, Japan and Australia.... In 1987, Waits received Rolling Stone magazine's Critic's Award for Best Live Performance, chosen over other noted performers such as Bruce Springsteen, U2, David Bowie, and Madonna. SPIN magazine listed him in its March 1990 issue as one of the ten most interesting recording artists of the last five years. Waits has appeared and performed on such television programs as "Saturday Night Live" and "Late Night with David Letterman," and has been the subject of numerous magazine and newspaper articles appearing in such publications as Time, Newsweek, and the Wall Street Journal. Tom Waits does not, however, do commercials. He has maintained this policy consistently ... rejecting numerous lucrative offers to endorse major products. Moreover, Waits' policy is a public one: in magazine, radio, and newspaper interviews he has expressed his philosophy that musical artists should not do commercials because it detracts from their artistic integrity.

Frito-Lay, Inc. is in the business of manufacturing, distributing, and selling prepared and packaged food products, including Doritos brand corn chips. Tracy-Locke, Inc. is an advertising agency which counts Frito-Lay among its clients. In developing an advertising campaign to introduce a new Frito-Lay product, SalsaRio Doritos, Tracy-Locke found inspiration in a 1976 Waits song, "Step Right Up." Ironically, this song is a jazzy parody of commercial hucksterism, and consists of a succession of humorous advertising pitches. The commercial the ad agency wrote echoed the rhyming word play of the Waits song....

The story of Tracy-Locke's search for a lead singer for the commercial suggests that nothing would do but a singer who could not only capture the feeling of "Step Right Up" but also imitate Tom Waits' voice....

Stephen Carter was among those who auditioned.... Over ten years of performing Waits songs as part of his band's repertoire, he had consciously perfected an imitation of Waits' voice. When Carter auditioned, members of the Tracy-Locke creative team "did a double take" over Carter's near-perfect imitation of Waits, and remarked to him how much he sounded like Waits. In fact, the commercial's musical director warned Carter that he probably wouldn't get the job because he sounded too much like Waits, which could pose legal problems. Carter, however, did get the job.

....

The commercial was broadcast in September and October 1988 on over 250 radio stations located in 61 markets nationwide.... Waits heard it during his appearance on a Los Angeles radio program, and was shocked. He realized "immediately that whoever was going to hear this and obviously identify the voice would also identify that [Tom Waits] in fact had agreed to do a commercial for Doritos."

In November 1988, Waits sued Tracy-Locke and Frito-Lay, alleging claims for voice misappropriation under California law and false endorsement under the Lanham Act. The case was tried before a jury in April and May 1990. The jury found in Waits' favor, awarding him $375,000 compensatory damages and $2 million punitive damages for voice misappropriation, and $100,000 damages for violation of the Lanham Act. The court awarded Waits attorneys' fees under the Lanham Act. This timely appeal followed.

DISCUSSION

....

II. *Lanham Act Claim*

Section 43(a) of the Lanham Act, 15 U.S.C. § 1125(a), prohibits the use of false designations of origin, false descriptions, and false representations in the advertising and sale of goods and services. *Smith v. Montoro*, 648 F.2d 602, 603 (9th Cir. 1981). Waits' claim under section 43(a) is premised on the theory that by using an imitation of his distinctive voice in an admitted parody of a Tom Waits song, the defendants misrepresented his association with and endorsement of SalsaRio Doritos.... On appeal, the defendants argue that Waits lacks standing to bring a Lanham Act claim, that Waits' false endorsement claim fails on its merits, that the damage award is duplicative, and that attorneys' fees are improper. Before we address these contentions, however, we turn to the threshold issue of whether false endorsement claims are properly cognizable under section 43(a) of the Lanham Act, a question of first impression in this circuit.

A. *False Endorsement*

At the time of the broadcast of the Doritos commercial, section 43(a) provided in pertinent part:

> Any person who shall affix, apply, or annex, or use in connection with any goods or services ... a false designation of origin, or any false designation or representation ... shall be liable to a civil action ... by any person who believes that he is or is likely to be damaged by the use of any such false designation or representation.

15 U.S.C. § 1125 note (Amendments) (1988). Courts in other jurisdictions have interpreted this language as authorizing claims for false endorsement. [Citations.] Moreover, courts have recognized false endorsement claims brought by plaintiffs, including celebrities, for the unauthorized imitation of their distinctive attributes, where those attributes amount to an unregistered commercial "trademark." *See Dallas Cowboys Cheerleaders, Inc. v. Pussycat Cinema, Ltd.*, 604 F.2d 200, 205 (2d Cir. 1979) (recognizing claim under § 43(a) because uniform worn by star of X-rated movie confusingly

similar to plaintiffs' trademark uniforms, falsely creating impression that plaintiffs "sponsored or otherwise approved the use" of the uniform); *Allen v. Men's World Outlet, Inc.*, 679 F. Supp. 360, 368 (S.D.N.Y. 1988) (celebrity states a claim under §43(a) by showing that advertisement featuring photograph of a look-alike falsely represented that advertised products were associated with him); *Allen v. National Video, Inc.*, 610 F. Supp. 612, 625–26 (S.D.N.Y. 1985) (recognizing celebrity's false endorsement claim under §43(a) because celebrity has commercial investment in name and face tantamount to interests of a trademark holder in distinctive mark); *see also Lahr v. Adell Chemical Co.*, 300 F.2d 256, 258 (1st Cir. 1962) (imitation of unique voice actionable as common law unfair competition); *cf. Sinatra v. Goodyear Tire & Rubber Co.*, 435 F.2d 711, 716 (9th Cir. 1970) (rejecting common law unfair competition claim because plaintiff's voice not sufficiently unique to be protectable), *cert. denied*, 402 U.S. 906 (1971).

The persuasiveness of this case law as to the cognizability of Waits' Lanham Act claim is reinforced by the 1988 Lanham Act amendments. See Trademark Law Revision Act of 1988, Pub. L. 100-667, §35, 102 Stat. 3946. The legislative history states that the amendments to section 43(a) codify previous judicial interpretation given this provision. S. Rep. No. 515, 100th Cong., 2d Sess., at 40, reprinted in 1988 U.S.C.C.A.N. 5577, 5603. Although these amendments did not take effect until November 1989, approximately a year after the broadcast of the defendants' Doritos commercial, as a codification of prior case law and in the absence of controlling precedent to the contrary, they properly inform our interpretation of the previous version of section 43(a). Specifically, we read the amended language to codify case law interpreting section 43(a) to encompass false endorsement claims. Section 43(a) now expressly prohibits, inter alia, the use of any symbol or device which is likely to deceive consumers as to the association, sponsorship, or approval of goods or services by another person. Moreover, the legislative history of the 1988 amendments also makes clear that in retaining the statute's original terms "symbol or device" in the definition of "trademark," Congress approved the broad judicial interpretation of these terms to include distinctive sounds and physical appearance. See S. Rep. No. 101-515 at 44, 1988 U.S.C.C.A.N. at 5607. In light of persuasive judicial authority and the subsequent congressional approval of that authority, we conclude that false endorsement claims, including those premised on the unauthorized imitation of an entertainer's distinctive voice, are cognizable under section 43(a).

....

C. *Merits*

The defendants next argue that Waits' false endorsement claim must fail on its merits because the Doritos commercial "did not represent that ... [Waits] sponsored or endorsed their product." We disagree. The court correctly instructed the jury that in considering Waits' Lanham Act claim, it must determine whether "ordinary consumers ... would be confused as to whether Tom Waits sang on the commercial ...

and whether he sponsors or endorses SalsaRio Doritos." The jury was told that in making this determination, it should consider the totality of the evidence, including the distinctiveness of Waits' voice and style, the evidence of actual confusion as to whether Waits actually sang on the commercial, and the defendants' intent to imitate Waits' voice. See generally, *Clamp Mfg. Co. v. Enco Mfg. Co.*, 870 F.2d 512, 517 (9th Cir.) (discussing factors to be considered in determining likelihood of confusion, including strength of mark, similarity of marks, evidence of actual confusion, marketing channels used, and intent in selecting marks), *cert. denied*, 493 U.S. 872 (1989).

At trial, the jury listened to numerous Tom Waits recordings, and to a recording of the Doritos commercial in which the Tom Waits impersonator delivered this "hip" endorsement of SalsaRio Doritos: "It's buffo, boffo, bravo, gung-ho, tally-ho, but never mellow ... try 'em, buy 'em, get 'em, got 'em." The jury also heard evidence, relevant to the likelihood of consumer confusion, that the Doritos commercial was targeted to an audience which overlapped with Waits' audience, males between the ages of 18 to 35 who listened to the radio. Finally, there was evidence of actual consumer confusion: the testimony of numerous witnesses that they actually believed it was Tom Waits singing the words of endorsement.

This evidence was sufficient to support the jury's finding that consumers were likely to be misled by the commercial into believing that Waits endorsed SalsaRio Doritos. [Citations.] The jury's verdict on Waits' Lanham Act claim must therefore stand.

....

Question

Rights of publicity cease in some states when a person dies and in others a specified number of years after a person's death. Is there any end to a false endorsement claim under section 43(a) after a celebrity dies? Consider the following ad that uses a quotation and name of deceased author William Faulkner.

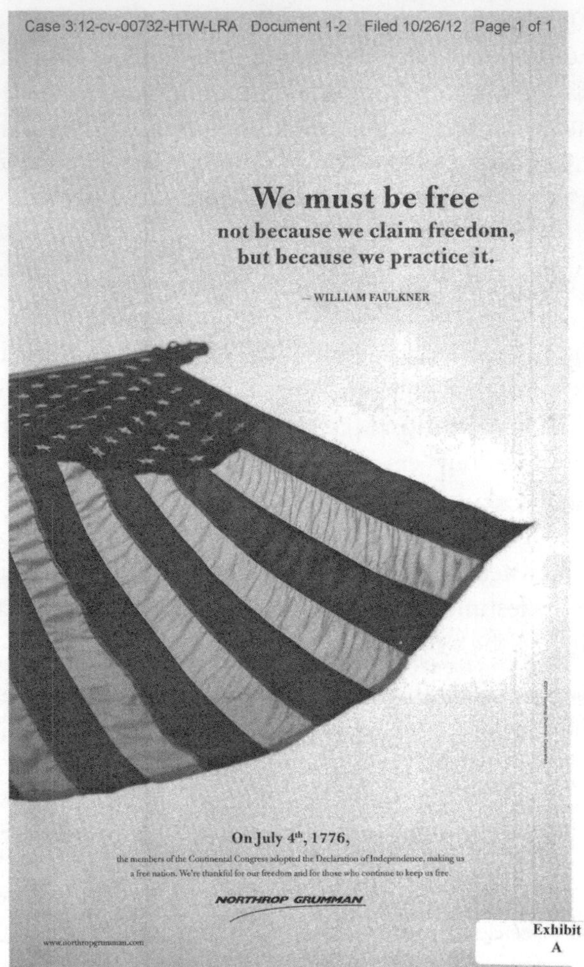

How should the court rule on the false endorsement claim by Faulkner's literary estate entity that also owns his publicity rights? *See* Complaint in *Faulkner Literary Rights, LLC v. Northrop Grumman Corp.*, 3:12 CV 732 HTW-LRA (S.D. Miss. Oct. 26, 2012).

White v. Samsung Electronics America, Inc.

971 F.2d 1395 (9th Cir.), *petition for rehearing and rehearing en banc denied*, 989 F.2d 1512 (9th Cir. 1992)

Goodwin, Circuit Judge:

....

Plaintiff Vanna White is the hostess of "Wheel of Fortune," one of the most popular game shows in television history. An estimated forty million people watch the program daily. Capitalizing on the fame which her participation in the show has bestowed on her, White markets her identity to various advertisers.

[A] series of advertisements prepared for Samsung by Deutsch ... ran in at least half a dozen publications with widespread, and in some cases national, circulation.... Each depicted a current item from popular culture and a Samsung electronic product. Each was set in the twenty-first century and conveyed the message that the Samsung product would still be in use by that time. By hypothesizing outrageous future outcomes for the cultural items, the ads created humorous effects....

The advertisement which prompted the current dispute was for Samsung videocassette recorders (VCRs). The ad depicted a robot, dressed in a wig, gown, and jewelry which Deutsch consciously selected to resemble White's hair and dress. The robot was posed next to a game board which is instantly recognizable as the Wheel of Fortune game show set, in a stance for which White is famous. The caption of the ad read: "Longest-running game show. 2012 A.D." Defendants referred to the ad as the "Vanna White" ad. Unlike the other celebrities used in the campaign, White neither consented to the ads nor was she paid.

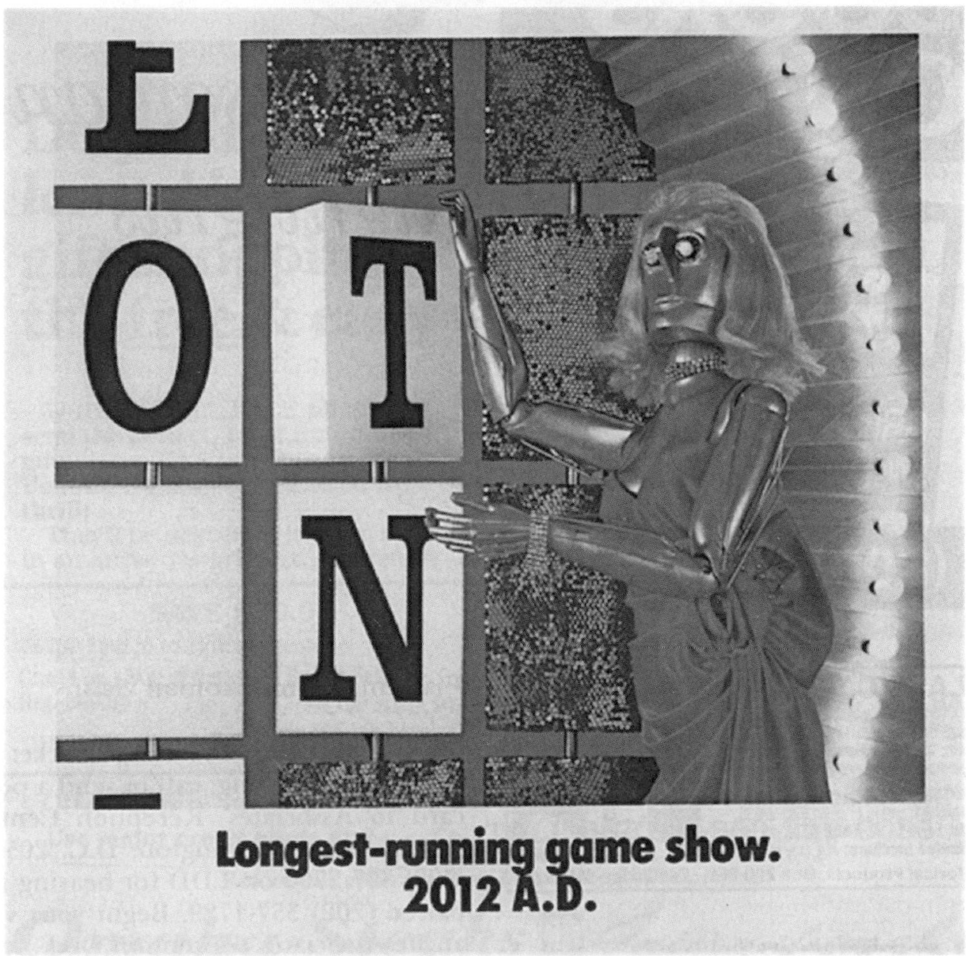

... White sued Samsung and Deutsch in federal district court under: (1) California Civil Code § 3344; (2) the California common law right of publicity; and (3) § 43(a) of the Lanham Act, 15 U.S.C. § 1125(a). The district court granted summary judgment against White on each of her claims. White now appeals.

....

... The female-shaped robot is wearing a long gown, blond wig, and large jewelry. Vanna White dresses exactly like this at times, but so do many other women. The robot is in the process of turning a block letter on a gameboard. Vanna White dresses like this while turning letters on a game-board but perhaps similarly attired Scrabble playing women do this as well. The robot is standing on what looks to be the Wheel of Fortune game show set. Vanna White dresses like this, turns letters, and does this on the Wheel of Fortune game show. She is the only one....

....

III. *The Lanham Act*

To prevail on her Lanham Act claim, White is required to show that ... running the robot ad..., created a likelihood of confusion, [citations], over whether White was endorsing Samsung's VCRs. [Citations].

... [W]e will look for guidance to the 8-factor test enunciated in *AMF, Inc. v. Sleekcraft Boats*, 599 F.2d 341 (9th Cir. 1979) ... [for] factors relevant to a likelihood of confusion....

In cases involving confusion over endorsement by a celebrity plaintiff, "mark" means the celebrity's persona. *See Allen v. National Video, Inc.*, 610 F. Supp. [612] at 627 [(S.D.N.Y. 1985)]. The "strength" of the mark refers to the level of recognition the celebrity enjoys among members of society. *See Academy [of Motion Picture Arts v. Creative House*,] 944 F.2d [1446] at 1455 [(9th Cir. 1991)]. If Vanna White is unknown to the segment of the public at whom Samsung's robot ad was directed, then that segment could not be confused as to whether she was endorsing Samsung VCRs. Conversely, if White is well-known, this would allow the possibility of a likelihood of confusion. For the purposes of the *Sleekcraft* test, White's "mark," or celebrity identity, is strong.

In cases concerning confusion over celebrity endorsement, the plaintiff's "goods" concern the reasons for or source of the plaintiff's fame. Because White's fame is based on her televised performances, her "goods" are closely related to Samsung's VCRs. Indeed, the ad itself reinforced the relationship by informing its readers that they would be taping the "longest-running game show" on Samsung's VCRs well into the future.

The third factor, "similarity of the marks," both supports and contradicts a finding of likelihood of confusion. On the one hand, all of the aspects of the robot ad identify White; on the other, the figure is quite clearly a robot, not a human. This ambiguity means that we must look to the other factors for resolution.

The fourth factor does not favor White's claim because she has presented no evidence of actual confusion.

Fifth, however, White has appeared in the same stance as the robot from the ad in numerous magazines, including the covers of some. Magazines were used as the marketing channels for the robot ad. This factor cuts toward a likelihood of confusion.

Sixth, consumers are not likely to be particularly careful in determining who endorses VCRs, making confusion as to their endorsement more likely.

Concerning the seventh factor, "defendant's intent,".... [t]hat defendants intended to spoof Vanna White and "Wheel of Fortune" ... does not preclude ... the possibility that defendants also intended to confuse consumers regarding endorsement.... Another ad in the series depicted Morton Downey Jr. as a presidential candidate in the year 2008. Doubtless, defendants intended to spoof presidential elections and Mr. Downey through this ad. Consumers, however, would likely believe, and would be correct in so believing, that Mr. Downey was paid for his permission and was endorsing Samsung products. Looking at the series of advertisements as a whole, a jury could reasonably conclude that beneath the surface humor of the series lay an intent to persuade consumers that celebrity Vanna White, like celebrity Downey, was endorsing Samsung products.

Finally, the eighth factor, "likelihood of expansion of the product lines," does not appear apposite to a celebrity endorsement case such as this.

Application of the *Sleekcraft* factors to this case indicates that the district court erred in rejecting White's Lanham Act claim at the summary judgment stage.... We hold only that White has raised a genuine issue of material fact concerning a likelihood of confusion as to her endorsement. [Citation.] Whether White's Lanham Act claim should succeed is a matter for the jury.... We note that the robot ad identifies White and was part of a series of ads in which other celebrities participated and were paid for their endorsement of Samsung's products.

....

On petition for rehearing and rehearing en banc:

....

The petition for rehearing is DENIED and the suggestion for rehearing en banc is REJECTED.

KOZINSKI, CIRCUIT JUDGE, with whom CIRCUIT JUDGES O'SCANNLAIN and KLEINFELD join, dissenting from the order rejecting the suggestion for rehearing en banc:

I

Saddam Hussein wants to keep advertisers from using his picture in unflattering contexts.[1] Clint Eastwood doesn't want tabloids to write about him.[2] Rudolf Valentino's

---

1. See Eben Shapiro, *Rising Caution on Using Celebrity Images*, N.Y. Times, Nov. 4, 1992, at D20 (Iraqi diplomat objects on right of publicity grounds to ad containing Hussein's picture and caption "History has shown what happens when one source controls all the information").

2. *Eastwood v. Superior Court*, 149 Cal. App. 3d 409, 198 Cal. Rptr. 342 (1983).

heirs want to control his film biography.[3] The Girl Scouts don't want their image soiled by association with certain activities.[4] George Lucas wants to keep Strategic Defense Initiative fans from calling it "Star Wars."[5] Pepsico doesn't want singers to use the word "Pepsi" in their songs.[6] Guy Lombardo wants an exclusive property right to ads that show big bands playing on New Year's Eve.[7] Uri Geller thinks he should be paid for ads showing psychics bending metal through telekinesis.[8] Paul Prudhomme, that household name, thinks the same about ads featuring corpulent bearded chefs.[9] And scads of copyright holders see purple when their creations are made fun of.[10]

Something very dangerous is going on here. Private property, including intellectual property, is essential to our way of life. It provides an incentive for investment and innovation; it stimulates the flourishing of our culture; it protects the moral entitlements of people to the fruits of their labors. But reducing too much to private property can be bad medicine. Private land, for instance, is far more useful if separated from other private land by public streets, roads and highways. Public parks, utility rights-of-way and sewers reduce the amount of land in private hands, but vastly enhance the value of the property that remains.

So too it is with intellectual property. Overprotecting intellectual property is as harmful as underprotecting it. Creativity is impossible without a rich public domain. Nothing today, likely nothing since we tamed fire, is genuinely new: Culture, like science and technology, grows by accretion, each new creator building on the works of those who came before. Overprotection stifles the very creative forces it's supposed to nurture.

The panel's opinion is a classic case of overprotection. Concerned about what it sees as a wrong done to Vanna White, the panel majority erects a property right of remarkable and dangerous breadth: Under the majority's opinion, it's now a tort for advertisers to *remind* the public of a celebrity. Not to use a celebrity's name, voice,

---

3. *Guglielmi v. Spelling-Goldberg Prods.*, 25 Cal. 3d 860, 160 Cal. Rptr. 352, 603 P.2d 454 (1979) (Rudolph Valentino); [citations].

4. *Girl Scouts v. Personality Posters Mfg.*, 304 F. Supp. 1228 (S.D.N.Y. 1969) (poster of a pregnant girl in a Girl Scout uniform with the caption "Be Prepared").

5. *Lucasfilm Ltd. v. High Frontier*, 622 F. Supp. 931 (D.D.C. 1985).

6. Pepsico Inc. claimed the lyrics and packaging of grunge rocker Tad Doyle's "Jack Pepsi" song were "offensive to [it] and [are] likely to offend [its] customers," in part because they "associate [Pepsico] and its Pepsi marks with intoxication and drunk driving." Russell, *Doyle Leaves Pepsi Thirsty for Compensation*, Billboard, June 15, 1991, at 43....

7. *Lombardo v. Doyle, Dane & Bernbach, Inc.*, 58 A.D.2d 620, 396 N.Y.S.2d 661 (1977).

8. *Geller v. Fallon McElligott*, No. 90-Civ-2839 (S.D.N.Y. July 22, 1991) (involving a Timex ad).

9. *Prudhomme v. Procter & Gamble Co.*, 800 F. Supp. 390 (E.D. La. 1992).

10. *E.g.*, *Acuff-Rose Music, Inc. v. Campbell*, 972 F.2d 1429 (6th Cir. 1992); *Cliffs Notes v. Bantam Doubleday Dell Publishing Group, Inc.*, 886 F.2d 490 (2d Cir. 1989); *Fisher v. Dees*, 794 F.2d 432 (9th Cir. 1986); *MCA, Inc. v. Wilson*, 677 F.2d 180 (2d Cir. 1981); *Elsmere Music, Inc. v. NBC*, 623 F.2d 252 (2d Cir. 1980); *Walt Disney Prods. v. The Air Pirates*, 581 F.2d 751 (9th Cir. 1978); *Berlin v. E.C. Publications, Inc.*, 329 F.2d 541 (2d Cir. 1964); *Lowenfels v. Nathan*, 2 F. Supp. 73 (S.D.N.Y. 1932).

signature or likeness; not to imply the celebrity endorses a product; but simply to evoke the celebrity's image in the public's mind. This Orwellian notion withdraws far more from the public domain than prudence and common sense allow. It conflicts with the Copyright Act and the Copyright Clause. It raises serious First Amendment problems. It's bad law, and it deserves a long, hard second look.

....

Consider how sweeping this new right is. What is it about the ad that makes people think of White? It's not the robot's wig, clothes or jewelry; there must be ten million blond women (many of them quasi-famous) who wear dresses and jewelry like White's. It's that the robot is posed near the "Wheel of Fortune" game board. Remove the game board from the ad, and no one would think of Vanna White. *See* Appendix. But once you include the game board, anybody standing beside it—a brunette woman, a man wearing women's clothes, a monkey in a wig and gown—would evoke White's image, precisely the way the robot did. It's the "Wheel of Fortune" set, not the robot's face or dress or jewelry that evokes White's image. The panel is giving White an exclusive right not in what she looks like or who she is, but in what she does for a living.

....

Questions

1. Judge Kozinski's dissent does not directly address the panel majority's decision concerning White's section 43(a) claim. In a footnote, he acknowledges that the Lanham Act covers false endorsement claims. Is a right of publicity claim more "dangerous" than a Lanham Act claim? Why would this be?

2. Does it make sense to say that Vanna White owns a trademark-like right in her letter-turning "persona"? Did she create the persona? If, as Judge Kozinski suggests, there is no persona without juxtaposition to the wheel, shouldn't the Wheel of Fortune producers enjoy the good-will built-up in the persona, including any trademark-like rights?

3. Like the courts in *Allen* and *Waits*, the majority in *White* analogized White's "persona" to a trademark and then applied the *Sleekcraft* factors. How useful are factors, such as the relatedness of the goods or similar trade channels, to a false endorsement claim? What if the product were ice cream sold to restaurants and hotels? Should it make a difference to the analysis of likely public deception?

4. The *Allen, Waits* and *White* cases all involve use of aspects of the celebrity's identities in commercial advertising. Should a false endorsement claim succeed where an aspect of identity is used in an artistic work? Consider the following lithograph of sports artist Rick Rush that commemorates golfer Tiger Woods' historic victory at the 1997 Masters Tournament in Augusta, Georgia:

Does use of Woods' likeness falsely suggest that he endorses the work? *See ETW Corp. v. Jireh Publishing, Inc.*, 332 F.3d 915 (6th Cir. 2003) and cases in Chapter 8[C], *infra.*

C. False Designation of Origin

America Online v. LCGM, Inc.

46 F. Supp. 2d 444 (E.D. Va. 1998)

Lee, J.

....

AOL, an Internet service provider located in the Eastern District of Virginia, provides a proprietary, content-based online service that provides its members (AOL members) access to the Internet and the capability to receive as well as send e-mail messages. AOL registered "AOL" as a trademark and service mark in 1996 and has registered its domain name "aol.com" with the InterNIC. At the time this cause of action arose, defendant LCGM, Inc. was a Michigan corporation which operated and transacted business from Internet domains offering pornographic web sites. Plaintiff alleges that defendant ... operates Internet domains offering pornographic web sites....

AOL alleges that defendants, in concert, sent unauthorized and unsolicited bulk e-mail advertisements ("spam") to AOL customers. AOL's Unsolicited Bulk E-mail Policy and its Terms of Service bar both members and nonmembers from sending bulk email through AOL's computer systems. Plaintiff estimates that defendants, in concert with their "site partners," transmitted more than 92 million unsolicited and bulk e-mail messages advertising their pornographic Web sites to AOL members from approximately June 17, 1997 to January 21, 1998....

Plaintiff alleges that defendants harvested, or collected, the email addresses of AOL members in violation of AOL's Terms of Service. Defendants have admitted to maintaining AOL memberships to harvest or collect the e-mail addresses of other AOL members....

Plaintiff alleges that defendants forged the domain information "aol.com" in the "from" line of e-mail messages sent to AOL members. Defendants have admitted to creating the domain information "aol.com" through an e-mail sending program, and to causing the AOL domain to appear in electronic header information of its commercial e-mails.... Plaintiffs assert that as a result, many AOL members expressed confusion about whether AOL endorsed defendants' pornographic Web sites or their bulk emailing practices. Plaintiff also asserts that defendants e-mail messages were sent through AOL's computer networks. Defendants have admitted to sending e-mail messages from their computers through defendants' network via e-mail software to AOL, which then relayed the messages to AOL members....

....

Plaintiff alleges that defendants' actions injured AOL by consuming capacity on AOL's computers, causing AOL to incur technical costs, impairing the functioning of AOL's e-mail system, forcing AOL to upgrade its computer networks to process authorized e-mails in a timely manner, damaging AOL's goodwill with its members, and causing AOL to lose customers and revenue. Plaintiff asserts that between the months of December 1997 and April 1998, defendants' unsolicited bulk e-mails generated more than 450,000 complaints by AOL members.

Count I: False Designation of Origin Under the Lanham Act

The undisputed facts establish that defendants violated 15 U.S.C. § 1125(a)(1) of the Lanham Act....

... The elements necessary to establish a false designation violation under the Lanham Act are as follows: (1) a defendant uses a designation; (2) in interstate commerce; (3) in connection with goods and services; (4) which designation is likely to cause confusion, mistake or deception as to origin, sponsorship, or approval of defendant's goods or services; and (5) plaintiff has been or is likely to be damaged by these acts....

Each of the false designation elements has been satisfied. First, defendants clearly used the "aol.com" designation, incorporating the registered trademark and service mark AOL in their email headers. Second, defendants' activities involved interstate commerce because all e-mails sent to AOL members were routed from defendants' computers in Michigan through AOL's computers in Virginia. Third, the use of AOL's designation was in connection with goods and services as defendants' e-mails advertised their commercial web sites. Fourth, the use of "aol.com" in defendants' e-mails was likely to cause confusion as to the origin and sponsorship of defendants' goods and services. Any e-mail recipient could logically conclude that a message containing the initials "aol.com" in the header would originate from AOL's registered Internet domain, which incorporates the registered mark "AOL." *AOL v. IMS*, 24 F. Supp. 2d 548 [(E.D. Va. 1998)]. The recipient of such a message would be led to conclude the sender was an AOL member or AOL, the Internet Service Provider. Indeed, plaintiff alleges that this designation did cause such confusion among many AOL members, who believed that AOL sponsored and authorized defendants' bulk e-mailing practices and pornographic web sites. Finally, plaintiff asserts that these acts damaged AOL's technical capabilities and its goodwill. The defendants are precluded from opposing these claims due to their failure to comply with discovery orders. Therefore, there is no genuine issue of material fact in regards to this Count, and the Court holds the plaintiff is entitled to summary judgment on Count I.

....

Questions

What is the nature of the likely confusion experienced by recipients of LCGM's unsolicited electronic mail? Are they likely to believe that AOL sent the spam, or that one of AOL's subscribers sent the spam? In what sense is a forged email return address a false designation of origin?

Note: Authors' and Performers' Moral Rights

The United States was late to join the Berne Convention, an international copyright treaty. One area of contention was the lack of protection of authors' moral rights afforded under the U.S. Copyright law. Article 6bis of the Convention provides:

> Even after transfer of [economic rights], the author shall have the right to claim authorship of the work and to object to any distortion, mutilation, or other modification of, or other derogatory action in relation to said work, which shall be prejudicial to his honor or reputation.

When the U.S. finally joined Berne in 1988, one of the justifications for compliance with *6bis* rights of integrity and attribution was the existence of state unfair competition laws, right of publicity laws and interpretations of section 43(a) of the Lanham Act that extended to integrity or attribution situations. Clint Carpenter, *Stepmother, May I?: Moral Rights, Dastar and the False Advertising Prong of Lanham Act Section 43(a)*, 63 Wash. & Lee L. Rev. 1601 (Fall 2006).

The Second Circuit in *Gilliam v. ABC, Inc.*, 538 F.2d 14 (2d Cir. 1976), implicitly recognized an integrity right under section 43(a). A group of British writers known as "Monty Python" wrote scripts for a television program entitled "Monty Python's Flying Circus." The BBC, with which the writers had a contract, licensed Time-Life Films to distribute the series in the U.S. and permitted editing for commercials, applicable censorship or governmental regulations, although there was no such clause in the agreement between the writers and the BBC. ABC agreed to broadcast two ninety-minute specials, each with three 30-minute programs. ABC deleted 24 minutes to fit in commercials or because ABC found certain material offensive. The Monty Python authors contended that the attribution of the truncated work to plaintiffs was false and misleading and harmful to their reputation. The Second Circuit reversed a denial of a preliminary injunction.

The Ninth Circuit in *Smith v. Montoro*, 648 F.2d 602 (9th Cir. 1981), interpreted section 43(a) to cover a right to prevent misattribution. An actor sued over the deletion of his name and the substitution of another actor's name in a movie's credits and advertising. The court found this to be a form of reverse passing off.

The U.S. relied in part on interpretations of section 43(a) like these as a basis for its contention that U.S. law sufficiently complied with the Berne integrity and attribution requirements. H.R. REP. NO. 100-609, at 34 (1988). As you read the next case, consider whether this basis still exists.

Dastar Corporation v. Twentieth Century Fox Film Corp.

539 U.S. 23 (2003)

JUSTICE SCALIA delivered the opinion of the Court.

In this case, we are asked to decide whether § 43(a) of the Lanham Act, 15 U.S.C. § 1125(a), prevents the unaccredited copying of a work ...

I

In 1948, three and a half years after the German surrender at Reims, General Dwight D. Eisenhower completed Crusade in Europe, his written account of the allied campaign in Europe during World War II. Doubleday published the book, registered it with the Copyright Office in 1948, and granted exclusive television rights to an affiliate of respondent Twentieth Century Fox Film Corporation (Fox). Fox, in turn, arranged for Time, Inc., to produce a television series, also called Crusade in Europe, based on the book, and Time assigned its copyright in the series to Fox. The television series, consisting of 26 episodes, was first broadcast in 1949. It combined a soundtrack based on a narration of the book with film footage from the United States Army, Navy, and Coast Guard, the British Ministry of Information and War Office, the National Film Board of Canada, and unidentified "Newsreel Pool Cameramen." In 1975, Doubleday renewed the copyright on the book.... Fox, however, did not renew the copyright on the Crusade television series, which expired in 1977, leaving the television series in the public domain.

In 1988, Fox reacquired the television rights in General Eisenhower's book, including the exclusive right to distribute the Crusade television series on video and to sub-license others to do so. Respondents SFM Entertainment and New Line Home Video, Inc., in turn, acquired from Fox the exclusive rights to distribute Crusade on video. SFM obtained the negatives of the original television series, restored them, and repackaged the series on videotape; New Line distributed the videotapes.

Enter petitioner Dastar. In 1995, Dastar decided to expand its product line from music compact discs to videos. Anticipating renewed interest in World War II on the 50th anniversary of the war's end, Dastar released a video set entitled World War II Campaigns in Europe. To make Campaigns, Dastar purchased eight beta cam tapes of the original version of the Crusade television series, which is in the public domain, copied them, and then edited the series. Dastar's Campaigns series is slightly more than half as long as the original Crusade television series. Dastar substituted a new opening sequence, credit page, and final closing for those of the Crusade television series; inserted new chapter-title sequences and narrated chapter introductions; moved the "recap" in the Crusade television series to the beginning and retitled it as a "preview"; and removed references to and images of the book. Dastar created new packaging for its Campaigns series and (as already noted) a new title.

Dastar manufactured and sold the Campaigns video set as its own product. The advertising states: "Produced and Distributed by: Entertainment Distributing" (which is owned by Dastar), and makes no reference to the Crusade television series. Similarly, the screen credits state "DASTAR CORP presents" and "an ENTERTAINMENT DISTRIBUTING Production," and list as executive producer, producer, and associate producer, employees of Dastar. The Campaigns videos themselves also make no reference to the Crusade television series, New Line's Crusade videotapes, or the book. Dastar sells its Campaigns videos to Sam's Club, Costco, Best Buy, and other retailers and mail-order companies for $25 per set, substantially less than New Line's video set.

In 1998, respondents Fox, SFM, and New Line brought this action alleging that Dastar's sale of its Campaigns video set infringes Doubleday's copyright in General Eisenhower's book and, thus, their exclusive television rights in the book. Respondents later amended their complaint to add claims that Dastar's sale of Campaigns "without proper credit" to the Crusade television series constitutes "reverse passing off"[1] in violation of §43(a) of the Lanham Act, 15 U.S.C. §1125(a)....

The Court of Appeals for the Ninth Circuit affirmed the judgment for respondents on the Lanham Act claim, but reversed as to the copyright claim and remanded. With respect to the Lanham Act claim, the Court of Appeals reasoned that "Dastar copied substantially the entire Crusade in Europe series created by Twentieth Century Fox, labeled the resulting product with a different name and marketed it without attribution to Fox[, and] therefore committed a 'bodily appropriation' of Fox's series." *Id.*, at 314. It concluded that "Dastar's 'bodily appropriation' of Fox's original [television] series is sufficient to establish the reverse passing off."

---

1. Passing off (or palming off, as it is sometimes called) occurs when a producer misrepresents his own goods or services as someone else's. *See, e.g., O. & W. Thum Co. v. Dickinson*, 245 F. 609, 621 (CA6 1917). "Reverse passing off," as its name implies, is the opposite: The producer misrepresents someone else's goods or services as his own. *See, e.g., Williams v. Curtiss-Wright Corp.*, 691 F.2d 168, 172 (CA3 1982).

II

The Lanham Act was intended to make "actionable the deceptive and misleading use of marks," and "to protect persons engaged in ... commerce against unfair competition." 15 U.S.C. § 1127. While much of the Lanham Act addresses the registration, use, and infringement of trademarks and related marks, § 43(a), 15 U.S.C. § 1125(a) is one of the few provisions that goes beyond trademark protection. As originally enacted, § 43(a) created a federal remedy against a person who used in commerce either "a false designation of origin, or any false description or representation" in connection with "any goods or services." 60 Stat. 441. As the Second Circuit accurately observed with regard to the original enactment, however—and as remains true after the 1988 revision—§ 43(a) "does not have boundless application as a remedy for unfair trade practices," *Alfred Dunhill, Ltd. v. Interstate Cigar Co.*, 499 F.2d 232, 237 (1974). "Because of its inherently limited wording, § 43(a) can never be a federal 'codification' of the overall law of 'unfair competition,'" 4 J. McCarthy Trademarks and Unfair Competition § 27:7, p. 27-14 (4th ed. 2002) (McCarthy), but can apply only to certain unfair trade practices prohibited by its text.

Although a case can be made that a proper reading of § 43(a), as originally enacted, would treat the word "origin" as referring only "to the geographic location in which the goods originated," *Two Pesos, Inc. v. Taco Cabana, Inc.*, 505 U.S. 763, 777 (1992) (Stevens, J., concurring in judgment), the Courts of Appeals considering the issue, beginning with the Sixth Circuit, unanimously concluded that it "does not merely refer to geographical origin, but also to origin of source or manufacture," *Federal-Mogul-Bower Bearings, Inc. v. Azoff*, 313 F.2d 405, 408 (1963), thereby creating a federal cause of action for traditional trademark infringement of unregistered marks. *See* 4 McCarthy § 27:14; *Two Pesos, supra*, at 768. Moreover, every Circuit to consider the issue found § 43(a) broad enough to encompass reverse passing off. [Citations.] The Trademark Law Revision Act of 1988 made clear that § 43(a) covers origin of production as well as geographic origin. Its language is amply inclusive, moreover, of reverse passing off—if indeed it does not implicitly adopt the unanimous court-of-appeals jurisprudence on that subject. [Citations.]

Thus, as it comes to us, the gravamen of respondents' claim is that, in marketing and selling Campaigns as its own product without acknowledging its nearly wholesale reliance on the Crusade television series, Dastar has made a "false designation of origin, false or misleading description of fact, or false or misleading representation of fact, which ... is likely to cause confusion ... as to the origin ... of his or her goods." That claim would undoubtedly be sustained if Dastar had bought some of New Line's Crusade videotapes and merely repackaged them as its own. Dastar's alleged wrongdoing, however, is vastly different: it took a creative work in the public domain—the Crusade television series—copied it, made modifications (arguably minor), and produced its very own series of videotapes. If "origin" refers only to the manufacturer or producer of the physical "goods" that are made available to the public (in this case the videotapes), Dastar was the origin. If, however, "origin" includes the creator of the underlying work that Dastar copied, then someone else (perhaps Fox) was the origin of Dastar's product. At bottom, we must decide what § 43(a)(1)(A) of the Lanham Act means by the "origin" of "goods."

III

The dictionary definition of "origin" is "the fact or process of coming into being from a source," and "that from which anything primarily proceeds; source." Webster's New International Dictionary 1720–1721 (2d ed. 1949). And the dictionary definition of "goods" (as relevant here) is "[w]ares; merchandise." *Id.*, at 1079. We think the most natural understanding of the "origin" of "goods"—the source of wares—is the producer of the tangible product sold in the marketplace, in this case the physical Campaigns videotape sold by Dastar. The concept might be stretched (as it was under the original version of § 43(a)) to include not only the actual producer, but also the trademark owner who commissioned or assumed responsibility for ("stood behind") production of the physical product. But as used in the Lanham Act, the phrase "origin of goods" is in our view incapable of connoting the person or entity that originated the ideas or communications that "goods" embody or contain. Such an extension would not only stretch the text, but it would be out of accord with the history and purpose of the Lanham Act and inconsistent with precedent.

Section 43(a) of the Lanham Act prohibits actions like trademark infringement that deceive consumers and impair a producer's goodwill. It forbids, for example, the Coca-Cola Company's passing off its product as Pepsi-Cola or reverse passing off Pepsi-Cola as its product. But the brand loyal consumer who prefers the drink that the Coca-Cola Company or PepsiCo sells, while he believes that that company produced (or at least stands behind the production of) that product, surely does not necessarily believe that that company was the "origin" of the drink in the sense that it was the very first to devise the formula. The consumer who buys a branded product does not automatically assume that the brand-name company is the same entity that came up with the idea for the product, or designed the product—and typically does not care whether it is. The words of the Lanham Act should not be stretched to cover matters that are typically of no consequence to purchasers.

It could be argued, perhaps, that the reality of purchaser concern is different for what might be called a communicative product—one that is valued not primarily for its physical qualities, such as a hammer, but for the intellectual content that it conveys, such as a book or, as here, a video. The purchaser of a novel is interested not merely, if at all, in the identity of the producer of the physical tome (the publisher), but also, and indeed primarily, in the identity of the creator of the story it conveys (the author). And the author, of course, has at least as much interest in avoiding passing-off (or reverse passing-off) of his creation as does the publisher. For such a communicative product (the argument goes) "origin of goods" in § 43(a) must be deemed to include not merely the producer of the physical item (the publishing house Farrar, Straus and Giroux, or the video producer Dastar) but also the creator of the content that the physical item conveys (the author Tom Wolfe, or—assertedly—respondents).

The problem with this argument according special treatment to communicative products is that it causes the Lanham Act to conflict with the law of copyright, which addresses that subject specifically. The right to copy, and to copy without attribution, once a copyright has expired, like "the right to make [an article whose patent has expired]—including the right to make it in precisely the shape it carried when patented—passes to the public." *Sears, Roebuck & Co. v. Stiffel Co.*, 376 U.S. 225, 230 (1964); *see also Kellogg Co. v. National Biscuit Co.*, 305 U.S. 111, 121–122 (1938). "In general, unless an intellectual property right such as a patent or copyright protects an item, it will be subject to copying." *TrafFix Devices, Inc. v. Marketing Displays, Inc.*, 532 U.S. 23, 29 (2001). The rights of a patentee or copyright holder are part of a "carefully crafted bargain," *Bonito Boats, Inc. v. Thunder Craft Boats, Inc.*, 489 U.S. 141, 150–151 (1989), under which, once the patent or copyright monopoly has expired, the public may use the invention or work at will and without attribution. Thus, in construing the Lanham Act, we have been "careful to caution against misuse or over-extension" of trademark and related protections into areas traditionally occupied by patent or copyright. *TrafFix*, 532 U.S., at 29. "The Lanham Act," we have said, "does not exist to reward manufacturers for their innovation in creating a particular device; that is the purpose of the patent law and its period of exclusivity." *Id.*, at 34. Federal trademark law "has no necessary relation to invention or discovery," *Trade-Mark Cases*, 100 U.S. 82, 94 (1879), but rather, by preventing competitors from copying "a source-identifying mark," "reduces the customer's costs of shopping and making purchasing decisions," and "helps assure a producer that it (and not an imitating competitor) will reap the financial, reputation-related rewards associated with a desirable product," *Qualitex Co. v. Jacobson Products Co.*, 514 U.S. 159, 163–164 (1995) (internal quotation marks and citation omitted). Assuming for the sake of argument that Dastar's representation of itself as the "Producer" of its videos amounted to a representation that it originated the creative work conveyed by the videos, allowing a cause of action under § 43(a) for that representation would create a species of mutant copyright law that limits the public's "federal right to 'copy and to use,'" expired copyrights, *Bonito Boats, supra*, at 165.

When Congress has wished to create such an addition to the law of copyright, it has done so with much more specificity than the Lanham Act's ambiguous use of "origin." The Visual Artists Rights Act of 1990, § 603(a), 104 Stat. 5128, provides that the author of an artistic work "shall have the right ... to claim authorship of that work." 17 U.S.C. § 106A(a)(1)(A). That express right of attribution is carefully limited and focused: It attaches only to specified "work[s] of visual art," § 101, is personal to the artist, §§ 106A(b) and (e), and endures only for "the life of the author," at § 106A(d)(1). Recognizing in § 43(a) a cause of action for misrepresentation of authorship of noncopyrighted works (visual or otherwise) would render these limitations superfluous. A statutory interpretation that renders another statute superfluous is of course to be avoided....

Reading "origin" in § 43(a) to require attribution of uncopyrighted materials would pose serious practical problems. Without a copyrighted work as the base point, the word "origin" has no discernable limits. A video of the MGM film Carmen Jones, after its copyright has expired, would presumably require attribution not just to MGM, but to Oscar Hammerstein II (who wrote the musical on which the film was based), to Georges Bizet (who wrote the opera on which the musical was based), and to Prosper Merimee (who wrote the novel on which the opera was based). In many cases, figuring out who is in the line of "origin" would be no simple task. Indeed, in the present case it is far from clear that respondents have that status. Neither SFM nor New Line had anything to do with the production of the Crusade television series—they merely were licensed to distribute the video version. While Fox might have a claim to being in the line of origin, its involvement with the creation of the television series was limited at best. Time, Inc., was the principal if not the exclusive creator, albeit under arrangement with Fox. And of course it was neither Fox nor Time, Inc., that shot the film used in the Crusade television series. Rather, that footage came from the United States Army, Navy, and Coast Guard, the British Ministry of Information and War Office, the National Film Board of Canada, and unidentified "Newsreel Pool Cameramen." If anyone has a claim to being the original creator of the material used in both the Crusade television series and the Campaigns videotapes, it would be those groups, rather than Fox. We do not think the Lanham Act requires this search for the source of the Nile and all its tributaries.

Another practical difficulty of adopting a special definition of "origin" for communicative products is that it places the manufacturers of those products in a difficult position. On the one hand, they would face Lanham Act liability for failing to credit the creator of a work on which their lawful copies are based; and on the other hand they could face Lanham Act liability for crediting the creator if that should be regarded as implying the creator's "sponsorship or approval" of the copy, 15 U.S.C. § 1125(a)(1)(A). In this case, for example, if Dastar had simply "copied [the television series] as Crusade in Europe and sold it as Crusade in Europe," without changing the title or packaging (including the original credits to Fox), it is hard to have confidence in respondents' assurance that they "would not be here on a Lanham Act cause of action," Tr. of Oral Arg. 35.

Finally, reading § 43(a) of the Lanham Act as creating a cause of action for, in effect, plagiarism—the use of otherwise unprotected works and inventions without attribution—would be hard to reconcile with our previous decisions. For example, in *Wal-Mart Stores, Inc. v. Samara Brothers, Inc.*, 529 U.S. 205 (2000), we considered whether product-design trade dress can ever be inherently distinctive. Wal-Mart produced "knockoffs" of children's clothes designed and manufactured by Samara Brothers, containing only "minor modifications" of the original designs. *Id.*, at 208. We concluded that the designs could not be protected under § 43(a) without a showing that they had acquired "secondary meaning," *id.*, at 214, so that they " 'identify the source of the product rather than the product itself,' " *id.*, at 211, (*quoting Inwood Laboratories, Inc. v. Ives Laboratories, Inc.*, 456 U.S. 844, 851, n.11 (1982)). This carefully considered limitation would be entirely pointless if the "original" producer could turn around and pursue a reverse-passing-off claim under exactly the same provision of the Lanham Act. Samara would merely have had to argue that it was the "origin" of the designs that Wal-Mart was selling as its own line. It was not, because "origin of goods" in the Lanham Act referred to the producer of the clothes, and not the producer of the (potentially) copyrightable or patentable designs that the clothes embodied.

. . . .

In sum, reading the phrase "origin of goods" in the Lanham Act in accordance with the Act's common-law foundations (which were not designed to protect originality or creativity), and in light of the copyright and patent laws (which were), we conclude that the phrase refers to the producer of the tangible goods that are offered for sale, and not to the author of any idea, concept, or communication embodied in those goods. *Cf.* 17 U.S.C. § 202 (distinguishing between a copyrighted work and "any material object in which the work is embodied"). To hold otherwise would be akin to finding that § 43(a) created a species of perpetual patent and copyright, which Congress may not do.

Questions

1. In *Gilliam v. ABC, Inc.*, 538 F.2d 14 (2d Cir. 1976), the Second Circuit found that showing truncated "Monty Python's Flying Circus" episodes under the original title was actionable under Section 43(a). After *Dastar*, would it matter that ABC retained the title "Monty Python's Flying Circus"? Would broadcasting an altered version thus be a "false designation of origin"? Would it be a "false or misleading description of fact ... which is likely to cause ... mistake or to deceive as to [Monty Python's] approval" of the ABC broadcast?

2. Would using Monty Python's name for ABC's truncated broadcast be a "misrepresentation of the nature" of the program? In the latter case, would that misrepresentation have occurred "in commercial advertising or promotion," as required by § 43(a)(1)(B)? *See infra* Chapter 10[A].

3. *Dastar* addressed a claim of "reverse passing off." Would it make a difference if the claim were for traditional passing off? Suppose the discovery of an obscure anonymous 16th-century English play, falsely published as a newly-unearthed work of Shakespeare. Has the publisher violated § 43(a)(1)(A)? Has it violated any other provision of the Lanham Act?

4. Plaintiff alleges that a CD falsely identified defendant as the owner of the copyright in the CD's contents. Is this a good claim after *Dastar*? *See also Best Hand Entertainment LLC v. Wideawake-Deathrow Entertainment, LLC*, 2014 U.S. Dist. LEXIS 43719 (E.D. Mich. 2014) (plaintiff's false attribution count under section 43(a) based on claim that CD falsely identified defendant as the owner of copyrights, causing confusion as to origin of CD, dismissed under *Dastar*).

Bretford Mfg., Inc. v. Smith System Mfg. Corp.

419 F.3d 576 (7th Cir. 2005)

EASTERBROOK, CIRCUIT JUDGE.

Bretford makes a line of computer tables that it sells under the name Connection TM. Since 1990 many of these tables have featured one rather than two legs on each end. The leg supports a sleeve attached to a V-shaped brace, making it easy to change the table's height while keeping the work surface stable. Although the sleeve and brace together look like a Y, Bretford calls it the V-Design table, and we employ the same usage.

This illustration, from Bretford's web site, shows the idea:

Between 1990 and 1997 Bretford was the only seller of computer tables with a V-shaped height-adjustment system. It sold about 200,000 V-Design tables during that period. Smith System, one of Bretford's competitors, decided to copy the sleeve and brace for its own line of computer tables. Smith System made its initial sales of the knockoff product to the Dallas school system in 1997, and this trademark litigation quickly followed.

Invoking § 43(a) of the Lanham Act, 15 U.S.C. § 1125(a), Bretford contends that the V-shaped design is its product's trade dress, which Smith System has infringed. It also contends that Smith System engaged in "reverse passing off" when it incorporated some Bretford hardware into a sample table that it showed purchasing officials in Dallas. The parties waived their right to a jury trial, and the district court held evidentiary hearings and issued opinions over a number of years. Although at one point the judge found Smith System liable and awarded damages in Bretford's favor, he reversed course in light of *Wal-Mart Stores, Inc. v. Samara Brothers, Inc.*, 529 U.S. 205 (2000), and *Dastar Corp. v. Twentieth Century Fox Film Corp.*, 539 U.S. 23 (2003). The appeal presents two principal questions: whether Smith System is entitled to copy Bretford's design, and, if yes, whether it was nonetheless wrongful for Smith System to use Bretford components in a sample table shown to the Dallas buyers.

....

The district court found that V-shaped legs do not signal Bretford as a source. The record supports this conclusion; indeed, Bretford has no evidence that the leg design prompts "Bretford" in buyers' minds. There are no surveys and no evidence of actual confusion. Both Bretford and Smith System sell through distributors and field representatives to sophisticated buyers who know exactly where their goods are coming from.

Many buyers ask for tables with V-shaped legs, and Bretford insists that this shows that they want its Connections TM furniture; quite the contrary, this form of specification does more to imply that the leg design is functional than to show that anyone cares who makes the table. In the end, all Bretford has to go on is the fact that it was the only maker of such tables for eight years and spent more than $4 million to promote sales. If that were enough to permit judgment in its favor, new entry would be curtailed unduly by the risk and expense of trademark litigation, for every introducer of a new design could make the same sort of claim. "Consumers should not be deprived of the benefits of competition with regard to the utilitarian and esthetic purposes that product design ordinarily serves by a rule of law that facilitates plausible threats of suit against new entrants based on alleged inherent distinctiveness." *Wal-Mart*, 529 U.S. at 213.

....

When Smith System decided to copy Bretford's table, it subcontracted the leg assemblies to a specialized metal fabricator, whose initial efforts were unsatisfactory. This left Smith System in a bind when the Dallas school system asked to see a table. Smith System cobbled a sample together by attaching the leg assembly from a Bretford table (which Smith System had repainted) to a top that Smith System had manufactured itself. (Who supplied other components, such as the cable guides and grommets, is disputed but irrelevant.) Dallas was satisfied and placed an order. All of the tables delivered to Dallas included legs manufactured by Smith System's subcontractor. Nonetheless, Bretford contends, by using its leg assemblies on even the one sample, Smith System engaged in reverse passing off and must pay damages.

Passing off or palming off occurs when a firm puts someone else's trademark on its own (usually inferior) goods; reverse passing off or misappropriation is selling someone else's goods under your own mark. *See Roho, Inc. v. Marquis*, 902 F.2d 356, 359 (5th Cir. 1990). It is not clear what's wrong with reselling someone else's goods, if you first buy them at retail. If every automobile sold by DeLorean includes the chassis and engine of a Peugeot, with DeLorean supplying only the body shell, Peugeot has received its asking price for each car sold and does not suffer any harm. Still, the Supreme Court said in *Dastar* that "reverse passing off" can violate the Lanham Act if a misdescription of goods' origin causes commercial injury....

Dastar added that the injury must be a trademark loss—which is to say, it must come from a misrepresentation of the goods' origin. *Dastar* thus had the right (so far as the Lanham Act is concerned) to incorporate into its videos footage taken and edited by others, provided that it manufactured the finished product and did not mislead anyone about who should be held responsible for shortcomings. No one makes a product from scratch, with trees and iron ore entering one end of the plant and a finished consumer product emerging at the other. Ford's cars include Fram oil filters, Goodyear tires, Owens-Corning glass, Bose radios, Pennzoil lubricants, and many other constituents; buyers can see some of the other producers' marks (those on the radio and tires for example) but not others, such as the oil and transmission fluid. Smith System builds tables using wood from one supplier, grommets (including Teflon from du Pont) from another, and vinyl molding and paint and bolts from any of a hundred more sources—the list is extensive even for a simple product such as a table. If Smith System does not tell duPont how the Teflon is used, and does not inform its consumers which firm supplied the wood, has it violated the Lanham Act? Surely not; the statute does not condemn the way in which all products are made.

Legs are a larger fraction of a table's total value than grommets and screws, but nothing in the statute establishes one rule for "major" components and another for less costly inputs. The right question, *Dastar* holds, is whether the consumer knows who has produced the finished product. In the *Dastar* case that was *Dastar* itself, even though most of the product's economic value came from elsewhere; just so when Smith System includes components manufactured by others but stands behind the finished product. The portion of § 43(a) that addresses reverse passing off is the one that condemns false designations of origin. "Origin" means, *Dastar* holds, "the producer of the tangible product sold in the marketplace." 539 U.S. at 31. As far as Dallas was concerned, the table's "origin" was Smith System, no matter who made any component or subassembly.

Much of Bretford's argument takes the form that it is just "unfair" for Smith System to proceed as it did, making a sale before its subcontractor could turn out acceptable leg assemblies. Businesses often think competition unfair, but federal law encourages wholesale copying, the better to drive down prices. Consumers rather than producers are the objects of the law's solicitude....

....

AFFIRMED.

Questions

1. In *Bretford*, Judge Easterbrook questions the policy justification for reading the Lanham Act to permit recovery for reverse passing off: "It's not clear what's wrong with reselling someone else's goods, if you first buy them at retail." If the trademark owner has already made a profit on a retail sale, why might it object to some other seller's reselling the product under a different trademark? Are those objections persuasive?

2. If Smith wants to use Bretford's V-shaped leg assemblies as components of its tables, may it advertise that it does so?

3. Strabala, an architect who had previously worked for Gensler & Associates, promoted his new business by stating on his website that he designed several famous buildings, including the Shanghai Tower, of which Gensler was the architect of record. Gensler sued, asserting a § 43(a) false designation of origin claim among others. The district court dismissed Gensler's complaint. On appeal, the court reversed, finding the district court improperly read *Dastar* to limit § 43(a) to false designations of goods' origins and not to reach services' origins. If Strabala worked in a large team of over one hundred while at Gensler, would his statement qualify as a false designation of origin? *Dastar* found that the defendants were in fact the origin of the videos at issue in that case. Was Strabala the origin of the design services for the famous buildings? *See M. Arthur Gensler Jr. & Assocs., Inc., v. Strabala*, 764 F.3d 735 (7th Cir. 2014).

4. Three well-known graffiti artists created a mural in San Francisco shown below:

The mural consists of two of the artists' pseudonyms painted over the other artist's signature "revolutions" images. The artists sued defendants who allegedly photographed the mural and used it on apparel and other items while obscuring the signatures of two of the artists. See below:

Defendants moved to dismiss the claim of false designation of origin under section 43(a). How should the court rule under *Dastar*? *See Williams v. Roberto Cavalli S.p.A.*, 113 U.S.P.Q.2d 1944 (C.D. Cal. 2015).

5. In an advertising campaign for its retirement account products, TD Ameritrade used elements reminiscent of the classic movie "Dirty Dancing." Instead of the movie line "Nobody puts Baby in a corner" uttered by the movie's male lead, the ad stated "No one puts your old 401(k) in a corner." In the final dance scene from the movie, the character Baby runs to the male lead at which point he lifts her in a dance lift while the music from the song "(I've Had) the Time of My Life" plays. In the TD ad, a piggy bank runs into a man's arms and he lifts it over his head, accompanied by the line "[b]ecause retirement should be the time of your life." The owner of rights in the film sued, among other things, for infringement of its common law trademark rights under section 43(a) in the line "Nobody puts Baby in a corner" and in the final dance lift scene. Should the court dismiss based on *Dastar*? *See Lions Gate Entertainment Inc. v. TD Ameritrade Services Co. Inc.*, 2016 U.S. Dist. LEXIS 101234 (C.D. Cal. August 1, 2016).

Phoenix Entertainment Partners, LLC v. Rumsey

829 F.3d 817 (7th Cir. July 21, 2016)

Rovner, Circuit Judge.

Slep-Tone Entertainment Corporation and its successor in interest, Phoenix Entertainment Partners, LLC (collectively, "Slep-Tone") contend in this litigation that the defendants, a pub and its owner, committed trademark infringement by passing off unauthorized digital copies of Slep-Tone karaoke files as genuine Slep-Tone tracks. [Citation.] Because we agree with the district court that Slep-Tone has not plausibly alleged that the defendants' conduct results in consumer confusion as to the source of any tangible good sold in the marketplace, we affirm the dismissal of its complaint.

[Plaintiffs alleged that they permitted purchasers of their karaoke files to make a copy in a different medium only if it followed plaintiffs' policies and also alleged that they audited such copies.]

....

Phoenix's two federal claims for trademark infringement are brought under sections 32 and 43 of the Lanham Act. 15 U.S.C. §§ 1114, 1125....

Slep-Tone is the owner of the Sound Choice trademark for "pre-recorded magnetic audio cassette tapes and compact discs containing musical compositions and compact discs containing video related to musical compositions" along with the display version of that mark. It is also the owner of distinctive and protectable trade dress associated with its graphical displays....

Slep-Tone's theory of the case proceeds as follows. When a person, without authorization from Slep-Tone, copies a Sound Choice karaoke track onto a different medium (a computer hard drive, for example) from the original CD+G or MP3+G medium distributed by Slep-Tone, that person creates a new good that is distinct from Slep-Tone's product. But the copy, when played, will still display both the registered Sound Choice marks along with each of the other elements of the trade dress.... This amounts to trademark infringement under section 32 and unfair competition under section 43(a) of the Lanham Act, in plaintiffs' view. Plaintiffs allege that the unauthorized use of their trademark and trade dress is likely to cause confusion or mistake among customers and patrons who view the unauthorized copy, or to deceive such customers and patrons, by leading them to believe that the track is a bona fide Sound Choice track manufactured by Slep-Tone and sold or licensed to the defendants. Viewers may also be led to believe, mistakenly, that Slep-Tone has sponsored or otherwise approved the defendants' services and commercial activities.

....

... [W]hat lies at the heart of the defendants' alleged wrongdoing is the unauthorized copying of Slep-Tone's karaoke tracks. It is undisputed that those tracks, the audio and visual components of which were arranged specifically for karaoke accompaniment, constitute derivative works that enjoy protection under the Copyright Act. [Citations.] And there is no doubt that, on the facts alleged, Slep-Tone would have a perfectly viable claim for copyright infringement against the defendants, *if* Slep-Tone owned the copyright on these tracks. We are told it does not. Slep-Tone *does* own the Sound Choice trademarks and associated trade dress, which explains why Slep-Tone has cast its lot with trademark rather than copyright law. But the fit between Slep-Tone's claims and trademark law is imperfect....

....

Although the rights protected by trademark and copyright laws are distinct, it can in some cases be challenging to identify which right is truly at issue when a claim of infringement is asserted. Not infrequently, the owner of the trademark for a particular good may not own the copyright on the expressive content of that good.... And where, as here, the protected mark (including the trade dress) is embedded in the good's creative content, such that the mark is invariably displayed along with the content, it can be particularly difficult to decide whether the unauthorized copying of the good presents a claim of trademark infringement or one of copyright infringement.

....

Dastar ... is not directly controlling of the result in this case. The defendants are not accused of putting their own mark on Slep-Tone's product and presenting it to the public as their own product, as was the charge in *Dastar*. Instead..., the defendants are accused of passing off their own "good"—the unauthorized copy of Slep-Tone's karaoke track—as Slep-Tone's good....

... *Dastar*'s rationale [nonetheless] informs our analysis in two important respects. First, *Dastar* ... cautions against allowing a trademark claim to substitute for what in real terms is a claim for copyright infringement. [Citations.] Second, *Dastar* considered and rejected a broader understanding of the "origin of goods" for communicative products that consumers will value more for the intellectual and creative content they convey than for their physical form. 539 U.S. at 33, 123 S. Ct. at 2047–48. That category of goods includes, in addition to the documentary videotapes at issue in *Dastar*, the karaoke tracks at issue in this case. Even as to these types of communicative goods, the Court made clear that the "good" whose "origin" is material for purposes of a trademark infringement claim is the "tangible product sold in the marketplace" rather than the creative content of that product. [Citations.]

....

Here, the good ... is the unauthorized digital copy of the Sound Choice karaoke track (duplicated from the original CD+G compact disc or MP3+G media supplied by Slep-Tone) made (or obtained from others) by the defendants. We shall assume, perhaps counter-intuitively, that a digital file counts as a tangible good for purposes of the trademark analysis. [Citations.] Any number of communicative products—books, music, movies, computer software—are now bought and sold in digital form, many of them exclusively so. But the question ... is what, if any, tangible "good" the consumer sees, and whether the use of the plaintiffs' trademark leads to confusion about the source of that particular good.

... [T]he defendants are not alleged to be ... selling copies of karaoke tracks.... The defendants instead are alleged to play the unauthorized copies for their bar patrons to encourage alcohol and food sales. So what the pub patrons see is the performance of the creative work contained on the copies: they hear the musical accompaniment and they see the corresponding lyrics and graphics.

... The patron sees only the performance of the creative content of the digital file. So far as the patron is concerned, the content could be played from a compact disc, the pub's karaoke hard drive, or from an internet streaming source. Whatever the source, the consumer sees and hears the same content and her perception of that content will be essentially the same.

It is true that the pub patron will see the Sound Choice mark and trade dress whenever the graphical component of the karaoke tracks is displayed. This, according to the plaintiffs, is what gives rise to confusion as to the source of the good containing those tracks: Patrons may assume it is a genuine, authorized Slep-Tone product when in fact it is a bootleg copy. But about *what* exactly is the patron confused? On seeing the Sound Choice mark, a patron may believe that she is seeing and hearing content that was created by Slep-Tone. And she is. [Citation.] But what *Dastar* makes clear is that a consumer's confusion must be confusion as to the source of the tangible good sold in the marketplace. [Citations;] *Bretford Mfg., Inc. v. Smith Sys. Mfg. Corp., supra*, 419 F.3d at 580; [citation].

A consumer of karaoke services like a patron of The Basket Case never sees a disc that is wrapped in Slep-Tone or Sound Choice packaging. He never sees a website offering downloads of Sound Choice tracks.... Any confusion, in short, is not about the source of the tangible good sold in the marketplace, as *Dastar* requires.

That the Sound Choice mark is embedded in the creative content of the karaoke track and is visible to the public whenever the track is played does not falsely suggest that Slep-Tone is endorsing the performance.... The producers of communicative goods often embed their marks not only on the packaging of the good but in its content. Cinematic films, for example, typically display the mark of the studio that made the film in the opening and/or closing credits—think of Metro-Goldwyn-Mayer Studios' roaring lion. When the copyright on such a creative work expires, enabling any member of the public to copy and use the work without license, it is not a trademark violation simply to display the work without first deleting the mark that was inserted into its content. Thus, as the district court pointed out in *Slep-Tone Entm't Corp. v. Canton-Phoenix Inc.*, a movie theater may freely exhibit a copy of Universal Studios' 1925 silent film, *The Phantom of the Opera*, which is now in the public domain, without fear of committing trademark infringement simply because Universal's registered trademark will be displayed when the film is played. 2014 U.S. Dist. LEXIS 159390, 2014 WL 5824787, at *11 (D. Ore. Sep. 4, 2014) (report & recommendation), *adopted as modified*, 2014 U.S. Dist. LEXIS 158851, 2014 WL 5817903 (D. Ore. Nov. 7, 2014), *appeal pending* (9th Cir.) (No. 14-36018). So long as Universal's mark is not overtly used to market the performance, there is no risk that a theater patron might think that Universal is sponsoring or endorsing the performance. *Id.* Likewise, another media company is free to make and sell copies of the film without deleting Universal's mark from the credits (or obtaining a license from Universal), so long as the packaging and advertisement of the tangible good on which the copy is fixed and offered to the consumer (a DVD or blu-ray disc, for example) does not use Universal's mark and thereby suggest that it is a Universal-produced or -endorsed copy. [Citations.] Because the creative content of the karaoke tracks at issue in this case presumably remains subject to copyright protection, the unauthorized display and performance of those tracks may well present an actionable claim of copyright violation, as we have said. But the routine display of Slep-Tone's embedded trademark during the performance of the tracks does not, without more, support a claim of trademark infringement or unfair competition under the Lanham Act.

Here, there is no allegation nor suggestion in the briefing that The Basket Case promotes itself as offering Sound Choice karaoke products—in its advertising or in its karaoke menus, for example. There is, consequently, no reason to believe that its patrons will think that Slep-Tone is sponsoring the performance of the copied karaoke tracks. And because patrons see only the creative content of the tracks rather than the particular medium from which the tracks are played, there is no reason to think that they believe that the digital file, wherever it resides, was itself produced or approved by Slep-Tone.

We have considered Slep-Tone's concern that if the data contained on one of its products is compressed excessively during the duplication process, the quality of an unauthorized copy may be poor and, when played, may lead viewers to think Slep-Tone products are of inferior quality. (Although the same danger may be present when a Slep-Tone customer makes an authorized copy, we shall assume that the auditing process referred to in the complaint takes care of this.) Quality is always a concern in passing-off cases: Not only is the trademark holder deprived of sales, but the counterfeit goods sold under its trademark place the holder's goodwill at risk to the extent the goods are of inferior quality. [Citation.] But the problem for Slep-Tone, apart from the fact that it does not affirmatively allege that the defendants' copies are noticeably inferior to their patrons, is that the defendants are not passing off a tangible good sold in the marketplace as a Slep-Tone good. As we have discussed, the defendants are not selling compact discs with karaoke tracks and billing them as genuine Slep-Tone tracks, in the way that a street vendor might hawk knock-off Yves Saint Laurent bags or Rolex watches to passers-by. Whatever wrong the defendants may have committed by making (or causing to be made) unauthorized copies of Slep-Tone's tracks, they are not alleged to have held out a tangible good sold in the marketplace as a Slep-Tone product. Consequently, the defendants' alleged conduct is not actionable as trademark infringement.

For all of the reasons we have discussed, we AFFIRM the dismissal of Slep-Tone's complaint.

Questions

1. Under the court's analysis, are there any claims other than Lanham Act claims that plaintiffs could assert in this case against unauthorized copying of their karaoke files?

2. Do you agree that patrons of the karaoke pub are not likely to believe that Slep-tone approved the use of the unauthorized copy?

Chapter 8

Defenses to Infringement

A. Statutory Defenses/Incontestability

Section 33 of the Lanham Act

We have already encountered a variety of defenses. For example, a defendant may raise as a defense to an infringement claim objections such as those that furnish the basis for rejecting an application for trademark registration. The grounds that the Lanham Act sets forth in section 14 as bases for cancelling a mark may also be invoked as defenses to infringement claims. These grounds include fraud, abandonment, genericism and functionality. Any mark, including one that has become incontestable, may be cancelled at any time if it is abandoned or functional, was obtained fraudulently or becomes generic.

Section 33(a) of the Lanham Act provides that a registration is prima facie evidence of the registrant's right to exclusive use of the registered mark in connection with the goods or services covered by the registration subject to legal and equitable defenses, including those set forth in section 33(b). An incontestable registration is "conclusive" of the owner's exclusive right to use of the marks, but incontestability only applies to the goods/services covered by the incontestable registration. *See, e.g., In re Best Software*, 63 U.S.P.Q.2d 1109, 1113 (T.T.A.B. 2002) ("ownership of an incontestable registration does not give the applicant a right to register the same or similar mark for different goods or services, even if they are closely related to the goods or services set forth in the incontestable registration."). *But see Synergistic Intern., LLC v. Korman*, 470 F.3d 162 (4th Cir. 2006) (plaintiff's incontestable GLASS DOCTOR mark registration for "installation of glass in buildings and vehicles" ruled to include defendant's glass repair business).

In addition to the nine defenses listed in section 33(b), that section refers to section 15 as a further limit on incontestable status. Section 33(b) begins: "To the extent that the right to use the registered mark has become incontestable under section 15." Section 15 in turn incorporates additional defenses through its reference to section 14(3) (which *inter alia* refers to genericism, required conditions for obtaining a collective or certification mark, and the statutory bars to registration set forth in section 2(a), (b), and (c)) and to section 14(5) (which refers to misuses of a certification mark).

Section 33(b) of the Lanham Act delineates nine exceptions to a registered mark's incontestable status as acquired under section 15. Because they are affirmative defenses, an alleged infringer has the burden of pleading and proving them. These defenses apply to contestable as well as incontestable marks.

As noted by the Supreme Court in *Park 'n Fly, Inc. v. Dollar Park and Fly, Inc.*, 469 U.S. 189 (1985), the effect of establishing a section 33(b) defense is evidentiary so that "registration constitutes only prima facie and not conclusive evidence of the owner's right to exclusive use of the mark." All legal and common law defenses are then applicable. *See* 15 U.S.C. § 1115. Courts nevertheless frequently treat an established defense as conclusive on the merits. This approach reaches the same result as long as the court does not interpret the statutory defense more narrowly than the common law defense which might otherwise be applied. *See generally*, J.T. McCarthy, McCarthy on Trademarks and Unfair Competition § 32:153 (4th ed.).

A brief review of the § 33(b) defenses follows:

(1) *Fraudulent acquisition of trademark registration or of incontestable right to use mark.*

This defense is explored in more detail *infra*, this Chapter, Section [2][a].

(2) *Abandonment of the mark.*

Abandonment is grounds for cancelling a mark at any time, and may also be raised as a defense in an infringement suit. Abandonment, which was explored in detail *supra*, Chapter 5, includes non-use with intent not to resume, allowing a mark to become generic, and uncontrolled licensing.

(3) *Use of the mark to misrepresent source.*

Similar to an unclean hands defense, this exception to incontestability includes intentionally false and misleading designations of origin, nature, or ingredients of registrant's goods. Courts have read this defense narrowly. In *General Motors Corp. v. Gibson Chemical & Oil Corp.*, 786 F.2d 105 (2d Cir. 1988), the court rejected the defendant's contention that GM's licensing separate organizations, subject to quality controls, to manufacture the trademarked transmission fluid amounted to section 33(b)(3) source misrepresentation.

(4) *Use of mark in a descriptive sense other than as a trademark (the so-called "fair use" defense).*

The trademark fair use defense privileges non-trademark descriptive uses under some conditions. It is explored in more detail *infra*, this Chapter, Section [2][b].

(5) *Limited territory defense.*

The limited territory defense was discussed in connection with concurrent use in Section [F] of Chapter 3, *supra.* This exception to an incontestable registration applies to a junior user who adopts a mark innocently before the senior user registers it, and who has used the mark continuously ever since. However, the benefits of the defense are restricted to the area of continuous use by the junior user prior to the plaintiff's registration (or application filing date for registrations resulting from applications filed after November 16, 1989, the effective date of The Trademark Revision Act of 1988). The area where continuous use by the defendant is established will thereafter be off-limits to the plaintiff and, conversely, use of the mark by the defendant in all other areas is barred. While the defendant may not subsequently extend the territory in which he uses the mark, he may be able to expand his business within his defined boundaries. *See, e.g. Peaches Entertainment Corp. v. Entertainment Repertoire Associates, Inc.*, 62 F.3d 690 (5th Cir. 1995).

(6) *Prior registration by defendant.*

Where the alleged infringer registered and used the mark prior to the registration of plaintiff and did not abandon it, the senior registrant may continue to use its mark, but only within the area where it was used prior to registration by plaintiff. This defense would seem to be useful only in situations in which two marks that were not confusingly similar when they were registered (because the products, geographic regions, or marks themselves were sufficiently dissimilar at the time to obviate confusion) later become confusingly similar. Even with that limitation, however, it seems peculiar to limit the senior registrant to a restricted geographic area at the behest of the junior registrant, even where the junior registrant has obtained a certificate of incontestability. Perhaps unsurprisingly, then, there is little case law invoking section 33(b)(6). However, in *Patsy's Italian Restaurant, Inc. v. Banas*, 658 F.3d 254 (2d Cir. 2011), the Second Circuit held that the prior use defense does not require use in interstate commerce.

(7) *Use of mark to violate anti-trust laws.*

The antitrust defense is rarely successful. *See, e.g., R.J. Reynolds Tobacco Co. v. Premium Tobacco Stores, Inc.*, 2001 U.S. Dist. LEXIS 8896 (N.D. Ill. June 29, 2001) (court strikes defendant's antitrust defense, finding it did not sufficiently allege that "the trademark ... was itself being used as the prime and effective instrument to effectuate the antitrust activity.") (*quoting Carl Zeiss Stiftung v. N.E.B. Carl Zeiss, Jena*, 298 F. Supp. 1309, 1314 (S.D.N.Y. 1969)).

(8) *Functionality.*

Although functionality was not initially enumerated as a separate defense to incontestability under section 33, courts and the Board treated it as one until the Fourth Circuit's decision in *Shakespeare Co. v. Silstar Corp.*, 9 F.3d 1091 (4th Cir. 1993), *cert. denied*, 511 U.S. 1127 (1994). *Silstar* held that functionality could not be asserted as a defense to an incontestable registration because the defense was not explicitly included in the statute. Sections 14 and 33 were amended in 1998 by Congress to include functionality explicitly both as a basis of cancellation and as a defense to incontestable marks. The amendment has been held to codify existing law in order to correct the reasoning in *Silstar. See Pudenz v. Littlefuse, Inc.*, 177 F.3d 1204 (11th Cir. 1999). For a discussion of the functionality defense, *see* Chapter 4[C], *supra*, and *infra* this Chapter, Section [2][c].

(9) *Equitable principles.*

Added in 1988, § 33(b)(9) explicitly makes "equitable principles, including laches, estoppel, and acquiescence" applicable defenses to incontestably registered marks. Laches, for purposes of objecting to registration of a mark, dates from the publication of the mark for opposition. *See Tillamook Country Smoker, Inc. v. Tillamook County Creamery Ass'n*, 333 F. Supp. 2d 975 (D. Or. 2004), *aff'd*, 465 F.3d 1102 (9th Cir. 2006), *citing Nat'l Cable Television Ass'n v. American Cinema Editors, Inc.*, 937 F.2d 1572 (Fed. Cir. 1991). Because of the public interest in avoiding confusion, however, where the marks and goods or services of the parties are substantially similar and confusion is inevitable, laches has been held unavailable even where established. *See, e.g., Ray Communications, Inc. v. Clear Channel Communications, Inc.*, 673 F.3d 294 (4th Cir. 2012). Laches is discussed in more detail in Section [2][d], *infra*.

1. Incontestability

15 U.S.C. § 1065 [Lanham Act § 15]

Except on a ground for which application to cancel may be filed at any time under paragraphs (3) and (5) of section 14 of this Act, and except to the extent, if any, to which the use of a mark registered on the principal register infringes a valid right acquired under the law of any State or Territory by use of a mark or trade name continuing from a date prior to the date of registration under this Act of such registered mark, the right of the registrant to use such registered mark in commerce for the goods or services on or in connection with which such registered mark has been in continuous use for five consecutive years subsequent to the date of such registration and is still in use in commerce, shall be incontestable: Provided, that—

(1) there has been no final decision adverse to registrant's claim of ownership of such mark for such goods or services, or to registrant's right to register the same or to keep the same on the register; and

(2) there is no proceeding involving said rights pending in the Patent and Trademark Office or in a court and not finally disposed of; and

(3) an affidavit is filed with the Commissioner within one year after the expiration of any such five-year period setting forth those goods or services stated in the registration on or in connection with which such mark has been in continuous use for such five consecutive years and is still in use in commerce, and the other matters specified in paragraphs (1) and (2) of this section; and

(4) no incontestable right shall be acquired in a mark which is the generic name for the goods or services or a portion thereof, for which it is registered.

Park 'n Fly, Inc. v. Dollar Park and Fly, Inc.

469 U.S. 189 (1985)

Justice O'Connor delivered the opinion of the Court:

In this case we consider whether an action to enjoin the infringement of an incontestable trade or service mark may be defended on the grounds that the mark is merely descriptive. We conclude that neither the language of the relevant statutes nor the legislative history supports such a defense.

I.

Petitioner operates long-term parking lots near airports. After starting business in St. Louis in 1967, petitioner subsequently opened facilities in Cleveland, Houston, Boston, Memphis, and San Francisco. Petitioner applied in 1969 to the United States Patent and Trademark Office (Patent Office) to register a service mark consisting of the logo of an airplane and the words "Park 'n Fly." The registration issued in August 1971. Nearly six years later, petitioner filed an affidavit with the Patent Office to establish the incontestable status of the mark. As required by § 15 of the Trademark Act of 1946 (Lanham Act), 60 Stat. 433, as amended, 15 U.S.C. § 1065, the affidavit stated that the mark had been registered and in continuous use for five consecutive years, that there had been no final adverse decision to petitioner's claim of ownership or right to registration, and that no proceedings involving such rights were pending. Incontestable status provides, subject to the provisions of § 15 and 33(b) of the Lanham Act, "conclusive evidence of the registrant's exclusive right to use the registered mark...." § 33(b), 15 U.S.C. § 1115(b).

Respondent also provides long-term airport parking services, but only has operations in Portland, Oregon. Respondent calls its business "Dollar Park and Fly." Petitioner filed this infringement action in 1978 in the United States District Court for the District of Oregon and requested the court permanently to enjoin respondent from using the words "Park and Fly" in connection with its business. Respondent counterclaimed and sought cancellation of petitioner's mark on the grounds that it is a generic term. *See* § 14(c), 15 U.S.C. § 1064(c). Respondent also argued that petitioner's mark is unenforceable because it is merely descriptive....

After a bench trial, the District Court found that petitioner's mark is not generic and observed that an incontestable mark cannot be challenged on the grounds that it is merely descriptive.

The Court of Appeals for the Ninth Circuit reversed. 718 F.2d 327 (1983). The District Court did not err, the Court of Appeals held, in refusing to invalidate petitioner's mark. *Id.*, at 331. The Court of Appeals noted, however, that it previously had held that incontestability provides a defense against the cancellation of a mark, but it may not be used offensively to enjoin another's use. *Ibid.* Petitioner, under this analysis, could obtain an injunction only if its mark would be entitled to continued registration without regard to its incontestable status.... Based on its own examination of the record, the Court of Appeals then determined that petitioner's mark is in fact merely descriptive, and therefore respondent should not be enjoined from using the name "Park and Fly." *Ibid.*

The decision below is in direct conflict with the decision of the Court of Appeals for the Seventh Circuit in *Union Carbide Corp. v. Ever-Ready, Inc.*, 531 F.2d 366, *cert. denied*, 429 U.S. 830 (1976). We granted certiorari to resolve this conflict, 465 U.S. 1078 (1984), and we now *reverse*.

II.

....

This case requires us to consider the effect of the incontestability provisions of the Lanham Act in the context of an infringement action defended on the grounds that the mark is merely descriptive. Statutory construction must begin with the language employed by Congress and the assumption that the ordinary meaning of that language accurately expresses the legislative purpose. [Citation.] With respect to incontestable trade or service marks, § 33(b) of the Lanham Act states that "registration shall be conclusive evidence of the registrant's exclusive right to use the registered mark" subject to the conditions of § 15 and certain enumerated defenses. Section 15 incorporates by reference subsections (c) and (e) of § 14, 15 U.S.C. § 1064. An incontestable mark that becomes generic may be canceled at any time pursuant to § 14(c). That section also allows cancellation of an incontestable mark at any time if it has been abandoned, if it is being used to misrepresent the source of the goods or services in connection with which it is used, or if it was obtained fraudulently or contrary to the provisions of § 4, 15 U.S.C. § 1054, or §§ 2(a)–(c), 15 U.S.C. §§ 1052(a)–(c).

One searches the language of the Lanham Act in vain to find any support for the offensive/defensive distinction applied by the Court of Appeals. The statute nowhere distinguishes between a registrant's offensive and defensive use of an incontestable mark. On the contrary, § 33(b)'s declaration that the registrant has an "exclusive right" to use the mark indicates that incontestable status may be used to enjoin infringement by others. A conclusion that such infringement cannot be enjoined renders meaningless the "exclusive right" recognized by the statute. Moreover, the language in three of the defenses enumerated in § 33(b) clearly contemplates the use of incontestability in infringement actions by plaintiffs. *See* §§ 33(b)(4)–(6), 15 U.S.C. §§ 1115(b)(4)–(6).

The language of the Lanham Act also refutes any conclusion that an incontestable mark may be challenged as merely descriptive. A mark that is merely descriptive of an applicant's goods or services is not registrable unless the mark has secondary meaning. Before a mark achieves incontestable status, registration provides prima facie evidence of the registrant's exclusive right to use the mark in commerce. § 33(a), 15 U.S.C. § 1115(a). The Lanham Act expressly provides that before a mark becomes incontestable an opposing party may prove any legal or equitable defense which might have been asserted if the mark had not been registered. *Ibid.* Thus, § 33(a) would have allowed respondent to challenge petitioner's mark as merely descriptive if the mark had not become incontestable. With respect to incontestable marks, however, § 33(b) provides that registration is conclusive evidence of the registrant's exclusive right to use the mark, subject to the conditions of § 15 and the seven defenses enumerated in § 33(b) itself. Mere descriptiveness is not recognized by either § 15 or § 33(b) as a basis for challenging an incontestable mark.

The Court of Appeals in discussing the offensive/defensive distinction observed that incontestability protects a registrant against cancellation of his mark. 718 F.2d, at 331. This observation is incorrect with respect to marks that become generic or which otherwise may be canceled at any time pursuant to §§ 14(c) and (e). Moreover, as applied to marks that are merely descriptive, the approach of the Court of Appeals makes incontestable status superfluous. Without regard to its incontestable status, a mark that has been registered five years is protected from cancellation except on the grounds stated in §§ 14(c) and (e). Pursuant to § 14, a mark may be canceled on the grounds that it is merely descriptive only if the petition to cancel is filed within five years of the date of registration. § 14(a), 15 U.S.C. § 1064(a). The approach adopted by the Court of Appeals implies that incontestability adds nothing to the protections against cancellation already provided in § 14. The decision below not only lacks support in the words of the statute, it effectively emasculates § 33(b) under the circumstances of this case.

III.

Nothing in the legislative history of the Lanham Act supports a departure from the plain language of the statutory provisions concerning incontestability. Indeed, a conclusion that incontestable status can provide the basis for enforcement of the registrant's exclusive right to use a trade or service mark promotes the goals of the statute. The Lanham Act provides national protection of trademarks in order to secure to the owner of the mark the goodwill of his business and to protect the ability of consumers to distinguish among competing producers. The opportunity to obtain incontestable status by satisfying the requirements of § 15 thus encourages producers to cultivate the goodwill associated with a particular mark. This function of the incontestability provisions would be utterly frustrated if the holder of an incontestable mark could not enjoin infringement by others so long as they established that the mark would not be registrable but for its incontestable status.

Respondent argues, however, that enforcing petitioner's mark would conflict with the goals of the Lanham Act because the mark is merely descriptive and should never have been registered in the first place. Representative Lanham, respondent notes, explained that the defenses enumerated in § 33(b) were "not intended to enlarge, restrict, amend, or modify the substantive law of trademarks either as set out in other sections of the act or as heretofore applied by the courts under prior laws." 92 Cong. Rec. 7524 (1946). Respondent reasons that because the Lanham Act did not alter the substantive law of trademarks, the incontestability provisions cannot protect petitioner's use of the mark if it were not originally registrable. Moreover, inasmuch as petitioner's mark is merely descriptive, respondent contends that enjoining others from using the mark will not encourage competition by assisting consumers in their ability to distinguish among competing producers.

These arguments are unpersuasive. Representative Lanham's remarks, if read in context, clearly refer to the effect of the defenses enumerated in § 33(b).[6] There is no

6. Representative Lanham made his remarks to clarify that the seven defenses enumerated in § 33(b) are not substantive rules of law which go to the validity or enforceability of an incontestable mark. 92 Cong.Rec. 7524 (1946). Instead, the defenses affect the evidentiary status of registration where the owner claims the benefit of a mark's incontestable status. If one of the defenses is established, registration constitutes only prima facie and not conclusive evidence of the owner's right to exclusive

question that the Lanham Act altered existing law concerning trademark rights in several respects.... Most significantly, Representative Lanham himself observed that incontestability was one of "the valuable new rights created by the act." 92 Cong. Rec. 7524 (1946).

The alternative of refusing to provide incontestable status for descriptive marks with secondary meaning was expressly noted in the hearings on the Lanham Act. Also mentioned was the possibility of including as a defense to infringement of an incontestable mark the "fact that a mark is a descriptive, generic, or geographical term or device." *Id.*, at 45, 47. Congress, however, did not adopt either of these alternatives. Instead, Congress expressly provided in §§ 33(b) and 15 that an incontestable mark could be challenged on specified grounds, and the grounds identified by Congress do not include mere descriptiveness.

The dissent echoes arguments made by opponents of the Lanham Act that the incontestable status of a descriptive mark might take from the public domain language that is merely descriptive.... Congress has already addressed concerns to prevent the "commercial monopolization" of descriptive language. The Lanham Act allows a mark to be challenged at any time if it becomes generic, and, under certain circumstances, permits the nontrademark use of descriptive terms contained in an incontestable mark. Finally, if "monopolization" of an incontestable mark threatens economic competition, § 33(b)(7), 15 U.S.C. § 1115(b)(7), provides a defense on the grounds that the mark is being used to violate federal antitrust laws. At bottom, the dissent simply disagrees with the balance struck by Congress in determining the protection to be given to incontestable marks.

....

We conclude that the holder of a registered mark may rely on incontestability to enjoin infringement and that such an action may not be defended on the grounds that the mark is merely descriptive.... Respondent urges that we nevertheless affirm the decision below based on the "prior use" defense recognized by 33(b)(5) of the Lanham Act. Alternatively, respondent argues that there is no likelihood of confusion and therefore no infringement justifying injunctive relief. The District Court rejected each of these arguments, but they were not addressed by the Court of Appeals. 718 F.2d, at 331–332, n.4. That court may consider them on remand. The judgment of the Court of Appeals is reversed, and the case is remanded for further proceedings consistent with this opinion.

It is so ordered.

---

use of the mark. *Ibid. See also* H.R. Conf. Rep. No. 2322, 79th Cong., 2d Sess., 6 (1946) (explanatory statement of House managers).

Questions

1. After eliminating the defenses that still can be asserted against an incontestable registration, are any useful defenses precluded apart from descriptiveness such as was involved in *Park 'n Fly*?

2. Plaintiff, your client, owns an incontestable Federal registration for LAWSTORE for providing general consumer legal services such as will-drafting, uncontested divorces, and title searches. Defendant has adopted LAWSTORE in connection with a similar business. The term at issue was invented by plaintiff and does not appear in any dictionary. Several legal practitioners had adopted LAWSTORE in connection with their legal services operations, but when advised of plaintiff's registration they agreed to stop using the term. What defense do you expect defendant to raise, and what arguments do you plan to make in response?

3. Can a challenge that an application was void *ab initio* because the mark was not in use at the time a use-based application was filed be made against an incontestable registration? Is this defense listed under section 1115(b)? *See Collectable Promotional Prods. Inc. v. Disney Enters., Inc.*, 92 U.S.P.Q.2d 1354 (W.D. Ok. 2009).

4. Can a challenge to an incontestable registration be made on the basis of the invalidity of an assignment of that registration? *See Federal Treasury Enterprise v. Spirits International N.V.*, 623 F.3d 61 (2d Cir. 2010).

Note: Incontestable Registration and Strength of the Mark

The *Park 'n Fly* majority held that once incontestable, a mark's registration may not be challenged on the ground that the mark is merely descriptive. Does the *Park 'n Fly* decision also mean that the distinctiveness of a mark is irrelevant to the analysis of likelihood of confusion? At first, courts unanimously distinguished defenses asserting the mere descriptiveness of a mark in order to challenge the validity of a registration, from arguments that the mark, as descriptive, was weak and therefore less prone to be confused with other, similar marks. For example, the court in *Source Services Corp. v. Source Telecomputing Corp.*, 635 F. Supp. 600 (N.D. Ill. 1986), observed:

> *Park 'n Fly* teach[es] the conclusive presumption of secondary meaning merely means an alleged infringer is not permitted to raise descriptiveness as a defense against the validity of plaintiff's mark. That says nothing about the expected reactions of actual marketplace consumers. [P]laintiffs must still provide a factual predicate showing consumers are likely to confuse defendants' products with their own. And the more descriptive a mark is in fact, the less likely that sort of confusion will be.

Some courts, however, expressed a contrary view. In *Dieter v. B & H Industries*, 880 F.2d 322 (11th Cir. 1989), *cert. denied*, 498 U.S. 950 (1990), the Eleventh Circuit noted that the question "[w]hether 'incontestable' status affects the strength of the mark for purposes of 'likelihood of confusion' determinations ... is an issue of first impression in this circuit." The court "decline[d] to follow" the *Source Services Corp.* decision (*supra*):

> We hold that incontestable status is a factor to be taken into consideration in likelihood of confusion analysis. Because [plaintiff's] mark is incontestable, then it is presumed to be at least descriptive with secondary meaning, and therefore a relatively strong mark.

Currently, the majority of courts have adopted the approach taken in *Source Services Corp. See, e.g., Renaissance Greeting Cards, Inc. v. Dollar Tree Stores*, 227 Fed. Appx. 239 (4th Cir. 2007); *American Society of Plumbing Engineers v. TMB Pub. Inc.*, 109 Fed. Appx. 781 (7th Cir. 2004); *Safer, Inc. v. OMS Investments, Inc.*, 94 U.S.P.Q.2d 1031, 1036 (T.T.A.B. 2010) ("the fact that opposer's federally-registered trademark has achieved incontestable status means that it is conclusively considered to be valid, but it does not dictate that the mark is 'strong' for purposes of determining likelihood of confusion."). *See also Entrepreneur Media, Inc. v. Smith*, 279 F.3d 1135 (9th Cir. 2002); *Oreck Corp. v. U.S. Floor Systems, Inc.*, 803 F.2d 166 (5th Cir. 1986), *cert. denied*, 481 U.S. 1069 (1987). ("*Park 'n Fly* says nothing to preclude this argument [of absence of likelihood of confusion]. Incontestable status does not make a weak mark strong.")

However, the minority position of *Dieter* is still followed, primarily in the Sixth and Eleventh Circuits. *See Sovereign Military Hospitaller Order of St. John of Jerusalem, of Rhodes and of Malta v. The Florida Priory of the Knights Hospitallers of the Sovereign Order of St. John of Jerusalem, Knights of Malta, The Ecumenical Order*, 809 F.3d 1171, 1178 (11th Cir. 2015) ("an incontestable mark is presumptively strong"); *Autozone, Inc. v. Tandy Corp.*, 373 F.3d 786 (6th Cir. 2004) (incontestable marks are presumed strong, but presumption can be overcome by showing widespread third-party use). *See also American Rice, Inc. v. Producers Rice Mill, Inc.*, 518 F.3d 321 (5th Cir. 2008) (affirming lower court's finding that plaintiff's "Girl Design" used on its rice is strong, relying in part on the incontestable status of the mark). *But see Therma-Scan, Inc. v. Thermoscan, Inc.*, 295 F.3d 623 (6th Cir. 2002) (finding a mark subject to an incontestable registration "not ... especially strong," and rejecting a presumption that a mark is strong because its registration is incontestable).

Which position makes more sense to you? Does the text of Section 33(b) of the Lanham Act, 15 U.S.C. § 1115(b), assist your determination? This provision states that once incontestability has been achieved, "the registration shall be conclusive evidence of the validity of the registered mark ... and of the registrant's exclusive right to use the registered mark in commerce." On its face, does the Lanham Act "make a weak mark strong"? Should it?

Question

Plaintiff owns an incontestable registration for VAIL for ski resort services. Defendant uses 1-800-SKI-VAIL for marketing services promoting services near Vail, Colorado. In determining the likelihood of confusion between the two marks, should the court presume that plaintiff's mark is strong due to its incontestability or can it also consider the geographic connotation of the term and third party uses in finding that, although protectable, the mark is relatively weak? *See Vail Associates, Inc. v. Vend-Tel-Co., Ltd.*, 516 F.3d 853 (10th Cir. 2008).

2. Particular Section 33(b) Defenses

a. Fraud on the Trademark Office

In order to establish fraud, the challenger must show that the registrant made a material and knowing misrepresentation. For example, the registrant's failure to reveal that a mark was commonly used in a generic or descriptive sense in the industry was held to be fraud in *G. Levor & Co., Inc. v. Nash, Inc.*, 123 U.S.P.Q. 234 (T.T.A.B. 1959). In *Hank Thorp, Inc. v. Minilite, Inc.*, 474 F. Supp. 228 (D. Del. 1979), the court found fraud by a registrant who knew he was not the owner of the mark. In *Kleven v Hereford*, 2015 U.S. Dist. LEXIS 111185 (C.D. Cal. Aug. 21, 2015), the court found fraud when the registrant of the Rin Tin Tin mark had entered into settlement agreements acknowledging that she was not the owner of the mark for the services for which she subsequently obtained registrations. In *Orient Express Trading Co. v. Federated Department Stores*, 842 F.2d 650 (2d Cir. 1988), the court noted that fraudulent statements made in a trademark registration application "may not be the product of mere error or inadvertence, but must indicate a deliberate attempt to mislead the PTO." New York City prevailed on summary judgment in its claim to cancel defendant's TAVERN ON THE GREEN registration on the ground of fraud where the defendant was aware of a previous license from New York City to use the mark and thus was aware it was not the owner of the mark at the time of filing the application. *City of New York v. Tavern on the Green, L.P.*, 427 B.R. 233 (S.D.N.Y. 2010). Under that standard, the court found that the registrant had fraudulently misrepresented its dates of first use and the scope of its subsequent use of its marks.

While an applicant must provide an oath that no other party, to the best of applicant's belief, has the right to use in commerce the applied-for mark, this oath does not impose a duty to investigate all other possible users, and an applicant need demonstrate only a good faith belief to escape cancellation. *See, e.g., Rosso and Mastracco, Inc. v. Giant Food Inc.*, 720 F.2d 1263 (Fed. Cir. 1983); *see also Sovereign Military Hospitaller Order of St. John of Jerusalem of Rhodes and of Malta v. The Florida Priory of the Knights Hospitallers of St. John of Jerusalem Knights of Malta, the Ecumenical Order*, 702 F.3d 1279 (11th Cir. 2012), *infra* this subsection.

Making intentionally false statements in the incontestability declaration was held to be fraud in *Robi v. Five Platters, Inc.*, 918 F.2d 1439 (9th Cir. 1990). *See also Daesang Corp. v. Rhee Bros., Inc.*, 77 U.S.P.Q.2d 1753 (D. Md. 2005) (failure of registrant to inform PTO that transliteration of mark meant Soon Chang, a place in Korea well known for sauces of the type covered by the application, and that registrant's customers would be aware of this association constituted fraud on the PTO).

Even if fraud in registration is proven, however, a trademark owner retains its common law rights, which can be used as a basis to challenge third parties.

In re Bose Corp.

580 F.3d 1240 (Fed. Cir. 2009)

Michel, Circuit Judge:

The Trademark Trial and Appeal Board ("Board") found that Bose Corporation ("Bose") committed fraud on the United States Patent and Trademark Office ("PTO") in renewing Registration No. 1,633,789 for the trademark WAVE. *Bose Corp. v. Hexawave, Inc.*, 88 USPQ2d 1332, 1338 (T.T.A.B. 2007). Bose appeals the Board's order cancelling the registration in its entirety. Because there is no substantial evidence that Bose intended to deceive the PTO in the renewal process, we reverse and remand.

I. BACKGROUND

Bose initiated an opposition against the HEXAWAVE trademark application by Hexawave, Inc. ("Hexawave"), alleging, inter alia, likelihood of confusion with Bose's prior registered trademarks, including WAVE. *Bose*, 88 USPQ2d at 1333. Hexawave counterclaimed for cancellation of Bose's WAVE mark, asserting that Bose committed fraud in its registration renewal application when it claimed use on all goods in the registration while knowing that it had stopped manufacturing and selling certain goods.

The fraud alleged by Hexawave involves Bose's combined Section 8 affidavit of continued use and Section 9 renewal application ("Section 8/9 renewal"), signed by Bose's general counsel, Mark E. Sullivan, and filed on January 8, 2001. In the renewal, Bose stated that the WAVE mark was still in use in commerce on various goods, including audio tape recorders and players. The Board found that (1) Bose stopped manufacturing and selling audio tape recorders and players sometime between 1996 and 1997; and (2) Mr. Sullivan knew that Bose discontinued those products when he signed the Section 8/9 renewal.

At the time Mr. Sullivan signed the Section 8/9 renewal, Bose continued to repair previously sold audio tape recorders and players, some of which were still under warranty. Mr. Sullivan testified that in his belief, the WAVE mark was used in commerce because "in the process of repairs, the product was being transported back to customers." The Board concluded that the repairing and shipping back did not constitute sufficient use to maintain a trademark registration for goods. It further found Mr. Sullivan's belief that transporting repaired goods constituted use was not reasonable. Finally, the Board found that the use statement in the Section 8/9 renewal was material. As a result, the Board ruled that Bose committed fraud on the PTO in maintaining the WAVE mark registration and ordered the cancellation of Bose's WAVE mark registration in its entirety....

Bose appealed. Because the original appellee Hexawave did not appear, the PTO moved, and the court granted leave to the Director, to participate as the appellee....

II. DISCUSSION

... "Fraud in procuring a trademark registration or renewal occurs when an applicant knowingly makes false, material representations of fact in connection with his application." *Torres v. Cantine Torresella S.r.l.*, 808 F.2d 46, 48 (Fed. Cir. 1986). A party seeking cancellation of a trademark registration for fraudulent procurement bears a heavy burden of proof. *W.D. Byron & Sons, Inc. v. Stein Bros. Mfg. Co.*, 377 F.2d 1001, 1004 (CCPA 1967). Indeed, "the very nature of the charge of fraud requires that it be proven to the hilt with clear and convincing evidence. There is no room for speculation, inference or surmise and, obviously, any doubt must be resolved against the charging party." *Smith Int'l, Inc. v. Olin Corp.*, 209 USPQ 1033, 1044 (T.T.A.B. 1981).

....

Mandated by the statute and case law, the Board had consistently and correctly acknowledged that there is "a material legal distinction between a false representation and a fraudulent one, the latter involving an intent to deceive, whereas the former may be occasioned by a misunderstanding, an inadvertence, a mere negligent omission, or the like." *Kemin Indus., Inc. v. Watkins Prods., Inc.*, 192 USPQ 327, 329 (T.T.A.B. 1976). In other words, deception must be willful to constitute fraud. *Smith Int'l*, 209 USPQ at 1043. [Citation.]

....

The Board stated in *Medinol v. Neuro Vasx, Inc.* that to determine whether a trademark registration was obtained fraudulently, "[t]he appropriate inquiry is ... not into the registrant's subjective intent, but rather into the objective manifestations of that intent." 67 USPQ2d 1205, 1209 (T.T.A.B. 2003). We understand the Board's emphasis on the "objective manifestations" to mean that "intent must often be inferred from the circumstances and related statement made." (internal quotation marks omitted) (*quoting First Int'l Serv.* [*Corp. v. Chuckles, Inc.*], 5 USPQ2d [1628] at 1636). We agree. However, despite the long line of precedents from the Board itself, from this court, and from other circuit courts, the Board went on to hold that "[a] trademark applicant commits fraud in procuring a registration when it makes material representations of fact in its declaration which it knows or *should know* to be false or misleading." (emphasis added). The Board has since followed this standard in several cancellation proceedings on the basis of fraud, including the one presently on appeal. *See Bose*, 88 USPQ2d at 1334.

By equating "should have known" of the falsity with a subjective intent, the Board erroneously lowered the fraud standard to a simple negligence standard....

We have previously stated that "[m]ere negligence is not sufficient to infer fraud or dishonesty." *Symbol Techs., Inc. v. Opticon, Inc.*, 935 F.2d 1569, 1582 (Fed. Cir. 1991). We even held that "a finding that particular conduct amounts to gross negligence does not of itself justify an inference of intent to deceive." *Kingsdown Med. Consultants, Ltd. v. Hollister Inc.*, 863 F.2d 867, 876 (Fed. Cir. 1988) (*en banc*). The principle that the standard for finding intent to deceive is stricter than the standard for negligence or gross negligence, even though announced in patent inequitable conduct cases, applies with equal force to trademark fraud cases. After all, an allegation of fraud in a trademark case, as in any other case, should not be taken lightly. [Citation.] Thus, we hold that a trademark is obtained fraudulently under the Lanham Act only if the applicant or registrant knowingly makes a false, material representation with the intent to deceive the PTO.

Subjective intent to deceive, however difficult it may be to prove, is an indispensable element in the analysis. Of course, "because direct evidence of deceptive intent is rarely available, such intent can be inferred from indirect and circumstantial evidence. But such evidence must still be clear and convincing, and inferences drawn from lesser evidence cannot satisfy the deceptive intent requirement." *Star Scientific, Inc. v. R.J. Reynolds Tobacco Co.*, 537 F.3d 1357, 1366 (Fed. Cir. 2008). When drawing an inference of intent, "the involved conduct, viewed in light of all the evidence ... must indicate sufficient culpability to require a finding of intent to deceive." *Kingsdown*, 863 F.2d at 876.

The Board in *Medinol* purportedly relied on this court's holding in *Torres* to justify a "should have known" standard. The Board read *Torres* too broadly. In that case, Torres obtained the trademark registration for "Las Torres" below a tower design. *Torres*, 808 F.2d at 47. The trademark was registered for use on wine, vermouth, and champagne. In the renewal application, Torres submitted an affidavit stating that the mark as registered was still in use in commerce for each of the goods specified in the registration. He even attached a specimen label with the registered mark displayed. In fact, Torres was not using the mark as registered. Instead, five years prior to the renewal application, Torres had admittedly altered the mark to "Torres" in conjunction with a different tower design. In addition, Torres knew that even the altered mark was in use only on wine. In other words, the registrant knowingly made false statements about the trademark and its usage when he filed his renewal application.

... [O]ne should not unduly focus on the phrase "should know" and ignore the facts of the case, i.e., the registrant "knows." Doing so would undermine the legal framework the court set out in *Torres.* Indeed, in *Torres*, the court cited various precedents—some persuasive, others binding on the court—and reemphasized several times that (1) fraud in trademark cases "occurs when an applicant knowingly makes false, material representations," (2) the Lanham Act imposes on an applicant the obligation not to "make knowingly inaccurate or knowingly misleading statements," and (3) a registrant must also "refrain from knowingly making false, material statements." *Id.* at 48. The "should know" language, if it signifies a simple negligence or a gross negligence standard, is not only inconsistent with the framework set out elsewhere in *Torres*, but would also have no precedential force as it would have conflicted with the precedents from CCPA. Certainly, the prior CCPA decisions cited in the *Torres* opinion were precedents binding on the *Torres* court. *See S. Corp. v. United States*, 690 F.2d 1368, 1369 (Fed. Cir. 1982). In fact, they still bind us because they have never been overturned en banc.[2]

....

Applying the law to the present case, Mr. Sullivan, who signed the application, knew that Bose had stopped manufacturing and selling audio tape recorders and players at the time the Section 8/9 renewal was filed. Therefore, the statement in the renewal application that the WAVE mark was in use in commerce on all the goods, including audio tape recorders and players, was false. Because Bose does not challenge

2. The PTO argues that under *Torres*, making a submission to the PTO with reckless disregard of its truth or falsity satisfies the intent to deceive requirement. We need not resolve this issue here. Before Sullivan submitted his declaration in 2001, neither the PTO nor any court had interpreted "use in commerce" to exclude the repairing and shipping of repaired goods. Thus, even if we were to assume that reckless disregard qualifies, there is no basis for finding Sullivan's conduct reckless.

the Board's conclusion that such a statement was material, we conclude that Bose made a material misrepresentation to the PTO.

However, Mr. Sullivan explained that in his belief, Bose's repairing of the damaged, previously-sold WAVE audio tape recorders and players and returning the repaired goods to the customers met the "use in commerce" requirement for the renewal of the trademark. The Board decided that Bose's activities did not constitute sufficient use to maintain a trademark registration. It also found Sullivan's belief not reasonable. We do not need to resolve the issue of the reasonableness as it is not part of the analysis. There is no fraud if a false misrepresentation is occasioned by an honest misunderstanding or inadvertence without a willful intent to deceive. *Smith Int'l*, 209 USPQ at 1043. Sullivan testified under oath that he believed the statement was true at the time he signed the renewal application. Unless the challenger can point to evidence to support an inference of deceptive intent, it has failed to satisfy the clear and convincing evidence standard required to establish a fraud claim.

We hold that Bose did not commit fraud in renewing its WAVE mark and the Board erred in canceling the mark in its entirety....

We agree with the Board, however, that because the WAVE mark is no longer in use on audio tape recorders and players, the registration needs to be restricted to reflect commercial reality. *See Bose*, 88 USPQ2d at 1338. We thus remand the case to the Board for appropriate proceedings....

Nationstar Mortgage v. Ahmad, 112 U.S.P.Q.2d 1361 (T.T.A.B. 2014). Ahmad filed a use-based application for registration of "Nationstar" for real estate services, submitting fabricated specimens of use (business cards falsely listing applicant as a mortgage broker). Nationstar opposed the registration, and Ahmad subsequently amended the application to an intent-to-use basis. The Board

> [took] the opportunity to confirm that once an opposition has been filed, fraud cannot be cured merely by amending the filing basis for those goods or services on which the mark was not used at the time of the signing of the use-based application. [Citations.] An applicant's statements as to its use of a mark for particular goods and services are unquestionably material to registrability. Moreover, "the law is clear that an applicant may not claim a Section 1(a) filing basis unless the mark was in use in commerce on or in connection with *all* the goods or services covered by the Section 1(a) basis as of the application filing date. 37 C.F.R. Section 2.34(a)(1)(i)." [Citation.] The applicant's statements are a fundamental statutory precondition to the issuance of a registration covering such goods and services and are relied upon by the USPTO's examining attorney in approving a use-based application for publication. Additionally, a fraud claim in an opposition notice is predicated on the opposer's belief in damage based on the application as published. See Section 13 of the Trademark Act, 15 U.S.C. § 1063. [Citation.] Thus, applicant's amendment, made after publication and institution of a challenge based on fraud, cannot aid applicant in defense of that claim.

See also Teal Bay Alliances v. Southbound One, 2015 U.S. Dist. LEXIS 10940 (D. Md. 2015) (ordering cancellation of mark when registrant submitted fabricated specimens of use: photographs of t-shirts that in fact had not been sold in commerce).

Question

The Federal Circuit in *Bose* left open the question of whether "reckless disregard" could satisfy the intent requirement to prove fraud on the PTO. If there had been clear case law that repairing and shipping of goods was not use in commerce at the time Bose's General Counsel signed the use declaration, would he be guilty of reckless disregard if he were unaware of such case law? Would a non-lawyer officer who signs the use declaration? Would outside trademark counsel, if that lawyer were unaware of the case law? *See generally*, L. Ritchie, *Is "Willful Blindness" the New 'Recklessness' After Global-Tech?*, 21 Fed. Cir. Bar J. 165 (2011) (discussing merits of "willful blindness" as a standard for the intent required to show fraud). The following decision addresses the relationship of "willful blindness" and fraud on the Trademark Office.

Sovereign Military Hospitaller Order of Saint John of Jerusalem of Rhodes and of Malta v. Florida Priory of the Knights Hospitallers of the Sovereign Order of Saint John of Jerusalem, Knights of Malta, The Ecumenical Order, 702 F.3d 1279 (11th Cir. 2012). Plaintiff Sovereign Military Hospitaller Order of Saint John of Jerusalem of Rhodes and of Malta is a religious order of the Roman Catholic Church dedicated to charitable work. Defendant, Florida Priory of the Knights Hospitallers of the Sovereign Order of Saint John of Jerusalem, Knights of Malta, The Ecumenical Order, is also a charitable organization, but is an expressly ecumenical, rather than Catholic, association. Although the defendant incorporated in Florida in 2005, it was associated with a parent organization, which was first incorporated in the United States in 1911. Meanwhile, the plaintiff began operating in the United States in 1926 or 1927. When, in the early 2000s, the plaintiff applied for its mark, a representative, Dean Francis Pace, swore in the application that:

> The undersigned, being hereby warned that willful false statements and the like so made are punishable by fine or imprisonment, or both, under 18 U.S.C. § 1001, and that such willful false statements may jeopardize the validity of the application or any resulting registration, declares that he/she is properly authorized to execute this application on behalf of the applicant; he/she believes the applicant to be the owner of the trademark/service mark sought to be registered, or, if the application is being filed under 15 U.S.C. § 1051(b), he/she believes applicant to be entitled to use such mark in commerce; to the best of his/her knowledge and belief no other person, firm, corporation, or association has the right to use the mark in commerce, either in the identical form thereof or in such near resemblance thereto as to be likely, when used on or in connection with the goods/services of such other person, to cause confusion, or to cause mistake, or to deceive; and that all statements made of his/her own knowledge are true; and that all statements made on information and belief are believed to be true.

The district court found that Plaintiff Order committed fraud on the PTO through execution of the oath that accompanied the service mark application by failing to disclose the existence of the Ecumenical Order to the PTO, despite finding that Pace was *personally unaware* of the existence of The Ecumenical Order at the time he signed the applications and the accompanying oath. *Sovereign Military Hospitaller*, 816 F. Supp. 2d at 1298, 1300. The Eleventh Circuit disagreed:

> ... To prove the fraud claim based on misrepresentations in the declaration oath, The Florida Priory was required to establish that Pace "was aware other organizations were using the ... mark (either in an identical form or a near resemblance) and 'knew or believed' those other organizations had a right to use the mark." *Angel Flight* [*of Ga., Inc. v. Angel Flight Am., Inc.*], 522 F.3d [1200] at 1211 [(11th Cir. 2008)] (analyzing a similar declaration). The declarant-focused text of the application oath requires the signatory's good-faith, subjective belief in the truth of its contents.... Pace had no awareness that any other organization was using the marks for which Plaintiff Order sought federal protection. This fact alone compels reversal of the fraud finding, as Pace could not have intended to deceive the PTO in attesting to an oath that he believed was entirely accurate.
>
> To support its finding of fraud, the district court analogized to the Supreme Court's recent decision in *Global-Tech Appliances, Inc. v. SEB S.A.*, 563 U.S. ___, 131 S. Ct. 2060, 179 L. Ed. 2d 1167 (2011). *Global-Tech* considered whether knowledge of infringement was required to sustain a claim that a party actively induced infringement of a patent under 35 U.S.C. § 271(b). *Id.* at 2063. The Supreme Court held that knowledge, rather than deliberate indifference, was required to sustain a claim under § 271 and that "willful blindness" was sufficient to satisfy that knowledge element. *Id.* at 2068. Utilizing this concept, the district court explained that "[t]o the extent that a willful blindness standard applies here, the Court concludes that [Plaintiff Order]'s failure to inform Pace of the existence of [T]he Ecumenical Order is evidence of willful blindness on [Plaintiff Order]'s part." 816 F. Supp. 2d at 1300.
>
> It was error to look to this case for the applicable standard to analyze a claim for fraud on the PTO. We have been admonished to exercise caution before importing standards from one area of intellectual-property law into another. *See Sony Corp. of Am. v. Universal City Studios, Inc.*, 464 U.S. 417, 439 n.19 (1984). The Florida Priory has not pointed to any authority to establish the sort of "historic kinship" that may justify translation of a patent-infringement standard into the mark-application context.... To the extent the district court relied on the inapplicable "willful blindness" standard to find the required intent to deceive the PTO, it erred.
>
> There is one additional aspect of the fraud analysis that the district court did not address. If the declarant subjectively believes the applicant has a superior right to use the mark, there is no fraud, even if the declarant was mistaken. *See Bose*, 580 F.3d at 1246 ("There is no fraud if a false misrepresentation is

> occasioned by an honest misunderstanding or inadvertence without a willful intent to deceive."). Here, The Florida Priory did not put forth any evidence to establish that Pace—or Plaintiff Order, for that matter—knew or believed that The Ecumenical Order or The Florida Priory had a superior right to the marks at issue ... Even assuming knowledge of The Ecumenical Order as of 1983, Plaintiff Order's relevant service mark registrations provide that the marks were first used in commerce in 1926 and 1927. The bare knowledge that The Ecumenical Order existed as of 1983 does not undermine Plaintiff Order's claim to be the senior user of those marks because, even knowing of The Ecumenical Order's existence, Plaintiff Order could justifiably believe that its marks were superior based on their first use dating back to the 1920s. *See Star Scientific, Inc. v. R.J. Reynolds Tobacco Co.*, 537 F.3d 1357, 1366 (Fed. Cir. 2008) (explaining that even though circumstantial evidence may be used to prove intent, the evidence "must still be clear and convincing, and inferences drawn from lesser evidence cannot satisfy the deceptive intent requirement"). In any event, The Florida Priory failed to proffer any evidence to show that Pace (or Plaintiff Order) believed that The Ecumenical Order had a right to use the objected-to marks in commerce. This is fatal to the claim of fraud. *See Angel Flight*, 522 F.3d at 1210.

The Eleventh Circuit reversed the cancellation of the plaintiff's marks, finding that the district court erred in finding that the plaintiff "fraudulently" obtained its marks. On remand, the district court again found fraud on the PTO and the 11th Circuit again reversed, 809 F.3d 1171 (11th Cir. 2015). The appellate court held that the registrant's awareness of a Delaware group's prior use of Knights of Malta and related marks as collective membership marks irrelevant to the Sovereign Military Hospitaller Order's registration of Knights of Malta and related marks as service marks.

Question

In *Boston Red Sox Club Limited Partnership v. Sherman*, 88 U.S.P.Q.2d 1581 (T.T.A.B. 2008), the Board found that Applicant's failure to produce any documents that evidenced a bona fide intent to use at the time the application was filed created a presumption of a lack of bona fide intent. Should such a showing be sufficient to make out a claim of fraud based on a lack of bona fide intent? *See Spin Master Ltd. v. Zobmondo Entertainment, LLC*, 778 F. Supp. 2d 1052 (C.D. Cal. 2011) (discusses the difference between the "objective" circumstances test of lack of bona fide intent and the "subjective" intent standard for fraud).

b. Fair Use: § 33(b)(4)

As we have seen, most of the defenses, including those to incontestably registered marks, concern the nature of the mark, or of the trademark owner's use of the mark. By contrast, two of the § 33(b) defenses focus on the other party's use. We have already examined one of these two defenses, the good-faith junior user exception, set forth at § 33(b)(5), in the materials on acquisition of trademark rights and concurrent use, *supra*, Chapter 3[F]. The other defense, trademark "fair use" (not to be confused with the eponymous, but quite different, exception to copyright infringement), applies when an alleged infringer has used a term in good faith primarily to describe a product, rather than to identify it with a particular source. In such a circumstance, the use will be held not to infringe the plaintiff's trademark that it resembles.

United States Shoe Corp. v. Brown Group Inc.

740 F. Supp. 196 (S.D.N.Y.), *aff'd*, 923 F.2d 844 (2d Cir. 1990)

LEVAL, J:

Plaintiff United States Shoe Corp. ("U.S. Shoe"), asserts trademark violation and unfair competition against Brown Group, Inc., in connection with the advertising and sale of women's dress shoes. Plaintiff advertises its women's dress pumps under the slogan and musical jingle, "Looks Like a Pump, Feels Like a Sneaker." Defendant has launched an advertising campaign that compares its pump to a sneaker and asserts that it "feels like a sneaker." Plaintiff seeks a preliminary injunction barring defendant from using the phrase. An evidentiary hearing was held on submission.

THINK OF IT AS A SNEAKER
WITH NO STRINGS ATTACHED.
Slip into the NaturalSport TownWalker. It has all the cushioning and support of our high performance walking shoes. And when we say it feels like a sneaker, we're not just stringing you along.

NATURAL SPORT
WALK OUR WAY
FROM NATURALIZER.

Background

The facts are largely undisputed. In August 1987, the plaintiff began to sell walking shoes under the Easy Spirit trademark. In or around October 1988, the plaintiff introduced under the same trademark a line of "comfortable women's dress pumps" which were intended to incorporate design and comfort elements of the plaintiff's walking shoes. Since that time, Easy Spirit pumps have been promoted and advertised by associating them with sneakers, and in particular by using the slogan or tag line, "Looks Like a Pump, Feels Like a Sneaker." This slogan has been prominently featured in plaintiff's print ads, point of purchase displays, catalog sheets and promotional brochures. It has also been used in a widely distributed television commercial, in which the slogan is sung while women are pictured playing basketball in Easy Spirit dress shoes. The plaintiff spent more than nine million dollars on advertising including the slogan in 1988 and 1989. During this time, sales increased dramatically. Sales of Easy Spirit pumps increased between 56% and 133% in the relevant market in the several weeks following runs of plaintiff's television commercial.

The defendant is the manufacturer and distributor of the NaturalSport line of walking shoes, and also of the Townwalker, a comfortable women's dress pump considered to be one of the key competitors of the Easy Spirit dress pump. In mid-1988, defendant retained the advertising agency D'Arcy, Masius, Benton & Bowles ("D'Arcy") to develop an ad campaign for the Townwalker and other NaturalSport shoes. D'Arcy recommended a campaign to communicate the basic product concept of the Townwalker: "a sneaker in a pump." D'Arcy submitted several proposed print ads for the Townwalker to the defendant, including some which used the slogan, "The pump that feels like a sneaker." The defendant rejected these ads, in part because of their similarity to plaintiff's advertising slogan, "Looks Like a Pump, Feels Like a Sneaker," of which defendant was aware....

The print advertisement ultimately selected by defendant features a photograph of a women's pump with the headline, "Think Of It As A Sneaker With No Strings Attached." The text of the ad includes the phrase, "And when we say it feels like a sneaker, we're not just stringing you along." The ad includes the NaturalSport logo, the slogan, "Walk Our Way" and the words "From Naturalizer," which defendant uses to advertise other styles of shoe in the NaturalSport line.

Plaintiff contends that the Townwalker ad's statement "And when we say it feels like a sneaker" is deliberately meant to mislead consumers into believing the Townwalker is the brand previously advertised by the slogan, "Looks Like a Pump, Feels Like a Sneaker," and thus cause consumers to purchase defendant's pump rather than plaintiff's. Plaintiff alleges that this constitutes a violation of the Lanham Act, as well as unfair competition and trademark violation under state common law.

....

Defendant's use of the words "feels like a sneaker" falls squarely within the "fair use" defense codified in Section 33(b)(4) of the Lanham Act. The fair use doctrine provides a statutory defense to a trademark infringement claim when "the use of the name, term or device charged to be an infringement is a use, otherwise than as a trade or service mark, ... of a term or device which is *descriptive of and used fairly and in good faith only to describe* to users the goods or services of such party, or their geographic origin." 15 U.S.C. § 1115(b)(4) (emphasis added). The purpose of the defense is to prevent the trademark rights of one party from being extended to preclude another party from the description of his product to the public. [Citation.] When the plaintiff chooses a mark with descriptive qualities, the fair use doctrine recognizes that "he cannot altogether exclude some kinds of competing uses," "particularly those which use words in their primary descriptive and non-trademark sense." *Abercrombie & Fitch Co. v. Hunting World, Inc.*, 537 F.2d 4, 12 (2d Cir. 1976). [Citation.]

An understanding of statutory fair use doctrine depends on the purposes and justifications of the trademark law. In general, the law disfavors the grant of exclusive monopoly rights. Exceptions exist, however, where the grant of monopoly rights results in substantial benefits to society. Because of the benefits to society resulting from the ability easily to recognize the goods or services of a purveyor or manufacturer, the trademark law grants the exclusive right to employ an identifying mark. A reciprocal benefit results. The merchant is thereby permitted to profit from a well earned reputation; the public is thereby enabled to choose the products produced by those who have satisfied them in the past, avoid those that have disappointed and recognize an unknown quantity as exactly that. The benefits are great, and because potential identifying marks exist in virtually inexhaustible supply, the cost of the monopoly to society is minimal.

The cost-free aspect of the trademark depends, however, on the exclusivity being practiced only over identifiers that are not needed by others for trade communication. If only one manufacturer of candy were permitted to call the product "candy"; if only one were permitted to say that it is "lemon flavored," then society would not be enriched but impoverished. Society would be deprived of useful information about competing products, and one supplier would receive an unfair and unjustified advantage over competitors. Thus the trademark law presumptively forbids the establishment of rights over "generic" or "descriptive" marks—marks that define or describe the product. An exception was permitted, however, to a user of a descriptive mark who over time had built up a customer recognition (secondary meaning) in the mark. It would be unfair to permit competitors to piggyback on the reputation earned by such a merchant. Thus a showing of acquired secondary meaning would overcome the presumptive ineligibility of descriptive words to exclusive reservation.

A user of a descriptive word may acquire the exclusive right to use that descriptive word as *an identifier* of the product or source. This, however, does not justify barring others from using the words in good faith *for descriptive purposes* pertinent to their products. Returning to the example of the candy manufacturers, the fact that one might acquire trademark rights over a descriptive identifier like "chewy" or "lemon flavored" cannot deprive society of the opportunity to be advised by other manufacturers that their candy is chewy or lemon flavored. Therefore, notwithstanding the establishment of trademark rights over a descriptive term by a showing that it has acquired secondary meaning, the statute preserves in others the right to the use of such terms "fairly and in good faith only to describe [and not to designate] the goods or services." 15 U.S.C. § 1115(b)(4). The purpose of this provision is to ensure that the according of monopoly trademark rights over descriptive marks (upon a showing of acquired secondary meaning) will not overbroadly deprive society of the use of those terms in their descriptive sense in commercial communication.

In this case, the defendant uses the phrase "feels like a sneaker" in a descriptive sense, claiming a virtue of the product. It essentially restates the key selling claim of defendant's product—that the Townswalker shoe was designed specifically to incorporate the comfort of athletic shoes.

Moreover, defendant is not using the phrase as an identifier or trademark to indicate origin or source. That function is performed in defendant's ad by the NaturalSport logo, which is prominently displayed, and by the slogan, "Walk our Way ... From Naturalizer." Defendant's use of the words "feels like a sneaker" is not even as a caption or slogan, but as a fragment of a sentence in small print. In short, defendant uses the words "otherwise than as a trade or service mark, ... fairly and in good faith only to describe to users the goods" marketed by defendant. 15 U.S.C. § 1115(b)(4). Under the fair use doctrine, such a use is not an infringement. There is no justification for permitting plaintiff to monopolize an essentially descriptive phrase which claims virtues, simply because plaintiff may have been the first to employ it in widely distributed advertisements.

Plaintiff, furthermore, has not demonstrated a sufficient likelihood of confusion as to source to justify a finding of infringement. Descriptive advertising claiming a product's virtues is likely to be understood as such rather than as an identifier of source. No confusion should be presumed from the defendant's use of descriptive words similar to plaintiff's, because the consumer is likely to understand that it is the claimed features of both products that are being discussed, and not their origin. Notwithstanding that plaintiff may have built up consumer recognition in its slogan and musical jingle, there is no reason to suppose that consumers will assume that any manufacturer who claims his shoes feel like a sneaker is the plaintiff. This is a standard descriptive approach to a claim of comfort and is unlikely to be understood as an identifier. Plaintiff has not met its burden of demonstrating that defendant's ad is likely to confuse consumers as to the source of defendant's product.

Questions

1. In *U.S. Shoe v. Brown Group*, the defendant's contested advertising copy "And when we say it feels like a sneaker, we're not just stringing you along" could be seen as a dig at the plaintiff's "feels like a sneaker" advertising campaign. But if the phrase were a snide reference to the plaintiff's advertisements, would the defendant be using it for reasons other than to describe its own product? Would such a use undermine the section 33(b)(4) defense? (As to whether it might call into play other defenses, see *infra* this Chapter, sections B.1 "nominative fair use"; C.2 parody.)

2. Simone Kelly-Brown ("Kelly-Brown") owns a motivational services business, Own Your Power Communications, Inc., that holds events and puts out publications under the registered service mark "Own Your Power." Oprah Winfrey produced a magazine, event, and website also employing the phrase "Own Your Power."

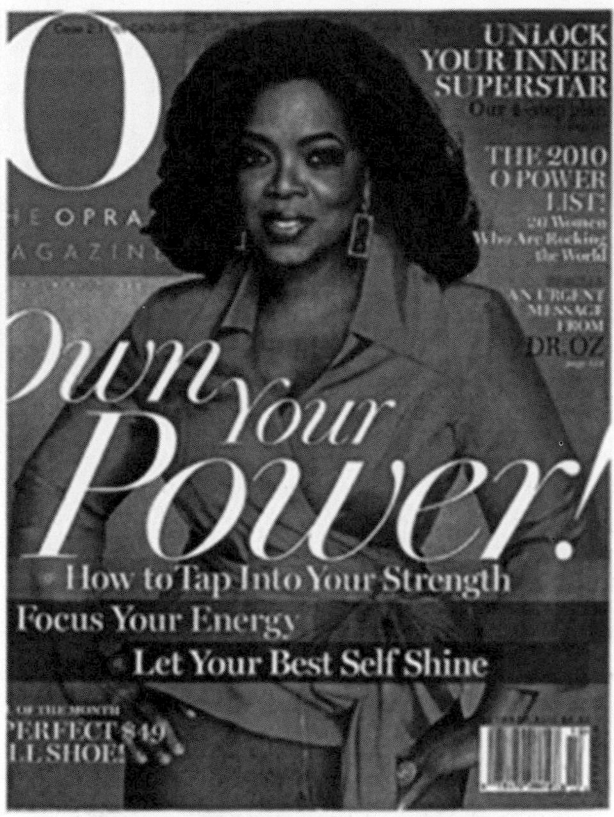

In response to Kelly-Brown's infringement action, Winfrey asserts that "Own Your Power" is a commonly-used phrase and that its use on the magazine cover and related events describes their contents and also "served as an exhortation for readers to take action to own their power and described a desired benefit of reading the Magazine Issue." How should the court rule? *See Kelly-Brown v Winfrey*, 717 F.3d 295 (2d Cir. 2013), *on remand*, 95 F. Supp. 3d 350 (S.D.N.Y. 2015).

3. Is there a difference between non trademark use and fair use under § 33(b)(4)? *See Kassa v. Detroit Metro Convention*, 117 U.S.P.Q.2d 1317 (E.D. Mich. 2015) (dismissing complaint by registrant of "Welcome to the D" for clothing and for entertainment services against Detroit Metro Convention and Visitors Bureau's use of the phrase on signs and banners connected with sporting events held in the city; holding defendants did not use the phrase as a trademark, and that their use was fair use).

Car-Freshner Corp. v. S.C. Johnson & Son Inc., 70 F.3d 267 (2d Cir. 1995).

This action for trademark infringement involves the principle that the public's right to use language and imagery for descriptive purposes is not defeated by the claims of a trademark owner to exclusivity.

Plaintiff Car-Freshner Corporation sells air fresheners for cars in the shape of a pine tree. Over a number of years, Car-Freshner has sold millions of such pine-tree-shaped fresheners. Its air fresheners are made of flat scented cardboard and come in a variety of colors and odors, including a green pine-scented version. They have a string attached to the top of the tree, so that they can be hung from the rear-view mirror of an automobile. We assume that plaintiff has established trademark rights in the pine-tree shape of its product and in the name "Little Tree," which it uses on some of its products.

Defendant S.C. Johnson & Son, Inc., sells air fresheners under the trademark name "Glade." Johnson's "Glade" products include a line of air fresheners called "Plug-Ins," designed to be plugged into electrical outlets. Glade Plug-Ins have a plastic casing that holds a replaceable fragrance cartridge of scented gel. When the unit is plugged in, the electrical current warms the gel, causing release of the fragrance into the air. During the Christmas holiday season, Johnson sells a pine-tree-shaped, plug-in air freshener called "Holiday Pine Potpourri" under its Glade Plug-Ins trademark.

Car-Freshner brought this action against Johnson, claiming that Johnson's sale of its pine-tree-shaped plug-in freshener violates Car-Freshner's trademark rights in the pine-tree shape of its air fresheners and in its mark "Little Tree." ... Johnson, in addition to denying that its use of a pine-tree shape creates a likelihood of confusion, asserted the affirmative defense known in trademark law as fair use.

....

The district court rejected Johnson's claim of fair use because it believed such a defense could be mounted only against a mark classed as "descriptive" in the four-tiered hierarchy of trademark law—generic, descriptive, suggestive, and arbitrary or fanciful. [Citation.] Although there is authority for that proposition, [citations], we believe that notion is misguided. It is true that the doctrine can apply only to marks consisting of terms or images with descriptive qualities. That is because only such terms or images are capable of being used by others in their primary descriptive sense. But it should make no difference whether the plaintiff's mark is to be classed on the descriptive tier of the trademark ladder (where protection is unavailable except on a showing of secondary meaning). What matters is whether the defendant is using the protected word or image descriptively, and not as a mark. [Citations.]

Whether the mark is classed as descriptive (and thus ineligible for protection without secondary meaning) depends on the relationship between the mark and the product described. Thus words like SWEET or CHEWY would be descriptive for a candy, but would be suggestive, or even arbitrary or fanciful, if used in connection with bed sheets, a computer, or an automobile. Regardless whether the protected mark is descriptive, suggestive, arbitrary, or fanciful as used in connection with the product or service covered by the mark, the public's right to use descriptive words or images in good faith in their ordinary descriptive sense must prevail over the exclusivity claims of the trademark owner. *See Dowbrands, L.P. v. Helene Curtis, Inc.*, 863 F. Supp. 963, 966–69 (D. Minn. 1994) (fair use defense is not limited to descriptive marks); Restatement (Third) of Unfair Competition § 28 cmt. a ("Trademark rights ... extend only to the source significance that has been acquired by such terms, not to their original descriptive meanings."). An auto manufacturer's use of the mark SWEET for its cars could not deprive anyone of the right to use that word in good faith in its ordinary descriptive sense and not as a trademark. Thus a candy manufacturer would remain free to advertise the sweetness of its candies without worry about the trademark owner's bridging the gap and going into the candy business. If any confusion results to the detriment of the markholder, that was a risk entailed in the selection of a mark with descriptive attributes.

Section 1115(b)(4) includes no prerequisite that the mark sought to be protected be on the descriptive tier....

In short, fair use permits others to use a protected mark to describe aspects of their own goods, provided the use is in good faith and not as a mark. *See* 15 U.S.C. § 1115(b)(4). That is precisely the case here. Johnson's use of the pine-tree shape describes two aspects of its product. The pine tree refers to the pine scent of its air freshening agent. Furthermore, as a Christmas tree is traditionally a pine tree, the use of the pine-tree shape refers to the Christmas season, during which Johnson sells this item. Johnson's use of the pine-tree shape is clearly descriptive. There is no indication that Johnson uses its tree shape as a mark. Its pine-tree-shaped air fresheners come in boxes prominently bearing the "Glade Plug-Ins" trademark as well as Johnson's corporate logo. Each unit has "Glade" imprinted across the front of the product itself.

....

We therefore reverse the district court's grant of summary judgment to Car-Freshner on the defense of fair use and direct entry of summary judgment in favor of Johnson on that issue. We thus affirm the dismissal of Car-Freshner's complaint.

Questions

1. Since 1996, THE RADIO CHANNEL website at "www.radiochannel.com" has offered a directory of radio stations and radio advertising information. Recently, an Internet webcaster has organized its live and on-demand television programming, radio programming, music and other media content offered to its subscribers at www.broadcast.com, into sixteen channels by content, including a "Radio Channel" for radio programming. When the words "radio channel" are typed into one popular search engine, the webcaster's site is listed before THE RADIO CHANNEL website in the list of hits. How would you decide the webcaster's fair use defense? Would it make a difference if, instead of sixteen content channels, the webcaster provided only one called "Radio Channel"? *Cf. Radio Channel Networks, Inc. v. Broadcast.Com, Inc.*, 1999 U.S. Dist. LEXIS 2577 (S.D.N.Y. Mar. 5, 1999), *aff'd w/out op.*, 201 F.3d 432 (2d Cir. 1999).

2. Consider a TV commercial for golf clubs with swing music in the background which, during 5 seconds of a 30 second commercial, shows three golfers in succession swinging their clubs preceded by the phrase on the screen "Swing, Swing, Swing." In a suit by the owner of the rights in the well-known swing song "Sing, Sing, Sing (with a Swing)," how would you decide a fair use defense? Would it affect your analysis if the advertising agency had initially approached the owner of the song, but decided not to use the song for reasons of costs? *EMI Catalogue Partnership v. Hill, Holliday, Connors, Cosmopulos, Inc.*, 228 F.3d 56 (2d Cir. 2000).

3. International Stamp Art, Inc. designs and produces note cards and greeting cards bearing reproductions of postage stamp art. For certain of these products, ISA used a perforation design to serve as a border for the card's design or illustration. ISA has obtained a trademark registration for the perforated border design. The U.S. Postal Service also issues greeting cards incorporating the designs of postage stamps, and which display a perforated border. In response to ISA's infringement action, the Postal Service contends that the perforated border is being used as an integral aspect of the image of a postage stamp. Is the Postal Service making a descriptive use "other than as a mark" that would qualify it for the § 33(b)(4) exception? *See International Stamp Art v. U.S. Postal Service*, 78 U.S.P.Q.2d 1116 (N.D. Ga. 2005), *aff'd* 456 F.3d 1270 (11th Cir. 2006).

4. Is use of the phrase "Ride Hard" by the motorcycle manufacturer Harley Davidson in its advertising and on some promotional merchandise (including T-shirts) that bear a Harley Davidson mark fair use where plaintiff owns the mark RIDE HARD for apparel? *See Bell v. Harley Davidson Motor Co.*, 539 F. Supp. 2d 1249 (S.D. Cal. 2008). Does it matter that Harley Davidson has not tried to register RIDE HARD as a mark and that third parties have used the phrase in advertising a variety of businesses?

5. Lettuce Entertain You Enterprises owns a family of LETTUCE marks for restaurant and catering services, although none of its restaurants use LETTUCE in the name of the restaurant. Defendant announced its intention to open a restaurant under the name LETTUCE MIX by placing a sign outside the intended premises. After Lettuce Entertain You brought suit, defendant covered the sign with another sign saying "Let Us Be!" with an image of a head of lettuce. Is this second sign a fair use? *See Lettuce Entertain You Enterprises, Inc. v. Leila Sophia AR, LLC*, 638 F. Supp. 2d 895 (E.D. Ill. 2009), *later decision* 703 F. Supp. 2d 777 (N.D. Ill. 2010).

6. Victoria's Secret used the term "Delicious" on pink tank tops as gifts with purchase during the launch of its BEAUTY RUSH personal care products as shown below:

The BEAUTY RUSH mark appears on the inside back collar area. Fortune Dynamic owns a registration for DELICIOUS for footwear. Should Victoria's Secret's fair use defense be successful? *See Fortune Dynamic, Inc. v. Victoria's Secret Stores Brand Management, Inc.*, 618 F.3d 1025 (9th Cir. 2010). Does it matter whether "Delicious" is intended to refer to the BEAUTY RUSH products or to the tank top wearer?

7. Where a company adopts the name of its founder as its mark and the founder then sells the company and its marks to a third party, is the founder precluded from using his name to describe his former relationship and the fact that he is connected with a new company? Is this fair use? Does it depend on how the use is made or what the contract of sale says? *See, e.g., Hensley Mfg, Inc. v. ProPride, Inc.*, 579 F.3d 603 (6th Cir. 2009); *JA Apparel Corp. v. Abboud*, 568 F.3d 390 (2d Cir. 2009), *on remand*, 682 F. Supp. 2d 294 (S.D.N.Y. 2010).

8. Village Voice publishes weekly newspapers in print and online versions for various cities throughout the United States. Annually, these newspapers publish "Best of" articles that rank local businesses in various categories, including restaurants, entertainment, shopping, and events. Village Voice owns registered marks for "Best of" services in the various cities in which Village Voice operates. Yelp, a website that allows users to rate restaurants and other services in various cities throughout the United States, has also published "Best of" lists of various categories of service providers in these cities. Recently, Village Voice brought suit alleging trademark infringement of its "Best of" marks. Does § 33(b)(4) protect Yelp's use of the "Best of" marks?

Pinterest, Inc. v. Pintrips, Inc., 140 F. Supp. 3d 997 (N.D. Cal. 2015). Pinterest holds federal registrations for PINTEREST and PIN for its service enabling users to view, post and organize content in which they are interested by creating "pins"—"pieces of digital content shaped like a vertical rectangular box, that contain a photo, caption, and various action buttons"—on their virtual Pinterest "Pinboard." Pinterest also uses, but has not registered "PIN IT." Pintrips is an online travel planning service that enables users to monitor fluctuating airline prices. "In order to use the Pintrips service, users must create an account on the Pintrips website and download a Google Chrome browser extension. Once installed, the Chrome browser extension inserts Pintrips' pin button next to airline itineraries when the user visits certain third-party travel websites. When a Pintrips user clicks on the pin button next to an itinerary, that itinerary is automatically 'pinned' to that user's 'Tripboard' on the Pintrips website. Once pinned, the price displayed next to the itinerary on the user's Tripboard will update to reflect the flight's real-time pricing and availability." The court found that Pintrips' use of the word "pin" on the website's pin button was a fair use under § 33(b)(4):

> *1. Pintrips Uses "Pin" to Describe a Feature of its Service, Not as a Mark*
>
> ....
>
> In this case, Pintrips has provided overwhelming evidence that its use of the word pin is used to describe the common act of pinning—*i.e.*, one of the services offered by the Pintrips website—and not to identify, distinguish, or indicate the source of those goods or services. Pintrips produced substantial evidence at trial that the terms pin and pinning have concrete and well-known

meanings in both the computing field generally and the social media field specifically. The Court credits the unrebutted testimony of Pintrips' expert Peter Kent, who explained that early software designers traditionally used real-world metaphors such as folders, files, desktops, and bulletin boards to describe new technological functions. Mr. Kent's testimony and the exhibits accepted into evidence demonstrate that the words pin and pinning have been used for over twenty years to describe the act of attaching one virtual object to another, much like one would use a physical pin to attach an object to a cork board....

Pintrips also presented evidence that some of the largest and most successful software and Internet companies have, for over a decade, used the word pin for this common and well-known purpose. For example, Microsoft's 2001 operating system, Windows XP, provided its users the ability to pin certain virtual objects—such as programs, folders, or files—to the operating system's start menu. Mr. Kent further testified that Microsoft also included the pinning functionality in its Word, Access, Excel, and PowerPoint programs, as well as its web browsers. In addition, Google offers its users a downloadable add-on toolbar for web browsers, which allows users to pin certain virtual buttons for easy access, and also included the pinning functionality in its Android smartphone and tablet operating system. In short, the Court found Mr. Kent's testimony (and the exhibits introduced during his testimony) to be credible and persuasive evidence that the word pin and the act of pinning are common and well-understood terms across virtually all major forms of computer technology purchased and used by the public.

Mr. Kent provided evidence that large social media websites similar to Pinterest use the term pin to describe the same functionality. For example, Facebook permits users to pin posts to a "group" and to pin messages, photos, and videos to each user's personal Facebook "timeline." Numerous media articles—many of which predate the genesis of Pinterest—report the terms pin and pinning as used in the same fashion by other companies.... In short, the words pin and pinning are regularly used to describe a particular, well-known, and decades-old computer operation.

Accordingly, Pintrips' pin button must be viewed in light of the long and pervasive use of similar pinning features and buttons employed by all manner of software and Internet companies. With that context in mind, no reasonable weighing of the evidence presented at trial could lead to the conclusion that Pintrips used the term pin as a way to identify, distinguish, or indicate the source of its goods or services. In fact, any attempt to *distinguish* Pintrips by use of its pin button would be futile, given that the words pin and pinning have been used to describe the same feature by many of the most popular and well-known software and Internet products since well before Pintrips' creation. The home page of the Pintrips website reinforces this interpretation.

> The Pintrips website expressly describes its pin button as a feature of the website that permits users to perform the same well-known pinning function offered by ... numerous software products and Internet websites....
>
> Pinterest argues that "[t]he existence of numerous alternatives for labeling content creation buttons like Pinterest's Pin It and Pintrips' 'pin' buttons confirms that Pintrips' use of 'pin' was not descriptive." But the *Fortune Dynamic* case cited by Pinterest does not support that broad statement. In *Fortune Dynamic*, the Court found that the word "delicious" was more suggestive than descriptive because the defendant had a number of alternative words that could adequately capture its goal of providing a "playful self-descriptor" on the front of its tank top. 618 F.3d at 1042. The Ninth Circuit's observation does not mean that any word with a synonym must be suggestive. For example, the term "copy and paste" is no less descriptive because other words, such as "reproduce and insert," could also be used to accurately describe the same computer operation. In fact, Pinterest's proposal that Pintrips use an alternative word for pin similar to "tweet," "stumble" or "luv"—none of which are descriptive terms of the kind contemplated by 15 U.S.C. § 1115(b)(4)—suggests that Pinterest's real argument is that Pintrips does not have a right to use the common descriptive word pin so long as it could create its own branded non-descriptive word as a stand-in. That position is flatly inconsistent with 15 U.S.C. § 1115(b)(4). Pintrips may avail itself of the fair use defense whether or not it could have dreamed up a non-descriptive word to use in place of pin.

Question

Should Pinterest's PIN mark be cancelled as generic? Given the testimony that the term has been used in connection with operating systems and social media for twenty years, would Pinterest's registration be vulnerable to cancellation for fraud on the trademark office (see *supra* this Chapter, section [A][2][b])?

KP Permanent Make-Up, Inc. v. Lasting Impression I, Inc.

543 U.S. 111 (2004)

Justice Souter delivered the opinion of the court:

The question here is whether a party raising the statutory affirmative defense of fair use to a claim of trademark infringement, 15 U.S.C. § 1115(b)(4), has a burden to negate any likelihood that the practice complained of will confuse consumers about the origin of the goods or services affected. We hold it does not.

I

Each party to this case sells permanent makeup, a mixture of pigment and liquid for injection under the skin to camouflage injuries and modify nature's dispensations, and each has used some version of the term "micro color" (as one word or two, singular or plural) in marketing and selling its product. Petitioner KP Permanent Make-Up, Inc., claims to have used the single-word version since 1990 or 1991 on advertising flyers and since 1991 on pigment bottles. Respondents Lasting Impression I, Inc., and its licensee, MCN International, Inc. (Lasting, for simplicity), deny that KP began using the term that early, but we accept KP's allegation as true for present purposes.... In 1992, Lasting applied to the United States Patent and Trademark Office (PTO) under 15 U.S.C. § 1051 for registration of a trademark consisting of the words "Micro Colors" in white letters separated by a green bar within a black square. The PTO registered the mark to Lasting in 1993, and in 1999 the registration became incontestable. § 1065.

It was also in 1999 that KP produced a 10-page advertising brochure using "microcolor" in a large, stylized typeface, provoking Lasting to demand that KP stop using the term. Instead, KP sued Lasting in the Central District of California, seeking, on more than one ground, a declaratory judgment that its language infringed no such exclusive right as Lasting claimed. Lasting counterclaimed, alleging, among other things, that KP had infringed Lasting's "Micro Colors" trademark.

KP sought summary judgment on the infringement counterclaim, based on the statutory affirmative defense of fair use, 15 U.S.C. § 1115(b)(4). After finding that Lasting had conceded that KP used the term only to describe its goods and not as a mark, the District Court held that KP was acting fairly and in good faith because undisputed facts showed that KP had employed the term "microcolor" continuously from a time before Lasting adopted the two-word, plural variant as a mark. Without enquiring whether the practice was likely to cause confusion, the court concluded that KP had made out its affirmative defense under § 1115(b)(4) and entered summary judgment for KP on Lasting's infringement claim.

On appeal, 328 F.3d 1061 (2003), the Court of Appeals for the Ninth Circuit thought it was error for the District Court to have addressed the fair use defense without delving into the matter of possible confusion on the part of consumers about the origin of KP's goods. The reviewing court took the view that no use could be recognized as fair where any consumer confusion was probable, and although the court did not pointedly address the burden of proof, it appears to have placed it on KP to show absence of consumer confusion. [Citation.] Since it found there were disputed material facts relevant under the Circuit's eight-factor test for assessing the likelihood of confusion, it reversed the summary judgment and remanded the case.

We granted KP's petition for certiorari, 540 U.S. 1099 (2004), to address a disagreement among the Courts of Appeals on the significance of likely confusion for a fair use defense to a trademark infringement claim, and the obligation of a party defending on that ground to show that its use is unlikely to cause consumer confusion. [Citation.]

... We now vacate the judgment of the Court of Appeals.

II

A

The holder of a registered mark (incontestable or not) has a civil action against anyone employing an imitation of it in commerce when "such use is likely to cause confusion, or to cause mistake, or to deceive." § 1114(1). Although an incontestable registration is "conclusive evidence ... of the registrant's exclusive right to use the ... mark in commerce," § 1115(b), the plaintiff's success is still subject to "proof of infringement as defined in section 1114," § 1115(b). And that, as just noted, requires a showing that the defendant's actual practice is likely to produce confusion in the minds of consumers about the origin of the goods or services in question. [Citation.] This plaintiff's burden has to be kept in mind when reading the relevant portion of the further provision for an affirmative defense of fair use, available to a party whose

> "use of the name, term, or device charged to be an infringement is a use, otherwise than as a mark, ... of a term or device which is descriptive of and used fairly and in good faith only to describe the goods or services of such party, or their geographic origin...." § 1115(b)(4).

Two points are evident. Section 1115(b) places a burden of proving likelihood of confusion (that is, infringement) on the party charging infringement even when relying on an incontestable registration. And Congress said nothing about likelihood of confusion in setting out the elements of the fair use defense in § 1115(b)(4).

Starting from these textual fixed points, it takes a long stretch to claim that a defense of fair use entails any burden to negate confusion. It is just not plausible that Congress would have used the descriptive phrase "likely to cause confusion, or to cause mistake, or to deceive" in § 1114 to describe the requirement that a markholder show likelihood of consumer confusion, but would have relied on the phrase "used fairly" in § 1115(b)(4) in a fit of terse drafting meant to place a defendant under a burden to negate confusion. "[W]here Congress includes particular language in one section of a statute but omits it in another section of the same Act, it is generally presumed that Congress acts intentionally and purposely in the disparate inclusion or exclusion." *Russello v. United States*, 464 U.S. 16, 23 (1983) (quoting *United States v. Wong Kim Bo*, 472 F.2d 720, 722 (CA5 1972)) (alteration in original).[4]

....

Finally, a look at the typical course of litigation in an infringement action points up the incoherence of placing a burden to show nonconfusion on a defendant. If a plaintiff succeeds in making out a prima facie case of trademark infringement, including the element of likelihood of consumer confusion, the defendant may offer rebutting evidence to undercut the force of the plaintiff's evidence on this (or any) element, or raise an affirmative defense to bar relief even if the prima facie case is

---

4. Not only that, but the failure to say anything about a defendant's burden on this point was almost certainly not an oversight, not after the House Subcommittee on Trademarks declined to forward a proposal to provide expressly as an element of the defense that a descriptive use be "'[un]likely to deceive the public.'" Hearings on H.R. 102 et al. before the Subcommittee on Trade-Marks of the House Committee on Patents, 77th Cong., 1st Sess., 167–168 (1941) (hereinafter Hearings) (testimony of Prof. Milton Handler).

sound, or do both. But it would make no sense to give the defendant a defense of showing affirmatively that the plaintiff cannot succeed in proving some element (like confusion); all the defendant needs to do is to leave the factfinder unpersuaded that the plaintiff has carried its own burden on that point. A defendant has no need of a court's true belief when agnosticism will do. Put another way, it is only when a plaintiff has shown likely confusion by a preponderance of the evidence that a defendant could have any need of an affirmative defense, but under Lasting's theory the defense would be foreclosed in such a case. "[I]t defies logic to argue that a defense may not be asserted in the only situation where it even becomes relevant." *Shakespeare Co. v. Silstar Corp.*, 110 F.3d at 243. Nor would it make sense to provide an affirmative defense of no confusion plus good faith, when merely rebutting the plaintiff's case on confusion would entitle the defendant to judgment, good faith or not.

....

B

Since the burden of proving likelihood of confusion rests with the plaintiff, and the fair use defendant has no free-standing need to show confusion unlikely, it follows (contrary to the Court of Appeals's view) that some possibility of consumer confusion must be compatible with fair use, and so it is. The common law's tolerance of a certain degree of confusion on the part of consumers followed from the very fact that in cases like this one an originally descriptive term was selected to be used as a mark, not to mention the undesirability of allowing anyone to obtain a complete monopoly on use of a descriptive term simply by grabbing it first. [Citation.] The Lanham Act adopts a similar leniency, there being no indication that the statute was meant to deprive commercial speakers of the ordinary utility of descriptive words. "If any confusion results, that is a risk the plaintiff accepted when it decided to identify its product with a mark that uses a well known descriptive phrase." *Cosmetically Sealed Industries, Inc. v. Chesebrough-Pond's USA Co.*, 125 F.3d at 30. *See also Park 'n Fly, Inc. v. Dollar Park & Fly, Inc.*, 469 U.S. 189, 201 (1985) (noting safeguards in Lanham Act to prevent commercial monopolization of language); *Car-Freshner Corp. v. S.C. Johnson & Son, Inc.*, 70 F.3d 267, 269 (CA2 1995) (noting importance of "protect[ing] the right of society at large to use words or images in their primary descriptive sense"). This right to describe is the reason that descriptive terms qualify for registration as trademarks only after taking on secondary meaning as "distinctive of the applicant's goods," 15 U.S.C. § 1052(f), with the registrant getting an exclusive right not in the original, descriptive sense, but only in the secondary one associated with the markholder's goods, 2 McCarthy, *supra*, § 11:45 ("The only aspect of the mark which is given legal protection is that penumbra or fringe of secondary meaning which surrounds the old descriptive word").

While we thus recognize that mere risk of confusion will not rule out fair use, we think it would be improvident to go further in this case, for deciding anything more would take us beyond the Ninth Circuit's consideration of the subject. It suffices to realize that our holding that fair use can occur along with some degree of confusion does not foreclose the relevance of the extent of any likely consumer confusion in assessing whether a defendant's use is objectively fair. Two Courts of Appeals have found it relevant to consider such scope, and commentators and *amici* here have urged us to say that the degree of likely consumer confusion bears not only on the fairness of using a term, but even on the further question whether an originally descriptive term has become so identified as a mark that a defendant's use of it cannot realistically be called descriptive. *See Shakespeare Co. v. Silstar Corp.*, 110 F.3d at 243 ("[T]o the degree that confusion is likely, a use is less likely to be found fair ..." (emphasis omitted)); *Sunmark, Inc. v. Ocean Spray Cranberries, Inc.*, 64 F.3d at 1059; Restatement (Third) of Unfair Competition § 28; [citations].

Since we do not rule out the pertinence of the degree of consumer confusion under the fair use defense, we likewise do not pass upon the position of the United States, as *amicus*, that the "used fairly" requirement in § 1115(b)(4) demands only that the descriptive term describe the goods accurately. Tr. of Oral Arg. 17. Accuracy of course has to be a consideration in assessing fair use, but the proceedings in this case so far raise no occasion to evaluate some other concerns that courts might pick as relevant, quite apart from attention to confusion. The Restatement raises possibilities like commercial justification and the strength of the plaintiff's mark. Restatement § 28. As to them, it is enough to say here that the door is not closed.

III

In sum, a plaintiff claiming infringement of an incontestable mark must show likelihood of consumer confusion as part of the prima facie case, 15 U.S.C. § 1115(b), while the defendant has no independent burden to negate the likelihood of any confusion in raising the affirmative defense that a term is used descriptively, not as a mark, fairly, and in good faith, § 1115(b)(4).

Because we read the Court of Appeals as requiring KP to shoulder a burden on the issue of confusion, we vacate the judgment and remand the case for further proceedings consistent with this opinion.

KP Permanent Make-Up, Inc. v. Lasting Impression I, Inc., 408 F.3d 596 (9th Cir. 2005). On remand, the Ninth Circuit interpreted the Supreme Court's statement that its holding did "not foreclose the relevance of the extent of any likely consumer confusion in assessing whether a defendant's use is objectively fair" and reversed summary judgment for the declaratory judgment plaintiff because there were genuine issues of fact as to likelihood of confusion:

> The fair use defense only comes into play once the party alleging infringement has shown by a preponderance of the evidence that confusion is likely. *See KP II*, 125 S. Ct. at 549. We hold in accordance with *Shakespeare Co.*, 110 F.3d at 243, that the degree of customer confusion remains a factor in evaluating fair use.
>
> Summary judgment on the defense of fair use is also improper. There are genuine issues of fact that are appropriate for the fact finder to determine in order to find that the defense of fair use has been established. Among the

> relevant factors for consideration by the jury in determining the fairness of the use are the degree of likely confusion, the strength of the trademark, the descriptive nature of the term for the product or service being offered by KP and the availability of alternate descriptive terms, the extent of the use of the term prior to registration of the trademark, and any differences among the times and contexts in which KP has used the term.

Is the Ninth Circuit's multifactor test for determining fair use a good one? Is it consistent with *Park & Fly*?

c. Functionality § 33(b)(8)

Jay Franco & Sons, Inc. v. Franek

615 F.3d 855 (7th Cir. 2010)

Easterbrook, Chief Judge:

The same year Huey Lewis and the News informed America that it's "Hip To Be Square", Clemens Franek sought to trademark the circular beach towel. His company, CLM Design, Inc., pitched the towel as a fashion statement—"the most radical beach fashion item since the bikini," declared one advertisement. "Bound to be round! Don't be square!" proclaimed another. CLM also targeted lazy sunbathers: "The round shape eliminates the need to constantly get up and move your towel as the sun moves across the sky. Instead merely reposition yourself."

The product enjoyed some initial success. Buoyed by an investment and promotional help from the actor Woody Harrelson (then a bartender on the TV show Cheers), CLM had sold more than 30,000 round beach towels in 32 states by the end of 1987. To secure its status as the premier circular-towel maker, the company in 1986 applied for a trademark on the towel's round design. The Patent and Trademark Office registered the "configuration of a round beach towel" as trademark No. 1,502,261 in 1988. But this was not enough to save CLM: Six years later it dissolved. The mark was assigned to Franek, who continues to sell circular towels.

In 2006 Franek discovered that Jay Franco & Sons, a distributor of bath, bedding, and beach accessories, was selling round beach towels. After settlement negotiations failed, Franek sued two of Jay Franco's customers, Target and Walmart, for unauthorized use of his registered trademark in violation of § 32 of the Lanham Act, 15 U.S.C. § 1114. Jay Franco had agreed to indemnify and defend its customers in such suits, so it sued Franek to invalidate his mark.... The district judge consolidated the two cases, granted summary judgment in Jay Franco's favor, and dismissed the remaining claims and counterclaims.... Franek appeals from that judgment; Target and Walmart are not part of the appeal.

One way to void a trademark is to challenge its distinctiveness. A valid trademark identifies the source of the good it marks. Designs do not inherently communicate that information, so to be valid a product-design mark must have acquired a "secondary meaning"—a link in the minds of consumers between the marked item and its source. *See Wal-Mart Stores, Inc. v. Samara Brothers, Inc.*, 529 U.S. 205

(2000); *Bretford Manufacturing, Inc. v. Smith System Manufacturing Corp.*, 419 F.3d 576, 578–80 (7th Cir. 2005). *Cf. Two Pesos, Inc. v. Taco Cabana, Inc.*, 505 U.S. 763 (1992). But this type of invalidation is unavailable to Jay Franco. Franek (and before him CLM) has continuously used the round-towel mark since its 1988 registration. That makes the mark "incontestable," 15 U.S.C. § 1065, a status that eliminates the need for a mark's owner in an infringement suit to show that his mark is distinctive. *See* 15 U.S.C. § 1115(b); *Park 'n Fly, Inc. v. Dollar Park and Fly, Inc.*, 469 U.S. 189 (1985).

Unfortunately for Franek, incontestable marks are not invincible. The Lanham Act lists a number of affirmative defenses an alleged infringer can parry with; one is a showing that the mark is "functional." *See* § 1115(b)(8).... The district judge [found] Franek's mark "functional" under the definition the Supreme Court gave that concept in *TrafFix Devices, Inc. v. Marketing Displays, Inc.*, 532 U.S. 23, 32–35 (2001). The judge got it right.

TrafFix says that a design is functional when it is "essential to the use or purpose of the device or when it affects the cost or quality of the device," 532 U.S. at 33, a definition cribbed from *Inwood Laboratories, Inc. v. Ives Laboratories, Inc.*, 456 U.S. 844, 850 n.10 (1982). So if a design enables a product to operate, or improves on a substitute design in some way (such as by making the product cheaper, faster, lighter, or stronger), then the design cannot be trademarked; it is functional because consumers would pay to have it rather than be indifferent toward or pay to avoid it. A qualification is that any pleasure a customer derives from the design's identification of the product's source—the joy of buying a marked good over an identical generic version because the consumer prefers the status conferred by the mark—doesn't count. That broad a theory of functionality would penalize companies for developing brands with cachet to distinguish themselves from competitors, which is the very purpose of trademark law. In short, a design that produces a benefit other than source identification is functional.

Figuring out which designs meet this criterion can be tricky. Utility patents serve as excellent cheat sheets because any design claimed in a patent is supposed to be useful. *See* 35 U.S.C. § 101; *Brenner v. Manson*, 383 U.S. 519, 528–36 (1966). For this reason, *TrafFix* held that expired utility patents provide "strong evidence that the features therein claimed are functional." 532 U.S. at 29. The parties in this case wrangle over the relevance of a handful of utility patents that claim circular towels. We need discuss only one (No. 4,794,029), which describes a round beach towel laced with drawstrings that can be pulled to turn the towel into a satchel. This patent's first two claims are:

> 1. A towel-bag construction comprising: a nonrectangular towel;
>
> a casing formed at the perimeter of said towel;
>
> a cord threaded through said casing; and
>
> a section of relatively non-stretchable fabric of a shape geometrically similar to that of said towel attached with its edges equidistant from the edges of said towel.

> 2. A towel-bag construction as set forth in claim 1 wherein said towel is circular in shape, whereby a user while sunbathing may reposition his or her body towards the changing angle of the sun while the towel remains stationary.

Claim 2 sounds like Franek's advertisements, which we quoted above. The patent's specification also reiterates, in both the summary and the detailed description, that a circular towel is central to the invention because of its benefit to lazy sunbathers.

Franek argues that claim 2 does not trigger the *TrafFix* presumption of functionality because his towel does not infringe the '029 patent....

Proving patent infringement can be sufficient to show that a trademarked design is useful, as it means that the infringing design is quite similar to a useful invention. *See Raytheon Co. v. Roper Corp.*, 724 F.2d 951, 959 (Fed. Cir. 1983). But such proof is unnecessary. Functionality is determined by a feature's usefulness, not its patentability or its infringement of a patent....

Nor does it matter that the '029 patent application was filed two years after Franek began selling round towels. As we've explained, a patent's invalidity for a reason other than uselessness says nothing about the claimed design's functionality. And a design patented yesterday can be as good evidence of a mark's functionality as a design patented 50 years ago. Indeed, more recent patents are often better evidence because technological change can render designs that were functional years ago no longer so. *See Eco Manufacturing LLC v. Honeywell International Inc.*, 357 F.3d 649, 653 (7th Cir. 2003). The Court in *TrafFix* may have dealt only with expired utility patents, but the logic it employed is not limited to them.

To put things another way, a trademark holder cannot block innovation by appropriating designs that undergird further improvements. Patent holders can do this, but a patent's life is short; trademarks can last forever, so granting trademark holders this power could permanently stifle product development. If we found Franek's trademark nonfunctional, then inventors seeking to build an improved round beach towel would be out of luck. They'd have to license Franek's mark or quell their inventiveness. That result does not jibe with the purposes of patent or trademark law. This "strong evidence" of the round towel's functionality is bolstered by Franek's own advertisements, which highlight two functional aspects of the round beach towel's design. One, also discussed in the '029 patent, is that roundness enables heliotropic sunbathers—tanners who swivel their bodies in unison with the sun's apparent motion in order to maintain an even tan—to remain on their towels as they rotate rather than exert the energy to stand up and reposition their towels every so often, as conventional rectangular towels require.

Franek responds that whatever its shape (golden-ratio rectangle, square, nonagon) any towel can satisfy a heliotropic tanner if it has enough surface area—the issue is size, not shape. That's true, and it is enough to keep the roundness of his towel from being functional under the first prong of *TrafFix*'s definition ("essential to the use or purpose of the device") but not the second. For heliotropic sunbathers, a circle surpasses other shapes because it provides the most rotational space without waste. Any non-circle polygon will either limit full rotations (spinning on a normal beach towel leads to sandy hair and feet) or not use all the surface area (a 6' tall person swiveling on a 6' by 6' square towel won't touch the corners). Compared to other shapes that permit full rotations, the round towel requires less material, which makes it easier to fold and carry. That's evidence that the towel's circularity "affects the … quality of the device." (The reduction in needed material also suggests that round towels are cheaper to produce than other-shaped towels, though Franek contends that cutting and hemming expenses make them costlier. We express no view on the matter.)

But let us suppose with Franek—who opposed summary judgment and who is thus entitled to all reasonable inferences—that round towels are not measurably better for spinning with the sun. After all, other shapes (squircles, regular icosagons) are similar enough to circles that any qualitative difference may be lost on tanners. Plus, the ability to rotate 180 degrees may be an undesired luxury. Few lie out from dawn 'til dusk (if only to avoid skin cancer) and the daily change in the sun's declination means it will rise due east and set due west just twice a year, during the vernal and autumnal equinoxes. A towel shaped like a curved hour-glass that allows only 150 or 120 degrees of rotation (or even fewer) may be all a heliotropic tanner wants. No matter. Franek's mark still is functional.

Franek's advertisements declare that the round towel is a fashion statement. Fashion is a form of function. A design's aesthetic appeal can be as functional as its tangible characteristics. *See Qualitex Co. v. Jacobson Products Co.*, 514 U.S. 159, 169–70 (1995); *Wal-Mart*, 529 U.S. at 214; *TrafFix*, 532 U.S. at 33; *W.T. Rogers Co. v. Keene*, 778 F.2d 334 (7th Cir. 1985).… And many cases say that fashionable designs can be freely copied unless protected by patent law. *See, e.g., Bonito Boats, Inc. v. Thunder Craft Boats, Inc.*, 489 U.S. 141 (1989); *Sears, Roebuck & Co. v. Stiffel Co.*, 376 U.S. 225 (1964); *Compco Corp. v. Day-Brite Lighting, Inc.*, 376 U.S. 234 (1964); *Kellogg Co. v. National Biscuit Co.*, 305 U.S. 111 (1938); *Singer Manufacturing Co. v. June Manufacturing Co.*, 163 U.S. 169 (1896).

The chief difficulty is distinguishing between designs that are fashionable enough to be functional and those that are merely pleasing. Only the latter group can be protected, because trademark law would be a cruel joke if it limited companies to tepid or repugnant brands that discourage customers from buying the marked wares. We discussed this problem at length in *Keene. See also Eco Manufacturing*, 357 F.3d at 654; *Schwinn Bicycle Co. v. Ross Bicycles, Inc.*, 870 F.2d 1176, 1188–91 (7th Cir. 1989). The Supreme Court broached the subject in *Qualitex* when it discussed the functionality of the green-gold color of a dry cleaning pad. Unwilling to say that the pad required a green-gold hue or was improved by it, the Court still thought that the color would be functional if its exclusive use by a single designer "would put competitors at a significant non-reputation-related disadvantage." 514 U.S. at 165. This is a problem for Franek's round-towel mark.

Franek wants a trademark on the circle. Granting a producer the exclusive use of a basic element of design (shape, material, color, and so forth) impoverishes other designers' palettes.... *Qualitex*'s determination that "color alone, at least sometimes, can meet the basic legal requirements for use as a trademark" (514 U.S. at 166), means that there is no per se rule against this practice. *See also Thomas & Betts Corp. v. Panduit Corp.*, 138 F.3d 277, 299 (7th Cir. 1998). The composition of the relevant market matters. But the more rudimentary and general the element—all six-sided shapes rather than an irregular, perforated hexagon; all labels made from tin rather than a specific tin label; all shades of the color purple rather than a single shade—the more likely it is that restricting its use will significantly impair competition. [Citation.] Franek's towel is of this ilk. He has trademarked the "configuration of a round beach towel." Every other beach towel manufacturer is barred from using the entire shape as well as any other design similar enough that consumers are likely to confuse it with Franek's circle (most regular polygons, for example).

Contrast Franek's mark with the irregular hexagon at issue in *Keene* or the green-gold hue in *Qualitex.* Those marks restrict few design options for competitors. Indeed, they are so distinctive that competitors' only reason to copy them would be to trade on the goodwill of the original designer.... That's not so here. A circle is the kind of basic design that a producer like Jay Franco adopts because alternatives are scarce and some consumers want the shape regardless of who manufactures it. There are only so many geometric shapes; few are both attractive and simple enough to fabricate cheaply. *Cf. Qualitex*, 514 U.S. at 168–69 (functionality doctrine invalidates marks that would create color scarcity in a particular market). And some consumers crave round towels—beachgoers who prefer curved edges to sharp corners, those who don't want to be "square," and those who relish the circle's simplicity. A producer barred from selling such towels loses a profitable portion of the market. The record does not divulge much on these matters, but any holes in the evidence are filled by the *TrafFix* presumption that Franek's mark is functional, a presumption he has failed to rebut.

Franek chose to pursue a trademark, not a design patent, to protect the stylish circularity of his beach towel.... He must live with that choice. We cannot permit him to keep the indefinite competitive advantage in producing beach towels this trademark creates.

If Franek is worried that consumers will confuse Jay Franco's round beach towels with his, he can imprint a distinctive verbal or pictorial mark on his towels. [Citation.] That will enable him to reap the benefits of his brand while still permitting healthy competition in the beach towel market.

AFFIRMED

Question

Clarin manufactures x-frame folding chairs, for which it held utility patents, now expired. It also secured a trademark registration for the following design.

Specialized Seating, one of Clarin's competitors, produces a very similar chair. Invoking *Traffix*, Specialized seating sought a declaratory judgment that its chairs did not infringe Clarin's rights under the Lanham Act. Clarin responded that there are many alternative designs for folding chairs; copying its design therefore is not necessary to compete in the folding chair market. If Clarin's design is one of many solutions to a design problem, is each solution susceptible to trademark protection (assuming secondary meaning is demonstrated), or are none of the solutions protectable by trademark law? *See Specialized Seating, Inc. v. Greenwich Industries, L.P*, 616 F.3d 722 (7th Cir. 2010); *cf. Pinterest v. Pintrips*, 140 F. Supp. 3d 997 (N.D. Cal. 2015), *supra* this Chapter, section [A][2][b].

Christian Louboutin, S.A. v. Yves St. Laurent America Holding, Inc.

696 F.3d 206 (2d Cir. 2012),
modification denied, 709 F.3d 140 (2d Cir. 2013)

Jose A. Cabranes, Circuit Judge:

The question presented is whether a single color may serve as a legally protected trademark in the fashion industry and, in particular, as the mark for a particular style of high fashion women's footwear. Christian Louboutin, a designer of high-fashion women's footwear and accessories, has since 1992 painted the "outsoles" of his women's high-heeled shoes with a high-gloss red lacquer. In 2008, he registered the red lacquered outsole as a trademark with the United States Patent and Trade Office ("PTO"). We are asked to decide whether that mark is protectable under federal trademark law....

The District Court, in addressing a difficult and novel issue of trademark law, held that, because a single color can never be protected by trademark in the fashion industry, Louboutin's trademark was likely not enforceable. It therefore declined to enter a preliminary injunction to restrain YSL's alleged use of the mark.

We conclude that the District Court's holding that a single color can never serve as a trademark in the fashion industry, *Christian Louboutin S.A. v. Yves Saint Laurent America, Inc.*, 778 F. Supp. 2d 445, 451, 457 (S.D.N.Y. 2011) ("*Louboutin*"), is inconsistent with the Supreme Court's decision in *Qualitex Co. v. Jacobson Products Co.*, 514 U.S. 159, 162 (1995) ("*Qualitex*"), and that the District Court therefore erred by resting its denial of Louboutin's preliminary injunction motion on that ground. We further conclude that Louboutin's trademark, which covers the red, lacquered outsole of a woman's high fashion shoe, has acquired limited "secondary meaning" as a distinctive symbol that identifies the Louboutin brand. As explained below, pursuant to Section 37 of the Lanham Act, 15 U.S.C. § 1119, we limit the trademark to uses in which the red outsole contrasts with the remainder of the shoe (known as the "upper"). We conclude that the trademark, as thus modified, is entitled to trademark protection. Finally, we conclude that, because the monochrome design employed by YSL is not a use of Louboutin's modified trademark, we need not, and indeed should not, address whether YSL's use of a red outsole risks consumer confusion or whether the Louboutin mark, as modified, is "functional." ...

BACKGROUND

This appeal arises out of an action for injunctive relief and enforcement of a trademark brought by Louboutin, together with the corporate entities that constitute his eponymous French fashion house, against YSL, a venerable French fashion institution. Louboutin is best known for his emphasis upon the otherwise-largely-ignored outsole of the shoe. Since their development in 1992, Louboutin's shoes have been characterized by their most striking feature: a bright, lacquered red outsole, which nearly always contrasts sharply with the color of the rest of the shoe.

Christian Louboutin introduced his signature footwear to the fashion market in 1992. Since then, his shoes have grown in popularity, appearing regularly on various celebrities and fashion icons. The District Court concluded, and YSL does not dispute, that "Louboutin [had] invested substantial amounts of capital building a reputation and good will, as well as promoting and protecting Louboutin's claim to exclusive ownership of the mark as its signature in women's high fashion footwear." *Louboutin*, 778 F. Supp. 2d at 447. The District Court further found that Louboutin had succeeded in promoting his shoes "to the point where, in the high-stakes commercial markets and social circles in which these things matter a great deal, the red outsole became closely associated with Louboutin. Leading designers have said it, including YSL, however begrudgingly." *Id.* at 447–48. As a result of Louboutin's marketing efforts, the District Court found, the "flash of a red sole" is today "instantly" recognizable, to "those in the know," as Louboutin's handiwork. *Id.* at 448.

On the strength of the fashion world's asserted recognition of the red sole, Louboutin on March 27, 2007 filed an application with the PTO to protect his mark (the "Red Sole Mark" or the "Mark"). The trademark was granted in January 2008, and stated: "The color(s) red is/are claimed as a feature of the mark. The mark consists of a lacquered red sole on footwear." *Id.* at 449 (capitalization altered). The written description was accompanied by a diagram indicating the placement of the color:

In 2011, YSL prepared to market a line of "monochrome" shoes in purple, green, yellow, and red. YSL shoes in the monochrome style feature the same color on the entire shoe, so that the red version is all red, including a red insole, heel, upper, and outsole. This was not the first time that YSL had designed a monochrome footwear line, or even a line of footwear with red soles; indeed, YSL maintains that since the 1970s it had sold such shoes in red and other colors.

In January 2011, Louboutin avers, his fashion house learned that YSL was marketing and selling a monochrome red shoe with a red sole. [This litigation followed.] ...

III. The "Functionality" Defense

....

B. "Aesthetic Functionality"

Generally, "[w]here [a product's] design is functional under the *Inwood* formulation there is no need to proceed further." *TrafFix Devices, Inc. v. Marketing Displays, Inc.*, 532 U.S. 23, 33 (2001) ("*TrafFix*"). Nevertheless, as the Supreme Court had held in 1995 in *Qualitex*, when the aesthetic design of a product is *itself* the mark for which protection is sought, we may also deem the mark functional if giving the markholder the right to use it exclusively "would put competitors at a significant non-reputation-related disadvantage," *Qualitex*, 514 U.S. at 165. This remains true even if there is "no indication that [the mark has] any bearing on the use or purpose of the product or its cost or quality." *TrafFix*, 532 U.S. at 33; [citation].

As set forth below, the test for aesthetic functionality is threefold: At the start, we address the two prongs of the *Inwood* test, asking whether the design feature is either "essential to the use or purpose" or "affects the cost or quality" of the product at issue. Next, if necessary, we turn to a third prong, which is the competition inquiry set forth in *Qualitex*. In other words, if a design feature would, from a traditional utilitarian perspective, be considered "essential to the use or purpose" of the article, or to affect its cost or quality, then the design feature is functional under *Inwood* and our inquiry ends.[15] But if the design feature is not "functional" from a traditional perspective, it must still pass the fact-intensive *Qualitex* test and be shown not to have a significant effect on competition in order to receive trademark protection.

---

15. *See, e.g., Industria Arredamenti Fratelli Saporiti v. Charles Craig, Ltd.*, 725 F.2d 18, 19 (2d Cir. 1984) (interlocking design of couch cushions was a visual "label" but served a utilitarian purpose by keeping cushions in place and was therefore functional).

i. The Development of the Aesthetic Functionality Doctrine

Although the theory of aesthetic functionality was proposed as early as 1938, the first court to adopt the theory as the basis for denial of protection of a design was the United States Court of Appeals for the Ninth Circuit in *Pagliero v. Wallace China Co.*, 198 F.2d 339 (9th Cir. 1952). In *Pagliero*, the Court of Appeals determined that the Wallace China Company was not entitled to the exclusive use of a particular floral design on hotel china, despite its "creat[ion of] a substantial market for its products bearing these designs by virtue of extensive advertising." *Id.* at 340. The design, the Court held, was "functional" because it satisfied "a demand for the aesthetic as well as for the utilitarian." *Id.* at 343–44. Because the "particular feature is an *important ingredient* in the commercial success of the product, the interest in free competition permits its imitation in the absence of a patent or copyright." *Id.* at 343 (emphasis added).

Despite its apparent counterintuitiveness (how can the purely aesthetic be deemed functional, one might ask?), our Court has long accepted the doctrine of aesthetic functionality. *See, e.g., Warner Bros., Inc.* [*v. Gay Toys, Inc.*], 724 F.2d [327] at 329–32 [(2d Cir. 1983)] (distinctive color and symbols on toy car were not functional, and so were protectable as trade dress).[17] We have rejected, however, the circular "important ingredient" test formulated by the *Pagliero* court, which inevitably penalized markholders for their success in promoting their product. Instead, we have concluded that "Lanham Act protection does not extend to configurations of ornamental features which would *significantly* limit the range of competitive designs available." *Coach Leatherware Co. v. AnnTaylor, Inc.*, 933 F.2d 162, 171 (2d Cir. 1991) (emphasis added). Accordingly, we have held that the doctrine of aesthetic functionality bars protection of a mark that is "necessary to compete in the [relevant] market." *Villeroy & Boch Keramische Werke K.G. v. THC Sys., Inc.*, 999 F.2d 619, 622 (2d Cir. 1993).

ii. A Modern Formulation of the Aesthetic Functionality Doctrine

In 1995, the Supreme Court in *Qualitex* gave its imprimatur to the aesthetic functionality doctrine, holding that "[t]he ultimate test of aesthetic functionality ... is whether the recognition of trademark rights [in an aesthetic design feature] would significantly hinder competition." *Qualitex*, 514 U.S. at 170 (quoting Restatement (Third) of Unfair Competition § 17, cmt. c, at 176 (1993)) (internal quotation marks

---

17. The doctrine of aesthetic functionality remains controversial in our sister circuits, which have applied the doctrine in varying ways (and some not at all). For example, the Seventh Circuit has applied the doctrine of aesthetic functionality liberally, holding that "[f]ashion is a form of function." *See Jay Franco & Sons, Inc. v. Franek*, 615 F.3d 855, 860 (7th Cir. 2010). The Sixth Circuit recently discussed the doctrine, but made clear that it has not yet decided whether or not to adopt it. *See Maker's Mark Distillery, Inc. v. Diageo N. Am., Inc.*, 679 F.3d 410, 417–19 (6th Cir. 2012). The Ninth Circuit has applied the doctrine inconsistently. *See* 1 McCarthy on Trademarks § 7:80 (4th ed.) (collecting cases). The Fifth Circuit rejects the doctrine of aesthetic functionality entirely. *Bd. of Supervisors for La. State Univ. Agric. & Mech. Coll. v. Smack Apparel Co.*, 550 F.3d 465, 487–88 (5th Cir. 2008) (arguing that the Supreme Court has recognized the aesthetic functionality doctrine only in *dicta*, and that therefore the Fifth Circuit's long-standing rejection of the doctrine was not abrogated by *Qualitex* and *TrafFix*).

omitted). Six years later, reiterating its *Qualitex* analysis, the Supreme Court in *TrafFix* declared that where "[a]esthetic functionality [is] the central question," courts must "inquire" as to whether recognizing the trademark "would put competitors at a significant non-reputation-related disadvantage." *TrafFix*, 532 U.S. at 32–33.

Although we have not recently had occasion to apply the doctrine of aesthetic functionality thus enunciated by the Supreme Court, it is clear that the combined effect of *Qualitex* and *TrafFix* was to validate the aesthetic functionality doctrine as it had already been developed by this Court ...

On the one hand, "'[w]here an ornamental feature is claimed as a trademark and trademark protection would significantly hinder competition by limiting the range of adequate alternative designs, the aesthetic functionality doctrine denies such protection.'" *Forschner Grp., Inc. v. Arrow Trading Co.*, 124 F.3d 402, 409–10 (2d Cir. 1997) (quoting *Wallace Int'l Silversmiths, Inc.*, 916 F.2d at 81). But on the other hand, "'distinctive and arbitrary arrangements of predominantly ornamental features that do *not* hinder potential competitors from entering the same market with differently dressed versions of the product are non-functional[,] and [are] hence eligible for [trademark protection].'" *Fabrication Enters., Inc.*, 64 F.3d at 59 (quoting *Stormy Clime* [*Ltd. v. ProGroup, Inc.*], 809 F.2d [971] at 977 [(2d Cir. 1987)] (emphasis added).

In short, a mark is aesthetically functional, and therefore ineligible for protection under the Lanham Act, where protection of the mark *significantly* undermines competitors' ability to compete in the relevant market. [Citations.] In making this determination, courts must carefully weigh "the competitive benefits of protecting the source-identifying aspects" of a mark against the "competitive costs of precluding competitors from using the feature." *Fabrication Enters., Inc.*, 64 F.3d at 59.

Finally, we note that a product feature's successful source indication can sometimes be difficult to distinguish from the feature's aesthetic function, if any. *See, e.g., Jay Franco & Sons, Inc. v. Franek*, 615 F.3d 855, 857 (7th Cir. 2010) (noting that "[f]iguring out which designs [produce a benefit other than source identification] can be tricky"). Therefore, in determining whether a mark has an aesthetic function so as to preclude trademark protection, we take care to ensure that the mark's very success in denoting (and promoting) its source does not itself defeat the markholder's right to protect that mark. [Citation.]

Because aesthetic function and branding success can sometimes be difficult to distinguish, the aesthetic functionality analysis is highly fact-specific. In conducting this inquiry, courts must consider both the markholder's right to enjoy the benefits of its effort to distinguish its product and the public's right to the "vigorously competitive market[]" protected by the Lanham Act, which an overly broad trademark might hinder. *Yurman Design, Inc.* [*v. PAJ, Inc.*], 262 F.3d [101], at 115 [(2d Cir. 2001)] (internal quotation mark omitted). In sum, courts must avoid jumping to the conclusion that an aesthetic feature is functional merely because it denotes the product's desirable source. *Cf. Pagliero*, 198 F.2d at 343.

iii. Aesthetic Functionality in the Fashion Industry

We now turn to the *per se* rule of functionality for color marks in the fashion industry adopted by the District Court—a rule that would effectively deny trademark protection to any deployment of a single color in an item of apparel. As noted above, the *Qualitex* Court expressly held that "sometimes[] a color will meet ordinary legal trademark requirements[, a]nd, when it does so, no special legal rule prevents color alone from serving as a trademark." *Qualitex*, 514 U.S. at 161. In other words, the Supreme Court specifically forbade the implementation of a *per se* rule that would deny protection for the use of a single color as a trademark in a particular industrial context. *Qualitex* requires an individualized, fact-based inquiry into the nature of the trademark, and cannot be read to sanction an industry-based *per se* rule. The District Court created just such a rule, on the theory that "there is something unique about the fashion world that militates against extending trademark protection to a single color." *Louboutin*, 778 F. Supp. 2d at 451.

Even if *Qualitex* could be read to permit an industry-specific *per se* rule of functionality (a reading we think doubtful), such a rule would be neither necessary nor appropriate here. We readily acknowledge that the fashion industry, like other industries, has special concerns in the operation of trademark law; it has been argued forcefully that United States law does not protect fashion design adequately. Indeed, the case on appeal is particularly difficult precisely because, as the District Court well noted, in the fashion industry, color can serve as a tool in the palette of a designer, rather than as mere ornamentation. *Louboutin*, 778 F. Supp. 2d at 452–53.

Nevertheless, the functionality defense does not guarantee a competitor "the greatest range for [his] creative outlet," *id.* at 452–53, but only the ability to fairly compete within a given market. [Citation.] The purpose of the functionality defense "is to prevent advances in functional design from being *monopolized* by the owner of [the mark] ... in order to encourage competition and the broadest dissemination of useful design features." *Fabrication Enters., Inc.*, 64 F.3d at 58 (internal quotation marks omitted) (emphasis added).

In short, "[b]y focusing upon hindrances to legitimate competition, the [aesthetic] functionality test, carefully applied, can accommodate consumers' somewhat conflicting interests in being assured enough product differentiation to avoid confusion as to source and in being afforded the benefits of competition among producers." [Citation.] ...

[The court held Louboutin's red sole a valid trademark, but not infringed by YSL's monochrome red shoe. "[T]he Mark has acquired secondary meaning—and thus the requisite "distinctness" to merit protection—when used as a red outsole *contrasting* with the remainder of the shoe. [But] in this case we determine that the Red Sole Mark merits protection only as modified, and ... YSL's use of a red outsole on monochromatic red shoes does not infringe on the Mark as modified...."]

Au-Tomotive Gold, Inc., v. Volkswagen of America, Inc., 457 F.3d 1062 (9th Cir. 2006). This case centered on the trademarks of two plaintiffs, well-known automobile manufacturer Volkswagen and Audi. Au-Tomotive Gold, Inc. (Auto Gold), a maker of automobile accessories, sold license plate frames and keyholders bearing the exact replicas of the trademarks of these brands. Auto Gold did not obtain a license to purvey these accessories, and though they were accompanied by disclaimers, the disclaimers were not visible or clear. Auto Gold argued that the logos and marks of Volkswagen and Audi were aesthetically functional elements of the product. The Ninth Circuit inquired whether protection of the feature as a trademark would impose a significant non-reputation-related competitive disadvantage.

> As an initial matter, Auto Gold's proffered rationale—that the trademarks "constitute[] the actual benefit the consumer wishes to purchase"—flies in the face of existing caselaw. We have squarely rejected the notion that "any feature of a product which contributes to the consumer appeal and saleability of the product is, as a matter of law, a functional element of that product." *Vuitton*, 644 F.2d at 773....
>
> ... The present case illustrates the point well, as the use of Volkswagen and Audi's marks is neither aesthetic nor independent of source identification. That is to say, there is no evidence that consumers buy Auto Gold's products solely because of their "intrinsic" aesthetic appeal. Instead, the alleged aesthetic function is indistinguishable from and tied to the mark's source-identifying nature.
>
> By Auto Gold's strident admission, consumers want "Audi" and "Volkswagen" accessories, not beautiful accessories. This consumer demand is difficult to quarantine from the source identification and reputation-enhancing value of the trademarks themselves. [Citation.] The demand for Auto Gold's products is inextricably tied to the trademarks themselves. [Citation.] Any disadvantage Auto Gold claims in not being able to sell Volkswagen or Audi marked goods is tied to the reputation and association with Volkswagen and Audi.

Reversing the district court's grant of summary judgment in favor of Auto Gold, the 9th Circuit concluded that were Auto Gold's position accepted, it would be a "death knell" for trademark protection. "It would mean that simply because a consumer likes a trademark, or finds it aesthetically pleasing, a competitor could adopt and use the mark on its own products. Thus, a competitor could adopt the distinctive Mercedes circle and tri-point star or the well-known golden arches of McDonald's, all under the rubric of aesthetic functionality."

Questions

1. In *Groeneveld Transport Efficiency, Inc. v. Lubecore Int'l.*, 730 F.3d 494 (6th Cir. 2013), a case involving the design of grease pumps, the court found that the plaintiff had failed to prove that functional considerations did not "substantially influence" the grease pump's appearance. Is the burden of proof always on the plaintiff to disprove functionality? Is the standard for functionality always "substantial influence," as opposed to "dictated by" functional considerations, or lack of alternative designs?

2. Cartier sells expensive luxury watches. It promotes its watches through extensive advertising campaigns. Globe Jewelry makes watches that resemble Cartier watches in outward appearance, but retail for significantly lower prices. Globe's watches are almost indistinguishable from Cartier watches in design and shape, but do not bear the Cartier mark. Cartier sues Globe for trade dress infringement, claiming that Globe has infringed the trade dress of these Cartier watches:

Globe contends that the designs of the watches are functional, and therefore cannot be protected as trade dress. How should the court rule? *See Cartier, Inc. v. Four Star Jewelry Creations, Inc.*, 348 F. Supp. 2d 217 (S.D.N.Y. 2004).

3. Wicked Lasers sells hand-held lasers, some of which have housings designed to look like Star Wars Light Sabers.

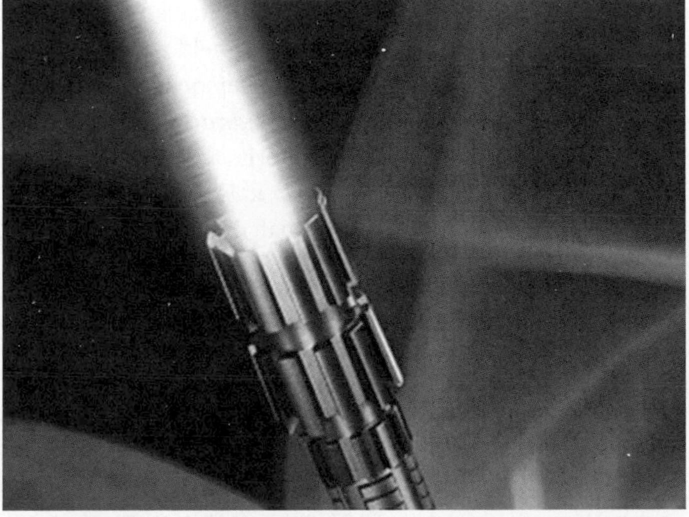

Lucasfilm objects. Is the design functional? *See* http://www.wickedlasers.com.

d. Laches § 33(b)(9)

Pro Football, Inc. v. Harjo

565 F.3d 880 (D.C. Cir. 2009)

Tatel, Circuit Judge:

At bottom, this case concerns whether various trademarks related to the Washington Redskins football team disparage Native Americans within the meaning of the Lanham Trademark Act, § 2, 15 U.S.C. § 1052(a). But that question has since been overshadowed by the defense of laches, the basis on which the district court first entered judgment for the Redskins six years ago. We reversed that decision, finding that the district court had misapplied the law of laches to the particular facts of the case. *Pro-Football, Inc. v. Harjo (Harjo II)*, 415 F.3d 44, 50 (D.C. Cir. 2005). On remand, the district court reconsidered the evidence in light of our instructions and again ruled for the team. *Pro-Football, Inc. v. Harjo (Harjo III)*, 567 F. Supp. 2d 46, 62 (D.D.C. 2008). Now appealing that decision, plaintiffs argue only that the district court improperly assessed evidence of prejudice in applying laches to the facts at issue. Limited to that question, we see no error and affirm.

I.

... Appellants, seven Native Americans, filed a 1992 action before the Patent and Trademark Office seeking cancellation of six Redskins trademarks that were, they argued, impermissibly disparaging towards members of their ethnic group. Pro-Football, the Redskins' corporate entity and the owner of the marks, argued to the Trademark Trial and Appeal Board that its long-standing use of the name, combined with plaintiffs' delay in bringing the case, called for application of laches, an equitable defense that applies where there is "(1) lack of diligence by the party against whom the defense is asserted, and (2) prejudice to the party asserting the defense," *Nat'l R.R. Passenger Corp. v. Morgan*, 536 U.S. 101, 121–22 (2002) (internal quotation marks omitted). The TTAB disagreed, observing that petitioners asserted an interest in preventing "a substantial segment of the population" from being held up "to public ridicule," and that insofar as that interest reached "beyond the personal interest being asserted by the present petitioners," laches was inappropriate. *Harjo v. Pro Football Inc.*, 30 U.S.P.Q. 2d 1828, 1831 (TTAB 1994). Finding on the merits that the marks were indeed disparaging, the TTAB cancelled them, *see Harjo v. Pro Football Inc.*, 50 U.S.P.Q. 2d 1705, 1749 (TTAB 1999), depriving Pro-Football of the ability to pursue infringers.

Pro-Football then exercised its option to dispute this holding by means of a civil action in the United States District Court for the District of Columbia. *See* 15 U.S.C. § 1071(b)(1), (4) (providing choice between district court action and Federal Circuit appeal). The district court sided with Pro-Football on the laches issue, holding that the 25-year delay between the mark's first registration in 1967 and the TTAB filing in 1992 indeed required dismissal of the action. *Pro-Football, Inc. v. Harjo*, 284 F. Supp. 2d 96, 144 (D.D.C. 2003). We reversed. "[L]aches," we said, "attaches only to parties who have unjustifiably delayed," *Harjo II*, 415 F.3d at 49, and the period of unjustifiable delay cannot start before a plaintiff reaches the age of majority, *id. at*

48–49. The youngest plaintiff, Mateo Romero, was only a year old in 1967. Because the correct inquiry would have assessed his delay and the consequent prejudice to Pro-Football only from the day of his eighteenth birthday in December 1984, we remanded the record to the district court to consider, in the first instance, the defense of laches with respect to Romero. *Id.* at 49–50.

On remand in this case, the district court again found the defense of laches persuasive. It held that the seven-year, nine-month "Romero Delay Period" evinced a lack of diligence on Romero's part, *Harjo III*, 567 F. Supp. 2d at 53–56, and following our instructions to consider both trial and economic prejudice, *see Harjo II*, 415 F.3d at 50, it found that that delay harmed Pro-Football, *Harjo III*, 567 F. Supp. 2d at 56–62. Now appealing from that decision, Romero challenges neither the applicability of laches *vel non* nor the district court's finding of unreasonable delay. We thus confine our review to the only question Romero does raise: whether the district court properly found trial and economic prejudice sufficient to support a defense of laches.

II.

... [W]e see no reason to reverse....

The district court relied primarily on two factors in finding trial prejudice: (1) the death of former Redskins president Edward Bennett Williams during the Romero Delay Period; and (2) the delay period's general contribution to the time lapse from the date of registration. *Cf. Harjo*, 50 U.S.P.Q. 2d at 1773–75 (disparagement is analyzed at the time of registration). According to the district court, both factors limited Pro-Football's ability to marshal evidence supporting its mark: Williams had met with Native American leaders close to the time of registration to discuss their views, while the nearly eight years of further delay made it more difficult to obtain any other contemporaneous evidence of public attitudes towards the mark. *See Harjo III*, 567 F. Supp. 2d at 56–58. Romero mainly argues that this "lost evidence" would have had minimal value. He believes that Williams' testimony would have reflected only a narrow set of views on the disparaging nature of the Redskins marks, and that any possibility that 1967 attitudes could have been better surveyed at the time of an earlier suit is outweighed by other overwhelming evidence of disparagement. We needn't cast doubt on Romero's view of the evidence to hold that there was no abuse of discretion. The lost evidence of contemporaneous public opinion is surely not entirely irrelevant, and weighing the prejudice resulting from its loss falls well within the zone of the district court's discretion. In reviewing that assessment, we cannot assume that legally relevant evidence possibly available in an earlier action would have lacked persuasive content.

Nor can we fault the district court's evaluation of economic prejudice. Undisputed record evidence reveals a significant expansion of Redskins merchandising efforts and sizable investment in the mark during the Romero Delay Period. Romero believes this investment is irrelevant absent some evidence that Pro-Football would have acted otherwise—by, say, changing the Redskins name—if Romero had sued earlier. But the district court repeatedly rejected this argument, citing the Federal Circuit's holding in *Bridgestone/Firestone Research, Inc. v. Automobile Club*, 245 F.3d 1359, 1363 (Fed.

Cir. 2001), that "[e]conomic prejudice arises from investment in and development of the trademark, and the continued commercial use and economic promotion of a mark over a prolonged period adds weight to the evidence of prejudice." *See Harjo III*, 567 F. Supp. 2d at 59. The court thus thought it sufficient that the team deployed investment capital toward a mark Romero waited too long to attack, whether or not the team could prove that it would necessarily have changed its name or employed a different investment strategy had Romero sued earlier.

This was no abuse of discretion. To be sure, a finding of prejudice requires at least some reliance on the absence of a lawsuit—if Pro-Football would have done exactly the same thing regardless of a more timely complaint, its laches defense devolves into claiming harm not from Romero's tardiness, but from Romero's success on the merits. But in contrast to the defense of estoppel—which requires evidence of specific reliance on a particular plaintiff's silence—laches requires only general evidence of prejudice, which may arise from mere proof of continued investment in the late-attacked mark alone. [Citation.] We have thus described as sufficient "a reliance interest resulting from the defendant's continued development of good-will during th[e] period of delay," and treated evidence of continued investment as proof of prejudice sufficient to bar injunctive relief. *NAACP v. NAACP Legal Def. & Educ. Fund, Inc.*, 753 F.2d 131, 137–38 (D.C. Cir. 1985). Such continued investment was unquestionably present here. The district court thus acted well within our precedent—as well as the precedent of the Federal Circuit, which directly reviews TTAB decisions—in finding economic prejudice on the basis of investments made during the delay period. The lost value of these investments was sufficient evidence of prejudice for the district court to exercise its discretion to apply laches, even absent specific evidence that more productive investments would in fact have resulted from an earlier suit.

In so holding, we stress two factors. First, as the district court correctly noted, the amount of prejudice required in a given case varies with the length of the delay. "If only a short period of time elapses between accrual of the claim and suit, the magnitude of prejudice required before suit would be barred is great; if the delay is lengthy, a lesser showing of prejudice is required." *Gull Airborne Instruments, Inc. v. Weinberger*, 694 F.2d 838, 843 (D.C. Cir. 1982). This reflects the view that "equity aids the vigilant and not those who slumber on their rights," *NAACP*, 753 F.2d at 137, as well as the fact that evidence of prejudice is among the evidence that can be lost by delay. Eight years is a long time—a delay made only more unreasonable by Romero's acknowledged exposure to the various Redskins trademarks well before reaching the age of majority. *See Harjo III*, 567 F. Supp. 2d at 54–55. The second point follows the first: because laches requires this equitable weighing of both the length of delay and the amount of prejudice, it leaves the district court very broad discretion to take account of the particular facts of particular cases. We have no basis for finding abuse of that discretion where, as here, the claim of error ultimately amounts to nothing more than a different take on hypothetical inquiries into what might have been.

....

IV.

Deciding only the questions presented, and finding no abuse of discretion in the district court's resolution of them, we affirm.

*So ordered.**

Oriental Fin. Group, Inc. v. Cooperativa de Ahorro y Credito Oriental, 698 F.3d 9 (1st Cir. 2012). The parties were competing financial institutions operating in Puerto Rico. Plaintiffs, collectively, "Oriental," used the ORIENTAL mark for many years in connection with their financial services. Oriental contended that the defendant, Cooperativa De Ahorro y Crédito Oriental ("Cooperativa"), began using a confusingly similar mark, COOP ORIENTAL, and a confusingly similar logo around 2009, in violation of Section 43(a) of the Lanham Act, 15 U.S.C. § 1125(a), and of Puerto Rico trademark law. The First Circuit held that Oriental's claims were not barred by laches because of the doctrine of progressive encroachment.

> As the Sixth Circuit noted in *Kellogg*, "Progressive encroachment is an offensive countermeasure to the affirmative defense[] of laches ... ; upon a finding of progressive encroachment, the delay upon which [laches is] premised is excused." *Kellogg Co. v. Exxon Corp.*, 209 F.3d 562, 571 (6th Cir. 2000). There is general agreement in other circuits that the doctrine of "progressive encroachment" can bar the defense of laches, and that "a trademark owner is not forced by the rule of laches to sue" where the doctrine applies. 6 McCarthy, *supra*, § 31:20.... We join our sister circuits in holding that the doctrine of progressive encroachment can bar the laches defense in a trademark case, and we conclude that, based on the undisputed facts, this doctrine is applicable here.
>
> As a general rule the progressive encroachment doctrine requires proof that (1) during the period of the delay the plaintiff could reasonably conclude that it should not bring suit to challenge the allegedly infringing activity; (2) the defendant materially altered its infringing activities; and (3) suit was not unreasonably delayed after the alteration in infringing activity. *See generally* 6 McCarthy, *supra*, § 31:20. Here, satisfaction of the second and third requirements are not open to serious dispute.
>
> The second requirement "turns ... on the likelihood of confusion resulting from the defendant's moving into the *same or similar market area* and placing itself more squarely in competition with the plaintiff." *Kellogg*, 209 F.3d at 573 (emphasis added). Put succinctly, we ask "whether [the] defendant, after

---

* *Editors' Note:* the laches defense barred the Harjo defendants' suit, but not the prospect of a suit by Native Americans too young to have sued during the time period of excessive delay. Accordingly, a new action was brought by a group of younger Native Americans who filed suit within a reasonable period after turning 18. See *Blackhorse v. Pro-Football, Inc.*, 111 U.S.P.Q.2d (T.T.A.B. 2014); 112 F.Supp.3d 439 (E.D. Va. 2015). Both the TTAB and the District Court rejected the laches defense. The District Court's analysis of the disparagement claim on the merits is excerpted *supra* Chapter 4[C].

beginning its use of the mark, *redirected its business* so that it more squarely competed with plaintiff and thereby increased the likelihood of public confusion of the marks."

... As to the third requirement, there is no doubt that Oriental brought suit shortly after these changes occurred.

The primary dispute in this case concerns the first requirement. This prong of the test asks first whether the right to relief was uncertain at an earlier time as to justify delay in bringing suit; that is, the defendant's activities did not present a clear case of infringement. Thus, the progressive encroachment doctrine allows the plaintiff to "wait[] until the 'likelihood of confusion looms large' to bring the action." *See, e.g., Kellogg*, 209 F.3d at 570–71 (quoting *Sara Lee Corp. v. Kayser-Roth Corp.*, 81 F.3d 455, 462 (4th Cir. 1996)); *Profitness Physical Therapy* [*Ctr. v. Pro-Fit Orthopedic & Sports Physical Therapy P.C.*, 314 F.3d [62] at 67 [(2d Cir. 2002)] (same). This is so because "the plaintiff [should have] some latitude in the timing of its bringing suit" where the infringement has not become clearly actionable. *Kellogg*, 209 F.3d at 570. This test requires the court to perform a likelihood of confusion analysis, "*determin[ing] ... whether and when any likelihood of confusion may have ripened into a claim.*" *Id.* at 571 (quoting *Kason Indus.*, 120 F.3d at 1206–07 (emphasis added)).

Alternatively, the inquiry under the first prong is whether the earlier infringement (in this case, the pre-2009 infringement), even if actionable, was so small in scope that a reasonable trademark owner could conclude that an infringement suit was not worth the costs of bringing suit. Specifically, the "trademark owner need not sue in the face of *de minimis* infringement by the junior user." *Tillamook Country Smoker*, 465 F.3d at 1110 (emphasis in original); *see also Grupo Gigante* [*SA De CV v. Dallo & Co., Inc.*], 391 F.3d [1088] at 1103 [(9th Cir. 2004)] ("The [progressive encroachment] doctrine allows a plaintiff to delay when a defendant engages in de minimis infringement at first, but then gradually encroaches on the plaintiff's market."); *AM Gen. Corp. v. DaimlerChrysler Corp.*, 311 F.3d 796, 823 (7th Cir. 2002) (noting that a trademark owner can " 'tolerate de minimis or low level infringements' and still have the right to 'act promptly' ") (quoting 6 McCarthy, *supra*, § 31:21); 6 McCarthy, *supra*, § 31:20 (noting that progressive encroachment does not require the trademark owner to sue immediately for a "low level infringement").

We agree that the progressive encroachment doctrine allows an infringement plaintiff to tolerate de minimis or low-level infringements prior to bringing suit (assuming that the other requirements of the doctrine are satisfied).

The First Circuit found that the national scope of Oriental's business, the limited geographic scope of Cooperativa's business, and the limited scope of the allegedly infringing uses meant that the allegedly infringing activity was de minimis before 2009. Thus, the doctrine of progressive encroachment was held to defeat the laches defense asserted by Cooperativa. The court vacated the district court's judgment and remanded to determine whether the COOP ORIENTAL mark and similar marks create a likelihood of confusion, and to fashion an appropriate injunction if a likelihood of confusion were established.

By contrast, in *Abraham v. Alpha Chi Omega*, 105 U.S.P.Q.2d 1692 (5th Cir. 2013), the Fifth Circuit upheld a jury determination that the "Greek Organizations" had unduly delayed in enforcing the trademarks in their insignia against Paddle Tramps, a company that had since the 1960s manufactured wooden paddles and decorations for fraternity and sorority members. The Organizations contacted Paddle Tramps several times beginning in the 1990s about obtaining a license, but did not initiate litigation until 2007. The court rejected the Organizations' contention that Paddle Tramps' infringement was too low-level to require prompt enforcement by the Organizations.

> Just under 2.5% of Paddle Tramps's revenue derives from the sale of infringing products, and the average royalty owed by Paddle Tramps to each of the Greek Organizations for the past few years of infringing conduct was only $140.78 annually. There is, however, evidence in the record to support the jury's finding. The creation of Paddle Tramps's website in 1997 and the sale of infringing products directly from that website in 2001 could be considered "an increase in the scope of the unlicensed user's business," which the district court correctly instructed could support a finding of progressive encroachment. The jury could have determined that the intervening six years between 2001 and 2007, when the Greek Organizations brought suit, is itself an unexcused delay sufficient to satisfy the lack-of-excuse element of laches.

Questions

1. If a trademark owner orders search reports that show a defendant's mark, should that start the period of delay for laches to commence? *See Saul Zaentz Co. v. Wozniak Travel, Inc.*, 627 F. Supp. 2d 1096 (N.D. Cal. 2008) (defendant's Hobbit Travel business first appeared in Tolkien rights owner's search reports 18 years before suit was brought).

2. In *Internet Specialties West, Inc. v. Milon-DiGiorgio Enterprises, Inc.*, 559 F.3d 985 (9th Cir. 2009), both plaintiff and defendant were Internet service providers. Although aware of defendant from 1998, plaintiff did not object until 2005, several months after defendant expanded to offer DSL service. Plaintiff argued that the period of delay for laches should start anew from this expansion. Do you agree or disagree with this position? Additionally, defendant argued it showed prejudice resulting from plaintiff's delay since in the meantime it had built its customer base from 2,000 to 13,000 and had built up goodwill through promoting its services through pay-per-click ads on the internet. Is this a sufficient showing of prejudice? See majority and dissenting opinions.

3. Recall the *Dawn Donut Co. v. Hart's Food Stores, Inc.*, 267 F.2d 358 (2d Cir. 1959), case, *supra* Chapter 3[F]. Suppose the trademark registrant years later began using the mark for donut shops in the Rochester NY area. Would the local junior user have a laches defense to the registrant's late assertion of its trademark rights in that locality?

4. What, if any, effect on a laches defense should a defendant's intentional copying and knowing exploitation of another's mark have? Should a trademark owner's delay become more undue when a third party exploits the mark with full knowledge of its ownership? Or should the exploiter's willful conduct disqualify a laches defense? *See D.C. Comics v. Towle*, 802 F.3d 1012 (9th Cir. 2015) (rejecting laches defense when defendant intentionally copied "Batmobile" trademark for replicas of the vehicle).

B. Judge-Made Defenses

1. Nominative Fair Use

Although "nominative fair use" is not a statutory defense to an incontestable registration, some courts have adopted the defense when a mark is used not to describe the defendant's product, but to refer fairly to another trademark owner or its goods or services. Devised in the Ninth Circuit, in the *New Kids on the Block* case, immediately below, the defense has been recognized in the Third and Fifth Circuits, *see, e.g., Century 21 Real Estate Corp. v. Lendingtree, Inc.*, 425 F.3d 211 (3d Cir. 2005); *Board of Supervisors for Louisiana State University Agricultural and Mechanical College v. Smack Apparel Co.*, 550 F.3d 465 (5th Cir. 2008). Other Circuits also hold such referential uses to be non infringing, without expressly labeling the lawful use "nominative fair use." *See, e.g., WCVB-TV v. Boston Athletic Ass'n*, 926 F.2d 42 (1st Cir. 1991); *Tiffany (NJ) Inc. v. eBay Inc.*, 600 F.3d 93 (2d Cir. 2010); *University of Florida v. KPB, Inc.*, 89 F.3d 773 (11th Cir. 1996). The Sixth Circuit and now the Second Circuit have expressly rejected the Ninth Circuit's elaboration of the defense, see *PACCAR Inc. v. TeleScan Technologies, L.L.C.*, 319 F.3d 243 (6th Cir. 2003); *International Info. Sys. Sec. Certification Consortium v. Sec. Univ., LLC*, 823 F.3d 153 (2d Cir. 2016), but the Second Circuit has integrated the Ninth Circuit's nominative fair use factors into the *Polaroid* factors, see edited case, *infra*. The Fourth Circuit has declined to rule one way or the other, *see Rosetta Stone, Inc. v. Google, Inc.*, 676 F.3d 144 (4th Cir. 2012). For a summary of the various Circuits' approaches to nominative uses, see Peter M. Brody & Alexandra J. Roberts, *What's in a Domain Name? Nominative Fair Use Online after* Toyota v. Tabari, 100 Trademark Reptr. 1290, 1299–1318 (2010). Congress has also recognized nominative fair use as exception to dilution protection in § 1125(c)(3), revised in 2006. *See infra*, Chapter 9[B].

New Kids On The Block v. News America Publishing

971 F.2d 302 (9th Cir. 1992)

Kozinski, Circuit Judge:

The individual plaintiffs perform professionally as The New Kids on the Block, reputedly one of today's hottest musical acts. This case requires us to weigh their rights in that name against the rights of others to use it in identifying the New Kids as the subjects of public opinion polls.

Background

No longer are entertainers limited to their craft in marketing themselves to the public. This is the age of the multi-media publicity blitzkrieg: Trading on their popularity, many entertainers hawk posters, T-shirts, badges, coffee mugs and the like—handsomely supplementing their incomes while boosting their public images. The New Kids are no exception; the record in this case indicates there are more than 500 products or services bearing the New Kids trademark. Among these are services taking advantage of a recent development in telecommunications: 900 area code numbers, where the caller is charged a fee, a portion of which is paid to the call recipient. Fans can call various New Kids 900 numbers to listen to the New Kids talk about themselves, to listen to other fans talk about the New Kids, or to leave messages for the New Kids and other fans. The defendants, two newspapers of national circulation, conducted separate polls of their readers seeking an answer to a pressing question: Which one of the New Kids is the most popular? USA Today's announcement contained a picture of the New Kids and asked, "Who's the best on the block?" The announcement listed a 900 number for voting, noted that "any USA Today profits from this phone line will go to charity," and closed with the following:

> New Kids on the Block are pop's hottest group. Which of the five is your fave? Or are they a turn off? ... Each call costs 50 cents. Results in Friday's Life section.

The Star's announcement, under a picture of the New Kids, went to the heart of the matter: "Now which kid is the sexiest?" The announcement, which appeared in the middle of a page containing a story on a New Kids concert, also stated:

> Which of the New Kids on the Block would you most like to move next door? STAR wants to know which cool New Kid is the hottest with our readers.

Readers were directed to a 900 number to register their votes; each call cost 95 cents per minute.

Fearing that the two newspapers were undermining their hegemony over their fans, the New Kids filed a shotgun complaint in federal court [alleging, *inter alia*, violations of the Lanham Act and of California unfair competition law]. The two papers raised the First Amendment as a defense, on the theory that the polls were part and parcel of their "news-gathering activities." The district court granted summary judgment for defendants.

Discussion

While the district court granted summary judgment on First Amendment grounds, we are free to affirm on any ground fairly presented by the record. Indeed, where we are able to resolve the case on nonconstitutional grounds, we ordinarily must avoid reaching the constitutional issue. Therefore, we consider first whether the New Kids have stated viable claims on their various causes of action.

... A trademark is a limited property right in a particular word, phrase or symbol. And although English is a language rich in imagery, we need not belabor the point that some words, phrases or symbols better convey their intended meanings than others. Indeed, the primary cost of recognizing property rights in trademarks is the removal of words from (or perhaps non-entrance into) our language. Thus, the holder of a trademark will be denied protection if it is (or becomes) generic, i.e., if it does not relate exclusively to the trademark owner's product. This requirement allays fears that producers will deplete the stock of useful words by asserting exclusive rights in them....

A related problem arises when a trademark also describes a person, a place or an attribute of a product. If the trademark holder were allowed exclusive rights in such use, the language would be depleted in much the same way as if generic words were protectable. Thus trademark law recognizes a defense where the mark is used only "to describe the goods or services of [a] party, or their geographic origin." 15 U.S.C. § 1115(b)(4). "The 'fair-use' defense, in essence, forbids a trademark registrant to appropriate a descriptive term for his exclusive use and so prevent others from accurately describing a characteristic of their goods." *Soweco, Inc. v. Shell Oil Co.*, 617 F.2d 1178, 1185 (5th Cir. 1980). Once again, the courts will hold as a matter of law that the original producer does not sponsor or endorse another product that uses his mark in a descriptive manner.

With many well-known trademarks, such as Jell-O, Scotch tape and Kleenex, there are equally informative non-trademark words describing the products (gelatin, cellophane tape and facial tissue). But sometimes there is no descriptive substitute, and a problem closely related to genericity and descriptiveness is presented when many goods and services are effectively identifiable only by their trademarks. For example, one might refer to "the two-time world champions" or "the professional basketball team from Chicago," but it's far simpler (and more likely to be understood) to refer to the Chicago Bulls. In such cases, use of the trademark does not imply sponsorship or endorsement of the product because the mark is used only to describe the thing, rather than to identify its source.

Indeed, it is often virtually impossible to refer to a particular product for purposes of comparison, criticism, point of reference or any other such purpose without using the mark. For example, reference to a large automobile manufacturer based in Michigan would not differentiate among the Big Three; reference to a large Japanese manufacturer of home electronics would narrow the field to a dozen or more companies. Much useful social and commercial discourse would be all but impossible if speakers were under threat of an infringement lawsuit every time they made reference to a person, company or product by using its trademark....

A good example of this is *Volkswagenwerk Aktiengesellschaft v. Church*, 411 F.2d 350 (9th Cir. 1969), where we held that Volkswagen could not prevent an automobile repair shop from using its mark. We recognized that in "advertising [the repair of Volkswagens, it] would be difficult, if not impossible, for [Church] to avoid altogether the use of the word 'Volkswagen' or its abbreviation 'VW,' which are the normal terms which, to the public at large, signify appellant's cars." *Id.* at 352. Church did not suggest to customers that he was part of the Volkswagen organization or that his repair shop was sponsored or authorized by VW; he merely used the words "Volkswagen" and "VW" to convey information about the types of cars he repaired. Therefore, his use of the Volkswagen trademark was not an infringing use.

The First Circuit confronted a similar problem when the holder of the trademark "Boston Marathon" tried to stop a television station from using the name.... Similarly, competitors may use a rival's trademark in advertising and other channels of communication if the use is not false or misleading. *See, e.g., Smith v. Chanel, Inc.*, 402 F.2d 562 (9th Cir. 1968) (maker of imitation perfume may use original's trademark in promoting product).

Cases like these are best understood as involving a non-trademark use of a mark—a use to which the infringement laws simply do not apply.... Indeed, we may generalize a class of cases where the use of the trademark does not attempt to capitalize on consumer confusion or to appropriate the cachet of one product for a different one. Such nominative use of a mark—where the only word reasonably available to describe a particular thing is pressed into service—lies outside the strictures of trademark law: Because it does not implicate the source-identification function that is the purpose of trademark, it does not constitute unfair competition; such use is fair because it does not imply sponsorship or endorsement by the trademark holder. "When the mark is used in a way that does not deceive the public we see no such sanctity in the word as to prevent its being used to tell the truth." *Prestonettes, Inc. v. Coty*, 264 U.S. 359, 368 (1924) (Holmes, J.).

To be sure, this is not the classic fair use case where the defendant has used the plaintiff's mark to describe the defendant's own product. Here, the New Kids trademark is used to refer to the New Kids themselves. We therefore do not purport to alter the test applicable in the paradigmatic fair use case. If the defendant's use of the plaintiff's trademark refers to something other than the plaintiff's product, the traditional fair use inquiry will continue to govern. But, where the defendant uses a trademark to describe the plaintiff's product, rather than its own, we hold that a commercial user is entitled to a nominative fair use defense provided he meets the following three requirements: First, the product or service in question must be one not readily identifiable without use of the trademark; second, only so much of the mark or marks may be used as is reasonably necessary to identify the product or service; and third, the user must do nothing that would, in conjunction with the mark, suggest sponsorship or endorsement by the trademark holder. The New Kids do not claim there was anything false or misleading about the newspapers' use of their mark. Rather, the first seven causes of action, while purporting to state different claims, all hinge on one key factual allegation: that the newspapers' use of the New Kids name in conducting the unauthorized polls somehow implied that the New Kids were sponsoring the polls. It is no more reasonably possible, however, to refer to the New Kids as an entity than it is to refer to the Chicago Bulls, Volkswagens or the Boston Marathon without using the trademark. Indeed, how could someone not conversant with the proper names of the individual New Kids talk about the group at all? While plaintiffs' trademark certainly deserves protection against copycats and those who falsely claim that the New Kids have endorsed or sponsored them, such protection does not extend to rendering newspaper articles, conversations, polls and comparative advertising impossible. The first nominative use requirement is therefore met.

Also met are the second and third requirements. Both The Star and USA Today reference the New Kids only to the extent necessary to identify them as the subject of the polls; they do not use the New Kids' distinctive logo or anything else that isn't needed to make the announcements intelligible to readers. Finally, nothing in the announcements suggests joint sponsorship or endorsement by the New Kids. The USA Today announcement implies quite the contrary by asking whether the New Kids might be "a turn off." The Star's poll is more effusive but says nothing that expressly or by fair implication connotes endorsement or joint sponsorship on the part of the New Kids.

The New Kids argue that, even if the newspapers are entitled to a nominative fair use defense for the announcements, they are not entitled to it for the polls themselves, which were money-making enterprises separate and apart from the newspapers' reporting businesses. According to plaintiffs, defendants could have minimized the intrusion into their rights by using an 800 number or asking readers to call in on normal telephone lines which would not have resulted in a profit to the newspapers based on the conduct of the polls themselves.

The New Kids see this as a crucial difference, distinguishing this case from *Volkswagenwerk*, *WCBV-TV* and other nominative use cases. The New Kids' argument in support of this distinction is not entirely implausible: They point out that their fans, like everyone else, have limited resources. Thus a dollar spent calling the newspapers' 900 lines to express loyalty to the New Kids may well be a dollar not spent on New Kids products and services, including the New Kids' own 900 numbers. In short, plaintiffs argue that a nominative fair use defense is inapplicable where the use in question competes directly with that of the trademark holder.

We reject this argument. While the New Kids have a limited property right in their name, that right does not entitle them to control their fans' use of their own money. Where, as here, the use does not imply sponsorship or endorsement, the fact that it is carried on for profit and in competition with the trademark holder's business is beside the point. *See, e.g., Universal City Studios, Inc. v. Ideal Publishing Corp.*, 195 U.S.P.Q. 761 (S.D.N.Y. 1977) (magazine's use of TV program's trademark "Hardy Boys" in connection with photographs of show's stars not infringing). Voting for their favorite New Kid may be, as plaintiffs point out, a way for fans to articulate their loyalty to the group, and this may diminish the resources available for products and services they sponsor. But the trademark laws do not give the New Kids the right to channel their fans' enthusiasm (and dollars) only into items licensed or authorized by them. *See International Order of Job's Daughters v. Lindeburg & Co.*, 633 F.2d 912 (9th Cir. 1990) (no infringement where unauthorized jewelry maker produced rings and pins bearing fraternal organization's trademark). The New Kids could not use the trademark laws to prevent the publication of an unauthorized group biography or to censor all parodies or satires which use their name. We fail to see a material difference between these examples and the use here.

Question

Although the court declares that "the trademark laws do not give the New Kids the right to channel their fans' enthusiasm (and dollars) only into items licensed or authorized by them," is such channeling not in fact the goal of a trademark licensing program? Moreover, some courts have protected such programs against unauthorized third-party merchandise. *See, e.g., Warner Bros. Inc. v. Gay Toys, Inc.*, 724 F.2d 327 (2d Cir. 1983); *Processed Plastic Co. v. Warner Communications, Inc.*, 675 F.2d 852 (7th Cir. 1982) (both finding trademark infringement by unlicensed toy cars bearing the Dukes of Hazzard "General Lee" insignia). Are these cases distinguishable from *New Kids*? *See also Dow Jones & Company, Inc. v. International Securities, Exchange, Inc.*, 451 F.3d 295 (2d Cir. 2006).

Kassbaum v. Steppenwolf Productions, Inc. 236 F.3d 487 (9th Cir. 2000). In 1967, John Kay, Jerry Edmonton, Michael Monarch and Goldie McJohn formed a musical band called "Steppenwolf." In 1968, Nicholas Kassbaum joined Steppenwolf as a bass player. From late 1968 until late April 1970, Steppenwolf toured the world in concerts and recorded music, with Kassbaum appearing prominently on record album covers and writing Steppenwolf compositions. However, in 1971, Kassbaum was excluded from the band. Kassbaum later signed an agreement acknowledging that Steppenwolf Productions, Inc. (SPI) owned the "Steppenwolf" service mark. Beginning in 1996, Kassbaum began performing with a group named the World Classic Rockers, using phrases such as "Formerly of Steppenwolf," "Original Member of Steppenwolf" and "Original Founding Member of Steppenwolf," in promotional materials. In response to these promotional claims, SPI sent Kassbaum cease and desist letters asserting that Kassbaum's historical references to Steppenwolf violated federal trademark law and the 1980 contract. Eventually, the district court granted SPI's motion for summary judgment on Kassbaum's complaint for declaratory relief, granted SPI's counterclaim for breach of contract, dismissed Kassbaum's complaint for declaratory relief, and granted SPI's request for a permanent injunction forbidding Kassbaum from using the designations. Kassbaum appealed.

> The purpose of a trademark is to allow customers to identify the manufacturer or sponsor of a good or the provider of a service. *New Kids on the Block v. News. Am. Pub., Inc.*, 971 F.2d 302, 305 (9th Cir. 1992). Actual consumer confusion is not required for profit recovery; it is sufficient to show a likelihood of confusion combined with willful infringement. [Citation.] For the reasons that follow, we believe that Kassbaum's references to himself in promotional materials as "Formerly of Steppenwolf," an "Original Member of Steppenwolf," and an "Original Founding Member of Steppenwolf," do not cause a likelihood of confusion.

> First, we believe the phrases "Formerly of," "Original Member of" and "Original Founding Member of," immediately preceding the name "Steppenwolf" in the promotional materials for World Classic Rockers greatly reduce the likelihood of confusion about the source of the band's music.
>
> Additionally, the context of the historical references to Kassbaum's affiliation with Steppenwolf in World Classic Rockers' promotional materials further reduces any likelihood of confusion between these two bands. In all promotional materials presented to the district court, references to World Classic Rockers are more prominent than are references to Steppenwolf. The materials display the title "World Classic Rockers" on the top or at the center of the page, while references to the band members' former groups, including Steppenwolf, are displayed on the bottom or around the edges of the page. Also, the title "World Classic Rockers" appears in large and bold lettering, while smaller and plainer lettering is used for the titles of the former groups, including Steppenwolf. Finally, while the materials mention multiple former groups, the materials promote only World Classic Rockers, not Steppenwolf, or any other former band.

The Ninth Circuit reversed and remanded the case.

International Info. Sys. Sec. Certification Consortium v. Security Univ., LLC

823 F.3d 153 (2d Cir. 2016)

POOLER, Circuit Judge:

Plaintiff-appellant International Information Systems Security Certification Consortium, Inc. ("ISC2") filed suit against defendants-appellees Security University ("SU") and Sondra Schneider, alleging that SU's use of ISC2's certification mark violated the Lanham Act, 15 U.S.C. § 1051 et seq., and constituted infringement under 15 U.S.C. § 1114, false designation of origin and false advertising under 15 U.S.C. § 1125(a), … Following cross-motions for summary judgment, the district court granted summary judgment to defendants on all grounds, holding that defendants' use of the certification mark constituted nominative fair use under the Ninth Circuit's test, which our Court has not, to this point, adopted. Critical to its determination that defendants' use of the mark constituted nominative fair use under the Ninth Circuit's test were the district court's misperceptions that the only type of confusion relevant to an infringement claim was confusion as to source and that a certification mark could not be infringed by a duly certified individual.

Having considered other circuits' nominative fair use tests as well as our own prior treatment of claims involving nominative use, we hold that nominative fair use is not an affirmative defense to a claim of infringement under the Lanham Act. We further hold that in cases involving nominative use, in addition to considering the *Polaroid* factors, courts are to consider (1) whether the use of the plaintiff's mark is necessary to describe both the plaintiff's product or service and the defendant's product or service, that is, whether the product or service is not readily identifiable without use of the mark; (2) whether the defendant uses only so much of the plaintiff's mark as is necessary to identify the product or service; and (3) whether the defendant did anything that would, in conjunction with the mark, suggest sponsorship or endorsement by the plaintiff holder, that is, whether the defendant's conduct or language reflects the true or accurate relationship between plaintiff's and defendant's products or services. When considering these factors, courts must be mindful of the different types of confusion relevant to infringement claims, including confusion as to sponsorship, affiliation, or connection, as well as, when considering a certification mark, the various ways such a mark can be infringed.

Because the district court failed to consider the *Polaroid* factors and because its consideration of the relevant nominative fair use factors was based on incorrect assumptions, we vacate the district court's grant of summary judgment on the infringement claims....

BACKGROUND

I. The CISSP® Mark

A. ISC2's Mark

ISC2 is a non-profit organization that was formed in 1989 to develop standards for the information security industry. In March 1990, ISC2 developed a certification program and began using the certification mark "CISSP®" to denote a "Certified Information Systems Security Professional" who has met certain requirements and standards of competency in the information security field, including passing the CISSP® certification examination that ISC2 administers.

On March 18, 1997, the United States Patent and Trademark Office registered ISC2's CISSP® certification mark. The registration stated: "The [CISSP®] certification mark is used by persons authorized by the certifier [ISC2] to certify completion of appropriate work experience and/or successfully passing examinations as established by the certifier in the field of security of information systems."

B. SU's Alleged Infringement

SU is a for-profit company that was formed in 1999 by defendant-appellee Sondra Schneider, a CISSP®-certified individual, to provide information security training. SU offers various classes, including a class to prepare individuals for ISC2's CISSP® certification examination. SU has used the CISSP® mark in connection with certification-specific training courses since 2001. It is undisputed that SU is allowed to use the CISSP® certification mark to indicate that its services are directed at preparing students for the CISSP® certification examination. Furthermore, given the nature of ISC2's certification mark, SU instructors may accurately identify themselves as being CISSP®-certified, so long as they follow ISC2's regulations governing the use of the mark.

However, ISC2 objects to some of SU's advertisements, run between 2010 and 2012, which, ISC2 argues, misleadingly suggested that SU's instructor, Clement

Dupuis, had attained some higher level of certification as a "Master CISSP" or "CISSP Master." ...

SU began using the term "Master" in May 2010. On June 9, 2010, ISC2's counsel wrote to Schneider asking that she cease using the phrase "Master CISSP" in SU's advertisements. On June 13, 2010, Schneider emailed Marc Thompson, an employee of a third party entity that oversees seminars on ISC2's behalf, stating that "SU will continue to use the word Master. Master Clement Dupuis is a Male Teacher [and] thus he is a Master according to the dictionary." [Citation.] On July 15, 2010, ISC2's counsel "again wrote to Ms. Schneider requesting that she and SU cease and desist their improper advertising." ...

....

DISCUSSION

I. Certification Marks

A "certification mark," such as CISSP®, is a special sub-category of marks which, unlike other trademarks, is intended to be used by those other than its owner, to indicate the quality, accuracy, or other characteristics of the goods or services.... The CISSP® mark is meant to certify quality and characteristics, that is, that the security information professional bearing the CISSP® mark meets ISC2's standards and has passed its competency test.

In spite of the differences between certification marks and other types of marks, the Lanham Act provides that certification marks are generally entitled to the same protection from infringement as are trademarks. [Citations.]

II. Infringement Claims

... Defendants do not dispute that ISC2's mark merits protection; they merely argue that their use of the mark is non-infringing.

...

A. Types of Confusion Relevant to Infringement Claims

The district court held that the only type of confusion relevant in determining infringement is confusion as to source. This is incorrect; protection is not exclusively limited for any type of mark to cases in which there may be confusion as to source.[3] Rather, "[t]he modern test of infringement is whether the defendant's use [is] likely to cause confusion *not just as to source*, but also as to sponsorship, affiliation or connection." 4 McCarthy on Trademarks and Unfair Competition [hereinafter "McCarthy"] § 23:76 (4th ed.) (emphasis added)....

...

3. Indeed, considering only source confusion would make little sense in the context of certification marks, as certification marks are generally not used to designate source at all.

C. Likelihood of Confusion in Nominative Use Cases

Having determined that the district court erred in considering only source confusion and erroneously limiting the ways in which certification marks can be infringed, we turn to the question of how the district court should assess likelihood of confusion on remand.

[O]ur Court's test for assessing likelihood of confusion is the *Polaroid* test.... This Court has repeatedly urged district courts to apply the *Polaroid* factors even "where a factor is irrelevant to the facts at hand." [Citation.]

The district court, rather than applying the Polaroid factors, applied the Ninth Circuit's test which applies in cases of nominative use of marks....

Other circuits have adopted variations of this test. [Citations.]

In the Ninth Circuit, nominative fair use is not an affirmative defense because it does not protect a defendant from liability if there is, in fact, a likelihood of consumer confusion. Rather, the nominative fair use test replaces the multi-factor test that the Ninth Circuit typically employs to determine consumer confusion, i.e., it replaces the Ninth Circuit's analogue to the *Polaroid* test. [Citations.]

By contrast, the Third Circuit, another court to have developed a nominative fair use doctrine, affords defendants broader protection. The Third Circuit treats nominative fair use as an affirmative defense that may be asserted by the defendant despite a likelihood of consumer confusion. To be entitled to protection based on the affirmative defense, a defendant must show

> (1) that the use of plaintiff's mark is necessary to describe both the plaintiff's product or service and the defendant's product or service; (2) that the defendant uses only so much of the plaintiff's mark as is necessary to describe plaintiff's product; and (3) that the defendant's conduct or language reflect the true and accurate relationship between plaintiff and defendant's products or services.

Century 21 Real Estate Corp., 425 F.3d at 222.

To this point, this Court has not adopted either the Ninth Circuit or the Third Circuit's rule on nominative fair use. [Citation.] Nonetheless, district courts within our Circuit frequently use the Ninth Circuit's formulation. [Citations.] Further, as discussed below we have endorsed the principles underlying the nominative fair use doctrine. [Citation.]

Having considered the case law, ... we reject the Third Circuit's treatment of nominative fair use as an affirmative defense.... The Third Circuit's basis for treating nominative fair use as an affirmative defense is that the Supreme Court has treated classic, or descriptive, fair use as an affirmative defense. [Citation.] But in treating descriptive fair use as an affirmative defense, the Supreme Court was interpreting a provision of the Lanham Act which provided that claims of infringement are subject to various defenses, including [the descriptive fair use defense,] see *KP Permanent Make-Up, Inc.*, 543 U.S. at 118–20 (analyzing 15 U.S.C. § 1115(b)(4) and ultimately concluding that Congress intended descriptive fair use to be an affirmative defense).

That is, under the Supreme Court's interpretation, the Lanham Act explicitly provides that descriptive fair use is an affirmative defense. And nominative fair use cannot fall within § 1115(b)(4)'s language, as nominative fair use is not the use of a name, term, or device otherwise than as a mark which is descriptive of and used merely to describe the goods or services of the alleged infringer. [Citation.] Nominative use involves using the mark at issue as a mark to specifically invoke the mark-holder's mark, rather than its use, other than as a mark, to describe the alleged infringer's goods or services. If Congress had wanted nominative fair use to constitute an additional affirmative defense, it would have provided as such. We therefore hold that nominative fair use is not an affirmative defense to an infringement claim.

We turn next to the question of whether we should adopt a nominative fair use test, either to supplant or to replace the *Polaroid* test. Although we see no reason to replace the *Polaroid* test in this context, we also recognize that many of the *Polaroid* factors are a bad fit here and that we have repeatedly emphasized that the *Polaroid* factors are non-exclusive. And although we have not expressly rejected or accepted other circuits' nominative fair use tests, we "have recognized that a defendant may lawfully use a plaintiff's trademark where doing so is necessary to describe the plaintiff's product and does not imply a false affiliation or endorsement by the plaintiff of the defendant." [Citations.]

Because we believe that the nominative fair use factors will be helpful to a district court's analysis, we hold that, in nominative use cases, district courts are to consider the Ninth Circuit and Third Circuit's nominative fair use factors, in addition to the *Polaroid* factors. When considering a likelihood of confusion in nominative fair use cases, in addition to discussing each of the *Polaroid* factors, courts are to consider: (1) whether the use of the plaintiff's mark is necessary to describe both the plaintiff's product or service and the defendant's product or service, that is, whether the product or service is not readily identifiable without use of the mark; (2) whether the defendant uses only so much of the plaintiff's mark as is necessary to identify the product or service; and (3) whether the defendant did anything that would, in conjunction with the mark, suggest sponsorship or endorsement by the plaintiff holder, that is, whether the defendant's conduct or language reflects the true or accurate relationship between plaintiff's and defendant's products or services.

When assessing the second nominative fair use factor, courts are to consider whether the alleged infringer "step[ped] over the line into a likelihood of confusion by using the senior user's mark too prominently or too often, in terms of size, emphasis, or repetition." McCarthy § 23:11; [citations]; *Brother Records, Inc. v. Jardine*, 318 F.3d 900, 908 (9th Cir. 2003) (considering the fact that the defendant used the mark "'The Beach Boys' more prominently and boldly" than the rest of its name "The Beach Boys Family and Friends" such that event organizers and members of the audience were confused about who was performing); [other citations].

Additionally, when considering the third nominative fair use factor, courts must not, as the district court did here, consider only source confusion, but rather must consider confusion regarding affiliation, sponsorship, or endorsement by the mark holder. [Citation.]

We therefore remand for reconsideration of the *Polaroid* factors in addition to the nominative fair use factors, keeping in mind the numerous types of confusion that are relevant to an infringement analysis other than mere source confusion and the numerous ways in which a certification mark may be infringed....

Questions

1. What difference does it make whether the nominative fair use factors are assessed as part of an affirmative defense, or instead are incorporated into the factors evaluating confusion as part of plaintiff's case in chief?

2. Williams Sonoma owns the Pottery Barn chain of furniture stores, and holds trademarks in both the "Pottery Barn" name and various furniture designs sold by these stores. Knock Off Wood is a blog run by a rural Alaskan housewife to teach readers how to build designer-looking furniture at home, including some products sold by Pottery Barn. Williams Sonoma sent the author of the Knock Off Wood blog a cease and desist letter claiming that the use of Pottery Barn names in the course of explaining how to make similar looking products was trademark infringement. Does the doctrine of nominative fair use protect Knock Off Wood's blog posts?

3. Fight for the Future is an advocacy group that focuses on free speech in the digital context. The group became concerned about proposed legislation that would extend criminal copyright liability to public performances in certain circumstances, and as a result would leave amateur musicians who post unauthorized covers of songs on websites like YouTube open to liability. In response, the group created FreeBieber.org because Justin Bieber became famous, in part, through posting covers of R&B songs on YouTube. Bieber's attorney sent a cease and desist letter to the group, claiming that the site's use of Bieber's name and depictions of him behind bars creates a false suggestion of endorsement on his part. The site, in turn, argues that their use of Bieber's name and likeness is nominative fair use. Who should prevail?

WCVB v. Boston Athletic Association, 926 F.2d 42 (1st Cir. 1991). The Boston Athletic Association (BAA) sponsors the Boston Marathon. It has licensed local television station Channel 4 to broadcast the race. Local station Channel 5, however, intends to broadcast the race as well, and to use the words "Boston Marathon" on the television screen in large letters before, during, and after the event. BAA sought to enjoin Channel 5 on the ground that broadcasting the words "Boston Marathon" violated federal trademark law. The district court denied the injunction and the First Circuit affirmed:

> In our view, the district court's refusal to grant the preliminary injunction was lawful. The dispositive legal issue concerns "customer confusion." A trademark, or service mark, is an "attention getting symbol" used basically, and primarily, to make clear to the customer the origin of the goods or the service. Trademark law prohibits the unauthorized use of such a mark, but only where doing so creates a "likelihood of confusion" about who produces the goods or provides the service in question. [Citations.] Unless a plaintiff can convince a district court that it will likely show such a "likelihood of confusion" on the merits of its trademark claim (or can convince a court of

appeals that the district court abused its discretion), it is not entitled to a preliminary injunction. Yet, we cannot find in the record before us sufficient evidence of relevant customer confusion, arising out of Channel 5's use of the words "Boston Marathon," to require the district court to issue the preliminary injunction that the appellants seek.

....

BAA argues that the confusion here involved is somewhat special. It points to cases where a defendant uses a plaintiff's trademark in connection with a different type of good or service and a plaintiff claims that the public will wrongly, and confusedly, think that the defendant's product somehow has the plaintiff's official "O.K." or imprimatur. The Eleventh Circuit, for example, found trademark law violated when the defendant, without authorization, used the plaintiff's football team mark, a bulldog, not in connection with a different football team, but, rather, on his beer mugs. *See University of Georgia Athletic Ass'n v. Laite*, 756 F.2d 1535 (11th Cir. 1985). This circuit has found trademark law violated, when the defendant, without authorization, used this very appellant's foot race mark, "Boston Marathon," on his t-shirts, sold during the event, permitting the customer to wrongly or confusedly think that his t-shirts were somehow "official." *See Sullivan, supra.* BAA goes on to say that Channel 5's use of those words will lead viewers, wrongly, and confusedly, to believe that Channel 5 (like the t-shirt seller) has a BAA license or permission or authorization to use the words, i.e., that it broadcasts with the BAA's official imprimatur. It also notes that this court, in *Sullivan*, listed circumstances that create a "rebuttable presumption" of confusion. And, it quotes language from *Sullivan*, in which this court, citing *International News Service v. Associated Press*, 248 U.S. 215 (1918), said that the defendant's t-shirts were "clearly designed to take advantage of the Boston Marathon and to benefit from the good will associated with its promotion by plaintiffs," and that defendants obtained a "free ride" at the plaintiffs' expense; they "reap where [they have] not sown." *Sullivan*, 867 F.2d at 33. Appellants say that Channel 5 is doing the same here.

In our view, the cases BAA cites, and *Sullivan* in particular, do not govern the outcome of this case. Nor can we find a likelihood of any relevant confusion here....

....

[T]he record provides us with an excellent reason for thinking that Channel 5's use of the words "Boston Marathon" would not confuse the typical Channel 5 viewer. That reason consists of the fact that those words do more than call attention to Channel 5's program; they also describe the event that Channel 5 will broadcast. Common sense suggests (consistent with the record here) that a viewer who sees those words flash upon the screen will believe simply that Channel 5 will show, or is showing, or has shown, the marathon, not that Channel 5 has some special approval from the BAA to do so. In technical trademark jargon, the use of words for descriptive purposes is called a "fair use," and the law usually permits it even if the words themselves also constitute a trademark.... As Justice Holmes pointed out many years ago, "when the mark is used in a way that does not deceive the public we see no such sanctity in the word as to prevent its being used to tell the truth." *Prestonettes, Inc. v. Coty*, 264 U.S. 359, 368 (1924).

This is not a case where it is difficult to decide whether a defendant is using particular words primarily as a mark, i.e., as an "attention getting symbol," or primarily as a description. Here there is little in the record before us to suggest the former (only the large size of the words on the screen); while there is much to show the latter (timing, meaning, context, intent, and surrounding circumstances). Consequently, the appellants have shown no real likelihood of relevant confusion.

We also note that the only federal court which has decided a case nearly identical to the one before us, a case in which a station planning to televise a public parade was sued by the parade's promoter who had granted "exclusive" rights to another station, reached a conclusion similar to the one we draw here. *See Production Contractors, Inc. v. WGN Continental Broadcasting Co.*, 622 F. Supp. 1500, 1504 (N.D. Ill. 1985). Reviewing the promoter's Lanham Act claim that the "unauthorized" broadcast would create a "false impression" of sponsorship, the court concluded that it fell "far short of establishing likelihood of confusion" among viewers that the defendant station was the "official" or "authorized" broadcaster of the parade. *See id.* at 1504–05. Similarly, we do not see how Channel 5's broadcast could likely confuse viewers that it bore the imprimatur of the BAA.

The district court's denial of the motion for preliminary injunction is AFFIRMED.

Question

Suppose that in addition to broadcasting the Boston Marathon itself, WCVB had flashed the Boston Marathon's logo on the screen during the broadcast. Would the court have reached the same conclusion?

Toyota Motor Sales U.S.A., Inc. v. Tabari, 610 F.3d 1171 (9th Cir. 2010). This trademark infringement action addressed the application of the nominative fair use doctrine to Internet domain names. The Tabaris, auto brokers, contacted authorized Lexus dealers, solicited bids and arranged for customers to buy a Lexus from the dealer offering the best combination of location, availability and price. These services were offered at <buy-a-lexus.com> and <buyorleaselexus.com>. When customers purchased a Lexus through the Tabaris, they received a genuine Lexus car sold by an authorized Lexus dealer. Applying the nominative fair use factors, the 9th Circuit inquired whether (1) the product was "readily identifiable" without use of the mark;

(2) defendant used more of the mark than necessary; or (3) defendant falsely suggested he was sponsored or endorsed by the trademark holder. The court assessed the third factor according to the supposed perspective of the "reasonably prudent customer in the marketplace." In this case, the reasonably prudent customer was one accustomed to shopping online, and the marketplace was the online marketplace.

> The district court reasoned that the fact that an internet domain contains a trademark will "generally" suggest sponsorship or endorsement by the trademark holder. When a domain name consists *only* of the trademark followed by.com, or some other suffix like.org or.net, it will typically suggest sponsorship or endorsement by the trademark holder. [Citation.].... But the case where the URL consists of nothing but a trademark followed by a suffix like.com or.org is a special one indeed. [Citation.] The importance ascribed to trademark.com in fact suggests that far less confusion will result when a domain making nominative use of a trademark includes characters in addition to those making up the mark. [Citation.] Because the official Lexus site is almost certain to be found at lexus.com (as, in fact, it is), it's far less likely to be found at other sites containing the word Lexus. On the other hand, a number of sites make nominative use of trademarks in their domains but are not sponsored or endorsed by the trademark holder: You can preen about your Mercedes at mercedesforum.com and mercedestalk.net, read the latest about your double-skim-no-whip latte at starbucksgossip.com and find out what goodies the world's greatest electronics store has on sale this week at frys-electronics-ads.com. Consumers who use the internet for shopping are generally quite sophisticated about such matters and won't be fooled into thinking that the prestigious German car manufacturer sells boots at mercedesboots.com, or homes at mercedeshomes.com, or that comcastsucks.org is sponsored or endorsed by the TV cable company just because the string of letters making up its trademark appears in the domain.
>
> ... When a domain name making nominative use of a mark does not actively suggest sponsorship or endorsement, the worst that can happen is that some consumers may arrive at the site uncertain as to what they will find. But in the age of FIOS, cable modems, DSL and T1 lines, reasonable, prudent and experienced internet consumers are accustomed to such exploration by trial and error. [Citation.] They skip from site to site, ready to hit the back button whenever they're not satisfied with a site's contents. They fully expect to find some sites that aren't what they imagine based on a glance at the domain name or search engine summary. Outside the special case of trademark.com, or domains that actively claim affiliation with the trademark holder, consumers don't form any firm expectations about the sponsorship of a website until they've seen the landing page—if then. This is sensible agnosticism, not consumer confusion. *See* Jennifer E. Rothman, *Initial Interest Confusion: Standing at the Crossroads of Trademark Law*, 27 Cardozo L. Rev. 105, 122–24, 140, 158 (2005). So long as the site as a whole does not suggest

sponsorship or endorsement by the trademark holder, such momentary uncertainty does not preclude a finding of nominative fair use.

> ... It is the wholesale prohibition of nominative use in domain names that would be unfair. It would be unfair to merchants seeking to communicate the nature of the service or product offered at their sites. And it would be unfair to consumers, who would be deprived of an increasingly important means of receiving such information. As noted, this would have serious First Amendment implications. The only winners would be companies like Toyota, which would acquire greater control over the markets for goods and services related to their trademarked brands, to the detriment of competition and consumers. The nominative fair use doctrine is designed to prevent this type of abuse of the rights granted by the Lanham Act.

The Ninth Circuit ruled that the injunction granted by the district court was too broad, implicating First Amendment concerns by impeding truthful communication between buyers and sellers in the marketplace. The court remanded, directing the district court to eschew application of the *Sleekcraft* factors and to "analyze the case solely under the rubric of nominative fair use." Following *KP Permanent Make-Up*, the 9th Circuit further ruled that a defendant seeking to assert nominative fair use as a defense need not disprove likelihood of confusion. Once the defendant has shown that it used the mark to refer to the trademarked good, "the burden then reverts to the plaintiff to show a likelihood of confusion."

Question

The Academy of Motion Picture Arts and Sciences awards Oscars annually for excellence in film. Sasha Stone was the owner and operator of "oscarwatch.com", a website that included commentary, predictions, analysis, a forum, and contests relating to the Oscars. In 2007, the Academy brought suit alleging trademark infringement and dilution for Stone's operation of the oscarwatch website. Soon thereafter, the parties settled, but had the litigation proceeded, who was likely to prevail?

Note: Failed Nominative Fair Use Defenses

In *Downing v. Abercrombie & Fitch*, 265 F.3d (9th Cir. 2001), Abercrombie had purchased a photo from a professional surf competition taken decades earlier of Downing and the three other plaintiffs. Without any of the plaintiffs' permission, Abercrombie had used the photo in a Quarterly catalog as part of a surfing theme. The plaintiffs then brought suit alleging violations of, among others, the Lanham Act. The lower court had granted Abercombie's motion for summary judgment, which was supported in the alternative by a finding that the Abercrombie's actions were nominative fair use. In rejecting this argument before remanding the case for trial, the court found:

> Abercrombie argues that its use of the photograph was nominative fair use in the same manner as the defendants' purported infringement in *New Kids.* We disagree. In *New Kids*, we stated that the test applies only "where the

> defendant uses a trademark to describe the plaintiff's product, rather than its own." [Citation.] Here, Abercrombie used the photograph in its catalog that was intended to sell its goods. As we have noted in this case involving a celebrity endorsement claim, the mark being protected is the Appellants' names and pictures....

In comparison, in *Horphag Research Ltd, v. Pellegrini*, 337 F.3d 1036 (9th Cir. 2003), Horphag owned the trademark for "Pycnogenol" for pine bark extract. Defendant Garcia's "healthierlife.com" website sold pharmaceutical products including "Pycnogenol" and "Masquelier's: the original French Pycnogenol." In rejecting Garcia's nominative fair use defense, the court ruled:

> [E]ven if Garcia could meet the first two [nominative fair use] criteria, he cannot meet the third requirement because, as evidenced by the record at trial, Garcia's references to Pycnogenol spawn confusion as to sponsorship and attempt to appropriate the cachet of the trademark Pycnogenol to his product.

Finally, in *Board of Supervisors v. Smack Apparel Co.*, 550 F.3d 465 (5th Cir. 2008), *see supra*, Chapter 2[B][2], the Fifth Circuit considered Smack's argument that its use of the trademarked colors and logos of the Universities was protected by nominative fair use:

> Smack used the Universities' colors and indicia in more than a nominative sense. It did not incorporate the colors and other inidcia to describe or compare its shirts with shirts licensed by the Universities, nor did it do so to tell the public what it had copied. Smack did incorporate the marks to identify the Universities as the subject of the shirts, but it did so in a way that improperly suggested affiliation, sponsorship, or endorsement.
>
> ....
>
> As noted by the district court, Smack copied the mark with "an intent to rely upon the drawing power in enticing fans of the particular universities to purchase their shirts." Such an attempt to capitalize on consumer confusion is not a nominative fair use....

Is there a difference between "capitalizing on consumer confusion" and "attempting to appropriate the cachet of the trademark"? Is the latter an inevitable consequence of invoking a trademark to sell competing goods?

2. Comparative Advertising

Smith v. Chanel, Inc.

402 F.2d 562 (9th Cir. 1968)

The Blindfold Test
ARPEGE
TA'RON
WE DARE YOU—
USE THIS TEST ON SKEPTICAL PROSPECTS
THERE HAVE BEEN MANY ATTEMPTS AT DUPLICATING PERFUMES BEFORE—HERE'S WHY THEY ALL FAILED
They have failed because the duplication was phony. Most anyone could detect the difference. Ta'ron's scientists have performed a masterful breakdown. It has taken years to find the secret of positive duplication. The results are paying off. This is not an ordinary event. The duplication of world famous aromas is now an absolute accomplishment. That's why Ta'ron cannot fail, and that's why you can get "into the bucks" quickly and easily by selling America's most sensational line.
TA'RON'S DECOR-DESIGNED BOTTLES, CONTAINERS AND GIFT BOXES WIN RAVES EVERY-WHERE SHOWN—
You'll be proud to show Ta'ron's bottles and containers. Every item is in keeping with the very finest boudoir appointments. The bottles are in gold and black. Individually gift boxed with protecting sleeve, ready for resale. Every perfume set is equipped with perfume funnel.

Browning, J:

Appellant R.G. Smith, doing business as Ta'Ron, Inc., advertised a fragrance called "Second Chance" as a duplicate of appellees' "Chanel No. 5," at a fraction of the latter's price. Appellees were granted a preliminary injunction prohibiting any reference to Chanel No. 5 in the promotion or sale of appellants' product. This appeal followed.

The action rests upon a single advertisement published in "Specialty Salesman," a trade journal directed to wholesale purchasers. The advertisement offered "The Ta'Ron Line of Perfumes" for sale. It gave the seller's address as "Ta'Ron Inc., 26 Harbor Cove, Mill Valley, Calif." It stated that the Ta'Ron perfumes "duplicate 100% perfect the exact scent of the world's finest and most expensive perfumes and colognes at prices that will zoom sales to volumes you have never before experienced!" It repeated the claim of exact duplication in a variety of forms.

The advertisement suggested that a "Blindfold Test" be used "on skeptical prospects," challenging them to detect any difference between a well-known fragrance and the Ta'Ron "duplicate." One suggested challenge was, "We dare you to try to detect any difference between Chanel #5* (25.00) and Ta'Ron's 2nd Chance. $7.00."

In an order blank printed as part of the advertisement each Ta'Ron fragrance was listed with the name of the well-known fragrance which it purportedly duplicated immediately beneath. Below "Second Chance" appeared "(Chanel #5*)." The asterisk referred to a statement at the bottom of the form reading "Registered Trade Name of Original Fragrance House."

Appellees conceded below and concede here that appellants "have the right to copy, if they can, the unpatented formula of appellees' products." Moreover, for the purposes of these proceedings, appellees assume that "the products manufactured and advertised by [appellants] are *in fact* equivalents of those products manufactured by appellees." (Emphasis in original.) Finally, appellees disclaim any contention that the packaging or labeling of appellants' "Second Chance" is misleading or confusing.

I

The principal question presented on this record is whether one who has copied an unpatented product sold under a trademark may use the trademark in his advertising to identify the product he has copied. We hold that he may, and that such advertising may not be enjoined under either the Lanham Act, 15 U.S.C. § 1125(a) (1964), or the common law of unfair competition, so long as it does not contain misrepresentations or create a reasonable likelihood that purchasers will be confused as to the source, identity, or sponsorship of the advertiser's product.

This conclusion is supported by direct holdings in *Saxlehner v. Wagner*, 216 U.S. 375 (1910); *Viavi Co. v. Vimedia Co.*, 245 F. 289 (8th Cir. 1917), and *Societe Comptoir de L'Industrie Cotonniere Etablissements Boussac v. Alexander's Dept. Stores, Inc.*, 299 F.2d 33, 1 A.L.R.3d 752 (2d Cir. 1962).

In *Saxlehner* the copied product was a "bitter water" drawn from certain privately owned natural springs. The plaintiff sold the natural water under the name "Hunyadi Janos," a valid trademark. The defendant was enjoined from using plaintiff's trademark to designate defendant's "artificial" water, but was permitted to use it to identify plaintiff's natural water as the product which defendant was copying.

Justice Holmes wrote:

> We see no reason for disturbing the finding of the courts below that there was no unfair competition and no fraud. The real intent of the plaintiff's bill, it seems to us, is to extend the monopoly of such trademark or trade name as she may have to a monopoly of her type of bitter water, by preventing manufacturers from telling the public in a way that will be understood, what they are copying and trying to sell. But the plaintiff has no patent for the water, and the defendants have a right to reproduce it as nearly as they can. *They have a right to tell the public what they are doing, and to get whatever share they can in the popularity of the water by advertising that they are trying to make the same article, and think that they succeed. If they do not convey, but, on the contrary, exclude, the notion that they are selling the plaintiff's goods, it is a strong proposition that when the article has a well-known name they have not the right to explain by that name what they imitate.* By doing so, they are not trying to get the good will of the name, but the good will of the goods. 216 U.S. at 380–381 [Citation.] (emphasis added).

In *Viavi Co. v. Vimedia Co.*, plaintiff sold unpatented proprietary medicinal preparations under the registered trademark "Viavi," and local sellers of defendant's medicinal preparations represented to prospective purchasers that Vimedia products "were the same or as good as Viavi" preparations. The court held, "[in] the absence of such a monopoly as a patent confers, any persons may reproduce the articles, if they can, and may sell them under the representation that they are the same article, if they exclude the notion that they are the plaintiff's goods." 245 F. at 292.

In *Societe Comptoir de L'Industrie Cotonniere Etablissements Boussac v. Alexander's Dept. Stores, Inc.*, the defendant used plaintiff's registered trademarks "Dior" and "Christian Dior" in defendant's advertising in identifying plaintiff's dresses as the original creations from which defendant's dresses were copied. The district court refused to grant a preliminary injunction.

The appellate court considered plaintiff's rights under both the Lanham Act and common law. Noting that the representation that defendant's dresses were copies of "Dior" originals was apparently truthful and that there was no evidence of deception or confusion as to the origin or sponsorship of defendant's garments (299 F.2d at 35), the court disposed of the claim of right under the Lanham Act as follows:

> In any proceeding under the Lanham Act the gist of the proceeding is a "false description or representation," 15 U.S.C.A. § 1125(a), or a use of the mark which "is likely to cause confusion or mistake or to deceive purchasers as to the source of origin of such goods or services," 15 U.S.C.A. § 1114(1).... Registration bestows upon the owner of the mark the limited right to protect his good will from possible harm by those uses of another as may engender a belief in the mind of the public that the product identified by the infringing mark is made or sponsored by the owner of the mark.... *The Lanham Act does not prohibit a commercial rival's truthfully denominating his goods a copy of a design in the public domain, though he uses the name of the designer to do so. Indeed it is difficult to see any other means that might be employed to inform the consuming public of the true origin of the design.* 299 F.2d at 36 (citations omitted) (emphasis added).
>
> ....

The rule rests upon the traditionally accepted premise that the only legally relevant function of a trademark is to impart information as to the source or sponsorship of the product. Appellees argue that protection should also be extended to the trademark's commercially more important function of embodying consumer good will created through extensive, skillful, and costly advertising. The courts, however, have generally confined legal protection to the trademark's source identification function for reasons grounded in the public policy favoring a free, competitive economy.

Preservation of the trademark as a means of identifying the trademark owner's products, implemented both by the Lanham Act and the common law, serves an important public purpose.[13] It makes effective competition possible in a complex,

13. It also serves two substantial private interests of the owner: It protects him from diversion of sales through a competitor's use of his trademark or one confusingly similar to it; and it protects his reputation from the injury that could occur if the competitor's goods were inferior.

impersonal marketplace by providing a means through which the consumer can identify products which please him and reward the producer with continued patronage. Without some such method of product identification, informed consumer choice, and hence meaningful competition in quality, could not exist.

....

A related consideration is also pertinent to the present case. Since appellees' perfume was unpatented, appellants had a right to copy it, as appellees concede. There was a strong public interest in their doing so, "[for] imitation is the life blood of competition. It is the unimpeded availability of substantially equivalent units that permits the normal operation of supply and demand to yield the fair price society must pay for a given commodity." *American Safety Table Co. v. Schreiber*, 269 F.2d 255, 272 (2d Cir. 1959). But this public benefit might be lost if appellants could not tell potential purchasers that appellants' product was the equivalent of appellees' product. "A competitor's chief weapon is his ability to represent his product as being equivalent and cheaper...." Alexander, *Honesty and Competition*, 39 So. Cal. L. Rev. 1, 4 (1966). The most effective way (and, where complex chemical compositions sold under trade names are involved, often the only practical way) in which this can be done is to identify the copied article by its trademark or trade name. To prohibit use of a competitor's trademark for the sole purpose of identifying the competitor's product would bar effective communication of claims of equivalence. Assuming the equivalence of "Second Chance" and "Chanel No. 5," the public interest would not be served by a rule of law which would preclude sellers of "Second Chance" from advising consumers of the equivalence and thus effectively deprive consumers of knowledge that an identical product was being offered at one third the price.

As Justice Holmes wrote in *Saxlehner v. Wagner*, the practical effect of such a rule would be to extend the monopoly of the trademark to a monopoly of the product. The monopoly conferred by judicial protection of complete trademark exclusivity would not be preceded by examination and approval by a governmental body, as is the case with most other government-granted monopolies. Moreover, it would not be limited in time, but would be perpetual.

Against these considerations, two principal arguments are made for protection of trademark values other than source identification.

The first of these, as stated in the findings of the district court, is that the creation of the other values inherent in the trademark require "the expenditure of great effort, skill and ability," and that the competitor should not be permitted "to take a free ride" on the trademark owner's "widespread goodwill and reputation."

....

A large expenditure of money does not in itself create legally protectable rights. Appellees are not entitled to monopolize the public's desire for the unpatented product, even though they themselves created that desire at great effort and expense. As we have noted, the most effective way (and in some cases the only practical way) in which others may compete in satisfying the demand for the product is to produce it and tell the public they have done so, and if they could be barred from this effort appellees would have found a way to acquire a practical monopoly in the unpatented product to which they are not legally entitled.

Disapproval of the copyist's opportunism may be an understandable first reaction, "[but] this initial response to the problem has been curbed in deference to the greater public good." *American Safety Table Co. v. Schreiber*, 269 F.2d at 272. By taking his "free ride," the copyist, albeit unintentionally, serves an important public interest by offering comparable goods at lower prices. On the other hand, the trademark owner, perhaps equally without design, sacrifices public to personal interests by seeking immunity from the rigors of competition.

Moreover, appellees' reputation is not directly at stake. Appellants' advertisement makes it clear that the product they offer is their own. If it proves to be inferior, they, not appellees, will bear the burden of consumer disapproval.

The second major argument for extended trademark protection is that even in the absence of confusion as to source, use of the trademark of another "creates a serious threat to the uniqueness and distinctiveness" of the trademark, and "if continued would create a risk of making a generic or descriptive term of the words" of which the trademark is composed.

The contention has little weight in the context of this case. Appellants do not use appellees' trademark as a generic term. They employ it only to describe appellees' product, not to identify their own. They do not label their product "Ta'Ron's Chanel No. 5," as they might if appellees' trademark had come to be the common name for the product to which it is applied. Appellants' use does not challenge the distinctiveness of appellees' trademark, or appellees' exclusive right to employ that trademark to indicate source or sponsorship. For reasons already discussed, we think appellees are entitled to no more....

We are satisfied, therefore, that both authority and reason require a holding that in the absence of misrepresentation or confusion as to source or sponsorship a seller in promoting his own goods may use the trademark of another to identify the latter's goods. The district court's contrary conclusion cannot support the injunction.*

Questions

1. It makes intuitive sense to permit defendant to label his goods truthfully to inform the consumer what the goods are, even if that label explicitly mentions a competing product. Defendant has a right to manufacture perfumes under the same

* *Editors' Note*: On remand after the decision in *Smith v. Chanel*, Chanel proved to the trial court's satisfaction that Smith's representations that Second Chance smelled like Chanel number 5 were, in fact, false, and obtained a broad injunction, restraining Smith from claiming in his advertising that "Second Chance" products duplicated or were the same as, or equivalent to, "Chanel No. 5" products with regard to "scent, smell, formulation, compounding, or otherwise." The Ninth Circuit affirmed on appeal, 528 F.2d 284. What would you need to show in order to rebut a defendant's claims of product equivalence?

unpatented formula as Chanel's; defendant therefore can inform the public of the identity of formulae and scents. But should truthful labeling necessarily extend to the use of a competitor's trademark? A second-comer may be entitled to make identical goods, but does it follow that he may sell them by reference to the mark, and goodwill, of another producer? Why not limit the second-comer to the truthful statement of the formula, or of other descriptive information, without identifying the rival producer's mark?

2. Competitors promoting their goods as desirable substitutes for the name-brand offering sometimes proclaim that if the consumer "likes" the name brand, her or she will "love" the competitor's, usually cheaper, version. *Compare Calvin Klein Cosmetics v. Parfums de Coeur*, 824 F.2d 665 (8th Cir. 1987) (rejecting challenges by the producers of "Calvin Klein's OBSESSION" scent against the like/love advertisements of the producers of CONFESS; the court found that the overall commercial context of the CONFESS promotion, including defendant's prominent use of the phrase "Designer Imposters by Parfums de Coeur" in connection with its like/love slogan, dispelled likelihood of consumer confusion), *with Charles of the Ritz Group Ltd. v. Quality King Distributors, Inc.*, 832 F.2d 1317 (2d Cir. 1987) (finding likelihood of confusion in slogans asserting "If you like OPIUM, you'll love OMNI," and "If you like OPIUM, a fragrance by Yves St. Laurent, you'll love OMNI, a fragrance by Deborah International Beauty."). Does it help to view "like/love" slogans as an "invitation to compare" the original goods and the proposed substitute? What information does the consumer need to make the comparison? *Cf. Ross Cosmetics Distribution Ctrs. v. United States*, 34 U.S.P.Q.2d 1758 (Ct Int'l. Trade 1994) (preventing importation of confusingly labeled "like/love" perfume substitute).

3. Suppose that Ta'Ron not only promoted "Second Chance" as identical to "Chanel No. 5," but offered customers, with each bottle of "Second Chance," an empty, recycled bottle of "Chanel No. 5," anticipating (but not expressly directing) that customers would fill the Chanel bottle with the Ta'Ron substitute, and discard the Ta'Ron bottle. Any liability under the Lanham Act? What if Ta'Ron did not supply the Chanel bottles, but its advertisements encouraged customers to transfer "Second Chance" to any leftover Chanel bottles the customers might have? What if Ta'Ron neither said nor supplied anything regarding refills of old Chanel bottles, but Ta'Ron were nonetheless aware (and expected) that many customers would do exactly that?

4. Davidoff manufactures premium cigars. JR Tobacco sells a "J*R Alternatives" line of copied cigars, which JR advertises as "duplicating as closely as possible the size, shape, taste, origin and wrapper cover" of the premium cigars from which they were copied, including several Davidoff cigars. Other ads for the entire J*R Alternatives line insist that "in many instances the cigars sold under the super premium label, the premium label, and our J*R label are the identical product!" Davidoff insists that the J*R cigars are far inferior, and that the only features of its premium cigars that JR actually copied were their size, shape and wrapper color. Are JR's ads actionable?

Who should bear the burden of proof regarding the comparability of the cigars and the steps taken to achieve it? *See JR Tobacco of America v. Davidoff of Geneva*, 957 F. Supp. 426 (S.D.N.Y. 1997).

5. Your client is a producer of smell-alike perfumes. He presents you with the following advertisement. What problems do you see?

3. First Sale

Once goods bearing the mark have been lawfully sold, may the trademark owner prohibit third parties from reselling the trademarked goods, or oblige the re-seller to remove the mark? We have already encountered one instance of resale, in the

Supreme Court's decision in *Champion Spark Plug Co. v. Sanders*, 331 U.S. 125 (1947), *supra*, Chapter 1. The Ninth Circuit discussed the first-sale doctrine as a defense to trademark infringement in **Au-Tomotive Gold Inc. v. Volkswagen of America, Inc.**, 603 F.3d 1133 (9th Cir. 2010). The defendant asserted the first sale doctrine, which allows the resale of legitimately purchased goods bearing the trademark, as a defense where it purchased genuine VW badges that it used to make marquee license plates. The Ninth Circuit, while recognizing the doctrine, rejected its applicability in that case:

> Auto Gold argues that because it purchased actual VW badges from a Volkswagen dealer for use on the marquee license plates, the "first sale" doctrine protects the sale of the plates. We hold that the "first sale" doctrine does not provide a defense because the plates create a likelihood of confusion as to their origin. We do not base our holding on a likelihood of confusion among purchasers of the plates. Rather, we base it on the likelihood of post-purchase confusion among observers who see the plates on purchasers' cars.
>
> ....
>
> Application of the "first sale" doctrine has generally focused on the likelihood of confusion among consumers. In *Sebastian Int'l, Inc. v. Longs Drug Stores Corp.*, 53 F.3d 1073, 1077 (9th Cir. 1995), we held that the "first sale" doctrine protected Longs when it purchased Sebastian hair products from a distributor and sold them in its own store despite Sebastian's efforts to allow only "Sebastian Collective Members" to sell the products. We recognized the principle that "the right of a producer to control distribution of its trademarked product does not extend beyond the first sale of the product." *Id.* at 1074. We emphasized that this rule "preserves an area of competition by limiting the producer's power to control the resale of its product," while ensuring that "the consumer gets exactly what the consumer bargains for, the genuine product of the particular producer." *Id.* at 1075.
>
> We also applied the "first sale" doctrine in *Enesco Corp. v. Price/Costco Inc.*, 146 F.3d 1083, 1084–85 (9th Cir. 1998), in which Costco purchased porcelain figurines manufactured by Enesco, repackaged them in allegedly inferior packaging, and sold them in its own stores. We held that Costco could repackage and sell the Enesco figurines, but that it was required to place labels on the packages that disclosed to the public that Costco had repackaged Enesco's original product. We rejected Enesco's argument that it would be harmed, even with this disclosure, because of the poor quality of the packaging. "The critical issue is whether the public is likely to be confused as a result of the lack of quality control." *Id.* at 1087.
>
> A number of district courts have applied the "first sale" doctrine in cases where the defendants incorporated the trademarked product into a new product. *See, e.g., Alexander Binzel Corp. v. Nu-Tecsys Corp.*, 785 F. Supp. 719 (N.D. Ill. 1992) (defendant manufactured welding gun using some parts bearing trademark of competitor); *Major League Baseball Players Ass'n v.*

Dad's Kid Corp., 806 F. Supp. 458 (S.D.N.Y. 1992) (defendant used three baseball trading cards bearing trademarks to create 3D playing card); *Scarves by Vera, Inc. v. Am. Handbags, Inc.*, 188 F. Supp. 255 (S.D.N.Y. 1960) (defendant used towels bearing plaintiff's trademark to create handbags). In these cases, the courts focused on the possibility of confusion as the dispositive factor. *See Alexander Binzel Corp.*, 785 F. Supp. at 724 (finding that "defendants did all that was required of them to diminish customer confusion by packaging their product with the Nu-Tecsys name and logo"); *Dad's Kid Corp.*, 806 F. Supp. at 460 (finding "no likelihood that anyone will be confused as to origin"); *Scarves by Vera, Inc.*, 188 F. Supp. at 258 (issuing injunction requiring further labeling because the court found "that the average purchaser would be misled" otherwise).

A separate line of cases further illustrates the central role of the likelihood of confusion, including post-purchase confusion, in trademark infringement claims. In this line of cases, we have held that producers committed trademark infringement by selling refurbished or altered goods under their original trademark. None of these cases directly addressed the "first sale" doctrine, but they establish that activities creating a likelihood of post-purchase confusion, even among non-purchasers, are not protected.

Questions

1. Did the Ninth Circuit treat the first sale doctrine as a true defense? Would it apply even if there were a likelihood of confusion?

2. Cecil McBee is a jazz musician. It is also a trademark registered and used in Japan for teenage girls' fashion. McBee failed in his attempts in Japan and in the U.S. to prevent the use of the Japanese mark. (*See supra* Chapter 6[A].) Suppose an American entrepreneur visiting Tokyo purchased several dozen "Cecil McBee" teenage fashion items and once back in the U.S. offered them for sale in her "cool Japanese fashion" boutique, advertising them truthfully as hot Japanese fashion goods acquired in and imported from Japan. Is her activity protected by the trademark exhaustion/first sale doctrine? Should it matter whether the resold item was made and purchased in the U.S., or instead the item is a genuine but different product made by a different foreign company which had (apparently legitimately) adopted a mark that might be confusingly similar to a U.S. mark?

4. Sovereign Immunity

College Savings Bank v. Florida Prepaid Postsecondary Education Expense Board

527 U.S. 666 (1999)

JUSTICE SCALIA delivered the opinion of the Court:

The Trademark Remedy Clarification Act (TRCA), 106 Stat. 3567, subjects the States to suits brought under § 43(a) of the Trademark Act of 1946 (Lanham Act) for false and misleading advertising, 60 Stat. 441, 15 U.S.C. § 1125(a). The question presented in this case is whether that provision is effective to permit suit against a State for its alleged misrepresentation of its own product—either because the TRCA effects a constitutionally permissible abrogation of state sovereign immunity, or because the TRCA operates as an invitation to waiver of such immunity which is automatically accepted by a State's engaging in the activities regulated by the Lanham Act.

I.

... [T]he Eleventh Amendment, ... provides:

> "The Judicial power of the United States shall not be construed to extend to any suit in law or equity, commenced or prosecuted against one of the United States by Citizens of another State, or by Citizens or Subjects of any Foreign State."

Though its precise terms bar only federal jurisdiction over suits brought against one State by citizens of another State or foreign state, we have long recognized that the Eleventh Amendment accomplished much more: It repudiated ... that the jurisdictional heads of Article III superseded the sovereign immunity that the States possessed before entering the Union....

While this immunity from suit is not absolute, we have recognized only two circumstances in which an individual may sue a State. First, Congress may authorize such a suit in the exercise of its power to enforce the Fourteenth Amendment—an Amendment enacted after the Eleventh Amendment and specifically designed to alter the federal-state balance. *Fitzpatrick v. Bitzer*, 427 U.S. 445 (1976). Second, a State may waive its sovereign immunity by consenting to suit. *Clark v. Barnard*, 108 U.S. 436, 447–448 (1883). This case turns on whether either of these two circumstances is present.

II.

... The TRCA amends § 43(a) by defining "any person" to include "any State, instrumentality of a State or employee of a State or instrumentality of a State acting in his or her official capacity." § 3(c), 106 Stat. 3568. The TRCA further amends the Lanham Act to provide that such state entities "shall not be immune, under the eleventh amendment of the Constitution of the United States or under any other doctrine of sovereign immunity, from suit in Federal court by any person, including any governmental or nongovernmental entity for any violation under this Act," and that remedies shall be available against such state entities "to the same extent as such remedies are available … in a suit against" a nonstate entity. § 3(b) (codified in 15 U.S.C. § 1122).

Petitioner College Savings Bank is a New Jersey chartered bank located in Princeton, New Jersey. Since 1987, it has marketed and sold CollegeSure certificates of deposit designed to finance the costs of college education.… College Savings filed the instant action [in United States District Court in New Jersey] alleging that Florida Prepaid violated § 43(a) of the Lanham Act by making misstatements about its own tuition savings plans in its brochures and annual reports.

… The District Court granted Florida Prepaid's motion to dismiss [on the ground of sovereign immunity]. The Court of Appeals affirmed. We granted *certiorari.*

III.

We turn first to the contention that Florida's sovereign immunity was validly abrogated. Our decision three Terms ago in *Seminole Tribe* [*of Fla. v. Florida*, 517 U.S. 44 (1996)], held that the power "to regulate Commerce" conferred by Article I of the Constitution gives Congress no authority to abrogate state sovereign immunity. As authority for the abrogation in the present case, petitioner relies upon § 5 of the Fourteenth Amendment, which we held … could be used for that purpose.

Section 1 of the Fourteenth Amendment provides that no State shall "deprive any person of … property … without due process of law." Section 5 provides that "the Congress shall have power to enforce, by appropriate legislation, the provisions of this article." We made clear in *City of Boerne v. Flores*, 521 U.S. 507 (1997), that the term "enforce" is to be taken seriously—that the object of valid § 5 legislation must be the carefully delimited remediation or prevention of constitutional violations. Petitioner claims that, with respect to § 43(a) of the Lanham Act, Congress enacted the TRCA to remedy and prevent state deprivations without due process of two species of "property" rights: (1) a right to be free from a business competitor's false advertising about its own product, and (2) a more generalized right to be secure in one's business interests. Neither of these qualifies as a property right protected by the Due Process Clause.

As to the first: The hallmark of a protected property interest is the right to exclude others. That is "one of the most essential sticks in the bundle of rights that are commonly characterized as property." *Kaiser Aetna v. United States*, 444 U.S. 164, 176 (1979). That is why the right that we all possess to use the public lands is not the "property" right of anyone—hence the sardonic maxim, explaining what economists call the "tragedy of the commons," *res publica, res nullius.* The Lanham Act may well contain provisions that protect constitutionally cognizable property interests—notably, its provisions dealing with infringement of trademarks, which are the "property" of the owner because he can exclude others from using them. [Citation.] The Lanham Act's false-advertising provisions, however, bear no relationship to any right to exclude; and Florida Prepaid's alleged misrepresentations concerning its own products intruded upon no interest over which petitioner had exclusive dominion.

... We turn next to the question whether Florida's sovereign immunity, though not abrogated, was voluntarily waived.

IV.

... [O]ur "test for determining whether a State has waived its immunity from federal-court jurisdiction is a stringent one." [Citation.] Generally, we will find a waiver either if the State voluntarily invokes our jurisdiction, [citations] or else if the State makes a "clear declaration" that it intends to submit itself to our jurisdiction....

There is no suggestion here that respondent Florida Prepaid expressly consented to being sued in federal court. Nor is this a case in which the State has affirmatively invoked our jurisdiction. Rather, petitioner College Savings and the United States both maintain that Florida Prepaid has "impliedly" or "constructively" waived its immunity from Lanham Act suit. They do so on the authority of *Parden v. Terminal R. Co. of Ala. Docks Dept.*, 377 U.S. 184 (1964)—an elliptical opinion that stands at the nadir of our waiver (and, for that matter, sovereign immunity) jurisprudence. In *Parden*, we permitted employees of a railroad owned and operated by Alabama to bring an action under the Federal Employers' Liability Act (FELA) against their employer....

... [I]n *Welch v. Texas Dept. of Highways and Public Transp.*, 483 U.S. 468 (1987), although we expressly avoided addressing the constitutionality of Congress's conditioning a State's engaging in Commerce-Clause activity upon the State's waiver of sovereign immunity, we said there was "no doubt that *Parden*'s discussion of congressional intent to negate Eleventh Amendment immunity is no longer good law," and overruled *Parden* "to the extent [it] is inconsistent with the requirement that an abrogation of Eleventh Amendment immunity by Congress must be expressed in unmistakably clear language," 483 U.S. at 478, and n.8.

....

We think that the constructive-waiver experiment of *Parden* was ill conceived, and see no merit in attempting to salvage any remnant of it.... *Parden* broke sharply with prior cases, and is fundamentally incompatible with later ones. We have never applied the holding of *Parden* to another statute, and in fact have narrowed the case in every subsequent opinion in which it has been under consideration. In short, *Parden* stands as an anomaly in the jurisprudence of sovereign immunity, and indeed in the jurisprudence of constitutional law. Today, we drop the other shoe: Whatever may remain of our decision in *Parden* is expressly overruled.

To begin with, we cannot square *Parden* with our cases requiring that a State's express waiver of sovereign immunity be unequivocal. The whole point of requiring a "clear declaration" by the State of its waiver is to be certain that the State in fact consents to suit. But there is little reason to assume actual consent based upon the State's mere presence in a field subject to congressional regulation....

Recognizing a congressional power to exact constructive waivers of sovereign immunity through the exercise of Article I powers would also, as a practical matter, permit Congress to circumvent the antiabrogation holding of *Seminole Tribe*. Forced waiver and abrogation are not even different sides of the same coin—they are the same side of the same coin....

Nor do we think that the constitutionally grounded principle of state sovereign immunity is any less robust where, as here, the asserted basis for constructive waiver is conduct that the State realistically could choose to abandon, that is undertaken for profit, that is traditionally performed by private citizens and corporations, and that otherwise resembles the behavior of "market participants." ... [I]t is hard to say that that limitation has any more support in text or tradition than, say, limiting abrogation or constructive waiver to the last Friday of the month. Since sovereign immunity itself was not traditionally limited by these factors, and since they have no bearing upon the voluntariness of the waiver, there is no principled reason why they should enter into our waiver analysis.

....

Concluding, for the foregoing reasons, that the sovereign immunity of the State of Florida was neither validly abrogated by the Trademark Remedy Clarification Act, nor voluntarily waived by the State's activities in interstate commerce, we hold that the federal courts are without jurisdiction to entertain this suit against an arm of the State of Florida. The judgment of the Third Circuit dismissing the action is *affirmed.*

JUSTICE STEVENS, *dissenting*:

....

The procedural posture of this case requires the Court to assume that Florida Prepaid is an "arm of the State" of Florida because its activities relate to the State's educational programs. But the validity of that assumption is doubtful if the Court's jurisprudence in this area is to be based primarily on present-day assumptions about the status of the doctrine of sovereign immunity in the 18th century. Sovereigns did not then play the kind of role in the commercial marketplace that they do today....

The majority ... assumes that petitioner's complaint has alleged a violation of the Lanham Act, but not one that is sufficiently serious to amount to a "deprivation" of its property. I think neither of those assumptions is relevant to the principal issue raised in this case, namely, whether Congress had the constitutional power to authorize suits against States and state instrumentalities for such a violation. In my judgment the Constitution granted it ample power to do so. Section 5 of the Fourteenth Amendment authorizes Congress to enact appropriate legislation to prevent deprivations of property without due process. Unlike the majority, I am persuaded that the Trademark Remedy Clarification Act was a valid exercise of that power, even if Florida Prepaid's allegedly false advertising in this case did not violate the Constitution. My conclusion rests on two premises that the Court rejects.

... [I]n my opinion "the activity of doing business, or the activity of making a profit," *ante* at 8, is a form of property. The asset that often appears on a company's balance sheet as "good will" is the substantial equivalent of that "activity." ... A State's deliberate destruction of a going business is surely a deprivation of property within the meaning of the Due Process Clause....

Note

Justice Scalia draws a distinction between the Lanham Act's trademark provisions, which he concedes involve property rights, and its false advertising provisions, which he holds do not. On that basis, might the Trademark Remedy Clarification Act effectively abrogate state sovereign immunity to suits for trademark infringement under section 32? It would appear not. On the same day the Court handed down its decision in *College Savings Bank v. Florida*, it issued a decision in the companion case, *Florida Prepaid Postsecondary Education Expense Board v. College Savings Bank*, 527 U.S. 627 (1999), involving the validity of the Patent Remedy Clarification Act, Pub. L. 102-560, 106 Stat. 4230 (1992). The Court of Appeals for the Federal Circuit held that Congress had properly exercised its power under the 14th Amendment to abrogate state sovereign immunity to patent infringement suits. The Supreme Court reversed. Justice Rehnquist's majority opinion agreed both that Congress had clearly intended to abrogate state sovereign immunity and that patents could be considered property. The court held however, that the legislative record contained scant support for the assertion that states avoiding patent infringement by pleading sovereign immunity amounted to "widespread and persisting deprivation of constitutional rights," and that the Patent Remedy Clarification Act swept too broadly:

> The historical record and the scope of coverage therefore make it clear that the Patent Remedy Act cannot be sustained under § 5 of the Fourteenth Amendment. The examples of States avoiding liability for patent infringement by pleading sovereign immunity in a federal-court patent action are scarce enough, but any plausible argument that such action on the part of the State deprived patentees of property and left them without a remedy under state law is scarcer still. The statute's apparent and more basic aims were to provide a uniform remedy for patent infringement and to place States on the same footing as private parties under that regime. These are proper Article I concerns, but that Article does not give Congress the power to enact such legislation after *Seminole Tribe.*

Has the Court left any room for abrogating state sovereign immunity to trademark suits? May state governments safely ignore the Lanham Act's infringement provisions? While Congress has not abrogated States' Eleventh Amendment immunity, and courts require express or unequivocal waiver of immunity, trademark infringement plaintiffs may nonetheless seek injunctive relief (but not damages) against state officials under the doctrine of *Ex parte Young*, 209 U.S. 123 (1908), so long as the official has "some connection with the enforcement of the act" (*id.* at 157) that allegedly violates the plaintiff's rights. In *Utah Republican Party v. Herbert*, 141 F.Supp.3d 1195 (D. Utah 2015), the District of Utah held that the Governor and the Lieutenant Governor of Utah could be sued in connection with the Utah Republican Party's trademark infringement action against the enforcement of a Utah law alleging that the law's authorization of candidates' appearance on the Republican Party ballot if they collected the requisite number of party member signatures, rather than exclusively by means of party caucuses or conventions, violated the Party's "rights to control and direct the use of its name, title, emblems, and endorsements...."

Question

When a state brings a trademark infringement action, does it voluntarily waive its immunity as to counterclaims? *See Virginia Polytechnic Institute v. Hokie Real Estate Inc.*, 813 F. Supp. 2d 745 (W.D. Va. 2011) (only compulsory counterclaims are waived). What if a state appeals a ruling about registrability from the TTAB to a federal district court? To the Federal Circuit? *See Bd. Of Regents of the Univ. of Wisconsin v. Phoenix Int'l Software Inc.*, 653 F.3d 448 (7th Cir. 2011) (compulsory counterclaims of infringement are not waived if appeal is to district court, but such counterclaims would be unavailable in an appeal to the Federal Circuit as the record consists only of proceedings before the Board).

C. Other Limitations on Trademark Protection: Expressive Use of Trademarks

1. Re-Weighing Likelihood of Confusion

Rogers v. Grimaldi

875 F.2d 994 (2d Cir. 1989)

NEWMAN, CIRCUIT JUDGE:

Appellant Ginger Rogers and the late Fred Astaire are among the most famous duos in show business history. Through their incomparable performances in Hollywood musicals, Ginger Rogers and Fred Astaire established themselves as paragons of style, elegance, and grace. A testament to their international recognition, and a key circumstance in this case, is the fact that Rogers and Astaire are among that small elite of the entertainment world whose identities are readily called to mind by just their first names, particularly the pairing "Ginger and Fred." This appeal presents a conflict between Rogers' right to protect her celebrated name and the right of others to express themselves freely in their own artistic work. Specifically, we must decide whether Rogers can prevent the use of the title "Ginger and Fred" for a fictional movie that only obliquely relates to Rogers and Astaire.

Rogers appeals from an order of the District Court for the Southern District of New York (Robert W. Sweet, Judge) dismissing on summary judgment her claims that defendants-appellees Alberto Grimaldi, MGM/UA Entertainment Co., and PEA Produzioni Europee Associate, S.R.L., producers and distributors of the motion picture "Ginger and Fred," violated the Lanham Act, 15 U.S.C. § 1125(a) (1982), and infringed her common law rights of publicity and privacy. *Rogers v. Grimaldi*, 695 F. Supp. 112 (S.D.N.Y. 1988). Although we disagree with some of the reasoning of the District Court, we affirm.

I. *Background*

Appellant Rogers has been an international celebrity for more than fifty years. In 1940, she won an Academy Award for her performance in the motion picture "Kitty Foyle." Her principal fame was established in a series of motion pictures in which she co-starred with Fred Astaire in the 1930s and 1940s, including "Top Hat" and "The Barkleys of Broadway."

There can be no dispute that Rogers' name has enormous drawing power in the entertainment world. Rogers has also used her name once for a commercial enterprise other than her show business career. In the mid-1970s, she licensed J.C. Penney, Inc. to produce a line of GINGER ROGERS lingerie. Rogers is also writing her autobiography, which she hopes to publish and possibly sell for adaptation as a movie.

In March 1986, appellees produced and distributed in the United States and Europe a film entitled "Ginger and Fred," created and directed by famed Italian film-maker Federico Fellini. The film tells the story of two fictional Italian cabaret performers, Pippo and Amelia, who, in their heyday, imitated Rogers and Astaire and became known in Italy as "Ginger and Fred." The film focuses on a televised reunion of Pippo and Amelia, many years after their retirement. Appellees describe the film as the bittersweet story of these two fictional dancers and as a satire of contemporary television variety shows.

The film received mixed reviews and played only briefly in its first run in the United States. Shortly after distribution of the film began, Rogers brought this suit, seeking permanent injunctive relief and money damages. Her complaint alleged that the defendants (1) violated section 43(a) of the Lanham Act, 15 U.S.C. §1125(a) (1982), by creating the false impression that the film was about her or that she sponsored, endorsed, or was otherwise involved in the film, [and] (2) violated her common law right of publicity....

After two years of discovery, the defendants moved for summary judgment. In opposition to the motion, Rogers submitted a market research survey purporting to establish that the title "Ginger and Fred" misled potential movie viewers as to Rogers' connection with the film. Rogers also provided anecdotal evidence of confusion, including the fact that when MGM/UA publicists first heard the film's title (and before they saw the movie), they began gathering old photographs of Rogers and Astaire for possible use in an advertising campaign.

The District Court granted summary judgment to the defendants. Judge Sweet found that defendants' use of Rogers' first name in the title and screenplay of the film was an exercise of artistic expression rather than commercial speech. 695 F. Supp. at 120. He then held that "[b]ecause the speech at issue here is not primarily intended to serve a commercial purpose, the prohibitions of the Lanham Act do not apply, and the Film is entitled to the full scope of protection under the First Amendment." *Id.* at 120–21. The District Judge also held that First Amendment concerns barred Rogers' state law right of publicity claim. *Id.* at 124....

II. *Discussion*

A. *Lanham Act*

....

The District Court ruled that because of First Amendment concerns, the Lanham Act cannot apply to the title of a motion picture where the title is "within the realm of artistic expression," 695 F. Supp. at 120, and is not "primarily intended to serve a commercial purpose," *id.* at 121. Use of the title "Ginger and Fred" did not violate the Act, the Court concluded, because of the undisputed artistic relevance of the title to the content of the film. *Id.* at 120. In effect, the District Court's ruling would create a nearly absolute privilege for movie titles, insulating them from Lanham Act claims as long as the film itself is an artistic work, and the title is relevant to the film's content. We think that approach unduly narrows the scope of the Act.

Movies, plays, books, and songs are all indisputably works of artistic expression and deserve protection. Nonetheless, they are also sold in the commercial marketplace like other more utilitarian products, making the danger of consumer deception a legitimate concern that warrants some government regulation. Poetic license is not without limits. The purchaser of a book, like the purchaser of a can of peas, has a right not to be misled as to the source of the product. Thus, it is well established that where the title of a movie or a book has acquired secondary meaning—that is, where the title is sufficiently well known that consumers associate it with a particular author's work—the holder of the rights to that title may prevent the use of the same or confusingly similar titles by other authors. Indeed, it would be ironic if, in the name of the First Amendment, courts did not recognize the right of authors to protect titles of their creative work against infringement by other authors. *Cf. Harper & Row, Publishers, Inc. v. Nation Enterprises*, 471 U.S. 539, 556–60 (1985) (noting that copyright law fosters free expression by protecting the right of authors to receive compensation for their work).

Though First Amendment concerns do not insulate titles of artistic works from all Lanham Act claims, such concerns must nonetheless inform our consideration of the scope of the Act as applied to claims involving such titles. Titles, like the artistic works they identify, are of a hybrid nature, combining artistic expression and commercial promotion. The title of a movie may be both an integral element of the film-maker's expression as well as a significant means of marketing the film to the public. The artistic and commercial elements of titles are inextricably intertwined. Film-makers and authors frequently rely on word-play, ambiguity, irony, and allusion in titling their works. Furthermore, their interest in freedom of artistic expression is shared by their audience. The subtleties of a title can enrich a reader's or a viewer's understanding of a work. Consumers of artistic works thus have a dual interest: They have an interest in not being misled and they also have an interest in enjoying the results of the author's freedom of expression. For all these reasons, the expressive element of titles requires more protection than the labeling of ordinary commercial products.[3]

---

3. In other respects, trademark law has also accorded greater leeway for the use of titles than for names of ordinary commercial products, thus allowing breathing space for free expression. A

Because overextension of Lanham Act restrictions in the area of titles might intrude on First Amendment values, we must construe the Act narrowly to avoid such a conflict. *See Silverman v. CBS*, 870 F.2d 40, 48 (2d Cir. 1989).

Rogers contends that First Amendment concerns are implicated only where a title is so intimately related to the subject matter of a work that the author has no alternative means of expressing what the work is about. This "no alternative avenues of communication" standard derives from *Lloyd Corp. v. Tanner*, 407 U.S. 551, 566–67 (1972), and has been applied by several courts in the trademark context.

In the context of titles, this "no alternative" standard provides insufficient leeway for literary expression. In *Lloyd*, the issue was whether the First Amendment provided war protesters with the right to distribute leaflets on a shopping center owner's property. The Supreme Court held that it did not. But a restriction on the *location* of a speech is different from a restriction on the *words* the speaker may use. *See* Denicola, [*Trademarks as Speech: Constitutional Implications of the Emerging Rationales for the Protection of Trade Symbols*, 1982 Wis. L. Rev. 158 (1982)], at 197. As the Supreme Court has noted, albeit in a different context, "[W]e cannot indulge the facile assumption that one can forbid particular words without running a substantial risk of suppressing ideas in the process." *Cohen v. California*, 403 U.S. 15, 26 (1971).

Thus, the "no alternative avenues" test does not sufficiently accommodate the public's interest in free expression, while the District Court's rule—that the Lanham Act is inapplicable to all titles that can be considered artistic expression—does not sufficiently protect the public against flagrant deception. We believe that in general the Act should be construed to apply to artistic works only where the public interest in avoiding consumer confusion outweighs the public interest in free expression. In the context of allegedly misleading titles using a celebrity's name, that balance will normally not support application of the Act unless the title has no artistic relevance to the underlying work whatsoever, or, if it has some artistic relevance, unless the title explicitly misleads as to the source or the content of the work.[4]

The reasons for striking the balance in this manner require some explanation. A misleading title with no artistic relevance cannot be sufficiently justified by a free expression interest. For example, if a film-maker placed the title "Ginger and Fred" on a film to which it had no artistic relevance at all, the arguably misleading suggestions

---

confusingly similar title will not be deemed infringing unless the title alleged to be infringed, even if arbitrary or fanciful, has acquired secondary meaning. *See* 1 J. McCarthy, *Trademarks and Unfair Competition* § 10.2 (1984).

4. This Circuit employed the "no alternative avenues of communication" standard in *Dallas Cowboys Cheerleaders, Inc. v. Pussycat Cinema, Ltd.*, 604 F.2d 200, 206 (2d Cir. 1979). As we stated in *Silverman*, however, that case involved a pornographic movie with blatantly false advertising. 870 F.2d at 48 n. 5. Advertisements for the movie were explicitly misleadingly, stating that the principal actress in the movie was a former Dallas Cowboys' cheerleader. We do not read *Dallas Cowboys Cheerleaders* as generally precluding all consideration of First Amendment concerns whenever an allegedly infringing author has "alternative avenues of communication."

as to source or content implicitly conveyed by the title could be found to violate the Lanham Act as to such a film.

....

Similarly, titles with at least minimal artistic relevance to the work may include explicit statements about the *content* of the work that are seriously misleading. For example, if the characters in the film in this case had published their memoirs under the title "The True Life Story of Ginger and Fred," and if the film-maker had then used that fictitious book title as the title of the film, the Lanham Act could be applicable to such an explicitly misleading description of content.[6] But many titles with a celebrity's name make no explicit statement that the work is about that person in any direct sense; the relevance of the title may be oblique and may become clear only after viewing or reading the work. As to such titles, the consumer interest in avoiding deception is too slight to warrant application of the Lanham Act. Though consumers frequently look to the title of a work to determine what it is about, they do not regard titles of artistic works in the same way as the names of ordinary commercial products. Since consumers expect an ordinary product to be what the name says it is, we apply the Lanham Act with some rigor to prohibit names that misdescribe such goods. But most consumers are well aware that they cannot judge a book solely by its title any more than by its cover. We therefore need not interpret the Act to require that authors select titles that unambiguously describe what the work is about nor to preclude them from using titles that are only suggestive of some topics that the work is not about. Where a title with at least some artistic relevance to the work is not explicitly misleading as to the content of the work, it is not false advertising under the Lanham Act.

This construction of the Lanham Act accommodates consumer and artistic interests. It insulates from restriction titles with at least minimal artistic relevance that are ambiguous or only implicitly misleading but leaves vulnerable to claims of deception titles that are explicitly misleading as to source or content, or that have no artistic relevance at all.

With this approach in mind, we now consider Rogers' Lanham Act claim to determine whether appellees are entitled to summary judgment....

Rogers essentially claims that the title "Ginger and Fred" is false advertising. Relying on her survey data, anecdotal evidence, and the title itself, she claims there is a likelihood of confusion that (1) Rogers produced, endorsed, sponsored, or approved the film, and/or (2) the film is about Rogers and Astaire, and that these contentions present triable issues of fact. In assessing the sufficiency of these claims, we accept Judge Sweet's conclusion, which is not subject to dispute, that the title "Ginger and Fred" surpasses the minimum threshold of artistic relevance to the film's content.

---

6. In offering this example and others in this opinion, we intend only to indicate instances where Lanham Act coverage might be available; whether in such instances a violation is established would depend on the fact-finder's conclusions in light of all the relevant facts and circumstances.

The central characters in the film are nicknamed "Ginger" and "Fred," and these names are not arbitrarily chosen just to exploit the publicity value of their real life counterparts but instead have genuine relevance to the film's story. We consider separately the claims of confusion as to sponsorship and content.

The title "Ginger and Fred" contains no explicit indication that Rogers endorsed the film or had a role in producing it. The survey evidence, even if its validity is assumed,[8] indicates at most that some members of the public would draw the incorrect inference that Rogers had some involvement with the film. But that risk of misunderstanding, not engendered by any overt claim in the title, is so outweighed by the interests in artistic expression as to preclude application of the Lanham Act. We therefore hold that the sponsorship and endorsement aspects of Rogers' Lanham Act claim raise no "genuine" issue that requires submission to a jury.

Rogers' claim that the title misleads consumers into thinking that the film is *about* her and Astaire also fails. Indeed, this case well illustrates the need for caution in applying the Lanham Act to titles alleged to mislead as to content. As both the survey and the evidence of the actual confusion among the movie's publicists show, there is no doubt a risk that some people looking at the title "Ginger and Fred" might think the film was about Rogers and Astaire in a direct, biographical sense. For those gaining that impression, the title is misleading. At the same time, the title is entirely truthful as to its content in referring to the film's fictional protagonists who are known to their Italian audience as "Ginger and Fred." Moreover, the title has an ironic meaning that is relevant to the film's content. As Fellini explains in an affidavit, Rogers and Astaire are to him "a glamorous and care-free symbol of what American cinema represented during the harsh times which Italy experienced in the 1930s and 1940s." In the film, he contrasts this elegance and class to the gaudiness and banality of contemporary television, which he satirizes. In this sense, the title is not misleading; on the contrary, it is an integral element of the film and the film-maker's artistic expression.

This mixture of meanings, with the possibly misleading meaning not the result of explicit misstatement, precludes a Lanham Act claim for false description of content in this case. To the extent that there is a risk that the title will mislead some consumers as to what the work is about, that risk is outweighed by the danger that suppressing an artistically relevant though ambiguous title will unduly restrict expression.

---

8. The survey sampled 201 people who said they were likely to go to a movie in the next six months. Half of those surveyed were shown a card with the title "Ginger and Fred" on it; the other half were shown an actual advertisement for the movie. Of these 201, 38 percent responded "yes" to the question: "Do you think that the actress, Ginger Rogers, had anything to do with this film, or not?" Of these respondents, a third answered yes to the question: "Do you think Ginger Rogers was involved in any way with making this film or not?" In other words, about 14 percent of the total 201 surveyed found that the title suggested that Rogers was involved in making the film.

Appellees contend that the survey used "leading" questions, making the survey results invalid. Without resolving this issue, we will assume for the purposes of this appeal that the survey was valid.

For these reasons, we hold that appellees are entitled to summary judgment on Rogers' claim that the title gives the false impression that the film is about Rogers and Astaire....

We therefore affirm the judgment of the District Court.

Louis Vuitton Malletier S.A. v. Warner Brothers Entertainment Inc.

868 F. Supp. 2d 172 (S.D.N.Y. 2012)

Carter, Jr., J:

On December 22, 2011, Louis Vuitton Malletier, S.A. ("Louis Vuitton") filed a complaint against Warner Bros. Entertainment Inc. ("Warner Bros."), focusing on Warner Bros.' use of a travel bag in the film "The Hangover: Part II" that allegedly infringes upon Louis Vuitton's trademarks. Plaintiff's complaint asserts three claims for relief: (1) false designation of origin/unfair competition in violation of §43(a) of the Lanham Act; (2) common law unfair competition; and (3) trademark dilution in violation N.Y. Gen. Bus. Law 360-*l*. On March 14, 2012, defendant filed a motion to dismiss the complaint with prejudice for failure to state a claim upon which relief can be granted pursuant to Fed. R. Civ. P. 12(b). The court has fully considered the parties' arguments, and for the reasons set forth below, defendant's motion is granted.

BACKGROUND

Louis Vuitton is one of the premier luxury fashion houses in the world, renowned for, among other things, its high-quality luggage, trunks, and handbags. Louis Vuitton's principle trademark is the highly-distinctive and famous Toile Monogram. Registered in 1932, this trademark, along with its component marks (collectively, the "LVM Marks"), are famous, distinctive, and incontestable....

....

Warner Bros. is one of the oldest and most respected producers of motion pictures and television shows in the country and the world. In the summer of 2011, Warner Bros. released "The Hangover: Part II" ("the Film"), the sequel to the 2009 hit bachelor-party-gone-awry-comedy "The Hangover." The Film has grossed roughly $580 million globally as of the date of the Complaint, becoming the highest-gross R-rated comedy of all time and one of the highest grossing movies in 2011.

Diophy is a company that creates products which use a monogram design that is a knockoff of the famous Toile Monogram (the "Knock-Off Monogram Design") ... Despite the inferior quality of Diophy's products, demand for its products bearing the Knock-Off Monogram Design remains high because they are far less expensive than genuine Louis Vuitton products.

A. The Airport Scene

As alleged in the complaint, in one early scene in the Film the "four main characters [are] in Los Angeles International Airport before a flight to Thailand for the character Stu's bachelor party and wedding." "[A]s the characters are walking through the airport, a porter is pushing on a dolly what appears to be Louis Vuitton trunks, some hard-sided luggage, and two Louis Vuitton Keepall travel bags." Alan, one of the characters, is carrying what appears to be a matching over-the-shoulder Louis Vuitton "Keepall" bag, but it is actually an infringing Diophy bag. Moments later, Alan is seen sitting on a bench in the airport lounge and places his bag (i.e., the Diophy bag) on the empty seat next to him. Stu, who is sitting in the chair to the other side of the bag, moves the bag so that Teddy, Stu's future brother-in-law, can sit down between him and Alan. Alan reacts by saying: "Careful that is ... that is a Lewis Vuitton." No other reference to Louis Vuitton or the Diophy bag is made after this point.

After the movie was released in theaters, Louis Vuitton sent Warner Bros. a cease and desist letter noting its objection to the use of the Diophy bag in the Film. Despite being informed of its objection, on December 6, 2011, Warner Bros. released the Film in the United States on DVD and Blu-Ray. The complaint alleges that "many consumers believed the Diophy [b]ag" used in the Film "was, in fact, a genuine Louis Vuitton," and that Louis Vuitton consented to Warner Bros.' "misrepresentation" that the Diophy bag was a genuine Louis Vuitton product....

....

Warner Bros. now moves to dismiss the complaint in its entirety on the ground that its use of the Diophy bag in the Film is protected by the First Amendment under the framework established by *Rogers v. Grimaldi*, 875 F.2d 994 (2d Cir. 1989).

DISCUSSION

....

B. Lanham Act claim

....

1. First Amendment

In *Rogers v. Grimaldi*, the Second Circuit held that the Lanham Act is inapplicable to "artistic works" as long as the defendant's use of the mark is (1) "artistically relevant" to the work and (2) not "explicitly misleading" as to the source or content of the work. 875 F.2d at 999; *Twin Peaks Prods., Inc. v. Publ'ns Int'l, Ltd.*, 996 F.2d 1366, 1379 (2d Cir. 1993). Louis Vuitton does not dispute that Warner Bros.' challenged use of the mark is noncommercial, placing it firmly within the purview of an "artistic work" under *Rogers*....

Louis Vuitton objects to the present motion on the following grounds: (1) whether the use was "artistically relevant" is an issue of fact that requires discovery; (2) the "explicitly misleading" prong is not limited to confusion as to the source or content of the defendant's work; (3) Warner Bros. is not afforded First Amendment protection for using an infringing product; and (4) disposing this case on a motion to dismiss is otherwise inappropriate.

a. Artistic Relevance

The threshold for "artistic relevance" is purposely low and will be satisfied unless the use "has no artistic relevance to the underlying work whatsoever." *Rogers*, 875 F.2d at 999; *see also* [*ESS Entertainment 2000, Inc. v.*] *Rock Star Videos Inc.*, 547 F.3d [1095] at 1100 [(9th Cir. 2008)] (holding that, under *Rogers*, "the level of relevance merely must be above zero"); *Dillinger, LLC v. Elec. Arts Inc.*, No. 09-cv-1236 (JMS) (DKL), 2011 U.S. Dist. LEXIS 64006 (S.D. Ind. June 16, 2011) ("[I]t is not the role of the Court to determine how meaningful the relationship between a trademark and the content of a literary work must be; consistent with *Rogers*, any connection whatsoever is enough."). The artistic relevance prong ensures that the defendant intended an artistic—i.e., noncommercial—association with the plaintiff's mark, as opposed to one in which the defendant intends to associate with the mark to exploit the mark's popularity and good will. *See Rogers*, 875 F.2d at 1001 (finding that the defendant satisfied the artistic relevance prong where its use of the trademark was "not arbitrarily chosen just to exploit the publicity value of [the plaintiffs' mark] but instead ha[d] genuine relevance to the film's story").

Warner Bros.' use of the Diophy bag meets this low threshold. Alan's terse remark to Teddy to "[be] [c]areful" because his bag "is a Lewis Vuitton" comes across as snobbish only because the public signifies Louis Vuitton—to which the Diophy bag looks confusingly similar—with luxury and a high society lifestyle. His remark also comes across as funny because he mispronounces the French "Louis" like the English "Lewis," and ironic because he cannot correctly pronounce the brand name of one of his expensive possessions, adding to the image of Alan as a socially inept and comically misinformed character. This scene also introduces the comedic tension between Alan and Teddy that appears throughout the Film.

Louis Vuitton contends that the Court cannot determine that the use of the Diophy bag was artistically relevant until after discovery. Specifically, Louis Vuitton maintains that it should be able to review the script and depose the Film's creators to determine whether Warner Bros. intended to use an authentic Louis Vuitton bag or Diophy's knock-off bag. However, the significance of the airport scene relies on Alan's bag—authentic or not—looking like a Louis Vuitton bag. Louis Vuitton does not dispute this was Warner Bros.' intention, and therefore the discovery it seeks is irrelevant. The Court is satisfied that Warner Bros.' use of the Diophy bag (whether intentional or inadvertent) was intended to create an artistic association with Louis Vuitton, and there is no indication that its use was commercially motivated. *See Rogers*, 875 F.2d at 1001.

Accordingly, the Court concludes that the use of the Diophy bag has some artistic relevance to the plot of the Film.

b. Explicitly Misleading

Since using the Diophy bag has some relevance to the Film, Warner Bros.' use of it is unprotected only if it "explicitly misleads as to the source or the content of the work." *Rogers*, 875 F.2d at 999. The Second Circuit has explained that the relevant question is whether the defendant's use of the mark "is misleading in the sense that it induces members of the public to believe [the work] was prepared or otherwise authorized" by the plaintiff. *Twin Peaks*, 996 F.2d at 1379. The explicitly misleading determination "must be made, in the first instance, by application of the venerable *Polaroid* [likelihood of confusion] factors." *Id.* (citing *Cliffs Notes*, 886 F.3d at 495 n. 3). Only a "particularly compelling" finding of likelihood of confusion can overcome the First Amendment interests. *Id.*

Rogers and the cases adopting its holding have consistently framed the applicable standard in terms of confusion as to the defendant's artistic work. *See Rogers*, 875 F.2d at 1001 ("The title 'Ginger and Fred' contains no explicit indication that Rogers endorsed the [defendant's] film or had a role in producing it."); *see also, e.g.*, [*Mattel Inc. v.*] *Walking Mountain* [*Productions*], 353 F.3d [792] at 807 [(9th Cir. 2003)] ("The photograph titles do not explicitly mislead as to [plaintiff] Mattel's sponsorship of [defendant's] works."); *Parks*, 329 F.3d at 459 ("[T]he title "Rosa Parks" makes no explicit statement that the [defendant's] work is about that person in any direct sense."); *Westchester Media v. PRL USA Holdings, Inc.*, 214 F.3d 658, 668 (5th Cir. 2000) (finding that consumers could plausibly believe "that [defendant's magazine] is associated with [plaintiffs goods]"); *Twin Peaks*, 996 F.2d at 1379 ("The question then is whether the title is misleading in the sense that it induces members of the public to believe [defendant's] Book was prepared or otherwise authorized by [the plaintiff]."); *Cliffs Notes*, 866 F.2d at 495 ("[W]e do not believe that there is a likelihood that an ordinarily prudent purchaser would think that [defendant's book] is actually a study guide produced by appellee.") (emphasis added); *Dillinger*, 2011 U.S. Dist. LEXIS 64006 (stating the legal issue as whether "[plaintiff's] label [is] explicitly misleading as to the source and content of the [defendant's] games").

It is not a coincidence that courts frame the confusion in relation to the defendant's artistic work, and not to someone else's. This narrow construction of the Lanham Act accommodates the public's interest in free expression by restricting its application to those situations that present the greatest risk of consumer confusion: namely, when trademarks are used to "dupe[] consumers into buying a product they mistakenly believe is sponsored by the trademark owner." *Rock Star Videos*, 547 F.3d at 1100 (*quoting Walking Mountain*, 353 F.3d at 806). When this concern is present it will generally outweigh the public's interest in free expression. *See Rogers*, 875 F.2d at 1000 ("If such explicit references [signifying endorsement] were used in a title and were false as applied to the underlying work, the consumer's interest in avoiding deception would warrant application of the Lanham Act, even if the title had some artistic relevance to the work."). However, if a trademark is not used, "in any direct sense," to designate the source or sponsorship of the defendant's work, then "the consumer interest in avoiding deception is too slight to warrant application of the Lanham Act." *Syler v. Woodruff*, 610 F. Supp. 2d 256, 266 (S.D.N.Y. 2009) (*quoting Rogers*, 875 F.2d at 1000); *see also* 4 McCarthy on Trademarks and Unfair Competition § 23:11.50 (4th ed.) ("[I]f the defendant does not use the accused designation as defendant's own identifying trademark, then confusion will usually be unlikely. Then there are not the requisite two similar marks confusing the viewer into believing that the two marks identify a single source.").

....

Here, the complaint alleges two distinct theories of confusion: (1) that consumers will be confused into believing that the Diophy bag is really a genuine Louis Vuitton bag; and (2) that Louis Vuitton approved the use of the Diophy bag in the Film. However, even drawing all reasonable inferences in the light most favorable to Louis Vuitton, as the Court is required to do, neither of these allegations involves confusion as to Warner Bros.' artistic work. Specifically, Louis Vuitton does not allege that Warner Bros. used the Diophy bag in order to mislead consumers into believing that Louis Vuitton produced or endorsed the Film. Therefore, the complaint fails to even allege the type of confusion that could potentially overcome the *Rogers* protection.

....

Louis Vuitton maintains that the *Rogers* test cannot be assessed on a motion to dismiss. The Court disagrees. Although many courts have considered the *Rogers* test on a summary judgment motion, not on a motion to dismiss, the circuit has never stated that a court cannot properly apply the *Rogers* test (or the likelihood of confusion factors) on a motion to dismiss. In fact, the Second Circuit has suggested that it would be appropriate "where the court is satisfied that the products or marks are so dissimilar that no question of fact is presented." *Pirone* [*v. MacMillian*, 894 F.2d 579 (2d Cir. 1990)], at 584 (affirming grant of summary judgment).... In the context of a motion to dismiss, courts have disposed of trademark claims where simply looking at the work itself, and the context in which it appears, demonstrates how implausible it is that a viewer will be confused into believing that the plaintiff endorsed the defendant's work (and without relying on the likelihood of confusion factors to do so). [Citations.]

Here, there is no likelihood of confusion that viewers would believe that the Diophy bag is a real Louis Vuitton bag just because a fictional character made this claim in the context of a fictional movie. Neither is there a likelihood of confusion that this statement would cause viewers to believe that Louis Vuitton approved of Warner Bros.' use of the Diophy bag. In a case such as this one, no amount of discovery will tilt the scales in favor of the mark holder at the expense of the public's right to free expression.

Therefore, even assuming, arguendo, that Louis Vuitton could state a cognizable claim of confusion, Warner Bros.' use of the Diophy bag is protected under *Rogers* because it has some artistic relevance to the Film and is not explicitly misleading.

Questions

1. Is the court correct in ruling that the *Rogers* analysis permits the dismissal of a complaint on a 12(b)(6) motion? If you were the lawyer for Louis Vuitton, what would you argue on appeal?

2. Did the court misread *Rogers* when it held that the only confusion that could overcome the protection of *Rogers* was evidence that Warner Bros. used the Diophy bag in order to mislead consumers into believing that Louis Vuitton produced or endorsed the film?

3. Does the *Rogers* decision suggest a limitation on Lanham Act claims regarding artistic uses of the names of celebrities whose fame has made them symbols of popular culture? Should a similar limitation be applied to artistic uses of trademarks whose fame has made them symbols of popular culture? Should that limitation extend to other uses of trademarks that are expressive, albeit not artistic? Consider the following (unauthorized) adaptation of the Starbucks logo, designed by arms salesman Jim Childers in appreciation for Starbucks' policy that its customers were welcome to carry their arms into Starbucks' locations (when permitted under state law).

4. Plaintiff Winchester Mystery House, LLC owns and operates the Winchester Mystery House, a historic Victorian-style mansion and surrounding gardens that operates as a tourist attraction. The house was owned by Sarah Winchester, widow of one of the heirs to the Winchester Repeating Arms Company, who allegedly became convinced that she was cursed by the spirits of those who had been killed by the Winchester rifle. The company owns trademark rights in "Winchester Mystery House" and the three-dimensional design of the Winchester mansion itself. Defendant recently released "Haunting of Winchester House", a film that, while not mentioning the "Winchester Mystery House," was shot in a Victorian-style structure, and includes the ghost of Sarah Winchester as a character. Applying the *Rogers* test, is the plaintiff likely to prevail in an analysis of likely confusion? *See Winchester Mystery House v. Global Asylum*, 148 Cal. Rptr. 3d 412 (Cal. Ct. App. 2012).

E.S.S. Entertainment 2000, Inc. v. Rock Star Videos, Inc.

547 F.3d 1095 (9th Cir. 2008)

O'Scannlain, Circuit Judge:

We must decide whether a producer of a video game in the "Grand Theft Auto" series has a defense under the First Amendment against a claim of trademark infringement.

I

A

Rockstar Games, Inc. ("Rockstar"), a wholly owned subsidiary of Take-Two Interactive Software, Inc., manufactures and distributes the Grand Theft Auto series of video games (the "Series"), including Grand Theft Auto: San Andreas ("San Andreas" or the "Game"). The Series is known for an irreverent and sometimes crass brand of humor, gratuitous violence and sex, and overall seediness.

Each game in the Series takes place in one or more dystopic, cartoonish cities modeled after actual American urban areas. The games always include a disclaimer stating that the locations depicted are fictional. Players control the game's protagonist, trying to complete various "missions" on a video screen. The plot advances with each mission accomplished until the player, having passed through thousands of cartoon-style places along the way, wins the game.

Consistent with the tone of the Series, San Andreas allows a player to experience a version of West Coast "gangster" culture. The Game takes place in the virtual cities of "Los Santos," "San Fierro," and "Las Venturas," based on Los Angeles, San Francisco, and Las Vegas, respectively.

Los Santos, of course, mimics the look and feel of actual Los Angeles neighborhoods. Instead of "Hollywood," "Santa Monica," "Venice Beach," and "Compton," Los Santos contains "Vinewood," "Santa Maria," "Verona Beach," and "Ganton." Rockstar has populated these areas with virtual liquor stores, ammunition dealers, casinos, pawn shops, tattoo parlors, bars, and strip clubs. The brand names, business names, and other aspects of the locations have been changed to fit the irreverent

"Los Santos" tone. Not especially saintly, Los Santos is complete with gangs who roam streets inhabited by prostitutes and drug pushers while random gunfire punctuates the soundtrack.

To generate their vision for Los Santos, some of the artists who drew it visited Los Angeles to take reference photographs. The artists took pictures of businesses, streets, and other places in Los Angeles that they thought evoked the San Andreas theme. They then returned home (to Scotland) to draw Los Santos, changing the images from the photographs as necessary to fit into the fictional world of Los Santos and San Andreas. According to Nikolas Taylor ("Taylor"), the Lead Map Artist for Los Santos, he and other artists did not seek to "re-creat[e] a realistic depiction of Los Angeles; rather, [they] were creating 'Los Santos,' a fictional city that lampooned the seedy underbelly of Los Angeles and the people, business and places [that] comprise it." One neighborhood in the fictional city is "East Los Santos," the Game's version of East Los Angeles. East Los Santos contains variations on the businesses and architecture of the real thing, including a virtual, cartoon-style strip club known as the "Pig Pen."

B

ESS Entertainment 2000, Inc. ("ESS"), operates a strip club, which features females dancing nude, on the eastern edge of downtown Los Angeles under the name Play Pen Gentlemen's Club ("Play Pen"). ESS claims that Rockstar's depiction of an East Los Santos strip club called the Pig Pen infringes its trademark and trade dress associated with the Play Pen.

The Play Pen's "logo" consists of the words "the Play Pen" (and the lower- and upper-case letters forming those words) and the phrase "Totally Nude" displayed in a publicly available font, with a silhouette of a nude female dancer inside the stem of the first "P." Apparently, ESS has no physical master or precise template for its logo. Different artists draw the nude silhouette in Play Pen's logo anew for each representation, although any final drawing must be acceptable to Play Pen's owners. There are several different versions of the silhouette, and some advertisements and signs for the Play Pen do not contain the nude silhouettes.

Although the artists took some inspiration from their photographs of the Play Pen, it seems they used photographs of other East Los Angeles locations to design other aspects of the Pig Pen. The Pig Pen building in Los Santos, for instance, lacks certain characteristics of the Play Pen building such as a stone facade, a valet stand, large plants and gold columns around the entrance, and a six-foot black iron fence around the parking lot. The Play Pen also has a red, white, and blue pole sign near the premises, which includes a trio of nude silhouettes above the logo and a separate "Totally Nude" sign below. The Pig Pen does not.

C

On April 22, 2005, ESS filed the underlying trademark violation action in district court against Rockstar. ESS asserted four claims: (1) trade dress infringement and unfair competition under section 43(a) of the Lanham Act, 15 U.S.C. § 1125(a); (2) trademark infringement under California Business and Professions Code § 14320;

(3) unfair competition under California Business and Professions Code §§ 17200 et seq.; and (4) unfair competition under California common law. The heart of ESS's complaint is that Rockstar has used Play Pen's distinctive logo and trade dress without its authorization and has created a likelihood of confusion among consumers as to whether ESS has endorsed, or is associated with, the video depiction.

In response, Rockstar moved for summary judgment on all of ESS's claims, arguing that the affirmative defenses of nominative fair use and the First Amendment protected it against liability. It also argued that its use of ESS's intellectual property did not infringe ESS's trademark by creating a "likelihood of confusion."

Although the district court rejected Rockstar's nominative fair use defense, it granted summary judgment based on the First Amendment defense. The district court did not address the merits of the trademark claim because its finding that Rockstar had a defense against liability made such analysis unnecessary.

II

Rockstar argues that, regardless of whether it infringed ESS's trademark under the Lanham Act or related California law, it is entitled to two defenses: one under the nominative fair use doctrine and one under the First Amendment. [The court held that "Since Rockstar did not use the trademarked logo to describe ESS's strip club, the district court correctly held that the nominative fair use defense does not apply in this case."]

B

Rockstar's second defense asks us to consider the intersection of trademark law and the First Amendment. The road is well traveled. We have adopted the Second Circuit's approach from *Rogers v. Grimaldi*, which "requires courts to construe the Lanham Act 'to apply to artistic works only where the public interest in avoiding consumer confusion *outweighs* the public interest in free expression.'" [*Mattel Inc. v.*] *Walking Mountain* [*Productions*], 353 F.3d [792] at 807 [(9th Cir. 2003)] (emphasis in original) (quoting *Rogers v. Grimaldi*, 875 F.2d 994, 999 (2d Cir. 1989)).... Although this test traditionally applies to uses of a trademark in the title of an artistic work, there is no principled reason why it ought not also apply to the use of a trademark in the body of the work. *See Walking Mountain*, 353 F.3d at 809 n.17 (implying that it would be acceptable to apply the *Rogers* test to non-titular trade dress claim). The parties do not dispute such an extension of the doctrine.

1

We first adopted the *Rogers* test in *MCA Records*, a case which is instructive for that reason. [*Mattel, Inc. v. MCA Records, Inc.*, 296 F.3d 894, 902 (9th Cir. 2002).] In *MCA Records*, the maker of the iconic "Barbie" dolls sued MCA for trademark infringement in the title of a song the record company had released, called "Barbie Girl." *Id.* at 899–900. The song was a commentary "about Barbie and the values ... she [supposedly] represents." *Id.* at 902. Applying *Rogers*, the court held that the First Amendment protected the record company. The first prong was straightforward. Because the song was about Barbie, "the use of Barbie in the song title clearly is relevant to the underlying work." *Id.; see also Walking Mountain*, 353 F.3d at 807 (holding that use of Barbie doll in photographic parody was relevant to the underlying work).

Moving to the second prong, we made an important point. "The *only* indication," we observed, "that Mattel might be associated with the song is the use of Barbie in the title; if this were enough to satisfy this prong of the *Rogers* test, it would render *Rogers* a nullity." *MCA Records*, 296 F.2d at 902 (emphasis in original). This makes good sense. After all, a trademark infringement claim presupposes a use of the mark. If that necessary element in every trademark case vitiated a First Amendment defense, the First Amendment would provide no defense at all.

2

Keeping *MCA Records* and related cases in mind, we now turn to the matter before us. ESS concedes that the Game is artistic and that therefore the *Rogers* test applies. However, ESS argues both that the incorporation of the Pig Pen into the Game has no artistic relevance and that it is explicitly misleading. It rests its argument on two observations: (1) the Game is not "about" ESS's Play Pen club the way that "Barbie Girl" was "about" the Barbie doll in *MCA Records*; and (2) also unlike the Barbie case, where the trademark and trade dress at issue was a cultural icon (Barbie), the Play Pen is not a cultural icon.

ESS's objections, though factually accurate, miss the point. Under *MCA Records* and the cases that followed it, only the use of a trademark with "'*no* artistic relevance to the underlying work *whatsoever*'" does not merit First Amendment protection. *Id.* (emphasis added) (quoting *Rogers*, 875 F.2d at 999). In other words, the level of relevance merely must be above zero. It is true that the Game is not "about" the Play Pen the way that Barbie Girl was about Barbie. But, given the low threshold the Game must surmount, that fact is hardly dispositive. It is also true that Play Pen has little cultural significance, but the same could be said about most of the individual establishments in East Los Angeles. Like most urban neighborhoods, its distinctiveness lies in its "look and feel," not in particular destinations as in a downtown or tourist district. And that neighborhood, with all that characterizes it, is relevant to Rockstar's artistic goal, which is to develop a cartoon-style parody of East Los Angeles. Possibly the only way, and certainly a reasonable way, to do that is to recreate a critical mass of the businesses and buildings that constitute it. In this context, we conclude that to include a strip club that is similar in look and feel to the Play Pen does indeed have at least "some artistic relevance." *See id.*

3

ESS also argues that Rockstar's use of the Pig Pen "'explicitly misleads as to the source or the content of the work.'" *Id.* (quoting *Rogers*, 875 F.2d at 999). This prong of the test points directly at the purpose of trademark law, namely to "avoid confusion in the marketplace by allowing a trademark owner to prevent others from duping consumers into buying a product they mistakenly believe is sponsored by the trademark owner." *Walking Mountain*, 353 F.3d at 806 (internal quotation marks and alteration omitted). The relevant question, therefore, is whether the Game would confuse its players into thinking that the Play Pen is somehow behind the Pig Pen or that it sponsors Rockstar's product. In answering that question, we keep in mind our observation in *MCA Records* that the mere use of a trademark alone cannot suffice to make such use explicitly misleading. *See MCA Records*, 296 F.3d at 902.

Both San Andreas and the Play Pen offer a form of lowbrow entertainment; besides this general similarity, they have nothing in common. The San Andreas Game is not complementary to the Play Pen; video games and strip clubs do not go together like a horse and carriage or, perish the thought, love and marriage. Nothing indicates that the buying public would reasonably have believed that ESS produced the video game or, for that matter, that Rockstar operated a strip club. A player can enter the virtual strip club in Los Santos, but ESS has provided no evidence that the setting is anything but generic. It also seems far-fetched that someone playing San Andreas would think ESS had provided whatever expertise, support, or unique strip-club knowledge it possesses to the production of the game. After all, the Game does not revolve around running or patronizing a strip club. Whatever one can do at the Pig Pen seems quite incidental to the overall story of the Game. A reasonable consumer would not think a company that owns one strip club in East Los Angeles, which is not well known to the public at large, also produces a technologically sophisticated video game like San Andreas.

Undeterred, ESS also argues that, because players are free to ignore the storyline and spend as much time as they want at the Pig Pen, the Pig Pen can be considered a significant part of the Game, leading to confusion. But fans can spend all nine innings of a baseball game at the hot dog stand; that hardly makes Dodger Stadium a butcher's shop. In other words, the chance to attend a virtual strip club is unambiguously *not* the main selling point of the Game.

III

Considering all of the foregoing, we conclude that Rockstar's modification of ESS's trademark is not explicitly misleading and is thus protected by the First Amendment. Since the First Amendment defense applies equally to ESS's state law claims as to its Lanham Act claim, the district court properly dismissed the entire case on Rockstar's motion for summary judgment.

AFFIRMED.

Questions

1. Should the *Rogers* test be applied in the same way to videogames as to movies? How about television series? Bravo Television's reality show *Top Chef* challenges chefs to cook gourmet meals in a series of competitive elimination challenges, until the final remaining chef claims the title "Top Chef." Commonly, a given contest features a particular commercial setting or ingredient. Some episodes have revolved around named high-end restaurants; others have required contestants to cook something yummy using Quaker® Oats or Baileys' Irish Cream® Liqueur. If the show's producers choose to use a branded ingredient whose producer declines to pay for placement, may they go ahead without permission? In the summer of 2009, NBC announced that it had signed a deal with Subway® restaurants to make Subway® an integral presence in its adventure series, *Chuck*. As such deals become more common, won't viewers naturally assume that a product that makes repeated appearances in a television series or film is there because its producer paid for them? If a different network airs an episode of a hospital drama in which multitudes come down with food poisoning after eating at a local Subway® restaurant, should Subway have any recourse?

2. How would it have changed the court's analysis if the Pig Pen had been named the "Play Pen," or if it had looked more like plaintiff's site, or both? Wouldn't the game version of the strip club still pass the test of non-zero artistic relevance?

3. Does the First Amendment provide a defense to right of publicity claims? In *Davis v. Electronic Arts, Inc.*, 775 F.3d 1172 (9th Cir. 2015), a controversy involving a videogame's use of the likenesses of former NFL football players, the Ninth Circuit reaffirmed its position in *Keller v. Elec. Arts. Inc.*, 724 F.3d 1268 (9th Cir. 2013), to hold the *Rogers* test, and its incorporation of First Amendment protections, inapplicable to right of publicity claims. By contrast, in *Brown v Electronic Arts, Inc.*, 724 F.3d 1235 (9th Cir. 2013), the same videogame producer's use of the likeness of former NCAA and NFL star Jim Brown, drew the latter's claim of false endorsement under Lanham Act section 43(a). The court upheld the dismissal of the action, holding that the *Rogers* test to hold that EA's use of Brown's likeness did not constitute an explicit attempt to signify that Brown endorsed the games, "is applicable when First Amendment rights are at their height—when expressive works are involved" and affirming the ruling. When the same expressive use gives rise to both section 43(a) and right of publicity claims, does it make sense to reach opposing outcomes? *See also Rosa and Raymond Parks Institute for Self Development v. Target Corp.*, 812 F.3d 824 (11th Cir. 2016) (Michigan's qualified privilege protecting matters of public interest overrides right of publicity claims against unlicensed use of Rosa Parks' name in books, a film, and a plaque, all concerning the civil rights movement, sold by Target).

4. In *Trademark: Champion of Free Speech*, 27 Colum. J. L. & Arts 187 (2004), Judge Pierre Leval suggests that courts have been too willing to invoke the First Amendment without first determining whether their cases present a real likelihood of consumer confusion. The trademark law, he argues, incorporates strong protection for free expression by limiting the scope of the trademark owner's right to control the unauthorized use of its mark:

> When lawsuits pit claims of exclusive trademark right against interests of free expression, courts should not run unnecessarily to the Constitution. The governing statutes charge the courts with a delegated duty to seek the answers first in the complex, intelligently balanced terms of the trademark laws themselves. Those terms are designed to balance the needs of merchants for identification as the provider of goods with the needs of society for free communication and discussion. Where the terms of the trademark law adequately protect an accused

infringer's use as falling outside the scope of the trademark owner's exclusive right, the court has no need to seek answers in the First Amendment.

Recall the cases you have read so far in which courts excused the unauthorized use of a mark on grounds informed by First Amendment considerations. Would any of these cases, in your view, have reached a different result if the courts had concentrated on limiting doctrines intrinsic to trademark law rather than relying on the First Amendment? Now recall the cases in which courts refused to give credence to a First Amendment defense. Did those cases reflect the nuanced understanding of the "intelligently balanced terms of the trademark laws" that Judge Leval invokes?

2. Parody

Dr. Seuss Enterprises, L.P. v. Penguin Books USA, Inc.

109 F.3d 1394 (9th Cir. 1997)

O'Scannlain, Circuit Judge:

We must decide whether a poetic account of the O.J. Simpson double murder trial entitled *The Cat NOT in the Hat! A Parody by Dr. Juice*, presents a sufficient showing of copyright and trademark infringement of the well-known *The Cat in the Hat* by Dr. Seuss.

I

Seuss, a California limited partnership, owns most of the copyrights and trademarks to the works of the late Theodor S. Geisel, the author and illustrator of the famous children's educational books written under the pseudonym "Dr. Seuss." Between 1931 and 1991, Geisel wrote, illustrated and published at least 47 books that resulted in approximately 35 million copies currently in print worldwide. He authored and illustrated the books in simple, rhyming, repetitive language, accompanied by characters that are recognizable by and appealing to children. The characters are often animals with human-like characteristics.

In *The Cat in the Hat*, first published in 1957, Geisel created a mischievous but well meaning character, the Cat, who continues to be among the most famous and well recognized of the Dr. Seuss creations. The Cat is almost always depicted with his distinctive scrunched and somewhat shabby red and white stove-pipe hat. Seuss owns the common law trademark rights to the words "Dr. Seuss" and "Cat in the Hat," as well as the character illustration of the Cat's stove-pipe hat. Seuss also owns the copyright registrations for the books *The Cat in the Hat, The Cat in the Hat Comes Back, The Cat in the Hat Beginner Book Dictionary, The Cat in the Hat Songbook*, and *The Cat's Quizzer.* In addition, Seuss has trademark registrations for the marks currently pending with the United States Trademark Office. Seuss has licensed the Dr. Seuss marks, including *The Cat in the Hat* character, for use on clothing, in interactive software, and in a theme park.

In 1995, Alan Katz and Chris Wrinn, respectively, wrote and illustrated *The Cat NOT in the Hat!* satirizing the O.J. Simpson double murder trial. Penguin and Dove, the publishers and distributors, were not licensed or authorized to use any of the works, characters or illustrations owned by Seuss. They also did not seek permission from Seuss to use these properties.

Seuss filed a complaint for copyright and trademark infringement, an application for a temporary restraining order and a preliminary injunction after seeing an advertisement promoting *The Cat NOT in the Hat!* prior to its publication. The advertisement declared:

> Wickedly clever author "Dr. Juice" gives the O.J. Simpson trial a very fresh new look. From Brentwood to the Los Angeles County Courthouse to Marcia Clark and the Dream Team. *The Cat Not in the Hat* tells the whole story in rhyming verse and sketches as witty as Theodore [sic] Geisel's best. This is one parody that really packs a punch!

Seuss alleged that *The Cat NOT in the Hat!* misappropriated substantial protected elements of its copyrighted works, used six unregistered and one registered Seuss trademarks, and diluted the distinctive quality of its famous marks. Katz subsequently filed a declaration stating that *The Cat in the Hat* was the "object for [his] parody" and portions of his book derive from *The Cat in the Hat* only as "necessary to conjure up the original."

... On March 21, 1996, the district court granted Seuss' request for a preliminary injunction. About 12,000 books, at an expense of approximately $35,500, had been printed to date but now were enjoined from distribution....

....

[The Ninth Circuit affirmed the district court's determination that the defendant's copying from *The Cat in the Hat* infringed Seuss' copyright, and was not a fair use parody.]

IV

....

A

The issue in trademark infringement actions is not the alleged appropriation of Seuss' creative expression, but rather, the likelihood of confusion in the market place as to the source of Penguin and Dove's *The Cat NOT in the Hat!*. "Likelihood of confusion" is the basic test for both common law trademark infringement and federal statutory trademark infringement. 3 J. Thomas McCarthy, *McCarthy on Trademarks and Unfair Competition*, § 23.01[1] (rev. ed.1994). A federal claim under Lanham Act § 43(a) for infringement of an unregistered mark is triggered by a use which "is likely to cause confusion, or to cause mistake, or to deceive as to the affiliation, connection, or association" of *The Cat NOT in the Hat!* with Seuss' *The Cat in the Hat.* Lanham Act § 43(a), 15 U.S.C. § 1125(a)(1)(A).

The eight-factor *Sleekcraft* test is used in the Ninth Circuit to analyze the likelihood of confusion question in all trademark infringement cases, both competitive and non-competitive. [Citation.]....

....

We agree with the district court's findings that under *Sleekcraft* many of the factors for analysis of trademark infringement were indeterminate and posed serious questions for litigation. First, Penguin and Dove do not dispute that the Cat's stove-pipe hat, the words "Dr. Seuss," and the title "The Cat in the Hat" are widely recognized trademarks. Second and third, the proximity and similarity between the marks and the infringing items are substantial: figures on the front and back of the infringing work; the Cat's stove-pipe hat; the narrator ("Dr. Seuss" versus "Dr. Juice"); and the title (*The Cat in the Hat* versus *The Cat NOT in the Hat!*). Below is one example:

Fourth, there is no evidence of actual confusion. Because *The Cat NOT in the Hat!* has been enjoined from distribution, there has been no opportunity to prove confusion in the market place. Fifth, the marketing channels used are indeterminate. Sixth, the use of the Cat's stove-pipe hat or the confusingly similar title to capture initial consumer attention, even though no actual sale is finally completed as a result of the confusion, may be still an infringement. *See Mobil Oil Corp. v. Pegasus Petroleum Corp.*, 818 F.2d 254, 257–58 (2d Cir. 1987). Seventh, Penguin and Dove's likely intent in selecting the Seuss marks was to draw consumer attention to what would otherwise be just one more book on the O.J. Simpson murder trial. Eighth and last, the likelihood of expansion of the product lines is indeterminate.

B

Even if Seuss establishes a likelihood of confusion, Penguin and Dove argue that their identical and confusingly similar use of Seuss' marks is offset by the work's parodic character. In a traditional trademark infringement suit founded on the likelihood of confusion rationale, the claim of parody is not really a separate "defense" as such, but merely a way of phrasing the traditional response that customers are not likely to be confused as to the source, sponsorship or approval. [Citation.] "Some parodies will constitute an infringement, some will not. But the cry of 'parody!' does not magically fend off otherwise legitimate claims of trademark infringement or dilution. There are confusing parodies and non-confusing parodies. All they have in common is an attempt at humor through the use of someone else's trademark. A non-infringing parody is merely amusing, not confusing." *McCarthy on Trademarks*, § 31.38[1], at 31-216 (rev. ed.1995).

In several cases, the courts have held, in effect, that poking fun at a trademark is no joke and have issued injunctions. Examples include: a diaper bag with green and red bands and the wording "Gucchi Goo," allegedly poking fun at the well-known Gucci name and the design mark, *Gucci Shops, Inc. v. R.H. Macy & Co.*, 446 F. Supp. 838 (S.D.N.Y. 1977); the use of a competing meat sauce of the trademark "A.2" as a "pun" on the famous "A.1" trademark, *Nabisco Brands, Inc. v. Kaye*, 760 F. Supp. 25 (D. Conn. 1991). Stating that, whereas a true parody will be so obvious that a clear distinction is preserved between the source of the target and the source of the parody, a court found that the "Hard Rain" logo was an infringement of the "Hard Rock" logo. In such a case, the claim of parody is no defense "where the purpose of the similarity is to capitalize on a famous mark's popularity for the defendant's own commercial use." *Hard Rock Cafe Licensing Corp. v. Pacific Graphics, Inc.*, 776 F. Supp. 1454, 1462 (W.D. Wash. 1991).

C

We are satisfied that the district court's determinations on the existence of serious questions for litigation and a balance of hardships favoring Seuss are not clearly erroneous. First, the district court properly found that serious questions exist for litigation because many of the factors for analysis of trademark infringement (i.e., likelihood of confusion) were indeterminate. Second, the good will and reputation associated with *The Cat in the Hat* character and title, the name "Dr. Seuss," and the Cat's Hat outweigh the $35,500 in expenses incurred by Penguin.

...

Question

In *Cliff's Notes, Inc. v. Bantam Doubleday Dell Pub. Group. Inc.*, 886 F.2d 490 (2d Cir. 1989), involving a Spy Magazine parody of the Cliff's Notes study guides, the Second Circuit acknowledged that the effectiveness of a parody lies in its ability to engender initial confusion between the parody and the parodied subject. So long as the initial misimpression is dispelled, then there is no actionable confusion. In *Cliffs Notes*, the parodist adopted a variety of disclaimers, which the court found sufficient to alleviate confusion. Why were similar disclaimers ineffective in the *Dr. Seuss* case?

Mattel, Inc. v. Universal Music International, 296 F.3d 894 (9th Cir. 2002). Mattel produces Barbie, the famous children's doll and associated Barbie-branded goods; over time Barbie has become a cultural icon, representing a certain conception of American young womanhood. Playing off of this status, the Danish band Aqua recorded the song "Barbie Girl," in which band members impersonate Barbie and Ken, singing about their desire to "go party." Mattel brought this suit alleging federal and state-law trademark infringement. The district court granted MCA, the band's record producer's motion for summary judgment, ruling that the song's use of Barbie was a parody and a nominative fair use, and was not likely to confuse consumers as to Mattel's affiliation with Aqua or to dilute the Barbie mark. The Ninth Circuit, through Judge Kozinski, after first considering the traditional commercial identifying purpose of trademarks, analyzed likelihood of confusion in the context of marks that convey social as well as commercial meanings:

> The problem arises when trademarks transcend their identifying purpose. Some trademarks enter our public discourse and become an integral part of our vocabulary. How else do you say that something's "the Rolls Royce of its class?" What else is a quick fix, but a Band-Aid? Does the average consumer know to ask for aspirin as "acetyl salicylic acid"? *See Bayer Co. v. United Drug Co.*, 272 F. 505, 510 (S.D.N.Y. 1921). Trademarks often fill in gaps in our vocabulary and add a contemporary flavor to our expressions. Once imbued with such expressive value, the trademark becomes a word in our language and assumes a role outside the bounds of trademark law.
>
> Our likelihood-of-confusion test, [citation], generally strikes a comfortable balance between the trademark owner's property rights and the public's expressive interests. But when a trademark owner asserts a right to control how we express ourselves—when we'd find it difficult to describe the product any other way (as in the case of aspirin), or when the mark (like Rolls Royce) has taken on an expressive meaning apart from its source-identifying function—applying the traditional test fails to account for the full weight of the public's interest in free expression.
>
> The First Amendment may offer little protection for a competitor who labels its commercial good with a confusingly similar mark, but "trademark rights do not entitle the owner to quash an unauthorized use of the mark by another who is communicating ideas or expressing points of view." *L.L. Bean, Inc. v. Drake Publishers, Inc.*, 811 F.2d 26, 29 (1st Cir. 1987). Were we to ignore the expressive value that some marks assume, trademark rights would grow to encroach upon the zone protected by the First Amendment. *See Yankee Publ'g, Inc. v. News Am. Publ'g, Inc.*, 809 F. Supp. 267, 276 (S.D.N.Y. 1992) ("When unauthorized use of another's mark is part of a communicative message and not a source identifier, the First Amendment is implicated in opposition to the trademark right."). Simply put, the trademark owner does not have the right to control public discourse whenever the public imbues his mark with a meaning beyond its source-identifying function. *See Anti-Monopoly, Inc. v. Gen. Mills Fun Group*, 611 F.2d 296, 301 (9th Cir. 1979) ("It is the source-denoting function which trademark laws protect, and nothing more.").

B.

There is no doubt that MCA uses Mattel's mark: Barbie is one half of Barbie Girl. But Barbie Girl is the title of a song about Barbie and Ken, a reference that—at least today—can only be to Mattel's famous couple. We expect a title to describe the underlying work, not to identify the producer, and Barbie Girl does just that.

The Barbie Girl title presages a song about Barbie, or at least a girl like Barbie. The title conveys a message to consumers about what they can expect to discover in the song itself; it's a quick glimpse of Aqua's take on their own song. The lyrics confirm this: The female singer, who calls herself Barbie, is "a Barbie girl, in [her] Barbie world." She tells her male counterpart (named Ken), "Life in plastic, it's fantastic. You can brush my hair, undress me everywhere/Imagination, life is your creation." And off they go to "party." The song pokes fun at Barbie and the values that Aqua contends she represents. *See Cliffs Notes, Inc. v. Bantam Doubleday Dell Publ'g Group*, 886 F.2d 490, 495–96 (2d Cir. 1989). The female singer explains, "I'm a blond bimbo girl, in a fantasy world/Dress me up, make it tight, I'm your dolly."

The song does not rely on the Barbie mark to poke fun at another subject but targets Barbie herself. *See Campbell v. Acuff-Rose Music, Inc.*, 510 U.S. 569, 580 (1994); *see also Dr. Seuss Ents., L.P. v. Penguin Books USA, Inc.*, 109 F.3d 1394, 1400 (9th Cir. 1997). This case is therefore distinguishable from *Dr. Seuss*, where we held that the book *The Cat NOT in the Hat!* Borrowed Dr. Seuss's trademarks and lyrics to get attention rather than to mock *The Cat in the Hat!* The defendant's use of the Dr. Seuss trademarks and copyrighted works had "no critical bearing on the substance or style of" *The Cat in the Hat!*, and therefore could not claim First Amendment protection. *Id.* at 1401. *Dr. Seuss* recognized that, where an artistic work targets the original and does not merely borrow another's property to get attention, First Amendment interests weigh more heavily in the balance. *See id.* at 1400–02; *see also Harley-Davidson, Inc. v. Grottanelli*, 164 F.3d 806, 812–13 (2d Cir. 1999) (a parodist whose expressive work aims its parodic commentary at a trademark is given considerable leeway, but a claimed parodic use that makes no comment on the mark is not a permitted trademark parody use).

The Second Circuit has held that "in general the [Lanham] Act should be construed to apply to artistic works only where the public interest in avoiding consumer confusion outweighs the public interest in free expression." *Rogers v. Grimaldi*, 875 F.2d 994, 999 (2d Cir. 1989); *see also Cliffs Notes*, 886 F.2d at 494 (quoting *Rogers*, 875 F.2d at 999). *Rogers* considered a challenge by the actress Ginger Rogers to the film *Ginger and Fred.* The movie told the story of two Italian cabaret performers who made a living by imitating Ginger Rogers and Fred Astaire. Rogers argued that the film's title created the false impression that she was associated with it.

At first glance, Rogers certainly had a point. Ginger was her name, and Fred was her dancing partner. If a pair of dancing shoes had been labeled Ginger and Fred, a dancer might have suspected that Rogers was associated with the shoes (or at least one of them), just as Michael Jordan has endorsed Nike sneakers that claim to make you fly through the air. But Ginger and Fred was not a brand of shoe; it was the title of a movie and, for the reasons explained by the Second Circuit, deserved to be treated differently.

A title is designed to catch the eye and to promote the value of the underlying work. Consumers expect a title to communicate a message about the book or movie, but they do not expect it to identify the publisher or producer. *See Application of Cooper*, 254 F.2d 611, 615–16, 45 C.C.P.A. 923 (C.C.P.A. 1958) (A "title ... identifies a specific literary work, ... and is not associated in the public mind with the ... manufacturer." (internal quotation marks omitted)). If we see a painting titled "Campbell's Chicken Noodle Soup," we're unlikely to believe that Campbell's has branched into the art business. Nor, upon hearing Janis Joplin croon "Oh Lord, won't you buy me a Mercedes-Benz?," would we suspect that she and the carmaker had entered into a joint venture. A title tells us something about the underlying work but seldom speaks to its origin?

Rogers concluded that literary titles do not violate the Lanham Act "unless the title has no artistic relevance to the underlying work whatsoever, or, if it has some artistic relevance, unless the title explicitly misleads as to the source or the content of the work." *Id.* at 999 (footnote omitted). We agree with the Second Circuit's analysis and adopt the *Rogers* standard as our own.

Applying *Rogers* to our case, we conclude that MCA's use of Barbie is not an infringement of Mattel's trademark. Under the first prong of *Rogers*, the use of Barbie in the song title clearly is relevant to the underlying work, namely, the song itself. As noted, the song is about Barbie and the values Aqua claims she represents. The song title does not explicitly mislead as to the source of the work; it does not, explicitly or otherwise, suggest that it was produced by Mattel. The *only* indication that Mattel might be associated with the song is the use of Barbie in the title; if this were enough to satisfy this prong of the *Rogers* test, it would render *Rogers* a nullity. We therefore agree with the district court that MCA was entitled to summary judgment on this ground. We need not consider whether the district court was correct in holding that MCA was also entitled to summary judgment because its use of Barbie was a nominative fair use.

Questions

1. Ignoring for the moment any First Amendment interest in recording a parody aimed at Barbie dolls, how likely is it that members of the public would be confused about the source or sponsorship of the Aqua song?

2. National Public Radio broadcasts "Science Friday," a popular show designed to make developments in science accessible to a broad public. Bob Enyart, a Protestant fundamentalist minister who contests evolution and other tenets of modern science, has created a series of podcasts and YouTube videos titled "Real Science Friday" attacking the NPR show and propagating creationist views. ScienceFriday, Inc., which holds trademark registrations for the "Science Friday" radio show and a related website, claims that consumers are likely to confuse "Real Science Friday" with "Science Friday." If the producers of "Real Science Friday" respond that they have employed that title in their podcasts and videos in order to parody and debunk the radio and related programs, how should the court rule? *See ScienceFriday, Inc. v. BobEnyart, Inc.*, Index N. 65389/2019 (N.Y. Sup. Ct., *complaint filed* November 9, 2012).

3. VIP produced "Buttwiper" squeaky rubber dog toys designed to parody a Budweiser beer bottle, depicted below.

Anheuser-Busch brought suit alleging trademark infringement, and introduced a survey of adult pet-owners indicating that 30% of those surveyed believed Buttwiper pet toys were sold with the approval or sponsorship of, or were affiliated with, the maker of Budweiser beer. Should a court credit evidence that the public believes parodies should be authorized? *See Anheuser-Busch v. VIP Products*, 666 F. Supp. 2d 974 (E.D. Mo. 2008).

4. Section 43(c) of the Lanham Act (as amended in 2006) (discussed *infra* Chapter 9), expressly excludes dilution liability for parodies:

> The following shall not be actionable as dilution by blurring or dilution by tarnishment under this subsection:

(A) Any fair use, including a nominative or descriptive fair use, or facilitation of such fair use, of a famous mark by another person other than as a designation of source for the person's own goods or services, including use in connection with—

....

(ii) identifying and parodying, criticizing, or commenting upon the famous mark owner or the goods or services of the famous mark owner.

Can the language of section 43(c) be read to exempt parodies from infringement and false designation of origin claims as well as dilution claims? Should it be?

3. Trademarks as Speech*

Rochelle Dreyfuss, *Reconciling Trademark Rights and Expressive Values: How to Stop Worrying and Learn to Love Ambiguity*

in Dinwoodie & Janis, Trademark Law and Theory (Edward Elgar 2008) (excerpt)**

Trademarks and free expression are on a collision course. In the early 90's, I wrote two articles examining the expansion of trademark law from its core focus on confusion about marketing signals, to cover such matters as dilution, implications of sponsorship, and rights of publicity. I suggested that these expansions were putting increasing pressure on speech interests. It seemed to me that signifiers drawn from mythology, history, and literature were losing their potency in a globalized environment in which the populace lacks a shared vocabulary or much interest in the classics. I posited that well-known marks were taking the place of these references. Used as metaphors, similes, and metonyms, trademarks were becoming the lingua franca of the communicative sphere. I was concerned, however, at the extent to which these "allusive uses" were coming under private control: judges were jumping ever more quickly from recognizing the value in a mark, to allowing the mark's proprietor to capture that value. I thought that, in fact, the significance of a mark was in large part generated by its audience, through the way in which it was recoded and recontextualized. Accordingly, it was incumbent upon courts to understand how signals functioned and to recognize the dual provenance of their value. While it was appropriate to give proprietors marketing control—rights over signaling value, other aspects—expressive value—belonged to the public. I admitted that separating these two dimensions would sometimes be difficult, but suggested techniques to make that division workable.

Over the last decade, a solution based on separating the spheres in which symbols operate has become increasingly less tractable. On the trademark holders' side, interest

---

* *Editors' Note*: The title of this subsection was coined by Prof. Robert Denicola. *See* Robert C. Denicola, *Trademarks as Speech: Constitutional Implications of the Emerging Rationales for the Protection of Trade Symbols*, 1982 Wis. L. Rev. 158.

** Copyright 2008. Reprinted by permission. [*Editors' Note:* Footnotes omitted.]

in and power over marks have expanded considerably. Proprietors use trademarks to maintain exclusivity after patents and copyrights have expired and trade secrets have been exposed; they also use them to leverage reputation across product categories. They engage in "lifestyle marketing"—offering goods across a range of sectors. In some cases, trademarks take on a life of their own: merchandising a mark through various licensing ventures can sometimes earn as much as sales of the underlying product.

Trademark holders have had remarkable success developing law responsive to these concerns: a range of new concepts, such as initial-interest and post-sale confusion; a new focus on trade dress protection; and new and improved rights of action: dilution protection has been federalized ... less conventional signs, such as scents, sounds, and color, are also becoming the subject matter of trademark protection. And moves are afoot to create new rights to control traditional knowledge, including tribal symbols.

Public use of trademarks has also multiplied. Fans have always put marks on tee shirts, sports caps, bumper stickers, buttons, mugs, posters—even birthday cakes—to express their affiliation with schools, teams, social organizations, and products. Some of these usages have become less complimentary. As one South African judge put it, tee shirts decorated with trademarks are now a focus for "young irreverent people who enjoy the idea of being gadflies." Nor is "gadflying" as limited as was once the case. Digitization reduces the cost of using trademarks in traditional media while the Internet offers fresh opportunities—the chance to create widely-available websites to sell marked products or to use trademarks artistically, politically, and humorously, or to critique the trademark holder's activities, politics, or products.

Most important, the dichotomy between marketing and expressive spheres, which was always somewhat indistinct, has collapsed entirely. In the absence of a means for communicating directly with customers, trademark holders use their marks to send not only traditional messages about the attributes of their products (source, quality and the like), but also a range of other, more expressive (and, as Jessica Litman says, "atmospheric") kinds of information. "Life style marketing," after all, requires transmission of life-style information—information about social values, ideals, and worldview. Other trademark usages are likewise becoming highly complex. Comparative ads, a staple of US marketing, have spread to other countries. Trade dress and trademarks are particularly useful in such ads because they can create forceful images and sound bites, calling one product to mind while marketing its rival.

Trademarks have also taken on a wholly new role: on the Internet, they are navigation tools, used by consumers to find merchants and by merchants to find consumers. Some shoppers look for goods on the Internet by using the trademark as a domain name. If they enter it correctly, they will likely find the trademark holder's website, but they may also discover that the same mark is used by merchants in remote locations, or incorporated into several Internet addresses. Even if they reach the right trademark holder's website, they may be treated to a competitor's ad, set to pop-up when the site is accessed. And, of course, if the mark is typed incorrectly, the consumer may encounter a "typosquatter"—the site of a rival, perhaps, or a griper. Another strategy is to "google" the trademark (enter it into a search engine); such key-word searches will present the consumer with a list of sites, some of which may hawk alternative products—a rival may be gaming the algorithm of the search engine or the listing-cum-ad may be keyed to appear whenever a search on the mark is conducted.

The result is a highly complicated picture. Images and trade symbols are increasing in cultural significance at exactly the time when protection is expanding. The exigencies of a global, on-line marketplace make stronger protection for trademarks necessary just when technology makes their widespread expressive use more feasible. Internet shopping requires *both* exclusivity *and* unrestricted availability—the former, to keep search costs down by ensuring that consumers find the right site; the latter to allow markets to work efficiently by ensuring that consumers receive information about comparable products. As the commercial/expressive duality of marks' meanings become salient, so too does the expressive/commercial duality of their use: many of those tee shirts, mugs, posters, and art works are sources of profits—profits that derive from the trademark but which are channeled back into efforts to destabilize its meaning.

It is not as though courts are unaware of these problems. In fact, cases with expressive claims to trademark usage have arisen in jurisdictions around the world and courts have developed a variety of responses. In some places, judges exploit statutory language and the facts of individual cases to limit the ambit of trademark protection and preserve space for free (or free-er) speech; other jurisdictions recognize very strong trademark claims, but courts will balance these rights against constitutive norms. Each approach has advantages and limitations. However, it is not always clear that the courts considering these issues have fully grappled with the reality of the problem. To many judges, the goal of trademark law is to safeguard the ability of a mark to "guarantee the identity ... of marked products ... without any possibility of confusion" (or tarnishment, or blurring, or on-line interference). In today's markets, however, that goal may be unattainable. Even if the problems noted above did not exist, cheap airline tickets and a taste for foreign food and culture expose consumers to familiar trademarks that signify unfamiliar merchants. Converging product functionalities (such as computers that play music) can similarly confer multiple meanings on a single mark. In short, conflicting uses of trademarks cannot be avoided.

....

In some ways, the response of the judiciary is surprising.... [T]he problem lies in the goals that courts are pursuing—avoiding all confusion and preventing all free riding. Thus, it may be that a more realistic understanding of possible outcomes is required. In an economy in which consumers have immediate access to products and services everywhere on the globe, in a legal environment in which symbols are protected in multiple ways, in a culture in which trademarks constitute a significant medium of expression, freedom from all sources of confusion or dilution is simply not achievable.

What can be achieved is a marketplace in which consumers understand what they are experiencing. Interpreting trademark legislation in a manner that is attentive to how encounters with multiple meanings are deciphered could lead to law that is protective of both trade and creativity. To be sure, there may be some expressive situations where confusion, dilution, or free-riding is so rampantly likely and destructive, trademark holders should win ... But a fuller understanding of how perception is shaped is likely to provide more durable protection for our shared expressive vocabulary.

....

Mattel Inc. v. Walking Mountain Productions, 353 F.3d 792 (9th Cir. 2003). Thomas Forsythe, aka "Walking Mountain Productions," is a self-taught photographer who resides in Kanab, Utah. He produces photographs with social and political overtones. In 1997, Forsythe developed a series of 78 photographs entitled "Food Chain Barbie," in which he depicted Barbie in various absurd and often sexualized positions. Forsythe uses the word "Barbie" in some of the titles of his works. While his works vary, Forsythe generally depicts one or more nude Barbie dolls juxtaposed with vintage kitchen appliances. For example, "Fondue a la Barbie" depicts Barbie heads in a fondue pot. "Barbie Enchiladas" depicts four Barbie dolls wrapped in tortillas and covered with salsa in a casserole dish in a lit oven. "Malted Barbie" features a nude Barbie placed on a vintage Hamilton Beach malt machine.

....

Mattel ... claims that Forsythe misappropriated its trade dress in Barbie's appearance, in violation of the Lanham Act, 15 U.S.C. § 1125. Mattel claims that it possesses a trade dress in the Superstar Barbie head and the doll's overall appearance. The district court concluded that there was no likelihood that the public would be misled into believing that Mattel endorsed Forsythe's photographs despite Forsythe's use of the Barbie figure.

Arguably, the Barbie trade dress also plays a role in our culture similar to the role played by the Barbie trademark—namely, symbolization of an unattainable ideal of femininity for some women. Forsythe's use of the Barbie trade dress, therefore, presumably would present First Amendment concerns similar to those that made us reluctant to apply the Lanham Act as a bar to the artistic uses of Mattel's Barbie trademark in both *MCA* and this case. But we need not decide how the *MCA/Rogers* First Amendment balancing might apply to Forsythe's use of the Barbie trade dress because we find, on a narrower ground, that it qualifies as nominative fair use.

....

Forsythe's use of the Barbie trade dress is nominative. Forsythe used Mattel's Barbie figure and head in his works to conjure up associations of Mattel, while at the same time to identify his own work, which is a criticism and parody of Barbie. [Citation.] Where use of the trade dress or mark is grounded in the defendant's desire to refer to the plaintiff's product as a point of reference for defendant's own work, a use is nominative.

....

We hold that Forsythe's use of Mattel's Barbie qualifies as nominative fair use. All three elements weigh in favor of Forsythe. Barbie would not be readily identifiable in a photographic work without use of the Barbie likeness and figure. Forsythe used only so much as was necessary to make his parodic use of Barbie readily identifiable, and it is highly unlikely that any reasonable consumer would have believed that Mattel sponsored or was affiliated with his work. The district court's grant of summary judgment to Forsythe on Mattel's trade dress infringement claim was, therefore, proper.

....

Radiance Foundation v. NAACP, 786 F.3d 316 (4th Cir. 2015). The Radiance Foundation published an article online titled "NAACP: National Association for the Abortion of Colored People" criticizing the NAACP's stance on abortion. In response to a cease-and-desist letter from the NAACP, Radiance sought a declaratory judgment that it had not infringed any NAACP trademarks. The NAACP then filed counterclaims alleging trademark infringement and dilution. The district court held for the NAACP and entered a permanent injunction. The Fourth Circuit reversed.

[T]rademark infringement is not designed to protect mark holders from consumer confusion about their positions on political or social issues. The evidence of "actual confusion" relied on by the district court consisted of phone calls to the NAACP by people who took issue with the NAACP supporting abortion. *Radiance Found.*, 25 F. Supp. 3d at 888–89. "[I]ndignation is not confusion," *Girl Scouts of U.S. v. Personality Posters, Mfg. Co.*, 304 F. Supp. 1228, 1231 (S.D.N.Y. 1969) [concerning poster reproducing Girl Scouts' slogan "Be Prepared" under a photograph depicting a pregnant teenager], at least not as pertains to trademark infringement, and at best the calls demonstrated confusion as to the NAACP's policy positions rather than any good or service. Policy stances are neither goods nor services, though the means of conveying them may be.

Political discourse is the grist of the mill in the marketplace of ideas. It may be that the only—but also the best—remedy available to a trademark holder is to engage in responsive speech.... The NAACP is a renowned civil rights organization with numerous mechanisms for connecting with its membership and the public. Organizations of its size and stature possess megaphones all their own. "Actual confusion" as to a non-profit's mission, tenets, and beliefs is commonplace, but that does not transform the Lanham Act into an instrument for chilling or silencing the speech of those who disagree with or misunderstand a mark holder's positions or views. *See Rogers v. Grimaldi*, 875 F.2d 994, 1001 (2d Cir. 1989).

....

It remains essential in any analysis of confusion to consider fully the purpose with which the mark was being used. The trial court did entertain the possibility of parody, but once it found that Radiance had not engaged in a successful parody, it ended its inquiry there. *Radiance Found.*, 25 F. Supp. 3d at 891–93. If not quite parody, the use of "National Association for the Abortion of Colored People" in this context may be more akin to satire, which "works by distort[ing] ... the familiar with the pretense of reality in order to convey an underlying critical message." [Citation.] ...

It is important moreover to pay sufficient attention to the full context in which the mark was used, which diminishes the likelihood of confusion about source even further. The domain names and webpage headings clearly denote other organizations: The Radiance Foundation or TooManyAborted. For each site, this post was one of dozens of articles on social and political issues.

....

We have identified individual difficulties with appellee's position, but it is well to understand the matter in its totality. The trial court found that using marks in a highly critical article that lambasts the NAACP for its views and actions constituted trademark infringement because the site solicits financial support for its activities, albeit attenuated from the use of the mark, and some consumers may be confused about the NAACP's true name and political positions. We need not go so far as to say that social commentary solicitations can never be the subject of a valid infringement claim in order to conclude that it will not be infringing so long as the use of the mark does

> not create confusion as to source, sponsorship, or affiliation. Any other holding would severely restrict all kinds of speakers from criticizing all manner of corporate positions and activities and propel the Lanham Act into treacherous constitutional terrain.

Gerlich v. Leath, 152 F.Supp.3d.1152 (S.D. Iowa 2016). Iowa State University's trademark licensing program allows student groups to use the university's name and insignia in connection with t-shirts and other student group allegiance goods. ISU NORML, a group advocating legalization of marijuana, is one of 800 ISU student groups subject to the university's Trademark Policy and Student Use Guidelines. Following ISU NORML's distribution of a t-shirt showing a cannabis leaf and incorporating the ISU mascot, Cy the Cardinal, the University came under political pressure to revise its Guidelines to prohibit licenses for student group designs that promote the use of drugs or alcohol. With the new Guidelines in place, the ISU Trademark Office denied ISU NORML's requests to use Cy on t-shirts that also displayed a marijuana leaf (the leaf design is part of the nationwide NORML's insignia). Student members of the ISU Chapter sought an injunction against the application of the new Guidelines on the ground that they constituted impermissible viewpoint discrimination. The University contended that its trademark licensing policies were "immune from First Amendment scrutiny under the government speech doctrine." The court rejected that defense:

> *b. Whether Defendants' Conduct was Government Speech*
>
> ... Under the government speech doctrine, the government may constitutionally discriminate among political viewpoints when expressing its own policies, directives, and preferred views. [Citation.] The government is afforded this immunity from First Amendment criticism because "'it is not easy to imagine how government could function if it lacked th[e] freedom' to select the messages it wishes to convey." [Citation.]
>
> In *Walker* [*v. Tex. Div., Sons of Confederate Veterans, Inc.*, 135 S. Ct. 2239 (2015)], the Supreme Court determined that specialty license plates issued by the State of Texas were government speech, and that the State's denial of a Confederate Flag plate was therefore not subject to First Amendment scrutiny. [Citation.] In so holding, the *Walker* Court cited its prior decision in *Pleasant Grove City v. Summum*, 555 U.S. at 470–73, where the Court concluded that permanent monuments privately donated for display in the city park constituted government speech, and therefore the government did not violate the First Amendment by selectively accepting those monuments. Applying the government speech test set forth in *Summum*, the *Walker* Court concluded that because (1) the States have historically used license plates to communicate with the public, (2) license plates are often closely identified in the public mind with the State, and (3) Texas effectively controlled the expressive content of the license plates by exercising final approval authority over submitted designs, Texas' specialty plates "are similar enough to the monuments in *Summum* to call for the same result." [Citation.] *Walker*

acknowledged that its holding applied only in limited circumstances, however, noting the unusually close connection between license plates and State directives. [Citation.] *Walker* held that license plates are government speech because they are government articles serving governmental purposes of vehicle registration and identification, are required by law for every Texas vehicle owner, are issued by the State, and are, "essentially, government IDs." [Citation.]

Defendants have not cited to any cases applying the government speech doctrine in the context of a university licensing program, nor have they cited any cases discussing government speech by a college or university. To the contrary, a number of other significant First Amendment cases instruct that speech by collegiate student organizations facilitated by a state university is not government speech. [Citations.]

Nonetheless, Defendants argue the *Walker* factors are satisfied here. First, Defendants assert that ISU speaks to the public with its trademarks in that it uses the trademarks to promote the ISU brand, which it uses to attract prospective students, garner public and private funding, and recruit employees. To support their contention that trademarks are fundamentally expressive tools for their owners, Defendants cite a number of trademark cases.... Second, Defendants argue that observers believe ISU licenses its marks to convey its preferred views, contending that [local politicians'] backlash to the [t-shirt] evinces public attribution of NORML ISU's advocacy to ISU itself. Finally, Defendants argue that the last criterion of the Walker test is satisfied because ISU has effectively controlled its trademark licensing program by its exercise of final approval authority.

After fully considering Defendants' arguments, the Court cannot conclude that ISU's trademark regime, used with permission by hundreds of varied student groups, qualifies for the unique and narrow status of the public monuments at issue in *Summum* or the license plates in *Walker*. Notably, the record is replete with statements by Defendants that they did not intend to communicate any message to the public by licensing ISU trademarks to student groups. [Citations.] Far from using its student group licensing program to communicate with the public, ISU remains staunchly neutral as to the professed views of its student groups, and exercises its power to deny licenses only when certain minimum standards of acceptability are not met (e.g., use of the marks on toilet paper and diapers). The Trademark Office's history of design approvals further demonstrates ISU does not license its trademarks to student groups to announce its political views, because the office has approved designs for an inchoate set of interest groups that are in one instance pro-life, then pro-BDSM, then pro-LGBTA, pro-Democrat, and pro-Republican. [Citation.] The Trademark Office's past practice thus makes clear that ISU does not grant licenses to political groups as a means of endorsing or expressing a particular view.

> To be sure, and as the cited trademark cases suggest, trademarks are frequently used to associate a product or image with the mark's owner. Unremarkably, ISU's images are associated in the public mind with ISU as an institution, which is why [the students] wanted to include ISU marks on her group's apparel. [Citation.] Yet to determine whether, in this case, the grant of a trademark license to a student group is intended as government speech, or whether the public would understand a student group's use of an ISU trademark as government speech, the Court must view ISU's trademark licensing program against the backdrop of America's educational culture and traditions.... In line with the university's traditional station in American society, when ISU licenses its trademarks to a multitude of student groups, the trademarks do not suggest ISU endorses any particular group's political views; rather, the use of the marks by a diverse and often intellectually opposed set of groups reflects the University's rightful commitment to fostering diverse forms of civic engagement and intellectual exploration and debate. Defendants' argument that ISU's licensed marks express the views of ISU itself runs counter to these traditions. Nonetheless, Defendants argue that as a matter of fact, the public did associate NORML ISU's t-shirt design with the government, pointing to responses from certain public officials and the few responses received from the general public. On this record, the Court cannot agree that the public believed ISU promoted marijuana law reform, because the record shows almost no reaction to the Article from the general public.

The court found that the University did exercise control over the licensing program, but that the third *Walker* factor was not determinative.

Questions

1. Recall *In re Tam*, 808 F.3d 1321 (Fed. Cir. 2015) (en banc), and *Blackhorse v. Pro-Football, Inc.*, 112 F. Supp. 3d 439 (E.D. Va. 2015), *supra* Chapter 4. Both cases addressed the argument that 2(a)'s exclusion of disparaging matter implemented a government speech policy and therefore was immune from First Amendment scrutiny. The full Federal Circuit rejected that contention, while the E.D. Va. accepted it.

The E.D. Va. held trademark registration government speech under the *Walker* criteria:

> The first *Walker* factor weighs in favor of government speech as registry with the federal trademark registration program communicates the message that the federal government has approved the trademark. The second *Walker* factor weighs in favor of government speech because the public closely associates federal trademark registration with the federal government as the insignia for federal trademark registration, ®, is a manifestation of the federal government's recognition of the mark.
>
> Finally, the third *Walker* factor weighs in favor of government speech because the federal government exercises editorial control over the federal trademark registration program.

By contrast, and like the *Gerlich* court's assessment of Iowa State's practices regarding student groups' use of university insignia, the Federal Circuit discerned no message of the government's own.

> The government's argument in this case that trademark registration amounts to government speech is at odds with the Supreme Court's analysis in *Walker* and unmoored from the very concept of government speech. When the government registers a trademark, the only message it conveys is that a mark is registered. The vast array of private trademarks are not created by the government, owned or monopolized by the government, sized and formatted by the government, immediately understood as performing any government function (like unique, visible vehicle identification), aligned with the government, or (putting aside any specific government-secured trademarks) used as a platform for government speech. There is simply no meaningful basis for finding that consumers associate registered private trademarks with the government.
>
> Indeed, the PTO routinely registers marks that no one can say the government endorses. [Citations.] As the government itself explains, "the USPTO does not endorse any particular product, service, mark, or registrant" when it registers a mark. Appellee's En Banc Br. 44. For decades, the government has maintained that:
>
>> [J]ust as the issuance of a trademark registration by this Office does not amount to government endorsement of the quality of the goods to which the mark is applied, the act of registration is not a government imprimatur or pronouncement that the mark is a "good" one in an aesthetic, or any analogous, sense.
>
> *In re Old Glory Condom Corp.*, 26 U.S.P.Q.2d 1216, 1219–20 n.3 (T.T.A.B. Mar. 3, 1993).

How discernible must the government's "message" be for the government speech doctrine to apply to a government entity's trademark licensing policies? Would it have made a difference if Iowa State University had sought to communicate a message through its trademark licensing program?

2. After his daughter was denied admission to her twin brother's Cub Scouts troop, Gregory Wrenn decided to start a non-discriminatory scouting organization under the name "Youthscouts." After his attempt to register the YOUTHSCOUTS service mark was successfully opposed by the Boy Scouts of America (BSA), Wrenn sought a declaratory judgment that his YOUTHSCOUTS mark did not infringe any Boy Scouts of America mark. He contended that the terms "scouts" and "scouting" are, and at the time of the BSA's trademark registration, were, generic terms when used in connection with scouting programs. The BSA responded that the terms, as a composite with the term "boy," were suggestive rather than generic because "scouts" and "scouting" do not of themselves identify the age of the participant. But if the mark is *BOY* SCOUTS, would *YOUTH* SCOUTS infringe? *See Wrenn v. Boy Scouts of America*, 89 U.S.P.Q.2d 1039 (N.D. Cal. 2008)

3. PissedConsumer.com is an advertising-supported website that invites consumers to post negative reviews of products and services. The site displays the reviews in a separate subdomain of the website based on the company offering the products or services involved, and the website uses metatags and other strategies to ensure that the site ranks high in search engine results for a reviewed company's name. Ascentive filed a Lanham Act suit against PissedConsumer, alleging infringement in the company's use of the marks in subdomain names and metatags. What result? *See Ascentive, LLC v. Opinion Corp.*, 842 F. Supp. 2d 450 (E.D.N.Y. 2011).

4. Since 1955, the Phillip Morris Company has featured cowboys in its Marlboro® cigarette ads, and the cowboy figure has become widely known as the "Marlboro Man." In 1997 the California State Health Department introduced a series of anti-smoking billboards, including the one below:

The billboard appeared on freeways throughout the state. It was reproduced in a variety of different news publications. A wall calendar featuring ad parodies used it for the month of October. The advertising agency that created the billboard features it on its website as an example of its work. Has Phillip Morris any recourse under the Lanham Act?

Chapter 9

Dilution

A. The Concept of Dilution

Barton Beebe, *The Suppressed Misappropriation Origins of Trademark Antidilution Law: The Landgericht Elberfeld's Odol Decision and Frank Schechter's the Rational Basis of Trademark Protection*

in ROCHELLE COOPER DREYFUSS AND JANE C. GINSBURG, EDS., INTELLECTUAL PROPERTY AT THE EDGE: THE CONTESTED CONTOURS OF IP (2013)*

In September, 1924, the Landgericht Elberfeld, an obscure German regional trial court just east of Dusseldorf, issued a brief, eight-paragraph decision resolving a dispute between the complainant, the longtime registrant of the nationally-famous trademark "Odol" for mouthwash, and the respondent, a recent registrant of the same mark for various steel products. The court found that the "respondent has registered the mark for its steel goods for the obvious purpose of deriving from [the mark's] selling power some advantage in marketing its own products," and ordered the cancellation of the respondent's registration on the ground that "[i]t is opposed to good morals to appropriate thus the fruits of another's labor in the consciousness that that other will or may thereby be damaged." The dissimilarity of mouthwash and steel products prompted the court to explain: "To be sure, the parties, on account of the wholly different goods put out by them are not in actual competition. That, however, is beside the point. The complainant has created a demand for its goods, while employing thereon a word having drawing power, for only through the year[s]-long and extended activity of the complainant was its selling power acquired." In light of this "year[s]-long and extended activity," the court reasoned that the plaintiff had "the utmost interest in seeing that its mark is not diluted [*verwässert*]: it would lose in selling power if everyone used it as the designation of his goods." And so, in the seminal *Odol* opinion, whose author remains unknown, the concept of trademark dilution was born.

The herald of a concept at the very edge of trademark law, the *Odol* decision soon made its way to America, and to the pages of the *Harvard Law Review*, and eventually, to the pages of the *U.S. Reports*. The journey began with the December 1924 issue of the German intellectual property law journal *Gewerblicher Rechtsschutz*

---

* Copyright 2013. Reprinted by permission. [*Editors' Note*: most footnotes omitted.]

und Urheberrecht, which reported the *Odol* decision in full. Four months later, in April 1925, the *Bulletin of the United States Trade-Mark Association* published a two-page discussion and partial translation of the *Odol* case by one Dr. Ludwig Wertheimer. Then, in 1927, came the main event. In that year, the young German-speaking American lawyer Frank Schechter published in the *Harvard Law Review* an article entitled *The Rational Basis of Trademark Protection* which relied heavily, though cagily, on the *Odol* case and which would eventually become the most cited law review article ever written on trademark law. The extraordinary influence of Schechter's article and, through it, of the *Odol* case was confirmed in 2003 in the U.S. Supreme Court opinion *Moseley v. V Secret Catalogue, Inc.* The *Moseley* Court quoted the thesis of Schechter's article that "the preservation of the uniqueness of a trademark should constitute the only rational basis for its protection," explained that Schechter "supported his conclusion by referring to a German case protecting the owner of the well-known trademark 'Odol,'" and dutifully quoted in a footnote from Schechter's discussion of the *Odol* case: "The German court 'held that the use of the mark, "Odol" even on non-competing goods was "*gegen die guten Sitten.*"'" Remarkably, the Supreme Court offered no translation of the meaning of the German: "opposed to good morals."

To be sure, the impact of *Rational Basis* has been profound, but it has also been scattered and confused. The article and the conception of trademark dilution that it set forth have generated an enormous amount of scholarly commentary both in the United States and abroad, not to mention two federal antidilution statutes, thirty-eight state antidilution statutes, and numerous foreign antidilution laws. Yet the "dauntingly elusive concept" of dilution remains essentially an enigma. As a leading American commentator attests,

> No part of trademark law that I have encountered in my forty years of teaching and practicing IP law has created so much doctrinal puzzlement and judicial incomprehension as the concept of dilution.... Few can successfully explain it without encountering stares of incomprehension or worse, nods of understanding which mask and conceal bewilderment and misinterpretation.[21]

If dilution is an enigma, even more so is *Rational Basis*. The article has produced a variety of conflicting interpretations of what its author thought dilution was, why he thought we should prevent it, and how he thought we should do so. Indeed, one wonders if even Schechter himself—who died only ten years after publishing *Rational Basis*, too young at the age of forty-seven, before he could further develop and clarify his ideas—ever fully understood what he intended when he used the term "dilution." The result is that now nearly a century since the *Odol* case and *Rational Basis*, we are still struggling to reach consensus on what exactly the Landgericht Elberfeld and Schechter meant—and, more importantly, what exactly we mean—by trademark dilution.

While the concept of trademark dilution, even in its pure and perfect form, whatever that may be, is no doubt quite subtle, dilution's theoretical elusiveness cannot

---

21. J. Thomas McCarthy, *Dilution of a Trademark: European and United States Law Compared*, 94 Trademark Rep. 1163, 1163 (2004)....

fully explain why the concept continues so thoroughly to befuddle trademark courts and commentators. This brief essay offers an additional explanation for the mystery surrounding the concept, an explanation grounded not in theory, but in history. It argues that Schechter deliberately sought in *Rational Basis* to obscure the true nature of the *Odol* case and of antidilution protection, and that even a century later, his effort at obfuscation remains more or less a success, at least in the United States. What Schechter sought to obscure in *Rational Basis* is that the *Odol* case was not, strictly speaking, a trademark case. Rather, it was a misappropriation case that happened to involve a trademark. Schechter sought to suppress this basic truth—that the concept of trademark dilution is essentially a misappropriation concept—in order to sell his proposed doctrinal reforms to an American audience altogether suspicious of misappropriation doctrine and increasingly under the sway of American Legal Realism. A highly-sophisticated trademark scholar and New York lawyer, a recent graduate of Columbia Law School, and the son of the great rabbi Solomon Schechter, Frank Schechter very likely understood in 1927 that his thinking—and the *Odol* decision—was in sync with the commercial realities of his time but strangely out of sync with its legal thought. Only nine years earlier, the Supreme Court had handed down its controversial majority opinion in the misappropriation case of *International News Service v. Associated Press.* In separate dissents, which would eventually become part of the canon of American Legal Realism, Justice Holmes and Justice Brandeis both criticized Justice Pitney's majority opinion for the empty formalism and circularity of its finding that the petitioner was "endeavoring to reap where it has not sown." Justice Brandeis in particular expressed concern that courts were ill-equipped to limit the reach of a broad misappropriation rule by which the respondent might "prevent appropriation of the fruits of its labor by another." Schechter needed to disassociate the *Odol* case from the *International News* majority; he needed somehow to clothe his essentially formalist misappropriation doctrine in the guise of legal realism. To do so required a great deal of finesse, or to but it more bluntly, of dissembling, and *Rational Basis* is full of it.... Schechter went so far as to delete from his lengthy quotation of Dr. Wertheimer's translation of the *Odol* opinion the opinion's central holding, that the respondent sought "to appropriate thus the fruits of another's labor."

Sara K. Stadler, *The Wages of Ubiquity in Trademark Law*

88 Iowa L. Rev. 731 (2003) (Excerpts)*

Introduction

... [D]ilution was born in 1927, when the Harvard Law Review published an article in which its author, Frank Schechter, warned that the distinctiveness of truly unique trademarks was in danger of being "whittled away" (diluted) by the use of those trademarks on unrelated goods, and proposed that if nothing else, trademark law should

 [*Editors' Note:* some footnotes omitted.]

be an instrument for the preservation of this uniqueness.[8] Courts initially were hostile to the radical theories that Schechter proposed, but in the end, scholars and practitioners convinced courts that Schechter had described a harm that deserved to be remedied—a harm that, in 1995, Congress defined as "the lessening of the capacity of a famous mark to identify and distinguish goods or services, regardless of the presence or absence of ... likelihood of confusion, mistake, or deception."[11]

Unfortunately, this harm was not the one that Schechter described. In promulgating and interpreting the trademark law, Congress and most courts have assumed that by "unique," Schechter meant "distinctive and famous"—in other words, that Schechter meant his dilution remedy to cover every famous word or phrase that happened to have acquired the ability to function as a trademark. A closer review of the Schechter text reveals, however, that Schechter intended his remedy to apply not to famous marks, but to a select class of highly distinctive (indeed, for the most part, inherently distinctive) trademarks that were, like most trademarks of his day, synonymous with a single product or product class. When viewed against the backdrop of modern marketing techniques, this definition of uniqueness reveals a growing state of what I term "ubiquity" in the trademark world—one in which trademark owners are deliberately destroying the uniqueness of their marks by using them to identify a diversity of products, or more generally, product myths and entire lifestyles. Worse, this ubiquity has gone unchecked, as courts often cite ubiquitous usage as evidence that a mark is famous and thus protectible under dilution law ...

....

I. Frank Schechter, Trademark Dilution, and the State of Ubiquity

... [T]he Trademark Act of 1905, even as amended in 1920, proscribed the use of an existing trademark only on "merchandise of substantially the same descriptive properties as those set forth in the registration," and as Schechter repeatedly (and unhappily) pointed out, courts tended to construe this language fairly narrowly....

Schechter ... saw plenty of harm in tolerating such peculiarities as "Kodak bath tubs," and he began to argue for making that harm actionable.... To [Schechter's] way of thinking, if asking whether consumers were misled failed to result in an injunction against, inter alia, "Kodak bath tubs," then courts needed to find another touchstone....

... Schechter['s] ... theory would rest on a simple, if unspoken, premise: owners of qualifying trademarks suffered injury whenever others used those marks without permission. For Schechter, this premise not only solved the "non-competing goods" problem, but it also compensated companies for making the investments that transformed words, phrases, and symbols into agents of "selling power." For Schechter, trademarks were not merely (or even primarily) the means by which producers

8. Frank I. Schechter, *The Rational Basis of Trademark Protection*, 40 Harv. L. Rev. 813 (1927).

11. Federal Trademark Dilution Act of 1995, Pub. L. No. 104-98, §4, 109 Stat. 985, 986 (1995), *amending* 15 U.S.C. 1127 (2000). [*Editors' Note*: The FTDA was subsequently amended in 2006. *See infra* Chapter 9[B] for the amended text.]

identified themselves as the sources of their goods. Trademarks had become part of the "goods" themselves.

... In [Schechter's] view, the value of a "symbol depended in large part upon its uniqueness." What did he mean by this? Were distinctiveness and uniqueness the same thing?

A close reading of Rational Basis indicates that the uniqueness ... consisted of classic trademark "distinctiveness" plus something more. Consider his examples: marks to which Schechter attributed "very little distinctiveness in the public mind" included the laudatory "Blue Ribbon" and "Gold Medal" and the descriptive "Simplex." None of these marks qualified as a technical trademark, but Schechter did not limit his reasoning to the question whether these marks were "coined" (i.e., fanciful), arbitrary, or suggestive on the one hand, or whether they were descriptive on the other. Blue Ribbon not only was laudatory, but it also had been "used, with or without registration, for all kinds of commodities or services, more than sixty times." Gold Medal, too, had been "as extensively and variously applied." Simplex had been registered, in whole or in part, "approximately sixty" times by numerous parties and had been "applied to so diversified a variety of products as windows, wires, concrete pilings, golf practice machines, letter openers, air brakes, inks and buttons." Contrast these marks with the ones Schechter meant to protect:

> "Rolls-Royce," "Aunt Jemima's," "Kodak," "Mazda," "Corona," "Nujol," and "Blue Goose," are coined, arbitrary or fanciful words or phrases that have been added to rather than withdrawn from the human vocabulary by their owners, and have, from the very beginning, been associated in the public mind with a particular product, not with a variety of products, and have created in the public consciousness an impression or symbol of the excellence of the particular product in question.

Schechter had painted a picture of what, to him, was a unique trademark: "arbitrary or fanciful words or phrases ... associated ... with a particular product." These were the types of trademarks Schechter proposed to protect under his new theory.

There are several concepts packed into this definition, but trademark fame—the headliner in litigation arising under the Federal Trademark Dilution Act—is not one of them. Instead, Schechter required the mark to possess, in ascending order of uniqueness components: (1) a level of distinctiveness in the marketplace, also known as secondary meaning, or the ability to indicate source to the public (a mark must "have created in the public consciousness an impression or symbol of the excellence of the particular product in question"); (2) a level of distinctiveness in the mark itself (a mark must be a "coined, arbitrary or fanciful word[] or phrase[]"); and (3) a singularity of association between the mark and the underlying product (a mark must be "associated in the public mind with a particular product, not with a variety of products"). The "and" in this construction is important. Schechter thought a trademark had to possess each one of these qualities before it was capable of being whittled away by offending uses.

... To Schechter, only ... highly distinctive marks, with their "impress upon the public consciousness," were capable of being vitiated by third party uses on unrelated goods. Because his "coined, arbitrary, or fanciful" language tracks the definition of a technical trademark, Schechter probably meant to limit his dilution remedy to those marks that would have qualified for federal registration under the 1905 Act. We must content ourselves with "probably" because Schechter made a mistake in characterizing the "Rolls-Royce" mark as a "coined, arbitrary or fanciful word"; the compound phrase "Rolls-Royce" was formed by combining two surnames, and thus the mark would properly have been categorized as a trade name—albeit, according to courts at the time, a highly protectible one. On the whole, though, the marks Schechter believed to possess uniqueness were those that courts would term "inherently distinctive" today....

... Schechter added one more layer to his definition of uniqueness. In order to qualify for protection against dilution, ... a mark must "have, from the very beginning, been associated in the public mind with a particular product, not with a variety of products."

Schechter understood that trademarks standing for one thing were both valuable and vulnerable to those who would make them stand for more than one thing. They were the trademarks he deemed "most in need of protection." Indeed, he wrote that "the preservation of the uniqueness of a trademark should constitute the only rational basis for its protection." As for marks standing for many things, they had already been vitiated—for them ... it was too late to preserve uniqueness through the application of the dilution doctrine.

....

Schechter believed it was high time for courts to remedy the "real injury in ... such [unrelated goods] cases," which was the gradual whittling away or dispersion of the identity and hold upon the public mind of the mark or name by its use upon non-competing goods. The more distinctive or unique the mark, the deeper is its impress upon the public consciousness, and the greater its need for protection against vitiation or dissociation from the particular product in connection with which it has been used.

As Schechter warned, if "'Kodak' may be used for bath tubs and cakes, 'Mazda' for cameras and shoes, or 'Ritz-Carlton' for coffee, these marks must inevitably be lost in the commonplace words of the language, despite the originality and ingenuity in their contrivance." Of equal concern, the "vast expenditures" each producer spent in advertising those marks would be lost as well. This set of harms would come to be known as trademark "dilution"—a remedy that Schechter termed "the very essence of any rational system of individual and exclusive trade symbols."

....

The years following the passage of the Lanham Act saw state legislatures in key states enact legislation prohibiting what they termed "injury to business reputation or of dilution of the distinctive quality" of a mark, notwithstanding the absence of consumer confusion "as to the source of goods or services." In enacting these dilution laws, state legislatures borrowed from Schechter, but (intentionally or not) failed to adopt the remedy he had prescribed. When Massachusetts passed such a law in 1947, it did so only after amending the original bill, in which the Massachusetts House of Representatives—like Schechter—had proposed to protect "only a 'coined or peculiar word' or 'unique symbol.'" [T]he Massachusetts Senate ... passed the much broader "dilution of the distinctive quality" language.... Illinois followed with a longer (but equally broad) version in 1953. In 1955, New York and Georgia followed.... And when a similar dilution provision found its way into the Model State Trademark Act in 1963, the floodgates opened. By 1994, the year before Congress enacted its federal dilution statute, 25 states had adopted some form of legislation outlawing the dilution of the "distinctive quality" of marks.

Legislation, of course, is not always synonymous with acceptance. With a few exceptions, courts refused to enforce the plain language of the dilution statutes. To judges comfortable with traditional trademark infringement, dilution was a radical remedy. Its most vocal critics charged that the dilution doctrine gave trademark owners "rights in gross"—i.e., exclusive rights in a trade symbol regardless of how (or even whether) it was being used to identify goods.

... Congress returned to dilution in 1995.... [T]he bill proscribed dilution of the "distinctive quality" of a famous mark, which was defined as "the lessening of the capacity of a famous mark to identify and distinguish goods or services." Schechter was invoked repeatedly throughout the proceedings. And if the language of the new section 43(c) indicated a preoccupation with fame, those involved in the legislative process clearly believed themselves to be enacting the remedy of which Schechter had conceived.

....

II. Will the Real Dilution Doctrine Please Stand Up?

A. Ubiquity as a Form of Dilution

... Marketing experts tell us not to worry about encountering a Pepsi brand single malt whisky or Chanel brand galoshes because Pepsico, Inc. and Chanel, Inc. would never market these products; single malt whisky and galoshes would be inconsistent with the "myths" surrounding Pepsi and Chanel, respectively. Some trademark scholars, taking their cue from the marketers, have defined dilution in terms of this myth disturbance. Dilution is, to them, "the impairment of brand equity caused by a use of the mark that creates associations and images inconsistent with the equity." Thus (the argument goes), if Pepsi were to make single malt whiskey, it would risk diluting its myth (youth), but if it made spandex "midriff" tops in candy colors, it would not. Not only is this interpretation of dilution inconsistent with the writings of Schechter, but more importantly, this interpretation ignores—and thus devalues—the product associations that the Pepsis of the world possess. When dilution, as Schechter conceived it, "happens," it not only disturbs the source signal broadcast by every distinctive mark, but it also disturbs the product signal—the one that links the Pepsi mark to carbonated cola beverages.

To be sure, a unique (and therefore dilutible) trademark does not possess only a product association. Unique trademarks are highly distinctive as well, which makes them able to identify a single, if anonymous, source. These trademarks thus possess the ability to create two types of associations in the minds of consumers: a source association (e.g., Pepsico, Inc.) and a product association (carbonated cola beverages). "Pepsi" is dilutible because, like Coke, Pepsi "means a single thing coming from a single source.... It hardly would be too much to say that the drink characterizes the name as much as the name the drink." [*Coca-Cola v. Koke Co.*, 254 U.S. 143, 146 (1920)]. This ability to create source and product associations is what Schechter termed "selling power." When a mark is diluted, both associations are disturbed. If, for example, the Pepsi mark were used by Company X in connection with a single malt whisky, "Pepsi" not only would come to mean two sources (Pepsico, Inc. and Company X), but it also would come to mean two products (carbonated cola beverages and single malt whisky). Pepsico, Inc. would be able to safeguard the source identification function of its mark under infringement law, of course, but it also would have recourse to dilution law, which would enable the company to protect the link between mark and "particular product" as well.

Schechter was right when he wrote that without uniqueness, there can be no "selling power"; without selling power, there can be no "dissociation from the particular product in connection with which [the mark] has been used"; and without this whittling away, there can be no dilution.... To the extent the distinctiveness of a mark alone is impaired, infringement offers a remedy (assuming, of course, the trademark owner can prove that consumer confusion is likely). But when a mark possesses "mere" distinctiveness, when a mark has plenty to say about source but nothing to say about product, when a mark does not possess uniqueness, there simply is nothing to "dilute."

... What if the trademark owner is the one transforming a unique symbol into a ubiquitous one? Judges, lawyers, and even scholars appear to have assumed that ... trademark owners are perfectly free to engage in acts that, if perpetrated by others, would be held to cause dilution under the doctrine as presently applied. Worse, courts have held that ubiquity only adds to the fame of the mark—an element of the modern dilution cause of action that, contrary to popular belief, never was part of the doctrine as Schechter conceived it. [I]f we believe what we have been saying about what dilution is, then we must acknowledge that the acts of trademark owners can have the same dilutive effects as can the acts of third parties. The source association that a mark possesses may be left intact, or even strengthened, when the owner of that mark engages in ubiquitous branding practices, but the product association is destroyed—and with it, uniqueness.

Ubiquity is dilution, for in each case, the "uniqueness" of the mark, as Schechter defined that term, is vitiated.... Hundreds, perhaps thousands of trademarks are in danger of losing their "unique distinctiveness" every day, and not because of anything trademark pirates are doing. Trademark owners are doing the damage themselves.

Questions

1. What marks today would Schechter's conception of dilution protect? MCDONALD'S? WINDOWS? ETCH-A-SKETCH? LEXUS?

2. Consider the mark VIRGIN, which has been used or licensed for diverse goods and services from a record label to airline services, or the Ralph Lauren POLO brand that has been promoted as synonymous with a trendy lifestyle and applied to numerous products from apparel and fragrances to home furnishings. Is the author suggesting that these famous marks should not be entitled to dilution protection? Do you agree?

3. What is the harm, if any, to consumers from dilution of a "unique" or "singular" mark of the type for which Schechter advocated? *See* Graeme Austin, *Trademarks and the Burdened Imagination*, 69 Brooklyn L. Rev. 827 (2004).

Ty Inc. v. Perryman

306 F.3d 509 (7th Cir. 2002)

Posner, Circuit Judge:

Ty Inc., the manufacturer of Beanie Babies, the well-known beanbag stuffed animals, brought this suit for trademark infringement against Ruth Perryman. Perryman sells second-hand beanbag stuffed animals, primarily but not exclusively Ty's Beanie Babies, over the Internet. Her Internet address ("domain name"), a particular focus of Ty's concern, is bargainbeanies.com. She has a like-named Web site (http://www.bargainbeanies.com) where she advertises her wares. Ty's suit is based on the federal antidilution statute, 15 U.S.C. § 1125(c), which protects "famous" marks from commercial uses that cause "dilution of the distinctive quality of the mark." *See Nabisco, Inc. v. PF Brands, Inc.*, 191 F.3d 208, 214–16 (2d Cir. 1999). The district court granted summary judgment in favor of Ty and entered an injunction that forbids the defendant to use "BEANIE or BEANIES or any colorable imitation thereof (whether alone or in connection with other terms) within any business name, Internet domain name, or trademark, or in connection with any non-Ty products." Perryman's appeal argues primarily that "beanies" has become a generic term for beanbag stuffed animals and therefore cannot be appropriated as a trademark at all, and that in any event the injunction (which has remained in effect during the appeal) is overbroad.

The fundamental purpose of a trademark is to reduce consumer search costs by providing a concise and unequivocal identifier of the particular source of particular goods. The consumer who knows at a glance whose brand he is being asked to buy knows whom to hold responsible if the brand disappoints and whose product to buy in the future if the brand pleases. This in turn gives producers an incentive to maintain high and uniform quality, since otherwise the investment in their trademark may be lost as customers turn away in disappointment from the brand. A successful brand, however, creates an incentive in unsuccessful competitors to pass off their inferior brand as the successful brand by adopting a confusingly similar trademark, in effect appropriating the goodwill created by the producer of the successful brand.

The traditional and still central concern of trademark law is to provide remedies against this practice.

Confusion is not a factor here, however, with a minor exception discussed at the end of the opinion. Perryman is not a competing producer of beanbag stuffed animals, and her Web site clearly disclaims any affiliation with Ty. But that does not get her off the hook. The reason is that state and now federal law also provides a remedy against the "dilution" of a trademark, though as noted at the outset of this opinion the federal statute is limited to the subset of "famous" trademarks and to dilutions of them caused by commercial uses that take place in interstate or foreign commerce. "Beanie Babies," and "Beanies" as the shortened form, are famous trademarks in the ordinary sense of the term: "everybody has heard of them".... Ty's trademarks are household words. And Perryman's use of these words was commercial in nature and took place in interstate commerce, and doubtless, given the reach of the aptly named World Wide Web, in foreign commerce as well.

But what is "dilution"? There are (at least) three possibilities relevant to this case, each defined by a different underlying concern. First, there is concern that consumer search costs will rise if a trademark becomes associated with a variety of unrelated products. Suppose an upscale restaurant calls itself "Tiffany." There is little danger that the consuming public will think it's dealing with a branch of the Tiffany jewelry store if it patronizes this restaurant. But when consumers next see the name "Tiffany" they may think about both the restaurant and the jewelry store, and if so the efficacy of the name as an identifier of the store will be diminished. Consumers will have to think harder—incur as it were a higher imagination cost—to recognize the name as the name of the store. [Citations.] So "blurring" is one form of dilution.

Now suppose that the "restaurant" that adopts the name "Tiffany" is actually a striptease joint. Again, and indeed even more certainly than in the previous case, consumers will not think the striptease joint under common ownership with the jewelry store. But because of the inveterate tendency of the human mind to proceed by association, every time they think of the word "Tiffany" their image of the fancy jewelry store will be tarnished by the association of the word with the strip joint. [Citations.] So "tarnishment" is a second form of dilution. Analytically it is a subset of blurring, since it reduces the distinctness of the trademark as a signifier of the trademarked product or service.

Third, and most far-reaching in its implications for the scope of the concept of dilution, there is a possible concern with situations in which, though there is neither blurring nor tarnishment, someone is still taking a free ride on the investment of the trademark owner in the trademark. Suppose the "Tiffany" restaurant in our first hypothetical example is located in Kuala Lumpur and though the people who patronize it (it is upscale) have heard of the Tiffany jewelry store, none of them is ever going to buy anything there, so that the efficacy of the trademark as an identifier will not be impaired. If appropriation of Tiffany's aura is nevertheless forbidden by an expansive concept of dilution, the benefits of the jewelry store's investment in creating a famous name will be, as economists say, "internalized"—that is, Tiffany will realize the full benefits of the investment rather than sharing those benefits with others—and as a result the amount of investing in creating a prestigious name will rise.

This rationale for antidilution law has not yet been articulated in or even implied by the case law, although a few cases suggest that the concept of dilution is not exhausted by blurring and tarnishment, *see Panavision Int'l, L.P. v. Toeppen*, 141 F.3d 1316, 1326 (9th Cir. 1998); *Intermatic, Inc. v. Toeppen*, 947 F. Supp. 1227, 1238–39 (N.D. Ill. 1996); *Rhee Bros., Inc. v. Han Ah Reum Corp.*, 178 F. Supp. 2d 525, 530 (D. Md. 2001), and the common law doctrine of "misappropriation" might conceivably be invoked in support of the rationale that we have sketched. [Citation.] The validity of the rationale may be doubted, however. The number of prestigious names is so vast (and, as important, would be even if there were no antidilution laws) that it is unlikely that the owner of a prestigious trademark could obtain substantial license fees if commercial use of the mark without his consent were forbidden despite the absence of consumer confusion, blurring, or tarnishment. Competition would drive the fee to zero since, if the name is being used in an unrelated market, virtually every prestigious name will be a substitute for every other in that market.

None of the rationales we have canvassed supports Ty's position in this case. Perryman is not producing a product, or a service, such as dining at a restaurant, that is distinct from any specific product; rather, she is selling the very product to which the trademark sought to be defended against her "infringement" is attached. You can't sell a branded product without using its brand name, that is, its trademark. Supposing that Perryman sold only Beanie Babies (a potentially relevant qualification, as we'll see), we would find it impossible to understand how she could be thought to be blurring, tarnishing, or otherwise free riding to any significant extent on Ty's investment in its mark. To say she was would amount to saying that if a used car dealer truthfully advertised that it sold Toyotas, or if a muffler manufacturer truthfully advertised that it specialized in making mufflers for installation in Toyotas, Toyota would have a claim of trademark infringement. Of course there can be no aftermarket without an original market, and in that sense sellers in a trademarked good's aftermarket are free riding on the trademark. But in that attenuated sense of free riding, almost everyone in business is free riding.

Ty's argument is especially strained because of its marketing strategy.... *Ty, Inc. v. GMA Accessories, Inc.*, 132 F.3d 1167, 1173 (7th Cir. 1997). Ty deliberately produces a quantity of each Beanie Baby that fails to clear the market at the very low price that it charges for Beanie Babies. The main goal is to stampede children into nagging their parents to buy the new Baby lest they be the only kid on the block who doesn't have it. A byproduct (or perhaps additional goal) is the creation of a secondary market, like the secondary market in works of art, in which prices on scarce Beanie Babies are bid up to a market-clearing level. Perryman is a middleman in this secondary market, the market, as we said, that came into existence as the result, either intended or foreseen, of a deliberate marketing strategy. That market is unlikely to operate efficiently if sellers who specialize in serving it cannot use "Beanies" to identify their business. Perryman's principal merchandise is Beanie Babies, so that to forbid it to use "Beanies" in its business name and advertising (Web or otherwise) is like forbidding a used car dealer who specializes in selling Chevrolets to mention the name in his advertising.

It is true that Web search engines do not stop with the Web address; if Perryman's Web address were www.perryman.com but her Web page mentioned Beanies, a search for the word "Beanies" would lead to her Web page. Yet we know from the events that led up to the passage in 1999 of the Anticybersquatting Consumer Protection Act, 15 U.S.C. § 1125(d), that many firms value having a domain name or Web address that signals their product. (The "cybersquatters" were individuals or firms that would register domain names for the purpose of selling them to companies that wanted a domain name that would be the name of their company or of their principal product.) After all, many consumers search by typing the name of a company in the Web address space (browser) on their home page rather than by use of a search engine. We do not think that by virtue of trademark law producers own their aftermarkets and can impede sellers in the aftermarket from marketing the trademarked product.

We surmise that what Ty is seeking in this case is an extension of antidilution law to forbid commercial uses that accelerate the transition from trademarks (brand names) to generic names (product names). Words such as "thermos," "yo–yo," "escalator," "cellophane," and "brassiere" started life as trademarks, but eventually lost their significance as source identifiers and became the popular names of the product rather than the name of the trademark owner's brand, and when that happened continued enforcement of the trademark would simply have undermined competition with the brand by making it difficult for competitors to indicate that they were selling the same product—by rendering them in effect speechless. Ty is doubtless cognizant of a similar and quite real danger to "Beanie Babies" and "Beanies." Notice that the illustrations we gave of trademarks that became generic names are all descriptive or at least suggestive of the product, which makes them better candidates for genericness than a fanciful trademark such as "Kodak" or "Exxon." Ty's trademarks likewise are descriptive of the product they denote; its argument that "Beanies" is "inherently distinctive" (like Kodak and Exxon), and therefore protected by trademark law without proof of secondary meaning, is nonsense. A trademark that describes a basic element of the product, as "Beanies" does, is not protected unless the owner can establish that the consuming public accepts the word as the designation of a brand of the product (that it has acquired, as the cases say, secondary meaning). [Citations omitted.] As the public does with regard to "Beanies"—for now. But because the word is catchier than "beanbag stuffed animals," "beanbag toys," or "plush toys," it may someday "catch on" to the point where the mark becomes generic, and then Ty will have to cast about for a different trademark.

Although there is a social cost when a mark becomes generic—the trademark owner has to invest in a new trademark to identify his brand—there is also a social benefit, namely an addition to ordinary language. A nontrivial number of words in common use began life as trademarks. An interpretation of antidilution law as arming trademark owners to enjoin uses of their mark that, while not confusing, threaten to render the mark generic may therefore not be in the public interest. Moreover, the vistas of litigation that such a theory of dilution opens up are staggering. Ty's counsel at argument refused to disclaim a right to sue the publishers of dictionaries should they include an entry for "beanie," lowercased and defined as a beanbag stuffed animal, thus accelerating the transition from trademark to generic term. He should have disclaimed such a right. [Citations omitted.]

We reject the extension of antidilution law that Ty beckons us to adopt, but having done so we must come back to the skipped issue of confusion. For although 80 percent of Perryman's sales are of Ty's products, this means that 20 percent are not, and on her Web page after listing the various Ty products under such names as "Beanie Babies" and "Teenie Beanies" she has the caption "Other Beanies" and under that is a list of products such as "Planet Plush" and "Rothschild Bears" that are not manufactured by Ty. This is plain misdescription, in fact false advertising, and supports the last prohibition in the injunction, the prohibition against using "Beanie" or "Beanies" "in connection with any non-Ty products." That much of the injunction should stand. But Ty has not demonstrated any basis for enjoining Perryman from using the terms in "any business name, Internet domain name, or trademark."

We can imagine an argument that merely deleting "Other Beanies" is not enough; that if the other beanbag stuffed animals look much like Ty's, consumers might assume they are "Beanies," or if not, that they still might associate "Beanies" with these other animals, causing the term to lose its distinctness as the name of Ty's products. But we do not understand Ty to be seeking a broadening of the injunction to require a disclaimer as to the source of the non-Ty products sold by Perryman. This however is a matter that can be pursued further on remand....

Questions

1. Did Judge Posner consider defendant's use of BEANIES in connection with non-Ty products to be dilution? Should he have?

2. Is Judge Posner's characterization of tarnishment as a sub-species of blurring persuasive?

3. Do you agree that use of "Beanies" as part of Perryman's domain and business names does not dilute the distinctiveness of plaintiff's BEANIE BABIES mark? Do uses that tend to genericize a mark dilute its distinctiveness? Should every business in the aftermarket for a product be entitled to use the brand name in its own name or domain name?

4. Recall Judge Posner's evocation of Tiffany to illustrate the concepts of blurring and tarnishment. In *Hugunin v. Land O' Lakes, Inc.*, 815 F.3d 1064 (7th Cir. 2016), in which the large dairy company claimed that a very small identically-named fishing tackle company was blurring its famous mark, in use since the 1920s, Judge Posner distinguished his earlier example:

> Everyone recognizes "Tiffany" as the name of a luxury jewelry store on Fifth Avenue in New York (with stores in other major cities), and seeing the

> name on a hotdog stand a passerby might think of the jewelry store and of the incongruity of a hot-dog stand's having the same name; he might think the jewelry store's cachet impaired by the coincidence and switch his patronage to Cartier or Harry Winston. Many consumers would recognize the name "LAND O LAKES" as referring to the dairy company, but we can't see how the company could be hurt by the use of the same name by a seller just of fishing tackle. The products of the two companies are too different, and the sale of fishing tackle is not so humble a business as the sale of hot dogs by street vendors. And so it is beyond unlikely that someone dissatisfied with LAND O LAKES fishing tackle would take revenge on the dairy company by not buying any of its products, or that a customer would have difficulty identifying Land O' Lakes' dairy products because he had seen the LAND O LAKES mark used on Hugunin's fishing tackle. Land O' Lakes products are advertised on their labels as dairy or other food products (such as instant cappuccino mixes), never as products relating to fishing.
>
> And the dairy company's mark is itself derivative from Minnesota's catchphrase "Land of 10,000 Lakes," see Wikipedia, "Minnesota," https://en.wikipedia.org/wiki/Minnesota (visited February 29, 2016), a phrase in such widespread use that the company could not insist that it was the sole lawful user of the phrase in advertising for all products.
>
> The disparity in size between the contenders deserves emphasis. In 2012, the last year for which we have statistics, Land O' Lakes' sales of dairy foods exceeded $4 billion, while Hugunin's sales were less than $30,000. It's hard to believe that a giant dairy company wants to destroy or annex Hugunin's tiny fishing-tackle business, or that Hugunin's tackle sales are being kept down by Land O' Lakes' having an identical trademark.

Are the differences between hot dog stands and fishing tackle companies persuasive? What, if anything, would justify different outcomes between the hypothetical hotdog stand and Hugunin's fishing tackle enterprise? Does this inquiry help illuminate the meaning of "dilution"?

Rebecca Tushnet, *Gone in 60 Milliseconds: Trademark Law and Cognitive Science*

86 Texas L. Rev. 507 (2008) (Excerpts)*

I. Introduction

....

Trademark dilution has been subjected to persistent criticisms: that it is not well defined and that as best as it can be identified, it still isn't harmful.

Cognitive models offer hope of answering these objections by conceiving of dilution as an increase in mental or internal search costs. Consumers allegedly have more difficulty

* Copyright 2008. Reprinted by permission. [*Editors' Note*: Some footnotes omitted.]

recalling, recognizing and producing a diluted trademark, and correspondingly are less likely to purchase products or services branded with that mark.

....

III The Appeal of the Internal-Search-Costs Model

....

[T]he cognitive processing model ... offers an attractive definition of dilution, one that creates a pleasing symmetry between dilution and the standard—now "external"—search cost model of infringement. Dilution imposes mental—"internal"—search costs on consumers, which is why dilution is harmful. Judge Posner has ably set forth the fundamentals of the cognitive model, and Jacob Jacoby, a prominent ... trademark expert, has seized on Posner's explanations as confirmation of his framework for measuring dilution experimentally.

A. Blurring

In *Ty, Inc. v. Perryman*, [306 F.3d 509 (7th Cir. 2002)], a case about a Web site that sold Beanie Babies and other stuffed bean-bag animals, Judge Posner ... contrasted infringement to dilution, which he saw as dealing with internal search costs—difficulties not in figuring out whether two products or services are from the same source, but in retrieving the mark from memory in the first place. In the cognitive model, blurring takes place when a single term activates multiple, non-confusing associations in a consumer's mind. Meanings or concepts ... are linked by mental networks. Concepts are activated through links in the network, triggering related concepts. Activation happens very fast, and if it does not continue, an unreinforced word or concept can die away....

Blurring involves relatively extended activation of two different meanings for a mark, until the consumer sorts out the proper referent. The basic theory is that an unrelated, nonconfusing mark similar to a famous mark adds new associations to a preexisting network, which slows processing time, especially if the junior mark has a very different meaning than the senior mark....

In 2000, Maureen Morrin and Jacob Jacoby conducted an experiment that can be used to bolster the internal search costs model.[56] The study had participants view diluting ads for Dogiva dog biscuits, Heineken popcorn, and Hyatt legal services. The ads were "tombstone" ads—print-only and highly informational.... Computers measured how long it took for participants to identify the senior marks after exposure to the junior marks. Morrin and Jacoby found that exposure to dilutive ads slowed participants' accuracy and response time in associating some brands with product categories and attributes, such as linking Godiva to chocolate and rich taste. Heineken beer was similarly affected by ads for Heineken popcorn, though Hyatt hotels were not affected by ads for Hyatt legal services.

---

56. [*See* Maureen Morrin & Jacob Jacoby, *Trademark Dilution: Empirical Measures for an Elusive Concept*, 19 J. PUB. POL'Y & MARKETING 265 (2000).]

… Other researchers conducted paper-and-pencil versions of the experiment using aided recall, in which respondents were required to retrieve distinctive aspects of a brand when presented with the brand name, and required to retrieve the brand name when presented with the brand's distinctive aspects.[65] The results also showed measurable dilutive effects.

Dilution proponents maintain that delayed responses, like decreased accuracy in linking brands to categories and products, are likely to affect purchasing decisions, given that advertisers often only have a few seconds—or even milliseconds—to catch consumers' attention. If a dilutive use defamiliarizes consumers with a mark, their positive emotional associations based on familiarity may be lost, giving them less reason to choose the underlying product. In the lab, dilution-generated delayed response times have been correlated with later decreases in the likelihood that subjects will choose a diluted brand from among competing alternatives.

B. Tarnishment

In Posner's model, dilution by tarnishment also involves interference with cognitive processing, but of a different kind. Judge Posner posited a strip joint named Tiffany's, and assumed that reasonable consumers do not think it has any connection with the jewelry store. Nevertheless, "because of the inveterate tendency of the human mind to proceed by association, every time [people who know about the strip joint think of the word 'Tiffany' their image of the fancy jewelry store will be tarnished by the association of the word with the strip joint." [*Ty*, 306 F.3d at 511]. This "inveterate tendency" can be equated to the psychological concept of activation discussed above.…

[D]ilution by tarnishment would mean that the idea of Tiffany's-the-strip-joint remains at least slightly activated after a reference to Tiffany's-the-jewelry-store, decreasing the overall positive value associated with Tiffany's-the-jewelry-store.…

Though it was decided on confusion grounds, *Anheuser-Busch, Inc. v. Balducci Publications*, [28 F.3d 769 (8th Cir. 1994)], a case against a humor magazine's parody ad for Michelob Oily, is one of Jacoby's prime examples of tarnishment. Participants in his study were shown either an ad for Michelob Dry or the mock ad for Michelob Oily. Thirty-seven percent of those shown the Michelob Oily ad "associated a negative meaning with Michelob or Anheuser-Busch," while no one who saw a Michelob Dry ad did so.[78] Such negative meanings attach to the senior mark directly, rather than being mediated through a second, unrelated product.…

C. Free Riding

Finally, Posner offers a third possible meaning of dilution, which is simply free riding. The example is a Tiffany's restaurant in Kuala Lumpur, which grabs some of the luster of Tiffany's-the-jeweler because of the same tendency to make associations

---

65. *See* Chris Pullig et al., *Brand Dilution: When Do New Brands Hurt Existing Brands?*, J. MARKETING, Apr. 2006, at 52, 61.

78. … Twenty-two percent said the Michelob Oily ad made them less likely to buy Michelob, and twenty percent said they were less likely to drink it, compared to seven and five percent, respectively, of those who saw the Michelob Dry ad.…

that explains tarnishment and blurring. People in Kuala Lumpur know about the jewelry store but would never patronize it, so no jewelry store customers have their mental models of Tiffany's distorted in any way. But non-customers now have multiple associations with Tiffany's, and their recognition of the famous mark is impaired. Posner is dubious about this rationale, and the new federal dilution law seems to have taken it off the table for federal claims, though it may still be viable under state law. This definition focuses on the mental processes of the junior user's customers, not the senior user's, but is otherwise quite similar to the definition of blurring.

....

IV. Critiquing the Cognitive Model of Dilution

....

A. Context Effects

In the *Perryman* case, Judge Posner did not explain why it was a problem for consumers to have to think harder to figure out the entity to which "Tiffany's" refers. In fact, he did not define what it means to think harder. With blurring, the result of the existence of Tiffany's-the-restaurant is that we need more context to figure out which Tiffany's someone is talking about, but we generally have that context. Product categories, images in ads, and even distinctive fonts can provide immediate context for a mark. Preexisting associations reinforce each other so that computer-related meanings of *apple* are more strongly and effectively activated in an Apple Computer ad, and fruit-related meanings are activated at the grocery store.

....

Product categories provide an important type of context. Robert Peterson and his confederates surveyed major product categories and trademarks, examining typicality (the extent to which naming a brand caused a respondent to produce its major product category, as McDonald's would produce "fast food") and dominance (the extent to which naming a product category caused a respondent to produce a brand as the first that came to mind). Leading brands' typicality was much greater than their dominance, on average three times greater. In other words, marks are easy to recognize as category members without being at the top of a respondent's mind in the category. Moreover, the differences between recognition when prompted with a brand and recognition when prompted with a category may have significant real-world effects. Even if the Heineken name in the abstract produces less association with beer because of Heineken popcorn, consumers may still identify it as a beer if they're prompted with the category, and when they go to the store to buy beer, it will be right there on the shelf.... Consumers just do not confront trademarks in the abstract very often....

....

Why, then, did laboratory studies reveal an apparent dilutive effect from a single exposure to Dogiva biscuits and Heineken popcorn? One possibility is that the test environment was itself decontextualizing, depriving subjects of the cues they'd ordinarily use to distinguish a dilutive use from a senior mark. Morrin and Jacoby told their test subjects, students who were taking marketing courses, that they'd be tested on the information provided in the ads, which themselves were not the image- and emotion-laden appeals to which consumers are generally subjected. This method made it likely that subjects would focus on information, not on the contextual, emotional associations that serve to distinguish brands in the real world....

B. Association Sets and Uncommon Words

....

Jerre Swann ... has been a major proponent of using cognitive theories to justify and define dilution. He cites psychological studies to show that adding unrelated associations to a famous mark causes dilution and interferes with consumers' ability to retrieve the mark because:

> "'[R]are words [like "Kodak"] are more distinctively encoded than (are) common words,'" and words that have a limited number of "association set[s]" (e.g., "Cheer" for an encouraging shout and an all-temperature detergent), can likewise be readily retrieved....
>
> "Some empirical research has shown[, on the other hand,] that the greater the number of associations a word has (the less distinctive it is)[,] the more difficult it is for the individual initially to encode the word in memory or later to recall the word."

Swann's citation to the work of Joan Meyers-Levy supposedly shows that increasing the association set size of a brand decreases the consumer's ability to retrieve brand-relevant information. There are at least three problems with this extrapolation. First, the underlying research uses a definition of "association set" ... as the number of words that are named by at least two people when a large number are asked the first word that comes to mind in response to a target word. Unless a dilutive use was the first thing that came to mind, it would not affect this measure of association. Second and relatedly, even if a dilutive use dominated some respondents' minds, it would only increase the set size by one. The underlying research does not come close to identifying any effect from an increase of one association. Third, Meyers-Levy does not measure change, though Swann applies her work to change over time; her research, like that of others in the field, compares words with existing high-and low-measured frequency and association set sizes.

Still, assuming those problems away, the Meyers-Levy research may have implications for famous brands. High-frequency words are easy to process, and thus we don't encode them distinctively, meaning that we don't pay much attention to them. If they are used as brand names, we will have trouble remembering the brand. Low-frequency words are relatively difficult to encode, and thus we process them more meaningfully. Given that advertisers have trouble getting consumers to pay attention to advertising in general, ... low-frequency words seem more desirable as marks. Meyers-Levy offers *ivory* as an example of a low-frequency word that therefore relates strongly to soap. When a word is low-frequency, a particular use will cause people to encode only relevant information presented in context, because their attention will be drawn to specific attributes of the word (for *ivory*, color and not elephants). Thus, with a low-frequency word, even a large association set size won't interfere with memory. "Indeed, it is possible that memory might be somewhat enhanced as the size of the association set increases [for low-frequency words] because more associations will be available to relate meaningfully to the brand in a distinctive manner." By contrast, Swann's reasoning is that a use that takes a mark from low to high frequency or increases the associations of a high-frequency mark creates a branding problem by making the mark harder to recognize.

Meyers-Levy experimented with fictitious antiperspirants, blemish medications, and disposable razors, choosing brand names from words with known frequencies and association-set sizes. Low-frequency words (fifteen or fewer uses per million words) were *crisp, moose, bribe, cork, shove*, and *dusk*. High-frequency words (one hundred or more per million) were *yard, lake, room, cloud, day*, and *round*. One might wonder about the selling power of Yard antiperspirant, Cloud blemish medication, and Round razors, but a more important thing to note is that low-frequency words are still quite recognizable.

Experimental subjects heard ads for products, which they were told were existing regional brands, and instructed to consider how clear, grammatical, and professionally written the ads were. Then they were asked to recall and write down all statements they could remember from the ads. Then, they were shown lists of brand names, instructed that some might be "impostors," and asked to indicate whether they recognized the brands. The results showed that, for high-frequency brand names, recall was poorer (both immediately and at 24 hours) for words with a large association-set size. With low-frequency brand names, recall was similar regardless of set size.

That sounds like good reason for marketers to minimize the associations evoked by their famous brands. The flaw is the assumption that famous brand names are high frequency, or can be made so by dilution.... In the 2003 release of the American National Corpus, ... only one of the top forty brands—[MICROSOFT]—in BusinessWeek's Best Global Brands 2006 had frequencies approaching one hundred per million words. Kodak, Swann's example of a famous mark subject to dilution, had a frequency of approximately seven per million, Hyatt and Godiva were slightly above one, and Heineken was below one. Thus, even dilutive uses that doubled the frequency of exposure to these marks would still leave them low-frequency. There just aren't that many high-frequency words.

The one study I have found that specifically addressed trademarks and frequency effects found that popular brands were recognized with a speed and accuracy similar to that of low-frequency words. Meyers-Levy's work, then, in fact suggest that dilution does not harm many famous trademarks, because adding associations to low-frequency words doesn't interfere with retrieval or recognition—and may even help.

C. Reaffirmation Effects

... [T]here are reasons to think that at least some dilutive uses can reinforce, rather than chip away at, the strength of a mark. Any delay in recognizing which Tiffany's or which Apple a particular use refers to may be compensated for by easier recall of the marks.

In essence, exposure to near variants or uses in other contexts makes the trademark more familiar and thus more easily retrieved from memory. This process can add value in the same way that marketers think preexisting associations carried by descriptive or suggestive terms add value to a trademark. Words with multiple associations may be more easily activated, or reference to one word may "prime" us to recall a similar word. Tiffany's-the-restaurant may make us think of Tiffany's-the-jeweler's when we are at lunch thinking of gifts for Mother's Day. In one experiment that was supposed to provide evidence for the cognitive model of tarnishment, exposure to ads for a Hyatt tattoo parlor actually increased preference for Hyatt hotels. (An important caveat, however, is that priming effects, like dilution effects, are typically small and could be unimportant to famous marks.)

Beyond priming, dilutive uses may increase the richness of a term's associations. Multiplication of associations can aid recall of trademarks comprising uncommon words. The cognitive model of dilution posits that consumers do not like to think hard.... Recall that low-frequency words are remembered better because they require more processing to encode in memory—an instance of "thinking hard" that's useful to trademark owners. In essence, there may be a tradeoff between ease and richness of processing. Some difficulty in retrieval prompts more mental processing, which itself leads to better long-term memory for the relevant concepts. The delayed response times that Morrin and Jacoby saw as evidence of dilution when they tested subjects with a single recognition test could have improved the strength of the diluted marks in the long run.

....

Priming also makes it particularly unlikely that a glancing exposure to a dilutive mark will cause harm to the senior brand. If a consumer is not paying attention and doesn't process the mark, it will just be a subliminal reminder, without generating new and inconsistent meanings. If a consumer's attention is caught, however, we simply don't know how that will play out in any particular case—whether it will ultimately reinforce the original, as the Hyatt tattoo parlor reinforces Hyatt hotels, or dilute it. When the effect can be either positive or negative, it is a mistake to adopt as the theory of dilution an explanation that always posits a negative effect.

D. What About Tarnishment?

....

There is very little empirical work in this area. Marketing researchers have, however, been extremely interested in a related question: when a strong existing brand introduces a new product extension that is bad, or enters into a marketing alliance with a partner who turns out to have reputation problems, does that reflect poorly on the originally strong and popular core brand? In bad partnerships and failed brand extensions, the trademark owner may have carefully attempted to maintain brand quality, but consumers judged the attempt a failure.

That brand-extension research suggests that dilution by tarnishment through the use of a similar mark on a shoddy product is unlikely in the absence of confusion, because consumers have relatively robust mental concepts of strong brands.[176] If they are given a reason to distinguish an authorized extension or co-branded product from the core brand—for example, a name like Courtyard by Marriott instead of Marriott Courtyard or Coke BlaK instead of "Coke"—they will do so, and negative opinions about the extension will not return to harm opinions of the core brand. If consumers seize on such fine distinctions for authorized line extensions, it seems implausible that, absent confusion, they will transfer negative opinions between unrelated products or services.

....

F. Summary

Given the available evidence ... the cognitive model of dilution lacks enough empirical support to justify its adoption as a general theory underlying dilution law. There is still too much we don't know about how consumers process marks in the marketplace. At a minimum, we cannot predict that any particular dilutive use will produce the difficulties posited by the cognitive model.

Questions

1. Is there anything left of Judge Posner's concept of dilution by blurring as protecting a consumer's mental search cost in light of the research examined by Professor Tushnet? How about dilution by tarnishment?

2. Could the concept of free riding support application of a dilution remedy? Should it? In what situations?

Barton Beebe, *Intellectual Property Law and The Sumptuary Code*

123 HARV. L. REV. 809, 848–59 (2010)*

... I first consider the failure of trademark antidilution law to live up to its name.

Since Schechter's time, trademark antidilution law has proved to be a dead letter both in the United States, as recent empirical work confirms, as well as abroad. This is largely due to the economistic turn in our understanding of this area of trademark doctrine. Most nations, including the United States, have codified some form of trademark antidilution law, as has the European Union. Yet the antidilution cause

176. *See, e.g.*, Stephen J. Hoch, *Product Experience Is Seductive*, 29 J. CONSUMER RES. 448, 451 (2002) ("Using a simple associative learning procedure, [researchers] showed that, in a few trials, people learn brand associations that later block the learning of new predictive attribute associations."); Deborah Roedder John et al., *The Negative Impact of Extensions: Can Flagship Products Be Diluted?*, J. MARKETING, Jan. 1998, at 19, 20 ("[B]eliefs about the flagship product [of a strong brand] are 'encapsulated' and extremely resistant to change ...")....

 [*Editors' Note*: Footnotes omitted.]

of action itself continues to meet with resistance—bordering on nullification—by courts around the world. There is a simple reason for this. Though we still dutifully cite to Schechter's 1926 article, trademark case law and commentary have transformed the concept of dilution from one based essentially on a theory of the fashion process to one based on a theory of "search costs." In an effort to fit the concept of dilution into an efficiency framework, we now speak of dilution in terms of "blurring," in which a defendant's use of a mark that is similar or identical to a plaintiff's mark is thought to "blur" the immediacy of the link between the plaintiff's mark and the plaintiff itself. This in turn is thought to require consumers to "think for a moment" before linking the mark to the plaintiff, which increases consumers' "imagination cost[s]," which is inefficient. Thus, a law that was originally designed to promote differentiation, both among branded goods and among the people who consume them, has been transformed into a law understood to promote identification of a brand with its goods. This allows trademark theorists to maintain the fiction that trademarks yield only absolute utility, that they do no more than denote the source of the goods to which they are affixed—a fiction that Schechter worked so hard to expose. But the result is that judges who might otherwise be willing to protect distinctiveness or uniqueness as something of social value (and we will see in a moment that they are certainly willing to do so) are instead hostile to the trademark antidilution cause of action because they see no harm worth enjoining in trivial increases in "internal search costs." Ironically, then, the very theorists who have sought with the search costs rationale to offer a strong defense of the antidilution cause of action and the added property rights that it yields have instead largely buried it.

....

Rather than resort to the rationale of preventing post-sale or sponsorship confusion, trademark courts will also enjoin a defendant's dilutive copying on vaguely reasoned theories of common law misappropriation. To the extent that these theories make little effort to ground themselves in any notion of search costs, they represent the clearest expression of courts' essentially normative commitment to policing the sumptuary code. An early and highly representative U.S. case in this regard involved the Atmos clock, a table clock that is wound solely by changes in atmospheric pressure. The manufacturer of the Atmos clock sued a competitor that produced an electric-powered simulation of the clock. Judge Jerome Frank was hardly an apologist for trademark law or for the "[n]on-economic snobbish desires of consumers (of the kind analyzed by Veblen) and the satisfaction of their desires engendered by ignorance." He nevertheless enjoined the simulation:

> [S]ome customers would buy plaintiff's cheaper clock for the purpose of acquiring the prestige gained by displaying what many visitors at the customers' homes would regard as a prestigious article.... Plaintiff's intention thus to reap financial benefits from poaching on the reputation of the Atmos clock is of major importance.

In a surprisingly persistent line of cases, all involving high-status goods, U.S. courts have since followed the reasoning of the Atmos clock case to hold that it is simply not fair for a person to acquire the prestige associated with a good—by using, for example, a product that "looks and sounds like the real thing"—without paying the customary price.

....

The irony of trademark antidilution law—that we are accomplishing the goals of Schechter's original formulation in ways unanticipated, if not rejected by Schechter—continues in one other and final respect. In speaking of dilution by blurring, I have spoken so far of only one of the two modes of trademark dilution conventionally recognized in current trademark doctrine. The other is dilution by "tarnishment," a mode of dilution that plaintiffs have traditionally invoked to address conduct that links their marks "to products of shoddy quality" or portrays their marks "in an unwholesome or unsavory context likely to evoke unflattering thoughts" about their marks. Standard examples of the latter form of tarnishment include defendants' use of marks in sexual, vulgar, or illicit contexts. Because such conduct does not affect the formal uniqueness of the targeted mark, Schechter himself never spoke of tarnishment as a form of dilution, and various trademark scholars, myself included, have questioned whether tarnishment is a form of dilution for the same reason. Yet with the Trademark Dilution Revision Act of 2006, the Lanham Act now explicitly provides relief for what it terms "dilution by tarnishment," which it defines broadly as "association arising from the similarity between a mark or trade name and a famous mark that harms the reputation of the famous mark." This revision brings the Lanham Act up to speed with the European Union's Trade Marks Directive, whose antidilution section has defined tarnishing conduct since the Directive's inception in 1988 as conduct that is "detrimental to ... the repute of the trade mark."

Latent within the concept of tarnishment, as within these statutory definitions, has always been an extraordinarily capacious notion of harm to the "reputation" or "repute" of the trademark, one that is now taking shape as the most effective means toward reaching the ultimate ends that Schechter sought—so that the stone Schechter ignored may very well become the chief cornerstone of the cause of action he envisioned. In *L'Oréal v. Bellure*, [Case C-487/07, 2009 ECJ EUR-Lex LEXIS 532 P 40 (June 18, 2009)], for example, the ECJ defined tarnishment as occurring when the defendant uses the plaintiff's trademark or a trademark similar to it in such a way that "the trade mark's power of attraction is reduced." The Supreme Court of Canada articulated a comparable standard in its 2006 opinion in *Veuve Clicquot Ponsardin v. Boutiques Cliquot Ltée* [[2006] 1 Supreme Court Reports [S.C.R.] 824 (Can.)]. There, the court addressed Canada's statutory trademark "depreciation" cause of action, which prohibits one party from using a mark "in a manner that is likely to have the effect of depreciating the value of the goodwill attaching" to another party's mark. In expanding upon the statutory language, the court opined that a trademark's "value can be lowered in other ways [than disparagement], as by the lesser distinctiveness that results when a mark is bandied about by different users." The Fourth Circuit, meanwhile, has recently stated that to establish tarnishment, the plaintiff merely "must show, in lieu of blurring, that [the defendant's use of its mark] harms the reputation of the [plaintiff's] mark."

On the basis of these statements, any uses of a trademark that reduce another mark's "selling power," lower the value of that mark's goodwill, or harm its reputation are potentially actionable as tarnishing uses. Such uses include, of course, dilutive copying that tarnishes the mark's reputation for uniqueness, regardless of whether that copying takes the form of "shoddy" copies, and regardless of whether that copying places the targeted mark in an "unwholesome or unsavory context." And where the plaintiff lacks persuasive evidence—as it almost always seems to do—that the defendant's mark has blurred the link between the plaintiff's mark and its source, the plaintiff may nevertheless contend that the defendant's mark tarnishes the reputation of the plaintiff's mark as being a mark that is used by one, or a few, sources and no others. The irony here is that, on this logic, while tarnishing conduct (such as placing the mark in an "unsavory context") does not necessarily dilute the uniqueness of the mark, the dilution of the uniqueness of the mark necessarily tarnishes it; and because tarnishment is now explicitly referenced in the U.S. statute as elsewhere, the form of protection that Schechter originally envisioned is now available, *mirabile dictu*, at the federal level. As with so much else in modern trademark law, if not in modern intellectual property law more generally, tarnishment doctrine is shifting from substance to form, from protecting and promoting the substantive meaning of the mark, to the extent that it has any, to protecting and promoting, more abstractly, the mark's formal "differential distinctiveness." Trademark law's expanding role as a modern form of sumptuary law has arguably precipitated this shift.

....

... A society's sumptuary is its system of consumption practices, akin to a language (or at least "a set of dialects"), by which individuals in the society signal through their consumption their differences from and similarities to others. Laws that seek to control and preserve this code are sumptuary laws. Historically, laws seeking to govern a society's system of consumption-based distinction have most commonly taken the form of direct controls on consumption—an example, by no means atypical, is the 1463 English ordinance limiting to two inches the extent to which the shoes of persons of rank could extend beyond their toes. Societies have regularly imposed such controls when their governing classes come to believe that too much of their society's wealth is being wasted on conspicuous or decadent forms of consumption or that their society's system of relative consumption no longer operates reliably to differentiate and distinguish—if not to discipline—the various members of the society. This latter problem—the breakdown of a society's consumption-based system of social distinction—has typically occurred when formerly rare commodities or their equivalents suddenly become abundant or when lower-status social groups gain the economic power to consume goods that formerly only upper-status social groups consumed. It has also occurred with urbanization, which tends to complicate the signaling and recognition of social position. The former problem—the squandering of national wealth—has been a constant concern but seems to be most acutely felt in times of war.

... We have recently undertaken a new round of sumptuary lawmaking, not just in the United States, but globally, and for reasons comparable to those that drove previous sumptuary turns. Sumptuary law did not disappear with industrialization and democratization, as is generally believed. Rather, it has taken on a new—though still quite eccentric—form: intellectual property law. To be sure, the express purpose and primary effect of intellectual property law remains the prevention of misappropriation and the promotion of technological and cultural progress. But for various reasons, we are increasingly investing intellectual property law with, and forcing the law to adapt to, a new purpose. This purpose is to preserve and stabilize our modern sumptuary code in the face of emerging social and technological conditions that threaten its viability and that intellectual property law is uniquely well-suited to address. We are thus increasingly relying on intellectual property law not so much to enforce social hierarchy as simply to conserve—or in Pierre Bourdieu's terminology, to "reproduce"—our system of consumption-based social distinction and the social structures and norms based upon it. The result is that intellectual property law now consists of two conflicting sides: the familiar progressive side of the law, which works, in the terms of the U.S. Constitution, "To promote the Progress of Science and useful Arts," and the unappreciated sumptuary side of the law, which is not progressive but rather socially and technologically reactionary.

Questions

1. In Professor Beebe's view, does antidilution law establish a special regime for particularly famous marks, or do its protections extend to all trademarks? Why should only famous marks bask in an aura of exclusivity?

2. What is "differential distinctiveness"? Is it a more useful, or ascertainable, concept than "blurring"?

B. Federal Dilution

1. Evolution of the Statutory Standards

Note: History of the Federal Dilution Statute

As noted in the Stadler excerpt *supra*, many state legislatures and courts adopted dilution remedies beginning in the 1940s. Massachusetts enacted an anti-dilution statute in 1947, followed, in the next decades, by Connecticut, Georgia, Illinois, and New York. In 1964, the United States Trademark Association (USTA) (now the International Trademark Association (INTA)) proposed a Model State Trademark Bill containing anti-dilution provisions. Many states, including Alabama, California, Delaware, Georgia, Louisiana, Maine, Massachusetts, Missouri, New Hampshire, New York, Oregon, Rhode Island and Texas, based their dilution statutes on the USTA model. However, trademark owners continued to press for a federal statute in light of the lack of uniformity of the state laws. Although Congress considered including dilution within its revision to the Lanham Act in 1988 as recommended in the *Report and Recommendations* of the USTA Trademark Review Commission, 77 T.M.R. 375 (1987), the federal anti-dilution proposal was not ultimately included in the Trademark Law Revision Act of 1988.

Congress did not enact an antidilution statute until the Federal Trademark Dilution Act of 1995 (FTDA), codified at 15 U.S.C. § 1125(c), § 43(c) of the Lanham Act (effective January 16, 1996). The FTDA added a new § 43(c) to the Lanham Act as well as a definition of dilution in § 45 as "the lessening of the capacity of a famous mark to identify and distinguish goods or services, regardless of the presence or absence of—(1) competition between the owner of the famous mark and other parities; or (2) likelihood of confusion, mistake or deception." The FTDA provided that owners of famous marks were entitled to relief against a "commercial use in commerce of a mark or trade name" that "causes dilution of the distinctive quality of the mark." The statute listed a number of factors to determine whether a mark "is distinctive and famous."

Uniformity, however, was not the result. Different interpretations of the FTDA included whether a mark qualified as famous if it possessed just niche or regional fame, whether marks had to be inherently distinctive to qualify as "distinctive" and whether tarnishment was even covered by the statute. *See generally* Clarisa Long, *Dilution*, 106 Colum. L. Rev. 1029 (2006). The most important split among courts, however, involved the standard for proving liability. Was likelihood of dilution enough or did a plaintiff need to prove actual dilution of its mark? The Supreme Court in *Moseley v. V. Secret Catalogue*, 537 U.S. 418 (2003), resolved the latter conflict among the circuits and held that the FTDA dictated the higher standard of proving actual dilution. Because trademark owners could establish a state anti-dilution violation based on a likelihood of dilution, some preferred, or at least joined, the state law claim to a federal action.

In response to the cries for reform by trademark owners, Congress passed the Trademark Dilution Revision Act of 2006 ("TDRA of 2006"), *infra*, which became effective on October 6, 2006. Congress endeavored to clarify the scope of anti-dilution protection in the 2006 Trademark Dilution Reform Act (TDRA), but did not preempt most State protections, except as against federally registered marks. Thus, state remedies generally remain available and retain relevance, particularly to the extent they offer protection where federal law does not. For example, while the TDRA of 2006 clarifies that only nationally famous marks qualify for federal protection, some states' anti-dilution laws cover marks famous in niche markets.

When the district court decided the *Moseley* case on remand, the revised dilution statute was in effect for prospective injunctive relief. In deciding that VICTOR'S SECRET and VICTOR'S LITTLE SECRET for the sale of sex toys and adult videos tarnished VICTORIA'S SECRET for lingerie, the court accordingly applied the likelihood of dilution standard set forth in the revised statute. *See V Secret Catalogue, Inc. v. Moseley*, 558 F. Supp. 2d 734 (W.D. Ky. 2008), *aff'd*, 605 F.3d 382 (6th Cir. 2010). The Sixth Circuit's decision appears *infra*.

15 U.S.C. § 1125(c) [Lanham Act § 43(c), as amended by the Trademark Dilution Revision Act of 2006, replacing section 43(c) in its entirety]

(c) dilution by Blurring; dilution by Tarnishment.

(1) Injunctive relief. Subject to the principles of equity, the owner of a famous mark that is distinctive, inherently or through acquired distinctiveness, shall be entitled to an injunction against another person who, at any time after the owner's mark has become famous, commences use of a mark or trade name in commerce that is likely to cause dilution by blurring or dilution by tarnishment of the famous mark, regardless of the presence or absence of actual or likely confusion, of competition, or of actual economic injury.

(2) Definitions.

(A) For purposes of paragraph (1), a mark is famous if it is widely recognized by the general consuming public of the United States as a designation of source of the goods or services of the mark's owner. In determining whether a mark possesses the requisite degree of recognition, the court may consider all relevant factors, including the following:

(i) The duration, extent, and geographic reach of advertising and publicity of the mark, whether advertised or publicized by the owner or third parties.

(ii) The amount, volume, and geographic extent of sales of goods or services offered under the mark.

(iii) The extent of actual recognition of the mark.

(iv) Whether the mark was registered under the Act of March 3, 1881, or the Act of February 20, 1905, or on the principal register.

(B) For purposes of paragraph (1), "dilution by blurring" is association arising from the similarity between a mark or trade name and a famous mark that impairs the distinctiveness of the famous mark. In determining whether a mark or trade name is likely to cause dilution by blurring, the court may consider all relevant factors, including the following:

(i) The degree of similarity between the mark or trade name and the famous mark.

(ii) The degree of inherent or acquired distinctiveness of the famous mark.

(iii) The extent to which the owner of the famous mark is engaging in substantially exclusive use of the mark.

(iv) The degree of recognition of the famous mark.

(v) Whether the user of the mark or trade name intended to create an association with the famous mark.

(vi) Any actual association between the mark or trade name and the famous mark.

(C) For purposes of paragraph (1), "dilution by tarnishment" is association arising from the similarity between a mark or trade name and a famous mark that harms the reputation of the famous mark.

(3) Exclusions. The following shall not be actionable as dilution by blurring or dilution by tarnishment under this subsection:

(A) Any fair use, including a nominative or descriptive fair use, or facilitation of such fair use, of a famous mark by another person other than as a designation of source for the person's own goods or services, including use in connection with—

(i) advertising or promotion that permits consumers to compare goods or services; or

(ii) identifying and parodying, criticizing, or commenting upon the famous mark owner or the goods or services of the famous mark owner.

(B) All forms of news reporting and news commentary.

(C) Any noncommercial use of a mark.

(4) Burden of proof. In a civil action for trade dress dilution under this Act for trade dress not registered on the principal register, the person who asserts trade dress protection has the burden of proving that—

(A) the claimed trade dress, taken as a whole, is not functional and is famous; and

(B) if the claimed trade dress includes any mark or marks registered on the principal register, the unregistered matter, taken as a whole, is famous separate and apart from any fame of such registered marks.

(5) Additional remedies. In an action brought under this subsection, the owner of the famous mark shall be entitled to injunctive relief as set forth in section 34. The owner of the famous mark shall also be entitled to the remedies set forth in sections 35(a) and 36 [15 USC §§ 1117(a) and 1118], subject to the discretion of the court and the principles of equity if—

(A) the mark or trade name that is likely to cause dilution by blurring or dilution by tarnishment was first used in commerce by the person against whom the injunction is sought after the date of enactment of the Trademark Dilution Revision Act of 2006 [enacted Oct. 6, 2006]; and

(B) in a claim arising under this subsection—

(i) by reason of dilution by blurring, the person against whom the injunction is sought willfully intended to trade on the recognition of the famous mark; or

(ii) by reason of dilution by tarnishment, the person against whom the injunction is sought willfully intended to harm the reputation of the famous mark.

(6) Ownership of valid registration a complete bar to action. The ownership by a person of a valid registration under the Act of March 3, 1881, or the Act of February 20, 1905, or on the principal register under this Act shall be a complete bar to an action against that person, with respect to that mark, that—

(A) is brought by another person under the common law or a statute of a State; and

(B)

(i) seeks to prevent dilution by blurring or dilution by tarnishment; or

(ii) asserts any claim of actual or likely damage or harm to the distinctiveness or reputation of a mark, label, or form of advertisement.

Questions

1. Must a mark be inherently distinctive for protection from dilution?

2. How helpful are the factors listed in the statute for determining "dilution by blurring"?

3. Does the statute define "tarnishment"?

4. Does the inclusion of protection against dilution in the federal statute sufficiently address the problem of checkerboard jurisprudence under state law?

5. Consider Lanham Act § 43(c)(6). Why do you suppose Congress preempted state dilution challenges to federally-registered marks?

6. Why do you suppose Congress limited the preemptive effect of federal law to the protection of federally-registered marks? Why tolerate a parallel state regime, especially where state protection exceeds the scope of federal protection?

7. Are the ubiquitous marks discussed in Professor Stadler's excerpted article, *supra* this chapter, such as PEPSI and CHANEL, likely to qualify for dilution protection under the federal statute?

8. Consider section 43(c)(3). How would the *New Kids on the Block v. News American Publishing*, 971 F.2d 302 (9th Cir. 1992), *supra* Chapter 8[B][1], be decided under the statute? Would defendant's use of the famous CHANEL #5 mark in *Smith v. Chanel, Inc.*, 402 F.2d 562 (9th Cir. 1968), *supra* Chapter 8[B][2] constitute actionable dilution?

9. In Disney's video "George of the Jungle 2," the villains drive bulldozers with recognizable CATERPILLAR trademarks to destroy Ape Mountain, and the narrator refers to the bulldozers as "deleterious dozers" and "maniacal machines." In the comedy film "Dickie Roberts: Former Child Star," the protagonist comically misuses a SLIP 'N SLIDE yellow water slide which results in his injury. This scene appears in advertisements and trailers for the film. Do the owners of the CATERPILLAR or SLIP 'N SLIDE marks have a viable federal dilution claim? *See Caterpillar Inc. v. Walt Disney*

Co., 287 F. Supp. 2d 913 (C.D. Ill. 2003); *Wham-O, Inc. v. Paramount Pictures Corp.*, 286 F. Supp. 2d 1254 (N.D. Cal. 2003).

10. The dilution statute requires that a mark be distinctive (either inherently or through secondary meaning) as well as famous in order to qualify for dilution protection. What if a famous mark is distinctive for plaintiff's goods or services but not for defendant's? Should it qualify for dilution protection for goods or services for which it is not distinctive? *See Hormel Foods Corp. v. Spam Arrest, LLC*, 2005 TTAB LEXIS 144 (T.T.A.B. Mar. 31, 2007) (SPAM held distinctive for food and merchandise but generic for unsolicited emails; defendant's SPAM ARREST mark covered software designed to protect against receipt of unwanted email).

11. The dilution statute applies to one who "commences use of a mark or trade name in commerce that is likely to cause dilution." Does a commercial printer use a mark in commerce if it "reproduces or offers to reproduce [another's] mark for customers" of its business? *See Nat'l Business Forms & Printing, Inc. v. Ford Motor Co.*, 671 F.3d 526 (5th Cir. 2012) (court looked to definition of a mark as "used by a person ... to identify and distinguish his or her own goods ... from those manufactured by another" to conclude that a commercial printer did not "use" Ford's marks to identify its printing business for dilution purposes).

Problem

Virgil's Sodas has developed a new product, which it has called "Dr. Better" and which its promotional website describes as follows:

> Virgil's Dr. Better is a classic Dr. Type soda recipe made naturally using the finest ingredients possible. We decided to make Dr. Better to rival with the super premium quality of our root beer. Our first step was to research the recipes used to make the original Dr. Type sodas from the early 1900's. Of course we found none since the recipe is a heavily guarded secret and our attempts to infiltrate and crack their safe failed. But we used our taste buds and knowledge of roots, spices and fruits to make a formula that surpasses any other Dr. type soda.

Were the producers of Dr. Pepper soda to bring a dilution action under section 43(c), how do you think the claim would fare?

a. Fame

National Pork Board v. Supreme Lobster and Seafood Company

96 U.S.P.Q.2d 1479 (T.T.A.B. 2010)

BUCHER, ADMINISTRATIVE TRADEMARK JUDGE:

Supreme Lobster and Seafood Company seeks registration on the Principal Register of the mark THE OTHER RED MEAT (*in standard character format*) for "fresh and frozen salmon" in International Class 29.

Registration has been opposed by National Pork Board (NPB) and National Pork Producers Council (NPPC). As their grounds for opposition, opposers assert that (1) applicant's mark when used in connection with its goods so resembles opposers' previously used and registered marks THE OTHER WHITE MEAT (*in standard character format*), for "association services namely, promoting the interests of members of the pork industry" in International Class 42, the "guitar pick" or "ham" design mark shown [below], registered for "promoting the interests of the members of the pork industry" in International Class 35, and "providing an Internet website featuring information about cooking and accompanying recipes" in International Class 43; THE OTHER WHITE MEAT (*in standard character format*), for "cookbooks, brochures about pork, pens, pencils, crayons, bumper stickers, and stickers" in International Class 16; shirts, t-shirts, sweatshirts, aprons, jackets, and hats" in International Class 25, and "providing an Internet website featuring food preparation/cooking information regarding pork and accompanying recipes" in International Class 43 as to be likely to cause confusion, to cause mistake or to deceive under Section 2(d) of the Lanham Act, 15 U.S.C. § 1052(d); and that (2) registration of applicant's mark will result in a likelihood of dilution under Section 43(c) of the Act, 15 U.S.C. § 1125(c).

Based upon the extensive evidence in this record, and for reasons discussed at length below, we sustain the opposition on the basis of a likelihood of dilution, and choose not to make a determination as to opposers' claim of likelihood of confusion.

....

From the beginning [in 1987], the national advertising campaign stressed that chicken and fish are not the only choices for a reduced-fat, balanced diet. The thrust of opposers' campaign was to create a positive effect on consumer attitudes about pork in the face of growing concerns about the health risks of eating red meat. Opposers' national print advertisements have for years stressed pork's nutritional benefits as well as its convenience. The advertising campaign for THE OTHER WHITE MEAT has also been waged on radio, television, billboards, taxi cabs and transit shelters....

As an example of added synergy, both retailers and food manufacturers have participated with opposers in co-branded advertising campaigns that promote the mark THE OTHER WHITE MEAT in conjunction with their own products and/or services. The examples include Campbell's food products, Miller Lite beer/Kraft food products and Kendall-Jackson wines. This is in addition to the regular and frequent advertising of the mark THE OTHER WHITE MEAT by supermarkets in their regular weekly newspaper circulars....

The mark is also promoted through advertising purchased by state pork producer associations that receive a portion of each year's total Pork Checkoff assessment funds.

Thus, in addition to the $500 million in demand enhancement activity that opposers have funded from 1987 to 2007, as much as an additional $50 million in promotional and marketing activities by the state associations (but supervised by NPB) has also enhanced the exposure of the mark THE OTHER WHITE MEAT.

Opposers have also scored public relations points through "earned media" activities designed to promote the pork industry under the mark THE OTHER WHITE MEAT, using celebrity spokespersons such as Peggy Fleming, Joan Lunden and Chicago's well-known Coach Mike Ditka, and by sponsoring race cars. Opposers' culinary marketing program garnered widespread news coverage through its "Celebrated Chefs" program and an annual "National Eat Dinner Together Week." Opposers promote the interests of the pork industry through numerous websites, some of which display the mark THE OTHER WHITE MEAT on every page of the site. During the month of July 2007, the dominant website, www.theotherwhitemeat.com, received almost a hundred thousand daily, unique visitors, with a total of almost six hundred thousand page views....

Similarly, opposers have run local and national advertising playing off the mark with tag-lines that read "The Other Backyard Barbecue," "The Other Stir-Fry," "The Other Romantic Dinner," "The Other Sunday Brunch," "The Other TV Dinner," "The Other Way to Spice Up Your Love Life," "The Other Steak Dinner," "The Other Prime Rib," and "The Other White Protein." In each case, these alternative slogans were always displayed in close conjunction with the central brand, THE OTHER WHITE MEAT, in an attempt to establish a close consumer perception around the phrase "The Other" in connection with promotion of the pork industry....

As part of its regular monitoring of its demand enhancement activities, as well as to comply with its obligation to report on such activities to the Agricultural Marketing Service of the USDA, opposers have since 1987 conducted semi-annual tracking surveys through independent research firms.... In response to the admittedly leading question "Have you read, seen or heard pork referred to as 'The Other White Meat?,'" these tracking studies have consistently shown public awareness of the mark THE OTHER WHITE MEAT at or above eighty-five percent of consumers nationwide.

In a separate study in the year 2000 ("the Northwestern Study"), ... researchers found that the mark THE OTHER WHITE MEAT was the fifth most recognized advertising slogan in America among the general adult population at that time....

Finally, in connection with this litigation, NPB engaged marketing research expert Robert Klein to conduct a survey testing the likelihood of dilution caused by applicant's intended mark. This research purported to show that more than thirty-five percent of the respondents, in response to an unaided question, associated applicant's slogan with NPB's slogan or the pork products it promotes.

Survey Evidence

Inasmuch as opposers and applicant have spent a great deal of time supporting and attacking, respectively, a prelitigation study and a litigation survey, we will discuss in detail the specifics of whether the results are probative to our determination herein.

Northwestern Study of 2000

....

[D]uring the last phase of the study (when twenty-five slogans were tested in more than a thousand telephone interviews), ... [t]he specific research goal was that of assessing the strength of THE OTHER WHITE MEAT in comparison with other well-known slogans. Respondents were asked whether they recognized a slogan and whether they could correctly attribute it to a brand, product or industry.[19]

Applicant attacks the aided awareness questioning used during the telephone survey. However, the methodology of this study did not lead respondents to a desired result by using inherently suggestive questions.... In assessing the proper evidentiary weight to be accorded to this evidence and testimony, we find the results to be probative of the public perceptions, and hence the renown, of opposers' claimed slogan.

....

Klein Dilution Survey of 2007

....

After playing a recording of applicant's slogan, the screener asked the respondents the following questions:

(4) "Thinking about the slogan you just heard THE OTHER RED MEAT, do any other advertising slogans or phrases come to mind?" [If answered "yes" continue to Q5]

(5) "What *other* advertising slogan or phrase comes to mind?"

Applicant charges that Question 4 is inappropriate "because it improperly suggests to survey respondents that another slogan or phrase exists that should be brought to mind" upon hearing applicant's slogan. However, the survey was intended to test the precise question of whether applicant's mark calls to mind opposers' mark or advertising campaigns.... We do not find this to an inappropriately leading question. An affirmative answer of another slogan is not presumed with the phrasing of " ... do any other advertising slogans ..." come to mind. We note that at no point in the survey did the screener ever mention opposers' mark or product. [Citations.] ...

Court opinions, ... as well as a leading commentator cited repeatedly by applicant, have confirmed that association queries are appropriate in light of the specific language of the current dilution provisions of the Lanham Act. Moreover, we find that the questions posed were clear and not leading. The survey was conducted by qualified persons following proper interview procedures, and in a manner that ensured objectivity.

19. The interviewer read each respondent a list of twenty-five advertising slogans. For each of the slogans, the respondent was asked if he/she recognized the slogan. If he/she responded affirmatively, the follow up question was to what brand, product or industry he/she attributed the slogan.

....

Finally, we note that the involved mark is an intent-to-use slogan with virtually no actual presence in the marketplace. Opposers' use of a well-designed telephone survey in this context appears to us totally appropriate. Applicant's adopted mark has not yet been used in commerce, and applicant could well choose to present the slogan visually in a myriad of ways, so there is no particular significance to visual stimuli in the case at hand.

Hence, we ... find the results of the survey to be probative on the issue of likelihood of dilution.

Dilution by blurring

....

A. Is the term THE OTHER WHITE MEAT famous?

... [T]he record is clear that NPPC, NPB and various state pork producer associations have spent more than $550 million dollars in Pork Checkoff funds on demand enhancement promotional activities over the more than twenty-year life of the mark, and that those dollars were spent on advertising and marketing activities that used the mark THE OTHER WHITE MEAT. In some instances, other marks and taglines were included, but every visual included in this extensive record shows that THE OTHER WHITE MEAT was the central focus of the advertising campaigns, not simply "wallpaper." The preponderance of the evidence in the record establishes that NPB's direct demand-enhancement campaign has expended, on average, more than $25 million per year during its lifetime....

... [S]ubstantial third-party advertising of the mark has taken place through cross-promotional and co-branded activities.

....

NPB's non-litigation consumer surveys—ranging from periodic tracking studies to the Northwestern Study of 2000—demonstrate a high degree of consumer and general public recognition of the mark. Tracking studies consistently have shown consumer recognition of the mark above the eighty-five percent level. Similarly, the Northwestern Study during the year 2000 showed nearly eighty percent awareness of the mark among the general adult population at that time. These researchers found that in terms of correct attribution between the slogan and the source, only four nationally known slogans ranked higher than THE OTHER WHITE MEAT Opposers point out that this means it was ranked higher than other well-known slogans such as JUST DO IT (Nike), DON'T LEAVE HOME WITHOUT IT (American Express), KING OF BEERS (Budweiser) and LIKE A GOOD NEIGHBOR (State Farm)....

Additionally, the record shows extensive references to the mark in the popular culture. The mark has made appearances on late night television shows, game shows, nationally syndicated comic strips, Hollywood box-office hits and as a variety of other references in the popular culture. Opposers argue that these cultural references are probative because they would not be so wide-spread if this slogan were not so famous to a substantial portion of the population.

Furthermore, the mark has been discussed in third-party publications, college textbooks on advertising and marketing, as a Harvard Business School Case Study, and in news reports in the nation's leading printed publications. The mark regularly shows up in published lists of famous marks, and is used as the instructional example by the Thomson Company on how to construct a trademark search for advertising slogans in the Thomson-Dialog database.

....

Accordingly, we find that the evidence demonstrates that THE OTHER WHITE MEAT is famous. It is among the most well-known advertising slogans in the U.S. given awareness rates at eighty to eighty-five percent of the general adult population and rates of correct source recognition at nearly seventy percent of the population. Awareness and recognition at this level has certainly supported a finding of fame in those rare instances where this Board has found a likelihood of dilution. *See 7-Eleven Inc. v. Wechler*, 83 USPQ2d 1715, 1727–28 (TTAB 2007) [fame for dilution purposes with survey showing awareness among seventy-three percent of general consumers]; and *Nasdaq Stock Market Inc. v. Antartica S.r.l.*, 69 USPQ2d 1718, 1737 (TTAB 2003) [fame for dilution purposes with survey showing awareness of the mark among eighty percent of investors].... All of this evidence taken together supports the conclusion that opposers' mark THE OTHER WHITE MEAT is famous among a broad spectrum of the general consuming public.

B. Was the mark THE OTHER WHITE MEAT famous before applicant's filing date?

The majority of the evidence in the record about the renown of opposers' slogan predates the involved application filing date of February 4, 2004. Therefore, we find that the fame of THE OTHER WHITE MEAT was well-established prior to the date that Supreme Lobster and Seafood Company filed the involved application.

[The Board went on to conclude that THE OTHER RED MEAT was likely to dilute THE OTHER WHITE MEAT through blurring].

Pinterest, Inc. v. Pintrips, Inc., 140 F. Supp. 3d 997 (N.D. Cal. 2015). (The case is described, *supra*, Chapter 8[A][2][b].) The court determined Pinterest was not a famous mark at the time Pintrips began using its mark in commerce in October 2011, or offering its services to the public in November 2012:

> Pinterest has provided no persuasive evidence that any of its marks were famous by October of 2011. Virtually all of the news articles offered by Pinterest were published after that date, and are thus irrelevant. Pinterest had approximately 1 million monthly users by August of 2011 (less than half a percent of the United States population), and, according to a Pinterest demonstrative summarizing data included in a Pinterest report, just less than 5 million monthly users by November 2011 (just under two percent of the

United States population). Neither figure comes close to suggesting that Pinterest had attained the level of prominence necessary for a brand to become part of the collective national consciousness. In fact, the Pinterest website was still operating as a closed, invitation-only website just several months before.... In addition, the "Pinterest" mark was not even registered until May of 2012. No reasonable weighing of these facts could satisfy the first element of the dilution analysis.

Moreover, Pinterest's dilution claim would fail on the same ground even were the Court to adopt Pinterest's proposed November 2012 date. Pinterest presented four types of evidence in support of its position: (1) contemporaneous news articles discussing Pinterest; (2) the volume of traffic on its website; (3) a survey conducted by a consulting service in July of 2012; and (4) the registration of its "Pinterest" mark. The Court will address each category in turn.

First, Pinterest presented approximately a dozen news articles published before November of 2012 that discuss Pinterest and its rapid growth. These articles were published by prominent newspapers and media outlets, including *The New York Times, The Wall Street Journal, The Los Angeles Times*, and *Fortune.* Of course, receiving publicity from the national media raises the awareness of a brand. However, it is clear from the content of these articles that Pinterest had not yet achieved the level of prominence necessary for a finding of fame at the time of publication. For example, many of the articles begin with a description of what Pinterest is and what it does, which would be unnecessary (or even baffling) for famous brands like Coca-Cola or Barbie. *See, e.g.*, TX160 (CNET article beginning with the sentence "Pinterest, an invitation-only site that describes itself as a pinboard to organize and share things you love, is growing at a phenomenal pace."); TX173 (*Wall Street Journal* article which begins by describing Pinterest as "the online scrapbooking website that has become a Silicon Valley darling because of its rapid user growth"). Other articles commented on how, until extremely recently, even local technology media barely knew of Pinterest's existence. *See* TX168 (CNN article observing that "[t]he web-based 'pinboard,' which launched almost two years ago, barely got a mention on Silicon Valley news sites until six months ago, when early adopters suddenly realized that a site with millions of monthly users had sprung up almost unnoticed by the tech press").

In short, these articles demonstrate that Pinterest had enjoyed rapid (and even unprecedented) growth in its user base in a very short period of time, which made the relatively new company a newsworthy subject for a number of publications. These articles also demonstrate that the articles' authors were not sure that their readership would know what Pinterest was without immediate explanation. A dozen (or even a few dozen) articles commenting on the newsworthy growth of a website does not suggest that the website has attained the level of fame necessary to prevail on a dilution claim. [Citation.] In fact, the tenor of the articles submitted strongly suggests the opposite.

Second, Pinterest presented evidence that its website drew 25 million monthly active users by October of 2012, which is about 8% of the U.S. population. However, the number of monthly users drawn by Pinterest in late 2012 is only a fraction of the number drawn by Yelp, the website at issue in the only case Pinterest cites in which a court referred to the number of monthly users as supporting a finding of fame. *See Yelp Inc. v. Catron*, 70 F. Supp. 3d 1082, 1096 (N.D. Cal. 2014) ("The reach of publicity of the Yelp Marks is extensive, as the Yelp Site averaged *102 million monthly unique visitors* between January and March 2013.") (emphasis added).

Third, Pinterest introduced a survey conducted in July of 2012, which found that 75% of the survey respondents recognized the name Pinterest. However, Pinterest did not call a witness with personal knowledge of how the survey was conducted or from where its pool of survey respondents was drawn. Accordingly, no testimony at trial established that the pool of survey respondents was drawn from the general public as opposed to a sub-group of individuals predisposed to be familiar with Pinterest.... In fact, there is a high likelihood that the survey pool was not drawn from the general public, given that it was comprised of a disproportionate percentage of female vs. male respondents: out of 837 interviews, 70% of respondents were female and 30% male. In addition, all respondents to the survey reported spending at least 90 minutes online in an average day for personal purposes alone, not including any time spent on work matters. *Id.* In short, Pinterest has not established that the July 2012 survey was conducted with a pool of respondents drawn from the general public, and, accordingly, the Court cannot consider its findings as evidence that the general public was familiar with Pinterest's marks.

Fourth, the Court agrees with Pinterest that the fact that its Pinterest mark was registered before November 2012—albeit only six months before—weighs slightly in favor of a finding of fame....

When these facts are weighed together, it is clear that Pinterest had not attained the status of a household name by November of 2012. The facts presented at trial suggest that Pinterest was a relatively new company that had received favorable media attention in response to its early growth. However, the number of Pinterest's monthly users in November of 2012 is dwarfed by the number of monthly users of Yelp, the company at issue in the only case cited by Pinterest on this point. That a sizeable (but still relatively small) sliver of the United States population used Pinterest in November of 2012 does not, without more, suggest that non-users would be familiar with its services. [Citation.] Pinterest simply has not demonstrated the extraordinarily high level of public awareness that a mark must reach in order to qualify as famous under the FTDA.... Accordingly, even if November 2012 were the appropriate date by which to measure fame, Pinterest's dilution claim still would fail.

Questions

1. Based on the *National Pork Board* decision, are brand awareness studies prior to an applicant's first use or constructive first use necessary to a finding that a mark is "famous" for dilution purposes?

2. Recall the considerations relevant to determining secondary meaning, *supra*, Chapter 2[B][2]. How differently do such considerations weigh in assessing fame for purposes of dilution?

3. Why is 8% of the U.S. population insufficient to establish fame? Should the court have inquired what proportion of the internet-using population 25 million persons represented? Is there a difference?

b. Blurring

Note: Surveying Dilution by "Blurring"

Parties in Lanham Act litigation offer consumer surveys to demonstrate (or contest) a variety of issues, from distinctiveness (secondary meaning or genericism), to likelihood of point-of-sale and post-sale confusion, to misrepresentations in false advertising actions. One would therefore expect surveys to play a role in litigating dilution claims. Whatever courts' skepticism of survey evidence in general, however, dilution surveys appear even more problematic. Section 43(c)(2)(B) defines "dilution by blurring" as "association arising from the similarity between a mark or trade name and a famous mark that impairs the distinctiveness of the famous mark." While "an association" seems not so vague as to resist testing, the meaning (much less the measurability) of "impairs the distinctiveness" is far more murky. Courts' uncertainty regarding the nature of the harm the parties' surveys purport to measure may well underlie their varying assessments of the weight to accord these surveys.

Because it is difficult to measure a harm without knowing what it is, perhaps the first task of the survey designer should be to identify what harm is caused by dilution (how a mark's distinctiveness might be impaired) and then to induce that harm under controlled and recordable conditions. Consider Schechter's seminal *The Rational Basis of Trademark Protection*, and Professor Stadler's restatement of Schechter, as well as Judge Posner's views on dilution harm in *Ty Inc. v. Perryman*, and Professor Beebe's characterization of antidilution law as modern sumptuary law. Does a consensus on the impairment of a mark's distinctiveness emerge from these authorities? If so, how would one go about demonstrating it to a court, by survey or other means?

As we have seen, 15 U.S.C. § 1125(c)(2)(B) lists six nonexclusive factors which courts may consider in deciding whether dilution by blurring is likely to occur.

Typically, rather than identifying "impairment," plaintiff's surveys attempt to assess "any actual association between the mark or trade name and the famous mark," although the "similarity of the marks" and "degree of recognition of the famous mark" factors are also amenable to survey proof. Plaintiffs have focused on the association prong of the statutory text of the TDRA, as if showing association dispensed them from demonstrating likely harm in a broader sense, because they appear to assume that impairment of distinctiveness would naturally follow from the association of defendant's mark with plaintiff's. For example, in *Gap, Inc. v. G.A.P. Adventures Inc.*, 100 U.S.P.Q.2d 1417 (S.D.N.Y. 2011), Gap, the clothing vendor, charged the G.A.P. Adventures travel agency with dilution.

> The population for both [of plaintiff's expert, Dr. Gerald Ford's] surveys consisted of men and women 18 years of age or older who reported that they were likely, within the next year, to use the Internet to search for information on travel tours outside the continental United States.
>
> This survey population was appropriate. Although G.A.P. Adventures' expert, Dr. Yoram Wind, gave the opinion that respondents should have been asked, more specifically, whether they were likely to search for information on adventure- and geo-tourism travel tours, because that is G.A.P. Adventures' target audience, Poon Tip [G.A.P. Adventures' co-founder] testified as to the wide variety of travel tours that G.A.P. Adventures now offers, to appeal to varying and extensive segments of the population. The survey population was therefore appropriate.
>
> Respondents for both of Ford's surveys were selected randomly and assigned to either a test cell or a control cell.
>
> Ford's survey addresses the likelihood of dilution using G.A.P. Adventures' old logo.
>
> 1. In the test cell, respondents were exposed to an abbreviated version of G.A.P. Adventures' website that used the old logo on the home page and that linked to hundreds of other G.A.P. Adventures web pages.
>
> 2. In the control cell, respondents were exposed to a website identical to that used in the test cell, except that "G.A.P." was replaced with the words "Great Adventure People" wherever it appeared. The "great adventure people" tagline was eliminated from the website as redundant. Otherwise, the questions and procedures for the test cell and the control cell were identical.
>
> 3. Respondents in both cells were asked, "What company or brand, if any, comes to mind when you see the name on this website?" If the respondent identified a company or brand, he or she was asked follow-up questions about that company or brand. Respondents were also asked what other companies or brands, if any, came to mind.
>
> 4. When shown the test cell website, 60.95% of respondents reported that Gap, either alone or in conjunction with another company or brand, came to mind.

> 5. When shown the control cell website, none of the respondents reported that Gap, alone or in conjunction with another company or brand, came to mind.
>
> 6. This survey demonstrates that exposure to G.A.P. Adventures' old logo caused an association with Gap's marks for 60.95% of adults in the relevant universe. This association was attributable to G.A.P. Adventures' use of "G.A.P." in its logo—the absence of "G.A.P." was the only difference between the test cell and the control cell.
>
> 7. Several of the verbatim responses demonstrate further that consumers associate G.A.P. Adventures' logo with plaintiffs.
>
> ....
>
> I accept the appropriateness and relevance of Dr. Ford's surveys. I find that they show a likelihood of association between G.A.P. Adventures and variants, with plaintiffs' trademark "Gap."

In *Visa International Service Ass'n v. JSL Corp.*, 590 F. Supp. 2d 1306 (D. Nev. 2008), *aff'd*, 610 F.3d 1088 (9th Cir. 2010), Ninth Circuit decision excerpted *infra* this Chapter, the court admitted a similar survey that Visa used to show a likelihood of dilution of the credit card service's mark through association with defendant's online English-language course. Visa's survey randomly selected the participants from a list of business owners, and exposed them either to an actual eVisa page or to a control page in which "ePassport" replaced "eVisa." Participants were then asked if the brand name on the webpage ("eVisa" or "ePassport") reminded them of any other company or brand name, and if yes, what company or brand name. The court rejected eVisa's challenge to the survey's admissibility (citations to record omitted):

> Defendant's arguments are without merit. The Blair survey in fact did present the EVISA mark in the context of Defendant's website as it appeared on February 1, 2001, forty-two days before this lawsuit began. Thus, the Blair survey presented the EVISA mark in its proper context. Moreover, Defendant has provided no authority for the proposition that a scientifically valid survey must replicate the process by which a person will come into contact with the relevant mark. In contrast, Plaintiff presented evidence that accepted scientific methods require only that consumers are shown the mark at issue in the context in which it appears in the marketplace.
>
> Finally, Defendant cannot complain that Blair's survey was directed at an inappropriate population. The only evidence provided by Defendant as to the identity of its customers indicates that, with one exception, they are businesses. The Blair survey is therefore admissible under Rule 702 and is strong evidence that there is actual association between the marks.

But, admitting a survey is one thing, concluding that the survey demonstrates association is another, and concluding that the association the survey shows also constitutes dilution by blurring yet another. The *Gap* and *Visa* courts reached opposite conclusions about a likelihood of blurring. The *Visa* court, equating association with impairment of distinctiveness through "whittling away," found a likelihood of dilution, ruling:

> With regard to the fifth factor—whether the user of the mark or trade name intended to create an association with the famous mark—the court agrees with Defendant that the factor weighs against a finding that Defendant has likely caused dilution of the VISA mark. However, the court also agrees with Plaintiff that the degree to which consumers actually associate the VISA and EVISA marks is more important to a finding of likely dilution than Defendant's intent. At bottom, trademark dilution is an objective inquiry into whether an alleged diluter's mark is likely to contribute to the gradual whittling away of a senior mark's value. *See Playboy Enterprises, Inc. v. Welles*, 279 F.3d 796, 805 (9th Cir. 2002). Therefore, because Plaintiff has made an exceptionally strong showing on the four other factors listed in § 1125(c)(2)(B), the court concludes as a matter of law that Defendant's use of the EVISA mark is likely to cause dilution by blurring of Plaintiff's VISA mark. Defendant has not presented evidence from which a rational fact finder could conclude otherwise.

By contrast, the *Gap* court found demonstration of association insufficient to prove blurring:

> Gap's marks are famous and widely recognized by the general consuming public. Gap's marks had achieved their fame by the time G.A.P. Adventures was founded, G.A.P. Adventures uses its marks in commerce, G.A.P. Adventures' marks and Gap's marks are similar; Gap's marks are strong in terms of both inherent and acquired distinctiveness; Gap's use of its marks is substantially exclusive in relation to the goods sold in its stores; Poon Tip intended to create an association with Gap (and he acted to strengthen that association over time); and Dr. Ford's surveys are probative of a likelihood of association between G.A.P. Adventures' marks and Gap's marks.
>
> However, I am not able to find that the association between the marks "impairs the distinctiveness of the famous mark." 15 U.S.C. § 1125(c)(2)(B); *see Starbucks Corp.* [*v. Wolfe's Borough Coffee, Inc.*], 588 F.3d [97] at 109 [2d Cir. 2009)]. Gap's proofs establish that consumers are likely to associate G.A.P. Adventures' marks with Gap's marks as a result of the similarities between the marks. However, "[t]he fact that people 'associate' the accused mark with the famous mark does not in itself prove the likelihood of dilution by blurring." 4 J. *Thomas McCarthy, McCarthy On Trademarks And Unfair Competition* § 24:120 (4th ed. 2011). Gap has not proved that, as a result of the likelihood that consumers will associate the marks, Gap is likely to suffer an impairment of the distinctiveness of its marks. Gap has not proved any injury to its trademarks. Because Gap has not proved a likelihood of dilution by blurring, I grant judgment for G.A.P. Adventures, dismissing Gap's federal dilution claim.

If you were Gap's counsel, how would you draw the link from association to "blurring"? What survey questions would (could) you devise? What other kinds of evidence would you adduce?

Visa International Service Association v. JSL Corp.

610 F.3d 1088 (9th Cir. 2010)

Kozinski, Chief Circuit Judge:

She sells sea shells by the sea shore. That's swell, but how about Shell espresso, Tide motor oil, Apple bicycles and Playboy computers? We consider the application of anti-dilution law to trademarks that are also common English words.

Facts

Joseph Orr runs eVisa, a "multilingual education and information business that exists and operates exclusively on the Internet," at www.evisa.com. At least he did, until the district court enjoined him. Orr traces the name eVisa back to an English language tutoring service called "Eikaiwa Visa" that he ran while living in Japan. "Eikaiwa" is Japanese for English conversation, and the "e" in eVisa is short for Eikaiwa. The use of the word "visa" in both eVisa and Eikaiwa Visa is meant to suggest "the ability to travel, both linguistically and physically, through the English-speaking world." Orr founded eVisa shortly before his return to America, where he started running it out of his apartment in Brooklyn, New York.

Visa International Service Association sued JSL Corporation, through which Orr operates eVisa, claiming that eVisa is likely to dilute the Visa trademark. The district court granted summary judgment for Visa, and JSL appeals.

Analysis

A plaintiff seeking relief under federal anti-dilution law must show that its mark is famous and distinctive, that defendant began using its mark in commerce after plaintiff's mark became famous and distinctive, and that defendant's mark is likely to dilute plaintiff's mark. *See Jada Toys, Inc. v. Mattel, Inc.*, 518 F.3d 628, 634 (9th Cir. 2008). JSL does not dispute that the Visa mark is famous and distinctive or that JSL began using the eVisa mark in commerce after Visa achieved its renown. JSL claims only that the district court erred when it found as a matter of law that eVisa was likely to dilute the Visa trademark.

There are two types of dilution, but here we are concerned only with dilution by blurring, which occurs when a mark previously associated with one product also becomes associated with a second. *See* 15 U.S.C. § 1125(c)(2)(B); *Mattel, Inc. v. MCA Records, Inc.*, 296 F.3d 894, 903–04 (9th Cir. 2002). This weakens the mark's ability to evoke the first product in the minds of consumers. "For example, Tylenol snowboards, Netscape sex shops and Harry Potter dry cleaners would all weaken the 'commercial magnetism' of these marks and diminish their ability to evoke their original associations." *Mattel*, 296 F.3d at 903. Dilution isn't confusion; quite the contrary. Dilution occurs when consumers form new and different associations with the plaintiff's mark. "Even if no one suspects that the maker of analgesics has entered into the snowboard business, the Tylenol mark will now bring to mind two products, not one." *Id.*

... Congress has enumerated factors courts may use to analyze the likelihood of dilution, including the similarity between the two marks and the distinctiveness and recognition of the plaintiff's mark. 15 U.S.C. § 1125(c)(2)(B)(i), (ii), (iv); *see also PerfumeBay.com, Inc. v. eBay, Inc.*, 506 F.3d 1165, 1181 n.9 (9th Cir. 2007)....

The marks here are effectively identical; the only difference is the prefix "e," which is commonly used to refer to the electronic or online version of a brand. That prefix does no more to distinguish the two marks than would the words "Corp." or "Inc." tacked onto the end. *See Horphag Research Ltd. v. Garcia*, 475 F.3d 1029, 1036 (9th Cir. 2007) (use of identical mark provides "circumstantial evidence" of dilution).

And Visa is a strong trademark. "In general, the more unique or arbitrary a mark, the more protection a court will afford it." *Nutri/System, Inc. v. Con-Stan Indus., Inc.*, 809 F.2d 601, 605 (9th Cir. 1987). The Visa mark draws on positive mental associations with travel visas, which make potentially difficult transactions relatively simple and facilitate new opportunities and experiences. Those are good attributes for a credit card. But those associations are sufficiently remote that the word visa wouldn't make people think of credit cards if it weren't for the Visa brand. "This suggests that any association is the result of goodwill and deserves broad protection from potential infringers." *Dreamwerks Prod. Grp., Inc. v. SKG Studio*, 142 F.3d 1127, 1130 n.7 (9th Cir. 1998). Visa also introduced uncontroverted evidence that Visa is the world's top brand in financial services and is used for online purchases almost as often as all other credit cards combined. This was enough to support the district court's summary judgment.

....

JSL claims the eVisa mark cannot cause dilution because, in addition to being an electronic payment network that's everywhere you want to be, a visa is a travel document authorizing the bearer to enter a country's territory. When a trademark is also a word with a dictionary definition, it may be difficult to show that the trademark holder's use of the word is sufficiently distinctive to deserve anti-dilution protection because such a word is likely to be descriptive or suggestive of an essential attribute of the trademarked good. Moreover, such a word may already be in use as a mark by third parties. For example, we rejected a dilution claim by Trek Bicycle Corporation for its "Trek" mark in part because it played heavily off the dictionary meaning of "trek," suggesting that the bicycles were designed for long or arduous journeys. *Thane Int'l, Inc. v. Trek Bicycle Corp.*, 305 F.3d 894, 912 n.14 (9th Cir. 2002). Additionally, the creators of the Star Trek series had already "incorporated this common English language word into their trademark," and the "glow of this celebrity ma[de] it difficult for Trek to obtain fame using the same word." *Id.* In our case, Visa's use of the word visa is sufficiently distinctive because it plays only weakly off the dictionary meaning of the term and JSL presented no evidence that a third party has used the word as a mark.

It's true that the word visa is used countless times every day for its common English definition, but the prevalence of such non-trademark use does not undermine the uniqueness of Visa as a trademark.... "The significant factor is not whether the word itself is common, but whether the way the word is used in a particular context is unique enough to warrant trademark protection." *Wynn Oil Co. v. Thomas*, 839 F.2d 1183, 1190 n.4 (6th Cir. 1988). In the context of anti-dilution law, the "particular context" that matters is use of the word in commerce to identify a good or service. There are, for instance, many camels, but just one Camel; many tides, but just one Tide. Camel cupcakes and Tide calculators would dilute the value of those marks. Likewise, despite widespread use of the word visa for its common English meaning, the introduction of the eVisa mark to the marketplace means that there are now two products, and not just one, competing for association with that word. This is the quintessential harm addressed by anti-dilution law.

JSL is not using the word visa for its literal dictionary definition, and this would be a different case if it were. Visa does not claim that it could enforce its Visa trademark to prevent JSL from opening "Orr's Visa Services," any more than Apple could shut down Orr's Apple Orchard or Camel could fold up Orr's Camel Breeders. Visa doesn't own the word "visa" and may not "deplete the stock of useful words" by asserting otherwise. [Citations.] Conferring anti-dilution rights to common English words would otherwise be untenable, as whole swaths of the dictionary could be taken out of circulation. Nor would a suit against Orr's Visa Services advance the purpose of anti-dilution law. Such use of the word would not create a new association for the word with a product; it would merely evoke the word's existing dictionary meaning, as to which no one may claim exclusivity.

JSL argues that its use of the word "visa" is akin to Orr's Visa Services because the eVisa mark is meant to "connote the ability to travel, both linguistically and physically, through the English-speaking world" and therefore employs the word's common English meaning. JSL's site depicted the eVisa mark next to a booklet that looks like a passport, and it divided the services offered into the categories "Travel Passport," "Language Passport" and "Technology Passport." But these allusions to the dictionary definition of the word visa do not change the fact that JSL has created a novel meaning for the word: to identify a "multilingual education and information business." This multiplication of meanings is the essence of dilution by blurring. Use of the word "visa" to refer to travel visas is permissible because it doesn't have this effect; the word elicits only the standard dictionary definition. Use of the word visa in a trademark to refer to a good or service other than a travel visa, as in this case, undoubtedly does have this effect; the word becomes associated with two products, rather than one. This is true even when use of the word also gestures at the word's dictionary definition.

JSL's allusions to international travel are more obvious and heavy-handed than Visa's, and JSL claims that its use of the word is therefore "different" from Visa's. That's true; Visa plays only weakly off the word's association with international travel, whereas JSL embraced the metaphor with gusto. But dilution always involves use of a mark by a defendant that is "different" from the plaintiff's use; the injury addressed by anti-dilution law in fact occurs when marks are placed in new and different contexts, thereby weakening the mark's ability to bring to mind the plaintiff's goods or services. *See Mattel*, 296 F.3d at 903. The only context that matters is that the marks are both used in commerce as trademarks to identify a good or service, as they undoubtedly are in this case.

The district court was quite right in granting summary judgment to Visa and enjoining JSL's use of the mark.

AFFIRMED.

Questions

1. Would it have made a difference in *Visa* if defendant's services were arranging foreign tours? Or arranging tours of New York City?

2. If the essence of dilution by blurring is that the "mark will now bring to mind two products, not one," does it follow that an action for blurring should lie only when the mark is used for a single product or service? Are brands that cover multiple products inherently incapable of being blurred—or, put another way, has the producer already blurred the mark by applying it to a variety of goods, especially if these are unrelated?

Starbucks Corp. v. Wolfe's Borough Coffee, Inc.

588 F.3d 97 (2d Cir. 2009)

Miner, Circuit Judge:

Plaintiffs-appellants, Starbucks Corporation and Starbucks U.S. Brands, LLC (together, "Starbucks"), appeal from a judgment entered on June 5, 2008, in the United States District Court for the Southern District of New York (Swain, J.), following a bench trial, in favor of defendant-appellee, Wolfe's Borough Coffee, Inc., d/b/a Black Bear Micro Roastery ("Black Bear"). The District Court found that Starbucks failed to demonstrate entitlement to relief on its (1) federal trademark infringement, dilution, and unfair competition claims brought pursuant to the Lanham Act, 15 U.S.C. §§ 1114(1), 1125, 1127; (2) state trademark dilution claims brought pursuant to New York Gen. Bus. Law § 360-l; and (3) unfair competition claim under New York common law. We vacate, in part, the District Court's decision and remand for further proceedings on the issue of whether Starbucks demonstrated a likelihood of dilution by "blurring" under federal trademark law. In all other respects, the judgment of the learned District Court is affirmed.

I. BACKGROUND

A. Preliminary Facts

... Since its founding, Starbucks has grown to over 8,700 retail locations in the United States, Canada, and 34 foreign countries and territories. In addition to operating its retail stores, Starbucks supplies its coffees to hundreds of restaurants, supermarkets, airlines, sport and entertainment venues, motion picture theaters, hotels, and cruise ship lines. Starbucks also maintains an internet site that generates over 350,000 "hits" per week from visitors.

In conducting all of its commercial activities, Starbucks prominently displays its registered "Starbucks" marks (the "Starbucks Marks") on its products and areas of business. The Starbucks Marks include, inter alia, the tradename "Starbucks" and its logo, which is circular and generally contains a graphic of a mermaid-like siren encompassed by the phrase "Starbucks Coffee." Starbucks "has been the subject of U.S. trademark registrations continuously since 1985" and has approximately 60 U.S. trademark registrations....

From fiscal years 2000 to 2003, Starbucks spent over $136 million on advertising, promotion, and marketing activities. These promotional activities included television and radio commercials, print advertising, and in-store displays, and "prominently feature[d] (or, in the case of radio, mention[ed]) the Starbucks Marks, which Starbucks considers to be critical to the maintenance of its positive public image and identity." Starbucks also enhanced its commercial presence by permitting the use of its products and retail stores in Hollywood films and popular television programs. These films and programs contained scenes in which the Starbucks Marks were also "prominently displayed."

....

Black Bear, also a company engaged in the sale of coffee products, has its principal place of business in Tuftonboro, New Hampshire.... Black Bear is a relatively small company owned by Jim Clark and his wife. It is a family-run business that "manufactures and sells ... roasted coffee beans and related goods via mail order, internet order, and at a limited number of New England supermarkets." Black Bear also sold coffee products from a retail outlet called "The Den," in Portsmouth, New Hampshire....

In April 1997, Black Bear began selling a "dark roasted blend" of coffee called "Charbucks Blend" and later "Mister Charbucks" (together, the "Charbucks Marks"). Charbucks Blend was sold in a packaging that showed a picture of a black bear above the large font "BLACK BEAR MICRO ROASTERY." The package informed consumers that the coffee was roasted and "Air Quenched" in New Hampshire and, in fairly large font, that "You wanted it dark ... You've got it dark!" Mister Charbucks was sold in a packaging that showed a picture of a man walking above the large font "Mister Charbucks." The package also informed consumers that the coffee was roasted in New Hampshire by "The Black Bear Micro Roastery" and that the coffee was "ROASTED TO THE EXTREME ... FOR THOSE WHO LIKE THE EXTREME."

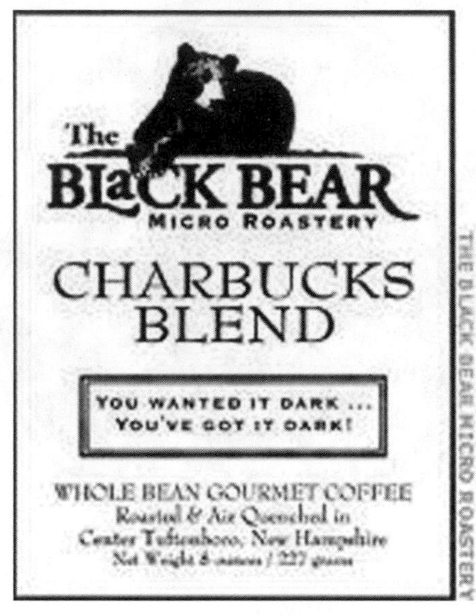

....

II. DISCUSSION

....

B. Federal Trademark Dilution

....

Federal law specifies six non-exhaustive factors for the courts to consider in determining whether there is dilution by blurring.... The District Court found that the second, third, and fourth factors favored Starbucks, and those findings are not challenged in this appeal.

With respect to the first factor—the degree of similarity between the marks—the District Court did not clearly err in finding that the Charbucks Marks were minimally similar to the Starbucks Marks. Although "Ch" arbucks is similar to "St" arbucks in sound and spelling, it is evident from the record that the Charbucks Marks—as they are presented to consumers—are minimally similar to the Starbucks Marks. The Charbucks line of products are presented as either "Mister Charbucks" or "Charbucks

Blend" in packaging that displays the "Black Bear" name in no subtle manner, and the packaging also makes clear that Black Bear is a "Micro Roastery" located in New Hampshire. *See Playtex Prods., Inc.* [*v. Georgia-Pacific Corp.*] 390 F.3d [158,] at 167–68 [2d Cir. 2004] (considering "the differences in the ways [the marks] are presented" in determining similarity in dilution action); *cf. Star Indus.* [*v. Bacardi & Co.*] 412 F.3d [373] at 386 [2d Cir. 2005] ("In assessing similarity [in the infringement context], courts look to the overall impression created by the logos and the context in which they are found and consider the totality of factors that could cause confusion among prospective purchasers"). Moreover, Black Bear's package design for Charbucks coffee is "different in imagery, color, and format from Starbucks' logo and signage."

For example, either a graphic of a bear or a male person is associated with Charbucks, and those marks are not comparable to the Starbucks graphic of a siren in pose, shape, art-style, gender, or overall impression.... To the extent the Charbucks Marks are presented to the public through Black Bear's website, the dissimilarity between the marks is still evident as the Charbucks brand of coffee is accompanied by Black Bear's domain name, www.blackbearcoffee.com, and other products, such as shirts and cups, displaying Black Bear's name.

Furthermore, we note that it is unlikely that "Charbucks" will appear to consumers outside the context of its normal use, since "Charbucks" is not directly identifiable with the actual product, i.e., coffee beans. *Cf. Nabisco v. PF Brands, Inc.*, 191 F.3d 208, 213, 218 (2d Cir. 1999) (observing that Pepperidge Farm's famous "goldfish" mark may be identified outside of the packaging because the goldfish cracker itself is the famous mark).... To be sure, consumers may simply refer to "Mister Charbucks" or "Charbucks Blend" in conversation; however, it was not clearly erroneous for the District Court to find that the "Mister" prefix or "Blend" suffix lessened the similarity between the Charbucks Marks and the Starbucks Marks in the court's overall assessment of similarity.

... Starbucks asserts that the District Court should have ignored the term "Mister" or "Blend" before or after "Charbucks" in assessing the "degree of similarity" factor because those terms are generic and "too weak to serve a brand-identifying function." This argument to ignore relevant evidence is unfounded in the law. [Citation.] And in any event, even if the core term "Charbucks" were used to identify a product as a stand-alone term, such finding would not be dispositive of the District Court's overall assessment of the degree of similarity. In this case, the District Court's reasons for a finding of minimal similarity between the Charbucks Marks and the Starbucks Marks were well supported by the record, as explained above.

Upon its finding that the marks were not substantially similar, however, the District Court concluded that "[t]his dissimilarity alone is sufficient to defeat [Starbucks'] blurring claim, and in any event, this factor at a minimum weighs strongly against [Starbucks] in the dilution analysis." We conclude that the District Court erred to the extent it required "substantial" similarity between the marks, and, in this connection, we note that the court may also have placed undue significance on the similarity factor in determining the likelihood of dilution in its alternative analysis.

... The current federal statute defines dilution by blurring as an "association arising from the similarity between a mark ... and a famous mark that impairs the distinctiveness of the famous mark," and the statute lists six non-exhaustive factors for determining the existence of an actionable claim for blurring. 15 U.S.C. § 1125(c)(2)(B). Although "similarity" is an integral element in the definition of "blurring," we find it significant that the federal dilution statute does not use the words "very" or "substantial" in connection with the similarity factor to be considered in examining a federal dilution claim. *See* 15 U.S.C. § 1125(c). [Citation.]

Indeed, one of the six statutory factors informing the inquiry as to whether the allegedly diluting mark "impairs the distinctiveness of the famous mark" is "[t]he degree of similarity between the mark or trade name and the famous mark." 15 U.S.C. § 1125(c)(2)(B)(i). Consideration of a "degree" of similarity as a factor in determining the likelihood of dilution does not lend itself to a requirement that the similarity between the subject marks must be "substantial" for a dilution claim to succeed. Moreover, were we to adhere to a substantial similarity requirement for all dilution by blurring claims, the significance of the remaining five factors would be materially diminished because they would have no relevance unless the degree of similarity between the marks are initially determined to be "substantial." ... Accordingly, the District Court erred to the extent it focused on the absence of "substantial similarity" between the Charbucks Marks and the Starbucks Marks to dispose of Starbucks' dilution claim. We note that the court's error likely affected its view of the importance of the other factors in analyzing the blurring claim, which must ultimately focus on whether an association, arising from the similarity between the subject marks, "impairs the distinctiveness of the famous mark."

Turning to the remaining two disputed factors—(1) whether the user of the mark intended to create an association with the famous mark, and (2) whether there is evidence of any actual association between the mark and the famous mark—we conclude that the District Court also erred in considering these factors.

The District Court determined that Black Bear possessed the requisite intent to associate Charbucks with Starbucks but that this factor did not weigh in favor of Starbucks because Black Bear did not act in "bad faith." The determination of an "intent to associate," however, does not require the additional consideration of whether bad faith corresponded with that intent. The plain language of section 1125(c) requires only the consideration of "[w]hether the user of the mark or trade name intended to create an association with the famous mark." *See* 15 U.S.C. § 1125(c)(2)(B)(v). Thus, where, as here, the allegedly diluting mark was created with an intent to associate with the famous mark, this factor favors a finding of a likelihood of dilution.

The District Court also determined that there was not an "actual association" favoring Starbucks in the dilution analysis. Starbucks, however, submitted the results of a telephone survey where 3.1% of 600 consumers responded that Starbucks was the possible source of Charbucks. The survey also showed that 30.5% of consumers responded "Starbucks" to the question: "[w]hat is the first thing that comes to mind when you hear the name 'Charbucks.'" In rejecting Starbucks' claim of actual association, the District Court referred to evidence supporting the absence of "actual confusion" to conclude that "the evidence is insufficient to make the ... factor weigh in [Starbucks'] favor to any significant degree." This was error, as the absence of actual or even of a likelihood of confusion does not undermine evidence of trademark dilution. *See* 15 U.S.C. § 1125(c)(2)(B); *accord Nabisco*, 191 F.3d at 221 (stating that while a showing of consumer confusion is relevant in determining dilution by blurring, the absence of confusion "has no probative value" in the dilution analysis).

Accordingly, in light of the foregoing, we remand to the District Court for consideration of Starbucks' claim of trademark dilution by blurring under 15 U.S.C. § 1125(c)(2)(B).

Starbucks Corp. v. Wolfe's Borough Coffee, Inc., 101 U.S.P.Q.2d 1212 (S.D.N.Y. 2011). On remand, the Southern District of New York declined to enter an injunction. Reviewing the evidence and applying the Second Circuit's analysis, the court cautioned that not every commercial reference to a famous mark is likely to "blur" it:

Likelihood of Dilution by Blurring

> The ultimate analytical question before the Court is not simply whether there has been an association between the marks. As the Second Circuit explained in *Starbucks IV*, the ultimate analytical question presented by a dilution-by-blurring claim is whether there is an association, arising from the similarity of the relevant marks, that impairs the distinctiveness of the famous mark. The Court evaluates the non-exclusive statutory factors in light of that ultimate question.
>
> The Court is also mindful of the purposes and core principles of trademark law when analyzing a blurring claim. It is settled law that trademarks do not create a "right-in-gross" or an unlimited right at large. [Citations.] Federal anti-dilution law should not be read to "prohibit all uses of a distinctive mark that the owner prefers not be made." *Nabisco Inc. v. P.F. Brands, Inc.*, 191 F.3d 208, 224 n.6; see also 4 McCarthy on Trademarks § 24:67 ("[N]o antidilution law should be so interpreted and applied as to result in granting the owner of a famous mark the automatic right to exclude any and all uses of similar marks in all product or service lines."). Antidilution law has been called "a scalpel, not a battle axe," and should be applied with care after rigorous evidentiary examination by the courts. 4 McCarthy § 24:67.
>
> ... [T]he distinctiveness, recognition, and exclusivity of use factors weigh in Plaintiff's favor. Indeed, Plaintiff's evidence on all three of these factors is strong. None of the three, however, is dependent on any consideration of the nature of the challenged marks or any defendant's use of any challenged mark. Thus, although these factors are significant insofar as they establish clearly Plaintiff's right to protection of its marks against dilution, they are

> not informative as to whether any association arising from similarity of the marks used by Defendant to Plaintiff's marks is likely to impair the distinctiveness of Plaintiff's marks.
>
> A fourth factor—intent to associate—also weighs in Plaintiff's favor, as Defendant's principal testified during trial that, by using the term Charbucks, he meant to evoke an image of dark-roasted coffee of the type offered by Starbucks.
>
> Similarity of the marks and association between the marks are obviously important factors. The statutory language leaves no doubt in this regard—dilution "is association arising from the similarity between a mark or trade name and a famous mark that impairs the distinctiveness of the famous mark." 15 U.S.C.A. § 1125 (c)(2)(B) (West 2009). It is thus appropriate to examine carefully, in considering the significance of both the evidence of similarity and the evidence of actual association, the degree to which any likelihood of dilution by blurring has been shown to arise from similarity between Defendant's marks and those of Plaintiff.... [T]he marks being compared in this case are only minimally similar as they are presented in commerce, and the evidence of association weighs no more than minimally in Plaintiff's favor.
>
> After considering all of the evidence and noting the dissimilarity of the marks as used in commerce, the weakness of the survey evidence, and the fact that consumers encounter Defendant's Charbucks term only in conjunction with other marks unique to Defendant, the Court holds that the Charbucks marks are only weakly associated with the minimally similar Starbucks marks and, thus, are not likely to impair the distinctiveness of the famous Starbucks marks. In other words, Plaintiff has failed to carry its burden of proving that Defendant's use of its marks, as evidenced on the record before the Court, is likely to cause dilution by blurring.

Emphasizing that plaintiff bore the burden of establishing likelihood of dilution, and the dissimilarity of the marks, the Second Circuit affirmed the District Court's rejection of a likelihood of dilution by blurring claim. *See Starbucks Corp. v. Wolfe's Borough Coffee, Inc.* 736 F.3d 198 (2d Cir. 2013).

Questions

1. Recall the "bridging the gap" factor in various Circuits' multi-factor tests for determining whether there is a likelihood of confusion. To what extent does the courts' evaluation of that factor for assessing likelihood of confusion resemble the courts' determinations of impairment by likelihood of blurring? Should the two inquiries be similar?

2. In *The Continuing Debacle of U.S. Antidilution Law: Evidence from One Year of Trademark Dilution Revision Act Case Law*, 24 Santa Clara Computer & High Tech. L.J. 449 (2008), Prof. Barton Beebe suggested that when dilution claims are pleaded together with infringement claims, a court will almost never find dilution if it has ruled that confusion is unlikely. Does it also follow that a successful dilution claim could have been brought as likelihood of confusion claim? To what extent do the above cases bear out either proposition?

3. The Starbucks court on remand found the dissimilarity of the Starbucks and Charbucks word marks determinative in assessing likelihood of blurring. How similar does trade dress need to be in order to be potentially dilutive? For example, Adidas uses the three-stripe design on footwear, which is registered as shown below. Would a competitor that uses a two or four-stripe design, such as the shoe shown below, be liable for dilution? For likelihood of confusion? *See Adidas-America, Inc. v. Payless Shoesource, Inc.*, 546 F. Supp. 2d 1029 (D. Or. 2008).

c. Tarnishment

Nordstrom, Inc. v. Nomorerack Retail Group, Inc., 2013 U.S. Dist. LEXIS 41810 (W.D. Wash., March 25, 2013). Nordstrom Rack first opened as a brick and mortar fashion retailer in the 1980s, selling slow-moving merchandise from flagship Nordstrom stores at clearance prices. Nordstrom Rack's business has grown significantly, including online under the URL http://www.nordstromrack.com. Nordstrom owns three federally registered trademarks in conjunction with this business: RACK; THE RACK and NORDSTROM RACK. NoMoreRack operates a members-only shopping website that offers steep discounts on clothing, accessories, fragrances, home products, appliances, electronics, software and toys. NoMoreRack is exclusively an online retail business, which operates under the URL "nomorerack.com." Customers shop the daily "events" listed on the site, which are deals that last for a limited time. In addition, NoMoreRack runs a member referral program on its site called "FriendRack." NoMoreRack's business has grown significantly through its U.S. customer base.

Nordstrom brought a variety of Lanham Act claims, including trademark infringement and dilution, against NoMoreRack. The court denied Nordstrom's motion for a preliminary injunction. After finding no likelihood of confusion between Nordstrom Rack and NoMoreRack, the court synthesized prior caselaw on dilution by tarnishment:

> Courts have found that harm "generally arises when the plaintiff's trademark is linked to products of shoddy quality, or is portrayed in an unwholesome or unsavory context likely to evoke unflattering thoughts about the owner's

> product." *Tiffany (NJ) Inc. v. eBay Inc.*, 600 F.3d 93, 111 (2d Cir. 2010) (*quoting Deere & Co. v. MTD Prods., Inc.*, 41 F.3d 39, 43 (2d Cir. 1994)). For example, there is some consensus among courts across jurisdictions that a famous mark is tarnished when it is semantically associated with a new mark used to sell sex-related products. See *V Secret Catalogue, Inc. v. Moseley*, 605 F.3d 382, 388 (6th Cir. 2010). A trademark may also be diluted by tarnishment if the mark loses its ability to serve as a "wholesome identifier" of the plaintiff's product. *Starbucks Corp. v. Wolfe's Borough Coffee, Inc.*, 588 F.3d 97, 110 (2d Cir. 2009) (*citing Hormel Foods Corp. v. Jim Henson Prods., Inc.*, 73 F.3d 497, 507 (2d Cir. 1996)). The Second Circuit found that the relevant inquiry is how the junior mark's product affects the positive impressions about the famous mark's product, and not whether a consumer simply associates a negative-sounding junior mark with the famous mark. *Starbucks*, 588 F.3d at 110.

The court then considered the evidence of tarnishment:

> In the present case, the Court must determine whether allegations of NoMoreRack's negative reputation, rises to the level of harm to Nordstrom Rack's reputation. Nordstrom submits the following evidence of NoMoreRack's reputation:
>
> 1) Better Business Bureau ("BBB") business review shows NoMoreRack's Vancouver office received 304 complaints beginning October 12, 2010, and NoMoreRack's New York business received 19 complaints beginning August 29, 2012.
>
> 2) Scambook.com lists 257 complaints about NoMoreRack from August 31, 2011 to November 19, 2012, with an estimated $120,228.84 in reported monetary damages.
>
> 3) Sitejabber.com lists 240 reviews on NoMoreRack from December 15, 2010 to November 19, 2012, listing the company as "Not Recommended" with a rating of 1.5 stars.
>
> 4) Complaintsboard.com lists 317 complaints against NoMoreRack as of November 19, 2012.
>
> 5) The Daily Goodie Bag, an online blog, captured over 50 negative comments that were initially posted on NoMoreRack's Facebook page, which were subsequently deleted from Facebook.
>
> 6) Third party Facebook pages devoted to providing a forum for NoMoreRack complaints, including "Nomorerack Consumer Complaints and Hate Page."
>
> 7) Since November 2012, the number of BBB complaints against NoMoreRack's Vancouver, New York and Delaware offices exceeds 1,500.
>
> Nordstrom alleges that NoMoreRack's "shoddy service" is in the form of fraudulent credit card charges, undelivered goods, damaged goods and

unfulfilled refunds. Other complaints include email spam and counterfeit merchandise. It alleges that NoMoreRack's reputation is further damaged through its affiliation with BidRack.com, a website that gained notoriety as a penny auction scam.

NoMoreRack admits that in February 2011, it displayed an offer from BidRack on its site, but denies any affiliation with the business. Since April 2011, NoMoreRack has severed all ties with BidRack. To counter Nordstrom's allegations of "shoddy service," NoMoreRack submits evidence of complaints lodged against Nordstrom on similar complaint forums, arguing that websites specifically designed to perpetuate complaints have little value or effect on the overall determination of a company's reputation. NoMoreRack further maintains that it has built a reputation for excellent customer service and that about 80 percent of NoMoreRack customers are repeat buyers and referrals. NoMoreRack submits evidence of its "positive" reputation through articles, customer reviews and social media examples.

The Court is cognizant that there is no steadfast rule on whether an association resulting from a company's "negative" reputation results in the type of "harm" embodied in the statute. A finding of harm is a fact-specific inquiry, and it is possible that the junior mark's overall negative reputation could place the famous mark's product or service in a bad light. See *Playmakers, LLC v. ESPN, Inc.*, 297 F.Supp.2d 1277, 1285 (W.D. Wash. 2003) ("'Tarnishment' is a form of dilution in which the junior user places the famous mark in a bad light, generally one that involves sexual activity, obscenity, or illegal activity."). The issue is whether the facts support a threshold finding that NoMoreRack's reputation for "shoddy service" places Nordstrom Rack in a bad light. The Court finds that it does not.

Considerations such as complaints, reduction in sales, loss of customers, and negative press are all relevant to the overall determination. In this case, Nordstrom only provides evidence of complaints against NoMoreRack to demonstrate its negative reputation. The majority of complaints are from anonymous Internet users that have posted on various blogs and forums online. Sites such as Sitejabber, Complaintsboard and Scambook are designed to facilitate negative feedback from disgruntled customers or even competitors, who can write multiple reviews across multiple forums. The evidence is not persuasive because there is no discerning whether the number of complaints actually correlates with the business' overall reputation. BBB complaints, while a little more credible, must be evaluated in light of all other considerations. NoMoreRack, on the other hand, provides evidence of positive reviews, increased growth and sales figures, and positive articles to rebut Nordstrom's argument. Upon balancing the evidence of both negative and positive associations, the facts are insufficient to show that NoMoreRack has a shoddy reputation. Thus, the use of NOMORERACK is not likely to cause dilution by tarnishment to NORDSTROM RACK.

Starbucks Corp. v. Wolfe's Borough Coffee, Inc.

588 F.3d 97 (2d Cir. 2009)

[The facts of this controversy are set out in section [B][1][b] ("blurring"), *supra* this Chapter.]

2. Dilution by Tarnishment

Dilution by tarnishment is an "association arising from the similarity between a mark or trade name and a famous mark that harms the reputation of the famous mark." 15 U.S.C. § 1125(c)(2)(C). "A trademark may be tarnished when it is linked to products of shoddy quality, or is portrayed in an unwholesome or unsavory context, with the result that the public will associate the lack of quality or lack of prestige in the defendant's goods with the plaintiff's unrelated goods." *Hormel Foods Corp. v. Jim Henson Productions, Inc.*, 73 F.3d 497, 507 (2d Cir. 1996). A trademark may also be diluted by tarnishment if the mark loses its ability to serve as a "wholesome identifier" of plaintiff's product. *Id.*; *accord Chemical Corp. v. Anheuser-Busch, Inc.*, 306 F.2d 433 (5th Cir. 1962) (finding that use of exterminator's slogan "where there's life, ... there's Bugs" tarnished the use of beer company's slogan "where there's life, ... there's Bud."); (citations).

Starbucks argues that the District Court "erred by failing to find that 'Charbucks' damages the positive reputation of Starbucks by evoking both 'Starbucks' and negative impressions in consumers, including the image of bitter, over-roasted coffee." Starbucks reasons that it has shown dilution by tarnishment because, pursuant to its survey, (1) 30.5% of persons surveyed "immediately associated 'Charbucks' with 'Starbucks' "; and (2) 62% of those surveyed who associated "Charbucks" with "Starbucks" "indicated that they would have a negative impression" of a "coffee named 'Charbucks.' " We are unpersuaded by Starbucks' reasoning.

To the extent Starbucks relies on the survey, a mere association between "Charbucks" and "Starbucks," coupled with a negative impression of the name "Charbucks," is insufficient to establish a likelihood of dilution by tarnishment. That a consumer may associate a negative-sounding junior mark with a famous mark says little of whether the consumer views the junior mark as harming the reputation of the famous mark. The more relevant question, for purposes of tarnishment, would have been how a hypothetical coffee named either "Mister Charbucks" or "Charbucks Blend" would affect the positive impressions about the coffee sold by Starbucks. We will not assume that a purportedly negative-sounding junior mark will likely harm the reputation of the famous mark by mere association when the survey conducted by the party claiming dilution could have easily enlightened us on the matter. Indeed, it may even have been that "Charbucks" would strengthen the positive impressions of Starbucks because it brings to the attention of consumers that the "Char" is absent in "Star" bucks, and, therefore, of the two "bucks," Starbucks is the "un-charred" and more appealing product. Juxtaposition may bring to light more appealing aspects of a name that otherwise would not have been brought to the attention of ordinary observers.

Starbucks also argues that "Charbucks" is a pejorative term for Starbucks' coffee, and, therefore, the Charbucks "name has negative associations that consumers are likely to associate with Starbucks' coffee." Although the term "Charbucks" was once used pejoratively during the so-called "coffee-war"[5] in Boston, Massachusetts, Black Bear is not propagating that negative meaning but, rather, is redefining "Charbucks" to promote a positive image for its brand of coffee.... "In short, Black Bear is promoting 'Charbucks' and not referring to it in a way as to harm the reputation of Starbucks' coffees." [Citation.]

Moreover, that the Charbucks line of coffee is marketed as a product of "[v]ery high quality"—as Starbucks also purports its coffee to be—is inconsistent with the concept of "tarnishment." *See Hormel Foods Corp.*, 73 F.3d at 507 (citing cases finding tarnishment where challenged marks were either "seamy" or substantially of lesser quality than the famous mark). Certainly, the similarity between Charbucks and Starbucks in that they are both "[v]ery high quality" coffees may be relevant in determining dilution, *see* 15 U.S.C. 1125(c)(2)(B), (c)(2)(C), but such similarity in this case undercuts the claim that Charbucks harms the reputation of Starbucks. *See Deere & Co. v. MTD Prods., Inc.*, 41 F.3d 39, 43 (2d Cir. 1994) ("'Tarnishment' generally arises when the plaintiff's trademark is linked to products of shoddy quality, or is portrayed in an unwholesome or unsavory context likely to evoke unflattering thoughts about the owner's product."). Accordingly, we conclude that the District Court did not err in rejecting Starbucks' claim of dilution by tarnishment.

Questions

1. The *Nordstrom* court observed that "there is some consensus among courts across jurisdictions that a famous mark is tarnished when it is semantically associated with a new mark used to sell sex-related products." Courts have announced a rebuttable presumption of tarnishment in cases of "semantic association" with such marks. Is a rebuttable presumption (or strong inference) of likely tarnishment justified in these cases? What type of evidence could a defendant submit that would rebut such a presumption?

2. What kind of evidence should a famous trademark owner show to demonstrate tarnishment by association with a business of shoddy repute?

3. Marketers of consumer products commonly pay for product placement in videogames. In 2005, the sportswear and shoe manufacturer Puma paid Activision to dress the characters in *True Crime New York City* in Puma® brand clothing and sneakers. In 2008, Barack Obama's presidential campaign purchased virtual billboard space in *Burnout Paradise* for the Xbox 360. Video game players might reasonably conclude that if a product shows up in a videogame, the producer has purchased the opportunity. How would you advise a producer who wants to keep tight control on

---

5. The name "Charbucks" was used publicly by the owner of a former chain of coffee bars, "Coffee Connection," to describe what the owner believed was the "over-roasted" type of coffee Starbucks was serving.

its product image to respond to an unlicensed videogame appearance? If a particularly violent serial killer in an M-rated blood-and-guts videogame were depicted swigging a Bud Lite® after every grisly murder, how should Anheuser-Busch respond?

4. Urban Gorilla sells a kit to fit onto a truck to make it resemble a HUMMER vehicle, the trade dress for which is a registered mark. Consider the HUMMER vehicle and the vehicle with an Urban Gorilla kit below. Assuming that the HUMMER trade dress is famous and distinctive, is the Urban Gorilla kit likely to cause dilution by blurring? By tarnishment? *See General Motors Corp. v. Urban Gorilla, LLC*, 500 F.3d 1222 (10th Cir. 2007), *on remand*, 2010 U.S. Dist. LEXIS 136711 (D. Utah Dec. 27, 2010).

HUMMER

URBAN GORILLA

5. Your client sells t-shirts through his "SkygraphX" website. His latest offering is pictured below. Philip Morris has sent a cease and desist letter, threatening to bring an action for trademark dilution. What is your advice?

d. Parody

Louis Vuitton Malletier S.A. v. Haute Diggity Dog, LLC

507 F.3d 252 (4th Cir. 2007)

NIEMEYER, J.:

Louis Vuitton Malletier S.A., a French corporation located in Paris, that manufactures luxury luggage, handbags, and accessories, commenced this action against Haute Diggity Dog, LLC, a Nevada corporation that manufactures and sells pet products nationally, alleging trademark infringement under 15 U.S.C. § 1114(1)(a), trademark dilution under 15 U.S.C. § 1125(c), copyright infringement under 17 U.S.C. § 501, and related statutory and common law violations....

On cross-motions for summary judgment, the district court concluded that Haute Diggity Dog's "Chewy Vuiton" dog toys were successful parodies of Louis Vuitton Malletier's trademarks, designs, and products, and on that basis, entered judgment in favor of Haute Diggity Dog on all of Louis Vuitton Malletier's claims.

On appeal, we agree with the district court that Haute Diggity Dog's products are not likely to cause confusion with those of Louis Vuitton Malletier and that Louis Vuitton Malletier's copyright was not infringed. On the trademark dilution claim, however, we reject the district court's reasoning but reach the same conclusion through a different analysis. Accordingly, we affirm.

I

....

LVM has registered trademarks for "LOUIS VUITTON," in connection with luggage and ladies' handbags (the "LOUIS VUITTON mark"); for a stylized monogram of "LV," in connection with traveling bags and other goods (the "LV mark"); and for a monogram canvas design consisting of a canvas with repetitions of the LV mark along with four-pointed stars, four-pointed stars inset in curved diamonds, and four-pointed flowers inset in circles, in connection with traveling bags and other products (the "Monogram Canvas mark"). In 2002, LVM adopted a brightly-colored version of the Monogram Canvas mark in which the LV mark and the designs were of various colors and the background was white (the "Multicolor design"), created in collaboration with Japanese artist Takashi Murakami.... In 2005, LVM adopted another design consisting of a canvas with repetitions of the LV mark and smiling cherries on a brown background (the "Cherry design").

... [T]he Multicolor design and the Cherry design attracted immediate and extraordinary media attention and publicity in magazines such as *Vogue, W, Elle, Harper's Bazaar, Us Weekly, Life and Style, Travel & Leisure, People, In Style*, and *Jane*. The press published photographs showing celebrities carrying these handbags, including Jennifer Lopez, Madonna, Eve, Elizabeth Hurley, Carmen Electra, and Anna Kournikova, among others. When the Multicolor design first appeared in 2003, the magazines typically reported, "The Murakami designs for Louis Vuitton, which were the hit of the summer, came with hefty price tags and a long waiting list." *People Magazine* said, "the wait list is in the thousands." The handbags retailed in the range of $995 for a medium handbag to $4500 for a large travel bag....

The original LOUIS VUITTON, LV, and Monogram Canvas marks ... have been used as identifiers of LVM products continuously since 1896.

During the period 2003–2005, LVM spent more than $48 million advertising products using its marks and designs, including more than $4 million for the Multicolor design.... LVM also advertises its products on the Internet through the specific websites www.louisvuitton.com and www.eluxury.com.

Although better known for its handbags and luggage, LVM also markets a limited selection of luxury pet accessories—collars, leashes, and dog carriers—which bear the Monogram Canvas mark and the Multicolor design. These items range in price from approximately $200 to $1600. LVM does not make dog toys.

Haute Diggity Dog, LLC, ... manufactures and sells nationally—primarily through pet stores—a line of pet chew toys and beds whose names parody elegant high-end brands of products such as perfume, cars, shoes, sparkling wine, and handbags. These include—in addition to Chewy Vuiton (LOUIS VUITTON)—Chewnel No. 5 (Chanel No. 5), Furcedes (Mercedes), Jimmy Chew (Jimmy Choo), Dog Perignonn (Dom Perignon), Sniffany & Co. (Tiffany & Co.), and Dogior (Dior). The chew toys and pet beds are plush, made of polyester, and have a shape and design that loosely imitate the signature product of the targeted brand.... The dog toys are generally sold for less than $20, although larger versions of some of Haute Diggity Dog's plush dog beds sell for more than $100.*

....

II

LVM contends first that Haute Diggity Dog's marketing and sale of its "Chewy Vuiton" dog toys infringe its trademarks because the advertising and sale of the "Chewy Vuiton" dog toys is likely to cause confusion. *See* 15 U.S.C. § 1114(1)(a)....

... [W]e agree with the district court that the "Chewy Vuiton" dog toys are successful parodies of LVM handbags and the LVM marks and trade dress.... First, the pet chew toy is obviously an irreverent, and indeed intentional, representation of an LVM handbag, albeit much smaller and coarser. The dog toy is shaped roughly like a handbag; its name "Chewy Vuiton" sounds like and rhymes with LOUIS VUITTON; its monogram CV mimics LVM's LV mark; the repetitious design clearly imitates the design on the LVM handbag; and the coloring is similar. In short, the dog toy is a small, plush imitation of an LVM handbag carried by women, which invokes the marks and design of the handbag, albeit irreverently and incompletely. No one can doubt that LVM handbags are the target of the imitation by Haute Diggity Dog's "Chewy Vuiton" dog toys.

....

* [*Editors' Note*: For an image of Haute Diggity Dog's CHEWY VUITTON dog bed, see *infra*, Question 2.]

... [T]he juxtaposition of the similar and dissimilar—the irreverent representation and the idealized image of an LVM handbag—immediately conveys a joking and amusing parody. The furry little "Chewy Vuiton" imitation, as something to be *chewed by a dog*, pokes fun at the elegance and expensiveness of a LOUIS VUITTON handbag, which must *not* be chewed by a dog. The LVM handbag is provided for the most elegant and well-to-do celebrity, to proudly display to the public and the press, whereas the imitation "Chewy Vuiton" "handbag" is designed to mock the celebrity and be used by a dog. The dog toy irreverently presents haute couture as an object for casual canine destruction. The satire is unmistakable. The dog toy is a comment on the rich and famous, on the LOUIS VUITTON name and related marks, and on conspicuous consumption in general. This parody is enhanced by the fact that "Chewy Vuiton" dog toys are sold with similar parodies of other famous and expensive brands—"Chewnel No. 5" targeting "Chanel No. 5"; "Dog Perignonn" targeting "Dom Perignon"; and "Sniffany & Co." targeting "Tiffany & Co."

[The court concluded that there is no likelihood of confusion]

III

LVM also contends that Haute Diggity Dog's advertising, sale, and distribution of the "Chewy Vuiton" dog toys dilutes its LOUIS VUITTON, LV, and Monogram Canvas marks, which are famous and distinctive, in violation of the Trademark Dilution Revision Act of 2006 ("TDRA"), 15 U.S.C.A. § 1125(c) (West Supp. 2007).... It also contends that "Chewy Vuiton" dog toys are likely to tarnish LVM's marks because they "pose a choking hazard for some dogs."

....

A

We address first LVM's claim for dilution by blurring.

The first three elements of a trademark dilution claim are not at issue in this case. LVM owns famous marks that are distinctive; Haute Diggity Dog has commenced using "Chewy Vuiton," "CV," and designs and colors that are allegedly diluting LVM's marks; and the similarity between Haute Diggity Dog's marks and LVM's marks gives rise to an association between the marks, albeit a parody. The issue for resolution is whether the association between Haute Diggity Dog's marks and LVM's marks is likely to impair the distinctiveness of LVM's famous marks.

...

To determine whether a junior mark is likely to dilute a famous mark through blurring, the TDRA directs the court to consider all factors relevant to the issue, including six factors that are enumerated in the statute: ...

Not every factor will be relevant in every case.... [A]fter we apply the factors as a matter of law, we reach the same conclusion reached by the district court.

... Although the TDRA does provide that fair use is a complete defense and allows that a parody can be considered fair use, it does not extend the fair use defense to parodies used as a trademark. As the statute provides:

> The following shall not be actionable as dilution by blurring or dilution by tarnishment under this subsection:
>
> (A) Any fair use ... *other than as a designation of source for the person's own goods or services*, including use in connection with ... parodying....

15 U.S.C.A. § 1125(c)(3)(A)(ii) (emphasis added). Under the statute's plain language, parodying a famous mark is protected by the fair use defense only if the parody is *not* "a designation of source for the person's own goods or services."

The TDRA, however, does not require a court to ignore the existence of a parody that is used as a trademark, and it does not preclude a court from considering parody as part of the circumstances to be considered for determining whether the plaintiff has made out a claim for dilution by blurring. Indeed, the statute permits a court to consider "all relevant factors," including the six factors supplied in § 1125(c)(2)(B).

Thus, it would appear that a defendant's use of a mark as a parody is relevant to the overall question of whether the defendant's use is likely to impair the famous mark's distinctiveness. Moreover, the fact that the defendant uses its marks as a parody is specifically relevant to several of the listed factors. For example, factor *(v)* (whether the defendant intended to create an association with the famous mark) and factor *(vi)* (whether there exists an actual association between the defendant's mark and the famous mark) directly invite inquiries into the defendant's intent in using the parody, the defendant's actual use of the parody, and the effect that its use has on the famous mark. While a parody intentionally creates an association with the famous mark in order to be a parody, it also intentionally communicates, if it is successful, that it is *not* the famous mark, but rather a satire of the famous mark. *See PETA* [*v. Doughney*, 263 F.3d 359], at 506 [(4th Cir. 2001)]. That the defendant is using its mark as a parody is therefore relevant in the consideration of these statutory factors.

Similarly, factors *(i)*, *(ii)*, and *(iv)*—the degree of similarity between the two marks, the degree of distinctiveness of the famous mark, and its recognizability—are directly implicated by consideration of the fact that the defendant's mark is a successful parody. Indeed, by making the famous mark an object of the parody, a successful parody might actually enhance the famous mark's distinctiveness by making it an icon. The brunt of the joke becomes yet more famous. *See Hormel Foods* [*v. Jim Henson Productions*, 73 F.3d 497], at 506 [(2d Cir. 1996)] (observing that a successful parody "tends to increase public identification" of the famous mark with its source); *see also Yankee Publ'g Inc. v. News Am. Publ'g Inc.*, 809 F. Supp. 267, 272–82 (S.D.N.Y. 1992) (suggesting that a sufficiently obvious parody is unlikely to blur the targeted famous mark).

....

In the case before us, when considering factors *(ii)*, *(iii)*, and *(iv)*, it is readily apparent, indeed conceded by Haute Diggity Dog, that LVM's marks are distinctive, famous, and strong. The LOUIS VUITTON mark is well known and is commonly identified as a brand of the great Parisian fashion house, Louis Vuitton Malletier. So too are its other marks and designs, which are invariably used with the LOUIS

VUITTON mark. It may not be too strong to refer to these famous marks as icons of high fashion.

While the establishment of these facts satisfies essential elements of LVM's dilution claim, *see* 15 U.S.C.A. § 1125(c)(1), the facts impose on LVM an increased burden to demonstrate that the distinctiveness of its famous marks is likely to be impaired by a successful parody. Even as Haute Diggity Dog's parody mimics the famous mark, it communicates simultaneously that it is not the famous mark, but is only satirizing it. [Citation.] And because the famous mark is particularly strong and distinctive, it becomes more likely that a parody will not impair the distinctiveness of the mark. In short, as Haute Diggity Dog's "Chewy Vuiton" marks are a successful parody, we conclude that they will not blur the distinctiveness of the famous mark as a unique identifier of its source.

It is important to note, however, that this might not be true if the parody is so similar to the famous mark that it likely could be construed as actual use of the famous mark itself. Factor *(i)* directs an inquiry into the "degree of similarity between the junior mark and the famous mark." If Haute Diggity Dog used the actual marks of LVM (as a parody or otherwise), it could dilute LVM's marks by blurring, regardless of whether Haute Diggity Dog's use was confusingly similar, whether it was in competition with LVM, or whether LVM sustained actual injury. *See* 15 U.S.C.A. § 1125(c)(1). Thus, "the use of DUPONT shoes, BUICK aspirin, and KODAK pianos would be actionable" under the TDRA because the unauthorized use of the famous marks *themselves* on unrelated goods might diminish the capacity of these trademarks to distinctively identify a single source. *Moseley*, 537 U.S. at 431 (quoting H.R. Rep. No. 104-374, at 3 (1995), *as reprinted in* 1995 U.S.C.C.A.N. 1029, 1030). This is true even though a consumer would be unlikely to confuse the manufacturer of KODAK film with the hypothetical producer of KODAK pianos.

But in this case, Haute Diggity Dog mimicked the famous marks; it did not come so close to them as to destroy the success of its parody and, more importantly, to diminish the LVM marks' capacity to identify a single source. Haute Diggity Dog designed a pet chew toy to imitate and suggest, but not *use*, the marks of a high-fashion LOUIS VUITTON handbag. It used "Chewy Vuiton" to mimic "LOUIS VUITTON"; it used "CV" to mimic "LV"; and it adopted *imperfectly* the items of LVM's designs. We conclude that these uses by Haute Diggity Dog were not so similar as to be likely to impair the distinctiveness of LVM's famous marks.

In a similar vein, when considering factors *(v)* and *(vi)*, it becomes apparent that Haute Diggity Dog intentionally associated its marks, but only partially and certainly imperfectly, so as to convey the simultaneous message that it was not in fact a source of LVM products. Rather, as a parody, it separated itself from the LVM marks in order to make fun of them.

In sum, when considering the relevant factors to determine whether blurring is likely to occur in this case, we readily come to the conclusion, as did the district court, that LVM has failed to make out a case of trademark dilution by blurring by failing to establish that the distinctiveness of its marks was likely to be impaired by Haute Diggity Dog's marketing and sale of its "Chewy Vuiton" products.

B

... To establish its claim for dilution by tarnishment, LVM must show, in lieu of blurring, that Haute Diggity Dog's use of the "Chewy Vuiton" mark on dog toys harms the reputation of the LOUIS VUITTON mark and LVM's other marks. LVM argues that the possibility that a dog could choke on a "Chewy Vuiton" toy causes this harm. LVM has, however, provided no record support for its assertion....

We agree with the district court that LVM failed to demonstrate a claim for dilution by tarnishment. *See Hormel Foods*, 73 F.3d at 507.

....

The judgment of the district court is

AFFIRMED.

Starbucks Corp. v. Wolfe's Borough Coffee, Inc., 588 F.3d 97 (2d Cir. 2009). After analyzing dilution by blurring (*supra* this Chapter, section [B][1][b]) and tarnishment (*supra* this Chapter, section [B][1][c]), the Second Circuit addressed Section 43(c)(3)'s parody exception:

> Even if its use of "Charbucks" constituted dilution by either blurring or tarnishment, Black Bear appears to argue in the alternative that Charbucks is a parody and thus falls under an exception to 15 U.S.C. § 1125(c).
>
> ... Black Bear's use of the Charbucks Marks cannot qualify under the parody exception because the Charbucks Marks are used "as a designation of source for [Black Bear's] own goods[, i.e., the Charbucks line of coffee]." Although Black Bear cites to several cases in support of its argument that the parody exception may still apply even if the parody were used to "identify the source of the defendants' goods," those cases were decided before the TDRA and are thus inapposite to the extent they are inconsistent with the amended section 1125(c)(3). *See Louis Vuitton Malletier S.A. v. Haute Diggity Dog, LLC*, 507 F.3d 252, 266 (4th Cir. 2007).
>
> Inasmuch as Black Bear's argument may be construed as advocating for consideration of parody in determining the likelihood of dilution by blurring—such as is recognized by the Fourth Circuit, *see id.* at 267—we need not adopt or reject *Louis Vuitton's* parody holding. We conclude that Black Bear's use of the Charbucks Marks is not a parody of the kind which would favor Black Bear in the dilution analysis even if we were to adopt the Fourth Circuit's rule.
>
> ....
>
> Here, unlike in *Louis Vuitton*, Black Bear's use of the Charbucks Marks is, at most, a subtle satire of the Starbucks Marks. Although we recognize some humor in "Char" bucks as a reference to the dark roast of the Starbucks coffees, Black Bear's claim of humor fails to demonstrate such a clear parody

as to qualify under the Fourth Circuit's rule. As the owner of Black Bear affirmed during his testimony, "[t]he inspiration for the term Charbucks comes directly from Starbucks' tendency to roast its products more darkly than that of other major roasters." The owner of Black Bear further testified that the Charbucks line of products "is the darkest roasted coffee that we do" and is of "[v]ery high quality." Thus, the Charbucks parody is promoted not as a satire or irreverent commentary of Starbucks but, rather, as a beacon to identify Charbucks as a coffee that competes at the same level and quality as Starbucks in producing dark-roasted coffees. *See Harley Davidson, Inc. v. Grottanelli*, 164 F.3d 806, 813 (2d Cir. 1999) ("[P]arodic use is sharply limited" in circumstances where "an alleged parody of a competitor's mark [is used] to sell a competing product."); *cf. Louis Vuitton*, 507 F.3d at 260–61 (permitting parodic use where the parody marketed its products to a significantly different class of consumers than the famous mark); *id.* ("The [Louis Vuitton] handbag is provided for the most elegant and well-to-do celebrity, to proudly display to the public and the press, whereas the imitation 'Chewy Vuiton' 'handbag' is designed to mock the celebrity and be used by a dog.").

Therefore, because the Charbucks Marks do not effect an "increase [in] public identification [of the Starbucks Marks with Starbucks]," the purported Charbucks parody plays no part in undermining a finding of dilution under the Fourth Circuit's rule.... Accordingly, we conclude that Black Bear's incantation of parody does nothing to shield it from Starbucks' dilution claim in this case.

Questions

1. Does the *Starbucks* court persuasively distinguish the CHEWY VUITON case?

2. Do you agree that the CHEWY VUITON, CV, and the designs shown below are sufficiently dissimilar from Louis Vuitton's marks that blurring is not likely? Does it matter that the plaintiff sells LOUIS VUITTON pet products? What if defendant used the same overall design pattern that plaintiff employs except that it used CV in place of the LV in the pattern?

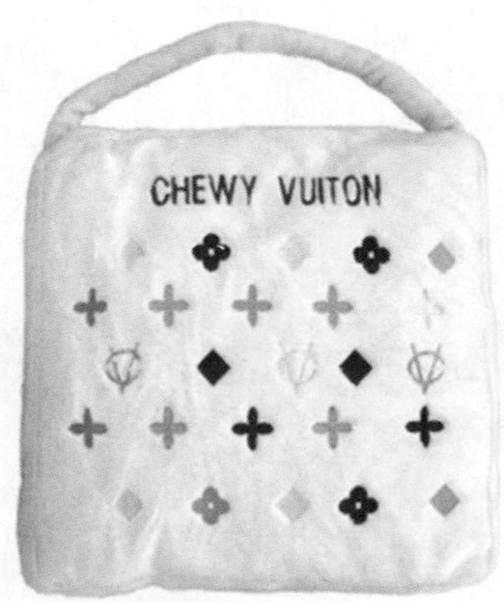

3. Fair use as a defense to trademark infringement under section 33(b)(4) requires good faith to establish the defense. Is there a similar requirement to establish a defense to dilution under section 43(c)(3)(A)? *See Rosetta Stone Ltd. v. Google, Inc.*, 676 F.3d 144 (4th Cir. 2012).

The Hershey Co. v. Art Van Furniture, Inc., 2008 U.S. Dist. LEXIS 87509 (E.D. Mich. Oct. 24, 2008). In this trademark infringement and dilution action, the court found no likelihood of confusion, but entered a preliminary injunction with respect to the dilution by blurring claim.

II. BACKGROUND

Plaintiff is a well-known maker of chocolate and confectionery goods, whose products are distributed and sold the world over. Defendant is Michigan's largest furniture retailer, operating 30 stores (all in-state), a website where customers may buy products online, and a fleet of about two dozen trucks for customer deliveries. The issue before the Court concerns Defendant's decoration of its delivery trucks.

On October 10, 2008, Defendant launched an advertising campaign. It posted ten truck decorations on its website and invited visitors to vote for their favorite design....

The first design on the contest page of Defendant's website is an image of a brown sofa emerging from a red and/or burgundy wrapper reminiscent of a candy bar. This "couch bar" is designed to bring to mind a candy or a chocolate bar, with its packaging torn open and mouth-watering contents exposed. Emblazoned across the wrapper are the words "ART VAN," spelled in white, block lettering, and on the bottom left of the wrapper, in smaller type, "Since 1959." On the right side of the image, where the sofa juts from the "candy bar," the torn wrapper has the appearance of crackled and ripped tinfoil. On the left, the same silver-colored foil is visible, protruding beneath the red and white wrapper.

Plaintiff contends that Defendant's design truck is an unauthorized and deliberate infringement of its trademarks and trade dress. Plaintiff claims that its trademark and trade dress packaging include:

1. a rectangular design;
2. silver, stylized lettering;
3. a brownish-maroon colored wrapper;
4. the name "Hershey's;" and
5. silver foil protruding from under the wrapper along the edges of the bar.

....

C. Likelihood of Success on Merits—Federal Dilution Claim

....

d. Defendant's use has/has not caused Dilution

...

Under the test established by the FDTA, the Court finds that a likelihood exists that Defendant's design will cause dilution of Plaintiff's mark.

[T]the second, third and fourth requirements of § 1125(c)(2)(B) are easily met. The evidence certainly supports an inference that Defendant intended to "create an association" with Plaintiff's mark (fifth factor), but whether such an association has actually been made is unclear (sixth factor). Finally, Defendant's "couch bar" design, with its stylized block lettering, its packaging in two elements, and especially its silver foil visible beneath the wrapper's sleeve, bears an unmistakable resemblance to some of Plaintiff's candy bars (first factor). *See Jada Toys*, [*Inc. v. Mattel, Inc.*], 518 F.3d at 635 (denying summary judgment because a reasonable trier of fact could find that two marks, "Hot Wheels" and "Hot Rigz," were "nearly identical" because both contained the word "hot," were accompanied by a flame, and used similar colors).

Plaintiff sustains its burden to show a reasonable likelihood of succeeding on the merits of its dilution by blurring claim.

D. Parody Defense

... Defendant relies heavily on the theory that its "couch bar" is merely a "clever parody" of an actual candy bar, and that the amusing nature of the design diffuses any risk that confused consumers would mistake its source or sponsorship. Defendant emphasizes that this image appears on its website next to nine other "whimsical" pictures, further reinforcing its satirical character. Defendant's reliance on the parody exception is misplaced.

The court quoted *Louis Vuitton Malletier v. Haute Diggety Dog* for the proposition that a parody must create two impressions, first of similarity bringing the target trademark to mind, second of difference, alerting the public that the parody is not purveyed by the trademark owner.

....

An important theme running through *Louis Vuitton* is that, while a parody may be nearly identical to the original in some respects, in others it is so different that no one could possibly mistake it for the real thing. *Id.* Defendant's design is neither similar nor different enough to convey a satirical message.

....

Questions

1. The *Art Van* court noted differences in the parties' trade dresses. Why did these differences not preclude a finding of blurring? *Cf. Starbucks v Wolfe's Borough Coffee, supra* this Chapter, Section [B][1][b].

2. Did the *Art Van* court persuasively distinguish the CHEWY VUITON parody? What did the court mean that Art Van's design "is neither similar nor different enough to convey a satirical message"?

New York Yankees Partnership v. IET Products and Services, Inc., 114 U.S.P.Q. 2d 1497 (T.T.A.B. 2015). The New York Yankees baseball club has long employed the logo pictured below on a variety of merchandising items, including apparel.

IET Products, Inc., intends to use the logo pictured below on t-shirts, jackets and baseball caps. It applied for trademark registration of the logo. The Yankees organization opposed the registration on grounds, inter alia, of dilution.

IET claimed that its logo was a fair use parody and was therefore *de jure* non dilutive, an assertion the Board found inconsistent with the text of Section 43(c):

> Applicant's argument ignores the language of Section 43(c)(3)(A)..., which limits the "fair use" exclusion as defined in the statute to use of a famous mark "other than as a designation of source for the person's own goods or services" (Section 43(c)(3)(A)). "Noncommercial" use also is excluded. (Section 43(c)(3)(C)). To obtain federal registration, an applicant's use of the applied-for matter must be as a designation of source—i.e., as a mark—and commercial—i.e., used in commerce. See Trademark Act Sections 1, 2, 17, 18, and 45, 15 U.S.C. §§1051, 1052, 1067, 1068, and 1127. This proceeding is before the Board because Applicant is not seeking merely to make ornamental, expressive, or noncommercial use of its marks, but because Applicant has applied to register its trademarks as designations of the source of Applicant's own T-shirts, baseball caps, hats, jackets, sweatshirts, and mugs. The fair use exclusion is typically inapplicable when registration is sought, and it does not apply here.

Questions

1. Would IET's fair use defense have fared better had IET not sought to register the steroids parody logo, but instead simply sold clothing bearing the logo?

2. As we have seen, to qualify under the fair use exemption to a dilution claim, a parody cannot be used as a trademark. Review section 43(c)(3)(C), which also exempts "noncommercial use of a mark." Can a parodic mark qualify as noncommercial use? *See Smith v. Wal-Mart Stores*, 537 F. Supp. 2d 1302 (N.D. Ga. 2008) (considered defendant's use of Wal-Queda and Walocaust on t-shirts and stickers as a parody of Wal-Mart). Should an applicant for a trademark registration be able to assert a parody or noncommercial defense to a dilution claim based on the statutory defense? *See American Express Marketing & Development Corp. v. Gilad Development Corp.*, 94 U.S.P.Q.2d 1294 (T.T.A.B. 2010); *Research In Motion Ltd. v. Defining Presence Marketing Group Inc*, 102 U.S.P.Q.2d 1187 (T.T.A.B. 2012) (CRACKBERRY for online and computer services dilutive of BLACKBERRY for smart phones); *Nike Inc. v. Maher*, 100 U.S.P.Q.2d 1018 (T.T.A.B. 2011) (JUST JESU IT for clothing dilutive of JUST DO IT slogan for Nike apparel). For an argument that a trademark that parodies a brand name should not be held to dilute the senior trademark, *see* Stacey L. Dogan & Mark A. Lemley, *Parody as Brand*, excerpted immediately below.

Stacey L. Dogan & Mark A. Lemley, *Parody as Brand*

47 U.C. Davis L. Rev. 473 (2013)*

I. Parodies, Brand Parodies, and the Law

A. Traditional Parodies

Parodies and their close kin satires are common in popular culture. So too are lawsuits filed against those parodies by irate trademark owners. Many of these cases involve classic examples of social commentary using—and targeting—brands.

. . . .

For traditional parodies . . . the legal rule should be simple, even if it is not always followed: Making fun of a trademark owner by doing something other than using their mark to brand your own products does not violate the Lanham Act.

B. Brand Parodies

Increasingly, however, we've witnessed a new phenomenon: lawsuits against parodies that serve as brands, titles, or taglines for commercial products. Haute Diggity Dog sells "Chewy Vuiton" dog toys, and Louis Vuitton is not happy about it. Macy's sells a diaper bag called "Gucchi Goo," and Gucci sues (and wins). The Utah tourism bureau describes the state as having the "Greatest Snow on Earth," a play on the Ringling Brothers' "Greatest Show on Earth" mark. Black Bear Roastery sells "Charbucks" coffee to poke fun at the famous brand's dark roast while cheekily offering its own dark-roast alternative. A Vermont hippie invites people to "Eat More Kale," and Chik-Fil-A thinks he's making fun of their "Eat More Chickin" mark. Hogg Wyld sells plus-size jeans under the name Lardache, and jeans-maker Jordache is not amused. A bar owner names its kitschy establishment the "Velvet Elvis," and gets a visit from the King's trademark attorneys. And so on.

In many ways, this new form of parody resembles the old. It's motivated by a desire to comment or criticize, and it's unlikely to confuse anyone about the source of the parody-branded product. In other ways, however, parody as brand differs from parody as product because the parody is being used as an indicator of source. Building a brand name around someone else's trademark looks, to some observers, like a classic case of "free riding," with the parodist taking advantage of the allure of the targeted brand. Trademark holders, not surprisingly, abhor the practice and sue to prevent it.

But trademark law is not—and has never been—about preventing all forms of free riding. Trademark law, even as it has expanded to prevent dilution, has always focused on preventing harm to the trademark holder or the public. Those who develop brands-as-parody may well be benefiting from the appeal of a famous brand, but if their use is an effective parody, it doesn't cause the kind of harm that trademark law is designed to address. These brands-as-parody, moreover, offer a valuable form of social commentary. Even more than non-commercial forms of parody, the subversive

---

* Copyright 2013. Reprinted by permission. [*Editors' Note*: Footnotes omitted.]

use of a parody *as* brand invites critical reflection on the role of brands in society and the extent to which we define ourselves by them.

Brands that parody, in other words, offer a unique platform for expression and pose little threat to trademark law's core values. As a matter of doctrine, however, the fact that a parody is also a brand complicates the trademark analysis. The trademark use doctrine is no longer a bar to an infringement suit; Black Bear *is* in fact using the term "Charbucks" as a mark to brand its products. Nominative use becomes harder, though not impossible, for the same reason. "Charbucks" is in fact nominative use in a sense; buyers presumably understand that it is a reference to Starbucks. But it is not *only* a nominative use; it is simultaneously a brand in its own right, and if it is memorable it may serve the traditional function of cementing Black Bear's product in people's minds. When a parody is also a brand, a number of courts have concluded that the analysis is the same as it is for any other trademark case: we ask whether confusion or dilution is likely, and if it is, the use is unlawful. In other words, those courts do not give parody a defense or any special treatment.

Perhaps it doesn't matter. Most parodies are unlikely to confuse consumers or to dilute the singularity of a famous trademark.... [M]aybe we don't need a defense to protect brand parodies; they will take care of themselves.

That answer seems unsatisfactory, and not merely because some brand parodies are in fact held illegal under questionable circumstances. Confusion is a fact-specific inquiry, often heavily reliant on manipulable survey evidence and subject to an ever-expanding notion of what it takes to confuse....

Dilution presents a different problem for brand parodies. While there is an explicit defense for parody in the Trademark Dilution Revision Act, it expressly applies only to parodies that use the mark "other than as a designation of source." Brand parodies, by contrast, do not benefit from the defense. That doesn't mean they are dilutive, of course; the Fourth Circuit found in *Louis Vuitton* that Chewy Vuiton was not. But it does mean that the parody is to be evaluated under the normal standards of blurring or tarnishment, a set of fact-intensive standards that map poorly to uses expressly intended to evoke a famous mark....

... Brand parodies, then, don't fit well within existing trademark infringement or dilution law. Parodies generally don't confuse consumers, and because they refer back to the plaintiff's mark directly they will not generally blur or tarnish that mark in the way dilution law prohibits. True parodies thus cause none of the harms that trademark law seeks to avoid. But because neither law is structured with parodies in mind, rote application of infringement and dilution standards can result in a condemnation of even obvious parodies. Lacking tools specifically designed for parody, courts treat it in an ad hoc way that reflects their own subjective assessment of the value or parody and the morality of free rides. The fact-intensive nature of the inquiry, moreover, means a long and costly process, which alone may deter parodies.

....

II. The Value of Brand Parodies

Whether or not they believe that a particular parody deserves legal protection, courts and commentators seem to agree that parody has social value as critical speech.... Despite their general appreciation of parody, however, courts show distinctly less enthusiasm for parodies that serve as brands. To some extent, their objection is doctrinal: both First Amendment and trademark jurisprudence give special status to non-commercial speech. But the trouble with brand parodies transcends doctrine; courts seem to struggle over their own intuitions about whether a defendant's commercial objectives undermine its speech interest in the parody. Given the malleability of confusion and dilution analysis, these judicial instincts often dictate the outcome in trademark litigation.

Yet there's a strong argument that, at least in the trademark context, incorporating a parody into a brand serves expressive goals that could not be realized through ordinary, non-branding speech. Many—perhaps most—branding parodies have a doubly subversive message. They are using a brand not only to lampoon the targeted brand, but also to call attention to the pervasiveness of branding in our society. Parodies, in general, replicate the central features of a particular work to "reference and ridicule" the work. Brand parodies do more: they not only borrow from the trademark itself, but they also appropriate the device of branding and employ it to make us think critically about the role of brands in our culture. The dog chew toy in *Louis Vuitton*, for example, "pokes fun at the elegance and expensiveness of a LOUIS VUITTON handbag" but also "irreverently presents haute couture as an object for casual canine destruction." Or so thought the Fourth Circuit, at least.

Trademark holders, of course, would prefer not to face this kind of ridicule of their brands or their branding practices. But trademark law does not exist to suit the needs of trademark holders; it aims to promote broader social objectives....

As discussed above, brands that parody have a dual target: the brand itself, and the phenomenon of branding. Given the prevalence of branding and its economic and social impact, commentary about both brands and branding is a matter of public concern. If they succeed in the market, moreover, these parodic brands must do so because they offer some utility to consumers. Just as prestige brands confer value to consumers who want to project an image of exclusivity, so brand parodies bring utility to consumers seeking to project a more rebellious or sardonic message. Absent some harm to the informational function of the underlying trademark, the availability of this new type of product likely increases social welfare. Further, if brands are part of a conversation between consumers, not just with trademark owners, brand parodies allow others to participate in that conversation with a different, unapproved message.

If the parody is effective, moreover—if consumers get the joke—it's hard to see how brand parodies pose any cognizable threat to trademark law's informational goals. Sure, the public might think less of the trademark holder as a result of the criticism, but trademark law has never addressed itself to that kind of harm. To the contrary, the fact that the defendant is using the plaintiff's brand to talk about the plaintiff, even for money, is a defense to infringement. Brand parodies, then, are a natural and desirable part of a social conversation that takes place through the phenomenon of branding. Trademark owners benefit from that conversation, but they are not the only ones with a right to speak.

Question

Do you agree that courts should treat nonconfusing brand parodies as no more dilutive than nonconfusing parodies that do not incorporate the target producer's trademark in the parodist's trademark? Was Congress' limitation of the 43(c) parody case to nontrademark use ill-considered? Irrelevant?

2. Use of a Famous Mark Other than as a Mark for Defendant's Goods or Services

MasterCard International Inc. v. Nader 2000 Primary Committee, Inc.

70 U.S.P.Q.2d 1046 (S.D.N.Y. 2004)

George B. Daniels, District Judge:

....

MasterCard, a Delaware corporation with its principal place of business in New York, is a large financial institution that engages in the interchange of funds by credit and debit payment cards through over 23,000 banks and other foreign and domestic member financial institutions. Since Fall of 1997, MasterCard has commissioned the authorship of a series of advertisements that have come to be known as the "Priceless Advertisements." These advertisements feature the names and images of several goods and services purchased by individuals which, with voice overs and visual displays, convey to the viewer the price of each of these items. At the end of each of the Priceless Advertisements a phrase identifying some priceless intangible that cannot be purchased (such as "a day where all you have to do is breathe") is followed by the words or voice over: "Priceless. There are some things money can't buy, for everything else there's MasterCard."

In August 2000, MasterCard became aware that Ralph Nader and his presidential committee were broadcasting an allegedly similar advertisement on television that promoted the presidential candidacy of Ralph Nader in the 2000 presidential election. That political ad included a sequential display of a series of items showing the price of each ("grilled tenderloin for fund-raiser; $1,000 a plate;" "campaign ads filled with half-truths: $10 million;" "promises to special interest groups: over $100 billion"). The advertisement ends with a phrase identifying a priceless intangible that cannot be purchased ("finding out the truth: priceless. There are some things that money can't buy"). The resulting ad (the "Nader ad") was shown on television during a two week period from August 6–17, during the 2000 presidential campaign, and also appeared on the defendants' web site throughout that campaign. Plaintiff sent defendants a letter explaining its concern over the similarity of the commercials, and suggested that defendants broadcast a more "original" advertisement. When plaintiff contacted representatives of defendants a few days later, plaintiff MasterCard advised defendants to cease broadcasting their political advertisement due to its similarity with MasterCard's own commercial advertisement and resulting infringement liability.

When the parties could not come to an agreement, on August 16, 2000, MasterCard filed a complaint alleging the following counts against Ralph Nader and his presidential committee; ... dilution in violation of Section 43(c) of the Lanham Act; copyright infringement in violation of the Copyright Act.... Plaintiff sought a preliminary injunction during the 2000 presidential campaign which was denied by this Court. Thereafter, defendants moved for summary judgment on all nine of plaintiff's counts.

DISCUSSION

....

3. Dilution

Counts Three and Eight of plaintiff's complaint allege against defendants federal and state dilution of plaintiff's trademarks. The Federal Trademark Dilution Act, 15 U.S.C. § 1125(c) and the New York anti-dilution law, New York Gen. Bus. Law § 360-1, protect against the unauthorized use of marks that impairs the goodwill and value of plaintiff's mark.... Under both federal and New York law, dilution can involve either blurring or tarnishment. [Citations.]

....

The Federal Trademark Dilution Act specifically exempts noncommercial uses of a mark from its coverage. Section 1125(c)(4) provides that "the following shall not be actionable under this section: ... (B) Noncommercial use of a mark." Therefore, prior to even addressing whether defendants have actually diluted plaintiff's marks under the federal law, the Court must first determine whether defendants' use of the marks is "commercial," and thereby, whether that use is even covered by the statute.

Plaintiff argues that Ralph Nader's Political Ad is commercial in nature even though it neither sells products or services, is not designed to entice consumers to buy products or services, and does not propose any kind of commercial transaction. MasterCard asserts that contributions to the Nader 2000 General Committee "increased from $5125 before the Ad ran to $818,000 in August 2000, after the Ad ran through the 'DONATE ON-LINE' icon or otherwise." ... Although the Nader Ad ran before a large sum of contributions were made to his campaign, plaintiff offers no evidence of a causal connection between the Ad and the contributions. There is nothing in the record other than the inference to be drawn from the proximity in time that advances the notion that the contributions Ralph Nader and his political committee received were a direct result of the Ad.

Even assuming the Nader Ad caused greater contributions to be made to his political campaign, this would not be enough to deem Ralph Nader's Ad "commercial." If so, then presumably, as suggested by defendants, all political campaign speech would also be "commercial speech" since all political candidates collect contributions. Ralph Nader's Political Ad attempts to communicate that other presidential candidates can be bought, but that the "truth," represented by himself, cannot. The Nader Ad is a strong political message which expresses his personal opinion on presidential campaigning. The legislative history of the Lanham Act clearly indicates that Congress did not intend for the Act to chill political speech. In speaking about the amendments to Section 43(a) that expanded what was actionable as deceptive advertisements, one of the new law's sponsors, United States Representative Robert Kastenmeier, pointed out that political advertising and promotion are not meant to be covered by the term "commercial." He stated that the statute

> uses the word "commercial" to describe advertising or promotion for business purposes, whether conducted by for-profit or non-profit organizations or individuals. *Political advertising and promotion is political speech, and therefore not encompassed by the term "commercial."* This is true whether what is being promoted is an individual candidacy for public office, or a particular political issue or point of view....

134 Cong. Rec. H. 1297 (daily ed. April 13, 1989) (statement of Wisconsin Rep. Kastenmeier) (emphasis added).

Plaintiff MasterCard urges the Court to rely on *United We Stand America, Inc. v. United We Stand, America New York, Inc.*, 128 F.3d 86 (2d Cir. 1997), to conclude that Ralph Nader's activities are "commercial" in nature. That case is not instructive in determining whether or not MasterCard has a basis to bring a claim against defendants under the Federal Trademark Dilution Act. In *United We Stand*, the Court was determining whether a certain political activity fell under the scope and the meaning of the word "services" and "use in commerce" of the Lanham Trademark Act, § 32(1)(a), 15 U.S.C.A. § 1114(1)(a). That particular section of the Lanham Act does not have a commercial activity requirement, nor does it exempt from liability noncommercial use of a mark. *See Planned Parenthood Federation of America Inc. v. U.S. District Court Southern District of New York*, 42 U.S.P.Q.2d 1430, 1434 (S.D.N.Y. 1997). However, the Federal Trademark Dilution Act, 15 U.S.C.A. § 1125(c), specifically exempts from the scope of all provisions of Section 1125 the "noncommercial use of a mark." *See id.*, at 1433.

Though not binding, this Court finds the analysis in *American Family Life Insurance Company v. Hagan*, 266 F. Supp. 2d 682 (N.D. Ohio 2002), to be relevant and persuasive. In that case, similar to the case at hand, the plaintiff, American Family Life Insurance Company, or AFLAC, ran well-known "AFLAC Duck" commercials which featured a white duck quacking the company's name "AFLAC." *Id.*, at 684. One of the defendants was a candidate for Governor of the State of Ohio running against the incumbent Governor Robert Taft. The candidate and his Campaign, developed internet commercials that "'borrow[ed]' from AFLAC's commercials. Specifically, the internet commercials included a crudely animated character made up of the incumbent Governor's head sitting on the body of a white cartoon duck; the duck quacks 'TaftQuack' several times during each commercial," which defendants ran on their website, www.taftquack.com. *Id.* Defendants' website also contained a link which visitors could use to make campaign contributions. *Id.* at 686–87. Among other claims, plaintiff sued defendants for federal trademark dilution and moved for a preliminary injunction.

In denying the plaintiff's motion for a preliminary injunction, and finding that the plaintiff was not likely to prevail on its dilution claim, the court also found that defendants' speech was political, rather than commercial. Specifically, the court stated that the candidate was "using a quacking cartoon character, which admittedly brings to mind AFLAC's marks, *as part of his communicative message*, in the context of expressing political speech." *Id.*, at 700 (emphasis in original). The court added that though "the consuming public may associate the AFLAC Duck and the TaftQuack character—a proposition the Court accepts—[this] is an insufficient predicate to support injunctive relief of political speech." *Id.*, at 701. The court further noted that though defendants included in their website a mechanism for visitors to make campaign contributions, "it is arguable whether [the candidate's] speech proposes a commercial transaction at all." *Id.*, at 697. The court stated that defendants' solicitation of contributions, and the resulting making of contributions, "is much more than merely a commercial transaction. Indeed, this exchange is properly classified not as a commercial transaction at all, but completely noncommercial, political speech." *Id.*

This Court finds that Ralph Nader's use of plaintiff's trademarks is not commercial, but instead political in nature and that therefore, it is exempted from coverage by the Federal Trademark Dilution Act. However, even if Ralph Nader's use of plaintiff's trademarks could be deemed commercial in nature, such use did not dilute plaintiff's marks. Defendants do not dispute that plaintiff's marks are famous, distinctive, or that they used plaintiff's marks after such marks became famous. However, there is no evidence in the record that defendants' use of plaintiff's marks actually caused dilution of the distinctiveness of plaintiff's marks. Plaintiff does not offer evidence that defendants' limited use of the Priceless marks lessened its value or the capacity of these marks to identify and distinguish plaintiff's goods or services. Further, plaintiff does not claim, nor is there any evidence in the record, that due to defendant's use of plaintiff's marks, plaintiff altered or lessened its use of the marks to identify MasterCard's products or services.

Count Three of plaintiff's complaint alleging dilution of plaintiff's trademarks is dismissed on defendants' motion for summary judgment. Ralph Nader's use of plaintiff's trademarks is political in nature, not within a commercial context, and is therefore exempted from coverage by the Federal Trademark Dilution Act. Furthermore, there is no evidence on the record that Ralph Nader's use of plaintiff's trademarks diluted plaintiff's trademarks.

Question

Steve Hershey's campaign for the Maryland state senate included signboards such as the one immediately below.

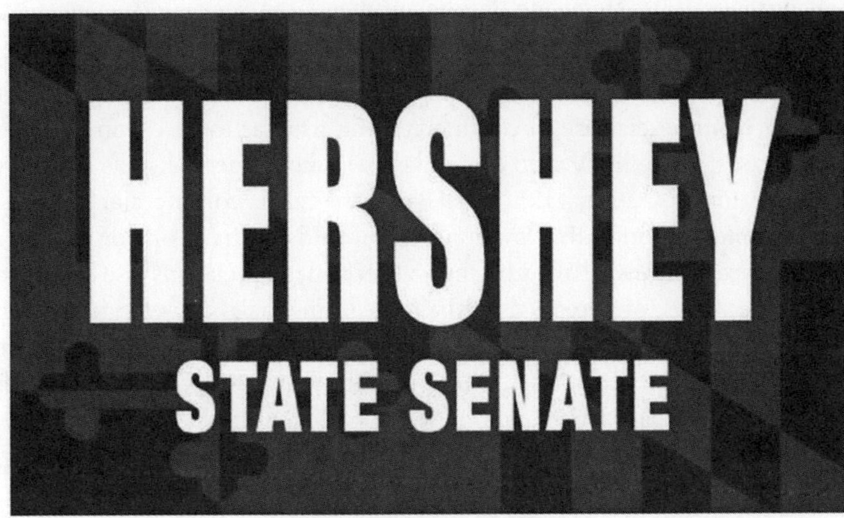

Friends of Steve Hershey
104 Wye View Road
Queenstown, Maryland 21658

AUTHORITY FRIENDS OF STEVE HERSHEY - WENDY HERSHEY, TREASURER

The Hershey Company objected, citing the similarity of Hershey's campaign signs to the trade dress of the Hershey chocolate bars. The similarity also drew the attention of several publications and members of the public. In response to the Hershey Co.'s motion for a preliminary injunction under Lanham Act sections 32 and 43(c), Steve Hershey asserted that his campaign materials were First Amendment-protected political speech. How should the court rule? *See Hershey Co. v. Friends of Steve Hershey*, 33 F. Supp. 3d 588 (D. Md. 2014).

Mattel, Inc. v. Universal Music International, 296 F.3d 894 (9th Cir. 2002). In 1997, Aqua, a Danish band, produced a song called "Barbie Girl," on their album Aquarium. The song was a success, making it onto the Top 40 music charts. Mattel, the owner of the toy doll Barbie, brought a lawsuit against the music companies who produced, marketed and sold Barbie Girl (collectively, "MCA"). Along with a traditional trademark infringement suit, excerpted *supra* in Chapter 8[C][2], Mattel separately argued that, under the Federal Trademark Dilution Act ("FTDA"), MCA's song diluted the Barbie mark in two ways: it diminished the mark's capacity to identify and distinguish Mattel products, and tarnished the mark because the song was inappropriate for young girls. *See* 15 U.S.C. § 1125(c). The 9th Circuit found that Barbie easily qualified under the FTDA as a famous and distinctive mark, and had reached this status long before MCA began to market the Barbie Girl song. The 9th Circuit also found that the song amounted to "commercial use in commerce" and that the use of the mark was dilutive, given that some consumers would think of both the doll and the song when hearing "Barbie." Then, the court turned to the FTDA's three statutory exemptions of comparative advertising, news reporting and commentary and noncommercial use, focusing on noncommercial use:

> A "noncommercial use" exemption, on its face, presents a bit of a conundrum because it seems at odds with the earlier requirement that the junior use be a "commercial use in commerce." If a use has to be commercial in order to be dilutive, how then can it also be noncommercial so as to satisfy the exception of section 1125(c)(4)(B)? If the term "commercial use" had the same meaning in both provisions, this would eliminate one of the three statutory exemptions defined by this subsection, because any use found to be dilutive would, of necessity, not be noncommercial.... Such a reading of the statute would also create a constitutional problem, because it would leave the FTDA with no First Amendment protection for dilutive speech other than comparative advertising and news reporting....
>
> Fortunately, the legislative history of the FTDA suggests an interpretation of the "noncommercial use" exemption that both solves our interpretive dilemma and diminishes some First Amendment concerns: "Noncommercial use" refers to a use that consists entirely of noncommercial, or fully constitutionally protected, speech. *See* 2 Jerome Gilson *et al., Trademark Protection and Practice* § 5.12[1][c][vi] at 5-240 (this exemption "is intended to prevent the courts from enjoining speech that has been recognized to be [fully] constitutionally protected," "such as parodies"). Where, as here, a statute's plain meaning "produces an absurd, and perhaps unconstitutional, result[, it is] entirely appropriate to consult all public materials, including the background of [the statute] and the legislative history of its adoption." *Green v. Bock Laundry Mach. Co.*, 490 U.S. 504, 527 (1989) (Scalia, J., concurring).
>
> The legislative history bearing on this issue is particularly persuasive. First, the FTDA's sponsors in both the House and the Senate were aware of the potential collision with the First Amendment if the statute authorized injunctions against protected speech. Upon introducing the counterpart bills, sponsors in each house explained that the proposed law "will not prohibit or threaten noncommercial expression, such as parody, satire, editorial and other forms of expression that are not a part of a commercial transaction." 141 Cong. Rec. S19306-10, S19310 (daily ed. Dec. 29, 1995) (statement of Sen. Hatch); 141 Cong. Rec. H14317-01, H14318 (daily ed. Dec. 12, 1995) (statement of Rep. Moorhead). The House Judiciary Committee agreed in its report on the FTDA. H.R. Rep. No. 104-374, at 4 (1995), *reprinted* in 1995 U.S.C.C.A.N. 1029, 1031 ("The bill will not prohibit or threaten 'noncommercial' expression, as that term has been defined by the courts.").

The FTDA's section-by-section analysis presented in the House and Senate suggests that the bill's sponsors relied on the "noncommercial use" exemption to allay First Amendment concerns. H.R. Rep. No. 104-374, at 8, *reprinted* in 1995 U.S.C.C.A.N. 1029, 1035 (the exemption "expressly incorporates the concept of 'commercial' speech from the 'commercial speech' doctrine, and proscribes dilution actions that seek to enjoin use of famous marks in 'non-commercial' uses (such as consumer product reviews)"); 141 Cong. Rec. S19306-10, S19311 (daily ed. Dec. 29, 1995) (the exemption "is consistent with existing case law[, which] recognizes that the use of marks in certain forms of artistic and expressive speech is protected by the First Amendment"). At the request of one of the bill's sponsors, the section-by-section analysis was printed in the Congressional Record. 141 Cong. Rec. S19306-10, S19311 (daily ed. Dec. 29, 1995). Thus, we know that this interpretation of the exemption was before the Senate when the FTDA was passed, and that no senator rose to dispute it.

To determine whether Barbie Girl falls within this exemption, we look to our definition of commercial speech under our First Amendment caselaw. See H.R. Rep. No. 104-374, at 8, *reprinted* in 1995 U.S.C.C.A.N. 1029, 1035 (the exemption "expressly incorporates the concept of 'commercial' speech from the 'commercial speech' doctrine"); 141 Cong. Rec. S19306-10, S19311 (daily ed. Dec. 29, 1995) (the exemption "is consistent with existing [First Amendment] case law"). "Although the boundary between commercial and noncommercial speech has yet to be clearly delineated, the 'core notion of commercial speech' is that it 'does no more than propose a commercial transaction.'" *Hoffman v. Capital Cities/ABC, Inc.*, 255 F.3d 1180, 1184 (9th Cir. 2001) (quoting *Bolger v. Youngs Drug Prods Corp.*, 463 U.S. 60, 66, 103 S. Ct. 2875, 77 L. Ed. 2d 469 (1983)). If speech is not "purely commercial"—that is, if it does more than propose a commercial transaction—then it is entitled to full First Amendment protection. *Id.* at 1185–86 (internal quotation marks omitted).

In *Hoffman*, a magazine published an article featuring digitally altered images from famous films. Computer artists modified shots of Dustin Hoffman, Cary Grant, Marilyn Monroe and others to put the actors in famous designers' spring fashions; a still of Hoffman from the movie "Tootsie" was altered so that he appeared to be wearing a Richard Tyler evening gown and Ralph Lauren heels. Hoffman, who had not given permission, sued under the Lanham Act and for violation of his right to publicity. *Id.* at 1183. The article featuring the altered image clearly served a commercial purpose: "to draw attention to the for-profit magazine in which it appeared" and to sell more copies. *Id.* at 1186. Nevertheless, we held that the article was fully protected under the First Amendment because it included protected expression: "humor" and "visual and verbal editorial comment on classic films and famous actors." *Id.* at 1185 (internal quotation marks omitted). Because its

> commercial purpose was "inextricably entwined with [these] expressive elements," the article and accompanying photographs enjoyed full First Amendment protection. *Id.*
>
> *Hoffman* controls: Barbie Girl is not purely commercial speech, and is therefore fully protected. To be sure, MCA used Barbie's name to sell copies of the song. However, as we've already observed, the song also lampoons the Barbie image and comments humorously on the cultural values Aqua claims she represents. Use of the Barbie mark in the song Barbie Girl therefore falls within the noncommercial use exemption to the FTDA. For precisely the same reasons, use of the mark in the song's title is also exempted.

The Court of Appeals affirmed the district court's ruling that Barbie Girl was a parody of Baribie and a nominative fair use, with Judge Kozinski advising the parties "to chill." (For an excerpt of the Ninth Circuit's analysis of the likelihood of confusion claim, see *supra*, Chapter 8[C].)

Louis Vuitton Malletier, S.A. v. My Other Bag, Inc.

117 U.S.P.Q.2d 537 (S.D.N.Y. 2016)

Jesse M. Furman, United States District Judge

Defendant My Other Bag, Inc. ("MOB") sells simple canvas tote bags with the text "My Other Bag ..." on one side and drawings meant to evoke iconic handbags by luxury designers, such as Louis Vuitton, Chanel, and Fendi, on the other. MOB's totes—indeed, its very name—are a play on the classic "my other car ..." novelty bumper stickers, which can be seen on inexpensive, beat up cars across the country informing passersby—with tongue firmly in cheek—that the driver's "other car" is a Mercedes (or some other luxury car brand). The "my other car" bumper stickers are, of course, a joke—a riff, if you will, on wealth, luxury brands, and the social expectations of who would be driving luxury and non-luxury cars. MOB's totes are just as obviously a joke, and one does not necessarily need to be familiar with the "my other car" trope to get the joke or to get the fact that the totes are meant to be taken in jest.

Louis Vuitton Malletier, S.A. ("Louis Vuitton"), the maker of Louis Vuitton bags, is perhaps unfamiliar with the "my other car" trope. Or maybe it just cannot take a joke. In either case, it brings claims against MOB with respect to MOB totes that are concededly meant to evoke iconic Louis Vuitton bags. More specifically, Louis Vuitton brings claims against MOB for trademark dilution ... under the Lanham Act.... For the reasons that follow, MOB's motion for summary judgment is granted ...

BACKGROUND

... Louis Vuitton is a world-renowned luxury fashion house known for its high-quality handbags and other luxury goods. Louis Vuitton bags often sell for thousands of dollars, and the company invests substantial sums in creating and maintaining a sense of exclusivity and luxury. As a result, several of Louis Vuitton's designs and trademarks are famous and well-recognized icons of wealth and expensive taste....

By all accounts, and as the discussion below will make clear, Louis Vuitton aggressively enforces its trademark rights.

MOB was founded by Tara Martin in 2011. As noted, the name "My Other Bag" was inspired by novelty bumper stickers, which can sometimes be seen on inexpensive cars claiming that the driver's "other car" is an expensive, luxury car, such as a Mercedes. MOB produces and sells canvas tote bags bearing caricatures of iconic designer handbags on one side and the text "My Other Bag ..." on the other. Several of MOB's tote bags—one of which is depicted in the appendix to this Opinion (*see* Op. App., Figs. C–D)—display images concededly designed to evoke classic Louis Vuitton bags. As the appendix illustrates, the drawings use simplified colors, graphic lines, and patterns that resemble Louis Vuitton's famous Toile Monogram, Monogram Multicolore, and Damier designs, but replace the interlocking "LV" and "Louis Vuitton" with an interlocking "MOB" or "My Other Bag." MOB markets its bags as "[e]co-friendly, sustainable tote bags playfully parodying the designer bags we love, but practical enough for everyday life." While Louis Vuitton sells its handbags for hundreds, if not thousands, of dollars apiece, MOB's totes sell at prices between thirty and fifty-five dollars. Its website and other marketing play up the idea that high-priced designer bags cannot be used to carry around, say, dirty gym clothes or messy groceries, while its casual canvas totes can.

A. Trademark Dilution

....

1. Fair Use

[T]he Court concludes as a matter of law that MOB's bags are protected as fair use—in particular, that its use of Louis Vuitton's marks constitutes "parody." As noted, a successful parody communicates to a consumer that "an entity separate and distinct from the trademark owner is poking fun at a trademark or the policies of its owner." [Citation.] In other words, a parody clearly indicates to the ordinary observer "that the defendant is not connected in any way with the owner of the target trademark." That is precisely what MOB's bags communicate. Indeed, the whole point is to play on the well-known "my other car ..." joke by playfully suggesting that the carrier's "*other* bag"—that is, *not* the bag that he or she is carrying—is a Louis Vuitton bag. That joke—combined with the stylized, almost cartoonish renderings of Louis Vuitton's bags depicted on the totes—builds significant distance between MOB's inexpensive workhorse totes and the expensive handbags they are meant to evoke, and invites an amusing comparison between MOB and the luxury status of Louis Vuitton. Further, the image of exclusivity and refinery that Louis Vuitton has so carefully cultivated is, at least in part, the brunt of the joke: Whereas a Louis Vuitton handbag is something wealthy women may handle with reverent care and display to communicate a certain status, MOB's canvas totes are utilitarian bags "intended to be stuffed with produce at the supermarket, sweaty clothes at the gym, or towels at the beach."

Louis Vuitton protests that, even if MOB's totes are a parody of *something*, they are not a parody of its handbags and, relatedly, that MOB's argument is a *post hoc* fabrication for purposes of this litigation. The company notes that MOB's Chief

Executive Officer, Tara Martin, has referred to its bags as "iconic" and stated that she never intended to disparage Louis Vuitton. Thus, Louis Vuitton argues, the "My Other Bag ..." joke mocks only MOB itself or, to the extent it has a broader target, "any humor is merely part of a larger social commentary, not a parody directed towards Louis Vuitton or its products." In support of those arguments, Louis Vuitton relies heavily on its victory in an unpublished 2012 opinion from this District: *Louis Vuitton Malletier, S.A. v. Hyundai Motor Am.*, No. 10-CV-1611 (PKC), 2012 U.S. Dist. LEXIS 42795, 2012 WL 1022247 (S.D.N.Y. Mar. 22, 2012). In that case, Hyundai aired a thirty-second commercial titled "Luxury," which included "a four-second scene of an inner-city basketball game played on a lavish marble court with a gold hoop." The scene also included a basketball bearing marks meant to evoke the Louis Vuitton Toile Monogram. The Court rejected Hyundai's parody defense based in large part on deposition testimony from Hyundai representatives that conclusively established that the car company had no intention for the commercial to make any statement about Louis Vuitton *at all. See* 2012 U.S. Dist. LEXIS 42795, [WL] at *17–19 (excerpting deposition testimony establishing that Hyundai did not mean to "criticize" or "make fun of" Louis Vuitton, or even "compare the Hyundai with [Louis Vuitton]"). On the basis of that testimony, the Court concluded that Hyundai had "disclaimed any intention to parody, criticize or comment upon Louis Vuitton" and that the ad was only intended to make a "broader social comment" about "what it means for a product to be luxurious." [Citation.]

The *Hyundai* decision is not without its critics [citation], but, in any event, this case is easily distinguished on its facts. Here, unlike in *Hyundai*, it is self-evident that MOB did mean to say something about Louis Vuitton specifically. That is, Louis Vuitton's handbags are an integral part of the joke that gives MOB its name and features prominently on every tote bag that MOB sells. In arguing otherwise, Louis Vuitton takes too narrow a view of what can qualify as a parody. The quip "My Other Bag ... is a Louis Vuitton," printed on a workhorse canvas bag, derives its humor from a constellation of features—including the features of the canvas bag itself, society's larger obsession with status symbols, *and* the meticulously promoted image of expensive taste (or showy status) that Louis Vuitton handbags have, to many, come to symbolize. The fact that MOB's totes convey a message about more than *just* Louis Vuitton bags is not fatal to a successful parody defense. *See Campbell v. Acuff-Rose Music, Inc.*, 510 U.S. 569, 580 (1994) (holding that a copyright parodist must show that his parody, "*at least in part*, comments on [the parodied] author's work" (emphasis added)); [citations].

In those regards, another decision from this District, *Tommy Hilfiger Licensing, Inc. v. Nature Labs, LLC*, 221 F. Supp. 2d 410, 415 (S.D.N.Y. 2002), is more on point. That case involved a line of parody perfume products for use on pets. In particular, the defendant had created a pet perfume called Tommy Holedigger, which resembled a Tommy Hilfiger fragrance in name, scent, and packaging. Hilfiger, like Louis Vuitton here, argued (albeit in connection with a claim of trademark infringement rather than dilution) that the defendant was not entitled to protection as a parody because "its product admittedly makes no comment about Hilfiger." In support of that argument,

Hilfiger cited testimony from the defendant's general partner that his product was not intended to make any comment about Hilfiger or its products. Noting that the general partner had also testified that "he was intending to create a 'parody ... target[ing] ... Tommy Hilfiger,' 'a fun play on words,' or 'spoof ... [t]o create enjoyment, a lighter side,'" Judge Mukasey rejected Hilfiger's argument as follows:

> Although [the general partner] had difficulty expressing the parodic content of his communicative message, courts have explained that:
>
> > Trademark parodies ... do convey a message. The message may be simply that business and product images need not always be taken too seriously; a trademark parody reminds us that we are free to laugh at the images and associations linked with the mark. The message also may be a simple form of entertainment conveyed by juxtaposing the irreverent representation of the trademark with the idealized image created by the mark's owner.
>
> *Id.* (quoting *L.L. Bean, Inc. v. Drake Publishers, Inc.*, 811 F.2d 26, 34 (1st Cir. 1987)). He added, in a comment that applies equally well here: "One can readily see why high-end fashion brands would be ripe targets for such mockery." *Id.*

Alternatively, relying principally on *Dallas Cowboys Cheerleaders, Inc. v. Pussycat Cinema, Ltd.*, 604 F.2d 200 (2d Cir. 1979), Louis Vuitton argues that MOB's totes cannot be a parody because they do not need to use Louis Vuitton's trademarks for the parody to make sense. Strictly speaking, that is true—to the extent that MOB could use any well-known luxury handbag brand to make its points. But, whereas the defendant in *Dallas Cowboys Cheerleaders*, a purveyor of a "gross and revolting sex film," [citation] did not have to use anyone else's trademark—let alone the plaintiff's specific trademark—to make its point (allegedly, "comment[ing] on 'sexuality in athletics,'" the same cannot be said here. MOB's tote bags would not make their point, and certainly would not be funny, if the obverse of the tote merely depicted some generic handbag. Such a tote would confusingly communicate only that "my other bag ... is some other bag." In other words, Louis Vuitton's argument distorts any "necessity" requirement beyond recognition, and myopically suggests that, where a parody must evoke at least one of a finite set of marks in order to make its point, it can evoke none of them because reference to any *particular* mark in the set is not absolutely necessary. The Court declines to create such an illogical rule.

...

[The court's rejection of Vuitton's blurring claim is omitted]

APPENDIX

. . . .

Fig. B.—Louis Vuitton SPEEDY® Toile Monogram

Fig. C.—My Other Bag's Zoey—Tonal Brown Tote (Front)

Fig. D.—My Other Bag's Zoey—Tonal Brown Tote (Back)

Questions

1. Should it matter whether defendant's parody pokes fun at a trademarked product or rather at a social condition that the mark symbolizes (in addition to a single source of origin)? Is it possible to draw a distinction? For those who have studied copyright law, how successful have federal courts been in applying a parody/satire distinction to guide the result in infringement cases?

2. Should it matter whether defendant's parody is communicated in a traditionally expressive medium, such as a motion picture, or instead in an everyday item of merchandise (such as a tote bag or pet paraphernalia)?

3. *Louis Vuitton Malletier, S.A. v. Hyundai*, referred to in *Louis Vuitton Malletier, S.A. v. My Other Bag*, involved a fleeting (4 seconds) copying of the LV logo on a basketball in a commercial for the Hyundai automobile; the court rejected a parody defense under the TDRA and under the First Amendment. Compare the decision in *Louis Vuitton Malletier, S.A. v. Warner Bros. Entertainment, Inc.*, *supra* Chapter 8[C][1], applying *Rogers v Grimaldi* and rejecting a claim of likelihood of confusion with respect to a similarly fleeting appearance of the LV logo. Is *Rogers* irrelevant to dilution cases? Is the use of the logo less artistically relevant in the Hyundai commercial than in the movie? Are viewers of the commercial more likely to be misled about who made or licensed the commercial than viewers of the movie? Or is the difference simply that movies may invoke the *Rogers* analysis and commercials may not? If that's the rule, does it make sense? How would such a rule apply to public service announcements, political campaign commercials, or political issue ads?

Chapter 10

False Advertising

Rebecca Tushnet, *Running the Gamut from A to B: Federal Trademark and False Advertising Law*

159 U. PENN. L. REV. 1305 (2011) (excerpt)*

....

The Lanham Act was conceived as a federal trademark statute, protecting marketplace participants against unfair competition. Consumers are generally presumed to care about the origin or the brand-specific characteristics of a product. A Snickers is not just any chocolate-peanut-nougat confection, and a buyer is entitled to get a genuine Snickers bar if she wants one, not a counterfeit. Thus, trademark infringement is a type of false advertising—a false claim of origin, or perhaps a false claim about a product's characteristics.

From the beginning, the Lanham Act prohibited false claims in language that extended beyond trademark. Some circuits initially limited the scope of the Act to cases in which an advertiser made false statements about its own products by analogizing to situations in which the advertiser used an infringing mark to identify its own products. In those circuits, false statements about a competitor's product were the province of state trade libel and product defamation law, which were and remain substantially more limited in scope than the Lanham Act because of their scienter requirements. In 1988, Congress amended the Lanham Act to make clear that false statements about anyone's products or services were actionable.

While courts limited the false advertising provisions of the Lanham Act, they simultaneously interpreted trademark law expansively by treating infringement as a strict liability cause of action, among other things. Courts generally construed the Lanham Act to follow common law concepts of infringement, and so it was with intent. Intent to confuse could justify an inference that consumer confusion was likely, but even innocent intent would not save a defendant whose use was likely to cause confusion. When courts then confronted nontrademark Lanham Act claims, they imposed strict liability for false advertising as well.

....

Treating trademark infringement as a specialized type of false advertising makes sense, not only because of the statutory language, but also because of the logical

---

 [*Editors' Note*: Footnotes omitted.]

affinity between the concepts. The drafters of the *Restatement (Third) of Unfair Competition* observed that infringement claims fell within the literal scope of deceptive marketing, though they recommended that plaintiffs bring their claims under the section more specifically dealing with trademark infringement. Still, the common foundation largely justified common treatment....

---

15 U.S.C. § 1125(a)(1)(B) [Lanham Act § 43(a)(1)(B)]

(1) Any person who, on or in connection with any goods or services, or any container for goods, uses in commerce any word, term, name, symbol, or device, or any combination thereof, or any false designation of origin, false or misleading description of fact, or false or misleading representation of fact, which—

....

(B) in commercial advertising or promotion, misrepresents the nature, characteristics, qualities, or geographic origin of his or her or another person's goods, services, or commercial activities,

shall be liable in a civil action by any person who believes that he or she is or is likely to be damaged by such act.

Questions

1. Note that section 43(a)(1)(B) does not address all false or misleading representations made in commerce, but only those made "in commercial advertising or promotion." As we have seen in Chapter 7[C], after *Dastar*'s restrictive interpretation of "origin of goods" in section 43(a)(1)(A), false or misleading information regarding only the intellectual origin of works of authorship, is not actionable section 43(a)(1)(A) of the Lanham Act. But might section 43(a)(1)(B) cover some misrepresentations of authorship? For example, if Pirate Press were to publish a book and advertise it, falsely, as "The next wizardly book by Harry Potter's author, J.K. Rowling," would that be an actionable false representation of the nature, characteristics or qualities of the book? Or would *Dastar* bar the claim?

2. The Department of Veterans Affairs has registered "GI Bill" as a trademark for goods and services including "providing education benefits, namely, financial assistance such as accelerated payment and tuition assistance for institutions of higher learning, non-college degree programs, on-the-job training and apprenticeship training ... to Veterans, Service members, National Guard members, Selected Reserve members, and eligible dependents." Responding to an Executive Order, the registration seeks to counter the advertising and recruitment efforts of for-profit schools looking to bring in GI Bill tuition dollars. According to the Veterans Affairs Department, "In some cases, these schools have ensnared Veterans looking for info by using official-looking websites, which funneled potential recruits to those schools without any balanced, objective information." How, if at all, does registering the trademark in "GI Bill" give the government tools to fight fraud that are more effective than 43(a)(1)(B)?

3. Section 43(a) of the Lanham Act was amended in 1988 to expand the realm of actionable deceptive advertisements to include statements about another's product in addition to previously covered statements about one's own product. Is this a positive development, or should the trademark law revision have taken the opposite approach, and have eliminated private law federal false advertising claims altogether? Is more speech, in the form of replies or counter statements by the aggrieved producer, a better way to combat allegedly false speech in the market than curtailing a competitor's claims?

4. How should a court determine whether a contested representation is true or false?

A. Commercial Advertising or Promotion

Gordon and Breach Science Publishers S.A., STBS, Ltd. v. American Institute of Physics, 859 F. Supp. 1521 (S.D.N.Y. 1994): Gordon & Breach (G & B) is a for-profit publisher of scholarly journals. American Institute of Physics (AIP) is a non-profit learned society that also publishes scientific journals. G & B brought a §43(a)(1)(B) claim based on two articles physics Professor Henry Barschall published in AIP journals, ranking scientific journals in terms of "cost-effectiveness" (price of the journal per 1000 characters), "impact" (frequency of citation in academic literature), and a "cost/impact ratio." G & B's journals ranked at or near the worst in all of the metrics, and AIP's ranked at or near the best. G & B alleged that AIG had engaged in the promotion of its publications through: (1) AIP's circulation to librarians at a conference in Denver of preprints summarizing the results of Barschall's work; (2) a press release, in response to G & B's press release attacking Barschall's articles, restating the results of the articles; (3) a letter to the editor of *CBE Views* defending and reiterating the results of Barschall's articles, after an earlier issue charged Barschall with bias and inaccuracy; and (4) AIP's meetings with and emails to librarians, as well as frequent quotes to the media. AIP responded that its conduct did not constitute "commercial advertising or promotion" under Lanham Act §43 (a)(1)(B).

The court first observed that the legislative history of the then recent amendment to the act stressed that new §43 (a)(1)(B) claims for product disparagement should not impinge on free speech. The court then turned to other cases in the Second Circuit that had interpreted "commercial advertising or promotion" in contexts other than in a "traditional ad campaign":

> The few cases that explore the meaning of "commercial advertising or promotion" make clear that, while the courts have not had the opportunity to apply the Act to a fact pattern similar to this case, the Act's reach is broader than merely the "classic advertising campaign" to which defendants would confine it, and it covers misrepresentations by non-profit and for-profit organizations alike. *See National Artists Mgmt. Co. v. Weaving*, 769 F. Supp. 1224, 1232 (S.D.N.Y. 1991) (citing legislative history for proposition that Section 43(a) applies to non-profit organizations). Section 43(a) has been found applicable, for example, to the fundraising letters of a non-profit pregnancy

counseling group, *Birthright v. Birthright, Inc.*, 827 F. Supp. 1114, 1138 (D.N.J. 1993); to the distribution of marketing information to retailers at a trade show, *American Needle & Novelty, Inc. v. Drew Pearson Marketing, Inc.*, 820 F. Supp. 1072, 1077–78 (N.D. Ill. 1993) (dicta); and even to an individual's "bad-mouthing" of her former company over the telephone in calls made to colleagues and friends, *National Artists*, 769 F. Supp. at 1234–36.

....

In *National Artists*, which contains perhaps the most thorough discussion of this issue, Judge Conboy examined the Act's application to various allegedly defamatory telephone calls made by the former president of a theatrical booking company and her husband regarding their reasons for leaving the company. Judge Conboy concluded:

> It is true that defendants' conduct—speaking by telephone with a number of friends, acquaintances, and colleagues about the reasons for terminating their relationships with [the company]—is not "commercial advertising and promotion" in the traditional sense of large-scale, nationwide commercial advertising campaigns. In the context of the theatre-booking industry, however, "services" are "promoted" by word-of-mouth and information is spread through a network of telephone contacts with producers, promoters, and presenters.

769 F. Supp. at 1235.

In *American Needle*, the court distinguished Judge Conboy's conclusion, noting that "[t]he level of circulation required to constitute advertising and promotion will undeniably vary from industry to industry and from case to case." 820 F. Supp. at 1078. *American Needle* concerned the "licensed headwear" industry, in which manufacturers are licensed by professional sports leagues to reproduce team logos on caps and hats. The court concluded that, in that industry, a single letter privately addressed to a non-consuming licensor did not rise to the requisite level; that is, it constituted an "isolated individualized written statement" rather than the kind of "public dissemination of information" necessary to state a claim under the Lanham Act. *Id.* at 1077–78.

The principles from the cases and legislative history may be summed up as follows: In order for representations to constitute "commercial advertising or promotion" under Section 43(a)(1)(B), they must be: (1) commercial speech; (2) by a defendant who is in commercial competition with plaintiff; (3) for the purpose of influencing consumers to buy defendant's goods or services. While the representations need not be made in a "classic advertising campaign," but may consist instead of more informal types of "promotion," the representations (4) must be disseminated sufficiently to the relevant purchasing public to constitute "advertising" or "promotion" within that industry.

The court ruled that AIP's publication of articles, as well as its press release and letter to the editor constituted protected speech, and dismissed the complaint with regard to those acts, but rejected the motion to dismiss with respect to AIP's dissemination of preprints and alleged campaign of sending emails to and meeting with librarians.

Neuros Co., Ltd. v. Kturbo, Inc.

698 F.3d 514 (7th Cir. 2012)

POSNER, CIRCUIT JUDGE.

This litigation, now in its fourth year, is between competing manufacturers of high-speed turbo blowers used by waste water treatment plants. The blowers maintain the oxygen dissolved in the water at a level needed by the aerobic (that is, oxygen-dependentbacteria that play a critical role in the treatment process by breaking down organic waste into carbon dioxide, nitrogen, and water. The plaintiffs operate in the United States as a joint venture under the name APG-Neuros, and to simplify exposition we'll pretend that APG-Neuros *is* the plaintiff and (for further simplification) call it Neuros.

Neuros was the first company to offer such blowers to waste water treatment facilities in North America. That was in 2006 and two years later the defendant, KTurbo, began offering its own blowers to those facilities, though with little success.

In 2008 Neuros won a bidding contest to supply high-speed turbo blowers to a waste water treatment plant in Utah. KTurbo came in third in the bidding—last, because there were only three bidders. Disappointed with the outcome of the bidding contest, the chief executive officer of KTurbo, HeonSeok Lee, prepared a series of PowerPoint slides and related tables that accused Neuros of fraud by representing to the Utah purchaser that its blowers would achieve a "total efficiency" that Lee claimed, probably correctly, was unattainable.

Waste water treatment plants hire consulting engineers to select, test, and install the turbo blowers. Lee's slides were aimed at those engineers. Here is a typical slide:

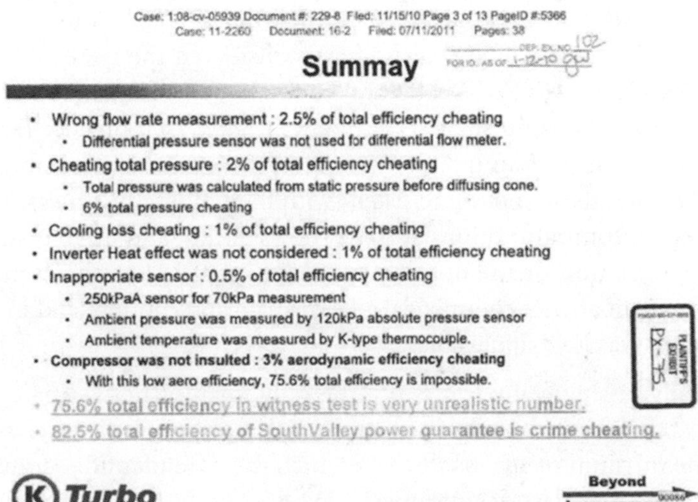

Lee made his PowerPoint presentation to a number of the engineering firms that advise waste water treatment plants on which turbo blowers to buy. Judging from the fact that KTurbo failed, so far as appears, to wrest any business from Neuros, the consulting engineers were not impressed by the slide show. Lee also published his accusations on one of KTurbo's websites and sent them to the sales representatives that the company uses to help market its blowers, doubtless hoping the representatives would convey the accusations to the engineers whom they visited on KTurbo's behalf.

[Neuros brought suit, alleging defamation and false advertising under the Lnham Act. After a bench trial, the district court found in Neuro's favor on the defamation claim, but dismissed the Lanham Act claim because the Power Point slides did not represent "commercial Advertising or promotion." KTurbo appealed the defamation judgment and Neuro cross-appealed the dismissal of its Lanham Act claim.]

....

[I]s the Lanham Act applicable? It's limited to misrepresentations "in commercial advertising or promotion," 15 U.S.C. § 1125(a)(1)(B), and in *Sanderson v. Culligan Int'l Co.*, 415 F.3d 620, 624 (7th Cir. 2005), we held that three person-to-person communications at trade shows did not constitute commercial advertising or promotion, while in *First Health Group Corp. v. BCE Emergis Corp.*, 269 F.3d 800, 803–04 (7th Cir. 2001), we said that the statutory term is limited to "promotional material disseminated to anonymous recipients" and that "an advertisement read by millions (or even thousands in a trade magazine) is advertising, while a person-to-person pitch by an account executive is not," before holding that in any event the defendant's promotional materials did not make false or misleading representations. In between those two decisions came *ISI Int'l, Inc. v. Borden Ladner Gervais, LLP*, 316 F.3d 731, 733 (7th Cir. 2003), which held that sending letters to the plaintiff's business partners, warning them (falsely) that if they continued dealing with the plaintiff they would be liable for patent infringement, was not commercial advertising or promotion.

These cases do not hold that "advertising or promotion" is always limited to published or broadcast materials—an interpretation that would put us at odds with all seven other federal courts of appeals to have considered the issue. [Citations.] All but one of these cases was decided before *Sanderson*, and four were decided before *First Health*, and there is no suggestion in either *Sanderson* or *First Health* (or for that matter in *ISI Int'l*) of an intention to create an intercircuit conflict. The cases from the other circuits are not inconsistent with the holding in *Sanderson* that three person-to-person communications at trade shows do not add up to commercial advertising or promotion or the holding in *ISI Int'l* that letters threatening suit for patent infringement are not commercial advertising or promotion; and in *First Health* the Lanham Act was held applicable.

A classic advertising campaign is not the only form of marketing embraced by the statutory term "commercial advertising or promotion." *Podiatrist Ass'n* required merely "some medium or means through which the defendant disseminated information to a particular class of consumers." 332 F.3d at 20. And the most recent case,

LidoChem, explained that "the required level of dissemination to the relevant purchasing public 'will vary according to the specifics of the industry.'" 2012 U.S. App. LEXIS 19266, at *6.

If "advertising or promotion" just meant "advertising," then "promotion" would do no work in the statute. More important (because of the frequency of redundant language in statutes, [citations], there are industries in which promotion—a systematic communicative endeavor to persuade possible customers to buy the seller's product—takes a form other than publishing or broadcasting. The de facto customers (de facto rather than de jure because they are the purchasers' agents, rather than the purchasers) for high-speed turbo blowers used in waste water treatment plants are the consulting engineers who manage the plants' bidding and purchasing. Lee's road show visited most of the engineering companies that do this, and each show presented promotional materials that trashed Neuros, KTurbo's most prominent competitor.

"Negative" ads—ads that denigrate a competitor—are a conventional though frequently disparaged form of commercial advertising. KTurbo's negative ads reached fewer customers than a conventional campaign of advertising or promotion would have done, but that was because there are fewer customers for high-speed turbo blowers in waste water treatment plants than there are for dog collars. Road shows are a common method of promotion; it is, for example, the standard method of promoting IPOs. And remember that some of KTurbo's false statements were posted on one of its websites—a reminder that methods of advertising and promotion are changing with innovations in communications media; they are no longer, if they ever were, confined to newspaper and magazine ads, radio and television commercials, and billboards.

The district court was troubled by the fact that "there is no evidence that the statements at issue were presented to any members of the general public." Well of course not; members of the general public do not buy high-speed turbo blowers or advise waste water treatment plants on the purchase of such blowers. There is no basis for limiting the Lanham Act to advertising or promotion directed to the *general* public, and the case law does not do that. *See, e.g., LidoChem, Inc. v. Stoller Enterprises, Inc., supra*, 2012 U.S. App. LEXIS 19266, at *8 (applying the Act to letters sent and statements made to distributors of farm chemicals); *Porous Media Corp. v. Pall Corp., supra*, 173 F.3d at 1114 (applying the Act to an "alert" sent only to large makers of air filters and to resellers of the filters); *Coastal Abstract Service, Inc. v. First American Title Ins. Co., supra*, 173 F.3d at 735 (to statements made only to one of two or three national refinancing companies); *Seven-Up Co. v. Coca-Cola Co., supra*, 86 F.3d at 1381 (only to independent soft drink bottlers). What advertising is *not* directed to subsets of the public (dog owners in our previous example) rather than to 314 million individuals and millions of firms? One of the subsets is engineering firms, and others are subsets of engineering firms such as the civil engineering firms that were faxed advertisements in *CE Design Ltd. v. King Architectural Metals, Inc.*, 637 F.3d 721 (7th Cir. 2011). No one doubted that those advertisements (challenged under a different statute) were—advertising.

Questions

1. The *Gordon & Breach* decision holds that in order for representations to constitute "commercial advertising or promotion" under Section 43(a)(1)(B), they must be made by a defendant who is in commercial competition with plaintiff. Should commercial advertising or promotion under Section 43(a)(1)(B) be actionable only if done by plaintiff's competitor? Why or why not?

2. Is it commercial advertising or promotion for defendant's sales force to make disparaging remarks about plaintiff to individual customers? In *Fashion Boutique v. Fendi USA*, 314 F.3d 48 (2d Cir. 2002), the court held that evidence of twenty-seven disparaging remarks made by sales staff to customers was "insufficient to satisfy the requirement that representations be disseminated widely in order to constitute 'commercial advertising or promotion' under the Lanham Act."

3. Is it commercial advertising or promotion for an employee who is leaving plaintiff's firm for a competing firm to send an email to 22 of her clients stating that plaintiff was merging with her new firm and moving its offices to the new firm's location? In *Grubbs v. Sheakly Group*, 807 F.3d 785 (6th Cir 2015), the court held that it was, because the email was disseminated to a substantial portion of the plaintiff's existing customer base.

4. Gnosis manufactures and sells a vitamin B product that is a mixture of both biologically active and inactive forms for use in nutritional supplements. However, at a trade show, Gnosis distributed product specification sheets that incorrectly listed the product as consisting only of the biologically active form. Merck, a competitor who does manufacture a pure biologically active vitamin B product, brought suit under §43(a)(1)(B). Is the distribution of the product specification sheets at the trade show "commercial advertising or promotion" within the meaning of the Act? After a bench trial, the district court concluded that it was. *See Merck Eprova AG v. Gnosis S.P.A.*, 901 F. Supp. 2d 436 (S.D.N.Y. 2012), *aff'd*, 760 F.3d 247 (2d Cir. 2014). In affirming the district court's judgment, the Second Circuit further ruled that "in a case where willful deception is proved, a presumption of injury may be used to award a plaintiff damages in the form of defendant's profits, and may, in circumstances such as those present here, warrant enhanced damages."

5. If unionized airline mechanics post a misleading review in yelp.com claiming that their airline's maintenance practices are unsafe, may the airline recover under the Lanham Act? Would your answer be different if the review were placed by a competing airline? Would it matter whether the reviewer's affiliation were disclosed?

6. Can you think of other kinds of non-advertising activities a company undertakes in support of its goods or services that would constitute "commercial ... promotion"? That would not constitute "commercial ... promotion"?

B. Literal Falsehood

Coca-Cola Co. v. Tropicana Prods., Inc.

690 F.2d 312 (2d Cir. 1982)

CARDAMONE, J:

A proverb current even in the days of ancient Rome was "seeing is believing." Today, a great deal of what people see flashes before them on their TV sets. This case involves a 30-second television commercial with simultaneous audio and video components. We have no doubt that the byword of Rome is as valid now as it was then. And, if seeing something on TV has a tendency to persuade a viewer to believe, how much greater is the impact on a viewer's credulity when he both sees and hears a message at the same time?

In mid-February of 1982 defendant Tropicana Products, Inc. (Tropicana) began airing a new television commercial for its Premium Pack orange juice. The commercial shows the renowned American Olympic athlete Bruce Jenner squeezing an orange while saying "It's pure, pasteurized juice as it comes from the orange," and then shows Jenner pouring the fresh-squeezed juice into a Tropicana carton while the audio states "It's the only leading brand not made with concentrate and water."

Soon after the advertisement began running, plaintiff Coca-Cola Company (Coke, Coca-Cola), maker of Minute Maid orange juice, brought suit in the United States District Court for the Southern District of New York against Tropicana for false advertising in violation of section 43(a) of the Lanham Act.... Coke claimed the commercial is false because it incorrectly represents that Premium Pack contains unprocessed, fresh-squeezed juice when in fact the juice is pasteurized (heated to about 200 degrees Fahrenheit) and sometimes frozen prior to packaging. The court below denied plaintiff's motion for a preliminary injunction to enjoin further broadcast of the advertisement pending the outcome of this litigation. In our view preliminary injunctive relief is appropriate.

....

II. *Irreparable Injury*

Perhaps the most difficult element to demonstrate when seeking an injunction against false advertising is the likelihood that one will suffer irreparable harm if the injunction does not issue. It is virtually impossible to prove that so much of one's sales will be lost or that one's goodwill will be damaged as a direct result of a competitor's advertisement. Too many market variables enter into the advertising-sales equation. Because of these impediments, a Lanham Act plaintiff who can prove actual lost sales may obtain an injunction even if most of his sales decline is attributable to factors other than a competitor's false advertising. In fact, he need not even point to an actual loss or diversion of sales.

The Lanham Act plaintiff must, however, offer something more than a mere subjective belief that he is likely to be injured as a result of the false advertising; he must submit proof which provides a reasonable basis for that belief. The likelihood of injury and causation will not be presumed, but must be demonstrated in some manner.

Two recent decisions of this Court have examined the type of proof necessary to satisfy this requirement. Relying on the fact that the products involved were in head-to-head competition, the Court in both cases directed the issuance of a preliminary injunction under the Lanham Act. *Vidal Sassoon*, 661 F.2d at 227; *Johnson & Johnson*, 631 F.2d at 189–91. In both decisions the Court reasoned that sales of the plaintiffs' products would probably be harmed if the competing products' advertising tended to mislead consumers in the manner alleged.[3] Market studies were used as evidence that some consumers were in fact misled by the advertising in issue. Thus, the market studies supplied the causative link between the advertising and the plaintiffs' potential lost sales; and thereby indicated a likelihood of injury.

Applying the same reasoning to the instant case, if consumers are misled by Tropicana's commercial, Coca-Cola probably would suffer irreparable injury. Tropicana and Coca-Cola are the leading national competitors for the chilled (ready-to-serve) orange juice market. If Tropicana's advertisement misleads consumers into believing that Premium Pack is a more desirable product because it contains only fresh-squeezed, unprocessed juice, then it is likely that Coke will lose a portion of the chilled juice market and thus suffer irreparable injury.

Evidence in the record supports the conclusion that consumers are likely to be misled in this manner. A consumer reaction survey conducted by ASI Market Research, Inc. and a Burke test, measuring recall of the commercial after it was aired on television, were admitted into evidence, though neither one was considered by the district court in reference to irreparable injury. The trial court examined the ASI survey regarding the issue of likelihood of success on the merits, and found that it contained various flaws which made it difficult to determine for certain whether a large number of consumers were misled. We do not disagree with those findings. We note, moreover, that despite these flaws the district court ruled that there were at least a small number of clearly deceived ASI interviewees. Our examination of the Burke test results leads to the same conclusion, *i.e.*, that a not insubstantial number of consumers were clearly misled by the defendant's ad. Together these tests provide sufficient evidence of a risk of irreparable harm because they demonstrate that a significant number of consumers would be likely to be misled. The trial court should have concluded, as did this Court in *Vidal Sassoon* and *Johnson & Johnson*, that the commercial will mislead consumers and, as a consequence, shift their purchases from plaintiff's product to defendant's. Coke, therefore, demonstrated that it is likely to suffer irreparable injury.

---

3. In *Vidal Sasoon* consumers were allegedly misled to believe that "Body on Tap" shampoo was an all-around superior product. In *Johnson & Johnson* consumers were allegedly misled into thinking that using NAIR depilatory with baby oil would obviate the need for using baby oil alone to moisturize the skin after shaving.

III. *Likelihood of Success on the Merits*

Once the initial requisite showing of irreparable harm has been made, the party seeking a preliminary injunction must satisfy either of the two alternatives regarding the merits of his case. We find that Coca-Cola satisfies the more stringent first alternative because it is likely to succeed on the merits of its false advertising action.

Coke is entitled to relief under the Lanham Act if Tropicana has used a false description or representation in its Jenner commercial. *See* 15 U.S.C. § 1125(a). When a merchandising statement or representation is literally or explicitly false, the court may grant relief without reference to the advertisement's impact on the buying public. When the challenged advertisement is implicitly rather than explicitly false, its tendency to violate the Lanham Act by misleading, confusing or deceiving should be tested by public reaction.

In viewing defendant's 30-second commercial at oral argument, we concluded that the trial court's finding that this ad was not facially false is an error of fact. Since the trial judge's finding on this issue was based solely on the inference it drew from reviewing documentary evidence, consisting of the commercial, we are in as good a position as it was to draw an appropriate inference. We find, therefore, that the squeezing-pouring sequence in the Jenner commercial is false on its face. The visual component of the ad makes an explicit representation that Premium Pack is produced by squeezing oranges and pouring the freshly-squeezed juice directly into the carton. This is not a true representation of how the product is prepared. Premium Pack juice is heated and sometimes frozen prior to packaging. Additionally, the simultaneous audio component of the ad states that Premium Pack is "pasteurized juice as it comes from the orange." This statement is blatantly false—pasteurized juice does not come from oranges. Pasteurization entails heating the juice to approximately 200 degrees Fahrenheit to kill certain natural enzymes and microorganisms which cause spoilage. Moreover, even if the addition of the word "pasteurized" somehow made sense and effectively qualified the visual image, Tropicana's commercial nevertheless represented that the juice is only squeezed, heated and packaged when in fact it may actually also be frozen.

Hence, Coke is likely to succeed in arguing that Tropicana's ad is false and that it is entitled to relief under the Lanham Act. The purpose of the Act is to insure truthfulness in advertising and to eliminate misrepresentations with reference to the inherent quality or characteristic of another's product. The claim that Tropicana's Premium Pack contains only fresh-squeezed, unprocessed juice is clearly a misrepresentation as to that product's inherent quality or characteristic. Since the plaintiff has satisfied the first preliminary injunction alternative, we need not decide whether the balance of hardships tips in its favor.

Because Tropicana has made a false representation in its advertising and Coke is likely to suffer irreparable harm as a result, we reverse the district court's denial of plaintiff's application and remand this case for issuance of a preliminary injunction preventing broadcast of the squeezing-pouring sequence in the Jenner commercial.

Questions

1. In *Coca-Cola v. Tropicana*, the Second Circuit distinguishes between explicitly and implicitly false statements. In the latter instance, no injunction will issue without evaluation of the advertisement's impact on the buying public. Why should plaintiffs complaining of explicitly false statements not also be required to demonstrate that the advertisement in fact tends to deceive?*

2. Johnson & Johnson, maker of Mylanta® antacid introduced Mylanta® Night Time Strength antacid, a formulation with more active ingredients per teaspoon than regular Mylanta. Ads for the new product described it as "made just for night-time heartburn," and "specially formulated for night time heartburn." The maker of Maalox® insists that the name of the product and the supporting ads are literally false, because they claim that Mylanta Night Time Strength is specially formulated, and therefore better than other antacids at reliving night-time heartburn, and that they claim that Mylanta Night Time Strength provides heartburn relief through the night. Maalox seeks to force Johnson and Johnson to stop running the ads and to rename its product. Johnson & Johnson concedes that the only difference between regular Mylanta and Mylanta Night Time Strength is that the latter is more concentrated, but it insists that neither the name of the product nor its ads contain any literal falsity. How should the court rule? *See Novartis Consumer Health v. Johnson & Johnson-Merck Consumer Pharmaceuticals*, 290 F.3d 578 (3d Cir. 2002).

3. United Industries produces Maxattrax cockroach bait. Its "Side by Side" commercial depicts a split-screen view of two roach bait products on two kitchen countertops. The lighting is dark. On the left, one sees the Maxattrax box; on the right, a generic "Roach Bait" box that is vaguely similar to the packaging of the Combat brand sold by Clorox. A voiceover asks: "Can you guess which bait kills roaches in 24 hours?" The lights then come up as the camera pans beyond the boxes to reveal a clean, calm, pristine kitchen, uninhabited by roaches, on the Maxattrax side. On the other side, the kitchen is in a chaotic state: cupboards and drawers are opening, items on the counter are turning over, paper towels are spinning off the dispenser, a spice rack is convulsing and losing its spices, all the apparent result of a major roach infestation. At the same time, the message "Based on lab tests" appear in small print at the bottom of the screen. The two roach bait boxes then reappear on the split-screen, and several computer-animated roaches on the "Roach Bait" side appear to kick over the generic box and dance gleefully upon it. The final visual is of the Maxattrax box

---

* *Editors' Note*: In *Merck Eprova AG v. Gnosis S.P.A.*, 760 F.3d 247 (2d Cir. 2014), the Second Circuit reaffirmed its rule that

> [W]here a defendant's advertising of products is literally false, a Lanham Act plaintiff need not "provide evidence of actual consumer confusion by resort to witness testimony, consumer surveys, or other such evidence in order to establish entitlement to damages under the Lanham Act." ... In light of this factual finding of literal falsity, the district court was correct to presume consumer confusion from Gnosis's marketing specification sheets, brochures, data sheets, and certificates of analysis.... Once literal falsity—an unchallenged factual finding—was proved, no further evidence of actual consumer confusion was necessary.

[Citations and internal quotations omitted.]

only, over which the announcer concluded, "to kill roaches in 24 hours, it's hot-shot Maxattrax. Maxattrax, it's the no-wait roach bait." Lab tests indicated that roaches died within 24 hours of contact with Maxattrax roach bait; they did not show that Maxattrax would clear up a roach infestation problem within 24 hours. Is the Maxattrax ad literally false? *See United Industries Corp. v. Clorox Co.*, 140 F.3d 1175 (8th Cir. 1998).

4. Gillette's television advertising for its M3 Power Razor System illustrates its claim that "micro-pulses raise hair up and away from skin," through a 1.8 second-long animated dramatization of hairs growing. In the animated cartoon, the oscillation produced by the M3 Power is shown as green waves moving over hairs. In response, the hairs shown extended in length in the direction of growth and changed angle towards a more vertical position. During the animation, the voice-over states: "Turn it on and micropulses raise the hair so the blades can shave closer." Gillette concedes that M3 Power's oscillations do not cause hair to change angle on the face, and it has ceased claiming that its razor changes the angle of the hair. But Gillette contends its razor does raise hairs, even if the hair extension effect shown in the animation is "somewhat exaggerated." Is the advertisement, without the explicit claim of angle-change, literally false? *See Schick Manufacturing, Inc. v. The Gillette Company*, 372 F. Supp. 2d 273 (D. Conn. 2005).

Clorox Co., Puerto Rico v. Proctor & Gamble Commercial Co.

228 F.3d 24 (1st Cir. 2000)

Lipez, Circuit Judge:

"Mas blanco no se puede" (Whiter is not possible) was the advertising tag line used by the defendant, the Proctor and Gamble Commercial Company, to sell its detergent, Ace con Blanqueador (Ace with whitener), in Puerto Rico. The Clorox Company Puerto Rico cried foul, complaining that no detergent brings out the white like its chlorine bleach when used with a detergent. Proctor & Gamble modified its pitch, inviting consumers to "Compare con su detergente ... Mas blanco no se puede" (Compare with your detergent ... Whiter is not possible). Unimpressed by this change, Clorox sued, alleging, inter alia, that the advertisements were false and misleading in violation of Section 43(a) of the Lanham Act, 15 U.S.C. § 1125(a). After Clorox moved for a preliminary injunction, the district court dismissed the false advertising claim sua sponte. Concluding that Clorox has stated a claim under § 43(a) of the Lanham Act, we vacate the dismissal and remand to the district court for further proceedings.

I.

We present the facts in the light most favorable to Clorox, the party opposing the dismissal of the complaint. *See Langadinos v. American Airlines, Inc.*, 199 F.3d 68, 69 (1st Cir. 2000). In 1989, Proctor & Gamble introduced in Puerto Rico Ace con Blanqueador, a powdered laundry detergent that contains a non-chlorine whitening agent described as a "color-safe oxygen bleach" with a patented "activator," the same formula used in powdered Tide with Bleach marketed in the continental United States. In 1997, Proctor & Gamble introduced a liquid version of Ace containing a "compound of high levels of sulfactants and enzymes which function as a whitener and a color enhancer," the same formula used in liquid Tide with Bleach Alternative.

The Original Doorstep Challenge Campaign

Proctor & Gamble conducted some consumer studies in 1997 and determined that an obstacle to obtaining an enhanced market share for Ace con Blanqueador was the public's perception that chlorine bleach was necessary to get clothes white. Using this new information, Proctor & Gamble implemented an advertising campaign to counter the perception of consumers that chlorine bleach was necessary, and to convince them that Ace was a superior option to using a lower-priced detergent in conjunction with chlorine bleach. This "Doorstep Challenge" included a series of television advertisements in which Francisco Zamora, a television celebrity in Puerto Rico, visited women in their homes to ask them about their laundry practices and to elicit their praise for Ace. In the commercials depicting powdered Ace, the overriding theme was that chlorine bleach was not necessary to get clothes white if washed with Ace. The commercials pitching liquid Ace also emphasized its enhanced whitening capacity, but did not specifically mention chlorine bleach. Each commercial closed with the tag line, "Whiter is not possible," a slogan Proctor & Gamble had been using since powdered Ace arrived on the market in 1989.

For instance, the "Evelyn" commercial for powdered Ace went as follows:

> Francisco: Do you use Ace?
>
> She: No....
>
> Fco: What is your laundry routine?
>
> She: I put in the three detergents I use, I throw in a bit of chlorine and I let it soak until the next day. I waste a lot of time ... but to accomplish what I want I have to do it that way.
>
> Fco: I dare you to wash your white garments with Ace and nothing else!
>
> She: Without chlorine?
>
> ....
>
> Fco: Without chlorine ... we're going to wash all these.
>
> She: I don't think so....
>
> She: The truth is ... that's whiteness, that's whiteness! So now I'm going to save money, time ...
>
> ....
>
> [VISUAL: Whiter is not possible.]

The Promotional Mailing

As part of its campaign to sell Ace, Proctor & Gamble sent a promotional brochure and product sample to consumers in Puerto Rico. The first page of the brochure depicted a bowling ball imprinted with the word "Ace" standing in front of several bowling pins that resembled Clorox bottles. The caption read: "Da en el blanco con una sola tirada," (hit the [white] spot with just one shot). The second and third pages of the brochure contained additional pictures surrounded by punchy statements in Spanish like, "Dare to pass the test. Wash with Ace and nothing else," "Say goodbye to the complications of chlorine and other cleaners," and "Resist the 'bombs.'[1] Put your ACE con Blanqueador to the test." Like the television commercials, the brochure ended with the tag line, "Whiter is not possible!"

The Modified Campaign

In January 1998, the Clorox Company, which markets in Puerto Rico a brand of chlorine-based liquid bleach called Clorox, sent a letter to Proctor & Gamble complaining that the Doorstep Challenge campaign was false and misleading, and demanding that Proctor & Gamble stop running the television advertisements. Although Proctor & Gamble would not alter the theme of its advertising, it agreed to soften the tag line by adding the qualification, "compare with your detergent," before the phrase "whiter is not possible."

The qualification did not satisfy Clorox. In March 1998, Clorox filed this lawsuit, alleging in its complaint violations of Section 43(a) of the Lanham Act, 15 U.S.C. § 1125(a)....

Clorox sought to permanently enjoin Proctor & Gamble from "making any claims that Ace gets clothes 'the whitest possible,' *without* the use of Clorox." (Emphasis in original). Additionally, Clorox sought damages and attorneys' fees under § 43(a) of the Lanham Act. Finally, Clorox moved for a preliminary injunction on its Lanham Act claim. In connection with the motion for a preliminary injunction, the parties conducted document production and depositions and submitted to the court relevant evidentiary materials, including consumer surveys, statements of experts, and the testimony of various witnesses. The district court did not hear oral argument.

In March 1999, ... the district court dismissed the Lanham Act claim sua sponte. This appeal followed....

II.

....

B. The Lanham Act False Advertising Claims

....

A plaintiff can succeed on a false advertising claim by proving either that an advertisement is false on its face or that the advertisement is literally true or ambiguous but likely to mislead and confuse consumers. *See Southland Sod Farms v. Stover Seed Co.*, 108 F.3d 1134, 1139 (9th Cir. 1997); *Castrol, Inc. v. Pennzoil Co.*, 987 F.2d 939, 943 (3d Cir. 1993); *Abbott Labs. v. Mead Johnson & Co.*, 971 F.2d 6, 13 (7th Cir. 1992).

1. The combination of detergent and chlorine bleach is called "la bomba" in Puerto Rico.

If the advertisement is literally false, the court may grant relief without considering evidence of consumer reaction. *See United Indus. Corp. v. Clorox Co.*, 140 F.3d 1175, 1180 (8th Cir. 1998). In the absence of such literal falsity, an additional burden is placed upon the plaintiff to show that the advertisement, though explicitly true, nonetheless conveys a misleading message to the viewing public. *See Sandoz Pharms. Corp. v. Richardson-Vicks, Inc.*, 902 F.2d 222, 228–29 (3d Cir. 1990). To satisfy its burden, the plaintiff must show how consumers have actually reacted to the challenged advertisement rather than merely demonstrating how they could have reacted. *See id.* at 229.

Clorox's amended complaint alleged that Proctor & Gamble's original and modified Doorstep Challenge television campaigns, as well as the promotional brochure, were false and misleading. Specifically, Clorox alleged that the Doorstep Challenge advertisements and promotions conveyed the false and misleading message to the Puerto Rican public that Ace con Blanqueador gets clothes as white or whiter than a detergent used with chlorine bleach. Clorox also alleged that the name "Ace con Blanqueador" is literally false with respect to Ace liquid detergent.

The district court's analysis of the Lanham Act claim consisted of two paragraphs in which it reasoned that Clorox "has failed to state a claim" under the Lanham Act because it could not establish that Proctor & Gamble's advertisements contained false or misleading statements. In particular, it found that the tag line appearing in the modified campaign commercials, "Compare with your detergent ... Whiter is not possible," was not false because it compared Ace only to other detergents, not to detergents used with chlorine bleach. The court also stated that, "Ace's comparison claim" was not actionable under the Lanham Act because it was "mere puffing."

....

We analyze Clorox's various allegations de novo, ... focusing on (1) the allegations of literal falsity, (2) the allegations of misleading advertising, and (3) the concept of "puffery."

1. *Claims of Literal Falsity*

Clorox challenged two features of Proctor & Gamble's advertising campaign as literally false. First, Clorox alleged that the television commercials that aired in the original and modified campaign claimed that Ace gets clothes as white or whiter than chlorine bleach. According to Clorox, that claim is literally false because tests prove that chlorine bleach whitens better than detergent used alone. Second, Clorox alleged that the name, "Ace con Blanqueador," is literally false with respect to Ace liquid detergent because it falsely suggests that Ace liquid contains whitener or bleach.

a. *The Television Advertisements*

Whether an advertisement is literally false is typically an issue of fact. *See Mead Johnson & Co. v. Abbott Labs.*, 209 F.3d 1032, 1034 (7th Cir. 2000) (denying petition for rehearing and amending prior panel opinion). At least two factual questions must be answered in evaluating the accuracy of any particular advertisement. First, a factfinder must determine the claim conveyed by the advertisement. *See United Indus. Corp.*, 140 F.3d at 1181 (applying clearly erroneous standard to review of district court's factual determination regarding the claim conveyed by an advertisement for roach bait); *Johnson & Johnson v. GAC Int'l, Inc.*, 862 F.2d 975, 979 (2d Cir. 1988). Once the claim made by the advertisement has been determined, the factfinder must then evaluate whether that claim is false. *See Castrol*, 987 F.2d at 944.

In the case at hand, the parties focus their attention solely upon the first of these factual determinations. The complaint asserts that in head-to-head whitening tests, Clorox achieved "by far, superior results" to Ace. Clorox also emphasizes that "Ace's own boxes" state that in certain cases, for better results, the consumers must use chlorine bleach. In reviewing the motion to dismiss, we therefore assume as true that chlorine bleach whitens better than Ace and that a contrary claim would be literally false. The primary dispute between the parties is not which product whitens better,[8] but rather whether any of Proctor & Gamble's advertisements make a claim of whitening superiority over chlorine bleach.

Although factfinders usually base literal falsity determinations upon the explicit claims made by an advertisement, they may also consider any claims the advertisement conveys by "necessary implication." [Citations.] A claim is conveyed by necessary implication when, considering the advertisement in its entirety, the audience would recognize the claim as readily as if it had been explicitly stated....

....

We conclude that Clorox has stated a claim that Proctor & Gamble's original Doorstep Challenge commercials are literally false. These commercials juxtapose a tag line, "Whiter is not possible," with images of consumers who normally used bleach to achieve white clothes and who are favorably impressed by the results obtained from using Ace alone. The overall theme of the commercials is that bleach is unnecessary if clothes are washed with Ace, and, in fact, many of the consumers visited by Zamora are congratulated at the end of the commercials for passing "the Ace whiteness challenge without chlorine." Some of the commercials also suggest that eliminating chlorine from the laundry process will save consumers time or money, or curtail the negative side effects of washing clothes with chlorine. A factfinder could reasonably conclude that, viewed in their entirety, these advertisements claim that Ace is equal or superior in whitening ability to a detergent and bleach combination.

The modified Doorstep Challenge campaign continued the same visual comparisons, as well as the congratulatory comments for passing the "Ace whiteness challenge without chlorine," but added the words "Compare your detergent" to the "Whiter is not possible" tag line shown at the bottom of the screen at the end of the commercials. Although this change may render the comparative claim of the advertisements more ambiguous, we nonetheless conclude that it remains reasonable to interpret these

8. Indeed, Proctor & Gamble does not challenge on appeal Clorox's assertion that chlorine bleach in combination with a detergent gets clothes whiter than its Ace detergent.

advertisements as making by necessary implication a superiority claim for Ace over chlorine bleach. Consequently, the court erred in dismissing Clorox's literal falsity claims with respect to both Doorstep Challenge campaigns.

b. *The Name "Ace con Blanqueador"*

Clorox also alleged that the name, "Ace con Blanqueador," as applied to liquid Ace, is literally false. According to Clorox, the word "blanqueador" implies that liquid Ace has whitening capabilities like bleach. Clorox alleged that this is literally false because in its liquid form Ace does not contain bleach or whitening agents. Instead, it contains only a "color enhancer." Clorox emphasizes that liquid Ace uses the same formula as "Tide with Bleach Alternative" whose name, unlike "blanqueador," clearly signifies the absence of bleach. Proctor & Gamble responds that "blanqueador" means "whitener," and that the name cannot be literally false because tests show that the agents added to liquid Ace produce greater whiteness than detergents without those agents.

Clorox's allegations about the use of the name "Ace con Blanqueador" for the liquid detergent state a claim for literal falsity. Although "blanqueador," meaning "whitener," is broad enough to encompass both bleach and non-bleach whitening agents, the question remains whether liquid Ace is properly described as containing "whitening agents" of any sort. Clorox has alleged that it is not, insisting that Ace's ingredients are properly termed "color enhancers." Although the distinction between a "whitening agent" and a "color enhancer" eludes us, we must credit that allegation in this appeal from a 12(b)(6) dismissal. If Clorox succeeds in proving that liquid Ace contains only an "enhancer," rather than a "whitener," and if it further establishes the other elements of a false advertising claim, see supra note 6, it will be entitled to relief under the Lanham Act because Proctor & Gamble's designation of Ace liquid detergent as "Ace con Blanqueador" would be literally false.

2. Claims of Misleading Advertising

In addition to its claims of literal falsity, Clorox has alleged in its complaint that the Ace advertising campaign, even if true or ambiguous, makes an implied claim that is misleading to consumers. This second theory of recovery under the Lanham Act is independent of a literal falsity theory. *See, e.g., Coca-Cola, Co. v. Tropicana Prods., Inc.*, 690 F.2d 312, 317 (2d Cir. 1982). Unlike the requirements of a claim of literal falsity, the plaintiff alleging a misleading advertisement has the burden of proving that a substantial portion of the audience for that advertisement was actually misled. *See Rhone-Poulenc Rorer*, 19 F.3d at 134 (citing *U.S. Healthcare v. Blue Cross*, 898 F.2d 914, 922 (3d Cir. 1990)). An advertisement's propensity to deceive the viewing public is most often proven by consumer survey data. *See id.* 19 F.3d at 129–30. Clorox appended to the amended complaint a consumer survey prepared by David Whitehouse of Gaither International/Puerto Rico, Inc. The survey consisted of a series of open-ended questions followed by several follow-up probes. In reliance on the survey, the complaint alleges that:

> In open-ended questions, 35% of respondents of its scientifically valid survey responded that the main message of the Doorstep Challenge Campaign was

> that, with ACE, there is no need to use other products for maximum whitening performance. In addition, when the respondents were asked if "the Detergent in the Ad (ACE) Leaves Clothes as White or Whiter than If One Uses Bleach," 47% totally agreed and 20% somewhat agreed with that statement. Plainly, the Doorstep Challenge Campaign has been amply shown to be likely to cause consumer deception.

Clorox has also alleged in its complaint that "in its promotional activities and advertisements," Proctor & Gamble "deceived and confused the public, causing consumers to wrongly believe they are buying a detergent that possesses the same qualities and characteristics as a detergent used with CLOROX."

The court was required to credit Clorox's allegations. It could not conduct its own evaluation of the advertising copy because whether advertising is misleading depends on "what message was actually conveyed to the viewing audience." *Smithkline Beecham Corp.*, 960 F.2d at 298; *see also Rhone-Poulenc Rorer*, 19 F.3d at 129. In deciding whether a message is "misleading," the message conveyed is discerned by "public reaction," not by judicial evaluation. [Citations.] That is, absent some other defect in its proof of the elements of a false advertising claim, ... if Clorox's consumer survey data (or Proctor & Gamble's own market research data) shows that the advertisements "deceived a substantial portion of the intended audience," *U.S. Healthcare*, 898 F.2d at 922, Clorox is entitled to relief under the Lanham Act. Hence, the claims asserting misleading advertising were improperly dismissed.

....

3. *Puffery*

Finally, the statements, "Compare with your detergent.... Whiter is not possible," and "Whiter is not possible," are not non-actionable puffing. "'Puffing' is exaggerated advertising, blustering, and boasting upon which no reasonable buyer would rely...." *McCarthy* § 27:38. "A specific and measurable advertisement claim of product superiority ... is not puffery." *Southland Sod Farms*, 108 F.3d at 1145 (claim that turfgrass seed requires "50% less mowing" was not puffery); *see also Castrol, Inc.*, 987 F.2d at 946 (claim that motor oil provides "longer engine life and better engine protection" was not puffery). Whether the "Doorstep Challenge" campaign conveys the message that Ace gets clothes whiter than chlorine bleach, or compares Ace with other detergents without implying that it whitens better than chlorine bleach, the claim is specific and measurable, not the kind of vague or subjective statement that characterizes puffery. Indeed, Proctor & Gamble concedes in its brief that its claim in its modified campaign, "Compare with your detergent ... Whiter is not possible," is not puffery. It contends that it is a true statement supported by its studies comparing Ace con Blanqueador with other detergents.

The original campaign tag line, "Whiter is not possible," is a closer call on the puffing issue. Standing alone, that statement might well constitute an unspecified boast, and hence puffing. In context, however, the statement invites consumers to compare Ace's whitening power against either other detergents acting alone or detergents used with chlorine bleach. Despite this ambiguity, it is a specific, measurable claim, and hence not puffing.

....

III.

Pursuant to § 43(a) of the Lanham Act, Clorox has stated a claim for literal falsity relating to the name of the Ace liquid detergent, "Ace con Blanqueador." Clorox has also stated claims for literal falsity and for misleading advertising with respect to the commercials aired in both the original and modified Doorstep Challenge advertising campaigns, as well as the promotional brochure. The district court erred by dismissing these claims pursuant to Rule 12(b)(6). We must vacate its judgment and remand the Lanham Act claims to the district court for further proceedings consistent with this decision.

Autodesk, Inc. v. Dassault Systemes Solidworks Corp., 685 F. Supp. 2d 1001 (N.D. Cal. 2009). Autodesk and Solidworks compete in the market for computer aided design software. Solidworks advertised its DWGgateway software as fully compatible with plaintiff's AutoCAD software. Plaintiff's advertising warned consumers of the perils of using competing CAD software, featuring comic strip depictions of character Jonnie Real who relies on "Won'tWorks" brand purportedly compatible software, which ruins his projects. Autodesk and Solidworks sued each other for false advertising. Both parties claimed that their opponent's ads were deceptive, but that their own ads were harmless puffery. The court ruled that Solidwork's statement that "*DWGgateway is the first free data translation plug-in that lets AutoCAD users work easily with DWG files created by any version of AutoCAD software*," made a measurable claim, but that the statement "*DWGseries is a set of FREE software tools created for current and former AutoCAD users to open, edit, and share DWG data more effectively with others*," was "a vague and unmeasurable claim of superiority that constitutes non-actionable puffery." The court also concluded that Autodesk's Jonny Real cartoons merely touted the general superiority of Autodesk's software, and were "too generalized and vague to be actionable":

> A claim based on "*real* interoperability" and a "*real* risk" conveys a subjective rather than objective message. Whether something is a "real" risk or provides "real" interoperability depends on what the consumer thinks "real" means in that context. Moreover, the entire message from these cartoons is that plaintiff's product is generally better and that competing products may produce defective designs. These are cartoons with no quantifiable statements. In fact, the advertisements make no specific allegations concerning defendant's products. Consumers would not rely on such advertisements.
>
> ....
>
> Consequently, both advertisements present specific general statements in a context that would not lead a reasonable consumer to rely on plaintiff's assertions. They are nonactionable puffery under the Lanham Act.

Questions

1. Mueller's is a regional brand of pasta available only in the North Eastern United States. The company labels packages of its pasta "America's favorite pasta." The best-selling brand of pasta in the U.S. is not Mueller's, but Barilla, which is available throughout the United States. The manufacturer of Barilla claims that the "America's Favorite Pasta" label is a false and misleading representation of fact. Mueller insists that the phrase is mere puffing, and therefore not actionable. How should the court rule? *See American Italian Pasta Co. v. New World Pasta*, 371 F.3d 387 (8th Cir. 2004).

2. In the 1860s, Piotr Arsenovitch Smirnov began a vodka trade house in Russia named "P.A. Smirnov in Moscow." During his lifetime, P.A. Smirnov built his trade house into a nationally and internationally renowned vodka distillery, winning numerous awards. In 1886, Smirnov was named the "Official Purveyor to the Russian Imperial Court." Smirnov died in 1898, leaving his distillery to his sons Piotr, Nikolai, Vladimir, Sergei, and Alexey. Piotr bought out his brothers' interest in the distillery, and he and his wife operated it until his death in 1910. Piotr's wife Eugenie continued to run the distillery until the Bolshevik government nationalized all distilleries in 1918. Meanwhile, Vladimir Smirnov emigrated to Europe, and opened a distillery under the name "Pierre Smirnoff & Sons. He later sold his rights in the name to Heublein, which introduced a Smirnoff brand vodka into the United States. That vodka was and continues to be distilled and bottled in the United States, and has become a best-selling brand. Bottles of Smirnoff vodka bear a label suggesting the vodka's Russian origin and imperial seal. Meanwhile, when the Soviet Union dissolved, Eugenie's daughter reopened a Smirnov distillery in Moscow. She sues Heublein under § 43(a), arguing that it falsely advertises its Smirnoff vodka as the prizewinning Russian vodka introduced in Moscow by P.A. Smirnov. What result? *See Joint Stock Society v. UDV North America*, 266 F.3d 164 (3d. Cir. 2001).

Church & Dwight Co. v. The Clorox Company

102 U.S.P.Q.2d (BNA) 1453 (S.D.N.Y. 2012)

Rakoff, J.:

By this action, plaintiff Church & Dwight Co. ("C & D") seeks, among other things, to preliminarily enjoin defendant Clorox Pet Products Company ("Clorox") from airing a commercial that makes allegedly misleading claims about the respective merits of each party's cat litter.... [T]he Court finds that Clorox's test is insufficiently reliable to meet the required legal standards and that the commercial is likely to cause C & D irreparable harm if not enjoined. [Citation.] Thus, for the reasons explained below, the Court grants C & D's request for a preliminary injunction enjoining further use of the commercial in issue.

C & D manufactures several kinds of cat litter that incorporate Arm & Hammer baking soda under the Arm & Hammer trademark. Those varieties include Arm & Hammer Double Duty Clumping Litter ("Double Duty") and Arm & Hammer Super Scoop Clumping Litter ("Super Scoop"). Clorox manufactures "Fresh Step" cat litter products, which utilize carbon instead of baking soda as an odor-fighting ingredient.

In the Fall of 2010, Clorox started airing certain commercials that immediately preceded the commercial here in dispute. In one commercial, cats were depicted choosing litter boxes filled with Fresh Step over litter boxes filled with Super Scoop. While this was occurring, the voiceover explained that "cats like boxes ... with Fresh Step litter inside ... because Fresh Step's scoopable litter with carbon is better at eliminating odors than Arm & Hammer." In another commercial, cats were first depicted stepping into the box containing Super Scoop and then stepping out of the box and choosing the box with Fresh Step. In January of 2011, Clorox began airing still another commercial that displayed cats engaging in "clever" behavior. As the videos played, the voiceover announced: "*Cats are smart. They can outsmart their humans. Their canines. Unlock doors. They're also smart enough to choose the litter with less odors.*"

C & D alleges that it then commissioned a test to replicate these situations and found that of the 158 cats tested, only six cats—less than four percent—rejected their litter box when the litter box was filled with Super Scoop. By contrast, eight cats—or five percent—allegedly rejected a litter box filled with Clorox's Fresh Step litter. As a result, on January 5, 2011, C & D filed a complaint against Clorox, claiming that the aforementioned commercials were literally false. Clorox agreed to permanently discontinue the commercials, and C & D voluntarily dismissed the complaint on February 2, 2011.

Sometime around February 14, 2011, Clorox began airing a new commercial, the one here in issue. In this commercial, cats are featured doing "clever" things and the voiceover announces: "*We get cats. They're smart. They can outsmart their humans. And their canines.*" Then a cat is seen entering a litter box and pawing through the litter as the voiceover continues, "*That's why they deserve the smartest choice in litter.*" The commercial then transitions to a demonstration that displays two laboratory beakers. One beaker is represented as Fresh Step and the bottom of it is filled with a black substance labeled "carbon." The other beaker is filled with a white substance labeled "baking soda." While the second beaker is not identified as any specific brand of cat litter, Arm & Hammer is the only major cat litter brand that uses baking soda. Green gas is then shown floating through the beakers and the voiceover continues: "*So we make Fresh Step scoopable litter with carbon, which is more effective at absorbing odors than baking soda.*" The green gas in the Fresh Step beaker then rapidly evaporates while the gas level in the baking soda beaker barely changes. During this dramatization, small text appears at the bottom of the screen informing the viewer that Clorox's claims are "[b]ased on [a] sensory lab test."

C & D alleges that the new commercial contains several false messages, including, inter alia, that cat litter products made with baking soda do not eliminate odors well and that cat litter products made with baking soda are less effective at eliminating odors than Clorox's Fresh Step cat litter.

... Success on the merits under § 43(a) of the Lanham Act requires a demonstration that the challenged advertisement is either (1) "literally false, i.e., false on its face," or (2) "while not literally false, ... nevertheless likely to mislead or confuse consumers." [Citations.] Where, as here, scientific or technical evidence is said to establish an advertiser's claim (a so-called "establishment claim"), a plaintiff can prove literal falsity by showing that the test "did not establish the proposition for which [it was] cited" because it is either "not sufficiently reliable to permit a conclusion" or "simply irrelevant." *Castrol, Inc. v. Quaker State Corp.*, 977 F.2d 57, 63 (2d Cir. 1992). Thus, C & D's likelihood of success on the merits depends upon its ability to show that Clorox's sensory lab test is "not sufficiently reliable" or "simply irrelevant."

To support its claim that carbon better eliminates cat malodor than baking soda, Clorox conducted an in-house test called the "Jar Test." In the Jar Test, Clorox prepared separate containers of: (i) fresh cat feces covered with carbon; (ii) fresh cat urine covered with carbon; (iii) fresh cat feces covered with baking soda; (iv) fresh cat urine covered with baking soda; (v) uncovered feces; and (vi) uncovered urine. After letting the sealed containers sit for twenty-two to twenty-six hours, the containers were placed in three sensory testing booths—one containing the carbon samples, one containing the baking soda samples, and one containing the uncovered feces and urine as a control—and eleven panelists rated the samples on a 0 to 15 scale. This experiment was repeated four times, for a total of forty-four samplings. Carbon was found to reduce odor from 2.72 to 0 while baking soda was found to reduce odor only from 2.72 to 1.85. Reducing odor from 2.72 to 1.85 represents a 32% decrease, precisely the decrease that is represented in the demonstration shown in Clorox's commercial.

Clorox trained the eleven panelists used in the Jar Test to evaluate odors on a specific scale, which its expert witness devised. According to Clorox, the sensory evaluation method here employed by Clorox has been reviewed in textbooks and peer-reviewed journals, and is taught in more than forty universities in the United States. Over the course of their training, panelists smelled identical smells at different levels of intensity in order to develop a common metric for pungency. Panelists also smelled different litter products, both with and without cat excrement, in order to learn to discriminate between cat malodor and other odors present in litter. Clorox taught its panelists that, when they could not detect a certain olfactory stimuli, they should note that absence by giving that odor a rating of zero. As it turned out, all eleven panelists gave a malodor rating of zero whenever cat excrement was treated with carbon, resulting in a score of zero for each of the forty-four trials.

C & D criticizes the reliability of the Jar Test in at least three respects. First, it argues that Clorox's commercial broadly claims that Fresh Step cat litter outperforms C & D's products in eliminating odor, a claim the Jar Test cannot support. Second, it argues that certain aspects of the Jar Test—particularly the uniformity of the panelists' findings that carbon completely eliminates cat malodor—are so suspicious as to render the Jar Test unreliable even for the narrower proposition that carbon better eliminates odor than baking soda. Third, it argues that the Jar Test is unreliable because it failed to use a ratio scale to compare degrees of malodor. The Court considers C & D's first two criticisms and, finding them meritorious, has no need to reach the third.

C & D's first criticism may be elaborated as follows. Under the doctrine of "falsity by necessary implication," a company's claims about particular aspects of its product may necessarily imply more sweeping claims about that product, and these implied claims may be "literally false" within the meaning of the Lanham Act. See *Castrol Inc. v. Pennzoil Co.*, 987 F.2d 939, 947 (3d Cir. 1993) ("The implication is that Pennzoil outperforms the other leading brands with respect to protecting against engine failure, because it outperforms them in protecting against viscosity breakdown, the cause of engine failure."); *Time Warner Cable, Inc. v. DIRECTV, Inc.*, 497 F.3d 144, 158 (2d Cir. 2007) (citing *Pennzoil*). A court must analyze the disputed message in its "full context," *Time Warner Cable*, 497 F.3d at 158 (quoting *Pennzoil*, 987 F.2d at 946), to determine whether its "words or images, considered in context, necessarily imply a false message." *Id.* Because an implication must be necessary in order to render the commercial's claims false, "if the language or graphic is susceptible to more than one reasonable interpretation, the advertisement cannot be literally false." *Id.*

C & D argues that under the doctrine of necessary implication, Clorox's claims about the superiority of carbon to baking soda necessarily imply that Fresh Step cat litter better eliminates odors than do Arm & Hammer litters that use baking soda. While Clorox responds that one could reasonably interpret its commercial as simply comparing the general odor-reducing properties of carbon and baking soda, Clorox has not identified any basis for believing that any consumer who pays attention to its commercial reasonably cares about how effectively carbon works compared with baking soda outside the context of cat litter and competing litter products.

The Jar Test cannot reasonably support the necessary implication that Clorox's litter outperforms C & D's products in eliminating odor in cat litters. As noted above, Clorox sealed the jars of cat waste for twenty-two to twenty-six hours before subjecting them to testing. In actual practice, however, cats do not seal their waste, and smells offend as much during the first twenty-two hours as they do afterwards. Thus, the Jar Test's unrealistic conditions say little, if anything, about how carbon performs in cat litter in circumstances highly relevant to a reasonable consumer. Moreover, to substantiate the commercial's implied claims, the Jar Test must prove not only that carbon eliminates odors in open cat litter (as opposed to sealed jars), but also (1) that it outperforms baking soda in that task and (2) that baking soda eliminates only thirty-two percent of odors, the amount by which, in the commercial, the gas dissipated in the beaker labeled "baking soda." Given that the Jar Test says little about how substances perform in litter as opposed to jars, it cannot possibly support Clorox's very specific claims with regard to litter. Consequently, the necessarily contrary implication of Clorox's commercials is literally false.

C & D's second criticism is that flaws in the methodology of the Jar Test render its conclusions unreliable. In particular, C & D notes that the uniformity with which panelists found that cat excrement treated with carbon contained "zero" malodor is highly implausible, and more likely reflects flaws in their in-house training or objectivity than any reliable result. C & D maintains that humans are "noisy instruments" that, for neurological reasons, perceive the exact same thing differently at different times and report the presence of olfactory stimuli even where they do not exist. Thus, given the variation even among the same person's reports at different times, C & D argues that eleven different people almost certainly would not uniformly report the same experience forty-four times.

C & D further notes that Clorox's own studies support this observation. First, in an internal panel validation test report—which involved cat litter—Clorox's panelists gave an average malodor score of greater than zero to a box of litter that admittedly contained no cat excrement. Second, in an earlier iteration of the Jar Test, eighteen percent of trials resulted in a report of some malodor in jars of excrement treated with carbon. Third, even Clorox's expert confirms that "[h]umans, even highly trained sensory panelists, are 'noisy' measuring instruments.... For a variety of physiological and psychological reasons, humans do not perceive and report exactly the same value when evaluating the same sample repeatedly."

Clorox responds that the mere fact that humans are noisy instruments does not preclude a uniform rating of zero where no malodor was in fact present. Moreover, according to Clorox, most of the studies showing that humans report experiencing stimuli even where none exists do not involve trained panelists such as those Clorox employed. These arguments misunderstand C & D's point. Clorox's own evidence acknowledges that humans, even trained panelists, report smells even when none are present. Thus, the Court agrees with C & D's expert that it is highly implausible that eleven panelists would stick their noses in jars of excrement and report forty-four independent times that they smelled nothing unpleasant. Accordingly, the Court concludes that the results of the Jar Test are "not sufficiently reliable to permit one to conclude with reasonable certainty that they established the proposition for which they were cited" in Clorox's commercial. [Citation.]

In short, because the Jar Test on which Clorox based its claims is unreliable and, even if it were reliable, could not possibly support Clorox's implied claims about the relative merits of carbon and baking soda in cat litter, the Court finds Clorox's claims are literally false. *Id.* Based on this literal falsity, C & D has met the requirement of likelihood of success on the merits.

....

[T]he Court concludes that ... C & D has proved a likelihood of irreparable harm on the facts of this case. One of the beakers in Clorox's commercial bore the label "baking soda," and, as noted, C & D is the only major manufacturer of cat litter that uses baking soda as a deodorizing ingredient. Consumers shopping for cat litter overwhelmingly identify baking soda with C & D's Arm & Hammer cat litter products. Finally, the commercial shares themes with Clorox's former commercials—e.g., reference to cats' intelligence and cleverness—recalling those former commercials' explicit mention of C & D's products....

Put simply, Clorox, cloaking itself in the authority of "a lab test," made literally false claims going to the heart of one of the main reasons for purchasing cat litter. In such circumstances, where the misrepresentation is so plainly material on its face, no detailed study of consumer reactions is necessary to conclude inferentially that Clorox is likely to divert customers from C & D's products to its own unless the offending commercial is enjoined. Thus, C & D has successfully shown a high likelihood of irreparable harm.

Because C & D has shown that it will likely succeed on the merits and that it will suffer irreparable harm if a preliminary injunction is not granted, the Court hereby grants C & D's request for a preliminary injunction. Specifically, Clorox is hereby enjoined, immediately, from further airing the commercial in question....

Chobani, LLC v. Dannon Co., 157 F.Supp.3d 190 (N.D.N.Y. 2016). Chobani and Dannon both produce "light" low-calorie Greek style yogurt. Chobani touts its products' absence of artificial sweeteners and preservatives. The court described the contested advertisement as follows:

> The Commercial's opening shot focuses on a cup of Dannon Light & Fit Greek Yogurt sitting on a table, which is immediately picked up by a young woman lounging in a pool chair. As she scrutinizes the product's ingredients label, a voiceover proclaims: "Dannon Light & Fit Greek actually uses artificial sweeteners like sucralose. Sucralose? Why? That stuff has chlorine added to it!" In response to this revelation, the woman scrunches her face in disgust and tosses the cup of Dannon yogurt into a distant receptacle, resembling a trash bin, labeled "towels."
>
> Instead, the young woman selects a cup of Chobani Simply 100 Greek Yogurt sitting on a table to her right as a swimming pool becomes visible in the background. The voiceover then states: "Now, there's Chobani Simply 100. It's the only 100 calorie light yogurt sweetened naturally." As she tears open the packaging, the Commercial pans to a wide shot of the swimming pool, where a child jumps in, making a big splash. The camera returns to the woman, now smiling contentedly, before finishing with a wide shot of the entire swimming pool scene. Text laid over this final shot includes a hashtag: "#NOBADSTUFF." ...

The court made the following findings regarding Sucralose:

> Sucralose, the artificial ingredient at the center of this dispute, is a "zero-calorie, non-nutritive sweetener" that has been approved by the U.S. Food and Drug Administration ("FDA") for human consumption since 1999. Sucralose has been extensively studied and the FDA has reviewed more than 110 safety studies in connection with its use as a general purpose sweetener for food.
>
> Sucralose is a molecule with twelve carbon, nineteen hydrogen, eight oxygen, and three chlorine atoms linked together in a stable form that is safe to consume. The molecule is manufactured through a process in which three atoms of chlorine are "substituted" for three hydrogen-oxygen groups on a sucrose molecule. This trio of chlorine atoms are known in the scientific community as a "chloride," a compound of chlorine that is bound to another element or group. Such chlorides are found throughout nature and in numerous natural food sources ranging from simple table salt to cow's milk.
>
> Pool chlorine, on the other hand, is a colloquial term for calcium hypochlorite, a powerful bleach and disinfectant that is harmful if added to

food or ingested. This substance is distinct both chemically and practically from the chlorine atoms found in sucralose. Calcium hypochlorite is not found in, or used to manufacture, any of Dannon's products.

The court ruled Chobani's advertisement "false by necessary implication."

Dannon contends it is likely to succeed on its claim that Chobani's Simply 100 Campaign is "literally false by necessary implication," because the statements about added chlorine convey the literally false message that the sucralose contained in Dannon's Light & Fit Greek renders it unsafe to eat.

Chobani defends its sweetener comparison claims by arguing that, not only is it literally true that sucralose has "chlorine added to it," but that the other challenged messages—that its products are "good" or that Dannon's artificial ingredients are "bad stuff"—are merely "puffery," statements of Chobani's own opinion about the superiority of its own natural products.

This argument is unpersuasive. "Puffery is an exaggeration or overstatement expressed in broad, vague, and commendatory language." [Citation] ...

"[B]ut an advertiser treads a far different line when it not only lauds its own products, but directly attacks a competitor." [Citation.] While the phrase "no bad stuff," if untethered to any comparison claim specifically referencing Dannon's product, may be considered the sort of commendatory overstatement incapable of deceiving a consumer, the Simply 100 Campaign employs that negative phrasing in connection with other statements and images that paint Dannon's products as a safety risk because they contain sucralose. [Citation.]

Putting aside the fact that Chobani's statements about "chlorine" may be literally true, courts regularly recognize that even where "no combination of words" found in the advertisement is untrue, the message conveyed by the advertisement may still be "literally false" if its clear meaning, considered in context, is false. [Citations.] ...

With these principles in mind, it is easy to conclude that Dannon, as counter-claimant here, has demonstrated a substantial likelihood of success on the merits of its false advertising claim, since it is likely that a factfinder would conclude that the challenged aspects of the Simply 100 Campaign unambiguously convey the literally false message that Dannon's product contains sucralose and is therefore unsafe to consume....

See also General Mills, Inc. v. Chobani, LLC, 158 F.Supp.3d 106 (N.D.N.Y. 2016) (similar claim of falsity by necessary implication successfully asserted against Chobani commercial describing preservative potassium sorbate in General Mills' Yoplait low-calorie Greek-style yogurt as a substance "used to kill bugs.").

Questions

1. In 2006, Quiznos sandwich shops launched an ad campaign comparing its PrimeRib Cheesesteak sandwich to Subway restaurant's Subway cheese steak sandwich, depicting the Subway sandwich as having less meat than the Quiznos sandwich. One commercial featured a man looking at the Subway and saying "I don't see any meat—oh, there it is." Another showed a man comparing the Quiznos and Subway sandwiches by describing them as "meat" and "no meat." Quiznos then posted a website at www.meatnomeat.com and announced a "Quiznos v. Subway TV ad challenge." The contest invited consumers to create and upload their own commercials comparing Quiznos steak subs to Subway steak subs; the winning commercial would be awarded a $10,000 prize. Throughout the contest, consumer-submitted commercials were available to the public on www.meatnomeat.com. Many of these commercials characterized the Subway steak sandwich as having little or no meat. Subway claims that both the Quiznos commercials and the consumer-created commercials are literally false, and has sued Quiznos under section 43(a) for false advertising. How should the court rule? *See Doctor's Associates, Inc. v. QIP Holder LLC*, 2010-1 Trade Cas. (CCH) P 76,956 (D. Conn. 2010).

2. Rose Art manufactures and sells magnetic building block sets, which it advertises as "entertainment for ages 3 to 100." The packages show pictures of elaborate structures, including a sphere, a tower, and an airplane, built from the magnetic blocks. A competing manufacturer sues for false representation, claiming that it is not possible for a child to build the pictured structures from the parts in the building sets. Plaintiff has no consumer survey evidence, but insists the packaging makes representations that are literally false. Rose Art insists that the pictures on the packages are literally true. In support of its motion for summary judgment on the literal falsity claim, Rose Art submits a video to the court showing an expert builder of construction toys putting together each of the structures pictured on its packages. How should the court rule? *See PlastWood SRL v. Rose Art Industries*, 90 U.S.P.Q.2d (BNA) 1241 (W.D. Wa. 2008).

3. Mead Johnson (maker of Enfamil brand infant formula) routinely advertises that generic store-brand infant formulas lack important nutrients found in Enfamil. PBM Products manufactures generic and store brand formulas that compete with Enfamil, and has filed false advertising suits under section 43(a)(1)(B) disputing Mead Johnson's ads and seeking to enjoin them. The prior suits have settled, with Mead Johnson agreeing to discontinue the allegedly false and misleading ads. PBM has recently sued Mead Johnson over direct mail advertising claiming that Enfamil contained ingredients important to infant brain and eye development and that store brands did not. PBM's store brands include these ingredients from the same supplier and in the same amounts as Enfamil does. In a jury trial of the false advertising claims, PBM seeks to introduce evidence of the earlier false advertising suits to help show that Mead Johnson intended to mislead consumers with the ad. Should the court admit the evidence of prior litigation? *See PBM Products v. Mead Johnson*, 639 F.3d 111 (4th Cir. 2011).

4. You represent Amazon.com. Its listings of items offered for sale often include succinct consumer reviews of the goods. Typical reviews give a 1–5 star rating and a short comment pinpointing the merits, or failings, of the goods. Your client has learned that a company called buyamazonreviews.com will, for $19 to $22 per review, place product reviews on the relevant pages of Amazon.com, touting the merits of the offered goods. Your client believes that the "reviewers" (employees of buyamazonreviews.com) may in fact never have used or even received the product they endorse. You have visited buyamazonreviews.com's website, which presents the following sales pitch:

> Are you tired of your products not being seen, tired of competitors leaving bad reviews? The solution is simple. Buy Amazon reviews. You can have unlimited 4 and 5 star reviews this week. Our skilled writers look at your product, look at your competitor's products and then write state of the art reviews that will be sure to generate sales for you.... We provide real reviews from aged accounts with real buying activity. Most products in the Amazon marketplace will never even be seen. The more positive reviews you have the better your chances are.... You can buy Amazon reviews for any type of product. We write reviews for music, eBooks, supplements, cosmetics etc. We won't just copy reviews from elsewhere and rewrite them. Your reviews will be 100% unique.

Assess the likelihood of success should Amazon.com bring a false representation action against buyamazonreviews.com.

C. Misleading Representations

Innovation Ventures, LLC v. N.V.E., Inc.

694 F.3d 723 (6th Cir. 2012)

Boggs, Circuit Judge:

[Innovation Ventures, LLC, d/b/a Living Essentials (LE), producer of the "5-hour ENERGY" energy shot, above [top] left, brought an action for trademark infringement under § 43(a) of the Lanham Act against N.V.E. Inc. (NVE), which markets the "6 Hour POWER" energy shot, above [top right]. In a separate action, LE successfully brought a trade dress infringement claim against N2G Distributing, Inc. (N2G) distributors of the "6 Hour ENERGY" energy shot, above [bottom center]; the court in that action ordered an injunction and a recall. Concerned that the recall notice did not adequately reach those who may have bought "6 Hour ENERGY" from resellers, LE released the following:

RECALL OF "6 HOUR" SHOT ORDERED

> *Court orders immediate stop to manufacturing, distributing and sale of 6 Hour Energy shot.*
>
> Dear Customer,
>
> We are pleased to announce that we won a decision against a "6 Hour" energy shot that closely mimicked 5-Hour Energy® The United States District Court, in Case No. 08-CV-10983, 2008 U.S. Dist. LEXIS 30047, issued a preliminary injunction ordering the immediate recall of the "6 Hour" product, and told its manufacturer to stop making, distributing and selling it.
>
> If you have any of the "6 Hour" energy shots in your store(s) or warehouse(s) contact the product's manufacturer or your distributor to return the product immediately.
>
> **DO NOT RETURN ANY 5-HOUR ENERGY®**. It can be difficult to tell 5-Hour Energy® apart from the "6 Hour" knockoff product. If you have any questions, please call us at 248-960-1700 ext. 217.
>
> We will vigorously protect the 5-Hour Energy® brand by pursuing all legal avenues against anyone encroaching on it, or creating confusion in the marketplace.

After the lower court granted cross-motions for summary judgment on LE's trademark infringement claim against NVE and NVE's false advertising counterclaim, the parties appealed. The Sixth Circuit reversed the grant of summary judgment on LE's trademark infringement claim because the infringement factors were evenly balanced at the pre-trial stage. The court then turned to the false advertising claim:]

B

1

NVE asserts on appeal that the recall notice LE distributed constituted false advertising....

NVE asserts that a jury could reasonably find that the notice: (1) was "literally false"; or (2) was "misleading" and deceived the intended audience. *See Balance Dynamics Corp. v. Schmitt Indus., Inc.*, 204 F.3d 683, 695–96 (6th Cir. 2000). The former theory focuses on the plain language of the notice, while the latter focuses on how the notice was perceived by its intended audience. The district court in the proceedings below in this case found that the notice was neither literally false nor misleading, disagreeing with the conclusion of the *BDI* court. District Judge Zatkoff found that "Judge Rosen's opinion and order adopting the Report and Recommendation did not state that the legal notice was *false*; rather, Judge Rosen concluded only that the legal notice was *misleading.*" District Ct. Op. at 11. Judge Zatkoff further disagreed with Magistrate Judge Pepe's conclusions in *BDI*:

> [I]t is undisputed that Plaintiff was awarded injunctive relief against the producer of an energy shot bearing the name "6-Hour," as stated in the notice. Stating that the decision was based on the use of an overall product image would have, perhaps, provided more clarity, but the absence of the explanation for the injunctive relief does not render the statement literally false.

Ibid. Parsing the language of the notice, Judge Zatkoff found that though the notice was ambiguous—"it did not state which product had been recalled"—it was not deceiving.

2

Where statements are literally true yet deceptive or too ambiguous to support a finding of literal falsity, a violation can only be established by proof of actual deception. A plaintiff relying on statements that are literally true yet misleading "cannot obtain relief by arguing how consumers could react; it must show how consumers actually do react." *Sandoz Pharm. Corp. v. Richardson-Vicks, Inc.*, 902 F.2d 222, 229 (3d Cir. 1990). On the other hand, where statements are literally false, a violation may be established without evidence that the statements actually misled consumers. [Citations.] Actual deception is presumed in such cases. *See U-Haul Int'l, Inc. v. Jartran, Inc.*, 793 F.2d 1034, 1040 (9th Cir. 1986). "A 'literally false' message may be either explicit or 'conveyed by necessary implication when, considering the advertisement in its entirety, the audience would recognize the claim as readily as if it had been explicitly stated.'" *Novartis*, 290 F.3d at 586–87 (quoting *Clorox Co. v. Proctor & Gamble Commercial Co.*, 228 F.3d 24, 35 (1st Cir. 2000)). "'The greater the degree to which a message relies upon the viewer or consumer to integrate its components and draw the apparent conclusion, however, the less likely it is that a finding of literal falsity will be supported.'" *Id.* at 587. (quoting *United Indus. Corp. v. Clorox Co.*, 140 F.3d 1175, 1181 (8th Cir. 1998)).

3

The language of the recall notice teeters on the cusp between ambiguity and literal falsity in two main respects—descriptive and grammatical.

First, the notice could be viewed as either ambiguous or false with respect to how the product is named. Towards the top, the notice simply referred to "'6 Hour' Energy shot"—in the notice "6 Hour" was in quotations, while "Energy shot" was not—without a prefatory article. At no point does the notice identify the name of the recalled product, "6 Hour Energy Shot." Read broadly, this could be considered ambiguous, as it does not specify which product was the subject of the recall; on further reflection, one could understand which products were and were not recalled. Read narrowly, this could be literally false—only a product specifically called "6 Hour Energy Shot" was recalled, not any energy shot whose name contained the words "6 Hour." The notice never referred to the product as "6 Hour Energy Shot" in one complete phrase.

Only one product, "6 Hour Energy Shot," and not other "6 Hour" products, such as "6 Hour POWER," were subject to the recall. At the time, there were several other energy shots, in addition to NVE's, with the phrase "6 Hour" in the title, such as "6 Hour Energy!" (made by BDI) and "Extreme Energy Six Hour Shot" (made by Ener Formulations Ltd.). None of these were recalled. Relatedly, LE wrote that it "w[o]n a decision against a '6 Hour' energy shot." This statement is not literally true—LE won a decision against N2G's use of an overall product image, *i.e.*, the label and bottle, that was confusingly similar to LE's overall product image.

Second, the notice uses different prefatory words to introduce the recalled product. At some points the notice uses an indefinite prefatory article, "a," to refer to "a '6 Hour' energy shot," suggesting that there may be more than one possible product at issue. At other points, the notice uses the prefatory pronoun "any": "If you have *any* of the '6 Hour' energy shots in your store(s) or warehouse(s) contact the product's manufacturer"—whoever they may be—"or your distributor to return the product immediately." (emphasis added). By saying "any" of the shots, the notice suggests that *any* shot bearing the name "6 Hour" was subject to recall. Elsewhere, the notice uses the prefatory definite article "the": "If you have any of *the* '6 Hour' energy shots in your store(s) or warehouse(s) contact the product's manufacturer or your distributor to return *the* product immediately." (emphasis added). This definite article suggests that there is only one specific product at issue, though the statement as a whole fails to specify exactly what product.

Justice Kagan recently had the occasion to opine on the subtle difference between "not an" and "not any":

> Truth be told, the answer to the general question "What does 'not an' mean?" is "It depends": The meaning of the phrase turns on its context. *See Johnson v. United States*, 559 U.S. 133, 130 S. Ct. 1265, 1270, 176 L. Ed. 2d 1 (2010) ("Ultimately, context determines meaning"). "Not an" sometimes means "not any," in the way Novo claims. If your spouse tells you he is late because he "did not take a cab," you will infer that he took no cab at all (but took the bus instead). If your child admits that she "did not read a book all summer," you will surmise that she did not read any book (but went to the movies a lot). And if a sports-fan friend bemoans that "the New York Mets do not have a chance of winning the World Series," you will gather that the team has no chance whatsoever (because they have no hitting). But now stop a moment. Suppose your spouse tells you that he got lost because he "did not make a turn." You would understand that he failed to make a particular turn, not that he drove from the outset in a straight line. Suppose your child explains her mediocre grade on a college exam by saying that she "did not read an assigned text." You would infer

> that she failed to read a specific book, not that she read nothing at all on the syllabus. And suppose a lawyer friend laments that in her last trial, she "did not prove an element of the offense." You would grasp that she is speaking not of all the elements, but of a particular one. The examples could go on and on, but the point is simple enough: When it comes to the meaning of "not an," context matters.

Caraco Pharm. Labs., Ltd. v. Novo Nordisk A/S, 132 S. Ct. 1670, 1681, 182 L. Ed. 2d 678 (2012). We answer this query the same way our Circuit Justice did: "it depends." And "it depends" cannot support a claim of literal falseness. "[O]nly an unambiguous message can be literally false." *Novartis*, 290 F.3d at 587. While it is a close question whether the notice is literally false, we cannot say that it is unambiguously so. However, we hold that a genuine dispute exists as to whether the notice was misleading and tended to deceive its intended audience.

C

1

Focusing on how the notice would have impacted retailers, rather than consumers, the district court excluded as inadmissible hearsay all evidence introduced by NVE to show that "various unidentified retailers contacted them because they were confused by the legal notice." District Ct. Op. at 11–12. The district court observed that NVE submitted only one named distributor who complained that he lost sales after the notice, "but given that the legal notice was distributed to over 100,000 retailers nationwide, this hardly constitutes evidence that a significant portion of the intended audience was actually deceived." The court held that NVE "failed to establish, with admissible evidence, sufficient facts demonstrating that the legal notice actually deceived a substantial portion of the intended audience."

2

NVE argues on appeal that the district court erroneously dismissed documentary and testimonial evidence from NVE, distributors, and brokers showing confusion as to whether NVE's product, "6 Hour POWER," had been recalled. Following the recall, NVE and its distributors received a number of calls from convenience stores and truck stop retailers—the very people that received the recall notice—who wanted to return "6 Hour POWER." One NVE employee stated that the notice caused a "huge nightmare" and the phones were "blowing off the hook" with calls to return the product. NVE claimed that at least one sales program—which involved a "road trip" to place corrugated display tops "all over New Jersey"—"just died" after the recall notice.

NVE's Michelle Canzone stated that she received "phone calls from brokers and customers and faxes of this legal notice sent to us and that's when the nightmare began.... [I]nitially, we started getting faxes and inquiries from our customer base, and then the phone calls just started pouring in from all little mom and pop shops all over the United States, you know, asking if they should pull our product." JR Merlau, Vice-President at Novelty, Inc., a distributor of "6 Hour POWER," testified: "[T]his notice was confusing to the marketplace. It caused a lot of issues within our customers.

We had to send out notices to our customers to advise them that none of the products we were selling was subject to this recall." Jim Green, Vice-President of Purchasing/Marketing for wholesaler Liberty USA, was "immediately inundated with calls from customers that were confused" and "wanted to return NVE's 6 HOUR [sic] POWER."

Karen McClellan was the Category Buyer responsible for energy shots at CoreMark, which distributes to more than 29,000 convenience stores nationwide. On June 16, 2008, she sent a notice to all United States division buyers to warn against spreading e-mails containing the recall and creating "panic." Asked about the last sentence of her notice—"I hope this clears up the confusion that this letter has created"—Ms. McClellan testified: "I was confused by the letter.... I had to read it thoroughly a few times and then I had to talk to Rise [Meguiar, LE's Sales Vice President,] and several other people to ask them exactly what it is about so I knew specifically." Still experiencing problems over a month later, on July 22, 2008, Ms. McClellan emailed LE for "help" to clear up continuing questions about returning "6 Hour POWER." Customers were calling with "questions" about sending back "perfectly good Stacker 26 Hour Power" because "the customer thinks it is this other stuff."

3

The district court, citing an opinion from the Southern District of Ohio, stated that NVE's proffered evidence of confusion constituted hearsay. *See Interactive Prods. Corp. v. A2Z Mobile Office Solutions, Inc.*, 195 F. Supp. 2d 1024, 1033 (S.D. Ohio 2001) ("[T]he only evidence of deception are the hearsay statements of a customer ... who told Comeaux that two of *his* customers were confused by the Announcement. Defendants argue correctly that the hearsay statements of [the] customer are inadmissible and, therefore, do not create a genuine issue of fact on deception."). The district court's reliance on *A2Z* was misplaced.

First, the strict application of the rules of evidence to a claim that depends on showing customer confusion places too heavy a burden on NVE. Should we expect a sworn statement or affidavit from a retailer who calls into a distributor and claims to have been confused? Second, the phone calls were not relied on to show the content of the conversations, but rather were introduced merely to show that the conversations occurred and the state of mind of the declarants. Fed. R. Evid. 803(3). The fact that so many people called NVE immediately after receiving the notice *at the very least* raises a genuine issue of material fact as to whether a significant portion of the recipients were misled.

Relatedly, on appeal LE characterizes these phone calls as "non-actionable customer inquiries." The phone calls at issue were not mere inquiries, such as the inquisitive letter at issue in *Balance Dynamics.* 204 F.3d at 694. To the contrary, many distributors called to stop buying "6 Hour POWER" after the notice was issued. NVE claims that after the recall, its sales growth for "6 Hour POWER dropped from 13.7% to 1.1%." NVE's damages expert estimated that NVE lost $3.4 million in sales as a result of the recall notice. A jury could find that these were not just inquiries; they were calls that resulted in lost sales. All of these calls evidence a belief that "6 Hour POWER" had been recalled. Had the callers lacked such a mistaken belief, such phone calls would not have occurred.

NVE sent out its first corrective notice to its distributor base on June 11, 2008, and sent another directly to convenience stores on September 15, 2008. Further, a number of distributors sent out their own corrective notices so retailers would not think "6 Hour POWER" had been recalled. NVE does not introduce evidence about these corrective notices for the truth of the matters asserted therein but rather to provide circumstantial evidence that some retailers believed that there was in fact a recall on "any of the '6 Hour' shots in your store," including "6 Hour POWER," and that NVE took actions to alleviate these concerns. There is more than enough evidence to survive summary judgment. Whether the evidence shows that the retailers were "tricked into believing an untruth about" "6 Hour POWER" is an issue for trial....

In a related case, *Innovation Ventures, LLC v. N2G Distributing, Inc.*, 763 F.3d 524 (6th Cir. 2014), the Sixth Circuit affirmed the entry of a permanent injunction against the producers of "6 Hour Energy Shot" (the third-party product referred to and pictured in *Innovation Ventures, LLC v. N.V.E., Inc.*). The court upheld the findings of likelihood of confusion with respect to both the word mark and the trade dress.

Questions

1. Robot-Coupe, which manufactures food processors, releases an ad that states: "Robot-Coupe: 21, Cuisinart: 0. WHEN ALL 21 OF THE THREE-STAR RESTAURANTS IN FRANCE'S MICHELIN GUIDE CHOOSE THE SAME PROFESSIONAL MODEL FOOD PROCESSOR, SOMEBODY KNOWS THE SCORE-SHOULDN'T YOU?" Cuisinart files suit under § 43(a) and demonstrates that Cuisinart does not make a professional model food processor. Is Robot-Coupe's ad literally false or impliedly so? *See Cuisinarts, Inc. v. Robot-Coupe Int'l Corp.*, 1982 U.S. Dist. LEXIS 13594 (S.D.N.Y June 9, 1982).

2. Polar Corp. manufactures carbonated beverages, releases a commercial which depicts an animated polar bear throwing a can of Coca-Cola into a trash barrel labeled "Keep the Arctic Pure" and then drinking a can of Polar Seltzer happily. After complaints from Coca-Cola Co., Polar files a declaratory judgment suit. What result? *See Polar Corp. v. Coca-Cola Co.*, 871 F. Supp. 1520 (D. Mass. 1994).

Coors Brewing Co. v. Anheuser-Busch Co.

802 F. Supp. 965 (S.D.N.Y. 1992)

MUKASKEY, J.:

Plaintiff, Coors Brewing Company, sues Anheuser-Busch Companies, Inc. and D'Arcy Masius Benton & Bowles, Anheuser-Busch's advertising agency, claiming that Anheuser-Busch's recent promotional campaign violates § 43(a) of the Lanham Act, New York unfair competition law, and §§ 349 and 350 of New York General Business Law. Plaintiff has sought a preliminary injunction prohibiting defendants' continued use of the advertisements at issue. For the reasons set forth below, plaintiff's application for a preliminary injunction is denied.

I.

Since 1978, Coors has been expanding from the western United States into a nationwide market. Also since 1978, Coors has marketed a reduced-calorie beer called Coors Light. Coors manufactures its line of beers, including Coors Light, using a process that the beer industry calls "high gravity brewing." During the 30 to 60 days it takes to produce the "high gravity" brew, it is cooled to about 4 to 5 degrees centigrade. When the aging process is completed, the brew is filtered to remove yeast and other microbes. The temperature of the brew then is reduced further, to approximately minus 1 degree centigrade. Finally, the high gravity brew, whose alcohol content exceeds the statutory maximum for beer, is "blended" with water.

Most Coors Light is processed fully, *i.e.*, brewed, blended, and bottled, in Golden, Colorado. However, somewhere between 65% (plaintiff's figure) and 85% (defendants' figure) of the Coors Light supplied to the Northeast is "blended" and bottled in Virginia. Using "special insulated railcars," plaintiff transports the high gravity brew from Colorado to Virginia, where plaintiff adds Virginia water to the brew, further filters the mixture, and then bottles it.

Defendant Anheuser-Busch produces a reduced-calorie beer called Natural Light. Like Coors Light, Natural Light is produced by a process of "high gravity" brewing. Apparently, the only material difference between the processes used to produce Coors Light and Natural eight is that Natural Light is pasteurized, a process that involves heating, whereas Coors Light is brewed at low temperatures.[1] In addition, Natural Light apparently is processed entirely—*i.e.*, brewed, blended, and bottled—in regional Anheuser-Busch breweries.

Defendants recently began an advertising campaign comparing Natural Light with Coors Light. That campaign includes radio, television, and point-of-sale advertisements, which, not surprisingly, promote Natural Light at the expense of Coors Light.

Defendants' 30-second television commercial consists of a series of images accompanied by the following narrative:

> *This is a railroad tanker. [flash the image of a railway tanker] This is the taste of the Rockies. [flash the image of a can of Coors Light] Tanker. [image of a railway tanker] Rockies. [image of a can of Coors Light]*
>
> *Actually, a concentrated form of Coors Light leaves Colorado in a tanker and travels to Virginia, where local water dilutes the Rockies concentrate before it's sent to you.*

1. The parties have disputed vigorously whether the taste of beer, unlike the taste of milk, is adversely affected by pasteurization. Coors says it is; Anheuser-Busch say it isn't. They have also disputed, in this forum and elsewhere, other features of their products and their advertising, defendants having gone so far as to accuse Coors of "*ad hominem* attacks on Natural Light." (Def. Mem. at 13) However, *de gustibus cerevesiae non scit lex.*

So what's it gonna be, the Rockies concentrate or an ice cold Natural Light that leaves our local breweries fresh and ready to drink? Like this [picture of a Natural Light delivery truck], not like this [picture of railway tanker].

So drink fresh, cold Natural Light and don't be railroaded.

The phrase "don't be railroaded" is accompanied by the image of a can of Coors Light atop a railroad car, over which is superimposed a circle with a diagonal line through its center—the international safety warning symbol.

Similarly, defendants' radio advertisements portray a dialogue between two (male) beer-drinkers. One beer-drinker asks the other, "Did you know that Coors Light ships beer concentrate in railroad tanker cars?" The first beer-drinker then continues: "Yeah, all the way from Colorado—1,500 miles to Virginia. That's where they add local water."

In addition, defendants have been distributing printed materials to be displayed by retailers. These point-of-sale materials assert that Coors Light is made from concentrate while Natural Light is fresh. These materials also contain the logo "Don't be railroaded" above the image a Coors Light inside the international safety warning symbol.

Plaintiff argues that the Natural Light advertisements imply that "differences in production make Natural Light 'fresh' in a way in which Coors Light is not." In other words, those advertisements imply that Natural Light is "fresher" than Coors Light because Natural Light leaves the factory ready to drink while Coors Light leaves Colorado in a "concentrate" form, which is diluted when it reaches Coors' plant in Virginia.

Plaintiff also contends that by broadcasting nationally the Natural Light advertisements, defendants lead consumers outside the Northeast to believe erroneously that their Coors Light is shipped to Virginia to be diluted before being shipped to their regional retailers.

II. *Lanham Act Claims*

The Second Circuit has held that in order to obtain injunctive relief against a false or misleading advertising claim[2] pursuant to section 43(a) of the Lanham Act, a plaintiff must demonstrate either: (1) that an advertisement is literally false; or (2) that the advertisement, though literally true, is likely to mislead and confuse customers.

1. *Literal Falsehoods*

In the case at hand, Coors contends that the challenged advertisements contain two literal falsehoods: (1) that "Coors Light is made from 'concentrate' that is 'diluted' with water"; and (2) that "Coors Light travels to Virginia 'before it's sent to you.'"

2. Under § 43(a), a merchant's false or misleading claim may relate either to its own product or another's product. [Citation.]

As to defendants' advertising claim that Coors Light is made from a concentrate, Coors has failed to prove literal falsehood. The challenged commercial states that Coors Light travels from Colorado to Virginia in "a concentrated form" and asks, "So what's it gonna be, the Rockies concentrate or an ice cold Natural Light ...?" Relying on 27 C.F.R. § 25.11, which provides that a "concentrate is produced from beer by the removal of water," plaintiff would define "concentrate" only as a substance from which water has been removed. However, defendants proffer another, equally plausible definition of "concentrate," namely, "a concentrated substance" or "concentrated form of something." In addition, when "concentrate" is used as an adjective, it means "concentrated." In turn, "concentrated" means "(1) rich in respect to a particular or essential element: strong, undiluted; (2) intense...." WEBSTER'S THIRD NEW INTERNATIONAL DICTIONARY 469 (1986). Because the term "concentrate" is equally open to either party's definition, defendants' advertising claim that Coors Light is made from a concentrate is ambiguous at most. Therefore, the commercial's reference to concentrate is not literally false.

In addition, plaintiff argues that the commercial's claim that Coors Light is diluted is literally false. However, dilute means, *inter alia*, "to make thinner or more liquid by admixture (as with water); to make less concentrated: diminish the strength, activity, or flavor of...." *Id.* 633. It is undisputed that water is added to the "high gravity" brew—or concentrate—to produce the final product. That process makes the concentrate less concentrated. Therefore, neither is defendants' use of the term dilute literally false.

Plaintiff also challenges as literally false, except as applied to the Northeast, defendants' claim that Coors Light travels to Virginia before it is distributed to consumers. However, Anheuser-Busch "represents that the commercials will not be broadcast on any 'superstations' or other media that can be received outside of the Northeast." Therefore, this portion of plaintiff's application for injunctive relief is moot.

2. *Implied Falsehoods*

Plaintiff contends that by repeatedly stating that Coors Light is made from concentrate and is diluted, and by showing Coors Light being shipped from Colorado in railway cars while stating that Natural Light leaves Anheuser-Busch factories fresh and ready to drink, defendants' commercial implies three falsehoods: (1) that Natural Light is not also made by a process of "high gravity" brewing; (2) that all of the Coors Light sold in the Northeast has been "blended" with Virginia water; and (3) that there is a difference between Colorado Coors and Virginia Coors.

A claim for implied falsehood rises or falls on a plaintiff's evidence of consumer confusion, *i.e.*, market surveys. In the case at hand, plaintiff retained a market research and behavioral consulting firm called Leo J. Shapiro and Associates ("Shapiro") to conduct market surveys. Philip Johnson, Shapiro's president, has submitted an affidavit setting forth the results of those surveys; he also testified—sort of—at the preliminary injunction hearing.

Between August 7 and 10, 1992, Shapiro conducted consumer surveys in shopping malls located in Boston, Philadelphia, Washington, D.C., New York, Los Angeles, and Kansas City. In all, Shapiro interviewed 200 men and 100 women who were over

21 years old and who had consumed beer in the preceding four weeks; 50 people were interviewed at each location.

Survey respondents were shown the challenged Natural Light television advertisement. After respondents had been shown the advertisement once, they were asked the following two questions:

> *Question 2a:* Now, tell me what you recall about the commercial I just showed you?
>
> Probe: What else was it about?
>
> *Question 2b*: And, what was the central theme or message in this commercial? What were they trying to tell you?

After respondents were asked, and answered, Questions 2a and 2b, the commercial was played a second time. Respondents then were asked six more questions:

> *Question 4*: What, if anything, did this commercial tell you about Coors Light beer?
>
> Probe: What else?
>
> *Question 5*: Based on this commercial, do you believe that Coors Light and Natural Light are made the same way, or are they made differently?
>
> If different: In what way is Coors Light made differently than Natural Light?
>
> *Question 6*: And, based on the commercial, do you believe there is any difference between Coors Light and Natural Light in terms of the freshness of the products?
>
> If yes: In what way is Coors Light different from Natural Light in terms of freshness?
>
> *Question 7*: Based on the commercial, do you believe there is any difference between Coors Light and Natural Light in terms of the purity or naturalness of the products?
>
> If yes: In what way is Coors Light different from Natural Light in terms of purity or naturalness?
>
> *Question 8*: Do you feel that seeing this commercial would encourage You to drink Coors Light beer, discourage you from drinking Coors Light beer, or would it make no difference? Why do you say that?
>
> Probe: Why else?
>
> *Question 9*: By the way, do you believe that this commercial is talking about the Coors Light beer that is available where you buy beer? Why do you say that?

In answer to Question 5, whether based on the commercial respondents believed that Coors Light and Natural Light were made the same way or different ways, 67% of all respondents answered that they believed the two beers were made in different ways while 21% of all respondents answered that they believed the two beers were made the same way. Of those respondents who answered that the two beers were made in different ways, (i) 29% stated that they believed that "Coors is diluted/watered down/Natural Light is not," (ii) 25% stated that "Coors/Coors Light made from concentrate/Natural Light is not," and (iii) 13% stated that "Coors made in two places/ Natural Light from one place." There were at least 20 other responses specifying differences between how the two beers are made, but those responses are not relevant to the case at hand.

Based on the answers to Question 5, plaintiff argues that 67% of all respondents falsely believed, based on the commercial in question, that Natural Light and Coors Light are made differently. Adding the category of respondents who said that they believed that "Coors is diluted/watered down/Natural Light is not" (29%), and the category of respondents who said that they believed that "Coors/Coors Light made from concentrate/Natural Light is not" (25%), the total percentage of the 67% of respondents who had been misled by the commercial into thinking that Natural Light is not made by a process of high gravity brewing is 54%. This means that, based on plaintiff's survey, 36.18% of *all* respondents were misled by defendants' commercial as to the differences between how the two beers are made.

In the case at hand, plaintiff's reliance on the answers elicited by Question 5 is misplaced because that question is leading and thus produced unreliable results. By asking whether, "based on the commercial," the respondent believes Coors Light and Natural Light are made the same way or different ways, Question 5 assumes that the commercial conveys some message comparing how the two beers are made. But, in response to the open-ended questions—Questions 2a and 2b—a statistically insignificant percentage of respondents remarked on differences between the processes by which the two beers are made. This jump in the percentage of respondents whose answers indicate a mistaken belief that Natural Light is not also made by a process of high gravity brewing from between 3% and 9% to 36.18% further suggests the leading nature of Question 5.

Question 5 is leading also in that it asks whether an obviously comparative advertisement, which disparages one product and promotes another, suggests or does not suggest a difference in the way the two products are made. This inquiry in itself implies, because the advertisement invidiously compares one product with another, that the advertisement does suggest a difference in the way the two products are made. Moreover, Question 5 failed to inform respondents that they also could respond that they did not know if the commercial implied that Coors Light and Natural Light are made by different processes. This omission further undermines the reliability of the answers elicited by Question 5. For the above reasons, I do not credit Question 5 with probative value.

By contrast, I find that the survey's open-ended questions, 2a and 2b, were generally reliable. Questions 2a and 2b elicited answers going principally to plaintiff's claims of literal falsehood, which I have rejected. In answer to Question 2a, the bulk of respondents remarked that Coors Light is made from concentrate (20%), is "diluted/ watered down" (32%), is transported by railway tanker (26%), and travels a long distance before it reaches customers (20%).

Because Johnson lumped together the percentage of respondents who said that Coors Light is diluted and the percentage of respondents who said that Coors Light is watered down, the 32% figure is uninformative. While I have found that it is literally true that in one sense Coors Light is "diluted," Coors Light does not appear to be "watered down," in the sense of containing more water than beer should or than Natural Light does. However, because I have no way of knowing what percentage of respondents said that Coors Light is diluted and what percentage said that Coors Light is watered down, this category of responses has no probative value. *See* Darrell Huff, *How to Statisticulate*, in HOW TO LIE WITH STATISTICS 110–20 (1954).

Plaintiff has invited me to enjoin the advertisement at issue despite any blemishes in Shapiro's survey technique based on the "general thrust of [the] survey rather than its quantitative results." Here, the "thrust" is to be found in the "quantitative results," or it is not to be found at all. I decline to imagine "thrust" in the absence of evidence. Nor is there significance in defendants' failure to conduct a survey of their own. The burden is plaintiff's, and defendants may rely on that if they choose. Accordingly, because I have found that the results of Question 5 are unreliable and that those results of Questions 2a and 2b that support plaintiff's claims are either ambiguous or are statistically insignificant, I find that plaintiff has failed to prove that the challenged commercial is likely to mislead consumers into believing that, unlike Coors Light, Natural Light is not made by a process of "high gravity" brewing.

As to plaintiff's two remaining implied falsehood claims, that (i) *all* of the Coors Light sold in the Northeast has been "blended" with Virginia water, and (ii) there is a difference between Colorado Coors and Virginia Coors, plaintiff has failed to support either of these claims with any extrinsic evidence; none of the survey questions even arguably addresses these claims. Moreover, I find that plaintiff is estopped to argue the third alleged falsehood, *i.e.*, that there is a difference between Colorado Coors and Virginia Coors. Plaintiff has promoted its beers, including Coors Light, as "the taste of the Rockies," based on use of water from the Rocky Mountains. After having advertised for years that Coors beers tasted better than other beers because Coors beers are made from Rocky Mountain water, Coors now cannot seek an equitable remedy that would prohibit defendants' hoisting Coors by its own petard.

For the above reasons, I find that plaintiff has failed to substantiate its implied falsehood claims with reliable extrinsic evidence.

It goes almost without saying that the balance of hardships between these major brewers seems evenly balanced. Certainly, plaintiff has made no showing that the balance tips decidedly in its favor.

For the above reasons, plaintiff's application for a preliminary injunction prohibiting defendants' continued use of the challenged Natural Light commercial is denied.

So ordered.

Lanham Act Liability of Advertising Agencies

Nestlé Purina Petcare Co. v. Blue Buffalo Co. Ltd., 2015 U.S. Dist. LEXIS 51273 (E.D. Mo. April 20, 2015). Nestle Purina PetCare Company alleged that Blue Buffalo falsely claimed that its dog food products, which it advertises as "grain free" and containing "no chicken by-product," do in fact contain those ingredients. Purina then issued press releases about the suit and launched a website, www.PetFoodHonesty.com (the "Honesty website") charging Blue Buffalo with false advertising. Blue Buffalo filed a counterclaim alleging that Purina's press releases and "Honesty website" constituted false advertising. Blue Buffalo also named the advertising agencies that assisted Purina with its challenged public statements and the Honesty website as defendants in the action. The advertising agencies moved to dismiss the claim against them. The court denied the motion.

> The language of the Act creates a cause of action against any person who engages in false advertising. Liability is not limited to direct competitors. [Citation.] Nor is liability limited to competitors who commission false advertisements. Rather, those who work with competitors to produce false advertisements may also be liable under the Lanham Act. [Citation.]
>
> Unfortunately, there is not much case law discussing the liability of advertising and public relations agencies for Lanham Act false advertising violations. However, a handful of district courts around the county have addressed this issue, and these courts have held that advertising agencies may be liable under the Lanham Act. See *Gillette v. Wilkinson Sword, Inc.*, 795 F. Supp. 662, 663–64 (S.D.N.Y. 1992) ("The analysis of *Noone* [*v. Banner Talent Associates, Inc.*, 398 F.Supp. 260 (S.D.N.Y. 1975),] is sound, and should apply generally to non-principal co-defendants who knowingly participate in false advertising. Thus, advertising agencies are liable under § 43(a) at least where they knowingly participate in the false advertising.") (citing *Noone*, 398 F.Supp. at 263); and *In re Century 21-RE/MAX Real Estate Adver. Claims Litig.*, 882 F. Supp. 915, 924–25 (C.D. Cal. 1994) (holding that "[j]oint tortfeasor liability is available only when the defendant has 'knowingly participated in the creation, development and propagation of the ... false advertising campaign'") (quoting *Gillette*, 795 F. Supp. at 664). See also *Maybelline Co. v. Noxell Corp.*, 813 F.2d 901 (8th Cir. 1987) (reviewing a false advertising claim under the Lanham Act which included advertising agency co-defendants who had carried out the challenged advertising campaign on behalf of Maybelline).
>
> The Advertising Defendants concede that advertising agencies may be liable under the Lanham Act, but argue that such is not the case here because liability will only be found where the agency "was an active participant in the preparation of the ad" and "knew or had reason to know that it was false or deceptive." [Citation.] The Advertising Defendants argue that Blue Buffalo has failed to sufficiently allege either of these elements. Blue Buffalo disagrees that the Lanham Act imposes a scienter or "knowing" requirement.

Although an older version of the Lanham Act included a "knowing" element, Congress amended the Act in 1988 to remove that element. Compare 15 U.S.C. § 1125(a) (1970) ("[A]ny person who shall *with knowledge of the falsity* of such designation of origin or description or representation cause or procure the same to be transported or used in commerce or deliver the same to any carrier to be transported or used, shall be liable to a civil action.") (emphasis added), with 15 U.S.C. § 1125(a) (1988) ("Any person who, on or in connection with any goods or services, or any container for goods, uses in commerce ... [any] false or misleading representation of fact ... shall be liable in a civil action....") (effective as of Nov. 1989). Indeed, courts agree that the elements of a false advertising claim under the current version of the Lanham Act are:

> (1) a false statement of fact by the defendant in a commercial advertisement about its own or another's product; (2) the statement actually deceived or has the tendency to deceive a substantial segment of its audience; (3) the deception is material, in that it is likely to influence the purchasing decision; (4) the defendant caused its false statement to enter interstate commerce; and (5) the plaintiff has been or is likely to be injured as a result of the false statement, either by direct diversion of sales from itself to defendant or by a loss of goodwill associated with its products.

Buetow v. A.L.S. Enterprises, Inc., 650 F.3d 1178, 1182–83 (8th Cir. 2011) (citing *United Indus. Corp. v. Clorox Co.*, 140 F.3d 1175, 1180 (8th Cir.1998).

Despite the clear language of the Lanham Act, the Advertising Defendants argue that the Lanham Act silently imposes a scienter requirement in actions against advertising agencies.... [The court distinguished prior cases on the ground that they relied on pre-amendment versions of the Lanham Act.]

Congress expressly removed the "knowing" element from the Lanham Act in the 1988 amendment, and the sparse case law cited by the parties has not convinced me that there is still a silent "knowing" requirement for claims against advertising agencies. As a result, I will not dismiss the complaint against the Advertising Defendants for failure to allege that the Advertising Defendants knew the advertisements they allegedly created were misleading or false.

Question

When Congress removed the knowledge requirement, do you think it had advertising agencies in mind? Why and under what circumstances should (or should not) advertising agencies be held to a different standard than their clients with respect to claims of false representation?

McNeil-PPC, Inc. v. Pfizer Inc.

351 F. Supp. 2d 226 (S.D.N.Y. 2005)

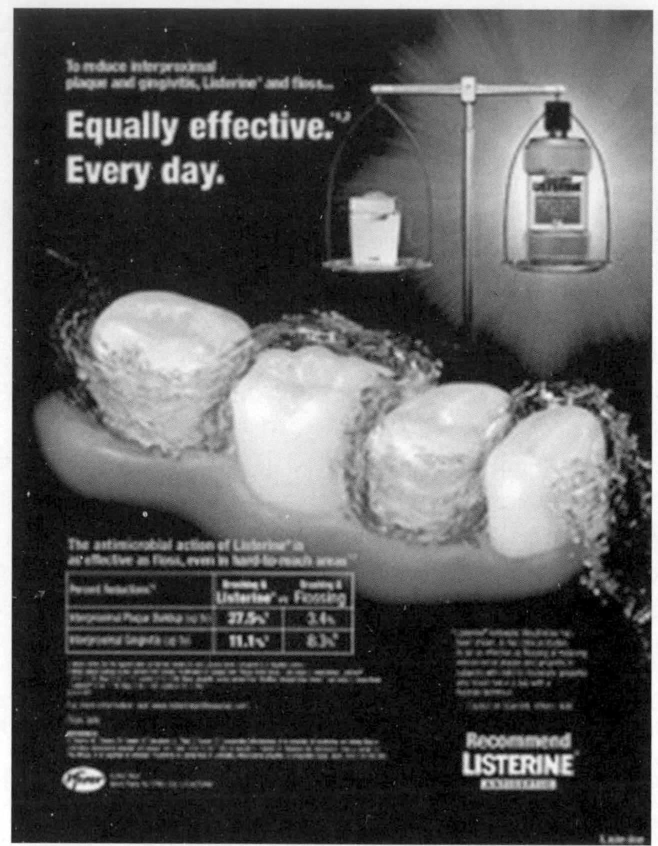

CHIN, J.:

In June 2004, defendant Pfizer Inc. ("Pfizer") launched a consumer advertising campaign for its mouthwash, Listerine Antiseptic Mouthrinse. Print ads and hang tags featured an image of a Listerine bottle balanced on a scale against a white container of dental floss, as shown above.

The campaign also featured a television commercial called the "Big Bang." In its third version, which is still running, the commercial announces that "Listerine's as effective as floss at fighting plaque and gingivitis. Clinical studies prove it." Although the commercial cautions that "there's no replacement for flossing," the commercial repeats two more times the message that Listerine is "as effective as flossing against plaque and gingivitis." The commercial also shows a narrow stream of blue liquid flowing out of a Cool Mint Listerine bottle, then tracking a piece of dental floss being pulled from a white floss container, and then swirling around and between teeth—bringing to mind an image of liquid floss.

In this case, plaintiff McNeil-PPC, Inc. ("PPC"), the market leader in sales of string dental floss and other interdental cleaning products, alleges that Pfizer has engaged in false advertising in violation of § 43(a) of the Lanham Act, 15 U.S.C. § 1125(a), and unfair competition in violation of state law. PPC contends that Pfizer's advertisements are false and misleading in two respects. First, PPC contends that Pfizer's literal (or explicit) claim that "clinical studies prove" that Listerine is "as effective as floss against plaque and gingivitis" is false. Second, PPC contends that Pfizer's advertisements also implicitly are claiming that Listerine is a replacement for floss—that all the benefits of flossing may be obtained by rinsing with Listerine—and that this implied message is false and misleading as well.

Before the Court is PPC's motion for a preliminary injunction enjoining Pfizer from continuing to make these claims in its advertisements. For the reasons set forth below, I conclude that Pfizer's advertisements are false and misleading. PPC's motion is granted and a preliminary injunction will be issued. My findings of fact and conclusions of law follow.

STATEMENT OF THE CASE

A. The Facts

1. The Parties and Their Products

PPC, a wholly-owned subsidiary of Johnson & Johnson ("J & J"), manufactures and markets consumer oral health products. PPC is the market leader in the sales of interdental cleaning products, including dental floss—waxed or unwaxed string used to mechanically remove food and debris from between the teeth and underneath the gumline....

J & J invented floss nearly 100 years ago. PPC's products include the Reach Access Daily Flosser (the "RADF"), a toothbrush-like device with a snap-on head (to be replaced after each use) containing a piece of string floss. The RADF was launched in August 2003. PPC also sells a battery-powered version of the RADF, called the Reach Access Power Flosser.

Pfizer manufactures and markets consumer and pharmaceutical products, including Listerine, an essential oil-containing antimicrobial mouthrinse. According to its label, Listerine:

> Kills germs that cause Bad Breath, Plaque & the gum disease Gingivitis.

Listerine has been "accepted" by the American Dental Association (the "ADA") and bears the ADA seal of acceptance on its label. The label instructs users to rinse with Listerine full strength for 30 seconds, each morning and night. Listerine also comes in several flavors, including Cool Mint, Fresh Burst, and Natural Citrus.

2. Oral Hygiene and Oral Diseases

Plaque is a biofilm comprised of a thin layer of bacteria that forms on teeth and other surfaces of the mouth. Food debris caught between teeth provides a source of nutrition for this bacteria and will help the bacteria multiply, grow, and persist. Plaque build-up may cause gingivitis, an inflammation of the superficial gum tissues surrounding the tooth. Gingivitis is common, affecting some two-thirds of the U.S. population. Its symptoms include red, inflamed, swollen, puffy, or bleeding gums.

Periodontitis is inflammation that develops in deeper tissues, and involves the bone and connection to the tooth (the periodontal ligament). Periodontitis is less common, affecting some 10–15% (more or less) of the population, although it becomes more prevalent with age. It is a major cause of tooth loss.

....

The removal of plaque and the prevention of plaque build-up are critical to addressing both gingivitis and periodontitis. In addition, although it is less clear, controlling plaque also helps prevent or reduce "caries"—cavities or dental decay. The ADA recognizes that "plaque is responsible for both tooth decay and gum disease."

The most common method of mechanically removing plaque is brushing, and today the use of toothbrushes and fluoridated toothpastes is "almost universal." Brushing, however, does not adequately remove plaque. In part, this is because many people do not brush properly or they brush less than the recommended two minutes twice a day. In part, it is also because for most people "toothbrushing alone cannot effectively control interproximal plaque," i.e., the plaque in the hard-to-reach places between the teeth. As a consequence, removal of plaque from the interproximal areas by additional methods is particularly important, for it is in these areas between the teeth that plaque deposits appear early and become more prevalent. The direct interproximal area is the area where there is "the most stagnation" and where "periodontal disease usually starts."

Traditionally, the "most widely recommended" mechanical device for removing interproximal plaque is dental floss.... Flossing provides a number of benefits. It removes food debris and plaque interdentally and it also removes plaque subgingivally. As part of a regular oral hygiene program, flossing helps reduce and prevent not only gingivitis but also periodontitis and caries.

Some 87% of consumers, however, floss either infrequently or not at all. Although dentists and dental hygienists regularly tell their patients to floss, many consumers do not floss or rarely floss because it is a difficult and time-consuming process.

As a consequence, a large consumer market exists to be tapped. If the 87% of consumers who never or rarely floss can be persuaded to floss more regularly, sales of floss would increase dramatically. PPC has endeavored, with products such as the RADF and the Power Flosser, to reach these consumers by trying to make flossing easier.

At the same time, Pfizer has recognized that there is enormous potential here for greater sales of Listerine as well. Pfizer has come to realize that if it could convince consumers who were reluctant flossers that they could obtain the benefits of flossing by rinsing with Listerine, it would be in a position to see its sales of Listerine increase dramatically.

In the context of this case, therefore, Pfizer and PPC are competitors.

3. The Listerine Studies

Pfizer sponsored two clinical studies involving Listerine and floss: the "Sharma Study" and the "Bauroth Study." These studies purported to compare the efficacy of

Listerine against dental floss in controlling plaque and gingivitis in subjects with mild to moderate gingivitis.

[Both studies divided subjects with mild to moderate gingivitis into three groups. One group received instruction in flossing and a supply of dental floss, and was directed to brush twice and floss once every day for six months. The second group was given a supply of Listerine and asked to brush twice and rinse twice every day for six months. The final group was given a supply of a placebo rinse and told to brush and rinse twice daily. The subjects returned to the clinic every month for a dental exam and new supplies. After three months, the Listerine and flossing groups had fewer symptoms of gingivitis than the control group. After six months, the Listerine results were better than the flossing results. The authors of both studies suggested that the most probable reason was that the subjects failed to floss consistently in the later months of the study.]

Neither the Bauroth Study nor the Sharma Study purported to examine whether Listerine could replace floss, and neither study examined the efficacy of Listerine with respect to severe gingivitis or periodontitis or tooth decay or the removal of food debris. In addition, neither study considered the adjunctive effects of Listerine when used in addition to brushing and flossing.

....

7. The Consumer Advertising Campaign

The consumer advertising campaign was launched in June 2004....

In the third version of the Big Bang, which continues to run, the commercial announces that "Listerine's as effective as floss at fighting plaque and gingivitis. Clinical studies prove it." The commercial cautions that "there's no replacement for flossing," but states that "if you don't floss like you should, you can get its plaque-fighting benefits by rinsing." The commercial goes on to repeat two more times the message that Listerine is "as effective as flossing against plaque and gingivitis."

The commercial also shows a narrow stream of blue liquid flowing out of a Cool Mint Listerine bottle, then tracking a piece of dental floss being pulled from a white floss container, and then swirling around and between teeth—bringing to mind an image of liquid floss. In a superscript that appears briefly on-screen, the commercial also tells viewers to "ask your dental professional."

Pfizer also published print ads, including a freestanding circular with a manufacturer's discount coupon featuring a bottle of Cool Mint Listerine balanced equally on a scale opposite a floss container (similar to the image used in the professional campaign). The ad proclaims that Listerine "Is Clinically Proven To Be As Effective as Floss at Reducing Plaque & Gingivitis between the Teeth." In small print near the bottom of the page, the ad states: "Floss Daily." There is no instruction telling consumers to consult their dentists.

Pfizer also used a hang tag and shoulder labels on its bottles of Listerine. The hang tag features the scale image and is similar to the print ad just described. The shoulder label has gone through three versions. The first version (which was red) stated: "Now Clinically Proven As Effective As Floss," with the words in much smaller print "Against Plaque and Gingivitis Between the Teeth." (PXs 98, 162). The second version (which is blue) reads the same as the first, with the addition in small print of the words: "Ask Your Dentist. Floss Daily." A third version (which is gold and red) is being or is about to be distributed and reads: "As Effective As Floss Against Plaque & Gingivitis Between Teeth," with the following words in smaller print: "Ask Your Dentist. Not a Replacement for Floss."

Pfizer has also featured the "as effective as flossing" claim on its website for Listerine. The first page of the website shows the Cool Mint Listerine bottle shaking, with the stream of blue liquid flowing out (as in the Big Bang commercial), and forming the words "Listerine Antiseptic is as effective as flossing," with a footnote to the words: "Against plaque and gingivitis between teeth. Use as directed. Ask your dentist. Not a replacement for floss." The first page also states:

> It's clinically proven.
>
> A quick easy rinse with Listerine Antiseptic, twice a day, is actually as effective as floss. Because Listerine Antiseptic gets between teeth to kill the germs that cause plaque and gingivitis. Ask your dentist. You'll find out that Listerine Antiseptic truly is the easy way to a healthy mouth.

The website has an entire section entitled "Effective As Floss," spanning many pages. In a question-and-answer section, the website addresses frequently asked questions, including the following:

> Question 3 Most people don't like to floss/don't make the time to floss. Isn't this new data telling people that they don't have to floss?
>
> Answer—No, flossing is essential in preventing gum disease because it helps remove food particles and plaque from between the teeth, areas where the toothbrush can't reach. However, optimal plaque control through brushing and flossing alone can sometimes be difficult to achieve. We believe that the results [of the two studies] suggest the importance of adding an antiseptic mouthwash to patients' daily oral healthcare....
>
> ....

8. The Surveys

In September and October 2004, at PPC's request, a consumer research firm, Bruno and Ridgway Research Associates, conducted three consumer surveys in connection with this case, in malls and shopping centers in ten different locations throughout the United States. The first was intended to determine the message that consumers took away from the Big Bang commercial. The second sought to determine the message that consumers took away from the first of the three shoulder labels. The third sought to measure the pre-existing beliefs of consumers regarding the use of Listerine and floss.

In the first survey, consumers were shown the third version of Big Bang twice and then asked a series of questions about the ideas that were communicated to them by the commercial. The survey found that 50% of the respondents took away the message that "you can replace floss with Listerine." ...

In the second survey, eligible consumers were shown a Listerine bottle with the first (or red) version of the shoulder label. They were asked essentially the same questions as were asked in the first survey. Some 45% of the consumers took away the message that Listerine could be used instead of floss....

In the third survey, a control survey, consumers were asked their "pre-existing beliefs" regarding Listerine and floss; the intent was to determine the number of people who did not recall seeing the commercials but who still believed that Listerine could be used instead of floss. A minority of those surveyed did not recall seeing Big Bang, and of those 19% stated the opinion that Listerine could be used in place of floss....

The surveyors then took the three surveys together, subtracted the 19% figure from the 50% and 45% figures, respectively, and concluded that 31% of those who saw the commercial and 26% of those who viewed the shoulder label took away a replacement message.

....

DISCUSSION

....

I conclude that PPC has demonstrated a likelihood of success on both its literal falsity claim and on its implied falsity claim. I address each claim in turn.

a. Literal Falsity

Pfizer's advertisements make the explicit claim that "clinical studies prove that Listerine is as effective as floss against plaque and gingivitis." As Pfizer purports to rely on "clinical studies," this is an "establishment claim" and PPC need only prove that "the [studies] referred to ... were not sufficiently reliable to permit one to conclude with reasonable certainty that they established the proposition for which they were cited." *Castrol* [*Inc. v. Quaker State Corp.*, 977 F.2d 57], at 62–63 [(2d Cir. 1992)]. Two questions are presented: first, whether the Sharma and Bauroth Studies stand for the proposition that "Listerine is as effective as floss against plaque and gingivitis"; and second, assuming they do, whether the studies are sufficiently reliable to permit one to draw that conclusion with "reasonable certainty."

First, even putting aside the issue of their reliability, the two studies do not stand for the proposition that "Listerine is as effective as floss against plaque and gingivitis." The two studies included in their samples only individuals with mild to moderate gingivitis. They excluded individuals with severe gingivitis or with any degree of periodontitis, and they did not purport to draw any conclusions with respect to these individuals. Hence, the literal claim in Pfizer's advertisements is overly broad, for the studies did not purport to prove that Listerine is as effective as floss "against plaque and gingivitis," but only against plaque and gingivitis in individuals with mild to moderate gingivitis. The advertisements do not specify that the "as effective as floss" claim is limited to individuals with mild to moderate gingivitis. Consequently, consumers who suffer from severe gingivitis or periodontitis (including mild periodontitis) may be misled by the ads into believing that Listerine is just as effective as floss in helping them fight plaque and gingivitis, when the studies simply do not stand for that proposition.

Second, the two studies were not sufficiently reliable to permit one to conclude with reasonable certainty that Listerine is as effective as floss in fighting plaque and gingivitis, even in individuals with mild to moderate gingivitis. What the two studies showed was that Listerine is as effective as floss when flossing is not done properly. The authors of both studies recognized that the plaque reductions in the flossing groups were lower than would be expected and hypothesized that "behavioral or technical causes" were the reason....

Hence, the studies did not "prove" that Listerine is "as effective as floss." Rather, they proved only that Listerine is "as effective as improperly-used floss." The studies showed only that Listerine is as effective as floss when the flossing is not performed properly....

Pfizer and its experts argue that the two studies are reliable, notwithstanding the indications that the participants in the flossing group did not floss properly, because these conditions reflect "real-world settings." But the ads do not say that "in the real world," where most people floss rarely or not at all and even those who do floss have difficulty flossing properly, Listerine is "as effective as floss." Rather, the ads make the blanket assertion that Listerine works just as well as floss, an assertion the two studies simply do not prove. Although it is important to determine how a product works in the real world, it is probably more important to first determine how a product will work when it is used properly.

....

Accordingly, I hold that PPC is likely to succeed on its claim of literal false advertisement.

b. Implied Falsity

In considering the claim of implied falsity, in accordance with Second Circuit law, I determine first the message that consumers take away from the advertisements and second whether that message is false.

(i) The Implicit Message

Pfizer argues that its advertisements do not implicitly send the message that Listerine is a replacement for floss. I disagree. Rather, I find that Pfizer's advertisements do send the message, implicitly, that Listerine is a replacement for floss—that the benefits of flossing may be obtained by rinsing with Listerine, and that, in particular, those consumers who do not have the time or desire to floss can switch to Listerine instead.

First, the words and images used in the advertisements confirm that this is the message being sent. The words ("as effective as floss") and images (a stream of blue liquid tracking floss as it is removed from a floss container and then swirling between and around teeth; a bottle of Listerine balanced equally on a scale against a container of floss) convey the impression that Listerine is the equal to floss.

Second, the Ridgway survey is convincing and was conducted in a generally objective and fair manner.... The Ridgway surveys show that 31% and 26% of the consumers who saw Big Bang and the shoulder label, respectively, took away the message that "you can replace floss with Listerine." Hence, a substantial percentage of the consumers who saw the advertisements took away a replacement message.

....

Accordingly, I conclude that the Pfizer ads send an implicit message that Listerine is a replacement for floss.

(ii) Falsity

The final inquiry, then, is whether the implicit message sent by the Pfizer ads is false. Pfizer argues that even assuming the advertisements do send a replacement message, the message is true: Listerine provides all the benefits of flossing.

Pfizer's position is based on two premises. First, Pfizer contends, the Sharma and Bauroth Studies prove that Listerine is as effective as floss in fighting plaque and gingivitis. Second, Pfizer contends, no clinical proof exists to show that flossing provides any benefit other than fighting plaque and gingivitis—there is no clinical proof that flossing reduces tooth decay or periodontitis. Indeed, Pfizer asserts, this notion is a "myth," and goes so far as to argue that there is no proof that reducing plaque will reduce caries or periodontitis. Hence, Pfizer continues, because Listerine does everything that floss can do, Listerine therefore provides all the benefits of floss—and consumers can "toss the floss" and replace it with Listerine.

These arguments are rejected. I conclude that the implicit message sent by Pfizer's advertisements is false, for Listerine is not a replacement for floss.

First, as discussed above, Pfizer's initial premise is wrong. The Sharma and Bauroth Studies do not prove that Listerine is just as effective as floss in fighting plaque and gingivitis. They prove only that Listerine is just as effective in fighting plaque and gingivitis as improperly-used floss. One simply cannot conclude from the two studies that Listerine is just as effective as flossing when the flossing is performed properly.

Second, Pfizer's second premise is wrong as well: there is substantial, convincing clinical, medical, and other proof to show that flossing does fight tooth decay and periodontitis and that Listerine is not a replacement for flossing.

Flossing provides certain benefits that Listerine does not. Floss penetrates subgingivally to remove plaque and biofilm below the gumline. Flossing, as part of a regular oral prevention program, also can reduce periodontitis. Flossing also reduces tooth decay and has an anti-caries effect. Finally, flossing removes food debris interdentally, including pieces of food trapped between the teeth that rinsing cannot dislodge. Numerous articles confirm that tooth decay and periodontitis can be reduced or prevented through interdental plaque control methods, including flossing....

Other substantial evidence also demonstrates, overwhelmingly, that flossing is important in reducing tooth decay and periodontitis and that it cannot be replaced by rinsing with a mouthwash....

Finally, of course, dentists and hygienists have been telling their patients for decades to floss daily. They have been doing so for good reason. The benefits of flossing are real—they are not a "myth." Pfizer's implicit message that Listerine can replace floss is false and misleading.

CONCLUSION

In sum, I find that PPC has demonstrated that it will suffer irreparable harm if a preliminary injunction is not issued, and I find further that PPC has demonstrated a likelihood of success on both its literal falsity claim and on its implied falsity claim.... In addition, I find that Pfizer's false and misleading advertising also poses a public health risk, as the advertisements present a danger of undermining the efforts of dental professionals—and the ADA—to convince consumers to floss on a daily basis.

Question

In the "pox on both your houses" department, scientists and health officials have concluded that there is no reliable scientific evidence to support the claim that flossing lowers the incidence of gum disease or reduces plaque. The U.S. government, moreover, has ceased to recommend daily flossing. *See* Annie Behr, *String of Lies: Our confusion over dental floss is the result of years of biased research, thanks to the war between floss and mouthwash*, Slate (Aug. 4, 2016), http://www.slate.com/articles/health_and_science/medical_examiner/2016/08/the_data_for_or_against_floss_is_biased_and_terrible.html. Given the new assessment of the evidence, would you advise Listerine that it may once again claim that its mouthwash is as effective as floss?

Eastman Chem. Co. v. PlastiPure, Inc.

775 F.3d 230 (5th Cir. 2014)

JENNIFER WALKER ELROD, CIRCUIT JUDGE:

After a jury found that PlastiPure, Inc. and CertiChem, Inc. violated the Lanham Act by making false statements of fact about their competitor's product, the district court entered an injunction against both companies. On appeal, PlastiPure and CertiChem challenge the jury verdict and the injunction on various grounds, including that their statements constituted non-actionable scientific opinions rather than actionable statements of fact. Because the Lanham Act prohibits false commercial speech even when that speech makes scientific claims, and because Appellants' other contentions lack merit, we AFFIRM.

I.

Eastman Chemical Company (Eastman) manufactures a plastic resin called Tritan and sells it to manufacturers of water bottles, baby bottles, food containers, and other consumer products. Eastman launched Tritan commercially in 2007 as an alternative to polycarbonate, which at that point was the primary plastic used in food contact applications. Shortly after Tritan's launch, consumers became concerned that an ingredient in polycarbonate, bisphenol A (BPA), could be harmful to humans. The concerns about BPA were premised on scientific studies purporting to show that BPA could activate estrogen receptors in the human body. Chemicals that mimic estrogen are said to possess estrogenic activity (EA), and they can trigger hormone-dependent cancers, reproductive abnormalities, and other negative health conditions. Eastman recognized that consumer fears about polycarbonate could be a boon to its sales of Tritan, provided that it could assure potential clients that Tritan does not exhibit EA. To that end, Eastman conducted a battery of tests on Tritan which, according to Eastman, showed that Tritan does not exhibit EA.

PlastiPure and CertiChem also hoped to seize on the opportunity created by the public's desire for BPA-free plastics. PlastiPure and CertiChem are companies founded by Dr. George Bittner, a professor of neurobiology at the University of Texas at Austin. PlastiPure developed a plastic resin that it claims does not exhibit EA and, like Eastman, PlastiPure sells its plastic resin to product manufacturers. CertiChem's primary focus is on testing materials for various sorts of hormonal activity.

In 2011, CertiChem published an article summarizing the results of its testing of more than 500 commercially available plastic products. The article was published in *Environmental Health Perspectives*, a peer-reviewed journal published by the National Institutes of Health. Although products made with Tritan were among the products tested, Tritan was not mentioned by name in the article.

After research on the article was completed, but prior to the article's publication, PlastiPure published a three-page sales brochure entitled "EA-Free Plastic Products: Beyond BPA-Free" and distributed the brochure at trade shows and directly to potential customers. The brochure contains a chart that depicts products containing "Eastman's Tritan" as having significant levels of EA. The caption to the chart states: "Examples of test results of products claiming to be EA-free or made from materials claiming to be EA-free are given in the figure to the right. Most examples are made from Eastman's TritanTM resin."

Based on the sales brochure and other marketing materials, Eastman filed suit against PlastiPure and CertiChem, alleging false advertising under the Lanham Act....

II.

....

Appellants argue that commercial statements relating to live scientific controversies should be treated as opinions for Lanham Act purposes. According to Appellants, enjoining statements that embrace one side of an open scientific debate would stifle academic freedom and inhibit the free flow of scientific ideas, contrary to the principles undergirding the First Amendment. Accordingly, they urge us to classify their statements about Tritan's EA content as opinions rather than actionable facts.

As primary support for their argument, Appellants offer the Second Circuit's opinion in *ONY, Inc. v. Cornerstone Therapeutics, Inc.*, 720 F.3d 490 (2d Cir. 2013). In *ONY*, the parties were rival producers of [a pharmaceutical product].... The defendants [published a peer-reviewed study showing the superiority of their product].... After the article's publication, the defendants "issued a press release touting its conclusions and distributed promotional materials that cited the article's findings." *Id.* at 495.

... After a thorough analysis [of the plaintiffs' Lanham Act claim], the Second Circuit concluded that the First Amendment places scientific debates unfolding within the scientific community beyond the reach of the Lanham Act. According to the Second Circuit, statements in scientific literature "are more closely akin to matters of opinion, and are so understood by the relevant scientific communities." *Id.* at 497.

Appellants insist that the present case is on "all fours" with *ONY*. We disagree. The plaintiff in *ONY* sought to enjoin statements made within the academic literature and directed at the scientific community. In that context, the Second Circuit concluded that the defendants' statements should be treated as opinions, else the prospect of defamation liability would stifle academic debate and trench upon First Amendment values. *See id.* at 497 ("[T]he trial of ideas plays out in the pages of peer-reviewed journals, and the scientific public sits as the jury."). Here, in contrast, ... [a]s the district court aptly summarized:

> This lawsuit is not about Dr. Bittner's scientific paper. It is about statements made in commercial advertisements or promotions, not statements made in a peer-reviewed journal. It is about statements made to consumers, not scientists. It is about statements made without the necessary context presented by a full scientific study, such as a description of the data, the experimental methodology, the potential conflicts of interest, and the differences between raw data and the conclusions drawn by the researcher.

....

Given the applicable binding precedent, it is of no moment that the commercial speech in this case concerned a topic of scientific debate. Advertisements do not become immune from Lanham Act scrutiny simply because their claims are open to scientific or public debate. Otherwise, the Lanham Act would hardly ever be enforceable ... The First Amendment ensures a robust discourse in the pages of academic journals, but it does not immunize false or misleading commercial claims. [Citations.]

Questions

1. Bacardi USA, Inc. produces HAVANA CLUB rum, in Puerto Rico. The bottles display the following information: On the front of the bottle, the phrase "Havana Club™" appears in large stylized letters, followed by the word "BRAND" in much smaller letters. Below that, in letters of prominent though slightly smaller size than those in the brand name and in a different font, the words "PUERTO RICAN RUM" appear. Beneath that, in smaller letters and different color ink, the label says "HAVANA CLUB™ RUM."

The words "Havana Club™" are also repeated several times around the neck of the bottle. The back of the bottle includes a statement in clearly legible type that reads:

> Havana Club™ Rum is a premium rum distilled and crafted in Puerto Rico using the original Arechabala family recipe. Developed in Cuba circa 1930, this finely crafted spirit uses black strap molasses, a slow fermentation process, five times distillation and white oak mellowing to create a velvet smoothness that is clean and round to the palate.

The words "HAVANA CLUB™ RUM" and the web address "www.havanaclubus.com" also appear on the back of the bottle above a government-mandated health warning, which is followed by a toll-free number containing the letters HAVANA and, in small print, the phrases "Produced by Havana Club, U.S.A., San Juan, P.R." and "Havana Club is a trademark."

Pernod-Ricard, one of Bacardi's competitors, asserts that the trademark HAVANA CLUB falsely represents the rum's geographic origin. It presented unrebutted survey evidence showing that 18% of consumers who looked at the Havana Club rum bottle believed that the rum was made in Cuba or from Cuban ingredients. Bacardi relies on the uncontested truthfulness of all the statements on the label. How should the court rule? *See Pernod Ricard USA, LLC v. Bacardi U.S.A., Inc.*, 653 F.3d 241 (3d Cir. 2011). If Bacardi sought to register HAVANA CLUB as a trademark for its Puerto Rican rum, would section 2(e) or section 2(a) bar the registration?

2. Lazar Khidekel was a Russian painter who died in 1986, leaving his unsold paintings to his son, Mark. Rene and Claude Boule are French art collectors who specialize in Russian art, and own paintings attributed to Lazar Khidekel. In the late 1980s, Rene and Claude met Mark. He examined their collection and, at their request (and in return for $8000), executed a certificate of authenticity attesting that sixteen of their paintings were authentic Lazar Khidekel works. In 1992, Rene and Claude loaned those paintings to the Musee d'art de Joliette in Canada for a special exhibit.

Several years later, Mark moved to New York City and sought to sell his late father's paintings. He arranged for the exhibition of his father's work at a gallery, and advertised the show as the "first ever North American exhibition" of Khidekel's work. He sent a letter to 25 important art galleries in which he claimed that the paintings shown in the 1992 exhibit at the Musee d'art de Jolliette were not authentic Khidekels. He later arranged to be interviewed by ARTnews magazine. In the interview as it appeared in the magazine, Mark complained that unscrupulous and dishonest art dealers had misrepresented thousands of fraudulent artworks as his father's paintings. He identified Rene and Claude's collection as a fraudulent one, and maintained that he had viewed their collection, and immediately advised them that none of the paintings they owned had been painted by his father.

The Boules are furious. They consult you to find out whether Mark's letter or the interview published in ARTnews might be actionable. Can they recover under § 43(a)? Why or why not? *See Boule v. Hutton*, 328 F.3d 84 (2d Cir. 2003).

3. Digital Widgets has secured several patents but not yet exploited them. To get the capital to take its inventions to market, Digital Widgets borrowed substantial sums of money from a venture capital firm, and assigned its patents as collateral for the loan. Unfortunately, in today's sluggish economy, Digital Widgets was unable to find the right marketing partner. It failed to market its inventions and defaulted on its loan payments. The venture capital firm informed it that it would therefore foreclose on the loan and take sole control of the collateral. In a desperate maneuver to stave off bankruptcy, Digital Widgets issued a press release and bought a full-page advertisement in *Investors Weekly* seeking additional funding. Both the press release and the advertisement claimed that Digital Widgets presented a unique and worthwhile investment opportunity because of the unrealized value of the patents that it owned. The venture capital firm sues for false advertising, claiming that it is the true owner of the patents, and Digital Widget's representations to the contrary are therefore false representations under 43(a)(1)(b). Digital Widgets concedes that it misrepresented the ownership of the patents, but argues that its only false representation was in connection with patents, not products, and it was therefore not actionable under section 43(a). How should the court rule? *See digiGAN, Inc. v. iValidate, Inc.*, 71 U.S.P.Q.2d 1455 (S.D.N.Y. 2004).

4. Professor Rebecca Tushnet has observed:

> Advertising persistently makes promises that will be nonmisleading or even helpful to some people, while misleading some other group. From a regulatory perspective, it may make sense to bar a claim when more people are misled than helped, or when the number of people misled is of sufficient absolute size regardless of the number helped. False advertising regulations and trademark law generally take the latter tack today.

Rebecca Tushnet, *It Depends on What the Meaning of "False" Is: Falsity and Misleadingness in Commercial Speech Doctrine*, 41 Loyola L.A. L. Rev. 227 (2008). How would limiting relief to cases in which plaintiff could show that more people were misled than informed change the shape of the law? How would plaintiff make such a showing? Would such a change make sense?

5. A recent study by marketing professors Priyali Rajagopal and Nicole Votolato Montgomery suggests that showing consumers a high-imagery commercial can actually persuade them that they have tried the advertised product and that they enjoyed it as much as the actors in the commercial seemed to. Experimental subjects seemed firmly convinced of the resulting memories of having used and liked the product, even when the product was completely imaginary. *See* Priyali Rajagopal and Nicole Votolato Montgomery, *I Imagine, I Experience, I Like: The False Experience Effect*, 38 J. Consumer Research 578 (2011). What implication should these findings have for analysis of implicitly false advertisements?

Pom Wonderful LLC v. Coca Cola Co.

134 S. Ct. 2228 (2014)

Justice Kennedy delivered the opinion of the Court

....

POM Wonderful LLC is a grower of pomegranates and a distributor of pomegranate juices. Through its POM Wonderful brand, POM produces, markets, and sells a variety of pomegranate products, including a pomegranate-blueberry juice blend.

POM competes in the pomegranate-blueberry juice market with the Coca-Cola Company. Coca-Cola, under its Minute Maid brand, created a juice blend containing 99.4% apple and grape juices, 0.3% pomegranate juice, 0.2% blueberry juice, and 0.1% raspberry juice. Despite the minuscule amount of pomegranate and blueberry juices in the blend, the front label of the Coca-Cola product displays the words "pomegranate blueberry" in all capital letters, on two separate lines. Below those words, Coca-Cola placed the phrase "flavored blend of 5 juices" in much smaller type. And below that phrase, in still smaller type, were the words "from concentrate with added ingredients"—and, with a line break before the final phrase—"and other natural flavors." The product's front label also displays a vignette of blueberries, grapes, and raspberries in front of a halved pomegranate and a halved apple.

Claiming that Coca-Cola's label tricks and deceives consumers, all to POM's injury as a competitor, POM brought suit under the Lanham Act. POM alleged that the name, label, marketing, and advertising of Coca-Cola's juice blend mislead consumers into believing the product consists predominantly of pomegranate and blueberry juice when it in fact consists predominantly of less expensive apple and grape juices. That confusion, POM complained, causes it to lose sales. POM sought damages and injunctive relief.

The District Court granted partial summary judgment to Coca-Cola on POM's Lanham Act claim, ruling that the FDCA and its regulations preclude challenges to the name and label of Coca-Cola's juice blend. The District Court reasoned that in the juice blend regulations the "FDA has directly spoken on the issues that form the basis of POM's Lanham Act claim against the naming and labeling of" Coca-Cola's product, but has not prohibited any, and indeed expressly has permitted some, aspects of Coca-Cola's label. 727 F. Supp. 2d 849, 871–873 (CD Cal. 2010).

The Court of Appeals for the Ninth Circuit affirmed in relevant part. Like the District Court, the Court of Appeals reasoned that Congress decided "to entrust matters of juice beverage labeling to the FDA"; the FDA has promulgated "comprehensive regulation of that labeling"; and the FDA "apparently" has not imposed the requirements on Coca-Cola's label that are sought by POM. 679 F.3d 1170, 1178 (2012). "[U]nder [Circuit] precedent," the Court of Appeals explained, "for a court to act when the FDA has not—despite regulating extensively in this area—would risk undercutting the FDA's expert judgments and authority." *Id.*, at 1177. For these reasons, and "[o]ut of respect for the statutory and regulatory scheme," the Court of Appeals barred POM's Lanham Act claim. *Id.*, at 1178.

....

Beginning with the text of the two statutes, it must be observed that neither the Lanham Act nor the FDCA [Food Drug and Cosmetic Act], in express terms, forbids or limits Lanham Act claims challenging labels that are regulated by the FDCA. By its terms, the Lanham Act subjects to suit any person who "misrepresents the nature, characteristics, qualities, or geographic origin" of goods or services. 15 U.S.C. § 1125(a). This comprehensive imposition of liability extends, by its own terms, to misrepresentations on labels, including food and beverage labels. No other provision in the Lanham Act limits that understanding or purports to govern the relevant interaction between the Lanham Act and the FDCA. And the FDCA, by its terms, does not preclude Lanham Act suits. In consequence, food and beverage labels regulated by the FDCA are not, under the terms of either statute, off limits to Lanham Act claims. No textual provision in either statute discloses a purpose to bar unfair competition claims like POM's.

This absence is of special significance because the Lanham Act and the FDCA have coexisted since the passage of the Lanham Act in 1946. [Citation.] If Congress had concluded, in light of experience, that Lanham Act suits could interfere with the FDCA, it might well have enacted a provision addressing the issue during these 70 years. [Citations.] Congress enacted amendments to the FDCA and the Lanham Act, *see, e.g.*, Nutrition Labeling and Education Act of 1990, 104 Stat. 2353; Trademark Law Revision

Act of 1988, § 132, 102 Stat. 3946, including an amendment that added to the FDCA an express pre-emption provision with respect to state laws addressing food and beverage misbranding, § 6, 104 Stat. 2362. Yet Congress did not enact a provision addressing the preclusion of other federal laws that might bear on food and beverage labeling. This is "powerful evidence that Congress did not intend FDA oversight to be the exclusive means" of ensuring proper food and beverage labeling. [Citation.]

....

The structures of the FDCA and the Lanham Act reinforce the conclusion drawn from the text. When two statutes complement each other, it would show disregard for the congressional design to hold that Congress nonetheless intended one federal statute to preclude the operation of the other.

....

The two statutes complement each other with respect to remedies in a more fundamental respect. Enforcement of the FDCA and the detailed prescriptions of its implementing regulations is largely committed to the FDA. The FDA, however, does not have the same perspective or expertise in assessing market dynamics that day-to-day competitors possess. Competitors who manufacture or distribute products have detailed knowledge regarding how consumers rely upon certain sales and marketing strategies. Their awareness of unfair competition practices may be far more immediate and accurate than that of agency rulemakers and regulators. Lanham Act suits draw upon this market expertise by empowering private parties to sue competitors to protect their interests on a case-by-case basis. By "serv[ing] a distinct compensatory function that may motivate injured persons to come forward," Lanham Act suits, to the extent they touch on the same subject matter as the FDCA, "provide incentives" for manufacturers to behave well. [Citation.] Allowing Lanham Act suits takes advantage of synergies among multiple methods of regulation. This is quite consistent with the congressional design to enact two different statutes, each with its own mechanisms to enhance the protection of competitors and consumers.

....

Finally, Coca-Cola urges that the FDCA, and particularly its implementing regulations, addresses food and beverage labeling with much more specificity than is found in the provisions of the Lanham Act. That is true. The pages of FDA rulemakings devoted only to juice-blend labeling attest to the level of detail with which the FDA has examined the subject. [Citation.] Because, as we have explained, the FDCA and the Lanham Act are complementary and have separate scopes and purposes, this greater specificity would matter only if the Lanham Act and the FDCA cannot be implemented in full at the same time. [Citations.] But neither the statutory structure nor the empirical evidence of which the Court is aware indicates there will be any difficulty in fully enforcing each statute according to its terms.

....

The position Coca-Cola takes in this Court that because food and beverage labeling is involved it has no Lanham Act liability here for practices that allegedly mislead and trick consumers, all to the injury of competitors, finds no support in precedent or the statutes.

D. Standing to Assert a § 43(a) Claim

Lexmark International, Inc. v. Static Control Components, Inc.

134 S. Ct. 1377 (2014)

Justice Scalia delivered the opinion of the Court

This case requires us to decide whether respondent, Static Control Components, Inc., may sue petitioner, Lexmark International, Inc., for false advertising under the Lanham Act, 15 U.S.C. § 1125(a).

I. Background

Lexmark manufactures and sells laser printers. It also sells toner cartridges for those printers (toner being the powdery ink that laser printers use to create images on paper). Lexmark designs its printers to work only with its own style of cartridges, and it therefore dominates the market for cartridges compatible with its printers. That market, however, is not devoid of competitors. Other businesses, called "remanufacturers," acquire used Lexmark toner cartridges, refurbish them, and sell them in competition with new and refurbished cartridges sold by Lexmark.

Lexmark would prefer that its customers return their empty cartridges to it for refurbishment and resale, rather than sell those cartridges to a remanufacturer. So Lexmark introduced what it called a "Prebate" program, which enabled customers to purchase new toner cartridges at a 20-percent discount if they would agree to return the cartridge to Lexmark once it was empty. Those terms were communicated to consumers through notices printed on the toner-cartridge boxes, which advised the consumer that opening the box would indicate assent to the terms—a practice commonly known as "shrinkwrap licensing," [citation]. To enforce the Prebate terms, Lexmark included a microchip in each Prebate cartridge that would disable the cartridge after it ran out of toner; for the cartridge to be used again, the microchip would have to be replaced by Lexmark.

Static Control is not itself a manufacturer or remanufacturer of toner cartridges. It is, rather, "the market leader [in] making and selling the components necessary to remanufacture Lexmark cartridges." 697 F.3d 387, 396 (CA6 2012) (case below). In addition to supplying remanufacturers with toner and various replacement parts, Static Control developed a microchip that could mimic the microchip in Lexmark's Prebate cartridges. By purchasing Static Control's microchips and using them to replace the Lexmark microchip, remanufacturers were able to refurbish and resell used Prebate cartridges.

Lexmark did not take kindly to that development. In 2002, it sued Static Control, alleging that Static Control's microchips violated both the Copyright Act of 1976, 17 U.S.C. § 101 *et seq.*, and the Digital Millennium Copyright Act, 17 U.S.C. § 1201 *et seq.* Static Control counterclaimed, alleging, among other things, violations of § 43(a) of the Lanham Act....

As relevant to its Lanham Act claim, Static Control alleged two types of false or misleading conduct by Lexmark. First, it alleged that through its Prebate program Lexmark "purposefully misleads end-users" to believe that they are legally bound by the Prebate terms and are thus required to return the Prebate-labeled cartridge to Lexmark after a single use. Second, it alleged that upon introducing the Prebate program, Lexmark "sent letters to most of the companies in the toner cartridge remanufacturing business" falsely advising those companies that it was illegal to sell refurbished Prebate cartridges and, in particular, that it was illegal to use Static Control's products to refurbish those cartridges. Static Control asserted that by those statements, Lexmark had materially misrepresented "the nature, characteristics, and qualities" of both its own products and Static Control's products....

[The District Court dismissed Static Control's counterclaim on the ground that it was an insufficiently direct competitor of Lexmark. The Sixth Circuit reversed.] Taking the lay of the land, it identified three competing approaches to determining whether a plaintiff has standing to sue under the Lanham Act. It observed that the Third, Fifth, Eighth, and Eleventh Circuits all refer to "antitrust standing ..." [Citations.] By contrast, "[t]he Seventh, Ninth, and Tenth [Circuits] use a categorical test, permitting Lanham Act suits only by an actual competitor." [Citations.] And the Second Circuit applies a " 'reasonable interest' approach," under which a Lanham Act plaintiff "has standing if the claimant can demonstrate '(1) a reasonable interest to be protected against the alleged false advertising and (2) a reasonable basis for believing that the interest is likely to be damaged by the alleged false advertising.' " [Citations.] The Sixth Circuit applied the Second Circuit's reasonable-interest test and concluded that Static Control had standing because it "alleged a cognizable interest in its business reputation and sales to remanufacturers and sufficiently alleged that th[o]se interests were harmed by Lexmark's statements to the remanufacturers that Static Control was engaging in illegal conduct." [Citation.]

We granted certiorari to decide "the appropriate analytical framework for determining a party's standing to maintain an action for false advertising under the Lanham Act."

....

III. Static Control's Right to Sue Under § 1125(a)

[T]his case presents a straightforward question of statutory interpretation: Does the cause of action in § 1125(a) extend to plaintiffs like Static Control? The statute authorizes suit by "any person who believes that he or she is likely to be damaged" by a defendant's false advertising. § 1125(a)(1). Read literally, that broad language might suggest that an action is available to anyone who can satisfy the minimum requirements of Article III. No party makes that argument, however, and the "unlikelihood that Congress meant to allow all factually injured plaintiffs to recover persuades us that [§ 1125(a)] should not get such an expansive reading." [Citation.] We reach that conclusion in light of two relevant background principles ... : zone of interests and proximate causality.

A. Zone of Interests

First, we presume that a statutory cause of action extends only to plaintiffs whose interests "fall within the zone of interests protected by the law invoked." [Citation.] ...

Identifying the interests protected by the Lanham Act ... requires no guesswork, since the Act includes an "unusual, and extraordinarily helpful," detailed statement of the statute's purposes. [The Court quoted the "intent of this chapter" provision in section 45.]

Most of the enumerated purposes are relevant to false-association cases; a typical false-advertising case will implicate only the Act's goal of "protect[ing] persons engaged in [commerce within the control of Congress] against unfair competition." Although "unfair competition" was a "plastic" concept at common law, [citation], it was understood to be concerned with injuries to business reputation and present and future sales. [Citations.]

We thus hold that to come within the zone of interests in a suit for false advertising under § 1125(a), a plaintiff must allege an injury to a commercial interest in reputation or sales. A consumer who is hoodwinked into purchasing a disappointing product may well have an injury-in-fact cognizable under Article III, but he cannot invoke the protection of the Lanham Act—a conclusion reached by every Circuit to consider the question. [Citations.] Even a business misled by a supplier into purchasing an inferior product is, like consumers generally, not under the Act's aegis.

B. Proximate Cause

Second, we generally presume that a statutory cause of action is limited to plaintiffs whose injuries are proximately caused by violations of the statute.... No party disputes that it is proper to read § 1125(a) as containing such a requirement, its broad language notwithstanding.

....

... [T]he proximate-cause requirement generally bars suits for alleged harm that is "too remote" from the defendant's unlawful conduct. That is ordinarily the case if the harm is purely derivative of "misfortunes visited upon a third person by the defendant's acts." [Citations.] In a sense, of course, all commercial injuries from false advertising are derivative of those suffered by consumers who are deceived by the advertising; but since the Lanham Act authorizes suit only for commercial injuries, the intervening step of consumer deception is not fatal to the showing of proximate causation required by the statute. [Citation.] That is consistent with our recognition that under common-law principles, a plaintiff can be directly injured by a misrepresentation even where "a third party, and not the plaintiff, ... relied on" it. [Citation.]

We thus hold that a plaintiff suing under § 1125(a) ordinarily must show economic or reputational injury flowing directly from the deception wrought by the defendant's advertising; and that that occurs when deception of consumers causes them to withhold trade from the plaintiff. That showing is generally not made when the deception produces injuries to a fellow commercial actor that in turn affect the plaintiff. For example, while a competitor who is forced out of business by a defendant's false advertising generally will be able to sue for its losses, the same is not true of the competitor's landlord, its electric company, and other commercial parties who suffer merely as a result of the competitor's "inability to meet [its] financial obligations." [Citation.]

C. Proposed Tests

... We hold ... that a direct application of the zone-of-interests test and the proximate-cause requirement supplies the relevant limits on who may sue.

The balancing test Lexmark advocates was first articulated by the Third Circuit in *Conte Bros.* [*Automotive, Inc. v. Quaker State-Slick 50, Inc.*, 165 F.3d 221 (3d Cir. 1998),] and later adopted by several other Circuits. *Conte Bros.* identified five relevant considerations:

> (1) The nature of the plaintiff's alleged injury: Is the injury of a type that Congress sought to redress in providing a private remedy for violations of the [Lanham Act]?
>
> (2) The directness or indirectness of the asserted injury.
>
> (3) The proximity or remoteness of the party to the alleged injurious conduct.
>
> (4) The speculativeness of the damages claim.
>
> (5) The risk of duplicative damages or complexity in apportioning damages. [Citation.]

This approach reflects a commendable effort to give content to an otherwise nebulous inquiry, but we think it slightly off the mark. The first factor can be read as requiring that the plaintiff's injury be within the relevant zone of interests and the second and third as requiring (somewhat redundantly) proximate causation; but it is not correct to treat those requirements, which must be met in every case, as mere factors to be weighed in a balance. And the fourth and fifth factors are themselves problematic. "[T]he difficulty that can arise when a court attempts to ascertain the damages caused by some remote action" is a "motivating principle" behind the proximate-cause requirement, [citation]; but potential difficulty in ascertaining and apportioning damages is not, as *Conte Bros.* might suggest, an independent basis for denying standing where it is adequately alleged that a defendant's conduct has proximately injured an interest of the plaintiff's that the statute protects. Even when a plaintiff cannot quantify its losses with sufficient certainty to recover damages, it may still be entitled to injunctive relief under § 1116(a) (assuming it can prove a likelihood of future injury) or disgorgement of the defendant's ill-gotten profits under § 1117(a). [Citations.] Finally, experience has shown that the *Conte Bros.* approach, like other open-ended balancing tests, can yield unpredictable and at times arbitrary results. *See, e.g.*, Tushnet, *Running the Gamut from A to B: Federal Trademark and False Advertising Law*, 159 U. Pa. L. Rev. 1305, 1376–1379 (2011).

In contrast to the multifactor balancing approach, the direct-competitor test provides a bright-line rule; but it does so at the expense of distorting the statutory language. To be sure, a plaintiff who does not compete with the defendant will often have a harder time establishing proximate causation. But a rule categorically prohibiting all suits by noncompetitors would read too much into the Act's reference to "unfair competition" in § 1127. By the time the Lanham Act was adopted, the common-law tort of unfair competition was understood not to be limited to actions between competitors. One leading authority in the field wrote that "there need be no competition in unfair competition," just as "[t]here is no soda in soda water, no grapes in grape fruit, no bread in bread fruit, and a clothes horse is not a horse but is good enough to hang things on." [Citations.] It is thus a mistake to infer that because the Lanham Act treats false advertising as a form of unfair competition, it can protect only the false-advertiser's direct competitors.

Finally, there is the "reasonable interest" test applied by the Sixth Circuit in this case. As typically formulated, it requires a commercial plaintiff to "demonstrate '(1) a reasonable interest to be protected against the alleged false advertising and (2) a reasonable basis for believing that the interest is likely to be damaged by the alleged false advertising.'" [Citation.] A purely practical objection to the test is that it lends itself to widely divergent application. Indeed, its vague language can be understood as requiring only the bare minimum of Article III standing. The popularity of the multifactor balancing test reflects its appeal to courts tired of "grappl[ing] with defining" the "'reasonable interest'" test "with greater precision." [Citation.] The theoretical difficulties with the test are even more substantial: The relevant question is not whether the plaintiff's interest is "reasonable," but whether it is one the Lanham Act protects; and not whether there is a "reasonable basis" for the plaintiff's claim of harm, but whether the harm alleged is proximately tied to the defendant's conduct. In short, we think the principles set forth above will provide clearer and more accurate guidance than the "reasonable interest" test.

IV. Application

Applying those principles to Static Control's false-advertising claim, we conclude that Static Control comes within the class of plaintiffs whom Congress authorized to sue under § 1125(a).

To begin, Static Control's alleged injuries—lost sales and damage to its business reputation—are injuries to precisely the sorts of commercial interests the Act protects. Static Control is suing not as a deceived consumer, but as a "perso[n] engaged in" "commerce within the control of Congress" whose position in the marketplace has been damaged by Lexmark's false advertising. § 1127. There is no doubt that it is within the zone of interests protected by the statute.

Static Control also sufficiently alleged that its injuries were proximately caused by Lexmark's misrepresentations. This case, it is true, does not present the "classic Lanham Act false-advertising claim" in which "'one competito[r] directly injur[es] another by making false statements about his own goods [or the competitor's goods] and thus inducing customers to switch.' " [Citation.] But although diversion of sales to a direct competitor may be the paradigmatic direct injury from false advertising, it is not the only type of injury cognizable under § 1125(a). For at least two reasons, Static Control's allegations satisfy the requirement of proximate causation.

First, Static Control alleged that Lexmark disparaged its business and products by asserting that Static Control's business was illegal. See 697 F.3d, at 411, n. 10 (noting allegation that Lexmark "directly target[ed] Static Control" when it "falsely advertised that Static Control infringed Lexmark's patents"). When a defendant harms a plaintiff's reputation by casting aspersions on its business, the plaintiff's injury flows directly from the audience's belief in the disparaging statements. Courts have therefore afforded relief under § 1125(a) not only where a defendant denigrates a plaintiff's product by name, [citation], but also where the defendant damages the product's reputation by, for example, equating it with an inferior product, [citations]. Traditional proximate-causation principles support those results: As we have observed, a defendant who " 'seeks to promote his own interests by telling a known falsehood to or about the plaintiff or his product' " may be said to have proximately caused the plaintiff's harm. [Citation.]

The District Court emphasized that Lexmark and Static Control are not direct competitors. But when a party claims reputational injury from disparagement, competition is not required for proximate cause; and that is true even if the defendant's aim was to harm its immediate competitors, and the plaintiff merely suffered collateral damage. Consider two rival carmakers who purchase airbags for their cars from different third-party manufacturers. If the first carmaker, hoping to divert sales from the second, falsely proclaims that the airbags used by the second carmaker are defective, both the second carmaker and its airbag supplier may suffer reputational injury, and their sales may decline as a result. In those circumstances, there is no reason to regard either party's injury as derivative of the other's; each is directly and independently harmed by the attack on its merchandise.

In addition, Static Control adequately alleged proximate causation by alleging that it designed, manufactured, and sold microchips that both (1) were necessary for, and (2) had no other use than, refurbishing Lexmark toner cartridges. It follows from that allegation that any false advertising that reduced the remanufacturers' business necessarily injured Static Control as well. Taking Static Control's assertions at face value, there is likely to be something very close to a 1:1 relationship between the number of refurbished Prebate cartridges sold (or not sold) by the remanufacturers and the number of Prebate microchips sold (or not sold) by Static Control. "Where the injury alleged is so integral an aspect of the [violation] alleged, there can be no question" that proximate cause is satisfied. [Citation.]

To be sure, on this view, the causal chain linking Static Control's injuries to consumer confusion is not direct, but includes the intervening link of injury to the remanufacturers. Static Control's allegations therefore might not support standing under a strict application of the " ' "general tendency" ' " not to stretch proximate causation " ""beyond the first step."" " [Citation.] But the reason for that general tendency is that there ordinarily is a "discontinuity" between the injury to the direct victim and the injury to the indirect victim, so that the latter is not surely attributable to the former (and thus also to the defendant's conduct), but might instead have resulted from "any number of [other] reasons." [Citation.] That is not the case here. Static Control's allegations suggest that if the remanufacturers sold 10,000 fewer refurbished cartridges because of Lexmark's false advertising, then it would follow more or less automatically that Static Control sold 10,000 fewer microchips for the same reason, without the need for any "speculative ... proceedings" or "intricate, uncertain inquiries." [Citation.] In these relatively unique circumstances, the remanufacturers are not "more immediate victim[s]" than Static Control. [Citation.]

Although we conclude that Static Control has alleged an adequate basis to proceed under § 1125(a), it cannot obtain relief without evidence of injury proximately caused by Lexmark's alleged misrepresentations. We hold only that Static Control is entitled to a chance to prove its case.

Questions

1. McDonald's ran a series of promotional games to attract customers. It advertised the games heavily, and represented that everyone who entered would have a fair chance to win. The ads gave the odds of winning the top prizes. Without McDonald's knowledge, the firm it had engaged to operate the games embezzled more than $20,000,000 in prize-winning game pieces. That operator was later caught and convicted, and McDonald's revised its prize security policies in the hope of preventing a recurrence. A group of local Burger King franchisees brought a false advertising claim against McDonald's, arguing that the ads misrepresented customers' chances of winning the contests. McDonald's concedes that the ads were misleading, but argues that the plaintiffs lack prudential standing. How should the court rule? *See Phoenix of Broward, Inc. v. McDonald's Corporation*, 489 F.3d 1156 (11th Cir. 2007).

2. In 2000, Natural Answers introduced HERBAQUIT smoking cessation lozenges, herbal lozenges containing no nicotine, which were advertised as helpful in reducing the urge to smoke. Natural Answers sold HERBAQUIT lozenges in drugstores, and health food stores and over the Internet. Between January of 2000 and March of 2002, customers bought 50,000 packages of HERBAQUIT. In March of 2002, though, Natural Answers discontinued the product. Six months later, SmithKline Beecham launched COMMIT, an FDA-approved nicotine lozenge. Defendant advertised COMMIT as "the first and only stop smoking lozenge." Natural Answers sued for false advertising, claiming that the representation was literally false, but SmithKline Beecham argues Natural Answers lacks prudential standing. What result? Would your answer change if Natural Answers has a bona fide intent to resume production and sale of HERBAQUIT? *See Natural Answers v. SmithKline Beecham Corp.*, 529 F.3d 1325 (11th Cir. 2008).

Chapter 11

Internet Domain Names

A. The Domain Name System

Jonathan Weinberg, *ICANN and the Problem of Legitimacy*

50 Duke L.J. 187 (2000) (Excerpt)*

....

I. How We Got Here

A. Early History of the Internet

For a long time after computers were developed, they were solitary objects; one computer could not talk with another. Researchers achieved a milestone in 1965 when they used an ordinary telephone line to connect a computer at the Massachusetts Institute of Technology with another in California, allowing them to share programs and data across a substantial distance. In order to allow computers to communicate effectively, though, computer scientists had to devise an entirely new way, known as packet switching, of transmitting information over phone lines.

A unit of the Department of Defense called the Defense Advanced Research Projects Agency, or DARPA, funded research into how to connect computers together into networks. With DARPA's support, scientists began to connect computers at various universities into a new network called the ARPANET. Data was transmitted over the ARPANET at a rate of 50,000 bits per second—blindingly fast at the time, but not too far off the speed any ordinary user with an off-the-shelf modem can achieve today.** In 1972, researchers developed the first e-mail program. This, for the first time, enabled the use of computers for long-distance person-to-person communication.

Computer networks began springing up wherever researchers could find someone to pay for them. The Department of Energy set up two networks, NASA set up another, and the National Science Foundation (NSF) provided seed money for yet another. In each case, far-flung researchers were able to use the network to communicate and share their work via e-mail.

---

* Copyright 2000. Reprinted by permission [*Editors' Note:* Footnotes omitted.]

** [*Editors' Note*: Current speeds are many times faster.According to Wikipedia, the average broadband connection speed in the United States in 2015 was 12.6 million bytes per second. *See* https://en.wikipedia.org/wiki/List_of_countries_by_Internet_connection_speeds.]

Scientists developed a technology called TCP/IP to connect all of these networks together. When the ARPANET adopted TCP/IP, people using ARPANET computers could communicate with people using computers on any other TCP/IP network. The technique of linking different networks together was referred to as internetworking or internetting, and the resulting "network of networks" was the Internet. By the mid-1980s, though, the number of interconnected hosts was still small.

The National Science Foundation saw the chance to change that. NSF helped fund a high-speed backbone to link networks serving thousands of research and educational institutions around the United States. By 1992, there were more than one million host computers connected to the Internet. At the same time, scientists were developing new ways to use an Internet connection. At a research center in Switzerland, scientists developed a key new application: the World Wide Web, which permitted users to link documents, programs, or video clips residing on different machines almost anywhere in the world.

B. Internet Addressing

In any system of networked computing, there has to be some mechanism enabling one computer to locate another. If I want to send e-mail to a buddy in Boise, the system needs to have some way to find his mail server so that it can direct the information there. Internet engineers came up with this solution: Each "host" computer connected to the Internet was assigned an Internet protocol (IP) address, which consisted of a unique 32-bit number, usually printed in dotted decimal form, such as 128.127.50.224. Dr. Jon Postel of the University of Southern California's Information Sciences Institute (ISI) assumed the task of assigning blocks of IP addresses to computer networks. Because no two computers had the same IP address, it was possible to locate any computer on the Internet simply by knowing its IP address. TCP/IP made possible a system of routing that permitted a user to dispatch a message onto the Internet, knowing only the IP address of the computer he wished to reach, with confidence that the message would eventually reach its intended destination.

In addition to an IP address, each host computer had a name, such as SRI-NIC. A Network Information Center maintained a hosts.txt table translating names to IP addresses for every host. A user could send e-mail specifying only the name of the relevant host; his computer would consult the hosts.txt table to determine the relevant IP address. There were two advantages to this dual system of names and addresses. First, IP addresses were opaque and hard to remember. Names were rather more user-friendly. It was inconvenient for a user to have to remember and type in a different IP address for every Internet resource he sought to access or e-mail message he wished to send. It was much easier to use a short name with semantic meaning. Second, the use of names made it possible for network operators to change the configuration of their networks, and therefore change the IP addresses associated with various machines, without disrupting communications with the outside world.

This system worked well so long as the number of computers attached to the Internet was small. As that number grew, however, it became clear that the Internet needed a more sophisticated addressing structure than the hosts.txt table could provide. By 1983, the size of that table and the frequency of its updates were "near the limit of manageability." Accordingly, scientists, including Postel and Paul Mockapetris, also of the Information Sciences Institute, developed the "domain name system" (DNS). The domain name system retains the user-friendliness of mapping each IP address to a domain name such as threecats.net or law.wayne.edu. The new system differs from the old approach, though, in key respects.

First, the DNS defines a hierarchical name space. That name space is divided into top-level domains, or TLDs. Each top-level domain is divided into second-level domains, and so on. Under the plan developed by Postel and Mockapetris, there were seven generic, three-letter top-level domains: .com, .net, .org, .edu, .gov, .mil, and .int. In addition, there were two-letter country code top-level domains such as .jp, .us, and .fr. At the outset, it was thought that .com would be used by commercial entities, .net by entities involved with the Internet networking infrastructure, .org by nonprofit organizations, and .edu by educational institutions. Today, the restrictions on the first three of these have long since fallen away. The largest top-level domain by far is .com, with more than sixteen million second-level domain names as of this writing; .net and .org come next.***

. . . .

Once the DNS got underway in 1985, the day-to-day job of registering second-level domains in the generic top-level domains was handled by the Stanford Research Institute (SRI) under contract to the U.S. Department of Defense. The Defense Department, which had long funded ISI as part of its funding of almost all of the Internet's early development, also entered into contracts under which it funded the activities of Dr. Postel and other Information Sciences Institute staff in coordinating IP address allocation and oversight of the domain name system. These activities came to be referred to as the Internet Assigned Numbers Authority (IANA). Later on, the National Science Foundation took over the role of funding the civilian part of the Internet infrastructure. The National Science Foundation entered into a cooperative agreement with a company named Network Solutions, Inc. (NSI) to perform the registration services that had been handled earlier by SRI. NSI agreed to register second-level domains in .com, .net, .org, and .edu and to maintain those top-level domains' master databases.**** Those services were underwritten by the National Science Foundation and were free to users.

*** *Editors' Note*: as of October 29, 2012, there were more than 105 million .com domain names, over 14 million .net, and over 10 million .org domain names. http://www.whois.sc/internet-statistics.

**** *Editors' Note*: Network Solutions, Inc. was acquired by Verisign, Inc. in 2000. Verisign still operates the .com and .net registries, *Verisign Domain Name Registries*, VeriSign, http://www.verisign.com/en_US/channel-resources/index.xhtml, as well as the .gov registry under a contract with the General Services Administration. Verisign's revenues from domain name services exceed $600 million annually. *See* Jonathan Weinberg, *Governments, Privatization, and "Privatization": ICANN and the GAC*, 18 MICH. TELECOMM. TECH. L. REV. 189, 191 n.7 (2011), *available at* http://www.mttlr.org/wp-content/journal/voleighteen/weinberg.pdf.

Internet Corporation for Assigned Names and Numbers (ICANN), *Basic TLD Information*

http://www.icann.org/en/resources/registries

The right-most label in a domain name is referred to as its "top-level domain" (TLD). TLDs with two letters have been established for over 250 countries and external territories and are referred to as "country-code" TLDs or "ccTLDs". TLDs with three or more characters are referred to as "generic" TLDs, or "gTLDs".

The responsibility for operating each TLD (including maintaining a registry of the domain names within the TLD) is delegated to a particular organization. These organizations are referred to as "registry operators" or "sponsors". Currently, domain names under the following gTLDs are available, and the corresponding registries are under contract with ICANN: .aero, .asia, .biz, .cat, .com, .coop, .info, .jobs, .mobi, .museum, .name, .net, .org, .pro, .tel and .travel.

Generally speaking, an unsponsored gTLD Registry operates under policies established by the global Internet community directly through the ICANN process .biz, .com, .info, .name, .net, .org, and .pro are unsponsored TLDs.

A sponsored TLD is a specialized TLD that has a sponsor representing a specific community that is served by the TLD. The sponsor thus carries out delegated policy-formulation responsibilities over many matters concerning the TLD .aero, .asia, .cat, .coop, .jobs, .mobi, .museum, .tel and .travel are sponsored TLDs.

Jessica Litman, *The DNS Wars*

4 J. Small & Emerging Bus. L. 149 (2000) (Excerpt)*

Until 1993, the National Science Foundation prohibited anyone from making commercial use of the Internet. When the NSF decommissioned the Internet backbone…, and stopped prohibiting commercial use, it foresaw a gradual increase in commercial Internet activity, and a growing, if still modest demand for commercial domain names in the.com top level domain, so it subcontracted the job of registering .com domain names to a small company named Network Solutions, which immediately put 2 1/2 employees on the job. Network Solutions registered .com domain names on a first-come first-served basis, just as all the Internet domain names had always been allocated.

Back in 1993 and 1994, nobody had any idea that the Internet was going to become the engine of electronic commerce within the next few years. People registered domain names in .com for a variety of reasons. There were some companies, like Clue Computing or Amazon.com, who registered their names as domain names because they planned to do business over the Internet. There were fans. A guy named Jef Poskanzer, for instance, registered acme.com because he'd always been a big fan of Wile E Coyote.

---

* [*Editors Note*: most footnotes omitted]

Then, there were domain name speculators: folks who believed that the Internet would be an important business tool some day, and domain names would be valuable commodities, and so they registered a whole slew of domain names they believed someone would someday pay money to own.

It's hard to know how to think about domain name speculators. These folks saw some unclaimed property that they believed would be valuable someday, and so they invested in it. Turns out they were right. Our society thinks about that sort of activity in different ways depending on the circumstances. Sometimes we encourage it: If the potentially valuable resource is land, or gold or pork bellies, or stock in some start-up company, we tend to think of the successful speculator as an admirable entrepreneur. Sometimes, we disapprove. If someone is stockpiling huge reserves of medicine or water or food in case the Y2K bug plunges society back into the dark ages, we tend to call it either greedy or silly. Sometimes, we simply won't permit it: If the potential valuable resource is a trademark, and someone tries to register it and put it in her trademark warehouse, in case she gets the chance to sell it to someone else some day, she can't.

In any event, there were domain name speculators, who were either business investors or cybersquatters, depending on your religion, and they registered potentially useful names like drugs.com, and also names they figured that businesses out there would want, like panavision.com. Some of them were planning on simply grabbing up unclaimed but commercially valuable domain names and selling them to the companies likely to want them at a substantial markup. A variation involved registering a slew of common surnames into the .com or .org domain on the theory that one could sell them to individuals who wanted domains named after their own surnames. Some of them went into it with honest intentions: they wanted to offer companies with no web presence web-hosting services, and went ahead and registered potential customers' marks as domain names as a initial step in their business plan. Others decided to use the domains they registered for porn sites, on the theory that someone would come along looking for the White House and type whitehouse.com, where they'd find all sorts of pornography that might entice them to stick around.

Whatever motives they had, though, during the couple of years between the time that Network Solutions started registering .com domain names on a first-come first-served basis and the moment that all the businesses in the Western World figured out that they wanted a domain name based on their trademarks, a fair number of domain names that someone else might also want got snapped up.

You can see that the whole situation was a collision waiting to happen: Out here in meat space, we can have a whole bunch of different owners of ACME as a trademark—the last time I counted there were more than 100 different trademark registrations, in addition to all the local unregistered ACME marks you can find by just looking in the telephone book. On the Internet, only one person can own acme.com. Jef Poskanzer, the Wile E Coyote fan I mentioned earlier, happens to be the lucky guy. He doesn't own *any* Acme trademarks, but he got there first.

That offends some people, who think that when Jef Poskanzer came knocking on Network Solutions' door, it should have done a quick trademark search, and when it discovered that Jef didn't own an ACME trademark and someone else did, it should have refused to give him acme.com, and instead hung onto it for the trademark owner.

Once it became clear that the Internet was important, even essential to business, a bunch of companies had decided to get themselves an Internet domain, and found that the ones they wanted had already been registered by someone else, under Network Solutions's first-come-first-served registration policy. They were outraged. They sued. Some won; some lost.

Hasbro toys was interested in offering an online version of its CLUE game at clue.com, but, it discovered that Clue Computing had gotten there first. Hasbro also considered putting together an online version of its CANDYLAND game, but then it found out that Candyland.com belonged to a company named the Internet Entertainment Group, which was using it for a pornographic website. The Amazon Bookstore, the oldest feminist bookstore in the United States, wanted to register amazon.com, but Amazon.com had gotten there first. Panavision, the movie camera company, went to Network Solutions to register panavision.com, and discovered it already belonged to a guy named Dennis Toeppen, and that Mr. Toeppen was willing to convey the domain name to Panavision, *if* Panavision forked over $13,000.

....

Hasbro sued Clue Computing. It lost.[21] It sued Internet Entertainment Group, and it won.[22] Panavision sued Mr. Toeppen, and it actually won a dilution claim, although the court had to do a fair amount of maneuvering to find commercial use in commerce—it decided that Toeppen's practice of selling domain names to the companies who owned the relevant trademarks was itself commercial use in commerce.[23]

There were a bunch of lawsuits, and the courts seemed to be working it out. Mr. Toeppen and other domain name speculators struck courts as profoundly offensive, so they called them cybersquatters and ruled against them. People who capitalized on famous trademarks to divert consumers to their sites, especially pornographic sites, also lost. Companies that had legitimate claim to their domain names, like Clue Computing, often didn't lose, but they spent millions of dollars in attorneys fees and court costs. The millions-of-dollars thing meant that some trademark owners offered to buy out domain name registrants rather than litigate. It also meant that when a number of different domain name registrants got bigfoot letters from trademark owners' lawyers, they decided to fold.

We had a system in which a trademark owner who wanted a domain name that had been registered by someone else might be able to get it by litigating but might not. For lots of trademark owners, that wasn't good enough. They felt *entitled* to

---

21. Hasbro, Inc. v. Clue Computing, CV 97 10065DPW (D Mass. 9/2/99), URL: http://www.clue.com/legal/hasbro/d2.html.

22. Hasbro, Inc. v. Internet Entertainment Group, 40 U.S.P.Q.2d 1479 (W.D. Wash. 1996).

23. Panavision International v. Toeppen, 141 F.3d 1316 (9th Cir. 1998).

occupy the domain names incorporating their trademarks, and if the system didn't give it to them, they needed to change the system.

Some of them sued *Network Solutions* for trademark infringement and dilution. That didn't work, and it shouldn't. If Dennis Toeppen isn't breaking the law when he registers panavision.com, Network Solutions surely isn't breaking the law when it lets him. Nonetheless, Network Solutions hated being dragged into court, and it lost it. I don't know who represented Network Solutions, but whoever it was must have frightened the company silly, because it set out to try to ensure that nobody could ever sue it for anything ever again. It adopted a new set of rules designed to placate trademark owners. The new rules first required all domain name registrants past and future to indemnify it for anything, and then insisted that if some trademark owner showed up with a certificate of registration complaining about a domain name, it could give the domain name registrant thirty days to prove that it's rights were superior to the trademark owner's, and, if it didn't, Network Solutions would suspend the domain name.

That didn't prevent Network Solutions from being sued; it just meant that domain name registrants had to go to court to stop Network Solutions from inactivating their domains.

. . . .

By now, this little company wasn't so little anymore, and it was pulling in millions and millions of dollars registering all these domain names. If other entities got into the registration business, folks figured, they could both offer a better alternative to NSI and make lots and lots of money doing so. An ad hoc International group of Internet organizations and trademark owners decided to replace the entire edifice with a new one, in which, incidentally, they would take over the registration business themselves, and introduce a bunch of new generic top level domains.

The crux of the proposal, for our purposes, is that it would have given companies who didn't get in in time to get a domain name based on their trademarks a new opportunity. Expanding the number of generic top level domains would give multiple claimants access to domains containing the same alphanumeric strings. Jef Poskanzer could keep acme.com, and Warner Brothers could take acme.biz, while the Acme glass company could have acme.glass and so forth. That proposal made the trademark bar unhappy. They argued that increasing the number of generic top level domains would just multiply the potential for confusion.[33]

As a prediction, that one is flawed. Consumers know that there are lots of different businesses named Acme, and don't expect any given Acme to be the particular Acme they have in mind. If consumers learned that there were lots of acme-based domain names on the web, they wouldn't expect any particular one to belong to

33. *See* International Trademark Association, *INTA Response to the U.S. Government Paper on the Improvement of Technical Management of Internet Names and Addresses* (March 18, 1998), URL: http://www.ntia.doc.gov/ntiahome/domainname/130dftmail/scanned/INTA.htm.

either Poskanzer or Warner Brothers. They wouldn't be confused. Yes, that might prevent Warner Brothers from grabbing a valuable marketing tool, but Warner Brothers doesn't have the acme.com domain as it is, so it isn't any worse off. Increasingly, however, the rhetoric about consumer confusion camouflaged efforts to leverage trademark rights into stronger property interests in the use of desirable alphanumeric strings on the Internet, even in the absence of any plausible likelihood of consumer confusion. In fact, the consumer confusion issues are not hard to solve, but some trademark interests perceived the domain name conundrum as an opportunity to expand their rights beyond the limits imposed by traditional trademark law. That trademark owners should pursue such a course is easy to understand, but there is no policy reason why we should design the architecture of the system to assist them.

The proposal to add new generic top level domains had additional potential advantages only tangentially related to trademark law. Because of successful advertising, a large segment of the public had come to view .com as the only "real" domain. The combined registration activities of businesses trying to do business on the World Wide Web and domain name speculators had led to the registration of essentially every word in a typical English-language dictionary as a second level domain in .com. New entrants into the world of e-commerce were necessarily settling for increasingly unwieldy domain names. The fact that there were few easy-to-remember alphanumeric strings left unregistered served as an entry barrier to new firms seeking to do business on the web, and gave their earlier competitors a marketing advantage that was difficult to overcome. In addition, it inflated the value of the resale market in .com domain names, encouraging the activities of domain name speculators. If the speculators were a significant part of the problem, parsimonious limits on the expansion of domain name space would only make the problem worse.

Most representatives of trademark owners were undoubtedly sincere in their efforts to protect trademarks from infringement and dilution, although their single-minded pursuit of that goal caused them to elevate trademark concerns over all others. (People who own trademarks appear to be doomed to perceive their marks as stronger and more valuable than their customers and competitors do.) Other trademark lobbyists may have gotten greedy, hoping to enshrine in domain name space the trademark rules that they felt should be the rules in meat space, but weren't.

The trademark bar started claiming that the only legitimate domain name use of a word that was also a trademark was a trademark use by the trademark owner, and demanded a system that allowed trademark owners to oust non-trademark owners of domain names incorporating their marks, and that permitted trademark owners to prevent any subsequent registration of any domain name incorporating their marks in any top level domain.

That's in a lot of ways an outrageous demand. This is not a particularly new problem. We have seen it in the United States with 1-800 telephone numbers, which are given out on a first-come first served basis, it's not that hard to solve. Trademark laws give businesses some powerful tools to prevent confusion and dilution, but they don't confer on anyone a right to own the phone number 1-800-trademark or the domain name trademark.com, much less trademark.net, trademark.org, or trademark.uk.

Moreover, a rule that a trademark owner had the right to any and all domain names of the form trademark.domain wouldn't make any sense and would be impossible to administer. For one thing, how are we supposed to pick which trademark owner? Dell Books has been around since 1943. Dell computers has been around since 1988. Both of them own trademark registrations for Dell. Which one is entitled to the domain name "dell.com"? And how do you decide? It gets worse if the dell you choose will presumptively have a claim on dell.org, dell.net, dell.us, dell.uk, dell.biz, and so forth. The BUDWEISER beer mark belongs to Anheuser-Busch in the United States and to the Budvar brewery in the Czech Republic. Anheuser-Busch's Budweiser beer is the more famous; Budvar's Budweiser was first. Only one of them, however, can own the domain name budweiser.com, and that domain will be accessible from computers in the United States, in the Czech Republic, and in any other country connected to the Internet. How should a domain name allocation system choose between them? The Apple Computer Company and Apple Records have shared the APPLE trademark without incident for more than 20 years, selling computers and recorded music, respectively, throughout the world. Only one of them can operate the apple.com domain. The British record company adopted the name first; the California computer company's business, however, is more intimately connected to the Internet. Does one of them have the superior claim, and, if so, which one?

....

Congress enacted the *Anticybersquatting Consumer Protection Act* [in 1999]. The new law establishes a new cause of action for registration, trafficking or use of a domain name confusingly similar to or dilutive of a trademark or personal name. It contains provisions for capturing domain names from registrants who are not subject to a federal court's *in personam* jurisdiction. It allows trademark owners to recover substantial statutory damages as well as an order for the transfer of a domain name when the domain name is registered or used "with a bad faith intent to profit" from its similarity to a trademark.

B. Anticybersquatting Consumer Protection Act

15 U.S.C. § 1125(d)(1) [Lanham Act § 43(d)(1)]

(1)(A) A person shall be liable in a civil action by the owner of a mark, including a personal name which is protected as a mark under this section, if, without regard to the goods or services of the parties, that person—

(i) has a bad faith intent to profit from that mark, including a personal name which is protected as a mark under this section; and

(ii) registers, traffics in, or uses a domain name that—

(I) in the case of a mark that is distinctive at the time of registration of the domain name, is identical or confusingly similar to that mark;

(II) in the case of a famous mark that is famous at the time of registration of the domain name, is identical or confusingly similar to or dilutive of that mark; or

(III) is a trademark, word, or name protected by reason of section 706 of title 18, United States Code, or section 220506 of title 36, United States Code.

(B) (i) In determining whether a person has a bad faith intent described under subparagraph (A), a court may consider factors such as, but not limited to—

(I) the trademark or other intellectual property rights of the person, if any, in the domain name;

(II) the extent to which the domain name consists of the legal name of the person or a name that is otherwise commonly used to identify that person;

(III) the person's prior use, if any, of the domain name in connection with the bona fide offering of any goods or services;

(IV) the person's bona fide noncommercial or fair use of the mark in a site accessible under the domain name;

(V) the person's intent to divert consumers from the mark owner's online location to a site accessible under the domain name that could harm the goodwill represented by the mark, either for commercial gain or with the intent to tarnish or disparage the mark, by creating a likelihood of confusion as to the source, sponsorship, affiliation, or endorsement of the site;

(VI) the person's offer to transfer, sell, or otherwise assign the domain name to the mark owner or any third party for financial gain without having used, or having an intent to use, the domain name in the bona fide offering of any goods or services, or the person's prior conduct indicating a pattern of such conduct;

(VII) the person's provision of material and misleading false contact information when applying for the registration of the domain name, the person's intentional failure to maintain accurate contact information, or the person's prior conduct indicating a pattern of such conduct;

(VIII) the person's registration or acquisition of multiple domain names which the person knows are identical or confusingly similar to marks of others that are distinctive at the time of registration of such domain names, or dilutive of famous marks of others that are famous at the time of registration of such domain names, without regard to the goods or services of the parties; and

(IX) the extent to which the mark incorporated in the person's domain name registration is or is not distinctive and famous within the meaning of subsection (c)(1) of section 43.

(ii) Bad faith intent described under subparagraph (A) shall not be found in any case in which the court determines that the person believed and had reasonable grounds to believe that the use of the domain name was a fair use or otherwise lawful.

(C) In any civil action involving the registration, trafficking, or use of a domain name under this paragraph, a court may order the forfeiture or cancellation of the domain name or the transfer of the domain name to the owner of the mark.

Question

What is a "domain name" under the ACPA? Only the character string immediately preceding the TLD? For example, wordpress.com is the domain name of a blog hosting site. Are the URLs of the hosted blogs also domain names? If a blog's URL includes a third party trademark without authorization, for example, https://ronkramermuscle beach.wordpress.com, is the blogger subject to suit under the ACPA? *See Thermolife Int'l. LLC v. https://ronkramermusclebeach.wordpress.com*, No. 5-15-cv-01616-HRL (N.D. Cal. June 18, 2015), https://scholar.google.com/scholar_case?q=ronkramer musclebeach&hl=en&as_sdt=80000006&case=14508712363050255245.

1. Bad Faith

Fagnelli Plumbing Company v. Gillece Plumbing And Heating, Inc.

98 U.S.P.Q.2d 1997 (W.D. Pa. 2011)

Schwab, United States District Judge:

I. INTRODUCTION

Currently pending before this Court are Cross-Motions for Summary Judgment filed by Plaintiff Fagnelli Plumbing Company, Inc. ("Fagnelli") and Defendants Gillece Plumbing and Heating, Inc., Gillece Services, LP, Thomas Gillece, and Joseph Benz (collectively referred to as "Defendants").... For the reasons which follow, the Court has determined that there are no genuine issues of material fact present, will grant Plaintiff's Motion for Summary Judgment as to Counts I–III, and will deny Defendants' Motion for Summary Judgment for the reasons set forth below.

II. FACTUAL BACKGROUND

... Fagnelli Plumbing and Gillece Plumbing directly compete to provide [plumbing heating and cooling] services to residential and commercial customers in Western Pennsylvania.

Plaintiff has been the registrant of the domain name "www.fagnelliplumbing.com" since 2000. On March 1, 2007, Gillece Plumbing purchased the domain name www.fagnelli.com ("fagnelli.com") from the domain registrar www.GoDaddy.com ("GoDaddy"). [Defendant] registered "fagnelli.com" with GoDaddy the same day. *Id.* Defendants purchased and registered the fagnelli.com domain name without Plaintiff's knowledge, permission, or consent. None of the Defendants were Plaintiff's authorized licensee to register the fagnelli.com domain name.

In March 2010, Lee Oleinick ("Oleinick"), a customer of Plaintiff for approximately ten years, attempted to locate Plaintiff's contact information online. Oleinick entered www.fagnelli.com into the URL bar on his web browser. Olenick was redirected to a website for Gillece Plumbing and Heating, Inc. which advertised its services.

On April 28, 2010, counsel for Plaintiff mailed a letter to Defendants requesting that they cease and desist from having fagnelli.com redirect internet traffic to its website and that Defendants transfer ownership and registration of fagnelli.com to Plaintiff. Redirection of internet traffic from fagnelli.com ceased on May 4, 2010. However, Defendants have not transferred ownership and registration of fagnelli.com to Plaintiff.

Plaintiff commenced the instant suit on May 18, 2010, alleging three causes of action against Defendants. Namely, Plaintiff alleged at Count I, cybersquatting in violation of the Anticybersquatting Consumer Protection Act ("ACPA"), 15 U.S.C. § 1125(d); at Count II, misleading description under Section 43(a)(1)(A) of the Lanham Act, 15 U.S.C. § 1125(a)(1)(A); and common law trademark infringement and unfair competition at Count III. Defendants filed their Answer and Affirmative Defenses on August 18, 2010. On February 1, 2011, both parties moved for summary judgment on all counts....

IV. DISCUSSION

A. COUNT I—CYBERSQUATTING

Plaintiff alleges that Defendant breached 15 U.S.C. § 1125(d), also known as the Anti-Cybersquatting Protection Act.

The Anti-Cybersquatting Protection Act ("ACPA") was intended to prevent "the bad faith, abusive registration and use of the distinctive trademarks of others as Internet domain names, with the intent to profit from the goodwill associated with those trademarks." *Shields v. Zuccarini*, 254 F.3d 476, 481 (3d Cir. 2001). In order to prove a claim under the ACPA, Plaintiff has the burden of establishing that: (1) the name "Fagnelli" is a distinctive mark entitled to protection; (2) Defendant's registration of fagnelli.com is identical or confusingly similar to Plaintiff's mark; and (3) Defendant registered fagnelli.com with the bad faith intent to profit from it. *Shields*, 254 F.3d at 482, *See also* 15 U.S.C. § 1125(d)(1)(A).

1. Fagnelli is a Distinctive Mark Entitled to Protection

The following factors under Section 1125(d)(1)(A)(ii)(I) may be considered in determining whether a mark is distinctive: (A) the degree of inherent or acquired distinctiveness of the mark; (B) the duration and extent of use of the mark in connection with the goods or services with which the mark is used; (C) the duration and extent of advertising and publicity of the mark; (D) the geographical extent of the trading area in which the mark is used; (E) the channels of trade for the goods and services with which the mark is used; (F) the degree of recognition of the mark in the trading areas and channels of trade used by the marks' owner and the person against whom the injunction is sought; and (G) the nature and extent of use of the same or similar mark by third parties. *Shields*, 254 F.3d at 482.

The duration of Plaintiff's business, more than 50 years, suggests the acquired distinctiveness of Plaintiff's name in the services of plumbing, heating, and cooling. It is undisputed that Plaintiff has been incorporated in Pennsylvania since 1974. Since that time, Plaintiff has been solely in the business of providing plumbing, heating, and cooling services to residential and commercial customers in Western Pennsylvania.

As to the duration and extent of advertising and publicity of the "Fagnelli" mark, Plaintiff has submitted evidence that its recent advertising expenditures have been: $40,000 in 2005; $51,000 in 2006, $62,000 in 2007, and $78,000 in 2008. Ernest Fagnelli testified that Fagnelli Plumbing has advertised its plumbing, heating, and cooling services in Western Pennsylvania since 1962 and was advertising on the radio, by direct mailings, and in the yellow pages many years before March 1, 2007. Fagnelli has also been featured on Plaintiff's own internet website, www.fagnelliplumbing.com, which has been registered since 2000, and prominently displays "Fagnelli" and advertises and offers its services to potential customers.

The degree of recognition of Plaintiff's mark also suggests the inherent and acquired distinctiveness of its mark. Plaintiff has submitted affidavits from four long-time customers who stated that "the Fagnelli name has become closely associated with plumbing, heating and cooling services in Allegheny County." The depositions were taken in January 2011 and demonstrate that for some members of the local public, Fagnelli, although a surname, has come to acquire the secondary meaning of a plumbing and heating business, rather than designating the actual people who bear the name. It is consistent with these depositions to conclude that Plaintiff's 5,000 prior customers and other members of the public have come to associate "Fagnelli" with plumbing, heating, and cooling services.

Plaintiff has also submitted an affidavit from Anthony H. Costa, Sr. (Costa) who testified that the "Fagnelli" has come to be closely associated with residential and commercial plumbing, heating and cooling services in Western Pennsylvania. Costa has not been Plaintiff's customer, but has come to associate its name with plumbing services through his work as a plumbing inspector for the Allegheny County Health Department and his position as the Chairman of the Allegheny County Plumbing Advisory Board. Costa also testified that he has seen Plaintiff's advertisements "for many years prior to 2007."

In light of the above, the Court concludes that "Fagnelli" is a distinctive mark entitled to protection.

2. Registration of "Fagnelli.com" is Confusingly Similar to Plaintiff's Mark

Plaintiff has the burden to demonstrate that its "mark and Defendant's domain are so similar in sight, sound or meaning that they could be confused." *Carnivale v. Staub Design, LLC*, 700 F. Supp. 2d 660, at 667 (D. Del. 2010). Plaintiff's burden is not, as Defendant argues, to produce evidence of actual confusion, but rather that there is the potential for confusion. Plaintiff has submitted an affidavit from one of its long-time customers that he was confused when trying to access Plaintiff's contact information online. Indeed, as demonstrated by Olenick's affidavit, "fagnelli.com", registered by Defendant, is similar in sight and meaning, and could be confused by potential customers attempting to access the Plaintiff's official website fagnelliplumbing.com. The likelihood of confusion is increased because potential customers were, at one point, redirected to another plumbing company advertising many of the same services to the same geographic area.

3. Defendant's Bad Faith Intent to Profit

15 U.S.C. § 1125(d)(1)(B)(i) provides a non-exhaustive list of nine factors that the Court may use to determine if Defendant acted with a bad faith intent to profit....

Here, the overwhelming number of the nine facts[sic] cut in Plaintiff's favor. It is undisputed that Defendant have[sic] no trademark or other intellectual property rights in the fagnelli.com domain name and such domain name is not consistent with Defendant's name, nor have Defendant legitimately used the domain name in connection with offering its services (factors I, II, III). Defendant's use of the Fagnelli domain name has not been used in a noncommercial or fair use in a site accessible through fagnelliplumbing.com (Factor IV).

Defendant contends that the Anti-Cybersquatting Consumer Protection Act was designed only to target individuals who register domain names in order to profit by extortion (See Factor VI). However, the Act's legislative history clearly addresses that "cybersquatters often register well-known marks to prey on consumer confusion by misusing the domain name to divert customers from the mark owner's site to the cybersquatter's own site...." S. REP. No. 106-140 (1999). Such a situation exists here, where it is undisputed that, at the very least, Defendant registered a domain name which was a variation of a direct competitor's official website (Factor V).

Although Defendant disputes that it intended to divert consumers from Plaintiff's website to the Gillece website, Defendant admits that it registered close to 100 other domain names containing in whole or in part the names of many other plumbing, heating, cooling, and electrical contractors in Western Pennsylvania. All such registrations were done without the knowledge, permission, or consent of the related business owners. Many such websites advertised and offered Defendants' services. Such registration establishes Defendant's pattern of behavior that may have kept potential customers from accessing the legitimate websites of competing businesses or divert customers to its own website. Such redirection could harm the goodwill represented by Plaintiff's mark and create in customers a likelihood of confusion as to the source, sponsorship, affiliation, or endorsement of the site. Defendant has not offered any evidence that registered the domain names for a bona fide reason other than to limit the parties' direct competition. Furthermore, previously discussed, Defendant incorporated "Fagnelli" into their domain name, which is distinctive in the Western District of Pennsylvania (Factor IX). As such, the undisputed material facts demonstrate Defendant's bad faith intent to profit from Plaintiff's goodwill, either for their own commercial gain or to deprive Plaintiff of potential customers.

Accordingly, because the record establishes that Fagnelli is a distinctive mark entitled to protection, Defendant's registration of fagnelli.com is confusingly similar to Plaintiff's mark, and Defendant's bad faith intent in registering the domain name, Plaintiff's Motion for Summary Judgment will be granted as to Count I.

Sporty's Farm L.L.C. v. Sportsman's Market, Inc., 202 F.3d 489 (2d Cir. 2000). Sportsman's Market, a well-known mail-order company for aviation accessories, adopted the mark SPORTY'S in the 1960s and registered it in 1985. Omega, a mail-order company selling scientific equipment, decided to launch Pilot Depot, which would compete directly with Sportsman's. Omega registered the domain name sportys.com. Omega later established a Christmas tree farm and sales business, named it "Sporty's Farm," and used the sportys.com domain to advertise its Christmas trees. Omega then sued for a declaratory judgment that it could continue to use the sportys.com domain name. Sportsman's counterclaimed for infringement and dilution. After a bench trial, the trial court entered judgment for Omega on the infringement claim and for Sportsman's on the dilution claim, and ordered Omega to surrender the domain name. Both parties appealed. While the appeal was pending, Congress enacted the AntiCybersquatting Consumer Protection Act. The Court of Appeals for the Second Circuit decided to apply the new law to the facts of the case on appeal, without first remanding the case to the district court to consider the applicability of the new law. (This enabled the Second Circuit to issue the very first court ruling interpreting the ACPA.) The court held that the facts found by the district court established that Sportsman's mark was distinctive, and that the sportys.com domain name was confusingly similar to the mark. The Court concluded that Omega had registered the domain name with a bad faith intent to profit. Analyzing the statutory factors, the Court concluded that Omega had no intellectual property rights in "sportys.com" at the time it registered the domain name, nor was "sportys" Omega's legal name. Omega made no use of the domain until after the litigation began. Moreover, Omega did not claim to be making fair or noncommercial use of the mark. All of these factors supported a finding of "bad faith intent to profit." The Court continued:

> The most important grounds for our holding that Sporty's Farm acted with a bad faith intent, however, are the unique circumstances of this case, which do not fit neatly into the specific factors enumerated by Congress but may nevertheless be considered under the statute. We know from the record and from the district court's findings that Omega planned to enter into direct competition with Sportsman's in the pilot and aviation consumer market. As recipients of Sportsman's catalogs, Omega's owners, the Hollanders, were fully aware that *sporty's* was a very strong mark for consumers of those products. It cannot be doubted, as the court found below, that Omega registered sportys.com for the primary purpose of keeping Sportsman's from using that domain name. Several months later, and after this lawsuit was filed, Omega created another company in an unrelated business that received the name Sporty's Farm so that it could (1) use the sportys.com domain name in some commercial fashion, (2) keep the name away from Sportsman's, and (3) protect itself in the event that Sportsman's brought an infringement claim alleging

that a "likelihood of confusion" had been created by Omega's version of cybersquatting. Finally, the explanation given for Sporty's Farm's desire to use the domain name, based on the existence of the dog Spotty, is more amusing than credible. Given these facts and the district court's grant of an equitable injunction under the FTDA, there is ample and overwhelming evidence that, as a matter of law, Sporty's Farm's acted with a "bad faith intent to profit" from the domain name sportys.com as those terms are used in the ACPA.

Questions

1. The ACPA limits liability to those domain name registrants who register, use or traffic in a domain name with "a bad faith intent *to profit.*" 15 U.S.C. § 1125(d)(1)(A). How does that differ from simple "bad faith intent"? In what sense was Omega's activity calculated to yield a "profit"? How does intent to profit differ from commercial use?

2. What would have been a "fair and noncommercial" use by Omega of the Sportys mark?

Southern Company v. Dauben, Inc., 324 Fed. Appx. 309 (5th Cir. 2009). The plaintiff, Southern Company ("Southern"), holds federal and state trademarks for "SOUTHERN COMPANY" and the domain name southerncompany.com. Southern instituted an action against the defendant Dauben Inc. for the domain names sotherncompany.com and southerncopany.com under the ACPA. These domain names were linked to a website that provided pay-per-click advertising for real estate and employment companies in the southern United States. The district court granted the plaintiff's motion for preliminary injunction to prevent Dauben's continued use of the domain names, which Dauben appealed. The Fifth Circuit noted that for a preliminary injunction to be granted, a court must consider a plaintiff's likelihood of success on the merits as well as any irreparable injury the plaintiff could face. The 5th Circuit first addressed Dauben's argument that the ACPA's fair use provision should apply when discussing the likelihood of success on the merits:

> Dauben ... argues that the district court abused its discretion by omitting any consideration of ACPA's fair use provision, which affects the bad faith finding, and we agree. Though ACPA explicitly provides a fair use safe harbor, the district court made no reference to this portion of ACPA in its analysis despite recognizing Dauben's invocations of the defense. ACPA's safe harbor provides a narrow berth for fair use arguments, and, on the merits, Dauben's claims may or may not hold up. *See Virtual Works, Inc.*, 238 F.3d at 270 ("A defendant who acts even partially in bad faith in registering a domain name is not, as a matter of law, entitled to benefit from the Act's safe harbor provision."). Nonetheless, where one is raised, a fair use defense bears on the likelihood of success on the merits. [Citations.] By failing to analyze this segment of the law pertinent to the parties' claims, the district court abused its discretion.

> Southern asserts that Dauben's fair use argument lacks merit because Dauben offered no evidence of "its business or about its intent in registering" the domain names and because Dauben cannot make a fair use of misspelled variations of SOUTHERN COMPANY. As to the former argument, we are unpersuaded because the district court had before it evidence concerning the content of the websites to which Dauben's domain names linked. As to Southern's latter argument, Dauben's using misspelled variations of "southern" and "company" (that is, "sothern" and "copany") certainly may weaken its fair use argument, but that is a question to be considered in the district court's evaluation of the facts and circumstances surrounding the claim—an evaluation that the court below failed to undertake.

Turning to irreparable injury, the 5th Circuit noted that the district court found Dauben's domain names confusingly similar to Southern's mark, and that the ensuing likelihood of consumer confusion as to the sponsorship of the websites linked to by the challenged domain names threatened irreparable injury to Southern. The 5th Circuit disagreed:

> The court's determination is flawed for two reasons. First, the likelihood of confusion test in trademark infringement law is different, and more comprehensive, than the test for "confusingly similar" under ACPA. *See N. Light Tech., Inc. v. N. Lights Club*, 236 F.3d 57, 66 n.14 (1st Cir. 2001) ("[T]he likelihood of confusion test of trademark infringement is more comprehensive than the identical or confusingly similar requirement of ACPA, as it requires considering factors beyond the facial similarity of the two marks." (internal quotation marks omitted)); *see also Coca-Cola Co.*,382 F.3d at 783 ("The inquiry under the ACPA is thus narrower than the traditional multifactor likelihood of confusion test for trademark infringement."); *Sporty's Farm*, 202 F.3d at 498 n.11 ("We note that 'confusingly similar' is a different standard from the 'likelihood of confusion' standard for trademark infringement....").
>
> Second, the court failed to describe how Dauben's confusingly similar domain names would injure Southern, let alone do so irreparably. Courts making this finding often describe how the content of a defendant's website threatens injury to the plaintiff.... Here, however, the district court pointed only to the likelihood that a consumer might accidentally come across Dauben's websites when seeking Southern's website, but it made no finding bearing on *how* this navigational miscue might injure Southern. Southern contends that the court properly determined that "[p]laintiff's evidence establishes ... a significant risk of irreparable injury." However, the court made clear that the only evidence it considered was Dauben's domain names and their similarity to Southern's mark. The court made no finding beyond the text of the domain names—such as the content of Dauben's websites—that suggests Southern may be irreparably harmed. For these two reasons, the district court abused its discretion in its analysis of whether there exists a threat of irreparable injury to Southern.

Accordingly, the 5th Circuit vacated the district court's order granting the preliminary injunction.

Question

On remand, Dauben will have the opportunity to persuade the trial court that its registration and use of the domain names "sotherncompany.com" and "southerncopany.com" is a fair use under section 33(b)(4) because it used the misspelled "sothern" and "copany" to represent the words "southern" and "company" in their descriptive sense. Flesh out that argument for Dauben. What's the most persuasive case it can make that it believed and had reasonable grounds to believe that its use was fair under the statute?

Lands' End, Inc. v. Remy, 447 F. Supp. 2d 941 (W.D. Wis. 2006). Plaintiff operates an online business selling clothing and accessories under the URL www.landsend.com.

> B. *Lands' End Affiliate Program*
>
> To increase the number of internet users who visit its website, plaintiff operates an affiliate program that allows owners of approved websites to link to plaintiff's website. When an internet user clicks on a link on an affiliate's website, connects to www.landsend.com and makes a purchase from plaintiff, the affiliate earns a 5% commission on the purchase. The Lands' End affiliate program is operated and administered by the LinkShare Affiliate Network, which provides tracking technology and administers the payment of referral fees from plaintiff to its affiliates.
>
> Defendants were Lands' End affiliates.
>
> ....
>
> C. *Defendants' Alleged Typosquatting Scheme*
>
> At all times relevant to this lawsuit, defendant Thinkspin owned the domain names www.lnadsend.com, www.klandsend.com, www.landsende.com, www.landdend.com, www.landswnd.com, www.landrnd.com, www.landsene.com, www.landsenc.com, www. landsennd.com, www.landse.com and www.landind.com. At all times relevant to this lawsuit, defendant Braderax owned the domain name www.landswend.com. At all times relevant to this lawsuit, defendant Seale owned the domain name www.landwend.com. Defendants no longer own or operate these websites.
>
> ... [I]f a user accidentally typed www.landenc.com into a web browser, the browser would appear to take the user immediately to the Lands' End website. In fact, however, the web browser would link the user "invisibly" to a URL associated with defendant Thinkspin's authorized affiliate website, www.savingsfinder.com. Although it would appear to the user as though he had accessed the Lands' End website directly, it would appear to Lands' End and LinkShare as though the user had accessed the website indirectly through

a link on savingsfinder.com. Consequently, defendant Thinkspin would receive a 5% commission on any Lands' End purchases made by the user.

A. *Anticybersquatting Consumer Protection Act*

Defendants contend that they did not act with bad faith because their typosquatting scheme directed traffic *to* plaintiff's website, rather than away from it. Plaintiff sees the matter differently and argues that defendants "hijacked Lands' End's own customers, sold them back to Lands' End, and collected a ransom for doing so." Dkt. # 83, at 19. Although "this is not the typical cybersquatting situation where a person registers a famous mark or name and then attempts to extort profits from the owner of the mark by selling the domain name," *Virtual Works, Inc., v. Volkswagen of America, Inc.*, 238 F.3d 264 (4th Cir. 2001), it is nevertheless a case in which defendants profited from their ownership of a domain name based on plaintiff's famous mark. The fact that defendants' conduct was not cybersquatting in its most "classic" form does not mean that it was not prohibited by the Anticybersquatting Consumer Protection Act.

"The key to a cybersquatting claim ... is bad faith intent to profit." *Bosley Medical Institute, Inc. v. Kremer*, 403 F.3d 672, 680–681 (9th Cir. 2005). How that profit is acquired matters less than the underlying bad faith. Although defendants contend that they provided a service to plaintiff, it is noteworthy that they took active steps to conceal their typosquatting scheme from plaintiff, and failed to disclose their "look alike" domain names to plaintiff when applying to become affiliates.

....

Defendants' conduct satisfies a number of these [bad faith] factors. Defendants have never used their infringing domain names as trademarks or service marks; thus, they had no intellectual property rights in them. The domain names did not contain any variation of defendants' names or of any name closely related to the defendants. Defendants have never used the infringing domain names in connection with the *bona fide* offering of goods or services; they have used them only to obtain commissions from the sale of plaintiff's products by surreptitiously redirecting users to plaintiff's website. Defendants did not use the domain names for a non-commercial or "fair use" purpose.

If defendants are to prevail on their motion for summary judgment, it must be clear from the undisputed facts that they acted in good faith. Plaintiff has adduced substantial evidence from which it might be inferred that defendants exploited plaintiff's mark for their own commercial gain by using the typosquatting domain names to obtain 5% commissions on sales for which plaintiff would otherwise have received 100% profit. Because a factfinder could reasonably infer that defendants acted in bad faith, defendants' motion will be denied with respect to plaintiff's claim under the Anticybersquatting Consumer Protection Act.

Questions

1. How was Lands' End harmed by the alleged typosquatting? Is harm an element of an ACPA claim?

2. Can you think of a legitimate interest for selecting a domain name that incorporates a typographical error?

3. Before mistyped URLs there were mistyped vanity phone numbers. In *Holiday Inns v. 800 Reservations, Inc.*, 86 F.3d 619 (6th Cir. 1996), Holiday Inn, which had the vanity telephone number 1-800-HOLIDAY [465–4329], was unsuccessful in its suit against a competitor that had acquired the telephone number 1-800-405-4329. Holiday Inns argued that because consumers frequently misdial zero instead of the letter "o", defendant's phone number would cause confusion in violation of section 43(a). The Sixth Circuit disagreed. 800 Reservations, it held, "did not create the consumers' confusion, but … merely took advantage of confusion already in existence." Moreover, since 800 Reservations didn't publicize the number, it did not use it in commerce. Similarly, in *DaimlerChrysler AG v. Bloom*, 315 F.3d 932 (8th Cir. 2003), defendant obtained the telephone number 1-800-637-2333 (1-800-MERCEDE) and used it to launch a commercial service for the benefit of Mercedes dealerships, but did not advertise the number to consumers. The court concluded that defendant had not used the Mercedes mark in commerce. Are the "typosquatting" cases consistent with this approach to likelihood of confusion? Are the typosquating cases likely to influence courts' assessments of likelihood of confusion in Lanham Act section 43(a) claims? See *Diller v. Barry Driller, Inc.*, 104 U.S.P.Q.2d 1676 (C.D. Cal. 2012) (awarding entertainer Barry Diller preliminary injunction on grounds of likelihood of confusion and false endorsement against registrant of <barrydriller.com> for site parodying Diller).

Gopets Ltd. v. Hise

657 F.3d 1024 (9th Cir. 2011)

W. Fletcher, Circuit Judge:

The Anticybersquatting Consumer Protection Act ("ACPA") prohibits "cybersquatters" from registering internet domain names that are identical or confusingly similar to registered service marks and trademarks. *See* 15 U.S.C. § 1125(d)(1). The prohibition contained in § 1125(d)(1) applies when a domain name is identical or confusingly similar to a mark that is distinctive "at the time of registration of the domain name." *Id.* The primary question before us is whether the term "registration" applies only to the initial registration of the domain name, or whether it also applies to a re-registration of a currently registered domain name by a new registrant. We hold that such re-registration is not a "registration" within the meaning of § 1125(d)(1).

I. Background

Defendant Edward Hise registered the domain name gopets.com in his own name in March 1999. He developed a business plan for gopets.com as part of a marketing class in which he was then enrolled. According to the business plan, Hise and a cousin who was a veterinarian would develop the site into "a pet owner resource covering health, safety, nutrition, animal behavior, training, competition, abuse, pets and children, free advice from veterinarians, and the pet industry."

Edward and his brother Joseph Hise own the corporation Digital Overture. Among other things, the Hises perform internet-related services for clients, including registering and maintaining domain names. The Hises and Digital Overture (collectively, "the Hises") have registered more than 1300 domain names in the last decade. Most appear to be plausible names for future internet sites rather than names of existing businesses. They frequently register similar domain names at the same time. For instance, they registered ehinges.com, ebenches.com, erivets.com, and esconces.com on the same day.

In 2004, Erik Bethke founded the company GoPets Ltd. in Korea. GoPets Ltd. created a game called GoPets featuring virtual pets that move between the computers of registered users. GoPets Ltd. filed an application to register the service mark "GoPets" in the United States on September 30, 2004. The mark was duly registered in November 2006. The registration shows that the first use of the term in commerce occurred on August 20, 2004.

Beginning in 2004, Bethke made several unsuccessful attempts to purchase the gopets.com domain name from the Hises. In response to Bethke's initial email inquiry about the domain name, Edward Hise wrote on September 1, 2004, that he had initially been "dedicated to building a business" at gopets.com, but because his other web businesses were thriving, he was open to selling the domain name to a "serious buyer []." He said he was holding an auction for the domain name and invited Bethke to submit a bid by September 15.

Bethke did not respond immediately. On October 11, he wrote to Edward Hise again, noting that Hise still owned the domain name—"so presumably you did not have any other serious offers." Bethke offered to pay $750 for the domain name. The Hises did not respond. In January 2005, Bethke again inquired about the domain name, this time through a friend. Edward Hise wrote back several months later, stating that he would not sell the domain name "for little or nothing" and that another group had offered to develop the site and share the profits. On May 16, 2005, Bethke wrote to Joseph Hise:

> Last year in October I offered you $750 for the domain after declining to participate in your blind bidding system.
>
> You also failed to answer our communications both in email as well as postal mail.
>
> We are proceeding with the ICA[N]N domain dispute claim....
>
> ....
>
> My very last offer is $100—the exact same cost as going through ICA[N]N, and frankly that is generous for I would far rather donate our money to ICA[N]N.

ICANN, the Internet Corporation for Assigned Names and Numbers, is an international group that offers non-binding arbitration for adjudicating disputes over domain names. A year later, on May 23, 2006, GoPets Ltd. filed a complaint against Edward Hise with the World Intellectual Property Organization ("WIPO"), which administers ICANN's Uniform Dispute Resolution Policy.

On July 26, 2006, a WIPO arbitrator decided in favor of Edward Hise. The arbitrator found that the gopets.com domain name was confusingly similar to GoPets Ltd.'s service mark, and he "wishe[d] ... to make it clear that [he was] unconvinced" that the Hises ever had serious plans to develop a website at gopets.com. Nevertheless, the arbitrator held that WIPO rules only compel the transfer of a disputed domain name if the name was initially registered in bad faith. Since Edward Hise had registered gopets.com five years before GoPets Ltd. was founded, gopets.com was not registered in bad faith.

On October 30, 2006, after the WIPO decision, Bethke offered to purchase gopets.com from the Hises for $5,000. After a telephone conversation, Bethke increased his offer to $40,000 on November 15. On November 20, Bethke emailed again, stating that his company owned the domain name gopetslive.com, and that they were about to begin a marketing campaign. They preferred to use gopets.com in the campaign and were still willing to pay $40,000 for it, but they needed to commit to a particular domain name by December 11. After December 11, "we would still be interested in gopets.com, but it loses all real urgency."

On December 12, Edward Hise sent Bethke an email, attaching a four-page letter. The email requested that Bethke forward the letter to GoPets Ltd.'s investors. The email stated that within forty-eight hours Hise would send the letter directly to the investors. The letter, signed by both Edward and Joseph Hise, presented what they called "Acquisition Considerations." It warned the investors that if GoPets Ltd. used the gopetslive.com domain name instead of gopets.com, the result would be to "continue to confuse newly adopted gopetslive.com" users. The letter noted that Bethke had said that some users were already confused. The letter stated, further, that if GoPets Ltd. bought gopets.com, "search engine results would be dramatically improved." ... The Hises ended the letter by offering to sell gopets.com to GoPets Ltd. for $5 million.

Two days after sending the email and letter, Edward Hise transferred the registration of gopets.com from himself to the brothers' corporation, Digital Overture.

While these exchanges between the Hises and GoPets Ltd. were taking place, the Hises added content to gopets.com. According to records from the Internet Archive, a non-profit organization that archives websites, content first appeared on gopets.com on September 26, 2004, approximately a month after Bethke's first inquiry about the site. Initially, the content consisted solely of a picture and description of a lost dog. The record does not reflect whether the website was updated at all during the next two years. By November 24, 2006, the site was updated with information about guide dogs. On January 6, 2007, the site contained a link to the GoPets.com WIPO arbitration decision. On March 16, 2007, the site contained a "GoPets.com" logo and text saying "Welcome to goPets.com the official online website. goAhead [sic] pet lovers tell your friends that GoPets.com will be arriving soon!"

Soon after the WIPO decision in their favor, the Hises began registering domain names ("Additional Domains") similar to gopets.com. On November 12, 2006, Edward Hise registered gopet.mobi, gopets.mobi, and gopets.name. On November 15, he registered gopetssite.com and goingpets.com. Between November 20 and the end of December, he registered gopet.biz, gopet.org, egopets.com, gopets.bz, gopets.ws, gopet.tv, gopet.ws, gopet.bz, gopet.de, gopet.eu, and gopet.name. He registered two additional domain names—mygopets.com and igopets.com—several months later.

In March 2007, a few months after the Hises offered to sell gopets.com for $5 million, GoPets Ltd. filed a complaint against the Hises in federal district court for the Central District of California. The complaint alleged cybersquatting under ACPA, service mark infringement and unfair competition under the Lanham Act and California law, service mark dilution under the Lanham Act and California law, and false advertising under California law. The complaint was amended to add similar claims with respect to the Additional Domains after GoPets Ltd. learned of their existence during discovery. GoPets Ltd. sought injunctive relief, transfer of all the domain names, statutory damages, accounting for wrongful profits, actual damages, and attorney's fees.

....

III. Discussion

....

B. ACPA Claims

1. The Text

... ACPA applies to all domain names, whether registered before or after the enactment of the statute. *See Sporty's Farm L.L.C. v. Sportsman's Market, Inc.*, 202 F.3d 489, 496–97 (2d Cir. 2000) (citing Pub. L. No. 106-113, § 3010, 113 Stat. 1536). To prevail on its ACPA claim, GoPets Ltd. must show (1) registration of a domain name, (2) that was "identical or confusingly similar to" a mark that was distinctive *at the time of registration*, and (3) "bad faith intent" at the time of registration. *See* 15 U.S.C. § 1125(d)(1). At issue in this case is what counts as "registration."

We first discuss the registration and re-registration of gopets.com. We then discuss the registration of the Additional Domains.

2. Gopets.com

GoPets Ltd. concedes that the gopets.com domain name was not "identical or confusingly similar to" a protected mark when Edward Hise registered it in 1999. GoPets Ltd. contends, however, that the term "registration" in ACPA includes re-registrations as well as initial registrations. It contends that the re-registration of the domain name by Digital Overture in December 2006, after Edward Hise transferred it, was a "registration" within the meaning of § 1125(d)(1). Since the service mark GoPets was distinctive in 2006, GoPets Ltd. argues that the 2006 re-registration violated ACPA....

The words "registration" and "register" are not defined in ACPA. It is obvious that, under any reasonable definition, the initial contract with the registrar constitutes a "registration" under ACPA. It is less obvious which later actions, if any, are also "registrations." After registering, a registrant can take a variety of actions that modify the registration. For instance, the registrant can update the registration if her contact or billing information changes. She can switch to "private" registration, where a third party's name is substituted for hers in the public databases of domain registrants. She can switch between registrars, but leave her contact and billing information unchanged. A registrant can change the name of the registrant without changing who pays for the domain, or a registrant can transfer both the domain and payment responsibilities to someone else. Even if the registrant does none of these things, she must still renew the registration periodically. All of these actions could conceivably be described as "registrations" within the meaning of § 1125(d)(1).

....

[T]he text of § 1125(d)(1) considered in isolation does not answer the question whether "registration" includes re-registration. Looking at ACPA in light of traditional property law, however, we conclude that Congress meant "registration" to refer only to the initial registration. It is undisputed that Edward Hise could have retained all of his rights to gopets.com indefinitely if he had maintained the registration of the domain name in his own name. We see no basis in ACPA to conclude that a right that belongs to an initial registrant of a currently registered domain name is lost when that name is transferred to another owner. The general rule is that a property owner may sell all of the rights he holds in property. GoPets Ltd.'s proposed rule would make rights to many domain names effectively inalienable, whether the alienation is by gift, inheritance, sale, or other form of transfer. Nothing in the text or structure of the statute indicates that Congress intended that rights in domain names should be inalienable.

We therefore hold that Digital Overture's re-registration of gopets.com was not a registration within the meaning of § 1125(d)(1). Because Edward Hise registered gopets.com in 1999, long before GoPets Ltd. registered its service mark, Digital Overture's re-registration and continued ownership of gopets.com does not violate § 1125(d)(1).

3. Additional Domains

We turn now to the Additional Domains. Unlike gopets.com, these domain names were registered at a time when the GoPets mark was distinctive. The question is whether they were registered in bad faith under § 1125(d)(1).

The district court found that the Hises' registration of the Additional Domains was in bad faith. The district court based its finding in part on the fact that the Hises had used the Additional Domains as leverage to increase the price they could obtain for gopets.com, a domain name whose re-registration, in the view of the district court, violated ACPA. As just discussed, the re-registration of gopets.com did not violate ACPA. However, we can affirm the district court on any ground supported by the record.... There is ample evidence in the record on which to base a finding of bad faith, even though the re-registration of gopets.com did not violate ACPA.

In determining whether a defendant has acted in bad faith within the meaning of § 1125(d)(1)(A), a court may consider, but is not limited to, nine factors. The two relevant factors here are:

> (V) the person's intent to divert consumers from the mark owner's online location to a site accessible under the domain name that could harm the goodwill represented by the mark ... for commercial gain ... by creating a likelihood of confusion as to the source, sponsorship, affiliation, or endorsement of the site; ...
>
> (VIII) the person's registration ... of multiple domain names which the person knows are identical or confusingly similar to marks of others that are distinctive at the time of registration of such domain names[.]

15 U.S.C. § 1125(d)(1)(B)(i). We take these two factors in reverse order.

First, it is undisputed that the service mark "GoPets" was "distinctive at the time of registration of [the additional] domain names." The Additional Domains are gopet.mobi, gopets.mobi, gopets.name, gopetssite.com, goingpets.com, gopet.biz, gopet.org, egopets.com, gopetz.bz, gopets.ws, gopet.tv, gopet.ws, gopet.bz, gopet.de, gopet.eu, gopet.name, mygopets.com and igopets.com. The Hises argue that these "multiple domain names" are not "confusingly similar" to "GoPets." The Hises' argument is implausible on its face....

Second, it is clear that the Hises intended the Additional Domains "to divert consumers from the mark owner's online location to a site accessible under [these] domain name[s] ... by creating a likelihood of confusion.".... The question is whether the registration of the Additional Domains was intended to achieve "commercial gain" by confusing consumers and diverting them from the website they intended to access. It clearly was so intended.

ACPA contains a safe harbor defense for registrants who "believed and had reasonable grounds to believe that the use of the domain name was a fair use or otherwise lawful." 15 U.S.C. § 1125(d)(1)(B)(ii). We have cautioned that the safe harbor defense should be invoked "very sparingly and only in the most unusual cases." *Lahoti v. VeriCheck, Inc.*, 586 F.3d 1190, 1203 (9th Cir. 2009) (internal quotation marks omitted). A defendant "who acts even partially in bad faith" cannot successfully assert a safe harbor defense. *Id.* (internal quotation marks omitted).

The Hises do not qualify for the safe harbor in their registration of the Additional Domains. The Hises argue that their victory in the WIPO arbitration led them to believe that their registration of the domain name gopets.com was proper. But the WIPO decision gave the Hises no reason to believe they had the right to register *additional* domain names that were identical or confusingly similar to GoPets. The WIPO arbitrator made clear that the Hises prevailed only because the service mark

GoPets had not been registered when Edward Hise registered the domain name gopets.com. The Additional Domains were registered well after GoPets was registered as a service mark.

....

We therefore affirm the district court's holding that the Hises violated ACPA in registering the Additional Domains.

....

C. Lanham Act

The district court granted summary judgment to GoPets Ltd. on its claim that the Hises and Digital Overture infringed on its service mark in violation of the Lanham Act.

Registration of a domain name without more does not constitute service mark or trademark infringement. *See Brookfield Commc'ns, Inc. v. W. Coast Entm't Corp.*, 174 F.3d 1036, 1052 (9th Cir. 1999). With respect to the Additional Domains, there is no evidence that the Hises did anything more than register them. Doing so did not violate the Lanham Act.

The same is not true with respect to gopets.com. The Hises did more than merely register the domain name; they also put text on the gopets.com website indicating that it was "GoPets.com the official online website." The district court properly held that in so doing the Hises violated the Lanham Act. *See Lockheed Martin Corp. v. Network Solutions, Inc.*, 985 F. Supp. 949, 957–58 (C.D. Cal. 1997).

Jysk Bed'N Linen v. Dutta-Roy, 810 F.3d 767 (11th Cir. 2015). The Eleventh Circuit declined to adopt the Ninth Circuit's ruling that the ACPA did not cover domain name re-registrations:

> Two of our sister circuits have provided divergent answers to this question. The Third Circuit, in *Schmidheiny v. Weber*, 319 F.3d 581 (3d Cir. 2003), found that a re-registration falls within the registration hook of the ACPA. [Citation.] It explained that "the language of the statute does not limit the word 'registration' to the narrow concept of 'creation registration'" and that "[t]he words 'initial' and 'creation' appear nowhere in [the statute]." [Citation.] The Third Circuit likened the registration of the domain name to a contract between the registrar and the registrant, and specifically held "that the word 'registration' includes a new contract at a different registrar and to a different registrant." [Citation.]
>
> The Ninth Circuit came to the opposite conclusion in *GoPets Ltd.v. Hise*, 657 F.3d 1024 (9th Cir. 2011), holding that a re-registration is not a registration for purposes of the ACPA. [Citation.] The Ninth Circuit viewed the domain-name registration through the lens of property law, rather than through the Third Circuit's analogy to contract law. [Citation.] It reasoned that a registrant owns a property right in the domain name when he registers

it, and therefore he is entitled to transfer that property to another owner. [Citation.] "The general rule is that a property owner may sell all of the rights he holds in property." [Citation.] The Ninth Circuit worried that if it were to hold that a re-registration fell within the purview of the Act, it "would make rights to many domain names effectively inalienable, whether the alienation is by gift, inheritance, sale or other form of transfer." [Citation.]

We agree with the Third Circuit. The Act does not define the term register. The Act nowhere contains the qualifications of initial or creation when it refers to the act of registering. It refers simply to a registration, and a re-registration is, by definition, a registration. To "re-register" is "[t]o register again." Re-register, v., Oxford English Dictionary (2015)....

Including re-registrations under the registration hook comports with the purpose of Congress in enacting the ACPA—to prevent cybersquatting. See *Southern Grouts & Mortars, Inc.*, 575 F.3d at 1246–47 ("Registering a famous trademark as a domain name and then offering it for sale to the trademark owner is exactly the wrong Congress intended to remedy when it passed the ACPA."). [Citation.] It would be nonsensical to exempt the bad-faith re-registration of a domain name simply because the bad-faith behavior occurred during a noninitial registration, thereby allowing the exact behavior that Congress sought to prevent.

We accordingly will not read additional words into the statute such as initial or creation. The plain meaning of register includes a re-registration. The District Court correctly held that a re-registration falls within the purview of the ACPA.

Questions

1. Newport News operates a chain of women's clothing stores under the NEWPORT NEWS mark. VCV owns more than 30 domain names incorporating the name of geographic locations. VCV originally populated those sites with information and links likely to be of interest to residents and visitors to those locations. VCV registered the domain name newportnews.com and put up a site with material relevant to the city of Newport News, Virginia. Newport News tried to buy the domain name, but VCV refused to sell it for a price Newport News was willing to pay. In 2007, VCV redesigned the site at newportnews.com to replace the city-specific focus with paid advertisements for women's fashions. The new site proved much more lucrative. Newport News claims that even if VCV initially registered the domain name in good faith, the recent website redesign should lead to liability under the ACPA. Does the *GoPets* decision support or undermine Newport's claim? *See Newport News Holdings Corp. v. Virtual City Vision*, 650 F.3d 423 (4th Cir. 2011). What would be the outcome under *Jysk Bed'N Linen*?

2. Southern Grouts & Mortars Company and the 3M Company compete in the swimming pool finishes market. Southern markets its quartz finish under the registered trademark DIAMOND BRITE; 3M sells its competing ceramic finish under the registered trademark COLORQUARTZ. In 2000, 3M purchased the American Electronic Sign Company. The company's assets included trademark registrations for DIAMOND BRITE in connection with the sale of electronic signs, and the domain name diamondbrite.com. 3M discontinued use of the DIAMONBRITE mark and retired the diamondbrite.com website. It has, however, continued to renew the domain name registration, although it has posted no content there. Southern sought to persuade 3M to transfer the domain name by polite request, by threat, and by offering money, but 3M steadfastly refused. Southern filed an ACPA suit, claiming that 3M's repeated renewal of the diamondbrite.com domain name reflected a bad faith intent to profit by preventing its competitor from using the domain name. Assume that Southern can prove that 3M's motive for renewing diamondbrite.com is to block Southern from using its domain name for its competing swimming pool finish. Is it entitled to relief under the ACPA? *See Southern Grouts & Mortars v. 3M Company*, 575 F.3d 1235 (11th Cir. 2009).

3. Paolo Dorigo designs, manufactures, and imports men's clothing under the EQ brand. In 1999, Paolo hired his friend Lucky to create a website for the business. Lucky and his brother designed the website in consultation with Paolo, and Lucky registered the domain name eq-italy.com in his own name and used it for the EQ site. Six years later, the website had become crucial to Paolo's business, and his friendship with Lucky had deteriorated. Lucky claimed that Paolo had failed to pay him commissions he had earned; Paolo disagreed. Ultimately, Lucky quit his job and went to work for a different business. He removed the EQ site from the Internet, and replaced it with a brief instruction to email Lucky for the answers to any fashion questions. Without the EQ website, Paolo's business lost thousands of dollars in the next several months. Paolo sued Lucky under the ACPA. Lucky argues that the evidence shows only that he used the domain name to gain leverage over Paolo's company in order to collect the unpaid commissions, and that that doesn't amount to "bad faith intent to profit" from Paolo's mark. Paolo insists that the statute says "registers, traffics in, or uses," with "or" between the terms, so use alone is enough to support a verdict, even in the absence of bad faith registration or trafficking, and that holding a domain name for ransom is evidence of bad faith under § 43(d)(1)(B)(VI). How should the court rule? *See DSPT International v. Naum*, 624 F.3d 1213 (9th Cir. 2010).

2. Gripe Sites

Lucas Nursery And Landscaping, Inc. v. Grosse

359 F.3d 806 (6th Cir. 2004)

R. Guy Cole, Jr., Circuit Judge:

. . . .

I. BACKGROUND

This case arises from a dispute related to landscaping work that was performed by Lucas Nursery at the residence of Michelle Grosse. In March 2000, Grosse hired

Lucas Nursery to correct a dip in the soil (known as a swale) that ran horizontally through the center of her front yard. Lucas Nursery's representative, Bob Lucas, Jr., stated that the swale could be corrected by using five large loads of topsoil. Lucas Nursery performed the work on May 16, 2000.

Grosse contends that the work was performed inadequately. After allegedly contacting Lucas Nursery on numerous occasions to express her displeasure with the work and to seek some repair, Grosse filed a complaint with the Better Business Bureau ("the BBB"). After the BBB ended its investigation without making a recommendation, Grosse remained dissatisfied by what she felt had been poor service by Lucas Nursery, and decided to inform others about her experience with the company.

On August 12, 2000, Grosse registered the domain name "lucasnursery.com." She then posted a web page for the sole purpose of relaying her story to the public. The web page was titled, "My Lucas Landscaping Experience." The web page included complaints regarding the poor preparation of the soil prior to Lucas Nursery's laying of the sod, the hasty nature of Lucas Nursery's work, the ineffectiveness of the BBB in addressing her complaint, and the fact that she had to pay an additional $5,400 to a second contractor to repair the work originally performed by Lucas Nursery.

On September 27, 2000, Grosse received a letter from Lucas Nursery's attorney demanding that she cease operating the web site. On October 2, 2000, Grosse removed the web site's content. However, after removing the web site's content, Grosse contacted the Michigan Bureau of Commercial Services Licensing Division and the U.S. Patent & Trademark Office to determine whether there was a registered trademark for Lucas Nursery. After learning that no trademark registration existed, Grosse concluded that Lucas Nursery could not prevent her from retaining the web site. On April 13, 2001, Grosse posted a new narrative on the web site, again describing her experience with Lucas Nursery.

Lucas Nursery filed suit against Grosse on August 17, 2001. Thereafter, each party moved for summary judgment. On April 23, 2002, the district court denied Lucas Nursery's motion for summary judgment and granted Grosse's motion for summary judgment.

II. ANALYSIS

....

In order for liability to attach under the ACPA a court must conclude that the defendant's actions constitute "bad faith." ACPA § 3002 (codified at 15 U.S.C. § 1125(d)(1)(A)–(B)). An analysis of whether a defendant's actions constitute bad faith within the meaning of the ACPA usually begins with consideration of several factors, nine of which are listed in the ACPA. *See Sporty's Farm v. Sportsman's Market, Inc.*, 202 F.3d 489, 498 (2d Cir. 2000). The first four factors are those that militate against a finding of bad faith by providing some reasonable basis for why a defendant might have registered the domain name of another mark holder. These factors focus on: whether the defendant has trademark or other rights in the domain name; the extent to which the domain name consists of the defendant's legal name or other common name; any prior use of the domain name for the offering of goods and services; and the bona fide noncommercial use of the site.

Each of the first three factors cuts against Grosse. She does not hold a trademark or other intellectual property rights to the domain name or names included in the registered domain name. The domain name neither consists of her legal name or any name used to refer to her. Grosse has also not used the domain name in connection with any offering of goods or services. The fourth factor cuts in Grosse's favor because the site was used for noncommercial purposes.

Factors five through eight are indicative of the presence of bad faith on the part of the defendant. These factors focus on: whether the defendant seeks to divert consumers from the mark holder's online location either in a way that could harm good will or tarnish or disparage the mark by creating a confusion regarding the sponsorship of the site; whether there has been an offer to transfer or sell the site for financial gain; whether the defendant provided misleading contact information when registering the domain name; and whether the defendant has acquired multiple domain names which may be duplicative of the marks of others.

....

None of these factors militates against Grosse. There is no dispute that Lucas Nursery did not have an online location, and hence Grosse's creation of a web site to complain about Lucas Nursery's services could not have been intended "to divert consumers from the mark owner's online location." Nor is there any evidence that Grosse ever sought to mislead consumers with regard to the site's sponsorship. The web site explicitly stated that the site was established by Grosse for the purposes of relaying her experience with Lucas Nursery. Moreover, Grosse never offered to sell the site to Lucas Nursery. She also did not provide misleading contact information when she registered the domain name. Finally, she has not acquired any additional domain names, which would be indicative of either an intent to sell such names to those entities whose trademarks were identical or similar, or exploit them for other uses.

....

Lucas Nursery seeks to buttress its argument with *Toronto-Dominion Bank v. Karpachev*, 188 F. Supp. 2d 110 (D. Mass. 2002). There, the district court granted Toronto-Dominion's motion for summary judgment against the defendant, concluding that there was sufficient evidence to show that the defendant had acted in bad faith under the ACPA. The defendant, a disgruntled customer, registered sixteen domain names composed of various misspellings of the name tdwaterhouse.com. *Id.* at 111. On the web sites associated with these names, the defendant attacked Toronto-Dominion for "webfacism" and involvement with white collar crime, among other things. *Id.* at 112. The court concluded that the defendant had acted in bad faith, citing four factors: (1) his intention to divert customers from the "tdwaterhouse" web site by creating confusion as to its source or sponsorship; (2) the fact that he had registered sixteen domain names; (3) the fact that he offered no goods or services on the site; and (4) the fact that he had no intellectual property rights in the site. *See id.* at 114.

Although Grosse's actions would arguably satisfy three of the four aforementioned factors, she does not fall within the factor that we consider central to a finding of bad faith. She did not register multiple web sites; she only registered one. Further, it is not clear to this Court that the presence of simply one factor that indicates a bad faith intent to profit, without more, can satisfy an imposition of liability within the meaning of the ACPA. The role of the reviewing court is not simply to add factors and place them in particular categories, without making some sense of what motivates the conduct at issue. The factors are given to courts as a guide, not as a substitute for careful thinking about whether the conduct at issue is motivated by a bad faith intent to profit. Perhaps most important to our conclusion are, Grosse's actions, which seem to have been undertaken in the spirit of informing fellow consumers about the practices of a landscaping company that she believed had performed inferior work on her yard. One of the ACPA's main objectives is the protection of consumers from slick internet peddlers who trade on the names and reputations of established brands. The practice of informing fellow consumers of one's experience with a particular service provider is surely not inconsistent with this ideal.

Conclusion

For the foregoing reasons, we AFFIRM the district court's grant of summary judgment in favor of Grosse.

Utah Lighthouse Ministry v. Foundation for Apologetic Information and Research, 527 F.3d 1045 (10th Cir. 2008). The Foundation of Apologetic Information and Research (FAIR), a volunteer organization responding to criticisms of the Church of Jesus Christ of Latter-day Saints (LDS) church, created a parody of a website run by the Utah Lighthouse Ministry (UTLM) that critiqued the LDS Church. In order to prevail on the cybersquatting claim, UTLM had to show that (1) that its trademark, UTAH LIGHTHOUSE, was distinctive at the time of registration of the domain name, (2) that the domain names registered by Wyatt (vice president of FAIR), including utahlighthouse.com and utahlighthouse.org, are identical or confusingly similar to the trademark, and (3) that Wyatt used or registered the domain names with a bad faith intent to profit. The Tenth Circuit found that UTLM did not meet its burden of showing that UTAH LIGHTHOUSE was distinctive, but found that the domain names utahlighthouse.com and utahlighthouse.org were virtually identical to the trademark. The Tenth Circuit then turned its attention to the third element:

> As to the third element, UTLM did not demonstrate that Defendants used the domain names with a bad faith intent to profit. The ACPA enumerates nine nonexclusive factors to assist the court in determining whether the use of a trademark involves a bad faith intent to profit. *See* 15 U.S.C. § 1125(d)(1)(B)(i). It is not necessary to evaluate all of the factors because several of the factors readily defeat an inference that the Defendants intended

to profit by using domain names similar to UTLM's trademark. The quintessential example of a bad faith intent to profit is when a defendant purchases a domain name very similar to the trademark and then offers to sell the name to the trademark owner at an extortionate price. A defendant could also intend to profit by diverting customers from the website of the trademark owner to the defendant's own website, where those consumers would purchase the defendant's products or services instead of the trademark owner's. Neither of these purposes is evident here.[10]

One factor is the domain name registrant's "bona fide noncommercial or fair use of the mark in a site accessible under the domain name." 15 U.S.C. § 1125(d)(1)(B)(i)(IV). The district court determined that Defendants' use was entirely noncommercial, and a fair use parody, and therefore found that Defendants did not use the mark in bad faith. This is consistent with the reasoning of several other courts that a website that critiques a product and uses the product's trademark as the website's domain name may be a fair use. *See Lucas Nursery & Landscaping, Inc. v. Grosse*, 359 F.3d 806, 809 (6th Cir. 2004) (consumer registering domain name "lucasnursery.com" and complaining about nursery's work was not liable under ACPA); *TMI, Inc. v. Maxwell*, 368 F.3d 433 (5th Cir. 2004) (holding that a website with the purpose of informing other consumers did not create the harm the ACPA intended to eliminate); *Mayflower Transit, L.L.C. v. Prince*, 314 F. Supp. 2d 362 (D.N.J. 2004) (finding no ACPA liability where Defendant registered "mayflowervanline.com," since the totality of circumstances demonstrated that registrant's motive was to express dissatisfaction in doing business with the mark's owner). Because Wyatt's parody offers an indirect critique and lacks an overt commercial purpose, it is similar to these consumer commentaries, and under the circumstances of this case, constitutes fair use.

Another critical factor is the defendant's intent to divert consumers to a website that "could harm the goodwill represented by the mark, either for commercial gain or with the intent to tarnish or disparage the mark, by creating a likelihood of confusion as to the source, sponsorship, affiliation, or endorsement of the site." 15 U.S.C. § 1125(d)(1)(B)(i)(V). The district court concluded, and we agree, that the Wyatt website created no likelihood of confusion as to its source, or whether it was affiliated with or endorsed by UTLM. In the trademark infringement context, the plaintiff has the burden of proving likelihood of confusion. *Australian Gold*, 436 F.3d at 1238–39. Applying this same burden of proof to the likelihood of confusion in the context of cybersquatting, we conclude that UTLM failed to raise a genuine issue of material fact as to Defendants' intent to cause confusion about the

10. UTLM did proffer evidence that during the time the Wyatt website was posted, the FAIR bookstore sold nine titles that were also offered by the UTLM bookstore. This is at most evidence that FAIR may have incidentally profited, but not that Wyatt intended to profit from the use of UTLM's trademark.

source of the Wyatt website as a means of harming the goodwill of the UTAH LIGHTHOUSE mark.

Our evaluation of the nine statutory factors along with other evidence submitted by UTLM leads us to conclude that Defendants lacked a bad faith intent to profit from the use of UTLM's trademark in several domain names linked with the Wyatt website. In addition, the ACPA contains a "safe harbor" provision, which precludes a finding of bad faith intent if "the court determines that the person believed and had reasonable grounds to believe that the use of the domain name was a fair use or otherwise lawful." 15 U.S.C. § 1125(d)(1)(B)(ii). The district court reasoned that because the Wyatt website was a parody, Defendants could have reasonably believed that use of the domain names was legal. UTLM contends that Defendants lacked such a reasonable belief because they did not contact an attorney to verify the legality of the Wyatt parody. UTLM cites to no authority that an attorney's opinion is necessary to forming a good faith, reasonable belief in this context. We conclude upon *de novo* review that the safe harbor provision applies to Defendants' use.

Thus the Tenth Circuit affirmed the district court, finding that the district court properly granted summary judgment on UTLM's cybersquatting claim.

Note: Section 43(d) and "Gripe" Sites

Subsequent cases have found the reasoning of *Lucas Nursery* persuasive. In *TMI v. Maxwell*, 368 F.3d 433, 70 U.S.P.Q.2d 1630 (5th Cir. 2004), the Court of Appeals for the 5th Circuit followed *Lucas Nursery* in dismissing both dilution and ACPA claims against a cyber-griper. After an unsatisfactory experience seeking to purchase a home from TrendMarker Homes, Defendant Maxwell had posted a site at <www.trendmakerhome.com> complaining about his experience. TrendMaker sued Maxwell for cybersquatting and dilution. The Fifth Circuit held that "Maxwell's conduct is not the kind of harm the ACPA is designed to prevent." In *Mayflower Transit, LLC v. Prince*, 314 F. Supp. 2d 362 (D.N.J. 2004), the court applied the reasoning of *Lucas Nursery* to a cyber-griping case involving the registration of multiple domain names. Brett Prince engaged Lincoln Storage, an intrastate moving company affiliated with Mayflower Van Lines, to move his worldly goods from West Orange, New Jersey to Freehold, New Jersey. Enroute, thieves broke in to the parked moving truck and stole much of Prince's property. Prince sued both the Lincoln and Mayflower, and registered the domain name <mayflowervanlinebeware.com>. He posted a website describing his moving experience under the headline "Beware of Lincoln Storage Warehouse. Beware of Mayflower Van Lines." The website urged consumers contemplating a move to avoid both companies. Prince subsequently registered the domain names:

<mayflowevanline.com>,

<lincolnstoragewarehouse.com>,

<newjerseymovingcompany.com>,

and posted similar material to those sites. Mayflower sued Prince under the ACPA. The court, relying on *Lucas Nursery*, held that Mayflower had failed to show that Prince had a "bad faith intent to profit," concluding that "genuine cyber-gripers … are not covered by the ACPA." Prince's registration and use of multiple domain names did not persuade the court that he acted in bad faith. In *A. Univ. of Antigua Coll. of Med. v. Woodward*, 837 F. Supp. 2d 686 (E.D. Mich. 2011), the court referenced *Lucas Nursery* to hold that Defendant Woodward, a former student of American University of Antigua College of Medicine created <aua-med.com> exclusively to complain about AUA and its medical program, and thus, AUA was not entitled to summary judgment on its ACPA claim.

In *Coca-Cola Company v. Purdy*, 382 F.3d 774 (8th Cir. 2004), however, the Court of Appeals for the Eighth Circuit distinguished *Lucas Nursery* and upheld a finding of bad faith intent to profit. The case involved the registration and use of domain names for a gripe site that was unrelated to the products or services sold by the owners of trademarks used in the contested domain names. William Purdy set up an anti-abortion web page at <www.abortionismurder.com>, where he posted antiabortion commentary and graphic photos of aborted fetuses. Purdy also posted links to a website offering to sell hats, neckties, and tee shirts adorned with antiabortion messages. Purdy registered the domains <drinkcoke.com>, <mycoca-cola.com>, <my-washingtonpost.com>, <mypepsi.org>, and others, and used those domain names to redirect browsers to <abortionismurder.com>. The trademark owners brought suit under the ACPA. In distinguishing *Lucas Nursery*, the Eighth Circuit emphasized that "[t]he content available at abortionismurder.com contained no references to plaintiffs, their products, or their alleged positions on abortion."

In *Bosley Medical Institute, Inc. v. Kremer*, 403 F.3d 672 (9th Cir. 2005), the Court of Appeals for the 9th Circuit dismissed a trademark infringement and dilution claim over a gripe site, but declined to dismiss the ACPA claim. Plaintiff Bosley Medical sued its former hair-transplant patient when he posted a site at <www.BosleyMedical.com> criticizing plaintiff's hair transplant services. The Ninth Circuit concluded that defendant's site did not violate the Lanham Act, because Kremer's actions were not "commercial use in commerce":

> The dangers that the Lanham Act was designed to address are simply not at issue in this case. The Lanham Act, expressly enacted to be applied in commercial contexts, does not prohibit all unauthorized uses of a trademark. Kremer's use of the Bosley Medical mark simply cannot mislead consumers into buying a competing product—no customer will mistakenly purchase a hair replacement service from Kremer under the belief that the service is being offered by Bosley. Neither is Kremer capitalizing on the good will Bosley has created in its mark. Any harm to Bosley arises not from a competitor's sale of a similar product under Bosley's mark, but from Kremer's criticism of their services. Bosley cannot use the Lanham Act either as a shield from Kremer's criticism, or as a sword to shut Kremer up.

The court remanded the ACPA claim for trial, however, noting that section 43(d) of the Lanham Act does not expressly require commercial use and that other circuits had interpreted it to make non-commercial as well as commercial cybersquatting actionable. In *Aviva USA Corp. v. Vazirani*, 902 F. Supp. 1246 (D. Ariz. 2012), the district court followed *Bosley*'s characterization of competitor-run criticism cites as non-commercial in an action between the plaintiff, Aviva, one of the largest insurance companies in the world, and the defendants, who once sold Aviva's life insurance and annuity products, and were now offering services in competition with Aviva. The defendants created a website to criticize Aviva and its business practices, using domain names such as insideaviva.com, avivaexposed.com, avivauncovered .com, and aviva-uncovered.com. The plaintiffs brought several claims, including under the Lanham Act and the ACPA. Despite defendants' competition with Aviva, the court not only found that the use was noncommercial under the Lanham Act, but, unlike *Bosley*, also granted summary judgment to defendants on the ACPA claim:

> Aviva also argues that "gripe sites," when operated by competitors, satisfy the commercial use requirement. Aviva cites two cases to support this proposition: *HER, Inc. v. Re/Max First Choice, LLC*, 468 F. Supp. 2d 964 (S.D. Ohio 2007) and *Sunlight Saunas v. Sundance Saunas*, 427 F. Supp. 2d 1032 (D. Kan. 2006). These cases, however, can be distinguished from the facts of this case. In *HER, Inc.*, the defendants specifically directed consumers to the defendants' own website in emails that allegedly infringed the plaintiff's marks, and the allegedly infringing domain names routed visitors to the defendants' website, which provided real estate searching services that directly competed with similar services provided on the plaintiff's website. *HER, Inc.*, 468 F. Supp. 2d at 968–71. Thus, that court concluded that "the marks were used by the Defendants in connection with the sale of goods and services." *Id.* at 978 n.6. Similarly, in *Sunlight Saunas*, the court found that the defendants "had no apparent reason to disparage [the plaintiff's] products except to promote their own." *Sunlight Saunas*, 427 F. Supp. 2d at 1057. In support of that conclusion, the court cited to evidence that the defendants' website temporarily "included direct links to competitors [and] also stated that 'other companies offer the same products without the fraudulent claims.'" *Id.* Thus, the court could not "find as a matter of law that [the] defendants' website speech, including the chosen domain name, [was] 'noncommercial' speech." *Id.*
>
> Here, in contrast, Defendants' Website did not contain any direct links to sites offering competing goods or services and did not promote any competing companies' goods or services. Nor did any of the domain names registered to Defendants route visitors to any commercial websites or other sites that competed with Aviva. Rather, all of the domain names routed visitors to Defendants' Website, which had a noncommercial purpose—that is, criticizing Aviva's business practices.
>
> ....

After analyzing the relevant factors, the Court finds that Aviva has failed to establish that Defendants acted with the required bad-faith intent to profit when they registered the domain names. Importantly, because the Website was not commercial, it was used only to criticize Aviva, and the Defendants never made any attempt to sell the domain names for profit, Defendants' actions do not fall within the scope of the ACPA. In other words, Defendants' "conduct is not the kind of harm that [the] ACPA was designed to prevent." *TMI [Inc. v. Maxwell]*, 368 F.3d [433] at 440 [(5th Cir. 2004)]. Therefore, the Court will grant Defendants' motion for summary judgment on Aviva's ACPA claim and deny Aviva's motion for summary judgment on that claim.

Question

Does/should it make a difference to the section 43(d) analysis whether the target business' unaltered trademark constitutes the gripe site full domain name, or whether the domain name incorporates some information that discloses the griping nature of the site, such as "[trademark]sucks.com" or '[trademark]beware.com"?

People for the Ethical Treatment of Animals v. Doughney, 263 F.3d 359 (4th Cir. 2001). Michael Doughney ("Doughney") registered the domain name peta.org and created a website called "People Eating Tasty Animals." PETA sued, alleging, among other claims cybersquatting under 15 U.S.C. § 1125(c). The Fourth Circuit affirmed the grant of summary judgment to PETA.

PETA is an animal rights organization with more than 600,000 members worldwide. PETA "is dedicated to promoting and heightening public awareness of animal protection issues and it opposes the exploitation of animals for food, clothing, entertainment and vivisection."

Doughney is a former internet executive who has registered many domain names since 1995. For example, Doughney registered domain names such as dubyadot.com, dubyadot.net, deathbush.com, RandallTerry.org (Not Randall Terry for Congress), bwtel.com (BaltimoreWashington Telephone Company), pmrc.org ("People's Manic Repressive Church"), and ex-cult.org (Ex-Cult Archive). At the time the district court issued its summary judgment ruling, Doughney owned 50–60 domain names.

Doughney registered the domain name peta.org in 1995 with Network Solutions, Inc. ("NSI"). When registering the domain name, Doughney represented to NSI that the registration did "not interfere with or infringe upon the rights of any third party," and that a "nonprofit educational organization" called "People Eating Tasty Animals" was registering the domain name. Doughney made these representations to NSI despite knowing that no corporation, partnership, organization or entity of any kind existed or traded under that name. Moreover, Doughney was familiar with PETA and its beliefs and had been for at least 15 years before registering the domain name.

After registering the peta.org domain name, Doughney used it to create a website purportedly on behalf of "People Eating Tasty Animals." Doughney claims he created the website as a parody of PETA. A viewer accessing the website would see the title "People Eating Tasty Animals" in large, bold type. Under the title, the viewer would see a statement that the website was a "resource for those who enjoy eating meat, wearing fur and leather, hunting, and the fruits of scientific research." The website contained links to various meat, fur, leather, hunting, animal research, and other organizations, all of which held views generally antithetical to PETA's views. Another statement on the website asked the viewer whether he/she was "Feeling lost? Offended? Perhaps you should, like, exit immediately." The phrase "exit immediately" contained a hyperlink to PETA's official website.

[Doughney refused PETA's request to transfer the domain name.]

In response to Doughney's domain name dispute with PETA, The Chronicle of Philanthropy quoted Doughney as stating that, "if they [PETA] want one of my domains, they should make me an offer." ...

....

Doughney does not dispute that the peta.org domain name engenders a likelihood of confusion between his web site and PETA. Doughney claims, though, that the inquiry should not end with his domain name. Rather, he urges the Court to consider his website in conjunction with the domain name because, together, they purportedly parody PETA and, thus, do not cause a likelihood of confusion.

....

Looking at Doughney's domain name alone, there is no suggestion of a parody. The domain name peta.org simply copies PETA's Mark, conveying the message that it is related to PETA. The domain name does not convey the second, contradictory message needed to establish a parody—a message that the domain name is not related to PETA, but that it is a parody of PETA.

Doughney claims that this second message can be found in the content of his website. Indeed, the website's content makes it clear that it is not related to PETA. However, this second message is not conveyed simultaneously with the first message, as required to be considered a parody. The domain name conveys the first message; the second message is conveyed only when the viewer reads the content of the website....

Thus, the messages are not conveyed simultaneously and do not constitute a parody. [Citations.] The district court properly rejected Doughney's parody defense and found that Doughney's use of the peta.org domain name engenders a likelihood of confusion....

....

B. Anticybersquatting Consumer Protection Act

The district court found Doughney liable under the Anticybersquatting Consumer Protection Act ("ACPA"), 15 U.S.C. § 1125(d)(1)(A). To establish an ACPA violation, PETA was required to (1) prove that Doughney had a bad faith intent to profit from using the peta.org domain name, and (2) that the peta.org domain name is identical or confusingly similar to, or dilutive of, the distinctive and famous PETA Mark. 15 U.S.C. § 1125(d)(1)(A).

....

Doughney does not dispute that the peta.org domain name engenders a likelihood of confusion between his web site and PETA. Doughney claims, though, that the inquiry should not end with his domain name. Rather, he urges the Court to consider his website in conjunction with the domain name because, together, they purportedly parody PETA and, thus, do not cause a likelihood of confusion.

....

Looking at Doughney's domain name alone, there is no suggestion of a parody. The domain name peta.org simply copies PETA's Mark, conveying the message that it is related to PETA. The domain name does not convey the second, contradictory message needed to establish a parody—a message that the domain name is not related to PETA, but that it is a parody of PETA.

Doughney claims that this second message can be found in the content of his website. Indeed, the website's content makes it clear that it is not related to PETA. However, this second message is not conveyed simultaneously with the first message, as required to be considered a parody. The domain name conveys the first message; the second message is conveyed only when the viewer reads the content of the website....

Thus, the messages are not conveyed simultaneously and do not constitute a parody. [Citations.] The district court properly rejected Doughney's parody defense and found that Doughney's use of the peta.org domain name engenders a likelihood of confusion....

Doughney's ... argument—that he did not seek to financially profit from registering a domain name using PETA's Mark—also offers him no relief. It is undisputed that Doughney made statements to the press and on his website recommending that PETA attempt to "settle" with him and "make him an offer." The undisputed evidence belies Doughney's argument.

Doughney's ... argument—that he did not act in bad faith—also is unavailing. Under 15 U.S.C. § 1125(d)(1)(B)(i), a court may consider several factors to determine whether a defendant acted in bad faith.... In addition to listing ... nine factors, the ACPA contains a safe harbor provision stating that bad faith intent "shall not be found in any case in which the court determines that the person believed and had reasonable grounds to believe that the use of the domain name was fair use or otherwise lawful." 15 U.S.C. § 1225(d)(1)(B)(ii).

The district court reviewed the factors listed in the statute and properly concluded that Doughney (I) had no intellectual property right in peta.org; (II) peta.org is not Doughney's name or a name otherwise used to identify Doughney; (III) Doughney had no prior use of peta.org in connection with the bona fide offering of any goods or services; (IV) Doughney used the PETA Mark in a commercial manner; (V) Doughney "clearly intended to confuse, mislead and divert internet users into accessing his web site which contained information antithetical and therefore harmful to the goodwill represented by the PETA Mark"; (VI) Doughney made statements on his web site and in the press recommending that PETA attempt to "settle" with him and "make him an offer"; (VII) Doughney made false statements when registering the domain name; and (VIII) Doughney registered other domain names that are identical or similar to the marks or names of other famous people and organizations. People for the Ethical Treatment of Animals, 113 F.Supp.2d at 920.

Doughney claims that the district court's later ruling denying PETA's motion for attorney fees triggers application of the ACPA's safe harbor provision. In that ruling, the district court stated that

> Doughney registered the domain name because he thought that he had a legitimate First Amendment right to express himself this way. The Court must consider Doughney's state of mind at the time he took the actions in question. Doughney thought he was within his First Amendment rights to create a parody of the plaintiff's organization.

People for the Ethical Treatment of Animals, Inc. v. Doughney, 2000 U.S. Dist. LEXIS 13421, *5, Civil Action No. 99-1336-A, Order at 4 (E.D. Va. Aug. 31, 2000). With its attorney's fee ruling, the district court did not find that Doughney "had reasonable grounds to believe" that his use of PETA's Mark was lawful. It held only that Doughney thought it to be lawful.

Moreover, a defendant "who acts even partially in bad faith in registering a domain name is not, as a matter of law, entitled to benefit from [the ACPA's] safe harbor provision." *Virtual Works, Inc.*, 238 F.3d at 270. Doughney knowingly provided false information to NSI upon registering the domain name, knew he was registering a domain name identical to PETA's Mark, and clearly intended to confuse Internet users into accessing his website, instead of PETA's official website. Considering the evidence of Doughney's bad faith, the safe harbor provision can provide him no relief....

Question

Is there a variant domain name Mr. Doughney might adopt that would signal that his web site criticizes or pokes fun at PETA, without running afoul of the Lanham Act?

Lamparello v. Falwell

420 F.3d 309 (4th Cir. 2005)

MOTZ, CIRCUIT JUDGE:

Christopher Lamparello appeals the district court's order enjoining him from maintaining a gripe website critical of Reverend Jerry Falwell. For the reasons stated below, we reverse.

I.

Reverend Falwell is "a nationally known minister who has been active as a commentator on politics and public affairs." *Hustler Magazine, Inc. v. Falwell*, 485 U.S. 46, 47, 108 S. Ct. 876, 99 L. Ed. 2d 41 (1988). He holds the common law trademarks "Jerry Falwell" and "Falwell," and the registered trademark "Listen America with Jerry Falwell." Jerry Falwell Ministries can be found online at "www.falwell.com," a website which receives 9,000 hits (or visits) per day.

Lamparello registered the domain name "www.fallwell.com" on February 11, 1999, after hearing Reverend Falwell give an interview "in which he expressed opinions about gay people and homosexuality that [Lamparello] considered ... offensive." Lamparello created a website at that domain name to respond to what he believed were "untruths about gay people." Lamparello's website included headlines such as "Bible verses that Dr. Falwell chooses to ignore" and "Jerry Falwell has been bearing false witness (Exodus 20:16) against his gay and lesbian neighbors for a long time." The site also contained in-depth criticism of Reverend Falwell's views. For example, the website stated:

> Dr. Falwell says that he is on the side of truth. He says that he will preach that homosexuality is a sin until the day he dies. But we believe that if the reverend were to take another thoughtful look at the scriptures, he would discover that they have been twisted around to support an anti-gay political agenda ... at the expense of the gospel.

Although the interior pages of Lamparello's website did not contain a disclaimer, the homepage prominently stated, "This website is NOT affiliated with Jerry Falwell or his ministry"; advised, "If you would like to visit Rev. Falwell's website, you may click here"; and provided a hyperlink to Reverend Falwell's website.

At one point, Lamparello's website included a link to the Amazon.com webpage for a book that offered interpretations of the Bible that Lamparello favored, but the parties agree that Lamparello has never sold goods or services on his website. The parties also agree that "Lamparello's domain name and web site at www.fallwell.com," which received only 200 hits per day, "had no measurable impact on the quantity of visits to [Reverend Falwell's] web site at www.falwell.com."

Nonetheless, Reverend Falwell sent Lamparello letters in October 2001 and June 2003 demanding that he cease and desist from using www.fallwell.com or any variation of Reverend Falwell's name as a domain name. Ultimately, Lamparello filed this action against Reverend Falwell and his ministries (collectively referred to hereinafter as

"Reverend Falwell"), seeking a declaratory judgment of noninfringement. Reverend Falwell counter-claimed, alleging trademark infringement under 15 U.S.C. § 1114 (2000), false designation of origin under 15 U.S.C. § 1125(a), unfair competition under 15 U.S.C. § 1126 and the common law of Virginia, and cybersquatting under 15 U.S.C. § 1125(d).

The parties stipulated to all relevant facts and filed cross-motions for summary judgment. The district court granted summary judgment to Reverend Falwell, enjoined Lamparello from using Reverend Falwell's mark at www.fallwell.com, and required Lamparello to transfer the domain name to Reverend Falwell. However, the court denied Reverend Falwell's request for statutory damages or attorney fees, reasoning that the "primary motive" of Lamparello's website was "to put forth opinions on issues that were contrary to those of [Reverend Falwell]" and "not to take away monies or to profit."

Lamparello appeals the district court's order; Reverend Falwell cross-appeals the denial of statutory damages and attorney fees. We review de novo a district court's ruling on cross-motions for summary judgment. *See People for the Ethical Treatment of Animals v. Doughney*, 263 F.3d 359, 364 (4th Cir. 2001) [hereinafter "PETA"].

II.

We first consider Reverend Falwell's claims of trademark infringement and false designation of origin.

A.

. . . .

Trademark law serves the important functions of protecting product identification, providing consumer information, and encouraging the production of quality goods and services. *See Qualitex Co. v. Jacobson Prods. Co.*, 514 U.S. 159, 164, 115 S. Ct. 1300, 131 L. Ed. 2d 248 (1995). But protections "'against unfair competition'" cannot be transformed into "'rights to control language.'" *CPC Int'l, Inc. v. Skippy Inc.*, 214 F.3d 456, 462 (4th Cir. 2000) (*quoting* Mark A. Lemley, *The Modern Lanham Act and the Death of Common Sense*, 108 Yale L.J. 1687, 1710–11 (1999)). "Such a transformation" would raise serious First Amendment concerns because it would limit the

> ability to discuss the products or criticize the conduct of companies that may be of widespread public concern and importance. Much useful social and commercial discourse would be all but impossible if speakers were under threat of an infringement lawsuit every time they made reference to a person, company or product by using its trademark.

Id. (internal quotation marks and citations omitted).

Lamparello and his amici argue at length that application of the Lanham Act must be restricted to "commercial speech" to assure that trademark law does not become a tool for unconstitutional censorship. The Sixth Circuit has endorsed this view, *see Taubman Co. v. Webfeats*, 319 F.3d 770, 774 (6th Cir. 2003), and the Ninth Circuit recently has done so as well, *see Bosley Med. Inst., Inc. v. Kremer*, 403 F.3d 672, 674 (9th Cir. 2005).

In its two most significant recent amendments to the Lanham Act, the Federal Trademark Dilution Act of 1995 ("FTDA") and the Anti-cybersquatting Consumer Protection Act of 1999 ("ACPA"), Congress left little doubt that it did not intend for trademark laws to impinge the First Amendment rights of critics and commentators. The dilution statute applies to only a "commercial use in commerce of a mark," 15 U.S.C. § 1125(c)(1), and explicitly states that the "noncommercial use of a mark" is not actionable. Id. § 1125(c)(4). Congress explained that this language was added to "adequately address[] legitimate First Amendment concerns," H.R. Rep. No. 104-374, at 4 (1995), *reprinted in* 1995 U.S.C.C.A.N. 1029, 1031, and "incorporated the concept of 'commercial' speech from the 'commercial speech' doctrine." *Id.* at 8, *reprinted in* 1995 U.S.C.C.A.N. at 1035.... Similarly, Congress directed that in determining whether an individual has engaged in cybersquatting, the courts may consider whether the person's use of the mark is a "bona fide noncommercial or fair use." 15 U.S.C. § 1125(d)(1)(B)(i)(IV). The legislature believed this provision necessary to "protect[] the rights of Internet users and the interests of all Americans in free speech and protected uses of trademarked names for such things as parody, comment, criticism, comparative advertising, news reporting, etc." S. Rep. No. 106-140 (1999).

In contrast, the trademark infringement and false designation of origin provisions of the Lanham Act (Sections 32 and 43(a), respectively) do not employ the term "noncommercial." They do state, however, that they pertain only to the use of a mark "in connection with the sale, offering for sale, distribution, or advertising of any goods or services," 15 U.S.C. § 1114(1)(a), or "in connection with any goods or services," *Id.* § 1125(a)(1). But courts have been reluctant to define those terms narrowly. Rather, as the Second Circuit has explained, "the term 'services' has been interpreted broadly" and so "the Lanham Act has ... been applied to defendants furnishing a wide variety of non-commercial public and civic benefits." *United We Stand Am., Inc. v. United We Stand, Am. N.Y., Inc.*, 128 F.3d 86, 89–90 (2d Cir. 1997). Similarly, in *PETA* we noted that a website need not actually sell goods or services for the use of a mark in that site's domain name to constitute a use "'in connection with' goods or services." *PETA*, 263 F.3d at 365; *see also Taubman Co.*, 319 F.3d at 775 (concluding that website with two links to websites of for-profit entities violated the Lanham Act).

Thus, even if we accepted Lamparello's contention that Sections 32 and 43(a) of the Lanham Act apply only to commercial speech, we would still face the difficult question of what constitutes such speech under those provisions. In the case at hand, we need not resolve that question or determine whether Sections 32 and 43(a) apply exclusively to commercial speech because Reverend Falwell's claims of trademark infringement and false designation fail for a more obvious reason. The hallmark of such claims is a likelihood of confusion—and there is no likelihood of confusion here.

B.

1.

"The use of a competitor's mark that does not cause confusion as to source is permissible." *Dorr-Oliver, Inc. v. Fluid-Quip, Inc.*, 94 F.3d 376, 380 (7th Cir. 1996). Accordingly, Lamparello can only be liable for infringement and false designation if his use of Reverend Falwell's mark would be likely to cause confusion as to the source of the website found at www.fallwell.com. This likelihood-of-confusion test "generally strikes a comfortable balance" between the First Amendment and the rights of markholders. *Mattel, Inc. v. MCA Records, Inc.*, 296 F.3d 894, 900 (9th Cir. 2002).

We have identified seven factors helpful in determining whether a likelihood of confusion exists as to the source of a work, but "not all these factors are always relevant or equally emphasized in each case." *Pizzeria Uno Corp. v. Temple*, 747 F.2d 1522, 1527 (4th Cir. 1984)....

Reverend Falwell's mark is distinctive, and the domain name of Lamparello's website, www.fallwell.com, closely resembles it. But, although Lamparello and Reverend Falwell employ similar marks online, Lamparello's website looks nothing like Reverend Falwell's; indeed, Lamparello has made no attempt to imitate Reverend Falwell's website. Moreover, Reverend Falwell does not even argue that Lamparello's website constitutes advertising or a facility for business, let alone a facility or advertising similar to that of Reverend Falwell. Furthermore, Lamparello clearly created his website intending only to provide a forum to criticize ideas, not to steal customers.

Most importantly, Reverend Falwell and Lamparello do not offer similar goods or services. Rather they offer opposing ideas and commentary. Reverend Falwell's mark identifies his spiritual and political views; the website at www.fallwell.com criticizes those very views. After even a quick glance at the content of the website at www.fallwell.com, no one seeking Reverend Falwell's guidance would be misled by the domain name—www.fallwell.com—into believing Reverend Falwell authorized the content of that website. No one would believe that Reverend Falwell sponsored a site criticizing himself, his positions, and his interpretations of the Bible. *See New Kids on the Block v. News Am. Publ'g, Inc.*, 971 F.2d 302, 308–09 (9th Cir. 1992) (stating that use of a mark to solicit criticism of the markholder implies the markholder is not the sponsor of the use).

Finally, the fact that people contacted Reverend Falwell's ministry to report that they found the content at www.fallwell.com antithetical to Reverend Falwell's views does not illustrate, as Reverend Falwell claims, that the website engendered actual confusion. To the contrary, the anecdotal evidence Reverend Falwell submitted shows that those searching for Reverend Falwell's site and arriving instead at Lamparello's site quickly realized that Reverend Falwell was not the source of the content therein.

For all of these reasons, it is clear that the undisputed record evidences no likelihood of confusion. In fact, Reverend Falwell even conceded at oral argument that those viewing the content of Lamparello's website probably were unlikely to confuse Reverend Falwell with the source of that material.

2.

Nevertheless, Reverend Falwell argues that he is entitled to prevail under the "initial interest confusion" doctrine. This relatively new and sporadically applied doctrine holds that "the Lanham Act forbids a competitor from luring potential customers away from a producer by initially passing off its goods as those of the producer's, even if confusion as to the source of the goods is dispelled by the time any sales are consummated." *Dorr-Oliver*, 94 F.3d at 382. According to Reverend Falwell, this doctrine requires us to compare his mark with Lamparello's website domain name, www.fallwell.com, without considering the content of Lamparello's website. Reverend Falwell argues that some people who misspell his name may go to www.fallwell.com assuming it is his site, thus giving Lamparello an unearned audience—albeit one that quickly disappears when it realizes it has not reached Reverend Falwell's site. This argument fails for two reasons.

First, we have never adopted the initial interest confusion theory; rather, we have followed a very different mode of analysis, requiring courts to determine whether a likelihood of confusion exists by "examining the allegedly infringing use *in the context in which it is seen by the ordinary consumer.*" *Anheuser-Busch, Inc. v. L & L Wings, Inc.*, 962 F.2d 316, 319 (4th Cir. 1992) (emphasis added) (citing cases); *see also What-A-Burger of Va., Inc. v. WHATABURGER, Inc.*, 357 F.3d 441, 450 (4th Cir. 2004).

Contrary to Reverend Falwell's arguments, we did not abandon this approach in *PETA*. Our inquiry in *PETA* was limited to whether Doughney's use of the domain name "www.peta.org" constituted a successful enough parody of People for the Ethical Treatment of Animals that no one was likely to believe www.peta.org was sponsored or endorsed by that organization. For a parody to be successful, it "must convey two simultaneous—and contradictory—messages: that it is the original, but also that it is not the original and is instead a parody." *PETA*, 263 F.3d at 366 (internal quotation marks and citation omitted). Doughney argued that his domain name conveyed the first message (that it was PETA's website) and that the content of his website conveyed the requisite second message (that it was not PETA's site). *Id.* Although "the website's content made it clear that it was not related to PETA," *id.*, we concluded that the website's content could not convey the requisite second message because the site's content "was not conveyed *simultaneously* with the first message, [i.e., the domain name itself,] as required to be considered a parody." *Id.* at 366. Accordingly, we found the "district court properly rejected Doughney's parody defense." *Id.* at 367.

PETA simply outlines the parameters of the parody defense; it does not adopt the initial interest confusion theory or otherwise diminish the necessity of examining context when determining whether a likelihood of confusion exists. Indeed, in *PETA* itself, rather than embracing a new approach, we reiterated that "to determine whether a likelihood of confusion exists, a court should not consider how closely a *fragment* of a given use duplicates the trademark, but must instead consider *whether the use in its entirety creates a likelihood of confusion.*" *Id.* at 366 (internal quotation marks and citation omitted) (emphasis added). When dealing with domain names, this means a court must evaluate an allegedly infringing domain name in conjunction with the content of the website identified by the domain name.[4]

Moreover, even if we did endorse the initial interest confusion theory, that theory would not assist Reverend Falwell here because it provides no basis for liability in circumstances such as these. The few appellate courts that have followed the Ninth Circuit and imposed liability under this theory for using marks on the Internet have done so only in cases involving a factor utterly absent here—one business's use of another's mark for its own financial gain. [Citations.]

Profiting financially from initial interest confusion is thus a key element for imposition of liability under this theory.[5] When an alleged infringer does not compete with the markholder for sales, "some initial confusion will not likely facilitate free riding on the goodwill of another mark, or otherwise harm the user claiming infringement. Where confusion has little or no meaningful effect in the marketplace, it is of little or no consequence in our analysis." *Checkpoint Sys. v. Check Point Software Techs., Inc.*, 269 F.3d 270, 296–97 (3d. Cir. 2001). For this reason, even the Ninth Circuit has stated that a firm is not liable for using another's mark in its domain name if it "could not financially capitalize on [a] misdirected consumer [looking for the markholder's site] even if it so desired." *Interstellar Starship Servs., Ltd. v. Epix, Inc.*, 304 F.3d 936, 946 (9th Cir. 2002).

This critical element—use of another firm's mark to capture the markholder's customers and profits—simply does not exist when the alleged infringer establishes a gripe site that criticizes the markholder. *See* Hannibal Travis, *The Battle For Mindshare: The Emerging Consensus that the First Amendment Protects Corporate Criticism and Parody on the Internet*, 10 Va. J.L. & Tech. 3, 85 (Winter 2005)....[6] Applying the initial interest confusion theory to gripe sites like Lamparello's would enable the markholder

4. Contrary to Reverend Falwell's suggestions, this rule does not change depending on how similar the domain name or title is to the mark. Hence, Reverend Falwell's assertion that he objects only to Lamparello using the domain name www.fallwell.com and has no objection to Lamparello posting his criticisms at "www.falwelliswrong.com," or a similar domain name, does not entitle him to a different evaluation rule. Rather it has long been established that even when alleged infringers use the *very marks at issue* in titles, courts look to the underlying *content* to determine whether the titles create a likelihood of confusion as to source. *See, e.g., Parks v. LaFace Records*, 329 F.3d 437, 452–54 (6th Cir. 2003); *Mattel*, 296 F.3d at 901–02; *Westchester Media v. PRL USA Holdings, Inc.*, 214 F.3d 658, 667–68 (5th Cir. 2000); *Rogers v. Grimaldi*, 875 F.2d 994, 1000–01 (2d Cir. 1989).

5. Offline uses of marks found to cause actionable initial interest confusion also have involved financial gain. *See Elvis Presley Enters., Inc. v. Capece*, 141 F.3d 188, 204 (5th Cir. 1998); *Mobil Oil Corp. v. Pegasus Petroleum Corp.*, 818 F.2d 254, 260 (2d Cir. 1987). And even those courts recognizing the initial interest confusion theory of liability but finding no actionable initial confusion involved one business's use of another's mark for profit. *See, e.g., Savin Corp. v. The Savin Group*, 391 F.3d 439, 462 n. 13 (2d Cir. 2004); *AM Gen. Corp. v. DaimlerChrysler Corp.*, 311 F.3d 796, 827–28 (7th Cir. 2002); *Checkpoint Sys., Inc. v. Check Point Software Techs., Inc.*, 269 F.3d 270, 298 (3d Cir. 2001); *Hasbro, Inc. v. Clue Computing, Inc.*, 232 F.3d 1, 2 (1st Cir. 2000); *Syndicate Sales, Inc. v. Hampshire Paper Corp.*, 192 F.3d 633, 638 (7th Cir. 1999); *Rust Env't & Infrastructure, Inc. v. Teunissen*, 131 F.3d 1210, 1217 (7th Cir. 1997); *Dorr-Oliver*, 94 F.3d at 383.

6. Although the appellate courts that have adopted the initial interest confusion theory have only applied it to profit-seeking uses of another's mark, the district courts have not so limited the application

to insulate himself from criticism—or at least to minimize access to it. We have already condemned such uses of the Lanham Act, stating that a markholder cannot "'shield itself from criticism by forbidding the use of its name in commentaries critical of its conduct.'" *CPC Int'l*, 214 F.3d at 462 (*quoting L.L. Bean, Inc. v. Drake Publishers, Inc.*, 811 F.2d 26, 33 (1st Cir. 1987)). "Just because speech is critical of a corporation and its business practices is not a sufficient reason to enjoin the speech." *Id.*

In sum, even if we were to accept the initial interest confusion theory, that theory would not apply in the case at hand. Rather, to determine whether a likelihood of confusion exists as to the source of a gripe site like that at issue in this case, a court must look not only to the allegedly infringing domain name, but also to the underlying content of the website. When we do so here, it is clear, as explained above, that no likelihood of confusion exists. Therefore, the district court erred in granting Reverend Falwell summary judgment on his infringement, false designation, and unfair competition claims.

....

IV.

For the foregoing reasons, Lamparello, rather than Reverend Falwell, is entitled to summary judgment on all counts. Accordingly, the judgment of the district court is reversed and the case is remanded for entry of judgment for Lamparello.

Question

Is the court's basis for distinguishing its decision in *PETA* persuasive? Is *PETA* still good law?

Jacqueline D. Lipton, *Bad Faith in Cyberspace: Grounding Domain Name Theory in Trademark, Property and Restitution*

23 Harv. J. L. & Tech. 447 (2010) (Excerpt)*

The current state of domain name regulation might be summarized as set out in Table 1. This table matches the various motivations for domain name registration against the most obvious categories of words and phrases that are commonly registered as domain names. The individual cells within the table identify the extent to which each pairing of market motivations with word type is regulated under existing rules.

---

of the theory. Without expressly referring to this theory, two frequently-discussed district court cases have held that using another's domain name to post content antithetical to the markholder constitutes infringement. *See Planned Parenthood Fed'n of Am., Inc. v. Bucci*, No. 97 Civ. 0629, 1997 U.S. Dist. LEXIS 3338 (S.D.N.Y. March 24, 1997), *aff'd*, 152 F.3d 920 (2d Cir. 1998) (table) (finding use of domain name "www.plannedparenthood.com" to provide links to passages of anti-abortion book constituted infringement); *Jews for Jesus v. Brodsky*, 993 F. Supp. 282 (D.N.J. 1998), *aff'd*, 159 F.3d 1351 (3d Cir. 1998) (table) (finding use of "www.jewsforjesus.org" to criticize religious group constituted infringement). We think both cases were wrongly decided to the extent that in determining whether the domain names were confusing, the courts did not consider whether the websites' content would dispel any confusion. In expanding the initial interest confusion theory of liability, these cases cut it off from its moorings to the detriment of the First Amendment.

The results evidence an inconsistent and unpredictable pastiche of regulations. There is no clear or consistent underlying theoretical basis for domain name regulation.

Table 1: Relationship between Registrants' Motivations and Categories of Domain Name Registered

	Sale Motive	Clickfarming Motive	Expressive Use Motive	Commercial Use Motive
Trademarks	Traditional cybersquatting	Potentially cybersquatting	Usually legitimate, particularly if the registrant does not use the ".com" version of the name	Competing TM interests—first come, first served
Personal Names	Traditional cybersquatting (if name is trademarked); 15 U.S.C. § 8131 (1)(A) liability (regardless of trademark)	Potentially cybersquatting (if name is trademarked); little recourse if no trademark	Usually legitimate use, particularly if registrant does not use ".com" version of trademarked personal name	Competing personal names—first come first served.
Cultural and Geographic Indicators	No regulation unless name is trademarked	No regulation unless term is trademarked	Presumptively legitimate use	Presumption of legitimate use
Generic Words & Phrases	Presumptively legitimate use	Presumptively legitimate use	Presumptively legitimate use	Presumption of legitimate use
Deliberate Misspellings of Trademarks	Cybersquatting (if name is trademarked); 15 U.S.C. § 8131(1)(A) liability (regardless of trademark)	Potentially cybersquatting (if name is trademarked); little recourse if no trademark	Unclear—potentially legitimate use	No legitimate use
Deliberate Misspellings of Personal Names	Cybersquatting (if name is trademarked); little recourse if no trademark	Potentially cybersquatting (if name is trademarked); little recourse if no trademark	Unclear—potentially legitimate use	No legitimate use
"Trademarksucks" Names	Potentially cybersquatting if domain name is substantially similar to trademark	Unclear—potentially trademark infringement, dilution or cybersquatting	Generally legitimate use	No legitimate use

The only conduct that is clearly sanctioned under current regulations is traditional cybersquatting on trademarks and personal names in the domain space. The regulation of other conduct is largely unclear. It is possible to discern some general principles about domain name regulation from this table, but at a fairly high level of abstraction. For example, purely expressive uses of domain names are for the most part regarded as being legitimate, regardless of the type of word or phrase registered [see Column 3]. Even expressive uses of trademarks [Column 3, Row 1] and of deliberate misspellings of trademarks [Column 3, Row 5] may be legitimate uses if the associated website is used for commentary, rather than commercial purposes.

Another general principle that may be derived from Table 1 is that registration of a deliberate misspelling of another person's trademark is presumptively illegitimate, at least if undertaken for a commercial purpose. In fact, it is difficult to conceive of a situation where someone registers a deliberate misspelling of another person's trademark for a purely expressive purpose, although it is possible that the operator of a purely expressive gripe site or parody site may want to engage in this conduct. In any event, the fifth and six rows of Column 4 are shaded out because it is difficult, if not impossible, to conceive of any legitimate commercial purpose for registering a deliberate misspelling of another's mark or name.

Table 1 also illustrates the confusion inherent with respect to "sucks"-type domain names. These are names that use a trademark with a pejorative word or phrase attached, such as "nikesucks.com". Typically, these domains are used for gripe sites—websites that include critical commentary about a trademark holder. However, these kinds of names are sometimes used for commercial purposes such as cybersquatting or clickfarming. Where pejorative domain names are used for commercial purposes, they are sometimes referred to as "sham speech" domain names. There is currently no clear regulatory approach to "sucks"-type domain names. Most commercial uses of such names are colorably illegitimate as they take advantage of the goodwill in a trademark to draw traffic for a non-related commercial purpose. However, some uses of "sucks"-type domain names are legitimately expressive and others combine expressive and commercial elements. The development of a more coherent theoretical framework for domain name regulation might assist in ascertaining what kinds of conduct concerning "sucks"-type domain names should be proscribed, and on what basis. A theoretical framework based on both trademark policy and unjust enrichment may be useful here to separate legitimate expressive uses of "sucks"-type domain names from bad faith commercial uses.

Another notable feature of Table 1 is that it highlights the position of clickfarming in the context of current domain name regulations. Most clickfarming involving trademarks or deliberate misspellings of trademarks is potentially regulated as a form of cybersquatting. This conduct may be considered cybersquatting because clickfarms that utilize other people's trademarks essentially use the marks for bad faith commercial profit motives. The commercial profit motive in clickfarming is different from traditional cybersquatting. For clickfarmers, the profit is not derived from a sale of the name, but rather from using the name to generate revenue from click-through advertisements. Nevertheless, most cybersquatting regulations are broad enough to encompass this kind of conduct. In the ACPA, for example, the notion of a bad faith intent to profit from a mark is not inextricably linked to a sale motive. The bad faith factors in the UDRP are likewise not limited to a sale motive. The intention to sell the domain name is only one of four non-exclusive bad faith factors in the UDRP.

Question

Is there a nominative fair use defense to section 43(d)? Consider the following: your client, "Ikeahackers" operates a website, under the domain name ikeahackers.com, for people who create new furniture (or improbable objects) by taking apart and recombining pieces of their Ikea furniture. "The ideas range from simply adding decorations to make a piece look unique to major revamps that require 'power tools and lots of ingenuity.'" http://arstechnica.com/tech-policy/2014/06/ikea-waits-8-years-then-shuts-down-ikeahackers-site-with-trademark-claim/. The site does not sell anything, but carries advertising. Ikea has sent a letter demanding that your client cease using "ikea" in its domain name. What do you advise?

3. Indirect Liability for Cybersquatting?

Petroliam Nasional Berhad v. GoDaddy.com, Inc.

737 F.3d 546 (9th Cir. 2013)

M. Smith, Circuit Judge:

In this appeal, Petroliam Nasional Berhad (Petronas) requests that we read a cause of action for contributory cybersquatting into the Anticybersquatting Consumer Protection Act (ACPA or Act), 15 U.S.C. § 1125(d). Because we conclude that neither the plain text nor the purpose of the ACPA provide support for such a cause of action, we hold that there is none. We therefore affirm the judgment of the district court.

FACTS AND PRIOR PROCEEDINGS

Petrolium Nasional Berhad (Petronas) is a major oil and gas company with its headquarters in Kuala Lumpur, Malaysia. Petronas owns the trademark to the name "PETRONAS." Godaddy.com, Inc. (GoDaddy) is the world's largest domain name registrar, maintaining over 50 million domain names registered by customers around the world. GoDaddy also provides domain name forwarding services, which, like its registration service, enables Internet users who type in a particular domain name to arrive at the target site specified by GoDaddy's customer, the registrant.

In 2003, a third party registered the domain names "petronastower.net" and "petronastowers.net" through a registrar other than GoDaddy. In 2007, the owner of those names transferred its registration service to GoDaddy. The registrant used GoDaddy's domain name forwarding service to direct the disputed domain names to the adult web site, "camfunchat.com," which was hosted on a web server maintained by a third party, and which had been associated with the disputed domain names, using the previous registrar.

....

Petronas sued GoDaddy in the United States District Court for the Northern District of California on a number of theories, including cybersquatting under 15 U.S.C. § 1125(d), and contributory cybersquatting....

Our first obligation in determining whether the ACPA includes a contributory cybersquatting claim is to examine the plain text of the statute. [Citation.] Established common law principles can be inferred into a cause of action where circumstances suggest that Congress intended those principles to apply. [Citations.]

We hold that the ACPA does not include a cause of action for contributory cybersquatting because: (1) the text of the Act does not apply to the conduct that would be actionable under such a theory; (2) Congress did not intend to implicitly include common law doctrines applicable to trademark infringement because the ACPA created a new cause of action that is distinct from traditional trademark remedies; and (3) allowing suits against registrars for contributory cybersquatting would not advance the goals of the statute.

I. The Plain Text of the ACPA Does Not Provide a Cause of Action for Contributory Cybersquatting

....

The ACPA imposes civil liability for cybersquatting on persons that "register[], traffic[] in, or use[] a domain name" with the "bad faith intent to profit" from that protected mark. 15 U.S.C. § 1125(d)(1)(A). The plain language of the statute thus prohibits the act of cybersquatting, but limits when a person can be considered to be a cybersquatter. *Id.* The statute makes no express provision for secondary liability. *Id.* Extending liability to registrars or other third parties who are not cybersquatters, but whose actions may have the effect of aiding such cybersquatting, would expand the range of conduct prohibited by the statute from a bad faith intent to cybersquat on a trademark to the mere maintenance of a domain name by a registrar, with or without a bad faith intent to profit. This cuts against finding a cause of action for contributory cybersquatting. [Citation.]

Furthermore, "Congress knew how to impose [secondary] liability when it chose to do so." [Citation.] Congress chose not to impose secondary liability under the ACPA, despite the fact that the availability of such remedies under traditional trademark liability should have increased the salience of that issue. [Citations.]

Petronas argues that the liability limiting language in Section 1114(2)(D)(iii) indicates that Congress intended 15 U.S.C. § 1125(d)(1)(A) to create a cause of action for secondary liability. Section 1114(2)(D)(iii) provides that "[a] domain name registrar, a domain name registry, or other domain name registration authority shall not be liable for damages under this section for the registration or maintenance of a domain name for another absent a showing of bad faith intent to profit from such registration or maintenance of the domain name." By its terms, Section 1114(2)(D)(iii), applies only to "this section," meaning Section 1114. Section 1114, in turn, sets out remedies for the entire Lanham Act, including actions brought under

Section 1125(a), which indisputably includes a cause of action for contributory infringement. [Citation.] Thus, the limitations on secondary liability in Section 1114 are equally consistent with the existence or absence of a cause of action for contributory cybersquatting under Section 1125(d). [Citation.]

Furthermore, the legislative history of the ACPA establishes that Section 1114(2)(D)(iii) was intended to codify the protection that we granted registrars in *Lockheed Martin Corp. v. Network Solutions, Inc.*, 194 F.3d 980, 984–985 (9th Cir. 1999), which considered secondary liability of registrars for trademark infringement under 15 U.S.C. § 1125(a). S. Rep. 106-140 at 11 ("The bill, as amended, also promotes the continued ease and efficiency users of the current registration system enjoy by codifying current case law limiting the secondary liability of domain name registrars and registries for the act of registration of a domain name." (*citing, inter alia, Lockheed,* 141 F. Supp. 2d 648)). Section 1114(2)(D)(iii) thus does not suggest that Congress intended to include a cause of action for contributory cybersquatting in Section 1125(d).

II. The ACPA Created a New and Distinct Cause of Action

Petronas next argues that Congress incorporated the common law of trademark, including contributory infringement, into the ACPA. Petronas observes that a number of district courts have relied on this reasoning in finding a cause of action for contributory cybersquatting. See *Verizon Cal., Inc. v. Above.com Pty Ltd.*, 881 F. Supp. 2d 1173, 1176–79 (C.D. Cal. 2011); *Microsoft Corp. v. Shah*, No. 10-0653, 2011 U.S. Dist. LEXIS 2995, 2011 WL 108954, at *1–3 (W.D. Wash. Jan. 12, 2011); *Solid Host, NL v. Namecheap, Inc.*, 652 F. Supp. 2d 1092, 1111–12 (C.D. Cal. 2009); *Ford Motor Co. v. Greatdomains.com, Inc.*, 177 F. Supp. 2d 635, 646–47 (E.D. Mich. 2001). We are not persuaded by such reasoning.

"[W]hen Congress enacts a statute under which a person may sue and recover damages from a private defendant for the defendant's violation of some statutory norm, there is no general presumption that the plaintiff may also sue aiders and abettors." [Citation.] Contributory liability has, however, been applied to trademark infringement under the Lanham Act. [Citation.] Petronas argues that by legislating against this background, and by placing the ACPA within the Lanham Act, Congress intended to include within the ACPA a cause of action for contributory cybersquatting. [Citation.] We disagree.

Although there is no general presumption of secondary liability, [citation], courts can infer such a cause of action where circumstances suggest that Congress intended to incorporate common law principles into a statute. The circumstances surrounding the passage of the Lanham Act support such an inference, as has been recognized by the Supreme Court. [Citation.] The circumstances surrounding the enactment of the ACPA, however, do not support the inference that Congress intended to incorporate theories of secondary liability into that Act. Accordingly, we conclude that the ACPA did not incorporate principles of secondary liability.

Prior to the enactment of the Lanham Act, the Supreme Court incorporated a common law theory of contributory liability into the law of trademarks and unfair competition. [Citation.] The Lanham Act then codified the existing common law of trademarks. [Citations.] In light of the Lanham Act's codification of common law principles, including contributory liability, the Supreme Court concluded that a plaintiff could re-cover under the Act for contributory infringement of a trademark. [Citation.]

By contrast, the ACPA did not result from the codification of common law, much less common law that included a cause of action for secondary liability. Rather, the ACPA created a new statutory cause of action to address a new problem: cybersquatting. S. Rep. 106-140 at 7 (noting that "[c]urrent law does not expressly prohibit the act of cybersquatting").

Consistent with their distinct purposes, claims under traditional trademark law and the ACPA have distinct elements. Traditional trademark law only restricts the commercial use of another's protected mark in order to avoid consumer confusion as to the source of a particular product. [Citations.] Cybersquatting liability, however, does not require commercial use of a domain name involving a protected mark. [Citation.] Moreover, to succeed on a claim for cybersquatting, a mark holder must prove "bad faith" under a statutory nine factor test. 15 U.S.C. § 1125(d)(1)(B). No analogous requirement exists for traditional trademark claims. [Citations.]

These differences highlight the fact that the rights created in the ACPA are distinct from the rights contained in other sections of the Lanham Act, and do not stem from the common law of trademarks. Accordingly we decline to infer the existence of secondary liability into the ACPA based on common law principles. [Citation.]

III. Finding a Cause of Action for Contributory Cybersquatting would not Further the Goals of the Statute

Congress enacted the ACPA in 1999 in order to "protect consumers ... and to provide clarity in the law for trademark owners by prohibiting the bad-faith and abusive registration of distinctive marks...." S. Rep. No. 106-140 at 4. The ACPA is a "carefully and narrowly tailored" attempt to fix this specific problem. Id. at 12–13. To this end, the statute imposes a number of limitations on who can be liable for cybersquatting and in what circumstances, including a bad faith requirement, and a narrow definition of who "uses" a domain name. 15 U.S.C. §§ 1125(d)(1)(A)(i), 1125(d)(1)(B), 1125(d)(1)(D). Imposing secondary liability on domain name registrars would expand the scope of the Act and seriously undermine both these limiting provisions.

Recognizing this risk, some of the district courts that have recognized a cause of action for contributory liability have required that a plaintiff show "exceptional circumstances" in order to hold a registrar liable under that theory. *See Above.com Pty Ltd.*, 881 F. Supp. 2d at 1178; *Shah*, 2011 U.S. Dist. LEXIS 2995, 2011 WL 108954, at *2; Greatdomains.com, Inc., 177 F. Supp. 2d at 647. This "exceptional circumstances" test has no basis in either the Act, or in the common law of trademark. Rather than attempt to cabin a judicially discovered cause of action for contributory cybersquatting with a limitation created out of whole cloth, we simply decline to recognize such a cause of action in the first place.

Limiting claims under the Act to direct liability is also consistent with the ACPA's goal of ensuring that trademark holders can acquire and use domain names without having to pay ransom money to cybersquatters. Because direct cybersquatting requires subjective bad faith, focusing on direct liability also spares neutral third party service providers from having to divine the intent of their customers. In order for a service provider like GoDaddy, with clients holding over 50 million domain names, to avoid contributory liability, it would presumably have to analyze its customer's subjective intent with respect to each domain name, using the nine factor statutory test. 15 U.S.C. § 1125(d)(1)(B). Despite that nearly impossible task, service providers would then be forced to inject themselves into trademark and domain name disputes. Moreover, imposing contributory liability for cybersquatting would incentivize "false positives," in which the lawful use of a domain name is restricted by a risk-averse third party service provider that receives a seemingly valid take-down request from a trademark holder. Entities might then be able to assert effective control over domain names even when they could not successfully bring an ACPA action in court.

When actionable cybersquatting occurs, mark holders have sufficient remedies under the ACPA without turning to contributory liability. In addition to the provisions imposing civil liability on cybersquatters, 15 U.S.C. § 1125(d)(1)(A), the ACPA authorizes an in rem action against a domain name if the registrant is not available to be sued personally. 15 U.S.C. § 1125(d)(2)(A). Finally, trademark holders may still bring claims for traditional direct or contributory trademark infringement that arises from cybersquatting activities. 15 U.S.C. § 1125(d)(3).

Questions

1. Even if claims against cybersquatting are only statutory, why does it follow that courts should not apply common law-based claims for derivative liability to statutory claims for primarily liability?

2. The Ninth Circuit emphasizes Congress' concern to immunize domain name registrars from liability, "absent a showing of bad faith intent to profit from such registration or maintenance of the domain name." Could such a showing be made with respect to a registrar? If so, could there be a claim for secondary liability?

3. Domain name registrar GoDaddy allows domain name registrants who have not yet developed content for their domains to take advantage of its parking program. GoDaddy arranges with its ad partner to populate the domain with paid advertising, and splits the revenue with the domain name registrant. The Motion Picture Academy, owner of service mark registrations for OSCAR and ACADEMY AWARDS sued GoDaddy under the ACPA for registering multiple infringing domain names such as "2011oscars.com," "oscarlist.com," and "academyawardz.com," and entering those domain names into its parking program. GoDaddy argues that it does not register, traffic in or use the domain names within the meaning of the ACPA, and that it has shown no bad faith intent. How should the court rule? *See Acad. of Motion Picture Arts & Scis. v. GoDaddy.com, Inc.*, 2015 U.S. Dist. LEXIS 120871 (C.D. Cal. September 10, 2015).

4. eNom provides domain name registration services and offers customers the opportunity to bid on soon-to-expire domain names under a program it calls "Club Drop." Five days before a domain name registration is due to expire, eNom invites customers to bid on the opportunity to acquire it. eNom then uses proprietary technology to attempt to register the domain name as soon as it becomes available; if it is successful, it allows the winning bidder to register the domain in its own name for the bid amount. A sporting goods store carelessly allows its domain name registration to lapse. eNom registers the domain name under its Club Drop program and conveys it to an unrelated sporting goods store in a different region. The initial owner of the domain name registration sues eNom under the ACPA. eNom argues that it lacks "bad faith intent to profit" as a matter of law, since it merely registered the domain name on a customer's behalf. How should the court rule? *See Philbrick v. eNom, Inc.*, 593 F. Supp. 2d 352 (D.N.H. 2009).

4. § 43(d)(2) and *in rem* Jurisdiction

The ACPA also includes a section 43(d)(2), which permits an *in rem* civil action to obtain forfeiture or cancellation of an infringing domain name:

15 U.S.C. § 1125(d)(2) [Lanham Act § 43(d)(2)]

....

(d) ....

(2) ....

(A) The owner of a mark may file an in rem civil action against a domain name in the judicial district in which the domain name registrar, domain name registry, or other domain name authority that registered or assigned the domain name is located if—

(i) the domain name violates any right of the owner of a mark registered in the Patent and Trademark Office, or protected under subsection (a) or (c); and

(ii) the court find that the owner—

(I) is not able to obtain in personam jurisdiction over a person who would have been a defendant in a civil action under paragraph (1); or

(II) through due diligence was not able to find a person who would have been a defendant in a civil action under paragraph (1)....

....

(D) (i) The remedies in an in rem action under this paragraph shall be limited to a court order for the forfeiture or cancellation of the domain name or the transfer of the domain name to the owner of the mark....

....

(4) The in rem jurisdiction established under paragraph (2) shall be in addition to any other jurisdiction that otherwise exists, whether in rem or in personam.

In *Caesars World v. Caesars-Palace.Com*, 112 F. Supp. 2d 502 (E.D. Va. 2000), the District Court for the Eastern District of Virginia upheld the constitutionality of §43(d)(2)'s *in rem* provision against a due process challenge. In *Lucent Technologies v. Lucentsucks.Com*, 95 F. Supp. 2d 528 (E.D. Va. 2000), however, the court held that a plaintiff could invoke the *in rem* action only after a reasonable, good faith effort to locate and obtain personal jurisdiction over the registrant of a disputed domain name. The court dismissed Lucent's *in rem* action against the lucentsucks.com domain name, noting that plaintiff had failed to wait a reasonable time for the registrant to respond to its notice before filing an *in rem* action, and had continued to proceed with its *in rem* suit after it became aware of the registrant's current address. Where the identity and address of the registrant is known and *in personam* jurisdiction is possible, the court held, a §43(d)(2) *in rem* cause of action is not available. Perhaps as a result of the limitation of the *in rem* claim to registrants who are either unlocatable or unamenable to jurisdiction, there have been few *in rem* actions since the ACPA's enactment.

Harrods Limited v. Sixty Internet Domain Names, 302 F.3d 214 (4th Cir. 2002). The plaintiff, Harrods Limited ("Harrods UK"), owner of the well-known Harrods of London department store, held trademarks in the name "Harrods" in much of the world, including the United States, and had launched a website under the domain name harrods.com. The defendants were 60 Internet domain names registered by Harrods (Buenos Aires) Limited ("Harrods BA"). Harrods BA, once affiliated with Harrods UK, was by then a completely separate corporate entity that owned "Harrods" as a trademark in many South American countries. Harrods BA had registered a number of Harrods-related domain names under the.com, .net, and .org domains (such as harrodsbuenosaires.com, harrodsbuenosaires.net, and harrodsbuenosaires.org). Harrods UK sued the 60 Domain Names under 15 U.S.C. §1125(d)(2), the in rem provision of the ACPA), alleging that the Domain Names infringed and diluted its American "Harrods" trademark and that Harrods BA registered the Names in bad faith in violation of 15 U.S.C. §1125(d)(1).

The Fourth Circuit first found that the district court's exercise of in rem jurisdiction was not a violation of the Due Process clause due to the situs of the disputed property (the domain name registration) in Virginia. The Fourth Circuit next addressed whether §1125(d)(2) provided for in rem jurisdiction against domain names for traditional infringement and dilution claims under §§1114, 1125(a) & (c) as well as for claims of bad faith registration with the intent to profit under §1125(d)(1), or whether the in rem provision was limited to claims under §1125(d)(1):

> On its face, subsection (d)(2)(A)(i) provides an in rem action for the violation of "any right" of a trademark owner, not just rights provided by subsection (d)(1). Moreover, subsection (d)(2)(A)(i) authorizes in rem jurisdiction for marks "protected under subsection (a) or (c)," the very

subsections underlying two of the claims that were dismissed by the district court as outside the scope of subsection (d)(2). While subsection (d)(2)(A)(ii) provides that the in rem action is available only if the plaintiff is unable to find or obtain personal jurisdiction over the "person who would have been a defendant in a civil action under paragraph (1)," we believe this language is best understood as a shorthand reference to the current registrant of the domain name, who would be the defendant in any trademark action involving a domain name. Finally, the legislative history of the ACPA specifically discussing the in rem provision speaks in terms of domain names that violate "substantive Federal trademark law" or that are "infringing or diluting under the Trademark Act." Sen. Rep. No. 106-140, at 10–11. This reinforces the language of subsection (d)(2)(A)(i), which suggests that the in rem provision is not limited to bad faith claims under subsection (d)(1). Thus, we conclude that the best interpretation of § 1125(d)(2) is that the in rem provision not only covers bad faith claims under § 1125(d)(1), but also covers infringement claims under § 1114 and § 1125(a) and dilution claims under § 1125(c).

Questions

1. Judge Michael dismisses the Domain Names' due process challenge to § 43(d)(2)'s in rem provisions because of the presence of the disputed property in the state of Virginia. In what sense are the domain names located in Virginia?

2. The court concludes that the in rem jurisdiction in section 43(d) allows suits for substantive trademark violations as well as claims for bad faith registration. If a traditional *in rem* action merely quiets title in land, what is the basis for adding claims that do not go to the ownership of the disputed property? What remedies are available in an in rem action for trademark infringement or dilution?

3. The court also found it significant that section 43(d)(2) "does not create a claim for the owner of *any* mark," but only for owners of marks that are registered in the PTO or protected under section 43(a) or 43(c). What trademarks does that exclude?

Note: In Rem *Actions Regarding U.S. Registrations of Foreign-Held Domain Names Corresponding to Foreign Trademarks*

Just as a domain name registrant need not be a U.S. business or resident, so the plaintiffs in these proceedings may be foreign enterprises. Sometimes neither the plaintiff nor the registrant are U.S. businesses or residents. Because the *in rem* proceeding concerns a *res* (the registration) localized in the U.S., the nationality or residence of the parties should not matter. Nonetheless, the role of U.S. law in providing a special procedural mechanism and a substantive norm may seem problematic when the parties not only are from countries other than the U.S., but also are both from the same foreign country. In *Heathmount A.E. Corp. v. Technodome.Com*, 106 F. Supp. 2d 860 (E.D. Va. 2000), the defendant, a Canadian corporation, urged the court to decline jurisdiction when the plaintiff was also a Canadian corporation, and the witnesses and documents were likely to be located in Canada. The court nonetheless retained jurisdiction:

> [P]ublic factors bearing on the question lean toward retaining the matter in this District. A Canadian court would be less familiar with the provisions of the ACPA than is this Court. Even if it prevailed, Plaintiff might face difficulties enforcing the Canadian court's judgment in the United States, which would arguably undercut its U.S. trademark rights in its "technodome" mark. A trademark holder seeking to enforce its U.S.-registered marks against infringing domain name registrants should not be penalized in the exercise of those rights merely because the parties involved are not United States citizens.
>
> On a more basic level, Plaintiff may not be able to assert the same rights in Canada, which lacks a body of law equivalent to the ACPA and whose enforcement of its trademark laws cannot extend into the United States. Defendants suggest that Canadian intellectual property law, drawing upon recent English case law, might view the registration of a trademark-infringing domain name as an actionable trademark violation. This outcome is particularly likely, Defendants argue, in a case like the one at bar, involving both registration and use of the mark. However, Defendants' prediction of what the Canadian courts will do when presented with this issue is necessarily speculative and provides little support for the argument that Canada is a satisfactory alternative forum for this lawsuit.

Questions

1. The *Heathmount* plaintiff was clearly "forum shopping" for the E.D. Va., whose *in rem* jurisdiction permits it to adjudicate cybersquatting claims against a domain name registrant not subject to U.S. courts' *in personam* jurisdiction. But, if a Canadian court has jurisdiction over the parties, and can apply the ACPA, why should plaintiff's forum choice be respected? How persuasive are the reasons the E.D. Va. offers for rejecting the registrant's arguments that the matter should be heard by a Canadian court? Are there more persuasive reasons?

2. Would the availability of an international administrative dispute resolution proceeding that allowed trademark owners to challenge registration of domain names that resembled their marks change the calculus? Why or why not?

Personal Jurisdiction in Cybersquatting Cases

Bittorent Inc. v. Bittorrent Mktg GmbH, 2014 U.S. Dist. LEXIS 157593 (N.D. Cal. Nov. 5, 2014). The ACPA's provisions on *in rem* jurisdiction provide a response to one of the jurisdictional problems arising out of alleged cybersquatting activity, enabling actions against a multiplicity of registrations of related domain names. Suits against individual cybersquatters remain governed by Federal Rule of Civil Procedure 4, which in turn references state long arm statutes and constitutional norms of minimum contacts. The application of these norms was tested in this case, involving a claim against a German national whom Bittorrent Inc. alleged had registered the domain name bittorent.net to compete with Bittorrent Inc.'s products and services by capitalizing on misdirected users, who paid for services that they did not in fact receive.

The Court notes that cybersquatting, as is alleged here, has always been subject to a somewhat different personal jurisdiction analysis:

> Although jurisdiction questions in most ordinary domain name disputes are analyzed according to the three-part [Calder] test ... a special jurisprudence seems to have developed for cases involving so-called "cybersquatters" or "cyberpirates." In a substantial number of cases, these so-called "cyberpirates" or "cybersquatters" will purposely register the trademark of a well-known corporation as a domain name with the intention of later selling that domain name to the corporation for an extraordinary profit.... [C]ybersquatting cases have developed their own statutory and court-made rules.

4A Charles Alan Wright & Arthur R. Miller, Federal Practice & Procedure Civil § 1073.1 (Personal Jurisdiction and the Internet) (3d ed. 2002). As such, courts have routinely found the existence of specific personal jurisdiction where the defendant's alleged conduct amounts to a scheme targeted at a trademark owner designed to extort money from the mark owner for domain names that capitalize on typographical errors and user confusion. [Citations.] Such is the case here.

Taking allegations in the Complaint as true and drawing reasonable inferences in Plaintiff's favor, there is no question that Plaintiff has alleged that Defendant intentionally engaged in a scheme to infringe Plaintiff's famous mark and force Plaintiff to pay ransom for the Infringing Domain Names. Even when Defendant offered digital download products and services on the Infringing Domain Names, such offers were deceptive because paying customers would not actually receive the purchased services. Such conduct evinces an intent to intentionally diminish the value of Plaintiff's trademark through customer confusion and frustration and, in turn, force Plaintiff to eliminate such blemishes on its trademark by acquiring the Infringing Domain Names from Defendant. Through this scheme, Defendant's use of the Infringing Domain Names put Plaintiff's "name and reputation at [its] mercy," thereby causing injury to Plaintiff in California. *Panavision*, 141 F.3d at 1327.

....

Exercising specific personal jurisdiction over a cybersquatter who, as here, knowingly registers confusingly similar domain names in a scheme to extort money from a trademark owner does not give rise to de facto universal jurisdiction. [Citation.] The cybersquatter is subject to suit in the forum where the trademark owner is located and experiences the brunt of the injury to its trademark. In this case, that would be California, where Plaintiff is incorporated and maintains its principal place of business. Because Plaintiff was the target of Defendant's scheme to extract money in exchange

> for domain names that incorporate Plaintiff's trademark, Defendant's contact with California is "not based on the 'random, fortuitous, or attenuated' contacts [it] makes by interacting with other persons affiliated with the State," but rather by its extortion scheme expressly aimed at Plaintiff in Plaintiff's principal place of business. [Citation.]
>
> Based on the foregoing, the Court concludes that Defendant has "purposefully directed" its conduct at California.

The court further found that Bittorent Inc.'s claims arose out of Bittorent GmbH's forum-related activities, and that exercising jurisdiction over Bittorent GmbH was reasonable "because Defendant interjected itself into California by targeting a California company through its elaborate cybersquatting and typosquatting scheme."

C. ICANN and the Uniform Trademark Domain Name Dispute Resolution Policy

By the mid-1990s, the explosive growth of the Internet had persuaded everyone that the extant method of administering the domain name system needed to change. Stakeholders began discussing alternative regimes, focusing heavily on proposals to add more generic top level domains and to introduce competition into the business of registering them. Meanwhile, intellectual property owners complained loudly that the domain name system needed to be more responsive to their concerns.

In 1997, the United States Government put together an interagency working group to formulate official U.S. policy on privatizing the Domain Name System. In June 1998, the Commerce Department released a proposal to turn over U.S. government involvement in the DNS system to a new non-profit corporation. The new corporation would decide whether to open new generic Top Level Domains [gTLDs], and how to do so. It would open up the business of registering gTLDs to multiple registrars, which could compete with Network Solutions, but it would make whatever changes it made gradually, with the first priority being stability of the Internet. The U.S. plan resorted to vague language on most of the controversial topics; resolving most disputes by delegating them to the yet-to-be-devised new corporation. Internet stakeholders had tentatively coalesced around a different plan to turn over oversight of the DNS to an international organization based in Europe, but most of the interested organizations agreed that they could accept the proposed U.S. framework, and began to try to exert their influence on the details. In response to intellectual property owner complaints, the U.S. government proposal had called upon the World Intellectual Property Organization (WIPO) to conduct a study of the intellectual property issues posed by the current domain name system, and to make recommendations for reform.

The idea of a new private non-profit corporation to administer the domain name system evolved into ICANN (the name is an acronym for Internet Corporation for Assigned Names and Numbers). The United States Department of Commerce signed an agreement with ICANN in the fall of 1998, which envisioned a gradual transition from U.S. government control of the DNS to autonomous ICANN control over a period of several years. The newly appointed ICANN interim Board met, elected officers, and began to try to figure out what it was the new organization was supposed to do, where it was going to get its funding and how it was supposed to behave.

Fifteen years later, Network Solution, now absorbed by Verisign, continues to control the .com and .net registries, but ICANN has accredited other registrars to compete with it in registering domain names. After a byzantine consideration process, ICANN between 1999 and 2010 also introduced 14 new gTLDs: .aero, .asia, .biz, .cat, .coop, .info, .jobs, .mobi, .museum, .name, .post, .pro, .tel, .travel.

Following a brief flirtation with allowing individual Internet users to become members of ICANN and elect the members of its Board of Directors, ICANN reorganized itself to eliminate Board elections. The Department of Commerce (DOC) had subjected ICANN to only minimal oversight, repeatedly extending its memorandum of understanding authorizing ICANN to continue to perform the functions it performs, without completely giving up its supervisory role. Meanwhile, the United Nations Working Group on Internet Governance urged a greater role for the United Nations in overseeing the DNS. In response, on September 30, 2009,

> the DOC allowed one of its main agreements with ICANN to lapse, thus surrendering the most formal and visible legal control the DOC had over ICANN. In so doing, the DOC gave up its reversionary interests in contracts ICANN had with third parties—the DOC's right to require ICANN to assign those contracts to someone else were the DOC ever to lose faith in ICANN. In exchange, ICANN promised to remain located in the U.S., thus remaining subject to U.S. jurisdiction. ICANN also committed itself to a lengthy round of accountability exercises, although whether these will amount to anything substantive is not obvious. Furthermore, ICANN again expanded the role of its Government Advisory Committee ("GAC"), a committee of government representatives open to every nation, which has a direct channel to the ICANN Board as well some agenda-setting powers.
>
> If these changes are less legally earthshaking than the parties might have sought to make them seem, their political import is nonetheless real. By allowing its most visible agreement with ICANN to expire, the DOC made a tangible—if still incomplete—response to growing international pressure for the U.S. to abandon the control over ICANN that other nations feared gave the U.S. a dominant role over the DNS. ICANN enjoys significantly more independence after the Affirmation than it had before. And the GAC, the only direct means by which non-U.S. governments can influence ICANN, emerges from the Affirmation stronger as well.

Michael Froomkin, *Almost Free: An Analysis of ICANN's Affirmation of Commitments*, 9 J. Telecom. & High Tech. L. 187, 188–89 (2011).

ICANN's most notable achievement so far is probably its imposition of a mandatory trademark dispute resolution policy on all domain name registrants. In April of 1999, the World Intellectual Property Association issued its report recommending changes to the domain name system to reduce conflicts between the domain name system and trademark rights. It suggested that domain name registrars collect and make publicly available reliable contact information for domain name registrants. It also suggested that ICANN adopt a mandatory administrative dispute resolution process to handle cases of alleged "cybersquatting" expeditiously without litigation. It recommended that ICANN introduce a procedure that allowed the owners of famous marks to prevent the registration of their marks in some or all top level domains by anyone other than the mark owner. Finally, it suggested caution in the introduction of new generic top level domains.

ICANN acted quickly to adopt a mandatory administrative dispute resolution procedure in the autumn of 1999.

Uniform Domain Name Dispute Resolution Policy

(As Approved by ICANN on October 24, 1999),
URL: http://www.icann.org/udrp/udrp-policy-24oct99.htm

1. *Purpose.* This Uniform Domain Name Dispute Resolution Policy (the "Policy") has been adopted by the Internet Corporation for Assigned Names and Numbers ("ICANN"), is incorporated by reference into your Registration Agreement, and sets forth the terms and conditions in connection with a dispute between you and any party other than us (the registrar) over the registration and use of an Internet domain name registered by you. Proceedings under Paragraph 4 of this Policy will be conducted according to the Rules for Uniform Domain Name Dispute Resolution Policy (the "Rules of Procedure"), which are available at <http://www.icann.org/udrp-rules-24oct99.htm>, and the selected administrative-dispute-resolution service provider's supplemental rules.

2. *Your Representations.* By applying to register a domain name, or by asking us to maintain or renew a domain name registration, you hereby represent and warrant to us that (a) the statements that you made in your Registration Agreement are complete and accurate; (b) to your knowledge, the registration of the domain name will not infringe upon or otherwise violate the rights of any third party; (c) you are not registering the domain name for an unlawful purpose; and (d) you will not knowingly use the domain name in violation of any applicable laws or regulations. It is your responsibility to determine whether your domain name registration infringes or violates someone else's rights.

3. *Cancellations, Transfers, and Changes.* We will cancel, transfer or otherwise make changes to domain name registrations under the following circumstances:

a. subject to the provisions of Paragraph 8, our receipt of written or appropriate electronic instructions from you or your authorized agent to take such action;

b. our receipt of an order from a court or arbitral tribunal, in each case of competent jurisdiction, requiring such action; and/or

c. our receipt of a decision of an Administrative Panel requiring such action in any administrative proceeding to which you were a party and which was conducted under this Policy or a later version of this Policy adopted by ICANN. (See Paragraph 4(i) and (k), below.)

We may also cancel, transfer or otherwise make changes to a domain name registration in accordance with the terms of your Registration Agreement or other legal requirements.

4. *Mandatory Administrative Proceeding.* This Paragraph sets forth the type of disputes for which you are required to submit to a mandatory administrative proceeding. These proceedings will be conducted before one of the administrative-dispute-resolution service providers listed at www.icann.org/udrp/approved-providers.htm (each, a "Provider").

a. *Applicable Disputes.* You are required to submit to a mandatory administrative proceeding in the event that a third party (a "complainant") asserts to the applicable Provider, in compliance with the Rules of Procedure, that

(i) your domain name is identical or confusingly similar to a trademark or service mark in which the complainant has rights; and

(ii) you have no rights or legitimate interests in respect of the domain name; and

(iii) your domain name has been registered and is being used in bad faith.

In the administrative proceeding, the complainant must prove that each of these three elements are present.

b. *Evidence of Registration and Use in Bad Faith.* For the purposes of Paragraph 4(a)(iii), the following circumstances, in particular but without limitation, if found by the Panel to be present, shall be evidence of the registration and use of a domain name in bad faith:

(i) circumstances indicating that you have registered or you have acquired the domain name primarily for the purpose of selling, renting, or otherwise transferring the domain name registration to the complainant who is the owner of the trademark or service mark or to a competitor of that complainant, for valuable consideration in excess of your documented out-of-pocket costs directly related to the domain name; or

(ii) you have registered the domain name in order to prevent the owner of the trademark or service mark from reflecting the mark in a corresponding domain name, provided that you have engaged in a pattern of such conduct; or

(iii) you have registered the domain name primarily for the purpose of disrupting the business of a competitor; or

(iv) by using the domain name, you have intentionally attempted to attract, for commercial gain, Internet users to your web site or other on-line location, by creating a likelihood of confusion with the complainant's mark as to the source, sponsorship, affiliation, or endorsement of your web site or location or of a product or service on your web site or location.

c. *How to Demonstrate Your Rights to and Legitimate Interests in the Domain Name in Responding to a Complaint.* When you receive a complaint, you should refer to Paragraph 5 of the Rules of Procedure in determining how your response should be prepared. Any of the following circumstances, in particular but without limitation, if found by the Panel to be proved based on its evaluation of all evidence presented, shall demonstrate your rights or legitimate interests to the domain name for purposes of Paragraph 4(a)(ii):

(i) before any notice to you of the dispute, your use of, or demonstrable preparations to use, the domain name or a name corresponding to the domain name in connection with a bona fide offering of goods or services; or

(ii) you (as an individual, business, or other organization) have been commonly known by the domain name, even if you have acquired no trademark or service mark rights; or

(iii) you are making a legitimate noncommercial or fair use of the domain name, without intent for commercial gain to misleadingly divert consumers or to tarnish the trademark or service mark at issue.

d. *Selection of Provider.* The complainant shall select the Provider from among those approved by ICANN by submitting the complaint to that Provider. The selected Provider will administer the proceeding, except in cases of consolidation as described in Paragraph 4(f).

e. *Initiation of Proceeding and Process and Appointment of Administrative Panel.* The Rules of Procedure state the process for initiating and conducting a proceeding and for appointing the panel that will decide the dispute (the "Administrative Panel").

f. *Consolidation.* In the event of multiple disputes between you and a complainant, either you or the complainant may petition to consolidate the disputes before a single Administrative Panel. This petition shall be made to the first Administrative Panel appointed to hear a pending dispute between the parties. This Administrative Panel may consolidate before it any or all such disputes in its sole discretion, provided that the disputes being consolidated are governed by this Policy or a later version of this Policy adopted by ICANN.

g. *Fees.* All fees charged by a Provider in connection with any dispute before an Administrative Panel pursuant to this Policy shall be paid by the complainant, except in cases where you elect to expand the Administrative Panel from one to three panelists as provided in Paragraph 5(b)(iv) of the Rules of Procedure, in which case all fees will be split evenly by you and the complainant.

h. *Our Involvement in Administrative Proceedings.* We do not, and will not, participate in the administration or conduct of any proceeding before an

Administrative Panel. In addition, we will not be liable as a result of any decisions rendered by the Administrative Panel.

i. *Remedies.* The remedies available to a complainant pursuant to any proceeding before an Administrative Panel shall be limited to requiring the cancellation of your domain name or the transfer of your domain name registration to the complainant.

j. *Notification and Publication.* The Provider shall notify us of any decision made by an Administrative Panel with respect to a domain name you have registered with us. All decisions under this Policy will be published in full over the Internet, except when an Administrative Panel determines in an exceptional case to redact portions of its decision.

k. *Availability of Court Proceedings.* The mandatory administrative proceeding requirements set forth in Paragraph 4 shall not prevent either you or the complainant from submitting the dispute to a court of competent jurisdiction for independent resolution before such mandatory administrative proceeding is commenced or after such proceeding is concluded. If an Administrative Panel decides that your domain name registration should be canceled or transferred, we will wait ten (10) business days (as observed in the location of our principal office) after we are informed by the applicable Provider of the Administrative Panel's decision before implementing that decision. We will then implement the decision unless we have received from you during that ten (10) business day period official documentation (such as a copy of a complaint, file-stamped by the clerk of the court) that you have commenced a lawsuit against the complainant in a jurisdiction to which the complainant has submitted under Paragraph 3(b)(xiii) of the Rules of Procedure. (In general, that jurisdiction is either the location of our principal office or of your address as shown in our Whois database. See Paragraphs 1 and 3(b)(xiii) of the Rules of Procedure for details.) If we receive such documentation within the ten (10) business day period, we will not implement the Administrative Panel's decision, and we will take no further action, until we receive (i) evidence satisfactory to us of a resolution between the parties; (ii) evidence satisfactory to us that your lawsuit has been dismissed or withdrawn; or (iii) a copy of an order from such court dismissing your lawsuit or ordering that you do not have the right to continue to use your domain name.

5. *All Other Disputes and Litigation.* All other disputes between you and any party other than us regarding your domain name registration that are not brought pursuant to the mandatory administrative proceeding provisions of Paragraph 4 shall be resolved between you and such other party through any court, arbitration or other proceeding that may be available.

Comparison of ACPA and UDRP Actions*

	ACPA	UDRP
Jurisdiction	Trademark owner suing under the ACPA selects the forum (subject to the usual rules of personal jurisdiction). The ACPA also provides for *in rem* proceedings in the forum of the registry, registrar, or other domain name authority that registered or assigned the domain name.	Complainant selects the dispute resolution provider from a list of ICANN accredited providers. (All registrants consent to UDRP resolution by any of ICANN's accredited providers when they register their domain names.)
Elements of Claim	Bad faith intent to profit from the mark; Registration, use or trafficking in a domain name identical or confusingly similar to the mark, or dilutive of a mark that was famous at the time of registration of the domain name.	Bad faith registration and use of a domain name identical or confusingly similar to mark in which complainant has rights and registrant has neither rights nor legitimate interests.
Bad Faith	Non-exclusive list of factors	Non-exclusive lists of bad faith and legitimate interests factors
Adjudicator	Tried before generalist federal district judges not specialized in trademark law.	ICANN-accredited arbitration organizations; arbitrators are private attorneys or law professors typically expert in trademark law.
Cost and Timing	Amount of time that a federal suit will take depends on whether the registrant appears and contests the complaint. As with other federal lawsuits, if the defendant does not respond at all, the plaintiff can seek entry of default judgment, which expedites the case and reduces the cost.	Quick and inexpensive compared to the ACPA. UDRP proceedings, which include only a complaint and answer with no additional discovery or motion practice, are much less expensive than filing a federal lawsuit. A domain name case filed with the WIPO Center normally concludes within two months, involving one round of limited pleadings and using mostly online procedures. Default judgments are also common in UDRP proceedings.
Remedies	Injunctive relief, election of actual or statutory damages, the possibility of attorney's fees, and forfeiture, cancellation, or transfer of the domain name.	UDRP is binding, but does not preclude subsequent resort to courts: parties involved can commence litigation under ACPA either before or after the proceeding. The only remedy available under the UDRP is the cancellation or transfer of the domain name.

* Comparisons adapted from Tenesa S. Scaturro, *The Anticybersquatting Consumer Protection Act and the Uniform Domain Name Dispute Resolution Policy the First Decade: Looking Back and Adapting Forward*, 11 NEV. L.J. 877 (2011).

....

Questions

1. How different is the UDRP from section 43(d) as a substantive matter? For example, § 43(d)(1)(A)(ii) appears to apply to anyone who registers, traffics in, *or* uses a domain name with bad faith intent to profit, while section 4(a)(iii) of the UDRP seems to require both bad faith registration *and* bad faith use. Is that difference likely to be determinative of the results in actual cases? What other provisions seem to be the principal substantive differences? In what sorts of cases is a court adjudicating a dispute under section 43(d) likely to reach a different result from an arbitrator adjudicating the same dispute under the UDRP?

2. To what degree should UDRP panels follow the law enunciated in decisions of United States federal or other national courts? In *Twitter, Inc. v. Geigo, Inc.*, WIPO Arbitration and Mediation Center Case No. D2011-1210 (Nov. 2, 2011), Twitter brought a complaint against a Panamanian domain name broker and parking business that had registered the domain name <twiter.com>, and used it for a website posting links to cell phone companies and chat room services. The domain name was first registered in 2004; Twitter did not begin its business until two years later. Geigo argued, therefore, that the initial registration could not have been in bad faith, and that, under *Gopets v. Hise*, later re-registrations were not unlawful. The panel found the reasoning of the 9th Circuit in *Gopets* to be unpersuasive:

> A UDRP panel owes great deference to the national courts. Their rulings may well be part of "applicable law" that a panel must consider (Rules, paragraph 15(a)), may become directly relevant in relation to mutual jurisdiction in the event of a court challenge (Policy, paragraph 4(k)), and are forged upon a record developed through full adversary proceedings. Nevertheless there are occasions when a Policy panel may decline to follow a court's interpretation....
>
> In any case, the language of paragraph 4 of the Policy differs markedly from that in the ACPA. Each subparagraph of paragraph 4(a) speaks expressly of "you"—the registrant. ACPA, in contrast, refers to a more general "any person." ACPA does not contain any counterpart to the affirmative representation the Policy (paragraph 2; emphasis supplied) requires from a registrant: "By applying to register a domain name, or by asking us to maintain or renew a domain name registration, you hereby represent and warrant to us that ... (b) to your knowledge, the registration of the domain name will not infringe upon or otherwise violate the rights of any third party". To this Panel, these differences are further reason to distinguish a single court case from longstanding Policy precedent.

3. In *Referee Enterprises v. Planet Ref*, National Arbitration Forum No. FA0004000 094707 (June 26, 2000), a UDRP panel dismissed a complaint filed by the owner of the registered mark REFEREE for magazines against the registrant of ereferee.com, noting that "Referee is generic for an official who serves as an umpire officiating at sports events and is a weak mark," and "Respondent has a legitimate interest in the Domain name in view of the sports background of the principal of Respondent and there is no bad faith use." Complainant then filed a Lanham Act suit in federal district court. Judge Clevert concluded that "the plaintiff is likely to establish that it is threatened with dilution, trademark infringement, unfair competition and false designation of origin," and enjoined the registrant from:

> using the mark REFEREE or any other mark confusingly similar to Referee Enterprise's REFEREE trademark, either alone or in combination with other words, specifically including, but not limited to: eReferee, ereferee.com, ereferee.net, ereferee.org, refereecamp.com, refereecamps .com, refereeclinics.com, refereeforum.com, refereeinsurance.com, refree mail.com and refereeresume.com; as a mark, domain name or highlighted term or in any way other than in common textual reference, any other mark or second-level domain name including the term "referee" in any form....

Referee Enterprises v. Planet Ref., 2001 U.S. Dist. LEXIS 9303 (E.D. Wi. Jan. 24, 2001). What arguments should the defendant make on appeal? How should REFEREE magazine respond?

ICANN's Uniform Dispute Resolution Policy took effect on January 1, 2000. By the following year, ICANN had approved four different administrative dispute resolution providers. Between January 1 and April 19, 2001, trademark owners filed 3499 proceedings under the UDRP, involving 6203 different domain names. By April 19, 2001, arbitrators had already resolved 2639 of those disputes. Arbitrators had ordered the transfer or cancellation of 3734 domain names in 2101 disputes. In 519 decisions, involving 658 domain names, arbitrators decided that the domain name registrants were entitled to retain their domain names under the policy. In statistics available in July 2016, the WIPO administrative dispute resolution provider, one of the largest and first ADR providers, had 44,589 UDRP proceedings filed before it involving .com domain names, constituting over 75% of its docket. *See* <http://www.wipo.int/amc/en/domains/statistics/gtlds_yr.jsp?year=>.

The total number of cases decided by WIPO through July 15, 2016 was 26,865, *see* <http://www.wipo.int/amc/en/domains/statistics/outcome.jsp>, of which 22,937 (or 86.17%) resulted in transfers of the domain name, and 32309 (or 12.13%) denials of the complaint. *See* <http://www.wipo.int/amc/en/domains/statistics/decision_rate.jsp?year=>. Administrative dispute panel decisions are posted on the Internet at the websites of the different approved dispute resolution providers. For example, WIPO decisions are indexed at <http://www.wipo.int/amc/en/domains/search/legalindex/>. The most notable advantage of the UDRP is that it provides a resolution that is both cheap and quick in comparison with litigation. However, the UDRP has come under attack for bias in favor of trademark-owner complainants over domain name registrant respondents and the absence of adequate due process protections. *See* Michael Geist, *Fair.com? An Examination of the Allegations of Systemic Unfairness in the ICANN UDRP*, 27 BROOK. J. INT'L LAW 903–38 (2002).

1. Bad Faith

Dial-A-Mattress Operating Corp. v. Christopher E. Moakely

WIPO Arbitration and Mediation Center Case No. D2005-0471
(July 1, 2005)

TOWNS, PANELIST:

1. The Parties

The Complainant is Dial-A-Mattress Operating Corp., Long Island City, New York, United States of America, represented by Sarah E. Greenless, Esq., Dial-A-Mattress Operating Corp., United States of America.

The Respondent is Christopher E. Moakely, Coplay, Pennsylvania, United States of America.

2. The Domain Name and Registrar

The disputed domain name <1-800mattress.com> is registered with Melbourne IT trading as Internet Name Worldwide.

....

4. Factual Background

The Complainant is a retailer in the field of mattresses and bedding products. Best known since 1988, as a telemarketer selling mattresses using the toll free number 1-800-MATTRESS, the Complainant also operates retail stores and sells mattresses and bedding products over the internet at "www.mattress.com". The Complainant has used the trade name "1-800-MATTRESS" since 1994, in connection with these activities.

The Complainant is the owner of the service marks 1-800-MATTRES, AND LEAVE OFF THE LAST S THAT'S THE S FOR SAVINGS, and 1-800-MATTRESS. The first mark was registered with the United States Patent and Trademark Office (PTO) on December 22, 1990, and the second mark obtained PTO registration on January 4, 2005. The PTO registration for 1-800-MATTRESS reflects that the mark was first used in commerce on December 31, 1995.

The Respondent, a former employee of the Complainant, registered the disputed domain name <1-800mattress.com> on February 7, 2000. The disputed domain name currently resolves to temporary website apparently maintained not by the Respondent but by the web host, and there is no indication in the record that the Respondent has ever made any commercial or noncommercial use of the domain name. On or about March 17, 2005, the Complainant contacted the Respondent, requesting that the Respondent cease and desist using the disputed domain name and transfer the domain name to the Complainant. The Respondent chose not to honor this request.

5. Parties' Contentions

A. Complainant

The Complainant contends that the disputed domain name <1-800mattress.com> is confusingly similar to its federally registered service marks, 1-800-MATTRES,

AND LEAVE OFF THE LAST S THAT'S THE S FOR SAVINGS, and 1-800-MATTRESS. The Complainant also maintains that the Respondent has no rights or legitimate interests with respect to the disputed domain name, because (1) the Complainant has not authorized the Respondent to use the domain name, (2) the Respondent has never been commonly known by the domain name, and (3) there is no evidence that the Respondent has used or made demonstrable preparations to use the domain name in connection with a *bona fide* offering of goods or services or for any legitimate noncommercial purpose. Further, the Complainant avers that the Respondent, a former employee of the Complainant, registered and is using the disputed domain name in bad faith. Accordingly, the Complainant seeks the transfer of the disputed domain name.

B. Respondent

The Respondent did not reply to the Complainant's contentions.

6. Discussion and Findings

A. Scope of the Policy

The Policy is addressed to resolving disputes concerning allegations of abusive domain name registration and use. *Milwaukee Electric Tool Corporation v. Bay Verte Machinery, Inc. d/b/a The Power Tool Store*, WIPO Case No. D2002-0774. Accordingly, the jurisdiction of this Panel is limited to providing a remedy in cases of "the abusive registration of domain names", also known as "cybersquatting". *Weber-Stephen Products Co. v. Armitage Hardware*, WIPO Case No. D2000-0187. *See* Report of the WIPO Internet Domain Name Process, Paragraphs 169 & 170. Paragraph 15(a) of the Rules provides that the Panel shall decide a complaint on the basis of statements and documents submitted and in accordance with the Policy, the Rules and any other rules or principles of law that the Panel deems applicable.

Paragraph 4(a) of the Policy requires that the Complainant prove each of the following three elements to obtain a decision that a domain name should be either cancelled or transferred:

> (i) The domain name registered by the Respondent is identical or confusingly similar to a trademark or service mark in which the Complainant has rights; and
>
> (ii) The Respondent has no rights or legitimate interests with respect to the domain name; and
>
> (iii) The domain name has been registered and is being used in bad faith.

Cancellation or transfer of the domain name are the sole remedies provided to the Complainant under the Policy, as set forth in Paragraph 4(i).

Paragraph 4(b) sets forth four situations under which the registration and use of a domain name is deemed to be in bad faith, but does not limit a finding of bad faith to only these situations.

Paragraph 4(c) in turn identifies three means through which a respondent may establish rights or legitimate interests in the domain name. Although the complainant bears the ultimate burden of establishing all three elements of Paragraph 4(a), a number of panels have concluded that Paragraph 4(c) shifts the burden to the respondent to come forward with evidence of a right or legitimate interest in the domain name, once the complainant has made a prima facie showing. *See, e.g., Document Technologies, Inc. v. International Electronic Communications Inc.*, WIPO Case No. D2000-0270.

B. Identical or Confusingly Similar

The Panel finds that the disputed domain name <1-800mattress.com> is confusingly similar to the Complainant's registered service marks 1-800-MATTRES, AND LEAVE OFF THE LAST S THAT'S THE S FOR SAVINGS, and 1-800-MATTRESS. For purposes of Paragraph 4(a)(i), a domain name incorporating a complainant's mark generally will be considered confusingly similar unless accompanied by other terms that effectively disclaim any association. *See Lockheed Martin Corporation. v. Dan Parisi*, WIPO Case No. D2000-1015; The *Salvation Army v. Info-Bahn, Inc.*, WIPO Case No. D2001-0463.1 The disputed domain name contains no additional terms that would distinguish it from the Complainant's service marks, and for this reason the Panel concludes that persons viewing the disputed domain name likely would think that the domain name is in some way connected to the Complainant. This is known as "initial interest confusion", which occurs when a member of the public sees the disputed domain name and thinks that it may lead to a website associated with the Complainant. *See Covance, Inc. and Covance Laboratories Ltd. v. The Covance Campaign*, WIPO Case No. D2004-0206.

The Complainant has established rights in the two service marks through registration and use. The Panel notes that the Complainant did not obtain registration of the 1-800-MATTRESS mark was until January 4, 2005, some five years after the Respondent registered the disputed domain name, but the federal registration indicates that the mark had been used in commerce since December 1995. Even had there been no use of this mark prior to the registration of the disputed domain name, a majority of Panels have held for purposes of Paragraph 4(a)(i) that a complainant can have rights in a trademark or service mark corresponding to the domain name even where those rights first arise after the registration of the domain name. *See, e.g., Digital Vision, Ltd. v. Advanced Chemill Systems*, WIPO Case No. D2001-0827; *Kangwon Land, Inc. v. Bong Woo Chun (K.W.L. Inc)*, WIPO Case No. D2003-0320; *AB Svenska Spel v. Andrey Zacharov*, WIPO Case No. D2003-0527; *Iogen Corporation v. Iogen*, WIPO Case No. D2003-0544; *Madrid 2012, S.A. v. Scott Martin-MadridMan Websites*, WIPO Case No. D2003-0598. *See PC Mall, Inc. v. Pygmy Computer Systems, Inc.*, WIPO Case No. D2004-0437.

C. Rights or Legitimate Interests

The Complainant has not authorized the Respondent to use its service marks or to register domain names reflecting these marks. There is no evidence that the Respondent has never been commonly known by the domain name. The record is not indicative of the Respondent's use of, or demonstrable preparations to use, the disputed domain name in connection with any offering of goods or services. Nor is there any indication that the Respondent is making any noncommercial use of the domain name.

Given the foregoing, the Panel finds that the Complainant has made a *prima facie* showing under Paragraph 4(a)(ii). The circumstances set forth in the Complaint are sufficiently evocative of cybersquatting to require the Respondent to come forward with evidence under Paragraph 4(c) of the Policy demonstrating rights to or legitimate interests in the disputed domain name. *See, e.g., Document Technologies, Inc. v. International Electronic Communications Inc.*, WIPO Case No. D2000-0270; *Compagnie de Saint Gobain v. Com-Union Corp.*, WIPO Case No. D2000-0020.

Pursuant to Paragraph 4(c) of the Policy, the Respondent may establish rights to or legitimate interests in the disputed domain name by demonstrating any of the following:

> (i) before any notice to it of the dispute, the respondent's use of, or demonstrable preparations to use, the domain name or a name corresponding to the domain name in connection with a *bona fide* offering of goods or services; or
>
> (ii) the respondent has been commonly known by the domain name, even if it has acquired no trademark or service mark rights; or
>
> (iii) the respondent is making a legitimate noncommercial or fair use of the domain name, without intent for commercial gain, to misleadingly divert consumers or to tarnish the trademark or service mark at issue.

The Respondent has not submitted a formal response to the Complaint, and in the absence of any such submission this Panel may accept all reasonable inferences and allegations included in the Complaint as true. *See, Talk City, Inc. v. Robertson*, WIPO Case No. D2000-0009.3 Nevertheless, the ultimate burden of proof on the legitimacy issue remains with the Complainant. *Document Technologies, Inc. v. International Electronic Communications Inc.*, WIPO Case No. D2000-0270. Accordingly, the Panel considers it appropriate to examine the record in its entirety to determine whether any evidence exists to support a claim by Respondent of rights or legitimate interests in the disputed domain name.

The record as a whole discloses nothing even remotely suggesting that the Respondent has been commonly known by the disputed domain name, nor any indication of any legitimate noncommercial or fair use of the domain name. The domain name currently resolves to a "temporary" website, apparently maintained by the website host to advertise its services, but there is no indication that the Respondent is using or has made demonstrable preparations to use the disputed domain name in connection with any offering of goods or services. In fact, the record reveals no plausible basis upon which the Respondent could claim any rights or legitimate interests in the disputed domain name. Accordingly, the Panel finds that the Complainant has met its burden under Paragraph 4(a)(ii).

D. Registered and Used in Bad Faith

Paragraph 4(b) of the Policy states that any of the following circumstances, in particular but without limitation, shall be considered evidence of the registration or use of a domain name in bad faith:

(i) circumstances indicating that the Respondent registered or acquired the domain name primarily for the purpose of selling, renting, or otherwise transferring the domain name registration to the Complainant (the owner of the trademark or service mark) or to a competitor of that Complainant, for valuable consideration in excess of documented out-of-pocket costs directly related to the domain name;

(ii) circumstances indicating that the Respondent registered the domain name in order to prevent the owner of the trademark or service mark from reflecting the mark in a corresponding domain name, provided that the Respondent has engaged in a pattern of such conduct;

(iii) circumstances indicating that the Respondent registered the domain name primarily for the purpose of disrupting the business of a competitor; or

(iv) circumstances indicating that the Respondent intentionally is using the domain name in an attempt to attract, for commercial gain, internet users to its website or other on-line location, by creating a likelihood of confusion with the Complainant's mark as to the source, sponsorship, affiliation, or endorsement of the Respondent's website or location or of a product or service on its website or location.

The overriding objective of the Policy is to prevent abusive domain name registration and use for the benefit of legitimate trademark owners, and the Panel notes that the examples of bad faith registration and use set forth in Paragraph 4(b) are not meant to be exhaustive of all circumstances from which such bad faith may be found. *See*, *Telstra Corporation Limited v. Nuclear Marshmallows*, WIPO Case No. D2000-0003. Under *Telstra*, passive holding of a domain name can be considered as bad faith where it is not possible to conceive of any plausible actual or contemplated active use of the disputed domain name that would not be illegitimate. *See, also Salomon Smith Barney, Inc. v. Salomon Internet Services*, WIPO Case No. D2000-0668.

The *Telstra* requirements are met where "the Complainant proves that the registration was undertaken in bad faith *and* that the circumstances of the case are such that Respondent is continuing to act in bad faith." *Telstra Corporation Limited v. Nuclear Marshmallows*, WIPO Case No. D2000-0003 (emphasis in original). A finding that the domain name "has been registered in bad faith" can be reached under *Telstra* where the totality of the circumstances persuades the panel that the primary motive for the respondent's acquisition of the disputed domain name was cybersquatting.

This Panel is persuaded from the circumstances of this case that the Respondent's primary motive in registering the disputed domain name was cybersquatting. The Respondent was employed by the Complainant during 1994 and 1995, and his wife also worked for the Complainant until her job position was eliminated in 2003. Clearly, the Respondent would have been aware of the Complainant's service marks at the time he registered the disputed domain name in February 2000. Moreover, the Respondent has failed to make any active use of the domain name, and the

Panel cannot conceive of any plausible actual or contemplated active use for which the Respondent could have registered the domain name that "would not be illegitimate, such as by being a passing off, an infringement of consumer protection legislation, or an infringement of the Complainant's rights under trademark law." *Telstra Corporation Limited v. Nuclear Marshmallows*, WIPO Case No. D2000-0003. The Panel therefore concludes that the Respondent's registration of the disputed domain name "was undertaken in bad faith *and* that the circumstances of the case are such that Respondent is continuing to act in bad faith." *Id.* (emphasis in original). Accordingly, the Panel finds that the Complainant has met its burden under Paragraph 4(a)(iii).

7. Decision

For all the foregoing reasons, in accordance with Paragraphs 4(i) of the Policy and 15 of the Rules, the Panel orders that the domain name <1-800mattress.com> be transferred to the Complainant.

Question

Jennifer Lopez holds federal service mark and trademark registrations for JENNIFER LOPEZ for entertainment services and associated merchandise, and has licensed an official website at www.jenniferlopez.com. Jeremiah Tieman has registered the domain names <jenniferlopez.net> and <jenniferlopez.org>, and uses the domain names for fan sites celebrating Ms Lopez. Tieman's sites contain paid advertising supplied by the Google AdSense program, as well as other links to commercial websites. The ads and paid links generate significant revenue. Lopez sent Tieman a cease and desist letter; Tieman's lawyer responded with a letter offering to sell Lopez the domain names for $80,000. Lopez argues that Tieman is exploiting her name to attract Internet users to his site in order to generate pay-per-click advertising revenues. Tieman insists that his fan site makes legitimate noncommercial use of Lopez's name, and that any ad revenue is incidental. Has the domain name been registered and used in bad faith? *See Jennifer Lopez Foundation v. Tieman*, WIPO Arbitration and Mediation Center Case No. D2009-0057 (March 24, 2009).

Deutsche Welle v. Diamondware Limited, WIPO Arbitation & Mediation Center Case No. D 2000-1202 (2001). Deutsche Welle, a German television broadcaster that used the registered mark "DW" brought a complaint over the domain name "dw.com." The domain had been registered by a U.S. software firm, which had done business under the "DW" acronym since 1994. Diamondware had registered the domain name in December of 1994 and operated an active business website at <www.dw.com>. In July, 2000, Deutsche Welle wrote to Diamondware and demanded the transfer of the domain name. Diamondware responded "Thank you for your interest in our domain name, dw.com. We are not currently offering this property for sale on the open market, however it has recently been attracting enquiries. Therefore, we would consider an offer above $3,750,000 (three million, seven hundred fifty thousand US Dollars) from an accredited buyer...." Deutsche Welle filed a UDRP complaint.

The three-member panel concluded that the dw.com domain name was identical to Deutsche Welle's registered trademark. It found, however, that Diamondware had provided ample evidence of its legitimate interest in the domain name. It also declined to find Diamondware's offer to consider selling the domain name for $3,750,000 to be evidence of bad faith:

> The Panel does not interpret the Policy to mean that a mere offer for sale of a domain name for a large sum of money is, of itself, proof of cybersquatting. It may, in certain circumstances, provide some evidence, but it is not conclusive evidence. Indeed, some of the largest sums of money paid for domain names have been for generic names and it is clear to anyone who follows reports of domain name sales that two-letter.com registrations are extremely prized. In any event, in this case the Respondent, with a substantial underlying business interest in the Domain Name, had every reason to demand a substantial sum of money for transfer of the Domain Name.
>
> The Panel finds that the Complainant has not met the burden of proving bad faith.

Finally, a majority of the panel upheld Diamondware's claim that Deutsche Welle's complaint amounted to "reverse domain name hijacking" under the UDRP:

> The Policy is only designed to deal with a very narrow category of case, namely cybersquatting. It was never intended to be a substitute for trade mark infringement litigation. Manifestly, … this was never a case of cybersquatting. The Policy is clear. To succeed in the Complaint, the Complainant has to prove, at the very least, that the Domain Name was registered in bad faith. When the Complainant conducted its Whois search and found that the Domain Name registration dated back nearly 6 years, it was alerted to the fact that registration of the Domain Name was most unlikely to have been undertaken "primarily" for any bad faith purpose directed at the Complainant. The Complainant has not produced one shred of evidence to suggest why the Respondent, a company in the United States, should have been aware of the existence of the Complainant, a German broadcasting service, back in 1994 when it registered the Domain Name. When the Complainant visited the Respondent's website (its letter of July 13, 2000 makes it clear that it was aware of the website) any doubts it may have had were removed. The Domain Name connects to an active website through which the Respondent conducts a bona fide business and in relation to which the acronym "DW" is apt. In such circumstances, the price the Respondent put on the Domain Name in the year 2000 was completely irrelevant to its motives when registering the Domain Name in 1994. None of this is addressed in the Complainant's response. In the view of [the majority], the Complainant's behaviour, which has wrongfully resulted in the Respondent having to incur what must be substantial legal fees, should be condemned as an abuse of the administrative procedure.

Plan.Net concept Spezialagentur für interactive Kommunikation GmbH v. Yikilmaz, WIPO Arbitration and Mediation Center Case No. D2006-0082 (March 24, 2006). The German Plan.Net, owner of both EU and German trademark registrations for PLAN.NET, brought a UDRP complaint against Turkish businessman Murat Yikilmaz over the registration of the domain "plan.net." Yikilmaz had registered a number of common English words as domain names, including <intelligence.net>, <dirtbike.com>, <airplane.com>, <matchmakers.com>, <graph.com>. The panel found that the domain name was confusingly similar to Plan Net's registered mark, but that the complainant had failed to prove either that Yikilmaz had no legitimate interests in the domain name or that he had registered and was using the domain name in bad faith:

> The Respondent makes no bones about registering domain names using generic terms and using them to generate commercial revenues, e.g., through "pay per click" advertising. The Respondent argues that, where a domain name consists of a generic term, the first person who registers it in good faith has rights or a legitimate interest in it. In this connection, the Respondent specifically denies any prior knowledge of the Complainant or its trademark....
>
> While a respondent's denial of knowledge of trademark rights often lacks credibility where the trademark is extremely well known or there are other compelling factors to the contrary, that is not this situation. The domain name here consists of a very plain English word plus a gTLD and there is nothing particularly about the Respondent's website that suggests any intention to pass off on the Complainant's rights or business. This is not a case where the Respondent's motives can be impugned solely on the papers.
>
> In these circumstances, the Panel is far from satisfied that a *prima facie* case of the absence of rights or legitimate interests has been made out. Even if it were, the Respondent has sufficiently explained its position. Accordingly, the Panel finds that the Complainant has not established the second requirement under the Policy.
>
> ....
>
> The Respondent, as already noted, freely admits he registers generic terms for the purposes of revenue generation. The problem for the Complainant is that such conduct breaches the Policy only if it is in bad faith and, in the absence of bad faith, the Respondent's conduct is perfectly legitimate....
>
> Here, there is no evidence of bad faith. The Respondent has plausibly in the circumstances of this case and the limited nature of these proceedings as proceedings on the papers denied any foreknowledge of the Complainant's trademark; the domain name consists of a plain English term and the Respondent has not sought to pass off on the Complainant's trademark or business.
>
> Accordingly, the Panel would find that this third requirement under the Policy is also not satisfied.

The panel refused to find reverse domain name hijacking:

> The mere failure of the Complaint is not sufficient to found a finding under paragraph 15(e) of the Rules; such a finding is intended only for the worst cases where there is bad faith such as malice or dishonesty or some other abuse of process.... It can be argued that the Complainant ought to have recognised the very speculative nature of the Complaint in the absence of any attempt to pass off on the Complainant's business or otherwise to hold the Complainant to ransom.... While the case is perhaps approaching the borderline, however, the Panel ultimately is not prepared to make such a finding in this case. Here, the Complainant does in fact have a registered Community Trademark. It is entitled to seek to protect that.

2. Nominative Use

The Orange Bowl Committee, Inc. v. Front and Center Tickets, Inc/Front and Center Entertainment

WIPO Arbitration and Mediation Center Case No. D2004-0947
(January 20, 2005)

PARTRIDGE, PRESIDING PANELIST:

1. The Parties

The Complainant is The Orange Bowl Committee, Inc, Miami, Florida, of United States of America, represented by Hunton & Williams, United States of America.

The Respondent is Front and Center Tickets, Inc/ Front and Center Entertainment, Fort Lauderdale, Florida, of United States of America, represented by Mark Halpern.

2. The Domain Names and Registrar

The disputed domain names <orangebowl.net> and <orangebowltickets.net> ("Domain Names") are registered with Dotster, Inc.

....

4. Factual Background

Complainant has used the ORANGE BOWL mark since 1935, for one of the nation's best-known college football tournaments. It has also expanded use of the mark to a variety of other goods and services, including a tennis tournament, a basketball championship, a golf tournament and various types of merchandise.

The ORANGE BOWL tournament has been the subject of extensive advertising and media attention and is watched annually by millions of spectators. The television rights alone to broadcast the ORANGE BOWL game involve fees in excess of $100,000,000.00.

Complainant sells millions of tickets and hundreds of thousands of goods under the ORANGE BOWL mark, some of which are sold via Complainant's websites at "www.orangebowl.com" and "www.orangebowl.org".

Complainant obtained a federal trademark registration for the mark ORANGE BOWL on December 12, 1995, but inadvertently allowed that registration to lapse on September 14, 2002, due an administrative error. Complainant is the co-owner federal trademark registrations for FEDEX ORANGE BOWL (Reg. No. 2,129,760; 2,037,172) and reapplied for federal registration of the mark ORANGE BOWL on December 10, 2002. Respondent admits that ORANGE BOWL is a famous name.

Respondent is engaged in the online resale of tickets for sporting and entertainment events. The domain name <orangebowltickets.net> was registered on April 14, 1999. The domain name <orangebowl.net> was registered on June 24, 1999.

....

At the time the Complainant in this action was filed, Respondent used the respective Domain Names for a site that offered tickets to various events, including college bowl game tickets and National Football League tickets, as well as "all concert tickets—all sporting event tickets—all theater tickets." The site included a disclaimer stating: "The National Collegiate Athletic Association (NCAA) has neither licensed or endorsed Front and Center Entertainment Group to sell goods and services in conjunction with NCAA and regular season or championship games." There was no disclaimer relating to Complainant.

The domain name <orangebowl.net> is no longer active, and Respondent has agreed to transfer it to Complainant.

The domain name <orangebowltickets.net> now leads to a modified site that prominently bears the heading "Orange Bowl National Championship Tickets." There is also a new disclaimer stating:

> "Orangebowltickets.net is a private ticket broker and the FedEx Orange Bowl has neither licensed nor endorsed Front and Center Entertainment Group to sell goods and services in conjunction with The FedEx Orange Bowl and regular season or championship games."

The page continues to offer tickets for other events, including other college bowl games, NFL games and the Superbowl, with several links from the site leading to Respondent's "frontrow.com" website where it offers tickets to other events, including tickets to Las Vegas Shows, Broadway Shows, NASCAR races, and concerts by performers such as Celine Dion, Elton John and Cher.

....

6. Discussion and Findings

The Respondent states that it has no argument regarding the domain name <orangebowl.net> and agrees to transfer the name to Complainant. Therefore, the entirety of the Panel finds in favor of Complainant on that domain name.

With respect to the domain name <orangebowltickets.net>, Paragraph 4(a) of the Policy requires the Complainant to establish each of the following elements:

> (i) that the domain name registered by the Respondent is identical or confusingly similar to a trademark or service mark in which the Complainant has rights;

(ii) that the Respondent has no rights or legitimate interest in respect of the domain name; and

(iii) that the domain name has been registered and is being used in bad faith.

The majority of the Panel finds as follows on these elements.

A. Identical or Confusingly Similar

Respondent does not dispute that Complainant owns trademark rights in the mark ORANGE BOWL. Respondent further concedes that the ORANGE BOWL name is famous.

The issue is whether the addition of "tickets" is sufficient to avoid a finding of confusingly similarity. In reaching a conclusion under this element of the Policy, prior decisions primarily base the test on a comparison of the mark and the domain name on their own, without regard to the content of the site. *See AT&T Corp. v. Amjad Kausar*, WIPO Case No. D2003-0327.

It is generally well-established the addition of merely descriptive or non-distinctive matter to another's mark is not sufficient to avoid confusion. *See NCAA v. Randy Pitkin*, WIPO Case No. D2000-0903. Thus, the addition of ".com" is held to be insufficient to avoid confusion. *Id.*

Similarly, in the other Panel decisions considering the issue, including decisions involving this Respondent, the addition of "tickets" to the name of an event has uniformly been held to be insufficient to avoid confusion. *See National Collegiate Athletic Association and March Madness Athletic Association, LLC v. Mark Helpern and Front & Center Entertainment*, WIPO Case No. D2000-0700 (transferring domain names including <finalfourtickets.net> to the complainant); *HBP, Inc. v. Front and Center Tickets, Inc.*, WIPO Case No. D2002-0802 (transferring the domain name <daytona500tickets.net> to the complainant); *ISL Worldwide and The Federal Internationale de Football Association v. Western States Ticket Service*, WIPO Case No. D2001-0070 (transferring <fifatickets.com>); *The Professional Golfers' Association of America v. 24/7 Ticket Service*, WIPO Case No. D2002-0258 (transferring <pgachampiontickets.com>); *NCAA v. Randy Pitkin*, WIPO Case No. D2000-0903 (finding in favor of complainant on this issue, but ruling in favor of respondent on other grounds); *Southwest Airlines Co. v. Patrick Orly*, WIPO Case No. D2003-0761 (transferring <southwestairlinestickets.com>).

Similarly, the Panel finds that Respondent's addition of "tickets" is not sufficient to avoid confusion since it is a generic or merely descriptive term for the goods offered by Complainant under the ORANGE BOWL mark. Accordingly, we conclude that the remaining domain name at issue is confusingly similar to a mark in which Complainant has rights under Paragraph 4(a)(i) of the Policy.

B. Rights or Legitimate Interests

Complainant contends that Respondent has no rights or legitimate interest in the Domain Name. The record shows that Respondent has no relationship with or authorization from Complainant for the use of the ORANGE BOWL mark. Further, it appears that Respondent is known as Front & Center Entertainment, not the name ORANGEBOWLTICKETS.NET.

Respondent contends that it is using the domain name for a bona fide offering of ORANGE BOWL tickets. Indeed, the record shows that Respondent sells ORANGE BOWL tickets, along with tickets for a wide range of other events. However, whether or not this use is a bona fide use depends on whether or not Respondent's use of the ORANGE BOWL is legitimate, non-infringing use. Otherwise, a respondent could rely on an intentional infringement to demonstrate a legitimate interest. *See Madonna Ciccone, p/k/a Madonna v. Dan Parisi and "Madonna.com"*, WIPO Case No. D2000-0847 (holding that infringing use of <madonna.com> to sell services did not create legitimate interest).

Respondent acknowledges that it is using Complainant's trademark in a domain name to promote its commercial ticket brokering services. Thus, our inquiry focuses on whether that use is permitted or not.

....

We conclude that the Respondent's use of Complainant's mark in Respondent's domain name fails to meet the test for fair use because the ORANGE BOWL mark is used in Respondent's domain name not merely to describe, but also as an attention-getting device to attract Internet users to Respondent's site to sell other products, and because the domain name is used to sell products that it does not describe (e.g., Broadway show tickets, Las Vegas tickets, NFL tickets and tickets for competing college bowl events). By using the mark in the domain name, Respondent is using Complainant's mark more prominently than is necessary merely to describe its services. Moreover, the Complainant's mark is used in a way that triggers initial interest confusion regarding the relationship with Complainant in a way that is not adequately dispelled, for reasons more fully discussed below.

....

Accordingly, for the reasons discussed above, we conclude that Respondent's use of Complainant's ORANGE BOWL mark in a domain name used in connection with the resale of tickets not only to the ORANGE BOWL game but also for tickets to a variety of unrelated and competing events is not fair use under the Policy. We further conclude, therefore, that Respondent lacks any right or legitimate interest in the use of ORANGE BOWL in its domain name and find in Complainant's favor on Paragraph 4(a)(ii) of the Policy.

C. Registered and Used in Bad Faith

The Policy lists several nonexclusive criteria to show bad faith registration and use of a domain name. Paragraph 4(b)(iv) indicates that bad faith use and registration may be found when the Respondent is intentionally attempting to attract, for commercial gain, Internet users to its website, by creating a likelihood of confusion with the complainant's mark.

Respondent concedes that it intentionally registered and is using Complainant's mark to attract Internet users to its website. It does this for commercial gain. We believe

Respondent does so by creating a likelihood of confusion with and by trading on Complainant's mark. Persons initially encountering Respondent's domain name are likely to be confused as to the source, sponsorship, affiliation or endorsement of the domain name due to the use of the famous ORANGE BOWL mark. They may thus be drawn into the site trusting that they may obtain tickets from an authorized source.

Respondent is using Complainant's well known mark as a principal means (i.e., via the domain name) to advertise and sell products of third parties. A disclaimer may or may not be sufficient to dispel confusion as to the source of products at the "point of sale" (i.e. on Respondent's website). However, at this point Respondent has already misused Complainant's mark to bring consumers into its shop. Once in the shop, consumers are offered competitors' products. In the words of the Seventh Circuit, this is "plain misdescription, in fact false advertising" (*Ty Inc. v. Perryman*, No. 02-1771, (7th Cir.), decided October 4, 2002). The panel majority does not consider that Respondent's disclaimer is adequate to cure this exercise of bad faith use of Complainant's famous and distinctive mark.

Even assuming that a disclaimer might be effective to remedy initial interest confusion in a way that would remedy the initial problematic use, Respondent's disclaimer does not dispel the initial interest confusion caused by the domain name itself and is inadequate to avoid likelihood of confusion at the site. Prior to this action, Respondent's website featured a disclaimer of affiliation with the NCAA that did not mention Complainant or the ORANGE BOWL mark. This was obviously inadequate to dispel confusion about the relationship of Respondent and its site with Complainant. Subsequent to the filing of this action, Respondent has modified its site and disclaimer.

The new disclaimer is also problematic. It states that "the FedEx Orange Bowl has neither licensed or endorsed Front and Center Entertainment Group to sell goods and services in conjunction with the FedEx Orange Bowl." The disclaimer is confusing in that it is limited the sale of "goods and services" in conjunction with the event and fails to address Respondent's relationship to Complainant with respect to the sale of "tickets." A person reading and understanding the disclaimer is not clearly informed whether or not Respondent as "a private ticket broker" is authorized by Complainant to resell ORANGE BOWL tickets.

We acknowledge that Respondent in part uses the domain name to resell ORANGE BOWL tickets, and in that limited sense persons are accurately informed about some of Respondent's products. However, they are not adequately informed about the relationship of Complainant to Respondent's site and tickets, and may incorrectly conclude Respondent's conduct, including pricing and sale of tickets to other events, is endorsed by Complainant, when in fact that is not the case.

In sum, as a result of Respondent's use of the famous and distinctive ORANGE BOWL mark in its domain name, consumers are likely to be brought to Respondent's website mistakenly believing it is authorized, "official" or endorsed by Complainant. Respondent is thereupon offering to sell tickets to events which compete with that of Complainant. This is a bad faith use of Complainant's mark. Once at the website, consumers are likely to continue to believe mistakenly that Complainant has authorized or endorsed Respondent's use of the ORANGE BOWL mark in connection with the resale of tickets to the ORANGE BOWL game and for other events.

Therefore, we conclude that Complainant has established bad faith registration and use under Paragraph 4(b)(iv) of the Policy.

7. Decision

For all the foregoing reasons, in accordance with Paragraphs 4(i) of the Policy and 15 of the Rules, we order that the domain name <orangebowl.net> and <orangebowltickets.net> be transferred to the Complainant.

Smith, Panelist, Dissenting

I believe that the Panel should rule for the Respondent for the reasons enunciated in the prior decision of the WIPO panel in *NCAA v. Randy Pitkin* WIPO Case No. D2000-0903.

In this case the portion of the domain name that is at issue is also the name of an event, which cannot otherwise easily be otherwise described, coupled with the word "tickets," where the website is being used for the purpose of advertising the sale of tickets to the event. It is my belief that the use of such a domain name including, as it does, the word "tickets" is not cybersquatting under the rules governing the Uniform Dispute Resolution Policy.

While the Internet domain name using only the trademark name of the event might be cybersquatting, and thus I agree with the award of the Internet domain name <orangebowl.net> to Complainant, a concession which apparently Respondent makes in its Reply Brief, without admission, I do not believe that this applies to the use of the name of the actual event coupled with the generic word "ticket."

When the trademark is also the name of an event, such as the Orange Bowl, use of the name of the event is not always a trademark use, but may be a nominative fair use, where the words "Orange Bowl" although they be a trademark, are being used for the name of the event. It is difficult to identify the event, particularly this one, since it is one of several "bowl" games, and cannot be identified by its date, which varies from year to year, and this year, for some reason, is on a Tuesday!

I submit that the Orange Bowl event is even harder to identify, without using the words which also are a trademark, then even the Super Bowl, since various words preceding the word Bowl are used to distinguish this game from others on nearby dates, which mark also apparently indicates a major product of the Florida location in which this particular bowl game is played. It cannot be distinguished by the identification of the teams, since USC, which often commands a seat at the Rose Bowl, this year is in the Orange Bowl.

To the extent that the Orange Bowl is the name of a venue, *i.e.*, the particular coliseum or stadium where the Orange Bowl game is played, then it is also the name of venue for which the ticket will provide a seat license for the holder to sit in, and likewise the identification of this venue, together with the generic word "tickets" where the sale of tickets for this event in this location is being held, is also not, in my view, an unfair use.

It is my belief therefore that it is not bad faith to register the domain name which is also the "name of the game," together with the generic word "tickets "in this circumstance. Respondent has also placed a prominent disclaimer of sponsorship or association with the Orange Bowl on the face of its website, and understands the need to avoid a likelihood of confusion or mistake, if such exists. It may well be that selling a plethora of tickets to the named event at much higher prices then are normally garnered for this game, will also help avoid any likelihood of confusion or mistake in the use of the Internet domain name <orangebowltickets.com>.

Finally, I take note of the decision of the United States Supreme Court in *KP Permanent Make Up v. Lasting Impressions*, ___ U.S. ___, No. 03-409 decided December 8, 2004 S.C. (December 2004), where the United States Supreme Court, in the jurisdiction where both respondent and complainant reside, and the jurisdiction where the tickets and event were sold and is held, determined that where a trademark is being used by a defendant fairly to describe, in this case, the event and/or the event tickets, then the possible existence of even actual confusion does not provide a basis for the finding of trademark infringement and unfair competition under United States law. The United States Supreme Court, specifically rejected the view of the United States Court of Appeals for the Ninth Circuit which had held that the existence of confusion might trump infringement, and/or that there would be a burden on one party or another to prove the existence of, or absence of, confusion, when a mark is being used fairly and descriptively.

The panel majority attempts to distinguish this case as one where the famous mark is being used by another "to attract Internet users to a website offering products in competition with the trademark holder's product." I do not believe this to be the case, since the tickets being offered are the trademark holder's product, and are to attend the trademark holder's product, its Orange Bowl games.

Finally, I note that the new phenomenon of corporate sponsorship has made even the trademark use of the Orange Bowl trademark, less likely to cause confusion, since it is now the, presumably "FedEx" or "Federal Express" "brand" Orange Bowl game, stadium, venue, and/or ticket therefor.

Questions

1. You represent Fiber Shield Ltd., a Canadian company that has not registered its corporate name as a trademark. When your client tried to register fibershield.com as a domain name, it discovered that fibershield.com was unavailable, and had been registered by Fiber-Shield Industries of New York. Your client therefore registered the domain name fibershield.net. Last week, it received a letter from Fiber-Shield industries attaching a copy of a U.S. Trademark registration for the mark "FIBER-SHIELD", and demanding that it surrender the domain name fibershield.net immediately. The letter insists that because your client knew of the prior registration of fibershield.com before it registered fibershield.net, it registered fibershield.net in

bad faith. What result under the UDRP? Under section 43(d)? *See Fiber-Shield Industries v. Fiber Shield (Toronto) Ltd*, National Arbitration Forum Case No. FA0001000092054 (Feb. 29, 2000).

2. CTA Computers has operated a computer resale business on the Internet at www.buypc.com for the past four years, and uses "BuyPC.com" as a common law service mark. Last year, CTA failed to pay the fees due for renewing the domain name, and its domain name registration lapsed. Recently, a domain name speculator registered buypc.com and offered it for sale at its website. CTA wishes to regain the buypc.com domain name without paying the domain name speculator's price. Is it likely to succeed in a dispute under the UDRP? Under § 43(d)? *See Cedar Trade Associates, Inc. v. Ricks*, Nat'l Arbitration Forum Case No. FA0002000093633 (Feb. 25, 2000).

3. Seth Sanders, a long time *Star Wars* fan, has registered the domain name obiwankenobi.com and operates an unauthorized *Star Wars* fan website at www.obiwankenobi.com, with special attention to the Obi-Wan Kenobi character from the original and most recent *Star Wars* movies. Lucasfilm, the producer of the *Star Wars* movies and the owner of seven registered trademarks for OBI-WAN KENOBI sent Mr. Sanders a cease-and-desist letter. Enraged that Lucasfilm would so mistreat a longstanding fan, Sanders redirected his obiwankenobi.com site to a randomly selected pornographic web business. Lucasfilm has now filed a UDRP complaint. What result should the panel reach? *Cf. Telaxis Communications Corp. v. Minkle*, WIPO Arbitration and Mediation Center Case No. D2000-0005 (March 5, 2000). Should a court deciding the dispute under § 43(d) reach a different result? Why or why not?

4. In *Google, Inc. v. Gillespie*, http://www.adrforum.com/domaindecisions/1434643.htm (NAF 2012), Google, Inc., succeeded in its UDRP action to cancel over 100 domain names incorporating the term "google." (A later stage of the controversy, in which Gillespie alleged that "google" had become generic for internet searching, appeared *supra* Chapter 5[A][1]. *See Elliot v. Google, Inc.*, 45 F. Supp. 3d 1156 (D. Az. 2014).) Should a domain name registrant's assertion that a trademark incorporated into a domain name has become generic figure in UDRP determinations? If so, how?

3. Gripe Sites

Zillow, Inc. v. Chris Storseth/Chris L Storseth, National Arbitraton Forum, Claim Number: FA1409001578264 (October 3, 2014), http://www.adrforum.com/domaindecisions/1578264.htm. Respondent Storseth registered 26 domain names incorporating the Zillow trademark. Disputed domain names included <zillowadvice.com>, <zillowinc.com>, <zillowinc.net>, <zillowleases.com>, <zillowlocal.com>, <zillowrents.com>, <zillowhomedesign.com>, <zillowrentalpro.com>, and <zillowhomerentals.com>. Storseth claimed shelter under UDRP 4(a)(ii), asserting rights and legitimate interests in the disputed domain names, on the ground that each website, albeit not itself a "gripe site," linked to a gripe site, <aclueforyou.com>, airing legitimate grievances against the Zillow real estate services. The panel rejected the defense:

The Panel finds that the submissions advanced by Respondent do not give rise to a right or legitimate interest in any of the disputed domain names. That is so essentially for two reasons.

First, the free speech defence that Respondent relies on could not on any interpretation of the general principle involved attract the benefit of that defence. None of the disputed domain names could ever form the basis of a claim to free speech as none of them suggest that they are devoted to free speech or criticism or have been composed in such a way as to indicate that they deal with or contain criticism and all of them simply adopt the name and trademark of Complainant, in many cases adding generic and other expressions such as "homerentals" and "premieragent" which give the false impression that they are Complainant's domain names dealing with Complainant's own business, which clearly they are not. If anything, the composition of the domain names underlines and emphasises the suggestion that they are Complainant's own official domain names, which they are not and that they will lead to a website dealing with Complainant's own business. For instance the domain name <**zillowinc.com**>, can mean only one thing, that it is a domain name of the incorporated Zillow company; and the domain name <**zillowhomerentals.com**> can mean only one thing, that it is a domain name of the Zillow company whose website will deal with Zillow's home rental business. All of the implications in the domain names are false and are really misleading assertions that the domain names are Complainant's domain names, the websites of which will speak for Complainant. *See Philip Morris USA Inc. v. DAVID DELMAN*, FA 155882 (Nat. Arb. Forum Apr. 29, 2014); *Philip Morris USA Inc. v. DAVID DELMAN / DAVID@DELMAN.TV*, FA 155881 (Nat. Arb. Forum Apr. 29, 2014); *Philip Morris USA Inc. v. Lori Wagner*, FA 1534894 (Nat. Arb. Forum Jan. 29, 2014). The Panel in this regard agrees with the remarks of the panelist in those cases when he said:

> "Respondent's free speech protections do not come into play with respect to the content of the Internet domain name itself. Free speech is only found to extend to the content of a website. Respondent cannot defend its use of the domain name by claiming that it has freedom of speech rights in the use of another party's trademarks in Internet domain names. Respondent ... may not be defended by any claim that using a confusingly similar domain name is protected by free speech rights. *See Watson Pharm., Inc. v. WhoisGuard*, FA 588321 (Nat. Arb. Forum Dec. 19, 2005) ("Even if the goal of providing a free speech forum for criticizing Complainant is commendable, that goal cannot be reached by usurping Complainant's marks and posing as Complainant.").

That is an apt description of what has happened in the present case, as Respondent has created domain names that usurp Complainant's marks, are confusingly similar to those marks and are the means of Respondent posing as Complainant. Accordingly, on the facts of the present case, the Panel finds that the disputed domain names, adopting and incorporating one or other of Complainant's trademarks as they do, cannot attract the benefit of free speech protection and are not protectable under Policy ¶ 4(a)(ii).

Secondly, even if the disputed domain names attracted any such protection, that protection would clearly be negated in the present case by the content of the website to which they lead. It has often been said that if a respondent establishes that a domain name is being used to support a genuine criticism site, known more popularly as a gripe site, it may be able to show that it has a right or legitimate interest in the domain name or may also be able to rebut an allegation of bad faith as in *Sutherland Institute v. Continuative LLC*, WIPO Case No. D2009-0693. Likewise, if a respondent establishes a genuine fan site or tribute site it may also be able to show a right or legitimate interest. That principle is often said in American cases to flow from the First Amendment to the United States Constitution and has been applied in several UDRP cases and by this Panelist. Freedom of speech is a valuable and important principle and when it is pleaded, as Respondent has done, it should be carefully considered, as the Panel has done in this case. However, an essential part of the principle is that the website in question must be a genuine gripe site, devoted solely to the subject under complaint and must not be used for commercial, financial or indeed any other purpose than promoting the issue which is the subject of the criticism. The Panel had occasion to consider this issue in *Ginn Real Estate Company LLC v. Hilton Wiener*, Nat. Arb.Forum, 1211342 (Aug. 20, 2008), a case that is not dissimilar to the present case and in which the Respondent used the domain name <ginnlawsuit.com> to resolve to a website where he engaged in trenchant criticism of the Complainant real estate developer. On that occasion, the Panel cited remarks in *Asset Loan Co. Pty Ltd v. Rogers*, D2006-0300 (WIPO May 2, 2006) that: "[w]hat is clear, however, from all of the discussion on this issue is that a respondent must not be seen to be using the criticism site for commercial gain. If that is really what the respondent is doing, the conduct is contrary to the plain words of paragraph 4(c)(iii) of the Policy and hence it cannot give rise to a legitimate interest." In the *Ginn Real Estate Case* the respondent had used the website in part to promote himself and the conclusion was reached that:

> "Accordingly, the website, at least in the past, has been used not solely as a criticism or 'gripe' site, but as a site to promote the Respondent's commercial and financial interests. It is not really too fine a point to say that at least one of the purposes of the website has been to solicit work for the Respondent."

Those remarks are equally applicable in the present case where Respondent has used the website to which the domain names resolve for the same purpose as in the *Ginn Real Estate Case,* namely to promote himself and to solicit business. Accordingly, the website cannot be relied on to excuse the unauthorised use by Respondent of Complainant's trademarks.

The website at <aclueforyou.com> carries criticism of Complainant's alleged business activities, detailed criticism which is expressed in graphic language and criticism which is repeated and elaborated on in both the Response and the additional submission. However, the content of the website goes well beyond that. On its home page is states that Respondent is a broker and realtor broker by using the words: "Chris Storseth Broker / Realtor MT FL" and contains a link to a segment of the website titled: "About Chris Storseth." When the internet user goes to that segment, the heading is seen to be "Chris Storseth, Realtor, Broker, Land Developer, Web Developer" with a description of Respondent's experience and success as a "Guru of Real Estate" and a link to a local newspaper describing him in that manner and also noting his success in several ventures and the fact that he runs a rental business called Queen City Property Management. One of the statements on Respondent's website is "Chris will not let you down, and exceeds expectations." This is a clear promotion of Respondent's business and a solicitation for business. The website also contains a blog which itself carries links to various commercial enterprises, one of which uses Complainant's Z trademark and advertises houses and apartments for rent. It also promotes Respondent as an experienced broker and as "Listing Agent, Consulting, Commercial R.E., Property Management." The website also carries a form for contacting Respondent which shows clearly that Respondent wants people to contact him if they wish to use his business services. This and other content is purely commercial as are many of the numerous links on the site and in the blog and are designed to promote Respondent and solicit business for him. This material would be legitimate advertising if it were carried by legitimate means, but what is fatal to Respondent's defence in the present case is that he uses Complainant's trademarks to promote himself and his various businesses and to solicit business. All of this is done under the guise of conducting an alleged gripe site which in the present case is a transparently false suggestion.

Questions

1. How would this dispute have been decided under the ACPA?

2. The Panelist cited prior panel decisions applying the UDRP; do these have precedential effect? What purpose does consulting prior panel decisions serve?

3. Wal-Mart is a well-known chain of discount stores. Harvey registers walmartsucks.com, and offers to sell it to Wal-Mart for 5 million dollars. Wal-Mart declines. Harvey then uses the domain name to operate a website, which solicits and posts criticism of Wal-Mart from disgruntled employees and dissatisfied customers. Wal-Mart files a complaint under the UDRP. What result? *See Wal-Mart Stores Inc. v. walmartcanadasucks.com*, WIPO Arbitation & Mediation Center Case No. D2000-1104 (Nov. 23, 2000); *Wal-Mart Stores, Inc. v. Walsucks*, WIPO Arbitation & Mediation Center Case No. D2000-0477 (July 20, 2000).

Since ICANN's UDRP took effect on January 1, 2000, dispute resolution providers have decided more than 50,000 disputes. The dispute resolution service provided by the World Intellectual Property Organization, WIPO, has by far the largest market share, and has come to dominate UDRP dispute resolution. In 2005, the WIPO Arbitration and Mediation Center posted an informal overview of the weight of WIPO panel authority on UDRP legal issues. The overview summarized WIPO panels' determinations on a number of recurrent legal questions. Where a majority of panelists had applied the policy to recurring fact patterns in a consistent way, the overview noted the majority position. Where a clear split of authority had emerged, the overview noted the split. Although the overview has no formal precedential weight, many panelists found it helpful, and chose to follow its restatement of prior decisions.

In 2011, WIPO posted edition 2.0 of the overview. The overview is available online at <http://www.wipo.int/amc/en/domains/search/overview2.0/index.html>.

For example, in connection with questions of confusing similarity under the UDRP, the overview presents these consensus views:

> **1.3 Is a domain name consisting of a trademark and a negative term confusingly similar to the complainant's trademark?** ("sucks cases")
>
> Consensus view: Generally, a domain name consisting of a trademark and a negative or pejorative term (such as [trademark]sucks.com) would be considered confusingly similar to the complainant's trademark for the purpose of satisfying the standing requirement under the first element of the UDRP (with the merits of such cases typically falling to be decided under subsequent elements). Panels have recognized that inclusion of a subsidiary word to the dominant feature of a mark at issue typically does not serve to obviate confusion for purposes of the UDRP's first element threshold requirement, and/ or that there may be a particular risk of confusion among Internet users whose first language is not the language of the domain name
>
> **1.4 Does the complainant have UDRP-relevant trademark rights in a trademark that was registered, or in which the complainant acquired unregistered rights, after the domain name was registered?**
>
> Consensus view: Registration of a domain name before a complainant acquires trademark rights in a name does not prevent a finding of identity or confusing similarity under the UDRP. The UDRP makes no specific reference to the date on which the holder of the trademark or service mark acquired rights. However, in such circumstances it may be difficult to prove that the domain name was registered in bad faith under the third element of the UDRP.

On the question of a registrant's rights and legitimate interests in a disputed domain name, Version 2.0 of the WIPO Overview notes this split of authority:

> **2.4 Can a criticism site generate rights and legitimate interests?**
>
> This section only concerns sites that practice genuine, noncommercial criticism. There are many UDRP decisions where the respondent argues that

the domain name is being used for a free speech purpose but the panel finds that it is primarily a pretext for commercial advantage.

See: *Wal-Mart Stores, Inc. v. Walsucks and Walmarket Puerto Rico*, WIPO Case No. D2000-0477, <walmartcanadasucks.com> *inter alia*, Transfer.

Rolex Watch U.S.A., Inc. v. Spider Webs, Ltd., WIPO Case No. D2001-0398, <relojesrolex.com> (*inter alia*, Transfer).

In the event that a domain name identical or confusingly similar to a trademark is being used for a genuine noncommercial free speech website, there are two main views. In cases involving only US parties or the selection of a US mutual jurisdiction, panelists tend to adopt the reasoning in View 2 (though not universally).

See: *Howard Jarvis Taxpayers Association v. Paul McCauley*, WIPO Case No. D2004-0014, Denial

Sermo, Inc. v. CatalystMD, LLC, WIPO Case No. D2008-0647, Denial.

View 1: The right to criticize does not necessarily extend to registering and using a domain name that is identical or confusingly similar to the complainant's trademark. That is especially the case if the respondent is using the trademark alone as the domain name (i.e, <trademark.tld>) as that may be understood by Internet users as impersonating the trademark owner. Where the domain name comprises the protected trademark plus an additional, typically derogatory term (*e.g.*, <trademarksucks.tld>), some panels have applied View 2 below.

View 2: Irrespective of whether the domain name as such connotes criticism, the respondent has a legitimate interest in using the trademark as part of the domain name of a criticism site if such use is fair and noncommercial.

Additional considerations: Some panels have opted to assess questions of whether a respondent may have a legitimate interest in using a trademark as part of the domain name of a criticism site by reference to additional considerations, including whether: (i) the domain name has been registered and is used genuinely for the purpose of criticizing the mark owner; (ii) the registrant believes the criticism to be well-founded and lacks intent for commercial gain; (iii) it is immediately apparent to Internet users visiting the website at the domain name that it is not operated by the owner of the mark; (iv) the respondent has refrained from registering all or most of the obvious domain names reasonably suitable for the owner of the mark; (v) where appropriate, a prominent and appropriate link is provided to the relevant trademark owner's website; and (vi) where there is a likelihood that email intended for the complainant will use the domain name in issue, senders are alerted in an appropriate way that their emails have been misaddressed.

The Overview describes a similar split in connection with purported fan sites:

> **2.5 Can a fan site generate rights or legitimate interests in the disputed domain name?**
>
> Many of the considerations used by panels in relation to criticism sites, as discussed in paragraph 2.4 above, also are applied by panels in relation to fan or tribute cites. Moreover, this section only deals with fan sites that are clearly active and noncommercial. There are many UDRP cases in which the respondent claims to have an active noncommercial fan site but the panel finds that it is primarily a pretext for commercial advantage.
>
> See: *Helen Fielding v. Anthony Corbert aka Anthony Corbett*, WIPO Case No. D2000-1000, <bridgetjones.com>.
>
> View 1: The registrant of an active and noncommercial fan site may have rights and legitimate interests in the domain name that includes the complainant's trademark. The site should be actually in use, clearly distinctive from any official site, and noncommercial in nature. Panels have found that a claimed fan site which includes pay-per-click (PPC) links or automated advertising would not normally be regarded as a legitimate non-commercial site. However, some panels have recognized that a degree of incidental commercial activity may be permissible in certain circumstances (*e.g.*, where such activity is of an ancillary or limited nature or bears some relationship to the site's subject).
>
> View 2: A respondent does not have rights or legitimate interests in expressing its view, even if positive, on an individual or entity by using an identical or confusingly similar domain name, if the respondent is intentionally misrepresenting itself as being (or as in some way associated with) that individual or entity, or seeks to derive commercial advantage from its registration and use. Also, where the domain name is identical to the trademark, panels have noted that such respondent action prevents the trademark holder from exercising its rights to the trademark and managing its presence on the Internet.

Hoteles Turísticos Unidos S.A., HOTUSA v. Jomar Technologies, WIPO Arbitration and Mediation Center Case No. D2008-0136 (April 3, 2008). Complainant owned trademark registrations for EUROSTARS, and operated a chain of Eurostar hotels, including the Eurostars Blue hotel in Tulum, Mexico. The respondent registered <eurostarsblue.com>, and posted a website headed "Boycott Eurostars Blue Hotel & Spa." Much of the material on the website protested the hotel's lax security and complained about an incident during a wedding at the hotel in which many guests' valuables were allegedly stolen. Panelist James Barker concluded that the complaint had succeeded in showing that the registrant had no rights or legitimate interests in the <eurostarsblue.com> domain name:

> B. Rights or Legitimate Interests
>
> To demonstrate that the Respondent lacks rights or legitimate interests, the Complainant refers to the use of the disputed domain name to promote

a boycott of the Eurostars Blue Tulum hotel. This, says the Complainant, is an attack on its reputation and prestige.

In this way, the Respondent's website is evidently designed for a dual, and related, purpose. Firstly, the Respondent's website operates as a forum for criticism of the Complainant's hotel at Tulum, specifically in relation to the incident of theft at the wedding in October 2007. Secondly, the Respondent's website incites the taking of a specific and negative action against the Complainant: in this case, the boycott of the Eurostars Blue Tulum hotel. That action is obviously designed to damage the Complainant's business.

Neither of these uses are 'commercial', in the sense that the Respondent is seeking to obtain some financial benefit from them. (Although the Respondent's use is clearly intended to have a commercial and detrimental effect on the Complainant.) For such non-commercial uses, the *WIPO Overview of WIPO Panel Views on Selected UDRP Questions* notes that there are two main views:

> "There is also some division between proceedings involving US parties and proceedings involving non-US parties, with few non-US panelists adopting the reasoning in View 2.
>
> *View 1:* The right to criticize does not extend to registering a domain name that is identical or confusingly similar to the owner's registered trademark or conveys an association with the mark....
>
> *View 2*: Irrespective of whether the domain name as such connotes criticism, the respondent has a legitimate interest in using the trademark as part of the domain name of a criticism site if the use is fair and non-commercial."

This Panel takes the view that it is consistent with the prior panel authority to apply 'View 2' where the parties are both resident in the United States of America. That is not the case here.

As such, the Panel has applied 'View 1'. That is, in this case, the use of the confusingly similar domain name for a criticism website does not confer a legitimate interest on the Respondent. And, as noted above, the Panel has found that the disputed domain name (which combines the trademark EUROSTARS with the word 'blue' in a context in which the Complainant operates a hotel called in part 'Eurostars Blue') is confusingly similar to the Complainant's mark.

This finding does not reflect on the Respondent's right to operate a website criticizing the Complainant. The Respondent has a right to do so and clearly believes that its criticisms are well-founded. However, as noted by the panel in *Triodos Bank NV v. Ashley Dobbs*, WIPO Case No. D2002-0776:

> "there is a world of difference between, on the one hand, a right to express (or a legitimate interest in expressing) critical views and, on the other hand, a right or legitimate interest in respect of a domain name. The two are completely different. The fact that use of the Domain Name enables

the Respondent to transmit his views more effectively is neither here nor there. Depriving the Respondent of the ability to deceive internet users by his use of the Domain Name does not in any way deprive him of his right to free speech. He could readily use a domain name which telegraphs to visitors precisely what his site contains and thereby obviate any risk of deception."

For these reasons, the Complainant has established this second element.

Questions

1. Should UDRP panelists treat prior panel decisions as precedent? As persuasive authority? Does the absence of an appellate review mechanism counsel against any binding effect? *See* Konstantinos Komaitis, The Current State of Domain Name Regulation: Domain Names as Second-Class Citizens in A Mark-Dominated World 175 (2010).

2. Given the UDRP panelists' expertise, and the high volume of decisions after twelve years (over 45,000) will UDRP decisions, even if binding neither subsequent panels nor national courts, nonetheless cumulatively constitute a body of domain name law that supersedes national trademark law in the domain name context? *See* Konstantinos Komaitis, *Trademark Law's Increment Through the Uniform Domain Name Dispute Resolution Policy*, Journal of Intellectual Property Law and Practice (2011), http://ssrn.com/abstract=1757964. If so, does it matter?

New Top Level Domains and New Rights Protections Mechanisms

ICANN has approved the introduction of new generic top level domains. When ICANN came on the scene in 1998, there were already eight gTLDs. (.com, .edu, .gov, .int, .mil, .net, .org, and .arpa). Subsequently, ICANN approved applications for fourteen new ones: .aero, .biz, .coop, .info, .museum, .name, .pro, .asia, .cat, .jobs, .mobi, .tel, .travel, and .xxx. Since June 11, 2011, when ICANN announced its plan to increase the number of new gTLDs, see http://www.icann.org/en/news/releases/release-20jun11-en.pdf, and January 12, 2012, when ICANN began accepting applications for new gTLDs, the expansion has grown to over 1000 new gTLDs. *See* Akram Atallah, ICANN Blog, *A "Grand" Milestone: New gTLD Program Reaches 1,000th Delegation*, https://www.icann.org/news/blog/a-grand-milestone-new-gtld-program-reaches-1-000th-delegation (May 25, 2016). Many of the new gTLDs are brand names, but some, such as .earth ("EARTH creates a unified space on the Internet where individuals and organizations can work together to solve our planet's most pressing issues"), and .BAR ("BAR is a simple and universal way of representing the online home for fun and social engagement") aim to create online communities. For examples of some of the new gTLDs, see case studies posted at https://newgtlds.icann.org/en/announcements-and-media/case-studies.

In response to complaints from trademark owners, ICANN agreed to require the registries for new gTLDs to put in place enhanced rights protection mechanisms.

These mechanisms include a Trademark Clearinghouse, a mandatory sunrise period, and a new Uniform Rapid Suspension System. *See* https://newgtlds.icann.org/en/applicants/urs. The Trademark Clearinghouse allows trademark owners to register their marks in a single unified database, and to receive notice of any domain name registrations in any domain that match their marks. The sunrise period requires the operator of any gTLD to offer trademark owners an opportunity to register their marks into the TLD before the domain is opened to general registration. The Uniform Rapid Suspension System is designed to be a faster, cheaper, streamlined version of the UDRP. Complaints are submitted electronically on a short form, reviewed by the dispute resolution provider within a few days, and immediately transmitted to the operator of the domain name registry. Within 24 hours of receiving the complaint, the registry must restrict any changes to the registration data, and notify the registrant. The current (March 1, 2013) version of the URS procedure requires the registrant to file a reply within 14 days. The complaint will then be decided by a single panelist, who may order the domain name suspended or may reject the complaint.

The elements required for suspension under the URS are, like the elements under the UDRP, that the complainant owns trademark rights, that the registered domain name is confusingly similar to the complainant's mark, that the registrant has no legitimate right or interest to the domain name; and that the domain was registered and is being used in bad faith. If there is no genuinely contestable issue of material fact on those issues, the domain name should be suspended. If there are contested material facts, the panelist is to reject the complaint. Disputes involving contested facts should be adjudicated according to the somewhat less summary process of the UDRP. Similarly, a trademark owner seeking a transfer of the domain name, rather than a suspension will need to proceed under the UDRP rather than the URS. *See ICANN Generic Top-Level Domains (gTLD) Oversight Hearing: Hearing Before the Subcommittee on Intellectual Property, Competition and the Internet of the House Committee on the Judiciary*, 112th Cong. (May 4, 2011); ICANN, *New gTLD Applicant Guidebook 4* (June 4, 2012), <https://newgtlds.icann.org/en/applicants/agb>.

D. The UDRP in the U.S. Courts

Sallen v. Corinthians Licenciamentos LTDA, 273 F.3d 14 (1st Cir. 2001). The owner of the Brazilian soccer team Corinthiao brought a successful UDRP proceeding against Jay Sallen, the registrant of the domain name <corinthians.com>. Sallen then filed suit under section 32(2)(D)(v) seeking the return of his domain name and a declaration that his registration and use of <corinthians.com> was not unlawful:

> Sallen asserts that (1) this provision of the ACPA creates an explicit cause of action for a declaration that a registrant who has lost a domain name under the UDRP has lawfully registered and used that domain name; (2) this declaration overrides the WIPO panel's decision to the contrary; and (3) federal courts may order the domain name reactivated or transferred

> back to the aggrieved registrant. Sallen's position is that, despite the terms of his domain name registration agreement, and despite the WIPO panel's interpretation of those terms, he is entitled to retain registration and use of corinthians.com if his registration and use of the domain name is consistent with the ACPA.
>
> This case raises an issue of first impression, requiring us to determine whether a domain name registrant, who has lost in a WIPO-adjudicated UDRP proceeding, may bring an action in federal court under § 1114(2)(D)(v) seeking to override the result of the earlier WIPO proceeding by having his status as a nonviolator of the ACPA declared and by getting an injunction forcing a transfer of the disputed domain name back to him. The answer to this question turns on the relationship between the ACPA, in particular § 1114(2)(D)(v), and decisions of administrative dispute resolution panels contractually empowered to adjudicate domain name disputes under the UDRP.
>
> The district court dismissed Sallen's complaint on the grounds that no actual controversy existed between the parties since CL never claimed that Sallen violated the ACPA. We hold that, although CL represented that it had "no intent to sue [Sallen] under the ACPA for his past activities in connection with corinthians.com," an actual controversy did exist between the parties concerning rights to corinthians.com, and that the district court incorrectly dismissed Sallen's complaint. Section 1114(2)(D)(v) grants domain name registrants who have lost domain names under administrative panel decisions applying the UDRP an affirmative cause of action in federal court for a declaration of nonviolation of the ACPA and for the return of the wrongfully transferred domain names. Accordingly, we reverse and remand to the district court.

Dluhos v. Strasberg, 321 F.3d 365 (3d Cir. 2003). The estate of Lee Strasberg, a famous acting teacher who died in 1982, filed a UDRP proceeding against Dluhos, the registrant of <leestrasberg.com>. Rather than contesting the UDRP proceeding, Dluhos filed an action in federal court challenging the constitutionality of the UDRP. After the UDRP panel ruled that the <leestrasberg.com> should be transferred to the Strasberg estate, Dluhos amended his complaint to add a count seeking the reinstatement of his domain. The district court dismissed Dluhos's constitutional challenge. In reviewing the UDRP decision, the court applied the deferential standard imposed by the Federal Arbitration Act, and upheld the award. On appeal, the Third Circuit held that UDRP decisions are not subject to review under the Federal Arbitration Act, but may be challenged under the ACPA:

> At issue before us then is whether the nonbinding domain name resolution policy (UDRP) proceeding that shifted Appellant's registered domain name to the Strasberg defendants constitutes arbitration under the FAA. If this proceeding qualifies as arbitration under the FAA, then the dispute resolution is subject to extremely limited review. If it does not fall under the

FAA umbrella, then the district court lacked jurisdiction to examine—and thus to affirm—the result under the lax FAA review standards.

IV.

We begin our analysis of the FAA's applicability by examining the specific arbitration agreement at issue, a contract-based arrangement for handling disputes between domain name registrants and third parties who challenge the registration and use of their trademarks. In our view, the UDRP's unique contractual arrangement renders the FAA's provisions for judicial review inapplicable.

A.

First, the UDRP obviously contemplates the possibility of judicial intervention, as no provision of the policy prevents a party from filing suit before, after or during the administrative proceedings. See UDRP § 4(k) (stating that domain-name resolution proceedings shall not stop either party from "submitting the dispute to a court of competent jurisdiction for independent resolution"); *Sallen v. Corinthians Licenciamentos Ltda.*, 273 F.3d 14, 26 (1st Cir. 2001) (discussing the likelihood that the "judicial outcome will override the UDRP one"). In that sense, this mechanism would not fall under the FAA because "the dispute will [not necessarily] be settled by this arbitration." *Harrison* [*v. Nissan Motor Corp.*, 111 F.3d 343], at 349 [(3d Cir. 1997)].

The UDRP was intended to ensure that the parties could seek independent judicial resolution of domain name disputes, regardless of whether its proceeding reached a conclusion. *See World Intellectual Property Organization, The Management of Internet Names and Addresses: Intellectual Property Issues: Final Reporter of the WIPO Internet Domain Name Process* 139, 150(iv), at http://wipo2.wipo.int/process1/report/finalreport.html (Apr. 30, 1999) (remarking that the parties should be permitted to seek "de novo review" of a UDRP-based dispute resolution); *see also Sallen*, 273 F.3d at 26 (affording independent complete review of a UDRP proceeding rather than addressing it under the FAA); *Weber-Stephen Prods. Co. v. Armitage Hardware & Bldg. Supply, Inc.*, 2000 U.S. Dist LEXIS 6335 (N.D. Ill. May 3, 2000) (concluding that the UDRP takes account of the possibility of parallel litigation in federal court, and that federal courts are "not bound by the outcome of the administrative proceedings").

Indeed, unlike methods of dispute resolution covered by the FAA, UDRP proceedings were never intended to replace formal litigation. *See Parisi* [*v. Netlearning, Inc.*, 139 F. Supp. 2d 745], at 752 [(E.D. Va. 2001)] (citing the FAA's requirement that parties to arbitration "agree[ ] that a judgment of the court shall be entered upon the award made pursuant to the arbitration," 9 U.S.C.S. 9, and noting the absence of such an agreement in the UDRP); David E. Sorkin, *Judicial Review of ICANN Domain Name Dispute Decisions*,

18 SANTA CLARA COMPUTER & HIGHTECH L.J. 35, 51–52 (2001) ("Unlike conventional arbitration, the UDRP is not meant to replace litigation, but merely to provide an additional forum for dispute resolution, with an explicit right of appeal to the courts."). Rather, the UDRP contemplates truncated proceedings. It "is fashioned as an 'online' procedure administered via the Internet," *Parisi*, 139 F. Supp. 2d at 747, which does not permit discovery, the presentation of live testimony (absent exceptional circumstances), or any remedy other than the transfer or cancellation of the domain name in question. [Citations.]

To shove Dluhos' square-peg UDRP proceeding into the round hole of the FAA would be to frustrate this aim, as judicial review of FAA-styled arbitration proceedings could be generously described only as extremely deferential.

B.

Second, because the trademark holder or the trademark holder's representative is not required to avail itself of the dispute resolution policy before moving ahead in the district court, these proceedings do not qualify as the type that would entail a court's compelling party participation prior to independent judicial review—thus removing the proceeding from the warmth of the FAA blanket. Under § 4 of the FAA, a district court may "stay the trial of the action until such arbitration has been had in accordance with the terms of the agreement." 9 U.S.C. § 4. Although "[s]ome courts, relying in part on their inherent equitable powers, have stayed litigation and compelled participation in non-binding procedures so long as there are 'reasonable commercial expectations' that the procedures would 'settle' disputed issues," *Parisi*, 139 F. Supp. 2d at 750 n.10 (*quoting AMF*, 621 F. Supp. at 460–461), a UDRP proceeding settles a domain-name dispute only to the extent that a season-finale cliffhanger resolves a sitcom's storyline—that is, it doesn't. It is true that the language of the resolution policy describes the dispute-resolution process as "mandatory," but "the process is not 'mandatory' in the sense that either disputant's legal claims accrue only after a panel's decision." *Parisi*, 139 F. Supp. 2d at 751 (*quoting Bankers Ins. Co.*, 245 F.3d at 319). Only the domain-name registrant is contractually obligated to participate in the proceeding if a complaint is filed. Even then, the panel may "decide the dispute based on the complaint" if the registrant declines to participate. UDRP § 5(e). That Dluhos could do precisely that by eschewing the NAF proceeding and filing suit in district court only demonstrates the dispute resolution policy's outcome's relative hollowness. Indeed, it is not the district court litigation that could be stayed pending dispute resolution, but rather the dispute-resolution mechanism itself. *See* UDRP § 18 (giving arbitration panel "the discretion to decide whether to suspend or terminate the administrative proceeding, or to proceed to a decision" while a lawsuit is pending). And that is exactly what the NAF panel did.

C.

The bottom line is that a registrant who loses a domain name to a trademark holder "can effectively suspend [a] panel's decision by filing a lawsuit in the specified jurisdiction and notifying the registrar in accordance with [UDRP § 4(k)]." *Parisi*, 139 F. Supp. 2d at 752. From that provision, it is evident that the UDRP provides "'parity of appeal,' affording a 'clear mechanism' for 'seeking judicial review of a decision of an administrative panel canceling or transferring the domain name.'" *Id.* (*quoting* ICANN, *Staff Report on Implementation Documents for the Uniform Dispute Resolution Policy* (Sept. 29, 1999)).

Accordingly, we hold that UDRP proceedings do not fall under the Federal Arbitration Act. More specifically, judicial review of those decisions is not restricted to a motion to vacate arbitration award under § 10 of the FAA, which applies only to binding proceedings likely to "realistically settle the dispute." The district court erred in reviewing the domain name proceeding under limitations of FAA standards.

V.

Because the UDRP—a private covenant—cannot confer federal jurisdiction where none independently exists, the remaining question is whether the Congress has provided a cause of action to challenge its decisions. In the Anticybersquatting Consumer Protection Act, we hold that it has.

The ACPA, 15 U.S.C. § 1114(2)(D)(v), "provide[s] registrants ... with an affirmative cause of action to recover domain names lost in UDRP proceedings." *Sallen*, 273 F.3d at 27. Under this modern amendment to the Lanham Act, a registrant whose domain name has been "suspended, disabled, or transferred" may sue for a declaration that the registrant is not in violation of the Act, as well as for an injunction returning the domain name. 15 U.S.C. § 1114(2)(D)(v). Congress' authorization of the federal courts to "grant injunctive relief to the domain name registrant, including the reactivation of the domain name or transfer of the domain name to the domain name registrant" gives the registrant an explicit cause of action through which to redress the loss of a domain name under the UDRP. *Id.*

Accordingly, as to the CMG and Strasberg defendants, we will reverse and remand the case for further proceedings consistent with this opinion. This decision in no way reflects an intimation that the NAP panel erred in its judgment, but merely that UDRP resolutions do not fall under the limited judicial review of arbitrators of the FAA.

Barcelona.Com, Inc. v. Excelentisimo Ayuntamiento de Barcelona

330 F.3d 617 (4th Cir. 2003)

Niemeyer, Circuit Judge:

Barcelona.com, Inc. ("Bcom, Inc."), a Delaware corporation, commenced this action under the Anticybersquatting Consumer Protection Act against Excelentisimo Ayuntamiento de Barcelona (the City Council of Barcelona, Spain) for a declaratory judgment that Bcom, Inc.'s registration and use of the domain name <barcelona.com> is not unlawful under the Lanham Act (Chapter 22 of Title 15 of the United States Code). The district court concluded that Bcom, Inc.'s use of <barcelona.com> was confusingly similar to Spanish trademarks owned by the City Council that include the word "Barcelona." Also finding bad faith on the basis that Bcom, Inc. had attempted to sell the <barcelona.com> domain name to the City Council for a profit, thc court ordered the transfer of the domain name to the City Council.

Because the district court applied Spanish law rather than United States law and based its transfer order, in part, on a counterclaim that the City Council never filed, we reverse the judgment of the district court denying Bcom, Inc. relief under the Anticybersquatting Consumer Protection Act, vacate its memorandum opinion and its order to transfer the domain name <barcelona.com> to the City Council, and remand for further proceedings consistent with this opinion.

I

In 1996, Mr. Joan Nogueras Cobo ("Nogueras"), a Spanish citizen, registered the domain name <barcelona.com> in the name of his wife, also a Spanish citizen, with the domain registrar, Network Solutions, Inc., in Herndon, Virginia. In the application for registration of the domain name, Nogueras listed himself as the administrative contact. When Nogueras met Mr. Shahab Hanif, a British citizen, in June 1999, they developed a business plan to turn <barcelona.com> into a tourist portal for the Barcelona, Spain, region. A few months later they formed Bcom, Inc. under Delaware law to own <barcelona.com> and to run the website, and Nogueras, his wife, and Hanif became Bcom, Inc.'s officers. Bcom, Inc. was formed as an American company in part because Nogueras believed that doing so would facilitate obtaining financing for the development of the website. Although Bcom, Inc. maintains a New York mailing address, it has no employees in the United States, does not own or lease office space in the United States, and does not have a telephone listing in the United States. Its computer server is in Spain.

Shortly after Nogueras registered the domain name <barcelona.com> in 1996, he placed some Barcelona-related information on the site. The site offered commercial services such as domain registry and web hosting, but did not offer much due to the lack of financing. Before developing the business plan with Hanif, Nogueras used a web-form on the City Council's official website to e-mail the mayor of Barcelona, Spain, proposing to "negotiate" with the City Council for its acquisition of the domain name <barcelona.com>, but Nogueras received no response. And even after the development of a business plan and after speaking with potential investors, Nogueras was unable to secure financing to develop the website.

In March 2000, about a year after Nogueras had e-mailed the Mayor, the City Council contacted Nogueras to learn more about Bcom, Inc. and its plans for the domain name <barcelona.com>. Nogueras and his marketing director met with City Council representatives, and after the meeting, sent them the business plan that was developed for Bcom, Inc.

On May 3, 2000, a lawyer for the City Council sent a letter to Nogueras demanding that Nogueras transfer the domain name <barcelona.com> to the City Council. The City Council owned about 150 trademarks issued in Spain, the majority of which included the word Barcelona, such as "Teatre Barcelona," "Barcelona Informacio I Grafic," and "Barcelona Informacio 010 El Tlefon Que Ho Contesta Tot." ...

....

Upon Bcom, Inc.'s refusal to transfer <barcelona.com> to the City Council, the City Council invoked the Uniform Domain Name Dispute Resolution Policy ("UDRP") promulgated by the Internet Corporation for Assigned Names and Numbers ("ICANN") to resolve the dispute.

The administrative complaint was resolved by a single WIPO panelist who issued a ruling in favor of the City Council on August 4, 2000. The WIPO panelist concluded that <barcelona.com> was confusingly similar to the City Council's Spanish trademarks, that Bcom, Inc. had no legitimate interest in <barcelona.com>, and that Bcom, Inc.'s registration and use of <barcelona.com> was in bad faith. To support his conclusion that Bcom, Inc. acted in bad faith, the WIPO panelist observed that the only purpose of the business plan was "to commercially exploit information about the City of Barcelona ... particularly ... the information prepared and provided by [the City Council] as part of its public service." The WIPO panelist ordered that Bcom, Inc. transfer the domain name <barcelona.com> to the City Council.

In accordance with the UDRP's provision that required a party aggrieved by the dispute resolution process to file any court challenge within ten business days, Bcom, Inc. commenced this action on August 18, 2000 under the provision of the Anticybersquatting Consumer Protection Act (the "ACPA") that authorizes a domain name owner to seek recovery or restoration of its domain name when a trademark owner has overstepped its authority in causing the domain name to be suspended, disabled, or transferred. *See* 15 U.S.C. § 1114(2)(D)(v). Bcom, Inc.'s complaint sought a declaratory judgment that its use of the name <barcelona.com> "does not infringe upon any trademark of defendant or cause confusion as to the origin, sponsorship, or approval of the website <barcelona.com>; ... [and] that [the City Council] is barred from instituting any action against [Bcom, Inc.] for trademark infringement."

Following a bench trial, the district court entered a memorandum opinion and an order dated February 22, 2002, denying Bcom, Inc.'s request for declaratory judgment and directing Bcom, Inc. to "transfer the domain name <barcelona.com> to the [City Council] forthwith." 189 F.Supp.2d 367, 377 (E.D. Va. 2002). Although the district court concluded that the WIPO panel ruling "should be given no weight and this case must be decided based on the evidence presented before the Court," the court proceeded in essence to apply the WIPO panelist opinion as well as Spanish law. *Id.* at 371. The court explained that even though the City Council did not own a trademark in the name "Barcelona" alone, it owned numerous Spanish trademarks that included the word Barcelona, which could, under Spanish law as understood by the district court, be enforced against an infringing use such as <barcelona.com>. *Id.* Adopting the WIPO panelist's decision, the court stated that "the WIPO decision was correct in its determination that [Bcom, Inc.] took 'advantage of the normal confusion' of an Internet user by using the 'Barcelona route' because an Internet user would 'normally expect to reach some official body ... for ... the information.'" *Id.* at 372. Referring to the facts that Bcom, Inc. engaged in little activity and attempted to sell the domain name to the City Council, the court concluded that "these factors clearly demonstrate a bad faith intent on the part of the Plaintiff and its sole shareholders to improperly profit from their registration of the domain name <barcelona.com>." At bottom, the court concluded that Bcom, Inc. failed to demonstrate, as required by 15 U.S.C. § 1114(2)(D)(v), that its use of <barcelona.com> was "not unlawful." *Id.* at 373.

....

From the district court's order of February 22, 2002, Bcom, Inc. filed this appeal.

II

....

[D]omain names are issued pursuant to contractual arrangements under which the registrant agrees to a dispute resolution process, the UDRP, which is designed to resolve a large number of disputes involving domain names, but this process is not intended to interfere with or modify any "independent resolution" by a court of competent jurisdiction. Moreover, the UDRP makes no effort at unifying the law of trademarks among the nations served by the Internet. Rather, it forms part of a contractual policy developed by ICANN for use by registrars in administering the issuance and transfer of domain names. Indeed, it explicitly anticipates that judicial proceedings will continue under various nations' laws applicable to the parties.

....

Moreover, any decision made by a panel under the UDRP is no more than an agreed-upon administration that is *not* given any deference under the ACPA. To the contrary, because a UDRP decision is susceptible of being grounded on principles foreign or hostile to American law, the ACPA authorizes reversing a panel decision if such a result is called for by application of the Lanham Act.

In sum, we conclude that we have jurisdiction over this dispute brought under the ACPA and the Lanham Act. Moreover, we give the decision of the WIPO panelist no deference in deciding this action under § 1114(2)(D)(v). [Citations.] Thus, for our purposes, the WIPO panelist's decision is relevant only to serve as the reason for

Bcom, Inc.'s bringing an action under § 1114(2)(D)(v) to reverse the WIPO panelist's decision.

III

Now we turn to the principal issue raised in this appeal. Bcom, Inc. contends that in deciding its claim under § 1114(2)(D)(v), the district court erred in applying the law of Spain rather than the law of the United States. Because the ACPA explicitly requires application of the Lanham Act, not foreign law, we agree.

Section 1114(2)(D)(v), the reverse domain name hijacking provision, states:

> A domain name registrant whose domain name has been suspended, disabled, or transferred under a policy described under clause (ii)(II) may, upon notice to the mark owner, file a civil action to establish that the registration or use of the domain name by such registrant is not unlawful under this chapter. The court may grant injunctive relief to the domain name registrant, including the reactivation of the domain name or transfer of the domain name to the domain name registrant.

15 U.S.C. § 1114(2)(D)(v). Thus, to establish a right to relief against an "overreaching trademark owner" under this reverse hijacking provision, a plaintiff must establish (1) that it is a domain name registrant; (2) that its domain name was suspended, disabled, or transferred under a policy implemented by a registrar as described in 15 U.S.C. § 1114(2)(D)(ii)(II); (3) that the owner of the mark that prompted the domain name to be suspended, disabled, or transferred has notice of the action by service or otherwise; and (4) that the plaintiff's registration or use of the domain name is not unlawful under the Lanham Act, as amended.

....

It is the last element that raises the principal issue on appeal. Bcom, Inc. argues that the district court erred in deciding whether Bcom, Inc. satisfied this element by applying Spanish law and then by concluding that Bcom, Inc.'s use of the domain name violated Spanish law.

It appears from the district court's memorandum opinion that it indeed did resolve the last element by applying Spanish law. Although the district court recognized that the City Council did not have a registered trademark in the name "Barcelona" alone, either in Spain or in the United States, it observed that "under Spanish law, when trademarks consisting of two or more words contain one word that stands out in a predominant manner, that dominant word must be given decisive relevance." *Barcelona.com, Inc.*, 189 F.Supp.2d at 371–72. The court noted that "the term 'Barcelona' has been included in many trademarks consisting of two or more words owned by the City Council of Barcelona. In most of these marks, the word 'Barcelona' is clearly the dominant word which characterizes the mark." 189 F.Supp.2d at 372. These observations regarding the substance and effect of Spanish law led the court to conclude that the City Council of Barcelona "owns a legally valid Spanish trademark for the dominant word 'Barcelona.'" *Id.* The district court then proceeded to determine whether Bcom's "use of the Barcelona trademark is not unlawful." *Id.* In this portion of its analysis, the district court determined that there was a "confusing similarity between the <barcelona.com> domain name and the marks held by the Council," *id.*, and that "the circumstances surrounding the incorporation of [Bcom, Inc.] and the actions taken by Nogueras in attempting to sell the domain name evidenced a bad faith intent to profit from the registration of a domain name containing the Council's mark," *id.* Applying Spanish trademark law in this manner, the court resolved that Bcom, Inc.'s registration and use of <barcelona.com> were unlawful.

It requires little discussion to demonstrate that this use of Spanish law by the district court was erroneous under the plain terms of the statute. The text of the ACPA explicitly requires application of the Lanham Act, not foreign law, to resolve an action brought under 15 U.S.C. § 1114(2)(D)(v). Specifically, it authorizes an aggrieved domain name registrant to "file a civil action to establish that the registration or use of the domain name by such registrant is *not unlawful under this chapter.*" 15 U.S.C. § 1114(2)(D)(v) (emphasis added). It is thus readily apparent that the cause of action created by Congress in this portion of the ACPA requires the court adjudicating such an action to determine whether the registration or use of the domain name violates the Lanham Act. Because the statutory language has a plain and unambiguous meaning that is consistent with the statutory context and application of this language in accordance with its plain meaning provides a component of a coherent statutory scheme, our statutory analysis need proceed no further. [Citation.]

By requiring application of United States trademark law to this action brought in a United States court by a United States corporation involving a domain name administered by a United States registrar, 15 U.S.C. § 1114(2)(D)(v) is consistent with the fundamental doctrine of territoriality upon which our trademark law is presently based....

When we apply the Lanham Act, not Spanish law, in determining whether Bcom, Inc.'s registration and use of <barcelona.com> is unlawful, the ineluctable conclusion follows that Bcom, Inc.'s registration and use of the name "Barcelona" is not unlawful. Under the Lanham Act, and apparently even under Spanish law, the City Council could not obtain a trademark interest in a purely descriptive geographical designation that refers only to the City of Barcelona. *See* 15 U.S.C. § 1052(e)(2); *see also* Spanish Trademark Law of 1988, Art. 11(1)(c) (forbidding registration of marks consisting exclusively of "geographical origin"). Under United States trademark law, a geographic designation can obtain trademark protection if that designation acquires secondary meaning. *See, e.g., Resorts of Pinehurst, Inc. v. Pinehurst Nat'l Corp.*, 148 F.3d 417, 421 (4th Cir. 1998). On the record in this case, however, there was no evidence that the public—in the United States or elsewhere—associates "Barcelona" with anything other than the City itself. Indeed, the Chief Director of the City Council submitted an affidavit stating that "the City does not own and is not using any trademarks in the United States, to identify any goods or services." Therefore, under United States trademark law, "Barcelona" should have been treated as a purely descriptive geographical term entitled to no trademark protection. *See* 15 U.S.C. § 1052(e)(2). It follows then that there was nothing unlawful about Nogueras' registration of

<barcelona.com>, nor is there anything unlawful under United States trademark law about Bcom, Inc.'s continued use of that domain name.

For these reasons, we conclude that Bcom, Inc. established entitlement to relief under 15 U.S.C. § 1114(2)(D)(v) with respect to the domain name <barcelona.com>, and accordingly we reverse the district court's ruling in this regard.

Question

Assume the district court was correct in concluding that Bcom's registration and use of <barcelona.com> violated the trademark law of Spain. Indeed, assume that the Barcelona City Council has obtained a Spanish court judgment to that effect. Should Bcom nonetheless be entitled to prevail in an action to recover the domain name on the ground that its registration and use of the domain name does not violate United States law?

Barcelona.com and *Sallen* remain the controlling authorities in US courts addressing UDRP decisions, *see, e.g.*, *Dynamis, Inc. v. Dynamis.com*, 780 F. Supp. 2d 465 (E.D. Va. 2011):

> As to Brenner's contention that a UDRP panel already rejected plaintiff's cyberquatting claim with respect to the DYNAMIS.COM domain name, it is well settled that "any decision made by a panel under the UDRP is no more than an agreed-upon administration that is not given any deference under the ACPA." *Barcelona.com, Inc. v. Excelentisimo Ayuntamiento de Barcelona*, 330 F.3d 617, 626 (4th Cir. 2003); *see also Sallen v. Corinthians Licenciamentos LTDA*, 273 F.3d 14, 28 (1st Cir. 2001) ("a federal court's interpretation of the ACPA supplants a WIPO panel's interpretation of the UDRP"); *Sallen v. Corinthians Licenciamentos Ltda.*, 273 F.3d 14, 26 (1st Cir. 2001) (affording complete, independent review of a UDRP proceeding rather than addressing it under the Federal Arbitration Act). Indeed, generally speaking, the UDRP panel's conclusion is inadmissible hearsay that cannot be considered in resolving this case. Thus, the UDRP's findings and recommendations are not dispositive here, and they cannot form the basis of a motion to dismiss. In sum, because the complaint alleges a sufficient, plausible basis for an *in rem* cybersquatting claim under the ACPA, Brenner's motion to dismiss must be denied.

Chapter 12

Remedies

Editors' Note: The student should consult 15 U.S.C. §§ 1116–19 (Lanham Act §§ 34–37), in Statutory Appendix A, *infra.*

A. Injunctive Relief

1. Injunctions

Herb Reed Enterprises, LLC v. Florida Entertainment Management, Inc.

736 F.3d 1239 (9th Cir. 2013)

McKeown, Circuit Judge:

"The Platters"—the legendary name of one of the most successful vocal performing groups of the 1950s—lives on. With 40 singles on the Billboard Hot 100 List, the names of The Platters' hits ironically foreshadowed decades of litigation—"Great Pretender," "Smoke Gets In Your Eyes," "Only You," and "To Each His Own." Larry Marshak and his company Florida Entertainment Management, Inc. (collectively "Marshak") challenge the district court's preliminary injunction in favor of Herb Reed Enterprises ("HRE"), enjoining Marshak from using the "The Platters" mark in connection with any vocal group with narrow exceptions. We consider an issue of first impression in our circuit: whether the likelihood of irreparable harm must be established—rather than presumed, as under prior Ninth Circuit precedent—by a plaintiff seeking injunctive relief in the trademark context. In light of Supreme Court precedent, the answer is yes, and we reverse the district court's order granting the preliminary injunction.

Background

The Platters vocal group was formed in 1953, with Herb Reed as one of its founders. Paul Robi, David Lynch, Zola Taylor, and Tony Williams, though not founders, have come to be recognized as the other "original" band members. The group became a "global sensation" during the latter half of the 1950s, then broke up in the 1960s as the original members left one by one. After the break up, each member continued to perform under some derivation of the name "The Platters." *Marshak v. Reed,* No. 96 CV 2292(NG)(MLO), 2001 U.S. Dist. LEXIS 880, 2001 WL 92225, at *4 (E.D.N.Y. and S.D.N.Y. Feb. 1, 2001) ("*Marshak I*").

Litigation has been the byproduct of the band's dissolution; there have been multiple legal disputes among the original members and their current and former managers over ownership of "The Platters" mark. Much of the litigation stemmed from employment contracts executed in 1956 between the original members and Five Platters, Inc. ("FPI"), the company belonging to Buck Ram, who became the group's manager in 1954. As part of the contracts, each member assigned to FPI any rights in the name "The Platters" in exchange for shares of FPI stock. *Marshak I,* 2001 U.S. Dist. LEXIS 880, 2001 WL 92225, at *3. According to Marshak, FPI later transferred its rights to the mark to Live Gold, Inc., which in turn transferred the rights to Marshak in 2009. Litigation over the validity of the contracts and ownership of the mark left a trail of conflicting decisions in various jurisdictions, which provide the backdrop for the present controversy....

....

Last year brought yet another lawsuit. HRE [the Manager of Herb Reed's business affairs] commenced the present litigation in 2012 against Marshak in the District of Nevada, alleging trademark infringement and seeking a preliminary injunction against Marshak's continued use of "The Platters" mark. The district court held that HRE was not precluded from asserting a right in "The Platters" mark.... The district court found that HRE had established a likelihood of success on the merits, a likelihood of irreparable harm, a balance of hardships in its favor, and that a preliminary injunction would serve public interest. Accordingly, the district court granted the preliminary injunction and set the bond at $10,000. Marshak now appeals from the preliminary injunction.

....

To obtain a preliminary injunction, HRE "must establish that [it] is likely to succeed on the merits, that [it] is likely to suffer irreparable harm in the absence of preliminary relief, that the balance of equities tips in [its] favor, and that an injunction is in the public interest." *Winter v. Natural Res. Def. Council, Inc.,* 555 U.S. 7, 20, 129 S. Ct. 365, 172 L. Ed. 2d 249 (2008). We review a district court's preliminary injunction for abuse of discretion, a standard of review that is "limited and deferential." *Johnson v. Couturier,* 572 F.3d 1067, 1078 (9th Cir. 2009). If the district court "identified and applied the correct legal rule to the relief requested," we will reverse only if the court's decision "resulted from a factual finding that was illogical, implausible, or without support in inferences that may be drawn from the facts in the record." *United States v. Hinkson,* 585 F.3d 1247, 1263 (9th Cir. 2009) (en banc).

Marshak's key arguments are that the district court erred in concluding that HRE had established a likelihood of success on the merits because Reed abandoned "The Platters" mark and that the district court erred in finding a likelihood of irreparable harm.

A. Likelihood of Success on the Underlying Trademark Dispute

As to its trademark infringement claim, to establish a likelihood of success on the merits HRE must show that it is "(1) the owner of a valid, protectable mark, and (2) that the alleged infringer is using a confusingly similar mark." *Grocery Outlet, Inc. v. Albertson's, Inc.*, 497 F.3d 949, 951 (9th Cir. 2007) (per curiam). Tellingly, Marshak does not challenge the district court's conclusions on these two points,[4] except by asserting the affirmative defense of abandonment on the alleged basis that Reed abandoned "The Platters" mark by signing [a prior] settlement. But "[a]bandonment of a trademark, being in the nature of a forfeiture, must be strictly proved." [Citation.] The district court did not err in concluding that Marshak failed to meet that burden.

Marshak has not established either of the two requirements of abandonment under 15 U.S.C. § 1127: (1) discontinuance of trademark use, and (2) intent not to resume use.... Non-use requires "*complete* cessation or discontinuance of trademark use," where "use" signifies any use in commerce and "includes the placement of a mark on goods sold or transported." *Electro Source, LLC v. Brandess-Kalt-Aetna Grp., Inc.*, 458 F.3d 931, 936, 938 (9th Cir. 2006) (emphasis in original). "Even a single instance of use is sufficient against a claim of abandonment of a mark if such use is made in good faith." *Carter-Wallace, Inc. v. Procter & Gamble Co.*, 434 F.2d 794, 804 (9th Cir. 1970).

HRE presented evidence that ... it continued to receive royalties from the sale of The Platters' previously recorded material.... The receipt of royalties is a genuine but limited usage of the mark that satisfies the "use" requirement, especially when viewed within the totality of the circumstances—namely, that Reed was constrained by the settlement." [Citation.] Receipt of royalties certainly qualifies as placement of "The Platters" mark on goods sold, and supports the finding that there was no abandonment. *See Marshak v. Treadwell*, 240 F.3d 184, 199 (3d Cir. 2001) ("A successful musical group does not abandon its mark unless there is proof that the owner ceased to commercially exploit the mark's secondary meaning in the music industry.") (internal quotation marks and citation omitted).

....

We conclude that the record supports the district court's determination that HRE did not abandon "The Platters" mark.

B. Likelihood of Irreparable Harm

... [T]wo recent Supreme Court cases have cast doubt on the validity of this court's previous rule that the likelihood of "irreparable injury may be presumed from a showing of likelihood of success on the merits of a trademark infringement claim." *Brookfield Communs., Inc. v. W. Coast Entm't Corp.*, 174 F.3d 1036, 1066 (9th Cir. 1999).

4. Marshak does not dispute the district court's finding that HRE is the senior user, or the district court's reasoning invaliding Marshak's claims of ownership. Nor does Marshak contest the district court's determination that Marshak's use of "The Platters" mark is confusingly similar to HRE's use of both "The Platters" and "Herb Reed and the Platters" marks according to the Ninth Circuit's test. *See AMF Inc. v. Sleekcraft Boats*, 599 F.2d 341, 348–49 & n.11 (9th Cir. 1979) (describing the factors relevant to determining whether the alleged infringer is using a confusingly similar mark), *abrogated in part on other grounds* by *Mattel, Inc. v. Walking Mountain Prods.*, 353 F.3d 792, 810 (9th Cir. 2003).

Since *Brookfield*, the landscape for benchmarking irreparable harm has changed with the Supreme Court's decisions in *eBay Inc. v. MercExchange, L.L.C.*, 547 U.S. 388, 126 S. Ct. 1837, 164 L. Ed. 2d 641, in 2006, and *Winter* in 2008.

In *eBay*, the Court held that the traditional four-factor test employed by courts of equity, including the requirement that the plaintiff must establish irreparable injury in seeking a permanent injunction, applies in the patent context. 547 U.S. at 391. Likening injunctions in patent cases to injunctions under the Copyright Act, the Court explained that it "has consistently rejected ... a rule that an injunction automatically follows a determination that a copyright has been infringed," and emphasized that a departure from the traditional principles of equity "should not be lightly implied." *Id.* at 391–93 (citations omitted). The same principle applies to trademark infringement under the Lanham Act. Just as "[n]othing in the Patent Act indicates that Congress intended such a departure," so too nothing in the Lanham Act indicates that Congress intended a departure for trademark infringement cases. *Id.* at 391–92. Both statutes provide that injunctions may be granted in accordance with "the principles of equity." 35 U.S.C. § 283; 15 U.S.C. § 1116(a).

In *Winter*, the Court underscored the requirement that the plaintiff seeking a preliminary injunction "demonstrate that irreparable injury is *likely* in the absence of an injunction." 555 U.S. at 22 (emphasis in original) (citations omitted). The Court reversed a preliminary injunction because it was based only on a "possibility" of irreparable harm, a standard that is "too lenient." *Id. Winter*'s admonition that irreparable harm must be shown to be likely in the absence of a preliminary injunction also forecloses the presumption of irreparable harm here.

Following *eBay* and *Winter*, we held that likely irreparable harm must be demonstrated to obtain a preliminary injunction in a copyright infringement case and that actual irreparable harm must be demonstrated to obtain a permanent injunction in a trademark infringement action. *Flexible Lifeline Sys. v. Precision Lift, Inc.*, 654 F.3d 989, 998 (9th Cir. 2011); *Reno Air Racing Ass'n, Inc., v. McCord*, 452 F.3d 1126, 1137–38 (9th Cir. 2006). Our imposition of the irreparable harm requirement for a permanent injunction in a trademark case applies with equal force in the preliminary injunction context. [Citation.] We now join other circuits in holding that the *eBay* principle—that a plaintiff must establish irreparable harm—applies to a preliminary injunction in a trademark infringement case. *See N. Am. Med. Corp. v. Axiom Worldwide, Inc.*, 522 F.3d 1211, 1228–29 (11th Cir. 2008); *Audi AG v. D'Amato*, 469 F.3d 534, 550 (6th Cir. 2006) (applying the requirement to a permanent injunction in a trademark infringement action).

Having anticipated that the Supreme Court's decisions in *eBay* and *Winter* signaled a shift away from the presumption of irreparable harm, the district court examined irreparable harm in its own right, explaining that HRE must "establish that remedies available at law, such as monetary damages, are inadequate to compensate" for the injury arising from Marshak's continuing allegedly infringing use of the mark. Although the district court identified the correct legal principle, we conclude that the record does not support a determination of the likelihood of irreparable harm.

Marshak asserts that the district court abused its discretion by relying on "unsupported and conclusory statements regarding harm [HRE] *might* suffer." We agree.

The district court's analysis of irreparable harm is cursory and conclusory, rather than being grounded in any evidence or showing offered by HRE. To begin, the court noted that it "cannot condone trademark infringement simply because it has been occurring for a long time and may continue to occur." The court went on to note that to do so "could encourage wide-scale infringement on the part of persons hoping to tread on the goodwill and fame of vintage music groups." Fair enough. Evidence of loss of control over business reputation and damage to goodwill could constitute irreparable harm. *See, e.g., Stuhlbarg Int'l Sales Co., Inc. v. John D. Brush and Co., Inc.*, 240 F.3d 832, 841 (9th Cir. 2001) (holding that evidence of loss of customer goodwill supports finding of irreparable harm). Here, however, the court's pronouncements are grounded in platitudes rather than evidence, and relate neither to whether "irreparable injury is *likely* in the absence of an injunction," *Winter*, 555 U.S. at 22, nor to whether legal remedies, such as money damages, are inadequate in this case. It may be that HRE could establish the likelihood of irreparable harm. But missing from this record is any such evidence.

....

Even if we comb the record for support or inferences of irreparable harm, the strongest evidence ... is an email from a potential customer complaining to Marshak's booking agent that the customer wanted Herb Reed's band rather than another tribute band. This evidence, however, simply underscores customer confusion, not irreparable harm.

The practical effect of the district court's conclusions, which included no factual findings, is to reinsert the now-rejected presumption of irreparable harm based solely on a strong case of trademark infringement. Gone are the days when "[o]nce the plaintiff in an infringement action has established a likelihood of confusion, it is ordinarily presumed that the plaintiff will suffer irreparable harm if injunctive relief does not issue." *Rodeo Collection, Ltd. v. W. Seventh*, 812 F.2d 1215, 1220 (9th Cir. 1987) (citing *Apple Computer, Inc. v. Formula International Inc.*, 725 F.2d 521, 526 (9th Cir.1984)). This approach collapses the likelihood of success and the irreparable harm factors. Those seeking injunctive relief must proffer evidence sufficient to establish a likelihood of irreparable harm. As in *Flexible Lifeline*, 654 F.3d at 1000, the fact that the "district court made no factual findings that would support a likelihood of irreparable harm," while not necessarily establishing a lack of irreparable harm, leads us to reverse the preliminary injunction and remand to the district court.

In light of our determination that the record fails to support a finding of likely irreparable harm, we need not address the balance of equities and public interest factors.

REVERSED and REMANDED.

Questions

1. What if a party waits for some time after learning of an infringing situation before bringing a motion for a preliminary injunction. Should that delay affect analysis of irreparable harm? Why or why not? *See, e.g. Citibank N.A. v. Citytrust*, 756 F.2d 273 (2d Cir. 1985). Are there any other factors that might undercut a finding of irreparable harm?

2. Can injunctive relief under the Lanham Act be obtained against infringements by state and/or federal government entities? See definition of "person" in section 45 of the Lanham Act, 15 U.S.C. § 1127, and *Preferred Risk Mutual Insurance Co. v. United States*, 86 F.3d 789 (8th Cir. 1996), *cert. denied*, 520 U.S. 1116 (1997). Do the Supreme Court's decisions in *College Savings Bank v. Florida Prepaid Postsecondary Education Expense Board* and in *Florida Prepaid Secondary Education Expense Board v. College Savings Bank* (Chapter 8[B][4], *supra*) change the analysis? Why or why not?

3. Once a permanent injunction is granted, are there any circumstances that would justify a modification of this relief? Consider the situation in which a registrant for a mark for Mexican cheese products was enjoined in 1988 in 4 states on the basis of the other party's prior common law rights in those states to a similar mark for Mexican cheese products. Do the facts that the Latino population has become more dispersed in the United States and that Spanish networks offering national advertising have emerged since the injunction issued justify a modification to the injunction allowing the defendant to advertise nationally in Spanish media? *See V&V Food Products, Inc. v. Cacique Cheese Co.*, 66 U.S.P.Q.2d 1179 (N.D. Ill. 2003).

Note: Presumption of Irreparable Harm

Many courts have applied a presumption that irreparable harm to a trademark owner ensues when a likelihood of confusion is shown because of the owner's loss of control over its goodwill and reputation, injuries difficult to quantify in a damage award. The Ninth Circuit in *Herb Reed, supra,* rejected the traditional presumption of irreparable harm and instead followed the Supreme Court's decisions in *eBay Inc. v. MercExchange, LLC*, 547 U.S. 388 (2006), involving a permanent injunction in a patent infringement claim, and *Winter v. Natural Resources Defense Council, Inc.*, 555 U.S. 7 (2008), involving a preliminary injunction against the Navy's use of sonar in exercises because of the impact on marine life. The Third Circuit has similarly found that the *eBay* and *Winter* rationale is "equally applicable in other contexts, including cases arising under the Lanham Act." *Ferring Pharm., Inc. v. Watson Pharm., Inc.*, 765 F.3d 205 (3d Cir. 2014) (involving denial of a preliminary injunction in a false advertising case).

In *Herb Reed,* the Ninth Circuit characterized the Eleventh Circuit's decision in *Axiom* as following *eBay* and *Winter*. In fact, the *Axiom* opinion noted the doubt cast on the presumption of irreparable harm, but declined to rule definitely. *North American Medical Corp. v. Axiom Worldwide, Inc.*, 522 F.3d 1211 (11th Cir. 2008); *see also Swarovski Aktiengesellschaft v. Building #19, Inc.*, 704 F.3d 44 (1st Cir. 2013) (no need to decide question as likely confusion had not been demonstrated); *Voice of the*

Arab World, Inc. v. MDTV Medical News Now, Inc., 645 F.3d 26 (1st Cir. 2011) (no need to decide question where delay in seeking preliminary relief made application of presumption inapplicable).

The Eleventh Circuit in *Axiom Worldwide* explained:

> Even though we hold that [plaintiffs] have established a substantial likelihood of success on the merits of their trademark infringement and false advertising claims, we must still evaluate whether [plaintiffs] have demonstrated, with respect to each claim, that they will suffer irreparable harm in the absence of an injunction. In reaching its conclusion that [plaintiffs] satisfied this element of the preliminary injunction test, the district court relied on two presumptions, one regarding the infringement claims and one regarding the false advertising claims. For the reasons that follow, we vacate the preliminary injunction with respect to both the trademark claims and the false advertising claims....
>
> ... [O]ur prior cases do extend a presumption of irreparable harm once a plaintiff establishes a likelihood of success on the merits of a trademark infringement claim....
>
> Nonetheless, ... a recent U.S. Supreme Court case calls into question whether courts may presume irreparable harm merely because a plaintiff in an intellectual property case has demonstrated a likelihood of success on the merits. *See generally eBay Inc. v. MercExchange, L.L.C.*, 547 U.S. 388, 126 S.Ct. 1837, 164 L.Ed.2d 641 (2006). In *eBay*, the Federal Circuit reversed the denial of injunctive relief, articulating a categorical rule that permanent injunctions shall issue once infringement is established. The Supreme Court reversed the Federal Circuit and admonished ... courts for applying categorical rules to the grant or denial of injunctive relief. The Court stressed that the Patent Act indicates "that injunctive relief 'may' issue only 'in accordance with the principles of equity.'" *Id.* at 393, 126 S. Ct. at 1839. Because the Court concluded "that neither court below correctly applied the traditional four-factor framework that governs the award of injunctive relief, [it] vacated the judgment of the Court of Appeals, so that the District Court may apply that framework in the first instance." *Id.* at 394, 126 S. Ct. at 1841....
>
> Similar to the Patent Act, the Lanham Act grants federal courts the "power to grant injunctions, according to the principles of equity and upon such terms as the court may deem reasonable." 15 U.S.C. § 1116(a) (2006).... Because the language of the Lanham Act ... is so similar to the language of the Patent Act, we conclude that the Supreme Court's *eBay* case is applicable to the instant case.
>
> However, we decline to express any further opinion with respect to the effect of *eBay* on this case. For example, we decline to decide whether the district court was correct in its holding that the nature of the trademark infringement gives rise to a presumption of irreparable injury. In other words,

> we decline to address whether such a presumption is the equivalent of the categorical rules rejected by the Court in *eBay* for several reasons ... [T]he district court has not addressed the effect of *eBay* ... [T]he district court may well conclude on remand that it can ... reach an appropriate decision by fully applying *eBay* without the benefit of a presumption of irreparable injury, or it may well decide that the particular circumstances of the instant case bear substantial parallels to previous cases such that a presumption of irreparable injury is an appropriate exercise of its discretion in light of the historical traditions. *See eBay*, 547 U.S. at 394–97, 126 S. Ct. at 1841–43 (concurring opinions of Chief Justice Roberts and Justice Kennedy, representing the views of seven Justices). Accordingly, we also vacate the preliminary injunction as it applies to the trademark infringement claim, and remand to the district court for further proceedings not inconsistent with this opinion, and with *eBay*.

Although the Second Circuit has found copyright plaintiffs must demonstrate irreparable harm to justify an injunction, *Salinger v. Colting*, 607 F.3d 68 (2d Cir. 2010), it has not yet held that *eBay* prohibits presuming irreparable harm when likely confusion has been shown. *See Barefoot Contessa Pantry, LLC v. Aqua Star (USA) Co.*, 2015 U.S. Dist. LEXIS 24013 (S.D.N.Y. Feb. 26, 2015). The district court in the *Barefoot Contessa* case granted a TRO without relying on the presumption, by finding irreparable harm in plaintiffs' loss of control over reputation. The plaintiffs are known for their celebrity chef TV show, cookbooks and high-end food products. They had licensed defendant's predecessor in interest to use their marks in connection with frozen dinners but terminated the license once it was assigned to a different company. The trade dress at issue in the case is shown below.

The district court noted:

> Courts have consistently "found irreparable harm to exist in situations where there is a likelihood of confusion between the marks, and where the reputation and goodwill cultivated by the party seeking the injunction would be out of the party's control because of the infringement." *Microban Prods. Co. v. API Indus., Inc.*, 2014 U.S. Dist. LEXIS 63883 (S.D.N.Y. May 8, 2014). That is because where "the party seeking the injunction shows that it will lose control over the reputation of its trademark ... loss of control over one's reputation is neither calculable nor precisely compensable." *NYP Holdings v. N.Y. Post Pub'g Inc.*, 63 F. Supp. 3d 328, [341 (S.D.N.Y. 2014)]. That is the case here. Plaintiffs ... have spent almost thirty-five years—and millions of dollars in advertisement and marketing—building the Barefoot Contessa brand. Additionally, Garten claims that she has been "extremely careful to associate the Barefoot Contessa brand with a handful of products for which [she has] total creative input and absolute control over design and quality, to ensure that any products bearing the brand and [her] name reflect [her] core values and high standards"—an assertion supported by her refusal to enter into a licensing agreement with Defendants after they acquired the assets of Contessa Premium because of her concerns regarding their inexperience in the frozen meals sector. Plaintiffs' control over products associated with Barefoot Contessa is imminently threatened by the "Contessa Chef Inspired" trade dress that is strongly similar—if not virtually identical to—the Frozen Dinner Trade Dress, particularly in light of the fact that the two products have appeared side-by-side in grocery stores, and have both been labeled "Barefoot Contessa" products by grocery stores.

The district court also concluded that the plaintiffs satisfied the *eBay* balance of hardships and public interest factors:

> Finally, assuming arguendo that Plaintiffs must show that the balance of hardships tips in their favor and that a temporary restraining order is in the public interest, they have done so. The Court is mindful that, after [defendant's predecessor's] liquidation in 2014, Defendants have been struggling to build a new consumer base, and that OFI may suffer financial and reputational harm from a cessation of production. At the same time, Defendants only started distribution of their "Contessa Chef Inspired" line of products last month. Moreover, as noted above, Plaintiffs also face a significant loss of consumer goodwill from continued sales of infringing products, as they have already received complaints regarding both counterfeit Barefoot Contessa frozen meals and "Contessa Chef Inspired" meals. And the temporary injunctive relief granted by the Court does not include a recall, one of the remedies Defendants contend would devastate their business; instead, the Court's order merely pauses existing production and shipping of infringing products—thereby restoring the parties to the status quo that existed before

Defendants began production of the allegedly infringing goods—pending the preliminary injunction hearing in two weeks.

Lastly, the harm Defendants face is, to a large extent, self-inflicted. After being refused a license from Plaintiffs, Defendants took a calculated risk in launching a product with a trade dress virtually identical to the trade dress that was used in the previously licensed line of products. In doing so, they proceeded at their peril. *Cf. SmithKline Beecham Consumer Healthcare, L.P. v. Watson Pharms., Inc.*, 63 F. Supp. 2d 467, 472 (S.D.N.Y. 1999), amended, No. 99-CV-9214 (DC), 1999 U.S. Dist. LEXIS 20221, (S.D.N.Y. Sept. 20, 1999) and order dissolved due to a change in circumstances, No. 99-CV-9214, (DC), 1999 U.S. Dist. LEXIS 19677, 1999 WL 1243894 (S.D.N.Y. Dec. 22, 1999) (finding that the balance of equities favored the plaintiff despite the fact that the defendant "would suffer substantial financial losses if its launch of the product is delayed," because "[a]ny harm that [defendant] would suffer by the issuance of a preliminary injunction is largely the result of its own doing."). As for whether a temporary restraining order is in the public interest, "[t]he consuming public has a protectable interest in being free from confusion, deception and mistake." *U.S. Polo Ass'n*, 800 F. Supp. 2d at 541; *see also Tecnimed*, 763 F. Supp. 2d at 417 (finding that the public interest is served "by removing confusing trade dress from the marketplace.").

Questions

1. Was the court in *Herb Reed* too quick to conclude that the decision whether to grant an injunction in trademark cases should be treated the same way as injunctions in patent and copyright cases? Arguably, trademark infringement claims differ from patent and copyright claims. Both patent law and copyright law seek to strike a balance between giving incentives to inventors and authors and protecting the public's interest in access to inventions and works in the public domain. Trademark law, in contrast, treats the owner's interest in avoiding a likelihood of confusion as congruent with the public's interest in not being confused. Does that difference suggest that courts should be less reluctant to presume irreparable harm in trademark infringement actions? *See, e.g., Champagne Louis Roederer v. J. Garcia Carrion, S.A.*, 732 F. Supp. 2d 836 (D. Minn. 2010) ("the public interest is served by preventing confusion in the marketplace").

2. Should courts be able to employ a rebuttable presumption of harm where a likelihood of confusion has been demonstrated? *See, e.g.*, David H. Bernstein & Andrew Gilden, *No Trolls Barred: Trademark Injunctions After* eBay?, 99 TMR 1037 (2009); *U.S. Polo Ass'n. Inc. v. PRL USA Holdings Inc.*, 800 F. Supp. 2d 515 (S.D.N.Y. 2011) (presumption should not apply but court found that irreparable harm was demonstrated because mark owner could lose control of its reputation); *Rebel Debutante LLC v. Forsythe Cosmetic Group Ltd.*, 799 F. Supp. 2d 558 (M.D.N.C. 2011) (*eBay* distinguishable in trademark context; court applies presumption of irreparable harm in preliminary injunction context). If a loss of control over one's reputation inevitably occurs when there is a likelihood of confusion, can a mark owner simply

point to this irreparable harm to satisfy the *eBay* standard? If so, is this analysis equivalent to presuming irreparable harm when a likelihood of confusion has been shown?

3. Injunctive relief can be the only relief a successful trademark plaintiff may realistically expect because of the difficulties of proving actual confusion, lost sales or willfulness, which can be critical predicates to receiving monetary awards. Even if *eBay* is determined to require a showing of irreparable harm, should the unavailability of monetary remedies in a case be considered in weighing the irreparability of harm factor? Otherwise, is a successful plaintiff in danger of obtaining no remedy? *Cf. Maker's Mark Distillery, Inc. v. Diageo North America, Inc.*, 703 F. Supp. 2d 671 (W.D. Ky. 2010) (court articulated four-factor test of *eBay*, but applied presumption of irreparable harm where no money damages were awarded), *infra*, this Chapter, *aff'd*, 679 F.3d 410 (6th Cir. 2012); *supra*, Chapter 6[B][1].

Note: The "Safe Distance" Rule

In determining whether a defendant is liable for contempt of a previously issued injunction against infringing conduct, courts frequently invoke the "safe distance" rule in cases where the previous infringer makes some modifications to the previously infringing mark or trade dress. Although the modified mark and/or trade dress may not have been found infringing in the first instance, it may violate the injunction if the modifications do not preserve a "safe distance" from the plaintiff's mark or trade dress. *See generally* 5 J. McCarthy on Trademarks and Unfair Competition § 30:21 (4th ed. 2016).

The Sixth Circuit recently applied this doctrine in *Innovation Ventures, LLC v. N2G Distributing, Inc.*, 763 F.3d 524 (6th Cir. 2014) a subsequent episode in the 5-HOUR ENERGY case encountered in Chapter 10[C], *supra*. The defendants in that case had been found liable for infringing plaintiff's 5-HOUR ENERGY mark and/or trade dress in a series of energy drink products sold by defendants. The plaintiff's 5-HOUR ENERGY product and defendant's initial 6-HOUR ENERGY product are shown below:

After a permanent injunction was entered, the defendants, through a new company, made some modifications to the products as shown below:

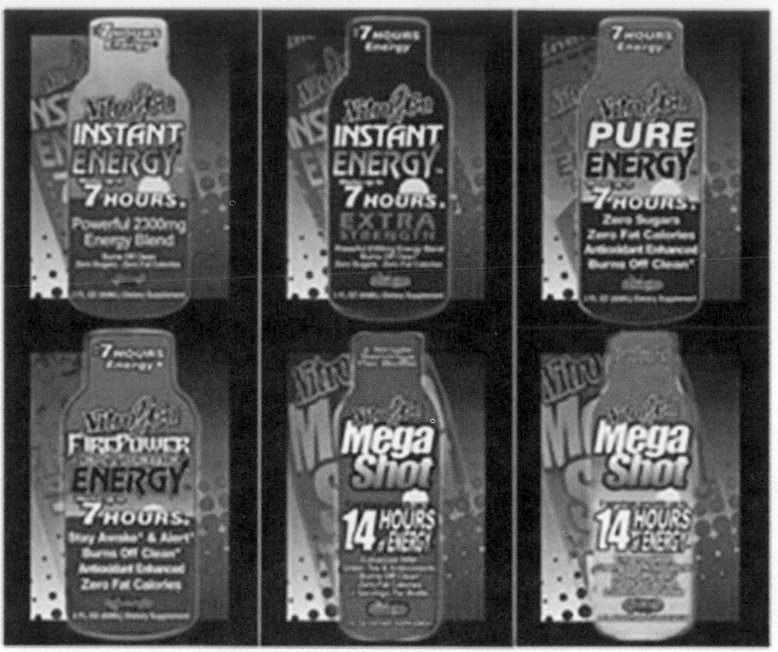

The plaintiff moved for a contempt order, which the district court granted. The district court did not engage in a likelihood of confusion analysis to determine whether the modified versions were infringing, but instead applied the "safe distance" rule. The Sixth Circuit affirmed, noting:

> A court's ability to issue injunctions, and then enforce those injunctions with a finding of contempt, springs from the court's inherent equitable powers. [Citations.] Equity allows courts, faced with recalcitrant parties who repeatedly violate the law, to craft permanent injunctions which "proscribe activities that, standing alone, would have been unassailable." *E.E.O.C. v. Wilson Metal Casket Co.*, 24 F.3d 836, 842 (6th Cir. 1994). This equitable principle goes by a specialized name in the context of permanent injunctions to protect intellectual property—the Safe Distance Rule....
>
> The Safe Distance Rule gives courts a ... useful tool in crafting and enforcing permanent injunctions. Once a party infringes on another's trademark or trade dress, the confusion sowed "is not magically remedied" by *de minimis* fixes. [Citation.] "Instead, the confusion lingers, creating the need for the infringer not only to secure a new non-infringing name (or other infringing characteristic) for his product, but one so far removed ... so as to put the public on notice that the two are not related." [Citation.] In contempt proceedings, the Safe Distance Rule "reliev[es] the reviewing court of the need to retry the entire range of issues that may be relevant in an infringement action for each small variation the defendant makes to the enjoined mark."

PRL USA Holdings, Inc. v. U.S. Polo Ass'n, Inc., 520 F.3d 109, 118 (2d Cir. 2008). If the law were otherwise, an enjoined party "could simply make a tiny change and start a new trademark contest all over again in the context of the contempt hearing as to use of the 'new' format." 5 McCarthy on Trademarks and Unfair Competition § 30:21 (4th ed. 2013).

The Safe Distance Rule is ... a specialized application of the courts' traditional equitable power to craft permanent injunctions tailored to the needs of each case, and then enforce them with the sanction of contempt. The district court's permanent injunction in this case barred Defendants, their agents, and their confederates from marketing products that use marks "confusingly similar" to the protected trademark and trade dress.... Once Plaintiff moved for contempt, the district court did not err by refusing to go through a full likelihood-of-confusion analysis with Defendants' modified products. The district court was within its rights to simply determine whether the modified products were confusingly similar. [Citation.]

Do you agree that the defendants' modified trade dress failed to keep a safe distance from plaintiff's?

Guthrie Healthcare Sys. v. ContextMedia, Inc., 826 F.3d 27 (2d Cir. 2016). As noted in Chapter 3[F], *supra*, after affirming a finding of infringement of Guthrie's registered logo, the appellate court discussed the limited injunctive relief that was confined to the small geographic area in which Guthrie had healthcare facilities and had shown a probability of confusion. Unlike *Dawn Donut* in which the defendant showed a lack of likely confusion outside plaintiff's territory of operation, the appellate court made the following observations on the proper scope of the injunction:

[A] senior user must prove a probability of confusion in order to win an injunction. But it does not follow that the injunction may extend only into areas for which the senior user has shown probability of confusion.... Once the senior user has proven entitlement to an injunction, the scope of the injunction should be governed by a variety of equitable factors—the principal concern ordinarily being providing the injured senior user with reasonable protection from the junior user's infringement. Of course, if the junior user demonstrates that in a particular geographic area there is no likelihood of confusion, ordinarily no useful purpose would be served by extending the injunction into that area, potentially inflicting great harm on the junior user without meaningful justification. [Citation.]

... The first problem with the injunction is that it allows Defendant to make substantial use of the marks *within* the Guthrie Service Area. The court's ruling leaves Defendant free to use the marks on the Internet, notwithstanding that Defendant's webpages are accessible in Plaintiff's Service Area, and are likely to cause confusion there. Secondly, the district court also expressly allowed Defendant unrestricted use of the marks in two counties (Tompkins and Schuyler) where Plaintiff maintained healthcare facilities, explaining that Plaintiff had "presented no evidence regarding the setup of these locations, in particular the patient waiting room experience there ... [and] [a]ccordingly ... ha[d] not proven that any patient exposure to [Defendant's] content in waiting rooms in those counties would occur or would be similar to exposure in the 11 counties discussed at trial." The court's explanation for excluding these counties where Plaintiff maintains patient care facilities from the scope of the injunction seems to us unpersuasive.

....

The district court relied primarily on the proposition ... that a permanent injunction must be "narrowly tailored to fit specific legal violations" and that a court "should not impose unnecessary burdens on lawful activity." *Starter Corp.*, 170 F.3d at 299. This proposition is without question a correct statement of the law. However, it does not follow from it that a senior user who has proven entitlement to an injunction affecting one geographic area by reason of the junior user's infringement must show the same high degree of probability of harm in every further area into which the injunction might extend, thus allowing the infringer free use of the infringing mark in all areas as to which the senior user has not shown a substantial probability of confusion. "[A] party who has once infringed a trademark may be required to suffer a position less advantageous than that of an innocent party ... and a court can frame an injunction which will keep a proven infringer safely away from the perimeter of future infringement." [Citation.]

....

In our case, in addition to proving that Defendant was infringing Plaintiff's mark, subjecting Plaintiff to a high probability of confusion in its main Service Area, Plaintiff has also shown that its activities and commercial relationships extended beyond that area....

Plaintiff recruits doctors, residents, and nursing students nationwide; it disseminates medical information over the Internet; it receives referrals from other physicians and medical professionals, who may be anywhere in the country; and, with respect to its medical research and clinical trials, it solicits funding beyond its Service Area. In all of these activities, Plaintiff is exposed to the risk of confusion and harm resulting from Defendant's use of the marks outside that area. For example, in order to avoid the fact or appearance of conflict of interest, which might harm its reputation with funders of its medical research or cause it to be disqualified by U.S. Government agencies from clinical trials, Plaintiff takes care not to endorse products or host advertisements for third-party products or services. If Defendant's transmissions [videos about medical issues, some of which contain ads] were to display advertising of pharmaceutical products or endorsements and this were observed outside the Guthrie Service Area by Plaintiff's potential funders or by government agencies, who would predictably believe that what they saw came from Plaintiff, Plaintiff could suffer serious harm to its reputation, impacting its receipt of funding grants or its eligibility to conduct clinical trials. Furthermore, potential doctors and nurses around the country whom Plaintiff seeks to recruit might well be affected in their employment decisions by what they see on Defendant's screens or transmissions. The same might apply to referrals of patients.

... Because the district court authorized Defendant to use what is in effect Plaintiff's mark as Defendant's mark outside the Service Area, Plaintiff, which now operates over 100 facilities in the Twin Tiers region, cannot expand beyond those borders without subjecting itself to a high risk of consumer confusion. This cloud affecting Plaintiff's mark beyond the counties where it presently maintains facilities might substantially impair its opportunity for growth and its eligibility as a prospective merger partner with entities operating outside its Service Area, diminishing its value as a commercial entity. *See Savin Corp.*, 391 F.3d at 459–60 (discussing the need to "protect the senior user's interest in being able to enter a related field at some future time").

No doubt, an injured senior user must show evidence of plausibly foreseeable confusion beyond its main area of injury before the trial court is required ... to consider extending the injunction into such additional areas.... Plaintiff easily satisfied that requirement.

... Every case turns on its particular facts, and in many instances it will be clear, for a variety of reasons, that an injunction of narrow geographic scope will grant the senior user completely adequate protection, and that an injunction going further would be not only unnecessary but unjust.... Plaintiff in our case made a showing of plausibly foreseeable confusion and harm resulting from Defendant's use of its marks beyond the area where confusion was probable. Even assuming it failed to show *probability* of confusion beyond its Service Area, that is not the governing standard in such circumstances. Plaintiff was entitled to have the district court consider extending the injunction beyond the area where confusion was probable upon proper consideration of all the equities.[10]

---

10. Nor do we imply that a prevailing plaintiff operating within a narrow service area is necessarily entitled to an injunction barring the infringing defendant from using its mark on the Internet ... The proper scope of the injunction depends on likelihood of confusion, which in turn depends on innumerable variable factors. The particular facts of this case lead us to conclude that Defendant's use of the logo on the Internet will cause sufficient likelihood of confusion to justify barring Defendant from Internet use. In other infringing circumstances, whether because of differences in the marks, geographic separation, differences between plaintiff's and defendant's commerce, or other reasons, a defendant's use of its mark on the Internet would cause little or no likelihood of confusion, and need not be enjoined.

We recognize further that the competing equities do not always favor a senior user that has shown infringement. Cases frequently arise in which imposition of a broad injunction on an innocent infringer, which had no realistic way of knowing that its mark was subject to a prior claim, would cause the junior user a catastrophic loss of goodwill acquired through investment of years of toil and large amounts of money. In such cases, notwithstanding that the legal right unquestionably belongs to the senior user, competing equities can complicate the issue of the breadth of injunctive relief. In our case, in contrast, a number of equitable considerations appear to favor Plaintiff.

Although Defendant did not act with bad faith . . . , Defendant could easily have avoided the problem that arose from its adoption of marks already reserved by another user. . . . Plaintiff had registered its mark with the PTO. Had Defendant exercised the precaution of running a trademark search before launching its marks, it would have learned that they were unavailable and would surely have had the good sense not to proceed with a logo so nearly identical to one for which trademark rights were already established. Defendant did not conduct a trademark search until it sought to register its marks and was notified by the PTO on February 28, 2012, that the marks it sought to register were "striking[ly] similar" to Plaintiff's already registered mark. Accordingly, while Defendant is not a "bad faith" infringer, nor is it an entirely . . . innocent infringer. The government had placed a convenient tool at its disposition, which it could have used to avoid this infringement, and it failed to utilize that tool.

Furthermore, this is not a case in which an injunction would have catastrophic effects on the infringer's business. . . . Defendant here had only recently begun using the logo. Nor is this a case in which the junior user is compelled to give up the name of its business. What is at stake is only the use of a decorative logo. No reason appears why Defendant cannot change its logo to one that is not confusingly similar to Plaintiff's without suffering major harm to its business.[11] Finally, Plaintiff is the injured party, and so far as we can see was without fault in the matter.

Finally, the equitable interests to be considered in fashioning an injunction are not only those of the parties to the litigation. . . . The public has a great interest in administration of the trademark law in a manner that protects against confusion. By perpetuating a highly confusing circumstance, the court's injunctive order harmed that public interest. The public interest would undoubtedly be better served by the elimination of this confusion.

---

11. The district court might contemplate diminishing any harm to Defendant caused by a mandatory logo change by allowing the change to be made in stages, perhaps beginning with the addition of a reasonably prominent disclaimer of connection to Plaintiff.

> ... The injunction ordered by the district court is affirmed to the extent that it enjoined Defendant from use of its marks. The scope of the injunction is hereby expanded to include Tompkins and Schuyler counties. We vacate the district court's order to the extent it leaves Defendant free to use its marks outside Plaintiff's Service Area, and in online applications. We leave it to the district court to determine whether the injunction can be tailored to allow Defendant some limited use of its marks outside Plaintiff's Service Area (expanded to include Tompkins and Schuyler counties) and on the Internet, giving due weight to Plaintiff's interest in protection from the risk of confusion in the marketplace and to all other appropriate equitable considerations. The matter is remanded for further proceedings in accordance with this ruling.

Questions

1. On remand in *Guthrie,* how should the district court re-fashion the injunction?

2. Georgia Pacific sells enMOTION towel dispensers along with paper towels designed to fit within them. Georgia Pacific commenced three separate trademark infringement suits in three different courts, one in North Carolina against von Drehle, which sold paper towels to fit within the enMOTION dispensers, and the other two in Arkansas and Ohio against Von Drehle's towel distributors. The actions in Arkansas and Ohio found no likelihood of confusion and were affirmed by the Eighth and Sixth Circuits respectively; whereas the action in North Carolina resulted in a finding of likelihood of confusion in which the district court entered a nationwide injunction against sales of the paper towels despite the opposite results in the other two proceedings. Was this proper? If not, should a geographically limited injunction have issued instead? *See Georgia-Pac. Consumer Prods. LP v. von Drehle Corp*., 781 F.3d 710 (4th Cir. 2015), *infra* this Chapter, and the district court opinion on remand, 2015 U.S. Dist. LEXIS 156723 (E.D.N.C. November 18, 2015).

3. Uber Technologies operates Uber, an app-based service that connects drivers with people who want a ride. Uber Promotions has operated a party bus/limo service to take multiple people to events in the Gainesville, Florida area prior to Uber Technologies' use and federal registrations. Uber Promotions, alarmed by Uber Technologies' expansion in Florida as well as by Uber Technologies' new service of UberEVENTS that allows an event host to purchase rides for attendees and some instances of actual confusion, sues and requests a preliminary injunction. Applying the *eBay* standard, do you think the court should issue a preliminary injunction? If so, in what geographical area? *See Uber Promotions, Inc. v. Uber Technologies, Inc.,* 162 F. Supp. 1253 (N.D. Fla. Feb. 16, 2016).

Note: Centrality of Injunctive Relief and Use of Alternate Dispute Resolution

Injunctive relief has been termed "the remedy of choice for trademark and unfair competition cases." *Century 21 Real Estate Corp. v. Sandlin*, 846 F.2d 1175, 1180 (9th

Cir. 1988). Injunctive relief is critical to trademark owners to halt infringing uses for which it has been held that "there is no adequate remedy at law for the injury caused." *Id.* A likelihood of confusion or dilution risks non-quantifiable damage to the trademark owner's reputation or to the goodwill or distinctiveness associated with its mark. As a result, trademark owners frequently seek preliminary injunctive relief as in *Herb Reed Enterprises, supra,* as well as permanent injunctive relief. Moreover, an injunction is often the only remedy trademark owners realistically can obtain in non-counterfeiting cases. Actual damages are difficult to prove, and an award of defendant's profits is not routine. Attorney's fees are awarded only in "exceptional cases." 15 U.S.C. § 1117(a).

Litigation can provide no certain answers in advance to many trademark, trade dress and related disputes. The "answer" may not be known until after there has been a motion for a temporary restraining order, followed by a motion for a preliminary injunction, an appeal to the Court of Appeals, then a trial, and a further appeal. Such litigation is not only enormously expensive but the uncertainty that lingers until a final decision issues can also destroy a business plan. Perhaps partly because there is no perceived likelihood of monetary compensation coupled with the uncertainty and expense of litigation, litigants sometimes resort to alternate methods of dispute resolution, including mediation and arbitration. These methods can reduce uncertainty by ensuring a rapid final decision, and can lower the cost of resolving disputes. They also avoid the gambling aspect of having such matters tried before a jury or a judge who is unfamiliar with trademarks.

In mediation, the disputing parties voluntarily meet with a neutral facilitator who tries to facilitate resolution. If the parties cannot agree on how to deal with their problem, either party can choose to litigate the issue in court, or to arbitrate. A number of the leading companies in the cereal industry, for example, have agreed that any trade dress dispute among them will be subject to mediation for a period of 90 days. If the matter is not resolved within that time, either party is free to fight it out in the courts.

The International Trademark Association (INTA) has established an international panel of mediators/arbitrators, all of whom are veteran lawyers in the trademark, trade dress, false advertising and unfair competition areas. The panelists are available either to mediate or to arbitrate disputes in these areas. An example of how the INTA panel can work is instructive. Two major consumer goods competitors were engaged in a dispute involving a 30-second commercial that had just appeared on national television. Among other things, the commercial referred to the competitor's principal trademark in a way that gave offense to the owner of the mark. The parties agreed to arbitrate before a single arbitrator from the CPR/INTA panel. The arbitration agreement provided that the hearing before the arbitrator would take place within 20 days and that the arbitrator would render the decision within 10 days. It was further agreed that pending the arbitrator's decision, the commercial would not be televised. Within 2 weeks of the signing of the arbitration agreement, a hearing was held, and 10 fact witnesses testified along with four experts. The arbitrator rendered a decision within 4 days after closing arguments. Thus, the parties, by this method, received a prompt and confidential resolution by a knowledgeable arbitrator. In addition, the cost of resolving the dispute was significantly reduced.

Recently, domain name disputes have become fertile ground for arbitration proceedings since the institution of ICANN's Dispute Resolution Policy. *See supra* Chapter 11[C]. Rather than undergoing the time and expense of bringing court actions for trademark infringement, dilution and/or cyberpiracy, many trademark owners are utilizing the relatively speedy and cost-effective arbitration procedure specified in ICANN's policy.

2. Disclaimers

Home Box Office v. Showtime

832 F.2d 1311 (2d Cir. 1987)

LUMBARD, CIRCUIT JUDGE:

....

I.

HBO and Showtime are competitors in the subscription television field. Both programming services offer a variety of movies, concerts, sporting events and other programs. Both sell their television services primarily to cable operators who then sell them to consumer subscribers.

HBO identifies its service through its federally registered service mark and trademark "HBO" which appears at the beginning of each program. HBO frequently promotes its companion "Cinemax" television service in tandem with its "HBO" service with slogans such as "HBO & CINEMAX." Showtime also frequently promotes its companion service, "The Movie Channel," along with its "Showtime" service with slogans such as "SHOWTIME/THE MOVIE CHANNEL."

At the National Cable Television Association Convention held in Las Vegas on May 17–20, 1987 (an industry trade show), Showtime launched a new advertising and promotional campaign using a new slogan as its theme. The primary slogan used was "SHOWTIME & HBO. It's Not Either/Or Anymore." (the "slogan"); the related slogans were: "THE MOVIE CHANNEL & HBO. Together is Better.", "Why SHOWTIME & HBO make such a perfect pair.", and "Play the Showtime PERFECT (HBO, Showtime) PAIR Instant Winner Game." The slogan was featured on a number of materials displayed or distributed at or near the Convention site. The materials included an outdoor highway billboard and a hot air balloon located outside the Convention Center; a rolling billboard that was driven around the Convention area; promotional videotapes played in public at the Las Vegas airport and in Convention hotel rooms; signs located in Showtime's Convention booth; promotional pens, tote bags, sunglasses, buttons and cookies distributed at Showtime's booth and/or to the hotel rooms of Convention attendees; advertisements that were distributed at the

Convention and which appeared in trade publications at or about the time of the Convention; packages of promotional material distributed to Showtime's cable affiliates at or about the time of the Convention; game cards; and a brochure emphasizing the value of subscribing to both HBO and Showtime. Some, but not all, of these materials contained disclaimers stating that HBO and Showtime were unrelated services.

....

HBO maintains that the slogan is confusing because it suggests that HBO and Showtime have merged or are engaged in a cooperative promotional campaign. To prove this, HBO produced evidence in the district court which tended to show that the slogan was the source of confusion because some observers perceived it to be part of a joint promotional campaign. The evidence presented by HBO included the promotional materials or representations of the materials used by Showtime at the Convention, a Boston Globe article that described the confusion caused by the slogan at the Convention among members of the cable television trade and a consumer reaction study in four cities that tested reactions to the videotaped commercial and the billboard that Showtime used at the Convention.

Showtime maintains that it adopted the slogan and undertook the related promotional campaign to educate consumers that Showtime has exclusive movies that are not available from HBO. Showtime asserts that its goal in using the slogan was to differentiate the two services and to convince consumers to subscribe to its service as well as to HBO. Showtime thus emphasizes that it sought to inform the public that Showtime and HBO are different, not to suggest any link between the services. It points to the disclaimers of any link between HBO and Showtime, and especially to the new promotional materials presented to the district court at the preliminary injunction hearing that featured disclaimers more prominently than did the materials that Showtime displayed and distributed at the Convention.

....

Although finding that the slogan was not "patently false," Judge Daranco credited the results of HBO's study and found that, if used alone without "adequate disclaiming information appropriate to the selected medium," it was ambiguous and likely to confuse and mislead consumers. Based on its findings, the district court enjoined Showtime from using the slogan and the related slogans "unless a prominent disclaimer, appropriate to the selected medium accompanies their use." The court thus enjoined the materials used at the Convention and any other materials not featuring an adequate disclaimer but it specifically exempted the materials presented at the hearing from the terms of the order. This court granted HBO's motion to hear this appeal on an expedited basis.

II.

Although we agree with the district court's application of the likelihood of confusion standard to Showtime's promotional materials, our view of the proper role of disclaimers in trademark infringement cases is somewhat different.... In many circumstances a disclaimer can avoid the problem of objectionable infringement by significantly reducing or eliminating consumer confusion by making clear the source of a product. *See Soltex Polymer Corporation v. Fortex Industries, Inc.*, No. 87-7245, slip op. (2d Cir. November 3, 1987) (minimal to moderate amount of consumer confusion found by district court could be cured effectively through the use of a disclaimer). We believe, however, that the record before us is not sufficient to support a finding that the disclaimers proposed by Showtime will be effective in substantially reducing consumer confusion. In fact, our examination of some of the promotional materials first submitted to the district court by Showtime as exhibits at the preliminary injunction hearing indicates to us that some of the potentially confusing statements are not effectively disclaimed because the disclaiming information does not appear in sufficiently close proximity to the infringing statements. As an example, we find Showtime's use of disclaimers to be especially problematic in the case of one of the multiple panel brochures submitted to the district court which had an infringing use on its back panel and a disclaimer only appearing on an inside panel …

Requiring infringing users such as Showtime to demonstrate the effectiveness of proposed disclaimers is supported by cases from other circuits in which the use of a disclaimer by an infringing user has been found not to be sufficient to avoid consumer confusion in the marketplace. *See, e.g., United States Jaycees v. Philadelphia Jaycees,* 639 F.2d 134, 142 (3d Cir. 1981); *Miss Universe, Inc. v. Flesher*, 605 F.2d 1130, 1134–35 (9th Cir. 1979). In addition, we note that there is a body of academic literature that questions the effectiveness of disclaimers in preventing consumer confusion as to the source of a product. *See* Jacoby & Raskoff, *Disclaimers as a Remedy for Trademark Infringement Litigation: More Trouble Than They Are Worth?*, 76 Trademark Rept. 35 (1986); Radin, *Disclaimers as a Remedy for Trademark Infringement: Inadequacies and Alternatives*, 76 Trademark Rept. 59 (1986). [Citation.]

These authors have concluded that disclaimers are frequently not effective. One discussion concluded that disclaimers, especially those (like the disclaimers in question in this case) which employ brief negator words such as "no" or "not," are generally ineffective. *See* Jacoby & Raskopf, *supra* at 54. This conclusion was based on a study of the effect of disclaimers on football jerseys, an example of the effect of corrective advertising, and a generalized framework involving behavioral science research. The authors recommended that courts should consider the effectiveness of a proposed disclaimer more carefully and "[w]henever disclaimers are considered, empirical studies should be used to evaluate their likely impact. At the very least, no disclaimer should issue without a full hearing regarding its likely effectiveness." *Id.* at 57–58 [citations], *see also* Radin, *supra* at 72. Radin also advocates the use of other methods either to make a disclaimer more effective or wholly unnecessary; the primary method he advocates is altering the context in which the infringing use occurs to make consumer confusion less likely. *Id.* at 71.

Although it is conceivable that a disclaimer could alleviate the likelihood of confusion that the district court found in this case, the court did not have before it sufficient evidence regarding the revised promotional materials to decide that their disclaimers rendered them significantly less likely to confuse consumers so that they might be exempted from the injunction. This is especially so as HBO had no opportunity to consider the proposed disclaimers and produce evidence as it had with respect to the slogans and disclaimers that Showtime used at the Convention.

In further proceedings before the district court, Showtime should be free to apply for relief from the injunction, on the basis of its use of disclaimers or otherwise, after it gives adequate notice to HBO.

Upon such an application, there would be a heavy burden on Showtime to come forward with evidence sufficient to demonstrate that any proposed materials would significantly reduce the likelihood of consumer confusion. We do not believe that Showtime, at any point in this litigation, has met this burden and until it satisfies the district court on the basis of proper showing, it may not use HBO's trademark in its slogan or the related slogans.

We appreciate that this assignment of the burden of proof unlike the method utilized by the district court might make it significantly more difficult for Showtime ever to use these slogans. Nevertheless, we believe that it is an appropriate allocation of burdens between these parties for several reasons. First, it acknowledges that by granting the preliminary injunction, the district court found that HBO had adequately proved that the slogan as Showtime first employed it was likely to cause consumer confusion. Second, it recognizes that by using the slogans as they were presented at the Convention, Showtime is infringing on HBO's trademark and, therefore, that Showtime has no right to use the mark unless and until it can demonstrate that, because of some change in the slogan or the context in which it is presented, its use will no longer constitute an infringement. Third, it alleviates the necessary hardship that could be imposed on HBO if it repeatedly had to catch up with Showtime's use of its trademark by adequately demonstrating that each new permutation of the slogan and its context was likely to mislead consumers. Fourth, and finally, it is the allocation of the burden of proof which best accords with our interpretation of the Lanham Act as a means of protecting trademark holders and the public from confusion as to the source and promotion of products.

... This case is remanded for further proceedings consistent with this opinion.

Soltex Polymer Corp. v. Fortex Industries, Inc., 832 F.2d 1325 (2d Cir. 1987). Although the district court found a likelihood of confusion between plaintiff's FORTIFLEX mark for raw materials sold to manufactures that make plastic products such as milk jugs and industrial containers and defendants FORTIFLEX mark for various containers, it refused to enjoin use of the mark and instead ordered defendants to use a disclaimer on certain containers. The Second Circuit affirmed, finding no abuse of discretion.

> *B. Appropriateness of the relief granted*
>
> ... Soltex argues that once the district court determined that there was any likelihood of confusion, it was entitled to injunctive relief as a matter of law in view of the Lanham Act's principal purpose to provide effective relief

against infringement and thereby protect trademarks and the goodwill associated with them. *See* S. Rep. No. 1333, 79th Cong., 2d Sess., *reprinted in* 1946 U.S. Code Cong. Serv. 1274.

A basic principle of the law of equitable remedies, however, is that the relief granted should be no broader than necessary to cure the effects of the harm caused. Defendants maintain that this principle supports their contention that the district court did not abuse its discretion in ordering a disclaimer in lieu of an injunction.

A district court has a "wide range of discretion in framing an injunction in terms it deems reasonable to prevent wrongful conduct." *Springs Mills, Inc. v. Ultracashmere House, Ltd.*, 724 F.2d 352, 355 (2d Cir. 1983) [citation]. We have emphasized before the "flexible approach" characteristic of our *Polaroid* decisions. *See Vitarroz Corp. v. Borden, Inc.*, 644 F.2d 960, 966 (2d Cir. 1981) [citations]. Indeed, we have rejected expressly an "all-or-nothing" or per se rule mandating the use of an absolute injunction whenever likelihood of confusion is found. *Id.* at 967–68; *see Springs Mills*, 724 F.2d at 355 ("district court did not err in devising an appropriate limited injunction"). This flexible approach also is in accord with the function of a court of equity.

The court's determination of whether to grant relief in the form of an absolute injunction or through the use of a disclaimer will not be disturbed on appeal, therefore, unless there has been an abuse of discretion. Although disclaimers may not always provide an effective remedy against an infringing use, a careful review of the record in this case satisfies us that the district court did not abuse its discretion. Several factors convinced the district court that an absolute prohibition against defendants' use of the FORTIFLEX mark was inappropriate. These included the court's factual findings that defendants adopted the FORTIFLEX mark in good faith, took substantial steps to present the mark only in conjunction with defendants' own stylized logo, and have a legitimate interest in preserving their rights in the "FORT" family of marks used by the [defendants] for many years. All of these findings are supported by the record.

In addition, given the undisputed fact that the market for defendants' industrial containers consists of relatively sophisticated buyers, the district court reasonably concluded that the minimal or moderate amount of potential confusion found could be cured effectively by use of a disclaimer. We find no abuse of discretion here, particularly in view of the district court's careful balancing of the equities to reach an appropriate result protective of the interests of both parties. Whether or not, as a matter of first impression, we would have reached the same result as the district court in refusing to enjoin defendants from using the FORTIFLEX mark on the industrial container line is beside the point. We simply cannot say that the district court abused its discretion in ordering a disclaimer instead of an absolute injunction. While we are aware that two other opinions filed today by panels of this court cast doubt on the effectiveness of disclaimers in trademark infringement

> cases involving a substantial likelihood of consumer confusion, *Home Box Office*, 832 F.2d at 1315, *Charles of the Ritz Group* [*v. Quality King Distributors, Inc.*], 832 F.2d [1317,] 1324 [(2d Cir. 1987)], where, as here, the likelihood of consumer confusion is far less than substantial, we believe that it is within the district court's discretion to grant disclaimer relief....

Questions

1. Can the reasoning in the *Home Box Office* and *Soltex* decisions, announced on the same day, be reconciled? Can the difference in result be explained by the effectiveness (or lack thereof) of the disclaimers at issue? Or by a balancing of the equities involved?

2. What kind of empirical evidence would be useful to a defendant trying to establish the effectiveness of a disclaimer in eliminating or substantially reducing a likelihood of confusion?

3. Should a disclaimer be more readily considered as an acceptable remedy if the mark at issue implicates First Amendment interests, such as a magazine title? *Cf. Westchester Media v. PRL USA Holdings, Inc.*, 214 F.3d 658 (5th Cir. 2000).

4. If a defendant uses a disclaimer, does it suggest that there is a likelihood of confusion that needs to be dispelled? May an adverse inference be drawn from such use?

5. Consider the facts in *Pebble Beach Co. v. Tour 18 I Ltd.*, 155 F.3d 526 (5th Cir. 1998). Tour 18 copied golf holes from well known golf courses, a fact which it promoted on the course and in advertising and promotional materials. Tour 18 employed disclaimers on the course and in some advertising materials. The appellate court permitted Tour 18 to make referential use of plaintiffs' marks, subject to use of conspicuous disclaimers, even though plaintiffs' survey of golfers who had played on defendant's Tour 18 course still evidenced some confusion. Should an absolute injunction have been granted? Is it necessary to tolerate some level of confusion in order to permit nominative fair use? *Cf. Toho Co. v. Wm. Morrow & Co.*, 33 F. Supp. 2d 1206 (C.D. Cal. 1998) (disclaimer on back cover of book prominently entitled GODZILLA! in stylized lettering similar to that used by plaintiff inadequate to render use a nominative fair use).

6. Where a domain name is found to be confusingly similar to a trademark, would a disclaimer of association with the trademark owner on the defendant's website be an adequate remedy? Why or why not? *See, e.g., OBH Inc. v. Spotlight Magazine Inc.*, 86 F. Supp. 2d 176 (W.D.N.Y. 2000); *Planned Parenthood Federation of America, Inc. v. Bucci*, 42 U.S.P.Q.2d 1430 (S.D.N.Y. 1997), *aff'd mem.*, 152 F.3d 920 (2d Cir. 1998).

3. Recalls and Destruction

Perfect Fit Indus. v. Acme Quilting Co.

646 F.2d 800 (2d Cir. 1981)

KEARSE, CIRCUIT JUDGE:

[The district court held that defendant's J-board trade dress for mattress pads violated plaintiff's common law unfair competition rights under N.Y. law and ordered defendant to deliver the infringing product inventory to plaintiff for destruction and to write to customers of the last 6 months requesting the return of the package inserts. Defendant appealed the order.]

....

We turn ... to the propriety of the recall provision of the district court's May 19 order. The recall provision is an unusual, and perhaps unprecedented, remedy for a violation of New York's law of unfair competition. Nonetheless, we conclude that the imposition of a recall requirement is well within the district court's broad powers as a court of equity, and that the district court properly exercised these powers in the present case.

It is well settled that the district court's equity jurisdiction empowers it "to mould each decree to the necessities of the particular case." ... State law does not govern the scope of the equity powers of the federal court; and this is so even when state law supplies the rule of decision.

... [T]here is federal precedent for use of the recall remedy in cases such as this. *See Kiki Undies Corp. v. Promenade Hosiery Mills*, Inc., 308 F. Supp. 489 (S.D.N.Y. 1969) (on remand from 411 F.2d 1097 (2d Cir. 1969), *cert. dismissed*, 396 U.S. 1054 (1970)). The circumstances in *Kiki Undies* were remarkably similar to those of the present case, except that the plaintiff's claim was decided under federal trademark laws rather than under state laws of unfair competition. The injunctive order fashioned by the district court required the defendant, inter alia, to use its best efforts, on a continuing basis, to withdraw the offending materials from all customers, retailers and other persons. The district court here had no less power to order Acme to make a single request to its distributees to return the offending J-boards.

We conclude that this was an appropriate case for the exercise of the court's power to require a recall. The district court found that Acme had intentionally copied Perfect Fit's trade dress, and on appeal we held that, as a matter of law, Acme's trade dress was likely to cause confusion among customers, *see* 618 F.2d at 954–55. Acme's infringing trade dress was therefore likely to divert customers from Perfect Fit's product to Acme's. Particularly because the first appeal had prolonged the litigation and therefore increased the probable injury to Perfect Fit, the district court was entirely justified in fashioning swift and complete relief for Perfect Fit. The recall procedure would naturally hasten the removal of the offending materials from public view and therefore seek to end quickly the injury to Perfect Fit.

Acme's argument that the recall provision is unduly burdensome is unpersuasive. Of course, a district court should carefully consider the likely burden and expense of a recall before it imposes the remedy. In some circumstances the imposition of a recall may be unduly onerous, as where the defendant's products are widely distributed and particularly expensive to ship. Or the probable benefit to the plaintiff from a recall may not outweigh the burden to the defendant in some cases even if that burden is relatively light. These are matters to be weighed in the first instance by the district court, and we see no abuse here of the district court's discretion. Nothing in the record developed below suggests that appropriate consideration was not given to these questions or indicates that Acme would suffer unduly under the May 19 order. The order did not require Acme to take extensive action to retrieve the J-boards. The company need only have written its customers requesting a return of the boards and paid the cost of the return for those customers who complied. *Compare Kiki Undies, supra.* Acme's evidence concerning the cost of this program was wholly speculative and was founded on the unwarranted assumption that every person contacted would return not only the J-boards, as requested, but the mattress covers as well. Given the flimsiness of Acme's showing of burden, we can hardly say that the district judge abused her discretion in granting the remedy.

....

Nikon, Inc. v. Ikon Corp., 987 F.2d 91 (2d Cir. 1993). After affirming that defendant's IKON mark for cameras infringed plaintiff's NIKON mark for cameras, the Second Circuit also affirmed the district court's recall order, reasoning as follows:

> [Defendant] claims that the recall order was unduly harsh under the circumstances, asserting that Nikon delayed the trial, causing it to last three years. IPC says that Nikon was in no hurry to get IPC products off the market and that a recall is not justified.
>
> We hold that the recall order was appropriate. The district court has broad discretion as to recall orders which are part of permanent injunctions. *Perfect Fit Industries v. Acme Quilting Co.*, 646 F.2d 800, 805 (2d Cir. 1981), *cert. denied*, 459 U.S. 832 (1982). As Nikon asserts, IPC was warned by its counsel that the trademarks were similar and that IPC should add to its mark to avoid confusion. IPC also withheld from its counsel its intention to enter the 35 mm market. This is evidence of bad faith on the part of IPC. Moreover, while affixing stickers on the cameras warning customers about Ikon's infringement might be said to be less harsh than a recall, there is no guarantee that retailers would affix the stickers. Further, IPC still could remove the trademark from the cameras and sell them to stores like Job Lot. Although IPC asserts it is a harsh remedy, there is no evidence in the record before us to show that the court abused its discretion in ordering the immediate recall.

Gucci America, Inc. v. Daffy's, Inc.

354 F.3d 228 (3d Cir. 2003)

McKee, Circuit Judge.

[The district court found defendant Daffy's, Inc., a discount retailer, liable for selling high quality counterfeit GUCCI handbags that defendant had acquired from its supplier without all the usual indicia of authenticity. Daffy's had taken a bag to a Gucci outlet store where the store clerk indicated that the bag was authentic. Daffy's also sent one bag to Gucci for repair, and it was repaired without comment. When

Gucci sent a cease and desist letter, Daffy's withdrew the few remaining bags from sale and also instituted a policy of not selling Gucci merchandise. Despite finding liability, the district court denied a recall order and a permanent injunction. Gucci appealed].

....

A. Recall Order

We review the district court's denial of Gucci's request for recall of the counterfeit handbags for an abuse of discretion. [Citations.]

Both Daffy's and Gucci agree that the propriety of the court's recall decision is governed by:

1. the willful or intentional infringement by the defendant;
2. whether the risk of confusion to the public and injury to the trademark owner is greater than the burden of the recall to the defendant; and
3. substantial risk of danger to the public due to the defendant's infringing activity.

See Theodore C. Max, *Total Recall: A Primer on a Drastic Form of Equitable Relief*, 84 Trademark Rep. 325, 327 (1994) (listing these factors); *see also Perfect Fit Industries v. Acme Quilting Co*, 646 F.2d 800, 807 (2d Cir. 1981) (weighing the first two factors in decision to order recall).

....

Gucci does not argue that Daffy's conduct created a substantial risk of danger to the public, nor does Gucci contest the district court's conclusion that Daffy's was "an innocent infringer".... Therefore, we may focus our discussion on the court's resolution of the balancing of harms required under the second factor set forth above....

... [W]e agree with the district court's determination that the public benefit of a recall does not outweigh the equities counseling against it. A recall would have a financial impact upon Daffy's. It would also likely injure the company's goodwill as consumers may well assume that Daffy's was guilty of intentional wrongdoing no matter how carefully Daffy's explained the circumstances leading to any recall. Since the counterfeit bags were virtually indistinguishable from Gucci manufactured bags, the district court quite reasonably concluded that "a recall would harm Daffy's with little real benefit to Gucci" or the public.

Gucci invokes a post-sale confusion theory, which presumes that "the senior user's potential purchasers or ongoing customers might mistakenly associate the inferior quality work of the junior user with the senior user and, therefore, refuse to deal with the senior user in the future." *Acxiom Corp. v. Axiom, Inc.*, 27 F. Supp. 2d 478, 497 (D. Del. 1998); [citation]. Yet, Gucci does not challenge the district court's conclusion that, given the quality of the counterfeit bags, third party observers would not perceive anything inferior about them. Accordingly, consumers would not attribute substandard merchandise to Gucci. Gucci does, however, claim that the district court gave short shrift to its concerns over ongoing confusion of Daffy's consumers who unknowingly possess a counterfeit "Gucci."

Although this position has some initial surface appeal, it does not withstand scrutiny. As we noted above, the district court considered the dangers of customer confusion. It gave "serious consideration to the fact that denying a recall will leave Daffy's customers under the continued misapprehension that they own a real Gucci product." However, the court was convinced that this did not justify a recall because the quality of the counterfeit bags and the relatively high price Daffy's customers were willing to pay for them undermined claims of a tarnished Gucci trademark. Finally, in the absence of sufficient evidence regarding the comparative durability of Daffy's bags and Gucci's bags, Gucci's conclusion that counterfeit bags would require greater maintenance rests upon pure speculation....

... The court's factual conclusions are not clearly erroneous. Given the careful application of the correct equitable standard to the evidence before it, it is clear to us that the district court did not abuse its discretion in refusing to order a recall.

[The majority also affirmed denial of injunctive relief.]

....

Rosenn, Circuit Judge, dissenting:

....

The District Court ignored the purpose of the trademark statute to protect the public from deceit and secure to the business community the advantages of its good name and reputation. It left the purchasers of 588 highly expensive counterfeit bags without any relief or even notice that the bags they were carrying were not genuine.... [T]he court denies the innocent trademark owner an injunction against future infringement and a recall of the spurious goods sold under the producer's trademark and good name. Because the majority affirms that decision, I respectfully dissent.

....

The District Court found that Daffy's unintentionally sold counterfeit bags. However, as between a sophisticated chain of discount stores in the high risk business of selling products acquired outside the customary chain of retail distribution and without the usual authenticating documentation and an innocent infringed, the District Court ... has favored and enriched the infringer and left the innocent and innovative creator of a famous product and trademark owner without any remedy whatsoever. Moreover, the court has denied protection against future infringement....

II.

Gucci is ... entitled to an injunction to protect it from future unintentional infringement by Daffy's. Although the District Court found that Daffy's infringement was unintentional, there is still a danger that Daffy's will harm Gucci in the future through an incident of unintentional infringement....

Although the majority acknowledges, as it must, that "trademark infringement amounts to irreparable injury as a matter of law," it jumps to an inexplicable conclusion that Gucci's failure to argue in the District Court that the "loss of control" over its trademarked goods by the infringement also amounts to a waiver of irreparable harm "for purposes of injunctive relief." This holding incredibly transforms the "control of quality" argument asserted by Gucci in its contention that the District Court committed legal error in failing to order a recall of the counterfeit goods into a general waiver of irreparable harm "for purposes of injunctive relief." Irreparable harm was and is a basic element of plaintiff's case from its inception. Implying a sub silent waiver, as the majority does, of the fundamental legal principal that "trademark infringement amounts to irreparable injury" is highly unwarranted and imprudent.

. . . .

By proving infringement, Gucci proved irreparable injury as a matter of law. Upon proving irreparable injury, the burden shifted to Daffy's to prove that the injury will not recur in the future. "It is well established that the voluntary discontinuance of challenged activities by a defendant does not necessarily moot a lawsuit." *Lyons P'ship, L.P. v. Morris Costumes, Inc.*, 243 F.3d 789, 800 (4th Cir. 2001) (internal quotation marks omitted). "That rule is subject to the caveat that an injunction is unnecessary when there is *no* reasonable expectation that the wrong will be repeated." *Id.* (citing *United States v. W.T. Grant Co.*, 345 U.S. 629, 633 (1953)) (emphasis in original) (internal quotation marks omitted).... To show that an injunction is unnecessary and further proceedings are mooted by Daffy's plans not to sell any more Gucci products, Daffy's must meet its "heavy burden" of showing that future infringement is "practically speaking, nearly impossible." *Lyons P'ship*, 243 F.3d at 800.

Daffy's argues that it now has a policy of not buying any Gucci goods. It points out that if it does not buy any Gucci branded goods, it cannot even unintentionally infringe Gucci's trademark. That is true as long as the policy lasts, but that is of little comfort to Gucci because Daffy's has the ability to change the policy at any time ... In response to our question at oral argument, Daffy's attorney would not stipulate that Daffy's will never sell Gucci's products. It merely claimed that its present policy is not to do so. No legal obligation prevents Daffy's from changing its mind tomorrow and immediately resuming sales of purported Gucci products.

Daffy's unwillingness to stipulate forbodes the possibility of future infringements, and once an infringement is shown, the trademark owner is not required to prove that the infringer is likely to infringe again. *Hard Rock Cafe Licensing Corp. v. Concession Services, Inc.*, 955 F.2d 1143, 1151 (7th Cir. 1992); *Basic Fun, Inc. v. X-Concepts, LLC.*, 157 F. Supp. 2d at 457 [(E.D. Pa. 2001)] ("If the infringers sincerely intended not to infringe, the injunction harms them little; if they do, it gives [the trademark owner] substantial protection of its trademark."). Once infringement has been proven, a "heavy burden" falls on the infringer to demonstrate that there is no possibility of further recurrence of the infringement. *Lyons P'ship*, 243 F.3d at 800. The unwillingness of Daffy's to stipulate that in the future it would not sell Gucci bags obviously inspires no confidence in its present policy.

. . . .

For the reasons set forth above, the denial of the injunction constituted reversible error

. . . .

Maker's Mark Distillery, Inc. v. Diageo North America, Inc., 703 F. Supp. 2d 671 (W.D. Ky. 2010), *aff'd*, 679 F.3d 410 (6th Cir. 2012). The appellate court's decision in this case is excerpted in Chapter 6[B], *supra.* The owner of MAKER'S MARK bourbon claimed rights in its red wax-like dripping seal and sued defendant in 2003 for using a similar seal in connection with a high-priced tequila product. Shortly after the lawsuit was brought, defendants ceased using the seal. The district court found the plaintiff had a protectable, non-functional mark that was infringed by the defendants' seal and, despite defendants' voluntary cessation of use for several years, entered an injunction.

> Cuervo argues that an injunction is inappropriate because it ceased use of the dripping wax seal more than five years ago and there is no proof that it intends to resume. While these precise facts may be true, the Court disagrees with Cuervo's conclusions drawn from them. At trial, Casa Cuervo Chief Executive Officer Juan Domingo Beckmann testified that he ceased use of the red dripping wax because he did not want a legal fight, but that he prefers to use the seal. "I like the way it looks, and I would like to be able to use the dripping wax because it looks more hand-crafted. But if I am going to be sued over it, or if I have to pay in order to use it, I simply wouldn't." Thus, Cuervo ceased using the mark based on a practical business judgment. That judgment is laudable but not conclusive here.
>
> In these circumstances, the Court finds that equity supports injunctive relief. *See Am. Bd. of Psychiatry and Neurology, Inc. v. Johnson-Powell*, 129 F.3d 1, 5 (1st Cir. 1997) (court does not abuse its discretion by affirming an injunction when the nonmoving party has voluntarily abated the use); *Lyons Partnership, L.P. v. Morris Costumes, Inc.*, 243 F.3d 789 (4th Cir. 2001) ("defendants face a heavy burden to establish mootness"). Moreover, there is an affirmative reason for the injunction. Equity also requires that Maker's Mark receive some tangible evidence of successfully protecting its trademark rights.

The *Gucci* majority saw no need for injunctive relief given the defendant's voluntary policy change not to sell Gucci products. By contrast, a voluntary cessation of use by the defendant in *Maker's Mark* did not stop the court from enjoining use. The Supreme Court addressed the effect of voluntary cessation in the context of a plaintiff facing a counterclaim. In **Already, LLC, d/b/a Yums v. Nike, Inc.**, 568 U.S. ___, 133 S. Ct. 721, 184 L. Ed. 2d 553 (2013), Nike, the manufacturer of a line of athletic shoes known as Air Force 1s, brought suit against Already, alleging that Already's

Sugars and Soulja Boys shoe lines infringed and diluted Nike's Air Force 1 trademark. Already counterclaimed that Nike's Air Force 1 trademark was invalid. Subsequently, Nike issued a "Covenant Not to Sue," which promised that Nike would not file trademark or unfair competition claims against Already or its affiliates based on Already's existing designs or "colorable imitation[s]" thereof. Arguing that the covenant extinguished any case or controversy between the parties, Nike moved to dismiss the case, but Already opposed the dismissal of its invalidity counterclaim, arguing that Nike's covenant did not moot the case. The District court ruled for Nike, placing the burden of sustaining subject matter jurisdiction on Already and construing the covenant broadly, so that any future shoe lines that arguably infringed Nike's Air Force 1 trademark would also be "colorable imitations" of Already's existing shoe lines and thus insulated from future Nike claims. The Second Circuit ruled that whether a "justiciable case or controversy" existed depended on the "totality of the circumstances," which includes "(1) the language of the covenant, (2) whether the covenant covers future, as well as past, activity and products, and (3) evidence of intention ... on the part of the party asserting jurisdiction" of a desire to engage in activities not covered by the covenant. Finding these three factors to weigh in favor of dismissal, the Second Circuit affirmed the District Court's conclusion.

The Supreme Court acknowledged that a defendant cannot moot a case simply by ceasing the allegedly unlawful conduct:

> We have recognized, however, that a defendant cannot automatically moot a case simply by ending its unlawful conduct once sued. [Citation.] Otherwise, a defendant could engage in unlawful conduct, stop when sued to have the case declared moot, then pick up where he left off, repeating this cycle until he achieves all his unlawful ends. Given this concern, our cases have explained that "a defendant claiming that its voluntary compliance moots a case bears the formidable burden of showing that it is absolutely clear the allegedly wrongful behavior could not reasonably be expected to recur." [Citation.]
>
> At the outset of this litigation, both parties had standing to pursue their competing claims in court. Nike had standing to sue because Already's activity was allegedly infringing its rights under trademark law. Already had standing to file its counterclaim because Nike was allegedly pressing an invalid trademark to halt Already's legitimate business activity. [Citation.] But then Nike dismissed its claims with prejudice and issued its covenant, calling into question the existence of any continuing case or controversy. Under our precedents, it was Nike's burden to show that it "could not reasonably be expected" to resume its enforcement efforts against Already. [Citation.]....
>
> Having determined that the voluntary cessation doctrine applies, we begin our analysis with the terms of the covenant:
>
> "[Nike] unconditionally and irrevocably covenants to refrain from making *any* claim(s) or demand(s) ... against Already or *any* of its ... related business entities ... [including] distributors ... and employees of such entities and

> *all* customers ... on account of any *possible* cause of action based on or involving trademark infringement, unfair competition, or dilution, under state or federal law ... relating to the NIKE Mark based on the appearance of *any* of Already's current and/or previous footwear product designs, and *any* colorable imitations thereof, regardless of whether that footwear is produced ... or otherwise used in commerce before or after the Effective Date of this Covenant." App. 96a–97a (emphasis added).
>
> The breadth of this covenant suffices to meet the burden imposed by the voluntary cessation test. The covenant is unconditional and irrevocable. Beyond simply prohibiting Nike from filing suit, it prohibits Nike from making any claim *or* any demand. It reaches beyond Already to protect Already's distributors and customers. And it covers not just current or previous designs, but any colorable imitations.
>
> In addition, Nike originally argued that the Sugars and Soulja Boys infringed its trademark; in other words, Nike believed those shoes were "colorable imitations" of the Air Force 1s. [Citation.] Nike's covenant now allows Already to produce all of its existing footwear designs—including the Sugar and Soulja Boy—and any "colorable imitation" of those designs. We agree with the Court of Appeals that "it is hard to imagine a scenario that would potentially infringe [Nike's trademark] and yet not fall under the Covenant." [Citation.] Nike, having taken the position in court that there is no prospect of such a shoe, would be hard pressed to assert the contrary down the road. [Citations.] If such a shoe exists, the parties have not pointed to it, there is no evidence that Already has dreamt of it, and we cannot conceive of it. It sits, as far as we can tell, on a shelf between Dorothy's ruby slippers and Perseus's winged sandals.

The Court then noted Already's failure to rebut the covenant with an expressed intention to create a shoe that might expose it to liability, and determined that Nike had demonstrated the invalidity counterclaim to be moot. Finally, the court considered Already's alternate grounds for maintaining jurisdiction, trepidation the litigation had caused in potential investors, the threat of litigation the company felt in putting forth new shoe lines, and simply because the two companies were market competitors. Ultimately, the Court found that these arguments failed to satisfy the requirements for a justiciable case or controversy and affirmed the Second Circuit's ruling.

Section 36 of the Lanham Act, 15 U.S.C. § 1118, also authorizes the destruction of articles that infringe a registered mark, section § 43(a) or section 43(c) (if willful).

Questions

1. As the *Perfect Fit* and *Nikon* cases illustrate, recall can be an extremely powerful remedy for trademark owners, and a corresponding calamity for infringers. While many considerations can support a recall order, one rationale is that recall acts as a deterrent to the defendant and to others against engaging in infringing conduct. Is this a proper consideration? What other reasons might support a recall order? In opposition to a recall, would it be wise for a defendant to stress the harm that such an order would cause to it as the defendant in *Gucci* did?

2. Is a recall order appropriate only when the infringement is willful? Is that why the *Gucci* court denied a recall remedy? Why would a court enjoin a use that has been stopped voluntarily as it had in *Maker's Mark*?

3. Was the majority or dissenting opinion in *Gucci* correct about the recall order? About the permanent injunction?

4. Entry of a destruction order is within the court's discretion, but only after plaintiff has established a violation of its rights after full trial, or after entry of summary judgment in its favor. If the infringing mark can be removed without destroying the product, should the court nonetheless order the destruction of the goods? What arguments would support an application for destruction in these circumstances?

5. Should a court ever order a recall at the preliminary injunction stage? If so, under what circumstances? *See Marlyn Nutraceuticals, Inc. v. Mucos Pharma GmbH & Co.*, 571 F.3d 873 (9th Cir. 2009).

4. Declaratory Relief: Defendants' Counterpart to Injunctive Relief

Classic Liquor Importers, Ltd. v. Spirits Int'l B.V.

151 F. Supp. 3d 451 (S.D.N.Y. 2015)

Rakoff, U.S.D.J.

....

The declaratory judgment procedure is of critical importance to new businesses that seek to clarify their rights before expending significant resources on activities that potentially infringe a more established business's trademarks. This case illustrates why.

Plaintiff Classic Liquor Importers, Ltd. ("Classic Liquor") is a newcomer to the liquor distribution business, established about two years ago "with the aim of becoming a leading developer, manufacturer, importer and seller of high quality spirits and wines. Defendant Spirits International B.V. ("SPI"), by contrast, is a leader in the industry; its vodka brands include STOLICHNAYA, ELIT BY STOLICHNAYA, and ELIT.

Classic Liquor asserts that it has committed millions of dollars to developing its first product, a vodka that it plans to market under the mark ROYAL ELITE. On October 30, 2014, Classic Liquor filed a trademark application in the United States Patent and Trademark Office ("USPTO") for the name ROYAL ELITE. In February

2015, the USPTO approved the ROYAL ELITE mark for publication, subject to third-party opposition.

In a cease-and-desist letter mailed to Classic Liquor on or about May 5, 2015, SPI alleged that Classic Liquor's proposed use of the ROYAL ELITE mark in connection with liquor and beverage products would infringe SPI's United States trademarks of variations of the term ELIT. The letter requested that SPI withdraw its application for the ROYAL ELITE mark and limit its application for a related mark to exclude wines, spirits, and other beverages. By letter dated May 21, 2015, Classic Liquor responded to SPI's letter, arguing that its proposed use of its ROYAL ELITE mark would not infringe SPI's ELIT marks. By letter dated July 10, 2015, SPI sought clarifications from Classic Liquor as to which products it planned to bring to market under the ROYAL ELITE mark. Without apparently responding to this last letter, Classic Liquor, on August 18, 2015, commenced this action.

In its Amended Complaint, filed on October 28, 2015, Classic Liquor seeks ... a declaratory judgment that its vodka bottles and the trademarks and trade dress used thereon do not infringe SPI's trademarks....

... Classic Liquor's president, Simon Alishaev, avers that "[s]ales and shipment of the ROYAL ELITE vodka to retailers commenced as early as September 2015, and the public has been purchasing [plaintiff's] ROYAL ELITE vodka[] product since then." Mr. Alishaev further avers that "Royal Elite is currently in approximately 100 retailers in the New York metro area and is expanding to over 10 states in January 2016—with further expansion to over 20 states through 2016."

... [T]he Amended Complaint asserts that on September 28, 2015, SPI filed an opposition to Classic Liquor's application for the ROYAL ELITE mark with the USPTO's Trademark Trial and Appeal Board ("TTAB"). However, in a letter to Classic Liquor dated October 28, 2015 (*i.e.*, well after this litigation commenced), SPI represented that it had no present intention to sue Classic Liquor for trademark infringement and purportedly did not have such an intention when it sent its cease-and-desist letter on May 5, 2015. Nonetheless, SPI reserved its right to pursue litigation "if and when Classic Liquor launches and has any actual sales, and depending on the iteration of the mark used, and if we observe or learn of any actual consumer confusion." ...

On November 16, 2015, SPI moved to dismiss Count[] One ... of the Amended Complaint [and] ... argued that the Court lacked subject-matter jurisdiction over Classic Liquor's declaratory judgment claim for non-infringement.

The Declaratory Judgment Act is properly invoked where "there is a substantial controversy, between parties having adverse legal interests, of sufficient immediacy and reality to warrant the issuance of a declaratory judgment." *Maryland Cas. Co. v. Pac. Coal & Oil Co.*, 312 U.S. 270, 273, 61 S. Ct. 510, 85 L. Ed. 826 (1941). The dispute must "admi[t] of specific relief through a decree of a conclusive character, as distinguished from an opinion advising what the law would be upon a hypothetical state of facts." *MedImmune, Inc. v. Genentech, Inc.*, 549 U.S. 118, 127, 127 S. Ct. 764, 166 L. Ed. 2d 604 (2007) (internal quotation marks omitted). While the "Act confers on federal courts unique and substantial discretion in deciding whether to declare the rights of litigants," *Peconic Baykeeper, Inc. v. Suffolk Cty.*, 600 F.3d 180, 187 (2d Cir. 2010) (internal quotation marks omitted), a "declaratory judgment action should be entertained when the judgment will serve a useful purpose in clarifying and settling the legal relations in issue, and ... when it will terminate and afford relief from the uncertainty, insecurity, and controversy giving rise to the proceeding." *Fort Howard Paper Co. v. William D. Witterf Inc.*, 787 F.2d 784, 790 (2d Cir. 1986) (internal quotation marks omitted).

The Second Circuit has explained that "[d]eclaratory judgment actions are particularly useful in resolving trademark disputes, in order to promptly resolve controversies where the alleged owner of a trademark right threatens to sue for infringement," and, as such "the finding of an actual controversy should be determined with some liberality" in such a case. *Starter Corp. v. Converse, Inc.*, 84 F.3d 592, 596 (2d Cir. 1996). "A more restrictive view," the Court of Appeals has explained, could require a party "to go to substantial expense in the manufacture, marketing, and sale of its [product], and subject itself to considerable liability for a violation of the Lanham Act before its right to even engage in this line of commerce could be adjudicated." *Id.*

....

... SPI argues that ... the claim is impermissibly hypothetical in nature ... [and] asserts (1) that Classic Liquor fails to adequately allege that it is imminently ready to market its product under the ROYAL ELITE mark; (2) that Classic Liquor has not sufficiently fixed its mark such that it can be compared to SPI's marks; (3) that evidence of actual consumer confusion is unavailable because Classic Liquor's products are supposedly not yet on the market; and (4) that SPI has no present intention, and has never threatened, to sue Classic Liquor for infringement.

The first three arguments are largely premised on the notion that Classic Liquor has not yet brought its product to market (or at least has not yet formally so alleged in its complaints). To the extent one goes beyond the pleadings, this premise is, obviously, undermined by Mr. Alishaev's sworn representation that Classic Liquor has, in fact, been shipping and selling products under the ROYAL ELITE mark since September 2015.

... SPI argues on reply that "even under the most generous interpretation [Classic Liquor's product] launch has been exceedingly minimal," noting that plaintiff's "papers do not state whether bottles, particularly in bars and restaurants, were placed there as promotions, or in fact were sold, and if so, with what resulting revenue." ... Because, on any reasonable interpretation of Mr. Alishaev's affidavit, Classic Liquor's products have entered the consumer marketplace, SPI's arguments that Classic Liquor has not sufficiently fixed its mark, has not sufficiently alleged concrete plans to launch its products, and has brought a suit in which evidence of actual consumer confusion will be unavailable are effectively without basis.

... [E]ven if the product launch had not occurred, the result ... would be the same. Courts routinely find subject-matter jurisdiction in declaratory judgment actions brought by businesses that are reasonably apprehensive that they will face infringement suits with respect to marks and products they are on the verge of introducing into commerce. *See Starter Corp.*, 84 F.3d at 596 (declaratory judgment available to plaintiff who can "demonstrate an actual intent and ability to imminently engage in the allegedly infringing conduct").[4]

. . . .

The claim that there was no prior threat of litigation is unpersuasive. In its letter of May 5, 2015, SPI stated that Classic Liquor's "proposed registration and use of the confusingly similar trademarks ROYAL ELITE will amount to unlawful infringement and dilution of [SPI's] registered trademark rights," and that if Classic Liquor does not cease and desist from using ROYAL ELITE, SPI will "vigorously protect[] its trademarks." This is clearly a threat of future litigation. . . .

While the May 5 letter was followed by a less aggressive letter dated July 10, 2015, seeking clarifications from Classic Liquor as to which products it planned to bring to market under the ROYAL ELITE marks, the July 10 letter by no means withdrew the substance of the May 5 letter. Defendant is not entitled to argue, after taking action that compelled plaintiff to sue to clarify its rights vis-a-vis defendant, that it did not really mean what it said in its May 5 letter. [Citations.]

SPI points to its self-serving representation in its October 28, 2015 letter to plaintiff—sent months after this litigation commenced—that it had no "present intent to sue Classic Liquor for trademark infringement." But Classic Liquor can hardly be blamed for taking little comfort in this litigation-induced disclaimer, insofar as SPI expressly reserved the right in that very same letter to sue Classic Liquor for trademark infringement "if and when Classic Liquor launches and has any actual sales, and depending on the iteration of the mark used, and if we observe or learn of any actual consumer confusion." The launch has now occurred. . . . Moreover, SPI has opposed Classic Liquor's applications to register the mark ROYAL ELITE in many countries, including the United States. Thus, even if one were to credit (which the Court does not) defendant's assertion that it has no intention of suing plaintiff, this action presents a "substantial controversy, between parties having adverse legal interests, of sufficient immediacy and reality to warrant the issuance of a declaratory judgment." *Maryland Cas. Co.*, 312 U.S. at 273.

---

4. *Starter Corp.* was abrogated by the Supreme Court's decision in *MedImmune* to the extent that *Starter Corp.* held that a declaratory judgment plaintiff must be under an imminent threat of liability. *See Vina Casa Tamaya S.A. v. Oakville Hills Cellar, Inc.*, 784 F. Supp. 2d 391, 395 (S.D.N.Y. 2011) ("*MedImmune* rejected lower courts' previous requirement that a declaratory judgment plaintiff seeking to establish federal jurisdiction must demonstrate 'a reasonable apprehension of imminent suit.'" (citation omitted)). *Starter Corp.*'s "actual intent and ability" requirement remains good law, however. *See Bruce Winston*, 2010 U.S. Dist. LEXIS 96974, 2010 WL 3629592, at *4 (finding that this prong of the *Starter Corp.* test "should survive because it is anchored in the requirement of the specificity and immediacy of the dispute which the Court reaffirmed in *MedImmune*").

In passing, it may be noted that SPI relied heavily in its briefing and at oral argument on the *Bruce Winston* case, in which [the court] found that he lacked subject-matter jurisdiction over plaintiff's declaratory judgment claim where defendant Harry Winston, Inc. did not object to plaintiff's present and planned uses of the BRUCE WINSTON mark—despite the fact that it was opposing plaintiff's application to register the mark with the TTAB. *See Bruce Winston,* 2010 U.S. Dist. LEXIS 96974, 2010 WL 3629592, at *1....

Specifically, in *Bruce Winston*, plaintiff had been using its marks for almost a decade and defendant had made clear that it took no issue with such uses. Rather, it was opposing plaintiff's attempt to register the BRUCE WINSTON mark because it would be tantamount to giving plaintiff (or a potential assignee of the mark) a "blank check" to use the mark in whatever potentially infringing way it wished going forward. [Citation.] Here, by contrast, SPI explicitly advised Classic Liquor in its May 5 letter—before Classic Liquor had even launched its products—that it viewed its proposed use of the ROYAL ELITE mark as infringing. And even though SPI's October 28 letter attempted to walk back that threat, the October 28 letter does not purport to give Classic Liquor any assurance that SPI will not view Classic Liquor's use of the ROYAL ELITE mark as infringing going forward. To the contrary, it reserves the right to sue if it observes consumer confusion. Thus, in sharp contrast to *Bruce Winston,* this action presents "a specific dispute about an imminent" or present activity. [Citation.]

....

At bottom, SPI is seeking to preserve an option to sue Classic Liquor at its discretion—potentially after Classic Liquor, an upstart in the industry, spends millions of dollars building brand recognition and establishing a foothold in the marketplace. While one can understand why holding this litigation in abeyance might be attractive to defendant, the Declaratory Judgment Act is designed precisely for situations like these where a party is put on notice by another that it may be infringing the noticing party's rights and seeks to "clarify[] and settl[e] the legal relations in issue," as well as "relief from the uncertainty, insecurity, and controversy giving rise to the proceeding." *Fort Howard Paper Co.,* 787 F.2d at 790. To state the obvious, the declaratory judgment procedure would be pointless in this context if a party had to wait to be sued for infringement before seeking a declaratory judgment of non-infringement.

....

In sum, ... the Court ... denie[s] [defendant's motion to dismiss] as to plaintiff's declaratory judgment claim.

Question

If a trademark owner wants another to stop using a mark but does not want to litigate over it, is there a danger in sending a cease and desist demand that the recipient will bring a declaratory judgment action? Should this possibility influence whether such a demand should be sent or, if sent, how it should be worded? What if the trademark owner has a preference for the jurisdiction where it resides in the event a suit must be brought, is there a danger that a recipient of a cease and desist demand will bring a declaratory judgment action in a different jurisdiction?

B. Monetary Relief

1. Assessing Profits and/or Damages

Taco Cabana Int'l, Inc. v. Two Pesos, Inc.

932 F.2d 1113 (5th Cir. 1991), *aff'd*, 505 U.S. 763 (1992)

Reavley, Circuit Judge:

[See the Supreme Court's decision, *supra* Chapter 7[A], for a discussion of the facts in the case.]

....

III. Remedies

The jury awarded $306,000 for lost profits, $628,300 for lost income, and nothing for loss of good will.... Finding intentional and deliberate infringement, the district court doubled the damages to $1,868,600 for the trade dress infringement, and awarded attorneys' fees of $937,550. The court further ordered Two Pesos to make several changes in the design of its Texas restaurants, and to dispel customer confusion by displaying a prominent sign for a year acknowledging that Two Pesos had unfairly copied Taco Cabana's restaurant concept.

Taco Cabana claims injury, under the so-called "headstart" theory, from Two Pesos' preemption of the Houston market and other areas. According to Two Pesos, the jury based damages on an initial franchise fee of $10,000 per store and continuing royalty of 1% (which is substantially below what Taco Cabana or Two Pesos requires of actual franchisees). The lost profits calculation apparently assumes a foreclosure of five restaurants in the Houston area at a 6% profit margin on sales of $1.7 million per store with an incremental fixed overhead of $204,000. The jury heard abundant evidence on the foregoing remedies, including detailed damage models yielding totals substantially exceeding the jury's award.

A. Trade-Dress Infringement Remedies

... Section 35 provides that a prevailing plaintiff may,

> subject to the principles of equity ... recover (1) defendant's profits, (2) any damages sustained by the plaintiff, and (3) the costs of the action.... In assessing damages the court may enter judgment, according to the circumstances of the case, for any sum above the amount found as actual damages, not exceeding three times such amount. Such sum ... shall constitute compensation and not a penalty. The court in exceptional cases may award reasonable attorney fees to the prevailing party.

15 U.S.C.A. § 1117(a) (West Supp. 1991)....

....

C. Profits and Damages

Two Pesos argues that a monetary award requires evidence of actual confusion, and that only diverted sales provide a proper measure of damages. We disagree, as we did in *Boston Professional Hockey* [*Ass'n v. Dallas Cap & Emblem Mfg., Inc.*], 597 F.2d [71], 76 [(5th Cir. 1979)] (plaintiff's failure to quantify any damages from diverted sales did not preclude recovery for deprivation of economic benefits that would have accrued from licensing); *see also Shen Mfg. Co. v. Suncrest Mills, Inc.*, 673 F. Supp. 1199, 1206 (S.D.N.Y. 1987) (defendant's intentional copying entitles plaintiff to profits based on unjust enrichment theory despite failure to prove any instance of actual confusion). Because we embrace the "headstart" theory as the apt framework for monetary recovery, we need not pursue the issue of actual diverted sales.

Especially given the volatility of the restaurant industry, and the significant value of securing the image of "market leader," we believe the "headstart" theory provides an apt framework for Taco Cabana's monetary recovery. Two Pesos' infringement foreclosed the Houston market, which Gabriel Gelb characterized as "one of the most affluent Mexican food markets in the country." Based on the Houston market alone, Gelb estimated lost profits of $4.4 million. Other damage models produced even higher figures. The jury award easily qualifies as reasonable compensation to Taco Cabana.

D. Enhanced Damages

Finding that Two Pesos' conduct was willful and deliberate, the district court doubled the jury award for infringement. Judge Singleton asserted that "[u]nder the facts of this case and listening to the witnesses and judging the credibility myself, I can come to no other conclusion than to find that Two Pesos' actions were willful in the sense that it was deliberate.... The evidence was overwhelming." Intentional imitation alone—as opposed to intentional infringement—would not suffice for the requisite bad faith, but as his Order recites, Judge Singleton found "that Two Pesos intentionally and deliberately infringed Taco Cabana's trade dress."

We must respect the fact that section 35 endows the district court with considerable discretion in fashioning an appropriate remedy for infringement. An enhancement of damages may be based on a finding of willful infringement, but cannot be punitive. *Playboy Enterprises, Inc. v. P.K. Sorren Export Co.*, 546 F. Supp. 987, 998 (S.D. Fla. 1982); *see* 15 U.S.C.A. § 1117(a) (West Supp. 1991) (any sum in excess of actual damages must "constitute compensation and not a penalty").

It is anomalous to say that an enhancement of damages, which implies an award exceeding the amount found "compensatory," must be "compensatory" and not "punitive." Responding to that anomaly, we have suggested that enhancement could, consistent with the "principles of equity" promoted in section 35, provide proper redress to an otherwise undercompensated plaintiff where imprecise damage calculations fail to do justice, particularly where the imprecision results from defendant's conduct.

Boston Professional Hockey, 597 F.2d at 77 (increased damages justified when defendant withholds or misrepresents available sales records or otherwise obstructs ascertainment of damages); *accord P.K. Sorren*, 546 F. Supp. at 998–99 (award of excess damages appropriate where "record strongly indicates that plaintiff's damages and defendant's profits were both greater than the amounts conclusively proven"). We find no evidence of information obstruction by Two Pesos, but we acknowledge the trial court's superior capacity to discern the elements of equitable compensation. Given the substantial evidence of willful infringement, the jury finding of trade secret misappropriation, and the evidence of substantial damages not reflected in the jury award, we cannot say that Judge Singleton abused his discretion.

....

Banjo Buddies, Inc. v. Renosky

399 F.3d 168 (3d Cir. 2005)

Roth, Circuit Judge:

This appeal requires us to decide whether a showing of willful infringement is a prerequisite to an accounting of a trademark infringer's profits for a violation of section 43(a) of the Lanham Act. We hold that willfulness is an important equitable factor but not a prerequisite to such an award, noting that our contrary position in *SecuraComm Consulting Inc. v. Securacom Inc.*, 166 F.3d 182, 190 (3d Cir. 1999), has been superseded by a 1999 amendment to the Lanham Act. We further affirm the District Court's resolution of several other damages issues, with a single exception explained below.

I. Factual Background and Procedural History

Joseph Renosky was a member of the board of directors of Banjo Buddies, Inc., ("Banjo Buddies" or "BBI") from February 1996 until May 1999. Banjo Buddies' principal product during that time was an extremely successful fishing lure called the Banjo Minnow, which Renosky helped develop.

The Banjo Minnow was principally advertised via "infomercial" broadcast, and was also sold in sporting goods catalogs and sporting goods stores. Tristar Products, Inc., obtained exclusive rights to advertise and sell the Banjo Minnow through all forms of "direct response marketing, ... print media, and retail distribution." BBI received 48% of Tristar's net profits in return. Renosky agreed to provide the manufactured Banjo Minnow lure kit through his corporation, Renosky Lures, Inc., to both Tristar and BBI at $5.20 per kit. Renosky received additional shares of BBI stock in exchange for producing the Banjo Minnow kits at a "fair price." ...

During the Banjo Minnow's early success in 1996, Renosky presented an idea to the BBI board for a "new and improved" Banjo Minnow called the Bionic Minnow. The board took no formal action on the proposal, and a month later Renosky advised one of BBI's directors that he would develop the new lure independently. At least two board members urged Renosky against this course of action, but Renosky could not be swayed. He immediately began developing the Bionic Minnow through Renosky Lures and ultimately marketed the new lure via infomercial and other means beginning in February 1999.

... BBI brought suit ... that Renosky violated section 43(a) of the Lanham Act, 15 U.S.C. § 1125(a), by developing and marketing the Bionic Minnow in such a way that customers would believe the Bionic Minnow was a Banjo Buddies product....

The District Court ... found that Renosky was liable for "false designation of origin" under § 43(a) of the Lanham Act ... [and] concluded that Renosky should be forced to disgorge the net profits of the Bionic Minnow project under section 35(a) of the Lanham Act, 15 U.S.C. § 1117(a), which provides for such accountings as an equitable remedy for Lanham Act violations....

Accordingly, the District Court ordered Renosky to pay to Banjo Buddies the net profits earned by the Bionic Minnow project, and to produce "verified financial records" attesting to this amount. Renosky never produced these records, despite numerous delays and court orders. Renosky did ultimately retain an independent financial analysis (the "Alpern Report"), which the District Court accepted for purposes of establishing the total sales of the Bionic Minnow through November 2002. However, the court rejected that report's conclusion that the Bionic Minnow project suffered a net loss. Accordingly, the court calculated Renosky's profits by multiplying the total sales figure by 16%, based on testimony from Renosky's business manager that Renosky Lures products typically earn a "bottom line" of between 15–17%. The court also determined that Renosky should be forced to disgorge all of the distributions (based on gross sales) made to him as a shareholder in the Bionic Minnow project. The court entered judgment in March 2003 against Renosky in the amount of $1,589,155.

....

III. Discussion

A. Willfulness Is a Factor, Not a Prerequisite.

....

The *Quick Technologies* court reaffirmed the factor-based approach elaborated in prior Fifth Circuit cases, including *Pebble Beach Co. v. Tour* 18 I, 155 F.3d 526, 554 (5th Cir. 1998), explaining that the infringer's intent was an important—but not indispensable—factor in evaluating whether equity supports disgorging the infringer's profits. *Quick Techs.*, 313 F.3d at 349. These factors "include, but are not limited to (1) whether the defendant had the intent to confuse or deceive, (2) whether sales have been diverted, (3) the adequacy of other remedies, (4) any unreasonable delay by the plaintiff in asserting his rights, (5) the public interest in making the misconduct unprofitable, and (6) whether it is a case of palming off." *Id.* (internal citations omitted).

... Relying on the *Quick Technologies* factor-based approach.... [W]e further conclude that the District Court did not abuse its discretion by ordering an accounting of Renosky's profits ... Because the District Court's findings concerning Renosky's intent are difficult to reconcile, see *supra* note 5, we will assume that factor is neutral. Nonetheless, all of the other *Quick Technologies* factors support an award of profits here.

It is likely that Renosky's conduct diverted sales from Banjo Buddies. *See Quick Techs.*, 313 F.3d at 349 (factor two). The District Court found that Renosky's marketing for the Bionic Minnow was confusingly similar to that of the Banjo Minnow, noting numerous material similarities in the infomercials used to market each product. The court also found that the two lure kits were "nearly identical" and were packaged identically. The court further found that the markets for the two products were "either the same or substantially overlapping." The District Court's observations concerning the close similarities of the products as well as their packaging and marketing schemes also strongly support the conclusion that Renosky was "palming off" the Bionic Minnow as a Banjo Buddies product. *See id.* (factor six). The public has an interest in discouraging this type of behavior, as it interferes with the consumer's ability to make informed purchasing decisions. *See id.* (factor five).

Next, there are no other adequate remedies. See *id.* (factor three). The District Court rejected Banjo Buddies' estimation of its damages (for both the Lanham Act claims and the state law claims) as too speculative. If Renosky's profits are not assessed, Banjo Buddies will be wholly uncompensated for Renosky's infringing actions. Finally, Banjo Buddies did not delay in bringing suit to stop Renosky's infringing actions. See *id.* (factor four). Accordingly, we conclude that the District Court did not abuse its discretion in deciding to order an accounting of Renosky's profits.

B. The District Court's Estimation of Profits.

....

Section 35(a) provides that "in assessing profits the plaintiff shall be required to prove defendant's sales only; defendant must prove all elements of cost or deduction claimed." 15 U.S.C. § 1117(a); [citation]. The District Court accepted the Alpern report's figure for total sales of the Bionic Minnow through November 22, 2002. Thus, Banjo Buddies' burden of proof was satisfied by Renosky's accountant's financial report.

However, the District Court held that Renosky failed to satisfy his burden of proof regarding costs and deductions ... [and] rejected the Alpern report's conclusion that Renosky suffered a loss of $492,699.00 for several reasons.... First, the court observed that the Alpern report's summary of direct expenses associated with the Bionic Minnow project—totaling almost five million dollars—was sorely lacking in detail, lumping costs into six broad categories with no explanation of what specific expenses those categories represented....

Renosky fails to address the District Court's remaining reasons for rejecting the Alpern report's analysis of costs associated with the Bionic Minnow project. Most important, Renosky makes no attempt to explain why he twice failed to produce verified financial records supporting his claimed costs and deductions as ordered by the court. The court also observed several unexplained discrepancies between the Alpern report's summary of direct expenses and other evidence in the record. Next, the court rejected the Alpern report's conclusion that "shared expenses" associated with the

Bionic Minnow project were $1,416,050. The court explained that the Alpern report did not show how "each item of general expense contributed to the production of the infringing items in issue and offer a fair and acceptable formula for allocating a given portion of overhead to the particular infringing items at issue." (citing *Design v. K-Mart Apparel Corp.*, 13 F.3d 559, 565–66 (2d Cir. 1994)). Finally, the court found that the Alpern report's "bottom line" lacked credibility. The court doubted that Renosky would allow the Bionic Minnow to lose nearly half a million dollars, and noted that Renosky's claimed loss was inconsistent with his attempt to secure clarification that profits accrued after November 22, 2002, would belong to him and not Banjo Buddies. Considering the collective strength of these arguments together with Renosky's failure to address most of them, we conclude that the District Court's rejection of the Alpern report's cost analysis was not clearly erroneous.

Because Renosky failed to meet his burden of proving costs and deductions, ... [t]he court decided to rely on the trial testimony of Renosky's business manager, Denice Altemus, who stated that Renosky Lures products "always [make] a bottom line of between 15 and 17%." Renosky argues that there is no direct evidence that the Bionic Minnow earned a profit in this range. While this is true, the onus of producing such evidence is clearly placed by § 35(a) on Renosky, not Banjo Buddies. 15 U.S.C. § 1117(a). The District Court has broad discretion in shaping remedies under § 35(a), [citation], and did not abuse that discretion by estimating ... a profit of 16%.

Renosky further argues that ... if Banjo Buddies had produced the Bionic Minnow, it would have received only 48% of the profits earned from the sale of the lure under its contract with TriStar....

[T]his argument ... fails as a matter of law, because there is no requirement that the defendant's profits approximate the plaintiff's damages. Section 35(a) permits a plaintiff to recover, "subject to the principles of equity ... (1) defendant's profits, (2) any damages sustained by the plaintiff, and (3) the costs of the action." 15 U.S.C. § 1117(a). As the Second Circuit observed in *George Basch*, 968 F.2d at 1537, an accounting of the infringer's profits is available if the defendant is unjustly enriched, if the plaintiff sustained damages, or if an accounting is necessary to deter infringement. These rationales are stated disjunctively; any one will do. *See id.* Allowing Renosky to keep half the estimated profits of his infringing activities would not serve the Congressional purpose of making infringement unprofitable—Renosky would be unjustly enriched and other would be infringers would be insufficiently deterred. [Citations.] Even if Banjo Buddies receives a windfall in this case—which, as discussed in the previous paragraph, is impossible for this court to determine—it is preferable that Banjo Buddies rather than Renosky receive the benefits of Renosky's infringement. [Citation.]

....

IV. Conclusion

For the reasons given above, we will affirm the District Court's award of Renosky's estimated profits on the Bionic Minnow project but reverse the District Court's decision to add Renosky's shareholder distributions to that amount. We will affirm the District Court's judgment in all other respects.

Romag Fasteners, Inc. v. Fossil, Inc., 817 F.3d 782 (Fed. Cir. 2016). The Federal Circuit took a different position from the Third Circuit in *Banjo Buddies, supra.* Applying Second Circuit law in an appeal from a denial of a profits award based on a finding of no willfulness in an infringement case, the Federal Circuit concluded that the 1999 amendments to the Lanham Act did not change the law as to whether willfulness could be a prerequisite to a profits award. Accordingly, the decision affirmed a finding that plaintiff could not recover profits. The decision noted the split in circuits concerning the willfulness requirement both before and after the 1999 amendments. The pre-1999 language of section 35(a) stated:

> "... provided that plaintiffs who had established "a violation of any right of the registrant of a mark registered in the Patent and Trademark Office, or a violation under section § 1125(a) of this title ... shall be entitled ... *subject to the principles of equity*, to recover (1) defendant's profits, (2) any damages sustained by the plaintiff, and (3) the costs of the action." 15 U.S.C. § 1117(a) (1996) (emphasis added) (amended 1999).
>
> ....
>
> Several courts of appeals determined that a finding of willfulness was required for an award of the defendant's profits. Among these was the Second Circuit, whose law governs here. The Second Circuit took the view that "under [15 U.S.C. § 1117(a)] of the Lanham Act, a plaintiff must prove that an infringer acted with willful deception before the infringer's profits are recoverable by way of an accounting." *George Basch Co. v. Blue Coral, Inc.*, 968 F.2d 1532, 1540 (2d Cir. 1992); [citation]. And, in the Second Circuit, while "a finding of willful deceptiveness is necessary in order to warrant an accounting for profits ... it may not be sufficient"—
>
>> generally, there are other factors to be considered. Among these are such familiar concerns as: (1) the degree of certainty that the defendant benefited from the unlawful conduct; (2) availability and adequacy of other remedies; (3) the role of a particular defendant in effectuating the infringement; (4) plaintiff's laches; and (5) plaintiff's unclean hands. The district court's discretion lies in assessing the relative importance of these factors and determining whether, on the whole, the equities weigh in favor of an accounting. As the Lanham Act dictates, every award is "subject to equitable principles" and should be determined "according to the circumstances of the case."

George Basch, 968 F.2d at 1540–41 (citations omitted).

The Federal Circuit noted that before the amendments, the District of Columbia, Third and Tenth Circuits also required willfulness; whereas, the Fifth and Eleventh Circuits did not. A review of the purpose of the 1999 amendments to differentiate profits and damages for the new dilution ground led the Federal Circuit to conclude that no change to existing law was intended as to infringement and section 43(a) claims.

> ... In 1996, Congress amended the Lanham Act to create a cause of action for trademark dilution, providing for injunctive relief and also monetary relief if the dilution was "wilfully intended." *See* Federal Trademark Dilution Act of 1995, Pub. L. No. 104-98, § 3, 109 Stat. 985, 985–86 (1996) (codified at 15 U.S.C. § 1125(c) (1997)).
>
> But the effort to award monetary relief for willful dilution was ineffective because the new dilution provision made available "the remed[y] set forth in section[] 1117(a)" without amending § 1117(a) to provide for such monetary remedies in the case of dilution. *Id.* In 1999, Congress amended § 1117(a) to correct this error. *See* Trademark Amendments Act of 1999, Pub. L. No. 106-43, § 3(b), 113 Stat. 218, 219. The current version of § 1117(a) reads,
>
> > [w]hen a violation of any right of the registrant of a mark registered in the Patent and Trademark Office, a violation under section 1125(a) or (d) of this title, or a willful violation under section 1125(c) of this title, shall have been established in any civil action arising under this chapter, the plaintiff shall be entitled, subject to the provisions of sections 1111 and 1114 of this title, and subject to the principles of equity, to recover (1) defendant's profits, (2) any damages sustained by the plaintiff, and (3) the costs of the action.
>
> 15 U.S.C. § 1117(a) (2014) (new language added by 1999 amendment underscored).
>
> ... After the 1999 amendment, the Fifth Circuit continued to hold that willfulness is not a prerequisite to an award of infringer's profits for violations of § 1125(a). *See Quick Techs., Inc. v. Sage Group PLC*, 313 F.3d 338, 349 (5th Cir. 2002) ("In accordance with our previous decisions, and in light of the plain language of § 1117(a), however, we decline to adopt a bright-line rule in which a showing of willful infringement is a prerequisite to an accounting of profits."). The Third Circuit reversed course, holding that the 1999 amendment barred a willfulness requirement, *see Banjo Buddies, Inc. v. Renosky*, 399 F.3d 168, 175 (3d Cir. 2005) ("By adding this word ['willful'] to the statute in 1999, but limiting it to [§ 1125(c)] violations, Congress effectively superseded the willfulness requirement as applied to [§ 1125(a)]."), and the Fourth Circuit held that a finding of willfulness is not required, *see Synergistic Int'l, LLC v. Korman*, 470 F.3d 162, 175 (4th Cir. 2006) ("[A]lthough willfulness is a proper and important factor in an assessment of whether to make a damages award, it is not an essential predicate thereto."); *see also Laukus v. Rio Brands, Inc.*, 391 F. App'x 416, 424 (6th Cir. 2010) ("Although showing willfulness is not required, willfulness is one element that courts may consider in weighing the equities.").
>
> Other courts of appeals considering the issue found a willfulness requirement for an award of the infringer's profits. *See Fifty-Six Hope Rd. Music,*

Ltd. v. A.V.E.L.A., Inc., 778 F.3d 1059, 1073–74 (9th Cir. 2015) ("Awarding profits is proper only where the defendant is attempting to gain the value of an established name of another. Willful infringement carries a connotation of deliberate intent to deceive.") [citation]; *see also Fishman Transducers, Inc. v. Paul*, 684 F.3d 187, 191 (1st Cir. 2012) ("[O]ur cases usually[, with the exception of direct competition cases,] require willfulness ... to allow either (1) more than single damages or (2) a recovery of the defendant's profits."); *W. Diversified Servs., Inc. v. Hyundai Motor Am., Inc.*, 427 F.3d 1269, 1270 (10th Cir. 2005) ("We hold that the willfulness required to support an award of profits under the Lanham Act typically requires an intent to appropriate the goodwill of another's mark."); 5 J. Thomas McCarthy, *McCarthy on Trademarks and Unfair Competition* § 30.62 (2015) ("Th[e] reading of Congressional intent [as removing the willfulness requirement] is inaccurate. In fact, the 1999 amendment of Lanham Act § 35(a) was not intended to change the law by removing willfulness as a requirement for an award of profits in a classic infringement case, but rather was meant to correct a drafting error.... The courts have leveraged this statutory change beyond its intended scope....").

... Contrary to Romag's argument, the willfulness rule was reaffirmed by the Second Circuit. In *Merck Eprova AG v. Gnosis S.p.A.*, a district court found that Gnosis had misrepresented the purity of certain nutritional supplement products and was liable for violating section 43(a) of the Lanham Act, 15 U.S.C. § 1125(a). 760 F.3d 247, 252–53 (2d Cir. 2014). The district court found that Gnosis had willfully deceived its customers and awarded Gnosis's profits to prevent its unjust enrichment, to compensate Merck for the business it lost as a result of Gnosis's false advertising, and to deter future unlawful conduct. *Id.* at 262. The Second Circuit restated its rule that "a finding of defendant's willful deceptiveness is a prerequisite for awarding profits," *id.* at 261 (quoting *George Basch*, 968 F.2d at 1537), and affirmed the district court's award of profits, as "willful, deliberate deception [had] been proved," *id.* at 262.

While the Second Circuit has not directly addressed the 1999 amendment, we see nothing in the 1999 amendment that permits us to declare that the governing Second Circuit precedent is no longer good law.

First, the limited purpose of the 1999 amendment was simply to correct an error in the 1996 Dilution Act. The legislative history of the Trademark Amendments Act of 1999 does not indicate that Congress contemplated its addition of "or a willful violation under section § 1125(c)," as affecting any change to the willfulness requirement for violations of § 1125(a). *See* H.R. Rep. No. 106-250, at 6 (1999). Rather, the legislative history indicates only that Congress sought to correct the mistaken omissions, from the text of 15 U.S.C. §§ 1117(a) and 1118, of willful violations of § 1125(c). *Id.* In short, there is no indication that Congress in 1999 intended to make a change in the law of trademark infringement as opposed to dilution. The history does

> not even acknowledge the pre-1999 split in the courts of appeals on the willfulness requirement for a recovery of infringer's profits, much less indicate a desire to change it. Given the alleged significance of the purported change, one would have expected to see an acknowledgement or discussion from Congress of the courts of appeals cases in the relevant area if Congress had intended to resolve the circuit conflict. [Citation.]
>
> Second, the language of the statute as to infringement liability remained unchanged with regard to the award of profits under the "principles of equity." 15 U.S.C. § 1117(a). By reenacting that standard, Congress could not have ratified a consistent judicial construction of § 1117(a) because there was a split in the courts of appeals, at the time of the 1999 amendment, as to the willfulness requirement. [Citations.]
>
> ....
>
> In any event, the "willful violation" language added in 1999 to cover dilution cannot simply be explained as a desire to distinguish dilution cases from violations of § 1125(a) for purposes of profits awards. The "willful violation" language was necessary to distinguish dilution cases from, *inter alia*, infringement cases in the area of damages (as opposed to profits), since it was established in the courts of appeals that willfulness was not required for damages recovery, *see* 5 J. Thomas McCarthy, *McCarthy on Trademarks and* Unfair *Competition* § 30.75 (2015), and Congress wished to limit damages awards for dilution to cases involving willfulness. So too, even with respect to awards of profits in dilution cases, the addition of "willful violation" was necessary to establish a uniform rule since the courts of appeals were divided as to the willfulness requirement in the infringement context, and silence might have generated a circuit split in the dilution area.

The Federal Circuit concluded:

> We conclude that the 1999 amendment to the Lanham Act left the law where it existed before 1999—namely, it left a conflict among the courts of appeals as to whether willfulness was required for recovery of profits. We accordingly follow the Second Circuit's decision in *George Basch* as reaffirmed in *Merck*. Under that standard, we agree with the district court that Romag is not entitled to recover Fossil's profits, as Romag did not prove that Fossil infringed willfully.

Questions

1. *Banjo Buddies* and *Romag* differ as to the effect of the 1999 Lanham Act amendments on whether willfulness can be a prerequisite to a profit award in an infringement or section 43(a) claim. Is the continuing split in circuits on this question an invitation to forum shopping?

2. Is there any way a victim of trademark infringement can gain an award of punitive damages? *See, e.g., Transgo, Inc. v. Ajac Transmission Parts Corp.*, 768 F.2d 1001

(9th Cir. 1985) (upholding award of punitive damages under California law); *Big O Tire Dealers, Inc. v. Goodyear Tire & Rubber Co., infra* (upholding award of punitive damages under Colorado law).

3. If the Lanham Act forbids punitive damage awards in a non-counterfeiting case, why should such relief continue to be available under state law?

4. Section 1117(a) provides that actual damages may be enhanced up to three times the amount and that profits may be adjusted up or down if the court finds that recovery is inadequate or excessive. Can a court add profits and damages together and apply a multiplier up to three times? *See Thompson v. Haynes*, 305 F.3d 1369 (Fed. Cir. 2002).

5. Section 1117(a) provides that in "assessing profits the plaintiff shall be required to prove defendant's sales only; defendant must prove all elements of cost or deduction claimed." Is it legitimate for a plaintiff to prove a defendant's gross sales of all products via defendant's tax returns or does a plaintiff need to prove gross sales of the infringing items? *See Venture Tape Corp. v. McGills Glass Warehouse*, 540 F.3d 56 (1st Cir. 2008).

2. Corrective Advertising

Big O Tire Dealers, Inc. v. Goodyear Tire & Rubber Co.

561 F.2d 1365 (10th Cir. 1977)

Lewis, Chief Judge:

[Big O, a $200,000 a year company, sued Goodyear Tire for a false designation under section 43(a) and for common law trademark infringement based on Goodyear's national campaign using the term "Bigfoot" to advertise one of its tires. Although Goodyear's search did not reveal Big O's prior common law use of BIGFOOT in connection with tires, the use came to Goodyear's attention shortly before the advertising launch. Despite Big O's insistence that it did not want money but only wanted Goodyear to halt the campaign as soon as possible, Goodyear refused. The jury rendered a verdict for Big O and Goodyear appealed.]

... Goodyear challenges the jury's verdict awarding Big O $2.8 million in compensatory damages.... Goodyear contends Big O failed to prove either the fact or the amount of damages. Big O asserts the evidence supporting the fact of damages falls into two categories: (1) Goodyear's enormous effort to adopt, use, and absorb Big O's trademark virtually destroyed Big O's ability to make any effective use of its "Big Foot" trademark and (2) Goodyear's false statements that "Bigfoot" was available only from Goodyear created the appearance of dishonesty and wrongful conduct by Big O thereby harming its reputation within the trade and with the public. We agree with the district court that there is sufficient evidence to support the jury's finding of the fact of damages.

... Big O claims the only way it can be restored to the position it was in before Goodyear infringed its trademark is to conduct a corrective advertising campaign ...

to dispel the public confusion caused by Goodyear's infringement. Goodyear spent approximately $10 million on its "Bigfoot" advertising campaign. Thus, Big O advances two rationales in support of the $2.8 million award: (1) there were Big O Tire Dealers in 28 percent of the states (14 of 50) and 28 percent of $10 million equals the amount of the award; and (2) the Federal Trade Commission generally orders businesses who engage in misleading advertising to spend approximately 25 percent of their advertising budget on corrective advertising and this award is roughly 25 percent of the amount Goodyear spent infringing on Big O's trademark. The district court used the first rationale in denying Goodyear's motion to set the verdict aside. The second rationale was presented by Big O at oral argument.

The purpose of general compensatory damages is to make the plaintiff whole. Big O concedes it was unable to prove with precision the amount necessary to make itself whole. However, the district court concluded "[the] damages awarded by the jury would enable Big O to do an equivalent volume of advertising in the states in which there are Big O dealers to inform their customers, potential customers, and the public as a whole about the true facts in this dispute or anything else necessary to eliminate the confusion." 408 F. Supp. 1232. Moreover, the Supreme Court has pointed out that a plaintiff's ability to prove with precision the amount necessary to make itself whole does not preclude recovery since

> "[the] most elementary conceptions of justice and public policy require that the wrongdoer shall bear the risk of the uncertainty which his own wrong has created."

Bigelow v. RKO Radio Pictures, Inc., 327 U.S. 251, 265.

There is precedent for the recovery of corrective advertising expenses incurred by a plaintiff to counteract the public confusion resulting from a defendant's wrongful conduct. [Here, however,] Big O did not spend any money prior to trial in advertising to counteract the confusion from the Goodyear advertising. It is clear from the record Big O did not have the economic resources to conduct an advertising campaign sufficient to counteract Goodyear's $9,690,029 saturation advertising campaign. We are thus confronted with the question whether the law should apply differently to those who have the economic power to help themselves concurrently with the wrong than to those who must seek redress through the courts. Under the facts of this case we are convinced the answer must be no. Goodyear contends the recovery of advertising expenses should be limited to those actually incurred prior to trial. In this case the effect of such a rule would be to recognize that Big O has a right to the exclusive use of its trademark but has no remedy to be put in the position it was in prior to September 16, 1974, before Goodyear effectively usurped Big O's trademark. The impact of Goodyear's "Bigfoot" campaign was devastating. The infringing mark was seen repeatedly by millions of consumers. It is clear from the record that Goodyear deeply penetrated the public consciousness. Thus, Big O is entitled to recover a reasonable amount equivalent to that of a concurrent corrective advertising campaign.

As the district court pointed out, the jury's verdict of $2.8 million corresponds to 28 percent of the approximately $10 million Goodyear spent infringing Big O's mark. Big O has dealers in 14 states which equals 28 percent of the 50 states. Big O also points out the jury's award is close to 25 percent of the amount Goodyear spent infringing on Big O's mark. Big O emphasizes that the Federal Trade Commission often requires businesses who engage in misleading advertising to spend 25 percent of their advertising budget on corrective advertising.

Taking cognizance of these two alternative rationales for the jury's award for compensatory damages we are convinced the award is not capable of support as to any amount in excess of $678,302. As the district court implied in attempting to explain the jury's verdict, Big O is not entitled to the total amount Goodyear spent on its nationwide campaign since Big O only has dealers in 14 states, thus making it unnecessary for Big O to run a nationwide advertising campaign. Furthermore, implicit in the FTC's 25 percent rule in corrective advertising cases is the fact that dispelling confusion and deception in the consuming public's mind does not require a dollar-for-dollar expenditure. In keeping with "[the] constant tendency of the courts ... to find some way in which damages can be awarded where a wrong has been done," we hold that the maximum amount which a jury could reasonably find necessary to place Big O in the position it was in before September 16, 1974, vis-a-vis its "Big Foot" trademark, is $678,302. We arrive at this amount by taking 28 percent of the $9,690,029 it was stipulated Goodyear spent on its "Bigfoot" campaign, and then reducing that figure by 75 percent in accordance with the FTC rule, since we agree with that agency's determination that a dollar-for dollar expenditure for corrective advertising is unnecessary to dispel the effects of confusing and misleading advertising.

....

U-Haul International, Inc. v. Jartran, Inc.

793 F.2d 1034 (9th Cir. 1986)

Sneed, Circuit Judge:

U-Haul International, Inc. (U-Haul) sued Jartran, Inc. (Jartran) for false comparative advertising under section 43(a) of the Lanham Act, 15 U.S.C. § 1125(a), and under the common law. The district court awarded U-Haul $40 million and attorney fees, as well as a permanent injunction against certain Jartran advertisements. *U-Haul International, Inc. v. Jartran, Inc.*, 601 F. Supp. 1140 (D. Ariz. 1984). Jartran appeals on several grounds.

I. FACTS

The U-Haul System has dominated the self-move consumer rental industry for many years. In mid-1979, Jartran entered that market on a national basis. It engaged in a nationwide newspaper advertising campaign comparing itself to U-Haul. The campaign lasted from the summer of 1979 to December of 1980 and included advertisements in forty-one states and the District of Columbia. While Jartran's revenues increased from $7 million in 1979 to $80 million in 1980, revenues of the U-Haul

System declined for the first time in its history, from $395 to $378 million. The tremendous success of the advertisements is demonstrated not only by the financial growth of Jartran, but also by Jartran's receipt of the prestigious "Gold Effie" award, which the American Marketing Association awards annually in recognition of effective advertising campaigns.

....

The district judge calculated damages with respect to each claim under two distinct methods ... The second theory relied on the cost of the advertising campaign to Jartran, $6 million, and the cost of corrective advertising by the U-Haul System, $13.6 million. This ... produced an award of $20 million. On the Lanham Act count, the district court doubled the $20 million under section 35 of the Lanham Act.... Because we affirm the calculation of the award based on advertising expenditures and the doubling of the award under section 35 of the Lanham Act, we need not address Jartran's challenges to the [alternative method]....

Jartran raises three challenges to the district judge's conclusion that Jartran is liable to U-Haul. First, it argues that the injury suffered by U-Haul was insufficiently direct to support a recovery under the Lanham Act. Second, it argues that the actual deception and reliance of consumers can be proved only by surveys of actual consumers. Finally, it argues that it is inappropriate to presume actual deception and reliance from proof of Jartran's intent to deceive. Because we reject the first and third challenges, we affirm the district court's findings of deception and reliance. Addressing the second challenge thus becomes unnecessary.

....

B. *Presumption of Consumer Deception and Reliance*

... [T]he district court held that "publication of deliberately false comparative claims gives rise to a presumption of actual deception and reliance...."

To support the district court's conclusion, U-Haul cites a false advertising case granting injunctive relief, *McNeilab, Inc. v. American Home Products Corp.*, 501 F. Supp. 517 (S.D.N.Y. 1980), and two of our "palming off" cases granting damages, *National Van Lines v. Dean*, 237 F.2d 688, 692 (9th Cir. 1956); *National Lead Co. v. Wolfe*, 223 F.2d 195, 202, 205 (9th Cir.), *cert. denied*, 350 U.S. 883, 76 S. Ct. 135, 100 L. Ed. 778, 107 U.S.P.Q. (BNA) 362 (1955). Jartran responds by pointing out that *McNeilab* was an injunction case, in which the burden of proof is substantially lower, and that the two "palming off" cases are not comparative advertising cases as is this one.

Jartran's distinctions do not undermine the force of U-Haul's argument. It is not easy to establish actual consumer deception through direct evidence. The expenditure by a competitor of substantial funds in an effort to deceive consumers and influence their purchasing decisions justifies the existence of a presumption that consumers are, in fact, being deceived. He who has attempted to deceive should not complain when required to bear the burden of rebutting a presumption that he succeeded.

The district judge's application of this presumption was fair and in keeping with our early "palming off" precedents. We hold that it was correct to apply it in this context.

CALCULATION OF THE AWARD

A. Calculation of Damages

Jartran does not dispute the propriety of basing a damage award on corrective advertising expenditures. *See, e.g., Otis Clapp & Son, Inc., v. Filmore Vitamin Co.*, 754 F.2d 738, 745 (7th Cir. 1985). Jartran does argue, however, that the district court did not have discretion to award damages for corrective advertising expenditures more than twice the size of the original advertising expenditures. Jartran relies on *Big O Tire Dealers, Inc. v. Goodyear Tire & Rubber Co.*, 561 F.2d 1365, 1375 (10th Cir. 1977), *cert. dismissed* under Sup. Ct. R. 60, 434 U.S. 1052 (1978). There the court reversed a jury verdict and held that the plaintiff's recovery for corrective advertising was limited to 25% of the defendant's wrongful expenditures. *Big O*, however, is plainly inapplicable. It explicitly distinguishes itself from the plentiful earlier precedent allowing recovery of actual corrective advertising expenditures. In *Big O* the plaintiff had not made any corrective advertising expenditures. *See id.*; *see also Cuisinarts, Inc. v. Robot-Coupe International Corp.*, 580 F. Supp. 634, 641 (S.D.N.Y. 1984) (limiting *Big O* in the same manner). It provides no basis for overturning the district court's award in this case of actual corrective advertising expenditures.

Jartran's complaints as to the propriety of U-Haul's corrective advertising campaign should have been addressed to the district court. That court did consider arguments that the advertising was not necessary to correct harm to the U-Haul trademark; but it rejected them. We agree with the district court's conclusion.

....

Questions

1. Do you agree with the *Big O* court's determination of the sum to award for corrective advertising? What other measures might you apply?

2. Once plaintiff has been awarded compensatory damages for corrective advertising, must it in fact devote that money to corrective advertising?

3. The jury in *Big O* also awarded plaintiff $16,800,000 in punitive damages under the state law claim. Under Colorado law, exemplary damages must bear some relation to the compensatory award. The jury award thus bore a 6:1 ratio to the jury's compensatory award. Is this "reasonable"? Should the appellate court apply a 6:1 ratio to the reduced compensatory award in determining exemplary damages?

4. Was the court in *U-Haul* correct in allowing plaintiff all of its expenses for corrective advertising even though the amount exceeded that incurred by the defendant for its advertising?

5. A rival court reporter acquired a URL incorporating the name of a competitor and then re-directed the domain name to her own website. When the competitor complained, the court reporter ceased re-directing the website but refused to transfer the domain name. The competitor successfully secured a transfer of the domain name through a WIPO arbitration and brought an action under §§ 43(a) and (d), claiming the cost of damage control spent on the WIPO arbitration. Should such damages be available when there are no claims of false advertising and the plaintiff has not engaged in any corrective advertising? *See Migliore & Assoc., LLC v. Kentuckiana Reporters, LLC*, 2015 U.S. Dist. LEXIS 19568 (D. Ky. Feb. 19, 2015).

3. Attorney's Fees

Nightingale Home Healthcare, Inc. v. Anodyne Therapy, LLC

626 F.3d 958 (7th Cir. 2010)

Posner, Circuit Judge.

After Anodyne successfully defended against Nightingale's suit, see 589 F.3d 881 (7th Cir. 2009), the district judge granted the defendant's request for an award of attorneys' fees in the amount of $72,747 ... based on 15 U.S.C. § 1117(a), which allows attorneys' fees to be awarded to prevailing parties in Lanham Act suits—but only in "exceptional cases," a term we shall try to clarify in this opinion because of the surprising lack of agreement among the federal courts of appeals concerning its meaning in the Act. [Citations.] The judge had granted summary judgment in favor of Anodyne on Nightingale's Lanham Act claim early in the litigation. Nightingale, which had not appealed that ruling, contends that no award of attorneys' fees is justified, because the case is not "exceptional."

The Fourth, Sixth, Tenth, and D.C. Circuits apply different tests of exceptionality depending on whether it was the plaintiff or the defendant who prevailed. In the Fourth and D.C. Circuits a prevailing plaintiff is entitled to an award of attorneys' fees if the defendant's infringement (most cases under the Lanham Act charge trademark infringement) was willful or in bad faith (these terms being regarded as synonyms), while a prevailing defendant "can qualify for an award of attorney fees upon a showing of 'something less than bad faith' by the plaintiff," such as "economic coercion, groundless arguments, and failure to cite controlling law." *Retail Services Inc. v. Freebies Publishing*, 364 F.3d 535, 550 (4th Cir. 2004); *Reader's Digest Ass'n, Inc. v. Conservative Digest, Inc.*, 821 F.2d 800, 808–09, 261 U.S. App. D.C. 312 (D.C. Cir. 1987).

In the Tenth Circuit the prevailing plaintiff has to prove that the defendant acted in bad faith, while the prevailing defendant need only show "(1) ... lack of any foundation [of the lawsuit], (2) the plaintiff's bad faith in bringing the suit, (3) the unusually vexatious and oppressive manner in which it is prosecuted, or (4) perhaps for other reasons as well." *National Ass'n of Professional Baseball Leagues, Inc. v. Very Minor Leagues, Inc.*, 223 F.3d 1143, 1147 (10th Cir. 2000). Given the fourth item in this list, the Tenth Circuit can hardly be said to have a test.

The Sixth Circuit asks in the case of a prevailing plaintiff whether the defendant's infringement of the plaintiff's trademark was "malicious, fraudulent, willful, or deliberate," and in the case of a prevailing defendant whether the plaintiff's suit was "oppressive." *Eagles, Ltd. v. American Eagle Foundation*, 356 F.3d 724, 728 (6th Cir. 2004). As factors indicating oppressiveness, Eagles quotes the Tenth Circuit's list but states in the alternative, quoting (see *id.* at 729) our opinion in *S Industries, Inc. v.*

Centra 2000, Inc., 249 F.3d 625, 627 (7th Cir. 2001), that "a suit is oppressive if it lacked merit, had elements of an abuse of process claim, and plaintiff's conduct unreasonably increased the cost of defending against the suit."

The Second, Fifth, and Eleventh Circuits require prevailing defendants, as well as prevailing plaintiffs, to prove that their opponent litigated in bad faith, or (when the defendant is the prevailing party) that the suit was a fraud. *Patsy's Brand, Inc. v. I.O.B. Realty, Inc.*, 317 F.3d 209, 221–22 (2d Cir. 2003); *Procter & Gamble Co. v. Amway Corp.*, 280 F.3d 519, 527–28 (5th Cir. 2002); *Lipscher v. LRP Publications, Inc.*, 266 F.3d 1305, 1320 (11th Cir. 2001); *Tire Kingdom, Inc. v. Morgan Tire & Auto, Inc.*, 253 F.3d 1332, 1335–36 (11th Cir. 2001) (per curiam). The Fifth Circuit adds that a court considering a prevailing defendant's application for an award of attorneys' fees should "consider the merits and substance of the civil action when examining the plaintiffs' good or bad faith." *Procter & Gamble Co. v. Amway Corp., supra*, 280 F.3d at 528.

The First, Third, Eighth, and Ninth Circuits, like the Second and the Eleventh, do not distinguish between prevailing plaintiffs and prevailing defendants; neither do they require a showing of bad faith. *Tamko Roofing Products, Inc. v. Ideal Roofing Co.*, 282 F.3d 23, 32 (1st Cir. 2002) ("willfulness short of bad faith or fraud will suffice when equitable considerations justify an award and the district court supportably finds the case exceptional"); *Securacomm Consulting, Inc. v. Securacom Inc.*, 224 F.3d 273, 280 (3d Cir. 2000) ("culpable conduct on the part of the losing party" is required but "comes in a variety of forms and may vary depending on the circumstances of a particular case"); *Stephen W. Boney, Inc. v. Boney Services, Inc.*, 127 F.3d 821, 827 (9th Cir. 1997) ("a finding that the losing party has acted in bad faith may provide evidence that the case is exceptional" but "other exceptional circumstances may [also] warrant a fee award"); *Hartman v. Hallmark Cards, Inc.*, 833 F.2d 117, 123 (8th Cir. 1987) ("bad faith is not a prerequisite" to an award). Yet a later Ninth Circuit decision interprets "exceptional" to mean "the defendant acted maliciously, fraudulently, deliberately, or willfully" (note the echo of the Sixth Circuit's *Eagles* decision) or the plaintiff's case was "groundless, unreasonable, vexatious, or pursued in bad faith." *Love v. Associated Newspapers, Ltd.*, 611 F.3d 601, 615 (9th Cir. 2010).

And where are we, the Seventh Circuit, in this jumble? In *Door Systems, Inc. v. Pro-Line Door Systems, Inc.*, 126 F.3d 1028, 1031 (7th Cir. 1997), we said that the test was whether the conduct of the party from which the payment of attorneys' fees was sought had been "oppressive," and that "whether the plaintiff's suit was oppressive" turned on whether the suit "was something that might be described not just as a losing suit but as a suit that had elements of an abuse of process, whether or not it had all the elements of the tort." But that, we said, "would not be the right question if the plaintiff had prevailed and was seeking the award of attorneys' fees. In such a case the focus would be on whether the defendant had lacked a solid justification for the defense or had put the plaintiff to an unreasonable expense in suing." *Id.*...

In later cases we said that oppressive conduct by a plaintiff ... would be conduct that "lacked merit, had elements of an abuse of process claim, and plaintiff's conduct in the litigation unreasonably increased the cost of defending against the suit,"

S Industries, Inc. v. Centra 2000, Inc., supra, 249 F.3d at 627; [citation], that oppressive conduct by defendants included not only willful infringement of the plaintiff's trademark but also "vexatious litigation conduct," *TE-TA-MA Truth Foundation-Family of URI, Inc. v. World Church of the Creator*, 392 F.3d 248, 261–63 (7th Cir. 2004); and that a finding that a suit was oppressive could be "based solely on the weakness" of the plaintiff's claims, *S Industries, Inc. v. Centra 2000, Inc., supra*, 249 F.3d at 627, or the plaintiff's "vexatious litigation conduct." *TE-TA-MA Truth Foundation-Family of URI, Inc. v. World Church of the Creator, supra*, 392 F.3d at 263. So "vexatious litigation conduct" by the losing party can justify the award of attorneys' fees to the winner, regardless of which side engages in such conduct, as long as it's the losing side.

....

It may be helpful ... to start with first principles, by asking why the Lanham Act makes an exception ... to the "American" rule that forbids shifting the litigation expenses of the prevailing party to the loser.

The reason has been said to be that "the public interest in the integrity of marks as a measure of quality of products" is so great that it would be "unconscionable not to provide a complete remedy including attorney fees for acts which courts have characterized as malicious, fraudulent, deliberate, and willful," and the award of fees "would make a trademark owner's remedy complete in enforcing his mark against willful infringers, and would give defendants a remedy against unfounded suits." S. Rep. No. 1400, 93d Cong., 2d Sess. 5–6 (1974)....

A more practical concern is the potential for businesses to use Lanham Act litigation for strategic purposes, not to obtain a judgment or defeat a claim but to obtain a competitive advantage independent of the outcome of the case by piling litigation costs on a competitor. Almost all cases under the Act ... whether they are suits for trademark infringement or for false advertising, 15 U.S.C. §§ 1114, 1125(a), are between competitors. The owner of a trademark might bring a Lanham Act suit against a new entrant into his market, alleging trademark infringement but really just hoping to drive out the entrant by imposing heavy litigation costs on him. *See, e.g., Peaceable Planet, Inc. v. Ty, Inc.*, 362 F.3d 986, 987 (7th Cir. 2004). "Trademark suits, like much other commercial litigation, often are characterized by firms' desire to heap costs on their rivals, imposing marketplace losses out of proportion to the legal merits." *Mead Johnson & Co. v. Abbott Laboratories*, 201 F.3d 883, 888 (7th Cir. 2000) ... Similarly, a large firm sued for trademark infringement by a small one might mount a scorched-earth defense to a meritorious claim in the hope of imposing prohibitive litigation costs on the plaintiff.

These, then, are the types of suit rightly adjudged "exceptional"; for in a battle of equals each contestant can bear his own litigation costs without impairing competition.

When the plaintiff is the oppressor, the concept of abuse of process provides a helpful characterization of his conduct. Unlike malicious prosecution, which involves filing a baseless suit to harass or intimidate an antagonist, abuse of process is the use of the litigation process for an improper purpose, whether or not the claim is colorable.... Abuse of process is a prime example of litigating in bad faith.

The term "abuse of process" is not used to describe behavior by defendants. *Id.*... If a defendant's trademark infringement or false advertising is blatant, his insistence on mounting a costly defense is the same misconduct as a plaintiff's bringing a case (frivolous or not) not in order to obtain a favorable judgment but instead to burden the defendant with costs likely to drive it out of the market. Predatory initiation of suit is mirrored in predatory resistance to valid claims.

We conclude that a case under the Lanham Act is "exceptional," in the sense of warranting an award of reasonable attorneys' fees to the winning party, if the losing party was the plaintiff and was guilty of abuse of process in suing, or if the losing party was the defendant and had no defense yet persisted in the trademark infringement or false advertising for which he was being sued, in order to impose costs on his opponent.

This approach captures the concerns that underlie the various tests and offers a pathway through the semantic jungle. It can account for most of the case outcomes in the various circuits with the exception of those that make it easier for prevailing defendants to obtain attorneys' fees than prevailing plaintiffs.... Plaintiffs and defendants in Lanham Act cases usually are symmetrically situated: they are businesses. Of course they may be very different in size, but this is not a reason for a general rule favoring prevailing plaintiffs or prevailing defendants, for there is no correlation between the size of a party and which side of the litigation he's on. Big businesses sue big and small businesses for trademark infringement and false advertising, and small businesses sue big and small businesses for the same torts. Disparity in size will often be relevant in evaluating the legitimacy of the suit or defense, but it is as likely to favor the defendant as the plaintiff.

....

... A tort is proved in a tort suit. But a proceeding for an award of attorneys' fees is not a suit; it is a tail dangling from a suit. We don't want the tail to wag the dog, and this means that an elaborate inquiry into the state of mind of the party from whom reimbursement of attorneys' fees is sought should be avoided. It should be enough to justify the award if the party seeking it can show that his opponent's claim or defense was objectively unreasonable—was a claim or defense that a rational litigant would pursue only because it would impose disproportionate costs on his opponent—in other words only because it was extortionate in character if not necessarily in provable intention. That should be enough to make a case "exceptional."

In this case, however, there is more. Nightingale, a provider of home healthcare services, had bought several infrared lamps from Anodyne that were designed to relieve pain and improve circulation, paying $6,000 for each lamp. Its Lanham Act claim was that Anodyne's sales representative had falsely represented that the lamp had been approved by the Food and Drug Administration for treatment of peripheral neuropathy. The device was FDA-approved and was intended for the treatment of peripheral neuropathy, and though the FDA had not approved it for that purpose this did not preclude a physician or other healthcare provider, such as Nightingale, from prescribing the device to patients as a treatment for that condition. The decision to prescribe such "off-label usage," as it is called, is deemed a professional judgment for the healthcare provider to make. 21 U.S.C. §396.

Nightingale told its patients that Anodyne's device was intended for treating peripheral neuropathy, but as far as appears did not tell them that it had been approved by the FDA for the treatment of that condition—a representation that could have gotten Nightingale into trouble with the agency. And when it replaced Anodyne's lamps with the virtually identical lamps of another company (apparently for reasons of price, unrelated to the scope of the FDA's approval), it advertised them just as it had advertised Anodyne's lamps—as devices for the treatment of peripheral neuropathy.

Not only had the Lanham Act claim no possible merit (which would not by itself demonstrate an abuse of process), but the district judge found that Nightingale had made the claim in an attempt to coerce a price reduction from Anodyne. Nightingale would have been content to continue buying Anodyne's lamps, as indicated by its purchasing lamps that were subject to the same limited FDA approval and advertising them the same way. The fact that the FDA had not approved Anodyne's lamps for treatment of peripheral neuropathy was thus of no consequence, for neither had it approved for that purpose the lamps that Nightingale bought to replace Anodyne's. To bring a frivolous claim in order to obtain an advantage unrelated to obtaining a favorable judgment is to commit an abuse of process.

....

We not only affirm the judgment of the district court but also grant Anodyne's motion for fees and costs pursuant to Rule 38 of the appellate rules....

Trafficschool.com Inc. v. Edriver Inc., 653 F.3d 820 (9th Cir. 2011). The appellate court reversed a denial of attorney's fees to plaintiffs who, although awarded no damages in challenging defendants' misleading practices on DMV.org website, were granted injunctive relief.

> Lanham Act cases generally consider whether defendants' conduct was "fraudulent, deliberate, or willful." *Horphag Research Ltd. v. Garcia*, 475 F.3d 1029, 1039 (9th Cir. 2007); [citation]. By examining only the relief awarded to plaintiffs, and failing to consider defendants' conduct, the district court applied the wrong legal standard. *See Lahoti v. Vericheck, Inc.*, 636 F.3d 501, 511 (9th Cir. 2011).
>
> No doubt, the court may take plaintiffs' failure to recover damages into account when exercising its discretion to award fees, but it must also consider that plaintiffs obtained a judgment and an injunction that ameliorate a serious public harm. In addition, the court must weigh the unlawfulness of defendants' conduct. It would be inequitable to force plaintiffs to bear the entire cost of enjoining defendants' willful deception when the injunction confers substantial benefits on the public. *See Comm. for Idaho's High Desert, Inc. v.*

> *Yost*, 92 F.3d 814, 818–19, 825 (9th Cir. 1996) (plaintiff was entitled to attorney's fees when district court awarded injunction but not damages); *Audi AG v. D'Amato*, 469 F.3d 534, 550–51 (6th Cir. 2006) (same). Plaintiffs put an end to the confusion created by DMV.org and stopped consumers from mistakenly transferring sensitive personal information to a commercial website. This conferred significant benefits on third parties and also vindicated plaintiffs' right to a "market free of false advertising." *Johnson & Johnson* [*v. Carter-Wallace, Inc.*], 631 F.2d [186,] 192 [(2d Cir. 1980)]. The district court abused its discretion by failing to consider these substantial benefits or defendants' bad acts in determining whether to award attorney's fees.

In **Georgia-Pacific Consumer Products LP v. von Drehle Corp.**, 781 F.3d 710 (4th Cir. 2015), the district court entered a nationwide injunction against defendant's distribution of paper towels designed to fit within plaintiff's enMOTION towel dispensers after a jury finding of contributory trademark infringement. It also trebled the jury's award of $791,431 to $2,374,293 and awarded attorney's fees of $2,225,782 after a finding that "exceptional" circumstances existed. The Fourth Circuit found that a nationwide injunction was improper because parallel actions had been brought against two of defendant's distributors that had resulted in prior findings of no infringement by the Sixth and Eighth Circuits. As a matter of comity, the Fourth Circuit limited the injunctive relief to the states within the Fourth Circuit. With respect to the trebling of damages, the appellate court found that the district court "conflated § 1117(a) and § 1117(b)." Section 1117(b) was inapplicable as the case did not involve a counterfeit mark, and the enhancement of damages available under section 1117(a) was inapplicable because there was no showing of the inadequacy of the award. With respect to the award of attorney's fees, the appellate court noted:

> ... Section 1117(a) provides, "The court in exceptional cases may award reasonable attorney fees to the prevailing party." The court based its willful-and-intentional finding on the fact that von Drehle specifically designed its 810-B paper towels for use in Georgia-Pacific's enMotion dispenser and knew that they would be stuffed in those dispensers.
>
> Von Drehle contends that this case is not "exceptional," as that term is used in § 1117(a), and that the district court erroneously relied on its purposeful conduct in distributing towels for use in Georgia-Pacific's enMotion machines, conflating willful and intentional conduct with willful and intentional infringement. We agree, especially since Von Drehle reasonably believed that its conduct was lawful.
>
> ....
>
> [A]fter the court had received the parties' briefs in this case, the Supreme Court handed down its decision in *Octane Fitness, LLC v. ICON Health & Fitness, Inc.*, 134 S. Ct. 1749, 188 L. Ed. 2d 816 (2014). While *Octane Fitness* did not construe § 1117(a), it did construe a parallel and identical provision in the Patent Act, which provides, "The court in exceptional cases may award

reasonable attorney fees to the prevailing party." 35 U.S.C. § 285. The Federal Circuit had previously given § 285 a narrow interpretation, concluding:

> A case may be deemed exceptional when there has been some material inappropriate conduct related to the matter in litigation, such as willful infringement, fraud or inequitable conduct in procuring the patent, misconduct during litigation, vexatious or unjustified litigation, conduct that violates Fed. R. Civ. P. 11, or like infractions. Absent misconduct in conduct of the litigation or in securing the patent, sanctions may be imposed against the patentee only if both (1) the litigation is brought in subjective bad faith, and (2) the litigation is objectively baseless.

Brooks Furniture Mfg., Inc. v. Dutailier Int'l, Inc., 393 F.3d 1378, 1381 (Fed. Cir. 2005); (citation omitted). But the Supreme Court rejected the Federal Circuit's interpretation of "exceptional," describing the Federal Circuit's test as "unduly rigid." *Octane Fitness*, 134 S. Ct. at 1755. Relying on the statute's simple text and dictionary definitions of "exceptional," the Court concluded:

> [A]n "exceptional" case is simply one that stands out from others with respect to the substantive strength of a party's litigating position (considering both the governing law and the facts of the case) or the unreasonable manner in which the case was litigated. District courts may determine whether a case is "exceptional" in the case-by-case exercise of their discretion, considering the totality of the circumstances.

Id. at 1756. The Court then pointed the district courts to the same nonexclusive list of factors that it had previously identified as relevant for use in determining whether to award attorneys fees under a similar provision of the Copyright Act, a list that included "frivolousness, motivation, objective unreasonableness (both in the factual and legal components of the case) and the need in particular circumstances to advance considerations of compensation and deterrence." *Id.* at 1756 n.6 (*quoting Fogerty v. Fantasy, Inc.*, 510 U.S. 517, 534 n.19, 114 S. Ct. 1023, 127 L. Ed. 2d 455 (1994)) (internal quotation marks omitted).

To be sure, the *Octane Fitness* Court did not interpret the attorneys fees provision of § 1117(a). But the language of § 1117(a) and § 285 is identical, and we conclude that there is no reason not to apply the *Octane Fitness* standard when considering the award of attorneys fees under § 1117(a). *See Fair Wind Sailing, Inc. v. Dempster*, 764 F.3d 303, 314–15 (3d Cir. 2014) ("While *Octane Fitness* directly concerns the scope of a district court's discretion to award fees for [an] 'exceptional' case under § 285 of the Patent Act, the case controls our interpretation of [§ 1117(a)]. Not only is § 285 identical to [§ 1117(a)], but Congress referenced § 285 in passing [§ 1117(a)]").

Thus, we conclude that a district court may find a case "exceptional" and therefore award attorneys fees to the prevailing party under § 1117(a) when it determines, in light of the totality of the circumstances, that (1) "there is an unusual discrepancy in the merits of the positions taken by the parties," *Fair Wind Sailing*, 764 F.3d at 315, based on the non-prevailing party's position as either frivolous or objectively unreasonable, *see Octane Fitness*, 134 S. Ct. at 1756 n.6; (2) the non-prevailing party "has litigated the case in an 'unreasonable manner,'" *Fair Wind Sailing*, 764 F.3d at 315 (*quoting Octane Fitness*, 134 S. Ct. at 1756); or (3) there is otherwise "the need in particular circumstances to advance considerations of compensation and deterrence," *Octane Fitness*, 134 S. Ct. at 1756 n.6 (*quoting Fogerty*, 510 U.S. at 534 n.19) (internal quotation marks omitted).

Because the district court did not have the benefit of the *Octane Fitness* standard when considering whether Georgia-Pacific was entitled to attorneys fees under § 1117(a), we vacate the court's award of attorneys fees and remand the question for further consideration in light of this standard.

Questions

1. Should a court consider the fact that a judgment is entered by default in determining whether circumstances are "exceptional" for purposes of awarding attorney's fees? *Cf. Reed Pub. B.V. v. Execulink, Inc.*, 1998 U.S. Dist. LEXIS 18245 (D.N.J. Nov. 17, 1998).

2. Where both federal and state infringement claims are brought and state law provides for the award of attorney's fees to a prevailing plaintiff without any showing of the "exceptional circumstances" required by the Lanham Act, is the state statute preempted? *See Attrezzi LLC v. Maytag Corp.*, 436 F.3d 32 (1st Cir. 2006).

3. Is Judge Posner's approach in *Nightingale Homes* better at defining "exceptional circumstances" than the approaches of the myriad circuit courts that he cites? Why/why not?

4. The Fifth Circuit has joined the Third and Fourth Circuits and has adopted the *Octane Fitness* standard of exceptionality. *See Baker v. DeShong*, 821 F.3d 620 (5th Cir. 2016). Is the *Octane* standard different from that articulated by the Seventh Circuit in *Nightingale*? Would the *Nightingale* result be different under the *Octane Fitness* standard?

5. A recent Seventh Circuit decision applied the *Nightingale* standard in assessing whether the circumstances were "exceptional" so as to require an award of attorney's fees. The opinion did not reference *Octane Fitness*. Should it have done so? *See Burford v. Accounting Practice Sales, Inc.*, 786 F.3d 582 (7th Cir. 2015); *see also Premium Balloon Accessories, Inc. v. Creative Balloons Mfg., Inc.*, 573 Fed. Appx. 547 (6th Cir. 2014) (not recommended for full-text publication) (applied *Octane Fitness* standard to attorney's fees question on patent issue, but applied Sixth Circuit standard on trade dress infringement issue).

6. Although the district court in *Georgia Pacific* originally awarded attorney's fees, on remand from the Fourth Circuit directing application of the *Octane* test of exceptionality, the court denied attorney's fees. *Georgia-Pacific Consumer Products LP v. Von Drehle Corp.*, 2015 U.S. Dist. LEXIS 156723 (E.D.N.C. Nov. 18, 2015). Does the *Octane* test raise the bar to granting a fee award?

C. Trademark Counterfeiting

Note: The Problem of Counterfeiting

Counterfeiting remedies present a marked contrast to those available for federal trademark infringement, dilution, unfair competition or cybersquatting and include criminal penalties, ex parte civil seizure orders, and statutory damages as well as mandatory attorney's fees and treble damages absent "extenuating circumstances" where there has been an "intentional" use of a counterfeit mark. The enhanced remedies exist to combat not only the normal harms trademark owners can suffer, such as diverted sales, reputation loss and potential injury to mark distinctiveness and goodwill, and that potential purchasers can suffer, such as obtaining the wrong goods or increased search costs, but also to redress other potential injuries to the public.

The International Chamber of Commerce estimates that counterfeit goods are worth $350 billion, representing about 7% of world trade. "Facts on Fakes," International Anticounterfeiting Coalition,

> http://4356049642aa3c99a6e91c99180a8219894d6198.gripelements.com/pdf/member-resources/facts_on_fakes.pdf

If accurate, this figure translates into a very substantial effect on the global economy, including lost jobs and tax revenues. For example, one estimate suggests that auto part counterfeiting costs the auto industry $12 billion in lost sales and could account for 200,000 lost jobs. *Id.*

Moreover, the Justice Department has noted the dangers that counterfeits can pose to public safety and health:

> Counterfeit marks ... can mask serious health or safety risks to consumers as in the case of counterfeit food products, batteries, prescription drugs, or auto parts ... Airline passengers are victims of counterfeit airplane parts, coronary patients are victims of counterfeit heart pumps, and children are victims of counterfeit infant formula....

"Computer Crimes & Intellectual Property Section," U.S. Dept. Of Justice, https://www.justice.gov/sites/default/files/criminal-ccips/legacy/2015/03/26/prosecuting_ip_crimes_manual_2013.pdf. The FAA, for example, estimates that 2% of airplane parts are counterfeit, and the World Health Organization estimates that about 10% of pharmaceuticals are counterfeit. "Facts On Fakes," *supra.* Resulting illness, death and crashes have been documented. *Id.*

Further, links have been reported between counterfeit operations and both organized crime and terrorist organizations, which have allegedly used counterfeiting as a money laundering or funding device. *Id.*

In reviewing the materials in this section, ask yourself whether the special remedies for counterfeiting are efficacious or necessary to protect against these harms.

1. What Is Counterfeiting?

15 U.S.C. § 1127 [Lanham Act § 45]

Counterfeit. A "counterfeit" is a spurious mark which is identical with, or substantially indistinguishable from, a registered mark.

Question

In order to be considered counterfeit, a mark must be identical or "substantially indistinguishable" from a registered mark. Under this standard, would COLDATE for toothpaste be a counterfeit of COLGATE for toothpaste? *See Colgate-Palmolive Co. v. J.M.D. All-Star Import and Export Inc.*, 486 F. Supp. 2d 286 (S.D.N.Y. 2007).

Rolex Watch, U.S.A., Inc. v. Michel Co.

179 F.3d 704 (9th Cir. 1999)

Tashima, Circuit Judge:

Micha Mottale, doing business as Michel Co. ("Mottale"), reconditions used Rolex watches with parts that are not provided or authorized by Rolex Watch, U.S.A., Inc. ("Rolex"), and sells the altered watches, as well as generic replacement parts fitting Rolex watches, to jewelry dealers and selected retail jewelers. In addition, Mottale provides the service of specially reconditioning used Rolex watches. The district court held that Mottale's retention of the original Rolex trademarks on the altered "Rolex" watches that he sells constituted trademark counterfeiting under section 32(1)(a) of the Trademark Act of 1946 ("Lanham Act"), 15 U.S.C. § 1114(1)(a), as interpreted by our decision in *Westinghouse Electric Corp. v. General Circuit Breaker & Electric Supply Inc.*, 106 F.3d 894, 899–900 (9th Cir.), *cert. denied*, 522 U.S. 857 (1997). On that basis, the district court permanently enjoined Mottale from selling such altered watches without (1) adding permanent independent marks on the non-Rolex parts, and (2) including a written disclosure concerning the generic replacement parts on tags, invoices, promotions, and advertising.

Rolex appeals ... because the changes that Mottale makes to used Rolex watches are so basic that they result in a different product. We agree, and accordingly direct the district court to enjoin Mottale from retaining Rolex's trademarks on the altered watches he sells. In addition, we reverse the district court's denial of Rolex's request for its attorney's fees on this claim and remand that request for consideration under section 35(b) of the Lanham Act, 15 U.S.C. § 1117(b).

For, to the extent that trademarks provide a means for the public to distinguish between manufacturers, they also provide incentives for manufacturers to provide quality goods. Traffickers of these counterfeit goods, however, attract some customers who would otherwise purchase the authentic goods. Trademark holders' returns to their investments in quality are thereby reduced. This reduction in profits may cause trademark holders to decrease their investments in quality below what they would spend were there no counterfeit goods. This in turn harms those consumers who wish to purchase higher quality goods.

I. FACTUAL AND PROCEDURAL BACKGROUND

....

... Rolex and official Rolex jewelers service Rolex watches. Rolex watches have a one-year warranty from Rolex; the addition of parts that are not provided or authorized by Rolex voids the watch's warranty. Rolex also will not service watches that have been modified with non-Rolex parts.

....

Mottale sells the following products related to Rolex watches: (1) used Rolex watches; (2) used Rolex watches that have been "reconditioned" or "customized" with non-Rolex parts, which we call "altered 'Rolex' watches;" (3) used Rolex watch replacement parts; and (4) generic replacement parts fitting Rolex watches. Mottale customizes used Rolex watches by replacing their bezels (the ring that surrounds the crystal and affixes it to the watch casing), dials, and bracelets, and/or by inserting diamonds into their dials. These replacement parts are not authorized or provided by Rolex. The altered "Rolex" watches retain their original Rolex trademarks on their dials and bracelets, except when Mottale replaces the bracelet. Some examples of the replacement bracelets used by Mottale bear an imitation of the Crown Device logo. The other replacement parts added by Mottale bear no independent mark.

....

The district court held that Mottale's sale of altered "Rolex" watches constituted counterfeit trademark use under section 32(1)(a) as construed in *Westinghouse*, 106 F.3d 894. In *Westinghouse*, we held that retaining the original Westinghouse trademarks on used, reconditioned circuit breakers sold by circuit breaker vendors constituted trademark counterfeiting under section 32(1)(a). *See id.* at 899–900. We rejected the vendors' suggestion that duplication of a trademark is necessary for trademark counterfeiting:

> [A] copy of a mark is no more likely to confuse the public than is the original; in fact, the public is more likely to be deceived by an original mark because it serves as a perfect imitation. In short, the distinction between using a duplication versus using an original has no relevance to the purposes of trademark law. When an original mark is attached to a product in such a way as to deceive the public, the product itself becomes a "counterfeit" just as it would if an imitation of the mark were attached.

Id. at 900.

Here the district court found that retention of the original Rolex marks on altered "Rolex" watches, in the absence of adequate disclosures that the altered watches contain non-Rolex parts, was deceptive and misleading as to the origin of the non-Rolex parts, and likely to cause confusion to subsequent or downstream purchasers, as well as to persons observing the product. Accordingly, under *Westinghouse*, the district court concluded that this confusing use of Rolex's trademarks in connection with the sale of altered "Rolex" watches constituted a counterfeit use of the trademarks.

Based on this finding of liability, the district court issued a permanent injunction. The district court found that the changes Mottale made to the used Rolex watches were not so extensive that Mottale should be completely enjoined from retaining Rolex's trademarks on the used Rolex watches he sells. Rather, the district court required Mottale to place an independent, permanent mark on the non-Rolex replacement parts that he adds to Rolex watches, such as "Michel Co.," and to include a written disclosure in tags, promotions, and advertising of his altered "Rolex" watches. The district court denied Rolex's request for attorneys' fees attributable to the prosecution of this claim, and for treble profits from Mottale's sales of altered "Rolex" watches.[4]

II. DISCUSSION

A. Adequacy of Injunctive Relief

....

Our analysis of Rolex's plea for greater injunctive relief begins with *Champion Spark Plug Co. v. Sanders*, 331 U.S. 125 (1947). In *Champion*, the manufacturer of Champion brand spark plugs brought a trademark infringement action against a business that repaired and reconditioned used Champion spark plugs and resold them. *See id.* at 126. The reconditioned spark plugs retained their original Champion trademark and were sold in boxes stamped with the word "Champion." *See id.* The Supreme Court upheld an injunction that permitted the business to continue to sell the reconditioned spark plugs bearing their original Champion trademark so long as the words "Used" or "Repaired" were also stamped on the plugs and the cartons included a more complete disclosure that the plugs were used and reconditioned. *See id.* 127–28, 130. The Court reasoned that it is permissible for a secondhand dealer to get some advantage from the trademark "so long as the manufacturer is not identified with the inferior qualities of the product resulting from wear and tear or the reconditioning by the dealer." *Id.* at 130 (citing *Prestonettes, Inc. v. Coty*, 264 U.S. 359 (1924)). In reaching the conclusion that stamping "Used" or "Repaired" on the plugs gave the manufacturer all the trademark protection to which it was entitled, the Court acknowledged that "cases may be imagined where the reconditioning or repair would be so extensive or so basic that it would be a misnomer to call the article by its original name, even though the words 'used' or 'repaired' were added." 331 U.S. at 129. *Champion* did not pose such as [sic] case because "the repair or reconditioning of the plugs does not give them a new design," but rather was no more than "a restoration, so far as possible, of their original condition." *Id.*

Rolex argues that this is a case where the alterations Mottale makes to Rolex's products are so basic that it is a misnomer ... to permit Mottale to retain Rolex's marks

---

4. The district court also found that Mottale sold two watches bearing Rolex trademarks that have no official Rolex parts, and one watch band bearing Rolex trademarks that is not a Rolex band at trade shows. It concluded that Mottale's sale of these completely counterfeit watches and bracelet violated section 32(1)(a) of the Lanham Act, and issued a permanent injunction, granted Rolex treble profits from these watches, and its attorneys' fees under 15 U.S.C. § 1117(b). Mottale did not appeal this ruling.

on the altered watches he sells. Mottale refurbishes the Rolex dial, sometimes adding diamonds to it, changes the watch bracelet, and/or replaces the Rolex watch bezel. Rolex asserts that the watch bezel as well as the workmanship involved in inserting diamonds into the face of the watch go to the basic performance and durability of the watch: The quality of the bezel and how it is attached affect the waterproofing of the watch; the insertion of diamonds on the face of the watch can affect the functioning of the watch hands. Rolex also contends that the durability of the watch bracelet and clasp affect the usefulness and longevity of the watch.

....

We ... conclude that the alterations that Mottale makes to the used Rolex watches he sells ... result in a new product, although one containing a Rolex movement and casing. In this light, the district court's requirement that Mottale put an independent mark, such as "Michel Co.," on the non-Rolex parts is [not] adequate to prevent consumer confusion ... Neither conveys basic changes that have been made to the watch. Nor would the face of the watch support a more adequate legend. Hence, under *Champion*, the retention of Rolex's trademarks on Mottale's altered watches is a misnomer—and a trademark infringement. We accordingly hold that the district court abused its discretion in not completely enjoining the use of Rolex's trademarks on the altered watches that Mottale sells.[8]

B. Attorney's Fees

....

There are two potential provisions under which the district court could have awarded Rolex attorney's fees for the prosecution of this claim. First, under 15 U.S.C. § 1117(a), "the court in exceptional cases may award reasonable attorney fees to the prevailing party." A trademark infringement is viewed as "exceptional" under § 1117(a) "when the infringement is malicious, fraudulent, deliberate or willful." [Citations.] Second, under 15 U.S.C. § 1117(b), in cases in which the violation of section 32(1)(a), 15 U.S.C. § 1114(1)(a), consists of "intentionally using a mark or designation, knowing such mark or designation is a counterfeit mark," the court shall grant the prevailing party a reasonable attorney's fee, unless it finds "extenuating circumstances." We have said that "in counterfeiting cases, 'unless the court finds extenuating circumstances,' treble damages and reasonable attorney's fees are available." [Citations.] Under both sections 1117(a) and 1117(b), awards are "never automatic and may be limited by equitable considerations." [Citation.]

The district court found that, except for Mottale's sale of three completely counterfeit items, Mottale's trademark violations were not exceptional under section 1117(a). The district court did not, however, make a determination of whether Rolex is entitled to attorney's fees under section 1117(b) for the prosecution of its claims

8. Rolex noted at oral argument that it did not seek, and had not sought in the district court, an injunction preventing individual owners of Rolex watches from altering their watches with non-Rolex parts. Neither the district court's injunction, nor the injunction we direct it to enter, enjoins Mottale from altering Rolex watches at the specific request of an individual watch owner.

that Mottale's altered "Rolex" watches violate trademark counterfeiting prohibitions. Where, as here, the district court finds trademark counterfeiting in violation of section 1114(1)(a), the district court must, when requested, address whether the prevailing party is entitled to the remedies provided by section 1117(b) for those violations. See 15 U.S.C. § 1117(b) (providing treble profits or damages and a reasonable attorney's fee for certain trademark counterfeit violations of 15 U.S.C. § 1114(1)(a)).

....

III. CONCLUSION

Because the changes that Mottale makes to used Rolex watches are so basic that they result in a different product, we reverse the permanent injunction entered by the district court to the extent that it permitted Mottale to retain Rolex's trademarks on the altered "Rolex" watches he sells, and remand with directions to enter a permanent injunction consistent with this opinion. We also reverse the district court's denial of Rolex's request for attorney's fees under its claim that Mottale's sale of altered "Rolex" watches violated its trademark rights, and remand this claim for consideration under 15 U.S.C. § 1117(b).

Hunting World, Inc. v. Reboans, 24 U.S.P.Q.2d 1844 (N.D. Cal. 1992). Defendant, who had been denied a license to sell Hunting World articles in the San Francisco area, went directly to the Italian manufacturer of Hunting World leather goods, and there acquired merchandise which it sold in San Francisco without plaintiff's permission. In response to plaintiff's action under the Trademark Counterfeiting Act, defendant asserted that, as a seller of genuine goods, it could not be engaged in counterfeiting under the Act. The court held for plaintiff:

> Regardless of whether [defendants'] story is true and the allegedly counterfeit bags were obtained from the [plaintiff's] factory, there is a fundamental problem with defendants' position. Defendants cite cases holding that the unauthorized sale of trademarked goods alone does not give rise to a claim for trademark infringement. However, none of the authorities cited by defendants support the proposition that goods subverted from the factory are not counterfeit and do not infringe plaintiff's trademark rights. As noted in *H.L. Hayden Co. v. Siemens Medical Systems, Inc.*, 879 F.2d 1005, one of the cases cited by defendants, although "the unauthorized sale of a genuine trademarked product does not in itself constitute trademark infringement ... identical goods sold in an unauthorized manner are not 'genuine' for purposes of the Lanham Act." *Id.* at 1023. [Citations.]
>
> In *El Greco Leather Products Co. v. Shoe World, Inc.*, 806 F.2d 392, 395 (2d Cir. 1986), the court held that even if the goods were originally ordered by the trademark owner, if the goods are not inspected by the trademark owner to insure quality, they are not genuine. In so holding, the court noted that "One of the most valuable and important protections afforded by the Lanham Act is the right to control the quality of the goods manufactured

and sold under the holder's trademark." *Id.* [Citations.] Similarly, in *Shell Oil Co. v. Commercial Petroleum, Inc.*, 928 F.2d 104 (4th Cir. 1991), the court held the use of Shell's trademark by a bulk oil wholesaler violated the Lanham Act because "a product in not truly 'genuine' unless it is manufactured and distributed under quality control established under the manufacturer." *Id.* at 107.

The court finds the reasoning in *El Greco* and *Shell* to be persuasive. Defendants claim to have purchased the merchandise at issue from the same factory that manufactures the goods for Hunting World. However, there has been no showing that Hunting World inspected or approved the goods at issue. Indeed, defendants' own experts admitted that the seized bags had certain defects. According to the testimony of Mr. Antognoli [plaintiff's factory production manager], defective or slightly imperfect bags are not sold, but are either destroyed or "cannibalized," i.e., the acceptable parts are used to make new bags. If the bags were not subjected to Hunting World's quality control procedures, they are not "genuine" for purposes of the Lanham Act.

In addition, the Ninth Circuit has held under similar facts that there is a likelihood of confusion. *Model Rectifier Corp. v. Takachiho Int'l, Inc.*, 709 F.2d 1517 (9th Cir. 1983). The use of the Hunting World marks implies that the goods are subject to the Hunting World quality control guidelines. Plaintiffs have presented evidence that the goods sold by defendants did not meet Hunting World's strict quality control standards. Thus, defendants' use of Hunting World's marks is likely to confuse consumers who rely on the trademarks as an indication of quality. Accordingly, the court finds that plaintiff has demonstrated a strong likelihood of success on the merits.

Century 21 Real Estate, LLC v. Destiny Real Estate Properties, 101 U.S.P.Q.2d 1423 (N.D. Ind. 2011). The court considered whether continued use of the licensed CENTURY 21 mark by a terminated franchisee constituted use of a counterfeit or spurious mark and thus constituted counterfeiting.

[D]oes the continued use of a formerly authorized mark by a hold-over franchisee constitute the use of a "counterfeit" mark?

The Court holds that it does, in light of the reasonable meaning of the statute and Seventh Circuit precedent, and notwithstanding split authority from other courts.

First, the Sixth Circuit has expressly held that a franchisee's hold over is not counterfeiting. In *U.S. Structures, Inc. v. J.P. Structures, Inc.*, 130 F.3d 1185 (6th Cir. 1997), the plaintiff sued its former franchisee, a deck-construction business, for continuing to use the plaintiff's trademark "Archadeck" and other related trademarks. *Id.* at 1187.... The Sixth Circuit ... [held] that "[a]lthough the [defendant's] use of an original trademark is without authorization, it is not the use of a counterfeit mark," and therefore attorney's fees were only available, if at all, under the more stringent standard of § 1117(a). *Id.* at 1192. The Court's holding did not explain why the defendant had not committed counterfeiting by attaching the plaintiff's trademark to unauthorized products and services.

Next, the Ninth Circuit held that in the context of certification marks—which differ in certain respects from ordinary trademarks—the continued use of a mark by a former licensee constitutes counterfeiting. In *State of Idaho Potato Comm'n v. G & T Terminal Packaging, Inc.*, 425 F.3d 708 (9th Cir. 2005), a state agency sued a former licensee of several certified marks including "Idaho" and "Grown in Idaho" for, inter alia, violating the Lanham Act by purchasing bags with the plaintiff's certification marks on them and using them to package potatoes after the license to use the mark had expired. *Id.* at 712.... The Ninth Circuit ... held that when a registered mark is used without license, whether it constitutes counterfeiting turns on whether the use of the mark was likely to cause confusion. And it reasoned that an ex-licensee's continued use of a certification mark, which implies that the goods or services meet certain standards, is likely to cause such confusion. *Id.* at 721....

Then, in *Pennzoil-Quaker State Co. v. Smith*, 2008 U.S. Dist. LEXIS 68445, (W.D. Pa. Sept. 2, 2008), the Western District of Pennsylvania held that the use of actual Pennzoil marks by a successor business to a formerly licensed distributor was not counterfeiting. There, the plaintiff sued the defendant oil-changing business for displaying, without authorization, signs that had been loaned by Pennzoil to the former business. The court concluded that the defendant was guilty of trademark infringement, but not counterfeiting, because the marks themselves (which actually belonged to the plaintiff) were genuine and thus that plaintiff could not satisfy the "counterfeit mark" element of counterfeiting. [Citations.] It reasoned that "[t]he plain language of the statute indicates that the term 'counterfeit' refers to the mark itself, not the nature of the goods or services associated with the mark." The Court distinguished the Ninth Circuit's decision in Idaho Potato Comm'n on the grounds that certification marks serve uniquely different purposes than ordinary trademarks, and instead found the Sixth Circuit's holding in *U.S. Structures* instructive. [Citation.]

Finally, while the Seventh Circuit has not expressly considered whether a hold-over franchisee's continued unauthorized use of a franchisor's mark constitutes counterfeiting, it has provided some guidance. In *General Elec. Co. v. Speicher*, 877 F.2d 531 (7th Cir. 1989), the court held that counterfeiting is not limited to reproduced (literally "counterfeit") marks and includes the use of a genuine mark on an unauthorized product. There, General Electric brought an infringement action against a company that was supplying customers its own inserts for industrial cutting tools in General Electric-labeled boxes. The defendant argued that the scheme involved no counterfeit marks because General Electric had itself placed the mark onto the boxes at issue....

The Seventh Circuit [stated]: "The happenstance of having trademarks made by the owner in one's possession, so that one doesn't have to copy them, has no relevance to the purposes of the statute. Indeed, the danger of confusion is even greater because the 'imitation' is not merely colorable, but perfect." *Id.* at 535. There are of course many differences between the deceptive packaging in *Speicher* and the situation of a hold-over franchisee. But the fundamental principles are the same and the analogy is instructive: the ex-franchisee sells a non-genuine service wrapped in the "package" stamped with the former franchisor's trademarks. The consumer associates the service with the franchisor's brand and may never know that the service provided was unauthorized. Profits are diverted that may have gone to sales of authorized services, and the franchisor loses control over its trademarks.

Thus, the Court concludes that the Sixth Circuit's rule from *U.S. Structures* is not viable in the Seventh Circuit in light of *Speicher.* Moreover, the Court would not likely adopt the holding of *U.S. Structures* even if circuit precedent did not foreclose it.... The Court can conceive of no reason why an ex-franchisee should escape liability for counterfeiting simply because that person had access to a franchisor's original marks because of the former relationship and therefore did not need to reproduce an identical or substantially similar mark. Indeed, as Speicher points out, the risk of confusion is greater when an original mark is used to designate inauthentic goods or services. Further, the Court is not convinced by Pennzoil's attempt to distinguish *Idaho Potato Comm'n.* While certification marks indeed serve unique purposes distinct from those of ordinary trademarks, the purposes of avoiding public confusion and safeguarding the value of trademarks are common to trademarks and certification marks. And it is these purposes, not some other unique public interests, that underlie the enhanced liability for trademark counterfeiting....

Questions

1. How, if at all, do the Trademark Counterfeiting Act and its judicial interpretation affect concepts of trademarks as "property?"

2. The *El Greco* decision cited in *Hunting World* found that, although originally ordered by the plaintiff, the shoes sold by the defendant were not "genuine" because they had not been inspected by plaintiff and thus did not satisfy plaintiff's quality control procedures. If a manufacturer sells its health supplement only to health care providers and approved retailers who agree not to sell the products over the internet or to the general public except through licensed pharmacies and health clinics, would the product be considered "genuine" if a doctor acquired the supplement from third parties and sold it over the Internet without any consultation? *See Standard Process, Inc. v. Banks*, 554 F. Supp. 2d 866 (E.D. Wis. 2008).

3. Could the defendant in *Hunting World* have been prosecuted for criminal counterfeiting? Why or why not? *See* 18 U.S.C. § 2320 directly below.

---

18 U.S.C. § 2320
(Trademark Counterfeiting Act of 1984, as amended)

§ 2320. Trafficking in counterfeit goods or services

(a) Offenses. Whoever intentionally—

(1) traffics in goods or services and knowingly uses a counterfeit mark on or in connection with such goods or services,

(2) traffics in labels, patches, stickers, wrappers, badges, emblems, medallions, charms, boxes, containers, cans, cases, hangtags, documentation, or packaging of any type or nature, knowing that a counterfeit mark has been applied thereto, the use of which is likely to cause confusion, to cause mistake, or to deceive, [or]

. . .

(4) traffics in a counterfeit drug,

or attempts or conspires to violate any of paragraphs (1) through (4) shall be punished as provided in subsection (b).

(b) Penalties.

(1) In general. Whoever commits an offense under subsection (a)—

(A) if an individual, shall be fined not more than $2,000,000 or imprisoned not more than 10 years, or both, and, if a person other than an individual, shall be fined not more than $5,000,000; and

(B) for a second or subsequent offense under subsection (a), if an individual, shall be fined not more than $5,000,000 or imprisoned not more than 20 years, or both, and if other than an individual, shall be fined not more than $15,000,000.

. . . .

(3) Counterfeit military goods or services and counterfeit drugs. Whoever commits an offense under subsection (a) involving a counterfeit military good or service or counterfeit drug—

(A) if an individual, shall be fined not more than $5,000,000, imprisoned not more than 20 years, or both, and if other than an individual, be fined not more than $15,000,000; and

(B) for a second or subsequent offense, if an individual, shall be fined not more than $15,000,000, imprisoned not more than 30 years, or both, and if other than an individual, shall be fined not more than $30,000,000.

(c) Forfeiture and destruction of property; restitution. Forfeiture, destruction, and restitution relating to this section shall be subject to section 2323, to the extent provided in that section, in addition to any other similar remedies provided by law.

(d) Defenses. All defenses, affirmative defenses, and limitations on remedies that would be applicable in an action under the Lanham Act shall be applicable in a prosecution under this section. In a prosecution under this section, the defendant shall have the burden of proof, by a preponderance of the evidence, of any such affirmative defense.

....

(f) Definitions. For the purposes of this section—

(1) the term "counterfeit mark" means—

(A) a spurious mark—

(i) that is used in connection with trafficking in any goods, services, labels, patches, stickers, wrappers, badges, emblems, medallions, charms, boxes, containers, cans, cases, hangtags, documentation, or packaging of any type or nature;

(ii) that is identical with, or substantially indistinguishable from, a mark registered on the principal register in the United States Patent and Trademark Office and in use, whether or not the defendant knew such mark was so registered;

(iii) that is applied to or used in connection with the goods or services for which the mark is registered with the United States Patent and Trademark Office, or is applied to or consists of a label, patch, sticker, wrapper, badge, emblem, medallion, charm, box, container, can, case, hangtag, documentation, or packaging of any type or nature that is designed, marketed, or otherwise intended to be used on or in connection with the goods or services for which the mark is registered in the United States Patent and Trademark Office; and

(iv) the use of which is likely to cause confusion, to cause mistake, or to deceive; ...

(2) the term "financial gain" includes the receipt, or expected receipt, of anything of value;

....

(5) the term "traffic" means to transport, transfer, or otherwise dispose of, to another, for purposes of commercial advantage or private financial gain, or to make, import, export, obtain control of, or possess, with intent to so transport, transfer, or otherwise dispose of; and

(6) the term "counterfeit drug" means a drug, as defined by section 201 of the Federal Food, Drug, and Cosmetic Act, that uses a counterfeit mark on or in connection with the drug.

(g) Limitation on cause of action. Nothing in this section shall entitle the United States to bring a criminal cause of action under this section for the repackaging of genuine goods or services not intended to deceive or confuse.

United States v. Torkington

812 F.2d 1347 (11th Cir. 1987)

Kravitch, J.:

The definition of the term "counterfeit mark" under section 2320(d)(1)(A) of the Trademark Counterfeiting Act of 1984 (the Act), 15 U.S.C. §§ 1116–1118, 18 U.S.C. § 2320, is at issue in this case of first impression. The district court held that a mark is not "counterfeit" under section 2320(d)(1)(A) unless the use of the mark in connection with the goods in question would be likely to cause direct purchasers to be confused, mistaken or deceived. The court found that, given the enormous price differential between the allegedly counterfeit goods and the authentic goods, it was unlikely, as a matter of law, that direct purchasers would be confused, mistaken or deceived. The court therefore dismissed the indictment.

We find that the district court's ruling ... is not supported by either the language or the legislative history of the section. Accordingly, we hold that section 2320(d)(1)(A) does not require a showing that direct purchasers would be confused, mistaken or deceived; rather, the section is satisfied where it is shown that members of the purchasing public would be likely to be confused, mistaken or deceived. Moreover, we find that this likely confusion test includes the likelihood of confusion in a post-sale context.

I. Background

On June 2, 1985, Edward Little, a private investigator with Rolex Watch U.S.A., Inc., visited a booth operated by appellee John Torkington at the Thunderbird Swap Shop Indoor Flea Market in Fort Lauderdale, Florida. Little noticed a salesman at the booth showing customers two watches bearing both the name "Rolex" and the Rolex crown trademark emblem. The watches were virtually indistinguishable from authentic Rolex watches. These allegedly counterfeit Rolex watches had been kept under the counter; there were no such watches on display.

Little asked to see those watches as well as other models of replica Rolex watches. The salesman showed him several. The salesman said that the watches were $27 each. Little asked the salesman whether the watches were guaranteed. The salesman responded that they were not guaranteed but said that Little could return any watch that broke to the booth and the salesman would fix it. Little purchased a watch. The salesman handed it to him in a pouch bearing the Rolex crown mark. It is undisputed that Little knew that he had purchased a replica Rolex watch and not an authentic one.

On June 23, 1985, a deputy marshal executed a search and seizure order on Torkington's booth at the Thunderbird Flea Market. He seized 742 replica Rolex watches bearing both the Rolex name and crown trademarks.

On October 3, 1985, a federal grand jury in the Southern District of Florida charged Torkington with two counts of trafficking and attempting to traffic in counterfeit Rolex watches, in violation of 18 U.S.C. § 2320(a). Count I of the indictment is based on the June 2, 1985 sale of the watch to Little. Count II is based on the 742 replica Rolex watches that were seized from Torkington's booth on June 23, 1985.

... Following hearings on the matter, the court issued an order on February 10, 1986 dismissing both counts of the indictment on the ground that the replica Rolex watches were not "counterfeit" under section 2320(d)(1)(A). The United States appealed.

II. Definition of "Counterfeit Mark"

....

Section 2320 of the Trademark Counterfeiting Act was enacted in order to increase the sanctions for the counterfeiting of certain registered trademarks above the purely civil remedies available under the Trademark Act of 1946, 15 U.S.C. §1051 *et seq.* [hereinafter the Lanham Act].

Section 2320 is narrower in scope than is the Lanham Act, however. In particular, its sanctions are available only where the defendant "knowingly uses a counterfeit mark on or in connection with" the goods or services in question. 18 U.S.C. §2320(a).

The section defines "counterfeit mark" as:

(A) a spurious mark—

(i) that is used in connection with trafficking in goods or services;

(ii) that is identical with, or substantially indistinguishable from, a mark registered for those goods or services on the principal register in the United States Patent and Trademark Office and in use, whether or not the defendant knew such mark was so registered; and

(iii) the use of which is likely to cause confusion, to cause mistake, or to deceive;

18 U.S.C. §2320(d)(1)(A) (emphasis added).

A. Confusion of the Purchasing Public

The "likely to cause confusion, to cause mistake, or to deceive" test of section 2320(d)(1)(A)(iii) is broadly worded. Nothing in the plain meaning of the section restricts its scope to the use of marks that would be likely to cause direct purchasers of the goods to be confused, mistaken or deceived.

The legislative history indicates that Congress intentionally omitted such limiting language. Congress easily could have inserted language restricting the scope of section 2320(d)(1)(A)(iii) to cases where it is likely that direct purchasers would be confused, mistaken or deceived. Congress in fact had used such limiting language in a similar context in the original version of section 1114(1) of the Lanham Act. Congress therefore had before it language it could have used to restrict section 2320(d)(1)(A)(iii) to situations where direct purchasers would be likely to be confused, mistaken, or deceived. Congress chose not to use either this or similar limiting language and we will not construe section 2320(d)(1)(A)(iii) in a way that adds a restriction that Congress chose not to include.

Moreover, not only did Congress omit the limiting language of the original version of section 1114(1) from section 2320(d)(1)(A)(iii), but it explicitly employed the language of the current version of section 1114(1) of the Lanham Act. In our view, Congress thereby manifested its intent that section 2320(d)(1)(A)(iii) be given the same interpretation as is given the identical language in section 1114(1) of the Lanham Act.

The current version of section 1114(1) of the Lanham Act differs from the original version in that it does not contain the likely to confuse direct purchasers requirement of the original section. Courts interpreting the current version of section 1114(1) have held that the section does not require a showing that direct purchasers would be likely to be confused, mistaken or deceived. Instead, they construe section 1114(1) to require simply the likely confusion of the purchasing public—a term that includes individuals who are potential purchasers of the trademark holders goods as well as those who are potential direct purchasers of the allegedly counterfeit goods.

Given our conclusion that section 2320(d)(1)(A)(iii) should be interpreted similarly to the identical language in section 1114(1), we hold that section 2320(d)(1)(A)(iii) also is satisfied when the use of the mark in connection with the goods or services in question would be likely to confuse the purchasing public.

B. Post-Sale Context

In its order the district court also concluded that the likelihood of postsale confusion is irrelevant to the section 2320(d)(1)(A)(iii) inquiry. We disagree.

Under section 1114(1) of the Lanham Act, the likely to confuse test is satisfied when potential purchasers of the trademark holder's products would be likely to be confused should they encounter the allegedly counterfeit goods in a post-sale context—for example, in a direct purchaser's possession. Consequently we conclude that the likely to confuse test of section 2320(d)(1)(A)(iii) also is satisfied by a showing that it is likely that members of the public would be confused, mistaken or deceived should they encounter the allegedly counterfeit goods in a post-sale context.

This conclusion is supported by the policy goals of the Trademark Counterfeiting Act. Like the Lanham Act, the Trademark Counterfeiting Act is not simply an anti-consumer fraud statute. Rather, a central policy goal of the Act is to protect trademark holders' ability to use their marks to identify themselves to their customers and to link that identify to their reputations for quality goods and services.[6]

It is essential to the Act's ability to serve this goal that the likely to confuse standard be interpreted to include post-sale confusion. A trademark holder's ability to use its mark to symbolize its reputation is harmed when potential purchasers of its goods see unauthentic goods and identify these goods with the trademark holder. This harm to trademark holders is no less serious when potential purchasers encounter these counterfeit goods in a post-sale context. Moreover, verbal disclaimers by sellers of counterfeit goods do not prevent this harm.

6. It also is important to recognize that the enforcement of trademark laws benefits consumers even in cases where there is no possibility that consumers will be defrauded.

III. Whether Dismissal is Appropriate

....

We therefore hold that the district court erred in dismissing the indictment because it was incorrect in concluding that the marks are not counterfeit as a matter of law. Accordingly, we reverse the dismissal of the indictment and remand.

REVERSED and REMANDED.

Questions

1. In footnote 6 of the *Torkington* decision, the court notes the consumer's interest in protecting even against post-sale confusion. How persuasive is this reasoning?

2. How does the consumer's interest in protecting against counterfeit ROLEX watches compare with the interest against counterfeit pharmaceuticals? Does the law recognize this difference?

3. Could a consumer who knowingly purchases a ROLEX watch for himself be prosecuted for criminal counterfeiting? Review the definition of "traffic" in section 2320(e)(2).

2. Ex Parte Seizure

15 U.S.C. § 1116(d) [Lanham Act § 34(d)], as amended by the Trademark Counterfeiting Act of 1984 and subsequent amendments

(d) Civil actions arising out of use of counterfeit marks.

(1)

(A) In the case of a civil action arising under section 32(1)(a) of this Act (15 U.S.C. 1114) or section 220506 of Title 36 with respect to a violation that consists of using a counterfeit mark in connection with the sale, offering for sale, or distribution of goods or services, the court may, upon ex parte application, grant an order under subsection (a) of this section pursuant to this subsection providing for the seizure of goods and counterfeit marks involved in such violation and the means of making such marks, and records documenting the manufacture, sale, or receipt of things involved in such violation.

(B) As used in this subsection the term "counterfeit mark" means—

(i) a counterfeit of a mark that is registered on the principal register in the United States Patent and Trademark Office for such goods or services sold, offered for sale, or distributed and that is in use, whether or not the person against whom relief is sought knew such mark was so registered; or

(ii) a spurious designation that is identical with, or substantially indistinguishable from, a designation as to which the remedies of this Act are made available by reason of section 220506 of Title 36; but such term does not include any mark or designation used on or in connection with goods or services of which the manufacturer or producer was, at the time of the manufacture or production in question authorized to use the mark or designation for the type of goods or services so manufactured or produced, by the holder of the right to use such mark or designation.

(2) The court shall not receive an application under this subsection unless the applicant has given such notice of the application as is reasonable under the circumstances to the United States attorney for the judicial district in which such order is sought. Such attorney may participate in the proceedings arising under such application if such proceedings may affect evidence of an offense against the United States. The court may deny such application if the court determines that the public interest in a potential prosecution so requires.

(3) The application for an order under this subsection shall—

(A) be based on an affidavit or the verified complaint establishing facts sufficient to support the findings of fact and conclusions of law required for such order; and

(B) contain the additional information required by paragraph (5) of this subsection to be set forth in such order.

(4) The court shall not grant such an application unless—

(A) the person obtaining an order under this subsection provides the security determined adequate by the court for the payment of such damages as any person may be entitled to recover as a result of a wrongful seizure or wrongful attempted seizure under this subsection; and

(B) the court finds that it clearly appears from specific facts that—

(i) an order other than ex parte seizure order is not adequate to achieve the purposes of section 1114 of this title;

(ii) the applicant has not publicized the requested seizure;

(iii) the applicant is likely to succeed in showing that the person against whom seizure would be ordered used a counterfeit mark in connection with the sale, offering for sale, or distribution of goods or services;

(iv) an immediate and irreparable injury will occur if such seizure is not ordered;

(v) the matter to be seized will be located at the place identified in the application;

(vi) the harm to the applicant of denying the application outweighs the harm to the legitimate interests of the person against whom seizure would be ordered of granting the application; and

(vii) the person against whom seizure would be ordered, or persons acting in concert with such person, would destroy, move, hide, or otherwise make such matter inaccessible to the court, if the applicant were to proceed on notice to such person.

(5) An order under this subsection shall set forth—

(A) the findings of fact and conclusions of law required for the order;

(B) a particular description of the matter to be seized, and a description of each place at which such matter is to be seized;

(C) the time period, which shall end not later than seven days after the date on which such order is issued, during which the seizure is to be made;

(D) the amount of security required to be provided under this subsection; and

(E) a date for the hearing required under paragraph (10) of this subsection.

(6) The court shall take appropriate action to protect the person against whom an order under this subsection is directed from publicity, by or at the behest of the plaintiff, about such order and any seizure under such order.

(7) Any materials seized under this subsection shall be taken into the custody of the court. The court shall enter an appropriate protective order with respect to discovery by the applicant of any records that have been seized. The protective order shall provide for appropriate procedures to assure that confidential information contained in such records is not improperly disclosed to the applicant.

(8) An order under this subsection, together with the supporting documents, shall be sealed until the person against whom the order is directed has an opportunity to contest such order, except that any person against whom such order is issued shall have access to such order and supporting documents after the seizure has been carried out.

(9) The court shall order that service of a copy of the order under this subsection shall be made by a Federal law enforcement officer (such as a United States marshall or an officer or agent of the United States Customs Service, Secret Service, Federal Bureau of Investigation, or Post Office) or may be made by a state or local law enforcement officer, who, upon making service, shall carry out the seizure under the order. The court shall issue orders, when appropriate, to protect the defendant from undue damage from the disclosure of trade secrets or other confidential information during the course of the seizure, including, when appropriate, orders restricting the access of the applicant (or any agent or employee of the applicant) to such secrets or information.

(10)

(A) The court shall hold a hearing, unless waived by all the parties, on the date set by the court in the order of seizure. That date shall be not sooner than ten days after the order is issued and not later than fifteen days after the order is issued, unless the applicant for the order shows good cause for another date or unless the party against whom such order is directed consents to another date for such hearing. At such hearing the party obtaining the order shall have the burden to prove that the facts supporting findings of fact and conclusions of law necessary to support such order are still in effect. If that party fails to meet that burden, the seizure order shall be dissolved or modified appropriately.

(B) In connection with a hearing under this paragraph, the court may make such orders modifying the time limits for discovery under the Rules of Civil Procedure as may be necessary to prevent the frustration of the purposes of such hearing.

(11) A person who suffers damage by reason of a wrongful seizure under this subsection has a cause of action against the applicant for the order under which such seizure was made, and shall be entitled to recover such relief as may be appropriate, including damages for lost profits, cost of materials, loss of good-will, and punitive damages in instances where the seizure was sought in bad faith, and, unless the court finds extenuating circumstances, to recover a reasonable attorney's fee. The court in its discretion may award prejudgment interest on relief recovered under this paragraph, at an annual interest rate established under section 6621 of Title 26, commencing on the date of service of the claimant's pleading setting forth the claim under this paragraph and ending on the date such recovery is granted, or for such shorter time as the court deems appropriate.

Questions

1. Do you believe that an ex parte seizure order would be available against an enterprise such as Wal-Mart were it selling counterfeit NIKE sneakers? Why or why not?

2. Suppose the Los Angeles Lakers team owns a federal registration for LAKERS for t-shirts, hats and sweatshirts. Would an ex parte seizure order be available against a factory making counterfeit LAKERS scarves that are being sold outside the Lakers' arena?

3. How successfully does the Trademark Counterfeiting Act respond to interests in both due process and effective protection of trademarks? Suppose you are a producer of designer luggage, or shirts, or watches, etc. You observe street vendors selling probable counterfeits on a major pedestrian thoroughfare. Does the Trademark Counterfeiting Act give you the means to pursue and seize the goods from the vendors? If you are a vendor whose goods have been wrongfully seized, do the provisions provide an adequate remedy? Consider *Waco Int'l, Inc. v. KHK Scaffolding Houston Inc.* and *Skierkewiecz v. Gonzalez, infra*, in answering this question.

Waco International, Inc. v. KHK Scaffolding Houston Inc.

278 F.3d 523 (5th Cir. 2002)

Restani, Circuit Judge:

The primary issues before the court are (1) whether the district court applied the proper standard for a Lanham Act wrongful seizure claim ... and (4) whether a cross-appellant is entitled to additional attorney fees. We affirm ... in all respects.

FACTUAL AND PROCEDURAL HISTORY

Plaintiff-Appellant Waco International Inc. ("Waco") ... manufactures scaffolding and shoring products. Waco owns the federally registered trademarks "WACO" and

"HI-LOAD." Waco's scaffolding and shoring products are marked with a decal bearing the Waco mark....

KHK Scaffolding Houston, Inc. ("KHK") ... sells scaffolding manufactured by its parent company in Dubai, United Arab Emirates ... KHK sells scaffolding that is compatible with products manufactured and sold by Waco and other companies. In its sales brochure, KHK indicates the compatibility of its scaffolding by abbreviated designations.... The scaffolds themselves do not bear the Waco mark or a KHK mark. The scaffolds are stamped "made in the U.A.E." ...

In early 1998, KHK mailed brochures and solicitation letters to prospective customers. Some of those materials stated that KHK was offering "Waco" products. On April 2, 1998, Waco sent a cease and desist letter to KHK. On April 20, 1998, Waco's investigator purchased scaffold frames from KHK. The investigator was given an original "sales report" that identified the frames as "WACO" frames. On April 20, 1998, KHK sent a letter to Waco's counsel stating that one of KHK's salespersons mistakenly quoted "Waco Red" and "Waco Blue" to six potential customers in the midst of his sales presentation, and that KHK would take measures to prevent such representations.

On April 30, 1998, Waco sued KHK ... and sought and obtained an ex parte seizure order under 15 U.S.C. § 1116(d)(1)(A). The seizure order permitted Waco to enter KHK's place of business and seize KHK's red and blue scaffolding and certain business records.

A post-seizure hearing was held on May 15, 1998, and a preliminary injunction hearing was held on June 8–10, 1998. The magistrate judge found that injunctive relief was not appropriate with respect to KHK's use of Waco Red and/or Waco Blue in describing the style or compatibility of its KHK products.[2] She found, however, that "invoices purporting to sell 'Waco Red' or 'Waco Blue' scaffolding ... demonstrate a likelihood of confusion, warranting injunctive relief." The magistrate judge recommended an injunction "enjoining KHK from quoting, describing, or purporting to sell, its products as 'Waco' products, 'Waco Red,' or 'Waco Blue'" [and] also recommended that the seizure order be dissolved pursuant to section 1116(d)(10)(A), reasoning that the products seized did not carry a "counterfeit mark." On July 20, 1998, the district court adopted the magistrate judge's recommendation in full.

KHK filed a counterclaim for compensatory and punitive damages for wrongful seizure under 15 U.S.C. § 1116(d)(11).... On August 16, 1999, the magistrate judge recommended ... that the court grant KHK's motion in part, reasoning that the seizure was wrongful as a matter of law because the KHK frames were "legitimate non-infringing merchandise." The judge recommended denial of summary judgment on KHK's claim for damages, noting that "evidence shows that the measure of damages allegedly sustained by KHK from the wrongful seizure is disputed." On September

2. The magistrate judge found that "in most cases, KHK is using the [Waco] mark in a descriptive sense, advertising its product as "Waco Red style" or "Waco Red compatible," or "interchangeable with Waco."

16, 1999, the district court adopted the magistrate judge's memorandum and recommendation in full.

....

The jury made the following findings, inter alia: (1) KHK had infringed Waco's trademarks, but that KHK's use constituted "fair use;" (2) KHK did not use a counterfeit mark in connection with the sale, offering for sale, or distribution of goods or services; ... (3) Waco had seized goods that were predominantly non-infringing and had acted in bad faith in seeking the seizure order. The jury also awarded KHK $730,687 in attorney fees, $185,196 in costs, and $250,000 in punitive damages. The jury found, however, that KHK suffered $0 in lost profits and $0 in lost goodwill from the seizure....

....

A. Wrongful Seizure Liability

....

... Congress intentionally left the definition of "wrongful seizure" to "case-by-case interpretation." See Joint Statement on Trademark Counterfeiting Legislation, 130 Cong. Rec. H12076, at 12083 (Oct. 10, 1984). Congress did identify, however, several guidelines for determining whether a seizure was wrongful. Congress indicated that a seizure may be wrongful: (1) where an applicant acted in "bad faith" in seeking the order; or (2) if the goods seized are predominately legitimate merchandise, even if the plaintiff acted in good faith. See Senate Comm. on the Judiciary, S. Rep. No. 98-526, at 8 (1984), reprinted in 1984 U.S.C.C.A.N. 3627, 3634 ...

... It is apparent that the district court referred to sections 1116(d)(1) and (d)(4) to indicate the authority under which the court granted the order. In fact, the district court specifically identified section 1116(d)(11) as the statutory provision under which it deemed the seizure wrongful:

> In seeking an ex parte seizure order, [Waco] assumed the risk imposed by section 1116(d)(11) that it would be liable for damages for a wrongful seizure if its position was not ultimately sustained upon completion of the adversarial process [i.e., the post-seizure hearings].

Waco claims error on the ground that the seizure was of "counterfeit goods" because the Waco mark was used on sales invoices issued "in connection with" the sale of KHK's scaffolding. Waco argues that the Lanham Act imposes liability for trademark counterfeiting on any person who shall, without the consent of the registrant, "use in commerce ... any counterfeit ... of a registered mark in connection with the sale, offering for sale, distribution, or advertising of any goods or services on or *in connection with* which such use is likely to cause confusion, or to cause mistake, or to deceive...." 15 U.S.C. § 1114(1)(a) (emphasis added). Waco's argument lacks merit.

First, that KHK may be liable under the Lanham Act for its representations in connection with the sale of its goods does not necessarily mean that the seizure was warranted. The ex parte seizure remedy must be narrowly construed, and is not coextensive with liability for any Lanham Act claim. *Martin's Herend Imports v. Diamond & Gem Trading*, 112 F.3d 1296, 1306 (5th Cir. 1997) ("*Martin's I*") (importation of gray market goods, although held to constitute infringement, was not an act of counterfeiting and thus ex parte seizure applicant could be liable under section 1116(d)(11) for wrongful seizure). Thus, even if Waco ultimately had prevailed at trial on its trademark infringement claim, its application for ex parte seizure still could be found wrongful.

Second, the primary focus of an ex parte seizure order is on the goods themselves, rather than any business practice or representation that may give rise to liability for trademark infringement or unfair competition. In light of this purpose, Congress has stated that "a seizure must be considered wrongful when the *material* to be seized is legitimate, non-infringing merchandise." 130 Cong. Rec. H-12076 (October 10, 1984) (emphasis added). Waco admits that the seized goods did not bear the Waco trademark. Waco also admits that the KHK scaffolding bore both an imprint of its country of origin (U.A.E.) and a safety label with KHK's name and telephone number. There is no support for the proposition that any unauthorized use of a mark not on the goods themselves precludes a finding that a seizure was sought wrongfully.

Even if use of the Waco mark "in connection with" the sale of unmarked goods could support a seizure order, the jury found that, as a factual matter, KHK did not "use a counterfeit of any of the listed Waco registered marks in connection with the sale, offering for sale, or distribution of goods or services." See Jury Question 4, RE1-3-5. We decline Waco's invitation to second-guess the jury's factual finding.

....

D. Whether KHK is "a person who suffers damage"

Waco contends that because the jury found that KHK had not suffered "lost profit" or "loss of good will," KHK suffered no actual damages and therefore it is not "a person who suffers damage" as required by section 1116(d)(11) ("A person who suffers damage by reason of a wrongful seizure under this subsection has a cause of action against the applicant ..."). Waco mischaracterizes a finding of lost profits and/or loss of good will as a statutory prerequisite for a wrongful seizure claim. McCarthy on Trademarks, at § 30:44 specifies that a claimant must prove as an element of a wrongful seizure claim that "Claimant was in fact damaged by reason of the seizure." McCarthy further explains that attorney fees are to be considered part of actual damage:

> One who proves damage from a wrongful seizure can recover all appropriate damages, including compensation for lost goods or materials, damage to good will and business reputation, and *all other elements of actual damage, including a reasonable attorney fee.*

Id.

Even if actual damages are, as Waco suggests, limited to lost profits and/or loss of good will, the statute does not, as Waco insists, apply only to claimants who have suffered "actual damages" but to those who have suffered "damage," which can include costs and fees incurred in bringing the wrongful seizure counterclaim. According to the legislative history, "the sponsors recognize that *ex parte* seizure orders are an extraordinary remedy, and that a person who is subject to a wrongful *ex parte* seizure should be *fully compensated* by the party who obtained the seizure order." 130 Cong. Rec., at H12082–83 (emphasis added). Thus, Congress apparently intended that wrongful seizure claimants be compensated for the attorney fees and costs expended in bringing the counterclaim, assuming the claimant prevails in establishing "bad faith" or that the goods were predominately legitimate. Failure to show lost profit or loss of good will does not necessarily preclude recovery of attorney's fees under the wrongful seizure statute.

E. Attorney Fees

Under section 1116(d)(11), "unless the court finds extenuating circumstances, [a claimant is entitled] to recover a reasonable attorney's fee...." Waco claims that such circumstances exist and that attorney fees must be denied. For example, Waco points to evidence that KHK was not awarded damages for lost profit or good will, that it produced "bogus" invoices in discovery, and that it altered business records. Even if such evidence could support a finding of "extenuating circumstances," there is no support for the proposition that the district court was under an affirmative obligation to make such a finding. The district court did not abuse its discretion in allowing KHK to recover attorney fees.

....

CONCLUSION

Accordingly, we AFFIRM the final judgment, the award of attorney's fees, the order denying prejudgment interest, and the order denying a permanent injunction.

Skierkewiecz v. Gonzalez

711 F. Supp. 931 (N.D. Ill. 1989)

Kocoras, J.:

This case comes before the Court on defendants John J. Brown's, David C. Hilliard's, Pattishall, McAuliffe, Newberry, Hilliard & Geraldson's, (hereinafter "Defendant Attorneys"), Charles Baley's, Mark Hinchy's, and Baley, Hinchy, Downes & Associates, Inc.'s, (hereinafter "Defendant Investigators"), Motion to Dismiss pursuant to Rule 12(b) of the Federal Rules of Civil Procedure. Defendants contend that Counts I through IV of the Complaint must be dismissed for failure to state a claim against these defendants and that the remaining counts must be dismissed because they name only defendants previously dismissed by plaintiffs. For the following reasons, the defendants' motion is granted in part and denied in part.

FACTS

....

On April 29, 1988, Defendant Attorneys appeared in chambers ... and presented their Motion for Ex Parte Seizure Order and affidavits in support. Judge Parsons entered the Ex Parte Temporary Restraining Order and Order for Seizure.

On May 4, 1988, two United States Marshals executed the Court's April 29, 1988, Order for Seizure at the ... Defendants' office and warehouse in Chicago. Subsequently, the ... Defendants brought a motion to vacate the seizure order to obtain the return of their goods.

On May 27, 1988, Judge Parsons addressed the defendants' motion to vacate and issued his Memorandum Opinion and Order in which he was highly critical of Defendant Attorneys. Judge Parsons detailed the numerous misrepresentations which had been made to him by the Defendant Attorneys at the Ex Parte hearing and made it clear that he would not have ordered the seizure in the absence of the false portrayal of the plaintiffs as counterfeiters. Nevertheless, Judge Parsons found it necessary to issue a preliminary injunction, enjoining the ... Defendants from selling tennis rackets marked with the word "Panther" or hang tags used as advertising pieces depicting a panther in any position.

On August 19, 1988, the plaintiffs filed the Complaint which is the subject of the Defendants' Motion to Dismiss. In Count I of plaintiffs' Complaint, plaintiffs seek damages against Defendant Attorneys for wrongful seizure pursuant to 15 U.S.C. § 1116(d)(11). In Count II, plaintiffs attempt to state a claim for abuse of process. Finally, Counts III and IV allege that Defendant Attorneys and Defendant Investigators committed trespass to chattel and trespass to land, respectively, during the execution of the April 29, 1988, Order for Seizure.

DISCUSSION

....

The defendants first contend that plaintiffs' claim for wrongful seizure (Count I) against the Defendant Attorneys must be dismissed. The defendants argue that the plaintiffs are merely seeking recovery for representations made by the Defendant Attorneys in the course of representing their client's legitimate trademark interest in obtaining the Order of Seizure and that these representations are protected under Illinois law. [Citation.] The defendants maintain that an attorney has a conditional privilege in advising and acting on behalf of his client which cannot be attacked absent a showing of malice, or the attorney's desire to harm which is separate and apart from the attorney's desire to protect his client. [Citation.]

The plaintiffs argue, however, that defendants have ignored the fact that plaintiffs' claim for wrongful seizure is brought pursuant to the federal cause of action created by 15 U.S.C. § 1116(d)(11) and have wrongfully read into this statute a conditional privilege for an attorney accused of obtaining a wrongful seizure. We agree.

When Congress passed 15 U.S.C. § 1116(d), it created an extraordinary remedy, an ex parte order authorizing seizure of alleged counterfeit marks.... However, ... Congress recognized that the remedy should only be used in extreme circumstances, and Congress expressly required the courts to use extreme caution before issuing a seizure order without first providing the targeted defendant with any measure of due process. The purpose behind such extraordinary action was to provide the plaintiff and the court with an effective weapon against those "fly-by-night" counterfeiters who will, if given notice of court proceedings, dispose of their goods to someone else in the counterfeit network or destroy them to escape legal liability. *See Slazengers Ltd. v. Stoller*, 1988 U.S. Dist. LEXIS 5194, No. 88 C 3722, at 4 (May 27, 1988) *citing* House Report to Trademark Counterfeiting Act of 1984, Rept. 98-997 p. 15, 98th Congress 2d Session, Sept. 7, 1984.

By enacting 15 U.S.C. § 1116(d)(11), Congress provided a means of preventing potential abuse by persons wishing to obtain ex parte seizure orders. The section allows recovery by the person who suffered damages by reason of a wrongful seizure where the seizure order was sought in bad faith. Section 1116(d)(11) does not explicitly or implicitly require the plaintiff to show the applicant acted with malice in obtaining the order, even where the applicant was an attorney allegedly acting on his client's behalf. Moreover, this Court believes that to read a malice requirement into the section would thwart its purpose of deterring applicants from requesting the seizure order except where absolutely necessary. Accordingly, no such conditional privilege recognized by the Illinois courts is applicable to a federal cause of action against an attorney who acted as an applicant for a seizure order in violation of 15 U.S.C. § 1116(d)(11).

In Count I, plaintiffs allege that Defendant Attorneys improperly sought and obtained the Ex Parte Seizure Order through the use of misleading statements presented to the Court. The Complaint further states that the Ex Parte Seizure Order was sought in bad faith in violation of 15 U.S.C. 1116(d)(11). The Court finds that these allegations are sufficient to state a claim against Defendant Attorneys, and consequently, defendants' motion to dismiss Count I is denied.

....

The defendants next contend that Counts III and IV of plaintiffs' Complaint, which allege trespass to land and trespass to chattel, must be dismissed because the Defendant Attorneys and Defendant Investigators were authorized by the Seizure Order to enter upon plaintiffs' premises and seize certain goods and records. The defendants maintain that such an entry upon land pursuant to court order cannot constitute a trespass.

... [A] party cannot be liable for trespass if acting pursuant to and within the scope of a valid court order. [Citation.] However, a party cannot stand behind a court order which was obtained through the party's own wrongful conduct. Thus, this Court believes that Count III must be dismissed as to the Defendant Investigators because they played no role in obtaining the Order of Seizure from Judge Parsons and they acted pursuant to and within the scope of a facially valid Order of Seizure in seizing certain goods and records. This Court will not, however, dismiss Count III as stated against the Defendant Attorneys. The facts, when taken as true, allege that the Defendant Attorneys wrongfully obtained and executed the Order of Seizure. These allegations are sufficient to state a claim for trespass to chattel against Defendant Attorneys.

With respect to plaintiffs' claim for trespass to land in Count IV, the Court believes the count should stand against both the Defendant Attorneys and Defendant

Investigators. First, for the reason stated in the preceding paragraph, the Court rejects defendants' argument that the Seizure Order immunizes the Defendant Attorneys from liability for trespass to land. In addition, both the Defendant Attorneys and the Defendant Investigators allegedly acted beyond the scope of the Order of Seizure when they remained on the premises without the U.S. Marshals. The Ex Parte Order of Seizure provides in pertinent part as follows:

> FURTHER ORDERED, that plaintiff's attorneys and representatives be allowed to accompany the Marshal, or other authorized persons, for the purpose of identifying goods and records subject to this Order;

Thus, the plaintiffs properly state a claim for trespass to land when they allege in Count IV that after the Marshal left the premises, Russell Stoller demanded that the Defendant Attorneys and Defendant Investigators leave the premises and they refused. Accordingly, defendants' motion to dismiss Count IV is denied.

Based on the foregoing discussion, the defendants' Motion to Dismiss is granted in part and denied in part....

3. Mandatory Treble Damages and Attorney's Fees

Section 35(b) requires imposition of treble damages and an award of attorney's fees where there has been an intentional use of a counterfeit mark or designation unless the court finds "extenuating circumstances." Consider the following decision's analysis of "intentional."

Chanel, Inc. v. Italian Activewear of Florida, Inc.

931 F.2d 1472 (11th Cir. 1991)

Edmonson, J.:

....

I.

Plaintiff-appellee Chanel, Inc. sells luxury items using registered well known trademarks. Defendant-appellant Italian Activewear was a Florida corporation selling imported goods under various labels, including Chanel. Defendant-appellant Mervyn Brody was president and chief operating officer of Italian Activewear. Defendant-appellant Myron Greenberg is a friend and business associate of Brody. Although not an employee, Greenberg sometime sold merchandise on behalf of Italian Activewear or Brody and would "keep an eye on things" at the store when Brody was out of town.

Italian Activewear, through Brody, imported and began marketing a shipment of handbags and belt buckles bearing Chanel trademarks. Brody purchased these goods from Sola, a European broker from whom Brody had earlier purchased other shipments of luxury items under various labels. Part of the shipment of Chanel-labeled goods was immediately resold to some California businessmen....

The Chanel-labeled goods purchased from Sola were counterfeit. In addition to minor differences in physical construction, these handbags lacked several indicia of authenticity possessed by genuine Chanel bags: each authentic Chanel bag has a uniquely numbered sticker affixed to an inconspicuous location inside the bag and comes with a separate "certificate of authenticity" bearing the same number; and each bag is packaged inside a felt bag and then inside a "shiny black box," both of which also bear Chanel trademarks. Authentic Chanel belt buckles, moreover, are not sold without Chanel belts, as these were.

In his deposition testimony, Brody stated that he did not know where Sola got the bags and buckles and that he did not ask. He also said he was aware the bags should have had certificates of authenticity but that these bags did not. He said he had made efforts to ensure the goods were genuine (by comparing them with products he knew to be genuine). Brody's verification efforts were further attested to by one of his employees at the preliminary injunction hearing.

Chanel first acted in California, seizing the counterfeit goods held by the Californians who received part of the Sola shipment. The Californians informed Greenberg—who was "minding the store" at Italian Activewear while Brody was away—of the seizure. Greenberg sent Brody the following facsimile:

> Att Merv. [Brody]
>
> Big trouble. Marshell (sic) & Chanel closed down Calif. Took bags and there will be lawsuit. They want to stop new shipments—and they are right. They know about this store and probably will be in here shortly. Trying to get your lawyer but I know he won't be able to do anything.
>
> Call back right away.
>
> Mike [Myron Greenberg]

He gathered up all the Chanel-labeled goods and removed them from the store, putting them in the trunk of a car which was then parked several blocks away.

Chanel sued Italian Activewear and Brody for trademark infringement in violation of 15 U.S.C.A. § 1114(1)(a). Greenberg was added as a defendant by later amendment. The district court granted plaintiff Chanel's motion for summary judgment in full, concluding as a matter of law not only that the trademark had been infringed, but also that the infringement had been intentional. It thus awarded the treble damages ($208,433.25) and attorneys' fees ($71,859.61) statutorily mandated in cases of intentional violation of 15 U.S.C.A. § 1114(1)(a). See 15 U.S.C.A. § 1117(b)....

II.

The Lanham Act prohibits, among other things, the use in commerce of a counterfeit trademark in a manner likely to cause confusion; and the Act further provides that anyone using a counterfeit trademark in such manner shall be liable in a civil action to the registrant of the trademark. See 15 U.S.C.A. § 1114(1)(a). The remedies available to the registrant are set forth in 15 U.S.C.A. § 1117. In addition to injunctive relief, a registrant whose rights are violated may generally recover the defendant's profits from the infringing activity (or its own damages or both) together with costs of the action. Based on equitable considerations, the trial court may, in its discretion, reduce or enhance the resulting award up to three times the original amount, and may, in exceptional cases, award attorneys' fees. 15 U.S.C.A. § 1117(a). If the infringement is intentional, however, § 1117(b) governs: unless the court finds extenuating circumstances, treble damages and attorneys' fees are mandated. 15 U.S.C.A. § 1117(b).

The interplay of these provisions demonstrates that a showing of intent or bad faith is unnecessary to establish a violation of § 1114(1)(a), or to seek remedies pursuant to § 1117(a). But where, as here, a registrant seeks the mandatory treble damages and attorneys' fees provided for in § 1117(b), the plaintiff must prove the defendants' intent to infringe.

....

III.

The district court's grant of summary judgment on this issue rested chiefly on two undisputed facts: (1) the counterfeit goods lacked all indicia of authenticity, and Brody knew that indicia of authenticity generally accompanied genuine Chanel products; and (2) Brody knew Sola was not an authorized distributor of Chanel products, yet failed to ask Sola the origin of his Chanel-labeled products. Based on these facts, the court concluded Brody had been willfully blind, and "[w]illful blindness is knowledge enough." *See Louis Vuitton S.A. v. Lee*, 875 F.2d 584, 590 (7th Cir. 1989). We accept this dicta from the Seventh Circuit: willful blindness could provide the requisite intent or bad faith. But whether a defendant has been willfully blind will depend on the circumstances[5] and, like intent itself, will generally be a question of fact for the factfinder after trial. The undisputed facts relied on by the district court could certainly support an inference of knowledge or willful blindness. But they do not so clearly compel that conclusion as to warrant finding intent as a matter of law.

Chanel ... points out Brody has been involved in trademark infringement litigation twice in the past (in the mid-1980's). Second, it points to Greenberg's actions after hearing of the seizure of Chanel-labeled goods in California: he sent a warning fax to Brody; and then removed all Chanel-labeled merchandise from the premises, putting it in the trunk of a car. But these additional facts are, at best, simply further circumstantial evidence strengthening the inference of knowledge or intent. That these facts do even this is uncertain; for they could cut both ways. Looking at the facts in the light most favorable to Brody and Greenberg as non-moving parties, Brody's past experiences with trademark infringement laws might in fact make his evidence of attempted verification of authenticity more believable. Greenberg's pointed-to actions all occurred after the infringing activities; and all are consistent with the possibility that he first heard about the infringement from the Californians after the raid and was simply taking actions to stop the infringing activities and minimize the damage.

5. In *Lee*, for example, the defendants had purchased obviously poorly crafted goods from an itinerant peddler at bargain-basement prices. 875 F.2d at 590.

... Chanel's evidence does not demonstrate lack of a genuine dispute on intent; so appellants did not have to present the significant, probative evidence Ferguson requires.

AFFIRMED in part, VACATED in part, and REMANDED for further proceedings.[7]

Lorillard Tobacco Co., Inc. v. A & E Oil, Inc.

503 F.3d 588 (7th Cir. 2007)

Manion, Circuit Judge.

[After finding that the defendants were selling counterfeit cigarettes, the Court addressed the question whether the defendants had knowledge that the cigarettes were counterfeit as a matter of law and thus were liable for attorney's fees absent extenuating circumstances.]

... To prove knowledge of the counterfeiting, Lorillard was not required to prove the defendants' actual knowledge; knowledge includes a willful blindness or a failure to investigate because one "was afraid of what the inquiry would yield." *Louis Vuitton v. Lee*, 875 F.2d 584, 590 (7th Cir. 1989). If willful blindness occurs, an award of attorneys' fees is required by the statutory language absent extenuating circumstances. 15 U.S.C. § 1117(b) ("the court shall ... enter judgment ... with a reasonable attorney's fee."); *see also Hard Rock Cafe Licensing v. Concession Servs., Inc.*, 955 F.2d 1143, 1151 ("Willful blindness is sufficient to trigger the mandatory provisions of subsection b." (*citing Lee*, 875 F.2d at 590)).

... [W]e find that the evidence demonstrates that the defendants acted with knowledge or willful blindness. Notably, the defendants do not contest on appeal the counterfeit nature of the cigarettes recovered from the station. *See* Def.-App. Br. at 8 ("Lorillard seized nine counterfeit Newport cigarette[ ] [packs] from the A & E mini-mart.... Each of the nine packets apparently bore fake tax-stamps."). Furthermore, the tax stamps on the counterfeit cigarettes were noticeably fraudulent. *Cf. Lee*, 875 F.2d at 590 (finding willfulness when shop owner failed to consider that "expensive brand-name goods [are] unlikely to display ... poor workmanship, to be lined with

7. Our conclusion that appellants' intent was not a proper subject for summary judgment is further confirmed by a brief look at other trademark infringement cases in which intent has been found. In *Louis Vuitton S.A. v. Lee*, for example, the "willful blindness" case discussed briefly above, the defendant had actually conceded knowledge in a pretrial stipulation. 875 F.2d 584 (7th Cir. 1989). And in *Louis Vuitton S. A. v. Spencer Handbags Corp.*, plaintiffs had a videotape of defendants bragging to a potential associate about their trademark infringement activities. 765 F.2d 966 (2d Cir. 1985). Intent was based on more circumstantial evidence (like that present in this case) in *Polo Fashions, Inc. v. Rabanne*, 661 F. Supp. 89 (S.D. Fla. 1986), and *Vuitton et Fils, S.A. v. Crown Handbags*, 492 F. Supp. 1071 (S.D.N.Y. 1979), *aff'd without opinion*, 622 F.2d 577 (2d Cir. 1980); but the findings of intent in these cases were made only after full bench trials, *see Rabanne*, 661 F. Supp. at 99; *Crown Handbags*, 492 F. Supp. at 1072. *See also Finity Sportswear v. Airnit, Inc.*, 631 F. Supp. 769 (S.D.N.Y. 1985) (knowledge or intent to infringe not appropriate subject of summary judgment). *But see Fendi S.A.S. Di Paola Fendi E. Sorelle v. Cosmetic World, Ltd.*, 642 F. Supp. 1143 (S.D.N.Y. 1986) (summary judgment on willfulness granted where defendant admitted in deposition that he told retail merchants to whom he sold products that the products were "imitations," but that retail merchants' customers would likely think they were buying genuine Fendi products).

purple vinyl, and to be sold by itinerant peddlers at bargain-basement prices."). Kuruvilla ... [w]hile stocking the cigarettes, ... checks for the tax stamps and examines each pack "every time," explaining that "before I put them in the counter, I—when I open up a carton, I do" check. Yet somehow he "never noticed" any discrepancies in the counterfeit tax stamps, notwithstanding the obviousness of the counterfeit. Later, however, in an affidavit submitted in opposition to the summary judgment motion, Kuruvilla denies checking tax stamps "most of the time," thus contradicting his deposition testimony. A defendant, however, cannot create "'sham' issues of fact with affidavits that contradict their prior depositions." [Citation.] Kuruvilla's attempt to create such a sham issue negates his feigned ignorance.

The record contains other contradictory evidence. For example, when Kuruvilla spoke with his brother, Kurian, about the seizure of the three packs of cigarettes, Kurian told Kuruvilla about the source of two of the packs. Specifically, one pack came from a customer returning a pack of bad-tasting cigarettes, and a second pack from Kurian testing a pack from the stock that likewise tasted "terrible." Kuruvilla, however, contradicted his brother and testified subsequently in a deposition that the cigarette packs belonged to Kurian personally. Kuruvilla attempted to retract his damaging deposition testimony by stating in the affidavit submitted in opposition to the summary judgment motion that "[t]he three open packs of cigarettes ... were stale cigarettes returned by customers." Again, this statement merely creates a sham issue of fact, since the defendants do not contest on appeal that the seized cigarettes were counterfeits, not just stale.

....

There is simply no evidence in the record to support defendants' claims of an innocent source for the counterfeit cigarettes. Furthermore, the defendants fail to present any evidence to counter Lorillard's evidence that the counterfeit cigarettes came from U.S.A. Cigarettes, a supplier connected to counterfeit cigarettes. Although the defendants denied in depositions ever purchasing cigarettes from U.S.A. Cigarettes, they admit that they could have done so. In fact, they acknowledge that they did purchase other products from this company whose name makes it an obvious source for cigarettes. One check written by A & E to U.S.A. Cigarettes bears the endorsement of Amin Arba, an alias for Amin Umar, who ... is a known source for counterfeit cigarettes. Umar would drive a green van around to various gas stations selling counterfeit cigarettes ... and, it can be reasonably inferred, receiving checks made out to U.S.A. Cigarettes. Many other checks to U.S.A. Cigarettes from other retailers also bear Umar's endorsement. In other related investigations and lawsuits, Lorillard has linked Umar specifically to sales of Newport counterfeit cigarettes. Joseph, the co-owner of A & E, also does business with U.S.A. Cigarettes at his other gas stations and, although Joseph denies ever speaking to Umar, Umar's telephone records indicate that he placed a call to Joseph's telephone number once. Finally, A & E's conduct during discovery suggests that it knew about the counterfeit cigarettes. Notably, A & E did not produce the checks written to U.S.A. Cigarettes until July 2004, after A & E had inaccurately represented to the district court that Lorillard already possessed "all business records in Defendant's possession." The district court found that "the individual Defendants in this case were less than forthcoming with Lorillard at the discovery stage of the litigation ... stalled ... and only cooperated after they were held in default."

....

When reviewing an appeal from summary judgment, we recognize that, in determining whether a defendant acted with willful blindness to counterfeit products, "[a]s a general rule, a party's state of mind (such as knowledge or intent) is a question of fact for the fact finder, to be determined after trial." *Chanel, Inc. v. Italian Activewear of Florida, Inc.*, 931 F.2d 1472, 1476 (11th Cir. 1991) [citations]. However, "we are not constrained to accept denials supported by a mere scintilla of evidence. Such bare denials—for example, where the defendant's alleged ignorance amounts to willful blindness, or where the owner's claims of ignorance are 'inconsistent with the uncontested facts'—are insufficient to create a genuine triable issue." *United States v. 16328 S. 43rd E. Ave., Bixby, Tulsa County, Okla.*, 275 F.3d 1281, 1285 (10th Cir. 2002) (affirming grant of summary judgment to United States in a forfeiture case based on legal conclusion that facts showed the defendant knew of and consented to criminal activities on property).

Similarly, in this case defendants must do more than baldly deny the reasonable inferences and facts presented by Lorillard to avoid the conclusion that they knowingly sold counterfeit cigarettes. [Citation.] Yet we reiterate that defendants offer no plausible explanation for the presence of the counterfeit cigarettes, the failure to notice the tax stamps when checked, implausible denials of knowledge of known counterfeit trafficker Umar and U.S.A. Cigarettes, and questionable discovery practices. As we have noted in the summary judgment context, "neither presenting a scintilla of evidence, ... nor the mere existence of some alleged factual dispute between the parties or some metaphysical doubt as to the material facts, is sufficient to oppose a motion for summary judgment.... The party must supply evidence sufficient to allow a jury to render a verdict in his favor." *Van Diest Supply Co. v. Shelby County State Bank*, 425 F.3d 437, 439 (7th Cir. 2005) (internal quotation and Citation.). The defendants have failed to do so. Accordingly, the district court did not err as a matter of law in determining that defendants knowingly sold counterfeit cigarettes and, therefore, the mandatory award for attorneys' fees under 15 U.S.C. § 1117(b) applied.

Questions

1. Do you agree with the district court or appellate court in *Chanel* concerning the plausible interpretations of Greenberg's actions after the raid?

2. Section 35(b) does not require mandatory treble damages and attorney's fees where "extenuating circumstances" are found. What might constitute such extenuating circumstances? *See Gucci America, Inc. v. Daffy's, Inc., supra* this Chapter.

3. What factors should a court consider in awarding statutory damages in lieu of actual damages in a case of counterfeiting? Is knowledge or "willful blindness" about

the counterfeit nature required? *See Diane Von Furstenberg Studio v. Snyder*, 2007 U.S. Dist. LEXIS 66633 (E.D. Va. Sept. 10, 2007).

4. Section 35(c) of the Lanham Act allows plaintiffs to elect statutory damages in cases involving the "use" of a counterfeit mark. Should such damages be available against a contributory infringer? *See Louis Vuitton Malletier SA v. Akanoc Solutions Inc.*, 658 F.3d 936 (9th Cir. 2011). If a plaintiff elects statutory damages, does it then forego the possibility of recovering attorney's fees under section 35(a), which provides for such an award in exceptional circumstances? Consider the language of section 35(c) which provides plaintiff the election "instead of actual damages and profits under subsection (a)." *See Louis Vuitton Malletier SA v. LY USA Inc.*, 676 F.3d 83 (2d Cir. 2012).

5. Both the *Chanel* and *Lorillard* decisions involved summary judgment motions but came out differently on willful blindness. Are they consistent?

4. Online Counterfeit Strategies

Stephen M. Gaffigan, *Online Anti-Counterfeiting Investigations and Enforcement*

Presented At 2012 AIPLA Annual Meeting (Oct. 2012) (excerpts)*

As recently as 2005, the bulk of counterfeiting occurred in bricks and mortar locations which were relatively easy to find and easy to raid.... That time of bliss was immediately followed by a short period of online counterfeiting conducted by individuals in the United States who built one or two websites and sold their infringing wares online in small quantities. Their goods were usually purchased from known distribution points like Canal Street, Santee Alley and the Harwin District. Investigators quickly learned how to identify and track these individuals online and, for the most part, when they were caught they would simply surrender their goods and go out of business....

Today, trademark owners charged with policing their marks online face a daunting task. The roots of the new online counterfeiting phenomenon can be traced back to (1) the rapid expansion of high speed Internet and English language skills in China, leading up to the 2008 Olympic Games in Beijing; and (2) the explosion of new web based technologies. No longer are there communication or technology barriers which prevent foreign distributors of counterfeit goods and their customers from doing business directly. In today's world, large scale turnkey operations pumping out tens of thousands of online shops are operated by small groups of individuals who contract out for everything from manufacturing to payment processing and website optimization. Today, the fake goods, the money, the criminals and the computer operations are rarely in the same place, making seizures much more difficult and much less rewarding. Rather than mass quantities of counterfeit goods entering the United States in shipping containers, even larger quantities are ordered via websites and shipped here 1 to 10 pieces at a time via EMS, UPS and FEDEX. The online environment sharply tilts the playing field in favor of the counterfeiters. Specifically, online infringers have the ability to operate anonymously and repeatedly set up and move their shops in a matter of minutes. The money for fake goods often moves through offshore payment processors and can transfer between foreign banks in minutes.

... [T]rademark owners have slowly developed some successful strategies ... regarding online enforcement....

... Specifically, in the last two years, the primary method of enforcing trademark rights against online counterfeiting organizations has been to seek an injunction transferring control of domain names used by defendants to support their illegal activities to the control of the Court and, ultimately, the trademark owner. The transfer of domain names has a twofold effect. First, the transfer immediately deprives the counterfeiter the ability to use the domain names as a means for continuing its illegal activities. Second, the transfer deprives the counterfeiter of the value of its costly search engine optimization efforts designed to make its domain names and associated websites appear at the top of various search engine results pages. The ordered injunctive relief is typically very effective.

Apparently, weary of losing domain names and associated page rank on search engines such as Google and Bing, counterfeiters have adopted a new plan.... [C]ounterfeiters have begun hacking into scores of legitimate websites and adding text or back end pages regarding counterfeit goods to those websites. The added pages are then optimized to appear at the top of search engine results pages and set to redirect a consumer clicking on the link or page to the counterfeiter's real website operating under a separate domain name. For example, recently when conducting a search for "Chanel Replica" on Google for example, one of the top search results returned was: http://marcct.org/Index.htm?yifoxew=Aaa+Quality+ Chanel+Replica+For+Sale&yifoxewp=550.

The base domain name, marcct.org belongs to MARC, Inc. of Manchester, an organization which serves the needs of developmentally disabled individuals in Connecticut. However, when the link was clicked on within the Google search result, the user was redirected to ipursevalley.co, a domain name and website operated by a counterfeiting organization....

....

Litigation is presently the best tool available to a brand owner when dealing with large scale, professional, online counterfeiting operations. Litigation is most effective in this field when conducted on an aggregate target or platform basis. The goal of the litigation should be to disrupt the target's business operations and cause the target economic harm. Most lawsuits are being filed on a John Doe basis since counterfeiters tend to operate anonymously....

....

Online enforcement often implicates third parties whose services are being used to facilitate the counterfeiting operation. In those instances, injunctive relief pursuant to 28 U.S.C § 1651(a), The All Writs Act may be considered. The All Writs Act allows the Court to enjoin non-parties and the traditional requirements for an injunction do not apply. The All Writs Act has recently been employed by Plaintiffs in trademark actions to require non-party payment processors, registrars, hosts, registries and even ICAAN to take action to disable domains and accounts supporting infringing activity.

Often, the only money a rights holder can hope to recover in an online enforcement action is whatever it can seize ex parte on the front end of the case. While pre-judgment asset restraint is often difficult, given the wide scale use of offshore payment processors, several strategies have emerged which increase the chances of a successful recovery:

- PayPal and other U.S. based payment processors typically comply quickly with asset restraint orders and often hold substantial funds. So, spending some time and effort locating such accounts in advance of filing can be very beneficial.

....

D. Border Control Measures

K Mart Corp. v. Cartier, Inc.

486 U.S. 281 (1988)

Justice Kennedy announced the judgment of the Court, and delivered the opinion of the Court with respect to Parts I and II-A which Rehnquist, C.J., and White, Blackmun, O'Connor, and Scalia, JJ., joined, an opinion with respect to Part II-B which White, J., joined, and an opinion for the Court with respect to Part II-C which Rehnquist, C.J., and Blackmun, O'Connor, and Scalia, JJ., joined:

A gray-market good is a foreign-manufactured good, bearing a valid United States trademark, that is imported without the consent of the U.S. trademark holder. These cases present the issue whether the Secretary of the Treasury's regulation permitting the importation of certain gray market goods, 19 C.F.R. § 133.21 (1987), is a reasonable agency interpretation of § 526 of the Tariff Act of 1930 (1930 Tariff Act), 46 Stat. 741, as amended, 19 U.S.C. § 1526.

I

A

The gray market arises in any of three general contexts. The prototypical gray-market victim (case 1) is a domestic firm that purchases from an independent foreign firm the rights to register and use the latter's trademark as a U.S. trademark and to sell its foreign-manufactured products here. Especially where the foreign firm has already registered the trademark in the United States or where the product has already earned a reputation for quality, the right to use that trademark can be very valuable. If the foreign manufacturer could import the trademarked goods and distribute them here, despite having sold the trademark to a domestic firm, the domestic firm would be forced into sharp intrabrand competition involving the very trademark it purchased. Similar intrabrand competition could arise if the foreign manufacturer markets its wares outside the United States, as is often the case, and a third party who purchases them abroad could legally import them. In either event, the parallel importation, if permitted to proceed, would create a gray market that could jeopardize the trademark holder's investment.

The second context (case 2) is a situation in which a domestic firm registers the U.S. trademark for goods that are manufactured abroad by an affiliated manufacturer. In its most common variation (case 2a), a foreign firm wishes to control distribution of its wares in this country by incorporating a subsidiary here. The subsidiary then registers under its own name (or the manufacturer assigns to the subsidiary's name) a U.S. trademark that is identical to its parent's foreign trademark. The parallel importation by a third party who buys the goods abroad (or conceivably even by the affiliated foreign manufacturer itself) creates a gray market. Two other variations on this theme occur when an American-based firm establishes abroad a manufacturing subsidiary corporation (case 2b) or its own unincorporated manufacturing division (case 2c) to produce its U.S. trademarked goods, and then imports them for domestic distribution. If the trademark holder or its foreign subsidiary sells the trademarked goods abroad, the parallel importation of the goods competes on the gray market with the holder's domestic sales.

In the third context (case 3), the domestic holder of a U.S. trademark authorizes an independent foreign manufacturer to use it. Usually the holder sells to the foreign manufacturer an exclusive right to use the trademark in a particular foreign location, but conditions the right on the foreign manufacturer's promise not to import its trademarked goods into the United States. Once again, if the foreign manufacturer or a third party imports into the United States, the foreign-manufactured goods will compete on the gray market with the holder's domestic goods.

B

Until 1922, the Federal Government did not regulate the importation of gray-market goods, not even to protect the investment of an independent purchaser of a foreign trademark, and not even in the extreme case where the independent foreign manufacturer breached its agreement to refrain from direct competition with the purchaser. That year, however, Congress was spurred to action by a Court of Appeals decision declining to enjoin the parallel importation of goods bearing a trademark that (as in case 1) a domestic company had purchased from an independent foreign manufacturer at a premium. *See A. Bourjois & Co. v. Katzel*, 275 F. 539 (C.A.2 1921), *rev'd*, 260 U.S. 689 (1923).

In an immediate response to *Katzel*, Congress enacted § 526 of the Tariff Act of 1922, 42 Stat. 975. That provision [was] later reenacted in identical form as § 526 of the 1930 Tariff Act, 19 U.S.C. § 1526 ...

The regulations implementing § 526 for the past 50 years have not applied the prohibition to all gray-market goods. The Customs Service regulation now in force provides generally that "[f]oreign-made articles bearing a trademark identical with one owned and recorded by a citizen of the United States or a corporation or association created or organized within the United States are subject to seizure and forfeiture as prohibited importations." 19 CFR § 133.21(b) (1987). But the regulation furnishes a "common-control" exception from the ban, permitting the entry of gray-market goods manufactured abroad by the trademark owner or its affiliate:

> (c) *Restrictions not applicable.* The restrictions ... do not apply to imported articles when:
>
> > (1) Both the foreign and the U.S. trademark or trade name are owned by the same person or business entity; [or]
> >
> > (2) The foreign and domestic trademark or trade name owners are parent and subsidiary companies or are otherwise subject to common ownership or control ...

The Customs Service regulation further provides an "authorized-use" exception, which permits importation of gray-market goods where

> (3) [t]he articles of foreign manufacture bear a recorded trademark or trade name applied under authorization of the U.S. owner ... 19 CFR § 133.21(c) (1987).

Respondents, an association of U.S. trademark holders and two of its members, brought suit in Federal District Court in February 1984, seeking both a declaration that the Customs Service regulation, 19 CFR § 133.21(c)(1)–(3) (1987), is invalid and an injunction against its enforcement. *Coalition to Preserve the Integrity of American Trademarks v. United States*, 598 F. Supp. 844 (D.D.C. 1984). They asserted that the common control and authorized-use exceptions are inconsistent with § 526 of the 1930 Tariff Act. Petitioners K Mart and 47th Street Photo intervened as defendants.

....

II

A

In determining whether a challenged regulation is valid, a reviewing court must first determine if the regulation is consistent with the language of the statute. "If the statute is clear and unambiguous 'that is the end of the matter, for the court, as well as the agency, must give effect to the unambiguously expressed intent of Congress.' ... The traditional deference courts pay to agency interpretation is not to be applied to alter the clearly expressed intent of Congress." In ascertaining the plain meaning of the statute, the court must look to the particular statutory language at issue, as well as the language and design of the statute as a whole. If the statute is silent or ambiguous with respect to the specific issue addressed by the regulation, the question becomes whether the agency regulation is a permissible construction of the statute. If the agency regulation is not in conflict with the plain language of the statute, a reviewing court must give deference to the agency's interpretation of the statute.

B

Following this analysis, I conclude that subsections (c)(1) and (c)(2) of the Customs Service regulation, 19 CFR § 133.21(c)(1) and (c)(2) (1987), are permissible constructions designed to resolve statutory ambiguities. All Members of the Court are in agreement that the agency may interpret the statute to bar importation of gray-market goods in what we have denoted case 1 and to permit the imports under case 2a. As these writings state, "owned by" is sufficiently ambiguous, in the context of the statute, that it applies to situations involving a foreign parent, which is case 2a. This ambiguity arises from the inability to discern, from the statutory language, which of the two entities involved in case 2a can be said to "own" the U.S. trademark if, as in some instances, the domestic subsidiary is wholly owned by its foreign parent.

A further statutory ambiguity contained in the phrase "merchandise of foreign manufacture," suffices to sustain the regulations as they apply to cases 2b and 2c. This ambiguity parallels that of "owned by," which sustained case 2a, because it is possible to interpret "merchandise of foreign manufacture" to mean (1) goods manufactured in a foreign country, (2) goods manufactured by a foreign company, or (3) goods manufactured in a foreign country by a foreign company. Given the imprecision in the statute, the agency is entitled to choose any reasonable definition and to interpret the statute to say that goods manufactured by a foreign subsidiary or division of a domestic company are not goods "of foreign manufacture."

(1)

Subsection (c)(3), 19 CFR § 133.21(c)(3) (1987), of the regulation, however, cannot stand. The ambiguous statutory phrases that we have already discussed, "owned by" and "merchandise of foreign manufacture," are irrelevant to the proscription contained in subsection (3) of the regulation. This subsection of the regulation denies a domestic trademark holder the power to prohibit the importation of goods made by an independent foreign manufacturer where the domestic trademark holder has authorized the foreign manufacturer to use the trademark. Under no reasonable construction of the statutory language can goods made in a foreign country by an independent foreign manufacturer be removed from the purview of the statute.

(2)

The design of the regulation is such that the subsection of the regulation dealing with case 3, § 133.21(c)(3), is severable. The severance and invalidation of this subsection will not impair the function of the statute as a whole, and there is no indication that the regulation would not have been passed but for its inclusion. Accordingly, subsection (c)(3) of section 133.21 must be invalidated for its conflict with the unequivocal language of the statute.

III

We hold that the Customs Service regulation is consistent with § 526 insofar as it exempts from the importation ban goods that are manufactured abroad by the "same person" who holds the U.S. trademark, 19 CFR § 133.21(c)(1) (1987), or by a person who is "subject to common ... control" with the U.S. trademark holder, § 133.21(c)(2). Because the authorized-use exception of the regulation, § 133.21(c)(3), is in conflict with the plain language of the statute, that provision cannot stand. The judgment of the Court of Appeals is, therefore, reversed insofar as it invalidated §§ 133.21(c)(1) and (c)(2), but affirmed with respect to § 133.21(c)(3).

It is so ordered.

Question

Are you persuaded that the Customs regulations at issue in *K Mart* reasonably construed an "ambiguity" in the statute?

---

15 U.S.C. § 1124 [Lanham Act § 42]

Except as provided in subsection (d) of section 1526 of title 19, no article of imported merchandise which shall copy or simulate the name of any domestic manufacture, or manufacturer, or trader, or of any manufacturer or trader located in any foreign country which, by treaty, convention, or law affords similar privileges to citizens of the United States, or which shall copy or simulate a trademark registered in accordance with the provisions of this Act or shall bear a name or mark calculated to induce the public to believe that the article is manufactured in the United States, or that it is manufactured in any foreign country or locality other than the country or locality in which it is in fact manufactured, shall be admitted to entry at any customhouse of the United States....

Note: Materially Different Goods Exception

The Customs affiliate exception that was upheld by the Supreme Court in *K-Mart* is not applicable in all situations. The District of Columbia Circuit found enforcement of the Customs' affiliate exception inapplicable under section 42 of the Lanham Act in cases in which the goods provided by the U.S. trademark owner differ materially from those produced by its affiliated foreign company if the goods of the foreign affiliate are imported into the U.S. by third parties (as opposed to the foreign affiliate itself). *See Lever Brothers Co. v. U.S.*, 877 F.2d 101 (D.C. Cir. 1989); *Lever Brothers Co. v. U.S.*, 981 F.2d 1330 (D.C. Cir. 1993). In such cases, Customs is required under section 42 to bar entry to the product. *Lever Brothers* involved a U.S. trademark holder and a UK affiliated company. Both sold deodorant soap under the SHIELD mark and liquid dishwashing detergent under the SUNLIGHT mark. Because the products produced by the two companies were tailored to their local markets, there were differences that were found to be material, e.g. the U.S. soap had more of certain ingredients to generate more lather given the preference for showers in the U.S. as compared with baths in the UK. The UK liquid dishwashing detergent was designed for water with a higher mineral content as compared with the US product. These differences were sufficient to cause likely confusion among U.S. consumers confronted with the U.K. products.

Bourdeau Bros. v. ITC

444 F.3d 1317 (Fed. Cir. 2006)

Clevenger, Senior Circuit Judge:

Appellants Bourdeau Bros., Inc. (Bourdeau), Sunova Implement Co. (Sunova), and OK Enterprises (OK), (collectively, appellants) appeal the decision of the United States International Trade Commission (ITC) affirming the Initial Determination and Recommended Remedy Determination (Initial Determination) of Administrative Law Judge Luckern (ALJ) that the importation of certain Deere European version forage harvesters infringed one or more of Deere's federally registered trademarks, Certain Agric. Vehicles & Components Thereof, Inv. No. 337-TA-487 (Jan. 13, 2004) (Initial Determination), and granting a general exclusion order covering those forage harvesters as well as cease and desist orders against Bourdeau, OK, and other respondents, Certain Agric. Vehicles & Components Thereof, Inv. No. 337-TA-487 (Int'l Trade Comm'n Sept. 24, 2004) (ITC Remedy Determination). We vacate and remand.

I

... Deere & Co. (Deere) filed a complaint with the ITC alleging violations of 19 U.S.C. § 1337 (section 1337) by the importation into the United States, and sale in the United States, of certain used agricultural vehicles that infringed United States Registered Trademark Nos. 1,503,576, 1,502,103, 1,254,339, and 91,860 (the Deere trademarks). In particular, Deere alleged that Deere forage harvesters that had been manufactured solely for sale in Europe (the European version forage harvesters) were being imported into the United States. Deere argued that the European version forage harvesters were materially different from the forage harvesters manufactured and authorized for sale in the United States (the North American version forage harvesters). Thus, Deere claimed that the European version forage harvesters constituted "gray market goods" such that they infringed Deere's trademarks....

....

III

Section 1337(a)(1)(c) forbids "[t]he importation into the United States, the sale for importation, or the sale within the United States after importation by the owner, importer, or consignee, of articles that infringe a valid and enforceable United States trademark registered under the Trademark Act of 1946." Thus, section 1337 grants the ITC the power to prevent the importation of goods that, if sold in the United States, would violate one of the provisions of the federal trademark statute, the Lanham Act.

Many of the goods that are forbidden from importation under section 1337 are what are referred to as "gray market goods": products that were "produced by the owner of the United States trademark or with its consent, but not authorized for sale in the United States." *Gamut Trading Co. v. Int'l Trade Comm'n*, 200 F.3d 775, 777 (Fed. Cir. 1999). The rationale behind preventing importation of these goods is that the public associates a trademark with goods having certain characteristics. *Id.* at

778–79. To the extent that foreign goods bearing a trademark have different characteristics than those trademarked goods authorized for sale in the United States, the public is likely to become confused or deceived as to which characteristics are properly associated with the trademark, thereby possibly eroding the goodwill of the trademark holder in the United States. *Id.* at 779.

Thus, gray market theory recognizes both the territorial boundaries of trademarks and a trademark owner's right to control the qualities or characteristics associated with a trademark in a certain territorial region. As such, the basic question in gray market cases "is not whether the mark was validly affixed" to the goods, "but whether there are differences between the foreign and domestic product and if so whether the differences are material." *Id.* We have applied "a low threshold of materiality, requiring no more than showing that consumers would be likely to consider the differences between the foreign and domestic products to be significant when purchasing the product." *Id.*

However, even though the threshold of materiality is low, "a plaintiff in a gray market trademark infringement case must establish that *all or substantially all* of its sales are accompanied by the asserted material difference in order to show that its goods are materially different." *SKF* [*USA, Inc. v. Int'l Trade Comm'n*,] 423 F.3d [1307,] 1315 [(Fed. Cir. 2005)] (emphasis added). As we noted in *SKF*, the sale by a trademark owner of the very same goods that he claims are gray market goods is inconsistent with a claim that consumers will be confused by those alleged gray market goods. *Id.* "To permit recovery by a trademark owner when less than 'substantially all' of its goods bear the material difference ... would allow the owner itself to contribute to the confusion by consumers that it accuses gray market importers of creating." *Id.* That is, a trademark owner has the right to determine the set of characteristics that are associated with his trademark in the United States; however, a trademark owner cannot authorize the sale of trademarked goods with a set of characteristics and at the same time claim that the set of characteristics should not be associated with the trademark.

This case involves the importation and sale of used forage harvesters manufactured by Deere. Deere sells 5000 and 6000 series forage harvesters in both the United States and Europe.... The 5000 series is manufactured exclusively in the United States, regardless of the market for which it is destined, while the 6000 series is manufactured exclusively in Germany. Both the 5000 and 6000 series forage harvesters fit generally into two categories: the North American version forage harvesters, which are manufactured for sale in the United States and North America, and the European version forage harvesters, which are manufactured for sale in Europe. Although the North American and European version forage harvesters are sold under the same series numbers, they have certain differences, including labeling differences and differences in certain safety features, discussed at greater length below.

Appellants are involved in the importation into the United States and the resale of used European version forage harvesters of both the 5000 and 6000 series. The ITC determined that the European versions of these forage harvesters are materially different from their North American counterparts and that the importation and sale of these forage harvesters violates section 1337.

IV

... [A]ppellants argue that, because the 5000 series forage harvesters are manufactured in the United States, they are not "gray market goods" and thus that importation and sale of these forage harvesters cannot violate section 1337. Appellants point to the Supreme Court's decision *K Mart Corp. v. Cartier, Inc.*, 486 U.S. 281 (1987), in which the Court ... noted that a gray market good is "a foreign-manufactured good, bearing a valid United States trademark, that is imported without the consent of the United States trademark holder." *K Mart*, 486 U.S. at 285.... Appellants argue that the Court did not include ... a case in which a domestic firm manufactures a product in the United States for sale abroad and that good is re-imported to the United States for later sale without the trademark owner's permission. Thus, appellants argue that a good manufactured domestically for export cannot be a "gray market good" and hence cannot violate section 1337.

However, *K Mart* did not address violations of either section 1337 or of the Lanham Act. Rather, the case discussed gray market theory as the background to an analysis of whether certain Customs regulations were consistent with section 526 of the Tariff Act of 1930, 19 U.S.C. § 1526, which attempted to regulate, for the first time, the importation of "gray market goods." *See K Mart*, 486 U.S. at 285–87. Both the regulation at issue, 19 C.F.R. § 133.21, and 19 U.S.C. § 1526 specifically refer to "[f]oreign-made articles" or "merchandise of foreign manufacture." *Id.* at 287–88 (quoting 19 C.F.R. § 133.21 (1987) and 19 U.S.C. § 1526). Thus, it is not surprising that the Court's description of gray market theory focused on goods of foreign manufacture. Further, the Court noted that "[t]he regulations implementing § 526 ... have not applied the prohibition to all gray-market goods." *Id.* at 288. Thus, *K Mart* should not be read to limit gray market theory, as it is applied in the context of section 1337, to goods of foreign manufacture.

In addition, the ITC has already determined that trademarked goods manufactured in the United States exclusively for sale in foreign countries may violate section 1337 if they are imported into the United States without the trademark owner's permission and if they are materially different from the trademarked goods authorized for sale in the United States. See Certain Cigarettes & Packaging, Thereof, Inv. No. 337-TA-424, USITC Pub. 3366, Commission Opinion at 2, n. 2 (Int'l Trade Comm'n, Oct. 16, 2000) (Cigarettes) (finding that cigarettes manufactured in the United States but intended for sale exclusively abroad violated section 1337). Although the ITC expressly declined to refer to the goods in Cigarettes as "gray market goods," using instead the terms "for-export" or "re-imported," the ITC analyzed whether the goods violated section 1337 using the "material difference" standard we applied in *Gamut.*

Indeed, section 1337(a)(1)(c) makes no reference to the term "gray market." In addition, unlike the statute at issue in *K Mart*, it does not distinguish between goods of domestic manufacture and goods of foreign manufacture. Rather, the statute simply declares unlawful "[t]he importation into the United States, the sale for importation, or the sale within the United States after importation by the owner, importer, or consignee, of articles that infringe a valid and enforceable United States trademark registered under the Trademark Act of 1946." 19 U.S.C. § 1337(a)(1)(c).

Finally, although this court noted in *Gamut* that "[t]he term 'gray market goods' refers to genuine goods that *in this case* are of foreign manufacture," we did not expressly limit the term "gray market goods" nor yet the reach of section 1337—to foreign-manufactured goods. 200 F.3d at 778 (emphasis added). Rather, we noted that "[t]he principle of gray market law is that the importation of a product that was produced by the owner of the United States trademark or with its consent, but not authorized for sale in the United States, may, in appropriate cases infringe the United States trademark." *Id.* at 777. Thus, gray market law is not concerned with where the good was manufactured, nor is it concerned with whether the trademark owner controlled the manufacture of the product or authorized the use of the trademark on that product in another country. Instead, gray market law is concerned with whether the trademark owner has authorized use of the trademark on that particular product in the United States and thus whether the trademark owner has control over the specific characteristics associated with the trademark in the United States.

As such, we agree with the ITC, and we hold that the importation and sale of a trademarked good of domestic manufacture, produced solely for sale abroad and not authorized by the owner of the trademark for sale in the United States, may violate section 1337 if the imported good is materially different from all or substantially all of those goods bearing the same trademark that are authorized for sale in the United States.

V

In order to find a violation of section 1337, the imported goods must be materially different from all or substantially all of those trademarked goods authorized for sale in the United States. The materiality threshold is low, "requiring no more than showing that consumers would be likely to consider the differences between the foreign and domestic products to be significant when purchasing the product, for such differences would suffice to erode the goodwill of the domestic source." *Gamut*, 200 F.3d at 779. Indeed, there need only be one material difference between a domestic and a foreign product in order to determine that the latter is a gray market good eligible for exclusion. *See, e.g., id.* at 780–82 (affirming ITC finding of material difference based solely on the absence of English-language warning and instructional labels on foreign goods). However, the "plaintiff ... must establish that all or substantially all of its sales are accompanied by the asserted material difference in order to show that its goods are materially different." *SKF*, 423 F.3d at 1315.

In this case, the ALJ found that there were numerous differences between the European and North American versions of both the 5000 and 6000 series forage harvesters that a customer in the United States would be likely to consider significant when purchasing the product. Initial Determination, slip op. at 19. While, for the most part, the appellants do not contest the existence of differences between the North American and European version forage harvesters, they argue that substantial evidence does not support the ALJ's findings that these differences are material.

However, substantial evidence supports the ALJ's determination that there are several differences between the North American and European version forage harvesters of both the 5000 and 6000 series that a customer would be likely to consider significant when purchasing the product. Both the 5000 and 6000 series harvesters contain differences in safety features that a customer would be likely to consider significant when purchasing the product. First of all, there are material differences between the lighting configuration and lighting functions of the North American and European forage harvesters, including the type of lights used during transport, the manner in which hazard lights and turn signals function, and whether safety warning lamps exist. There are also material differences between the warning labels and safety decals on the North American forage harvesters, which carry pictures and English writing, and European forage harvesters, which carry only pictures. *See In re Certain Agric. Tractors Under 50 Power Takeoff Horsepower Investigation*, 44 U.S.P.Q.2d 1385, 1402 (Int'l Trade Comm'n 1997) ("*Tractors*") (finding that the absence of English language warning and instructional labels on foreign goods constituted a material difference), *aff'd, Gamut*, 200 F.3d 775.

There are several other material differences between the North American and European versions of both the 5000 and 6000 series forage harvesters. There is a material difference in the hitch mechanism of the North American and European forage harvesters, as the mechanism in the European forage harvesters is not compatible with wagons used in North America. In addition, the operator's manuals of the European version forage harvesters are in the language of the target country, while the American forage harvesters' manuals are in English. Although appellants claim that North American manuals are often provided to purchasers of European version forage harvesters, this only serves to heighten confusion, as the North American and European manuals contain different information due to other differences in the products.

Finally, there are differences in the services provided along with the machines, including the Deere Product Improvement Programs (PIPs) and Service Information System (SIS). Although all three types of Deere's PIPs—mechanical, fix-it fail, and safety—are free to customers who have purchased American forage harvesters, the owners of European forage harvesters only qualify for safety PIPs. Further, the SIS, which records details about past PIPs, differs depending on the PIPs for which a machine is available, such that more information is available for North American forage harvesters than European forage harvesters. [The court vacated and remanded the case, however, for a determination whether Deere had itself sold the European forage harvesters in the U.S.]

Editors' Note: On remand, the ITC found that Deere & Company was not entitled to an exclusion order because not all or substantially all of Deere's authorized sales in the U.S. were of its North American version harvesters. On a further appeal, the Federal Circuit vacated and remanded, finding that the ITC had misapplied the all or substantially all test. *Deere & Co. v. ITC*, 605 F.3d 1350 (Fed. Cir. 2010). On the second remand, the ITC found that an exclusion order was justified. 2012 ITC LEXIS 118 (Int'l Trade Comm'n, Jan. 13, 2012).

Questions

1. Can genuine goods become spurious? Suppose that a licensee has been manufacturing and selling trademarked goods. When the license terminates or is otherwise revoked, may the licensee continue selling its inventory of trademarked goods, or will doing so violate the Lanham Act? *Compare Glovaroma, Inc. v. Maljack Productions, Inc.*, 71 F. Supp. 2d 846 (N.D. Ill. 1999), *with Rogers v. HSN Direct Joint Venture*, 1999 U.S. Dist. LEXIS 14392 (S.D.N.Y. 1999). *See also Abercrombie & Fitch v. Fashion Shops of Ky.*, 363 F. Supp. 2d 952 (S.D. Ohio 2005) (licensed Abercrombie & Fitch clothing that failed U.S. quality standards, but whose sale abroad was permitted, was resold by unlicensed third party in the U.S.); *American Circuit Breaker Corp. v. Oregon Breakers Inc.*, 406 F.3d 577 (9th Cir. 2005) (resale in U.S. of circuit breakers made under license for the Canadian market; only difference between U.S.-destined and Canada-destined goods is the nonfunctional color of the plastic housing).

2. Would differences in the warranties offered for gray market auto parts sold to auto dealers be a "material" difference so as to make such goods infringing? Does it matter that the auto dealers are aware of the warranty differences? Should post-sale confusion of the dealers' customers be considered in determining materiality? *See Kia Motors America, Inc. v. Autoworks Distributing*, 90 U.S.P.Q.2d 1598 (D. Minn. 2009).

3. Hokto USA grows its mushrooms in a special growing medium to satisfy U.S. organic standards; whereas its Japanese parent Hokto Japan does not use this medium for its mushrooms intended for the Japanese market. Additionally, the Japanese parent uses Japanese language packaging for mushrooms intended for the Japanese market; whereas, Hokto USA's packages are also in English. The labeling provides information about calorie count, serving size and nutritional information. Concord Farms imports Hokto Japan's mushrooms intended for the Japanese market. Should the differences with Hokto USA's mushrooms be considered material? *See Hokto Kinoko Co. v. Concord Farms, Inc.*, 738 F.3d 1085 (9th Cir. 2013) (affirms summary judgment for the plaintiff).

Appendix A

Lanham Trademark Act of 1946, as Amended through February 1, 2016 and codified in Chapter 22 of Title 15 of the United States Code

NOTE: The headings used for sections and subsections or paragraphs in the following reprint of the Act are not part of the Act but have been added for convenience. Prior trademark statutes may be found in Title 15, Chapter 3, of the U.S. Code and in the Statutes at Large. The present Act forms Chapter 22 of Title 15 of the U.S. Code. Lanham Act section numbers appear at the beginning of each section, followed by the U.S. Code cite in parentheses.

CHAPTER 22—TRADEMARKS

SUBCHAPTER I—THE PRINCIPAL REGISTER

Sec.

16 (15 U.S.C. § 1066). Interference; declaration by Director.

17 (15 U.S.C. § 1067). Interference, opposition, and proceedings for concurrent use registration or for cancellation; notice; Trademark Trial and Appeal Board.

18 (15 U.S.C. § 1068). Action of Director in interference, opposition, and proceedings for concurrent use registration or for cancellation.

19 (15 U.S.C. § 1069). Application of equitable principles in inter partes proceedings.

20 (15 U.S.C. § 1070). Appeals to Trademark Trial and Appeal Board from decisions of examiners.

21 (15 U.S.C. § 1071). Appeal to courts.

22 (15 U.S.C. § 1072). Registration as constructive notice of claim of ownership.

SUBCHAPTER II—THE SUPPLEMENTAL REGISTER

23 (15 U.S.C. § 1091). Supplemental register.

24 (15 U.S.C. § 1092). Publication; not subject to opposition; cancellation.

25 (15 U.S.C. § 1093). Registration certificates for marks on principal and supplemental registers to be different.

26 (15 U.S.C. § 1094). Provisions of chapter applicable to registrations on supplemental register.

27 (15 U.S.C. § 1095). Registration on principal register not precluded.

28 (15 U.S.C. § 1096). Registration on supplemental register not used to stop importations.

SUBCHAPTER III—GENERAL PROVISIONS

29 (15 U.S.C. § 1111). Notice of registration; display with mark; recovery of profits and damages in infringement suit.

30 (15 U.S.C. § 1112). Classification of goods and services; registration in plurality of classes.

31 (15 U.S.C. § 1113). Fees.

32 (15 U.S.C. § 1114). Remedies; infringement; innocent infringement by printers and publishers.

33 (15 U.S.C. § 1115). Registration on principal register as evidence of exclusive right to use mark; defenses.

34 (15 U.S.C. § 1116). Injunctive relief.

35 (15 U.S.C. § 1117). Recovery for violation of rights.

36 (15 U.S.C. § 1118). Destruction of infringing articles.

37 (15 U.S.C. § 1119). Power of court over registration.

38 (15 U.S.C. § 1120). Civil liability for false or fraudulent registration.

39 (15 U.S.C. § 1121).	Jurisdiction of Federal courts; State and local requirements that registered trademarks be altered or displayed differently; prohibition.
40 (15 U.S.C. § 1122).	Liability of United States and States, and instrumentalities and officials thereof.
41 (15 U.S.C. § 1123).	Rules and regulations for conduct of proceedings in Patent and Trademark Office.
42 (15 U.S.C. § 1124).	Importation of goods bearing infringing marks or names forbidden.
43 (15 U.S.C. § 1125).	False designations of origin, false descriptions, and dilution forbidden.
44 (15 U.S.C. § 1126).	International conventions.
45 (15 U.S.C. § 1127).	Construction and definitions; intent of chapter.
15 U.S.C. § 8131.	Cyberpiracy protections for individuals.

SUBCHAPTER IV—THE MADRID PROTOCOL

60 (15 U.S.C. § 1141).	Definitions.
61 (15 U.S.C. § 1141a).	International applications based on United States applications or registrations.
62 (15 U.S.C. § 1141b).	Certification of the international application.
63 (15 U.S.C. § 1141c).	Restriction, abandonment, cancellation, or expiration of a basic application or basic registration.
64 (15 U.S.C. § 1141d).	Request for extension of protection subsequent to international registration.
65 (15 U.S.C. § 1141e).	Extension of protection of an international registration to the United States under the Madrid Protocol.
66 (15 U.S.C. § 1141f).	Effect of filing a request for extension of protection of an international registration to the United States.
67 (15 U.S.C. § 1141g).	Right of priority for request for extension of protection to the United States.
68 (15 U.S.C. § 1141h).	Examination of and opposition to request for extension of protection; notification of refusal.
69 (15 U.S.C. § 1141i).	Effect of extension of protection.
70 (15 U.S.C. § 1141j).	Dependence of extension of protection to the United States on the underlying international registration.
71 (15 U.S.C. § 1141k).	Affidavits and fees.
72 (15 U.S.C. § 1141l).	Assignment of an extension of protection.
73 (15 U.S.C. § 1141m).	Incontestability.
74 (15 U.S.C. § 1141n).	Rights of extension of protection.

SUBCHAPTER I—THE PRINCIPAL REGISTER

§1 (15 U.S.C. §1051). Application for registration; verification

(a) Application for use of trademark

(1) The owner of a trademark used in commerce may request registration of its trademark on the principal register hereby established by paying the prescribed fee and filing in the Patent and Trademark Office an application and a verified statement, in such form as may be prescribed by the Director, and such number of specimens or facsimiles of the mark as used as may be required by the Director.

(2) The application shall include specification of the applicant's domicile and citizenship, the date of the applicant's first use of the mark, the date of the applicant's first use of the mark in commerce, the goods in connection with which the mark is used, and a drawing of the mark.

(3) The statement shall be verified by the applicant and specify that—

(A) the person making the verification believes that he or she, or the juristic person in whose behalf he or she makes the verification, to be the owner of the mark sought to be registered;

(B) to the best of the verifier's knowledge and belief, the facts recited in the application are accurate;

(C) the mark is in use in commerce; and

(D) to the best of the verifier's knowledge and belief, no other person has the right to use such mark in commerce either in the identical form thereof or in such near resemblance thereto as to be likely, when used on or in connection with the goods of such other person, to cause confusion, or to cause mistake, or to deceive, except that, in the case of every application claiming concurrent use, the applicant shall—

(i) state exceptions to the claim of exclusive use; and

(ii) shall 1 specify, to the extent of the verifier's knowledge—

(I) any concurrent use by others;

(II) the goods on or in connection with which and the areas in which each concurrent use exists;

(III) the periods of each use; and

(IV) the goods and area for which the applicant desires registration.

(4) The applicant shall comply with such rules or regulations as may be prescribed by the Director. The Director shall promulgate rules prescribing the requirements for the application and for obtaining a filing date herein.

(b) Application for bona fide intention to use trademark

(1) A person who has a bona fide intention, under circumstances showing the good faith of such person, to use a trademark in commerce may request registration of its trademark on the principal register hereby established by paying the prescribed

fee and filing in the Patent and Trademark Office an application and a verified statement, in such form as may be prescribed by the Director.

(2) The application shall include specification of the applicant's domicile and citizenship, the goods in connection with which the applicant has a bona fide intention to use the mark, and a drawing of the mark.

(3) The statement shall be verified by the applicant and specify—

(A) that the person making the verification believes that he or she, or the juristic person in whose behalf he or she makes the verification, to be entitled to use the mark in commerce;

(B) the applicant's bona fide intention to use the mark in commerce;

(C) that, to the best of the verifier's knowledge and belief, the facts recited in the application are accurate; and

(D) that, to the best of the verifier's knowledge and belief, no other person has the right to use such mark in commerce either in the identical form thereof or in such near resemblance thereto as to be likely, when used on or in connection with the goods of such other person, to cause confusion, or to cause mistake, or to deceive. Except for applications filed pursuant to section 1126 [§ 44] of this title, no mark shall be registered until the applicant has met the requirements of subsections (c) and (d) of this section.

(4) The applicant shall comply with such rules or regulations as may be prescribed by the Director. The Director shall promulgate rules prescribing the requirements for the application and for obtaining a filing date herein.

(c) Amendment of application under subsection (b) to conform to requirements of subsection (a)

At any time during examination of an application filed under subsection (b) of this section, an applicant who has made use of the mark in commerce may claim the benefits of such use for purposes of this chapter, by amending his or her application to bring it into conformity with the requirements of subsection (a) of this section.

(d) Verified statement that trademark is used in commerce

(1) Within six months after the date on which the notice of allowance with respect to a mark is issued under section 1063(b)(2) [§ 13(b)(2)] of this title to an applicant under subsection (b) of this section, the applicant shall file in the Patent and Trademark Office, together with such number of specimens or facsimiles of the mark as used in commerce as may be required by the Director and payment of the prescribed fee, a verified statement that the mark is in use in commerce and specifying the date of the applicant's first use of the mark in commerce and those goods or services specified in the notice of allowance on or in connection with which the mark is used in commerce. Subject to examination and acceptance of the statement of use, the mark shall be registered in the Patent and Trademark Office, a certificate of registration shall be issued for those goods or services recited in the statement of use for which the mark is entitled to registration, and

notice of registration shall be published in the Official Gazette of the Patent and Trademark Office. Such examination may include an examination of the factors set forth in subsections (a) through (e) of section 1052 [§2] of this title. The notice of registration shall specify the goods or services for which the mark is registered.

(2) The Director shall extend, for one additional 6-month period, the time for filing the statement of use under paragraph (1), upon written request of the applicant before the expiration of the 6-month period provided in paragraph (1). In addition to an extension under the preceding sentence, the Director may, upon a showing of good cause by the applicant, further extend the time for filing the statement of use under paragraph (1) for periods aggregating not more than 24 months, pursuant to written request of the applicant made before the expiration of the last extension granted under this paragraph. Any request for an extension under this paragraph shall be accompanied by a verified statement that the applicant has a continued bona fide intention to use the mark in commerce and specifying those goods or services identified in the notice of allowance on or in connection with which the applicant has a continued bona fide intention to use the mark in commerce. Any request for an extension under this paragraph shall be accompanied by payment of the prescribed fee. The Director shall issue regulations setting forth guidelines for determining what constitutes good cause for purposes of this paragraph.

(3) The Director shall notify any applicant who files a statement of use of the acceptance or refusal thereof and, if the statement of use is refused, the reasons for the refusal. An applicant may amend the statement of use.

(4) The failure to timely file a verified statement of use under paragraph (1) or an extension request under paragraph (2) shall result in abandonment of the application, unless it can be shown to the satisfaction of the Director that the delay in responding was unintentional, in which case the time for filing may be extended, but for a period not to exceed the period specified in paragraphs (1) and (2) for filing a statement of use.

(e) Designation of resident for service of process and notices

If the applicant is not domiciled in the United States the applicant may designate, by a document filed in the United States Patent and Trademark Office, the name and address of a person resident in the United States on whom may be served notices or process in proceedings affecting the mark. Such notices or process may be served upon the person so designated by leaving with that person or mailing to that person a copy thereof at the address specified in the last designation so filed. If the person so designated cannot be found at the address given in the last designation, or if the registrant does not designate by a document filed in the United States Patent and Trademark Office the name and address of a person resident in the United States on whom may be served notices or process in proceedings affecting the mark, such notices or process may be served on the Director.

§ 2 (15 U.S.C. § 1052). Trademarks registrable on principal register; concurrent registration

No trademark by which the goods of the applicant may be distinguished from the goods of others shall be refused registration on the principal register on account of its nature unless it—

(a) Consists of or comprises immoral, deceptive, or scandalous matter; or matter which may disparage or falsely suggest a connection with persons, living or dead, institutions, beliefs, or national symbols, or bring them into contempt, or disrepute; or a geographical indication which, when used on or in connection with wines or spirits, identifies a place other than the origin of the goods and is first used on or in connection with wines or spirits by the applicant on or after one year after the date on which the WTO Agreement (as defined in section 3501(9) of title 19) enters into force with respect to the United States.

(b) Consists of or comprises the flag or coat of arms or other insignia of the United States, or of any State or municipality, or of any foreign nation, or any simulation thereof.

(c) Consists of or comprises a name, portrait, or signature identifying a particular living individual except by his written consent, or the name, signature, or portrait of a deceased President of the United States during the life of his widow, if any, except by the written consent of the widow.

(d) Consists of or comprises a mark which so resembles a mark registered in the Patent and Trademark Office, or a mark or trade name previously used in the United States by another and not abandoned, as to be likely, when used on or in connection with the goods of the applicant, to cause confusion, or to cause mistake, or to deceive: *Provided*, That if the Director determines that confusion, mistake, or deception is not likely to result from the continued use by more than one person of the same or similar marks under conditions and limitations as to the mode or place of use of the marks or the goods on or in connection with which such marks are used, concurrent registrations may be issued to such persons when they have become entitled to use such marks as a result of their concurrent lawful use in commerce prior to (1) the earliest of the filing dates of the applications pending or of any registration issued under this chapter; (2) July 5, 1947, in the case of registrations previously issued under the Act of March 3, 1881, or February 20, 1905, and continuing in full force and effect on that date; or (3) July 5, 1947, in the case of applications filed under the Act of February 20, 1905, and registered after July 5, 1947. Use prior to the filing date of any pending application or a registration shall not be required when the owner of such application or registration consents to the grant of a concurrent registration to the applicant. Concurrent registrations may also be issued by the Director when a court of competent jurisdiction has finally determined that more than one person is entitled to use the same or similar marks in commerce. In issuing concurrent registrations, the Director shall prescribe conditions and limitations as to the mode or place of use of the mark or the goods on or in connection with which such mark is registered to the respective persons.

(e) Consists of a mark which (1) when used on or in connection with the goods of the applicant is merely descriptive or deceptively misdescriptive of them, (2) when used on or in connection with the goods of the applicant is primarily geographically descriptive of them, except as indications of regional origin may be registrable under section 1054 [§4] of this title, (3) when used on or in connection with the goods of the applicant is primarily geographically deceptively misdescriptive of them, (4) is primarily merely a surname, or (5) comprises any matter that, as a whole, is functional.

(f) Except as expressly excluded in subsections (a), (b), (c), (d), (e)(3), and (e)(5) of this section, nothing in this chapter shall prevent the registration of a mark used by the applicant which has become distinctive of the applicant's goods in commerce. The Director may accept as prima facie evidence that the mark has become distinctive, as used on or in connection with the applicant's goods in commerce, proof of substantially exclusive and continuous use thereof as a mark by the applicant in commerce for the five years before the date on which the claim of distinctiveness is made. Nothing in this section shall prevent the registration of a mark which, when used on or in connection with the goods of the applicant, is primarily geographically deceptively misdescriptive of them, and which became distinctive of the applicant's goods in commerce before December 8, 1993.

A mark which would be likely to cause dilution by blurring or dilution by tarnishment under section 1125(c) [§43(c)] of this title, may be refused registration only pursuant to a proceeding brought under section 1063 [§13] of this title. A registration for a mark which would be likely to cause dilution by blurring or dilution by tarnishment under section 1125(c) [§43(c)] of this title, may be canceled pursuant to a proceeding brought under either section 1064 [§14] of this title or section 1092 [§19] of this title.

§3 (15 U.S.C. §1053). Service marks registrable

Subject to the provisions relating to the registration of trademarks, so far as they are applicable, service marks shall be registrable, in the same manner and with the same effect as are trademarks, and when registered they shall be entitled to the protection provided in this chapter in the case of trademarks. Applications and procedure under this section shall conform as nearly as practicable to those prescribed for the registration of trademarks.

§4 (15 U.S.C. §1054). Collective marks and certification marks registrable

Subject to the provisions relating to the registration of trademarks, so far as they are applicable, collective and certification marks, including indications of regional origin, shall be registrable under this chapter, in the same manner and with the same effect as are trademarks, by persons, and nations, States, municipalities, and the like, exercising legitimate control over the use of the marks sought to be registered, even though not possessing an industrial or commercial establishment, and when registered they shall be entitled to the protection provided in this chapter in the case of trademarks, except in the case of certification marks when used so as to represent falsely that the owner or a user thereof makes or sells the goods or performs the services on or in connection with which such mark is used. Applications and procedure under this section shall conform as nearly as practicable to those prescribed for the registration of trademarks.

§ 5 (15 U.S.C. § 1055). Use by related companies affecting validity and registration

Where a registered mark or a mark sought to be registered is or may be used legitimately by related companies, such use shall inure to the benefit of the registrant or applicant for registration, and such use shall not affect the validity of such mark or of its registration, provided such mark is not used in such manner as to deceive the public. If first use of a mark by a person is controlled by the registrant or applicant for registration of the mark with respect to the nature and quality of the goods or services, such first use shall inure to the benefit of the registrant or applicant, as the case may be.

§ 6 (15 U.S.C. § 1056). Disclaimer of unregistrable matter

(a) Compulsory and voluntary disclaimers

The Director may require the applicant to disclaim an unregistrable component of a mark otherwise registrable. An applicant may voluntarily disclaim a component of a mark sought to be registered.

(b) Prejudice of rights

No disclaimer, including those made under subsection (e) of section 1057 [§ 7] of this title, shall prejudice or affect the applicant's or registrant's rights then existing or thereafter arising in the disclaimed matter, or his right of registration on another application if the disclaimed matter be or shall have become distinctive of his goods or services.

§ 7 (15 U.S.C. § 1057). Certificates of registration

(a) Issuance and form

Certificates of registration of marks registered upon the principal register shall be issued in the name of the United States of America, under the seal of the Patent and Trademark Office, and shall be signed by the Director or have his signature placed thereon, and a record thereof shall be kept in the Patent and Trademark Office. The registration shall reproduce the mark, and state that the mark is registered on the principal register under this chapter, the date of the first use of the mark, the date of the first use of the mark in commerce, the particular goods or services for which it is registered, the number and date of the registration, the term thereof, the date on which the application for registration was received in the Patent and Trademark Office, and any conditions and limitations that may be imposed in the registration.

(b) Certificate as prima facie evidence

A certificate of registration of a mark upon the principal register provided by this chapter shall be prima facie evidence of the validity of the registered mark and of the registration of the mark, of the owner's ownership of the mark, and of the owner's exclusive right to use the registered mark in commerce on or in connection with the goods or services specified in the certificate, subject to any conditions or limitations stated in the certificate.

(c) Application to register mark considered constructive use

Contingent on the registration of a mark on the principal register provided by this chapter, the filing of the application to register such mark shall constitute constructive use of the mark, conferring a right of priority, nationwide in effect, on or in connection with the goods or services specified in the registration against any other person except for a person whose mark has not been abandoned and who, prior to such filing—

(1) has used the mark;

(2) has filed an application to register the mark which is pending or has resulted in registration of the mark; or

(3) has filed a foreign application to register the mark on the basis of which he or she has acquired a right of priority, and timely files an application under section 1126(d) [§ 44(d)] of this title to register the mark which is pending or has resulted in registration of the mark.

(d) Issuance to assignee

A certificate of registration of a mark may be issued to the assignee of the applicant, but the assignment must first be recorded in the United States Patent and Trademark Office. In case of change of ownership the Director shall, at the request of the owner and upon a proper showing and the payment of the prescribed fee, issue to such assignee a new certificate of registration of the said mark in the name of such assignee, and for the unexpired part of the original period.

(e) Surrender, cancellation, or amendment by owner

Upon application of the owner the Director may permit any registration to be surrendered for cancellation, and upon cancellation appropriate entry shall be made in the records of the United States Patent and Trademark Office. Upon application of the owner and payment of the prescribed fee, the Director for good cause may permit any registration to be amended or to be disclaimed in part: *Provided*, That the amendment or disclaimer does not alter materially the character of the mark. Appropriate entry shall be made in the records of the United States Patent and Trademark Office and upon the certificate of registration.

(f) Copies of United States Patent and Trademark Office records as evidence

Copies of any records, books, papers, or drawings belonging to the United States Patent and Trademark Office relating to marks, and copies of registrations, when authenticated by the seal of the United States Patent and Trademark Office and certified by the Director, or in his name by an employee of the Office duly designated by the Director, shall be evidence in all cases wherein the originals would be evidence; and any person making application therefor and paying the prescribed fee shall have such copies.

(g) Correction of Patent and Trademark Office mistake

Whenever a material mistake in a registration, incurred through the fault of the United States Patent and Trademark Office, is clearly disclosed by the records of the Office a certificate stating the fact and nature of such mistake, shall be issued without charge and recorded and a printed copy thereof shall be attached to each printed copy of the registration and such corrected registration shall thereafter have the same effect as if the same had been originally issued in such corrected form, or in the discretion of the Director a new certificate of registration may be issued without charge. All certificates of correction heretofore issued in accordance with the rules of the United States Patent and Trademark Office and the registrations to which they are attached shall have the same force and effect as if such certificates and their issue had been specifically authorized by statute.

(h) Correction of applicant's mistake

Whenever a mistake has been made in a registration and a showing has been made that such mistake occurred in good faith through the fault of the applicant, the Director is authorized to issue a certificate of correction or, in his discretion, a new certificate upon the payment of the prescribed fee: *Provided*, That the correction does not involve such changes in the registration as to require republication of the mark.

§ 8 (15 U.S.C. § 1058). Duration, affidavits and fees

(a) Time Periods for Required Affidavits

Each registration shall remain in force for 10 years, except that the registration of any mark shall be canceled by the Director unless the owner of the registration files in the United States Patent and Trademark Office affidavits that meet the requirements of subsection (b), within the following time periods:

(1) Within the 1-year period immediately preceding the expiration of 6 years following the date of registration under this Act or the date of the publication under section 1062(c) [§ 12(c)].

(2) Within the 1-year period immediately preceding the expiration of 10 years following the date of registration, and each successive 10-year period following the date of registration.

(3) The owner may file the affidavit required under this section within the 6-month grace period immediately following the expiration of the periods established in paragraphs (1) and (2), together with the fee described in subsection (b) and the additional grace period surcharge prescribed by the Director.

(b) Requirements for Affidavit

The affidavit referred to in subsection (a) shall—

(1)(A) state that the mark is in use in commerce;

(B) set forth the goods and services recited in the registration on or in connection with which the mark is in use in commerce;

(C) be accompanied by such number of specimens or facsimiles showing current use of the mark in commerce as may be required by the Director; and

(D) be accompanied by the fee prescribed by the Director; or

(2)(A) set forth the goods and services recited in the registration on or in connection with which the mark is not in use in commerce;

(B) include a showing that any nonuse is due to special circumstances which excuse such nonuse and is not due to any intention to abandon the mark; and

(C) be accompanied by the fee prescribed by the Director.

(c) Deficient Affidavit

If any submission filed within the period set forth in subsection (a) is deficient, including that the affidavit was not filed in the name of the owner of the registration, the deficiency may be corrected after the statutory time period, within the time prescribed after notification of the deficiency. Such submission shall be accompanied by the additional deficiency surcharge prescribed by the Director.

(d) Notice of Requirement

Special notice of the requirement for such affidavit shall be attached to each certificate of registration and notice of publication under section 1062(c) [§ 12(c)].

(e) Notification of Acceptance or Refusal

The Director shall notify any owner who files any affidavit required by this section of the Director's acceptance or refusal thereof and, in the case of a refusal, the reasons therefor.

(f) Designation of Resident for Service of Process and Notices

If the owner is not domiciled in the United States, the owner may designate, by a document filed in the United States Patent and Trademark Office, the name and address of a person resident in the United States on whom may be served notices or process in proceedings affecting the mark. Such notices or process may be served upon the person so designated by leaving with that person or mailing to that person a copy thereof at the address specified in the last designation so filed. If the person so designated cannot be found at the last designated address, or if the owner does not designate by a document filed in the United States Patent and Trademark Office the name and address of a person resident in the United States on whom may be served notices or process in proceedings affecting the mark, such notices or process may be served on the Director.

§ 9 (15 U.S.C. § 1059). Renewal of registration

(a) Period of renewal; time for renewal

Subject to the provisions of section 1058 [§ 8] of this title, each registration may be renewed for periods of 10 years at the end of each successive 10-year period following the date of registration upon payment of the prescribed fee and the filing of a written application, in such form as may be prescribed by the Director. Such application may be made at any time within 1 year before the end of each successive 10-year period for which the registration was issued or renewed, or it may be made within a grace period of 6 months after the end of each successive 10-year period, upon payment of a fee and surcharge prescribed therefor. If any application filed under this section is deficient, the deficiency may be corrected within the time prescribed after notification of the deficiency, upon payment of a surcharge prescribed therefor.

(b) Notification of refusal of renewal

If the Director refuses to renew the registration, the Director shall notify the registrant of the Director's refusal and the reasons therefor.

(c) Designation of resident for service of process and notices

If the registrant is not domiciled in the United States the registrant may designate, by a document filed in the United States Patent and Trademark Office, the name and address of a person resident in the United States on whom may be served notices or process in proceedings affecting the mark. Such notices or process may be served upon the person so designated by leaving with that person or mailing to that person a copy thereof at the address specified in the last designation so filed. If the person so designated cannot be found at the address given in the last designation, or if the registrant does not designate by a document filed in the United States Patent and Trademark Office the name and address of a person resident in the United States on whom may be served notices or process in proceedings affecting the mark, such notices or process may be served on the Director.

§ 10 (15 U.S.C. § 1060). Assignment

(a)(1) A registered mark or a mark for which an application to register has been filed shall be assignable with the good will of the business in which the mark is used, or with that part of the good will of the business connected with the use of and symbolized by the mark. Notwithstanding the preceding sentence, no application to register a mark under section 1051(b) [§ 1(b)] of this title shall be assignable prior to the filing of an amendment under section 1051(c) [§ 1(c)] of this title to bring the application into conformity with section 1051(a) [§ 1(a)] of this title or the filing of the verified statement of use under section 1051(d) [§ 1(d)] of this title, except for an assignment to a successor to the business of the applicant, or portion thereof, to which the mark pertains, if that business is ongoing and existing.

(2) In any assignment authorized by this section, it shall not be necessary to include the good will of the business connected with the use of and symbolized by any other mark used in the business or by the name or style under which the business is conducted.

(3) Assignments shall be by instruments in writing duly executed. Acknowledgment shall be prima facie evidence of the execution of an assignment, and when the prescribed information reporting the assignment is recorded in the United States Patent and Trademark Office, the record shall be prima facie evidence of execution.

(4) An assignment shall be void against any subsequent purchaser for valuable consideration without notice, unless the prescribed information reporting the

assignment is recorded in the United States Patent and Trademark Office within 3 months after the date of the assignment or prior to the subsequent purchase.

(5) The United States Patent and Trademark Office shall maintain a record of information on assignments, in such form as may be prescribed by the Director.

(b) An assignee not domiciled in the United States may designate by a document filed in the United States Patent and Trademark Office the name and address of a person resident in the United States on whom may be served notices or process in proceedings affecting the mark. Such notices or process may be served upon the person so designated by leaving with that person or mailing to that person a copy thereof at the address specified in the last designation so filed. If the person so designated cannot be found at the address given in the last designation, or if the assignee does not designate by a document filed in the United States Patent and Trademark Office the name and address of a person resident in the United States on whom may be served notices or process in proceedings affecting the mark, such notices or process may be served upon the Director.

§ 11 (15 U.S.C. § 1061). Execution of acknowledgments and verifications

Acknowledgments and verifications required under this chapter may be made before any person within the United States authorized by law to administer oaths, or, when made in a foreign country, before any diplomatic or consular officer of the United States or before any official authorized to administer oaths in the foreign country concerned whose authority is proved by a certificate of a diplomatic or consular officer of the United States, or apostille of an official designated by a foreign country which, by treaty or convention, accords like effect to apostilles of designated officials in the United States, and shall be valid if they comply with the laws of the state or country where made.

§ 12 (15 U.S.C. § 1062). Publication

(a) Examination and publication

Upon the filing of an application for registration and payment of the prescribed fee, the Director shall refer the application to the examiner in charge of the registration of marks, who shall cause an examination to be made and, if on such examination it shall appear that the applicant is entitled to registration, or would be entitled to registration upon the acceptance of the statement of use required by section 1051(d) [§ 1(d)] of this title, the Director shall cause the mark to be published in the Official Gazette of the Patent and Trademark Office: *Provided*, That in the case of an applicant claiming concurrent use, or in the case of an application to be placed in an interference as provided for in section 1066 [§ 16] of this title the mark, if otherwise registrable, may be published subject to the determination of the rights of the parties to such proceedings.

(b) Refusal of registration; amendment of application; abandonment

If the applicant is found not entitled to registration, the examiner shall advise the applicant thereof and of the reasons therefor. The applicant shall have a period of six months in which to reply or amend his application, which shall then be reexamined. This procedure may be repeated until (1) the examiner finally refuses registration of the mark or (2) the applicant fails for a period of six months to reply or amend or appeal, whereupon the application shall be deemed to have been abandoned, unless it can be shown to the satisfaction of the Director that the delay in responding was unintentional, whereupon such time may be extended.

(c) Republication of marks registered under prior acts

A registrant of a mark registered under the provisions of the Act of March 3, 1881, or the Act of February 20, 1905, may, at any time prior to the expiration of the registration thereof, upon the payment of the prescribed fee file with the Director an affidavit setting forth those goods stated in the registration on which said mark is in use in commerce and that the registrant claims the benefits of this chapter for said mark. The Director shall publish notice thereof with a reproduction of said mark in the Official Gazette, and notify the registrant of such publication and of the requirement for the affidavit of use or nonuse as provided for in subsection (b) of section 1058 [§ 8] of this title. Marks published under this subsection shall not be subject to the provisions of section 1063 [§ 13] of this title.

§ 13 (15 U.S.C. § 1063). Opposition to registration

(a) Any person who believes that he would be damaged by the registration of a mark upon the principal register, including the registration of any mark which would be likely to cause dilution by blurring or dilution by tarnishment under section 1125(c) [§ 43(c)] of this title, may, upon payment of the prescribed fee, file an opposition in the Patent and Trademark Office, stating the grounds therefor, within thirty days after the publication under subsection (a) of section 1062 [§ 12] of this title of the mark sought to be registered. Upon written request prior to the expiration of the thirty-day period, the time for filing opposition shall be extended for an additional thirty days, and further extensions of time for filing opposition may be granted by the Director for good cause when requested prior to the expiration of an extension. The Director shall notify the applicant of each extension of the time for filing opposition. An opposition may be amended under such conditions as may be prescribed by the Director.

(b) Unless registration is successfully opposed—

(1) a mark entitled to registration on the principal register based on an application filed under section 1051(a) [§ 1(a)] of this title or pursuant to section 1126 [§ 44] of this title shall be registered in the Patent and Trademark Office, a certificate of registration shall be issued, and notice of the registration shall be published in the Official Gazette of the Patent and Trademark Office; or

(2) a notice of allowance shall be issued to the applicant if the applicant applied for registration under section 1051(b) [§ 1(b)] of this title.

§ 14 (15 U.S.C. § 1064). Cancellation of registration

A petition to cancel a registration of a mark, stating the grounds relied upon, may, upon payment of the prescribed fee, be filed as follows by any person who believes that he is or will be damaged, including as a result of a likelihood of dilution by blurring or dilution by tarnishment under section 1125(c) [§ 43(c)] of this title, by the registration of a mark on the principal register established by this chapter, or under the Act of March 3, 1881, or the Act of February 20, 1905:

(1) Within five years from the date of the registration of the mark under this chapter.

(2) Within five years from the date of publication under section 1062(c) [§12(c)] of this title of a mark registered under the Act of March 3, 1881, or the Act of February 20, 1905.

(3) At any time if the registered mark becomes the generic name for the goods or services, or a portion thereof, for which it is registered, or is functional, or has been abandoned, or its registration was obtained fraudulently or contrary to the provisions of section 1054 [§4] of this title or of subsection (a), (b), or (c) of section 1052 [§2] of this title for a registration under this chapter, or contrary to similar prohibitory provisions of such prior Acts for a registration under such Acts, or if the registered mark is being used by, or with the permission of, the registrant so as to misrepresent the source of the goods or services on or in connection with which the mark is used. If the registered mark becomes the generic name for less than all of the goods or services for which it is registered, a petition to cancel the registration for only those goods or services may be filed. A registered mark shall not be deemed to be the generic name of goods or services solely because such mark is also used as a name of or to identify a unique product or service. The primary significance of the registered mark to the relevant public rather than purchaser motivation shall be the test for determining whether the registered mark has become the generic name of goods or services on or in connection with which it has been used.

(4) At any time if the mark is registered under the Act of March 3, 1881, or the Act of February 20, 1905, and has not been published under the provisions of subsection (c) of section 1062 [§12] of this title.

(5) At any time in the case of a certification mark on the ground that the registrant

(A) does not control, or is not able legitimately to exercise control over, the use of such mark, or

(B) engages in the production or marketing of any goods or services to which the certification mark is applied, or

(C) permits the use of the certification mark for purposes other than to certify, or

(D) discriminately refuses to certify or to continue to certify the goods or services of any person who maintains the standards or conditions which such mark certifies:

Provided, That the Federal Trade Commission may apply to cancel on the grounds specified in paragraphs (3) and (5) of this section any mark registered on the principal register established by this chapter, and the prescribed fee shall not be required. Nothing in paragraph (5) shall be deemed to prohibit the registrant from using its certification mark in advertising or promoting recognition of the certification program or of the goods or services meeting the certification standards of the registrant. Such uses of the certification mark shall not be grounds for cancellation under paragraph (5), so long as the registrant does not itself produce, manufacture, or sell any of the certified goods or services to which its identical certification mark is applied.

§ 15 (15 U.S.C. § 1065). Incontestability of right to use mark under certain conditions

Except on a ground for which application to cancel may be filed at any time under paragraphs (3) and (5) of section 1064 [§ 14] of this title, and except to the extent, if any, to which the use of a mark registered on the principal register infringes a valid right acquired under the law of any State or Territory by use of a mark or trade name continuing from a date prior to the date of registration under this chapter of such registered mark, the right of the owner to use such registered mark in commerce for the goods or services on or in connection with which such registered mark has been in continuous use for five consecutive years subsequent to the date of such registration and is still in use in commerce, shall be incontestable: *Provided*, That—

(1) there has been no final decision adverse to the owner's claim of ownership of such mark for such goods or services, or to the owner's right to register the same or to keep the same on the register; and

(2) there is no proceeding involving said rights pending in the United States Patent and Trademark Office or in a court and not finally disposed of; and

(3) an affidavit is filed with the Director within one year after the expiration of any such five-year period setting forth those goods or services stated in the registration on or in connection with which such mark has been in continuous use for such five consecutive years and is still in use in commerce, and other matters specified in paragraphs (1) and (2) of this section; and

(4) no incontestable right shall be acquired in a mark which is the generic name for the goods or services or a portion thereof, for which it is registered.

Subject to the conditions above specified in this section, the incontestable right with reference to a mark registered under this chapter shall apply to a mark registered under the Act of March 3, 1881, or the Act of February 20, 1905, upon the filing of the required affidavit with the Director within one year after the expiration of any period of five consecutive years after the date of publication of a mark under the provisions of subsection (c) of section 1062 [§ 12] of this title. The Director shall notify any registrant who files the above-prescribed affidavit of the filing thereof.

§ 16 (15 U.S.C. § 1066). Interference; declaration by Director

Upon petition showing extraordinary circumstances, the Director may declare that an interference exists when application is made for the registration of a mark which so resembles a mark previously registered by another, or for the registration of which another has previously made application, as to be likely when used on or in connection with the goods or services of the applicant to cause confusion or mistake or to deceive.

No interference shall be declared between an application and the registration of a mark the right to the use of which has become incontestable.

§ 17 (15 U.S.C. § 1067). Interference, opposition, and proceedings for concurrent use registration or for cancellation; notice; Trademark Trial and Appeal Board

(a) In every case of interference, opposition to registration, application to register as a lawful concurrent user, or application to cancel the registration of a mark, the Director shall give notice to all parties and shall direct a Trademark Trial and Appeal Board to determine and decide the respective rights of registration.

(b) The Trademark Trial and Appeal Board shall include the Director, the Commissioner for Patents, the Commissioner for Trademarks, and administrative trademark judges who are appointed by the Director.

(c) **Authority of the Secretary**

The Secretary of Commerce may, in his or her discretion, deem the appointment of an administrative trademark judge who, before the date of the enactment of this subsection, held office pursuant to an appointment by the Director to take effect on the date on which the Director initially appointed the administrative trademark judge.

(d) **Defense to Challenge of Appointment**

It shall be a defense to a challenge to the appointment of an administrative trademark judge on the basis of the judge's having been originally appointed by the Director that the administrative trademark judge so appointed was acting as a de facto officer.

§ 18 (15 U.S.C. § 1068). Action of Director in interference, opposition, and proceedings for concurrent use registration or for cancellation

In such proceedings the Director may refuse to register the opposed mark, may cancel the registration, in whole or in part, may modify the application or registration by limiting the goods or services specified therein, may otherwise restrict or rectify with respect to the register the registration of a registered mark, may refuse to register any or all of several interfering marks, or may register the mark or marks for the person or persons entitled thereto, as the rights of the parties under this chapter may be established in the proceedings: *Provided*, That in the case of the registration of any mark based on concurrent use, the Director shall determine and fix the conditions and limitations provided for in subsection (d) of section 1052 [§ 2] of this title. However, no final judgment shall be entered in favor of an applicant under section 1051(b) [§ 1(b)] of this title before the mark is registered, if such applicant cannot prevail without establishing constructive use pursuant to section 1057(c) [§ 7(c)] of this title.

§ 19 (15 U.S.C. § 1069). Application of equitable principles in inter partes proceedings

In all inter partes proceedings equitable principles of laches, estoppel, and acquiescence, where applicable may be considered and applied.

§ 20 (15 U.S.C. § 1070). Appeals to Trademark Trial and Appeal Board from decisions of examiners

An appeal may be taken to the Trademark Trial and Appeal Board from any final decision of the examiner in charge of the registration of marks upon the payment of the prescribed fee.

§ 21 (15 U.S.C. § 1071). Appeal to courts

(a) Persons entitled to appeal; United States Court of Appeals for the Federal Circuit; waiver of civil action; election of civil action by adverse party; procedure

(1) An applicant for registration of a mark, party to an interference proceeding, party to an opposition proceeding, party to an application to register as a lawful concurrent user, party to a cancellation proceeding, a registrant who has filed an affidavit as provided in section 1058 or section 71 of this title, or an applicant for renewal, who is dissatisfied with the decision of the Director or Trademark Trial and Appeal Board, may appeal to the United States Court of Appeals for the Federal Circuit thereby waiving his right to proceed under subsection (b) of this section: *Provided*, That such appeal shall be dismissed if any adverse party to the proceeding, other than the Director, shall, within twenty days after the appellant has filed notice of appeal according to paragraph (2) of this subsection, files notice with the Director that he elects to have all further proceedings conducted as provided in subsection (b) of this section. Thereupon the appellant shall have thirty days thereafter within which to file a civil action under subsection (b) of this section, in default of which the decision appealed from shall govern the further proceedings in the case.

(2) When an appeal is taken to the United States Court of Appeals for the Federal Circuit, the appellant shall file in the United States Patent and Trademark Office a written notice of appeal directed to the Director, within such time after the date of the decision from which the appeal is taken as the Director prescribes, but in no case less than 60 days after that date.

(3) The Director shall transmit to the United States Court of Appeals for the Federal Circuit a certified list of the documents comprising the record in the United States Patent and Trademark Office. The court may request that the Director forward the original or certified copies of such documents during pendency of the appeal. In an ex parte case, the Director shall submit to that court a brief explaining the grounds for the decision of the United States Patent and Trademark Office, addressing all the issues involved in the appeal. The court shall, before hearing an appeal, give notice of the time and place of the hearing to the Director and the parties in the appeal.

(4) The United States Court of Appeals for the Federal Circuit shall review the decision from which the appeal is taken on the record before the United States Patent and Trademark Office. Upon its determination the court shall issue its mandate and opinion to the Director, which shall be entered of record in the United States Patent and Trademark Office and shall govern the further proceedings in the case.

However, no final judgment shall be entered in favor of an applicant under section 1051(b) [§1(b)] of this title before the mark is registered, if such applicant cannot prevail without establishing constructive use pursuant to section 1057(c) [§7(c)] of this title.

(b) Civil action; persons entitled to; jurisdiction of court; status of Director; procedure

(1) Whenever a person authorized by subsection (a) of this section to appeal to the United States Court of Appeals for the Federal Circuit is dissatisfied with the decision of the Director or Trademark Trial and Appeal Board, said person may, unless appeal has been taken to said United States Court of Appeals for the Federal Circuit, have remedy by a civil action if commenced within such time after such decision, not less than sixty days, as the Director appoints or as provided in subsection (a) of this section. The court may adjudge that an applicant is entitled to a registration upon the application involved, that a registration involved should be canceled, or such other matter as the issues in the proceeding require, as the facts in the case may appear. Such adjudication shall authorize the Director to take any necessary action, upon compliance with the requirements of law. However, no final judgment shall be entered in favor of an applicant under section 1051(b) [§1(b)] of this title before the mark is registered, if such applicant cannot prevail without establishing constructive use pursuant to section 1057(c) [§7(c)] of this title.

(2) The Director shall not be made a party to an inter partes proceeding under this subsection, but he shall be notified of the filing of the complaint by the clerk of the court in which it is filed and shall have the right to intervene in the action.

(3) In any case where there is no adverse party, a copy of the complaint shall be served on the Director, and, unless the court finds the expenses to be unreasonable, all the expenses of the proceeding shall be paid by the party bringing the case, whether the final decision is in favor of such party or not. In suits brought hereunder, the record in the United States Patent and Trademark Office shall be admitted on motion of any party, upon such terms and conditions as to costs, expenses, and the further cross-examination of the witnesses as the court imposes, without prejudice to the right of any party to take further testimony. The testimony and exhibits of the record in the United States Patent and Trademark Office, when admitted, shall have the same effect as if originally taken and produced in the suit.

(4) Where there is an adverse party, such suit may be instituted against the party in interest as shown by the records of the United States Patent and Trademark Office at the time of the decision complained of, but any party in interest may become a party to the action. If there be adverse parties residing in a plurality of districts not embraced within the same State, or an adverse party residing in a foreign country, the United States District Court for the District of Columbia shall have jurisdiction and may issue summons against the adverse parties directed to the marshal of any district in which any adverse party resides. Summons against adverse parties residing in foreign countries may be served by publication or otherwise as the court directs.

§ 22 (15 U.S.C. § 1072). Registration as constructive notice of claim of ownership

Registration of a mark on the principal register provided by this chapter or under the Act of March 3, 1881, or the Act of February 20, 1905, shall be constructive notice of the registrant's claim of ownership thereof.

SUBCHAPTER II—THE SUPPLEMENTAL REGISTER

§ 23 (15 U.S.C. § 1091). Supplemental register

(a) Marks registerable

In addition to the principal register, the Director shall keep a continuation of the register provided in paragraph (b) of section 1 of the Act of March 19, 1920, entitled "An Act to give effect to certain provisions of the convention for the protection of trademarks and commercial names, made and signed in the city of Buenos Aires, in the Argentine Republic, August 20, 1910, and for other purposes", to be called the supplemental register. All marks capable of distinguishing applicant's goods or services and not registrable on the principal register provided in this chapter, except those declared to be unregistrable under subsections (a), (b), (c), (d), and (e)(3) of section 1052 [§ 2] of this title, which are in lawful use in commerce by the owner thereof, on or in connection with any goods or services may be registered on the supplemental register upon the payment of the prescribed fee and compliance with the provisions of subsections (a) and (e) of section 1051 [§ 1] of this title so far as they are applicable. Nothing in this section shall prevent the registration on the supplemental register of a mark, capable of distinguishing the applicant's goods or services and not registrable on the principal register under this chapter, that is declared to be unregistrable under section 1052(e)(3) [§ 2(e)(3)] of this title, if such mark has been in lawful use in commerce by the owner thereof, on or in connection with any goods or services, since before December 8, 1993.

(b) Application and proceedings for registration

Upon the filing of an application for registration on the supplemental register and payment of the prescribed fee the Director shall refer the application to the examiner in charge of the registration of marks, who shall cause an examination to be made and if on such examination it shall appear that the applicant is entitled to registration, the registration shall be granted. If the applicant is found not entitled to registration the provisions of subsection (b) of section 1062 [§ 12] of this title shall apply.

(c) Nature of mark

For the purposes of registration on the supplemental register, a mark may consist of any trademark, symbol, label, package, configuration of goods, name, word, slogan, phrase, surname, geographical name, numeral, device, any matter that as a whole is not functional, or any combination of any of the foregoing, but such mark must be capable of distinguishing the applicant's goods or services.

§ 24 (15 U.S.C. § 1092). Publication; not subject to opposition; cancellation

Marks for the supplemental register shall not be published for or be subject to opposition, but shall be published on registration in the Official Gazette of the Patent and Trademark Office. Whenever any person believes that such person is or will be damaged by the registration of a mark on the supplemental register—

(1) for which the effective filing date is after the date on which such person's mark became famous and which would be likely to cause dilution by blurring or dilution by tarnishment under section 1125(c) [§ 43(c)] of this title; or

(2) on grounds other than dilution by blurring or dilution by tarnishment, such person may at any time, upon payment of the prescribed fee and the filing of a petition stating the ground therefor, apply to the Director to cancel such registration. The Director shall refer such application to the Trademark Trial and Appeal Board which shall give notice thereof to the registrant. If it is found after a hearing before the Board that the registrant is not entitled to registration, or that the mark has been abandoned, the registration shall be canceled by the Director. However, no final judgment shall be entered in favor of an applicant under section 1051(b) [§ 1(b)] of this title before the mark is registered, if such applicant cannot prevail without establishing constructive use pursuant to section 1057(c) [§ 7(c)] of this title.

§ 25 (15 U.S.C. § 1093). Registration certificates for marks on principal and supplemental registers to be different

The certificates of registration for marks registered on the supplemental register shall be conspicuously different from certificates issued for marks registered on the principal register.

§ 26 (15 U.S.C. § 1094). Provisions of chapter applicable to registrations on supplemental register

The provisions of this chapter shall govern so far as applicable applications for registration and registrations on the supplemental register as well as those on the principal register, but applications for and registrations on the supplemental register shall not be subject to or receive the advantages of sections 1051(b), 1052(e), 1052(f), 1057(b), 1057(c), 1062(a), 1063 to 1068, inclusive, 1072, 1115 and 1124 [§§ 1(b), 2(e), 2(f), 7 (b), 7(c), 12(a), 13–18, 22, 33, 42] of this title.

§ 27 (15 U.S.C. § 1095). Registration on principal register not precluded

Registration of a mark on the supplemental register, or under the Act of March 19, 1920, shall not preclude registration by the registrant on the principal register established by this chapter. Registration of a mark on the supplemental register shall not constitute an admission that the mark has not acquired distinctiveness.

§ 28 (15 U.S.C. § 1096). Registration on supplemental register not used to stop importations

Registration on the supplemental register or under the Act of March 19, 1920, shall not be filed in the Department of the Treasury or be used to stop importations.

SUBCHAPTER III—GENERAL PROVISIONS

§29 (15 U.S.C. §1111). Notice of registration; display with mark; recovery of profits and damages in infringement suit

Notwithstanding the provisions of section 1072 [§22] of this title, a registrant of a mark registered in the Patent and Trademark Office, may give notice that his mark is registered by displaying with the mark the words "Registered in U.S. Patent and Trademark Office" or "Reg. U.S. Pat. & Tm. Off." or the letter R enclosed within a circle, thus ®; and in any suit for infringement under this chapter by such a registrant failing to give such notice of registration, no profits and no damages shall be recovered under the provisions of this chapter unless the defendant had actual notice of the registration.

§30 (15 U.S.C. §1112). Classification of goods and services; registration in plurality of classes

The Director may establish a classification of goods and services, for convenience of Patent and Trademark Office administration, but not to limit or extend the applicant's or registrant's rights. The applicant may apply to register a mark for any or all of the goods or services on or in connection with which he or she is using or has a bona fide intention to use the mark in commerce: *Provided*, That if the Director by regulation permits the filing of an application for the registration of a mark for goods or services which fall within a plurality of classes, a fee equaling the sum of the fees for filing an application in each class shall be paid, and the Director may issue a single certificate of registration for such mark.

§31 (15 U.S.C. §1113). Fees

(a) Applications; services; materials

The Director shall establish fees for the filing and processing of an application for the registration of a trademark or other mark and for all other services performed by and materials furnished by the Patent and Trademark Office related to trademarks and other marks. Fees established under this subsection may be adjusted by the Director once each year to reflect, in the aggregate, any fluctuations during the preceding 12 months in the Consumer Price Index, as determined by the Secretary of Labor. Changes of less than 1 percent may be ignored. No fee established under this section shall take effect until at least 30 days after notice of the fee has been published in the Federal Register and in the Official Gazette of the Patent and Trademark Office.

(b) Waiver; Indian products

The Director may waive the payment of any fee for any service or material related to trademarks or other marks in connection with an occasional request made by a department or agency of the Government, or any officer thereof. The Indian Arts and Crafts Board will not be charged any fee to register Government trademarks of genuineness and quality for Indian products or for products of particular Indian tribes and groups.

§32 (15 U.S.C. §1114). Remedies; infringement; innocent infringement by printers and publishers

(1) Any person who shall, without the consent of the registrant—

(a) use in commerce any reproduction, counterfeit, copy, or colorable imitation of a registered mark in connection with the sale, offering for sale, distribution, or advertising of any goods or services on or in connection with which such use is likely to cause confusion, or to cause mistake, or to deceive; or

(b) reproduce, counterfeit, copy, or colorably imitate a registered mark and apply such reproduction, counterfeit, copy, or colorable imitation to labels, signs, prints, packages, wrappers, receptacles or advertisements intended to be used in commerce upon or in connection with the sale, offering for sale, distribution, or advertising of goods or services on or in connection with which such use is likely to cause confusion, or to cause mistake, or to deceive,

shall be liable in a civil action by the registrant for the remedies hereinafter provided. Under subsection (b) hereof, the registrant shall not be entitled to recover profits or damages unless the acts have been committed with knowledge that such imitation is intended to be used to cause confusion, or to cause mistake, or to deceive.

As used in this paragraph, the term "any person" includes the United States, all agencies and instrumentalities thereof, and all individuals, firms, corporations, or other persons acting for the United States and with the authorization and consent of the United States, and any State, any instrumentality of a State, and any officer or employee of a State or instrumentality of a State acting in his or her official capacity. The United States, all agencies and instrumentalities thereof, and all individuals, firms, corporations, other persons acting for the United States and with the authorization and consent of the United States, and any State, and any such instrumentality, officer, or employee, shall be subject to the provisions of this chapter in the same manner and to the same extent as any nongovernmental entity.

(2) Notwithstanding any other provision of this chapter, the remedies given to the owner of a right infringed under this chapter or to a person bringing an action under section 1125 [§43] (a) or (d) of this title shall be limited as follows:

(A) Where an infringer or violator is engaged solely in the business of printing the mark or violating matter for others and establishes that he or she was an innocent infringer or innocent violator, the owner of the right infringed or person bringing the action under section 1125(a) of this title shall be entitled as against such infringer or violator only to an injunction against future printing.

(B) Where the infringement or violation complained of is contained in or is part of paid advertising matter in a newspaper, magazine, or other similar periodical or in an electronic communication as defined in section 2510(12) of title 18, the remedies of the owner of the right infringed or person bringing the action under section 1125(a) of this title as against the publisher or distributor of such newspaper, magazine, or other similar periodical or electronic communication shall be limited to an injunction against the presentation of such advertising matter in future issues of such newspapers, magazines, or other similar periodicals or in future transmissions of such electronic communications. The limitations of this subparagraph shall apply only to innocent infringers and innocent violators.

(C) Injunctive relief shall not be available to the owner of the right infringed or person bringing the action under section 1125(a) of this title with respect to an issue of a newspaper, magazine, or other similar periodical or an electronic communication containing infringing matter or violating matter where restraining the dissemination of such infringing matter or violating matter in any particular issue of such periodical or in an electronic communication would delay the delivery of such issue or transmission of such electronic communication after the regular time for such delivery or transmission, and such delay would be due to the method by which publication and distribution of such periodical or transmission of such electronic communication is customarily conducted in accordance with sound business practice, and not due to any method or device adopted to evade this section or to prevent or delay the issuance of an injunction or restraining order with respect to such infringing matter or violating matter.

(D)(i)(I) A domain name registrar, a domain name registry, or other domain name registration authority that takes any action described under clause (ii) affecting a domain name shall not be liable for monetary relief or, except as provided in subclause (II), for injunctive relief, to any person for such action, regardless of whether the domain name is finally determined to infringe or dilute the mark.

(II) A domain name registrar, domain name registry, or other domain name registration authority described in subclause (I) may be subject to injunctive relief only if such registrar, registry, or other registration authority has—

(aa) not expeditiously deposited with a court, in which an action has been filed regarding the disposition of the domain name, documents sufficient for the court to establish the court's control and authority regarding the disposition of the registration and use of the domain name;

(bb) transferred, suspended, or otherwise modified the domain name during the pendency of the action, except upon order of the court; or

(cc) willfully failed to comply with any such court order.

(ii) An action referred to under clause (i)(I) is any action of refusing to register, removing from registration, transferring, temporarily disabling, or permanently canceling a domain name—

(I) in compliance with a court order under section 1125(d) of this title; or

(II) in the implementation of a reasonable policy by such registrar, registry, or authority prohibiting the registration of a domain name that is identical to, confusingly similar to, or dilutive of another's mark.

(iii) A domain name registrar, a domain name registry, or other domain name registration authority shall not be liable for damages under this section for the registration or maintenance of a domain name for another absent a showing of bad faith intent to profit from such registration or maintenance of the domain name.

(iv) If a registrar, registry, or other registration authority takes an action described under clause (ii) based on a knowing and material misrepresentation by any other person that a domain name is identical to, confusingly similar to, or dilutive of a mark, the person making the knowing and material misrepresentation shall be liable for any damages, including costs and attorney's fees, incurred by the domain name registrant as a result of such action. The court may also grant injunctive relief to the domain name registrant, including the reactivation of the domain name or the transfer of the domain name to the domain name registrant.

(v) A domain name registrant whose domain name has been suspended, disabled, or transferred under a policy described under clause (ii)(II) may, upon notice to the mark owner, file a civil action to establish that the registration or use of the domain name by such registrant is not unlawful under this chapter. The court may grant injunctive relief to the domain name registrant, including the reactivation of the domain name or transfer of the domain name to the domain name registrant.

(E) As used in this paragraph—

(i) the term "violator" means a person who violates section 1125(a) [§ 43(a)] of this title; and

(ii) the term "violating matter" means matter that is the subject of a violation under section 1125(a) of this title.

(3)(A) Any person who engages in the conduct described in paragraph (11) of section 110 of title 17 and who complies with the requirements set forth in that paragraph is not liable on account of such conduct for a violation of any right under this chapter. This subparagraph does not preclude liability, nor shall it be construed to restrict the defenses or limitations on rights granted under this chapter, of a person for conduct not described in paragraph (11) of section 110 of title 17, even if that person also engages in conduct described in paragraph (11) of section 110 of such title.

(B) A manufacturer, licensee, or licensor of technology that enables the making of limited portions of audio or video content of a motion picture imperceptible as described in subparagraph (A) is not liable on account of such manufacture or license for a violation of any right under this chapter, if such manufacturer, licensee, or licensor ensures that the technology provides a clear and conspicuous notice at the beginning of each performance that the performance of the motion picture is altered from the performance intended by the director or copyright holder of the motion picture. The limitations on liability in subparagraph (A) and this subparagraph shall not apply to a manufacturer, licensee, or licensor of technology that fails to comply with this paragraph.

(C) The requirement under subparagraph (B) to provide notice shall apply only with respect to technology manufactured after the end of the 180-day period beginning on April 27, 2005.

(D) Any failure by a manufacturer, licensee, or licensor of technology to qualify for the exemption under subparagraphs (A) and (B) shall not be construed to create an inference that any such party that engages in conduct described in paragraph (11) of section 110 of title 17 is liable for trademark infringement by reason of such conduct.

§ 33 (15 U.S.C. § 1115). Registration on principal register as evidence of exclusive right to use mark; defenses

(a) Evidentiary value; defenses

Any registration issued under the Act of March 3, 1881, or the Act of February 20, 1905, or of a mark registered on the principal register provided by this chapter and owned by a party to an action shall be admissible in evidence and shall be prima facie evidence of the validity of the registered mark and of the registration of the mark, of the registrant's ownership of the mark, and of the registrant's exclusive right to use the registered mark in commerce on or in connection with the goods or services specified in the registration subject to any conditions or limitations stated therein, but shall not preclude another person from proving any legal or equitable defense or defect, including those set forth in subsection (b) of this section, which might have been asserted if such mark had not been registered.

(b) Incontestability; defenses

To the extent that the right to use the registered mark has become incontestable under section 1065 of this title, the registration shall be conclusive evidence of the validity of the registered mark and of the registration of the mark, of the registrant's ownership of the mark, and of the registrant's exclusive right to use the registered mark in commerce. Such conclusive evidence shall relate to the exclusive right to use the mark on or in connection with the goods or services specified in the affidavit filed under the provisions of section 1065 [§ 15] of this title, or in the renewal application filed under the provisions of section 1059 [§ 9] of this title if the goods or services specified in the renewal are fewer in number, subject to any conditions or limitations in the registration or in such affidavit or renewal application. Such conclusive evidence of the right to use the registered mark shall be subject to proof of infringement as defined in section 1114 [§ 32] of this title, and shall be subject to the following defenses or defects:

(1) That the registration or the incontestable right to use the mark was obtained fraudulently; or

(2) That the mark has been abandoned by the registrant; or

(3) That the registered mark is being used by or with the permission of the registrant or a person in privity with the registrant, so as to misrepresent the source of the goods or services on or in connection with which the mark is used; or

(4) That the use of the name, term, or device charged to be an infringement is a use, otherwise than as a mark, of the party's individual name in his own business, or of the individual name of anyone in privity with such party, or of a term or device which is descriptive of and used fairly and in good faith only to describe the goods or services of such party, or their geographic origin; or

(5) That the mark whose use by a party is charged as an infringement was adopted without knowledge of the registrant's prior use and has been continuously used by such party or those in privity with him from a date prior to (A) the date of constructive use of the mark established pursuant to section 1057(c) [§7(c)] of this title, (B) the registration of the mark under this chapter if the application for registration is filed before the effective date of the Trademark Law Revision Act of 1988, or (C) publication of the registered mark under subsection (c) of section 1062 [§12] of this title: *Provided, however,* That this defense or defect shall apply only for the area in which such continuous prior use is proved; or

(6) That the mark whose use is charged as an infringement was registered and used prior to the registration under this chapter or publication under subsection (c) of section 1062 of this title of the registered mark of the registrant, and not abandoned: *Provided, however,* That this defense or defect shall apply only for the area in which the mark was used prior to such registration or such publication of the registrant's mark; or

(7) That the mark has been or is being used to violate the antitrust laws of the United States; or

(8) That the mark is functional; or

(9) That equitable principles, including laches, estoppel, and acquiescence, are applicable.

§34 (15 U.S.C. §1116). Injunctions; enforcement; notice of filing suit given Director

(**a**) The several courts vested with jurisdiction of civil actions arising under this chapter shall have power to grant injunctions, according to the principles of equity and upon such terms as the court may deem reasonable, to prevent the violation of any right of the registrant of a mark registered in the Patent and Trademark Office or to prevent a violation under subsection (a), (c), or (d) of section 1125 [§43] of this title. Any such injunction may include a provision directing the defendant to file with the court and serve on the plaintiff within thirty days after the service on the defendant of such injunction, or such extended period as the court may direct, a report in writing under oath setting forth in detail the manner and form in which the defendant has complied with the injunction. Any such injunction granted upon hearing, after notice to the defendant, by any district court of the United States, may be served on the parties against whom such injunction is granted anywhere in the United States where they may be found, and shall be operative and may be enforced by proceedings to punish for contempt, or otherwise, by the court by which such injunction was granted, or by any other United States district court in whose jurisdiction the defendant may be found.

(**b**) The said courts shall have jurisdiction to enforce said injunction, as herein provided, as fully as if the injunction had been granted by the district court in which it is sought to be enforced. The clerk of the court or judge granting the injunction shall, when required to do so by the court before which application to enforce said injunction is made, transfer without delay to said court a certified copy of all papers on file in his office upon which said injunction was granted.

(**c**) It shall be the duty of the clerks of such courts within one month after the filing of any action, suit, or proceeding involving a mark registered under the provisions of this chapter to give notice thereof in writing to the Director setting forth in order so far as known the names and addresses of the litigants and the designating number or numbers of the registration or registrations upon which the action, suit, or proceeding has been brought, and in the event any other registration be subsequently included in the action, suit, or proceeding by amendment, answer, or other pleading, the clerk shall give like notice thereof to the Director, and within one month after the judgment is entered or an appeal is taken the clerk of the court shall give notice thereof to the Director, and it shall be the duty of the Director on receipt of such notice forthwith to endorse the same upon the file wrapper of the said registration or registrations and to incorporate the same as a part of the contents of said file wrapper.

(**d**) (1)(A) In the case of a civil action arising under section 1114(1)(a) [§32(1)(a)] of this title or section 220506 of title 36 with respect to a violation that consists of using a counterfeit mark in connection with the sale, offering for sale, or distribution of goods or services, the court may, upon ex parte application, grant an order under subsection (a) of this section pursuant to this subsection providing for the seizure of goods and counterfeit marks involved in such violation and the means of making such marks, and records documenting the manufacture, sale, or receipt of things involved in such violation.

(B) As used in this subsection the term "counterfeit mark" means—

(i) a counterfeit of a mark that is registered on the principal register in the United States Patent and Trademark Office for such goods or services sold, offered for sale, or distributed and that is in use, whether or not the person against whom relief is sought knew such mark was so registered; or

(ii) a spurious designation that is identical with, or substantially indistinguishable from, a designation as to which the remedies of this chapter are made available by reason of section 220506 of title 36;

but such term does not include any mark or designation used on or in connection with goods or services of which the manufacture or producer was, at the time of the manufacture or production in question authorized to use the mark or designation for the type of goods or services so manufactured or produced, by the holder of the right to use such mark or designation.

(2) The court shall not receive an application under this subsection unless the applicant has given such notice of the application as is reasonable under the circumstances to the United States attorney for the judicial district in which such order

is sought. Such attorney may participate in the proceedings arising under such application if such proceedings may affect evidence of an offense against the United States. The court may deny such application if the court determines that the public interest in a potential prosecution so requires.

(3) The application for an order under this subsection shall—

(A) be based on an affidavit or the verified complaint establishing facts sufficient to support the findings of fact and conclusions of law required for such order; and

(B) contain the additional information required by paragraph (5) of this subsection to be set forth in such order.

(4) The court shall not grant such an application unless—

(A) the person obtaining an order under this subsection provides the security determined adequate by the court for the payment of such damages as any person may be entitled to recover as a result of a wrongful seizure or wrongful attempted seizure under this subsection; and

(B) the court finds that it clearly appears from specific facts that—

(i) an order other than an ex parte seizure order is not adequate to achieve the purposes of section 1114 [§32] of this title;

(ii) the applicant has not publicized the requested seizure;

(iii) the applicant is likely to succeed in showing that the person against whom seizure would be ordered used a counterfeit mark in connection with the sale, offering for sale, or distribution of goods or services;

(iv) an immediate and irreparable injury will occur if such seizure is not ordered;

(v) the matter to be seized will be located at the place identified in the application;

(vi) the harm to the applicant of denying the application outweighs the harm to the legitimate interests of the person against whom seizure would be ordered of granting the application; and

(vii) the person against whom seizure would be ordered, or persons acting in concert with such person, would destroy, move, hide, or otherwise make such matter inaccessible to the court, if the applicant were to proceed on notice to such person.

(5) An order under this subsection shall set forth—

(A) the findings of fact and conclusions of law required for the order;

(B) a particular description of the matter to be seized, and a description of each place at which such matter is to be seized;

(C) the time period, which shall end not later than seven days after the date on which such order is issued, during which the seizure is to be made;

(D) the amount of security required to be provided under this subsection; and

(E) a date for the hearing required under paragraph (10) of this subsection.

(6) The court shall take appropriate action to protect the person against whom an order under this subsection is directed from publicity, by or at the behest of the plaintiff, about such order and any seizure under such order.

(7) Any materials seized under this subsection shall be taken into the custody of the court. The court shall enter an appropriate protective order with respect to discovery by the applicant of any records that have been seized. The protective order shall provide for appropriate procedures to assure that confidential information contained in such records is not improperly disclosed to the applicant.

(8) An order under this subsection, together with the supporting documents, shall be sealed until the person against whom the order is directed has an opportunity to contest such order, except that any person against whom such order is issued shall have access to such order and supporting documents after the seizure has been carried out.

(9) The court shall order that service of a copy of the order under this subsection shall be made by a Federal law enforcement officer (such as a United States marshal or an officer or agent of the United States Customs Service, Secret Service, Federal Bureau of Investigation, or Post Office) or may be made by a State or local law enforcement officer, who, upon making service, shall carry out the seizure under the order. The court shall issue orders, when appropriate, to protect the defendant from undue damage from the disclosure of trade secrets or other confidential information during the course of the seizure, including, when appropriate, orders restricting the access of the applicant (or any agent or employee of the applicant) to such secrets or information.

(10)(A) The court shall hold a hearing, unless waived by all the parties, on the date set by the court in the order of seizure. That date shall be not sooner than ten days after the order is issued and not later than fifteen days after the order is issued, unless the applicant for the order shows good cause for another date or unless the party against whom such order is directed consents to another date for such hearing. At such hearing the party obtaining the order shall have the burden to prove that the facts supporting findings of fact and conclusions of law necessary to support such order are still in effect. If that party fails to meet that burden, the seizure order shall be dissolved or modified appropriately.

(B) In connection with a hearing under this paragraph, the court may make such orders modifying the time limits for discovery under the Rules of Civil Procedure as may be necessary to prevent the frustration of the purposes of such hearing.

(11) A person who suffers damage by reason of a wrongful seizure under this subsection has a cause of action against the applicant for the order under which such seizure was made, and shall be entitled to recover such relief as may be appropriate, including damages for lost profits, cost of materials, loss of good will,

and punitive damages in instances where the seizure was sought in bad faith, and, unless the court finds extenuating circumstances, to recover a reasonable attorney's fee. The court in its discretion may award prejudgment interest on relief recovered under this paragraph, at an annual interest rate established under section 6621(a)(2) of the Internal Revenue Code of 1986, commencing on the date of service of the claimant's pleading setting forth the claim under this paragraph and ending on the date such recovery is granted, or for such shorter time as the court deems appropriate.

§ 35 (15 U.S.C. § 1117). Recovery of profits, damages, and costs

(a) When a violation of any right of the registrant of a mark registered in the Patent and Trademark Office, a violation under section 1125 (a) or (d) [§ 43(a) or (d)]of this title, or a willful violation under section 1125(c) [§ 43(c)] of this title, shall have been established in any civil action arising under this chapter, the plaintiff shall be entitled, subject to the provisions of sections 1111 [§ 29] and 1114 [§ 32] of this title, and subject to the principles of equity, to recover (1) defendant's profits, (2) any damages sustained by the plaintiff, and (3) the costs of the action. The court shall assess such profits and damages or cause the same to be assessed under its direction. In assessing profits the plaintiff shall be required to prove defendant's sale[s] only; defendant must prove all elements of cost or deduction claimed. In assessing damages the court may enter judgment, according to the circumstances of the case, for any sum above the amount found as actual damages, not exceeding three times such amount. If the court shall find that the amount of the recovery based on profits is either inadequate or excessive the court may in its discretion enter judgment for such sum as the court shall find to be just, according to the circumstances of the case. Such sum in either of the above circumstances shall constitute compensation and not a penalty. The court in exceptional cases may award reasonable attorney fees to the prevailing party.

(b) In assessing damages under subsection (a) for any violation of section 32(1)(a) [§ 1114(a)] of this Act or section 220506 of title 36, United States Code, in a case involving use of a counterfeit mark or designation (as defined in section 34(d) [§ 1116(d)] of this Act), the court shall, unless the court finds extenuating circumstances, enter judgment for three times such profits or damages, whichever amount is greater, together with a reasonable attorney's fee, if the violation consists of—

(1) intentionally using a mark or designation, knowing such mark or designation is a counterfeit mark (as defined in section 34(d) [§ 1116(d)] of this Act), in connection with the sale, offering for sale, or distribution of goods or services; or

(2) providing goods or services necessary to the commission of a violation specified in paragraph (1), with the intent that the recipient of the goods or services would put the goods or services to use in committing the violation.

In such a case, the court may award prejudgment interest on such amount at an annual interest rate established under section 6621(a)(2) of the Internal Revenue Code of 1986, beginning on the date of the service of the claimant's pleadings setting forth the claim for such entry of judgment and ending on the date such entry is made, or for such shorter time as the court considers appropriate.

(c) In a case involving the use of a counterfeit mark (as defined in section 1116(d) [§ 34] of this title) in connection with the sale, offering for sale, or distribution of goods or services, the plaintiff may elect, at any time before final judgment is rendered by the trial court, to recover, instead of actual damages and profits under subsection (a) of this section, an award of statutory damages for any such use in connection with the sale, offering for sale, or distribution of goods or services in the amount of—

(1) not less than $1000 or more than $200,000 per counterfeit mark per type of goods or services sold, offered for sale, or distributed, as the court considers just; or

(2) if the court finds that the use of the counterfeit mark was willful, not more than $2,000,000 per counterfeit mark per type of goods or services sold, offered for sale, or distributed, as the court considers just.

(d) In a case involving a violation of section 1125(d)(1) [§ 43(d)(1)] of this title, the plaintiff may elect, at any time before final judgment is rendered by the trial court, to recover, instead of actual damages and profits, an award of statutory damages in the amount of not less than $1,000 and not more than $100,000 per domain name, as the court considers just.

(e) In the case of a violation referred to in this section, it shall be a rebuttable presumption that the violation is willful for purposes of determining relief if the violator, or a person acting in concert with the violator, knowingly provided or knowingly caused to be provided materially false contact information to a domain name registrar, domain name registry, or other domain name registration authority in registering, maintaining, or renewing a domain name used in connection with the violation. Nothing in this subsection limits what may be considered a willful violation under this section.

§ 36 (15 U.S.C. § 1118). Destruction of infringing articles

In any action arising under this chapter, in which a violation of any right of the registrant of a mark registered in the Patent and Trademark Office, a violation under section 1125(a) [§ 43(a)] of this title, or a willful violation under section 1125(c) [§ 43(c)] of this title, shall have been established, the court may order that all labels, signs, prints, packages, wrappers, receptacles, and advertisements in the possession of the defendant, bearing the registered mark or, in the case of a violation of section 1125(a) [§ 43(a)] of this title or a willful violation under section 1125(c) [§ 43(c)] of this title, the word, term, name, symbol, device, combination thereof, designation, description, or representation that is the subject of the violation, or any reproduction, counterfeit, copy, or colorable imitation thereof, and all plates, molds, matrices, and other means of making the same, shall be delivered up and destroyed. The party seeking an order under this section for destruction of articles seized under section 1116(d) [§ 34(d)] of this title shall give ten days' notice to the United States attorney for the judicial district in which such order is sought (unless good cause is shown for lesser notice) and such United States attorney may, if such destruction may affect evidence of an offense against the United States, seek a hearing on such destruction or participate in any hearing otherwise to be held with respect to such destruction.

§ 37 (15 U.S.C. § 1119). Power of court over registration

In any action involving a registered mark the court may determine the right to registration, order the cancelation of registrations, in whole or in part, restore canceled registrations, and otherwise rectify the register with respect to the registrations of any party to the action. Decrees and orders shall be certified by the court to the Director, who shall make appropriate entry upon the records of the Patent and Trademark Office, and shall be controlled thereby.

§ 38 (15 U.S.C. § 1120). Civil liability for false or fraudulent registration

Any person who shall procure registration in the Patent and Trademark Office of a mark by a false or fraudulent declaration or representation, oral or in writing, or by any false means, shall be liable in a civil action by any person injured thereby for any damages sustained in consequence thereof.

§ 39 (15 U.S.C. § 1121). Jurisdiction of Federal courts; State and local requirements that registered trademarks be altered or displayed differently; prohibition

(a) The district and territorial courts of the United States shall have original jurisdiction and the courts of appeal of the United States (other than the United States Court of Appeals for the Federal Circuit) shall have appellate jurisdiction, of all actions arising under this chapter, without regard to the amount in controversy or to diversity or lack of diversity of the citizenship of the parties.

(b) No State or other jurisdiction of the United States or any political subdivision or any agency thereof may require alteration of a registered mark, or require that additional trademarks, service marks, trade names, or corporate names that may be associated with or incorporated into the registered mark be displayed in the mark in a manner differing from the display of such additional trademarks, service marks, trade names, or corporate names contemplated by the registered mark as exhibited in the certificate of registration issued by the United States Patent and Trademark Office.

§ 40 (15 U.S.C. § 1122). Liability of United States and States, and instrumentalities and officials thereof

(a) Waiver of sovereign immunity by the United States

The United States, all agencies and instrumentalities thereof, and all individuals, firms, corporations, other persons acting for the United States and with the authorization and consent of the United States, shall not be immune from suit in Federal or State court by any person, including any governmental or nongovernmental entity, for any violation under this chapter.

(b) Waiver of sovereign immunity by States

Any State, instrumentality of a State or any officer or employee of a State or instrumentality of a State acting in his or her official capacity, shall not be immune, under the eleventh amendment of the Constitution of the United States or under any other doctrine of sovereign immunity, from suit in Federal court by any person, including any governmental or nongovernmental entity for any violation under this chapter.

(c) Remedies

In a suit described in subsection (a) or (b) of this section for a violation described therein, remedies (including remedies both at law and in equity) are available for the violation to the same extent as such remedies are available for such a violation in a suit against any person other than the United States or any agency or instrumentality thereof, or any individual, firm, corporation, or other person acting for the United States and with authorization and consent of the United States, or a State, instrumentality of a State, or officer or employee of a State or instrumentality of a State acting in his or her official capacity. Such remedies include injunctive relief under section 1116 [§ 34] of this title, actual damages, profits, costs and attorney's fees under section 1117 [§ 35] of this title, destruction of infringing articles under section 1118 [§ 36] of this title, the remedies provided for under sections 1114 [§ 32], 1119 [§ 37], 1120 [§ 38], 1124 [§ 42] and 1125 [§ 43] of this title, and for any other remedies provided under this chapter.

§ 41 (15 U.S.C. § 1123). Rules and regulations for conduct of proceedings in Patent and Trademark Office

The Director shall make rules and regulations, not inconsistent with law, for the conduct of proceedings in the Patent and Trademark Office under this chapter.

§ 42 (15 U.S.C. § 1124). Importation of goods bearing infringing marks or names forbidden

Except as provided in subsection (d) of section 1526 of title 19, no article of imported merchandise which shall copy or simulate the name of any domestic manufacture, or manufacturer, or trader, or of any manufacturer or trader located in any foreign country which, by treaty, convention, or law affords similar privileges to citizens of the United States, or which shall copy or simulate a trademark registered in accordance with the provisions of this chapter or shall bear a name or mark calculated to induce the public to believe that the article is manufactured in the United States, or that it is manufactured in any foreign country or locality other than the country or locality in which it is in fact manufactured, shall be admitted to entry at any customhouse of the United States; and, in order to aid the officers of the customs in enforcing this prohibition, any domestic manufacturer or trader, and any foreign manufacturer or trader, who is entitled under the provisions of a treaty, convention, declaration, or agreement between the United States and any foreign country to the advantages afforded by law to citizens of the United States in respect to trademarks and commercial names, may require his name and residence, and the name of the locality in which his goods are manufactured, and a copy of the certificate of registration of his trademark, issued in accordance with the provisions of this chapter, to be recorded in books which shall be kept for this purpose in the Department of the Treasury, under such regulations as the Secretary of the Treasury shall prescribe, and may furnish to the Department facsimiles of his name, the name of the locality in which his goods are manufactured, or of his registered trademark, and thereupon the Secretary of the Treasury shall cause one or more copies of the same to be transmitted to each collector or other proper officer of customs.

§ 43 (15 U.S.C. § 1125). False designations of origin, false descriptions, and dilution forbidden

(a) Civil action

(1) Any person who, on or in connection with any goods or services, or any container for goods, uses in commerce any word, term, name, symbol, or device, or any combination thereof, or any false designation of origin, false or misleading description of fact, or false or misleading representation of fact, which—

(A) is likely to cause confusion, or to cause mistake, or to deceive as to the affiliation, connection, or association of such person with another person, or as to the origin, sponsorship, or approval of his or her goods, services, or commercial activities by another person, or

(B) in commercial advertising or promotion, misrepresents the nature, characteristics, qualities, or geographic origin of his or her or another person's goods, services, or commercial activities,

shall be liable in a civil action by any person who believes that he or she is or is likely to be damaged by such act.

(2) As used in this subsection, the term "any person" includes any State, instrumentality of a State or employee of a State or instrumentality of a State acting in his or her official capacity. Any State, and any such instrumentality, officer, or employee, shall be subject to the provisions of this chapter in the same manner and to the same extent as any nongovernmental entity.

(3) In a civil action for trade dress infringement under this chapter for trade dress not registered on the principal register, the person who asserts trade dress protection has the burden of proving that the matter sought to be protected is not functional.

(b) Importation

Any goods marked or labeled in contravention of the provisions of this section shall not be imported into the United States or admitted to entry at any customhouse of the United States. The owner, importer, or consignee of goods refused entry at any customhouse under this section may have any recourse by protest or appeal that is given under the customs revenue laws or may have the remedy given by this chapter in cases involving goods refused entry or seized.

(c) Dilution by blurring; dilution by tarnishment

(1) Injunctive relief

Subject to the principles of equity, the owner of a famous mark that is distinctive, inherently or through acquired distinctiveness, shall be entitled to an injunction against another person who, at any time after the owner's mark has become famous, commences use of a mark or trade name in commerce that is likely to cause dilution by blurring or dilution by tarnishment of the famous mark, regardless of the presence or absence of actual or likely confusion, of competition, or of actual economic injury.

(2) Definitions

(A) For purposes of paragraph (1), a mark is famous if it is widely recognized by the general consuming public of the United States as a designation of source of the goods or services of the mark's owner. In determining whether a mark possesses the requisite degree of recognition, the court may consider all relevant factors, including the following:

(i) The duration, extent, and geographic reach of advertising and publicity of the mark, whether advertised or publicized by the owner or third parties.

(ii) The amount, volume, and geographic extent of sales of goods or services offered under the mark.

(iii) The extent of actual recognition of the mark.

(iv) Whether the mark was registered under the Act of March 3, 1881, or the Act of February 20, 1905, or on the principal register.

(B) For purposes of paragraph (1), "dilution by blurring" is association arising from the similarity between a mark or trade name and a famous mark that impairs the distinctiveness of the famous mark. In determining whether a mark or trade name is likely to cause dilution by blurring, the court may consider all relevant factors, including the following:

(i) The degree of similarity between the mark or trade name and the famous mark.

(ii) The degree of inherent or acquired distinctiveness of the famous mark.

(iii) The extent to which the owner of the famous mark is engaging in substantially exclusive use of the mark.

(iv) The degree of recognition of the famous mark.

(v) Whether the user of the mark or trade name intended to create an association with the famous mark.

(vi) Any actual association between the mark or trade name and the famous mark.

(C) For purposes of paragraph (1), "dilution by tarnishment" is association arising from the similarity between a mark or trade name and a famous mark that harms the reputation of the famous mark.

(3) Exclusions

The following shall not be actionable as dilution by blurring or dilution by tarnishment under this subsection:

(A) Any fair use, including a nominative or descriptive fair use, or facilitation of such fair use, of a famous mark by another person other than as a designation of source for the person's own goods or services, including use in connection with—

(i) advertising or promotion that permits consumers to compare goods or services; or

(ii) identifying and parodying, criticizing, or commenting upon the famous mark owner or the goods or services of the famous mark owner.

(B) All forms of news reporting and news commentary.

(C) Any noncommercial use of a mark.

(4) Burden of proof

In a civil action for trade dress dilution under this chapter for trade dress not registered on the principal register, the person who asserts trade dress protection has the burden of proving that—

(A) the claimed trade dress, taken as a whole, is not functional and is famous; and

(B) if the claimed trade dress includes any mark or marks registered on the principal register, the unregistered matter, taken as a whole, is famous separate and apart from any fame of such registered marks.

(5) Additional remedies

In an action brought under this subsection, the owner of the famous mark shall be entitled to injunctive relief as set forth in section 1116 [§ 34] of this title. The owner of the famous mark shall also be entitled to the remedies set forth in sections 1117(a) [§ 35(a)] and 1118 [§ 36] of this title, subject to the discretion of the court and the principles of equity if—

(A) the mark or trade name that is likely to cause dilution by blurring or dilution by tarnishment was first used in commerce by the person against whom the injunction is sought after October 6, 2006; and

(B) in a claim arising under this subsection—

(i) by reason of dilution by blurring, the person against whom the injunction is sought willfully intended to trade on the recognition of the famous mark; or

(ii) by reason of dilution by tarnishment, the person against whom the injunction is sought willfully intended to harm the reputation of the famous mark.

(6) Ownership of valid registration a complete bar to action

The ownership by a person of a valid registration under the Act of March 3, 1881, or the Act of February 20, 1905, or on the principal register under this chapter shall be a complete bar to an action against that person, with respect to that mark, that—

(A) is brought by another person under the common law or a statute of a State; and

(B) (i) seeks to prevent dilution by blurring or dilution by tarnishment; or

(ii) asserts any claim of actual or likely damage or harm to the distinctiveness or reputation of a mark, label, or form of advertisement.

(7) Savings clause

Nothing in this subsection shall be construed to impair, modify, or supersede the applicability of the patent laws of the United States.

(d) Cyberpiracy prevention

(1)(A) A person shall be liable in a civil action by the owner of a mark, including a personal name which is protected as a mark under this section, if, without regard to the goods or services of the parties, that person—

(i) has a bad faith intent to profit from that mark, including a personal name which is protected as a mark under this section; and

(ii) registers, traffics in, or uses a domain name that—

(I) in the case of a mark that is distinctive at the time of registration of the domain name, is identical or confusingly similar to that mark;

(II) in the case of a famous mark that is famous at the time of registration of the domain name, is identical or confusingly similar to or dilutive of that mark; or

(III) is a trademark, word, or name protected by reason of section 706 of title 18 or section 220506 of title 36.

(B)(i) In determining whether a person has a bad faith intent described under subparagraph (A), a court may consider factors such as, but not limited to—

(I) the trademark or other intellectual property rights of the person, if any, in the domain name;

(II) the extent to which the domain name consists of the legal name of the person or a name that is otherwise commonly used to identify that person;

(III) the person's prior use, if any, of the domain name in connection with the bona fide offering of any goods or services;

(IV) the person's bona fide noncommercial or fair use of the mark in a site accessible under the domain name;

(V) the person's intent to divert consumers from the mark owner's online location to a site accessible under the domain name that could harm the goodwill represented by the mark, either for commercial gain or with the intent to tarnish or disparage the mark, by creating a likelihood of confusion as to the source, sponsorship, affiliation, or endorsement of the site;

(VI) the person's offer to transfer, sell, or otherwise assign the domain name to the mark owner or any third party for financial gain without having used, or having an intent to use, the domain name in the bona fide offering of any goods or services, or the person's prior conduct indicating a pattern of such conduct;

(VII) the person's provision of material and misleading false contact information when applying for the registration of the domain name, the person's intentional failure to maintain accurate contact information, or the person's prior conduct indicating a pattern of such conduct;

(VIII) the person's registration or acquisition of multiple domain names which the person knows are identical or confusingly similar to marks of others that are distinctive at the time of registration of such domain names, or dilutive of famous marks of others that are famous at the time of registration of such domain names, without regard to the goods or services of the parties; and

(IX) the extent to which the mark incorporated in the person's domain name registration is or is not distinctive and famous within the meaning of subsection (c).

(ii) Bad faith intent described under subparagraph (A) shall not be found in any case in which the court determines that the person believed and had reasonable grounds to believe that the use of the domain name was a fair use or otherwise lawful.

(C) In any civil action involving the registration, trafficking, or use of a domain name under this paragraph, a court may order the forfeiture or cancellation of the domain name or the transfer of the domain name to the owner of the mark.

(D) A person shall be liable for using a domain name under subparagraph (A) only if that person is the domain name registrant or that registrant's authorized licensee.

(E) As used in this paragraph, the term "traffics in" refers to transactions that include, but are not limited to, sales, purchases, loans, pledges, licenses, exchanges of currency, and any other transfer for consideration or receipt in exchange for consideration.

(2)(A) The owner of a mark may file an in rem civil action against a domain name in the judicial district in which the domain name registrar, domain name registry, or other domain name authority that registered or assigned the domain name is located if—

(i) the domain name violates any right of the owner of a mark registered in the Patent and Trademark Office, or protected under subsection (a) or (c) of this section; and

(ii) the court finds that the owner—

(I) is not able to obtain in personam jurisdiction over a person who would have been a defendant in a civil action under paragraph (1); or

(II) through due diligence was not able to find a person who would have been a defendant in a civil action under paragraph (1) by—

(aa) sending a notice of the alleged violation and intent to proceed under this paragraph to the registrant of the domain name at the postal and e-mail address provided by the registrant to the registrar; and

(bb) publishing notice of the action as the court may direct promptly after filing the action.

(B) The actions under subparagraph (A)(ii) shall constitute service of process.

(C) In an in rem action under this paragraph, a domain name shall be deemed to have its situs in the judicial district in which—

(i) the domain name registrar, registry, or other domain name authority that registered or assigned the domain name is located; or

(ii) documents sufficient to establish control and authority regarding the disposition of the registration and use of the domain name are deposited with the court.

(D)(i) The remedies in an in rem action under this paragraph shall be limited to a court order for the forfeiture or cancellation of the domain name or the transfer of the domain name to the owner of the mark. Upon receipt of written notification of a filed, stamped copy of a complaint filed by the owner of a mark in a United States district court under this paragraph, the domain name registrar, domain name registry, or other domain name authority shall—

(I) expeditiously deposit with the court documents sufficient to establish the court's control and authority regarding the disposition of the registration and use of the domain name to the court; and

(II) not transfer, suspend, or otherwise modify the domain name during the pendency of the action, except upon order of the court.

(ii) The domain name registrar or registry or other domain name authority shall not be liable for injunctive or monetary relief under this paragraph except in the case of bad faith or reckless disregard, which includes a willful failure to comply with any such court order.

(3) The civil action established under paragraph (1) and the in rem action established under paragraph (2), and any remedy available under either such action, shall be in addition to any other civil action or remedy otherwise applicable.

(4) The in rem jurisdiction established under paragraph (2) shall be in addition to any other jurisdiction that otherwise exists, whether in rem or in personam.

§44 (15 U.S.C. §1126). International conventions

(a) Register of marks communicated by international bureaus

The Director shall keep a register of all marks communicated to him by the international bureaus provided for by the conventions for the protection of industrial property, trademarks, trade and commercial names, and the repression of unfair competition to which the United States is or may become a party, and upon the payment of the fees required by such conventions and the fees required in this chapter may place the marks so communicated upon such register. This register shall show a facsimile of the mark or trade or commercial name; the name, citizenship, and address of the registrant; the number, date, and place of the first registration of the mark, including the dates on which application for such registration was filed and granted and the term of such registration; a list of goods or services to which the mark is applied as shown by the registration in the country of origin, and such other data as may be useful concerning the mark. This register shall be a continuation of the register provided in section 1(a) of the Act of March 19, 1920.

(b) Benefits of section to persons whose country of origin is party to convention or treaty

Any person whose country of origin is a party to any convention or treaty relating to trademarks, trade or commercial names, or the repression of unfair competition, to which the United States is also a party, or extends reciprocal rights to nationals of the United States by law, shall be entitled to the benefits of this section under the conditions expressed herein to the extent necessary to give effect to any provision of such convention, treaty or reciprocal law, in addition to the rights to which any owner of a mark is otherwise entitled by this chapter.

(c) Prior registration in country of origin; country of origin defined

No registration of a mark in the United States by a person described in subsection (b) of this section shall be granted until such mark has been registered in the country of origin of the applicant, unless the applicant alleges use in commerce. For the purposes of this section, the country of origin of the applicant is the country in which he has a bona fide and effective industrial or commercial establishment, or if he has not such an establishment the country in which he is domiciled, or if he has not a domicile in any of the countries described in subsection (b) of this section, the country of which he is a national.

(d) Right of priority

An application for registration of a mark under section 1051 [§ 1], 1053 [§ 3], 1054 [§ 4], or 1091 [§ 23] of this title or under subsection (e) of this section, filed by a person described in subsection (b) of this section who has previously duly filed an application for registration of the same mark in one of the countries described in subsection (b) of this section shall be accorded the same force and effect as would be accorded to the same application if filed in the United States on the same date on which the application was first filed in such foreign country: *Provided*, That—

(1) the application in the United States is filed within six months from the date on which the application was first filed in the foreign country;

(2) the application conforms as nearly as practicable to the requirements of this chapter, including a statement that the applicant has a bona fide intention to use the mark in commerce;

(3) the rights acquired by third parties before the date of the filing of the first application in the foreign country shall in no way be affected by a registration obtained on an application filed under this subsection;

(4) nothing in this subsection shall entitle the owner of a registration granted under this section to sue for acts committed prior to the date on which his mark was registered in this country unless the registration is based on use in commerce.

In like manner and subject to the same conditions and requirements, the right provided in this section may be based upon a subsequent regularly filed application in the same foreign country, instead of the first filed foreign application: *Provided*, That any foreign application filed prior to such subsequent application has been withdrawn, abandoned, or otherwise disposed of, without having been laid open to public inspection and without leaving any rights outstanding, and has not served, nor thereafter shall serve, as a basis for claiming a right of priority.

(e) Registration on principal or supplemental register; copy of foreign registration

A mark duly registered in the country of origin of the foreign applicant may be registered on the principal register if eligible, otherwise on the supplemental register in this chapter provided. Such applicant shall submit, within such time period as may be prescribed by the Director, a true copy, a photocopy, a certification, or a certified copy of the registration in the country of origin of the applicant. The application must state the applicant's bona fide intention to use the mark in commerce, but use in commerce shall not be required prior to registration.

(f) Domestic registration independent of foreign registration

The registration of a mark under the provisions of subsections (c), (d), and (e) of this section by a person described in subsection (b) of this section shall be independent of the registration in the country of origin and the duration, validity, or transfer in the United States of such registration shall be governed by the provisions of this chapter.

(g) Trade or commercial names of foreign nationals protected without registration

Trade names or commercial names of persons described in subsection (b) of this section shall be protected without the obligation of filing or registration whether or not they form parts of marks.

(h) Protection of foreign nationals against unfair competition

Any person designated in subsection (b) of this section as entitled to the benefits and subject to the provisions of this chapter shall be entitled to effective protection against unfair competition, and the remedies provided in this chapter for infringement of marks shall be available so far as they may be appropriate in repressing acts of unfair competition.

(i) Citizens or residents of United States entitled to benefits of section

Citizens or residents of the United States shall have the same benefits as are granted by this section to persons described in subsection (b) of this section.

§45 (15 U.S.C. §1127). Construction and definitions; intent of chapter

In the construction of this chapter, unless the contrary is plainly apparent from the context—

United States. The United States includes and embraces all territory which is under its jurisdiction and control.

Commerce. The word "commerce" means all commerce which may lawfully be regulated by Congress.

Principal Register. The term "principal register" refers to the register provided for by sections 1051 [§ 1] to 1072 [§ 22] of this title, and the term "supplemental register" refers to the register provided for by sections 1091 [§ 23] to 1096 [§ 28] of this title.

Person. The term "person" and any other word or term used to designate the applicant or other entitled to a benefit or privilege or rendered liable under the provisions of this chapter includes a juristic person as well as a natural person. The term "juristic person" includes a firm, corporation, union, association, or other organization capable of suing and being sued in a court of law.

The term "person" also includes the United States, any agency or instrumentality thereof, or any individual, firm, or corporation acting for the United States and with the authorization and consent of the United States. The United States, any agency or instrumentality thereof, and any individual, firm, or corporation acting for the United States and with the authorization and consent of the United States, shall be subject to the provisions of this chapter in the same manner and to the same extent as any nongovernmental entity.

The term "person" also includes any State, any instrumentality of a State, and any officer or employee of a State or instrumentality of a State acting in his or her official capacity. Any State, and any such instrumentality, officer, or employee, shall be subject to the provisions of this chapter in the same manner and to the same extent as any nongovernmental entity.

Applicant, registrant. The terms "applicant" and "registrant" embrace the legal representatives, predecessors, successors and assigns of such applicant or registrant.

Director. The term "Director" means the Under Secretary of Commerce for Intellectual Property and Director of the United States Patent and Trademark Office.

Related Company. The term "related company" means any person whose use of a mark is controlled by the owner of the mark with respect to the nature and quality of the goods or services on or in connection with which the mark is used.

Trade name, commercial name. The terms "trade name" and "commercial name" mean any name used by a person to identify his or her business or vocation.

Trademark. The term "trademark" includes any word, name, symbol, or device, or any combination thereof—

(1) used by a person, or

(2) which a person has a bona fide intention to use in commerce and applies to register on the principal register established by this chapter,

to identify and distinguish his or her goods, including a unique product, from those manufactured or sold by others and to indicate the source of the goods, even if that source is unknown.

Service mark. The term "service mark" means any word, name, symbol, or device, or any combination thereof—

(1) used by a person, or

(2) which a person has a bona fide intention to use in commerce and applies to register on the principal register established by this chapter,

to identify and distinguish the services of one person, including a unique service, from the services of others and to indicate the source of the services, even if that source is unknown. Titles, character names, and other distinctive features of radio or television programs may be registered as service marks notwithstanding that they, or the programs, may advertise the goods of the sponsor.

Certification mark. The term "certification mark" means any word, name, symbol, or device, or any combination thereof—

(1) used by a person other than its owner, or

(2) which its owner has a bona fide intention to permit a person other than the owner to use in commerce and files an application to register on the principal register established by this chapter, to certify regional or other origin, material, mode of manufacture, quality, accuracy, or other characteristics of such person's goods or services or that the work or labor on the goods or services was performed by members of a union or other organization.

Collective mark. The term "collective mark" means a trademark or service mark—

(1) used by the members of a cooperative, an association, or other collective group or organization, or

(2) which such cooperative, association, or other collective group or organization has a bona fide intention to use in commerce and applies to register on the principal register established by this chapter, and includes marks indicating membership in a union, an association, or other organization.

Mark. The term "mark" includes any trademark, service mark, collective mark, or certification mark.

Use in commerce. The term "use in commerce" means the bona fide use of a mark in the ordinary course of trade, and not made merely to reserve a right in a mark. For purposes of this chapter, a mark shall be deemed to be in use in commerce—

(1) on goods when—

(A) it is placed in any manner on the goods or their containers or the displays associated therewith or on the tags or labels affixed thereto, or if the nature of the goods makes such placement impracticable, then on documents associated with the goods or their sale, and

(B) the goods are sold or transported in commerce, and

(2) on services when it is used or displayed in the sale or advertising of services and the services are rendered in commerce, or the services are rendered in more than one State or in the United States and a foreign country and the person rendering the services is engaged in commerce in connection with the services.

Abandonment. A mark shall be deemed to be "abandoned" if either of the following occurs:

(1) When its use has been discontinued with intent not to resume such use. Intent not to resume may be inferred from circumstances. Nonuse for 3 consecutive years shall be prima facie evidence of abandonment. "Use" of a mark means the bona fide use of such mark made in the ordinary course of trade, and not made merely to reserve a right in a mark.

(2) When any course of conduct of the owner, including acts of omission as well as commission, causes the mark to become the generic name for the goods or services on or in connection with which it is used or otherwise to lose its significance as a mark. Purchaser motivation shall not be a test for determining abandonment under this paragraph.

Colorable imitation. The term "colorable imitation" includes any mark which so resembles a registered mark as to be likely to cause confusion or mistake or to deceive.

Registered mark. The term "registered mark" means a mark registered in the United States Patent and Trademark Office under this chapter or under the Act of March 3, 1881, or the Act of February 20, 1905, or the Act of March 19, 1920. The phrase "marks registered in the Patent and Trademark Office" means registered marks.

Prior Acts. The term "Act of March 3, 1881", "Act of February 20, 1905", or "Act of March 19, 1920", means the respective Act as amended.

Counterfeit. A "counterfeit" is a spurious mark which is identical with, or substantially indistinguishable from, a registered mark.

Domain name. The term "domain name" means any alphanumeric designation which is registered with or assigned by any domain name registrar, domain name registry, or other domain name registration authority as part of an electronic address on the Internet.

Internet. The term "Internet" has the meaning given that term in section 230(f)(1) of title 47.

Singular and plural. Words used in the singular include the plural and vice versa.

Intent of Act. The intent of this chapter is to regulate commerce within the control of Congress by making actionable the deceptive and misleading use of marks in such commerce; to protect registered marks used in such commerce from interference by State, or territorial legislation; to protect persons engaged in such commerce against unfair competition; to prevent fraud and deception in such commerce by the use of reproductions, copies, counterfeits, or colorable imitations of registered marks; and to provide rights and remedies stipulated by treaties and conventions respecting trademarks, trade names, and unfair competition entered into between the United States and foreign nations.

15 U.S.C. § 8131. Cyberpiracy protections for individuals*

(1) In general

(A) Civil liability

Any person who registers a domain name that consists of the name of another living person, or a name substantially and confusingly similar thereto, without that person's consent, with the specific intent to profit from such name by selling the domain name for financial gain to that person or any third party, shall be liable in a civil action by such person.

(B) Exception

A person who in good faith registers a domain name consisting of the name of another living person, or a name substantially and confusingly similar thereto, shall not be liable under this paragraph if such name is used in, affiliated with, or related to a work of authorship protected under title 17, including a work made for hire as defined in section 101 of title 17, and if the person registering the domain name is the copyright owner or licensee of the work, the person intends to sell the domain name in conjunction with the lawful exploitation of the work, and such registration is not prohibited by a contract between the registrant and the named person. The exception under this subparagraph shall apply only to a civil action brought under paragraph (1) and shall in no manner limit the protections afforded under the Trademark Act of 1946 (15 U.S.C. 1051 et seq.) or other provision of Federal or State law.

(2) Remedies

In any civil action brought under paragraph (1), a court may award injunctive relief, including the forfeiture or cancellation of the domain name or the transfer of the domain name to the plaintiff. The court may also, in its discretion, award costs and attorneys fees to the prevailing party.

(3) Definition

In this section, the term "domain name" has the meaning given that term in section 45 of the Trademark Act of 1946 (15 U.S.C. 1127).

(4) Effective date

This section shall apply to domain names registered on or after November 29, 1999.

SUBCHAPTER IV — THE MADRID PROTOCOL

§ 60 (15 U.S.C. § 1141). Definitions

In this subchapter:

(1) Basic application

The term "basic application" means the application for the registration of a mark that has been filed with an Office of a Contracting Party and that constitutes the basis for an application for the international registration of that mark.

---

* [*Editors' Note*: This section was enacted as part of the *Anticybersquatting Consumer Protection Act*, and was originally codified at 15 U.S.C. § 1129.]

(2) Basic registration

The term "basic registration" means the registration of a mark that has been granted by an Office of a Contracting Party and that constitutes the basis for an application for the international registration of that mark.

(3) Contracting Party

The term "Contracting Party" means any country or inter-governmental organization that is a party to the Madrid Protocol.

(4) Date of recordal

The term "date of recordal" means the date on which a request for extension of protection, filed after an international registration is granted, is recorded on the International Register.

(5) Declaration of bona fide intention to use the mark in commerce

The term "declaration of bona fide intention to use the mark in commerce" means a declaration that is signed by the applicant for, or holder of, an international registration who is seeking extension of protection of a mark to the United States and that contains a statement that—

(A) the applicant or holder has a bona fide intention to use the mark in commerce;

(B) the person making the declaration believes himself or herself, or the firm, corporation, or association in whose behalf he or she makes the declaration, to be entitled to use the mark in commerce; and

(C) no other person, firm, corporation, or association, to the best of his or her knowledge and belief, has the right to use such mark in commerce either in the identical form of the mark or in such near resemblance to the mark as to be likely, when used on or in connection with the goods of such other person, firm, corporation, or association, to cause confusion, mistake, or deception.

(6) Extension of protection

The term "extension of protection" means the protection resulting from an international registration that extends to the United States at the request of the holder of the international registration, in accordance with the Madrid Protocol.

(7) Holder of an international registration

A "holder" of an international registration is the natural or juristic person in whose name the international registration is recorded on the International Register.

(8) International application

The term "international application" means an application for international registration that is filed under the Madrid Protocol.

(9) International Bureau

The term "International Bureau" means the International Bureau of the World Intellectual Property Organization.

(10) International Register

The term "International Register" means the official collection of data concerning international registrations maintained by the International Bureau that the Madrid Protocol or its implementing regulations require or permit to be recorded.

(11) International registration

The term "international registration" means the registration of a mark granted under the Madrid Protocol.

(12) International registration date

The term "international registration date" means the date assigned to the international registration by the International Bureau.

(13) Madrid Protocol

The term "Madrid Protocol" means the Protocol Relating to the Madrid Agreement Concerning the International Registration of Marks, adopted at Madrid, Spain, on June 27, 1989.

(14) Notification of refusal

The term "notification of refusal" means the notice sent by the United States Patent and Trademark Office to the International Bureau declaring that an extension of protection cannot be granted.

(15) Office of a Contracting Party

The term "Office of a Contracting Party" means—

(A) the office, or governmental entity, of a Contracting Party that is responsible for the registration of marks; or

(B) the common office, or governmental entity, of more than 1 Contracting Party that is responsible for the registration of marks and is so recognized by the International Bureau.

(16) Office of origin

The term "office of origin" means the Office of a Contracting Party with which a basic application was filed or by which a basic registration was granted.

(17) Opposition period

The term "opposition period" means the time allowed for filing an opposition in the United States Patent and Trademark Office, including any extension of time granted under section 1063 of this title.

§61 (15 U.S.C. §1141a). International applications based on United States applications or registrations

(a) In general

The owner of a basic application pending before the United States Patent and Trademark Office, or the owner of a basic registration granted by the United States Patent and Trademark Office may file an international application by submitting to the

United States Patent and Trademark Office a written application in such form, together with such fees, as may be prescribed by the Director.

(b) Qualified owners

A qualified owner, under subsection (a) of this section, shall—

(1) be a national of the United States;

(2) be domiciled in the United States; or

(3) have a real and effective industrial or commercial establishment in the United States.

§62 (15 U.S.C. §1141b). Certification of the international application

(a) Certification procedure

Upon the filing of an application for international registration and payment of the prescribed fees, the Director shall examine the international application for the purpose of certifying that the information contained in the international application corresponds to the information contained in the basic application or basic registration at the time of the certification.

(b) Transmittal

Upon examination and certification of the international application, the Director shall transmit the international application to the International Bureau.

§63 (15 U.S.C. §1141c). Restriction, abandonment, cancellation, or expiration of a basic application or basic registration

With respect to an international application transmitted to the International Bureau under section 1141b [§62] of this title, the Director shall notify the International Bureau whenever the basic application or basic registration which is the basis for the international application has been restricted, abandoned, or canceled, or has expired, with respect to some or all of the goods and services listed in the international registration—

(1) within 5 years after the international registration date; or

(2) more than 5 years after the international registration date if the restriction, abandonment, or cancellation of the basic application or basic registration resulted from an action that began before the end of that 5-year period.

§64 (15 U.S.C. §1141d). Request for extension of protection subsequent to international registration

The holder of an international registration that is based upon a basic application filed with the United States Patent and Trademark Office or a basic registration granted by the Patent and Trademark Office may request an extension of protection of its international registration by filing such a request—

(1) directly with the International Bureau; or

(2) with the United States Patent and Trademark Office for transmittal to the International Bureau, if the request is in such form, and contains such transmittal fee, as may be prescribed by the Director.

§65 (15 U.S.C. §1141e). Extension of protection of an international registration to the United States under the Madrid Protocol

(a) In general

Subject to the provisions of section 1141h [§68] of this title, the holder of an international registration shall be entitled to the benefits of extension of protection of that international registration to the United States to the extent necessary to give effect to any provision of the Madrid Protocol.

(b) If the United States is office of origin

Where the United States Patent and Trademark Office is the office of origin for a trademark application or registration, any international registration based on such application or registration cannot be used to obtain the benefits of the Madrid Protocol in the United States.

§66 (15 U.S.C. §1141f). Effect of filing a request for extension of protection of an international registration to the United States

(a) Requirement for request for extension of protection

A request for extension of protection of an international registration to the United States that the International Bureau transmits to the United States Patent and Trademark Office shall be deemed to be properly filed in the United States if such request, when received by the International Bureau, has attached to it a declaration of bona fide intention to use the mark in commerce that is verified by the applicant for, or holder of, the international registration.

(b) Effect of proper filing

Unless extension of protection is refused under section 1141h [§68] of this title, the proper filing of the request for extension of protection under subsection (a) of this section shall constitute constructive use of the mark, conferring the same rights as those specified in section 1057(c) [§7(c)] of this title, as of the earliest of the following:

(1) The international registration date, if the request for extension of protection was filed in the international application.

(2) The date of recordal of the request for extension of protection, if the request for extension of protection was made after the international registration date.

(3) The date of priority claimed pursuant to section 1141g [§67] of this title.

§67 (15 U.S.C. §1141g). Right of priority for request for extension of protection to the United States

The holder of an international registration with a request for an extension of protection to the United States shall be entitled to claim a date of priority based on a right of priority within the meaning of Article 4 of the Paris Convention for the Protection of Industrial Property if—

(1) the request for extension of protection contains a claim of priority; and

(2) the date of international registration or the date of the recordal of the request for extension of protection to the United States is not later than 6 months after the date of the first regular national filing (within the meaning of Article 4(A)(3) of the Paris Convention for the Protection of Industrial Property) or a subsequent application (within the meaning of Article 4(C)(4) of the Paris Convention for the Protection of Industrial Property).

§ 68 (15 U.S.C. § 1141h). Examination of and opposition to request for extension of protection; notification of refusal

(a) Examination and opposition

(1) A request for extension of protection described in section 1141f(a) [§ 66(a)] of this title shall be examined as an application for registration on the Principal Register under this chapter, and if on such examination it appears that the applicant is entitled to extension of protection under this subchapter, the Director shall cause the mark to be published in the Official Gazette of the United States Patent and Trademark Office.

(2) Subject to the provisions of subsection (c) of this section, a request for extension of protection under this subchapter shall be subject to opposition under section 1063 [§ 13] of this title.

(3) Extension of protection shall not be refused on the ground that the mark has not been used in commerce.

(4) Extension of protection shall be refused to any mark not registrable on the Principal Register.

(b) Notification of refusal

If, a request for extension of protection is refused under subsection (a) of this section, the Director shall declare in a notification of refusal (as provided in subsection (c) of this section) that the extension of protection cannot be granted, together with a statement of all grounds on which the refusal was based.

(c) Notice to International Bureau

(1) Within 18 months after the date on which the International Bureau transmits to the Patent and Trademark Office a notification of a request for extension of protection, the Director shall transmit to the International Bureau any of the following that applies to such request:

(A) A notification of refusal based on an examination of the request for extension of protection.

(B) A notification of refusal based on the filing of an opposition to the request.

(C) A notification of the possibility that an opposition to the request may be filed after the end of that 18-month period.

(2) If the Director has sent a notification of the possibility of opposition under paragraph (1)(C), the Director shall, if applicable, transmit to the International Bureau a notification of refusal on the basis of the opposition, together with a

statement of all the grounds for the opposition, within 7 months after the beginning of the opposition period or within 1 month after the end of the opposition period, whichever is earlier.

(3) If a notification of refusal of a request for extension of protection is transmitted under paragraph (1) or (2), no grounds for refusal of such request other than those set forth in such notification may be transmitted to the International Bureau by the Director after the expiration of the time periods set forth in paragraph (1) or (2), as the case may be.

(4) If a notification specified in paragraph (1) or (2) is not sent to the International Bureau within the time period set forth in such paragraph, with respect to a request for extension of protection, the request for extension of protection shall not be refused and the Director shall issue a certificate of extension of protection pursuant to the request.

(d) Designation of agent for service of process

In responding to a notification of refusal with respect to a mark, the holder of the international registration of the mark may designate, by a document filed in the United States Patent and Trademark Office, the name and address of a person residing in the United States on whom notices or process in proceedings affecting the mark may be served. Such notices or process may be served upon the person designated by leaving with that person, or mailing to that person, a copy thereof at the address specified in the last designation filed. If the person designated cannot be found at the address given in the last designation, or if the holder does not designate by a document filed in the United States Patent and Trademark Office the name and address of a person residing in the United States for service of notices or process in proceedings affecting the mark, the notice or process may be served on the Director.

§ 69 (15 U.S.C. § 1141i). Effect of extension of protection

(a) Issuance of extension of protection

Unless a request for extension of protection is refused under section 1141h [§ 68] of this title, the Director shall issue a certificate of extension of protection pursuant to the request and shall cause notice of such certificate of extension of protection to be published in the Official Gazette of the United States Patent and Trademark Office.

(b) Effect of extension of protection

From the date on which a certificate of extension of protection is issued under subsection (a) of this section—

(1) such extension of protection shall have the same effect and validity as a registration on the Principal Register; and

(2) the holder of the international registration shall have the same rights and remedies as the owner of a registration on the Principal Register.

§ 70 (15 U.S.C. § 1141j). Dependence of extension of protection to the United States on the underlying international registration

(a) Effect of cancellation of international registration

If the International Bureau notifies the United States Patent and Trademark Office of the cancellation of an international registration with respect to some or all of the goods and services listed in the international registration, the Director shall cancel any extension of protection to the United States with respect to such goods and services as of the date on which the international registration was canceled.

(b) Effect of failure to renew international registration

If the International Bureau does not renew an international registration, the corresponding extension of protection to the United States shall cease to be valid as of the date of the expiration of the international registration.

(c) Transformation of an extension of protection into a United States application

The holder of an international registration canceled in whole or in part by the International Bureau at the request of the office of origin, under article 6(4) of the Madrid Protocol, may file an application, under section 1051 [§ 1] or 1126 [§ 44] of this title, for the registration of the same mark for any of the goods and services to which the cancellation applies that were covered by an extension of protection to the United States based on that international registration. Such an application shall be treated as if it had been filed on the international registration date or the date of recordal of the request for extension of protection with the International Bureau, whichever date applies, and, if the extension of protection enjoyed priority under section 1141g [§ 67] of this title, shall enjoy the same priority. Such an application shall be entitled to the benefits conferred by this subsection only if the application is filed not later than 3 months after the date on which the international registration was canceled, in whole or in part, and only if the application complies with all the requirements of this chapter which apply to any application filed pursuant to section 1051 [§ 1] or 1126 [§ 44] of this title.

§ 71 (15 U.S.C. § 1141k). Duration, affidavits and fees

(a) Time periods for required affidavits

Each extension of protection for which a certificate has been issued under section 69 [15 USC § 1141i] shall remain in force for the term of the international registration upon which it is based, except that the extension of protection of any mark shall be canceled by the Director unless the holder of the international registration files in the United States Patent and Trademark Office affidavits that meet the requirements of subsection (b), within the following time periods:

(1) Within the 1-year period immediately preceding the expiration of 6 years following the date of issuance of the certificate of extension of protection.

(2) Within the 1-year period immediately preceding the expiration of 10 years following the date of issuance of the certificate of extension of protection, and each successive 10-year period following the date of issuance of the certificate of extension of protection.

(3) The holder may file the affidavit required under this section within a grace period of 6 months after the end of the applicable time period established in paragraph (1) or (2), together with the fee described in subsection (b) and the additional grace period surcharge prescribed by the Director.

(b) Requirements for affidavit

The affidavit referred to in subsection (a) shall—

(1)(A) state that the mark is in use in commerce;

(B) set forth the goods and services recited in the extension of protection on or in connection with which the mark is in use in commerce;

(C) be accompanied by such number of specimens or facsimiles showing current use of the mark in commerce as may be required by the Director; and

(D) be accompanied by the fee prescribed by the Director; or

(2)(A) set forth the goods and services recited in the extension of protection on or in connection with which the mark is not in use in commerce;

(B) include a showing that any nonuse is due to special circumstances which excuse such nonuse and is not due to any intention to abandon the mark; and

(C) be accompanied by the fee prescribed by the Director.

(c) Deficient affidavit

If any submission filed within the period set forth in subsection (a) is deficient, including that the affidavit was not filed in the name of the holder of the international registration, the deficiency may be corrected after the statutory time period, within the time prescribed after notification of the deficiency. Such submission shall be accompanied by the additional deficiency surcharge prescribed by the Director.

(d) Notice of requirement

Special notice of the requirement for such affidavit shall be attached to each certificate of extension of protection.

(e) Notification of acceptance or refusal

The Director shall notify the holder of the international registration who files any affidavit required by this section of the Director's acceptance or refusal thereof and, in the case of a refusal, the reasons therefor.

(f) Designation of resident for service of process and notices

If the holder of the international registration of the mark is not domiciled in the United States, the holder may designate, by a document filed in the United States Patent and Trademark Office, the name and address of a person resident in the United States on whom may be served notices or process in proceedings affecting the mark. Such notices or process may be served upon the person so designated by leaving with that person or mailing to that person a copy thereof at the address specified in the last designation so filed. If the person so designated cannot be found at the last designated address, or if the holder does not designate by a document filed in the United

States Patent and Trademark Office the name and address of a person resident in the United States on whom may be served notices or process in proceedings affecting the mark, such notices or process may be served on the Director.

§72 (15 U.S.C. §1141*l*). Assignment of an extension of protection

An extension of protection may be assigned, together with the goodwill associated with the mark, only to a person who is a national of, is domiciled in, or has a bona fide and effective industrial or commercial establishment either in a country that is a Contracting Party or in a country that is a member of an intergovernmental organization that is a Contracting Party.

§73 (15 U.S.C. §1141m). Incontestability

The period of continuous use prescribed under section 1065 [§15] of this title for a mark covered by an extension of protection issued under this subchapter may begin no earlier than the date on which the Director issues the certificate of the extension of protection under section 1141i [§69] of this title, except as provided in section 1141n [§74] of this title.

§74 (15 U.S.C. §1141n). Rights of extension of protection

When a United States registration and a subsequently issued certificate of extension of protection to the United States are owned by the same person, identify the same mark, and list the same goods or services, the extension of protection shall have the same rights that accrued to the registration prior to issuance of the certificate of extension of protection.

Appendix B

Restatement of the Law (Third) of Unfair Competition, §§ 1, 9, 13, 16–17, 20–27

Section

1. General Principles
9. Definitions of Trademark and Service Mark
13. Distinctiveness; Secondary Meaning
16. Configurations of Packaging and Products: Trade Dress and Product Designs
17. Functional Designs
20. Standard of Infringement
21. Proof of Likelihood of Confusion: Market Factors
22. Proof of Likelihood of Confusion: Intent of the Actor
23. Proof of Likelihood of Confusion: Evidence of Actual Confusion
24. Use of Another's Trademark on Genuine Goods
25. Liability Without Proof of Confusion: Dilution and Tarnishment
26. Contributory Infringement by Printers, Publishers, and Other Suppliers
27. Contributory Infringement by Manufacturers and Distributors

§ 1. General Principles

One who causes harm to the commercial relations of another by engaging in a business or trade is not subject to liability to the other for such harm unless:

(a) the harm results from acts or practices of the actor actionable by the other under the rules of this Restatement relating to:

(1) deceptive marketing, as specified in Chapter Two;

(2) infringement of trademarks and other indicia of identification, as specified in Chapter Three;

(3) appropriation of intangible trade values including trade secrets and the right of publicity, as specified in Chapter Four;

or from other acts or practices of the actor determined to be actionable as an unfair method of competition, taking into account the nature of the conduct and its likely effect on both the person seeking relief and the public; or

(b) the acts or practices of the actor are actionable by the other under federal or state statutes, international agreements, or general principles of common law apart from those considered in this Restatement.

§ 9. Definitions of Trademark and Service Mark

A trademark is a word, name, symbol, device, or other designation, or a combination of such designations, that is distinctive of a person's goods or services and that is used in a manner that identifies those goods or services and distinguishes them from the goods or services of others. A service mark is a trademark that is used in connection with services.

§ 13. Distinctiveness; Secondary Meaning

A word, name, symbol, device, or other designation, or a combination of such designations, is "distinctive" under the rules stated in §§ 9–12 if:

(a) the designation is "inherently distinctive," in that, because of the nature of the designation and the context in which it is used, prospective purchasers are likely to perceive it as a designation that, in the case of a trademark, identifies goods or services produced or sponsored by a particular person, whether known or anonymous, or in the case of a trade name, identifies the business or other enterprise of a particular person, whether known or anonymous, or in the case of a collective mark, identifies members of the collective group or goods or services produced or sponsored by members, or in the case of a certification mark, identifies the certified goods or services; or

(b) the designation, although not "inherently distinctive," has become distinctive, in that, as a result of its use, prospective purchasers have come to perceive it as a designation that identifies goods, services, businesses, or members in the manner described in Subsection (a). Such acquired distinctiveness is commonly referred to as "secondary meaning."

§ 16. Configurations of Packaging and Products: Trade Dress and Product Designs

The design of elements that constitute the appearance or image of goods or services as presented to prospective purchasers, including the design of packaging, labels, containers, displays, decor, or the design of a product, a product feature, or a combination of product features, is eligible for protection as a mark under the rules stated in this Chapter if:

(a) the design is distinctive under the rule stated in § 13; and

(b) the design is not functional under the rule stated in § 17.

§ 17. Functional Designs

A design is "functional" for purposes of the rule stated in § 16 if the design affords benefits in the manufacturing, marketing, or use of the goods or services with which the design is used, apart from any benefits attributable to the design's significance as an indication of source, that are important to effective competition by others and that are not practically available through the use of alternative designs.

§ 20. Standard of Infringement

(1) One is subject to liability for infringement of another's trademark, trade name, collective mark, or certification mark if the other's use has priority under the rules stated in § 19 and in identifying the actor's business or in marketing the actor's goods or services the actor uses a designation that causes a likelihood of confusion:

(a) that the actor's business is the business of the other or is associated or otherwise connected with the other; or

(b) that the goods or services marketed by the actor are produced, sponsored, certified, or approved by the other; or

(c) that the goods or services marketed by the other are produced, sponsored, certified, or approved by the actor.

(2) One is also subject to liability for infringement of another's collective membership mark if the other's use has priority under the rules stated in § 19 and the actor uses a designation that causes a likelihood of confusion that the actor is a member of or otherwise associated with the collective group.

§ 21. Proof of Likelihood of Confusion: Market Factors

Whether an actor's use of a designation causes a likelihood of confusion with the use of a trademark, trade name, collective mark, or certification mark by another under the rule stated in § 20 is determined by a consideration of all the circumstances involved in the marketing of the respective goods or services or in the operation of the respective businesses. In making that determination the following market factors, among others, may be important:

(a) the degree of similarity between the respective designations, including a comparison of

(i) the overall impression created by the designations as they are used in marketing the respective goods or services or in identifying the respective businesses;

(ii) the pronunciation of the designations;

(iii) the translation of any foreign words contained in the designations;

(iv) the verbal translation of any pictures, illustrations, or designs contained in the designations;

(v) the suggestions, connotations, or meanings of the designations;

(b) the degree of similarity in the marketing methods and channels of distribution used for the respective goods or services;

(c) the characteristics of the prospective purchasers of the goods or services and the degree of care they are likely to exercise in making purchasing decisions;

(d) the degree of distinctiveness of the other's designation;

(e) when the goods, services, or business of the actor differ in kind from those of the other, the likelihood that the actor's prospective purchasers would expect a person in the position of the other to expand its marketing or sponsorship into the product, service, or business market of the actor;

(f) when the actor and the other sell their goods or services or carry on their businesses in different geographic markets, the extent to which the other's designation is identified with the other in the geographic market of the actor.

§ 22. Proof of Likelihood of Confusion: Intent of the Actor

(1) A likelihood of confusion may be inferred from proof that the actor used a designation resembling another's trademark, trade name, collective mark, or certification mark with the intent to cause confusion or to deceive.

(2) A likelihood of confusion should not be inferred from proof that the actor intentionally copied the other's designation if the actor acted in good faith under circumstances that do not otherwise indicate an intent to cause confusion or to deceive.

§ 23. Proof of Likelihood of Confusion: Evidence of Actual Confusion

(1) A likelihood of confusion may be inferred from proof of actual confusion.

(2) An absence of likelihood of confusion may be inferred from the absence of proof of actual confusion if the actor and the other have made significant use of their respective designations in the same geographic market for a substantial period of time, and any resulting confusion would ordinarily be manifested by provable facts.

§ 24. Use of Another's Trademark on Genuine Goods

One is not subject to liability under the rule stated in § 20 for using another's trademark, trade name, collective mark, or certification mark in marketing genuine goods or services the source, sponsorship, or certification of which is accurately identified by the mark unless:

(a) the other uses a different mark for different types or grades of goods or services and the actor markets one of the types or grades under a mark used for another type or grade; or

(b) the actor markets under the mark genuine goods of the other that have been repaired, reconditioned, altered, or used, or genuine services that do not conform to the standards imposed by the other, and the actor's use of the mark causes a likelihood of confusion that the goods are new or unaltered or that the repair, reconditioning, or alteration was performed, authorized, or certified by the other, or that the services conform to the other's standards.

§ 25. Liability Without Proof of Confusion: Dilution and Tarnishment

(1) One may be subject to liability under the law of trademarks for the use of a designation that resembles the trademark, trade name, collective mark, or certification mark of another without proof of a likelihood of confusion only under an applicable antidilution statute. An actor is subject to liability under an antidilution statute if the actor uses such a designation in a manner that is likely to associate the other's mark with the goods, services, or business of the actor and:

(a) the other's mark is highly distinctive and the association of the mark with the actor's goods, services, or business is likely to cause a reduction in that distinctiveness; or

(b) the association of the other's mark with the actor's goods, services, or business, or the nature of the actor's use, is likely to disparage the other's goods, services, or business or tarnish the images associated with the other's mark.

(2) One who uses a designation that resembles the trademark, trade name, collective mark, or certification mark of another, not in a manner that is likely to associate the other's mark with the goods, services, or business of the actor, but rather to comment on, criticize, ridicule, parody, or disparage the other or the other's goods, services, business, or mark, is subject to liability without proof of a likelihood of confusion only if the actor's conduct meets the requirements of a cause of action for defamation, invasion of privacy, or injurious falsehood.

§ 26. Contributory Infringement by Printers, Publishers, and Other Suppliers

(1) One who, on behalf of a third person, reproduces or imitates the trademark, trade name, collective mark, or certification mark of another on goods, labels, packaging, advertisements, or other materials that are used by the third person in a manner that subjects the third person to liability to the other for infringement under the rule stated in § 20 is subject to liability to that other for contributory infringement.

(2) If an actor subject to contributory liability under the rule stated in Subsection (1) acted without knowledge that the reproduction or imitation was intended by the third person to confuse or deceive, the actor is subject only to appropriate injunctive relief.

§ 27. Contributory Infringement by Manufacturers and Distributors

One who markets goods or services to a third person who further markets the goods or services in a manner that subjects the third person to liability to another for infringement under the rule stated in § 20 is subject to liability to that other for contributory infringement if:

(a) the actor intentionally induces the third person to engage in the infringing conduct; or

(b) the actor fails to take reasonable precautions against the occurrence of the third person's infringing conduct in circumstances in which the infringing conduct can be reasonably anticipated.

Appendix C

Uniform Domain Name Dispute Resolution Policy

(As Approved by ICANN on October 24, 1999)

1. Purpose. This Uniform Domain Name Dispute Resolution Policy (the "Policy") has been adopted by the Internet Corporation for Assigned Names and Numbers ("ICANN"), is incorporated by reference into your Registration Agreement, and sets forth the terms and conditions in connection with a dispute between you and any party other than us (the registrar) over the registration and use of an Internet domain name registered by you. Proceedings under Paragraph 4 of this Policy will be conducted according to the Rules for Uniform Domain Name Dispute Resolution Policy (the "Rules of Procedure"), which are available at www.icann.org/udrp/udrp-rules-24oct99.htm, and the selected administrative-dispute-resolution service provider's supplemental rules.

2. Your Representations. By applying to register a domain name, or by asking us to maintain or renew a domain name registration, you hereby represent and warrant to us that (a) the statements that you made in your Registration Agreement are complete and accurate; (b) to your knowledge, the registration of the domain name will not infringe upon or otherwise violate the rights of any third party; (c) you are not registering the domain name for an unlawful purpose; and (d) you will not knowingly use the domain name in violation of any applicable laws or regulations. It is your responsibility to determine whether your domain name registration infringes or violates someone else's rights.

3. Cancellations, Transfers, and Changes. We will cancel, transfer or otherwise make changes to domain name registrations under the following circumstances:

(a) subject to the provisions of Paragraph 8, our receipt of written or appropriate electronic instructions from you or your authorized agent to take such action;

(b) our receipt of an order from a court or arbitral tribunal, in each case of competent jurisdiction, requiring such action; and/or

(c) our receipt of a decision of an Administrative Panel requiring such action in any administrative proceeding to which you were a party and which was conducted under this Policy or a later version of this Policy adopted by ICANN. (See Paragraph 4(i) and (k) below.)

We may also cancel, transfer or otherwise make changes to a domain name registration in accordance with the terms of your Registration Agreement or other legal requirements.

4. **Mandatory Administrative Proceeding.** This Paragraph sets forth the type of disputes for which you are required to submit to a mandatory administrative proceeding. These proceedings will be conducted before one of the administrative-dispute-resolution service providers listed at www.icann.org/udrp/approved-providers.htm. (each, a "Provider").

(a) **Applicable Disputes.** You are required to submit to a mandatory administrative proceeding in the event that a third party (a "complainant") asserts to the applicable Provider, in compliance with the Rules of Procedure, that

(i) your domain name is identical or confusingly similar to a trademark or service mark in which the complainant has rights; and

(ii) you have no rights or legitimate interests in respect of the domain name; and

(iii) your domain name has been registered and is being used in bad faith.

In the administrative proceeding, the complainant must prove that each of these three elements are present.

(b) **Evidence of Registration and Use in Bad Faith.** For the purposes of Paragraph 4(a)(iii), the following circumstances, in particular but without limitation, if found by the Panel to be present, shall be evidence of the registration and use of a domain name in bad faith:

(i) circumstances indicating that you have registered or you have acquired the domain name primarily for the purpose of selling, renting, or otherwise transferring the domain name registration to the complainant who is the owner of the trademark or service mark or to a competitor of that complainant, for valuable consideration in excess of your documented out-of-pocket costs directly related to the domain name; or

(ii) you have registered the domain name in order to prevent the owner of the trademark or service mark from reflecting the mark in a corresponding domain name, provided that you have engaged in a pattern of such conduct; or

(iii) you have registered the domain name primarily for the purpose of disrupting the business of a competitor; or

(iv) by using the domain name, you have intentionally attempted to attract, for commercial gain, Internet users to your web site or other on-line location, by creating a likelihood of confusion with the complainant's mark as to the source, sponsorship, affiliation, or endorsement of your web site or location or of a product or service on your web site or location.

(c) **How to Demonstrate Your Rights to and Legitimate Interests in the Domain Name in Responding to a Complaint.** When you receive a complaint, you should refer to Paragraph 5 of the Rules of Procedure in determining how your response should be prepared. Any of the following circumstances, in particular but without limitation, if found by the Panel to be proved based on its evaluation of all evidence presented, shall demonstrate your rights or legitimate interests to the domain name for purposes of Paragraph 4(a)(ii):

(i) before any notice to you of the dispute, your use of, or demonstrable preparations to use, the domain name or a name corresponding to the domain name in connection with a bona fide offering of goods or services; or

(ii) you (as an individual, business, or other organization) have been commonly known by the domain name, even if you have acquired no trademark or service mark rights; or

(iii) you are making a legitimate noncommercial or fair use of the domain name, without intent for commercial gain to misleadingly divert consumers or to tarnish the trademark or service mark at issue.

(d) Selection of Provider. The complainant shall select the Provider from among those approved by ICANN by submitting the complaint to that Provider. The selected Provider will administer the proceeding, except in cases of consolidation as described in Paragraph 4(f).

(e) Initiation of Proceeding and Process and Appointment of Administrative Panel. The Rules of Procedure state the process for initiating and conducting a proceeding and for appointing the panel that will decide the dispute (the "Administrative Panel").

(f) Consolidation. In the event of multiple disputes between you and a complainant, either you or the complainant may petition to consolidate the disputes before a single Administrative Panel. This petition shall be made to the first Administrative Panel appointed to hear a pending dispute between the parties. This Administrative Panel may consolidate before it any or all such disputes in its sole discretion, provided that the disputes being consolidated are governed by this Policy or a later version of this Policy adopted by ICANN.

(g) Fees. All fees charged by a Provider in connection with any dispute before an Administrative Panel pursuant to this Policy shall be paid by the complainant, except in cases where you elect to expand the Administrative Panel from one to three panelists as provided in Paragraph 5(b)(iv) of the Rules of Procedure, in which case all fees will be split evenly by you and the complainant.

(h) Our Involvement in Administrative Proceedings. We do not, and will not, participate in the administration or conduct of any proceeding before an Administrative Panel. In addition, we will not be liable as a result of any decisions rendered by the Administrative Panel.

(i) Remedies. The remedies available to a complainant pursuant to any proceeding before an Administrative Panel shall be limited to requiring the cancellation of your domain name or the transfer of your domain name registration to the complainant.

(j) Notification and Publication. The Provider shall notify us of any decision made by an Administrative Panel with respect to a domain name you have registered with us. All decisions under this Policy will be published in full over the Internet, except when an Administrative Panel determines in an exceptional case to redact portions of its decision.

(k) **Availability of Court Proceedings.** The mandatory administrative proceeding requirements set forth in Paragraph 4 shall not prevent either you or the complainant from submitting the dispute to a court of competent jurisdiction for independent resolution before such mandatory administrative proceeding is commenced or after such proceeding is concluded. If an Administrative Panel decides that your domain name registration should be canceled or transferred, we will wait ten (10) business days (as observed in the location of our principal office) after we are informed by the applicable Provider of the Administrative Panel's decision before implementing that decision. We will then implement the decision unless we have received from you during that ten (10) business day period official documentation (such as a copy of a complaint, file-stamped by the clerk of the court) that you have commenced a lawsuit against the complainant in a jurisdiction to which the complainant has submitted under Paragraph 3(b)(xiii) of the Rules of Procedure. (In general, that jurisdiction is either the location of our principal office or of your address as shown in our Whois database. See Paragraphs 1 and 3(b)(xiii) of the Rules of Procedure for details.) If we receive such documentation within the ten (10) business day period, we will not implement the Administrative Panel's decision, and we will take no further action, until we receive (i) evidence satisfactory to us of a resolution between the parties; (ii) evidence satisfactory to us that your lawsuit has been dismissed or withdrawn; or (iii) a copy of an order from such court dismissing your lawsuit or ordering that you do not have the right to continue to use your domain name.

5. All Other Disputes and Litigation. All other disputes between you and any party other than us regarding your domain name registration that are not brought pursuant to the mandatory administrative proceeding provisions of Paragraph 4 shall be resolved between you and such other party through any court, arbitration or other proceeding that may be available.

6. Our Involvement in Disputes. We will not participate in any way in any dispute between you and any party other than us regarding the registration and use of your domain name. You shall not name us as a party or otherwise include us in any such proceeding. In the event that we are named as a party in any such proceeding, we reserve the right to raise any and all defenses deemed appropriate, and to take any other action necessary to defend ourselves.

7. Maintaining the Status Quo. We will not cancel, transfer, activate, deactivate, or otherwise change the status of any domain name registration under this Policy except as provided in Paragraph 3 above.

8. Transfers During a Dispute.

(a) **Transfers of a Domain Name to a New Holder.** You may not transfer your domain name registration to another holder (i) during a pending administrative proceeding brought pursuant to Paragraph 4 or for a period of fifteen (15) business days (as observed in the location of our principal place of business) after such proceeding is concluded; or (ii) during a pending court proceeding or arbitration commenced regarding your domain name unless the party to whom the domain name registration is being transferred agrees, in writing, to be bound by the decision of the court or arbitrator. We reserve the right to cancel any transfer of a domain name registration to another holder that is made in violation of this subparagraph.

(b) Changing Registrars. You may not transfer your domain name registration to another registrar during a pending administrative proceeding brought pursuant to Paragraph 4 or for a period of fifteen (15) business days (as observed in the location of our principal place of business) after such proceeding is concluded. You may transfer administration of your domain name registration to another registrar during a pending court action or arbitration, provided that the domain name you have registered with us shall continue to be subject to the proceedings commenced against you in accordance with the terms of this Policy. In the event that you transfer a domain name registration to us during the pendency of a court action or arbitration, such dispute shall remain subject to the domain name dispute policy of the registrar from which the domain name registration was transferred.

9. Policy Modifications. We reserve the right to modify this Policy at any time with the permission of ICANN. We will post our revised Policy … at least thirty (30) calendar days before it becomes effective. Unless this Policy has already been invoked by the submission of a complaint to a Provider, in which event the version of the Policy in effect at the time it was invoked will apply to you until the dispute is over, all such changes will be binding upon you with respect to any domain name registration dispute, whether the dispute arose before, on or after the effective date of our change. In the event that you object to a change in this Policy, your sole remedy is to cancel your domain name registration with us, provided that you will not be entitled to a refund of any fees you paid to us. The revised Policy will apply to you until you cancel your domain name registration.

Appendix D

Paris Convention for the Protection of Industrial Property (excerpts)

of March 20, 1883,
as revised
at BRUSSELS on December 14, 1900, at WASHINGTON on June 2, 1911, at THE HAGUE on November 6, 1925, at LONDON on June 2, 1934, at LISBON on October 31, 1958, and at STOCKHOLM on July 14, 1967, and as amended on September 28, 1979

Note: Headings enclosed in brackets are supplied by the World Intellectual Property Organization.

Article 1 [Establishment of the Union; Scope of Industrial Property]

(1) The countries to which this Convention applies constitute a Union for the protection of industrial property.

(2) The protection of industrial property has as its object patents, utility models, industrial designs, trademarks, service marks, trade names, indications of source or appellations of origin, and the repression of unfair competition.

(3) Industrial property shall be understood in the broadest sense and shall apply not only to industry and commerce proper, but likewise to agricultural and extractive industries and to all manufactured or natural products, for example, wines, grain, tobacco leaf, fruit, cattle, minerals, mineral waters, beer, flowers, and flour.

(4) Patents shall include the various kinds of industrial patents recognized by the laws of the countries of the Union, such as patents of importation, patents of improvement, patents and certificates of addition, etc.

Article 2 [National Treatment for Nationals of Countries of the Union]

(1) Nationals of any country of the Union shall, as regards the protection of industrial property, enjoy in all the other countries of the Union the advantages that their respective laws now grant, or may hereafter grant, to nationals; all without prejudice to the rights specially provided for by this Convention. Consequently, they shall have the same protection as the latter, and the same legal remedy against any infringement of their rights, provided that the conditions and formalities imposed upon nationals are complied with.

(2) However, no requirement as to domicile or establishment in the country where protection is claimed may be imposed upon nationals of countries of the Union for the enjoyment of any industrial property rights.

(3) The provisions of the laws of each of the countries of the Union relating to judicial and administrative procedure and to jurisdiction, and to the designation of an address for service or the appointment of an agent, which may be required by the laws on industrial property are expressly reserved.

Article 3 [Same Treatment for Certain Categories of Persons as for Nationals of Countries of the Union]

Nationals of countries outside the Union who are domiciled or who have real and effective industrial or commercial establishments in the territory of one of the countries of the Union shall be treated in the same manner as nationals of the countries of the Union.

Article 4 [A to D, F. *Patents, Utility Models, Industrial Designs, Marks* ... : Right of Priority ...]

A.—(1) Any person who has duly filed an application for a patent, or for the registration of a utility model, or of an industrial design, or of a trademark, in one of the countries of the Union, or his successor in title, shall enjoy, for the purpose of filing in the other countries, a right of priority during the periods hereinafter fixed.

(2) Any filing that is equivalent to a regular national filing under the domestic legislation of any country of the Union or under bilateral or multilateral treaties concluded between countries of the Union shall be recognized as giving rise to the right of priority.

(3) By a regular national filing is meant any filing that is adequate to establish the date on which the application was filed in the country concerned, whatever may be the subsequent fate of the application.

B.—Consequently, any subsequent filing in any of the other countries of the Union before the expiration of the periods referred to above shall not be invalidated by reason of any acts accomplished in the interval, in particular, another filing, the publication or exploitation of the invention, the putting on sale of copies of the design, or the use of the mark, and such acts cannot give rise to any third-party right or any right of personal possession. Rights acquired by third parties before the date of the first application that serves as the basis for the right of priority are reserved in accordance with the domestic legislation of each country of the Union.

C.—(1) The periods of priority referred to above shall be twelve months for patents and utility models, and six months for industrial designs and trademarks.

(2) These periods shall start from the date of filing of the first application; the day of filing shall not be included in the period.

(3) If the last day of the period is an official holiday, or a day when the Office is not open for the filing of applications in the country where protection is claimed, the period shall be extended until the first following working day.

(4) A subsequent application concerning the same subject as a previous first application within the meaning of paragraph (2), above, filed in the same country of the Union shall be considered as the first application, of which the filing date shall be the starting point of the period of priority, if, at the time of filing the subsequent application, the said previous application has been withdrawn, abandoned, or refused, without having been laid open to public inspection and without leaving any rights outstanding, and if it has not yet served as a basis for claiming a right of priority. The previous application may not thereafter serve as a basis for claiming a right of priority.

D.—(1) Any person desiring to take advantage of the priority of a previous filing shall be required to make a declaration indicating the date of such filing and the country in which it was made. Each country shall determine the latest date on which such declaration must be made.

(2) These particulars shall be mentioned in the publications issued by the competent authority, and in particular in the patents and the specifications relating thereto.

(3) The countries of the Union may require any person making a declaration of priority to produce a copy of the application (description, drawings, etc.) previously filed. The copy, certified as correct by the authority which received such application, shall not require any authentication, and may in any case be filed, without fee, at any time within three months of the filing of the subsequent application. They may require it to be accompanied by a certificate from the same authority showing the date of filing, and by a translation.

(4) No other formalities may be required for the declaration of priority at the time of filing the application. Each country of the Union shall determine the consequences of failure to comply with the formalities prescribed by this Article, but such consequences shall in no case go beyond the loss of the right of priority.

(5) Subsequently, further proof may be required.

Any person who avails himself of the priority of a previous application shall be required to specify the number of that application; this number shall be published as provided for by paragraph (2), above.

....

Article 5 [... C. *Marks:* Failure to Use; Different Forms; Use by Co-proprietors.—D. *Patents, Utility Models, Marks, Industrial Designs;* Marking]

C.—(1) If, in any country, use of the registered mark is compulsory, the registration may be cancelled only after a reasonable period, and then only if the person concerned does not justify his inaction.

(2) Use of a trademark by the proprietor in a form differing in elements which do not alter the distinctive character of the mark in the form in which it was registered in one of the countries of the Union shall not entail invalidation of the registration and shall not diminish the protection granted to the mark.

(3) Concurrent use of the same mark on identical or similar goods by industrial or commercial establishments considered as co-proprietors of the mark according to

the provisions of the domestic law of the country where protection is claimed shall not prevent registration or diminish in any way the protection granted to the said mark in any country of the Union, provided that such use does not result in misleading the public and is not contrary to the public interest.

D.—No indication or mention of the patent, of the utility model, of the registration of the trademark, or of the deposit of the industrial design, shall be required upon the goods as a condition of recognition of the right to protection.

Article 5bis [*All Industrial Property Rights:* Period of Grace for the Payment of Fees for the Maintenance of Rights ...]

(1) A period of grace of not less than six months shall be allowed for the payment of the fees prescribed for the maintenance of industrial property rights, subject, if the domestic legislation so provides, to the payment of a surcharge.

....

Article 6 [*Marks*: Conditions of Registration; Independence of Protection of Same Mark in Different Countries]

(1) The conditions for the filing and registration of trademarks shall be determined in each country of the Union by its domestic legislation.

(2) However, an application for the registration of a mark filed by a national of a country of the Union in any country of the Union may not be refused, nor may a registration be invalidated, on the ground that filing, registration, or renewal, has not been effected in the country of origin.

(3) A mark duly registered in a country of the Union shall be regarded as independent of marks registered in the other countries of the Union, including the country of origin.

Article 6bis [*Marks:* Well-Known Marks]

(1) The countries of the Union undertake, ex officio if their legislation so permits, or at the request of an interested party, to refuse or to cancel the registration, and to prohibit the use, of a trademark which constitutes a reproduction, an imitation, or a translation, liable to create confusion, of a mark considered by the competent authority of the country of registration or use to be well known in that country as being already the mark of a person entitled to the benefits of this Convention and used for identical or similar goods. These provisions shall also apply when the essential part of the mark constitutes a reproduction of any such well-known mark or an imitation liable to create confusion therewith.

(2) A period of at least five years from the date of registration shall be allowed for requesting the cancellation of such a mark. The countries of the Union may provide for a period within which the prohibition of use must be requested.

(3) No time limit shall be fixed for requesting the cancellation or the prohibition of the use of marks registered or used in bad faith.

Article 6ter [*Marks:* Prohibitions concerning State Emblems, Official Hallmarks, and Emblems of Intergovernmental Organizations]

(1)(a) The countries of the Union agree to refuse or to invalidate the registration, and to prohibit by appropriate measures the use, without authorization by the competent authorities, either as trademarks or as elements of trademarks, of armorial bearings, flags, and other State emblems, of the countries of the Union, official signs and hallmarks indicating control and warranty adopted by them, and any imitation from a heraldic point of view.

(b) The provisions of subparagraph (a), above, shall apply equally to armorial bearings, flags, other emblems, abbreviations, and names, of international intergovernmental organizations of which one or more countries of the Union are members, with the exception of armorial bearings, flags, other emblems, abbreviations, and names, that are already the subject of international agreements in force, intended to ensure their protection.

(c) No country of the Union shall be required to apply the provisions of subparagraph (b), above, to the prejudice of the owners of rights acquired in good faith before the entry into force, in that country, of this Convention. The countries of the Union shall not be required to apply the said provisions when the use or registration referred to in subparagraph (a), above, is not of such a nature as to suggest to the public that a connection exists between the organization concerned and the armorial bearings, flags, emblems, abbreviations, and names, or if such use or registration is probably not of such a nature as to mislead the public as to the existence of a connection between the user and the organization.

(2) Prohibition of the use of official signs and hallmarks indicating control and warranty shall apply solely in cases where the marks in which they are incorporated are intended to be used on goods of the same or a similar kind.

(3)(a) For the application of these provisions, the countries of the Union agree to communicate reciprocally, through the intermediary of the International Bureau, the list of State emblems, and official signs and hallmarks indicating control and warranty, which they desire, or may hereafter desire, to place wholly or within certain limits under the protection of this Article, and all subsequent modifications of such list. Each country of the Union shall in due course make available to the public the lists so communicated.Nevertheless such communication is not obligatory in respect of flags of States.

(b) The provisions of subparagraph (b) of paragraph (1) of this Article shall apply only to such armorial bearings, flags, other emblems, abbreviations, and names, of international intergovernmental organizations as the latter have communicated to the countries of the Union through the intermediary of the International Bureau.

(4) Any country of the Union may, within a period of twelve months from the receipt of the notification, transmit its objections, if any, through the intermediary of the International Bureau, to the country or international intergovernmental organization concerned.

(5) In the case of State flags, the measures prescribed by paragraph (1), above, shall apply solely to marks registered after November 6, 1925.

(6) In the case of State emblems other than flags, and of official signs and hallmarks of the countries of the Union, and in the case of armorial bearings, flags, other emblems, abbreviations, and names, of international intergovernmental organizations, these provisions shall apply only to marks registered more than two months after receipt of the communication provided for in paragraph (3), above.

(7) In cases of bad faith, the countries shall have the right to cancel even those marks incorporating State emblems, signs, and hallmarks, which were registered before November 6, 1925.

(8) Nationals of any country who are authorized to make use of the State emblems, signs, and hallmarks, of their country may use them even if they are similar to those of another country.

(9) The countries of the Union undertake to prohibit the unauthorized use in trade of the State armorial bearings of the other countries of the Union, when the use is of such a nature as to be misleading as to the origin of the goods.

(10) The above provisions shall not prevent the countries from exercising the right given in paragraph (3) of Article 6^{quinquies}, Section B, to refuse or to invalidate the registration of marks incorporating, without authorization, armorial bearings, flags, other State emblems, or official signs and hallmarks adopted by a country of the Union, as well as the distinctive signs of international intergovernmental organizations referred to in paragraph (1), above.

Article 6^{quater} [*Marks:* Assignment of Marks]

(1) When, in accordance with the law of a country of the Union, the assignment of a mark is valid only if it takes place at the same time as the transfer of the business or goodwill to which the mark belongs, it shall suffice for the recognition of such validity that the portion of the business or goodwill located in that country be transferred to the assignee, together with the exclusive right to manufacture in the said country, or to sell therein, the goods bearing the mark assigned.

(2) The foregoing provision does not impose upon the countries of the Union any obligation to regard as valid the assignment of any mark the use of which by the assignee would, in fact, be of such a nature as to mislead the public, particularly as regards the origin, nature, or essential qualities, of the goods to which the mark is applied.

Article 6^{quinquies} [*Marks:* Protection of Marks Registered in One Country of the Union in the Other Countries of the Union]

A.—(1) Every trademark duly registered in the country of origin shall be accepted for filing and protected as is in the other countries of the Union, subject to the reservations indicated in this Article. Such countries may, before proceeding to final registration, require the production of a certificate of registration in the country of origin, issued by the competent authority. No authentication shall be required for this certificate.

(2) Shall be considered the country of origin the country of the Union where the applicant has a real and effective industrial or commercial establishment, or, if he has no such establishment within the Union, the country of the Union where he has his domicile, or, if he has no domicile within the Union but is a national of a country of the Union, the country of which he is a national.

B.—Trademarks covered by this Article may be neither denied registration nor invalidated except in the following cases:

(i). when they are of such a nature as to infringe rights acquired by third parties in the country where protection is claimed;

(ii). when they are devoid of any distinctive character, or consist exclusively of signs or indications which may serve, in trade, to designate the kind, quality, quantity, intended purpose, value, place of origin, of the goods, or the time of production, or have become customary in the current language or in the bona fide and established practices of the trade of the country where protection is claimed;

(iii). when they are contrary to morality or public order and, in particular, of such a nature as to deceive the public. It is understood that a mark may not be considered contrary to public order for the sole reason that it does not conform to a provision of the legislation on marks, except if such provision itself relates to public order.

This provision is subject, however, to the application of Article 10bis.

C.—(1) In determining whether a mark is eligible for protection, all the factual circumstances must be taken into consideration, particularly the length of time the mark has been in use.

(2) No trademark shall be refused in the other countries of the Union for the sole reason that it differs from the mark protected in the country of origin only in respect of elements that do not alter its distinctive character and do not affect its identity in the form in which it has been registered in the said country of origin.

D.—No person may benefit from the provisions of this Article if the mark for which he claims protection is not registered in the country of origin.

E.—However, in no case shall the renewal of the registration of the mark in the country of origin involve an obligation to renew the registration in the other countries of the Union in which the mark has been registered.

F.—The benefit of priority shall remain unaffected for applications for the registration of marks filed within the period fixed by Article 4, even if registration in the country of origin is effected after the expiration of such period.

Article 6sexies [*Marks:* Service Marks]

The countries of the Union undertake to protect service marks. They shall not be required to provide for the registration of such marks.

Article 6septies [*Marks:* Registration in the Name of the Agent or Representative of the Proprietor Without the Latter's Authorization]

(1) If the agent or representative of the person who is the proprietor of a mark in one of the countries of the Union applies, without such proprietor's authorization, for the registration of the mark in his own name, in one or more countries of the Union, the proprietor shall be entitled to oppose the registration applied for or demand its cancellation or, if the law of the country so allows, the assignment in his favor of the said registration, unless such agent or representative justifies his action.

(2) The proprietor of the mark shall, subject to the provisions of paragraph (1), above, be entitled to oppose the use of his mark by his agent or representative if he has not authorized such use.

(3) Domestic legislation may provide an equitable time limit within which the proprietor of a mark must exercise the rights provided for in this Article.

Article 7 [*Marks:* Nature of the Goods to which the Mark is Applied]

The nature of the goods to which a trademark is to be applied shall in no case form an obstacle to the registration of the mark.

Article 7bis [*Marks:* Collective Marks]

(1) The countries of the Union undertake to accept for filing and to protect collective marks belonging to associations the existence of which is not contrary to the law of the country of origin, even if such associations do not possess an industrial or commercial establishment.

(2) Each country shall be the judge of the particular conditions under which a collective mark shall be protected and may refuse protection if the mark is contrary to the public interest.

(3) Nevertheless, the protection of these marks shall not be refused to any association the existence of which is not contrary to the law of the country of origin, on the ground that such association is not established in the country where protection is sought or is not constituted according to the law of the latter country.

Article 8 [*Trade Names*]

A trade name shall be protected in all the countries of the Union without the obligation of filing or registration, whether or not it forms part of a trademark.

Article 9 [*Marks, Trade Names:* Seizure, on Importation, etc., of Goods Unlawfully Bearing a Mark or Trade Name]

(1) All goods unlawfully bearing a trademark or trade name shall be seized on importation into those countries of the Union where such mark or trade name is entitled to legal protection.

(2) Seizure shall likewise be effected in the country where the unlawful affixation occurred or in the country into which the goods were imported.

(3) Seizure shall take place at the request of the public prosecutor, or any other competent authority, or any interested party, whether a natural person or a legal entity, in conformity with the domestic legislation of each country.

(4) The authorities shall not be bound to effect seizure of goods in transit.

(5) If the legislation of a country does not permit seizure on importation, seizure shall be replaced by prohibition of importation or by seizure inside the country.

(6) If the legislation of a country permits neither seizure on importation nor prohibition of importation nor seizure inside the country, then, until such time as the legislation is modified accordingly, these measures shall be replaced by the actions and remedies available in such cases to nationals under the law of such country.

Article 10 [*False Indications:* Seizure, on Importation, etc., of Goods Bearing False Indications as to Their Source or the Identity of the Producer]

(1) The provisions of the preceding Article shall apply in cases of direct or indirect use of a false indication of the source of the goods or the identity of the producer, manufacturer, or merchant.

(2) Any producer, manufacturer, or merchant, whether a natural person or a legal entity, engaged in the production or manufacture of or trade in such goods and established either in the locality falsely indicated as the source, or in the region where such locality is situated, or in the country falsely indicated, or in the country where the false indication of source is used, shall in any case be deemed an interested party.

Article 10bis [*Unfair Competition*]

(1) The countries of the Union are bound to assure to nationals of such countries effective protection against unfair competition.

(2) Any act of competition contrary to honest practices in industrial or commercial matters constitutes an act of unfair competition.

(3) The following in particular shall be prohibited:

(i). all acts of such a nature as to create confusion by any means whatever with the establishment, the goods, or the industrial or commercial activities, of a competitor;

(ii). false allegations in the course of trade of such a nature as to discredit the establishment, the goods, or the industrial or commercial activities, of a competitor;

(iii). indications or allegations the use of which in the course of trade is liable to mislead the public as to the nature, the manufacturing process, the characteristics, the suitability for their purpose, or the quantity, of the goods.

Article 10ter [*Marks, Trade Names, False Indications, Unfair Competition*: Remedies, Right to Sue]

(1) The countries of the Union undertake to assure to nationals of the other countries of the Union appropriate legal remedies effectively to repress all the acts referred to in Articles 9, 10, and 10bis.

(2) They undertake, further, to provide measures to permit federations and associations representing interested industrialists, producers, or merchants, provided that the existence of such federations and associations is not contrary to the laws of their countries, to take action in the courts or before the administrative authorities, with a view to the repression of the acts referred to in Articles 9, 10, and 10bis, in so far as the law of the country in which protection is claimed allows such action by federations and associations of that country.

Article 11 [*Inventions, Utility Models, Industrial Designs, Marks:* Temporary Protection at Certain International Exhibitions]

(1) The countries of the Union shall, in conformity with their domestic legislation, grant temporary protection to patentable inventions, utility models, industrial designs, and trademarks, in respect of goods exhibited at official or officially recognized international exhibitions held in the territory of any of them.

(2) Such temporary protection shall not extend the periods provided by Article 4. If, later, the right of priority is invoked, the authorities of any country may provide that the period shall start from the date of introduction of the goods into the exhibition.

(3) Each country may require, as proof of the identity of the article exhibited and of the date of its introduction, such documentary evidence as it considers necessary.

Article 12 [Special National Industrial Property Services]

(1) Each country of the Union undertakes to establish a special industrial property service and a central office for the communication to the public of patents, utility models, industrial designs, and trademarks.

(2) This service shall publish an official periodical journal. It shall publish regularly:

(a) the names of the proprietors of patents granted, with a brief designation of the inventions patented;

(b) the reproductions of registered trademarks.

Appendix E

Agreement on Trade-Related Aspects of Intellectual Property Rights (TRIPS) (excerpts)

PART I

GENERAL PROVISIONS AND BASIC PRINCIPLES

Article 1 Nature and Scope of Obligations

1. Members shall give effect to the provisions of this Agreement. Members may, but shall not be obliged to, implement in their law more extensive protection than is required by this Agreement, provided that such protection does not contravene the provisions of this Agreement. Members shall be free to determine the appropriate method of implementing the provisions of this Agreement within their own legal system and practice.

2. For the purposes of this Agreement, the term "intellectual property" refers to all categories of intellectual property that are the subject of Sections 1 through 7 of Part II.

3. Members shall accord the treatment provided for in this Agreement to the nationals of other Members.[1] In respect of the relevant intellectual property right, the nationals of other Members shall be understood as those natural or legal persons that would meet the criteria for eligibility for protection provided for in the Paris Convention (1967), the Berne Convention (1971), the Rome Convention and the Treaty on Intellectual Property in Respect of Integrated Circuits, were all Members of the WTO members of those conventions.[2] Any Member availing itself of the possibilities provided in paragraph 3 of Article 5 or paragraph 2 of Article 6 of the Rome Convention shall make a notification as foreseen in those provisions to the Council for Trade-Related Aspects of Intellectual Property Rights (the "Council for TRIPS").

1. When "nationals" are referred to in this Agreement, they shall be deemed, in the case of a separate customs territory Member of the WTO, to mean persons, natural or legal, who are domiciled or who have a real and effective industrial or commercial establishment in that customs territory.

2. In this Agreement, "Paris Convention" refers to the Paris Convention for the Protection of Industrial Property; "Paris Convention (1967)" refers to the Stockholm Act of this Convention of 14 July 1967. "Berne Convention" refers to the Berne Convention for the Protection of Literary and Artistic Works; "Berne Convention (1971)" refers to the Paris Act of this Convention of 24 July 1971. "Rome Convention" refers to the International Convention for the Protection of Performers, Producers of Phonograms and Broadcasting Organizations, adopted at Rome on 26 October 1961. "Treaty on Intellectual Property in Respect of Integrated Circuits" (IPIC Treaty) refers to the Treaty on Intellectual Property in Respect of Integrated Circuits, adopted at Washington on 26 May 1989. "WTO Agreement" refers to the Agreement Establishing the WTO.

Article 2 Intellectual Property Conventions

1. In respect of Parts II, III and IV of this Agreement, Members shall comply with Articles 1 through 12, and Article 19, of the Paris Convention (1967).

2. Nothing in Parts I to IV of this Agreement shall derogate from existing obligations that Members may have to each other under the Paris Convention, the Berne Convention, the Rome Convention and the Treaty on Intellectual Property in Respect of Integrated Circuits.

Article 3 National Treatment

1. Each Member shall accord to the nationals of other Members treatment no less favourable than that it accords to its own nationals with regard to the protection[3] of intellectual property, subject to the exceptions already provided in, respectively, the Paris Convention (1967), the Berne Convention (1971), the Rome Convention or the Treaty on Intellectual Property in Respect of Integrated Circuits. In respect of performers, producers of phonograms and broadcasting organizations, this obligation only applies in respect of the rights provided under this Agreement. Any Member availing itself of the possibilities provided in Article 6 of the Berne Convention (1971) or paragraph 1(b) of Article 16 of the Rome Convention shall make a notification as foreseen in those provisions to the Council for TRIPS.

2. Members may avail themselves of the exceptions permitted under paragraph 1 in relation to judicial and administrative procedures, including the designation of an address for service or the appointment of an agent within the jurisdiction of a Member, only where such exceptions are necessary to secure compliance with laws and regulations which are not inconsistent with the provisions of this Agreement and where such practices are not applied in a manner which would constitute a disguised restriction on trade.

Article 4 Most-Favoured-Nation Treatment

With regard to the protection of intellectual property, any advantage, favour, privilege or immunity granted by a Member to the nationals of any other country shall be accorded immediately and unconditionally to the nationals of all other Members. Exempted from this obligation are any advantage, favour, privilege or immunity accorded by a Member:

(a) deriving from international agreements on judicial assistance or law enforcement of a general nature and not particularly confined to the protection of intellectual property;

(b) granted in accordance with the provisions of the Berne Convention (1971) or the Rome Convention authorizing that the treatment accorded be a function not of national treatment but of the treatment accorded in another country;

3. For the purposes of Articles 3 and 4, "protection" shall include matters affecting the availability, acquisition, scope, maintenance and enforcement of intellectual property rights as well as those matters affecting the use of intellectual property rights specifically addressed in this Agreement.

(c) in respect of the rights of performers, producers of phonograms and broadcasting organizations not provided under this Agreement;

(d) deriving from international agreements related to the protection of intellectual property which entered into force prior to the entry into force of the WTO Agreement, provided that such agreements are notified to the Council for TRIPS and do not constitute an arbitrary or unjustifiable discrimination against nationals of other Members.

Article 5 Multilateral Agreements on Acquisition or Maintenance of Protection

The obligations under Articles 3 and 4 do not apply to procedures provided in multilateral agreements concluded under the auspices of WIPO relating to the acquisition or maintenance of intellectual property rights.

Article 6 Exhaustion

For the purposes of dispute settlement under this Agreement, subject to the provisions of Articles 3 and 4 nothing in this Agreement shall be used to address the issue of the exhaustion of intellectual property rights.

Article 7 Objectives

The protection and enforcement of intellectual property rights should contribute to the promotion of technological innovation and to the transfer and dissemination of technology, to the mutual advantage of producers and users of technological knowledge and in a manner conducive to social and economic welfare, and to a balance of rights and obligations.

Article 8 Principles

1. Members may, in formulating or amending their laws and regulations, adopt measures necessary to protect public health and nutrition, and to promote the public interest in sectors of vital importance to their socio-economic and technological development, provided that such measures are consistent with the provisions of this Agreement.

2. Appropriate measures, provided that they are consistent with the provisions of this Agreement, may be needed to prevent the abuse of intellectual property rights by right holders or the resort to practices which unreasonably restrain trade or adversely affect the international transfer of technology.

PART II
STANDARDS CONCERNING THE AVAILABILITY, SCOPE AND USE OF INTELLECTUAL PROPERTY RIGHTS

....

SECTION 2: TRADEMARKS

Article 15 Protectable Subject Matter

1. Any sign, or any combination of signs, capable of distinguishing the goods or services of one undertaking from those of other undertakings, shall be capable of constituting a trademark. Such signs, in particular words including personal names, letters, numerals, figurative elements and combinations of colours as well as any combination

of such signs, shall be eligible for registration as trademarks. Where signs are not inherently capable of distinguishing the relevant goods or services, Members may make registrability depend on distinctiveness acquired through use. Members may require, as a condition of registration, that signs be visually perceptible.

2. Paragraph 1 shall not be understood to prevent a Member from denying registration of a trademark on other grounds, provided that they do not derogate from the provisions of the Paris Convention (1967).

3. Members may make registrability depend on use. However, actual use of a trademark shall not be a condition for filing an application for registration. An application shall not be refused solely on the ground that intended use has not taken place before the expiry of a period of three years from the date of application.

4. The nature of the goods or services to which a trademark is to be applied shall in no case form an obstacle to registration of the trademark.

5. Members shall publish each trademark either before it is registered or promptly after it is registered and shall afford a reasonable opportunity for petitions to cancel the registration. In addition, Members may afford an opportunity for the registration of a trademark to be opposed.

Article 16 Rights Conferred

1. The owner of a registered trademark shall have the exclusive right to prevent all third parties not having the owner's consent from using in the course of trade identical or similar signs for goods or services which are identical or similar to those in respect of which the trademark is registered where such use would result in a likelihood of confusion. In case of the use of an identical sign for identical goods or services, a likelihood of confusion shall be presumed. The rights described above shall not prejudice any existing prior rights, nor shall they affect the possibility of Members making rights available on the basis of use.

2. Article 6bis of the Paris Convention (1967) shall apply, *mutatis mutandis*, to services. In determining whether a trademark is well-known, Members shall take account of the knowledge of the trademark in the relevant sector of the public, including knowledge in the Member concerned which has been obtained as a result of the promotion of the trademark.

3. Article 6bis of the Paris Convention (1967) shall apply, *mutatis mutandis*, to goods or services which are not similar to those in respect of which a trademark is registered, provided that use of that trademark in relation to those goods or services would indicate a connection between those goods or services and the owner of the registered trademark and provided that the interests of the owner of the registered trademark are likely to be damaged by such use.

Article 17 Exceptions

Members may provide limited exceptions to the rights conferred by a trademark, such as fair use of descriptive terms, provided that such exceptions take account of the legitimate interests of the owner of the trademark and of third parties.

Article 18 Term of Protection

Initial registration, and each renewal of registration, of a trademark shall be for a term of no less than seven years. The registration of a trademark shall be renewable indefinitely.

Article 19 Requirement of Use

1. If use is required to maintain a registration, the registration may be cancelled only after an uninterrupted period of at least three years of non-use, unless valid reasons based on the existence of obstacles to such use are shown by the trademark owner. Circumstances arising independently of the will of the owner of the trademark which constitute an obstacle to the use of the trademark, such as import restrictions on or other government requirements for goods or services protected by the trademark, shall be recognized as valid reasons for non-use.

2. When subject to the control of its owner, use of a trademark by another person shall be recognized as use of the trademark for the purpose of maintaining the registration.

Article 20 Other Requirements

The use of a trademark in the course of trade shall not be unjustifiably encumbered by special requirements, such as use with another trademark, use in a special form or use in a manner detrimental to its capability to distinguish the goods or services of one undertaking from those of other undertakings. This will not preclude a requirement prescribing the use of the trademark identifying the undertaking producing the goods or services along with, but without linking it to, the trademark distinguishing the specific goods or services in question of that undertaking.

Article 21 Licensing and Assignment

Members may determine conditions on the licensing and assignment of trademarks, it being understood that the compulsory licensing of trademarks shall not be permitted and that the owner of a registered trademark shall have the right to assign the trademark with or without the transfer of the business to which the trademark belongs.

SECTION 3: GEOGRAPHICAL INDICATIONS

Article 22 Protection of Geographical Indications

1. Geographical indications are, for the purposes of this Agreement, indications which identify a good as originating in the territory of a Member, or a region or locality in that territory, where a given quality, reputation or other characteristic of the good is essentially attributable to its geographical origin.

2. In respect of geographical indications, Members shall provide the legal means for interested parties to prevent:

(a) the use of any means in the designation or presentation of a good that indicates or suggests that the good in question originates in a geographical area other than the true place of origin in a manner which misleads the public as to the geographical origin of the good;

(b) any use which constitutes an act of unfair competition within the meaning of Article 10bis of the Paris Convention (1967).

3. A Member shall, *ex officio* if its legislation so permits or at the request of an interested party, refuse or invalidate the registration of a trademark which contains or consists of a geographical indication with respect to goods not originating in the territory indicated, if use of the indication in the trademark for such goods in that Member is of such a nature as to mislead the public as to the true place of origin.

4. The protecton under paragraphs 1, 2 and 3 shall be applicable against a geographical indication which, although literally true as to the territory, region or locality in which the goods originate, falsely represents to the public that the goods originate in another territory.

Article 23 Additional Protection for Geographical Indications for Wines and Spirits

1. Each Member shall provide the legal means for interested parties to prevent use of a geographical indication identifying wines for wines not originating in the place indicated by the geographical indication in question or identifying spirits for spirits not originating in the place indicated by the geographical indication in question, even where the true origin of the goods is indicated or the geographical indication is used in translation or accompanied by expressions such as "kind," "type," "style," "imitation" or the like.[4]

2. The registration of a trademark for wines which contains or consists of a geographical indication identifying wines or for spirits which contains or consists of a geographical indication identifying spirits shall be refused or invalidated, *ex officio* if a Member's legislation so permits or at the request of an interested party, with respect to such wines or spirits not having this origin.

3. In the case of homonymous geographical indications for wines, protection shall be accorded to each indication, subject to the provisions of paragraph 4 of Article 22. Each Member shall determine the practical conditions under which the homonymous indications in question will be differentiated from each other, taking into account the need to ensure equitable treatment of the producers concerned and that consumers are not misled.

4. In order to facilitate the protection of geographical indications for wines, negotiations shall be undertaken in the Council for TRIPS concerning the establishment of a multilateral system of notification and registration of geographical indications for wines eligible for protection in those Members participating in the system.

Article 24 International Negotiations; Exceptions

1. Members agree to enter into negotiations aimed at increasing the protection of individual geographical indications under Article 23. The provisions of paragraphs 4–8 below shall not be used by a Member to refuse to conduct negotiations or to conclude

---

4. Notwithstanding the first sentence of Article 42, Members may, with respect to these obligations, instead provide for enforcement by administrative action.

bilateral or multilateral agreements. In the context of such negotiations, Members shall be willing to consider the continued applicability of these provisions to individual geographical indications whose use was the subject of such negotiations.

2. The Council for TRIPS shall keep under review the application of the provisions of this Section; the first such review shall take place within two years of the entry into force of the WTO Agreement. Any matter affecting the compliance with the obligations under these provisions may be drawn to the attention of the Council, which, at the request of a Member, shall consult with any Member or Members in respect of such matter in respect of which it has not been possible to find a satisfactory solution through bilateral or plurilateral consultations between the Members concerned. The Council shall take such action as may be agreed to facilitate the operation and further the objectives of this Section.

3. In implementing this Section, a Member shall not diminish the protection of geographical indications that existed in that Member immediately prior to the date of entry into force of the WTO Agreement.

4. Nothing in this Section shall require a Member to prevent continued and similar use of a particular geographical indication of another Member identifying wines or spirits in connection with goods or services by any of its nationals or domiciliaries who have used that geographical indication in a continuous manner with regard to the same or related goods or services in the territory of that Member either (a) for at least 10 years preceding 15 April 1994 or (b) in good faith preceding that date.

5. Where a trademark has been applied for or registered in good faith, or where rights to a trademark have been acquired through use in good faith either:

(a) before the date of application of these provisions in that Member as defined in Part VI; or

(b) before the geographical indication is protected in its country of origin;

measures adopted to implement this Section shall not prejudice eligibility for or the validity of the registration of a trademark, or the right to use a trademark, on the basis that such a trademark is identical with, or similar to, a geographical indication.

6. Nothing in this Section shall require a Member to apply its provisions in respect of a geographical indication of any other Member with respect to goods or services for which the relevant indication is identical with the term customary in common language as the common name for such goods or services in the territory of that Member. Nothing in this Section shall require a Member to apply its provisions in respect of a geographical indication of any other Member with respect to products of the vine for which the relevant indication is identical with the customary name of a grape variety existing in the territory of that Member as of the date of entry into force of the WTO Agreement.

7. A Member may provide that any request made under this Section in connection with the use or registration of a trademark must be presented within five years after

the adverse use of the protected indication has become generally known in that Member or after the date of registration of the trademark in that Member provided that the trademark has been published by that date, if such date is earlier than the date on which the adverse use became generally known in that Member, provided that the geographical indication is not used or registered in bad faith.

8. The provisions of this Section shall in no way prejudice the right of any person to use, in the course of trade, that person's name or the name of that person's predecessor in business, except where such name is used in such a manner as to mislead the public.

9. There shall be no obligation under this Agreement to protect geographical indications which are not or cease to be protected in their country of origin, or which have fallen into disuse in that country.

Index

[References are to sections.]

U

W